The
Bible Commentary

F. C. Cook, *Editor*

Abridged and Edited by

J. M. Fuller

PROVERBS
ECCLESIASTES
SONG OF SOLOMON
JEREMIAH
EZEKIEL

BAKER BOOK HOUSE
Grand Rapids, Michigan 49506

BARNES' NOTES

Heritage Edition   Fourteen Volumes 0834-4

When ordering by ISBN (International Standard Book Number), numbers listed above should be preceded by 0-8010-.

Reprinted from the 1879 edition published by John Murray, London, under the title, *The Student's Commentary on the Holy Bible*

Reprinted 1983 by Baker Book House Company

ISBN : 0-8010-0839-5

Printed and bound in the United States of America

PROVERBS.

INTRODUCTION.

1. The opening words of the Book (i. 1) give us its current Hebrew title; of which the first word has been adopted by translators, and "Proverbs" has become in the LXX., the Vulgate, and the Authorized Version, the common heading of the Book. At one time a title of honour, the Book of Wisdom, or the "all-excellent wisdom," was applied by both Jews and Christians to this Book, indicating that the Book took its place, as the representative of the Wisdom of which the Hebrews thought so much, at the head of the whole class of books, Canonical or Apocryphal, which were known as Sapiential.

The Hebrew word for "proverb" (*mashâl*) has a much more definite significance than the Greek παροιμία, and the Latin *proverbium*. Its root-meaning is that of comparison, the putting this and that together, noting likeness in things unlike; it answers, *i.e.*, to the Greek παραβολή rather than παροιμία. That it was applied also to moral apophthegms of varying length, pointed and pithy in their form, even though there might be no similitude, is evident enough throughout the Book.[1]

Proverbs are characteristic of a comparatively early stage in the mental growth of most nations. A single startling or humorous fact serving as the type of all similar facts (*e.g.* 1 S. x. 12); the mere result of an induction to which other instances may be referred (*e.g.* 1 S. xxiv. 13); a law, with or without a similitude, or explaining in this manner the course of events in the lives of men or in the history of their nation (Jer. xxxi. 29 ; Ezek. xviii. 2):—these things furnish proverbs found in the history of all nations, generally in its earlier stages. There is little or no record of their birth. No one knows their author. They find acceptance with men from their inherent truth or semblance of truth. Afterwards, commonly at a much later period, men make collections of them.

2. The Book of Proverbs, however, is not such a collection. So far as it includes what had previously been current in familiar sayings, there was a process of selection, guided by a distinct didactic aim, excluding all that were local, personal, or simply humorous, and receiving those which

---

[1] The word has sometimes a more extended meaning. Discourses of more or less poetic character, without formal comparison, and with no didactic result, are, as in the case of that of Balaam (Num. xxiii. 7, 18, xxiv. 3, 15, 20, 21, 23), and Job (xxvii. 1, xxix. 1), and Ezekiel (xvii. 2, xx. 49, xxiv. 3), described as "parables." The triumph-song of Num. xxi. 27-30, uttered by those who "speak in proverbs," serves as another instance of the wider meaning.

fell in with the ethical purpose of the teacher. As in the history of other nations, so among the Hebrews (cp. 1 K. iv. 31), there rose up, at a certain stage of culture, those to whom the proverb was the most natural mode of utterance, who embodied in it all that they had observed or thought out as to the phenomena of nature or of human life. Such pre-eminently was the sage to whose authorship the Book of Proverbs is assigned, Solomon, the son of David.

The definite precision of 1 K. iv. 32 leads to the inference that there was at the time when that Book was written a known collection of sayings ascribed to Solomon far longer than the present Book, and of songs which are almost, or altogether, lost to us. The scope of that collection may probably have included a far wider range of subjects (such as trees, creatures, &c.), than the present Book, which is from first to last ethical in its scope, deals but sparingly, through the larger portion of its contents, with the world of animals and plants, and has nothing that takes the form of fable.

3. The structure of the Book shews, however, that it is a compilation from different sources as well as a selection from the sayings of one man only; and a compilation which, in its present form, was made some three centuries after the time of Solomon. One considerable section of the book consists of proverbs that were first arranged and written out under Hezekiah (xxv. 1). Agur (xxx. 1) and Lemuel (xxxi. 1) are named as the authors of the last two chapters. The Book is, therefore, analogous in its composition to the Psalms; it is an anthology from the sayings of the sages of Israel, taking its name from him who was the chiefest of them, as the Book of Psalms is an anthology from the hymns not of David only, but of the sons of Korah and others.

The question how far the Book gives us the teaching of Solomon himself, what portions of it may be assigned to him, and what to some later writers, has been very differently answered : but certain landmarks present themselves, dividing the Book into sections, each of which is a complete whole.

(*a*) i. 1–6 ; the title and introduction to the Book, describing its contents and aim. There seems good reason for believing that while *v.* 1 gave the original title of the Book, the other verses were added by the last compiler, in whose hands it took its present shape.

(*b*) i. 7 ; something of a motto, laying down the principle which is the basis of the whole Book. This may be assigned to the same compiler.

(*c*) i. 8–ix. 18 ; one long exhortation, addressed by the teacher to his scholar, and each sub-section opening with the words, "my son" or "my children." In ch. viii. there is a change to a higher strain. Wisdom herself speaks, and not to the individual seeker, but to the sons of men at large (viii. 4). This personification of Wisdom as a living power, and the stress laid upon her greatness and beauty, contrasted with the "strange woman," the "foreigner," *i.e.*, the harlot or adulteress, whose fascination is most perilous to the soul entering on its time of trial, are the characteristic features of this portion.

The whole of this section has

been ascribed by some commentators to a later author than Solomon, on grounds which are, to say the least, very uncertain.[2] Arguments, in favour of identity of authorship, are not wanting.[3]

(d) x. 1–xxii. 16. The title indicates that the section had an independent origin. The continuous teaching is replaced by a series of isolated maxims, short, pithy, antithetic, the true type of the Hebrew proverbs, hardly ever carried beyond the limits of a single verse, dealing with the common facts of life, and viewing them from the point of prudence. This is the kernel of the whole Book, representing the wisdom which made Solomon famous among men. Containing about 400 of these maxims, it may be thought of as probably a selection from the larger number referred to in 1 K. iv. 32, made

possibly under the direction of the king himself, and prefaced by the more homiletic teachings of chs. i.-ix. Though there is no systematic order, here and there two or more verses in succession deal with the same topic[4] in a way which throws some light on the process by which the selection had been made, as though there had been something like a commonplace book, in which, though there was no systematic arrangement, there was a certain degree of grouping under different heads or catchwords. Certain phrases too are characteristic of this section.[5] As regards the substance of the teaching; stress is laid[6] on the thought that Jehovah, the "Lord," is the supreme Giver of all good, the Judge and Ruler of mankind, all-knowing, and ordering all things; that the king, thought of in the ideal

---

[2] (1) It has been inferred from e.g. x. 1, that the compiler wished to indicate that chs. i.-ix. were by another writer; an inference thought to be confirmed by the contrast between the styles of writing. (2) The warnings (e.g. i. 10 &c.) against the life of robbers as a besetting danger for the young are affirmed to point to a time of greater disorder than the reign of Solomon. (3) New words or forms are alleged to fall in with the same theory. (4) Traces of the influence of the Book of Job are adduced to place the composition of this portion after the beginning of the seventh century, to which the Book of Job is referred.

To which it may be answered: (1) The difference of style is not greater than would be natural in one who in maturer age was writing a preface to maxims which had been noted down separately from time to time. (2) The life of the outlaw was one of constant recurrence in the earlier history of Israel (e.g. Judg. ix. 4), and there is no ground for supposing that it was entirely suppressed under Solomon. (3) The argument from peculiar words, always more or less fallacious, is traversed by the far larger number of words, which are common in nearly the same proportion to all parts of the Book. (4) The uncertainty as to the date of Job

makes any argument based upon it of very doubtful weight.

[3] (1) There are no warnings against idolatry, such as would have been natural in one who lived under the later kings of Judah; (2) the danger of contamination from foreign vices was precisely that which began to be felt under Solomon; (3) the forms of luxury, described in vii. 16, 17, are such as were conspicuous in his reign (1 K. x. 28).

[4] E.g. x. 6 and 7, 8 and 9, 13 and 14, 16 and 17, 18 and 19, xi. 25 and 26, 30 and 31, and especially the recurrence of the name "Jehovah," xv. 33, xvi. 1-9, 11, and of the word "king" in xvi. 10, 12-15.

[5] E.g. the "fountain" or "well of life" (x. 11, xiii. 14, xiv. 27, xvi. 22), the "tree of life" (xi. 30, xiii. 12, xv. 4), the "snares of death" (xiii. 14, xiv. 27), the "destruction" that follows upon evil-doing (x. 14, 15, xiii. 3, xiv. 28, xviii. 7), the use of a peculiar word for "speaking" or "uttering" either truth or falsehood (xii. 17, xiv. 5, 25, xix. 5, 9), of another for "perverting" or "overthrowing" (xiii. 6, xix. 3, xxii. 12), the use of a peculiar form of an unusual verb for "meddling" (xvii. 14, xviii. 1, xx. 3, and nowhere else in the Old Testament), &c.

[6] Especially in xv. 3, 8, 9, 11, 16, 25, 26, 29, 33, and xvi. 1-7, 9, 11, 33.

greatness which was natural in the time of Solomon, and hardly so at a later period, was as the counterpart and representative of Jehovah, an earthly Providence (xvi. 10-15, xix. 6, 12, xx. 8, 26, 28, xxi. 1).

(e) xxii. 17–xxiv. 22 : a section containing the more continuous teaching, the personal address, of the teacher to his " son " (xxiii. 15, 19, 26, xxiv. 13, 21), the same warnings against sins of impurity (xxiii. 27, 28), the same declaration of the end which the teacher has in view (xxii. 17–21), as are met with in chs. i.–ix. It may seem a natural hypothesis that the same writer, having made the selection which forms the central portion of the book, wrote both prologue and epilogue to it, and that this, with the short section (f), was the form in which the Book was current until it received its last additions in the reign of Hezekiah.

(f) xxiv. 23–34 : a section with a new title. " These things also belong to the wise," i.e. are spoken by them, fulfil the promise of the title (i. 6) that it would include the " words of the wise," wherever the compiler found them. Short as the section is, it presents in the parable of the field of the slothful (xxiv. 30–34) some characteristic features not to be found in the other portions of the Book. What had been spoken before barely and briefly (vi. 9) is now reproduced with pictorial vividness. What was before a general maxim, becomes sharper and more pointed as a lesson of experience.

(g) xxv.—xxix. 27. The superscription of this section pre-supposes the existence of a previous collection, known as the Proverbs of Solomon, and recognized as at once authentic and authoritative. It shews that there were also current, orally, or in writing, other proverbs not included in that collection. It brings before us a marked instance of the activity of that period in collecting, arranging, and editing the writings of an earlier age. It is a distinct statement, that both the collection that precedes, and that which follows, were at that time, after careful inquiry, recognized to be by Solomon himself. The chapters to which it is prefixed present a general resemblance to the portion (x.–xxii. 16) which all critics have regarded as the oldest portion of the Book. There is the same stress laid on the ideal excellence of the kingly office (cp. xxv. 2–7 with xvi. 10–15), the same half-grouping under special words and thoughts.[7] The average length of the proverbs is about the same, in most there is the same general parallelism of the clauses. There is a freer use of direct similitudes. In one passage (xxvii. 23–27) there is, as an exceptional case, instruction which seems to be economic rather than ethical in its character, designed, it may be, to uphold the older agricultural life of the Israelites as contrasted with the growing tendency to seek wealth by commerce, and so fall into the luxury and profligacy of the Phœnicians.

(h) xxx, xxxi. These two chapters present problems of greater difficulty, and open a wider field for conjecture. The word trans-

---

[7] E.g. in xxv. 2-7 referring to kings, in the words "take away" (xxv. 4, 5), in the use of the same word (in Hebrew) for "strife," or "cause" (xxv. 9), of "gold" (xxv. 11, 12), of the "fool" in the first twelve verses of ch. xxvi., of the "slothful" in xxvi. 13-16, of the "righteous" in xxix. 2, 7, 16.

lated "prophecy"[8] (xxx. 1, xxxi. 1 ; *massa*) is elsewhere, with scarcely an exception, rendered "burden," either in its literal sense, or, as denoting a solemn speech or oracle, uttered by a Prophet (cp. the titles of Isaiah xiii.–xxiii.). If this meaning be received here, it indicates a marked difference between these chapters and the hortative addresses, or the collections of apophthegms of which, up to this time, the Book had been composed.[9]

The "prophecy" is addressed to two disciples, Ithiel (cp. Neh. xi. 7) and Ucal. Some take these names to be two ideal names, the first meaning "God is with me," and the second "I am strong," both names of the same ideal person, the representative of a Divine wisdom, meeting (*vv.* 4, 5) the confession of ignorance and blindness. By others the words are treated as not being names at all, but part of the opening words of Agur himself, the introduction to the strange complaint, or confession, which opens so abruptly (*v.* 2).

The leading features of the section are less didactic, more enigmatic in character, as though it corresponded specially to the "dark sayings" of i. 6. The phenomena are grouped into quaternions, and show a strange intermingling of facts belonging to the brute and to the human world ; in this, whensoever and by whomsoever written, shewing the influence of the Book of Job as clearly as the earlier sections did. Probably, the section is a fragment of a work written by one belonging originally to the country to which many critics have been led to refer the Book of Job itself, a proselyte to the faith which the occurrence of the name Jehovah (*v.* 9) proves that the writer had received. The reign of Hezekiah was conspicuous for the re-opening of intercourse with these neighbouring nations (2 Chr. xxxii. 23), for the admission of converts from them among the citizens of Zion (Ps. lxxxvii.), and for the zeal shown in collecting and adding to the canon whatever bore upon it the stamp of a lofty and heavenly wisdom.

(*i*) xxxi. 1–9. Most Jewish and some Patristic commentators have conjectured that Lemuel is a name for Solomon, and that the words of his mother's reproof were spoken when the first promise of his reign was beginning to pass into sensuality and excess ; others have suggested that Lemuel is simply an ideal name, he who is "for God," the true king who leads a life consecrated to the service of Jehovah. We must be

---

[8] The Vulgate in both passages gives "visio." The LXX. substitutes an entirely different verse for xxx. 1, and in xxxi. 1 gives χρηματισμός.

[9] Some have maintained that allusion is here made to a "land" of Massa (Gen. xxv. 14; 1 Chr. i. 30) ; that its inhabitants were among the "children of the East," whose wisdom had become proverbial (1 K. iv. 30) ; and that their words were therefore thought worthy of being appended to those of the sage by whom they were surpassed. With the help of some changes in the vowel-points of the original, xxx. 1 is transformed into "Agur the son of her to whom Massa is obedient," *i.e.* the queen of Massa ; and xxxi. 1 appears as "The words of (or "for") Lemuel, king of Massa, which his mother taught him." Agur and Lemuel are thus made out to be brothers, and the queen is made the possessor of a wisdom which places her on a level with the queen of the South, or with the son of David himself. The hypothesis is ingenious rather than satisfying.

content to confess our ignorance who Lemuel was, and what was the occasion of the "prophecy." It probably belongs to the same period as ch. xxx. and was added to the Book not earlier than the time of Hezekiah.

(j) xxxi. 10–31. The last portion of the Book forms, more distinctly, perhaps, than any other, a complete whole in itself. From beginning to end there is but one subject, the delineation of a perfect wife. The section is alphabetic in its structure. The form may have been adopted, as in the case of the alphabetic Psalms, partly as a help to memory, partly from the delight which, in certain stages, generally comparatively late in the history of literature, is felt in choosing a structure which presents difficulties and requires ingenuity to overcome them. The absence of any historical allusions makes it impossible to fix any precise date for it.

4. The ethical teaching of the Book of Proverbs rests on principles which have their application to the varying circumstances of life.

The Book belongs to a period when men had been taught to see more clearly than before the relative importance of the moral and the ceremonial precepts which seemed, in the Law of Moses, to stand on the same level as enjoined by Divine authority. The language of Samuel (1 Sam. xv. 22), of Asaph (Ps. l. 13, 14), of David (Ps. li. 16, 17), had impressed itself on the minds of the people at large, and on one who, like the writer of the Book of Proverbs, had grown up under the immediate influence of the teacher (Nathan) who, after the death of Samuel, stood at the

head of the prophetic order. The tendency to discriminate between moral and positive obligations thus originated, would be fostered by intercourse with other Semitic nations, such as Edom and Sheba, standing on the same footing as regards the fundamental principles of ethics, but not led, as Israel had been, through the discipline of typical or symbolic ordinances. If the Book of Job was already known to the Israelite seekers after wisdom, the grandeur of its thoughts and the absence in it of any reference to the Law as such, would strengthen the conviction that instruction might be given, leading to a life of true wisdom and holiness and yet not including any direct reference to ceremonial or ritual precepts. These would be preserved in the traditions of household life, the example of parents, the teaching of priests and Levites; while a teacher such as the writer of the Book of Proverbs could aim at laying the foundation of a godly life independently of them, and exhibit that life in its completeness.

This accounts for the absence from the Proverbs of all mention of obligations on which devout Israelites at all times must have laid stress, and to which Pharisaism in its later developments gave an exaggerated prominence.[1]

It was this negative characteristic which fitted the Book to do a

---

[1] There is no reference to the law of the Sabbath, nor to the payment of tithes, nor to the observance of the Passover and other Feasts. What is true of the Book of Job, that, with the exception of the frequent occurrence of Jehovah as the distinctive name of God, it contains but little that would indicate any knowledge of the Law, or an Israelitish origin, is true, to nearly the same extent, here.

work which could not otherwise have been done so well, both for the education of Israel, and for that of mankind at large. The Jew was to be taught to recognize a common ground on which he and they alike stood (Mark xii. 33). The Greek, when the sacred books of Israel were brought before him in his own language, could find in such a Book as Proverbs, that which he could understand and sympathize with,—teaching as to life and its duties, vices and their penalties, not unlike that which he found in his own literature. It was significant of the attractive power which this Book exercised on the minds of men during the period between the Old and New Testaments, when there was no " open vision," and the gift of prophecy was for a time withdrawn, that the two most prominent books in the collection which we know as the Apocrypha, the only two, indeed, that have a marked didactic character, the Wisdom of Solomon and Ecclesiasticus, were based upon its model, and to a large extent reproduced its precepts.

The teaching of the Book of Proverbs was, however, in its essence, identical with that which formed the basis of the faith of Israel. Its morality was not merely the result of a wide observation of the consequences of good and evil conduct, but was essentially religious. The constant occurrence of the Divine name in the form (Jehovah), which was the characteristic inheritance of Israel, and which is more frequently used than that of God (*Elohim*), is in itself a sufficient proof that there was no surrender of the truth of which that name was the symbol.

The fear of Jehovah (i. 7) stood in the very front of its teaching as the beginning of wisdom. The temper thus indicated, that of awe and reverence, rooted in the consciousness of man's littleness and weakness in the presence of the Eternal and the Infinite, was at once the motive and the crown (ii. 5) of the life of obedience to the laws of duty which the teaching of the Book enjoins. If outward prosperity, "length of days," and "riches and honour" (iii. 16, x. 27), attach to those who keep His commandments, men are taught also that He educates and trains them by "chastening" and "correction" (iii. 11, 12). All powers of intellect and speech, all efforts after holiness, are thought of as His gifts (xvi. 1, 9), even as men are taught to recognize His bounty in all the outward blessings of their lives, and in the family relationships which make up the happiness of home (xix. 14). When men are told to seek wisdom, they are led on to think of it as clothed with a personal life, in closest fellowship with the Eternal, inseparably one with Him (viii. 22, 30). And as the wisdom which the Book inculcates is thus raised far above the level of earthly prudence, so also the reward is more than outward prosperity. "Righteousness delivereth from death" (xi. 4), turns, *i.e.*, the inevitable end of life into an euthanasia. In contrast with the wicked, of whom it is true that "when he dieth his expectation shall perish" (xi. 7), it is written of the righteous that he "hath hope in his death" (xiv. 32).

5. The application of these principles to practical and social life presupposes a state of society in

which the simplicity of village life is giving way to the sudden development of the wealth and luxury which belong to cities. The dangers against which the young are warned with oft-repeated earnestness are those of extravagance, indebtedness, drunkenness, impurity leading to open lawlessness, and the life of the freebooter. Other faults incident to different temperaments are each, in their turn, held up to reprobation.[2] With the practical wisdom which is characteristic of the Book, appealing, as it does, to those that are halting between two opinions, and inclining to the worse, stress is laid not chiefly on the sin but on the folly of the vice, not on its eternal, but its temporal consequences. Men are urged to act first from secondary, prudential motives, to shun the poverty, wretchedness, ignominy, which are the consequences of self-indulgence, that so they may learn the habits of self-restraint which will make them capable of higher thoughts, and obedient to the Divine Law, as finding in that obedience itself their exceeding great reward. The remedies for these evils the writer or writers of the Book of Proverbs saw were to be found in education. Individuals and nations alike needed discipline and restraint. Individuals would find this in the training of home, in the counsels, warnings, and, if necessary, the chastisements also, by which the unruly will is checked and guided ; nations, in the stern, inflexible, incorruptible administration of jus-

tice controlled by a wise and righteous king (xvi. 10, 12-14, xx. 8, 26, 28). Hence kings are counselled no less than subjects (xxviii. 16, xxix. 12, xxxi. 4) : the king is advised not to rely too much on his own unaided judgment, but to surround himself with wise and prudent counsellors (xxiv. 6), and to refer all to that wisdom, which is the gift of God (viii. 15).

No ethical manual would be complete, unless it assigned to woman, as well as man, her right position in the social order. From her folly (xi. 22) and degradation (ii. 16-19, v. 3-14, vii. 6-27) spring the worst evils ; in her excellence is the crown and glory of a man's life (xi. 16, xii. 4). No picture of ideal happiness is brighter than that of a home which is thus made perfect with the clear brightness of true union (v. 15-20). The "prudent wife" is thought of as one of God's best gifts (xix. 14), "building her house" (xiv. 1) on the only true foundation. Her influence on her children is as great as that of their father, if not greater (i. 8, vi. 20). They owe what they have of goodness to her loving persuasion. Their sins and follies are a heaviness and reproach to her (x. 1, xvii. 25). They are bound to render to her a true and loving obedience (i. 8, vi. 20). The teaching on this subject culminates in ch. xxxi., consisting as it does, (1) of prophecy or oracular speech as to the office of a king and the special temptations incident to it, which comes from one who was herself the mother of a king, and (2) of the picture of a perfect wife, wise, active, liberal, largehearted, the ideal which the young man, seeking for the true blessedness of life, was to keep in view.

---

[2] *E.g.* idleness (xv. 19, xix. 15, 24, xxiv. 30-34, xxvi. 13-16), pride (xvi. 18, xviii. 12), uncontrolled speech (x. 10, 19, xviii. 7), want of reverence for parents and for the aged (xiii. 1, xv. 5, xix. 26).

6. The LXX., or Greek Version of the Book of Proverbs, presents several points of interest. What was true of the LXX. translation as a whole, that it seemed to bridge over the chasm that had divided the Jew from the Greek, holds good in a special degree of this part of it. In making that translation the Jew would have to familiarize himself with the terminology of Greek ethical writers, and to note the precise equivalents for the attributes, moral and intellectual, of which the Book treats so fully. In reading it the Greek would find himself, far more than he would in reading Law or Psalm or Prophet, on common ground on which he and the Jew could meet. The very words with which the Greek version of the Book abounds, such as σοφία, φρόνησις, σύνεσις, δικαιοσύνη, were those which were echoing in every lecture-room in Alexandria. As the Book itself, according to its traditional authorship, was the first-fruits of that largeness of heart which admitted intercourse with other nations and familiarity with their modes of thought and speech, so the translation tended to give prominence to that side of Judaism in which it presented itself to men, not as prophetic, typical, ceremonial, but wholly or chiefly as a monotheistic system of pure ethics.

Hence this Book, almost alone of the Books of the Old Testament, served as a model for the Hellenistic writers of the two centuries B.C. The Wisdom of Solomon, the Wisdom of Sirach or the son of Sirach (cp. the prologue), probably also other lost books of the same kind, confessed in their very titles, yet more in their whole structure and tone, that the Proverbs of Solomon (especially ch. viii.) had left their stamp upon them.

Philo's language, descriptive of the Logos,[3] is a reflection of the Greek words in which Wisdom is personified.[4] In the teaching of St. John, may be traced, in the highest aspects of Christian theology, the influence of the vivid portraiture of the personified *Sophia* of the Proverbs.[5]

It lay in the nature of the case, both as to the thoughts of Philo, and yet more as to the higher teaching of St. John, that, so far as the Divine Wisdom was personified, the masculine, not the feminine, word should gain the ascendancy. A system in which Σοφία had been the dominant word might have led to an earlier development of that attractive power of the " ever-feminine," of which Mariolatry was a later growth ; or might have become one in which, as in the Rabbinic exegesis of Prov. viii., Wisdom was identified with the Law given by Moses, and yet existing before the world was.

An instance, hardly less striking,

---

[3] Μιμούμενος τὰς τοῦ πατρὸς ὁδοὺς, πρὸς παραδείγματα ἀρχέτυπα ἐκείνου βλέπων.—Philo, "De Conf. Ling." III. 342.

[4] Ὡς ἰσχυρὰ ἐποίει τὰ θεμέλια τῆς γῆς ἤμην παρ' αὐτῷ ἁρμόζουσα· ἐγὼ ἤμην ᾗ προσέχαιρεν, καθ' ἡμέραν δὲ εὐφραινόμην ἐν προσώπῳ αὐτοῦ ἐν παντὶ καιρῷ.—viii. 29, 30.

[5] The phrases which came to express the eternal generation of the Λόγος as the μονογενὴς υἱὸς (John i. 14, 18), such, e.g., as πρὸ τοῦ αἰῶνος, ἐν ἀρχῇ, were used of her. The doxology which ascribes to the Lamb that was slain πλοῦτον καὶ σοφίαν καὶ ἰσχὺν καὶ τιμὴν καὶ δόξαν (Rev. v. 12) is all but an echo of the words in which Wisdom speaks of herself (ἐμὴ φρόνησις, ἐμὴ δὲ ἰσχὺς... πλοῦτος καὶ δόξα ἐμοὶ ὑπάρχει, viii. 14, 18). Even the ἐσκήνωσεν ἐν ἡμῖν of John i. 14 can hardly be separated altogether from the ἐγὼ ἡ σοφία, κατεσκήνωσα βουλὴν καὶ γνῶσιν of Prov. viii. 12.

of the influence exercised by the teaching of the Greek Version is seen in Luke xi. 49. If our Lord was speaking of Himself as ἡ σοφία τοῦ θεοῦ that sent its Prophets and Apostles into the world and sent them in vain, then we have a direct indication that He sought to lead His disciples to identify Him with the personal Wisdom of whom such great things are said in Prov. viii., and who utters a like complaint (Prov. i. 20–33). If, however, the Wisdom of God be taken as the title of some lost book, the inference is that the teaching of the Book of Proverbs had impressed itself so deeply on the minds of the Jews of Palestine no less than on those of Alexandria as to give rise there also to a "Sapiential" literature in which Wisdom appeared as the sender of those Apostles and Prophets, on whom, as its foundation, the Church was to be built. If, further, we take in the thought that our Lord's representations of His work, as they were determined, on one side, by the Messianic language of Isaiah, were influenced, on another, by the teaching of chs. viii., ix., the invitation in ix. 5 may be the source from whence flowed the deeper parable of John vi. and of the Last Supper; the "house" which Wisdom built, with its στῦλοι ἑπτὰ (ix. 1), the starting-point of the thought that the Church is the "house of God" (1 Tim. iii. 15), "built" upon the rock (Matt. xvi. 18) of the Apostles as the στῦλοι of that house (Gal. ii. 9 ; 1 Tim. iii. 15) ; and the feast which she prepared (ix. 2, 3) the origin of the parable of the Wedding Feast.

Thus, also, may be explained the stress which St. Paul lays on the fact that Christ Jesus ἐγενήθη ἡμῖν σοφία ἀπὸ θεοῦ (1 Cor. i 30), that He is θεοῦ σοφία (1 Cor. i. 24), that in Him are hid "all the treasures of wisdom and knowledge" (Col. ii. 3). Its influence on Patristic theology is shewn by the prominence given to Prov. viii. 22 (see note) throughout the Arian controversy ; and more remote after-growths of the Greek version of this book, may be noted in the Achamoth, or Σοφία, of the Gnostic systems of Basilides and Valentinus, in the church dedicated by Constantine to the Divine Wisdom, in the retention of that name by Justinian when he built the temple which, as the Mosque of Santa Sophia, still attracts the admiration of Christendom, and lastly, in the commonness of the personal name Sophia, the only one of its class that has become popular, while others, such as Irene, Agape, Pistis, Dikaiosyne, have fallen almost or altogether into oblivion.

The direct use of the Book of Proverbs in the New Testament presents some peculiar features. Quotations from it are not very numerous, and are brought in, not with such words as γέγραπται, ἡ γραφὴ λέγει, or as coupled with the name of Solomon, but as current and familiar sayings, as if the Book had been used generally in education and its maxims impressed upon the memory. In almost all cases the quotations are from the LXX. Version, in some instances even where it differs widely from the Hebrew. It will be worth while, as the circumstances just mentioned often hinder the quotations or allusive references from attracting the attention of the English reader, to refer to some, at least, of the more striking examples in parallel columns.[6]

The familiarity of the New Testament writers with the Greek version of the Book is, however, shewn in other ways. Over and above their use of the same ethical terminology (σοφία, σύνεσις, φρόνησις, ἐπίγνωσις θεοῦ, αἴσθησις), its influence is to be traced in their choice of a word which occupies a prominent position in the vocabulary of Christendom. In Proverbs prophetic stress is laid on the φόβος θεοῦ as the ἀρχὴ σοφίας, the groundwork of all virtues : the word occurs thirteen times, to say nothing of the parallel passages in Pss. xix. 9, xxxiv. 11, cxi. 10. It might have been expected that it would be found not less prominent in the teaching of the New Testament. There, however, it is found but seldom (Acts ix. 31 ; 2 Cor. v. 11 ; 2 Cor. vii. 1 ; Eph. v. 21). It is not difficult to see why the old phrase was felt to be no longer adequate. In proportion as Κύριος came to be identified in men's minds with the Lord Jesus, and love in return for His love the one constraining motive, would there seem something harsh and jarring in a phrase which would come to them as equivalent to "the fear of

Christ." Happily the LXX. version of the Book of Proverbs supplied also the synonym that was needed. In Prov. i. 7 there is an alternative rendering, standing in juxtaposition to the other, viz., εὐσέβεια ; εὐσέβεια εἰς θεὸν ἀρχὴ αἰσθήσεως. The word occurs also in xiii. 11, and in Isai. xi. 2, where also it stands together with an alternative rendering πνεῦμα φόβου θεοῦ. The substantive, and yet more the adjective εὐσεβὴς, occurs with greater frequency in the Apocryphal books, especially in Ecclesiasticus. The way was thus prepared for the prominence which the word gains, just as the necessity was beginning to be felt, in the latest Epistles of the New Testament. It occurs ten times in the Pastoral Epistles of St. Paul, and four times in 2 Peter ; Acts iii. 12 (where the A.V. gives "holiness"), being the only other passage. The temper of devoutness, reverence, godliness, had thus taken the place in Christian terminology of the older "fear of the Lord."

For the most part the choice of the Greek equivalents for the more prominent ethical or philosophical terms of the Proverbs is singularly felicitous. The history of the dominant word of the Book (Chochmah, or more commonly in the plural, Chochmoth, Wisdom) is indeed almost an exact parallel to that of the Σοφία by which it was rendered. As used in the earlier Books of the Old Testament (Exod. xxviii. 3, xxxv. 10, 31, 35, xxxvi. 1) it, or its cognate adjective, is applied to the wisdom of those who had the skill or art which was required for the ornamentation of the Tabernacle. We have traces of a higher application in Deut. iv. 6, xxxiv. 9. As used of the wisdom of Solomon in 1 Kings,

---

[6] The student should compare the Greek of

iii. 11, 12	with	Heb. xii. 5, 6.
iii. 34	,,	Jas. iv. 6.
iv. 26	,,	Heb. xii. 13.
xi. 31	,,	1 Pet. iv. 18.
xiii. 7	,,	2 Cor. vi. 10.
xxii. 8	,,	2 Cor. ix. 7.
xxii. 8	,,	Gal. vi. 7.
xxiv. 21	,,	1 Pet. ii. 17.
xxv. 7	,,	Luke xiv. 10.
xxv. 21	,,	Rom. xii. 20.
xxvi. 11	,,	2 Pet. ii. 22.
xxvii. 1.	,,	James iv. 14, 16.

xxx. 4 (xxiv. 27 in LXX.). τίς ἀνέβη εἰς τὸν οὐρανὸν καὶ κατέβη with John iii. 13.

and throughout Job and the Psalms, as in the Proverbs, the higher prevails exclusively. So, in like manner, Aristotle describes the gradual elevation of the Greek σοφὸς, how it was first applied to sculptors like Pheidias and Polycleitos, how σοφία thus came to be known as ἀρετὴ τέχνης, then became equivalent to the highest accuracy in all things, and finally was thought of as οὐδεμίας γενέσεως, separated altogether from the idea of art-production. So too the use of φρόνησις for a Hebrew word indicating the power which divides, discerns, distinguishes, is appropriate if the chief office of φρόνησις be τὰ καθ' ἕκαστα γνωρίζειν. The general choice of αἴσθησις rather than ἐπιστήμη for the rendering of the equivalent Hebrew word shewed that they recognized the essentially practical character of the knowledge of which the Proverbs spoke, as perceiving the right thing to be done, and the right word to be said, in each detail of life.

Lastly, may be noted here some salient features of this Greek Version.

(a) In not a few places it adds to the existing Hebrew; the addition sometimes having the character of an alternative rendering, sometimes consisting of entirely new matter.[7]

(b) Sometimes the insertions or variations have the character of an exegetical gloss, toning down or making more explicit what might seem doubtful or misleading in the original.[8]

The arrangement of the closing chapters in the Greek Version also presents striking peculiarities, the whole of ch. xxx. and xxxi. ,1–9 being inserted after ch. xxiv. 22, as part of the same chapter, and the acrostic description of the true wife ending the book as ch. xxix. The most probable explanation of the transposition is that it originated in some accidental dislocation in the MS. from which the translation was made.

---

[7] *E.g.* consult the Greek of i. 7 ; iv. 27; vi. 8 ; vii. 22 : after ix. 12 ; ix. ad fin.; xi. 14 ; xvi. 5 ; xviii. 8 (substituted for the Hebrew); xix. 13 (do.) ; xxiii. 31 ; xxiv. 21 ; xxvii. 16 (substituted for the Hebrew); xxx. 31 (apparently a paraphrase for the Hebrew).

[8] *E.g.* i. 28; ii. 16; iii. 9; xiii. 11; xvi. 4 (as an alternative rendering); xvii. 1; xxi. 9; xxvii. 19; xxvii. 22; xxx. 19.

THE

PROVERBS.

Chap. 1. THE [a]proverbs of Solomon the son of David, king of Israel;

2 To know wisdom and instruction;
To perceive the words of understanding;

3 To [b]receive the instruction of wisdom,
Justice, and judgment, and [1]equity;

4 To give subtilty to the [c]simple,
To the young man knowledge and [2]discretion.

5 [d]A wise *man* will hear, and will increase learning;
And a man of understanding shall attain unto wise counsels:

6 To understand a proverb, and [3]the interpretation;
The words of the wise, and their [e]dark sayings.

a 1 K. 4. 32.
ch. 10. 1.
& 25. 1.
Eccl. 12. 9.

b ch. 2. 1, 9.

c ch. 9. 4.

d ch. 9. 9.

e Ps. 78. 2.

---

[1] Heb. *equities.*   [2] Or, *advisement.*   [3] Or, *an eloquent speech.*

I.-IX. This long exhortation, characterized by the frequent recurrence of the words "My son," is of the nature of a preface to the collection of the "Proverbs of Solomon" (x. 1). On i. 1-7, see Introd. p. 340.

2. The writer's purpose is to educate. He is writing what might be called an ethical handbook for the young, though not for the young only. Of all Books in the Old Testament this is the one which we may think of as most distinctively educational. A comparison of it with a like manual, the "Sayings of the Fathers," in the Mishna, would help the student to measure the difference between Scriptural and Rabbinic teaching.

wisdom] The power by which human personality reaches its highest spiritual perfection, by which all lower elements are brought into harmony with the highest, is presently personified as life-giving and creative. Cp. Job xxviii. 23 &c., notes.

instruction] i.e. Discipline or training, the practical complement of the more speculative wisdom.

understanding] The power of distinguishing right from wrong, truth from its counterfeit. The three words σοφία, παιδεία, φρόνησις (LXX.), express very happily the relation of the words in the Heb.

3. *wisdom*] Not the same word as in *v.* 2; better, perhaps, **thoughtfulness.**

justice] Rather, **righteousness.** The word in the Hebrew includes the ideas of truth and beneficence as well as "justice."

judgment] The teaching of the Proverbs is to lead us to pass a right sentence upon human actions, whether our own or another's.

equity] In the Heb. (see marg.) the plural is used, and expresses the many varying forms and phases of the one pervading principle.

4. This verse points out the two classes for which the Book will be useful: (1) the "simple," literally the "open," the openhearted, the minds ready to receive impressions for good or evil (*v.* 22); and (2) the "young," who need both knowledge and discipline. To these the teacher offers the "subtilty," which may turn to evil (Exod. xxi. 14) and become as the wisdom of the serpent (Gen. iii. 1), but which also takes its place, as that wisdom does, among the highest moral gifts (Matt. x. 16); the "knowledge" of good and evil; and the "discretion," or **discernment,** which sets a man on his guard, and keeps him from being duped by false advisers. The LXX. renderings, πανουργία for "subtilty," αἴσθησις for "knowledge," ἔννοια for "discretion," are interesting as shewing the endeavour to find exact parallels for the Hebrew in the terminology of Greek ethics.

5. But it is not for the young only that he writes. The "man of understanding" may gain "wise counsels," literally, the power to "steer" his course rightly on the dangerous seas of life. This "steersmanship," it may be noted, is a word almost peculiar to Proverbs (cp. "counsel" in xi. 14, xii. 5, xxiv. 6).

6. The Book has yet a further scope; these proverbs are to form a habit of mind. To gain through them the power of entering into the deeper meaning of other proverbs, is the end kept in view. Cp. Matt. xiii.

The rendering "interpretation" spoils the parallelism of the two clauses, and fails to express the Hebrew. In Hab. ii. 6, it is rendered "taunting proverb." Here "riddle" or "enigma" would better express the meaning.

f ch. 9. 10.
Eccl. 12. 13.

g ch. 4. 1.
& 6. 20.

h ch. 3. 22.

i Gen. 39. 7,
&c.
Ps. 1. 1.
Eph. 5. 11.
k Jer. 5. 26.

l Ps. 28. 1.
& 143. 7.

m Ps. 1. 1.
ch. 4. 14.
n Ps.119.101.
o Isai. 59. 7.
Rom. 3. 15.

p ch. 15. 27.
1 Tim. 6. 10.

7 *f*The fear of the LORD *is* ¹the beginning of knowledge:
But fools despise wisdom and instruction.
8 *g*My son, hear the instruction of thy father,
And forsake not the law of thy mother:
9 For *h*they *shall be* ²an ornament of grace unto thy head,
And chains about thy neck.

10 My son, if sinners entice thee, *i*consent thou not.
11 If they say, Come with us, let us *k*lay wait for blood,
Let us lurk privily for the innocent without cause:
12 Let us swallow them up alive as the grave;
And whole, *l*as those that go down into the pit:
13 We shall find all precious substance,
We shall fill our houses with spoil:
14 Cast in thy lot among us;—let us all have one purse:
15 My son, *m*walk not thou in the way with them;
*n*Refrain thy foot from their path:
16 *o*For their feet run to evil,—and make haste to shed blood.
17 Surely in vain the net is spread ³in the sight of any bird.
18 And they lay wait for their *own* blood;
They lurk privily for their *own* lives.
19 *p*So *are* the ways of every one that is greedy of gain;
Which taketh away the life of the owners thereof.

¹ Or, *the principal part.*
² Heb. *an adding.*
³ Heb. *in the eyes of every thing that hath a wing.*

---

7. The beginning of wisdom is found in the temper of reverence and awe. The fear of the finite in the presence of the Infinite, of the sinful in the presence of the Holy (cp. Job xlii. 5, 6), this for the Israelite was the starting-point of all true wisdom. In the Book of Job (xxviii. 28) it appears as an oracle accompanied by the noblest poetry. In Ps. cxi. 10 it comes as the choral close of a Temple hymn. Here it is the watchword of a true ethical education. This fear has no "torment," and is compatible with child-like love. But this and not love is the "*beginning*" of wisdom." Through successive stages and by the discipline of life, love blends with it and makes it perfect.

9. To the Israelite's mind no signs or badges of joy or glory were higher in worth than the garland round the head, the gold chain round the neck, worn by kings and the favourites of kings (Gen. xli. 42; Dan. v. 29).

10. The first great danger which besets the simple and the young is that of evil companionship. The only safety is to be found in the power of saying,—"No," to all such invitations.

11. The temptation against which the teacher seeks to guard his disciple is that of joining a band of highway robbers. The "vain men" who gathered round Jephthah (Judg. xi. 3), the lawless or discontented who came to David in Adullam (1 S. xxii. 2), the bands of robbers who infested every part of the country in the period of the New Testament, and against whom every Roman governor had to wage incessant war, shew how deeply rooted the evil was in Palestine. Cp. Ps. x. 7, 10 note.

without cause] Better, **in vain;** most modern commentators join the words with "innocent," and interpret them after Job i. 9. The evil-doers deride their victims as being righteous "in vain." They get nothing by it. It does them no good.

12. *i.e.* "We will be as all-devouring as Sheol. The destruction of those we attack shall be as sudden as that of those who go down quickly into the pit." Some render the latter clause, **and upright men as those that go down to the pit.** "Pit" here is a synonym for Sheol, the great cavernous depth, the shadow-world of the dead.

13, 14. The second form of temptation (see *v.* 10 note) appeals to the main attraction of the robber-life, its wild communism, the sense of equal hazards and equal hopes.

17. Strictly speaking, this is the first proverb (*i.e.* similitude) in the Book; a proverb which has received a variety of interpretations. The true meaning seems to be as follows: "For in vain, to no purpose, is the net spread out openly. Clear as the warning is, it is in vain. The birds still fly in. So the great net of God's judgments is spread out, open to the eyes of all, and yet the doers of evil, wilfully blind, still rush into it." Others take the words as pointing to the failure of the plans of the evil-doers against the innocent (the "bird"): others, again, interpret the proverb of the young man who thinks that he at least shall not fall into the snares laid for him, and so goes blindly into them.

19. Not robbery only, but all forms of covetousness are destructive of true life.

20 [1]q Wisdom crieth without ; — she uttereth her voice in the
  streets :
21 She crieth in the chief place of concourse, in the openings of the
  gates :
In the city she uttereth her words, *saying*,
22 How long. ye simple ones, will ye love simplicity ?
And the scorners delight in their scorning,
And fools hate knowledge ?
23 Turn you at my reproof :
Behold, r I will pour out my spirit unto you,
I will make known my words unto you.
24 s Because I have called, and ye refused ;
I have stretched out my hand, and no man regarded ;
25 But ye t have set at nought all my counsel,
And would none of my reproof :
26 u I also will laugh at your calamity ;
I will mock when your fear cometh ;
27 When x your fear cometh as desolation,
And your destruction cometh as a whirlwind ,
When distress and anguish cometh upon you.
28 y Then shall they call upon me, but I will not answer ;
They shall seek me early, but they shall not find me :
29 For that they z hated knowledge,
And did not a choose the fear of the LORD :
30 b They would none of my counsel :
They despised all my reproof.
31 Therefore c shall they eat of the fruit of their own way,
And be filled with their own devices.

Marginal references: q ch. 8. 1, &c. & 9. 3. John 7. 37. r Joel 2. 28. s Isai. 65. 12. & 66. 4. Jer. 7. 13. Zech. 7. 11. t Ps. 107. 11. ver. 30. Luke 7. 30. u Ps. 2. 4. x ch. 10. 24. y Job 27. 9. & 35. 12. Isai. 1. 15. Jer. 11. 11. & 14. 12. Ezek. 8. 18. Mic. 3. 4. Zech. 7. 13, Jam. 4. 3. z Job 21. 14. ver. 22. a Ps.119.173. b ver. 25. Ps. 81. 11. c Job 4. 8. ch. 14. 14. & 22. 8. Isai. 3. 11. Jer. 6. 19.

[1] Heb. *Wisdoms*, that is, *Excellent wisdom*.

20. Wisdom is personified. In the Hebrew the noun is a feminine plural (see p. 349), as though this Wisdom were the queen of all wisdoms, uniting in herself all their excellences. She lifts up her voice, not in solitude, but in the haunts of men "without," *i.e.* outside the walls, in the streets, at the highest point of all places of concourse, in the open space of the gates where the elders meet and the king sits in judgment, in the heart of the city itself (*v.* 21) ; through sages, lawgivers, teachers, and yet more through life and its experiences, she preaches to mankind. Socrates said that the fields and the trees taught him nothing, but that he found the wisdom he was seeking in his converse with the men whom he met as he walked in the streets and *agora* of Athens.

22. Cp. Ps. i. 1 note. (1) The "simple," lit. *open*, fatally open to evil ; (2) the "scorners," mocking at all good ; lastly (3) the "fools" in the sense of being hardened, obstinate, perverse, hating the knowledge they have rejected.

23. The teaching of Divine Wisdom is essentially the same as that of the Divine Word (John vii. 38, 39). "Turning," repentance and conversion, this is what she calls the simple to. The promise of the Spirit is also like His (John xiv. 26). And

with the spirit there are to be also the "words" of Wisdom. Not the "spirit" alone, nor "words" alone, but both together, each doing its appointed work—this is the divine instrumentality for the education of such as will receive it.

24. The threats and warnings of Wisdom are also foreshadowings of the teaching of Jesus. There will come a time when "too late" shall be written on all efforts, on all remorse. Cp. Matt. xxv. 10, 30.

26. Cp. marg. ref. The scorn and derision with which men look on pride and malice, baffled and put to shame, has something that answers to it in the Divine Judgment. It is, however, significant that in the fuller revelation of the mind and will of the Father in the person of the Son no such language meets us. Sadness, sternness, severity, there may be, but, from first to last, no word of mere derision.

27. *desolation*] Better, **tempest**. The rapid gathering of the clouds, the rushing of the mighty winds, are the fittest types of the suddenness with which in the end the judgment of God shall fall on those who look not for it. Cp. Matt. xxiv. 29 &c. ; Luke xvii. 24.

29–31. This is no arbitrary sentence. The fault was all along their own. The fruit of their own ways is death.

32 For the ¹turning away of the simple shall slay them,
   And the prosperity of fools shall destroy them.
d Ps. 25. 12,
13.
33 But *ᵈ*whoso hearkeneth unto me shall dwell safely,
e Ps. 112. 7.
   And *ᵉ*shall be quiet from fear of evil.

CHAP. 2. MY son, if thou wilt receive my words,
a ch. 4. 21.
& 7. 1.
   And *ᵃ*hide my commandments with thee;
2 So that thou incline thine ear unto wisdom,
   And apply thine heart to understanding;
3 Yea, if thou criest after knowledge,
   And ²liftest up thy voice for understanding;
b ch. 3. 14.
4 *ᵇ*If thou seekest her as silver,
   And searchest for her as *for* hid treasures;
5 Then shalt thou understand the fear of the LORD,
   And find the knowledge of God.
c 1 K. 3. 9,
12.
Jam. 1. 5.
6 *ᶜ*For the LORD giveth wisdom:
   Out of his mouth *cometh* knowledge and understanding.
7 He layeth up sound wisdom for the righteous:
d Ps. 84. 11.
ch. 30. 5.
   ᵈHe is a buckler to them that walk uprightly.
8 He keepeth the paths of judgment,
e 1 Sam. 2. 9.
Ps. 66. 9.
   And *ᵉ*preserveth the way of his saints.
9 Then shalt thou understand righteousness, and judgment,
   And equity; *yea*, every good path.
10 When wisdom entereth into thine heart,
   And knowledge is pleasant unto thy soul;
11 Discretion shall preserve thee,
f ch. 6. 22.
   *f*Understanding shall keep thee ·
12 To deliver thee from the way of the evil *man*,
   From the man that speaketh froward things;
13 Who leave the paths of uprightness,

¹ Or, *ease of the simple.*   ² Heb. *givest thy voice.*

---

32. *turning*] Wisdom had called the simple to "turn," and they had turned, but it was "away" from her. For "prosperity" read **carelessness**. Not outward prosperity, but the temper which it too often produces, the easy-going indifference to higher truths, is that which destroys.

II. Now in the Divine order comes the promise (*v.* 5). The conditions of its fulfilment are stated in *vv.* 1–4 in four sets of parallel clauses, each with some shade of distinct meaning. Thus not "receiving" only, but "hiding" or treasuring up—not the "ear" only, but the "heart"— not the mere "cry," but the eager "lifting up the voice."

4. Note the illustrations. (1) Contact with Phœnician commerce, and joint expeditions in ships of Tarshish (see Ps. lxxii. 10 note), had made the Israelites familiar with the risks and the enterprise of the miner's life. Cp. Job xxviii. (2) The treasure hid in a field, is the second point of comparison. Such treasure-seeking has always been characteristic of the East. Cp. Matt. xiii. 44.

5. The promise. The highest blessedness is to know God (John xvii. 3). If any distinction between "the LORD" (Jehovah)

and "God" (Elohim) can be pressed here, it is that in the former the personality, in the latter the glory, of the Divine nature is prominent.

6. Men do not gain wisdom by any efforts of their own, but God gives it according to the laws of His own goodness.

7. *sound wisdom*] "Soundness," an idea which passes on into that of health and safety. Cp. "sound doctrine" in 1 Tim. i. 10; 2 Tim. iv. 3.

8. *saints*] The devout and God-fearing. Cp. Ps. lxxxv. 8 &c. The occurrence of the word here, in a Book that became more and more prominent as prophetic utterances ceased, probably helped to determine its application in the period of the Maccabean struggles to those who specially claimed for themselves the title of "devout" (*Chasidim* the Ἀσιδαῖοι of 1 Macc. vii. 13).

10. Another picture of the results of living in the fear of the Lord. Not that to which it leads a man, but that from which it saves him, is brought into view. Notice also that it is one thing for wisdom to find entrance into the soul, another to be welcomed as a "pleasant" guest.

12–15. The evil-doers here include not robbers and murderers only (i. 10–16), but

To ^gwalk in the ways of darkness;
14 Who ^hrejoice to do evil,
  And ⁱdelight in the frowardness of the wicked;
15 ^kWhose ways *are* crooked,
  And *they* froward in their paths:
16 To deliver thee from ^lthe strange woman,
  ^m*Even* from the stranger *which* flattereth with her words:
17 ⁿWhich forsaketh the guide of her youth,
  And forgetteth the covenant of her God.
18 For ^oher house inclineth unto death,
  And her paths unto the dead.
19 None that go unto her return again,
  Neither take they hold of the paths of life.
20 That thou mayest walk in the way of good *men*,
  And keep the paths of the righteous.
21 ^pFor the upright shall dwell in the land,
  And the perfect shall remain in it.
22 ^qBut the wicked shall be cut off from the earth,
  And the transgressors shall be ¹rooted out of it.

Chap. 3. MY son, forget not my law;
  ^aBut let thine heart keep my commandments:
2 For length of days, and ²long life,

g John 3. 19, 20.
h ch. 10. 23.
Jer. 11. 15.
i Rom. 1. 32.
k Ps. 125. 5.

l ch. 5. 20.

m ch. 5. 3.
& 6. 24.
& 7. 5.
n See Mal. 2. 14, 15.
o ch. 7. 27.

p Ps. 37. 29.

q Job 18. 17.
Ps. 37. 28.
& 104. 35.

a Deut. 8. 1.
& 30. 16, 20.

¹ Or, *plucked up.*   ² Heb. *years of life.*

all who leave the straight path and the open day for crooked ways, perverse counsels, deeds of darkness. " To delight &c." (*v.* 14) is the lowest depth of all.

16. The second great evil, the warnings against which are frequent (see marg. reff.). Two words are used to describe the class. (1) " The strange woman" is one who does not belong to the family, one who by birth is outside the Covenant of Israel. (2) "The stranger" is none other than a foreigner. It is the word used of the "strange" wives of Solomon (1 K. xi. 1, 8), and of those of the Jews who returned from Babylon (Ezra x. *passim*). The two words together, in connexion with those which follow, and which imply at once marriage and a profession of religious faith, point to some interesting facts in the social history of Israel. Whatever form the sin here referred to had assumed before the monarchy (and the Book of Judges testifies to its frequency), the intercourse with Phœnicians and other nations under Solomon had a strong tendency to increase it. The king's example would naturally be followed, and it probably became a fashion to have *foreign* wives and concubines. At first, it would seem, this was accompanied by some show of proselytism (*v.* 17); but the old heathen leaven presently broke out; the sensual worship of other gods led the way to a life of harlotry. The stringent laws of the Mosaic code (Lev. xix. 29, xxi. 9; Deut. xxiii. 18) probably deterred the women of Israel from that sin, and led to a higher standard of purity among them than prevailed among other nations.

Most interpreters have, however, gene-ralized the words as speaking of any adulteress. The LXX. as if reluctant to speak of facts so shameful, has allegorized them, and seen in the temptress the personification of "evil counsel."

17. *the guide of her youth*] Better, **the familiar friend** (cp. xvi. 28, xvii. 9). The "friend" is, of course, the husband, or the man to whom the strange woman first belonged as a recognized concubine. Cp. Jer. iii. 4

the covenant of her God] The sin of the adulteress is not against man only but against the Law of God, against His Covenant. The words point to some religious formula of espousals. Cp. Mal. ii. 14.

18. The house of the adulteress is as Hades, the realm of death, haunted by the spectral shadows of the dead (Rephaim, see Ps. lxxxviii. 10 note), who have perished there.

19. The words describe more than the fatal persistency of the sinful habit when once formed. A resurrection from that world of the dead to "the paths of life" is all but impossible.

20. The previous picture of shame and sin is brought before the disciple as an incentive to a better course.

21, 22. Noticeable here is the Hebrew love of home and love of country. To "dwell in the land " is (cp. Ex. xx. 12; Levit. xxv. 18 &c.) the highest blessing for the whole people and for individual men. In contrast with it is the life of the sinner cut off from the **land** (not "earth ") of his fathers.

III. 2. Three words carry on the chain

b Ps. 119.
165.

c Ex. 13. 9.
Deut. 6. 8.
ch. 6. 21.
& 7. 3.
d Jer. 17. 1.
2 Cor. 3. 3.
e Ps. 111. 10.
See 1 Sam.
2. 26.
Acts 2. 47.
Rom. 14. 18.
f Ps. 37. 3, 5.
g Jer. 9. 23.
h 1 Ch. 28. 9.
i Jer. 10. 23.
k Rom. 12. 16.
l Job 1. 1.
ch. 16. 6.
m Job 21. 24.
n Ex. 22. 29.
& 23. 19.
& 34. 26.
Deut. 26, 2.
Mal. 3. 10,
Luke 14. 13.
o Deut. 28. 8.
p Ps. 94. 12.
Rev. 3. 19.
q Deut. 8. 5.
r ch. 8. 34,
35.

And *b*peace, shall they add to thee.

3 Let not mercy and truth forsake thee :
  *c*Bind them about thy neck ;
  *d*Write them upon the table of thine heart :
4 *e*So shalt thou find favour and ¹good understanding
  In the sight of God and man.

5 *f*Trust in the LORD with all thine heart ;
  *g*And lean not unto thine own understanding.
6 *h*In all thy ways acknowledge him,
  And he shall *i*direct thy paths.
7 *k*Be not wise in thine own eyes :
  *l*Fear the LORD, and depart from evil.
8 It shall be ²health to thy navel,
  And ³*m*marrow to thy bones.

9 *n*Honour the LORD with thy substance,
  And with the firstfruits of all thine increase :
10 *o*So shall thy barns be filled with plenty,
  And thy presses shall burst out with new wine.

11 *p*My son, despise not the chastening of the LORD ;
  Neither be weary of his correction :
12 For whom the LORD loveth he correcteth ;
  *q*Even as a father the son *in whom* he delighteth.

13 *r*Happy *is* the man *that* findeth wisdom,
  And ⁴the man *that* getteth understanding.

¹ Or, *good success.*   ³ Heb. *watering*, or, *mois-*   ⁴ Heb. *the man* that *draweth*
² Heb. *medicine.*   *tening.*   *out understanding.*

---

of blessings ; (1) "Length of days" (see Ps. xci. 16 note) ; (2) "Years of *life*," *i.e.* of a life worth living (cp. Pss. xxx. 5, xli. 8) ; (3) "Peace ;" tranquillity inward and outward, the serenity of life continuing through old age till death. Cp. 1 Tim. iv. 8.

3. The two elements of a morally perfect character. (1) "Mercy," shutting out all forms of selfishness and hate. (2) "Truth," shutting out all deliberate falsehood, all hypocrisy, conscious or unconscious. The words that follow possibly refer to the Eastern custom of writing sacred names on pieces of papyrus or parchment, and wearing them round the neck, as charms and talismans against evil. Cp., however, 1 Pet. iii. 3, 4.

4. Cp. Luke ii. 52. These are the two conditions of true human growth.

5. In preaching "trust in God" the moralist anticipates the teaching that man is justified by faith. To confide in God's will, the secret of all true greatness, is to rise out of all our anxieties and plans and fears when we think of ourselves as the arbiters of our own fortunes, and so "lean to our own understanding."

6. Not in acts of solemn worship or great crises only, but "in *all* thy ways ;" and then God will make the "path" straight and even.

7. The great hindrance to all true wisdom is the thought that we have already attained it.

8. *navel*] The central region of the body

is taken as the representative of all the vital organs. For "health" we should read **healing**, or, as in the marg. There is probably a reference to the local applications used by the surgery of the period as means of healing.

9. "Substance" points to capital, "increase" to revenue. The LXX. as if to guard against ill-gotten gains being offered as an atonement for the ill-getting, inserts the qualifying words, "honour the Lord from thy *righteous* labours."

10. Cp. marg. ref. This fulness of outward blessings does not exclude the thought of the "chastening" (*v.* 11), without which the discipline of life would be incomplete. "Presses" are the vats of a Roman vineyard, into which the wine flowed through a pipe from the wine-press.

11. *despise...be weary*] The temper is not that of contempt. To struggle impatiently, to fret and chafe, when suffering comes on us, is the danger to which we are exposed when we do not accept it as from the hands of God. Cp. Jonah iv. 9 ; Job v. 17.

12. The first distinct utterance of a truth which has been so full of comfort to many thousands ; it is the summing up of all controversies (cp. John ix. 2) as to the mystery of suffering. The Apostle writing to the Hebrews can find no stronger comfort (Heb. xii. 6) than this ; the Church, in her Visitation Service, has no truer message for the sufferer.

13. The first beatitude of the Proverbs

14 *For the merchandise of it *is* better than the merchandise of silver,
And the gain thereof than fine gold.

15 She *is* more precious than rubies :
And *all the things thou canst desire are not to be compared unto her.

16 *Length of days *is* in her right hand ;
And in her left hand riches and honour.

17 *Her ways *are* ways of pleasantness,
And all her paths *are* peace.

18 She *is* *a tree of life to them that lay hold upon her :
And happy *is every one* that retaineth her.

19 *The LORD by wisdom hath founded the earth ;
By understanding hath he ¹established the heavens.

20 *By his knowledge the depths are broken up,
And *the clouds drop down the dew.

21 My son, let not them depart from thine eyes :
Keep sound wisdom and discretion :

22 So shall they be life unto thy soul,—and *grace to thy neck.

23 *Then shalt thou walk in thy way safely,
And thy foot shall not stumble.

24 *When thou liest down, thou shalt not be afraid :
Yea, thou shalt lie down, and thy sleep shall be sweet.

25 *Be not afraid of sudden fear,
Neither of the desolation of the wicked, when it cometh.

s Job 28. 13.
Ps. 19, 10.
ch. 8. 11, 19.
& 16. 16.

t Matt. 13.
44.

u ch. 8. 18.
1 Tim. 4. 8.

x Matt. 11.
29, 30.

y Gen. 2. 9.
& 3. 22.

z Ps. 104. 24.
& 136. 5.
ch. 8. 27.
Jer. 10. 12.
& 51. 15.
a Gen. 1. 9.
b Deut.33.28.
Job 36. 28.

c ch. 1. 9.

d Ps. 37. 24.
& 91. 11, 12.
ch. 10. 9.
e Lev. 26. 6.
Ps. 3. 5.
& 4. 8.
f Ps. 91. 5.
& 112. 7.

¹ Or, *prepared.*

introduces a new lesson. "Getteth understanding," lit. as in the margin, probably in the sense of "drawing forth from God's store, from the experience of life" (as in viii. 35, xviii. 22). The preciousness of wisdom is dwelt on here, not the use to be made of it.

14. Cp. ii. 4. "Fine gold " is apparently a technical word of that commerce, the native gold in the nugget or the dust.

15. *rubies*] The *peninim* were among the costly articles of traffic, and red or rose-coloured (Lam. iv. 7). The last fact has led some to identify them with coral, or (as in the A.V.) with "rubies." Most commentators, however, have identified them with pearls, which may connect this passage with Matt. vii. 6, xiii. 45. The words of the promise here are almost the echo of 1 K. iii. 11-13.

17. "Ways" and "paths" describe the two kinds of roads, the "highway" and the "byway." In both these he who was guided by Wisdom would walk securely.

18. This and the other references in Proverbs (xi. 30, xiii. 12, xv. 4) are the only allusions in any Book of the Old Testament, after Genesis, to the "tree" itself, or to its spiritual significance. Further, there is the tendency to a half-allegorizing application of that history. "The tree of life" which Adam was not to taste lies open to his children. Wisdom is the "tree of life," giving a true immortality. The symbol entered largely into the religious imagery of Assyria, Egypt, and Persia. Philo, going

a step further, found in the two trees the ideal representatives of speculative knowledge and moral wisdom ; and the same image subserves a higher purpose in the promises and the visions of Rev. ii. 7, xxii. 2.

19. Hitherto Wisdom has been thought of in relation to men. Now the question comes, What is she in relation to God ? and the answer is, that the creative act implies a Divine Wisdom, through which the Divine Will acts. This thought, developed in ch. viii., is the first link in the chain which connects this "Wisdom" with the Divine Word, the LOGOS of St. John's Gospel. Cp. Ps. xxxiii. 6 ; John i. 3. The words of the writer of the Proverbs take their place among the proofs of the dogmatic statements of the Nicene Creed.

20. Cp. Gen. i. 7, vii. 11 ; Job xxxviii. Looking upon the face of Nature, men see two storehouses of the living water, without which it would be waste and barren. From the "depths" rush forth the surging waves, from the "clouds" falls the gentle rain or "dew ;" but both alike are ordered by the Divine Wisdom.

21. *let not them depart*] *i.e.* The wisdom and discretion of the following clause. Keep thine eye on them, as one who watches over priceless treasures.

25. Under the form of this strong prohibition there is an equally strong promise. So safe will all thy ways be that to fear will be a sin.

26 For the LORD shall be thy confidence,
    And shall keep thy foot from being taken.

g Rom. 13.7.
Gal. 6. 10.

27 *g*Withhold not good from ¹them to whom it is due,
    When it is in the power of thine hand to do *it*.

h Lev. 19.13.
Deut. 24. 15.

28 *h*Say not unto thy neighbour,
    Go, and come again, and to morrow I will give;
    When thou hast it by thee.

29 ²Devise not evil against thy neighbour,
    Seeing he dwelleth securely by thee.

i Rom.12.18.

30 *i*Strive not with a man without cause,
    If he have done thee no harm.

k Ps. 37. 1.
& 73. 3.
ch. 24. 1.
l Ps. 25. 14.

31 *k*Envy thou not ³the oppressor,—and choose none of his ways.
32 For the froward *is* abomination to the LORD :
    *l*But his secret *is* with the righteous.

m Lev. 26.
14, &c.
Ps. 37. 22.
Mal. 2. 2.
n Ps. 1. 3.
o Jam. 4. 6.
1 Pet. 5. 5.

33 *m*The curse of the LORD *is* in the house of the wicked :
    But *n*he blesseth the habitation of the just.
34 *o*Surely he scorneth the scorners :
    But he giveth grace unto the lowly.
35 The wise shall inherit glory :
    But shame ⁴shall be the promotion of fools.

a Ps. 34. 11.
ch. 1. 8.

CHAP. 4. HEAR, *a*ye children, the instruction of a father,
    And attend to know understanding.
2 For I give you good doctrine,—forsake ye not my law.
3 For I was my father's son,

b 1 Ch. 29. 1.

    *b*Tender and only *beloved* in the sight of my mother.

---

¹ Heb. *the owners thereof*.
² Or, *Practise no evil*.
³ Heb. *a man of violence*.
⁴ Heb. *exalteth the fools*.

27-35. A marked change in style. The continuous exhortation is replaced by a series of maxims.

from them to whom it is due] Lit. as in the marg. The precept expresses the great Scriptural thought that the so-called possession of wealth is but a stewardship; that the true owners of what we call our own are those to whom, with it, we may do good. Not to relieve them is a breach of trust.

28. Procrastination is specially fatal to the giving impulse. The LXX. adds the caution, " for thou knowest not what the morrow will bring forth."

29. *securely*] *i.e.* " With full trust," without care or suspicion. Cp. Judg. xviii. 7, 27.

31. A protest against the tendency to worship success, to think the lot of the " man of violence " enviable, and therefore to be chosen.

32. The true nature of such success. That which men admire is to Jehovah an abomination. His "secret," *i.e.* His close, intimate communion as of "friend with friend," is with the righteous.

33. The thought, like that which appears in Zech. v. 3, 4, and pervades the tragedies of Greek drama, is of a curse, an Atè, dwelling in a house from generation to generation, the source of ever-recurring woes. There is, possibly, a contrast between the " house " or " palace " of the rich oppressor and the lowly shepherd's hut, the

" sheep-cote " (2 S. vii. 8) ennobled only by its upright inhabitants.

34. *Surely*] Better, **If he scorneth the scorners**, *i.e.* Divine scorn of evil is the complement, and, as it were, the condition, of Divine bounty to the lowly (cp. marg. reff. and i. 26 note).

35. The marg. conveys the thought that " fools " glory in that which is indeed their shame. Others take the clause as meaning " every fool takes up shame," *i.e.* gains nothing but that.

IV. 1. The words " ye children " indicate as usual a new section returning, after the break of iii. 27-35, to the old strain of fatherly counsel.

2. *doctrine*] Knowledge orally given and received.

3. Probably the words of Solomon himself, who looks back from his glorious throne and his matured wisdom to the training which was the starting point. The part taken by Bathsheba in 1 K. i., no less than the friendship between her and Nathan, indicates that a mother's training might well have laid the foundation of the king's future wisdom. Among the Israelites and Egyptians alone, of the nations of the old world, was the son's reverence for the mother placed side by side with that which he owed to his father.

" Only *beloved*," lit. " only," but the word is used apparently (as in Gen. xxii. 2, 12)

4 ^cHe taught me also, and said unto me,
Let thine heart retain my words:
^dKeep my commandments, and live.

5 ^eGet wisdom, get understanding:
Forget *it* not; neither decline from the words of my mouth.

6 Forsake her not, and she shall preserve thee:
^fLove her, and she shall keep thee.

7 ^gWisdom *is* the principal thing; *therefore* get wisdom:
And with all thy getting get understanding.

8 ^hExalt her, and she shall promote thee:
She shall bring thee to honour, when thou dost embrace her.

9 She shall give to thine head ⁱan ornament of grace:
¹A crown of glory shall she deliver to thee.

10 Hear, O my son, and receive my sayings;
^kAnd the years of thy life shall be many.

11 I have taught thee in the way of wisdom;
I have led thee in right paths.

12 When thou goest, ^lthy steps shall not be straitened;
^mAnd when thou runnest, thou shalt not stumble.

13 Take fast hold of instruction; let *her* not go:
Keep her; for she *is* thy life.

14 ⁿEnter not into the path of the wicked,
And go not in the way of evil *men*.

15 Avoid it, pass not by it,—turn from it, and pass away.

16 ^oFor they sleep not, except they have done mischief;
And their sleep is taken away, unless they cause *some* to fall.

17 For they eat the bread of wickedness,
And drink the wine of violence.

18 ^pBut the path of the just ^q*is* as the shining light,
That shineth more and more unto the perfect day.

19 ^rThe way of the wicked *is* as darkness:
They know not at what they stumble.

20 My son, attend to my words;
Incline thine ear unto my sayings.

21 ^sLet them not depart from thine eyes;
^tKeep them in the midst of thine heart.

Marginal references:

c Eph. 6. 4.

d ch. 7. 2.
e ch. 2. 2, 3.

f 2 Thess. 2. 10.
g Matt. 13. 44.
Luke 10. 42.
h 1 Sam. 2. 30.

i ch. 1. 9.
& 3. 22.

k ch. 3. 2.

l Ps. 18. 36.
m Ps. 91. 11, 12.

n Ps. 1. 1.
ch. 1. 10. 15.

o Ps. 36. 4.
Isai. 57. 20.

p Matt. 5. 14. 45.
Phil. 2. 15.
q 2 Sam. 23. 4.
r 1 Sam. 2. 9.
Job 18. 5, 6.
Isai. 59. 9, 10.
Jer. 23. 12.

s ch. 3. 3, 21.
t ch. 2. 1.

¹ Or, *she shall compass thee with a crown of glory.*

---

in its derived sense, " beloved like an only son." The Vulg. gives " unigenitus." Cp. the words applied to our Lord, as the " only begotten" (John i. 14), the " beloved " (Eph. i. 6).

4-20. The counsel which has come to him, in substance, from his father. Cp. it with 2 S. xxiii. 2 &c.; 1 Chr. xxviii. 9, xxix. 17; Pss. xv., xxiv., xxxvii.

7. Or, "**The beginning of wisdom is**—get wisdom." To seek is to find, to desire is to obtain.

12. The ever-recurring parable of the journey of life. In the way of wisdom the path is clear and open, obstacles disappear; in the quickest activity (" when thou runnest ") there is no risk of falling.

13. *she is thy life*] Another parallel between personified Wisdom in this Book and the Incarnate Wisdom in John i. 4.

16. A fearful stage of debasement. Sin is the condition without which there can be no repose.

17. *i.e.* Bread and wine gained by unjust deeds. Cp. Amos ii. 8. A less probable interpretation is, "They eat wickedness as bread, and drink violence as wine." Cp. Job xv. 16, xxxiv. 7.

18. *shining...shineth*] The two Hebrew words are different; the first having the sense of **bright** or clear. The beauty of a cloudless sunshine growing on, shining as it goes, to the full and perfect day, is chosen as the fittest figure of the ever-increasing brightness of the good man's life. Cp. marg. reff.

19. Cp. our Lord's teaching (John xi. 10, xii. 35).

20. The teacher speaks again in his own person.

22 For they *are* life unto those that find them,
And ^{u1}health to all their flesh.

u ch. 3. 8.
& 12. 18.

23 Keep thy heart ^{2}with all diligence;
For out of it *are* the issues of life.
24 Put away from thee ^{3}a froward mouth,
And perverse lips put far from thee.
25 Let thine eyes look right on,
And let thine eyelids look straight before thee.
26 Ponder the path of thy feet,
And ^{4}let all thy ways be established.

x Deut. 5. 32.
& 28. 14.
Josh. 1. 7.
y Isai. 1. 16.
Rom. 12. 9.

27 ^{x}Turn not to the right hand nor to the left:
^{y}Remove thy foot from evil.

CHAP. 5. MY son, attend unto my wisdom,
And bow thine ear to my understanding:
2 That thou mayest regard discretion,

a Mal. 2. 7.

And *that* thy lips may ^{a}keep knowledge.

b ch. 2. 16.
& 6. 24.
c Ps. 55. 21.
d Eccl. 7. 26.
e Heb. 4. 12.
f ch. 7. 27.

3 ^{b}For the lips of a strange woman drop *as* an honeycomb,
And her ^{5}mouth *is* ^{c}smoother than oil:
4 But her end is ^{d}bitter as wormwood,
^{e}Sharp as a twoedged sword.
5 ^{f}Her feet go down to death;—her steps take hold on hell.
6 Lest thou shouldest ponder the path of life,
Her ways are moveable, *that* thou canst not know *them.*
7 Hear me now therefore, O ye children,
And depart not from the words of my mouth.
8 Remove thy way far from her,
And come not nigh the door of her house:
9 Lest thou give thine honour unto others,
And thy years unto the cruel:
10 Lest strangers be filled with ^{6}thy wealth;
And thy labours *be* in the house of a stranger;

---

^{1} Heb. *medicine.*
^{2} Heb. *above all keeping.*
^{3} Heb. *frowardness of*
*mouth, and perverseness
of lips.*
^{4} Or, *all thy ways shall be*
ordered aright.
^{5} Heb. *palate.*
^{6} Heb. *thy strength.*

---

22. *health*] See iii. 8 note.
23. Better, as in the marg., *i.e.* with more vigilance than men use over aught else. The words that follow carry on the same similitude. The fountains and wells of the East were watched over with special care. The heart is such a fountain, out of it flow the "issues" of life. Shall men let those streams be tainted at the fountainhead?
24–26. Speech turned from its true purpose, the wandering eye that leads on to evil, action hasty and inconsiderate, are the natural results where we do not "above all keeping keep our heart" (*v.* 23).
27. The ever-recurring image of the straight road on which no one ever loses his way represents here as elsewhere the onward course through life of the man who seeks and finds wisdom.
V. 1. The formula of a new counsel, introducing another warning against the besetting sin of youth (ii. 16).
2. *And that thy lips may keep*] Lit. "and thy lips shall keep."
3. *smoother than oil*] The same comparison

is used in marg. ref. to describe the treachery of a false friend.
4. *wormwood*] In Eastern medicine this herb, the Absinthium of Greek and Latin botanists, was looked upon as poisonous rather than medicinal. Cp. Rev. viii. 11.
6. Or (with the LXX. and Vulg.), **Lest she should ponder** (or "She ponders not") **the way of life, her paths move to and fro** (unsteady as an earthquake); **she knows not.** The words describe with a terrible vividness the state of heart and soul which prostitution brings upon its victims; the reckless blindness that will not think, tottering on the abyss, yet loud in its defiant mirth, ignoring the dreadful future.
9. *thine honour*] *i.e.* "The grace and freshness of thy youth" (cp. Hosea xiv. 6: Dan. x. 8). The thought of this is to guard the young man against the sins that stain and mar it. The slave of lust sacrifices "years" that might have been peaceful and happy to one who is merciless.
10. *strangers*] The whole gang of those into whose hands the slave of lust yields himself. The words are significant as

11 And thou mourn at the last,
    When thy flesh and thy body are consumed,
12 And say, How have I *g*hated instruction,
    And my heart *h*despised reproof;
13 And have not obeyed the voice of my teachers,
    Nor inclined mine ear to them that instructed me!
14 I was almost in all evil
    In the midst of the congregation and assembly.
15 Drink waters out of thine own cistern,
    And running waters out of thine own well.
16 Let thy fountains be dispersed abroad,
    And rivers of waters in the streets.
17 Let them be only thine own,—and not strangers' with thee.
18 Let thy fountain be blessed:
    And rejoice with *i*the wife of thy youth.
19 *k Let her be as* the loving hind and pleasant roe;
    Let her breasts ¹satisfy thee at all times;
    And ²be thou ravished always with her love.
20 And why wilt thou, my son, be ravished with *l*a strange woman,
    And embrace the bosom of a stranger?
21 *m*For the ways of man *are* before the eyes of the LORD,
    And he pondereth all his goings.
22 *n*His own iniquities shall take the wicked himself,
    And he shall be holden with the cords of his ³sins.
23 *o*He shall die without instruction;
    And in the greatness of his folly he shall go astray.

CHAP. 6. MY son, *a*if thou be surety for thy friend,
    If thou hast stricken thy hand with a stranger,

g ch. 1. 29.
h ch. 1. 25.
& 12. 1.

i Mal. 2. 14.
k See Cant.
2. 9.
& 4. 5.
& 7. 3.
l ch. 7. 5.
m 2 Chr.16.9.
Job 31. 4.
& 34. 21.
ch. 15. 3.
Jer. 16. 17.
& 32. 19.
Hos. 7. 2.
Heb. 4. 13.
n Ps. 9. 15.
o Job 4. 21.
& 36. 12.
a ch. 11. 15.
& 20. 16.
& 27. 13.

¹ Heb. *water thee.*   ² Heb. *err thou always in her love.*   ³ Heb. *sin.*

shewing that the older punishment of death
(Deut. xxii. 21; Ezek. xvi. 38; John viii. 5)
was not always inflicted, and that the detected adulterer was exposed rather to
indefinite extortion. Besides loss of purity
and peace, the sin, in all its forms, brings
poverty.

11. Yet one more curse is attendant on
impurity. Then, as now, disease was the
penalty of this sin.

12. Bitterer than slavery, poverty, disease, will be the bitterness of self-reproach,
the hopeless remorse that worketh death.

14. The conscience-stricken sinner had
been "almost" given up to every form of
evil in the sight of the whole assembly of
fellow-townsmen; "almost," therefore, condemned to the death which that assembly
might inflict (Lev. xx. 10; Deut. xxii. 22).
The public scandal of the sin is brought in
as its last aggravating feature.

15. The teacher seeks to counteract the
evils of mere sensual passion chiefly by
setting forth the true blessedness of which
it is the counterfeit. The true wife is as a
fountain of refreshment, where the weary
soul may quench its thirst. Even the joy
which is of the senses appears, as in the
Song of Solomon, purified and stainless (see
v. 19 marg. reff.).

16. Wedded love streams forth in blessing

on all around, on children and on neighbours
and in the streets, precisely because the
wife's true love is given to the husband
only.

19. Better, "A loving hind (is she) and
pleasant roe." As in the whole circle of
Arab and Persian poetry the antelope and
the gazelle are the chosen images of beauty,
so they served with equal fitness for the
masculine and feminine types of it. Cp.
the names Tabitha and Dorcas (Acts ix. 36).

20. Emphasis is laid (see ii. 16 note) on
the origin of the beguiler.

21. One more warning. The sin is not
against man, nor dependent on man's detec-
tion only. The secret sin is open before the
eyes of Jehovah. In the balance of His
righteous judgment are weighed all human
acts.

pondereth] Note the recurrence of the
word used of the harlot herself (see *v.* 6
note): she ponders not, God does.

23. The end of the sensual life :—to
"die without instruction," life ended, but
the discipline of life fruitless; to "go astray,"
as if drunk with the greatness of his folly
(the same word is used as for "ravished"
in *v.* 19, see marg.), even to the end. This
is the close of what might have gone **on**
brightening to the perfect day (iv. 18).

VI. 1. *surety*] The "pledge," or security

2 Thou art snared with the words of thy mouth,
  Thou art taken with the words of thy mouth.
3 Do this now, my son, and deliver thyself,
  When thou art come into the hand of thy friend;
  Go, humble thyself ¹and make sure thy friend.

b Ps. 132. 4.   4 *b*Give not sleep to thine eyes,—nor slumber to thine eyelids.
5 Deliver thyself as a roe from the hand *of the hunter*,
  And as a bird from the hand of the fowler.

c Job 12. 7.   6 *c*Go to the ant, thou sluggard;—consider her ways, and be
     wise:
7 Which having no guide, overseer, or ruler,
8 Provideth her meat in the summer,
  And gathereth her food in the harvest.

d ch. 24. 33,   9 *d*How long wilt thou sleep, O sluggard?
31.   When wilt thou arise out of thy sleep?
10 *Yet* a little sleep, a little slumber,
   A little folding of the hands to sleep:

e ch. 10. 4.   11 *e*So shall thy poverty come as one that travelleth,
& 13. 4.   And thy want as an armed man.
& 20. 4.

¹ Or, *so shalt thou prevail with thy friend.*

---

for payment, which *e.g.* David was to bring
back from his brothers (1 Sam. xvii. 18).
So the word was used in the primitive trade
transactions of the early Israelites.

In the warnings against this suretyship in
the Book of Proverbs we may trace the influence of intercourse with the Phœnicians.
The merchants of Tyre and Zidon seem to
have discovered the value of credit as an
element of wealth. A man might obtain
goods, or escape the pressure of a creditor
at an inconvenient season, or obtain a loan
on more favourable terms, by finding security. To give such security might be one
of the kindest offices which one friend could
render to another. Side by side, however,
with a legitimate system of credit there
sprang up, as in later times, a fraudulent
counterfeit. Phœnician or Jewish money-
lenders (the "stranger") were ready to
make their loans to the spendthrift. He
was equally ready to find a companion (the
"friend") who would become his surety.
It was merely a form, just writing a few
words, just "a clasping of the hands" (see
marg. reff.) in token that the obligation was
accepted, and that was all. It would be
unfriendly to refuse. And yet, as the
teacher warns his hearers, there might be,
in that moment of careless weakness, the
first link of a long chain of ignominy, gall-
ing, fretting, wearing, depriving life of all
its peace. The Jewish law of debt, hard
and stern like that of most ancient nations,
might be enforced against him in all its
rigour. Money and land might go, the very
bed under him might be seized, and his garment torn from his back (xx. 16, xxii. 27),
the older and more lenient law (Ex. xxii. 25–
27) having apparently fallen into disuse.
He might be brought into a life-long bondage, subject only to the possible relief of

the year of Jubilee, when the people were
religious enough to remember and observe
it. His wives, his sons, his daughters
might be sharers in that slavery (Neh. v.
3–5). It was doubtful whether he could claim
the privilege which under Ex. xxi. 2 belonged to an Israelite slave that had been
bought. Against such an evil, no warnings
could be too frequent or too urgent.

stricken thy hand] The natural symbol of
the promise to keep a contract; in this case,
to pay another man's debts. Cp. xvii. 18,
xxii. 26; Job xvii. 3; Ezek. xvii. 18.

2. Or, "If thou art snared...if thou art
taken," &c.

3. Better, "Do this now, O my son, and
free thyself when thou hast come into thy
friend's house; go, **bow thyself down** (perhaps "stamp with thy foot," or "hasten"),
press hotly upon thy friend. By persuasion, and if need be, by threats, get back the
bond which thou hast been entrapped
into signing." The "friend" is, as before,
the companion, not the creditor.

6. The warning against the wastefulness
of the prodigal is followed by a warning as
emphatic against the wastefulness of sloth.
The point of comparison with the ant is not
so much the foresight of the insect as its un-
wearied activity during the appointed season, rebuking man's inaction at a special
crisis (*v.* 4). In xxx. 25, the storing, provi-
dent habit of the ant is noticed.

7. The words express the wonder with
which the Hebrew observer looked on the
phenomena of insect-life. "Guide," better
captain, as in Josh. x. 24. The LXX. introduces here a corresponding reference to
the industry of the bee.

11. The similitude is drawn from the two
sources of Eastern terror: the "traveller,"
i.e. "the thief in the night," coming sud-

12 A naughty person, a wicked man,
Walketh with a froward mouth.
13 *f* He winketh with his eyes,—he speaketh with his feet,
14 He teacheth with his fingers;—frowardness *is* in his heart,
g He deviseth mischief continually;—*h* he ¹soweth discord.
15 Therefore shall his calamity come suddenly;
Suddenly shall he *i* be broken *k* without remedy.

16 These six *things* doth the LORD hate:
Yea, seven *are* an abomination ²unto him:
17 ¹³ A proud look, *m* a lying tongue,
And *n* hands that shed innocent blood.
18 *o* An heart that deviseth wicked imaginations,
p Feet that be swift in running to mischief,
19 *q* A false witness *that* speaketh lies,
And he *r* that soweth discord among brethren.

20 *s* My son, keep thy father's commandment,
And forsake not the law of thy mother:
21 *t* Bind them continually upon thine heart,
And tie them about thy neck.
22 *u* When thou goest, it shall lead thee;
When thou sleepest, *x* it shall keep thee;
And *when* thou awakest, it shall talk with thee.
23 *y* For the commandment *is* a ⁴lamp; and the law *is* light;
And reproofs of instruction *are* the way of life:
24 *z* To keep thee from the evil woman,
From the flattery ⁵of the tongue of a strange woman.
25 *a* Lust not after her beauty in thine heart;
Neither let her take thee with her eyelids.
26 For *b* by means of a whorish woman *a man is brought* to a piece of bread:
c And ⁶the adulteress will *d* hunt for the precious life.

f Job 15. 12.
Ps. 35. 19.
ch. 10. 10.
g Mic. 2. 1.
h ver. 19.
i Jer. 19. 11.
k 2 Chr. 36. 16.

l Ps. 18. 27.
& 101. 5.
m Ps. 120. 2, 3.
n Isai. 1. 15.
o Gen. 6. 5.
p Isai. 59. 7.
Rom. 3. 15.
q Ps. 27. 12.
ch. 19. 5, 9.
r ver. 14.
s ch. 1. 8.
Eph. 6. 1.
t ch. 7. 3.
u ch. 3. 23, 24.
x ch. 2. 11.

y Ps. 19. 8.

z ch. 2. 16.
& 5. 3.
& 7. 5.
a Matt. 5. 28.

b ch. 29. 3.

c Gen. 39. 14.
d Ezek. 13. 18.

¹ Heb. *casteth forth.*
² Heb. *of his soul.*
³ Heb. *Haughty eyes.*
⁴ Or, *candle.*
⁵ Or, *of the strange tongue.*
⁶ Heb. *the woman of a man,* or, *a man's wife.*

denly to plunder; the "armed man," lit. "the man of the shield," the armed robber. The habit of indolence is more fatally destructive than these marauders.

12. *A naughty person*] Lit. "a man of Belial," *i.e.* a worthless man (see Deut. xiii. 13 note). This is the portrait of the man who is not to be trusted, whose look and gestures warn against him all who can observe. His speech is tortuous and crafty; his wink tells the accomplice that the victim is already snared; his gestures with foot and hand are half in deceit, and half in mockery.

15. The duper and the dupe shall share the same calamity.

16-19. A new section, but not a new subject. The closing words, "he that soweth discord" (*v.* 19, cp. *v.* 14), lead us to identify the sketch as taken from the same character. With the recognized Hebrew form of climax (see xxx. 15, 18, 24; Amos i. ii.; Job v. 19), the teacher here enumerates six qualities as detestable, and the seventh as worse than all (seven repre-

senting completeness), but all the seven in this instance belong to one man, the man of Belial (*v.* 12).

21-22. The thought of iii. 3 carried a step further. No outward charm, but the law of obedience, shall give safety to the traveller, when he sleeps or when he wakes.

23. Cp. Ps. cxix. 105.

24. *evil woman*] Lit. "woman of evil." In reading what follows, it must be remembered that the warning is against the danger of the sin of the adulterous wife.

25. *eyelids*] Possibly pointing to the Eastern custom of painting the eyes on the outside with *kohl* so as to give brightness and languishing expression.

26. The two forms of evil bring, each of them, their own penalty. By the one a man is brought to such poverty as to beg for "a piece of bread" (cp. 1 S. ii. 36): by the other and more deadly sin he incurs a peril which may affect his life. The second clause is very abrupt and emphatic in the original; "but as for a man's wife;—she hunts for the precious life."

27 Can a man take fire in his bosom,
 And his clothes not be burned?
28 Can one go upon hot coals,—and his feet not be burned?
29 So he that goeth in to his neighbour's wife;
 Whosoever toucheth her shall not be innocent.
30 *Men* do not despise a thief, if he steal
 To satisfy his soul when he is hungry;

e Ex.22.1, 4. 31 But *if* he be found, *e*he shall restore sevenfold;
 He shall give all the substance of his house.

f ch. 7. 7. 32 *But* whoso committeth adultery with a woman *f*lacketh [1]under-
 standing:
 He *that* doeth it destroyeth his own soul.
33 A wound and dishonour shall he get;
 And his reproach shall not be wiped away.
34 For jealousy *is* the rage of a man:
 Therefore he will not spare in the day of vengeance.
35 [2]He will not regard any ransom;
 Neither will he rest content, though thou givest many gifts.

CHAP. 7. MY son, keep my words,

a ch. 2. 1. And *a*lay up my commandments with thee.
b Lev. 18. 5. 2 *b*Keep my commandments, and live;
ch. 4. 4.
Isai. 55. 3. *c*And my law as the apple of thine eye.
c Deut.32.10. 3 *d*Bind them upon thy fingers,
d Deut. 6. 8.
& 11. 18. Write them upon the table of thine heart.
ch. 3. 3.
& 6. 21. 4 Say unto wisdom, Thou *art* my sister;
 And call understanding *thy* kinswoman:
e ch. 2. 16. 5 *e*That they may keep thee from the strange woman,
& 5. 3.
& 6. 24. From the stranger *which* flattereth with her words.
6 For at the window of my house—I looked through my casement,
7 And beheld among the simple ones,
f ch. 6. 32. I discerned among [3]the youths, a young man *f*void of under-
& 9. 4, 16. standing,
8 Passing through the street near her corner;
 And he went the way to her house,
g Job 24. 15. 9 *g*In the twilight, [4]in the evening,—in the black and dark night:
10 And, behold, there met him a woman
 With the attire of an harlot, and subtil of heart.
h ch. 9. 13. 11 (*h*She *is* loud and stubborn;—*i*her feet abide not in her house:
i 1 Tim.5.13. 12 Now *is she* without, now in the streets,
Tit. 2. 5. And lieth in wait at every corner.)
13 So she caught him, and kissed him,
 And [5]with an impudent face said unto him,

[1] Heb. *heart.* [3] Heb. *the sons.* [5] Heb. *she strengthened her*
[2] Heb. *He will not accept* [4] Heb. *in the evening of the* *face, and said.*
 the face of any ransom. *day.*

VII. The harlot adulteress of an Eastern city is contrasted with the true feminine ideal of the Wisdom who is to be the "sister" and "kinswoman" (*v.* 4) of the young man as he goes on his way through life. See ch. viii. introduction.

6. *casement*] The latticed opening of an Eastern house, overlooking the street (cp. Judg. v. 28).

7. *simple*] In the bad sense of the word (i. 22 note); "open" to all impressions of evil, empty-headed and empty-hearted;

lounging near the house of ill-repute, not as yet deliberately purposing to sin, but placing himself in the way of it at a time when the pure in heart would seek their home. There is a certain symbolic meaning in the picture of the gathering gloom (*v.* 9). Night is falling over the young man's life as the shadows deepen.

11. *loud and stubborn*] Both words describe the half-animal signs of a vicious nature. Cp. Hos. iv. 16.

14 ¹*I have* peace offerings with me ;
    This day have I paid my vows.
15 Therefore came I forth to meet thee,
    Diligently to seek thy face, and I have found thee.
16 I have decked my bed with coverings of tapestry,
    With carved *works*, with *ᵏ*fine linen of Egypt.   *ᵏ* Isai. 19. 9.
17 I have perfumed my bed—with myrrh, aloes, and cinnamon.
18 Come, let us take our fill of love until the morning :
    Let us solace ourselves with loves.
19 For the goodman *is* not at home,—he is gone a long journey :
20 He hath taken a bag of money ²with him,
    And will come home at ³the day appointed.
21 With *ˡ*her much fair speech she caused him to yield,   *ˡ* ch. 5. 3.
    *ᵐ*With the flattering of her lips she forced him.   *ᵐ* Ps. 12. 2.
22 He goeth after her ⁴straightway,
    As an ox goeth to the slaughter,
    Or as a fool to the correction of the stocks ;
23 Till a dart strike through his liver;
    *ⁿ*As a bird hasteth to the snare,   *ⁿ* Eccl. 9. 12.
    And knoweth not that it *is* for his life.
24 Hearken unto me now therefore, O ye children,
    And attend to the words of my mouth.
25 Let not thine heart decline to her ways,
    Go not astray in her paths.
26 For she hath cast down many wounded :
    Yea, *ᵒ*many strong *men* have been slain by her.   *ᵒ* Neh. 13. 26.
27 *ᵖ*Her house *is* the way to hell,   *ᵖ* ch. 2. 18.
    Going down to the chambers of death.   & 5. 5.
                     & 9. 18.

¹ Heb. *Peace offerings* are ² Heb. *in his hand.* ⁴ Heb. *suddenly.*
 upon me.   ³ Or, *the new moon.*

---

14. This pretence of a religious feast gives us an insight into some strange features of popular religion under the monarchy of Judah. The harlot uses the technical word (Lev. iii. 1) for the "peace-offerings," and makes them the starting-point for sin. They have to be eaten on the same day that they are offered (Lev. vii. 15, 16), and she invites her victim to the feast. She who speaks is a "foreigner" who, under a show of conformity to the religion of Israel, still retains her old notions (see ii. 16 note), and a feast-day to her is nothing but a time of self-indulgence, which she may invite another to share with her. If we assume, as probable, that these harlots of Jerusalem were mainly of Phœnician origin, the connexion of their worship with their sin would be but the continuation of their original *cultus*.

16. The words point to the art and commerce which flourished under Solomon.

carved works] Most commentators take the original as meaning "striped coverlets of linen of Egypt."

17. The love of perfumes is here, as in Isai. iii. 24, a sign of luxurious vice.

cinnamon] The Hebrew word is identical with the English. The spice imported by the Phœnician traders from the further East, probably from Ceylon, has kept its name through all changes of language.

19. The reference to the husband is probably a blind. The use of the word "goodman" is due to the wish of the English translators to give a colloquial character to this part of their Version. The Heb. is merely "the man." A touch of scorn may be noticed in the form of speech : not "*my* husband," but simply "the man."

21. *fair speech*] The Hebrew word is usually translated "doctrine," or "learning" (i. 5, iv. 2, ix. 9) ; possibly it is used here in keen irony.

22. *as a fool* &c.] Lit. "As a fetter to the correction of a fool," the order of which is inverted in the A.V. The LXX., followed by the Syriac Version, has another reading, and interprets the clause : "As a dog, enticed by food, goes to the chain that is to bind him, so does the youth go to the temptress." None of the attempts of commentators to get a meaning out of the present text are in any degree satisfactory.

23. The first clause does not connect itself very clearly with the foregoing, and is probably affected by the corrupt text which makes it perplexing.

26. The house of the harlot is now likened to a field of battle strewn with the corpses of the many slain.

a ch. 1. 20.
& 9. 3.

CHAP. 8. DOTH not *a*wisdom cry?
 And understanding put forth her voice?
2 She standeth in the top of high places,
 By the way in the places of the paths.
3 She crieth at the gates, at the entry of the city,
 At the coming in at the doors.
4 Unto you, O men, I call;—and my voice *is* to the sons of man.
5 O ye simple, understand wisdom:
 And, ye fools, be ye of an understanding heart.

b ch. 22. 20.

6 Hear; for I will speak of *b*excellent things;
 And the opening of my lips *shall be* right things.
 For my mouth shall speak truth;
 And wickedness *is* ¹an abomination to my lips.
8 All the words of my mouth *are* in righteousness;
 There is nothing ²froward or perverse in them.
9 They *are* all plain to him that understandeth,
 And right to them that find knowledge.
10 Receive my instruction, and not silver;
 And knowledge, rather than choice gold.

c Job 28. 15,
&c.
Ps. 19. 10.
& 119. 127.
ch. 3. 14, 15.
& 4. 5, 7.
& 16. 16.

11 *c*For wisdom *is* better than rubies;
 And all the things that may be desired are not to be compared
 to it.
12 I wisdom dwell with ³prudence,
 And find out knowledge of witty inventions.

d ch. 16. 6.

13 *d*The fear of the LORD *is* to hate evil:
 *e*Pride, and arrogancy, and the evil way,

e ch. 6. 17.
f ch. 4. 24.

 And *f*the froward mouth, do I hate.
14 Counsel *is* mine, and sound wisdom:
 I *am* understanding; *g*I have strength.

g Eccl. 7. 19.
h Dan. 2. 21.
Rom. 13. 1.

15 *h*By me kings reign,—and princes decree justice.
16 By me princes rule,
 And nobles, *even* all the judges of the earth.

¹ Heb. *the abomination of*   ² Heb. *wreathed.*
  my lips.   ³ Or, *subtilty.*

VIII. A companion picture to that in ch. vii., and serving in some measure to generalize and idealize it. Wisdom also calls (*v.* 5) to the "simple" and the "fools," and they have to choose between her voice and that of the Temptress.

2, 3. The full enumeration of localities points to the publicity and openness of Wisdom's teaching (see i. 20 note), as contrasted with the stealth and secrecy and darkness which shroud the harlot's enticements (vii. 9).

4. *men...sons of man*] The two words are used, which, like *viri* and *homines*, describe the higher and the lower, the stronger and the weaker. Cp. Ps. xlix. 2 note.

6. *excellent*] Lit. "princely things." The word is not the same as in marg. ref., and is elsewhere always used of persons (cp. "captain" in 1 Sam. ix. 16, 2 Sam. v. 2). The poetic style of this part of the Book applies it here to the things taught, or to the character of the teaching.

8, 9. Words of the ideal Wisdom, which find their highest fulfilment in that of the Incarnate Word. Cp. Luke iv. 22; Matt. xi. 19.

12. Wisdom first speaks warnings (i. 24 note), next promises (ii. 1 note); but here she neither promises nor threatens, but speaks of her own excellence. "Prudence" is the "subtilty" (see marg.), the wiliness of the serpent (Gen. iii. 1), in itself neutral, but capable of being turned to good as well as evil. Wisdom, occupied with things heavenly and eternal, also "dwells with" the practical tact and insight needed for the life of common men. "Witty inventions" are rather **counsels**. The truth intended is, that all special rules for the details of life spring out of the highest Wisdom as their source.

15. Not only the common life of common men, but the exercise of the highest sovereignty, must have this Wisdom as its ground. Cp. with this passage (*vv.* 15-21) the teaching of 1 K. iii. 5-14. The word rendered "princes" (*v.* 15) is different from that in *v.* 16; the first might, perhaps, be rendered "rulers."

17 *I love them that love me;
And *those that seek me early shall find me.
18 *Riches and honour *are* with me;
Yea, durable riches and righteousness.
19 *My fruit *is* better than gold, yea, than fine gold;
And my revenue than choice silver.
20 I *lead in the way of righteousness,
In the midst of the paths of judgment:
21 That I may cause those that love me to inherit substance;
And I will fill their treasures.

22 *The LORD possessed me in the beginning of his way,
Before his works of old.
23 *I was set up from everlasting,
From the beginning, or ever the earth was.
24 When *there were* no depths, I was brought forth;
When *there were* no fountains abounding with water.
25 *Before the mountains were settled,
Before the hills was I brought forth:
26 While as yet he had not made the earth, nor the ²fields,
Nor ³the highest part of the dust of the world.

i 1 Sam.2.30.
Ps. 91. 14.
John 14. 21.
k Jam. 1. 5.
l ch. 3. 16.
Matt. 6. 33.
m ch. 3. 14.
ver. 10.

n ch. 3. 19.

o Ps. 2. 6.

p Job 15. 7, 8.

¹ Or, *walk.*   ² Or, *open places.*   ³ Or, *the chief part.*

---

18. *durable riches*] *i.e.* Treasure piled up for many years, *ancient* wealth.

19. *gold*] The "choice, fine gold" of marg. reff. The "fine gold" in the second clause is a different word, and perhaps represents gold extracted from the ore.

22. A verse which has played an important part in the history of Christian dogma. Wisdom reveals herself as preceding all creation, stamped upon it all, one with God, yet in some way distinguishable from Him as the object of His love (*v.* 30). St. John declares that all which Wisdom here speaks of herself was true in its highest sense of the Word that became flesh (John i. 1-14) : just as Apostles afterwards applied Wisd. vii. 22-30 to Christ (cp. Col. i. 15 ; Heb. i. 3).

possessed] The word has acquired a special prominence in connexion with the Arian controversy. The meaning which it usually bears is that of "getting" (Gen. iv. 1), "buying" (Gen. xlvii. 22), "possessing" (Jer. xxxii. 15). In this sense one of the oldest Divine names was that of "Possessor of heaven and earth" (Gen. xiv. 19, 22). But the idea of thus "getting" or "possessing" involved, as a Divine act in relation to the universe, the idea of creation, and thus in one or two passages the word might be rendered, though not accurately, by "created" (*e.g.* Ps. cxxxix. 13). It would seem accordingly as if the Greek translators of the Old Testament oscillated between the two meanings; and in this passage we find the various renderings ἔκτισε "created" (LXX.), and ἐκτήσατο "possessed" (Aquila). The text with the former word naturally became one of the stock arguments of the Arians against the eternal co-existence of the Son, and the

other translation was as vehemently defended by the orthodox Fathers. Athanasius receiving ἔκτισεν, took it in the sense of appointing, and saw in the LXX. a declaration that the Father had made the Son the "chief," the "head," the "sovereign," over all creation. There does not seem indeed any ground for the thought of creation either in the meaning of the root, or in the general usage of the word. What is meant in this passage is that we cannot think of God as ever having been without Wisdom. She is "as the beginning of His ways." So far as the words bear upon Christian dogma they accord with the words of John i. 1, "the Word was with God." The next words indeed assert priority to all the works of God, from the first starting-point of time.

23. *I was set up*] Rather, "I was anointed" (cp. Ps. ii. 6 marg. : 2 Chr. xxviii. 15). The image is that of Wisdom anointed, as at her birth, with "the oil of gladness."

or ever the earth was] Lit. "from the times before the earth."

24. Cp. Gen. i. ; Job xxii., xxvi., xxxviii. A world of waters, "great deeps" lying in darkness, this was the picture of the remotest time of which man could form any conception, and yet the co-existence of the uncreated Wisdom with the eternal Jehovah was before that.

25. Cp. Ps. xc. 2. What the Psalmist said of Jehovah, the teacher here asserts of Wisdom; she was before the everlasting hills.

26. *the highest part of the dust of the world*] Lit. "the head of the dusts of the world;" an image of either (1) the dry land, habitable, fit for cultivation, as con-

27 When he prepared the heavens, I *was* there :
    When he set [1]a compass upon the face of the depth :
28 When he established the clouds above :
    When he strengthened the fountains of the deep :

q Gen. 1. 9.   29 *q*When he gave to the sea his decree,
Job 38. 10.
Ps. 33. 7.   That the waters should not pass his commandment :
& 104. 9.   When *r*he appointed the foundations of the earth :
Jer. 5. 22.   30 *s*Then I was by him, *as* one brought up *with him :*
r Job 38. 4.   *t*And I was daily *his* delight,—rejoicing always before him ;
s John 1. 1,
2, 18.   31 Rejoicing in the habitable part of his earth ;
t Matt. 3. 17.   And *u*my delights *were* with the sons of men.
Col. 1. 13.
u Ps. 16. 3.   32 Now therefore hearken unto me, O ye children :
x Ps. 119. 1.   For *x*blessed *are they that* keep my ways.
& 128. 1, 2.   33 Hear instruction, and be wise,—and refuse it not.
Luke 11. 28.
y ch. 3. 13,18. 34 *y*Blessed *is* the man that heareth me,
           Watching daily at my gates,—waiting at the posts of my doors.
       35 For whoso findeth me findeth life,
z ch. 12. 2.   And shall [2]*z*obtain favour of the LORD.
a ch. 20. 2.   36 But he that sinneth against me *a*wrongeth his own soul :
           All they that hate me love death.

a Matt.16.18.
Eph. 2. 20,   **CHAP. 9.** WISDOM hath *a*builded her·house,
21, 22.
1 Pet. 2. 5.   She hath hewn out her seven pillars :
b Matt. 22.   2 *b*She hath killed [3]her beasts ; *c*she hath mingled her wine ;
3, &c.   She hath also furnished her table.
c ver. 5.
ch. 23. 30.   3 She hath *d*sent forth her maidens :
d Rom.10.15.   *e*She crieth *f*upon the highest places of the city,
e ch. 8. 1, 2. 4 *g*Whoso *is* simple, let him turn in hither :
f ver. 14.
g ver. 16.   *As for* him that wanteth understanding, she saith to him,
ch. 6. 32.
Matt. 11. 25.   [1] Or, *a circle.*   [2] Heb. *bring forth.*   [3] Heb. *her killing.*

---

trasted with the waters of the chaotic deep; or (2) man himself. Cp. Eccles. iii. 20.

27. *a compass*] Better as in the marg. and Job xxii. 14 (see note), *i.e.* the great vault of heaven stretched over the deep seas.

30. *as one brought up with him*] *i.e.* As his foster child. Others take the word in the original in another sense, " I was as his artificer," a rendering which falls in best with the special point of the whole passage, the creative energy of Wisdom. Cp. Wisd. vii. 21, 22.

daily] Heb. " day by day." As the Creator rejoiced in His workmanship (Gen. i. 4, 10, 12, 13), so Wisdom rejoiced in the exuberance of her might and strength.

31. Wisdom rejoices yet more in the world as inhabited by God's rational creatures (cp. Isai. xlv. 18). Giving joy and delight to God, she finds her delight among the sons of men. These words, like the rest, are as an unconscious prophecy fulfilled in the Divine Word, in whom were "hid all the treasures of Wisdom." Cp. marg. reff. : in Him the Father was well pleased ; and yet His "joy also is fulfilled," not in the glory of the material universe, but in His work among the sons of men.

32. The old exhortation with a new force. The counsels are no longer those of

prudence and human experience, but of a Wisdom eternal as Jehovah, ordering all things.

34. The image is suggested probably by the Levites who guarded the doors of the sanctuary (Pss. cxxxiv. 1, cxxxv. 2). Not less blessed than theirs is the lot of those who wait upon Wisdom in the Temple not made with hands.

35. Wisdom then is the only true life. The Word, the Light, is also the Life of man (John i. 4). The eternal life is to know God and Christ (John xvii. 3).

IX. **1.** A parable full of beauty, and interesting in its parallelism to the parables of our Lord (Matt. xxii. 3, 4 ; Luke xiv 16).

seven pillars] The number is chosen as indicating completeness and perfection. God revealing Himself in nature, resting in His work, entering into covenant with men,— these were the ideas conveyed by it.

2. *mingled her wine*] *i.e.* with myrrh and other spices, to give flavour and strength.

3. Wisdom and the "foolish woman" (*v.* 13) speak from the same places and to the same class — the simple, undecided, wavering, standing at the diverging point of the two paths that lead to life or death.

5 [h]Come, eat of my bread,
And drink of the wine *which* I have mingled.
6 Forsake the foolish, and live;
And go in the way of understanding.
7 He that reproveth a scorner getteth to himself shame :
And he that rebuketh a wicked *man getteth* himself a blot.
8 [i]Reprove not a scorner, lest he hate thee :
[k]Rebuke a wise man, and he will love thee.
9 Give *instruction* to a wise *man*, and he will be yet wiser :
Teach a just *man*, [l]and he will increase in learning.
10 [m]The fear of the LORD *is* the beginning of wisdom :
And the knowledge of the holy *is* understanding.
11 [n]For by me thy days shall be multiplied,
And the years of thy life shall be increased.
12 [o]If thou be wise, thou shalt be wise for thyself :
But *if* thou scornest, thou alone shalt bear *it*.

13 [p]A foolish woman *is* clamorous :
She is simple, and knoweth nothing.
14 For she sitteth at the door of her house,
On a seat [q]in the high places of the city,
15 To call passengers—who go right on their ways :
16 [r]Whoso *is* simple, let him turn in hither :
And *as for* him that wanteth understanding, she saith to him,
17 [s]Stolen waters are sweet,—and bread [1]*eaten* in secret is pleasant.
18 But he knoweth not that [t]the dead *are* there ;
And that her guests *are* in the depths of hell.

CHAP. 10. THE proverbs of Solomon.
[a]A wise son maketh a glad father :
But a foolish son *is* the heaviness of his mother.

[1] Heb. *of secrecies.*

Marginal references:
[h] ver. 2.
Cant. 5. 1.
Isai. 55. 1.
[i] Matt. 7. 6.
[k] Ps. 141. 5.
[l] Matt. 13. 12.
[m] Job 28. 28.
Ps. 111. 10.
ch. 1. 7.
[n] ch. 3. 2, 16.
& 10. 27.
[o] Job 35. 6, 7.
ch. 16. 26.
ch. 7. 11.
[q] ver. 3.
[r] ver. 4.
[s] ch. 20. 17.
[t] ch. 2. 18.
& 7. 27.
[a] ch. 15. 20.
& 17. 21, 25.
& 19. 13.
& 29. 3, 15.

---

5. A parallel to the higher teaching of the Gospels (cp. John vi. 27; Matt. xxvi. 26).

7–9. These verses seem somewhat to interrupt the continuity of the invitation which Wisdom utters. The order of thought is, however, this : "I speak to you, the simple, the open ones, for you have yet ears to hear : but from the scorner or evil doer, as such, I turn away." The words are illustrated by Matt. xiii. 11 &c.

10. *the holy*] The word in the Heb. is plural, agreeing, probably, with *Elohim* understood (so in xxx. 3). The knowledge of the Most Holy One stands as the counterpart of the fear of Jehovah.

12. The great law of personal retribution (cp. Matt. vii. 2). The LXX. makes a curious addition to this verse, "My son, if thou wilt be wise for thyself, thou shalt be wise also for thy neighbours ; but if thou turn out evil, thou alone shalt bear evil. He who resteth on lies shall guide the winds, and the same shall hunt after winged birds ; for he hath left the ways of his own vineyard, and has gone astray with the wheels of his own husbandry. He goeth through a wilderness without water, and over a land set in thirsty places, and with his hands he gathereth barrenness."

13. The picture of the harlot as the representative of the sensual life, the Folly between which and Wisdom the young man has to make his choice (*v.* 3 note). "Simple," in the worst sense, as open to all forms of evil. "Knoweth nothing," ignorant with the ignorance which is wilful and reckless.

14. Contrast with *v.* 1 &c. The foolish woman has her house, but it is no stately palace with seven pillars, like the home of Wisdom. No train of maidens wait on her, and invite her guests, but she herself sits at the door, her position as prominent as that of Wisdom, counterfeiting her voice, making the same offer to the same class (cp. *v.* 16 with *v.* 4).

17. The besetting sin of all times and countries, the one great proof of the inherent corruption of man's nature. Pleasures are attractive *because* they are forbidden (cp. Rom. vii. 7).

18. Cp. marg. reff. With this warning the long introduction closes, and the collection of separate proverbs begins. Wisdom and Folly have each spoken ; the issues of each have been painted in life-like hues. The learner is left to choose.

X. 1. See Introduction, p. 341.

b Ps. 49. 6, &c.
ch. 11. 4.
Luke 12. 19, 20.
c Dan. 4. 27.
d Ps. 10. 14.
& 34. 9, 10.
& 37. 25.
e ch. 12. 24.
& 19. 15.
f ch. 13. 4.
& 21. 5.
g ch. 12. 4.
& 17. 2.
& 19. 26.
h ver. 11.
i Ps. 9. 5, 6.
& 112. 6.
Eccl. 8. 10.

k ver. 10.

l Ps. 23. 4.
ch. 28. 18.
Isai. 33. 15, 16.
m ch. 6. 13.
n ver. 8.

o Ps. 37. 30.
ch. 13. 14.
& 18. 4.
p Ps. 107. 42.
q ch. 17. 9.
1 Cor. 13. 4.
1 Pet. 4. 8.
r ch. 26. 3.

s ch. 18. 7.
& 21. 23.

2 *b*Treasures of wickedness profit nothing:
　*c*But righteousness delivereth from death.

3 *d*The LORD will not suffer the soul of the righteous to famish:
　But he casteth away ¹the substance of the wicked.

4 *e*He becometh poor that dealeth *with* a slack hand:
　But *f*the hand of the diligent maketh rich.

5 He that gathereth in summer *is* a wise son:
　But he that sleepeth in harvest *is* *g*a son that causeth shame.

6 Blessings *are* upon the head of the just:
　But *h*violence covereth the mouth of the wicked.

7 *i*The memory of the just *is* blessed:
　But the name of the wicked shall rot.

8 The wise in heart will receive commandments:
　*k*But ²a prating fool ³shall fall.

9 *l*He that walketh uprightly walketh surely:
　But he that perverteth his ways shall be known.

10 *m*He that winketh with the eye causeth sorrow:
　*n*But a prating fool ⁴shall fall.

11 *o*The mouth of a righteous *man is* a well of life:
　But *p*violence covereth the mouth of the wicked.

12 Hatred stirreth up strifes:—but *q*love covereth all sins.

13 In the lips of him that hath understanding wisdom is found:
　But *r*a rod *is* for the back of him that is void of ⁵understanding.

14 Wise *men* lay up knowledge:
　But *s*the mouth of the foolish *is* near destruction.

¹ Or, *the wicked for* their *wickedness.*
² Heb. *a fool of lips.*
³ Or, *shall be beaten.*
⁴ Or, *shall be beaten.*
⁵ Heb. *heart.*

---

2. *righteousness*] Including, perhaps, the idea of benevolence. Cp. the use of δικαιοσύνη, in Matt. vi. 1 (the older reading), and 2 Cor. ix. 9, 10.

3. *casteth away* &c.] Better, "overturns, disappoints the strong desire of the wicked." Tantalus-like, they never get the enjoyment they thirst after.

4. *slack*] The word is elsewhere translated as "deceitful" (Job xiii. 7; Ps. cxx. 2, 3; Hos. vii. 16; Jer. xlviii. 10). The two thoughts run easily into each other.

5. The son is called upon to enter on the labours of others, and reap where they have sown. To sleep when the plenteous harvest lies ready for the sickle is the extremest sloth.

6. *covereth* &c.] The meaning is perhaps, the violence which the wicked has done is as a bandage over his mouth, reducing him to a silence and shame, like that of the leper (Lev. xiii. 45; Mic. iii. 7) or the condemned criminal (Esth. vii. 8), whose "face is covered."

8. *a prating...fall*] Better, as in the marg. Inward self-contained wisdom is contrasted with self-exposed folly.

9. *shall be known*] Lit. "shall be made

to know" (see Jer. xxxi. 19; Judg. viii. 16 marg.) in the sense of exposed.

10. In *v.* 8 the relation between the two clauses was one of contrast, here of resemblance. Cunning, reticence, and deceit (vi. 12 note) bring sorrow no less than garrulity.

11. Cp. *v.* 6. Streams of living water (like the "fountain of living waters" of Jer. ii. 13, xvii. 13, and the "living water" of John iv. 10), flow from the mouth of the righteous, but that of the wicked is "covered," *i.e.* stopped and put to silence by their own violence.

12. *love covereth all sins*] *i.e.* First hides, does not expose, and then forgives and forgets all sins.

13. *i.e.* The wisdom of the wise is seen in the words that issue from his lips; the folly of the fool is not only seen in his speech, but brings upon him the chastisement which he well deserves.

14. *lay up*] The point of the maxim is that the wise man reserves what he has to say for the right time, place, and persons (cp. Matt. vii. 6), as contrasted with the foolish, ever giving immediate utterance to what destroys himself and others.

15 *The rich man's wealth *is* his strong city :
   The destruction of the poor *is* their poverty.

16 The labour of the righteous *tendeth* to life :
   The fruit of the wicked to sin.

17 He *is in* the way of life that keepeth instruction :
   But he that refuseth reproof [1]erreth.

18 He that hideth hatred *with* lying lips,
   And *u* he that uttereth a slander, *is* a fool.

19 *x* In the multitude of words there wanteth not sin .
   But *y* he that refraineth his lips *is* wise.

20 The tongue of the just *is as* choice silver :
   The heart of the wicked *is* little worth.

21 The lips of the righteous feed many :
   But fools die for want [2] of wisdom.

22 *z* The blessing of the LORD, it maketh rich,
   And he addeth no sorrow with it.

23 *a It is* as sport to a fool to do mischief :
   But a man of understanding hath wisdom.

24 *b* The fear of the wicked, it shall come upon him :
   But *c* the desire of the righteous shall be granted.

25 As the whirlwind passeth, *d* so *is* the wicked no *more :*
   But *e* the righteous *is* an everlasting foundation.

[1] Or, *causeth to err.*   [2] Heb. *of heart.*

t Job 31. 24.
Ps. 52. 7.
1 Tim. 6. 17.

u Ps. 15. 3.

x Eccl. 5. 3.
y Jam. 3. 2.

z Gen. 24. 35.
& 26. 12.
Ps. 37. 22.
a ch. 14. 9.
& 15. 21.
b Job 15. 21.
c Ps. 145. 19.
Matt. 5. 6.
1 John 5.
14, 15.
d Ps. 37. 9,
10.
e Ps. 15. 5.
ver. 30.
Matt. 16. 18.

15. *destruction*] That which crushes, throws into ruins. Wealth secures its possessors against many dangers ; poverty exposes men to worse evils than itself, meanness, servility, and cowardice. Below the surface there lies, it may be, a grave irony against the rich ; see xviii. 11.

16. A warning against the conclusion to seek wealth first of all, which men of lower natures might draw from *v.* 15.

" Quærenda pecunia primum est ;
Virtus post nummos !"
                    Horace, 'Ep.' 1. i. 53.

Such an inference is met by the experience, that while wealth gotten by honest industry is not only, like inherited riches a defence, but also a blessing, the seeming **profit** (rather than " fruit ") of the wicked tends to further sin (1 Tim. vi. 10), and so to punishment. Cp. Rom. vi. 21.

17. Lit. **A way of life is he that keepeth instruction.** The verb " erreth " is better rendered in the margin. The influence for good or evil spreads beyond the man himself.

18. Better, **He who hideth hatred is of lying lips.** He who cherishes hatred, is either a knave, or a fool—a knave if he hides, a fool if he utters it.

19. *there wanteth not sin*] Some render this, "Sin shall not cease," &c., *i.e.* many words do not mend a fault. Silence on the part both of the reprover and the offender is often better. The A. V. is, however, preferable.

20. The tongue, the instrument of the mind is contrasted with the heart or mind itself, the just with the wicked, the choice silver with the worthless "little," the Heb. word being possibly taken in its primary sense as a " filing " or " scraping " of dross or worthless metal. If the tongue is precious, how much more the mind ! If the heart is worthless, how much more the speech !

21. *feed*] The Heb. word, like ποιμαίνειν, includes the idea of guiding as well as nourishing ; doing a shepherd's work in both.
for want of wisdom] Some prefer, **through him who wanteth understanding,** referring to a person. The wise guides others to safety ; the fool, empty-headed, and empty-hearted, involves others like himself in destruction.

23. As the fool finds his sport in doing mischief, so the man of understanding finds in wisdom his truest refreshment and delight.

24. *The fear*] *i.e.* The thing feared (cp. marg. ref.).
shall be granted] Or, **He (Jehovah) giveth the desire of the righteous.**

25. Or, **when the whirlwind is passing, then the wicked is no more.** Cp. Matt. vii. 24–27.
the righteous &c.] In the later Rabbinic interpretation this was applied to the Messiah as being the Just One, the Everlasting Foundation, on Whom the world was established.

26 As vinegar to the teeth, and as smoke to the eyes,
　　So *is* the sluggard to them that send him.

f ch. 9. 11.　　27 *f*The fear of the LORD [1]prolongeth days :
g Job 15. 32,　　　　But *g*the years of the wicked shall be shortened.
33.
& 22. 16.　　28 The hope of the righteous *shall be* gladness :
Ps. 55. 23.　　　　But the *h*expectation of the wicked shall perish.
Eccl. 7. 17.
h Job 8. 13.　　29 The way of the LORD *is* strength to the upright :
& 11. 20.　　　　*i*But destruction *shall be* to the workers of iniquity.
Ps. 112. 10.
ch. 11. 7.　　30 *k*The righteous shall never be removed :
i Ps. 1. 6.　　　　But the wicked shall not inhabit the earth.
& 37. 20.
k Ps. 37. 22,　　31 *l*The mouth of the just bringeth forth wisdom :
29.　　　　But the froward tongue shall be cut out.
& 125. 1.
ver. 25.
l Ps. 37. 30.　　32 The lips of the righteous know what is acceptable :
　　　　But the mouth of the wicked *speaketh* [2]frowardness.

a Lev. 19. 35,　　**CHAP. 11.** A *a*[3]FALSE balance *is* abomination to the LORD :
36.　　　　But [4]a just weight *is* his delight.

b ch. 15. 33.　　2 *b*When pride cometh, then cometh shame :
& 16. 18.　　　　But with the lowly *is* wisdom.
& 18. 12.
Dan. 4. 30,　　3 *c*The integrity of the upright shall guide them :
31.　　　　But the perverseness of transgressors shall destroy them.
c ch. 13. 6.

d ch. 10. 2.　　4 *d*Riches profit not in the day of wrath :
Ezek. 7. 19.　　　　But *e*righteousness delivereth from death.
e Gen. 7. 1.

　　5 The righteousness of the perfect shall [5]direct his way :
　　　　But the wicked shall fall by his own wickedness.

　　6 The righteousness of the upright shall deliver them :
f ch. 5. 22.　　　　But *f*transgressors shall be taken in *their own* naughtiness.
Eccl. 10. 8.

[1] Heb. *addeth.*　　　　[3] Heb. *Balances of deceit.*　　　[5] Heb. *rectify.*
[2] Heb. *frowardnesses.*　　[4] Heb. *a perfect stone.*

---

26. The teeth set on edge by the sour wine used by peasants (Ruth ii. 14 ; Ps. lxix. 21), the eye irritated by wood-smoke, these shadow the annoyance of having a messenger who *will* loiter on the way.

28. Transpose "hope" and "expectation." The expectant waiting of the righteous is joyful at the time, and ends in joy : the eager hope of the wicked comes to nought.

29. Omit "shall be." The meaning is : "The Way of Jehovah," *i.e.* the Divine Order of the world, has its two sides. It is "strength to the upright, destruction to the workers of iniquity."

30. *the wicked shall not inhabit*] The other and higher side of the same law of the Divine Government appears in Matt. v. 5.

31. *bringeth forth &c.*] As a tree full of life and sap brings forth its fruit. So the "froward tongue" is like a tree that brings forth evil and not good fruit ; it "shall be cut down." The abuse of God's gift of speech will lead ultimately to its forfeiture. There shall, at last, be the silence of shame and confusion.

32. *know*] *i.e.* "Know, and *therefore* utter." So, in like manner, the "mouth

of the wicked " knows, and therefore speaks frowardness, and that only.

XI. 1. This emphatic reproduction of the old rule of Deut. xxv. 13, 14 is perhaps a trace of the danger of dishonesty incidental to the growing commerce of the Israelites. The stress laid on the same sin in xvi. 11, xx. 10, bears witness to the desire of the teacher to educate the youth of Israel to a high standard of integrity, just as the protest of Hosea against it (xii. 7) shews the zeal of the prophet in rebuking what was becoming more and more a besetting sin.

a just weight] Lit., as in the marg., indicating a time when stones rather than metal were used as a standard of weight. Cp. Deut. xxv. 13.

2. A Rabbinic paraphrase of the second clause is : "Lowly souls become full of wisdom as the low place becomes full of water."

4. *the day of wrath*] Words true in their highest sense of the great " dies iræ " of the future, but spoken in the first instance (cp. Zeph. i. 15–18) of *any* "day of the Lord," any time of judgment, when men or nations receive the chastisement of their sins. At such a time " riches profit not."

7 *g*When a wicked man dieth, *his* expectation shall perish: *g* ch. 10. 28.
And the hope of unjust *men* perisheth.

8 *h*The righteous is delivered out of trouble,   *h* ch. 21. 18.
And the wicked cometh in his stead.

9 An *i*hypocrite with *his* mouth destroyeth his neighbour: *i* Job 8. 13.
But through knowledge shall the just be delivered.

10 *k*When it goeth well with the righteous, the city rejoiceth: *k* Esth. 8. 15.
And when the wicked perish, *there is* shouting.   ch. 28. 12, 28.

11 *l*By the blessing of the upright the city is exalted: *l* ch. 29. 8.
But it is overthrown by the mouth of the wicked.

12 He that is ¹void of wisdom despiseth his neighbour:
But a man of understanding holdeth his peace.

13 *m2*A talebearer revealeth secrets: *m* Lev. 19. 16.
But he that is of a faithful spirit concealeth the matter.   ch. 20. 19.

14 *n*Where no counsel *is*, the people fall: *n* ch. 15. 22.
But in the multitude of counsellors *there is* safety.   & 24. 6.

15 *o*He that is surety for a stranger ³shall smart *for it:*   *o* ch. 6. 1.
And he that hateth ⁴suretiship is sure.

16 *p*A gracious woman retaineth honour: *p* ch. 31. 30.
And strong *men* retain riches.

17 *q*The merciful man doeth good to his own soul: *q* Matt. 5. 7.
But *he that is* cruel troubleth his own flesh.   & 25. 34, &c.

18 The wicked worketh a deceitful work:
But *r*to him that soweth righteousness *shall be* a sure reward.   *r* Hos. 10. 12.
    Gal. 6. 8, 9.

19 As righteousness *tendeth* to life: Jam. 3. 18.
So he that pursueth evil *pursueth it* to his own death.

20 They that are of a froward heart *are* abomination to the LORD:
But *such as are* upright in *their* way *are* his delight.

21 *s*Though hand *join* in hand, the wicked shall not be unpunished: *s* ch. 16. 5.
But *t*the seed of the righteous shall be delivered.   *t* Ps. 112. 2.

---

¹ Heb. *destitute of heart.*	being *a talebearer.*	⁴ Heb. *those that strike*
² Heb. *He that walketh,*	³ Heb. *shall be sore broken.*	hands.

---

7. Significant words, as showing the belief that when the righteous died, his "expectation" (*i.e.* his hope for the future) did *not* perish. The second clause is rendered by some, "the expectation that brings sorrow."

9. *through knowledge*] Better, **By the knowledge of the just, shall they** (*i.e.* the neighbours) **be delivered.**

11. *the blessing of the upright*] Probably the prayers which he offers for the good of the city in which he dwells, and which avail to preserve it from destruction (cp. Gen. xviii. 23–33); or "the blessing which God gives the upright."

12. None but the man "void of wisdom" will show contempt for those about him. The wise man, if he cannot admire or praise, will at least know how to be silent.

13. The man who comes to us with tales about others will reveal our secrets also. Faithfulness is shown, not only in doing what a man has been commissioned to do, but in doing it quietly and without garrulity.

14. *counsel*] See i. 5 note. This precept may well be thought of as coming with special force at the time of the organization of the monarchy of Israel. Cp. 1 K. xii. 6.

15. See marg. ref. The play upon "sure" and "suretiship" in the A.V. (though each word is rightly rendered) has nothing corresponding to it in the Hebrew, and seems to have originated in a desire to give point to the proverb.

16. Or, "The gracious woman wins and keeps honour, *as* (the conjunction may be so rendered) strong men win riches."

18. *deceitful work*] Work which deceives and disappoints the worker; in contrast with the "sure reward" of the second clause. Omit "shall be" and render, "but he that soweth righteousness worketh a sure reward."

21. Lit. "hand to hand." The meaning of which is, "Hand may plight faith to hand, men may confederate for evil, yet punishment shall come at last;" or "From

22 *As* a jewel of gold in a swine's snout,
   So is a fair woman which [1] is without discretion.

23 The desire of the righteous *is* only good :

u Rom. 2.
8, 9.
x Ps. 112. 9.

   But the expectation of the wicked *u is* wrath.

24 There is that *x* scattereth, and yet increaseth ;
   And *there is* that withholdeth more than is meet, but *it tendeth* to
   poverty.

y 2 Cor. 9. 6,
7, 8, 9, 10.
z Matt. 5. 7.

25 *y* 2 The liberal soul shall be made fat :
   z And he that watereth shall be watered also himself.

a Amos 8.
5, 6.
b Job 29. 13.

26 *a* He that withholdeth corn, the people shall curse him :
   But *b* blessing *shall be* upon the head of him that selleth *it*.

27 He that diligently seeketh good procureth favour :

c Esth. 7. 10.
Ps. 7. 15.
& 57. 6.
d Job 31. 24.
Ps. 52. 7.

   c But he that seeketh mischief, it shall come unto him.

28 *d* He that trusteth in his riches shall fall :
   But *e* the righteous shall flourish as a branch.

Mark 10. 24.
Luke 12. 21.
1 Tim. 6. 17.
e Ps. 52. 8.
& 92. 12.
Jer. 17. 8.
f Eccl. 5. 16.

29 He that troubleth his own house *f* shall inherit the wind :
   And the fool *shall be* servant to the wise of heart.

30 The fruit of the righteous *is* a tree of life ;
   And *g* he that [3] winneth souls *is* wise.

g Dan. 12. 3.
1 Cor. 9. 19,
&c.
Jam. 5. 20.
h Jer. 25. 29.

31 *h* Behold, the righteous shall be recompensed in the earth :
   Much more the wicked and the sinner.

CHAP. 12. WHOSO loveth instruction loveth knowledge :
   But he that hateth reproof *is* brutish.

---

[1] Heb. *departeth from*.   [2] Heb. *The soul of blessing*.   [3] Heb. *taketh*.

---

hand to hand, from one generation to another, punishment shall descend on the evil doers."

22. The most direct proverb, in the sense of "similitude," which has as yet met us.

jewel of gold] Better, **ring ;** *i.e.* the nose-ring (Gen. xxiv. 22, 47 ; Isai. iii. 21).

without discretion] Lit. "without taste," void of the subtle tact and grace, without which mere outward beauty is as ill-bestowed as the nose-ring in the snout of the unclean beast. If we may assume that in ancient Syria, as in modern Europe, swine commonly wore such a ring to hinder them doing mischief, the similitude receives a fresh vividness.

24. *withholdeth more than is meet*] *i.e.* Is sparing and niggardly where he ought to give. The contrast is stated in the form of a paradox, to which the two following verses supply the answer. Some render, "There is that withholdeth from what is due," *i.e.* from a just debt, or from the generosity of a just man.

25. *liberal soul*] Lit. "the soul that blesses," *i.e.* gives freely and fully. The similitudes are both of them essentially Eastern. Fatness, the sleek, well-filled look of health, becomes the figure of prosperity, as leanness of misfortune (xiii. 4, xxviii. 25 ; Ps. xxii. 29 ; Isai. x. 16). Kindly acts come as the refreshing dew and soft rain from heaven upon a thirsty land.

26. In the early stages of commerce there seems no way of making money rapidly so sure as that of buying up corn in time of dearth, waiting till the dearth presses heavily, and then selling at famine prices. Men hate this selfishness, and pour blessings upon him who sells at a moderate profit.

27. *procureth*] Better, **striveth after.** He who desires good, absolutely, for its own sake, is also unconsciously striving after the favour which attends goodness.

28. *branch*] Better, **leaf,** as in Ps. i. 3 ; Isai. xxxiv. 4.

29. *He that troubleth* &c.] The temper, niggardly and worrying, which leads a man to make those about him miserable, and proves but bad economy in the end.

30. *winneth souls*] Better, **a wise man winneth souls.** He that is wise draws the souls of men to himself, just as the fruit of the righteous is to all around him a tree of life, bearing new fruits of healing evermore. The phrase is elsewhere translated by "taketh the life" (1 K. xix. 4 ; Ps. xxxi. 13). The wise man is the true conqueror. For the Christian meaning given to these words see N. T. reff. in marg.

31. The sense would appear to be, "The righteous is requited, *i.e.* is punished for his lesser sins, or as a discipline ; much more the wicked, &c." Cp. 1 Pet. iv. 18.

XII. 1. *brutish*] Dumb as a brute beast. The difference between man and brute lies

2 ^aA good *man* obtaineth favour of the LORD :
But a man of wicked devices will he condemn.

3 A man shall not be established by wickedness :
But the ^broot of the righteous shall not be moved.

4 ^cA virtuous woman *is* a crown to her husband :
But she that maketh ashamed *is* ^das rottenness in his bones.

5 The thoughts of the righteous *are* right :
But the counsels of the wicked *are* deceit.

6 ^eThe words of the wicked *are* to lie in wait for blood :
^fBut the mouth of the upright shall deliver them.

7 ^gThe wicked are overthrown, and *are* not :
But the house of the righteous shall stand.

8 A man shall be commended according to his wisdom :
^hBut he that is ¹of a perverse heart shall be despised.

9 ⁱ*He that is* despised, and hath a servant,
Is better than he that honoureth himself, and lacketh bread.

10 ^kA righteous *man* regardeth the life of his beast :
But the ²tender mercies of the wicked *are* cruel.

11 ^lHe that tilleth his land shall be satisfied with bread :
But he that followeth vain *persons* ^m*is* void of understanding.

12 The wicked desireth ³the net of evil *men :*
But the root of the righteous yieldeth *fruit.*

13 ⁴ⁿThe wicked is snared by the transgression of *his* lips :
^oBut the just shall come out of trouble.

a ch. 8. 35.

b ch. 10. 25.

c ch. 31. 23.
1 Cor. 11. 7.
d ch. 14. 30.

e ch. 1. 11,
18.
f ch. 14. 3.
g Ps. 37. 36,
37.
ch. 11. 21.
Matt. 7. 24,
25, 26, 27.
h 1 Sam. 25.
17.
i ch. 13. 7.

k Deut. 25. 4.

l Gen. 3. 19.
ch. 28. 19.
m ch. 6. 32.

n ch. 18. 7.
o 2 Pet. 2. 9.

---

¹ Heb. *perverse of heart.*   ³ Or, *the fortress.*   *wicked* is *in the trans-*
² Or, *bowels.*   ⁴ Heb. *The snare of the*   *gression of lips.*

---

chiefly in the capacity of the former for progress and improvement, and that capacity depends upon his willingness to submit to discipline and education. Cp. Ps. xlix. 12.

4. *virtuous*] The word implies the virtue of earnestness, or strength of character, rather than of simple chastity.

a crown] With the Jews the sign, not of kingly power only, but also of joy and gladness. Cp. S. of S. iii. 11.

6. *shall deliver them*] *i.e.* The righteous themselves.

9. Two interpretations are equally tenable ; (1) as in the A.V., He whom men despise, or who is "lowly" in his own eyes (cp. 1 S. xviii. 23), if he has a slave, *i.e.* if he is one step above absolute poverty, and has some one to supply his wants, is better off than the man who boasts of rank or descent and has nothing to eat. Respectable mediocrity is better than boastful poverty. (2) He who, though despised, is a servant to himself, *i.e.* supplies his own wants, is better than the arrogant and helpless.

10. *regardeth*] Lit. "knoweth." All true sympathy and care must grow out of knowledge. The duty of a man to animals (1) rests upon direct commandments in the Law (Ex. xx. 10, xxiii. 4, 5) ; (2) connects itself with the thought that the mercies of God are over all His works, and that man's mercy, in proportion to its excellence, must be like His (Jonah iv. 11) ; and (3) has perpetuated its influence in the popular morality of the East.

tender mercies] Better, "the feelings, the emotions," all that should have led to mercy and pity towards man.

11. The contrast is carried on between the life of industry and that of the idle, "vain person" of the "baser sort" (the "Raca" of Matt. v. 22). We might have expected that the second clause would have ended with such words as "shall lack bread," but the contrast goes deeper. Idleness leads to a worse evil than that of hunger.

12. The meaning seems to be : — The "net of evil men" (cp. i. 17) is that in which they are taken, the judgment of God in which they are ensnared. This they run into with such a blind infatuation, that it seems as if they were in love with their own destruction. The marginal rendering gives the thought that the wicked seek the protection of others like themselves, but seek in vain ; the "root of the just" (*i.e.* that in them which is fixed and stable) alone yields that protection.

p ch. 18. 20.
q Isai. 3. 10, 11.

r ch. 3. 7.
Luke 18. 11.

s ch. 29. 11.

t ch. 14. 5.

u Ps. 57. 4.
& 59. 7.
& 64. 3.

x Ps. 52. 5.
ch. 19. 9.

y ch. 6. 17.
& 11. 20.
Rev. 22. 15.

z ch. 13. 16.
& 15. 2.

a ch. 10. 4.

b ch. 15. 13.
c Isai. 50. 4.

14 *p*A man shall be satisfied with good by the fruit of *his* mouth :
   *q*And the recompence of a man's hands shall be rendered unto
   him.

15 *r*The way of a fool *is* right in his own eyes :
   But he that hearkeneth unto counsel *is* wise.

16 *s*A fool's wrath is [1]presently known :
   But a prudent *man* covereth shame.

17 *t*He that speaketh truth sheweth forth righteousness :
   But a false witness deceit.

18 *u*There is that speaketh like the piercings of a sword :
   But the tongue of the wise *is* health.

19 The lip of truth shall be established for ever :
   *x*But a lying tongue *is* but for a moment.

20 Deceit *is* in the heart of them that imagine evil :
   But to the counsellors of peace *is* joy.

21 There shall no evil happen to the just :
   But the wicked shall be filled with mischief.

22 *y*Lying lips *are* abomination to the LORD :
   But they that deal truly *are* his delight.

23 *z*A prudent man concealeth knowledge :
   But the heart of fools proclaimeth foolishness.

24 *a*The hand of the diligent shall bear rule :
   But the [2]slothful shall be under tribute.

25 *b*Heaviness in the heart of man maketh it stoop :
   But *c*a good word maketh it glad.

26 The righteous *is* more [3]excellent than his neighbour :
   But the way of the wicked seduceth them.

27 The slothful *man* roasteth not that which he took in hunting :
   But the substance of a diligent man *is* precious.

28 In the way of righteousness *is* life ;
   And *in* the pathway *thereof there is* no death.

[1] Heb. *in that day.*   [2] Or, *deceitful.*   [3] Or, *abundant.*

---

14. See xiii. 2 note.
16. The " fool " cannot restrain his wrath ; it rushes on " presently " (as in the margin, **on the same day**), however uselessly. The prudent man knows that to utter his indignation at reproach and shame will but lead to a fresh attack, and takes refuge in reticence.
17. The thought which lies below the surface is that of the inseparable union between truth and justice. The end does not justify the means, and only he who breathes and utters truth makes the righteous cause clear.
20. The " deceit " of "those who imagine evil " can work nothing but evil to those whom they advise. The " counsellors of peace" have joy in themselves, and impart it to others also.
23. Another aspect of the truth of x. 14.
24. *under tribute*] The comparison is pro-

bably suggested by the contrast between the condition of a conquered race (cp. Josh. xvi. 10 ; Judg. i. 30–33), and that of the freedom of their conquerors from such burdens. The proverb indicates that beyond all political divisions of this nature there lies an ethical law. The " slothful " descend inevitably to pauperism and servitude. The prominence of compulsory labour under Solomon (1 K. ix. 21) gives a special significance to the illustration.
26. *is more excellent than*] Rather, **the just man guides his neighbour.**
27. The word rendered "roasteth" occurs nowhere else ; but the interpretation of the A.V. is widely adopted. Others render the first clause thus : " The slothful man will not *secure* (keep in his net) what he takes in hunting," *i.e.* will let whatever he gains slip from his hands through want of effort and attention.

Chap. 13. A WISE son *heareth* his father's instruction :
 a But a scorner heareth not rebuke.

2 *b* A man shall eat good by the fruit of *his* mouth :
But the soul of the transgressors *shall eat* violence.

3 *c* He that keepeth his mouth keepeth his life :
But he that openeth wide his lips shall have destruction.

4 *d* The soul of the sluggard desireth, and *hath* nothing :
But the soul of the diligent shall be made fat.

5 A righteous *man* hateth lying :
But a wicked *man* is loathsome, and cometh to shame.

6 *e* Righteousness keepeth *him that is* upright in the way :
But wickedness overthroweth [1] the sinner.

7 *f* There is that maketh himself rich, yet *hath* nothing :
There is that maketh himself poor, yet *hath* great riches.

8 The ransom of a man's life *are* his riches :
But the poor heareth not rebuke.

9 The light of the righteous rejoiceth :
g But the [2] lamp of the wicked shall be put out.

10 Only by pride cometh contention :
But with the well advised *is* wisdom.

11 *h* Wealth *gotten* by vanity shall be diminished :
But he that gathereth [3] by labour shall increase.

12 Hope deferred maketh the heart sick :
But *i* when the desire cometh, *it is* a tree of life.

13 Whoso *k* despiseth the word shall be destroyed :
But he that feareth the commandment [4] shall be rewarded.

a 1 Sam. 2. 25.
b ch. 12. 14.
c Ps. 39. 1. ch. 21. 23. Jam. 3. 2.
d ch. 10. 4.
e ch. 11. 3, 5, 6.
f ch. 12. 9.
g Job 18. 5, 6. & 21. 17. ch. 24. 20.
h ch. 10. 2. & 20. 21.
i ver. 19.
k 2Chr.36.16.

[1] Heb. *sin.*
[2] Or, *candle.*
[3] Heb. *with the hand.*
[4] Or, *shall be in peace.*

XIII. **1.** *heareth*] The verb of the second clause is inserted in the first, just as in the next verse that of the first is inserted in the second. Stress is laid on the obstinacy of the scorner refusing to hear, not "instruction" only, but the much stronger "rebuke."

2. *the fruit of his mouth*] Speech rightly used is itself good, and must therefore bring good fruit.

eat violence] *i.e.* Bring upon itself repayment in kind for its deeds of evil.

7. Cp. xi. 24. There is a seeming wealth behind which there lies a deep spiritual poverty and wretchedness. There is a poverty which makes a man rich for the kingdom of God.

8. On the one side is the seeming advantage of wealth. The rich man gets out of many troubles, escapes often from a just retribution, by his money. But then the poor man in his turn is free from the risk of the threats and litigation that beset the rich. He "hears no rebuke" (the words are not used as in *v.* 1) just as the dead "hear not the voice of the op-

pressor" (Job iii. 18) or the abuse of the envious.

9. Very beautiful in its poetry is the idea of the light "rejoicing" in its brightness (cp. Ps. xix. 5 ; Job xxxviii. 7). Note also the distinction between the "light" and the "lamp." The righteous have the true light in them. That which belongs to the wicked is but derived and temporary, and shall be extinguished before long. Cp. a like distinction in John i. 8, v. 35.

10. Either (1) "By pride alone comes contention" — that is the one unfailing spring of quarrels ; or (2) "By pride comes contention only"—it, and it alone, is the fruit of pride.

11. *by vanity*] Lit. "by a breath," *i.e.* by a windfall, or sudden stroke of fortune, not by honest labour. The general meaning seems to be that the mere possession of riches is as nothing ; they come and go, but the power to gain by skill of hand ("labour") is everything.

12. *when the desire cometh*] The desire comes, it is a tree of life : *i.e.* the object of our desires is attained. Cp. iii. 18.

l ch. 10. 11.
& 14. 27.
& 16. 22.

m 2 Sam.
22. 6.

n ch. 12. 23.
& 15. 2.

o ch. 25. 13.

p ch. 15. 5,
31.
q ver. 12.

r Ps. 32. 10.

s Job 27. 16,
17.
ch. 28. 8.
Eccl. 2. 26.
t ch. 12. 11.

u ch. 19. 18.
& 22. 15.
& 23. 13.
& 29. 15, 17.
x Ps. 34. 10.
& 37. 3.

a ch. 24. 3.
b Ruth 4. 11.

c Job 12. 4.

d ch. 12. 6.

14 *l*The law of the wise *is* a fountain of life,
To depart from *m* the snares of death.

15 Good understanding giveth favour :
But the way of transgressors *is* hard.

16 *n*Every prudent *man* dealeth with knowledge :
But a fool ¹layeth open *his* folly.

17 A wicked messenger falleth into mischief :
But *o*²a faithful ambassador *is* health.

18 Poverty and shame *shall be to* him that refuseth instruction :
But *p*he that regardeth reproof shall be honoured.

19 *q*The desire accomplished is sweet to the soul :
But *it is* abomination to fools to depart from evil.

20 He that walketh with wise *men* shall be wise :
But a companion of fools ³shall be destroyed.

21 *r*Evil pursueth sinners :
But to the righteous good shall be repayed.

22 A good *man* leaveth an inheritance to his children's children :
And *s*the wealth of the sinner *is* laid up for the just.

23 *t*Much food *is in* the tillage of the poor :
But there is *that is* destroyed for want of judgment.

24 *u*He that spareth his rod hateth his son :
But he that loveth him chasteneth him betimes.

25 *x*The righteous eateth to the satisfying of his soul :
But the belly of the wicked shall want.

CHAP. 14. EVERY *a* wise woman *b*buildeth her house :
But the foolish plucketh it down with her hands.

2 He that walketh in his uprightness feareth the LORD :
*c*But *he that is* perverse in his ways despiseth him.

3 In the mouth of the foolish *is* a rod of pride :
*d*But the lips of the wise shall preserve them.

4 Where no oxen *are*, the crib *is* clean :
But much increase *is* by the strength of the ox.

¹ Heb. *spreadeth*.   ² Heb. *an ambassador of*   ³ Heb. *shall be broken*.
                        faithfulness.

---

15. *hard*] The primary meaning of the original word is permanence (cp. Deut. xxi. 4; Mic. vi. 2). This may be applied as here to the hard dry rock, to running streams, or to stagnant pools. In either case, the idea is that of the barren dry soil, or the impassable marsh, in contrast with the fountain of life, carrying joy and refreshment with it.

19. The connexion is somewhat obscure. Either, "Satisfied desire is pleasant, *therefore* it is an abomination to fools to depart from the evil on which their minds are set ;" or, "Sweet is the satisfaction of desire, yet the wicked will not depart from the evil which makes that satisfaction impossible."

22. An expression of trust, that in the long run the anomalies of the world are rendered even (cp. marg. reff.). The heaped-up treasures of the wicked find their way at last into the hands of better men.

23. The contrast is the ever-recurring one between honest poverty and dishonest wealth. "The new-ploughed field of the poor is much food, but there are those, who, though rich, perish through their disregard of right."

XIV. **1.** *Every wise woman*] Lit. **Wise women.** The fullest recognition that has as yet met us of the importance of woman, for good or evil, in all human society.

3. *a rod of pride*] *i.e.* The pride shown in his speech is as a rod with which he strikes down others and himself.

4. *i.e.* Labour has its rough, unpleasant side, yet it ends in profit. So also, the life of contemplation may seem purer, "cleaner" than that of action. The outer

5 *e* A faithful witness will not lie:
But a false witness will utter lies.

6 A scorner seeketh wisdom, and *findeth* it not:
But *f* knowledge *is* easy unto him that understandeth.

7 Go from the presence of a foolish man,
When thou perceivest not *in him* the lips of knowledge.

8 The wisdom of the prudent *is* to understand his way:
But the folly of fools *is* deceit.

9 *g* Fools make a mock at sin:
But among the righteous *there is* favour.

10 The heart knoweth [1] his own bitterness;
And a stranger doth not intermeddle with his joy.

11 *h* The house of the wicked shall be overthrown:
But the tabernacle of the upright shall flourish.

12 *i* There is a way which seemeth right unto a man,
But *k* the end thereof *are* the ways of death.

13 Even in laughter the heart is sorrowful;
And *l* the end of that mirth *is* heaviness.

14 The backslider in heart shall be *m* filled with his own ways:
And a good man *shall be satisfied* from himself.

15 The simple believeth every word:
But the prudent *man* looketh well to his going.

16 *n* A wise *man* feareth, and departeth from evil:
But the fool rageth, and is confident.

17 *He that is* soon angry dealeth foolishly:
And a man of wicked devices is hated.

e Ex. 20. 16.
& 23. 1.
ch. 6. 19.
& 12. 17.
ver. 25.
f ch. 8. 9.
& 17. 24.

g ch. 10. 23.

h Job 8. 15.

i ch. 16. 25.

k Rom. 6. 21.

l ch. 5. 4.
Eccl. 2. 2.
m ch. 1. 31.
& 12. 14.

n ch. 22. 3.

[1] Heb. *the bitterness of his soul.*

---

business of the world brings its cares and disturbances, but also "much increase." There will be a sure reward of that activity in good works for him who goes, as with "the strength of the ox," to the task to which God calls him.

6. *findeth it not*] Lit. **there is none.** The successful pursuit of wisdom presupposes at least earnestness and reverence. The scoffer shuts himself out from the capacity of recognizing truth.

8. The Hebrew counterpart to the Greek "Know thyself." "The highest wisdom is for a man to understand his own way. The extremest folly is *self*-deceit." The word "deceit" may, however, involve fraud practised upon others. The folly of fools shows itself then in their ceaseless effort to deceive.

9. *Fools make a mock*] The verb in the Heb. is singular, the noun plural. The A.V. assumes that the number is altered to individualize the application of the maxim. Others translate, "Sin mocks the fools who are its victims," *i.e.* disappoints and ruins them; or, "A sin-offering does but mock the worshippers when they are wilfully

wicked:" they expect to gain God's favour, and do not gain it. So taken it becomes parallel to xv. 8, xxi. 7.

10. A striking expression of the ultimate solitude of each man's soul at all times, and not merely at the hour of death. Something there is in every sorrow, and in every joy, which no one else can share. Beyond that range it is well to remember that there is a Divine Sympathy, uniting perfect knowledge and perfect love.

12. *a way* &c.] The way of the fool, the way of self-indulgence and self-will.

13. Sorrow of some kind either mingles itself with outward joy, or follows hard upon it.

14. *shall be satisfied*] These words are not in the original. Repeat the verb from the first clause, "He who falls away from God in his heart, shall be filled with his own ways; and the good man (shall be filled) with that which belongs to him."

15. *simple*] In the bad sense (cp. i. 22).

17. The contrast lies between two forms of evil. Hasty anger acts foolishly, but the "man of wicked devices," vindictive and insidious, incurs all men's hatred.

18 The simple inherit folly:
But the prudent are crowned with knowledge.

19 The evil bow before the good;
And the wicked at the gates of the righteous.

o ch. 19. 7.

20 *o*The poor is hated even of his own neighbour:
But ¹the rich *hath* many friends.

21 He that despiseth his neighbour sinneth:

p Ps. 41. 1.
& 112. 9.

*p*But he that hath mercy on the poor, happy *is* he.

22 Do they not err that devise evil?
But mercy and truth *shall be* to them that devise good.

23 In all labour there is profit:
But the talk of the lips *tendeth* only to penury.

24 The crown of the wise *is* their riches:
But the foolishness of fools *is* folly.

q ver. 5.

25 *q*A true witness delivereth souls:
But a deceitful *witness* speaketh lies.

26 In the fear of the LORD *is* strong confidence:
And his children shall have a place of refuge.

r ch. 13. 14.

27 *r*The fear of the LORD *is* a fountain of life,
To depart from the snares of death.

28 In the multitude of people *is* the king's honour:
But in the want of people *is* the destruction of the prince.

s ch. 16. 32.
Jam. 1. 19.

29 *s*He *that is* slow to wrath *is* of great understanding:
But *he that is* ²hasty of spirit exalteth folly.

30 A sound heart *is* the life of the flesh:

t Ps. 112. 10.
u ch. 12. 4.

But *t*envy *u*the rottenness of the bones.

---

¹ Heb. *many* are *the lovers of the rich.*   ² Heb. *short of spirit.*

---

18. *crowned*] The teacher anticipates the truth, and the paradox, of the Stoic saying, "The wise is the only king."

20. The maxim, jarring as it is, represents the generalization of a wide experience; but the words which follow (*v.* 21) show that it is not to be taken by itself. In spite of all the selfish morality of mere prudence, the hearer is warned that to despise his "neighbour" (Christians must take the word in all the width given to it by the parable of the Good Samaritan) is to sin. The fulness of blessing comes on him who sees in the poor the objects of his mercy.

22. *err*] In the sense of wandering from the right way, the way of life.

23. The contrast between a single, thorough deed, and the mere emptiness of speech.

24. "The crown," *i.e.* the glory of the wise man constitutes his wealth. He alone is truly rich even as he alone (cp. *v.* 18 note) is truly king.

The seeming tautology of the second clause is really its point. Turn "the foolishness of fools" as you will, it comes back to "foolishness" at last.

25. In the second clause, "destroyeth life" might have been expected as the antithesis to "delivereth souls." But what worse could be said? "A deceitful witness speaketh lies." All destruction is implied in falsehood.

26. *his children*] Probably, the children whom the LORD adopts, and who are true to their adoption.

27. See marg. ref. and x. 11 note.

28. A protest against the false ideal of national greatness to which Eastern kings, for the most part, have bowed down. Not conquest, or pomp, or gorgeous array, but a happy and numerous people form the true glory of a king. The word translated "prince" is of doubtful meaning; but the translation is supported by the LXX., Vulg., and most commentators.

29. *exalteth folly*] Lifts it up, as it were, on high, and exposes it to the gaze of all men.

30. *sound heart*] Lit. "heart of health," that in which all emotions and appetites are in a healthy equilibrium. The contrast with this is the envy which eats, like a consuming disease, into the very bones and marrow of a man's moral life.

31 [x]He that oppresseth the poor reproacheth [y]his Maker :
But he that honoureth him hath mercy on the poor.

32 The wicked is driven away in his wickedness :
But [z]the righteous hath hope in his death.

33 Wisdom resteth in the heart of him that hath understanding :
But [a]*that which is* in the midst of fools is made known.

34 Righteousness exalteth a nation :
But sin *is* a reproach [1]to any people.

35 [b]The king's favour *is* toward a wise servant :
But his wrath is *against* him that causeth shame.

CHAP. 15. A [a]SOFT answer turneth away wrath :
But [b]grievous words stir up anger.

2 The tongue of the wise useth knowledge aright :
[c]But the mouth of fools [2]poureth out foolishness.

3 [d]The eyes of the LORD *are* in every place,
Beholding the evil and the good.

4 [3]A wholesome tongue *is* a tree of life :
But perverseness therein *is* a breach in the spirit.

5 [e]A fool despiseth his father's instruction :
[f]But he that regardeth reproof is prudent.

6 In the house of the righteous *is* much treasure :
But in the revenues of the wicked is trouble.

7 The lips of the wise disperse knowledge :
But the heart of the foolish *doeth* not so.

8 [g]The sacrifice of the wicked *is* an abomination to the LORD :
But the prayer of the upright *is* his delight.

9 The way of the wicked *is* an abomination unto the LORD :
But he loveth him that [h]followeth after righteousness.

[x] ch. 17. 5.
Matt. 25. 40, 45.
[y] See Job 31. 15, 16.
ch. 22. 2.
[z] Job 13. 15.
& 19. 26.
Ps. 23. 4.
& 37. 37.
2 Cor. 1. 9.
& 5. 8.
2 Tim. 4. 18.
[a] ch. 12. 16.
& 29. 11.
[b] Matt. 24. 45, 47.
[a] Judg. 8. 1, 2, 3.
ch. 25. 15.
[b] 1 Sam. 25. 10, &c.
1 K. 12. 13, 14, 16.
[c] ver. 28.
ch. 12. 23.
& 13. 16.
[d] Job 34. 21.
ch. 5. 21.
Jer. 16. 17.
& 32. 19.
Heb. 4. 13.
[e] ch. 10. 1.
[f] ch. 13. 18.
ver. 31. 32.

[g] ch. 21. 27.
Isai. 1. 11.
& 61. 8.
& 66. 3.
Jer. 6. 20.
Amos 5. 22.
[h] ch. 21. 21.
1 Tim. 6. 11.

[1] Heb. *to nations.*   [2] Heb. *belcheth*, or, *bubbleth.*   [3] Heb. *The healing of the tongue.*

---

31. *honoureth him*] *i.e.* God, Who is the Maker of poor and rich alike.

32. Consult marg. reff. The hope which abides even "in death" must look beyond it.

33. Omit "that which is." "Wisdom" is the subject of both clauses. She is "made known," *i.e.* by the very force of contrast, in the midst of fools; or she is reserved and reticent in the one, noisy and boastful in the other. The LXX. and some other Versions get over the difficulty by reading "Wisdom is not made known."

34. *reproach*] The word so rendered has this sense in the Targum of Lev. xx. 17. Its more usual meaning is "mercy," "piety;" hence some have attached to the word rendered "sin" the sense of "sin-offering," and so get the maxim "piety is an atonement for the people."

XV. 2. *useth knowledge aright*] Rather, **makes knowledge goodly.** The power of well-considered speech to commend true wisdom, is contrasted with the pouring (lit. as in marg.) forth of folly.

3. The teaching which began with the fear of the Lord (i. 7) would not be complete without this assertion of His omnipresent knowledge.

4. *A wholesome tongue*] Lit. as in marg., the same word as "sound" in xiv. 30 (see note). A more literal rendering would be **soundness of speech.**
tree of life] Cp. iii. 18 note.
breach in the spirit] With the sense of **vexation** (cp. Isai. lxv. 14).

7. *not so*] The word translated "so" is taken by some in its etymological force as "strong," "firm," and the passage is rendered "the heart of the fool *disperseth* (supplied from the first clause) what is weak and unsteady," *i.e.* "falsehood and unwisdom." The LXX. takes it as an adjective, "the heart of the fool is unstedfast." The phrase as it stands in the A.V. is, however, of frequent occurrence (Gen. xlviii. 18 ; Exod. x. 11 ; Num. xii. 7).

10 [1]Correction *is* [i]grievous unto him that forsaketh the way:
And [k]he that hateth reproof shall die.

11 [l]Hell and destruction *are* before the LORD :
How much more then [m]the hearts of the children of men ?

12 [n]A scorner loveth not one that reproveth him :
Neither will he go unto the wise.

13 [o]A merry heart maketh a cheerful countenance :
But [p]by sorrow of the heart the spirit is broken.

14 The heart of him that hath understanding seeketh knowledge :
But the mouth of fools feedeth on foolishness.

15 All the days of the afflicted *are* evil :
[q]But he that is of a merry heart *hath* a continual feast.

16 [r]Better *is* little with the fear of the LORD
Than great treasure and trouble therewith.

17 [s]Better *is* a dinner of herbs where love is,
Than a stalled ox and hatred therewith.

18 [t]A wrathful man stirreth up strife :
But *he that is* slow to anger appeaseth strife.

19 [u]The way of the slothful *man is* as an hedge of thorns :
But the way of the righteous [2]*is* made plain.

20 [x]A wise son maketh a glad father :
But a foolish man despiseth his mother.

21 [y]Folly *is* joy to *him that is* [3]destitute of wisdom :
[z]But a man of understanding walketh uprightly.

22 [a]Without counsel purposes are disappointed :
But in the multitude of counsellors they are established.

23 A man hath joy by the answer of his mouth :
And [b]a word *spoken* [4]in due season, how good *is it* !

---

[1] Or, *Instruction.*   [2] Heb. is *raised up as a causey.*   [3] Heb. *void of heart.*   [4] Heb. *in his season.*

---

10. Better, **There is a grievous correction,** *i.e.* nothing less than death, to him that forsaketh the way.

13. Some prefer to render the last clause, " In sorrow of heart the breath is oppressed."

15. *afflicted*] The affliction meant here is less that of outward circumstances than of a troubled and downcast spirit. Life to the cheerful is as one perpetual banquet, whether he be poor or rich. That which disturbs the feast is anxiety, the "taking (anxious) thought" of Matt. vi. 34.

16. This proverb has its completion in the teaching of Matt. vi. 33.

17. *a dinner of herbs*] The meals of the poor and the abstemious. The " stalled ox," like the "fatted calf " of Luke xv. 23, would indicate a stately magnificence.

19. The slothful goes on his journey, and for him the path is thick set with thorns, briars, fences, through which he cannot force his way. For the " righteous " (better, upright), the same path is as the broad raised causeway of the king's highway. Cp. Isai. xl. 3.

20. To "despise " a mother is to cause her the deepest grief, and is therefore not unfitly contrasted with "making a glad father."

21. *i.e.* The empty-hearted, rejoicing in folly, goes the wrong way ; the man of understanding, rejoicing in wisdom, goes the right way.

22. *counsellors*] The Hebrew word, used almost as an official title (1 Chr. xxvii. 32; Isai. i. 26, xix. 11), brings before us the picture of the council-chamber of Eastern countries, arranged for a solemn conference of the wise.

23. Probably, a special reference to debates in council (*v.* 22). They bring before us the special characteristic of the East, the delight in ready, improvised answers, solving difficulties, turning aside anger. Cp. the effect on the scribe (Mark xii. 28).

24 ^cThe way of life *is* above to the wise,
    That he may depart from hell beneath.

c Phil. 3. 20.
Col. 3. 1, 2.

25 ^dThe LORD will destroy the house of the proud :
    But ^ehe will establish the border of the widow.

d ch. 12. 7.
& 14. 11.
e Ps. 146. 9.

26 ^fThe thoughts of the wicked *are* an abomination to the LORD :
    ^gBut *the words* of the pure *are* [1]pleasant words.

f ch. 6. 16,
18.
g Ps. 37. 30.

27 ^hHe that is greedy of gain troubleth his own house ;
    But he that hateth gifts shall live.

h ch. 11. 19.
Isai. 5. 8.
Jer. 17. 11.

28 The heart of the righteous ⁱstudieth to answer :
    But the mouth of the wicked poureth out evil things.

i 1 Pet. 3. 15.

29 ^kThe LORD *is* far from the wicked :
    But ^lhe heareth the prayer of the righteous.

k Ps. 10. 1.
& 34. 16.
l Ps. 145. 18,
19.

30 The light of the eyes rejoiceth the heart :
    And a good report maketh the bones fat.

31 ^mThe ear that heareth the reproof of life
    Abideth among the wise.

m ver. 5.

32 He that refuseth [2]instruction despiseth his own soul :
    But he that [3]heareth reproof [4]getteth understanding.

33 ⁿThe fear of the LORD *is* the instruction of wisdom ;
    And ^obefore honour *is* humility.

n ch. 1. 7.
o ch. 18. 12.

CHAP. 16. THE ^a[5]preparations of the heart in man,
    ^bAnd the answer of the tongue, *is* from the LORD.

2 ^cAll the ways of a man *are* clean in his own eyes ;
    But ^dthe LORD weigheth the spirits.

a ch. 19. 21.
& 20. 24.
Jer. 10. 23.
b Matt. 10.
19, 20.
c ch. 21. 2.
d 1 Sam. 16. 7.

---

[1] Heb. *words of pleasant-ness.*
[2] Or, *correction.*
[3] Or, *obeyeth.*
[4] Heb. *possesseth an heart.*
[5] Or, *disposings.*

---

24. *above...beneath*] The one path is all along upward, leading to the highest life. It rescues the "wise" from the other, which is all along downward, ending in the gloom of Sheol.

25. *the widow*] Here, as elsewhere (Deut. x. 18 ; Ps. lxviii. 5), the widow, as the extremest type of desolation, stands as the representative of a class safer in their poverty under the protection of the Lord, than the proud in the haughtiness of their strength.

26. Some prefer the marg., and render, **words of pleasantness are pure.** Gracious words are to God as a pure acceptable offering, the similitude being taken from the Levitical ritual, and the word "pure" in a half ceremonial sense (cp. Mal. i. 11).

27. *gifts*] There is a special application to the office of the judge. The Chaldee Targum paraphrases the first words of this passage, "he who gathers the mammon of unrighteousness," using the words with special reference to wealth obtained by unjust judgments. May we infer that Christ's adoption of that phrase (Luke xvi. 9) had a point of contact with this proverb, through the Version then popularly used in the synagogues of Palestine ?

28. Contrast the "studying" of the wise before he answers and the hasty babbling of the foolish. The teaching of our Lord (Matt. x. 19) presents us with a different and higher precept, resting upon different conditions.

29. Cp. John ix. 31.

30. *the light of the eyes*] The brightness which shines in the eyes of one whose heart and face are alike full of joy. Such a look acts with a healing and quickening power. Cp. xvi. 15.

a good report] *i.e.* Good news.

31. *the reproof of life*] *i.e.* The reproof that leads to, or gives life, rather than that which comes from life and its experience.

33. *the instruction of wisdom*] *i.e.* The discipline that leads to wisdom.

XVI. The proverbs in *vv.* 1–7 have, more than any other group, a specially religious character impressed on them. The name of Jehovah as Giver, Guide, Ruler, or Judge, meets us in each of them.

1. Better, **The plans of the heart belong to man, but the utterance of the tongue is from Jehovah.** Thoughts come and go, as it were, spontaneously ; but true, well-ordered speech is the gift of God. Cp. *v.* 9.

2. We are blind to our own faults, do not see ourselves as others see us. There is One Who tries not the "ways" only, but the

Marginal references:

- *e* Ps. 37. 5.
- & 55. 22.
- Matt. 6. 25.
- Luke 12. 22.
- Phil. 4. 6.
- 1 Pet. 5. 7.
- *f* Isai. 43. 7.
- Rom. 11. 36.
- *g* Job 21. 30.
- Rom. 9. 22.
- *h* ch. 6. 17.
- & 8. 13.
- *i* ch. 11. 21.
- *k* Dan. 4. 27.
- Luke 11. 41.
- *l* ch. 14. 16.
- *m* Ps. 37. 16.
- ch. 15. 16.
- *n* ver. 1.
- ch. 19. 21.
- *o* Ps. 37. 23.
- Prov. 20. 24.
- Jer. 10. 23.
- *p* Lev. 19. 36.
- *q* ch. 25. 5.
- & 29. 14.
- *r* ch. 14. 35.
- & 22. 11.
- *s* ch. 19. 12.
- & 20. 2.
- *t* ch. 19. 12.
- *u* Job 29. 23.
- Zech. 10. 1.
- *x* ch. 8. 11, 19.

3 *e* Commit thy works unto the LORD,
And thy thoughts shall be established.

4 *f* The LORD hath made all *things* for himself:
g Yea, even the wicked for the day of evil.

5 *h* Every one *that is* proud in heart *is* an abomination to the LORD:
Though hand *join* in hand, he shall not be ²unpunished.

6 *k* By mercy and truth iniquity is purged:
And *l* by the fear of the LORD *men* depart from evil.

7 When a man's ways please the LORD,
He maketh even his enemies to be at peace with him.

8 *m* Better *is* a little with righteousness
Than great revenues without right.

9 *n* A man's heart deviseth his way:
o But the LORD directeth his steps.

10 ³A divine sentence *is* in the lips of the king:
His mouth transgresseth not in judgment.

11 *p* A just weight and balance *are* the LORD's:
⁴All the weights of the bag *are* his work.

12 *It is* an abomination to kings to commit wickedness:
For *q* the throne is established by righteousness.

13 *r* Righteous lips *are* the delight of kings;
And they love him that speaketh right.

14 *s* The wrath of a king *is as* messengers of death:
But a wise man will pacify it.

15 In the light of the king's countenance *is* life;
And *t* his favour *is* *u* as a cloud of the latter rain.

16 *x* How much better *is it* to get wisdom than gold!
And to get understanding rather to be chosen than silver!

---

¹ Heb. *Roll.*
² Heb. *held innocent.*
³ Heb. *Divination.*
⁴ Heb. *All the stones.*

"spirits" (Heb. iv. 12): this is the true remedy against self-deceit.

3. *Commit*] Lit. as in marg., as a man transfers a burden from his own back to one stronger and better able to bear it. Cp. marg. reff.

thy thoughts] *i.e.* The plans or counsels out of which the works spring.

4. *for himself*] Better, **The Lord hath wrought everything for its own end;** and this includes the appointment of an "evil day" for "the wicked" who deserve it.

5. See marg. ref. note.

6. Cp. xv. 8. "By mercy and truth," not by sacrifices and burnt-offerings, "iniquity is purged," atoned for, expiated." The teaching is the same as that of the Prophets.

7. Goodness has power to charm and win even enemies to itself.

9. *deviseth his way*] *i.e.* Thinks it out with anxious care; yet it is the Lord and He only Who directs the steps. Cp. *v.* 1.

10. *A divine sentence*] See marg., *i.e.* "soothsaying" in its darker aspect as contrasted with prophecy. The true oracle is to be sought, not from soothsayers and diviners, but "at the lips of the king," who is ideally the representative, the προφήτης of Jehovah, in His government of mankind.

11. See xi. 1 note. Men are not to think that trade lies outside the Divine Law. God has commanded there also all that belongs to truth and right.

14. While *v.* 13 depicts the king as he ought to be, this verse reminds us of the terrible rapidity with which, in the despotic monarchies of the East, punishment, even death, follows royal displeasure.

15. The "latter rain" is that which falls in March or April just before the harvest. The "cloud" which brings it, at once screening men from the scorching sun, and bringing plenty and blessing, is a fit type of the highest favour.

17 The highway of the upright *is* to depart from evil :
He that keepeth his way preserveth his soul.

18 *ᵛ*Pride *goeth* before destruction,
And an haughty spirit before a fall.

19 Better *it is to be* of an humble spirit with the lowly,
Than to divide the spoil with the proud.

20 *¹*He that handleth a matter wisely shall find good :
And whoso *ᶻ*trusteth in the LORD, happy *is* he.

21 The wise in heart shall be called prudent :
And the sweetness of the lips increaseth learning.

22 *ᵃ*Understanding *is* a wellspring of life unto him that hath it :
But the instruction of fools *is* folly.

23 *ᵇ*The heart of the wise *²*teacheth his mouth,
And addeth learning to his lips.

24 Pleasant words *are as* an honeycomb,
Sweet to the soul, and health to the bones.

25 *ᶜ*There is a way that seemeth right unto a man,
But the end thereof *are* the ways of death.

26 *ᵈ³*He that laboureth laboureth for himself ;
For his mouth *⁴*craveth it of him.

27 *⁵*An ungodly man diggeth up evil :
And in his lips *there is* as a burning fire.

28 *ᵉ*A froward man *⁶*soweth strife :
And *ᶠ*a whisperer separateth chief friends.

29 A violent man *ᵍ*enticeth his neighbour,
And leadeth him into the way *that is* not good.

30 He shutteth his eyes to devise froward things :
Moving his lips he bringeth evil to pass.

31 *ʰ*The hoary head *is* a crown of glory,
If it be found in the way of righteousness.

ᵛ ch. 11. 2.
& 17. 19.
& 18. 12.

ᶻ Ps. 2. 12.
& 34. 8.
& 125. 1.
Isai. 30. 18.
Jer. 17. 7.
ᶜ ch. 13. 14.
& 14. 27.

ᵇ Ps. 37. 30.
Matt. 12. 34.

ᶜ ch. 14. 12.

ᵈ See ch. 9.
12.
Eccl. 6. 7.

ᵉ ch. 6. 14,
19.
& 15. 18.
& 26. 21.
& 29. 22.
ᶠ ch. 17. 9.
ᵍ ch. 1. 10,
&c.

ʰ ch. 20. 29.

---

¹ Or, *He that understandeth a matter.*
² Heb. *maketh wise.*
³ Heb. *The soul of him that laboureth.*
⁴ Heb. *boweth unto him.*
⁵ Heb. *A man of Belial.*
⁶ Heb. *sendeth forth.*

---

20. Good as it is to "handle a matter wisely," it is far better to "trust in the Lord." The former is really impossible except through the latter.

21. The words point to the conditions of all true growth in wisdom ; and he who has the gift of uttering it in winning speech increases it in himself and others.

22. *wellspring of life*] Cp. x. 11 note.

the instruction of fools] Not that which they give, but that which they receive. Cp. xiv. 24. "Folly" is its own all-sufficient punishment.

24. Honey took its place not only among the luxuries, but among the medicines of the Israelites. This two-fold use made it all the fitter to be an emblem both of the true Wisdom which is also true obedience, and of the "pleasant words" in which that Wisdom speaks.

26. *He that laboureth*] Lit., as in the marg., *i.e.* "The desire of the labourer labours

for him" (or, helps him in his work), "for his mouth urges him on." Hunger of some kind is the spring of all hearty labour. Without that the man would sit down and take his ease. So also, unless there is a hunger in the soul, craving to be fed, there can be no true labour after righteousness and wisdom (cp. Matt. v. 6).

27–30. The four verses speak of the same thing, and the well-known opprobrious name, the "man of Belial," stands at the head as stigmatizing the man who delights in causing the mischief of which they treat.

diggeth up evil] *i.e.* Digs an evil pit for others to fall into. Cp. Ps. vii. 15.

30. The physiognomy of the man of Belial, the half-closed eyes that never look you straight in the face, the restlessness or cunning of which biting the lips is the surest indication. Cp. vi. 13.

31. Omit "if." Lit. "it (*i.e.* the hoary head) is found in the way of righteous-

*ch. 19. 11.	32 *He that is* slow to anger *is* better than the mighty; And he that ruleth his spirit than he that taketh a city. 33 The lot is cast into the lap; But the whole disposing thereof *is* of the LORD.
a ch. 15. 17.	**CHAP. 17.** BETTER *is* *a* dry morsel, and quietness therewith, Than an house full of *1* sacrifices *with* strife.
b ch. 10. 5. & 19. 26.	2 A wise servant shall have rule over *b* a son that causeth shame, And shall have part of the inheritance among the brethren.
c Ps. 26. 2. ch. 27. 21. Jer. 17. 10.	3 *c* The fining pot *is* for silver, and the furnace for gold: But the LORD trieth the hearts.
	4 A wicked doer giveth heed to false lips; *And* a liar giveth ear to a naughty tongue.
d ch. 14. 31. *e* Obad. 12.	5 *d* Whoso mocketh the poor reproacheth his Maker, *And* *e* he that is glad at calamities shall not be *2* unpunished.
f Ps. 127. 3. & 128. 3.	6 *f* Children's children *are* the crown of old men; And the glory of children *are* their fathers.
	7 *3* Excellent speech becometh not a fool: Much less do *4* lying lips a prince.
g ch. 18. 16. & 19. 6.	8 *g* A gift *is as* *5* a precious stone in the eyes of him that hath it: Whithersoever it turneth, it prospereth.
h ch. 10. 12. *i* ch. 16. 28.	9 *h* He that covereth a transgression *6* seeketh love; But *i* he that repeateth a matter separateth *very* friends.

1 Or, *good cheer.*   *3* Heb. *A lip of excellency.*   *5* Heb. *a stone of grace.*
2 Heb. *held innocent.*   *4* Heb. *a lip of lying.*   *6* Or, *procureth.*

---

ness," comes as the reward of righteousness.

33. *disposing*] Better, the **judgment** or sentence which depends upon the lot. The lots were thrown into the gathered folds of a robe, and then drawn out. Where everything seemed the merest chance, there the faithful Israelite teacher recognized the guidance of a higher Will. Cp. the case of Achan (Josh. vii. 18), and of Jonathan (1 Sam. xiv. 37–42). The process here described would seem to have been employed ordinarily in trials where the judges could not decide on the facts before them (cp. xviii. 18).

XVII. **1.** *sacrifices*] The feast accompanied the offerings (vii. 14). Part of the victims were burnt upon the Altar, the rest was consumed by the worshipper and his friends. The "house full of sacrifices" was therefore one abounding in sumptuous feasts.

2. The "servant," it must be remembered, was a slave, but (as in such cases as Gen. xv. 2; '2 Sam. xvi. 4) might succeed to the inheritance.

3. Wonderful as is the separation of the pure metal from the dross with which it has mingled, there is something yet more wonderful in the Divine discipline which purifies the good that lies hid, like a grain of gold, even in rough and common natures, and frees it from all admixture of evil. Cp. Mal. iii. 2; 1 Pet. i. 7.

4. The two clauses describe two phases of the mutual affinities of evil. The evil-doer delights in lies, the liar in bad words.

5. *he that is glad at calamities*] A temper common at all times as the most hateful form of evil; the Greek ἐπιχαιρεκακία. The sins spoken of in both clauses occur also in Job's vindication of his integrity (xxxi. 13, 29).

6. The reciprocity of good in sustained family relationships. A long line of children's children is the glory of old age, a long line of ancestors the glory of their descendants.

7. The marg. renderings are more literal and give greater emphasis. What is pointed out is not the unfitness of lying lips for the princely-hearted, but the necessity of harmony, in each case, between character and speech.

8. A half-satirical description of the power of bribery in palaces and among judges. The precious stone (lit. as in marg.) is probably a gem, thought of as a talisman, which, "wherever it turns," will ensure "prosperity" to him who, being the possessor, has the power to give it.

9. *seeketh love*] *i.e.* Takes the course which leads to his gaining it.

he that repeateth a matter] The warning is directed against that which leads a man to dwell with irritating iteration on a past offence instead of burying it in oblivion.

10 [1]A reproof entereth more into a wise man
Than an hundred stripes into a fool.

11 An evil *man* seeketh only rebellion :
Therefore a cruel messenger shall be sent against him.

12 Let [k]a bear robbed of her whelps meet a man,
Rather than a fool in his folly.

13 Whoso [l]rewardeth evil for good,
Evil shall not depart from his house.

14 The beginning of strife *is as* when one letteth out water :
Therefore [m]leave off contention, before it be meddled with.

15 [n]He that justifieth the wicked, and he that condemneth the just,
Even they both *are* abomination to the LORD.

16 Wherefore *is there* a price in the hand of a fool
To get wisdom, [o]seeing *he hath* no heart *to it ?*

17 [p]A friend loveth at all times,
And a brother is born for adversity.

18 [q]A man void of [2]understanding striketh hands,
And becometh surety in the presence of his friend.

19 He loveth transgression that loveth strife :
And [r]he that exalteth his gate seeketh destruction.

20 [3]He that hath a froward heart findeth no good :
And he that hath [s]a perverse tongue falleth into mischief.

21 [t]He that begetteth a fool *doeth it* to his sorrow :
And the father of a fool hath no joy.

22 [u]A merry heart doeth good [4]*like* a medicine :
[x]But a broken spirit drieth the bones.

k Hos. 13. 8.

l Ps. 109. 4.
Jer. 18. 20.
See Rom.
12. 17.
1 Thess. 5. 15.
1 Pet. 3. 9.
m ch. 20. 3.
1 Thess. 4. 11.
n Ex. 23. 7.
ch. 24. 24.
Isai. 5. 23.

o ch. 21. 25, 26.
p Ruth 1. 16.
ch. 18. 24.

q ch. 6. 1.
& 11. 15.

r ch. 16. 18.

s Jam. 3. 8.
t ch. 10. 1.
& 19. 13.
ver. 25.
u ch. 12. 25.
& 15. 13, 15.
x Ps. 22. 15.

[1] Or, *A reproof aweth more*
a wise man, than to strike
a fool an hundred times.
[2] Heb. *heart.*
[3] Heb. *The froward of*
heart.
[4] Or, *to a medicine.*

---

separateth very friends] Better, **alienateth
his chief friend.** The tale-bearer works injury to himself.

11. The proverb expresses the reverence of the East for the supreme authority of the king. The "cruel messenger" is probably the king's officer despatched to subdue and punish. The LXX. renders "The Lord will send a pitiless Angel."

12. The large brown bear of Syria, in her rage at the loss of her whelps, was to the Israelites the strongest type of brute ferocity. Cp. 2 Sam. xvii. 8 ; 2 K. ii. 24.

14. The figure is taken from the great tank or reservoir upon which Eastern cities often depended for their supply of water. The beginning of strife is compared to the first crack in the mound of such a reservoir. At first a few drops ooze out, but after a time the whole mass of waters pour themselves forth with fury, and it is hard to set limits to the destruction which they cause.

before it be meddled with] Lit. "before it rolls, or rushes forward."

15. Men need to be warned against an unjust acquittal, no less than against unjust condemnation. The word "justifieth" has its forensic sense, "to declare righteous," to acquit.

16. More literally : **Why is there a price
in the hand of a fool ? Is it to get wisdom
when he has no heart for it ?** No money will avail without the understanding heart.

17. Some take the proverb to describe (as in xviii. 24) the "friend that sticketh closer than a brother : " and render : **At all times
a friend loveth, but in adversity he is born**
(*i.e.* becomes) **a brother.**

18. Cp. marg. reff. As nothing is nobler than the self-sacrifice of the true friend (*v.* 17), so nothing is more contemptible than the weakness which allows itself to be sacrificed for the sake of worthless associates.

in the presence of his friend] *i.e.* "On behalf of " or "to his friend for some third person."

19. *he that exalteth his gate*] *i.e.* Builds a stately house, indulges in arrogant ostentation.

22. *doeth good like a medicine*] Better, **worketh a good healing.** Omit "like."

23 A wicked *man* taketh a gift out of the bosom
   *v*To pervert the ways of judgment.

24 *z*Wisdom *is* before him that hath understanding;
   But the eyes of a fool *are* in the ends of the earth.

25 *a*A foolish son *is* a grief to his father,
   And bitterness to her that bare him.

26 Also *b*to punish the just *is* not good,
   Nor to strike princes for equity.

27 *c*He that hath knowledge spareth his words :
   And a man of understanding is of ¹an excellent spirit.

28 *d*Even a fool, when he holdeth his peace, is counted wise :
   And he that shutteth his lips *is esteemed* a man of understanding.

CHAP. 18. THROUGH ²desire a man, having separated himself,
seeketh
   And intermeddleth with all wisdom.

2 A fool hath no delight in understanding,
   But that his heart may discover itself.

3 When the wicked cometh, *then* cometh also contempt,
   And with ignominy reproach.

4 *a*The words of a man's mouth *are as* deep waters,
   b And the wellspring of wisdom *as* a flowing brook.

---

¹ Or, *a cool spirit.*
² Or, *He that separateth*   *himself seeketh according*   *meddleth in every busi-*
                              to his *desire,* and *inter-*   *ness :* See Jude 19.

---

23. The words "out of the bosom," from
the fold of the garment, rather than from
the bag or girdle in which money was usually
carried, possibly point to the stealthiness
with which the "gift" (or, bribe) is offered
to the judge.

24. *before him*] Set straight before his
eyes as the mark to which they look.
Others, following the LXX. and Vulg., interpret the verse, Wisdom is seen in the
clear, stedfast look of the wise man as contrasted with the wandering gaze of the
fool.

25. Cp. *v.* 21. Here is added a reference
to the sorrow which the folly of a child
brings specially to the mother.

26. *Nor to strike* &c.] Better, **and to strike
the noble** (in character rather than in rank)
is against right. Cp. John xviii. 23.

27. Better, **A man of calm** (or noble)
spirit is a man of understanding.

28. *is esteemed*] Or, "is" (simply). The
maxim would imply that silence is in any
case good.

XVIII. 1. The text and the marginal
readings indicate the two chief construc-
tions of this somewhat difficult verse. Other
renderings are

(1) **He who separateth himself from
others seeks his own desire, and rushes
forward against all wise counsel :** a warning against self-will and the self-assertion

which exults in differing from the received
customs and opinions of mankind.

(2) He who separates himself (from the
foolish, unlearned multitude) seeks his own
desire (that which is worthy to be desired),
and mingleth himself with all wisdom. So
the Jewish commentators generally.

Between (1) blaming and (2) commending
the life of isolation, the decision must be
that (1) is most in harmony with the temper
of the Book of Proverbs ; but it is not
strange that Pharisaism, in its very name,
separating and self-exalting, should have
adopted (2).

2. Another form of egotism. In "understanding," *i.e.* self-knowledge, the "fool"
finds no pleasure ; but self-assertion, talking
about himself and his own opinions, is his
highest joy.

3. *with ignominy*] Better, "together with
baseness comes reproach.' The outer shame
follows close upon the inner.

4. The parallelism of the two clauses is
probably one of contrast. If so, the proverb is a comparison between all teaching
from without and that of the light within.
"The words of a man's mouth " are dark as
the "deep waters" of a pool, or tank
("deep waters " being associated in the Old
Testament with the thought of darkness
and mystery; cp. xx. 5 ; Ps. lxix. 2 ; Eccles.
vii. 24); but "the wellspring of wisdom is

5 *It is* not good to accept the person of the wicked,
To overthrow the righteous in judgment.

6 A fool's lips enter into contention,
And his mouth calleth for strokes.

7 *A fool's mouth *is* his destruction,
And his lips *are* the snare of his soul.

8 *The words of a ¹talebearer *are* ²as wounds,
And they go down into the ³innermost parts of the belly.

9 He also that is slothful in his work
Is *brother to him that is a great waster.

10 *The name of the LORD *is* a strong tower :
The righteous runneth into it, and ⁴is safe.

11 *The rich man's wealth *is* his strong city,
And as an high wall in his own conceit.

12 *Before destruction the heart of man is haughty,
And before honour *is* humility.

13 He that ⁵answereth a matter *before he heareth *it*,
It *is* folly and shame unto him.

14 The spirit of a man will sustain his infirmity ;
But a wounded spirit who can bear ?

15 The heart of the prudent getteth knowledge ;
And the ear of the wise seeketh knowledge.

16 *A man's gift maketh room for him,
And bringeth him before great men.

17 *He that is* first in his own cause *seemeth* just ;
But his neighbour cometh and searcheth him.

18 The lot causeth contentions to cease,
And parteth between the mighty.

c Lev. 19. 15.
Deut. 1. 17.
& 16. 19.
ch. 24. 23.
& 28. 21.

d ch. 10. 14.
& 12. 13.
& 13. 3.
Eccl. 10. 12.
e ch. 12. 18.

f ch. 28. 24.

g 2 Sam. 22.
3, 51.
Ps. 27. 1.
& 61. 3, 4.
& 91. 2.
& 144. 2.
h ch. 10. 15.
i ch. 11. 2.
& 15. 33.
& 16. 18.
k John 7. 51.

l Gen. 32. 20.
1 Sam. 25.
27.
ch. 17. 8.
& 21. 14.

---

¹ Or, *whisperer.*
² Or, *like as when men are*   *wounded.*
³ Heb. *chambers.*
⁴ Heb. *is set aloft.*
⁵ Heb. *returneth a word.*

---

as a flowing brook," bright and clear. The verse presents a contrast like that of Jer. ii. 13.

6–8. The first verse speaks of the immediate, the others of the remote, results of the "fool's" temper. First, "contention," then "strokes" or blows, then "destruction," and last, "wounds."

8. *wounds*] The word so rendered occurs here and in xxvi. 22 only. Others render it "dainties," and take the verse to describe the avidity with which men swallow in tales of scandal. They find their way to the innermost recesses of man's nature.

10. *safe*] Lit. as in the marg. *i.e.* is exalted. Cp. Ps. xviii. 2, 33.

11. What the name of the Lord is to the righteous (*v.* 10), that wealth is to the rich. He flees to it for refuge as to a strong city ; but it is so only "in his own conceit" or imagination.

high] In the Hebrew the same word as "safe" (*v.* 10), and manifestly used in reference to it.

12. *before*] In the sense of priority of time.

14. *infirmity*] Bodily pain or trouble. "Spirit" in the Heb. is masculine in the first clause, feminine in the second, as though used in the latter as having lost its strength.

15. With the wise and prudent there is no loss of time. "Heart" and "ear"—the mind working within, or gathering from without materials for its thought — are, through this channel or that, ever gaining knowledge.

16. The "gift" (or, bribe), by a bold personification, appears as the powerful "friend at court," who introduces another, and makes him welcome in high places.

17. A protest against another fault in judging. Haste is hardly less evil than corruption. "Audi alteram partem" should be the rule of every judge.

his neighbour] The other party to the suit "searcheth," *i.e.* scrutinizes and detects him.

18. Cp. xvi. 33 note. A tacit appeal to

19 A brother offended *is harder to be won* than a strong city:
And *their* contentions *are* like the bars of a castle.

m ch. 12. 14. & 13. 2.

20 *m*A man's belly shall be satisfied with the fruit of his mouth;
And with the increase of his lips shall he be filled.

n See Matt. 12. 37.

21 *n*Death and life *are* in the power of the tongue:
And they that love it shall eat the fruit thereof.

o ch. 19. 14. & 31. 10.

22 *oWhoso* findeth a wife findeth a good *thing*,
And obtaineth favour of the LORD.

p Jam. 2. 3.

23 The poor useth intreaties;—but the rich answereth *p*roughly.

q ch. 17. 17.

24 A man *that hath* friends must shew himself friendly:
*q*And there is a friend *that* sticketh closer than a brother.

a ch. 28. 6.

CHAP. 19. BETTER *ais* the poor that walketh in his integrity,
Than *he that is* perverse in his lips, and is a fool.

2 Also, *that* the soul *be* without knowledge, *it is* not good;
And he that hasteth with *his* feet sinneth.

3 The foolishness of man perverteth his way.
*b*And his heart fretteth against the LORD.

b Ps. 37. 7.

c ch. 14. 20.

4 *c*Wealth maketh many friends;
But the poor is separated from his neighbour.

d ver. 9.
Ex. 23. 1.
Deut. 19. 16, 19.
ch. 6. 19.
& 21. 28.
e ch. 29. 26.
f ch. 17. 8.
& 18. 16.
& 21. 14.
g ch. 14. 20.
h Ps. 38. 11.

5 *d*A false witness shall not be [1]unpunished,
And *he that* speaketh lies shall not escape.

6 *e*Many will intreat the favour of the prince:
And *f*every man *is* a friend to [2]him that giveth gifts.

7 *g*All the brethren of the poor do hate him:
How much more do his friends go *h*far from him?
He pursueth *them with* words, *yet* they *are* wanting *to him*.

[1] Heb. *held innocent.*   [2] Heb. *a man of gifts.*

---

the Divine Judge gave a fairer prospect of a just decision than corruption (*v.* 16) or hasty onesidedness (*v.* 17).

19. The meaning of the first clause is obtained in the A.V. by the insertion of the words in italics, and it seems on the whole to be the best. The LXX. and Vulg. give an entirely different rendering, based, apparently, upon a different text.

20. The general sense is plain. A man must for good or evil take the consequence of his words, as well as his deeds. Cp. marg. reff.

22. The sense seems to require, "Whoso findeth a good wife," as in some Chaldee MSS.; but the proverb-writer may be looking at marriage in its ideal aspect, and sees in every such union the hands of God joining together man and woman for their mutual good. The LXX. adds "He who casts out a good wife, casts away that which is good: but he that keepeth an adulteress is foolish and ungodly."

23. Note the paradox. The poor man, of whom one might expect roughness, supplicates; the rich, well-nurtured, from whom one might look for courtesy, answers harshly and brusquely.

24. Better, "**A man of many companions is so to his own destruction**, but there is a friend (the true, loving friend) &c." It is not the multitude of so-called friends that helps us. They may only embarrass and perplex. What we prize is the one whose love is stronger and purer even than all ties of kindred.

XIX. 1. The "perverse" man is the rich fool, as contrasted with the poor man who is upright.

Both *vv.* 1 and 2 are wanting in the LXX.

3. The unwisdom which, having brought about disasters by its own perverseness, then turns round and "fretteth," *i.e.* angrily murmurs against the Providence of God.

perverteth] Rather, "overturneth," "maketh to fail."

6. *intreat the favour* &c.] Lit. "stroke the face" of the man of princely nature, who gives munificently.

7. It seems best to follow the Vulgate in taking the last clause as a separate maxim, "He who pursues words, nought are they;" *i.e.* the fair speeches and promises of help come to nothing. A various reading in the

8 He that getteth [1]wisdom loveth his own soul:
He that keepeth understanding [i]shall find good.

9 [k]A false witness shall not be unpunished,
And *he that* speaketh lies shall perish.

10 Delight is not seemly for a fool;
Much less [l]for a servant to have rule over princes.

11 [m]The [2]discretion of a man deferreth his anger;
[n]And *it is* his glory to pass over a transgression.

12 [o]The king's wrath *is* as the roaring of a lion;
But his favour *is* [p]as dew upon the grass.

13 [q]A foolish son *is* the calamity of his father:
[r]And the contentions of a wife *are* a continual dropping.

14 [s]House and riches *are* the inheritance of fathers:
And [t]a prudent wife *is* from the LORD.

15 [u]Slothfulness casteth into a deep sleep;
And an idle soul shall [x]suffer hunger.

16 [y]He that keepeth the commandment keepeth his own soul;
But he that despiseth his ways shall die.

17 [z]He that hath pity upon the poor lendeth unto the LORD;
And [3]that which he hath given will he pay him again.

18 [a]Chasten thy son while there is hope,
And let not thy soul spare [4]for his crying.

19 A man of great wrath shall suffer punishment:
For if thou deliver *him*, yet thou must [5]do it again.

[i] ch. 16. 20.
[k] ver. 5.
[l] ch. 30. 22. Eccl. 10. 6, 7.
[m] ch. 14. 29. Jam. 1. 19.
[n] ch. 16. 32.
[o] ch. 16. 14. & 20. 2. & 28. 15.
[p] Hos. 14. 5.
[q] ch. 10. 1. & 15. 20. & 17. 21, 25.
[r] ch. 21. 9. & 27. 15.
[s] 2 Cor. 12. 14.
[t] ch. 18. 22.
[u] ch. 6. 9.
[x] ch. 10. 4. & 20. 13. & 23. 21.
[y] Luke 10. 28. & 11. 28.
[z] ch. 28. 27. Eccl. 11. 1. Matt. 10. 42. 2 Cor. 9. 6, 7, 8. Heb. 6. 10.
[a] ch. 13. 24. & 23. 13. & 29. 17.

[1] Heb. *an heart.*
[2] Or, *prudence.*
[3] Or, *his deed.*
[4] Or, *to his destruction:* or, *to cause him to die.*
[5] Heb. *add.*

Hebrew gives, "he pursues after words, and these he shall have"—*i.e.* these, and nothing else.

This and other like maxims do not in reality cast scorn and shame on a state which Christ has pronounced "blessed." Side by side with them is *v.* 1, setting forth the honour of an upright poverty. But as there is an honourable poverty, so there is one which is altogether inglorious, caused by sloth and folly, leading to shame and ignominy, and it is well that the man who wishes to live rightly should avoid this. The teaching of Christ is, of course, higher than that of the Book of Proverbs, being based upon a fuller revelation of the Divine Will, pointing to a higher end and a nobler standard of duty, and transcending the common motives and common facts of life.

8. *wisdom*] Lit., as in the marg., to gain a "heart," *i.e.* the higher faculties both of reason and feeling, is identical with gaining wisdom, *i.e.* the faculty which seeks and finds.

10. "Delight," high unrestrained enjoyment, is to the "fool" who lacks wisdom but a temptation and a snare. The second clause carries the thought on to what the despotism of Eastern monarchies often presented, the objectionable rule of some favoured slave, it might be, of alien birth, over the princes and nobles of the land.

13. *calamity*] The Hebrew word is plural (as in Pss. lvii. 1, xci. 3), and seems to express the multiplied and manifold sorrow caused by the foolish son.

continual dropping] The irritating, unceasing, sound of the fall, drop after drop, of water through the chinks in the roof.

15. *casteth into a deep sleep*] Better, **causeth deep sleep to fall.**

16. *keepeth his own soul*] *i.e.* His life in the truest and highest sense.

17. Note the original greatness of the thought. We give to the poor. Have we lost our gift? No, what we gave, we have lent to One Who will repay with usury. Cp. the yet nobler truth of our Lord's teaching (Matt. xxv. 40).

18. *while there is hope*] While he is still young, and capable of being reformed.

crying] Better, as in the margin, **Do not set thy soul on his destruction**; words which either counsel forbearance in the act of chastisement (cp. Eph. vi. 4; Col. iii. 21); or urge that a false clemency is a real cruelty. The latter sense is preferable. The father is warned that to forbear from chastising is virtually to expose the son who needs it to a far worse penalty.

19. The sense of the last words seems to be that the connexion between wrath and punishment is so invariable, that all efforts

20 Hear counsel, and receive instruction,
That thou mayest be wise [b]in thy latter end.

b Ps. 37. 37.

21 [c]There are many devices in a man's heart ;
Nevertheless the counsel of the LORD, that shall stand.

c Job 23. 13.
Ps. 33. 10.
ch. 16. 1.
Isai. 14. 26.
& 46. 10.
Acts 5. 39.
Heb. 6. 17.

22 The desire of a man *is* his kindness :
And a poor man *is* better than a liar.

23 [d]The fear of the LORD *tendeth* to life :
And *he that hath it* shall abide satisfied ;
He shall not be visited with evil.

d 1 Tim. 4. 8.

24 [e]A slothful *man* hideth his hand in *his* bosom,
And will not so much as bring it to his mouth again.

e ch. 15. 19.
& 26. 13, 15.

25 [f]Smite a scorner, and the simple [1][g]will beware :
And [h]reprove one that hath understanding, *and* he will understand knowledge.

f ch. 21. 11.
g Deut. 13. 11.
h ch. 9. 8.

26 He that wasteth *his* father, *and* chaseth away *his* mother,
Is [i]a son that causeth shame, and bringeth reproach.

i ch. 17. 2.

27 Cease, my son, to hear the instruction
That causeth to err from the words of knowledge.

28 [2]An ungodly witness scorneth judgment :
And [k]the mouth of the wicked devoureth iniquity.

k Job 15. 16.
& 20. 12.
& 34. 7.
l ch. 10. 13.
& 26. 3.

29 Judgments are prepared for scorners,
[l]And stripes for the back of fools.

CHAP. 20. WINE [a]*is* a mocker, strong drink *is* raging .
And whosoever is deceived thereby is not wise.

a Gen. 9. 21.
ch. 23. 29.
Isai. 28. 7.
Hos. 4. 11.
b ch. 16. 14.
& 19. 12.
c ch. 8. 36.

2 [b]The fear of a king *is* as the roaring of a lion :
Whoso provoketh him to anger [c]sinneth *against* his own soul.

[1] Heb. *will be cunning.*   [2] Heb. *A witness of Belial.*

---

to save the passionate man from the disas-
trous consequences which he brings on his
own head are made in vain.

21. Contrast the *many* purposes of man,
shifting, changing, from good to better, from
bad to worse, and the one unchanging
righteous "counsel" of Jehovah.

22. The "liar" is probably the man,
who makes false excuses for not giving, and
so is inferior to the poor man, whose "desire," the wish to do good, is taken, in the
absence of means to carry it into effect, for
the act of kindness itself.

23. *shall abide satisfied*] Better, **one that
is satisfied hath a sure abiding-place.**
The word "abide" has, most probably,
here as elsewhere, its original sense of
"passing the night." Even in the hour of
darkness he shall be free from fear.

24. *hideth his hand in his bosom*] Better,
dippeth his hand in the dish (cp. 2 K. xxi.
13). The scene brought before us is that of
an Eastern feast. There are no knives, or
forks, or spoons. Every guest has to help
himself, or be helped by the host. Cp.
John xiii. 26.

25. Words which embrace nearly the
whole theory of punishment. If the man

who offends is a "scorner," hardened beyond all hope of reformation, then punish
him by way of retribution and example,
and let the penalty be sharp, that even
the unwary and careless may beware. If
the man be "understanding," then let the
punishment take the form of discipline.
Admonish, reprove, educate.

26. Or, **A son that causeth shame, and
bringeth reproach, is one that wasteth
his father, and chaseth away his mother.**

27. Lit. **Cease, my son, to hear instruction, that thou mayest err from the words
of knowledge ;** advice given ironically
to do that to which his weakness leads
him, with a clear knowledge of the evil
to which he is drifting.

28. *ungodly witness*] Lit. "Witness of
Belial," "worthless," "untruthful."

devoureth iniquity] Seizes on it eagerly,
as a dainty, lives on it.

XX. 1. "Wine" and "strong drink"
are personified as themselves doing what
they make men do. The latter (see Lev. x.
9 note) is here, probably, the "palm-wine"
of Syria.

2. *sinneth against his own soul*] *i.e.* Against
his own life (cp. Hab. ii. 10).

3 *It is* an honour for a man to cease from strife:
But every fool will be meddling.

4 *The sluggard will not plow by reason of the ¹cold;
*Therefore shall he beg in harvest, and *have* nothing.

5 *Counsel in the heart of man *is like* deep water;
But a man of understanding will draw it out.

6 *Most men will proclaim every one his own ²goodness:
But *a faithful man who can find?

7 *The just *man* walketh in his integrity:
*His children *are* blessed after him.

8 *A king that sitteth in the throne of judgment
Scattereth away all evil with his eyes.

9 *Who can say, I have made my heart clean,
I am pure from my sin?

10 *³Divers weights, *and* ⁴divers measures,
Both of them *are* alike abomination to the LORD.

11 Even a child is *known by his doings,
Whether his work *be* pure, and whether *it be* right.

12 *The hearing ear, and the seeing eye,
The LORD hath made even both of them.

13 *Love not sleep, lest thou come to poverty;
Open thine eyes, *and* thou shalt be satisfied with bread.

14 *It is* naught, *it is* naught, saith the buyer:
But when he is gone his way, then he boasteth.

15 There is gold, and a multitude of rubies:
But *the lips of knowledge *are* a precious jewel.

16 *Take his garment that is surety *for* a stranger:
And take a pledge of him for a strange woman.

---

¹ Or, *winter.*
² Or, *bounty.*
³ Heb. *A stone and a stone.*
⁴ Heb. *An ephah and an ephah.*

d ch. 17. 14.

e ch. 10. 4.
& 19. 24.
- ch. 19. 15.

g ch. 18. 4.

h ch. 25. 14.
Matt. 6. 2.
Luke 18. 11.
i Ps. 12. 1.
Luke 18. 8.
k 2 Cor. 1. 12.
l Ps. 37. 26.
& 112. 2.
m ver. 26.
n 1 K. 8. 46.
2 Chr. 6. 36.
Job 14. 4.
Ps. 51. 5.
Eccl. 7. 20.
1 Cor. 4. 4.
1 John 1. 8.
o Deut. 25.
13, &c.
& 16. 11.
Mic. 6. 10.
p Matt. 7. 16.
q Ex. 4. 11.
r ch. 6. 9.
& 12. 11.
& 19. 15.
Rom. 12. 11.

s Job 28. 12,
16–19.
ch. 3. 15.
& 8. 11.
t ch. 22. 26,
27.

---

3. *meddling*] See xvii. 14 note.

4. Ploughing-time in Palestine is in November and December, when the wind blows commonly from the North.

5. The contest between reticence on the one side and pertinacity in search on the other is represented as by a parable. The well may be very deep (cp. marg. ref.), but the "man of understanding" has skill enough to draw up the water even to the last drop. Every question is, as it were, a turning of the windlass.

6. *goodness*] With the special sense of bounty, beneficence. Contrast promise and performance. Men boast of their liberality, and we look in vain for the fulfilment of actual obligations.

9. A warning voice against the spirit, which, ignorant of its own guilt, is forward to condemn others.

10. See xi. 1: Here perhaps, as a companion to *v.* 9, with a wider application to all judging one man by rules which we do not apply to ourselves or to another.

11. The graces or the faults of children are not trifles. "The child is father of the man;" and the earliest actions are prophecies of the future, whether it will be pure and right, or unclean and evil.

12. Not only do we owe the gifts of sight and hearing to Jehovah, but He, being the giver, will also call us to account for them (cp. Ps. xciv. 9).

13. *open thine eyes*] Be vigilant and active. That is the secret of prosperity.

14. *naught*] Bad, worthless (2 K. ii. 19).

15. *a precious jewel*] Lit. "A vessel of preciousness," *i.e.* most precious of all are "the lips of knowledge."

16. The warning against suretiship and lust are here repeated and combined (cp. xxvii. 13). The judge tells the creditor to seize the goods of the surety who has been weak enough to pledge himself for those who are alien to him, instead of those of the actual debtor. The reading of the A. V. recalls in the second clause the history of Tamar (Gen. xxxviii. 17, 18). The Hebrew

u ch. 9. 17.

x ch. 15. 22.
& 24. 6.
y Luke14.31.
z ch. 11. 13.
a Rom. 16.
18.
b Ex. 21. 17.
c Job18.5,6.
ch. 24. 20.
d ch. 28. 20.
e Hab. 2. 6.

f Deut.32.35.
ch. 17. 13.
& 24. 29.
1 Thess. 5.
15.
1 Pet. 3. 9.
g 2 Sam. 16.
12.
h ver. 10.
i Ps. 37. 23.
ch. 16. 9.
Jer. 10. 23.
k Eccl.5.4,5.
l Ps. 101.5.
ver. 8.

m 1 Cor. 2.
11.

17 u1Bread of deceit is sweet to a man;
But afterwards his mouth shall be filled with gravel.

18 x Every purpose is established by counsel:
y And with good advice make war.

19 z He that goeth about as a talebearer revealeth secrets:
Therefore meddle not with him a that 2 flattereth with his lips.

20 b Whoso curseth his father or his mother,
c His 3 lamp shall be put out in obscure darkness.

21 d An inheritance may be gotten hastily at the beginning;
e But the end thereof shall not be blessed.

22 f Say not thou, I will recompense evil;
But g wait on the LORD, and he shall save thee.

23 h Divers weights are an abomination unto the LORD;
And 4 a false balance is not good.

24 i Man's goings are of the LORD;
How can a man then understand his own way?

25 It is a snare to the man who devoureth that which is holy,
And k after vows to make enquiry.

26 l A wise king scattereth the wicked,
And bringeth the wheel over them.

27 m The spirit of man is the 5 candle of the LORD,
Searching all the inward parts of the belly.

1 Heb. Bread of lying, or,
falsehood.
2 Or, enticeth.
3 Or, candle.
4 Heb. balances of deceit.
5 Or, lamp.

---

text, however, gives "strangers" in the masculine plural, and is probably right, the feminine being the reading of the margin, probably adopted from xxvii. 13.

17. "To eat gravel" was a Hebrew (Lam. iii. 16), and is an Arabic, phrase for getting into trouble. So "bread," got by deceit, tastes sweet at first, but ends by leaving the hunger of the soul unsatisfied. There is a pleasure in the sense of cleverness felt after a hard bargain or a successful fraud, which must be met by bidding men look on the after consequences.

19. flattereth] Lit. "The man who opens his lips," who has no reticence; such a man, with or without intending it, does the work of a talebearer.

20. A connecting link between Lev. xx. 9 and Matt. xv. 4. The words, "his lamp shall be put out," describe the failure of outward happiness.

21. Or, An inheritance gotten hastily (greedily sought after by unjust means) at the beginning, the end thereof shall not be blessed. Another reading gives, "an inheritance loathed, (cp. Zech. xi. 8), or with a curse upon it." The A.V. agrees with the Versions.

22. God's awarding to everyone according to his works, is the true check to the spirit of vindictiveness (cp. Rom. xii. 17, 19). Note that man is not told to wait on the Lord in expectation of seeing vengeance on his

enemies, but "He shall save thee." The difference of the two hopes, in their effect upon the man's character, is incalculable.

24. The order of a man's life is a mystery even to himself. He knows not whither he is going, or for what God is educating him.

25. Better, It is a snare to a man to utter a vow (of consecration) rashly, and after vows to enquire whether he can fulfil them. Both clauses are a protest against the besetting sin of rash and hasty vows. Cp. marg. ref.

26. the wheel] The threshing-wheel (Isai. xxviii. 27, 28), which passes over the corn and separates the grain from the chaff. The proverb involves therefore the idea of the division of the good from the evil, no less than that of the punishment of the latter.

27. The spirit of man] The "breath" of Gen. ii. 7, the higher life, above that which he has in common with lower animals, coming to him direct from God. Such a life, with all its powers of insight, consciousness, reflection, is as a lamp which God has lighted, throwing its rays into the darkest recesses of the heart. A yet higher truth is proclaimed in the Prologue of St. John's Gospel. The candle, or lamp of Jehovah, derives its light from "the Light that lighteth every man," even the Eternal Word.

28 [n]Mercy and truth preserve the king:
And his throne is upholden by mercy.

[n] Ps. 101. 1.
ch. 29. 14.

29 The glory of young men *is* their strength:
And [o]the beauty of old men *is* the grey head.

[o] ch. 16. 31.

30 The blueness of a wound [1]cleanseth away evil:
So *do* stripes the inward parts of the belly.

CHAP. 21. THE king's heart *is* in the hand of the LORD, *as* the
rivers of water:
He turneth it whithersoever he will.

2 [a]Every way of a man *is* right in his own eyes:
[b]But the LORD pondereth the hearts

[a] ch. 16. 2.

[b] ch. 24. 12.
Luke 16. 15.

3 [c]To do justice and judgment
Is more acceptable to the LORD than sacrifice.

[c] 1 Sam. 15. 22.
Ps. 50. 8.
ch. 15. 8.
Isai. 1. 11, &c.

4 [d][2]An high look, and a proud heart,
And [3]the plowing of the wicked, *is* sin.

[d] ch. 6. 17.

5 [e]The thoughts of the diligent *tend* only to plenteousness;
But of every one *that is* hasty only to want.

[e] ch. 10. 4.
& 13. 4.

6 [f]The getting of treasures by a lying tongue
Is a vanity tossed to and fro of them that seek death.

[f] ch. 10. 2.
& 13. 11.
& 20. 21.
2 Pet. 2. 3.

7 The robbery of the wicked shall [4]destroy them;
Because they refuse to do judgment.

8 The way of man *is* froward and strange:
But *as for* the pure, his work *is* right.

9 [g]*It is* better to dwell in a corner of the housetop,
Than with [5]a brawling woman in [6]a wide house.

[g] ver. 19.
ch. 19. 13.
& 25. 24.
& 27. 15.

[1] Heb. is *a purging medicine against evil.*
[2] Heb. *Haughtiness of eyes.*
[3] Or, *the light of the wicked.*
[4] Heb. *saw them,* or, *dwell with them.*
[5] Heb. *a woman of contentions.*
[6] Heb. *an house of society.*

---

30. Better, **The blueness of a wound is a cleansing of evil, so are the stripes that go down to the inward parts of the belly.**
The open sores of wounds left by the scourge, unclean and foul as they seem, are yet a cleansing, purifying process for evil; so also are the stripes that reach the inward parts of the belly, *i.e.* the sharp reproofs, the stings of conscience, which penetrate where no scourge can reach, into the inner life of man. Chastisement, whatever be its nature, must be real; the scourge must leave its mark, the reproof must go deep.

XXI. 1. *rivers of water*] See Ps. i. 3 note. As the cultivator directs the stream into the channels where it is most wanted, so Jehovah directs the thoughts of the true king, that his favours may fall, not at random, but in harmony with a Divine order.

3. Cp. marg. reff. The words have a special significance as coming from the king who had built the Temple, and had offered sacrifices that "could not be numbered for multitude" (1 K. viii. 5).

4. *the plowing*] The Heb. word, with a change in its vowel-points, may signify either (1) the "fallow-field," the "tillage" of xiii. 23, or (2) the **lamp.** According to (1) the verse would mean, "The outward signs of pride, the proud heart, the broad lands of the wicked, all are evil." (2) however belongs, as it were, to the language of the time and of the Book (xiii. 9, xxiv. 20). The "lamp of the wicked" is their outwardly bright prosperity.

5. Here diligence is opposed, not to sloth but to haste. Undue hurry is as fatal to success as undue procrastination.

6. *vanity*] Or, "**a breath** driven to and fro of those that are seeking death." Another reading of the last words is, "of the snares of death" (cp. 1 Tim. vi. 9). Some commentators have suggested that the "vapour" or "mist" is the mirage of the desert, misleading those who follow it, and becoming a "net of death."

7. *robbery*] Probably the "violence" which the wicked practise.
shall destroy them] More literally, **carries them away.**

8. Or, "Perverse is the way of a sin-burdened man."

9. *a wide house*] Lit. "a house of companionship," *i.e.* **a house shared with her.** The flat roof of an Eastern house was

h Jam. 4. 5.	10 *h* The soul of the wicked desireth evil: His neighbour ¹findeth no favour in his eyes.
i ch. 19. 25.	11 *i* When the scorner is punished, the simple is made wise: And when the wise is instructed, he receiveth knowledge.
	12 The righteous *man* wisely considereth the house of the wicked: *But God* overthroweth the wicked for *their* wickedness.
k Matt. 7. 2. & 18. 30, &c. Jam. 2. 13.	13 *k* Whoso stoppeth his ears at the cry of the poor, He also shall cry himself, but shall not be heard.
l ch. 17. 8, 23. & 18. 16.	14 *l* A gift in secret pacifieth anger: And a reward in the bosom strong wrath.
m ch. 10. 29.	15 *It is* joy to the just to do judgment: *m* But destruction *shall be* to the workers of iniquity.
	16 The man that wandereth out of the way of understanding Shall remain in the congregation of the dead.
	17 He that loveth ²pleasure *shall be* a poor man: He that loveth wine and oil shall not be rich.
n ch. 11. 8. Isai. 43. 3, 4.	18 *n* The wicked *shall be* a ransom for the righteous, And the transgressor for the upright.
o ver. 9.	19 *o It is* better to dwell ³in the wilderness, Than with a contentious and an angry woman.
p Ps. 112. 3.	20 *p There is* treasure to be desired and oil in the dwelling of the wise; But a foolish man spendeth it up.
q ch. 15. 9. Matt. 5. 6.	21 *q* He that followeth after righteousness and mercy Findeth life, righteousness, and honour.
r Eccl. 9. 14, &c.	22 *r* A wise *man* scaleth the city of the mighty, And casteth down the strength of the confidence thereof.
s ch. 12. 13. & 13. 3. & 18. 21. Jam. 3. 2.	23 *s* Whoso keepeth his mouth and his tongue Keepeth his soul from troubles.

¹ Heb. *is not favoured.*
² Or, *sport.*
³ Heb. *in the land of the desert.*

often used for retirement by day, or in summer for sleep by night. The corner of such a roof was exposed to all changes of weather, and the point of the proverb lies in the thought that all winds and storms which a man might meet with there are more endurable than the tempest within.

12. Or, **The Righteous One** (Jehovah) **regardeth well the house of the wicked, and maketh the wicked fall into mischief.**

16. *congregation of the dead*] The Rephaim (cp. ii. 18 note).

remain] *i.e.* "He shall find a resting-place, but it shall be in Hades."

17. *wine and oil*] *i.e.* The costly adjuncts of a princely banquet. The price of oil or precious unguent was about equal to the 300 days' wages of a field labourer (Matt. xx. 2). Indulgence in such a luxury would thus become the type of all extravagance and excess.

18. Cp. marg. reff. Evil doers seem to draw down the wrath of God upon their heads, and so become, as it were, the scape-goats of the comparatively righteous.

20. *spendeth it up*] Lit. **swalloweth it.** The wise man keeps a store in reserve. He gains uprightly, spends moderately, never exhausts himself. But the proverb may have also a higher application. The wise man stores up all "treasure to be desired" of wisdom, all "oil" of divine influence, which strengthens and refreshes, and so is ready at all times for the work to which the Master calls him. Cp. Matt. xxv. 1-13.

21. The man who keeps "righteousness" will assuredly find it, but he will find besides it the "life" and the "honour" which he was not seeking. Cp. 1 K. iii. 13; Matt. vi. 33.

22. Even in war, counsel does more than brute strength. So of the warfare which is carried on in the inner battle-field of the soul. There also wisdom is mighty to the "pulling down of strongholds" (2 Cor. x. 4,

24 Proud *and* haughty scorner *is* his name,
Who dealeth [1]in proud wrath.

25 [t]The desire of the slothful killeth him;
For his hands refuse to labour.

26 He coveteth greedily all the day long:
But the [u]righteous giveth and spareth not.

27 [x]The sacrifice of the wicked *is* abomination:
How much more, *when* he bringeth it [2]with a wicked mind?

28 [y3]A false witness shall perish:
But the man that heareth speaketh constantly.

29 A wicked man hardeneth his face:
But *as for* the upright, he [4]directeth his way.

30 [z] *There is* no wisdom nor understanding
Nor counsel against the LORD.

31 [a]The horse *is* prepared against the day of battle:
But [b5] safety *is* of the LORD.

CHAP. 22. A [a]*GOOD* name *is* rather to be chosen than great riches,
And [6]loving favour rather than silver and gold.

2 [b]The rich and poor meet together:
[c]The LORD *is* the maker of them all.

3 [d]A prudent *man* foreseeth the evil, and hideth himself:
But the simple pass on, and are punished.

4 [e7]By humility *and* the fear of the LORD
Are riches, and honour, and life.

5 [f]Thorns *and* snares *are* in the way of the froward:
[g] He that doth keep his soul shall be far from them.

t ch. 13. 4.

u Ps. 37. 26.
& 112 9.
x Ps. 50. 9.
Isai. 66. 3.
Jer. 6. 20.
Amos 5. 22.
y ch. 19. 5, 9.

z Isai. 8. 9,
10.
Jer. 9. 23.
Acts 5. 39.
a Ps. 20. 7.
& 33. 17.
Isai. 31. 1.
b Ps. 3. 8.
a Eccl. 7. 1.

b ch. 29. 13.
1 Cor. 12. 21.
c Job 31. 15.
ch. 14. 31.
d ch. 14. 16.
& 27. 12.

e Ps. 112. 3.
Matt. 6. 33.

f ch. 15. 19.
g 1 John 5.
18.

[1] Heb. *in the wrath of pride.*
[2] Heb. *in wickedness?*
[3] Heb. *A witness of lies.*
[4] Or, *considereth.*
[5] Or, *victory.*
[6] Or, *favour is better than, &c.*
[7] Or, *The reward of humility, &c.*

where St. Paul uses the very words of the LXX. Version of this passage), and the wise man scales and keeps the city which the strong man armed has seized and made his own.

25. *killeth him*] He wastes his strength and life in unsatisfied longings for something which he has not energy to gain. The wish to do great or good things may sometimes be taken for the deed, but if the hindrance is from a man's own sloth, it does but add to his condemnation.

26. *all the day long*] Better, **every day.** The wish of the slothful man passes into restless, covetous, dissatisfied desire; the righteous, free from that desire, gives without grudging.

27. A lower depth even than xv. 8. The wicked man may connect his devotion with his guilt, offer his sacrifice and vow his vow (as men have done under heathenism or a corrupted Christianity) for success in the perpetration of a crime.

28. *speaketh constantly*] His testimony abides evermore who repeats simply what he has heard, whether from the lips of men or from the voice within, in contrast with "the false witness."

29. *directeth*] *i.e.* Makes straight and firm. On one side it is the callousness of guilt, on the other the confidence of integrity.

30, 31. Two companion-proverbs. Nothing avails against, nothing without, God. The horse is the type of warlike strength, used chiefly or exclusively in battle. 1 K. iv. 26, x. 26-28, may be thought of as having given occasion to the latter of the two proverbs.

XXII. 1. Omit "good." The word is an insertion. To the Hebrew, "name" by itself conveyed the idea of good repute, just as "men without a name" (cp. Job xxx. 8 marg.) are those sunk in ignominy. The marg. gives a preferable rendering of the second clause of this verse.

2. Cp. marg. reff. Another recognition of the oneness of a common humanity, overriding all distinctions of rank.

4. Better, (cp. marg.) **The reward of humility** (is) the fear of the Lord, "riches, and honour, and life."

^h Eph. 6. 4.
2 Tim. 3. 15.

6 ^{h 1} Train up a child ² in the way he should go :
And when he is old, he will not depart from it.

ⁱ Jam. 2. 6.

7 ⁱ The rich ruleth over the poor,
And the borrower *is* servant ³ to the lender.

^k Job 4. 8.
Hos. 10. 13.

8 ^k He that soweth iniquity shall reap vanity :
⁴ And the rod of his anger shall fail.

^l 2 Cor. 9. 6.

9 ^{l 5} He that hath a bountiful eye shall be blessed ;
For he giveth of his bread to the poor.

^m Gen. 21.
9, 10.
Ps. 101. 5.
ⁿ Ps. 101. 6.
ch. 16. 13.

10 ^m Cast out the scorner, and contention shall go out ;
Yea, strife and reproach shall cease.

11 ⁿ He that loveth pureness of heart,
⁶ *For* the grace of his lips the king *shall be* his friend.

12 The eyes of the LORD preserve knowledge,
And he overthroweth ⁷ the words of the transgressor.

^o ch. 26. 13.

13 ^o The slothful *man* saith, *There is* a lion without,
I shall be slain in the streets.

^p ch. 2. 16.
& 5. 3.
& 7. 5.
& 23. 27.
^q Eccl. 7. 26.
^r ch. 13. 24.
& 19. 18.
& 23. 13, 14.
& 29. 15, 17.

14 ^p The mouth of strange women *is* a deep pit :
^q He that is abhorred of the LORD shall fall therein.

15 Foolishness *is* bound in the heart of a child ;
But ^r the rod of correction shall drive it far from him.

16 He that oppresseth the poor to increase his *riches*,
And he that giveth to the rich, *shall* surely *come* to want.

17 Bow down thine ear, and hear the words of the wise,
And apply thine heart unto my knowledge.

18 For *it is* a pleasant thing if thou keep them ⁸ within thee ;
They shall withal be fitted in thy lips.

---

¹ Or, *Catechise.*
² Heb. *in his way.*
³ Heb. *to the man that lendeth.*
⁴ Or, *and with the rod of his anger he shall be consumed.*
⁵ Heb. *Good of eye.*
⁶ Or, and hath *grace in his lips.*
⁷ Or, *the matters.*
⁸ Heb. *in thy belly.*

---

6. *Train*] Initiate, and so, educate.

the way he should go] Or, **according to the tenor of his way**, *i.e.* the path specially belonging to, specially fitted for, the individual's character. The proverb enjoins the closest possible study of each child's temperament and the adaptation of "his way of life" to that.

8. *the rod of his anger*] That with which he smites others (cp. Isai. xiv. 6). The A.V. describes the final impotence of the wrath of the wicked.

9. *He that hath a bountiful eye*] Lit., as in the marg., contrasted with the "evil eye" of xxviii. 22.

11. More lit., "He that loveth pureness of heart, his lips are gracious, the king is his friend."

13. The point of the satire is the ingenuity with which the slothful man devises the most improbable alarms. He hears that "there is a lion without," *i.e.*, in the broad open country ; he is afraid of being slain in the very streets of the city.

14. The fall of the man into the snare of the harlot seems to be the consequence of the abhorrence or wrath of Jehovah. That abhorrence is, however, the result of previous evil. The man is left to himself, and sin becomes the penalty of sin.

16. Better, **He who oppresses the poor for his own profit gives** (*i.e.* will, in the common course of things, be compelled to give) **to a rich man, and that only to his own loss.** Ill-gotten gains do not prosper, and only expose the oppressor to extortion and violence in his turn.

17. This is the commencement of a new and entirely distinct section, opening, after the fashion of iii. 1, 21, iv. 1, vii. 1, with a general exhortation (*vv.* 17-21) and passing on to special precepts. The "words of the wise" may be a title to the section : cp. xxiv. 23. The general characteristics of this section appear to be (1) a less close attention to the laws of parallelism, and (2) a tendency to longer and more complicated sentences. Cp. Introduction, p. 342.

18. What is "pleasant" in the sight of God and man is the union of two things, belief passing into profession, profession resting on belief.

19 That thy trust may be in the LORD,
    I have made known to thee this day, ¹ even to thee.
20 Have not I written to thee ˢ excellent things   ˢ ch. 8. 6.
    In counsels and knowledge,
21 ᵗ That I might make thee know the certainty of the words of truth ;   ᵗ Luke 1. 3,4.
    ᵘ That thou mightest answer the words of truth ² to them that   ᵘ 1 Pet. 3. 15.
        send unto thee ?

22 ˣ Rob not the poor, because he *is* poor :   ˣ Ex. 23. 6.
    ʸ Neither oppress the afflicted in the gate :   Job 31. 16.
                                                      21.
23 ᶻ For the LORD will plead their cause,   ʸ Zech. 7. 10.
    And spoil the soul of those that spoiled them.   Mal. 3. 5.
                                                      ᶻ 1 Sam. 24.
24 Make no friendship with an angry man ;   12.
    And with a furious man thou shalt not go :   & 25. 39.
                                                      Ps. 12. 5.
25 Lest thou learn his ways,—and get a snare to thy soul.   & 35. 1, 10.
                                                      & 68. 5.
26 ᵃ Be not thou *one* of them that strike hands,   & 140. 12.
    Or of them that are sureties for debts.   ch. 23. 11.
                                                      Jer. 51. 36.
27 If thou hast nothing to pay,   ᵃ ch. 6. 1.
    Why should he ᵇ take away thy bed from under thee ?   & 11. 15.
                                                      ᵇ ch. 20. 16.
28 ᶜ Remove not the ancient ³ landmark,   ᶜ Deut. 19.
    Which thy fathers have set.   14.
                                                      & 27. 17.
29 Seest thou a man diligent in his business ?   ch. 23. 10.
    He shall stand before kings ;
    He shall not stand before ⁴ mean *men*.

CHAP. 23. WHEN thou sittest to eat with a ruler,
    Consider diligently what *is* before thee :
2 And put a knife to thy throat,
    If thou *be* a man given to appetite.

¹ Or, trust *thou also.*   ² Or, *to those that send thee?*   ⁴ Heb. *obscure* men.
                              ³ Or, *bound.*

---

19. *even to thee*] The wide general character of the teaching does not hinder its being a personal message to every one who reads it.

20. *excellent things*] A meaning of the word derived from "the third," *i.e.* "the chief of three warriors in a chariot" (cp. Exod. xiv. 7 note). Another reading of the Hebrew text gives "Have I not written to thee long ago?" and this would form a natural antithesis to "this day" of *v.* 19. The rendering of the LXX. is "write them for thyself three times;" that of the Vulgate, "I have written it (*i.e.* my counsel) in three-fold form;" the "three times" or "three-fold form" being referred either to the Proverbs, Ecclesiastes, the Song of Solomon, or to the division of the Old Testament into the Law, the Prophets, and the Hagiographa.

21. *to them that send unto thee*] Better as in the marg. ; cp. x. 26. The man who has learnt the certainty of the words of truth will learn to observe it in all that men commit to him.

22. *i.e.* "Do not be tempted by the helplessness of the poor man to do him wrong :" some prefer, "Refrain from doing him wrong through pity for his helplessness."

the gate] The place where the rulers of the

city sit in judgment. The words point to the special form of oppression of which unjust judges are the instruments.

26. *strike hands*] *i.e.* Bind themselves as surety for what another owes (cp. marg. reff.).

27. *he*] *i.e.* The man to whom the surety has been given. The practice of distraining for payment of a debt, seems, though prohibited (Ex. xxii. 27), to have become common.

28. A protest against the grasping covetousness (Isai. v. 8) which is regardless of the rights of the poor upon whose inheritance men encroach (cp. marg. reff.). The not uncommon reference of the words to the "landmarks" of thought or custom, however natural and legitimate, is foreign to the mind of the writer.

29. The gift of a quick and ready intellect is to lead to high office, it is not to be wasted on a work to which the obscure are adequate.

XXIII. 1. *what is before thee*] Beware lest dainties tempt thee to excess. Or, "consider diligently **who is** before thee," the character and temper of the ruler who invites thee.

2. *i.e.* "Restrain thy appetite, eat as if the knife were at thy throat." Others render the words "thou wilt put a knife to

3 Be not desirous of his dainties :—for they *are* deceitful meat.

a ch. 28. 20.
1 Tim. 6. 9, 10.
b ch. 3. 5.
Rom. 12. 16.

4 *a* Labour not to be rich :—*b* cease from thine own wisdom.
5 [1] Wilt thou set thine eyes upon that which is not ?
    For *riches* certainly make themselves wings;
    They fly away as an eagle toward heaven.

c Ps. 141. 4.
d Deut. 15. 9.

6 *c* Eat thou not the bread of *him that hath* *d* an evil eye,
    Neither desire thou his dainty meats :
7 For as he thinketh in his heart, so *is* he :

e Ps. 12. 2.

    Eat and drink, *e* saith he to thee ;
    But his heart *is* not with thee.
8 The morsel *which* thou hast eaten shalt thou vomit up,
    And lose thy sweet words.

f ch. 9. 8.
Matt. 7. 6.

9 *f* Speak not in the ears of a fool :
    For he will despise the wisdom of thy words.

g Deut. 19. 14.
& 27. 17.
ch. 22. 28.
h Job 31. 21.
ch. 22. 23.

10 *g* Remove not the old [2] landmark ;
    And enter not into the fields of the fatherless :
11 *h* For their redeemer *is* mighty ;
    He shall plead their cause with thee.

12 Apply thine heart unto instruction,
    And thine ears to the words of knowledge.

i ch. 13. 24.
& 19. 18.
& 22. 15.
& 29. 15.
k 1 Cor. 5. 5.

13 *i* Withhold not correction from the child :
    For *if* thou beatest him with the rod, he shall not die.
14 Thou shalt beat him with the rod,
    And *k* shalt deliver his soul from hell.

l ver. 24. 25.
ch. 29. 3.

15 My son, *l* if thine heart be wise,
    My heart shall rejoice, [3] even mine.
16 Yea, my reins shall rejoice,—when thy lips speak right things.

[1] Heb. *Wilt thou cause thine eyes to fly upon.*

[2] Or, *bound.*
[3] Or, *even I* will rejoice.

---

thy throat " &c., *i.e.* "indulgence at such a time may endanger thy very life."

3. *dainties...deceitful meat*] Such as "savoury meat," venison (Gen. xxvii. 4), offered not from genuine hospitality, but with some by-ends.

4. *cease from thine own wisdom*] *i.e.* "Cease from the use of what is in itself most excellent, if it only serves to seek after wealth, and so ministers to evil." There is no special contrast between "thine own wisdom " and that given from above, though it is of course implied that in ceasing from his own prudence the man is on the way to attain a higher wisdom.

5. *set thine eyes*] Lit. as in the marg., *i.e.* "gaze eagerly upon ; " and then we get an emphatic parallelism with the words that follow, "they fly away as an eagle towards heaven ; " "certainly make themselves wings."

6. A different danger from that of *v.* 1. The hazard here is the hospitality of the purse-proud rich, avaricious or grudging even in his banquets.

evil eye] Not with the later associations of a mysterious power for mischief, but simply, as in marg. ref. and in Matt. xx. 15.

7. *thinketh*] The Hebrew verb is found here only, and probably means, "as he is all along in his heart, so is he (at last) in act.''

9. The "fool" here is one wilfully and persistently deaf to it, almost identical with the scorner.

11. The reason is given for the precept (*v.* 10).

their redeemer] See Job xix. 25 note. It was the duty of the *Goel*, the next of kin, to take on himself, in case of murder, the office of avenger of blood (Num. xxxv. 19). By a slight extension the word was applied to one who took on himself a like office in cases short of this. Here, therefore, the thought is that, destitute as the fatherless may seem, there is One Who claims them as His next of kin, and will avenge them. Jehovah Himself is in this sense their *Goel*, their Redeemer.

13, 14. *i.e.*, "You will not kill your son by scourging him, you may kill him by withholding the scourge."

14. *hell*] Sheol, the world of the dead.

15–35. Another continuous exhortation rather than a collection of maxims.

16. The teacher rejoices when the disciple's heart (*v.* 15) receives wisdom, and yet more when his lips can utter it.

17 ^m Let not thine heart envy sinners:
But ⁿ *be thou* in the fear of the LORD all the day long.
18 ^o For surely there is an ¹ end;
And thine expectation shall not be cut off.

19 Hear thou, my son, and be wise,
And ^p guide thine heart in the way.
20 ^q Be not among winebibbers ;— among riotous eaters ² of
flesh :
21 For the drunkard and the glutton shall come to poverty:
And ^r drowsiness shall clothe *a man* with rags.
22 ^s Hearken unto thy father that begat thee,
And despise not thy mother when she is old.
23 ^t Buy the truth, and sell *it* not;
Also wisdom, and instruction, and understanding.
24 ^u The father of the righteous shall greatly rejoice :
And he that begetteth a wise *child* shall have joy of him.
25 Thy father and thy mother shall be glad,
And she that bare thee shall rejoice.

26 My son, give me thine heart,
And let thine eyes observe my ways.
27 ^x For a whore *is* a deep ditch ;
And a strange woman *is* a narrow pit.
28 ^y She also lieth in wait ³ as *for* a prey,
And increaseth the transgressors among men.

29 ^z Who hath woe ? who hath sorrow ?
Who hath contentions ? who hath babbling ?
Who hath wounds without cause ?
Who ^a hath redness of eyes ?
30 ^b They that tarry long at the wine ;
They that go to seek ^c mixed wine.
31 Look not thou upon the wine when it is red,
When it giveth his colour in the cup,
When it moveth itself aright.

m ch. 3. 31.
& 24. 1.
n ch. 28. 14.
o Ps. 37. 37.
ch. 24. 14.
Luke 16. 25.

p ch. 4. 23.

q Isai. 5. 22.
Matt. 24. 49.
Rom 13. 13.
Eph. 5. 18.

r ch. 19. 15.
s ch. 1. 8.
& 30. 17.
Eph. 6. 1, 2.
t ch. 4. 5, 7.
Matt. 13. 44.
u ch. 10. 1.
& 15. 20.
ver. 15.

x ch. 22. 14.

y ch. 7. 12.
Eccl. 7. 26.

z Isai. 5. 11,
22.

a Gen. 49. 12.

b ch. 20. 1.
Eph. 5. 18.
c Ps. 75. 8.
ch. 9. 2.

Or, *reward.*　　　² Heb. *of their flesh.*　　　³ Or, *as a robber.*

reins] See Job xix. 27 note.

17. *envy sinners*] Cp. in Pss. xxxvii. 1, lxxiii. 3, the feeling which looks half longingly at the prosperity of evil doers. Some connect the verb "envy" with the second clause, "envy not sinners, but envy, emulate, the fear of the Lord."

18. Or, **For if there is an end** (hereafter), **thine expectations shall not be cut off.** There is an implied confidence in immortality.

20. *riotous eaters of flesh*] The word is the same as "glutton" in *v.* 21 and Deut. xxi. 20.

21. The three forms of evil that destroy reputation and tempt to waste are brought together.

drowsiness] Specially the drunken sleep, heavy and confused.

26. *observe*] Another reading gives, "let thine eyes *delight* in my ways."

28. *as for a prey*] Better as in the marg.

the transgressors] Better, "the treacherous," those that attack men treacherously.

29. *woe...sorrow*] The words in the original are interjections, probably expressing distress. The sharp touch of the satirist reproduces the actual inarticulate utterances of drunkenness.

30. *mixed wine*] Wine flavoured with aromatic spices, that increase its stimulating properties (Isai. v. 22). There is a touch of sarcasm in "go to seek." The word, elsewhere used of diligent search after knowledge (xxv. 2 ; Job xi. 7 ; Ps. cxxxix. 1), is here used of the investigations of connoisseurs in wine meeting to test its qualities.

31. *his colour*] Lit. "its eye," the clear **brightness**, or the beaded bubbles on which the wine-drinker looks with complacency.

it moveth itself aright] The Hebrew word describes the pellucid stream flowing pleasantly from the wine-skin or jug into the goblet or the throat (cp. Song of Sol. vii. 9), rather than a sparkling wine.

32 At the last it biteth like a serpent,
　　And stingeth like [1] an adder.
33 Thine eyes shall behold strange women,
　　And thine heart shall utter perverse things.
34 Yea, thou shalt be as he that lieth down [2] in the midst of the sea,
　　Or as he that lieth upon the top of a mast.

d ch. 27. 22.
Jer. 5. 3.
e Eph. 4. 19.
f See Deut. 29. 19.

35 *d* They have stricken me, *shalt thou say, and* I was not sick;
　　They have beaten me, *and* [3] *e* I felt *it* not:
　　f When shall I awake?—I will seek it yet again.

Isai. 56. 12.
a Ps. 37. 1, &c.
& 73. 3.
ch. 3. 31.
& 23. 17.
ver. 19.
b Prov. 1. 15.
c Ps. 10. 7.

CHAP. 24. BE not thou *a* envious against evil men,
　　b Neither desire to be with them.
2 *c* For their heart studieth destruction,
　　And their lips talk of mischief.
3 Through wisdom is an house builded;
　　And by understanding it is established:
4 And by knowledge shall the chambers be filled
　　With all precious and pleasant riches.

d ch. 21. 22.
Eccl. 9. 16.

5 *d* A wise man [4] *is* strong;
　　Yea, a man of knowledge [5] increaseth strength.

e ch. 11. 14.
& 20. 18.
Luke 14. 31.

6 *e* For by wise counsel thou shalt make thy war:
　　And in multitude of counsellors *there is* safety.

f Ps. 10. 5.
ch. 14. 6.

7 *f* Wisdom *is* too high for a fool:
　　He openeth not his mouth in the gate.

g Rom. 1. 30.

8 He that *g* deviseth to do evil
　　Shall be called a mischievous person.
9 The thought of foolishness *is* sin:
　　And the scorner *is* an abomination to men.

h Ps. 82. 4.
Isai. 58. 6, 7.
1 John 3. 16.

10 *If* thou faint in the day of adversity,—thy strength *is* [6] small.
11 *h* If thou forbear to deliver *them that are* drawn unto death,
　　And *those that are* ready to be slain;
12 If thou sayest, Behold, we knew it not;

i ch. 21. 2.

　　Doth not *i* he that pondereth the heart consider *it?*

---

[1] Or, *a cockatrice.*　　[3] Heb. *I knew it not.*　　[5] Heb. *strengtheneth might.*
[2] Heb. *in the heart of the sea.*　　[4] Heb. is *in strength.*　　[6] Heb. *narrow.*

---

32. *adder*] Said to be the Cerastes, or horned snake.

34. The passage is interesting, as showing the increased familiarity of Israelites with the experiences of sea-life (cp. Pss. civ. 25, 26, cvii. 23–30).

in the midst of the sea] *i.e.* When the ship is in the trough of the sea and the man is on the deck. The second clause varies the form of danger, the man is in the "cradle" at the top of the mast, and sleeps there, regardless of the danger.

35. The picture ends with the words of the drunkard on waking from his sleep. Unconscious of the excesses of the night, his first thought is to return to his old habit.

When shall I awake, &c.] Better, **when I shall awake I will seek it yet again.**

XXIV. 1. A lesson given before, now combined with another. True followers

after wisdom will admit neither envy of evil on the one hand, nor admiration or fellowship with it on the other.

3, 4. The "house" is figurative of the whole life, the "chambers" of all regions, inward and outward, of it.

5. *is strong*] Lit. as in marg.; *i.e.* rooted and established in strength.

7. *in the gate*] Cp. xxii. 22 note.

11. Lit.

" Deliver those that are drawn unto death,
　And those who totter to the slaughter—if thou withdraw..."

i.e. "O withdraw them," save them from their doom; in contrast to *v.* 10. The structure and meaning are both somewhat obscure; but the sentence is complete in itself, and is not a mere hypothesis concluded in the following verses.

12. As *v.* 11 warned men against acqui-

And he that keepeth thy soul, doth *not* he know *it ?*
And shall *not* he render to *every* man [k] according to his works ?

13 My son, [l] eat thou honey, because *it is* good ;
And the honeycomb, *which is* sweet [1] to thy taste :
14 [m] So *shall* the knowledge of wisdom *be* unto thy soul :
When thou hast found *it*, [n] then there shall be a reward,
And thy expectation shall not be cut off.

15 [o] Lay not wait, O wicked *man*, against the dwelling of the righteous ;
Spoil not his resting place :
16 [p] For a just *man* falleth seven times, and riseth up again :
[q] But the wicked shall fall into mischief.

17 [r] Rejoice not when thine enemy falleth,
And let not thine heart be glad when he stumbleth :
18 Lest the LORD see *it*, and [2] it displease him,
And he turn away his wrath from him.

19 [s][3] Fret not thyself because of evil *men*,
Neither be thou envious at the wicked ;
20 For [t] there shall be no reward to the evil *man ;*
[u] The [4] candle of the wicked shall be put out.

21 My son, [x] fear thou the LORD and the king :
And meddle not with [5] them that are given to change :
22 For their calamity shall rise suddenly ;
And who knoweth the ruin of them both ?

23 These *things* also *belong* to the wise.
[y] *It is* not good to have respect of persons in judgment.
24 [z] He that saith unto the wicked, Thou *art* righteous ;
Him shall the people curse, nations shall abhor him :

[k] Job 34. 11.
Ps. 62. 12.
Jer. 32. 19.
Rom. 2. 6.
Rev. 2. 23.
[l] Cant. 5. 1.
[m] Ps. 19. 10.
& 119. 103.
[n] ch. 23. 18.

[o] Ps. 10. 9, 10.

[p] Ps. 34. 19.
& 37. 24.
Mic. 7. 8.
[q] Esth. 7. 10.
Amos 5. 2.
Rev. 18. 21.
[r] Job 31. 29.
Ps. 35. 15.
ch. 17. 5.
Obad. 12.
[s] Ps. 37. 1.
& 73. 3.
ch. 23. 17.
ver. 1.
[t] Ps. 11. 6.
[u] Job 18. 5.
& 21. 17.
ch. 13. 9.
& 20. 20.
[x] Rom. 13. 7.
1 Pet. 2. 17.

[y] Lev. 19. 15.
Deut. 1. 17.
ch. 18. 5.
& 28. 21.
John 7. 24.
[z] ch. 17. 15.
Isai. 5. 23.

[1] Heb. *upon thy palate.*
[2] Heb. *it be evil in his eyes.*
[3] Or, *Keep not company with the wicked.*
[4] Or, *lamp.*
[5] Heb. *changers.*

escing in an unrighteous tyranny, so this denounces the tendency to hush up a wrong with the false plea of ignorance. Cp. Eccles. v. 8. Verses 10–12 thus form a complete and connected whole.

13. Honey entered largely into the diet of Hebrew children (Isai. vii. 15), so that it was as natural an emblem for the purest and simplest wisdom, as the "sincere milk of the word" was to the New Testament writers. The learner hears what seems a rule of diet—then (*v.* 14) the parable is explained.

14. *the knowledge of wisdom*] Better, **Know that thus** (like the honey) **is wisdom to thy soul.**

15, 16. The teaching of the proverb warns men not to attack or plot against the righteous. They will lose their labour, "Though the just man fall (not into sin, but into calamities), yet he riseth up." The point of the teaching is not the liability of good men to err, but God's providential care over them (cp. marg. reff.). "Seven times" is a certain for an uncertain number (cp. Job v. 19). In contrast with this is the

fate of the evil-doers, who fall utterly even in a single distress.

18. See marg. The meaning is "Thy joy will be suicidal, the wrath of the righteous Judge will be turned upon thee, as the greater offender, and thou wilt have to bear a worse evil than that which thou exultest in."

20. *no reward*] Lit. "no future," no life worthy to be called life, no blessing.

21. *them that are given to change*] Those that seek to set aside the worship of the true God, or the authority of the true king, who represents Him.

22. *both*] Those who fear not God, and those who fear not the king.

23. *belong to the wise*] Either "are fitting for the wise, addressed to them," or (as in the superscriptions of many of the Psalms) "are written by the wise." Most recent commentators take it in the latter sense, and look on it as indicating the beginning of a fresh section, containing proverbs not ascribed to Solomon's authorship. Cp. Introduction, p. 342.

25 But to them that rebuke *him* shall be delight,
And [1] a good blessing shall come upon them.

26 *Every man* shall kiss *his* lips
[2] That giveth a right answer.

a 1 K. 5. 17, 18. Luke 14. 28.

27 *a* Prepare thy work without,
And make it fit for thyself in the field ;
And afterwards build thine house.

b Eph. 4. 25.

28 *b* Be not a witness against thy neighbour without cause ;
And deceive *not* with thy lips.

c ch. 20. 22. Matt. 5. 39, 44. Rom. 12. 17, 19.

29 *c* Say not, I will do so to him as he hath done to me :
I will render to the man according to his work.

30 I went by the field of the slothful,
And by the vineyard of the man void of understanding ;

d Gen. 3. 18.

31 And, lo, *d* it was all grown over with thorns,
And nettles had covered the face thereof,
And the stone wall thereof was broken down.

32 Then I saw, *and* [3] considered *it* well :
I looked upon *it, and* received instruction.

e ch. 6. 9.

33 *e* Yet a little sleep, a little slumber,
A little folding of the hands to sleep :

34 So shall thy poverty come *as* one that travelleth ;
And thy want as [4] an armed man.

a 1 K. 4. 32.

CHAP. 25. *a* THESE *are* also proverbs of Solomon, which the men of Hezekiah king of Judah copied out.

b Deut. 29. 29. Rom. 11. 33. *c* Job 29. 16.

2 *b* It is* the glory of God to conceal a thing :
But the honour of kings *is* *c* to search out a matter.

3 The heaven for height, and the earth for depth,
And the heart of kings [5] *is* unsearchable.

[1] Heb. *a blessing of good.*
[2] Heb. *that answereth right words.*
[3] Heb. *set my heart.*
[4] Heb. *a man of shield.*
[5] Heb. there is *no searching.*

---

25. There is no surer path to popularity than a righteous severity in punishing guilt.
26. Better, **He shall kiss lips that giveth a right answer,** *i.e.* he shall gain the hearts of men as much as by all outward signs of sympathy and favour. Cp. 2 Sam. xv. 1–6.
27. *i.e.* Get an estate into good order before erecting a house on it. To "build a house" may, however, be equivalent (cp. Ex. i. 21 ; Deut. xxv. 9 ; Ruth iv. 11) to "founding a family ;" and the words a warning against a hasty and imprudent marriage. The young man is taught to cultivate his land before he has to bear the burdens of a family. Further, in a spiritual sense, the "field" may be the man's outer common work, the "house" the dwelling-place of his higher life. He must do the former faithfully in order to attain the latter. Neglect in one is fatal to the other. Cp. Luke xvi. 10, 11.
28. *deceive not with thy lips*] Better, **wilt thou deceive with thy lips ?**
29. A protest against vindictiveness in every form. Cp. marg. reff.
30. The chapter ends with an apologue,

which may be taken as a parable of something yet deeper. The field and the vineyard are more than the man's earthly possessions. His neglect brings barrenness or desolation to the garden of the soul. The "thorns" are evil habits that choke the good seed, and the "nettles" are those that are actually hurtful and offensive to others. The "wall" is the defence which laws and rules give to the inward life, and which the sluggard learns to disregard, and the "poverty" is the loss of the true riches of the soul, tranquillity, and peace, and righteousness.
33, 34. See vi. 11 note.
XXV. **1.** A new section. See p. 342.
copied out] In the sense of a transfer from oral tradition to writing.
2. The earthly monarch might be, in some respects, the type of the heavenly, but here there is a marked contrast. The king presses further and further into all knowledge ; God surrounds Himself as in "thick darkness," and there are secrets unrevealed even after the fullest revelation.
3. The other side of the thought of *v.* 2. What the mind of God is to the searchers

4 ^d Take away the dross from the silver,
And there shall come forth a vessel for the finer.
5 ^e Take away the wicked *from* before the king,
And ^f his throne shall be established in righteousness.
6 ¹ Put not forth thyself in the presence of the king,
And stand not in the place of great *men :*
7 ^g For better *it is* that it be said unto thee, Come up hither;
Than that thou shouldest be put lower in the presence of the
prince
Whom thine eyes have seen.
8 ^h Go not forth hastily to strive,
Lest *thou know not* what to do in the end thereof,
When thy neighbour hath put thee to shame.
9 ⁱ Debate thy cause with thy neighbour *himself;*
And ² discover not a secret to another :
10 Lest he that heareth *it* put thee to shame,
And thine infamy turn not away.
11 ^k A word ³ fitly spoken
Is like apples of gold in pictures of silver.
12 *As* an earring of gold, and an ornament of fine gold,
So is a wise reprover upon an obedient ear.
13 ^l As the cold of snow in the time of harvest,
So is a faithful messenger to them that send him :
For he refresheth the soul of his masters.

d 2Tim. 2. 21.

e ch. 20. 8.
f ch. 16. 12.
& 29. 14.

g Luke 14. 8,
9, 10.

h ch. 17. 14.
Matt. 5. 25.

i Matt. 5. 25.

k ch. 15. 23.
Isai. 50. 4.

l ch. 13. 17.

¹ Heb. *Set not out thy glory.*   ² Or, *discover not the secret of another.*   ³ Heb. *spoken upon his wheels.*

after knowledge, that the heart of the true and wise king is to those who try to guess its counsels.

5. The interpretation of the proverb of *v.* 4. The king himself, like the Lord Whom he represents, is to sit as " a refiner of silver" (Mal. iii. 3).

6, 7. The pushing, boastful temper is, in the long run, suicidal. It is wiser as well as nobler to take the lower place at first in humility, than to take it afterwards with shame. Cp. marg. ref. *g*, which is one of the few instances in which our Lord's teaching was fashioned, as to its outward form, upon that of this Book.

8. The general meaning is, it is dangerous to plunge into litigation. At all times there is the risk of failure, and, if we fail, of being at the mercy of an irritated adversary. Without the italics, the clause may be rendered, "lest thou do something (*i.e.* something humiliating and vexatious) at the end thereof."

9. An anticipation of the highest standard of ethical refinement (Matt. xviii. 15), but with a difference. Here the motive is prudential, the risk of shame, the fear of the irretrievable infamy of the betrayer of secrets. In the teaching of Christ the precept rests on the Divine Authority and the perfect Example.

11. *apples of gold*] Probably the golden-coloured fruit set in **baskets** (*i.e.* chased vessels of open-worked silver) ; so is **a word**

spoken upon its wheels (*i.e.* moving quickly and quietly on its way). The proverb may have had its origin in some kingly gift to the son of David, the work of Tyrian artists, like Hiram and his fellows. Others gazed on the cunning work and admired, but the wise king saw in the costly rarity a parable of something higher. "A word well set upon the wheels of speech" excelled it. Ornamentation of this kind in the precious metals was known, even as late as in the middle ages, as *œuvre de Salomon*.

12. The theme of this proverb being the same as that of *v.* 11, its occurrence suggests the thought that rings used as ornaments for ears, or nose, or forehead, and other trinkets formed part of the works of art spoken of in the foregoing note, and that the king had something at once pointed and wise to say of each of them.

13. A picture of the growing luxury of the Solomonic period. The "snow in harvest" is not a shower of snow or hail, which would be terrifying and harmful rather than refreshing (cp. 1 Sam. xii. 17, 18) ; but, rather, the snow of Lebanon or Hermon put into wine or other drink to make it more refreshing in the scorching heat of May or June at the king's summer-palace on Lebanon (1 K. ix. 19; S. of S. vii. 4 notes). More reviving even than the iced wine-cup was the faithful messenger. Contrast x. 26.

ᵐ ch. 20. 6.
ⁿ Jude 12.

ᵒ Gen. 32. 4,
&c.
1 Sam. 25.
24, &c.
ch. 15. 1.
& 16. 14.
ᵖ ver. 27.

ᵠ Ps. 57. 4.
& 120. 3, 4.
ch. 12. 18.

ʳ Dan. 6. 18.
Rom. 12. 15.
ˢ Ex. 23. 4, 5.
Matt. 5. 44.

ᵗ 2 Sam. 16.
12.
ᵘ Job 37. 22.
ˣ Ps. 101. 5.

14 *ᵐ*Whoso boasteth himself ¹of a false gift
Is like *ⁿ*clouds and wind without rain.

15 *ᵒ*By long forbearing is a prince persuaded,
And a soft tongue breaketh the bone.

16 *ᵖ*Hast thou found honey? eat so much as is sufficient for thee,
Lest thou be filled therewith, and vomit it.

17 ²Withdraw thy foot from thy neighbour's house;
Lest he be ³weary of thee, and *so* hate thee.

18 *ᵠ*A man that beareth false witness against his neighbour
Is a maul, and a sword, and a sharp arrow.

19 Confidence in an unfaithful man in time of trouble
Is like a broken tooth, and a foot out of joint.

20 *As* he that taketh away a garment in cold weather,
And as vinegar upon nitre,
So *is* he that *ʳ*singeth songs to an heavy heart.

21 *ˢ*If thine enemy be hungry, give him bread to eat;
And if he be thirsty, give him water to drink:

22 For thou shalt heap coals of fire upon his head,
*ᵗ*And the LORD shall reward thee.

23 *ᵘ*⁴The north wind driveth away rain:
So *doth* an angry countenance *ˣ*a backbiting tongue.

¹ Heb. *in a gift of falsehood.*
² Or, *Let thy foot be seldom*
in thy neighbour's house.
³ Heb. *full of thee.*
⁴ Or, *The north wind bringeth forth rain: so doth a backbiting tongue an angry countenance.*

---

14. The disappointment caused by him who promises much and performs little or nothing, is likened to the phenomena of an eastern climate; the drought of summer, the eager expectation of men who watch the rising clouds and the freshening breeze, the bitter disappointment when the breeze dies off, and the clouds pass away, and the wished-for rain does not come.

15. *a soft tongue*] Winning and gentle speech does what it seems at first least capable of doing; it overcomes obstacles which are as bones that the strongest jaws would fail to crush.

16. *Hast thou found honey?*] Cp. Judg. xiv. 8; 1 Sam. xiv. 27. The precept extends to the pleasure of which honey is the symbol.

17. Let thy foot be seldom in the house of thy friend, &c. Though thy visits were sweet as honey, he may soon learn to loathe them.

18. *maul*] A heavy sledge hammer. The word is connected with "malleus:" its diminutive "mallet" is still in use.

19. Stress is to be laid on the uselessness of the "broken tooth" and the "foot out of joint," or **tottering,** rather than on the pain connected with them. The A.V. loses the emphasis and point of the Hebrew by inverting the original order, which is "a broken...joint is confidence" &c.

20. Examples of unwisdom and incongruity sharpen the point of the proverb. Pouring vinegar upon nitre or potash utterly spoils it. The effervescence caused by the mixture is perhaps taken as a type of the irritation produced by the "songs" sung out of season to a heavy heart.

The verb rendered "taketh away" may have the sense (as in Ezek. xvi. 11) of "adorning one's-self," and the illustration would then be, "as to put on a fine garment in time of cold is unseasonable, so is singing to a heavy heart."

21, 22. A precept reproduced by St. Paul (Rom. xii. 20); the second clause of which seems at first sight to suggest a motive incompatible with a true charity. Lev. xvi. 12 suggests an explanation. The High Priest on the Day of Atonement was to take his censer, to fill it with "coals of fire," and then to put the incense thereon for a sweet-smelling savour. So it is here. The first emotion in another caused by the good done to him may be one of burning shame, but the shame will do its work and the heart also will burn, and prayer and confession and thanksgiving will rise as incense to the throne of God. Thus, "we shall overcome evil with good."

23. The marginal reading is far more accurate and gives a better sense. The N.W. wind in Palestine commonly brings rain, and this was probably in the thought of the writer.

24 *It is* better to dwell in the corner of the housetop,
Than with a brawling woman and in a wide house.

25 *As* cold waters to a thirsty soul,
So *is* good news from a far country.

26 A righteous man falling down before the wicked
Is as a troubled fountain, and a corrupt spring.

27 *It is* not good to eat much honey:
So *for men* *to search their own glory *is not* glory.

28 *He that *hath* no rule over his own spirit
Is like a city *that is* broken down, *and* without walls.

CHAP. 26. AS snow in summer, *and as rain in harvest,
So honour is not seemly for a fool.

2 As the bird by wandering, as the swallow by flying,
So *the curse causeless shall not come.

3 *A whip for the horse, a bridle for the ass,
And a rod for the fool's back.

4 Answer not a fool according to his folly,
Lest thou also be like unto him.

5 *Answer a fool according to his folly,
Lest he be wise in ¹his own conceit.

6 He that sendeth a message by the hand of a fool
Cutteth off the feet, *and* drinketh ²damage.

7 The legs of the lame ³are not equal:
So *is* a parable in the mouth of fools.

y ch. 19. 13.
& 21. 9, 19.

z ver. 16.

a ch. 27. 2.

b ch. 16. 32.

a 1 Sam. 12. 17.

b Num. 23. 8.
Deut. 23. 5.
c Ps. 32. 9.
ch. 10. 13.

d Matt. 16. 1-4.
& 21. 24-27.

¹ Heb. *his own eyes.*   ² Or, *violence.*   ³ Heb. *are lifted up.*

---

24. Cp. xxi. 9 note.
25. The craving of wanderers for tidings from the home they have left is as a consuming thirst, the news that quenches it as a refreshing fountain.
26. *falling down before*] *i.e.* Yielding and cringing. To see this instead of stedfastness, is as grievous as for the traveller to find the spring at which he hoped to quench his thirst turbid and defiled.
27. *So for men* &c.] A difficult sentence, the text of which is probably defective. The words are not in the original. Many commentators render: **so to search into weighty matters is itself a weight,** *i.e.* men soon become satiated with it as with honey. Possibly a warning against an over-curious searching into the mysteries of God's word or works.
XXVI. 1. In Palestine there is commonly hardly any rain from the early showers of spring to October. Hence "rain in harvest" became sometimes (see marg. ref.) a supernatural sign, sometimes, as here, a proverb for whatever was strange and incongruous.
2. *i.e.* "Vague as the flight of the sparrow, aimless as the wheelings of the swallow, is the causeless curse. It will never reach its goal." The marginal reading in the Hebrew, however, gives "to him" instead

of "not" or "never;" *i.e.* "The causeless curse, though it may pass out of our ken, like a bird's track in the air, will come on the man who utters it." Cp. the English proverb, "Curses, like young chickens, always come home to roost."
4, 5. Two sides of a truth. To "answer a fool according to his folly" is in *v.* 4 to bandy words with him, to descend to his level of coarse anger and vile abuse; in *v.* 5 it is to say the right word at the right time, to expose his unwisdom and untruth to others and to himself, not by a teaching beyond his reach, but by words that he is just able to apprehend. The apparent contradiction between the two verses led some of the Rabbis to question the canonical authority of this Book. The Pythagoreans had maxims expressing a truth in precepts seemingly contradictory.
6. *cutteth off the feet*] Mutilates him, spoils the work which the messenger ought to fulfil.
drinketh damage] *i.e.* "has to drink full draughts of shame and loss" (cp. Job xv. 16).
7. Or, **Take away the legs of the lame man, and the parable that is in the mouth of fools:** both are alike useless to their possessors. Other meanings are (1) "The legs of the lame man are feeble, so is a

8 [1]As he that bindeth a stone in a sling,
    So *is* he that giveth honour to a fool.

9 *As* a thorn goeth up into the hand of a drunkard,
    So *is* a parable in the mouth of fools.

10 [2]The great *God* that formed all *things*
    Both rewardeth the fool, and rewardeth transgressors.

c 2 Pet. 2. 22.   11 *e*As a dog returneth to his vomit,
f Ex. 8. 15.   *f* So a fool [3]returneth to his folly.

g ch. 29. 20.   12 *g*Seest thou a man wise in his own conceit?
Luke 18. 11.   *There is* more hope of a fool than of him.
Rom. 12. 16.
Rev. 3. 17.   13 *h*The slothful *man* saith, *There is* a lion in the way;
h ch. 22. 13.   A lion *is* in the streets.

14 *As* the door turneth upon his hinges,
    So *doth* the slothful upon his bed.

i ch. 19. 24.   15 *i*The slothful hideth his hand in *his* bosom;
                      [4]It grieveth him to bring it again to his mouth.

16 The sluggard *is* wiser in his own conceit
    Than seven men that can render a reason.

17 He that passeth by, *and* [5]meddleth with strife *belonging* not to
        him,
    Is like one that taketh a dog by the ears.

18 As a mad *man* who casteth [6]firebrands, arrows, and death,
19 So *is* the man *that* deceiveth his neighbour,
k Eph. 5. 4.   And saith, *k*Am not I in sport?

20 [7]Where no wood is, *there* the fire goeth out:
l ch. 22. 10.   So *l*where *there is* no [8]talebearer, the strife [9]ceaseth.

m ch. 15. 18.   21 *m*As coals *are* to burning coals, and wood to fire;
& 29. 22.   So *is* a contentious man to kindle strife.

---

[1] Or, *As he that putteth a*   *fool, he hireth also trans-*   [6] Heb. *flames,* or, *sparks.*
    precious stone in an heap   *gressors.*   [7] Heb. *Without wood.*
    of stones.   [3] Heb. *iterateth his folly.*   [8] Or, *whisperer.*
[2] Or, *A great* man *grieveth*   [4] Or, *he is weary.*   [9] Heb. *is silent.*
    all, and he hireth the   [5] Or, *is enraged.*

---

parable in the mouth of fools." (2) "The
lifting up of the legs of a lame man, *i.e.* his
attempts at dancing, are as the parable in
the mouth of fools."

8. *i.e.* "To give honour to the fool is like
binding a stone in a sling; you can-
not throw it." In each case you misapply
and so waste. Others render in the sense
of the marg.: To use a precious stone where
a pebble would be sufficient, is not less
foolish than to give honour to a fool.

9. Better, "As a thorn which is lifted
up in the hand of the drunkard" &c. As
such a weapon so used may do mischief to
the man himself or to others, so may the
sharp, keen-edged proverb when used by
one who does not understand it.

10. The word "God" is not in the original, and the adjective translated "great"
is never used elsewhere absolutely in that
sense. The simplest and best interpretation

is, **As the archer that woundeth every one,
so is he who hireth the fool, and he who
hireth every passer-by.** Acting at random,
entrusting matters of grave moment to men
of bad repute, is as likely to do mischief as
to shoot arrows at every one.

13. Cp. marg. ref. note. Here there is
greater dramatic vividness in the two words
used: (1) A roaring one, (2) a lion, more
specifically.

15. *grieveth him*] Better, **wearieth him.**

16. *seven*] The definite number used for
the indefinite (cp. xxiv. 16).

reason] Better, **a right judgment.**

18, 19. The teacher cuts off the plea
men make when they have hurt their neighbour by lies, that they "did not mean mischief," that they were "only in fun." Such
jesting is like that of the madman flinging
firebrands or arrows.

21. *coals*] Charcoal.

22 [n]The words of a talebearer *are* as wounds,
And they go down into the [1]innermost parts of the belly.

23 Burning lips and a wicked heart
Are like a potsherd covered with silver dross.

24 He that hateth [2]dissembleth with his lips,
And layeth up deceit within him;

25 [o]When he [3]speaketh fair, believe him not:
For *there are* seven abominations in his heart.

26 *Whose* [4]hatred is covered by deceit,
His wickedness shall be shewed before the *whole* congregation.

27 [p]Whoso diggeth a pit shall fall therein:
And he that rolleth a stone, it will return upon him.

28 A lying tongue hateth *those that are* afflicted by it;
And a flattering mouth worketh ruin.

CHAP. 27. BOAST [a]not thy self of [5]to morrow;
For thou knowest not what a day may bring forth.

2 [b]Let another man praise thee, and not thine own mouth;
A stranger, and not thine own lips.

3 A stone *is* [6]heavy, and the sand weighty:
But a fool's wrath *is* heavier than them both.

4 [7]Wrath *is* cruel, and anger *is* outrageous;
But [c]who *is* able to stand before [8]envy?

5 [d]Open rebuke *is* better than secret love.

6 [e]Faithful *are* the wounds of a friend;
But the kisses of an enemy *are* [9]deceitful.

7 The full soul [1]loatheth an honeycomb;
But [f]to the hungry soul every bitter thing is sweet.

[n] ch. 18. 8.

[o] Ps. 28. 3.
Jer. 9. 8.

[p] Ps. 7. 15.
& 9. 15.
ch. 28. 10.
Eccl. 10. 8.

[a] Luke 12.
19, 20.
Jam. 4. 13,
&c.
[b] ch. 25. 27.

[c] 1 John 3.
12.
[d] ch. 28. 23.
Gal. 2. 14.
[e] Ps. 141. 5.

[f] Job 6. 7.

---

[1] Heb. *chambers*.
[2] Or, *is known*.
[3] Heb. *maketh his voice gracious*.
[4] Or, *hatred is covered in secret*.
[5] Heb. *to morrow day*.
[6] Heb. *heaviness*.
[7] *Wrath* is *cruelty, and anger an overflowing.*
[8] Or, *jealousy?* ch. 6. 34.
[9] Or, *earnest*, or, *frequent*.
[1] Heb. *treadeth under foot*.

---

22. Cp. marg. ref. note.

23. *Burning lips*] *i.e.* "Lips glowing with affection, uttering warm words of love," joined with a malignant heart, are like a piece of broken earthenware from the furnace, which glitters with the silver drops that stick to it, but is itself worthless.

25. *seven abominations*] Cp. *v.* 16 note. Here "seven" retains, perhaps, its significance as the symbol of completeness. Evil has, as it were, gone through all its work, and holds its accursed Sabbath in the heart in which all things are "very evil."

26. Better, "Hatred is covered by deceit, but in the midst of the congregation his wickedness will be made manifest," *i.e.* then, in the time of need, the feigned friendship will pass into open enmity.

27. *rolleth a stone*] The illustration refers, probably, to the use made of stones in the rough warfare of an earlier age. Cp. Judg. ix. 53; 2 Sam. xi. 21. The man is supposed to be rolling the stone up to the heights.

28. The lying tongue hates its victims.

XXVII. 2. *another*] An "*alienus*" rather than "*alius*." Praise to be worth anything must be altogether independent.

3. Cp. Ecclus. xxii. 15; a like comparison between the heaviest material burdens and the more intolerable load of unreasoning passion.

4. *envy*] Better, as in the marg., the violence of passion in the husband who thinks himself wronged (cp. vi. 34).

5. *secret love*] Better, **love that is hidden;** *i.e.* love which never shows itself in this one way of rebuking faults. Rebuke, whether from friend or foe, is better than such love.

6. *deceitful*] Better, **abundant.** Very lavish is the enemy of the kisses that cover perfidy, but lavish of them only. His courtesy goes no deeper.

7. The special instance covers the general law, that indulgence in pleasure of any kind brings on satiety and weariness, but self-

8 As a bird that wandereth from her nest,
So *is* a man that wandereth from his place.

9 Ointment and perfume rejoice the heart:
So *doth* the sweetness of a man's friend [1]by hearty counsel.

10 Thine own friend, and thy father's friend, forsake not;
Neither go into thy brother's house in the day of thy calamity:
For [g]better *is* a neighbour *that is* near than a brother far off.

g ch. 17. 17.
& 18. 24.
See ch. 19. 7.
h ch. 10. 1.
& 23. 15, 24.
i Ps. 127. 5.
k ch. 22. 3.

11 [h]My son, be wise, and make my heart glad,
[i]That I may answer him that reproacheth me.

12 [k]A prudent *man* foreseeth the evil, *and* hideth himself;
But the simple pass on, *and* are punished.

l See Ex.
22. 26.
ch. 20. 16.

13 [l]Take his garment that is surety for a stranger,
And take a pledge of him for a strange woman.

14 He that blesseth his friend with a loud voice, rising early in the morning,
It shall be counted a curse to him.

m ch. 19. 13.

15 [m]A continual dropping in a very rainy day
And a contentious woman are alike.

16 Whosoever hideth her hideth the wind,
And the ointment of his right hand, *which* bewrayeth *itself*.

17 Iron sharpeneth iron;
So a man sharpeneth the countenance of his friend.

n 1 Cor. 9.
7, 13.

18 [n]Whoso keepeth the fig tree shall eat the fruit thereof:
So he that waiteth on his master shall be honoured.

19 As in water face *answereth* to face,
So the heart of man to man.

[1] Heb. *from the counsel of the soul.*

restraint multiplies the sources of enjoyment.

8. Change of place is thought of as in itself an evil. It is not easy for the man to find another home or the bird another nest. The maxim is characteristic of the earlier stages of Hebrew history, before exile and travel had made change of country a more familiar thing. Cp. the feeling which made the thought of being "a fugitive and a vagabond" (Gen. iv. 12, 13) the most terrible of all punishments.

10. "Better is a neighbour" who is really "near" in heart and spirit, than a brother who though closer by blood, is "far off" in feeling.

11. The voice of the teacher to his true disciple. He pleads with him that the uprightness of the scholar will be the truest answer to all attacks on the character or teaching of the master.

12, 13. Cp. marg. reff.

14. The picture of the ostentatious flatterer going at daybreak to pour out blessings on his patron. For any good that he does, for any thanks he gets, he might as well utter curses.

15. *continual dropping*] Here, as in marg. ref., the flat earthen roof of Eastern houses, always liable to cracks and leakage, supplies the ground-work of the similitude.

16. The point is the impossibility of concealment or restraint. A man cannot hide the wind, or clasp it in his hands. If he takes an unguent in his right hand, the odour betrays him, or it slips out. So in like manner, the "contentious woman" is one whose faults it is impossible either to hide or check. The difficulty of the proverb led to a different reading, adopted by the Versions, "The north wind is rough, and yet it is called propitious:" it clears off the clouds and brings fine weather.

17. The proverb expresses the gain of mutual counsel as found in clear, well-defined thoughts. Two minds, thus acting on each other, become more acute. This is better than to see in "sharpening" the idea of provoking, and the point of the maxim in the fact that the quarrels of those who have been friends are bitter in proportion to their previous intimacy.

18. *waiteth*] Lit. "keepeth," "observeth." As the fig-tree requires constant care but yields abundant crops, so the ministrations of a faithful servant will not be without their due reward. Cp. 2 Tim. ii. 6.

19. As we see our own face when we

20 [o]Hell and destruction are [1]never full; [o] ch. 30. 16. Hab. 2. 5.
So [p] the eyes of man are never satisfied. [p] Eccl. 1. 8. & 6. 7.
21 [q]*As* the fining pot for silver, and the furnace for gold; [q] ch. 17. 3.
So *is* a man to his praise.
22 [r]Though thou shouldest bray a fool in a mortar among wheat with a pestle, [r] ch. 23. 35. Isai. 1. 5. Jer. 5. 3.
Yet will not his foolishness depart from him.
23 Be thou diligent to know the state of thy flocks,
And [2]look well to thy herds.
24 For [3]riches *are* not for ever:
And doth the crown *endure* [4]to every generation?
25 [s]The hay appeareth, and the tender grass sheweth itself, [s] Ps. 104. 14.
And herbs of the mountains are gathered.
26 The lambs *are* for thy clothing,
And the goats *are* the price of the field.
27 And *thou shalt have* goats' milk enough for thy food,
For the food of thy household,
And *for* the [5]maintenance for thy maidens.

Chap. 28. THE [a]wicked flee when no man pursueth: [a] Lev. 26. 17, 36 Ps. 53. 5.
But the righteous are bold as a lion.
2 For the transgression of a land many *are* the princes thereof:
But [6]by a man of understanding *and* knowledge the state *thereof* shall be prolonged.

[1] Heb. *not.*
[2] Heb. *set thy heart.*
[3] Heb. *strength.*
[4] Heb. *to generation and generation?*
[5] Heb. *life.*
[6] Or, *by men of understanding* and *wisdom shall they likewise be prolonged.*

---

look on the mirror-like surface of the water, so in every heart of man we may see our own likeness. In spite of all diversities we come upon the common human nature in which we all alike share. Others see in the reference to the reflection in the water the thought that we judge of others by ourselves, find them faithful or the reverse, as we ourselves are.

20. Hades, the world of the dead, and Destruction (Death, the destroying power, personified) have been at all times and in all countries thought of as all-devouring, insatiable (cp. marg. ref.). Yet one thing is equally so, the lust of the eye, the restless craving which grows with what it feeds on (Eccles. i. 8).

21. *so is* &c.] Better, **So let a man be to his praise,** let him purify it from all the alloy of flattery and baseness with which it is too probably mixed up.

22. *bray*] To pound wheat in a mortar with a pestle, in order to free the wheat from its husks and impurities, is to go through a far more elaborate process than threshing. But the folly of the fool is not thus to be got rid of. It sticks to him to the last; all discipline, teaching, experience seem to be wasted on him.

23–27. The verses sing the praises of the earlier patriarchal life, with its flocks and herds, and tillage of the ground, as compared with the commerce of a later time, with money as its chief or only wealth.

23. *the state*] Lit. **face.** The verse is an illustration of John x. 3, 14.

24. *riches*] The money which men may steal, or waste, is contrasted with the land of which the owner is not so easily deprived. Nor will the crown (both the "crown of pure gold" worn on the mitre of the High-priest, Exod. xxix. 6, xxxix. 30, and the kingly diadem, the symbol of power generally) be transmitted (as flocks and herds had been) "from one generation to another."

25. *appeareth*] Better, **When the grass disappeareth,** the "tender grass sheweth itself." Stress is laid on the regular succession of the products of the earth. The "grass" ("hay") of the first clause is (cp. Pss. xxxvii. 2, xc. 5, ciii. 15; 2 K. xix. 26) the proverbial type of what is perishable and fleeting. The verse gives a picture of the pleasantness of the husbandman's calling; compared with this what can wealth or rank offer? With this there mingles (cp. *v.* 23) the thought that each stage of that life in its season requires care and watchfulness.

XXVIII. **2.** *transgression*] Better, **rebellion.** A revolt against a ruler leads to rapid changes of dynasty (the whole history of the kingdom of Israel was a proof

b Matt. 18.
28.

Ps. 10. 3.
& 49. 18.
Rom. 1. 32.
d 1 K. 18. 18,
21.
Matt. 3. 7.
& 14. 4.
Eph. 5. 11.
e Ps. 92. 6.
f John 7. 17.
1 Cor. 2. 15.
1 John 2. 20.
27.
g ch. 19. 1.
ver. 18.
h ch. 29. 3.
i Job 27. 16,
17.
ch. 13. 22.
Eccl. 2. 26.
k Zech. 7. 11.
l Ps. 66. 18.
& 109. 7.
ch. 15. 8.
m ch. 26. 27.
n Matt. 6. 33.

o ver. 28.
ch. 11. 10.
& 29. 2.
Eccl. 10. 6.
p Ps. 32. 3, 5.
1 John 1. 8,
9, 10.
q Ps. 16. 8.
ch. 23. 17.
r Rom. 2. 5.
& 11. 20.

3 ^bA poor man that oppresseth the poor
Is *like* a sweeping rain ¹which leaveth no food.

4 ^cThey that forsake the law praise the wicked:
^dBut such as keep the law contend with them.

5 ^eEvil men understand not judgment:
But ^fthey that seek the LORD understand all *things*.

6 ^gBetter *is* the poor that walketh in his uprightness,
Than *he that is* perverse *in his* ways, though he *be* rich.

7 ^hWhoso keepeth the law *is* a wise son:
But he that ²is a companion of riotous *men* shameth his father.

8 ⁱHe that by usury and ³unjust gain increaseth his substance,
He shall gather it for him that will pity the poor.

9 ^kHe that turneth away his ear from hearing the law,
^lEven his prayer *shall be* abomination.

10 ^mWhoso causeth the righteous to go astray in an evil way,
He shall fall himself into his own pit:
ⁿBut the upright shall have good *things* in possession.

11 The rich man *is* wise ⁴in his own conceit;
But the poor that hath understanding searcheth him out.

12 ^oWhen righteous *men* do rejoice, *there is* great glory:
But when the wicked rise, a man is ⁵hidden.

13 ^pHe that covereth his sins shall not prosper:
But whoso confesseth and forsaketh *them* shall have mercy.

14 Happy *is* the man ^qthat feareth alway:
^rBut he that hardeneth his heart shall fall into mischief.

¹ Heb. *without food.*   ³ Heb. *by increase.*   ⁴ Heb. *in his eyes.*
² Or, *feedeth gluttons.*   ⁵ Or, *sought for.*

of this), but "with men of understanding and knowledge thus shall he (the prince) continue." True wisdom will lead men to maintain an existing order. The A.V. implies that political disorders may come as the punishment of any national sin.

the state] Better, **it** (the land) **shall surely prolong its days in stability.**

3. Men raise a man of the people, poor like themselves, to power. They find him the worst oppressor of all, plundering them to their last morsels, like the storm-rain which sweeps off the seed-corn instead of bringing fertility.

5. The deep inter-dependence of morality and intellect. We have a right judgment in all things in proportion as our hearts seek to know God. Cp. James i. 23, 24.

6. *perverse in his ways*] Lit. "Perverse in his *double* ways." Cp. Ecclus. ii. 12; James i. 8.

8. *unjust gain*] Omit "unjust": "usury and gain" make up the notion of "gain derived from usury." Ill-gotten gains do not prosper, after a time they pass into hands that know how to use them better.

10. When the wicked succeed in tempt-

ing the righteous, Vice seems to win a triumph. But the triumph is suicidal. The tempter will suffer the punishment he deserves, and the blameless, if true to themselves, will be strengthened and ennobled by the temptation.

11. Wealth blunts, poverty sharpens, the critical power of intellect.

12. *there is great glory*] Men array themselves in festive apparel, and show their joy conspicuously.

a man is hidden] Better, **men hide themselves,** they shrink and cower for fear, and yet are hunted out.

13. The conditions of freedom are confession and amendment, confession to God of sins against Him, to men of sins against them. The teaching of ethical wisdom on this point is identical with that of Psalmist, Prophet, Apostles, and our Lord Himself.

14. The "fear" here is not so much reverential awe, as anxious, or "nervous" sensitiveness of conscience. To most men this temperament seems that of the self-tormentor. To him who looks deeper it is a condition of blessedness, and the callousness which is opposed to it ends in misery.

15 *As* a roaring lion, and a ranging bear;
    So is a wicked ruler over the poor people.

16 The prince that wanteth understanding *is* also a great oppressor:
    But he that hateth covetousness shall prolong *his* days.

17 A man that doeth violence to the blood of *any* person
    Shall flee to the pit; let no man stay him.

18 Whoso walketh uprightly shall be saved:
    But *he that is* perverse *in his* ways shall fall at once.

19 He that tilleth his land shall have plenty of bread:
    But he that followeth after vain *persons* shall have poverty enough.

20 A faithful man shall abound with blessings:
    But he that maketh haste to be rich shall not be [1]innocent.

21 To have respect of persons *is* not good:
    For for a piece of bread *that* man will transgress.

22 [2]He that hasteth to be rich *hath* an evil eye,
    And considereth not that poverty shall come upon him.

23 He that rebuketh a man afterwards shall find more favour
    Than he that flattereth with the tongue.

24 Whoso robbeth his father or his mother, and saith, *It is* no transgression;
    The same *is* the companion of [3]a destroyer.

25 He that is of a proud heart stirreth up strife:
    But he that putteth his trust in the LORD shall be made fat.

26 He that trusteth in his own heart is a fool:
    But whoso walketh wisely, he shall be delivered.

27 He that giveth unto the poor shall not lack:
    But he that hideth his eyes shall have many a curse.

s 1 Pet. 5. 8.
t Ex. 1. 14, 16, 22.
Matt. 2. 16.
u Gen. 9. 6.
Ex. 21. 14.
x ch. 10. 9, 25.
y ver. 6.
s ch. 12. 11.
a ch. 13. 11 & 20. 21.
& 23. 4.
ver. 22.
1 Tim. 6. 9.
b ch. 18. 5.
& 24. 23.
c Ezek. 13. 19.
d ver. 20.
e ch. 27. 5, 6.
f ch. 18. 9.
g ch. 13. 10.
h 1 Tim. 6. 6.
i Deut. 15. 7, &c.
ch. 19. 17.

---

[1] Or, *unpunished.*
[2] Or, *He that hath an evil* eye hasteth to be rich.
[3] Heb. *a man destroying.*

---

15. The form of political wretchedness, when the poverty of the oppressed subjects not only embitters their sufferings, but exasperates the brutal ferocity of the ruler.

17. The case of wilful murder, not the lesser crime of manslaughter for which the cities of refuge were appointed. One, with that guilt on his soul, is simply hasting on to his own destruction. Those who see him must simply stand aloof, and let God's judgments fulfil themselves.

18. *in his ways*] Rather "in his double ways" (as in *v.* 6). The evil of vacillation rather than that of craft, the want of the one guiding principle of right, is contrasted with the straightforwardness of the man that "walketh uprightly."

shall fall at once] Better, **shall fall in one of them** (his ways). The attempt to combine incompatibilities is sure to fail. Men cannot serve God and Mammon.

20. Not the possession of wealth, nor even the acquisition of it, is evil, but the eager haste of covetousness.

shall not be innocent] Better, as in the margin, in contrast with the many "blessings" of the "faithful."

21. Dishonest partiality leads men who have enslaved themselves to it to transgress, even when the inducement is altogether disproportionate. A "piece of bread" was proverbial at all times as the extremest point of poverty (cp. marg. ref.).

22. The covetous temper leads not only to dishonesty, but to the "evil eye" of envy; and the temper of grudging, carking care, leads him to poverty.

24. *is the companion of a destroyer*] *i.e.* He stands on the same footing as the open, lawless robber. Cp. this with our Lord's teaching as to Corban (Mark vii. 10–13).

25. *shall be made fat*] He shall enjoy the two-fold blessing of abundance and tranquillity (cp. xi. 25).

26. The contrast between the wisdom of him who trusts in the Lord, and the folly of self-trust.

27. *hideth his eyes*] *i.e.* Turns away from, disregards, the poor. Cp. Isai. i. 15.

k ver. 12.
ch. 29. 2.
l Job 24. 4.

a 1 Sam. 2.
25.
2 Chr. 36. 16.
ch. 1. 24-27.
b Esth. 8. 15.
ch. 11. 10.
& 28. 12, 28.
c Esth. 3. 15.
d ch. 10. 1.
& 15. 20.
& 27. 11.
e ch. 5. 9, 10.
Luke 15. 13,
30.

28 *k* When the wicked rise, *l* men hide themselves:
 But when they perish, the righteous increase.

Chap. 29. 1 *a* HE, that being often reproved hardeneth *his* neck,
 Shall suddenly be destroyed, and that without remedy.

2 *b* When the righteous are 2 in authority, the people rejoice :
 But when the wicked beareth rule, *c* the people mourn.

3 *d* Whoso loveth wisdom rejoiceth his father :
 e But he that keepeth company with harlots spendeth *his* substance.

4 The king by judgment establisheth the land :
 But 3 he that receiveth gifts overthroweth it.

5 A man that flattereth his neighbour
 Spreadeth a net for his feet.

6 In the transgression of an evil man *there is* a snare :
 But the righteous doth sing and rejoice.

f Job 29. 16.
& 31. 13.
Ps. 41. 1.

7 *f* The righteous considereth the cause of the poor :
 But the wicked regardeth not to know *it.*

g ch. 11. 11.

h Ezek. 22.
30.

8 *g* Scornful men 4 bring a city into a snare :
 But wise *men* *h* turn away wrath.

9 *If* a wise man contendeth with a foolish man,
 i Whether he rage or laugh, *there is* no rest.

i Matt. 11. 17.

k Gen. 4. 5, 8.
1 John 3. 12.

10 5 *k* The bloodthirsty hate the upright,
 But the just seek his soul.

l Judg. 16.
17.
ch. 12. 16.
& 14. 33.

11 A *l* fool uttereth all his mind :
 But a wise *man* keepeth it in till afterwards.

12 If a ruler hearken to lies,—all his servants *are* wicked.

m ch. 22. 2.

n Matt. 5. 45.

13 The poor and 6 the deceitful man *m* meet together :
 n The LORD lighteneth both their eyes.

 1 Heb. *A man of reproofs.* 3 Heb. *a man of oblations.* 5 Heb. *Men of blood.*
 2 Or, *increased.* 4 Or, *set a city on fire.* 6 Or, *the usurer.*

XXIX. 1. *shall be destroyed*] Lit. "shall
be broken " (vi. 15). Stress is laid on the
suddenness in such a case of the long-de-
layed retribution.

3. *spendeth* &c.] The laws of parallelism
would lead us to expect " troubleth his
father ; " but that is passed over as a thing
about which the profligate would not care,
and he is reminded of what comes home to
him, that he is on the road to ruin.

The king] The ruler, as the supreme
fountain of all justice, and as the ideal
judge, is contrasted with the taker of
bribes.

6. While the offence of the wicked, rising
out of a confirmed habit of evil, becomes a
snare for his destruction ; the righteous,
even if he offend, is forgiven and can still
rejoice in his freedom from condemnation.
The second clause is taken by some as entirely contrasted with the first ; it expresses
the joy of one whose conscience is void of
offence, and who is in no danger of falling
into the snare.

8. *Scornful men*] The men who head
political or religious revolutions, who inflame
(lit. as in the marg.) the minds of the people
against the powers that be.

9. All modes of teaching—the stern rebuke or the smiling speech—are alike useless with the " foolish " man ; there is " no
rest." The ceaseless cavilling goes on still.

10. *seek his soul*] *i.e.* "Care for, watch
over, his life " (cp. Ps. cxlii. 4).

11. *mind*] The Hebrew word is used
sometimes for "mind" or "reason," sometimes for "passion," or "wrath." The reticence commended would include both ;
but the verb "keepeth it in" (rendered
"stilleth," in Ps. lxv. 7) is slightly in
favour of the second of the two senses.

12. *all his servants are wicked*] They
know what will please, and they become
informers and backbiters.

13. Better, The poor and the **oppressor.**
"Usurer," as in the marg. expresses the
special form of oppression from which the
poor suffer most at the hands of the rich.

14 [o] The king that [p] faithfully judgeth the poor,
His throne shall be established for ever.

15 [q] The rod and reproof give wisdom :
But [r] a child left *to himself* bringeth his mother to shame.

16 When the wicked are multiplied, transgression increaseth :
[s] But the righteous shall see their fall.

17 [t] Correct thy son, and he shall give thee rest ;
Yea, he shall give delight unto thy soul.

18 [u] Where *there is* no vision, the people [1] perish :
But [x] he that keepeth the law, happy *is* he.

19 A servant will not be corrected by words :
For though he understand he will not answer.

20 Seest thou a man *that is* hasty [2] in his words ?
[y] *There is* more hope of a fool than of him.

21 He that delicately bringeth up his servant from a child
Shall have him become *his* son at the length.

22 [z] An angry man stirreth up strife,
And a furious man aboundeth in transgression.

23 [a] A man's pride shall bring him low :
But honour shall uphold the humble in spirit.

24 Whoso is partner with a thief hateth his own soul :
[b] He heareth cursing, and bewrayeth *it* not.

25 [c] The fear of man bringeth a snare :
But whoso putteth his trust in the LORD [3] shall be safe.

26 [d] Many seek [4] the ruler's favour ;
But *every* man's judgment *cometh* from the LORD.

[1] Or, *is made naked.*   [2] Or, *in his matters ?*   [4] Heb. *the face of a ruler.*
[3] Heb. *shall be set on high.*

o ch. 20. 28.
& 25. 5.
p Ps. 72. 2, 4,
13, 14.
q ver. 17.
r ch. 10. 1.
& 17. 21, 25.

s Ps. 37. 36.
& 58. 10.
t ch. 13. 24.
& 19. 18.

u 1 Sam. 3. 1.
Amos 8. 11,
12.
x John 13. 17.
Jam. 1. 25.

y ch. 26. 12.

z ch. 15. 18.
& 26. 21.

a Job 22. 29.
ch. 15. 33.
Isai. 66. 2.
Dan. 4. 30.
Matt. 23. 12.
Luke 14. 11.
Acts 12. 23.
Jam. 4. 6.
1 Pet. 5. 5.
b Lev. 5. 1.
c Gen. 12. 12.
& 20. 2, 11.
d See Ps.
20. 9.
ch. 19. 6.

God has made them both and bestows His light equally on both.

15. *left to himself*] The condition of one who has been pampered and indulged. The mother who yields weakly is as guilty of abandoning the child she spoils, as if she cast him forth ; and for her evil neglect, there shall fall upon her the righteous punishment of shame and ignominy.

18. *vision*] The word commonly used of the revelation of God's will made to prophets. Cp. Isai. i. 1 ; Nah. i. 1.

When prophetic vision fails, obedience to the Law is the best or only substitute for it, both being forms through which Divine wisdom is revealed. Very striking in the midst of ethical precepts is this recognition of the need of a yet higher teaching, without which morality passes into worldly prudence or degenerates into casuistry. The "wise man," the son of David, has seen in the prophets and in their work the condition of true national blessedness. The darkest time in the history of Israel had been when there "was no open vision (1 Sam. iii. 1) ; at such a time the people "perish," are let loose, "are left to run wild."

19. *servant*] *i.e.* A slave, whose obedience

is reluctant. He may "understand" the words, but they produce no good effect. There is still lacking the true "answer" of obedience.

21. *son*] The Hebrew word occurs here only and is therefore of doubtful meaning. The favoured slave, petted and pampered from boyhood, will claim at last the privilege, perhaps the inheritance, of sonship.

23. *honour shall uphold the humble in spirit*] Better, **the lowly in spirit shall lay hold on honour.**

24. On the first discovery of the theft, the person wronged (Judg. xvii. 2), or the judge of the city (marg. ref.), pronounced a solemn curse on the thief and on all who, knowing the offender, were unwilling to give evidence against him. The accomplice of the thief hears that curse, and yet is silent, and so falls under it, and "destroys his own soul."

25. The confusion and wretchedness in which the fear of what men can do entangles us, is contrasted with the security of one, who not only "fears" the Lord, so as to avoid offending Him, but trusts in Him as his protector and guide.

26. To trust in the favour of princes is to

27 An unjust man *is* an abomination to the just:
And *he that is* upright in the way *is* abomination to the wicked.

a ch. 31. 1.   CHAP. 30. THE words of Agur the son of Jakeh, *even* *a*the prophecy: the man spake unto Ithiel, even unto Ithiel and
Ucal,

b Ps. 73. 22.   2 *b*Surely I *am* more brutish than *any* man,
And have not the understanding of a man.
3 I neither learned wisdom,
Nor ¹have the knowledge of the holy.

c John 3. 13.   4 *c*Who hath ascended up into heaven, or descended?
d Job 38. 4.   *d*Who hath gathered the wind in his fists?
Ps. 104. 3.   Who hath bound the waters in a garment?
Isai. 40. 12,   Who hath established all the ends of the earth?
&c.   What *is* his name, and what *is* his son's name, if thou canst
tell?

e Ps. 12. 6.   5 *e*Every word of God *is* ²pure:
& 18. 30.   *f* He *is* a shield unto them that put their trust in him.
& 19. 8.
f Ps. 18. 30.   6 *g*Add thou not unto his words,
& 115. 9.   Lest he reprove thee, and thou be found a liar.
10, 11.
g Deut. 4. 2.   7 Two *things* have I required of thee;
& 12. 32.   ³Deny me *them* not before I die:
Rev. 22. 18,
19.   8 Remove far from me vanity and lies:
Give me neither poverty nor riches;
h Matt. 6. 11.   *h* Feed me with food ⁴convenient for me:

¹ Heb. *know*.   ³ Heb. *withhold not from*   ⁴ Heb. *of my allowance*.
² Heb. *purified*.   *me*.

build upon the sands. The judgment which
will set right all wrong will come from the
Lord. It is better to wait for that than to
run hither and thither, canvassing, bribing,
flattering.

27. The words point out not only the
antagonism between the doers of good and
evil, but the instinctive antipathy which
the one feels towards the other.

XXX. 1. See the Introduction, p. 342.
According to the different reading, there
noted, the inscription ends with, "the man
spake," and the words that follow, are the
beginning of the confession, "I have wearied
myself after God and have fainted."

spake] The Hebrew word is that commonly used of the utterance of a Divine
oracle.

2. A confession of ignorance, with which
cp. the saying of Socrates that he was wise
only so far as he knew that he knew nothing, or that of Asaph (Ps. lxxiii. 22).

3. He found, when he looked within, that
all his learning was as nothing. He had
heard of God only "by the hearing of the
ear" (Job xlii. 5), and now he discovered
how little that availed.

the holy] The Holy One. Cp. ix. 10.

4. Man is to be humbled to the dust by
the thought of the glory of God as seen in
the visible creation.

*Who hath ascended up into heaven, or de-
scended?*] The thought is obviously that of

the all-embracing Providence of God, taking
in at once the greatest and the least, the
highest and the lowest. The mysteries of
the winds and of the waters baffle men's researches.

what is his son's name] The primary
thought is that man knows so little of the
Divine nature that he cannot tell whether
he may transfer to it the human relationships with which he is familiar, or must
rest in the thought of a unity indivisible
and incommunicable. If there be such an
Only-begotten of the Father (cp. viii. 30),
His nature, until revealed, must be as incomprehensible by us as that of the Father
Himself.

5. Out of this consciousness of the impotence of all man's efforts after the knowledge of God rises the sense of the preciousness of every living word that God has Himself revealed, whether through "the Law
and the Prophets" or through "wise men
and scribes."

6. Men are not to mingle revealed truth
with their own imaginations and traditions.
In speculating on the unseen, the risk of
error is indefinitely great, and that error God
reproves by manifesting its falsehoods.

7. *Two things*] The limitation of man's desires follows naturally upon his consciousness of the limits of his knowledge.

8. The order of the two requests is significant. The wise man's prayer is first and

9 ⁱ Lest I be full, and ¹ deny *thee*,—and say, Who *is* the LORD?
  Or lest I be poor, and steal,
  And take the name of my God *in vain*.

ⁱ Deut. 8. 12,
14, 17.
Neh. 9. 25.
Job 31. 24.
Hos. 13. 6.

10 ² Accuse not a servant unto his master,
  Lest he curse thee, and thou be found guilty.

11 *There is* a generation *that* curseth their father,
  And doth not bless their mother.

12 *There is* a generation ^k*that are* pure in their own eyes,
  And *yet* is not washed from their filthiness.

^k Luke 18.
11.

13 *There is* a generation, O how ^l lofty are their eyes!
  And their eyelids are lifted up.

^l Ps. 131. 1.
ch. 6. 17.

14 ^m *There is* a generation, whose teeth *are as* swords,
  And their jaw teeth *as* knives,
  ⁿ To devour the poor from off the earth,
  And the needy from *among* men.

^m Job 29. 17.
Ps. 52. 2.
ch. 12. 18.
ⁿ Ps. 14. 4.
Amos 8. 4.

15 The horseleach hath two daughters, *crying*, Give, give.
  There are three *things that* are never satisfied,
  Yea, four *things* say not, ³ *It is* enough:

16 ^o The grave; and the barren womb;
  The earth *that* is not filled with water;
  And the fire *that* saith not, *It is* enough.

^o ch. 27. 20.
Hab. 2. 5.

17 ^p The eye *that* mocketh at *his* father,
  And despiseth to obey *his* mother,
  The ravens of ⁴ the valley shall pick it out,
  And the young eagles shall eat it.

^p Gen. 9. 22.
Lev. 20. 9.
ch. 20. 20.
& 23. 22.

18 There be three *things which* are too wonderful for me,
  Yea, four which I know not:

---

¹ Heb. *belie* thee.   ² Heb. *Hurt not with thy tongue*.   ³ Heb. *wealth*.   ⁴ Or, *the brook*.

---

chiefly, "truth in the inward parts," the removal of all forms of falsehood, hollowness, hypocrisy.

neither poverty &c.] The evil of the opposite extremes of social life is that in different ways they lead men to a false standard of duty, and so to that forgetfulness of God which passes into an absolute denial.

food convenient for me] Lit. "give me for food the bread of my appointed portion." The prayer foreshadows that which we have been taught by the Divine Wisdom, "Give us, day by day, our daily bread."

9. The special dangers of the two extremes. Wealth tempts to pride, unbelief, and a scorn like that of Pharaoh (Exod. v. 2); poverty to dishonesty, and then to perjury, or to the hypocritical profession of religion which is practically identical with it.

10. *Accuse not a servant*] The prayer in *v.* 8 does not shut out sympathy with those who are less favoured. Even the slave has a right to protection against frivolous or needless accusation. Others, however, render the words **Make not a slave to accuse his master**, *i.e.* Do not make him discontented with his lot, lest he afterwards curse thee for having made it worse than it was.

11. As the teacher had uttered what he most desired, so now he tells what he most abhorred; and in true harmony with the teaching of the Ten Commandments places in the foremost rank those who rise against the Fifth.

12. The Pharisee temper (cp. marg. ref.).

15, 16. Note the numeration mounting to a climax, the two, the three, the four (Amos i. 3 &c.). The word rendered "horseleach" is found nowhere else, and its etymology is doubtful; but there are good grounds for taking the word in its literal sense, as giving an example, in the natural world, of the insatiable greed of which the next verse gives other instances. Its voracious appetite is here represented, to express its intensity, as two daughters, uttering the same ceaseless cry for more.

16. *The grave*] Heb. *Sheol*. The "Hell" or Hades of xxvii. 20, all-consuming yet never full.

18-20. Another enigma. The four things of *v.* 16 agreed in the common point of insatiableness; the four now mentioned

19 The way of an eagle in the air;—the way of a serpent upon a
     rock;
   The way of a ship in the [1] midst of the sea;
   And the way of a man with a maid.
20 Such *is* the way of an adulterous woman;
   She eateth, and wipeth her mouth,
   And saith, I have done no wickedness.
21 For three *things* the earth is disquieted,
   And for four *which* it cannot bear:
22 [q] For a servant when he reigneth;
   And a fool when he is filled with meat;
23 For an odious *woman* when she is married;
   And an handmaid that is heir to her mistress.
24 There be four *things which are* little upon the earth,
   But they *are* [2] exceeding wise:
25 [r] The ants *are* a people not strong,
   Yet they prepare their meat in the summer;
26 [s] The conies *are but* a feeble folk,
   Yet make they their houses in the rocks;
27 The locusts have no king,
   Yet go they forth all of them [3] by bands;
28 The spider taketh hold with her hands,
   And is in kings' palaces.
29 There be three *things* which go well,
   Yea, four are comely in going:
30 A lion *which is* strongest among beasts,
   And turneth not away for any;
31 A [4][5] greyhound; an he goat also;
   And a king, against whom *there is* no rising up.

[q] ch. 19. 10.
Eccl. 10. 7.

[r] ch. 6. 6, &c.

[s] Ps. 104. 18.

---

[1] Heb. *heart*.   [3] Heb. *gathered together*.   [5] Heb. *girt in the loins*.
[2] Heb. *wise, made wise*.   [4] Or, *horse*.

---

agree in this, that they leave no trace behind them.

19. *the way of a man with a maid*] The
act of sin leaves no outward mark upon the
sinners.

21. *for four which it cannot bear*] Better,
four it cannot bear. Here the common
element is that of being intolerable, and the
four examples are divided equally between
the two sexes. Each has its examples of
power and prosperity misused because they
fall to the lot of those who have no training for them, and are therefore in the wrong
place.

23. *odious woman*] One in whom there
is nothing loveable. Marriage, which to
most women is the state in which they find
scope for their highest qualities, becomes
to her only a sphere in which to make herself and others miserable.

24. *exceeding wise*] Some prefer the reading of the LXX. and Vulg., "wiser than
the wise." The thought, in either case,
turns upon the marvels of instinct, which,
in their own province, transcend the more
elaborate results of human wisdom.

25. See marg. ref. note. Note the word
"people" applied here to ants, as to locusts

in Joel i. 6. The marvel lies in their collective, and, as it were, organized action.

26. *conies*] See marg. ref. note.

27. Cp. Joel ii. 7, 8; the most striking
fact in the flight of the locust-swarms was
their apparent order and discipline, sweeping over the land like the invasion of a
great army.

28. *spider*] Rather, the Gecko (or Stellio),
a genus of the lizard tribe, many species of
which haunt houses, make their way through
crevices in the walls, and with feet that se-
crete a venomous exudation catch the spiders
or the flies they find there.

31. *A greyhound*] The Heb. word occurs
nowhere else in the O.T. The literal meaning is, "one with loins girded;" and some
have referred this to the stripes of the
zebra, others to the "war-horse" (cp. Job
xxxix. 19, 25), as he is represented in the
sculptures of Persepolis, with rich and
stately trappings.

a king, against whom there is no rising up]
i.e. A king irresistible. Others prefer, "a
king in the midst of his people," and the
sense, as giving a more vivid picture, is certainly more satisfactory.

32 If thou hast done foolishly in lifting up thyself,
  Or if thou hast thought evil,—[t] *lay* thine hand upon thy mouth.
33 Surely the churning of milk bringeth forth butter,
  And the wringing of the nose bringeth forth blood :
  So the forcing of wrath bringeth forth strife.

Chap. 31. THE words of king Lemuel, [a] the prophecy that his
  mother taught him.
2 What, my son ? and what, [b] the son of my womb ?
  And what, the son of my vows ?
3 [c] Give not thy strength unto women,
  Nor thy ways [d] to that which destroyeth kings.
4 [e] *It is* not for kings, O Lemuel, *it is* not for kings to drink wine ;
  Nor for princes strong drink :
5 [f] Lest they drink, and forget the law,
  And [1] pervert the judgment [2] of any of the afflicted.
6 [g] Give strong drink unto him that is ready to perish,
  And wine unto those that be [3] of heavy hearts.
7 Let him drink, and forget his poverty,
  And remember his misery no more.
8 [h] Open thy mouth for the dumb
  [i] In the cause of all [4] such as are appointed to destruction.
9 Open thy mouth, [k] judge righteously,
  And [l] plead the cause of the poor and needy.
10 (א) [m] Who can find a virtuous woman ?
  For her price *is* far above rubies.
11 (ב) The heart of her husband doth safely trust in her,
  So that he shall have no need of spoil.

[t] Job 21. 5.
& 40. 4.
Eccl. 8. 2.
Mic. 7. 16.

[a] ch. 30. 1.

[b] Isai. 40. 15.

[c] ch. 5. 9.

[d] Deut. 17.
17.
Neh. 13. 26.
ch. 7. 26.
[e] Eccl. 10. 17.
[f] Hos. 4. 11.

[g] Ps. 104. 15.

[h] See Job
29. 15, 16.
[i] 1 Sam. 19 4.
Esth. 4. 16.
[k] Lev. 19. 15.
Deut. 1. 16.
[l] Job 29. 12.
Isai. 1. 17.
Jer. 22. 16.
[m] ch. 12. 4.
& 18. 22.
& 19. 14.

[1] Heb. *alter.*
[2] Heb. *of all the sons of affliction.*
[3] Heb. *bitter of soul,* 1 Sam. 1. 10.
[4] Heb. *the sons of destruction.*

---

32. *lay thine hand upon thy mouth*] The act expresses the silence of humiliation and repentance after the sin has been committed, and that of self-restraint, which checks the haughty or malignant thought before it has passed even into words.

33. *churning...wringing...forcing*] In the Heb. one and the same word. "The pressure of milk produces curds, the pressure of the nose produces blood, the pressure of wrath (*i.e.* brooding over and, as it were, condensing it) produces strife."

XXXI. See Introduction, p. 343.

1. *that his mother taught him*] Cp. i. 8, vi. 20. If we refer the chapter to Israelite authorship, we may remember the honour paid to the wisdom of Miriam, Deborah, and Huldah; if to Edomite or Arabian, we may think of the Queen of Sheba, whose love of wisdom led her to sit at the feet of the son of David.

2. The repetitions are emphatic ; expressive of anxious love.

son of my vows] Like Samuel, and Samson, the child often asked for in prayer, the prayer ratified by a vow of dedication. The name Lemuel (lit. "for God," consecrated to Him) may be the expression of that dedication ; and the warning against indulging in wine (*v.* 4) shews that it had something of the Nazarite or Rechabite idea in it.

3. *to that which destroyeth*] The temptations of the harem were then, as now, the curse of all Eastern kingdoms.

4. Some read, "nor for princes to say, Where is strong drink ?" The "strong drink" (xx. 1) was distilled from barley, or honey, or dates.

6. The true purpose of the power of wine over man's mind and body, as a restorative and remedial agent. Cp. marg. ref. The same thought shewed itself in the Jewish practice of giving a cup of wine to mourners, and (as in the history of the Crucifixion) to criminals at their execution.

8. In contrast with the two besetting sins of Eastern monarchs stands their one great duty, to give help to those who had no other helper.

such as are appointed to destruction] Lit. "children of bereavement," with the sense, either, as in the text, of those "destined to be bereaved of life or goods," or of "bereaved or fatherless children."

10. See Introduction, p. 344.

rubies] Better **pearls.** See iii. 15 note.

11. *no need of spoil*] Better, **no lack of gain,** lack of honest gain.

12 (ב) She will do him good and not evil all the days of her life.
13 (ד) She seeketh wool, and flax,
And worketh willingly with her hands.
14 (ה) She is like the merchants' ships;
She bringeth her food from afar.
15 (ו) *n*She riseth also while it is yet night,
And *o*giveth meat to her household,
And a portion to her maidens.
16 (ז) She considereth a field, and ¹buyeth it:
With the fruit of her hands she planteth a vineyard.
17 (ח) She girdeth her loins with strength,
And strengtheneth her arms.
18 (ט) ²She perceiveth that her merchandise *is* good:
Her candle goeth not out by night.
19 (י) She layeth her hands to the spindle,
And her hands hold the distaff.
20 (כ) ³*p* She stretcheth out her hand to the poor;
Yea, she reacheth forth her hands to the needy.
21 (ל) She is not afraid of the snow for her household:
For all her household *are* clothed with ⁴scarlet.
22 (מ) She maketh herself coverings of tapestry;
Her clothing *is* silk and purple.
23 (נ) *q*Her husband is known in the gates,
When he sitteth among the elders of the land.
24 (ס) She maketh fine linen, and selleth *it;*
And delivereth girdles unto the merchant.
25 (ע) Strength and honour *are* her clothing;
And she shall rejoice in time to come.
26 (פ) She openeth her mouth with wisdom;
And in her tongue *is* the law of kindness.
27 (צ) She looketh well to the ways of her household,
And eateth not the bread of idleness.
28 (ק) Her children arise up, and call her blessed;
Her husband *also,* and he praiseth her

¹ Heb. *taketh.*   ² Heb. *She tasteth.*   ⁴ Or, *double garments.*
³ Heb. *She spreadeth.*

13. *worketh willingly with her hands*] Or, **Worketh with willing hands.** The stress laid on the industrial habits of Israelite matrons may perhaps belong to a time when, as under the monarchy of Judah, those habits were passing away.

14. The comparison points to the enlarged commerce of the Israelites consequent on their intercourse with the Phœnicians under David and Solomon; cp. *v.* 24.

15. *a portion to her maidens*] The daily task assigned to each at the same time as the daily food. Cp. xxx. 8; Ex. v. 14.

16. The verse points to a large sphere of feminine activity, strikingly in contrast with the degradation to which woman in the East has now fallen.

20. The industry is not selfish, but bears the fruit of an open-handed charity.

21. *scarlet*] Probably some well-known articles of dress, at once conspicuous for their colour, or, as some think, for their double texture and warmth.

22. *silk*] Better, **fine linen,** the *byssus* of Egypt.

23. The industry of the wife leaves the husband free to take his place among the elders that sit in councils.

24. *fine linen*] Not the same word as in *v.* 22 note; it describes a made-up garment (Isai. iii. 23).
merchant] Lit. "Canaanite," *i.e.* the Phœnician merchant.

25. *shall rejoice in time to come*] Better, **rejoiceth over the time to come**; *i.e.* looks forward to the future, not with anxious care, but with confident gladness.

26. *law of kindness*] The words which come from the lips of the true wife are as a law giving guidance and instruction to those that hear them; but the law is not proclaimed in its sterner aspects, but as one in which "mercy tempers justice," and love, the fulfilling of the law, is seen to be the source from which it springs.

29 (ר) Many daughters [1]have done virtuously,
But thou excellest them all.
30 (ש) Favour *is* deceitful, and beauty *is* vain :
But a woman *that* feareth the LORD, she shall be praised.
31 (ת) Give her of the fruit of her hands ;
And let her own works praise her in the gates.

[1] Or, *have gotten riches.*

29. The words of praise which the husband (*v.* 28) is supposed to have addressed to the ideal wife.

virtuously] The Hebrew word has primarily (like "virtus") the idea of "strength," but is used with various shades of meaning. Here (as in xii. 4; Ruth iii. 11) the strength is that of character stedfast in goodness.

In other passages (*e.g.* Gen. xxxiv. 29; Ps. xlix. 10) it has the sense of "riches," and is so taken here by the LXX. and Vulg., see also the marg. rendering.

30. The last lesson of the Book is the same as the first. The fear of the Lord is the condition of all womanly, as well as of all manly, excellence.

ECCLESIASTES.

INTRODUCTION.

I. This Book is placed, in the most ancient Jewish and Christian lists, between the other two Books (Proverbs and the Song of Songs) attributed to Solomon, and the constant tradition of the Jewish and Christian Churches has handed down Solomon without question as the author.

Some modern critics have indeed alleged that Solomon could not have written it, (a) because the language is such as no Jew in his age could have used, (b) because the language differs from that of Proverbs and the Song of Songs, and (c) because the historical allusions in the Book do not agree with the period and the circumstances of Solomon.

(a) In answer to this, it would appear that every word quoted from Ecclesiastes as impossible to be used before the Captivity has been shewn either (1) to be used in Books written, as is generally believed, before the Captivity; or (2) to be formed from words, and by a grammatical process, in use before the Captivity; or (3) to be represented in such Books by a derivative; or (4) to be undoubtedly common to other Semitic dialects besides Chaldee, and therefore, presumably, to Hebrew before the Captivity, although not found in extant writings of earlier date than Ecclesiastes. The allegation, therefore, that the language of this Book shews distinct traces of the Chaldean invasion, of the Babylonian Captivity, or of any later event which affected the Hebrew tongue, may be considered sufficiently answered.[1]

(b) The dissimilarity in style and diction between this Book and Proverbs or the Song of Songs is admitted; but it has been accounted for to some extent, first, by the difference of subject. Abstract ideas may be expressed up to a certain point by words which originally denoted something else: but philosophic thought such as distinguishes this Book from the other two, gradually forms its own terminology. Next, it is argued, that there was an interval of many years between the composition of the two former Books and of this; and that in that time there was a natural change in the temperament, views, and style of the writer; a change which may be traced partly to Solomon's familiarity with foreign women sprung from various Semitic races, partly also to his extensive negotiations and personal intercourse with the representatives of other nations, some of whom were

---

[1] Writers who maintain that the language of Ecclesiastes could not have been used by a Jew in Solomon's age, diverge so widely from one another on the question of date as to suggest a serious doubt whether such grammatical knowledge of Hebrew as is now attainable ought to be allowed all the weight that is claimed for it in deciding the date of the composition of this Book. If the majority place it between the 4th and 6th centuries B.C., some place it as high as the 10th and some as low as the 1st.

not of Semitic origin (1 K. x. 22).[2]
Lastly, to balance the differences, it is to be noted that
there are some characteristic re-
semblances between these Books.
It is reasonable to regard these as
an indication of a common origin.

(c) It is alleged that the particular mention of Jerusalem (i. 1,
12) as the seat of Solomon's reign,
implies that the Book was written
at a time when there was more
than one seat of kingly authority
in Israel, *i.e.* after the separation
of the ten tribes and the erection
of another capital, Samaria. The
answer is that there is an obvious
fitness in the specific mention of
Jerusalem previous to the account
of Solomon's labours in chs. i., ii.,
for it was the scene of his peculiar
work for many years, and the place
which he had made the chief monument of his grandeur.

It is alleged that the expression,
" I was king " (i. 12), implies that
at the time when these words were
written Solomon was no longer
king, and that consequently the
passage must have been written by
some one personating him after his
death. But, in Hebrew the preterite
is used with strict grammatical
propriety in describing a past

which extends into the present.
Solomon is as a speaker who views
the action or state expressed by
the verb as then first about coming
to pass, in progress, or perhaps occurring at the instant. The phrase
therefore would be both gram-
matically correct if used by Solomon before the close of his reign,
and a natural expression of his
feelings in his old age.

It is argued that such a state of
violence, popular oppression and
despotic rule, as that which is in-
stanced in iv. 1 did not exist in
Palestine in the peaceful reign of
Solomon. This allegation has no
foundation in fact. The significant
statements of historians (*e.g.* 1 K.
xii. 4 and 2 Chr. ii. 17, 18, viii. 7–
9) and the numerous unmistakeable
allusions in the Book of Proverbs
(*e.g.* i. 10–13, vi. 16–19, xi. 26, xiv.
20, xxii. 22, 23, xxiv. 21, xxv. 5,
xxviii. 2, 16) agree with the descriptions in Ecclesiastes in shewing that the kingdom of Israel,
even in its most prosperous days,
afforded grievous instances of the
common evils of Asiatic despotism.[3]

It is stated that such passages as
xii. 7, 14 shew a knowledge of revealed truth beyond what was
given prior to the Captivity.[4]   But

[2] The history of literature supplies
many instances of the same writer expressing his thoughts in different styles.
Cp. the difference between the speeches
and the narrative of the Greek historian
Thucydides ; and cp. the difference
in the dialect, diction, and metre of the
chorus with the dialogue of Greek tra-
gedy. The style of Milton in his " Ode
on the Nativity," written in his 21st year,
differs widely from "Samson Agonistes,"
a product of his old age. Holy Scripture
itself supplies a striking instance of the
same kind ; the Revelation of St. John
presents some remarkable differences of
style and language if compared with the
Gospel and Epistles ; yet this dissimilarity

does not prevent critics, after taking all
the facts into account, from considering
the whole of these Books as the work of
the same author.
[3] It has also been argued that Solomon,
as the supreme ruler of the people, and
therefore responsible for the oppression,
would not have placed on record a description of it. But, even supposing that
Solomon's own subjects are here referred
to by him ; yet all sovereigns, inti-
mately acquainted with the condition of
their people, are aware of and must de-
plore the infliction of much misery which
they are unable to prevent or to avenge.
[4] See Introduction to the Psalms, p.
100.

if the exact words of Ecclesiastes be compared with the obscure intimations given by Moses on the one hand, and with the later utterances of Daniel on the other, this Book appears to hold a middle place. It tallies very closely with some of the Psalms which were probably written about the age of Solomon.[5] After all, does not the argument above mentioned proceed on an assumption that we are more competent than we really are to find out the ways of the Author of Revelation? Are we qualified to decide positively that so much as is recorded on those subjects in Ecclesiastes came out of its proper season if it was given to Solomon?

On the whole, therefore, it seems the most reasonable course to accept as a simple statement of fact the words with which Ecclesiastes begins; and, in accordance with the voice of the Church from the beginning, to regard Solomon as the author of this Book.

II. What was the object of the writer in composing this Book?

The method of Greek philosophy and its principles, Epicurean, Stoic, and Cynic, have been attributed to the author of Ecclesiastes; but on no better ground than might be found in the writings of any thoughtful and sensitive man who has felt, contemplated, and described the perplexities of human life.

The author was evidently a man of profound faith in God, of large and varied personal experience, of acute observation of men and things, and of deep sensibility.

Probably he was first moved to write by a mind painfully full of the disappointing nature of all things viewed apart from God: next by deep sympathy with fellow-men touched by the same natural feelings as himself, and suffering like him, though each in their several ways; and thirdly, by the evident desire to lead other men, and specially young men, out of the temptations which he had felt, and out of the perplexities which once entangled and staggered him. Whether his heart was chilled by old age or by the cold shadow of some former eclipse of faith can only be conjectured; but there is in Ecclesiastes an absence of that fervour of zeal for the glory of God which glows in other Books, and which we are justified in regarding as a feature of Solomon's character in his early days. His immediate object would seem then to be to relieve his mind by pouring out the results of his own life, to comfort those who bore the same burden of humanity, and to lift up those who were naturally feeble or depressed by circumstances and to lead them in the way of God's commandments.

As regards plan, the writer of the Book evidently regarded it as complete in itself; the first part of the Book being contemplative or doctrinal, and the latter part practical.

First, there is the writer's statement of his subject, and his detailed account of his personal experience of the influence of vanity pervading human proceedings (chs. i. ii.). Then, there is the announcement of an external law to which also human affairs are subject, i.e. the will of God, Whose plan, incom-

---

[5] e.g. with regard to the judgment of the world, Pss. i. 5, ix. 8, xcvi. 13, and with regard to the souls of the dead being with God, Ps. xvi. 8-11.

prehensible in its extent, is found by all to be more or less in conflict with man's will (chs. iii. iv.), the result of such conflict being disappointment and perplexity to man. Then there is the commencement (ch. v.) of personal practical advice, followed by a mixture of reflections, maxims, and exhortations, in which the vanity of riches, the practical superiority of wisdom and patience, and the supreme power of God, are the prominent topics set forth in various ways (chs. vi., vii., viii.). In ch. ix. the writer's reflections, in ch. x. his maxims, are brought to an end ; and in chs. xi. and xii. we have a concluding exhortation to such conduct and sentiments as are most likely to alleviate the vanity of this life, viz. to charity, industry, patience and the fear of God.

If the Book was composed, as seems probable, towards the end of Solomon's reign, its direct tendency is obvious. In an age when "silver was as stones in Jerusalem" no lesson was more necessary, and none would tell with deeper effect, than those powerful and touching declarations of the vanity of wealth and grandeur which are perhaps the most conspicuous feature in this Book. Further, if the Book appealed then, as it has ever since appealed, to an inner circle of more thoughtful readers, they especially who in those days discerned the signs of the approaching dismemberment of the kingdom and the diminution of the glory of Jerusalem would find their comfort in its lessons of patient endurance and resignation to the sovereign will of God. Whenever the Church has been threatened with approaching calamity this Book has always shewn its consolatory effect upon devout believers.[6] It served, before Christ came, to lighten for Jews the darkness of those "crooked" ways of God which have exercised the Christian penetration of Pascal and Butler. To the desolation of religious doubt, Ecclesiastes brings a special message of consolation and direction : for it shews that a cry of perplexity finds a place even in the sacred Books ; and it indicates a nearer approach to the living God in reverent worship (v. 1), in active service (xi. 6), in humble acknowledgment of His power (iii. 10–17), in reliance on His final justice (v. 8, xii. 13, 14), as the means by which that cry has been, and may again be, hushed.

---

[6] Augustine refers to it as setting forth the vanity of this life, only that we may desire that life wherein, instead of vanity beneath the sun, there is truth under Him Who made the sun. It was the same tendency which induced the author of the "De Imitatione Christi" to borrow from Ecclesiastes the key-note of his golden book.

ECCLESIASTES;

OR,

THE PREACHER.

Chap. 1. THE words *a*of the Preacher, the son of David, king in Jerusalem.

2 *b*Vanity of vanities, saith the Preacher, vanity of vanities;
3 *c*all *is* vanity. *d*What profit hath a man of all his labour which
4 he taketh under the sun? *One* generation passeth away, and *another* generation cometh: *e*but the earth abideth for ever.
5 *f*The sun also ariseth, and the sun goeth down, and ¹hasteth to

¹ Heb. *panteth.*

a ver. 12.
ch. 7. 27.
& 12. 8, 9, 10.
b Ps. 39. 5, 6.
& 62. 9.
& 144. 4.
c ch. 12. 8.
c Rom. 8. 20.
d ch. 2. 22.
& 3. 9.
e Ps. 104. 5.
& 119. 90.
f Ps. 19. 5, 6.

I. **1–3.** These introductory verses serve to describe the writer, and to state the subject of his Book.

1. *Preacher*] Lit. **Convener.** No one English word represents adequately the Heb. *Koheleth.* Though capable, according to Hebrew usage, of being applied to men in office, it is strictly a feminine participle, and describes a person in the act of calling together an assembly of people as if with the intention of addressing them. The word thus understood refers us to the action of Wisdom personified (Prov. i. 20, viii. 8). In Prov. and here Solomon seems to support two characters, speaking sometimes in the third person as Wisdom instructing the assembled people, at other times in the first person. So our Lord speaks of Himself (cp. Luke xi. 49 with Matt. xxiii. 34) as Wisdom, and as desiring (Luke xiii. 34) to gather the people together for instruction. It is unfortunate that the word "Preacher" does not bring this personification before English minds, but a different idea.

2. *Vanity*] This word (*Hebel*, or, when used as a proper name, in Gen. iv. 2, *Abel*), occurs no less than 37 times in Ecclesiastes, and has been called the key of the Book. Primarily it means "breath," "light wind;" and denotes that which (1) passes away more or less quickly and completely, (2) leaves either no result or no adequate result behind, and therefore (3) fails to satisfy the mind of man, which naturally craves for something permanent and progressive: it is also applied to (4) idols, as contrasted with the Living, Eternal, and Almighty God, and thus in the Hebrew mind it is connected with sin. In this Book it is applied to all works on earth, to pleasure, grandeur, wisdom, the life of man, childhood, youth, and length of days, the oblivion of the grave, wandering and unsatisfied desires, unenjoyed possessions, and anomalies in the moral government of the world.

Solomon speaks of the world-wide existence of "vanity," not with bitterness or scorn, but as a fact, which forced itself on him as he advanced in knowledge of men and things, and which he regards with sorrow and perplexity. From such feelings he finds refuge by contrasting this with another fact, which he holds with equal firmness, viz. that the whole universe is made and is governed by a God of justice, goodness, and power. The place of vanity in the order of Divine Providence—unknown to Solomon, unless the answer be indicated in vii. 29—is explained to us by St. Paul, Romans viii., where its origin is traced to the subjugation and corruption of creation by sin as a consequence of the fall of man; and its extinction is declared to be reserved till after the Resurrection in the glory and liberty of the children of God.

Vanity of vanities] A well-known Hebrew idiom signifying vanity in the highest degree. Cp. the phrase, "Holy of Holies."

all] Solomon includes both the courses of nature and the works of man (*vv.* 4–11). Cp. Rom. viii. 22.

3. *What profit* &c.] The question often repeated is the great practical inquiry of the Book; it receives its final answer in xii. 13, 14. When this question was asked the Lord had not yet spoken (Matt. xi. 28). The word "profit" (or preeminence) is opposed to "vanity."

hath a man] Rather, **hath man.**

4–11. "Vanity" is shown in mankind, the elements, and all that moves on earth; the same course is repeated again and again without any permanent result or real progress; and events and men are alike forgotten.

4. *abideth*] The apparent permanence of the earth increases by contrast the transitory condition of its inhabitants.

ever] The word does not here absolutely signify "eternity" (cp. iii. 11 note), but a certainly short period (cp. Ex. xxi. 6): here it might be paraphrased "as long as this world, this present order of things, lasts."

5. *hasteth* &c.] Lit. **at his place panting** (in his eagerness) **riseth he there.**

v John 3. 8.

h Job 38. 10.

i Prov. 27. 20.

k ch. 3. 15.

l ver. 1.

m Gen. 3. 19.
ch. 3. 10.

6 his place where he arose. *v*The wind goeth toward the south, and turneth about unto the north; it whirleth about continually, and the wind returneth again according to his circuits.

7 *h*All the rivers run into the sea; yet the sea *is* not full; unto the place from whence the rivers come, thither they ¹return

8 again. All things *are* full of labour; man cannot utter *it*: ¹the eye is not satisfied with seeing, nor the ear filled with hearing.

9 *k*The thing that hath been, it *is that* which shall be; and that which is done *is* that which shall be done: and *there is* no new

10 *thing* under the sun. Is there *any* thing whereof it may be said, See, this *is* new? it hath been already of old time, which was

11 before us. *There is* no remembrance of former *things;* neither shall there be *any* remembrance of *things* that are to come with *those* that shall come after.

12, 13 *l*I the Preacher was king over Israel in Jerusalem. And I gave my heart to seek and search out by wisdom concerning all *things* that are done under heaven: *m*this sore travail hath God given to the sons of man ²to be exercised therewith.

14 I have seen all the works that are done under the sun; and, be-

---

¹ Heb. *return to go.*   ² Or, *to afflict them.*

---

6. More lit. **Going towards the south and veering towards the north, veering, veering goes the wind; and to its veerings the wind returns.**

7. *the place*] *i.e.* The spring or river-head. It would seem that the ancient Hebrews regarded the clouds as the immediate feeders of the springs (Prov. viii. 28, and Ps. civ. 10, 13). Gen. ii. 6 indicates some acquaintance with the process and result of evaporation.

8. *All things...utter it*] This clause, as here translated, refers to the immensity of labour. Others translate it, "all words are full of labour; they make weary the hearers," or "are feeble or insufficient" to tell the whole; and are referred to the impossibility of adequately describing labour.

9. *hath been...is done*] *i.e.* Hath happened in the course of nature...is done by man.

11. *things*] Rather, **men.**

12. Solomon relates his personal experience (ch. ii.); the result of which was "no profit," and a conviction that all, even God's gifts of earthly good to good men, in this life are subject to vanity. His trial of God's first gift, wisdom, is recounted in *vv.* 12–18.

was] This tense does not imply that Solomon had ceased to be king when the word was written. See Introduction, p. 424. He begins with the time of his accession to the throne, when the gifts of wisdom and riches were specially promised to him (1 K. iii. 12, 13).

13. *wisdom*] As including both the powers of observation and judgment, and the knowledge acquired thereby (1 K. iii. 28, iv. 29, x. 8 &c.). It increases by exercise. Here is noted its application to men and their actions.

travail] In the sense of toil; the word is here applied to all human occupations.

God] Thirty-nine times in this Book, God is named as Elohim; a name common to the true God and to false gods, and used by believers and by idolators: but the name Jehovah, by which He is known peculiarly to the people who are in Covenant with Him, is never once used.

Perhaps the chief reason for this is that the evil which is the object of inquiry in this Book is not at all peculiar to the chosen people. All creation (Rom. viii.) groans under it. The Preacher does not write of, or to, the Hebrew race exclusively. There is no express and obvious reference to their national expectations, the events of their national history, or even to the divine oracles which were deposited with them. Hence it was natural for the wisest and largest-hearted man of his race to take a wider range of observation than any other Hebrew writer before or after him. It became the sovereign of many peoples whose religions diverged more or less remotely from the true religion, to address himself to a more extensive sphere than that which was occupied by the twelve tribes, and to adapt his language accordingly. See v. 1 note.

14. *vexation of spirit*] A phrase which occurs 7 times, and may be otherwise translated, **feeding on wind.** Modern Heb. grammarians assert that the word rendered "vexation" must be derived from a root signifying "to feed," "follow," "strive after." This being admitted, it remains to choose between two translations: (1) "Striving after wind," or "windy effort;" adopted by the LXX. and the majority of modern interpreters; or (2) **feeding on wind.** Cp. Hos. xii. 1: and similar phrases in Prov. xv. 14; Isai. xliv. 20; Ps. xxxvii. 3.

15 hold, all *is* vanity and vexation of spirit. ⁿ*That which is* crooked
    cannot be made straight: and ¹that which is wanting cannot be
16 numbered. I communed with mine own heart, saying, Lo, I am
    come to great estate, and have gotten ^omore wisdom than all
    they that have been before me in Jerusalem : yea, my heart ²had
17 great experience of wisdom and knowledge. ^pAnd I gave my
    heart to know wisdom, and to know madness and folly : I per-
18 ceived that this also is vexation of spirit. For ^qin much wisdom
    is much grief : and he that increaseth knowledge increaseth
    sorrow.

CHAP. 2. ^aI SAID in mine heart, Go to now, I will prove thee with
    mirth, therefore enjoy pleasure : and, behold, ^bthis also *is* va-
2 nity. ^cI said of laughter, *It is* mad : and of mirth, What doeth it ?
3 ^dI sought in mine heart ³to give myself unto wine, yet acquaint-
    ing mine heart with wisdom ; and to lay hold on folly, till I
    might see what *was* that good for the sons of men, which they
4 should do under the heaven ⁴all the days of their life. I made
    me great works ; I builded me houses ; I planted me vineyards :
5 I made me gardens and orchards, and I planted trees in them
6 of all *kind of* fruits. I made me pools of water, to water there-
7 with the wood that bringeth forth trees : I got *me* servants and
    maidens, and had ⁵servants born in my house ; also I had great
    possessions of great and small cattle above all that were in Jeru-

Marginal references:
n ch. 7. 13.

o 1 K. 3. 12,
13.
& 4. 30.
& 10. 7, 23.
ch. 2. 9.
p ch. 2. 3. 12.
& 7. 23, 25.
1 Thess. 5.
21.
q ch. 12. 12.
a Luke 12.
19.
b Isai. 50. 11.
c Prov. 14.
13.
ch. 7. 6.
d ch. 1. 17.

---

¹ Heb. *defect.*
² Heb. *had seen much.*
³ Heb. *to draw my flesh with wine.*
⁴ Heb. *the number of the days of their life.*
⁵ Heb. *sons of my house.*

---

15. He saw clearly both the disorder and incompleteness of human actions (cp. marg. ref.), and also man's impotence to rectify them.

16. *I am come* &c.] Rather, **I have accumulated** (lit. "enlarged and added") **wisdom more than** &c.

they that have been &c.] The reference is probably to the line of Canaanitish kings who lived in Jerusalem before David took it, such as Melchizedek (Gen. xiv. 18), Adonizedec (Josh. x. 1), and Araunah (2 Sam. xxiv. 23); or, it may be, to Solomon's contemporaries of his own country (1 K. iv. 31) and of other countries who visited him (1 K. iv. 34, x. 24). For "in" Jerusalem render **over.**

17. *to know madness and folly*] A knowledge of folly would help him to discern wisdom, and to exercise that chief function of practical wisdom—to avoid folly.

18. We become more sensible of our ignorance and impotence, and therefore sorrowful, in proportion as we discover more of the constitution of nature and the scheme of Providence in the government of the world ; every discovery serving to convince us that more remains concealed of which we had no suspicion before.

II. 1–11. Solomon's trial of God's second gift, viz. riches, and the enjoyment which riches supply; this brought him to the same result (cp. i. 12).

Comparing Solomon's action with Luke xii. 16–21, it must be remembered that Solomon's object was the acquisition of wisdom, not self-indulgence, and that he did not fail to look forward to the certainty of death overtaking him.

3. *I sought* &c.] Rather, **I resolved** (lit. "I turned in my heart") **to draw my flesh with wine** (see marg.), **my heart guiding me with wisdom.** In the course of his attempt to answer the question of i. 3, whilst his heart was directing him (as a charioteer directs his horses or a shepherd his sheep) with wisdom, and whilst he was following that guidance, he determined to draw with him his flesh by wine, thus making his flesh, which he speaks of as distinct from himself (cp. Rom. vii. 25), a confederate and subsidiary in his attempt.

4–10. Cp. 1 K. vii. 1-12, ix. 15-19, x. 14-27, and 2 Chr. viii. 4.

5. *orchards*] Lit. "paradises," *i.e.* parks or pleasure-grounds (cp. Neh. ii. 8 note). Indications of at least three of these have been pointed out ; one at Jerusalem near the pool of Siloam, called "the king's garden" (Neh. iii. 15 ; Jer. lii. 7) ; a second near Bethlehem (cp. *v.* 6) ; and a third in the remote north, on the heights of Hermon (Song of Sol. iv. 8, viii. 11).

6. *pools*] A short distance south of Bethlehem, in a valley in the defile of Urtas, three "Pools of Solomon" are still shewn and an adjoining hill still bears the name of the "Little Paradise."

7. *I got*] Rather, **I bought,** in distinction from those born in the house. The "chil-

e 1 K. 9.28.
& 10. 10.
14. 21, &c.

f ch. 1. 16.

g ch. 3. 22.
& 5. 18.
& 9. 9.

h ch. 1. 3, 14.

i ch. 1. 17.
& 7. 25.

k Prov.17.24.
ch. 8. 1.

l Ps. 49. 10.

8 salem before me : *e* I gathered me also silver and gold, and the peculiar treasure of kings and of the provinces : I gat me men singers and women singers, and the delights of the sons of men,

9 as ¹ musical instruments, and that of all sorts. So *f* I was great, and increased more than all that were before me in Jerusalem :

10 also my wisdom remained with me. And whatsoever mine eyes desired I kept not from them, I withheld not my heart from any joy ; for my heart rejoiced in all my labour : and *g* this was

11 my portion of all my labour. Then I looked on all the works that my hands had wrought, and on the labour that I had laboured to do : and, behold, all *was* *h* vanity and vexation of spirit, and *there was* no profit under the sun.

12 And I turned myself to behold wisdom, *i* and madness, and folly : for what *can* the man *do* that cometh after the king ?

13 ² *even* that which hath been already done. Then I saw ³ that

14 wisdom excelleth folly, as far as light excelleth darkness. *k* The wise man's eyes *are* in his head ; but the fool walketh in darkness : and I myself perceived also that *l* one event happeneth to

15 them all. Then said I in my heart, As it happeneth to the fool, so it ⁴ happeneth even to me ; and why was I then more wise ?

16 Then I said in my heart, that this also *is* vanity. For *there is* no remembrance of the wise more than of the fool for ever ; seeing that which now *is* in the days to come shall all be for-

17 gotten. And how dieth the wise *man* ? as the fool. Therefore

---

¹ Heb. *musical instrument and instruments.*
² Or, *in those things which*
  have been already done.
³ Heb. *that there is an excellency in wisdom more*
⁴ Heb. *happeneth to me, even to me.*

---

dren of Solomon's servants" (cp. Ezra ii. 55, 58) were more probably of Canaanitish origin (1 K. ix. 20, 21, v. 15) than Hebrews (1 K. ix. 22).

possessions of great and small cattle] Rather, **herds of oxen and sheep.**

all...before me] King David's herds and flocks are mentioned in 1 Chr. xxvii. 29, 31 : but we have no specific account of the wealth of other Canaanitish or Hebrew inhabitants of Jerusalem before Solomon.

8. *kings*] Both tributary (1 K. x. 15) and independent (1 K. v. 1, ix. 14, x. 2) ; the "provinces" probably correspond to the kingdoms mentioned in 1 K. iv. 21.

as musical...sorts] Rather, **Many women** (cp. 1 K. xi. 1-3).

10. *portion*] A word of frequent occurrence. By it Solomon describes the pleasure found in the act of working and also perhaps the pleasure felt in the process of acquiring wisdom ; this pleasure is admitted to be good, if received from God (v. 26, v. 18 ; cp. 1 Tim. iv. 4) ; but being transitory it is subject to vanity, and therefore does not afford a sufficient answer to the repeated question, "What profit &c. ? " (i. 3).

12—26. Solomon having found that wisdom and folly agree in being subject to vanity, now contrasts one with the other (v. 13). Both are brought under vanity by events (v. 14) which come on the wise man and the fool alike from without—death and oblivion (v. 16), uncertainty (v. 19), disap-

pointment (v. 21)—all happening by an external law beyond human control. Amidst this vanity, the good (see v. 10 note) that accrues to man, is the pleasure felt (24-26) in receiving God's gifts, and in working with and for them.

12. *what can the man do &c.*] i.e. "What is any man — in this study of wisdom and folly — after one like me, who, from my position, have had such peculiar advantages (see i. 16, and cp. ii. 25) for carrying it on ? That which man did of old he can but do again : he is not likely to add to the result of my researches, nor even to equal them." Some hold that the "man" is a reference to Solomon's successor—not in his inquiries, but in his kingdom, i.e. Jeroboam.

14. *event*] Or, "hap" (Ruth ii. 3). The verb from which it is derived seems in this Book to refer specially to death. The word does not mean chance (cp. ix. 1, 2), independent of the ordering of Divine Providence : the Gentile notion of "mere chance," or "blind fate," is never once contemplated by the writer of this Book, and it would be inconsistent with his tenets of the unlimited power and activity of God.

16. *seeing that &c.*] Cp. i. 11. Some render, "as in time past, so in days to come, all will be forgotten ; " others, " because in the days to come all will have been long before forgotten."

17. *I hated life*] Cp. this expression, ex-

I hated life; because the work that is wrought under the sun *is*
18 grievous unto me: for all *is* vanity and vexation of spirit. Yea,
I hated all my labour which I had [1] taken under the sun: because [m] I should leave it unto the man that shall be after me. [m] Ps. 49. 10.
19 And who knoweth whether he shall be a wise *man* or a fool? yet
shall he have rule over all my labour wherein I have laboured,
and wherein I have shewed myself wise under the sun. This *is*
20 also vanity. Therefore I went about to cause my heart to de-
21 spair of all the labour which I took under the sun. For there
is a man whose labour *is* in wisdom, and in knowledge, and in
equity; yet to a man that hath not laboured therein shall he
[2] leave it *for* his portion. This also *is* vanity and a great evil.
22 [n] For what hath man of all his labour, and of the vexation of his [n] ch. 1. 3. & 3. 9.
23 heart, wherein he hath laboured under the sun? For all his
days *are* [o] sorrows, and his travail grief; yea, his heart taketh [o] Job 5. 7. & 14. 1.
not rest in the night. This is also vanity.
24 [p] *There is* nothing better for a man, *than* that he should eat [p] ch. 3. 12, 13, 22. & 5. 18. & 8. 15.
and drink, and *that* he [3] should make his soul enjoy good in his
labour. This also I saw, that it *was* from the hand of God.
25 For who can eat, or who else can hasten *hereunto*, more than I?
26 For *God* giveth to a man that *is* good [4] in his sight wisdom, and
knowledge, and joy: but to the sinner he giveth travail, to
gather and to heap up, that [q] he may give to *him that is* good [q] Job 27. 16, 17. Prov.28.8.
before God. This also *is* vanity and vexation of spirit.

CHAP. 3. TO every *thing there is* a season, and a [a] time to every pur- [a] ver. 17. ch. 8. 6.
pose under the heaven:

[1] Heb. *laboured.*
[2] Heb. *give.*
[3] Or, *delight his senses.*
[4] Heb. *before him,* Gen. 7. 1. Luke 1. 6.

---

torted from Solomon by the perception of the vanity of his wisdom and greatness, with Rom. viii. 22, 23. The words of Moses (Num. xi. 15), and of Job (iii. 21, vi. 9), are scarcely less forcible. This feeling is with some men a powerful motive to conversion (Luke xiv. 26).

19. *labour*] Cp. *vv.* 4-8.

20. *I went about*] *i.e.* I turned from one course of action to another.

23. *are sorrows...grief*] Rather, **sorrows and grief are his toil.** See i. 13.

24. *nothing better for a man, than that* &c.] Lit. **no good in man that** &c. The one joy of working or receiving, which, though it be transitory, a man recognizes as a real good, even that is not in the power of man to secure for himself: that good is the gift of God.

26. The doctrine of Retribution, or, the revealed fact that God is the moral Governor of the world, is here stated for the first time (cp. iii. 15, 17, &c.) in this Book.

This also is vanity] Not only the travail of the sinner. Even the best gifts of God, wisdom, knowledge, and joy, so far as they are given in this life, are not permanent, and are not always (see ix. 11) efficacious for the purpose for which they appear to be given.

III. **1-15.** It follows from ii. 26 that the works of men are subject in their results to another will (God's) besides that of the doer. Here is the germ of the great question of later times—how to reconcile man's freewill with God's decrees. Solomon's way of stating it is that to every separate work, which goes to make up the great aggregate of human activity (the "travail," *v.* 10), there is a season, an appropriate time which God appoints for its being done (*vv.* 1-8). To the question (*v.* 9) What profit? he answers that the works of men, if done according to God's appointment, are a part of that beautifully arranged scheme of Divine Providence which, as a whole, is, by reason of its extent and duration, incomprehensible to us (*v.* 11). Man's good is to rejoice and do good in his lifetime, which he can do only as God appoints (*vv.* 12, 13). God's work, of which this would be a part, is for ever, is perfect (and so not subject to vanity), and is calculated to teach men to fear Him (*v.* 14). His work, which was begun long ago, is now going on to completion; His work hereafter will be a complement of something which was done previously; and He recalls the past in order to add to it what shall make it complete and perfect (*v.* 15). The principle of Divine government—that every work in order to be permanent and successful must be God's work as well as man's work—is also declared in Ps. cxxvii. 1, 2 (attributed to Solomon).

1. *every thing*] More particularly the actions of men (*e.g.* his own, ii. 1-8) and

b Heb. 9. 27.	2 A time ¹to be born, and *b* a time to die ; A time to plant, and a time to pluck up *that which is* planted ; 3 A time to kill, and a time to heal ; A time to break down, and a time to build up ; 4 A time to weep, and a time to laugh ; A time to mourn, and a time to dance ; 5 A time to cast away stones, and a time to gather stones together ;
c Joel 2. 16. 1 Cor. 7. 5.	A time to embrace, and *c* a time ²to refrain from embracing ; 6 A time to ³get, and a time to lose ; A time to keep, and a time to cast away ; 7 A time to rend, and a time to sew ;
d Amos 5. 13.	*d* A time to keep silence, and a time to speak ;
e Luke 14. 26.	8 A time to love, and a time to *e* hate ; A time of war, and a time of peace.
f ch. 1. 3.	9 *f* What profit hath he that worketh in that wherein he la- boureth ?
g ch. 1. 13.	10 *g* I have seen the travail, which God hath given to the sons of 11 men to be exercised in it. He hath made every *thing* beautiful in his time : also he hath set the world in their heart, so that
h ch. 8. 17. Rom. 11. 33. *i* ver. 22. *k* ch. 2. 24.	*h* no man can find out the work that God maketh from the be- 12 ginning to the end. *i* I know that *there is* no good in them, but 13 for *a man* to rejoice, and to do good in his life. And also *k* that every man should eat and drink, and enjoy the good of all his 14 labour, it *is* the gift of God. I know that, whatsoever God doeth,
l Jam. 1. 17.	it shall be for ever : *l* nothing can be put to it, nor any thing taken from it : and God doeth *it*, that *men* should fear before
m ch. 1. 9.	15 him. *m* That which hath been is now ; and that which is to be hath already been ; and God requireth ⁴ that which is past.

¹ Heb. *to bear.*   ³ Or, *seek.*
² Heb. *to be far from.*   ⁴ Heb. *that which is driven away.*

---

events which happen to men, the world of Providence rather than the world of creation.   It would seem that most of his own works described in ii. 1-8 were present to his mind. The rare word translated "season" means emphatically "fitting time" (cp. Neh. ii. 6 ; Esth. ix. 27, 31).

5. Stones may be regarded either as materials for building, or as impediments to the fertility of land (see 2 K. iii. 19, 25 ; Isai. v. 2).

6. *get...lose*] Rather, **seek, and a time to give up for lost.**

7. *rend*] *i.e.* Tear garments in sign of mourning or anger.   See 2 Sam. i. 2, 11 &c.

11. Rather, **He hath made all** (the travail, *v.* 10) **beautiful** (fit, in harmony with the whole work of God) **in its time ;** also **He hath set eternity in their heart** (*i.e.* the heart of the sons of men, *v.* 10).

The word, translated "world" in the text, and "eternity" in this note, is used seven times in Ecclesiastes.

The interpretation "eternity," is conceived in the sense of a long indefinite period of time, in accordance with the use of the word throughout this Book, and the rest of the Old Testament. God has placed in the inborn constitution of man the capa-

bility of conceiving of eternity, the struggle to apprehend the everlasting, the longing after an eternal life.

With the other meaning "the world," *i.e.* the material world, or universe, in which we dwell, the context is explained as referring either to the knowledge of the objects with which this world is filled, or to the love of the pleasures of the world. This meaning seems to be less in harmony with the context than the other : but the principal objection to it is that it assigns to the word in the original a sense which, although found in Rabbinical Hebrew, it never bears in the language of the Old Testament.

so...find] *i.e.* Without enabling man to find. Cp. vii. 13, viii. 17.

12. *in them*] *i.e.* in the sons of men.

to do good] In a moral sense. Physical enjoyment is referred to in *v.* 13.

14. The last clause of this verse goes beyond a declaration of the fact of God's government of the world (ii. 26) by adding the moral effect which that fact is calculated to produce on those who see it. It is the first indication of the practical conclusion (xii. 13) of the Book.

15. Rather, **What has been—that *was* before, and that which shall be has been**

16 And moreover [n]I saw under the sun the place of judgment, *that* wickedness *was* there; and the place of righteousness, *that*
17 iniquity *was* there. I said in mine heart, [o]God shall judge the righteous and the wicked: for *there is* [p]a time there for every purpose and for every work.
18 I said in mine heart concerning the estate of the sons of men, [1]that God might manifest them, and that they might see that
19 they themselves are beasts. [q]For that which befalleth the sons of men befalleth beasts; even one thing befalleth them: as the one dieth, so dieth the other; yea, they have all one breath; so that a man hath no preeminence above a beast: for all *is* vanity.
20 All go unto one place; [r]all are of the dust, and all turn to dust
21 again. [s]Who knoweth the spirit [2]of man that [3]goeth upward, and the spirit of the beast that goeth downward to the
22 earth? [t]Wherefore I perceive that *there is* nothing better, than that a man should rejoice in his own works; for [u]that *is*

[n] ch. 5. 8.

[o] Rom. 2.
6, 7, 8.
2 Cor.5.10.
2 Thess. 1.
6, 7.
[p] ver. 1.

[q] Ps. 49. 12,
20. & 73.22.
ch. 2. 16.

[r] Gen. 3. 19.

[s] ch. 12. 7.

[t] ver. 12.
ch. 2. 24.
& 5. 18.
& 11. 9.
[u] ch. 2. 10.

---

[1] Or, *that they might clear God, and see, &c.*   [2] Heb. *of the sons of man.*   [3] Heb. *is ascending.*

---

before. The word "is" in our A.V. is erroneously printed in Roman letters: it does not exist in the Hebrew; and the word there translated "now" is the same which is translated "already."

requireth] *i.e.* requireth for judgment, as the word specially means in 2 Sam. iv. 11; Ezek. iii. 18 &c. It is obvious from the context of the last clause of *v.* 14, and *vv.* 16, 17, that this is the meaning here.

past] Lit. "put to flight." The meaning of the verse is that there is a connexion between events, past, present and future, and that this connexion exists in the justice of God Who controls all.

16-22. That great anomaly in the moral government of this world, the seemingly unequal distribution of rewards and punishments, will be rectified by God, Who has future times and events under His control (*vv.* 16, 17). As for men, they are placed by God, Who is their teacher, in a humble condition, even on a level with inferior animals, by death, that great instance of their subjection to vanity (*vv.* 18, 19), which reduces to its original form all that was made of the dust of the ground (*v.* 20). And though the destinies of man and beast are different, yet in our present want of knowledge as to God's future dealing with our spirits (*v.* 21), man finds his portion (see ii. 10 note) in such labour and such joy as God assigns to him in his lifetime (*v.* 22).

16. *I saw* &c.] Rather, **I have seen** (as in *v.* 10) **under the sun the place** &c. The place of judgment means the seat of the authorized judge. Compare "the place of the holy" (viii. 10).

17. *a time there*] *i.e.* a time with God.

18. Lit. **I said in my heart with regard to the sons of men,** *it is* **that God may prove them and shew them that they are**

beasts, they themselves. "Shewing" is the reading of the LXX. and Syriac: the present Hebrew text reads "seeing." The meaning is that the long delay of God's judgment (*vv.* 16, 17) is calculated to shew men that the brevity of their life renders them incapable of following out and understanding His distributive justice.

19. *that which befalleth the sons of men*] Lit. the event or hap of the sons of men, *i.e.* that which comes upon them from without, in virtue of the ordinance of God. See ii. 14 note. Death in particular (*vv.* 2, 11) is a part of the "work that God doeth."

21. The A.V. of this verse is the only rendering which the Hebrew text, as now pointed, allows. It is in accordance with the best Jewish and many modern interpreters. A slightly different pointing would be requisite to authorize the translation, "Who knows the spirit of the sons of man whether it goes above, and the spirit of the beast whether it goes down below?" &c., which, though it seems neither necessary nor suitable, is sanctioned by the LXX. and other Versions and by some modern interpreters.

Who knoweth] This expression (used also in ii. 19, vi. 12) does not necessarily imply complete and absolute ignorance. In Ps. xc. 11, it is applied to that which is partially understood: compare similar forms of expression in Prov. xxxi. 10; Ps. xciv. 16; Isai. liii. 1. Moreover it is evident from marg. ref. that Solomon did not doubt the future existence and destination of the soul. This verse can only be construed as a confession of much ignorance on the subject.

22. *what shall be after him*] *i.e.* What shall become of the results of his work after he is dead. Cp. ii. 19, vi. 12.

x ch. 6. 12.
& 8. 7.
& 10. 14.
a ch. 3. 16.
& 5. 8.

b Job 3. 17,
&c.

c Job 3. 11,
16, 21.
ch. 6. 3.

d Prov. 6. 10.
& 24. 33.
e Prov. 15.
16, 17.
& 16. 8.

f Prov. 27.
20.
1 John 2. 16.
g Ps. 39. 6.

his portion : ^xfor who shall bring him to see what shall be after him?

CHAP. 4. SO I returned, and considered all the ^aoppressions that are done under the sun : and behold the tears of *such as were* oppressed, and they had no comforter ; and on the ¹side of their oppres- 2 sors *there was* power ; but they had no comforter. ^bWherefore I praised the dead which are already dead more than the living 3 which are yet alive. ^cYea, better *is* he than both they, which hath not yet been, who hath not seen the evil work that is done under the sun.

4   Again, I considered all travail, and ²every right work, that ³for this a man is envied of his neighbour. This *is* also vanity 5 and vexation of spirit. ^dThe fool foldeth his hands together, 6 and eateth his own flesh. ^eBetter *is* an handful *with* quietness, than both the hands full *with* travail and vexation of spirit.

7, 8   Then I returned, and I saw vanity under the sun. There is one *alone*, and *there is* not a second ; yea, he hath neither child nor brother : yet *is there* no end of all his labour ; neither is his ^feye satisfied with riches ; ^gneither *saith he*, For whom do I labour, and bereave my soul of good ? This *is* also vanity, yea, it *is* a sore travail.

9   Two *are* better than one ; because they have a good reward 10 for their labour. For if they fall, the one will lift up his fellow : but woe to him *that is* alone when he falleth ; for *he hath* not 11 another to help him up. Again, if two lie together, then they 12 have heat : but how can one be warm *alone ?* And if one pre- vail against him, two shall withstand him ; and a threefold cord is not quickly broken.

13   Better *is* a poor and a wise child than an old and foolish king,

---

¹ Heb. *hand.*
² Heb. *all the rightness of work.*

³ Heb. *this* is *the envy of a man from his neighbour.*

IV. Having arrived (iii. 22) at a partial answer to his question (i. 3) ; viz. that there is positive good (= a portion) in that satisfaction which is found in working, Solomon now turns to the case of such happiness being interrupted and reduced to vanity by various contingencies—by oppres- sion (*vv.* 1–3) ; by envy (*vv.* 4–6) ; by loneli- ness (*vv.* 7–12) ; and by decay of working power (*vv.* 13–16). The first two instances seem taken from the lower ranks of life, the last two from the higher.

1. *So I returned, and considered*] Rather, **And I returned and saw.** He turns to look on other phenomena, and to test by them his previous conclusion.

oppressed] See Introduction, p. 424.

4. *every right work*] Rather, **every success in work.**

for this &c.] *i.e.* "This successful work makes the worker an object of envy." Some understand the meaning to be, " this work is the effect of the rivalry of man with his neighbour."

5. *foldeth his hands*] The envious man is here exhibited in the attitude of the sluggard (marg. reff.).

eateth his own flesh] *i.e.* "Destroys him-

self :" cp. a similar expression in Isai. xlix. 26 ; Ps. xxvii. 2 ; Mic. iii. 3.

6. Either the fool's sarcasm on his success- ful but restless neighbour ; or the comment of Solomon recommending contentment with a moderate competence. The former mean- ing seems preferable.

7-12. The spectacle of a prosperous man whose condition is rendered vain by his brotherless, childless isolation.

8. *a second*] Any one associated or con- nected with him.

9-12. Cp. a saying from the Talmud, " A man without companions is like the left hand without the right."

13-16. These verses set forth the vanity of earthly prosperity even on a throne. Opinion as to their application is chiefly divided between considering them a parable or fiction like that of the childless man in *v.* 8 : or as setting forth first the vicissitudes of royal life in two proverbial sayings (*vv.* 13, 14), and then (*vv.* 15, 16), the vicissitudes or procession of the whole human race, one generation giving place to another, which in its turn will be forgotten by its successor. On the whole, the first appears to have the better claim.

13. *child*] Rather, **young man.**

14 ¹who will no more be admonished. For out of prison he cometh to reign; whereas also *he that is* born in his kingdom becometh
15 poor. I considered all the living which walk under the sun,
16 with the second child that shall stand up in his stead. *There is* no end of all the people, *even* of all that have been before them: they also that have come after shall not rejoice in him. Surely this also *is* vanity and vexation of spirit.

CHAP. 5. KEEP ªthy foot when thou goest to the house of God, and be more ready to hear, ᵇthan to give the sacrifice of fools:
2 for they consider not that they do evil. Be not rash with thy mouth, and let not thine heart be hasty to utter *any* ²thing before God: for God *is* in heaven, and thou upon earth: there-
3 fore let thy words ᶜbe few. For a dream cometh through the multitude of business; and ᵈa fool's voice *is known* by multitude
4 of words. ᵉWhen thou vowest a vow unto God, defer not to pay it; for *he hath* no pleasure in fools: ᶠpay that which thou
5 hast vowed. ᵍBetter *is it* that thou shouldest not vow, than that
6 thou shouldest vow and not pay. Suffer not thy mouth to cause thy flesh to sin; ʰneither say thou before the angel, that it *was* an error: wherefore should God be angry at thy voice,

a See Ex.3.5.
Isai.1.12,&c.
b 1 Sam. 15.
22.
Ps. 50. 8.
Prov.15. 8.
Hos. 6. 6.
c Prov.10.19.
Matt. 6. 7.
d Prov. 10.
19.
e Num. 30.2.
Deut. 23. 21,
22, 23.
Ps. 50. 14.
f Ps. 66. 13.
g Prov. 20.
25.
Acts 5. 4.
h 1 Cor. 11.
10.

---

¹ Heb. *who knoweth not to be admonished.*   ² Or, *word.*

---

14. Rather, **For out of the house of bondage he goes forth to be a king;** although **he was born poor in his kingdom,** *i.e.* in the country over which he became king.

15. *I considered* &c.] Lit. **I saw** "all the population of the young man's kingdom."

the second child] This **second youth** is generally understood to be identical with the one mentioned in *v.* 13.

16. *There is*] Rather, **There was.**

that have been before them] Rather, **before whom he was,** *i.e.* at the head of whom the young king was. Cp. Micah ii. 13.

they also that...him] *i.e.* The next generation shall forget this chosen king.

V. The Preacher now begins to address his hearer in the second person. The soliloquy, hitherto unbroken, is henceforth interrupted by personal addresses, which are repeated with increasing frequency from this place to the end of the Book. They who divide the whole Book into two parts, the first theoretical, the second practical, begin the second division here.

There is a striking resemblance between the line of thought pursued in this Book and that of Asaph in Psalm lxxiii. As the Psalmist, so the Preacher, after setting forth his view of human life, takes his hearer into the house of God for an explanation and directions. If the expression "goest to the house of God" (*v.* 1) has also the spiritual sense of entering into communion with God, Solomon here admonishes generally that reverence is due to God, and particularly that the "vanity" which is mingled with the "portion" that God assigns to every man, ought to be treated as a divine

mystery, not to be made an occasion of idle thought, hasty words, and rash resolutions, but to be considered in the fear of God (*vv.* 1–7); that the spectacle of unjust oppression is to be patiently referred to God's supreme judgment (*vv.* 8, 9); that mere riches are unsatisfying, bring care with them, and if hoarded are transitory (*vv.* 10–17); and that a man's enjoyment of his portion in life, including both labour and riches, is the gift of God (*vv.* 18–20).

1. *Keep thy foot*] *i.e.* Give thy mind to what thou art going to do.

the house of God] It has been said that here an ordinary devout Hebrew writer might have been expected to call it "the house of Jehovah;" but to those who accept this Book as the work of Solomon after his fall into idolatry, it will appear a natural sign of the writer's self-humiliation, an acknowledgment of his unworthiness of the privileges of a son of the Covenant, that he avoids the name of the Lord of the Covenant (see i. 13 note).

be more ready to hear] Perhaps in the sense that, "to draw near for the purpose of hearing (and obeying) is better than &c."

6. *Suffer not thy mouth* &c.] *i.e.* Do not make rash vows which may hereafter be the cause of evasion and prevarication, and remain unfulfilled.

before the angel] The LXX. and some other Versions render "before the face of God," meaning a spiritual being representing the Presence of God, a minister of divine justice (Exod. xxiii. 21), such an one as inflicted judgment upon David (2 Sam. xxiv. 17). Others, with less probability, understand

i ch. 12. 13.

k ch. 3. 16.

l Ps. 12. 5.
& 58. 11.
& 82. 1.

m ch. 6. 1.

n Job 1. 21.
Ps. 49. 17.
1 Tim. 6. 7.

o ch. 1. 3.
p Prov. 11. 29.
q Ps. 127. 2.

r ch. 2. 24.
& 3. 12.
1 Tim. 6. 17.

s ch. 2. 10.
& 3. 22.
t ch. 2. 24.
& 3. 13.
& 6. 2.

a ch. 5. 13.

7 and destroy the work of thine hands? For in the multitude of dreams and many words *there are* also *divers* vanities: but *i*fear thou God.

8 If thou *k*seest the oppression of the poor, and violent perverting of judgment and justice in a province, marvel not ¹at the matter: for *l*he that *is* higher than the highest regardeth; and 9 *there be* higher than they. Moreover the profit of the earth is for all: the king *himself* is served by the field.

10 He that loveth silver shall not be satisfied with silver; nor he 11 that loveth abundance with increase: this *is* also vanity. When goods increase, they are increased that eat them: and what good *is there* to the owners thereof, saving the beholding *of them* 12 with their eyes? The sleep of a labouring man *is* sweet, whether he eat little or much: but the abundance of the rich will not suffer him to sleep.

13 *m*There is a sore evil *which* I have seen under the sun, *namely*, 14 riches kept for the owners thereof to their hurt. But those riches perish by evil travail: and he begetteth a son, and *there* 15 *is* nothing in his hand. *n*As he came forth of his mother's womb, naked shall he return to go as he came, and shall take nothing of his labour, which he may carry away in his hand. 16 And this also *is* a sore evil, *that* in all points as he came, so shall he go: and *o*what profit hath he *p*that hath laboured for 17 the wind? all his days also *q*he eateth in darkness, and *he hath* much sorrow and wrath with his sickness.

18 Behold *that* which I have seen: *r*²it *is* good and comely *for* one to eat and to drink, and to enjoy the good of all his labour that he taketh under the sun ³all the days of his life, which God 19 giveth him: *s*for it *is* his portion. *t*Every man also to whom God hath given riches and wealth, and hath given him power to eat thereof, and to take his portion, and to rejoice in his labour; 20 this *is* the gift of God. ⁴For he shall not much remember the days of his life; because God answereth *him* in the joy of his heart.

CHAP. 6. *a*THERE is an evil which I have seen under the sun,

---

¹ Heb. *at the will*, or, *purpose.*
² Heb. there is *a good which*
³ Heb. *the number of the days.*
is comely, &c.
⁴ Or, *Though* he give *not much*, yet he *remembereth, &c.*

---

the Angel to be a priest, and refer to Mal. ii. 7.

7. *For...vanities*] Or, **For** *so it happens* **through many dreams and vanities and many words.**

8. *matter*] Rather, **purpose** (as in marg., and iii. 1), referring either to the will of God or to the edict of an oppressive ruler.

for he...they] Lit. **for high watches over high and the Highest over them**, *i.e.* the king in the capital watches over the judge or governor in the province, and God over both. This seems more in harmony with the preceding verses, and more agreeable to the scope of this passage than to understand the passage only of earthly rulers.

9. *the king himself is served by the field*] Rather, **the king** *is* **subject to the field,** *i.e.* is dependent on its cultivation. The higher ranks, if they oppress the lower, lose thereby their own means of subsistence.

11. *they...that eat them*] *i.e.* The labourers employed, and the household servants.

12. *labouring man*] Not a slave (LXX.), but every one who, according to the divine direction, earns his bread in the sweat of his brow.

14. *evil travail*] Adverse accident, or unsuccessful employment (cp. i. 13, iv. 8).

17. *hath much sorrow* &c.] Rather, **is very sad and hath pain and vexation.**

18. Rather, **Behold what I have seen to be good, it is pleasant for a man to eat.** Such thankful enjoyment is inculcated by the Law (Deut. xii. 7, 18).

20. The days will pass smoothly and pleasantly, whilst he lives in the consciousness of God's favour.

answereth him] *i.e.* grants his prayers.

VI. The Preacher in this chapter contemplates the case of men to whom God gives wealth, honour, success, children, and

2 and it *is* common among men: a man to whom God hath given
riches, wealth, and honour, *b* so that he wanteth nothing for his
soul of all that he desireth, *c* yet God giveth him not power to
eat thereof, but a stranger eateth it: this *is* vanity, and it *is* an
3 evil disease. If a man beget an hundred *children*, and live
many years, so that the days of his years be many, and his soul
be not filled with good, and *d* also *that* he have no burial; I say,
4 *that* *e* an untimely birth *is* better than he. For he cometh in
with vanity, and departeth in darkness, and his name shall be
5 covered with darkness. Moreover he hath not seen the sun,
6 nor known *any thing*: this hath more rest than the other. Yea,
though he live a thousand years twice *told*, yet hath he seen no
good: do not all go to one place?
7 *f* All the labour of man *is* for his mouth, and yet the ¹appetite
8 is not filled. For what hath the wise more than the fool? what
9 hath the poor, that knoweth to walk before the living? Better
is the sight of the eyes ²than the wandering of the desire: this
10 *is* also vanity and vexation of spirit. That which hath been is
named already, and it is known that it *is* man: *g* neither may he
11 contend with him that is mightier than he. Seeing there be

b Job 21. 10,
&c.
Ps. 17. 14.
& 73. 7.
c Luke12.

d 2 K. 9. 35.
Isai. 14. 19,
20.
Jer. 22. 19.
e Job 3. 16.
Ps. 58. 8.
ch. 4. 3.

f Prov. 16.
26.

g Job 9. 32.
Isai. 45. 9.
Jer. 49. 19.

¹ Heb. *soul*.   ² Heb. *than the walking of the soul*.

---

long life, yet withholds from them the capacity of enjoyment, rest, permanence or contentment (*vv.* 1–9). What then is good for
man to do, whose lot in life is so thoroughly
subject to vanity? (*vv.* 10–12).

1. *common among*] Rather, **great** (heavy)
upon men.

3. *no burial*] For a corpse to lie un-
buried was a circumstance in itself of peculiar ignominy and dishonour (cp. marg.
reff.).

4. *he...his*] Rather, **it...its.** The untimely
birth is spoken of.

5. Rather, **it hath not seen nor known
the sun: this** (the untimely birth) **hath
rest rather than the other.**

6. *he live*] Rather, **he hath lived.** "He"
refers to the man (*v.* 3). His want of satisfaction in life, and the dishonour done to
his corpse, are regarded as such great evils
that they counterbalance his numerous children, and length of days, and render his
lot viewed as a whole no better than the
common lot of all.

7–9. Connect these verses with *vv.* 2, 3 :—
"All labour is undertaken with a view to
some profit, but as a rule the men who
labour are never satisfied. What advantage then has he who labours if (being rich)
he is wise, or if being poor he knows how
to conduct himself properly; what advantage have such labourers above a fool?
(None, so far as they are without contentment; for) a thing present before the eyes
is preferable to a future which exists only
in the desire."

8. *what*] Lit. **what profit** (as in i. 3).

knoweth...living] *i.e.* "Knows how to
conduct himself rightly among his contemporaries."

10. Or, "That which has been named—
i.e. events past or current, either (i. 9)
as they present themselves to man, or (iii.
15) as they are ordered by God—was long ago
(*i.e.* was decreed, its nature and place were
defined by the Almighty), and was known
that it is man;" *i.e.* the course of events
shapes the conduct and character of man,
so that what he does and suffers is said to
be or constitute the man. God from the
beginning definitely ordained the course
of events external to man, and constituted man in such a way that events materially affect his conduct and his destiny.
Hence God, by withholding from certain
men the gift of contentment, and thus sub-
jecting them to vanity, is acting according
to the predetermined course of His Providence which man cannot alter (cp. Rom.
viii. 20). Others translate, "What there is,
its name is named long ago and known, that
it is man;" *i.e.* "What hath been and is,
not only came into existence long ago (i.
9, iii. 15), but also has been known and
named, and is acknowledged that it, besides other things, is specially man; that
man always remains the same, and cannot
go beyond his appointed bounds."

him that is mightier] *i.e.* God; cp. ix. 1;
1 Cor. x. 22, and marg. reff.

11. *things*] Namely, the various circumstances detailed in the foregoing chapters,
from the Preacher's personal experience,
and his observation of other men, ending
with the comprehensive declaration in *v.* 10
to the effect that vanity is an essential part
of the constitution of creation as it now
exists, and was foreknown.

what is man the better?] Rather, **what is
profitable to man?**

12 many things that increase vanity, what *is* man the better? For
who knoweth what *is* good for man in *this* life, ¹all the days of

his vain life which he spendeth as *ᵸ*a shadow? for *ⁱ*who can tell
a man what shall be after him under the sun?

CHAP. 7. A *ᵃ*GOOD name *is* better than precious ointment;
And the day of death than the day of one's birth.

2 *It is* better to go to the house of mourning,
Than to go to the house of feasting:
For that *is* the end of all men;
And the living will lay *it* to his heart.

3 ²Sorrow *is* better than laughter:
*ᵇ*For by the sadness of the countenance the heart is made
better.

4 The heart of the wise *is* in the house of mourning;
But the heart of fools *is* in the house of mirth.

5 *ᶜIt is* better to hear the rebuke of the wise,
Than for a man to hear the song of fools.

6 *ᵈ*For as the ³crackling of thorns under a pot,
So *is* the laughter of the fool: this also *is* vanity.

7 Surely oppression maketh a wise man mad;
*ᵉ*And a gift destroyeth the heart.

marginal references:
ᵸ Ps. 102.11.
& 109. 23.
Jam. 4. 14.
ⁱ Ps. 39. 6.
ch. 8. 7.
ᵃ Prov.15.30.
& 22. 1.

ᵇ 2 Cor. 7.10.

ᶜ See
Ps. 141. 5.
Prov. 13. 18.
ᵈ Ps.118.12.
ch. 2. 2.

ᵉ Ex. 23. 8.
Deut. 16. 19.

¹ Heb. *the number of the
days of the life of his
vanity.*

² Or, *Anger.*
³ Heb. *sound.*

---

12. *after him*] *i.e.* On earth, in his own
present sphere of action, after his departure hence (cp. ii. 19, iii. 22).

VII. Chs. vii. and x. shew a striking resemblance to the style of the writer of the
Book of Proverbs. Hitherto the principal
object has been to state the vanity of the
conditions of human life: henceforth the
principal object will be to direct man how
to conduct himself under those conditions.

The general drift of the writer's counsels
throughout the last six chapters, and particularly in vii. 1–22, points to wisdom
united with the fear of God as the "good
for man in this life." It is illustrated by
frequent reference to, and contrast with,
that evil which consists of folly allied with
wickedness.

1. *name...ointment*] The likeness between
reputation and odour supplies a common
metaphor : the contrast is between reputation, as an honourable attainment which
only wise men win, and fragrant odour, as
a gratification of the senses which all men
enjoy.

The connexion of this verse with the preceding verses is this :—the man, who wants
to know what is profitable for man and
good in this life, is here told to act in such
a way as ordinarily secures a good reputation (*i.e.* to act like a wise man), and to
teach himself this hard lesson,—to regard
the day of death as preferable to the day of
birth. Though Solomon seems in some
places to feel strongly (ii. 16, iii. 19, 20
&c.) that natural fear of death which is,
in a great measure, mistrust founded on

the ignorance which Christ dispelled; yet
he states the advantage of death over life
in respect of its freedom from toil, oppression, restlessness (ii. 17, iv. 2, vi. 5), and in
respect of its implying an immediate and
a nearer approach to God (iii. 21, xii. 7).
While Solomon preferred the day of death,
he might still (with Luther here) have regarded birth as a good thing, and as having
its place in the creation of God.

2. *that*] Namely, what is seen in the
house of mourning.
lay it to his heart] Consider it attentively.

3. *Sorrow*] Rather, **Seriousness.**
the heart is made better] *i.e.* is made bright
and joyful (cp. 2 Cor. vi. 10). The mind
which bears itself equally in human concerns, whether they be pleasant or sorrowful, must always be glad, free, and at peace.

4. *house of mourning...house of mirth*]
These phrases acquire a forcible significance from the Eastern custom of prolong-
ing both festive and mournful celebrations
through several days. See Gen. l. 10; Judg.
xiv. 17. This verse indicates that a life of
enjoyment, does not mean the abandonment
of ourselves to pleasures, but the thankful
and sober use of the beautiful things which
God gives us.

6. *as the crackling of thorns*] Noisy while
it lasts, and quickly extinguished. See Ps.
lviii. 9 note.

7. Rather, **oppression** (or *extortion*) **maketh a wise man foolish; and a bribe** &c.
If a wise man, being in a high position,
exercises oppression (see Ps. lxii. 10), or
practises extortion, he becomes a fool in

8 Better *is* the end of a thing than the beginning thereof:
And *ʃ* the patient in spirit *is* better than the proud in spirit.

9 *g* Be not hasty in thy spirit to be angry:
For anger resteth in the bosom of fools.

10 Say not thou, What is *the cause* that the former days were better
than these?
For thou dost not enquire ¹wisely concerning this.

11 Wisdom *is* ²good with an inheritance:
And *by it there is* profit *h* to them that see the sun.

12 For wisdom *is* a ³defence, *and* money *is* a defence:
But the excellency of knowledge *is, that* wisdom giveth life to
them that have it.

13 Consider the work of God:
For *i* who can make *that* straight, which he hath made crooked?

14 *k* In the day of prosperity be joyful,
But in the day of adversity consider:
God also hath ⁴set the one over against the other,
To the end that man should find nothing after him.

15 All *things* have I seen in the days of my vanity: *l* there is a
just *man* that perisheth in his righteousness, and there is a

Prov.14.29.

g Prov. 14.
17.
Jam. 1. 19.

h ch. 11. 7.

i See Job
12. 14.
ch. 1. 15.
Isai. 14. 27.
k ch. 3. 4.
Deut. 28. 47.

l ch. 8. 14.

---

¹ Heb. *out of wisdom.*   ² Or, *as good as an inherit-*   ³ Heb. *shadow.*
ance, yea, better too.   ⁴ Heb. *made.*

---

so doing. This verse is a warning against impatience in the exercise of power or the acquisition of riches.

8. *Better*] Inasmuch as something certain is attained, man contemplates the end throughout an entire course of action, and does not rest upon the beginning.

patient...proud] Lit. "Long," long-suffering..." high," in the sense of impatient.

11. *And by it there is profit* &c.] Lit. **And is profitable to the living.** The same word as in vi. 11, to the question in which it looks like an answer.

12. *wisdom is a defence* &c.] See marg. and Ps. cxxi. 5, *i.e.*, He who is defended from adversity by his wisdom is in as good a position as he who is defended by his riches.

excellency] Lit. **Profit.**

giveth life to] Lit. " Causes to live," "makes alive" (Prov. iii. 18); the deeper meaning of which is elicited by comparing these words with John vi. 63; Matt. iv. 4.

13. *the work of God*] The scheme of Divine Providence, the course of events which God orders and controls (cp. iii. 11). It comprises both events which are "straight," *i.e.* in accordance with our expectation, and events which are "crooked," *i.e.* which by their seeming inequality baffle our comprehension.

14. Good and prosperous days are in God's design peculiar times of comfort and rejoicing: the days of affliction and trouble, are in God's design the proper seasons of recollection and serious consideration. The Providence of God hath so contrived it, that our good and evil days should be intermingled each with the other. This mix-

ture of good and evil days is by the Divine Providence so proportioned, that it sufficiently justifies the dealings of God towards the sons of men, and obviates all their discontent and murmurings against Him.

set the one over against the other] Rather, **made this as well as that,** *i.e.* the day of adversity, as well as the day of prosperity. The seeming imitation of this passage in Ecclesiasticus (xxxvi. 13-15) affords a strong presumption that this Book was written before the days of the son of Sirach.

to the end &c.] God hath constituted the vicissitude of prosperity and adversity in such a way that no man can forecast the events that shall follow when he is removed from his present state. Cp. vi. 12 note.

15. *the days of my vanity*] This does not imply that those days of vanity were ended (see i. 12 note).

15–17. The meaning may be best explained by a paraphrase. Solomon states how the wise man should regard the "crooked (*v.* 13) work of God" when it bears upon him. He says in effect, "Do not think that thou couldest alter the two instances (described in *v.* 15) of such crooked work so as to make it straight, that thou art more righteous or more wise than He is Who ordained these events. To set up thy judgment in opposition to His would imply an excess of wickedness and folly, deserving the punishment of premature death. But rather it is good for thee to grasp these seeming anomalies; if thou ponder them they will tend to impress on thee that fear of God which is a part of wisdom, and will guide thee safely through all the perplexities

m Prov. 25. 16.
n Rom. 12. 3.

o Job 15. 32.
Ps. 55. 23.
Prov. 10. 27.

p Prov.21.22.
ch. 9. 16.
q 1 K. 8. 46.
2 Chr. 6. 36.
Prov. 20. 9.
Rom. 3. 23.
1 John 1. 8.

r Rom. 1. 22.
s Job 28. 12, 20.
1 Tim. 6. 16.
t Rom.11.33.
u ch. 1. 17.

x Prov.5.3,4.

y ch. 1. 1, 2

z Job 33. 23.
Ps. 12. 1.

a Gen. 1. 27.
b Gen. 3. 6, 7.

16 wicked *man* that prolongeth *his life* in his wickedness. *m* Be not righteous over much; *n* neither make thyself over wise: why
17 shouldest thou ¹ destroy thyself? Be not over much wicked, neither be thou foolish: *o* why shouldest thou die ² before thy
18 time? *It is* good that thou shouldest take hold of this; yea, also from this withdraw not thine hand: for he that feareth
19 God shall come forth of them all. *p* Wisdom strengtheneth the
20 wise more than ten mighty *men* which are in the city. *q* For *there is* not a just man upon earth, that doeth good, and sinneth
21 not. Also ³ take no heed unto all words that are spoken; lest
22 thou hear thy servant curse thee: for oftentimes also thine own heart knoweth that thou thyself likewise hast cursed others.
23 All this have I proved by wisdom: *r* I said, I will be wise;
24 but it *was* far from me. *s* That which is far off, and *t* exceeding
25 deep, who can find it out? ⁴ *u* I applied mine heart to know, and to search, and to seek out wisdom, and the reason *of things*, and to know the wickedness of folly, even of foolishness *and*
26 madness: *x* and I find more bitter than death the woman, whose heart *is* snares and nets, *and* her hands *as* bands: ⁵ whoso pleaseth God shall escape from her; but the sinner shall be taken by
27 her. Behold, this have I found, saith *y* the preacher, ⁶ *counting*
28 one by one, to find out the account: which yet my soul seeketh, but I find not: *z* one man among a thousand have I found; but a woman among all those have I not found.
29 Lo, this only have I found, *a* that God hath made man upright; but *b* they have sought out many inventions.

CHAP. 8. WHO *is* as the wise *man?* and who knoweth the inter-

---

¹ Heb. *be desolate?*
² Heb. *not in thy time?*
³ Heb. *give not thine heart.*

⁴ Heb. *I and my heart compassed.*
⁵ Heb. *he that is good before God.*

⁶ Or, weighing *one thing after another, to find out the reason.*

---

of this life" (cp. viii. 12, 13). The suggestion that these verses are intended to advocate a middle course between sin and virtue is at variance with the whole tenor of the Book.

16. *destroy thyself*] LXX. and Vulg. render, "be amazed." Cp. "marvel not" (v. 8).

20. The connexion of this verse with *vv.* 18, 19 becomes clearer if it is borne in mind that the fear of God, wisdom, and justice, are merely different sides of one and the same character, the formation of which is the aim of all the precepts in this chapter. The words "just" (*vv.* 15, 20) and "righteous" (*v.* 16) are exactly the same in Hebrew.

21, 22. *curse...cursed*] Rather, **speak evil of...spoken evil of.**

23. *I will be*] Or, **I am.** There was a time when Solomon thought himself wise enough to comprehend the work of God, and therefore needed for himself the self-humbling conviction declared in this verse.

it i.e.] Wisdom. Cp. viii. 17.)

24. Lit. **Far off** *is* **that which hath been** *i.e.* events as they have occurred in the order of Divine Providence), **and deep, deep, who can find it out?**

25. *reason*] The same word is translated "account" (*v.* 27), "invention" (*v.* 29), and "device" (ix. 10): it is derived from a root signifying "to count."

26. Cp. the account of Solomon's wives (1 K. xi. 1-8): see also Prov. ii. 16-19, v. 3 &c.

28. *one man*] One whose good qualities quite satisfy our expectation. Cp. the expression "one among a thousand" (marg. ref.).

a woman] The number of Solomon's wives and concubines (1 K. xi. 3) was a thousand.

29. *God hath made*] Rather, **God made.** A definite allusion to the original state of man: in which he was exempt from vanity.

VIII. Although in some degree baffled in his own pursuit of wisdom, Solomon yet regards wisdom as the nearest approach to "that good for man" which he is seeking; and presses here, as a part of that wisdom, a spirit of obedience (*vv.* 1-5). In the face of the incomprehensible course of external events, he determined to abide in the fear and trust of God (*vv.* 6-14), and to acknowledge the natural incompetence of every man to find out the unsearchable ways of God (*vv.* 15-17).

1. *and who*] Rather, **and as he who knoweth.** The possessor of wisdom excels

pretation of a thing ? *a* a man's wisdom maketh his face to shine, and [1] [b] the boldness of his face shall be changed.

2 I *counsel thee* to keep the king's commandment, *c* and *that* in
3 regard of the oath of God. *d* Be not hasty to go out of his sight: stand not in an evil thing; for he doeth whatsoever pleaseth
4 him. Where the word of a king *is, there is* power: and *e* who
5 may say unto him, What doest thou ? Whoso keepeth the commandment [2] shall feel no evil thing: and *a wise man's heart* discerneth both time and judgment.

6 Because *f* to every purpose there is time and judgment, there-
7 fore the misery of man *is* great upon him. *g* For he knoweth not that which shall be : for who can tell him [3] when it shall be?
8 *h There is* no man that hath power *i* over the spirit to retain the spirit; neither *hath he* power in the day of death: and *there is* no [4] discharge in *that* war ; neither shall wickedness deliver those that are given to it.

9 All this have I seen, and applied my heart unto every work that is done under the sun : *there is* a time wherein one man
10 ruleth over another to his own hurt. And so I saw the wicked buried, who had come and gone from the place of the holy, and they were forgotten in the city where they had so done : this *is* also vanity.

11 *k* Because sentence against an evil work is not executed speed-
12 ily, therefore the heart of the sons of men is fully set in them to do evil. *l* Though a sinner do evil an hundred times, and his *days* be prolonged, yet surely I know that *m* it shall be well with
13 them that fear God, which fear before him : but it shall not be well with the wicked, neither shall he prolong *his* days, which *are* as a shadow ; because he feareth not before God.

a Prov.4.8,9.
See Acts
6. 15.
b Deut. 28.
50.
c Ezek. 17.
18.
Rom. 13. 5.
d ch. 10. 4.
e Job 34. 18.

f ch. 3. 1.

g Prov. 24.
22.
ch. 6. 12.
& 10. 4.
h Ps. 49. 6, 7.
i Job 14. 5.

k Ps. 10. 6.
& 50. 21.
Isai. 26. 10.
l Isai. 65. 20.
Rom. 2. 5.
m Ps. 37. 11.
18, 19.
Prov. 1. 32,
33.
Isai. 3. 10.
Matt. 25. 34,
41.

[1] Heb. *the strength.*
[2] Heb. *shall know.*
[3] Or, *how it shall be?*
[4] Or, *casting off weapons.*

---

other men : it imparts serenity to his countenance, and removes the expression of gloom or fierceness (see marg. ref.).

2. *oath*] A reference to the oath of allegiance taken to Solomon at his accession to the throne (1 Chr. xxix. 24 marg.).

3. *stand not* &c.] *i.e.* "Do not persist in rebellion."

5. *feel*] Lit. **know.** The meaning is, "He who obeys the commandment (*i.e.* the word of the king, *v.* 4), will not be an accomplice in any act of rebellion ; and if he be a wise man he discerns (lit. knows) that the king's commandment or action is liable to correction, if it be wrong, in God's time and by God's judgment." Cp. iii. 11, 17.

6. *Because, therefore*] Or, as in *v.* 7, "for."

The possibility of God's time and judgment being in opposition to a king's purpose or commandment (*v.* 5), suggests the thought that such discord is a misery (=evil, vi. 1) common to man (or, mankind).

7. *when*] Or, as in marg. For the meaning of this verse, cp. marg. reff.

8. *neither hath he power*] Rather, **and** *there is* **no power.** Cp. iii. 19.

no discharge &c.] *i.e.* "No exemption from

the final hour of struggle between life and death."

wickedness] Though the life of the wicked may be prolonged (vii. 15), yet wickedness itself has no inherent power to prolong that life.

9. *to his own hurt*] Or, "to the hurt of the subject." The case is still that of an unwise king whose command is obeyed (*v.* 2) even to the hurt of the wise man who obeys him.

10. *i.e.* "I saw wicked (rulers) buried, who came into the world and went from the Holy Place (the seat of authority and justice, Deut. xix. 17 ; 2 Chr. xix. 6), and they were forgotten in the city where they had so ruled to the hurt of their subjects : this—their death and oblivion—shews their lot also to be vanity." Others interpret the verse: "I have seen wicked men buried ; and (others) came into the world, and from the Holy Place they went out of the world, and were forgotten in the city where they had done rightly" (cp. 2 K. vii. 9).

12. *his days be prolonged*] *i.e.* in his wickedness (*v.* 8).

I is emphatic, as if to mark the opposition to the "sons of men" (*v.* 11).

n Ps. 73. 14. ch. 2. 14. & 7. 15. & 9. 1, 2. o ch. 2. 24. & 3. 12, 22. & 5. 18. & 9. 7.

14 There is a vanity which is done upon the earth; that there be
just *men*, unto whom it [n] happeneth according to the work of
the wicked; again, there be wicked *men*, to whom it happeneth
according to the work of the righteous: I said that this also *is*
15 vanity. [o] Then I commended mirth, because a man hath no
better thing under the sun, than to eat, and to drink, and to be
merry: for that shall abide with him of his labour the days of
his life, which God giveth him under the sun.

p Job 5. 9. ch. 3. 11. Rom. 11. 33. q Ps. 73. 16.

16 When I applied mine heart to know wisdom, and to see the
business that is done upon the earth: (for also *there is that* nei-
17 ther day nor night seeth sleep with his eyes:) then I beheld all
the work of God, that [p] a man cannot find out the work that is
done under the sun: because though a man labour to seek *it*
out, yet he shall not find *it*; yea farther; though a wise *man*
think to know *it*, [q] yet shall he not be able to find *it*.

a ch. 8. 14. b Job. 21. 7, &c. Ps. 73. 3, 12, 13. Mal. 3. 15.

Chap. 9. FOR all this [1] I considered in my heart even to declare all
this, [a] that the righteous, and the wise, and their works, *are* in the
hand of God: no man knoweth either love or hatred *by* all *that is*
2 before them. [b] All *things come* alike to all: *there is* one event to
the righteous, and to the wicked; to the good and to the clean,
and to the unclean; to him that sacrificeth, and to him that
sacrificeth not: as *is* the good, so *is* the sinner; *and* he that
3 sweareth, as *he* that feareth an oath. This *is* an evil among all
things that are done under the sun, that *there is* one event unto
all: yea, also the heart of the sons of men is full of evil, and
madness *is* in their heart while they live, and after that *they go*

[1] Heb. *I gave*, or, *set to my heart.*

---

14. *which is done upon the earth*] The instance of vanity, to which these words are applied, is the seeming inequality of God's justice; but if they are considered in connexion with the profession of personal faith in God's absolute justice (*v.* 12), the conclusion is irresistible, that, whatever reason the Preacher had for reserve in declaring his belief, he certainly looked forward to a final judgment in a future state of existence (cp. iii. 17, xii. 14).

15. *mirth*] Better, **Gladness**, or "joy" (as in ii. 10). The Hebrew word is applied not only to the pleasures arising from the bodily senses, but also frequently to religious joy. The sentiment of this verse is a frequent conclusion of the writer's personal experience (cp. marg. reff.), and is unfairly charged with Epicureanism. The Preacher is careful to set forth pleasure as a gift from God, to be earned by labour, and received with thankfulness to the Giver, and to be accounted for to Him. His estimate of the pleasures of the senses is recorded in vii. 2-6.

16, 17. These verses supplement *v.* 15 with the reflection that the man who goes beyond that limited sphere within which he can labour and be contented, and investigates the whole work of God, will find that his finite intelligence cannot grasp it.

16. *business*] Or, "travail" (i. 13, iii. 10). The sleeplessness noted probably refers to the writer himself.

IX. In *vv.* 1-12 reasons are adduced for the universal conclusion (viii. 17) that no man can understand the works of God. This does not, however, prevent the assertion of the practical advantage in this life of that wisdom which includes the fear of God (*v.* 13 &c.). Cp. *vv.* 1-10 with Wisd. ii. 1-9.

1. A good man's trust in God is set forth as a counterpoise to our ignorance of the ways of Providence.

in the hand of God] Under His special protection (Deut. xxxiii. 3 &c.) as righteous, and under His direction (Prov. xxi. 1) as men.

no man &c.] Lit. **both love** *and* **also hatred man knoweth not: all** *are* **before them.** Love and hatred here mean the ordinary outward tokens of God's favour or displeasure, *i.e.* prosperity and adversity. "Man knoweth not" probably means: "man knows not whether to expect prosperity or adversity from God; all his earthly future is in obscurity."

2. *event*] See ii. 14 note.

sweareth] *i.e.* Swears lightly or profanely.

3. Cp. viii. 11. The seeming indiscriminateness of the course of events tends to encourage evil-disposed men in their folly.

4 to the dead. For to him that is joined to all the living there
5 is hope: for a living dog is better than a dead lion. For the
living know that they shall die: but *c*the dead know not any
thing, neither have they any more a reward; for *d*the memory
6 of them is forgotten. Also their love, and their hatred, and their
envy, is now perished : neither have they any more a portion for
ever in any *thing* that is done under the sun.

7 Go thy way, *e*eat thy bread with joy, and drink thy wine with
8 a merry heart; for God now accepteth thy works. Let thy garments be always white; and let thy head lack no ointment.
9 ¹Live joyfully with the wife whom thou lovest all the days of the
life of thy vanity, which he hath given thee under the sun, all the
days of thy vanity : *f*for that *is* thy portion in *this* life, and in thy
10 labour which thou takest under the sun. Whatsoever thy hand
findeth to do, do *it* with thy might; for *there is* no work, nor
device, nor knowledge, nor wisdom, in the grave, whither thou
goest.

11 I returned, *g*and saw under the sun, that the race *is* not to
the swift, nor the battle to the strong, neither yet bread to the
wise, nor yet riches to men of understanding, nor yet favour to
12 men of skill; but time and chance happeneth to them all. For
*h*man also knoweth not his time : as the fishes that are taken in
an evil net, and as the birds that are caught in the snare;
so *are* the sons of men *i*snared in an evil time, when it falleth
suddenly upon them.

13 This wisdom have I seen also under the sun, and it *seemed* great

c Job 14. 21.
Isai. 63. 16.
d Job 7. 8,
9, 10.
Isai. 26. 14.

e ch. 8. 15.

f ch. 2. 10.
24. & 3. 13,
22. & 5. 18.

g Amos 2.
14, 15.
Jer. 9. 23.

h ch. 8. 7.

i Prov. 29. 6.
Luke 12.
20, 39.
1 Thess. 5. 3.

¹ Heb. *See,* or, *Enjoy life.*

---

4. *For to him*] Rather, **Yet to him.** Notwithstanding evils, life has its advantage,
and specially when compared with death.

dog] To the Hebrews a type of all that
was contemptible (1 Sam. xvii. 43).

5, 6. See viii. 12, 14 note. The living
are conscious that there is a future before
them : but the dead are unconscious ; they
earn nothing, receive nothing, even the
memory of them soon disappears ; they are
no longer excited by the passions which
belong to men in this life ; their share in its
activity has ceased. Solomon here describes
what he sees, not what he believes ; there
is no reference here to the fact or the mode
of the existence of the soul in another world,
which are matters of faith.

The last clause of *v.* 6 indicates that the
writer confines his observations on the dead
to their portion in, or relation to, this
world.

6. *now*] Rather, **long ago.**

7-12. Read these six verses connectedly,
in order to arrive at the meaning of the
writer ; and cp. ii. 1-12.

After the description (*vv.* 5, 6) of the
portionless condition of the dead, the next
thought which occurs is that the man who
is prosperous and active should simply
enjoy his portion all through this life (*vv.* 7-
10); and then (*vv.* 11, 12) follows the correct-

ing thought (see iii. 1-15 note), introduced
as usual (ii. 12, iv. 1, 7) by "I returned,"
viz. that the course of events is disposed
and regulated by another Will than that of
man.

The person addressed is one whose life of
labour is already pleasing to God, and who
bears visible tokens of God's favour.

7. *now accepteth*] Rather, **already has
pleasure in.** Joy (marg. ref. note) is regarded as a sign of the approbation and
favour of God.

8. White garments and perfume are simply an expressive sign of joy.

10. The works which we carry on here
with the combined energies of body and
soul come to an end in the hour of death,
when the soul enters a new sphere of existence, and body and soul cease to act together. Cp. John ix. 4.

device] See vii. 25 note.

11. *chance*] Or, "incident," that which
comes to us from without, one of the external
events described in ch. iii. Cp. ii. 14 note.

12. *time*] See iii. 1 &c.

13. Or, **Also this have I seen—wisdom
under the sun, and great it** *seemed* **to me.**

From this verse to the end of ch. x., the
writer inculcates, in a series of proverbs, wisdom in contrast to folly, as the best remedy
in the present life to the evil of vanity.

k See
2 Sam. 20.
16-22.

14 unto me: *k There was* a little city, and few men within it; and
there came a great king against it, and besieged it, and built
15 great bulwarks against it: now there was found in it a poor
wise man, and he by his wisdom delivered the city; yet no

l Prov. 21.
22. & 24, 5.
ch. 7. 19.
ver. 18.
m Mark 6.
2, 3.

16 man remembered that same poor man. *l*Then said I, Wisdom
is better than strength: nevertheless *m*the poor man's wisdom
is despised, and his words are not heard.

17   The words of wise *men are* heard in quiet
More than the cry of him that ruleth among fools.

n ver. 16.
o Josh. 7. 1,
11, 12.

18 *n*Wisdom *is* better than weapons of war:
But *o*one sinner destroyeth much good.

Chap. 10. DEAD *1*flies cause the ointment of the apothecary to
send forth a stinking savour:
So doth a little folly him that is in reputation for wisdom *and*
honour.

2 A wise man's heart *is* at his right hand;
But a fool's heart at his left.

3 Yea also, when he that is a fool walketh by the way, *2*his wisdom
faileth *him*,

a Prov. 13.
16. & 18. 2.
b ch. 8. 3.

*a*And he saith to every one *that* he *is* a fool.

4 If the spirit of the ruler rise up against thee, *b*leave not thy
place;
For *c*yielding pacifieth great offences.

c 1 Sam. 25.
24, &c.
Prov. 25. 15.

5 There is an evil *which* I have seen under the sun,
As an error *which* proceedeth *3*from the ruler:

d Esth. 3. 1.

6 *d*Folly is set *4*in great dignity,—and the rich sit in low place.

---

1 Heb. *Flies of death.*   *2* Heb. *his heart.*   *4* Heb. *in great heights.*
3 Heb. *from before.*

14, 15. A parable probably without foundation in fact. Critics who ascribe this Book to a late age offer no better suggestion than that the "little city" may be Athens delivered B.C. 480 from the host of Xerxes through the wisdom of Themistocles, or Dora besieged B.C. 218 by Antiochus the Great.

Verses 16, 17 are comments on the two facts—the deliverance of the city and its forgetfulness of him who delivered it—stated in *v.* 15.

18. *sinner*] The word in the original indicates intellectual as well as moral error.

X. This chapter resembles a portion of the Book of Proverbs, consisting entirely of rhythmical sentences giving advice, more or less direct, as to conduct. It is part of the writer's answer to the question (ii. 3, vi. 12) "What is good for men to do?" The thought which underlies the whole chapter is the advantage of that wisdom which includes piety and patience, as practical guidance through all the perplexities of life: various traits of wisdom are set forth in a favourable light, heightened by contrast with folly. A great part of the advice seems, in addition to its general application, to have a special reference to servants of a king.

1. This verse is by its meaning so closely connected with ix. 18 that the selection of it for the beginning of a new chapter seems unfortunate.

apothecary] Rather, **dealer in spices** and perfumes (cp. Ex. xxx. 25). The swarms of flies in the East very soon corrupt and destroy any moist unguent or mixture left uncovered, and pollute a dish of food in a few minutes.

so doth &c.] Lit. **more weighty than wisdom, than honour, is a little folly.**

2. The metaphor perhaps means "A wise man's sense is in its place, ready to help and protect him; but a fool's is missing when it is wanted, and so is useless."

3. "Way" may be understood either literally (cp. *v.* 15), or figuratively, of the course of action which he follows.

he saith &c.] He exposes his folly to every one he meets.

4. *If the spirit* &c.] *i.e.* If he be angry.

leave not thy place] *i.e.* Do not lose thy self-control and quit his presence. Gentleness on thy part will calm both thyself and him, and prevent great wrongs being committed by either.

6, 7. The "evil" of *v.* 5 is here specified as that caprice of a king by which an unworthy favourite of low origin is promoted to successive dignities, while a noble person is degraded or neglected.

7 I have seen servants *upon horses,
And princes walking as servants upon the earth.

8 *He that diggeth a pit shall fall into it ;
And whoso breaketh an hedge, a serpent shall bite him.
9 Whoso removeth stones shall be hurt therewith ;
And he that cleaveth wood shall be endangered thereby.
10 If the iron be blunt, and he do not whet the edge,
Then must he put to more strength :
But wisdom *is* profitable to direct.

11 Surely the serpent will bite *without enchantment ;
And ¹a babbler is no better.
12 ʰThe words of a wise man's mouth *are* ²gracious ;
But ⁱthe lips of a fool will swallow up himself.
13 The beginning of the words of his mouth *is* foolishness :
And the end of ³his talk *is* mischievous madness.
14 ᵏA fool also ⁴is full of words :
A man cannot tell what shall be ;
And ˡwhat shall be after him, who can tell him ?
15 The labour of the foolish wearieth every one of them,
Because he knoweth not how to go to the city.

16 ᵐWoe to thee, O land, when thy king *is* a child,
And thy princes eat in the morning !
17 Blessed *art* thou, O land, when thy king *is* the son of nobles,
And ⁿthy princes eat in due season, for strength, and not for
drunkenness !

18 By much slothfulness the building decayeth ;
And through idleness of the hands the house droppeth through.

19 A feast is made for laughter, and ᵒwine ⁵maketh merry :
But money answereth all *things*.

20 ᵖCurse not the king, no not in thy ⁶thought ;

Marginal references:
e Prov. 19.
10. & 30. 22.
f Ps. 7. 15.
Prov. 26. 27.
g Ps. 58. 4, 5.
Jer. 8. 17.
h Prov. 10.
32.
& 12. 13.
i Prov. 10.
14.
& 18. 7.
k Prov. 15. 2.
l ch. 3. 22.
& 6. 12.
& 8. 7.
m Isai. 3. 4,
5, 12.
n Prov. 31. 4.
o Ps. 104. 15.
p Ex. 22. 28
Acts 23. 5.

¹ Heb. *the master of the tongue.*
² Heb. *grace.*
³ Heb. *his mouth.*
⁴ Heb. *multiplieth words.*
⁵ Heb. *maketh glad the life.*
⁶ Or, *conscience,* figure like, Luke 19. 40.

8–10. The figures seem to be taken from the work of building up and pulling down houses. In their general application, they recommend the man who would act wisely to be cautious when taking any step in life which involves risk.

8. *breaketh an hedge*] Rather, **breaks through a wall.**

serpent] The habit of snakes is to nestle in a chink of a wall, or among stones (cp. Amos v. 19).

9. *be endangered*] Rather, **cut himself.**

11. Rather, **If a serpent without enchantment** (*i.e.* not being enchanted) **bites, then there is no advantage to the charmer:** *i.e.* if the charmer is unwisely slack in exercising his craft, he will be bitten like other people. See Ps. lviii. 4 note.

14. *full of words*] Confident talking of the future is indicated rather than mere loquacity. Cp. Jas. iv. 13.

15. The sense is, "The fool wearies himself with ineffectual attempts, he has

not sufficient knowledge for the transaction of ordinary business."

16–20. Foolish rulers, by their weakness, self-indulgence and sloth, bring decay upon the state : nobleness and temperance insure prosperity : yet the subject must not rebel in word or thought against his king.

16. *a child*] Rather, **young.** The word is applied to Rehoboam (2 Chr. xiii. 7) at the time of his accession to the throne, when he was 41 years old.

eat in the morning] A sign of intemperance (cp. Isai. v. 11).

17. *son of nobles*] *i.e.* of a noble disposition.

18. The "building" or "house" represents the state. Cp. Isai. iii. 6 ; Amos ix. 10.

droppeth through] *i.e.* Lets the rain through the roof.

19. Lit. **For merriment they make a feast** (= bread), **and wine gladdens the living, and money supplies all things.**

20. *Curse*] Cp. vii. 21, 22.

And curse not the rich in thy bedchamber :
For a bird of the air shall carry the voice,
And that which hath wings shall tell the matter.

a See Isai.
32. 20.
b Deut. 15.
10.
Prov. 19. 17.
Matt. 10. 42.
2 Cor. 9. 8.
Gal. 6. 9.
Heb. 6. 10.
c Ps. 112. 9.
Luke 6. 30.
1 Tim. 6.
18, 19.
d Mic. 5. 5.
e Eph. 5. 16.
f John 3. 8.
g Ps. 139.
14, 15.

CHAP. 11. CAST thy bread *a* ¹upon the waters :
  b For thou shalt find it after many days.
2 *c* Give a portion *d* to seven, and also to eight ;
  e For thou knowest not what evil shall be upon the earth.
3 If the clouds be full of rain, they empty *themselves* upon the
    earth :
  And if the tree fall toward the south, or toward the north,
  In the place where the tree falleth, there it shall be.
4 He that observeth the wind shall not sow ;
  And he that regardeth the clouds shall not reap.
5 As *f* thou knowest not what *is* the way of the spirit,
  g Nor how the bones *do grow* in the womb of her that is with
    child :
  Even so thou knowest not the works of God who maketh all.
6 In the morning sow thy seed,
  And in the evening withhold not thine hand :
  For thou knowest not whether ²shall prosper, either this or
    that,
  Or whether they both *shall be* alike good.

h ch. 7. 11.

7 Truly the light *is* sweet,
  And a pleasant *thing it is* for the eyes *h* to behold the sun :
8 But if a man live many years, *and* rejoice in them all ;

---

¹ Heb. *upon the face of the waters.*   ² Heb. *shall be right.*

XI. There ought to be no division between x. 20 and xi. 1.

1, 2. As if in contrast to the self-indulgence described in x. 16–19, the opposite
virtue, readiness to give to others, is inculcated. The use of the word " bread " in
both x. 19 (see note) and xi. 1 points the
contrast.

1. The verse means, "Shew hospitality,
even though the corresponding return of
hospitality to you seem improbable ; yet be
hospitable in faith." Cp. Luke xiv. 13, 14 ;
Heb. xiii. 2. Some interpreters not un-
reasonably understand by "bread" the seed
from the produce of which bread is made.
Seed cast upon the fertile soil flooded by the
early rains would be returned to the sower
in autumn with large increase.

2. The verse means, "Let your hospitality and your alms be extensive : for you
know not what reverses may befall either
that person who by your liberality will be
strengthened to meet them, or yourself who
may come to need grateful friends." Cp.
Luke xvi. 9.

seven, and also to eight] A definite number
for an indefinite (cp. marg. ref.).

3-6. "Unforeseen events come from God ;
and the man who is always gazing on the
uncertain future will neither begin nor complete any useful work : but do thou bear in
mind that times and circumstances, the
powers of nature and the results to which

they minister, are in the hand of God ; and
be both diligent and trustful." The images
are connected chiefly with the occupation of
an agricultural labourer : the discharge of
rain from the cloud, and the inclination of
the falling tree, and the direction of the
wind, are beyond his control, though the
result of his work is affected by them. The
common application of the image of the
fallen tree to the state of departed souls was
probably not in the mind of the inspired
writer.

5. *spirit*] The same Hebrew word (like
Pneuma in Greek and *Ghost* in English)
signifies both the wind (*v.* 4) and the
Spirit (cp. marg. ref.). The Old Testament in many places recognizes the special
operation of God (Job x. 8–12 ; Ps. cxxxix.
13–16 ; Jer. i. 5), and distinctly of the
Spirit of God (Job xxxi. 15) in the origina-
tion of every child. Cp. Gen. ii. 7.

7-xii. 7. The preceding exhortation to a
life of labour in the sight of God is now addressed specially to the active and the
young ; and is enforced by another consideration, namely, the transitory character
of all that sustains youth.

7. *the light,...the sun*] Gifts of God which
cheer man's toil, but which he almost ceases
to appreciate in his old age.

8. *days of darkness*] The time of old age,
and perhaps any time of sorrow or misfortune. Cp. xii. 2.

Yet let him remember the days of darkness;
For they shall be many. All that cometh *is* vanity.

9 Rejoice, O young man, in thy youth;
And let thy heart cheer thee in the days of thy youth,
'And walk in the ways of thine heart, and in the sight of thine eyes :
But know thou, that for all these *things* *k*God will bring thee into judgment.
10 Therefore remove ¹sorrow from thy heart,
And *l*put away evil from thy flesh :
*m*For childhood and youth *are* vanity.

i Num. 15. 39.

k ch. 12. 14. Rom. 2. 6. —11.

l 2 Cor. 7. 1. 2 Tim. 2. 22. *m* Ps. 39. 5.

CHAP. 12. REMEMBER *a*now thy Creator in the days of thy youth,
While the evil days come not, nor the years draw nigh,
*b*When thou shalt say, I have no pleasure in them ;
2 While the sun, or the light, or the moon, or the stars, be not darkened,
Nor the clouds return after the rain :
3 In the day when the keepers of the house shall tremble,
And the strong men shall bow themselves,
And ²the grinders cease because they are few,
And those that look out of the windows be darkened,
4 And the doors shall be shut in the streets,
When the sound of the grinding is low,
And he shall rise up at the voice of the bird,
And all *c*the daughters of musick shall be brought low ;

a Prov. 22. 6. Lam. 3. 27.

b See 2 Sam. 19. 35.

c 2 Sam. 19. 35.

¹ Or, *anger.*   ² Or, *the grinders fail, because they* grind *little.*

All that cometh] *i.e.* "The future," which must not be reckoned on by the active man, as if his present state of healthy energy were to continue.

9. *Rejoice...cheer...walk*] The imperative mood is used to encourage one who possesses certain gifts from God to remember that they come from God and are to be used in accordance with His will.

in the ways &c.] The words are probably used in an innocent sense (ii. 10; Prov. xvi. 9).

judgment] This includes a judgment beyond the grave ; though the writer's view of it was dim and indefinite if compared with a Christian's.

10. The sense appears to be, "Let the timely recollection of God's judgment, and of the fleeting character of youth, so influence your conduct that you will refrain from acts which entail future remorse and pain."

XII. 1. *Remember now*] Rather, **And remember.** The connexion between this verse and the preceding one is unfortunately interrupted by our division of chapters.

Creator] Gratitude to God as Creator is here inculcated, as just previously (xi. 9) fear of God as Judge. Godliness, acquired as a habit in youth, is recommended as the proper compensation for that natural cessation of youthful happiness which makes the *days*

of old age more or less *evil ;* more evil in proportion as there is less of godliness in the heart, and less evil where there is more godliness.

while the evil days come not] Rather, **before the evil days come.**

2. *While...not*] Or, **Before.** The darkening of the lights of heaven denotes a time of affliction and sadness. Cp. Ezek. xxxii. 7, 8 ; Job iii. 9 ; Isai. v. 30. Contrast this representation of old age with 2 Sam. xxiii. 4, 5.

3—6. The body in old age and death is here described under the figure of a decaying house with its inmates and furniture.

3. This verse is best understood as referring to the change which old age brings to four parts of the body, the arms ("the keepers"), the legs ("the strong men"), the teeth ("the grinders"), and the eyes.

4. *And the doors...is low*] The house is viewed from without. The way of entry and exit is stopped : little or no sound issues forth to tell of life stirring within. The old man as he grows older has less in common with the rising generation; mutual interest and intercourse decline. Some take the doors and the sound of the mill as figures of the lips and ears and of the speech.

he shall rise &c.] Here the metaphor of the house passes out of sight. The verb may

5 Also *when* they shall be afraid of *that which is* high,
And fears *shall be* in the way,
And the almond tree shall flourish,
And the grasshopper shall be a burden,
And desire shall fail:

d Job 17. 13.
e Jer. 9. 17.

Because man goeth to *e*his long home, and *e*the mourners go about the streets:

6 Or ever the silver cord be loosed, or the golden bowl be broken,
Or the pitcher be broken at the fountain, or the wheel broken at the cistern.

f Gen. 3. 19.
Job 34. 15.
Ps. 90. 3.
g ch. 3. 21.
h Num. 16.
22.
Job 34. 14.
Isai. 57. 16.
Zech. 12. 1.
i Ps. 62. 9.
ch. 1. 2.
k 1 Kin. 4.
32.

7 *f*Then shall the dust return to the earth as it was:
*g*And the spirit shall return unto God *h*who gave it.

8 *i*Vanity of vanities, saith the preacher; all *is* vanity.

9 And ¹moreover, because the preacher was wise, he still taught the people knowledge; yea, he gave good heed, and sought out,

10 *and* *k*set in order many proverbs. The preacher sought to find out ²acceptable words: and *that which was* written *was* upright,

¹ Or, *the more wise the preacher was, &c.*

² Heb. *words of delight.*

---

either be taken impersonally (= "they shall rise," compare the next verse): or as definitely referring to an old man, who as the master of the house rises out of sleep at the first sound in the morning.

all the daughters of musick] *i.e.* Singing women (ii. 8).

be brought low] *i.e.* Sound faintly in the ears of old age.

5. *high*] The powerful and the proud, such persons as an old man in his timidity might shrink from opposing or meeting: or, high ground which old men would avoid ascending.

fears...in the way] Cp. Prov. xxvi. 13.

the almond tree] The type of old age. Many modern critics translate "The almond shall be despised," *i.e.* pleasant food shall be no longer relished.

the grasshopper] Rather, **the locust.** The clause means, heaviness and stiffness shall take the place of that active motion for which the locust is conspicuous.

desire] Lit. **the caper-berry**; which, eaten as a provocative to appetite, shall fail to take effect on a man whose powers are exhausted.

long home] Lit. "eternal (see i. 4 note) house;" man's place in the next world. Without attributing to the author of Ecclesiastes that deep insight into the future life which is shewn by the writer of the Epistles to the Corinthians, we may observe that He by Whom both writers were inspired sanctions in both Books (see 2 Cor. v. 1–6) the use of the same expression "eternal house." In 2 Cor. it means that spiritual body which shall be hereafter ; and it is placed, as it is here (see *v.* 3), in contrast with that earthly dissolving house which clothes the spirit of man in this world.

mourners] The singing women who attend funerals for hire (see Matt. ix. 23).

6. *be loosed*] The termination of life is signified generally by the snapping of the silver cord by which the lamp hangs from the ceiling ; by the dashing in pieces of the cup or reservoir of oil ; by the shattering of the pitcher used to bring water from the spring ; and by the breaking of the wheel by which a bucket is let down into the well. Others discern in the silver cord, the soul which holds the body in life ; in the bowl, the body ; and in the golden oil (cp. Zech. iv. 12) within it, the spirit.

the spirit] *i.e.* The spirit separated unto God from the body at death. No more is said here of its future destiny. To return to God, Who is the fountain (Ps. xxxvi. 9) of Life, certainly means to continue to live. The doctrine of life after death is implied here as in Exod. iii. 6 (cp. Mark xii. 26), Ps. xvii. 15 (see note), and in many other passages of Scripture earlier than the age of Solomon. The inference that the soul loses its personality and is absorbed into something else has no warrant in this or any other statement in this Book, and would be inconsistent with the announcement of a judgment after death (*v.* 14).

8–14. This passage is properly regarded as the Epilogue of the whole Book ; a kind of apology for the obscurity of many of its sayings. The passage serves therefore to make the Book more intelligible and more acceptable.

Here, as in the beginning of the Book (i. 1, 2), the Preacher speaks of himself (*vv.* 8, 9, 10) in the third person. He first repeats (*v.* 8) the mournful, perplexing theme with which his musings began (i. 2) ; and then states the encouraging practical conclusion (*vv.* 13, 14) to which they have led him. It

11 *even* words of truth. The words of the wise *are* as goads, and
as nails fastened *by* the masters of assemblies, *which* are given
12 from one shepherd. And further, by these, my son, be admonished: of making many books *there is* no end; and [1]much   [1] ch. 1. 18.
[1]study *is* a weariness of the flesh.
13   [2]Let us hear the conclusion of the whole matter: [m]Fear God,   [m] Deut. 6. 2.
and keep his commandments: for this *is* the whole *duty* of man.   & 10. 12.
14 For [n]God shall bring every work into judgment, with every   [n] ch. 11. 9.
secret thing, whether *it be* good, or whether *it be* evil.   Matt. 12. 36.
Acts 17. 30, 31.
Rom. 2. 16.
1 Cor. 4. 5.

[1] Or, *reading*.   even *all that hath been*
[2] Or, *The end of the matter,*   *heard,* is.

---

has been pointed out that the Epilogue assumes the identity of the Preacher with
the writer of the Book of Proverbs.

11. Lit. **Words of wise men are as goads,
and as nails driven in (***by***) masters of assemblies; they are given from one shepherd:** "goads," because they rouse the
hearer and impel him to right actions;
"nails" (perhaps tent-spikes), because they
remain fixed in the memory: "masters
of assemblies" are simply "teachers" or
"preachers" (see i. 1 note), instructors
of such assemblies as Wisdom addresses
(Prov. i. 20).

one shepherd] *i.e.* GOD, Who is the supreme Giver of wisdom (Prov. ii. 6), and
the chief Shepherd (Jer. xxiii. 1-4). Cp. 1
Cor. ii. 12, 13.

12. *by these*] *i.e.* "By the words of wise
men."

books] Rather, "Writings." Probably
the proverbs current in the Preacher's age,
including, though not specially indicating,
his own.

The Preacher protests against the folly of
protracted, unprofitable, meditation.

13. Lit. "The conclusion of the discourse" (or "word," = words, i. 1), "the
whole, let us hear."

the whole duty of man] Rather, **the whole
man.** To fear God and to obey Him is the
whole man, constitutes man's whole being;
that only is conceded to Man; all other
things, as this Book again and again teaches,
are dependent on a Higher Incomprehensible Being.

14. *judgment with*] Rather, judgment (*which
shall be held*) **upon** &c.: *i.e.*, an appointed judgment which shall take place in another world,
as distinct from that retribution which frequently follows man's actions in the course
of this world, and which is too imperfect
(cp. ii. 15, iv. 1, vii. 15, ix. 2 &c.) to be described by these expressions. He that is
fully convinced that there is no solid happiness to be found in this world, and that
there is a world to come wherein God will
adjudge men to happiness or misery respectively, as they have made their choice and
acted here, must necessarily subscribe to
the truth of Solomon's conclusion, that true
religion is the only way to true happiness.

THE

SONG OF SOLOMON.

INTRODUCTION.

1. "The Song of Songs which is Solomon's," so designated by its most ancient (Hebrew) title, holds an unique position in sacred literature. It may be said to be the enigma of the Old Testament, as the Apocalypse is of the New.

The Song was regarded as an integral and venerated portion of the Hebrew canon before the commencement of the Christian era, and passed as such into the canon of the primitive Church : it has been always held both by the Church and by the Synagogue in the highest and most reverent estimation.[1]

One or two allusions have been found in the Song to at least one older canonical Book (Genesis) ; and a few references to it occur in Books of later composition (Proverbs, Isaiah, Hosea) ; while two or three doubtful allusions have been thought to be made to it by writers of the New Testament. These references are sufficient to establish the recognition of the Song as a part of Holy Scripture by some among the canonical writers.

2. The difficulties of the interpreter of the Song are unusually great. One lies in the peculiar form of composition. The Song of Songs might be called a lyrico-dramatic poem, but it is not a drama in the sense that it was either intended or adapted for representation.

Though the Song is a well-organized poetical whole, its unity [2] is made up of various parts and sections, of which several have so much independence and individuality as to have been not inaptly called Idylls, i.e. short poetic pieces of various forms containing each

---

[1] Rabbi Akiba as reported in the Mishnah, expressing the general judgment of Jewish schools and doctors in the first and second centuries, exclaimed: "No man in Israel ever doubted the canonicity of the Song of Songs, for the course of ages cannot vie with the day on which the Song of Songs was given to Israel; all the Kethubim (Hagiographa) are indeed a holy thing, but the Song of Songs is a holy of holies." Origen, after enumerating six of the chief songs of Holy Scripture, e,g., the songs of the Red Sea (Exod. xv.), of the Well (Num. xxi. 17, 18), of Moses (Deut. xxxii.), of Deborah (Judg. v.), of David (Ps. xviii.), of Isaiah (Isai. v.), and assigning to each its special significance in reference to the spiritual life, thus proceeds : "When thou hast passed through all these, thou must mount yet higher to sing with the Bridegroom this Song of Songs." In the Book of Proverbs, according to St. Jerome, the young are taught the duties of life ; in Ecclesiastes the middle-aged the vanity of earthly things ; in the Song of Songs the perfected, who have the world beneath their feet, are joined to the embraces of the heavenly Bridegroom.

[2] Almost all recent critics now assume that the Song is not an anthology or collection of poems and fragments by various authors, but (as its Hebrew title indicates) a single poem, the work of one author. The old popular renderings of this title, "Cantica," "Canticles," or "Songs of Solomon," were consequently—as to the plural form—inexact and misleading.

a distinct subject of representation. These shorter pieces are all, however, so closely linked by a common purpose, as to form, when viewed in their right connexion, constituent parts of a larger and complete poem.

The earliest Jewish expositor of the Song as a whole, the author of the so-called Chaldee Targum, divides it in his historico-prophetic interpretation into two nearly equal halves at v. 1. All that precedes the close of that verse he makes refer to the times of the Exodus and of the first Temple, and all that follows to times subsequent to the deportation to Babylon down to the final restoration of Israel and the glories of the latter day. Whatever we may think of this allegorical interpretation, the division itself may, with other divisions—suggested by refrains and recurrent phrases, used it would seem of set purpose to indicate the commencement or the close of various sections,—prove a valuable clue to the true significance of the whole.

The two most important of these refrains are, first, the bride's threefold adjuration to the Chorus (ii. 7, iii. 5, and viii. 4), marking at each place, as most interpreters agree, the close of one division of the poem; secondly, the question asked three times by a Chorus on as many distinct appearances of the bride (iii. 6, vi. 10, and viii. 5), marking, in like manner, a fresh commencement. These two refrains enable us to divide each half of the Song into three parts of nearly equal length, and make the whole poem consist of six parts; an arrangement which, in its main features, has obtained a majority of

suffrages among modern interpreters.[3]

The Song is throughout so far dramatic in form that it consists entirely of dialogue or monologue, the writer nowhere speaking in his own person; and the dialogue is connected with the development of a certain action. There are, we believe, only three chief speakers, "the bride," "the beloved," and a Chorus of "virgins" or "daughters of Jerusalem," having each their own manner and peculiar words and phrases, and these so carefully adhered to as to help us, in some cases of doubt, to determine the particular speaker (see i. 8 note)[4].

If in other Scriptures are found words of indignation and wrath

---

[3] Each of these parts, on a closer view, will be found to break up into two or three smaller sections, some quite idyllic in their character, and capable of being regarded as distinct little poems (*e.g.* ii. 8–17, iii. 1–5, v. 2–8). Here occur other recurrent phrases, *e.g.* "Behold, thou art fair" &c. (i. 15, iv. 1, 7, vi. 4, vii. 6), which is a formula of commencement; and the following formulæ of conclusion, "His left hand underneath my head" &c. (ii. 6, viii. 3); "Flee, my beloved" &c.; and "I am my beloved's" &c. (ii. 16, 17, vii. 10, viii. 14).

[4] Origen adds a fourth speaker, a Chorus of young men, companions of the bridegroom (iii. 11). The bride constantly repeats her favourite phrases; *e.g.* the adjuration (ii. 7 &c., v. 8); "I am my beloved's" &c. (ii. 16, vi. 3, vii. 10, cp. viii. 10); "Flee (or "turn") my beloved," &c. (ii. 17, viii. 14); her beloved is a "shepherd" who "feeds" his flock (i. 7) "among lilies" (ii. 16, vi. 3). The beloved repeatedly employs the same terms in addressing the bride; *e.g.* "My love" or "friend" (i. 9, 15, ii. 2, 10, 13, iv. 1, 7, v. 2, vi. 4); "My dove" (ii. 14, v. 2, vi. 9); "My sister" (iv. 9, 10, v. 2); "Let me hear thy voice" (ii. 14, viii. 13); "Thou hast doves' eyes" (i. 15, iv. 1). Cp. also iv. 1–3 with vi. 5–7, and iv. 4, 5, with vii. 3, 4.

and terrible threatenings, the characteristics of this Book are sweetness, cheerfulness, and joy, characteristics somewhat at variance with "the hypothesis" so-called "of the shepherd lover."[5] According to the view taken in this Commentary, there is but one lover in the Song, and one object of his affection, without rival or disturbing influence on either side. The beloved of the bride is in truth a king, and if she occasionally speaks of him as a shepherd, she intimates (vi. 2, 3) that she is speaking figuratively. Being herself a rustic maiden of comparatively lowly station she, by such an appellation, seeks to draw down him "whom her soul loveth" (i. 7, iii. 1-4), though he be the king of Israel, within her narrower circle of thoughts and aspirations. And, therefore, while the whole poem breathes of almost more than regal splendour and magnificence, the bride is nowhere represented as dwelling with any pride or satisfaction on the riches or grandeur of her beloved, but only on what he is to her in his own person as "chiefest among ten thousand" and "altogether lovely" (v. 10, 16 notes).

3. Most recent critics have agreed in assigning to the Song an early date.

The diction of the Song (on the character of which several critics

have insisted when arguing for a later date) is unquestionably peculiar. The poem is written in pure Hebrew of the best age, but with a large sprinkling of uncommon idioms and some very remarkable and apparently foreign words. Diction apart, most of the references and allusions in the Song would lead us to assign it, in accordance with its title, to the age of Solomon, nor does there seem to be sufficient reason for departing from the traditional belief that Solomon was himself the author; unless it be considered a panegyric composed in his honour by a prophet or poet of the king's own circle. In that case some of the peculiarities of diction and phraseology might be accounted for by assuming the author to have been a native of the Northern part of Solomon's dominions.

One striking characteristic of the writer of the Song is a love of natural scenes and objects, and familiarity with them as they would be presented, in the wide area[6] of the Hebrew monarchy, to an observant eye in the age of Solomon. Thus it has been observed that this short poem contains 18 names of plants and 13 of animals. Not less delight is exhibited in the enumeration of those works of human art and labour and those articles of commerce, which in the time of Solo-

---

[5] This hypothesis, held by many distinguished critics, assumes that there are two lovers in the Song, one a faithful simple-minded shepherd, the other a magnificent voluptuous king, by each of whom the affections of a Shulamite maiden are alternately solicited; while she, faithful in her allegiance to her shepherd-lover, rejects with scorn the monarch's blandishments, and finally compels him to abandon his pursuit.

[6] Thus, allusions to the north of Palestine, in which the writer seems to take particular delight, are found in iv. 8, 11, 15, i. 16, 17. Allusions to the east of Jordan occur in ii. 17, iv. 1, vi. 5, 13; and allusions to the fields and valleys, the flowers and animals, on the west of the river in ii. 1, 12, 14, iv. 5, v. 12, vii. 13; The furthest south is alluded to in i. 14, iv. 4, 6, 12-14, vi. 4, vii. 4 &c.

mon so largely ministered to royal pomp and luxury.[7]

The time in which the Song was written was unquestionably one of peace and general prosperity, such as occurred but very rarely in the chequered history of Israel. All the indications named above concur with this in fixing that time as the age of Solomon.

4. The interpretation of the Song of Songs followed in this Commentary proceeds on the assumption that the primary subject and occasion of the poem was a real historical event, of which we have here the only record, the marriage union of Solomon with a shepherd-maiden of northern Palestine, by whose beauty and nobility of soul the great king had been captivated. Starting from this historical basis, the Song of Songs is in its essential character an ideal representation of human love in the relation of marriage (viii. 6, 7).[8]

5. According to this literal and historical interpretation, Parts I.–III. constitute the first half or one main division of the Poem, which may be called: THE BRIDE AND HER ESPOUSALS WITH THE KING (i. 2—v. 1). The three parts represent each a different scene and distinct action.

Part I. THE BRIDE IN THE KING'S CHAMBERS (i. 2–ii. 7) subdivisible into four sections, corresponding to so many pauses in the action or dialogue.[9]

The scene is laid apparently in a wooded district of northern Palestine near the bride's home, where the king is spending part of the summer season in tents. The three chief speakers of the poem are now introduced in succession : first, A female Chorus (the "daughters of Jerusalem") commence by singing a short ode of two stanzas in praise of the absent king (i. 2–4). The next speaker, the Shulamite maiden ("the bride"), appears to have been recently brought from her country home to the king's pavilion, to be there affianced to him. A brief dialogue ensues between her and the Chorus (i. 5–7). The king himself appears, in the third place, and commending the beauty of the bride, receives from her in return words of praise and affection (i. 16, ii. 7). Throughout

---

[7] *E.g.* the tower of Lebanon (vii. 4), David's tower in Jerusalem (iv. 4), rings and jewels (v. 14), crowns and necklaces (iii. 11, i. 10), palanquins and chariots (iii. 7, 9, i. 9), pillars of marble (v. 15), and every kind of spice and costly perfume (iv. 6, 14, i. 12, 13).

[8] The allegorical method of interpretation depicts the Song to have been in its original purpose an ideal representation of the Communion of love between the Holy One and His Church as first exhibited in the election of Israel, not following, however, any actual developments of that relation in the changing fortunes of the chosen people, but representing (in accordance with the ideal truth of things) any transient disturbance of communion as resulting in the drawing of a closer bond. This is thought to be done by

means of a succession of lyrico-dramatic songs, and under the allegory of the bridal love of the Shulamite and Solomon. The whole conception is thus based on the image referred to in Ex. xxxiv. 14 &c., and Lev. xxvi. 5 &c. (cp. Ex. xx. 5 ; Lev. xviii. 7 ; Num. xiv. 33 ; Deut. xxxii. 16, 31). That such a conception should suddenly spring up in the mind or age of Solomon into this full and vigorous life, is considered possible when the analogous development of the "Chokhmah" (or Hebrew Philosophy) in the same generation, is considered and compared with Pss. xlv. and lxxii. which equally belong to it.

[9] 1. "The Prologue" (i. 2–4) ; 2. "The bride and the daughters of Jerusalem" (i. 5–8) ; 3. "The entrance of the king" (i. 9–14) ; 4. "The bride and the beloved" (i. 15–ii. 7).

this part the bride is represented as of inferior rank to him whom she calls her "beloved," shrinking at times from the splendours of the royal station that awaits her. She speaks of him both as a shepherd and as a king; but, in either character, as of one in whose favour and society she finds supreme satisfaction and entire rest. It is a day of early love, but not that of their first meeting.

Part II. MONOLOGUES OF THE BRIDE (ii. 8–iii. 5), comprising two sections.[1] This part carries us back to an earlier period than the former, and affords a glance at the previous history of the Shulamite in her relations to the king. She describes to the Chorus in two monologues how the beloved had visited her on a spring morning, and how she had afterwards dreamed of him at night.

Part III. ROYAL ESPOUSALS (iii. 6–v. 1), subdivisible into three sections.[2] The scene changes to Jerusalem, whither the bride is brought in royal state to be united to the king in marriage.

Parts IV.–VI. THE BRIDE THE KING'S WIFE (v. 2–viii. 14). The once lowly Shulamite, though now sharing with her beloved the high places of Israel, yet retains that sweetness, humility, and devoted affection, which in other scenes and circumstances had gained his heart. She invites him to revisit with her rural scenes, and share once more their simple pleasures (vii. 11–13).

Part IV. SEEKING AND FINDING

(v. 2–vi. 9) may be divided into three sections.[3] The scene of this part is still Jerusalem. The bride after relating to the chorus a second dream concerning her beloved, pours forth a stream of richest fancies in his praise, who, as she complains, has departed from her. The Chorus offering to aid her in her search of him, suddenly the beloved reappears and gives in his turn the noblest commendations to the bride.

Part V. HOMEWARD THOUGHTS (vi. 10–viii. 4), subdivisible into four sections.[4] The scene is still Jerusalem, or a palace-garden in the neighbourhood; but the bride's thoughts are now reverting to her northern home. She relates how in early spring she had first met the king in a walnut-garden in her own country. The Chorus ask her to perform a sacred dance seemingly well known to the bride and her country-folk. The bride complies, and while she is dancing and the Chorus are singing some stanzas in her praise, the king himself appears. The bride invites him to return with her into the country and to her mother's house.

Part VI. THE RETURN HOME (viii. 5–14), containing three very brief sections.[5] The scene changes to the bride's birthplace, to which she has now returned with the

---

[1] 1. "The visit of the beloved" (ii. 8–17); 2. "The bride's first dream" (iii. 1–5).
[2] 1. "Bridal procession and royal entry" (iii. 6–11); 2. "The bridegroom's commendation of the bride" (iv. 1–7); 3. "The king's invitation" (iv. 8–v. 1).

[3] 1. "The bride's second dream" (v. 2 –8); 2. "The bride's commendation of the beloved" (v. 9–vi. 3); 3. "The beloved's commendation of the bride" (vi. 4–9).
[4] 1. "The Shulamite" (vi. 10–13); 2. "The dance of Mahanaim" (vii. 1–5); 3. "The king and the bride" (vii. 6–10); 4. "The bride's invitation" (vii. 11–viii. 4).
[5] 1. "Last vows sealed" (viii. 5–7); 2. "The bride's intercession" (viii. 8–12); 3. "The Epilogue" (viii. 13, 14).

king. The bride commends her brothers to the good graces of the king, and ends, at his request, by charming his ear with one last song, recalling to his memory a strain of other days (see viii. 14 note).

The history, which forms its groundwork is, however, throughout the poem, contemplated from an ideal point of view ; and the fundamental idea expressed and illustrated is the awful all-constraining, the at once levelling and elevating power of the mightiest and most universal of human affections. The refrains and phrases, to which allusion has been already made, give expression at regular intervals to this idea.[6]

The ideal character of the whole poem is further evidenced by the way in which the chief points whereon the action turns are indicated ;[7] and it will be found that the two halves, or main divisions of the Song have throughout numerous well-balanced contrasts and correspondences.[8]

These and other peculiarities,

---

[6] *E.g.* ii. 7, iii. 5, viii. 4, 7 ; vii. 6 ; viii. 6.

[7] *E.g.* The question of the Chorus (iii. 6, vi. 10, viii. 5).

[8] In the one the bride ascends to Jerusalem and at the king's invitation remains with him there, in the other at her request he returns with her to Shunem ; in the one, the beloved seeks and wins the bride, in the other she seeks and obtains her will from him ; in the one he claims her self-surrender, in the other she demands his vow of fidelity. In the first half of the Song the Chorus sing the praise of the king, in the second they celebrate the beauty of the bride and her triumph over him. Finally, in each of these main divisions the bride relates to her companions a significant dream in order more fully to express her feelings towards the beloved (iii. 1-5, v. 2-8), and in each she sings at his request a strain of peculiar import which seems to have a special music for his ear (ii. 17, viii. 14).

which impart to the Song of Songs its unique and enigmatical character, seem chiefly due to its idealizing treatment of an actual history felt at the time, and especially by the writer, to be profoundly interesting and significant.

Further, that the history thus idealized and the form in which it is presented have meanings beyond themselves and point to something higher, has ever been a deep-seated conviction in the mind both of the Church and of the Synagogue.

The two axes, so to speak, on which the main action of the poem appears alternately to revolve, may be found in the king's invitation to the bride on bringing her to Jerusalem (iv. 8), and in the bride's to the king in recalling him to Shunem (vii. 11–13, viii. 2) ; in these two invitations and their immediate consequences — the willing obedience of the bride and the ready condescension of the king, the first surrender on her part and the final vow on his—the writer of the Song seems to have intended to exhibit the two-fold energy, both for elevation and abasement, of that affection, to the delineation of which his work is dedicated. The omnipotent, transforming, and yet conserving power of faithful love is here seen in like yet diverse operation in the two personalities through whom it is exhibited. In the case of the bride we see the lowly rejoicing in unforeseen elevation without loss of virginal simplicity, in that of the beloved the highest is made happy through self-abasement without compromise of kingly honour.

It is then no mere fancy, which for so many ages past has been wont to find in the pictures and melodies of the Song of Songs types and echoes of the actings and emotions of the highest Love, of Love Divine, in its relations to Humanity. Christians may trace in the noble and gentle history thus presented foreshadowings of the infinite condescensions of Incarnate Love ; — that Love which, first stooping in human form to visit us in our low estate in order to seek out and win its object (Ps. cxxxvi. 23), and then raising along with itself a sanctified Humanity to the Heavenly Places (Eph. ii. 6), is finally awaiting there an invitation from the mystic Bride to return to earth once more and seal the Union for Eternity (Rev. xxii. 17).

THE
SONG OF SOLOMON.

^a 1 Kin. 4. 32. **CHAP. 1.** THE ^asong of songs, which *is* Solomon's.

2 Let him kiss me with the kisses of his mouth:

^b ch. 4. 10.   ^bFor ¹thy love *is* better than wine.

3 Because of the savour of thy good ointments
Thy name *is as* ointment poured forth,
Therefore do the virgins love thee.

^c Hos. 11. 4.
John 6. 44.
& 12. 32.
^d Phil. 3. 12,
13, 14.
^e Ps. 45. 14,
15.
John 14. 2.
Eph. 2. 6.

4 ^cDraw me, ^dwe will run after thee:
The king ^ehath brought me into his chambers:
We will be glad and rejoice in thee,
We will remember thy love more than wine:
²The upright love thee.

5 I *am* black, but comely, O ye daughters of Jerusalem,
As the tents of Kedar, as the curtains of Solomon.

6 Look not upon me, because I *am* black,
Because the sun hath looked upon me:
My mother's children were angry with me;
They made me the keeper of the vineyards;

¹ Heb. *thy loves.*   ² Or, *they love thee uprightly.*

I. 1. The "Song of songs," *i.e.* the best or most excellent of songs.

which is Solomon's] Literally, "to" or "for Solomon," *i.e.* belonging to Solomon as its author or concerning him as its subject. In a title or inscription, the former interpretation is to be preferred.

FIRST PART. I. 2—II. 7.

2–4. THE PROLOGUE. — The Song commences with two stanzas in praise of the king (now absent) by a Chorus of virgins belonging to the royal household. Expositors, Jewish and Christian, interpret the whole as spoken by the Church of the Heavenly Bridegroom.

2. *Let him kiss me*] Christian expositors have regarded this as a prayer of the Church under the old Covenant for closer communion with the Godhead through the Incarnation. Thus St. Gregory, "Every precept of Christ received by the Church is as one of His kisses."

thy love] Better as margin, *i.e.* thy endearments or tokens of affection are more desired than any other delights.

3. *Because* &c.] Better, **For fragrance are thine ointments good,** making with the clause that follows two steps of a climax: "thy perfumes are good, thy name the best of all perfumes." "Ointments" here are unguents or fragrant oils largely used for anointing at entertainments (cp. Ps. xxiii. 5; Luke vii. 46; John xii. 3).

thy name—poured forth] As unguents are

the sweeter for diffusion, so the king's name the wider it is known.

4. *the king hath brought me*] Made me a member of his household. This is true of every member of the Chorus as well as of the bride.

the upright love thee] Better as in marg., **uprightly do they** (*i.e.* "the virgins" of *v.* 3) **love thee.** Cp. the use of the same word in Ps. lviii. 1; Prov. xxiii. 31.

5–8. This section is made by the Targumist and other Jewish interpreters to adumbrate the condition of Israel in the wilderness; by some Christian expositors, that of the Gentile Church on her first conversion.

5. *I am black* &c.] Dark-hued, as the tents of Kedar with their black goats' hair coverings, rough and weather-stained, "but comely" (beautiful) as the rich hangings which adorn the pavilion of Solomon. Kedar was the name of an Arab tribe (Gen. xxv. 13; Ps. cxx. 5). The word itself signifies "dark" or "black." Possibly "tents of Kedar" stand here poetically for shepherds' tents in general (Isai. lx. 7).

6. *Look not upon me*] In wonder or scorn at my **swarthy** hue. It was acquired in enforced but honest toil: **the sun hath scanned me** (or "glared upon me") with his burning eye. The second word rendered "looked" is a word twice found in Job (xx. 9, xxviii. 7), and indicates in the latter place the piercing glance of a bird of prey.

But mine own vineyard have I not kept.

7 Tell me, O thou whom my soul loveth, where thou feedest,
Where thou makest *thy flock* to rest at noon :
For why should I be ¹as one that turneth aside by the flocks of
thy companions?

8 If thou know not, *f* O thou fairest among women,
Go thy way forth by the footsteps of the flock,
And feed thy kids beside the shepherds' tents.

9 I have compared thee, *g* O my love,
ᵸTo a company of horses in Pharaoh's chariots.

10 ⁱThy cheeks are comely with rows *of jewels*,
Thy neck with chains *of gold*.

11 We will make thee borders of gold with studs of silver.

12 While the king *sitteth* at his table,
My spikenard sendeth forth the smell thereof.

13 A bundle of myrrh *is* my wellbeloved unto me ;
He shall lie all night betwixt my breasts.

¹ Or, *as one that is veiled.*

f ch. 5. 9.
& 6. 1.

g ch. 2. 2, 10,
13.
& 4. 1, 7.
& 5. 2.
& 6. 4.
John 15. 14,
15.
ᵸ 2 Chr. 1.
16, 17.
ⁱ Ezek. 16.
11, 12, 13.

my mother's children] Or, **sons** ; a more affectionate designation than "brothers," and implying the most intimate relationship.

angry] This anger was perhaps but a form of jealous care for their sister's safety (cp. viii. 12). By engaging her in rustic labours they preserved her from idleness and temptation, albeit with a temporary loss of outward comeliness.

mine own vineyard] A figurative expression for herself or her beauty.

7. *whom my soul loveth*] A phrase recurring several times. It expresses great intensity of affection.

feedest] *i.e.* "Pursuest thy occupation as a shepherd ;" so she speaks figuratively of the Son of David. Cp. ii. 16, vi. 3 ; Ps. xxiii. 1.

rest] Or, **lie down** ; a term properly used of the couching of four-footed animals : "thy flock" is here therefore easily understood. Cp. Ezek. xxxiv. 14, 15 ; Ps. xxiii. 2 ; Jer. l. 6.

as one that turneth aside] Or, **goeth astray** like an outcast.

8. The Chorus, and not the king, are the speakers here. Their meaning seems to be : If thy beloved be indeed a shepherd, then seek him yonder among other shepherds, but if a king, thou wilt find him here in his royal dwelling.

9-14. This and the next (i. 15-ii. 7) sections are regarded by ancient commentators (Jewish and Christian) as expressing "the love of espousals" (Jer. ii. 2) between the Holy One and His Church, first in the wilderness of the Exodus, and then in the wilderness of the world (Ezek. xx. 35, 36).

9. Or, **to a mare of mine in the chariots of Pharaoh I liken thee, O my friend.** (The last word is the feminine form of that rendered "friend" at v. 16.) The comparison of the bride to a beautiful horse is singularly like one in Theocritus, and some

have conjectured that the Greek poet, having read at Alexandria the Septuagint Version of the Song, may have borrowed these thoughts from it. If so, we have here the first instance of an influence of sacred on profane literature. The simile is peculiarly appropriate on the lips, or from the pen, of Solomon, who first brought horses and chariots from Egypt (1 K. x. 28, 29). As applied to the bride it expresses the stately and imposing character of her beauty.

10, 11. *rows...borders*] The same Heb. word in both places ; ornaments forming part of the bride's head-dress, probably strings of beads or other ornaments descending on the cheeks. The introduction of "jewels" and "gold" in *v.* 10 injures the sense and destroys the climax of *v.* 11, which was spoken by a chorus (hence "we," not "I," as when the king speaks, *v.* 9). They promise the bride ornaments more worthy and becoming than the rustic attire in which she has already such charms for the king : "Ornaments of gold will we make for thee with studs (or ' points ') of silver." The "studs" are little silver ornaments which it is proposed to affix to the golden (cp. Prov. xxv. 12), or substitute for the strung beads of the bride's necklace.

12-14. The bride's reply (*v.* 12) may mean, "While the king reclines at the banquet I anoint him with my costliest perfume, but he has for me a yet sweeter fragrance" (*vv.* 13, 14). According to Origen's interpretation, the bride represents herself as anointing the king, like Mary (John xii. 3), with her most precious unguents.

spikenard] An unguent of great esteem in the ancient world, retaining its Indian name in Hebrew, Greek and Latin. It is obtained from an Indian plant now called *jatamansi*.

13. Render : **A bag of myrrh is my beloved to me, which lodgeth in my bosom.**

14 My beloved *is* unto me *as* a cluster of [1]camphire in the vineyards
of En-gedi.

k ch. 4. 1.
& 5. 12.

15 [k]Behold, thou *art* fair, [2]my love;
Behold, thou *art* fair; thou *hast* doves' eyes.

16 Behold, thou *art* fair, my beloved, yea, pleasant:
Also our bed *is* green.

17 The beams of our house *are* cedar,—*and* our [3]rafters of fir.

CHAP. 2. I *AM* the rose of Sharon,—*and* the lily of the valleys.

2 As the lily among thorns,—so *is* my love among the daughters.

3 As the apple tree among the trees of the wood,
So *is* my beloved among the sons.
[4]I sat down under his shadow with great delight,

a Rev. 22.
1, 2.

*a*And his fruit *was* sweet to my [5]taste.

4 He brought me to the [5]banqueting house,
And his banner over me *was* love.

---

[1] Or, *cypress*, ch. 4. 13.　　[3] Or, *galleries.*　　[5] Heb. *palate.*
[2] Or, *my companion.*　　[4] Heb. *I delighted and sat down, &c.*　　[6] Heb. *house of wine.*

---

14. *camphire*] Rather, *Copher*, from which "cyprus" is probably derived (in marg. mis-spelt "cypress"), the name by which the plant called by the Arabs *henna* was known to the Greeks and Romans. It is still much esteemed throughout the East for the fragrance of its flowers and the dye extracted from its leaves. Engedi was famous for its vines, and the henna may have been cultivated with the vines in the same inclosures.

15.—II. 7. A dialogue ensues between the king and the bride, in which each in succession develops the thought or returns the commendations of the other. Almost every term of praise and endearment here employed may be exactly paralleled by those elsewhere made use of in Scripture to describe the relations of Israel or the Church to the Heavenly Bridegroom.

15. Outward beauty is of course the first here thought of; but this outward fairness is the symbol and accompaniment of an inward beauty indicated in the words **thine eyes are doves,** *i.e.* innocent, meek, and loving. The bride is herself called "a dove" (ii. 14 and vi. 9), as is the Church of Israel (Ps. lxxiv. 19; cp. Ps. lxviii. 13).

16. The bride's reply. Cp. Isai. v. 1 and xxxiii. 17, both, perhaps, conscious references to this Song, Isaiah being the only prophet who thus speaks of the Holy One of Israel by the term constantly employed by the bride throughout the Song to designate him "whom her soul loveth."

yea, pleasant] More than corporeally beautiful, full of moral grace and charm (cp. 2 Sam. i. 23; Pss. xxvii. 4, xc. 17). "Christ is beautiful," says Bede, "in His Divinity, pleasant in His Humanity."

our bed is green] The epithet is appropriate for a bank or natural bed of grass and flowers.

17. The king replies, "The tall umbrageous forest-trees shut us in, as we sit together on this grassy bed, like the roof and walls of a many-chambered house, while cypress avenues on every side seem like the long-drawn corridors of a stately palace."

II. 1. The division of the chapters is unfortunate; ch. ii. ought to have begun at i. 15, or ch. i. to have been continued to ii. 7. The bride replies, "And I am like a lovely wild flower springing at the root of the stately forest-trees." The majority of Christian fathers assigned this verse to the king (Christ). Hebrew commentators generally assign it to the bride. It is quite uncertain what flower is meant by the word rendered (here and Isai. xxxv. 1) "rose." The etymology is in favour of its being a bulbous plant [the white narcissus, Conder]. "Sharon" is usually the proper name of the celebrated plain from Joppa to Cæsarea, between the hill-country and the sea, and travellers have remarked the abundance of flowers with which this plain is still carpeted in spring. But in the time of Eusebius and Jerome there was a smaller plain of Sharon (Saron) situated between Mount Tabor and the sea of Tiberias, which would be very near the bride's native home if that were Shunem.

2. The king resumes, taking up the bride's comparison: "As the lily excels in beauty the thorny shrubs among which it grows, so my friend excels her companions."

3-7. The bride's answer: "As the 'tappuach' with its fragrant fruit excels the barren trees of the wild wood, so my beloved his associates and friends &c." "Tappuach" may in early Hebrew have been a generic name for apple, quince, citron, orange &c.

4. *his banner*] As the standard is the rallying-point and guide of the individual sol-

5 Stay me with flagons, [1]comfort me with apples :
  For I *am* sick of love.
6 [b]His left hand *is* under my head,   [b] ch. 8. 3.
  And his right hand doth embrace me.
7 [2][c]I charge you, O ye daughters of Jerusalem,   [c] ch. 3. 5.
  By the roes, and by the hinds of the field,   & 8. 4.
  That ye stir not up, nor awake *my* love, till he please.
8 The voice of my beloved ! behold, he cometh
  Leaping upon the mountains, skipping upon the hills.
9 [d]My beloved is like a roe or a young hart :   [d] ver. 17.
  Behold, he standeth behind our wall,
  He looketh forth at the windows,
  [3]Shewing himself through the lattice.
10 My beloved spake, and said unto me,
  [e]Rise up, my love, my fair one, and come away.   [e] ver. 13.
11 For, lo, the winter is past,—the rain is over *and* gone ;

---

[1] Heb. *straw me with*   [2] Heb. *I adjure you.*   [3] Heb. *flourishing.*
    apples.

---

dier, so the bride, transplanted from a lowly station to new scenes of unwonted splendour, finds support and safety in the known attachment of her beloved. His "love" is her "banner." The thought is similar to that expressed in the name "Jehovah-nissi" (Ex. xvii. 15 note).

5. *flagons*] More probably **cakes of raisins** or dried grapes (2 Sam. vi. 19 note ; 1 Chr. xvi. 3 ; Hos. iii. 1). For an instance of the reviving power of dried fruit, see 1 Sam. xxx. 12.

6. Render as a wish or prayer : "O that his left hand were under my head, and that his right hand did embrace me ! " Let him draw me to him with entire affection. Cp. Deut. xxxiii. 27 ; Prov. iv. 8.

7. Render : **I adjure you...by the gazelles, or by the hinds of the field, that ye stir not up nor awaken love until it please.** The A.V., "my love," is misleading. The affection or passion in itself, not its object, is here meant. This adjuration, three times significantly introduced as a concluding formula (marg. reff.), expresses one of the main thoughts of the poem ; namely, that genuine love is a shy and gentle affection which dreads intrusion and scrutiny ; hence the allusion to the gazelles and hinds, shy and timid creatures.
The complementary thought is that of viii. 6, 7, where love is again described, and by the bride, as a fiery principle.

SECOND PART. II. 8—III. 5.

8-17. The bride relates to the Chorus a visit which the beloved had paid her some time previously in her native home. He on a fair spring morning solicits her company. The bride, immersed in rustic toils, refuses for the present, but confessing her love, bids him return at the cool of day. It is a spring-time of affection which is here

described, still earlier than that of the former chapter, a day of pure first-love, in which, on either side, all royal state and circumstance is forgotten or concealed. Hence, perhaps, the annual recitation of the Song of Songs by the Synagogue with each return of spring, at the Feast of Passover, and special interpretations of this passage by Hebrew doctors, as referring to the paschal call of Israel out of Egypt, and by Christian fathers, as foreshadowing the evangelic mysteries of Easter—Resurrection and Regeneration. The whole scene has also been thought to represent the communion of a newly-awakened soul with Christ, He gradually revealing Himself to her, and bidding her come forth into fuller communion.

8. *voice*] Better, **sound.** Not a voice, but the sound of approaching footsteps is meant (cp. "noise," Isai. xiii. 4).

9. *like a roe*] Gazelle (cp. Prov. v. 19 note). The points of comparison here are beauty of form, grace, and speed of movement. In 2 Sam. ii. 18 ; 1 Chr. xii. 8, princes are compared to "gazelles."

wall] The clay-built wall of the house or vineyard of the bride's family, different from the strong wall of a city or fortress (v. 7, viii. 9, 10).

looketh forth at the windows] The meaning evidently is, that he is looking in at, or through, the window from the outside. Cp. v. 4 note.

shewing himself] Or, peering. Some, taking the marginal rendering, imagine that the radiant face of the beloved is thus compared to some beautiful flower entangled in the lattice-work which protects the opening of the window, whence he gazes down upon the bride.

10-13. Arise, my friend, my beautiful one, and come away. The stanza begins

12 The flowers appear on the earth;
     The time of the singing *of birds* is come,
     And the voice of the turtle is heard in our land;
13 The fig tree putteth forth her green figs,
     And the vines *with* the tender grape give a *good* smell.
     f Arise, my love, my fair one, and come away.
14 O my dove, *that art* in the clefts of the rock, in the secret *places*
     of the stairs,
     Let me see thy countenance, *g* let me hear thy voice;
     For sweet *is* thy voice, and thy countenance *is* comely.
15 Take us *h* the foxes, the little foxes, that spoil the vines:
     For our vines *have* tender grapes.
16 *i* My beloved *is* mine, and I *am* his:—He feedeth among the
     lilies.
17 *k* Until the day break, and the shadows flee away,
     Turn, my beloved,
     And be thou *l* like a roe or a young hart
     Upon the mountains ¹of Bether.

CHAP. 3. BY *a* night on my bed I sought him whom my soul loveth:
     I sought him, but I found him not.
2 I will rise now, and go about the city

f ver. 10.

g ch. 8. 13.

h Ps. 80. 13.
Ezek. 13, 4.
Luke 13. 32.

i ch. 6. 3.
& 7. 10.

k ch. 4. 6.

l ver. 9.
ch. 8. 14.

a Is. 26. 9.

¹ Or, *of division.*

---

and ends with this refrain, in which the bride reports the invitation of the beloved that she should come forth with him into the open champaign, now a scene of verdure and beauty, and at a time of mirth and mutual affection. The season indicated by six signs (*vv* 11–13) is that of spring after the cessation of the latter rain in the first or paschal month (Joel ii. 23), *i.e.* Nisan or Abib, corresponding to the latter part of March and early part of April. Cyril interpreted *vv*. 11, 12 of our Lord's Resurrection in the spring.

12. *The time of the singing* &c.] *i.e.* The song of pairing birds. This is better than the rendering of the ancient Versions, " the pruning time is come."

13. *The vines* &c.] **The vines in blossom give forth fragrance.** The fragrance of the vine blossom ("semadar"), which precedes the appearance of "the tender grape," is very sweet but transient.

14. *the secret places of the stairs*] A hidden nook approached by a zig-zag path. The beloved urges the bride to come forth from her rock-girt home.

15. The bride answers by singing what appears to be a fragment of a vine-dresser's ballad, insinuating the vineyard duties imposed on her by her brethren (i. 6), which prevent her from joining him. The destructive propensities of foxes or jackals in general are referred to, no grapes existing at the season indicated. Allegorical interpretations make these foxes symbolize "false teachers " (cp. Ezek. xiii. 4).

16. *feedeth among the lilies*] Pursues his occupation as a shepherd among congenial scenes and objects of gentleness and beauty.

17. *Until the day break*] Or, rather, **until the day breathe,** *i.e.* until the fresh evening breeze spring up in what is called (Gen. iii. 8) "the cool" or **breathing time of the day.**

and the shadows flee] *i.e.* Lengthen out, and finally lose their outlines with the sinking and departure of the sun (cp. Jer. vi. 4). As the visit of the beloved is most naturally conceived of as taking place in the early morning, and the bride is evidently dismissing him till a later time of day, it seems almost certain that this interpretation is the correct one which makes that time to be evening after sunset. The phrase recurs in iv. 6.

mountains of Bether] If a definite locality, identical with Bithron, a hilly district on the east side of the Jordan valley (2 Sam. ii. 29), not far from Mahanaim (vi. 13 marg.). If used in a symbolical sense, mountains of "separation," dividing for a time the beloved from the bride. This interpretation seems to be the better, though the local reference need not be abandoned.

III. 1–5. The bride relates to the Chorus what appears to be an imaginary occurrence transacted in a dream (like that of v. 2–8). The Targum takes this section to be typical of the wanderings of Israel after the Holy One in the wilderness, as the next (*vv*. 6–11) is made to represent their entrance into the land.

1. *By night*] *i.e.* In the night-hours.

In the streets, and in the broad ways
I will seek him whom my soul loveth:
I sought him, but I found him not.
3 [b]The watchmen that go about the city found me: [b] ch. 5. 7.
 To whom I said, Saw ye him whom my soul loveth?
4 *It was* but a little that I passed from them,
 But I found him whom my soul loveth:
 I held him, and would not let him go,
 Until I had brought him into my mother's house,
 And into the chamber of her that conceived me.
5 [c]I charge you, O ye daughters of Jerusalem,   [c] ch. 2. 7.
 By the roes, and by the hinds of the field,   & 8. 4.
 That ye stir not up, nor awake *my* love till he please.

6 [d]Who *is* this that cometh out of the wilderness like pillars of   [d] ch. 8. 5.
    smoke,
 Perfumed with myrrh and frankincense,
 With all powders of the merchant?
7 Behold his bed, which *is* Solomon's;
 Threescore valiant men *are* about it, of the valiant of Israel.
8 They all hold swords, *being* expert in war:
 Every man *hath* his sword upon his thigh because of fear in the
    night.
9 King Solomon made himself [1]a chariot of the wood of Lebanon.
10 He made the pillars thereof *of* silver,
 The bottom thereof *of* gold,—the covering of it *of* purple,
 The midst thereof being paved *with* love,
 For the daughters of Jerusalem.

[1] Or, *a bed.*

---

3. *the city*] One near the bride's native home, possibly Shunem.

4. *I held him*] This begins the fourth stanza. The bride's mother is mentioned again in vi. 9, and viii. 2.

5. See ii. 7 note.

THIRD PART.—III. 6-V. 1.

The principal and central action of the Song; the bride's entry into the city of David, and her marriage there with the king. Jewish interpreters regard this part of the poem as symbolizing the "first" entrance of the Church of the Old Testament into the land of promise, and her spiritual espousals, and communion with the King of kings, through the erection of Solomon's Temple and the institution of its acceptable worship. Christian Fathers, in a like spirit, make most things here refer to the espousals of the Church with Christ in the Passion and Resurrection, or the communion of Christian souls with Him in meditation thereon.

6-11. Two or more citizens of Jerusalem, or the Chorus of youths, companions of the bridegroom, describe the magnificent appearance of the bride borne in a royal litter, and then that of the king in festive joy wearing a nuptial crown.

6. "Wilderness" is here pasture-land in contrast with the cultivated districts and garden-enclosures round the city. Cp. Jer. xxiii. 10; Joel ii. 22; Isai. xlii. 11; Ps. lxv. 12.

pillars of smoke] Here an image of delight and pleasure. Frankincense and other perfumes are burned in such abundance round the bridal equipage that the whole procession appears from the distance to be one of moving wreaths and columns of smoke.

all powders of the merchant] Every kind of spice forming an article of commerce.

7. *bed*] Probably the royal litter or palanquin in which the bride is borne, surrounded by his own body-guard consisting of **sixty mighties of the mighty men of Israel.**

8. *because of fear in the night*] i.e. Against night alarms. Cp. Ps. xci. 5.

9, 10. A stately bed hath king Solomon made for himself of woods (or *trees*) **of the Lebanon.** The word rendered "bed" occurs nowhere else in Scripture, and is of doubtful etymology and meaning. It may denote here (1) the bride's car or litter ; or (2) a more magnificent vehicle provided for her reception on her entrance into the city, and in which perhaps the king goes forth to meet her. It has been made under Solomon's own directions of the costliest woods (ceda and pine) of the Lebanon ; it is furnished with "pillars of silver" supporting

11 Go forth, O ye daughters of Zion,
   And behold king Solomon with the crown wherewith his mother
      crowned him
   In the day of his espousals,
   And in the day of the gladness of his heart.

^a ch. 1. 15.
& 5. 12.

CHAP. **4**. BEHOLD, ^athou *art* fair, my love; behold, thou *art* fair;
   Thou *hast* doves' eyes within thy locks:

^b ch. 6. 5.

   Thy hair *is* as a ^bflock of goats, ¹that appear from mount
      Gilead.

^c ch. 6. 6.

2 ^cThy teeth *are* like a flock *of sheep that are even* shorn, which
      came up from the washing;
   Whereof every one bear twins, and none *is* barren among them.

3 Thy lips *are* like a thread of scarlet, and thy speech *is* comely:

^d ch. 6. 7.

   ^dThy temples *are* like a piece of a pomegranate within thy locks.

^e ch. 7. 4.
^f Neh. 3. 19.

4 ^eThy neck *is* like the tower of David builded ^ffor an armoury,
   Whereon there hang a thousand bucklers, all shields of mighty
      men.

^g See Prov.
5. 19.
ch. 7. 3.
^h ch. 2. 17.

5 ^gThy two breasts *are* like two young roes that are twins,
   Which feed among the lilies.

6 ^hUntil the day ²break, and the shadows flee away,
   I will get me to the mountain of myrrh, and to the hill of
      frankincense.

ⁱ Eph. 5. 27.

7 ⁱThou *art* all fair, my love;—*there is* no spot in thee.

8 Come with me from Lebanon, *my* spouse, with me from
      Lebanon:

¹ Or, *that eat of, &c.*   ² Heb. *breathe.*

---

a "baldachin" or "canopy of gold" (not "bottom" as in A.V.), and with "a seat (not 'covering') of purple cushions," while "its interior is paved with (mosaic work, or tapestry of) love from (not 'for') the daughters of Jerusalem;" the meaning being that this part of the adornment is a gift of love, whereby the female Chorus have testified their goodwill to the bride, and their desire to gratify the king.

11. *daughters of Zion*] So called here to distinguish them from the bride's companions, who are always addressed by her as "daughters of Jerusalem."

his mother] Bathsheba (1 K. i. 11). This is the last mention of her in sacred history.

IV. 1–6. The king in a lyric song of five stanzas commends the beauty of the bride.

1. *Thou hast doves' eyes* &c.] **Thine eyes are doves behind thy veil.** So also in *v.* 3, vi. 7; Isai. xlvii. 2, "veil" is better than "locks."

that appear from &c.] Or, "that couch upon Mount Gilead." The point of comparison seems to be the multitudinousness of the flocks seen browsing on the verdant slopes of the rich pasture-lands (Num. xxxii. 1; Mic. vii. 14).

2. *Whereof* &c.] Or, "all of them are equal pairs, and none is bereft among

them," *i.e.* none has lost her mate. The points of comparison in this simile are of course brilliant whiteness, regularity, and completeness of number.

3. *thy speech is comely*] Perhaps, "thy mouth," *i.e.* the organ of speech.

4. The "tower of David" may be that mentioned in Neh. iii. 25–27; Mic. iv. 8. For the custom of hanging shields and other weapons in and upon buildings suited for the purpose, see Ezek. xxvii. 10, 11.

7—V. 1. The king meeting the bride in the evening of the same day, expresses once more his love and admiration in the sweetest and tenderest terms and figures. He calls her now "bride" (spouse, *v.* 8) for the first time, to mark it as the hour of their espousals, and "sister-bride" (spouse, *vv.* 9, 10, 12, v. 1), to express the likeness of thought and disposition which henceforth unites them. At the same time he invites her to leave for his sake her birthplace and its mountain neighbourhood, and live henceforth for him alone.

8. The order and collocation of words in the Hebrew is grand and significant. **With me from Lebanon, O bride, with me from Lebanon thou shalt come, shalt look around (or wander forth) from the height** (lit. "head") **of Amana, from the height of Shenir and Hermon, from dens of lions, from mountain-haunts of leopards.** It is

Look from the top of Amana, from the top of Shenir [k]and
Hermon,
From the lions' dens, from the mountains of the leopards.

9 Thou hast [1]ravished my heart, my sister, *my* spouse;
Thou hast ravished my heart with one of thine eyes,
With one chain of thy neck.

10 How fair is thy love, my sister, *my* spouse!
[l]How much better is thy love than wine!
And the smell of thine ointments than all spices!

11 Thy lips, O *my* spouse, drop *as* the honeycomb:
[m]Honey and milk *are* under thy tongue;
And the smell of thy garments *is* [n]like the smell of Lebanon.

12 A garden [2]inclosed *is* my sister, *my* spouse;
A spring shut up, a fountain sealed.

13 Thy plants *are* an orchard of pomegranates, with pleasant
fruits;

14 [3]Camphire, with spikenard, spikenard and saffron;
Calamus and cinnamon, with all trees of frankincense;
Myrrh and aloes, with all the chief spices:

15 A fountain of gardens, a well of [o]living waters,
And streams from Lebanon.

16 Awake, O north wind; and come, thou south;
Blow upon my garden, *that* the spices thereof may flow out.

[k] Deut. 3. 9.

[l] ch. 1. 2.

[m] Prov. 24.
13, 14.
ch. 5. 1.

[n] Gen. 27. 27.
Hos. 14. 6, 7.

[o] John 4. 10.
& 7. 38.

---

[1] Or, *taken away my heart.*   [2] Heb. *barred.*   [3] Or, *cypress,* ch. 1. 14.

---

evidently a solemn invitation from the king in the sense of Ps. xlv. 10, 11. Four peaks in the same mountain-system are here named as a poetical periphrasis for northern Palestine, the region in which is situated the native home of the bride. (1) Amana (or Abana, 2 K. v. 12), that part of the Anti-libanus which overlooks Damascus. (2) Shenir or Senir, another peak of the same range (according to Deut. iii. 9, the Amorite name for Hermon, but spoken of here and 1 in Chro. v. 23 as distinct from it). (3) Hermon, the celebrated mountain which forms the culminating point of the Anti-libanus, on the north-eastern border of the Holy Land. (4) Lebanon, properly the western range overlooking the Mediterranean, but here used as a common designation for the whole mountain-system. Leopards are still not unfrequently seen there, but the lion has long since disappeared.

9—11. The similes employed refer to the graces of adornment, speech, and gesture, as expressions of inward character and sentiment.

9. *with one of thine eyes*] Rather, **with one look of thine.**

11. *honeycomb*] Lit. **Thy lips distil a dropping** (of pure honey). Cp. marg. reff.

12—15. The loveliness and purity of the bride are now set forth under the image of a paradise or garden fast barred against intruders, filled with rarest plants of excellent fragrance, and watered by abundant streams. Cp. Prov. v. 15-20.

12. *a fountain sealed*] *i.e.* A well-spring

covered with a stone (Gen. xxix. 3), and sealed with "the king's own signet" (Dan. vi. 17; cp. Matt. xxvii. 66).

13. *orchard*] This is the rendering here and in Eccles. ii. 5 of "pardes" (see Neh. ii. 8 note). The pomegranate was for the Jews a sacred fruit, and a characteristic product of the Land of Promise (cp. Exod. xxviii. 33, 34; Num. xx. 5; Deut. viii. 8; 1 K. vii. 18, 20). It is frequently mentioned in the Song, and always in connexion with the bride. It abounds to this day in the ravines of the Lebanon.

camphire] **Cyprus.** See i. 14 note.

13-15. Seven kinds of spices (some of them with Indian names, *e.g.* aloes, spikenard, saffron) are enumerated as found in this symbolic garden. They are for the most part pure exotics which have formed for countless ages articles of commerce in the East, and were brought at that time in Solomon's ships from southern Arabia, the great Indian Peninsula, and perhaps the islands of the Indian Archipelago. The picture here is best regarded as a purely ideal one, having no corresponding reality but in the bride herself. The beauties and attractions of both north and south,—of Lebanon with its streams of sparkling water and fresh mountain air, of En-gedi with its tropical climate and henna plantations, of the spice-groves of Arabia Felix, and of the rarest products of the distant mysterious Ophir,—all combine to furnish one glorious representation, "Thou art all fair!"

16. The bride's brief reply, declaring her

p ch. 5. 1.

> *p*Let my beloved come into his garden,
> And eat his pleasant fruits.

a ch. 4. 16.

Chap. 5. I *a*AM come into my garden, my sister, *my* spouse:
I have gathered my myrrh with my spice;

b ch. 4. 11.

*b*I have eaten my honeycomb with my honey;
I have drunk my wine with my milk:

c Luke 15. 7, 10.
John 3. 29. & 15. 14.
d Rev. 3. 20.

Eat, O *c*friends; drink, ¹yea, drink abundantly, O beloved.

2 I sleep, but my heart waketh:
It is the voice of my beloved *d*that knocketh, *saying,*
Open to me, my sister, my love, my dove, my undefiled:
For my head is filled with dew,
And my locks with the drops of the night.

3 I have put off my coat; how shall I put it on?
I have washed my feet; how shall I defile them?

4 My beloved put in his hand by the hole *of the door*
And my bowels were moved ²for him.

5 I rose up to open to my beloved;
And my hands dropped *with* myrrh,
And my fingers *with* ³sweet smelling myrrh,
Upon the handles of the lock.

---

¹ Or, *and be drunken* with   ² Or, (as some read) *in me.*   ³ Heb. *passing,* or, *running*
loves.   *about.*

---

affection for the king and willingness to belong to him.

V. **1.** *my honeycomb*] Lit. "my reed," or "my wood," *i.e.* the substance itself, or portions of it in which the comb is formed. The bees in Palestine form their combs not only in the hollows of trees and rocks, but also in reeds by the river-banks. The king's meaning appears to be: "All pleases me in thee, there is nothing to despise or cast away."

Eat, O friends] A salutation from the king to his assembled guests, or to the Chorus of young men his companions, bidding them in the gladness of his heart (iii. 11) partake of the banquet. So ends this day of outward festivity and supreme heart-joy. The first half of the Song of Songs is fitly closed. The second half of the poem commences (*v.* 2) with a change of tone and reaction of feeling similar to that of iii. 1. It terminates with the sealing (viii. 6, 7) of yet deeper love.

Fourth Part. V. 2—VI. 9.

Some time may be supposed to have elapsed since the bride's solemn espousals with the king (iv. 7–v. 1). A transient cloud of doubt or estrangement is now passing over her soul, as by the relation of this dream she intimates to her friends. Ancient allegorical interpreters find here a symbol of the condition and feelings of Israel during the Babylonian Captivity, when the glories and privileges of Solomon's Temple were no more, and the manifested Presence of the Holy One had been withdrawn. Israel in exile seeks the Lord (*v.* 8), and will find Him again in the second Temple (vi. 3–9).

2. *I sleep, but my heart waketh*] A poetical periphrasis for "I dream." Cp. the ancient saying: "Dreams are the vigils of those who slumber, hopes are waking dreams."

the voice] Or, "sound." Cp. ii. 8, note. She hears him knocking before he speaks.

my undefiled] Lit. "my perfect one." Vulg. "immaculata mea." Cp. iv. 7.

3. She makes trivial excuses, as one in a dream.

4. *put in his hand*] **Through** (lit. "from") **the hole** (of the lock), in order to raise the pins by which the bolt was fastened. The Oriental lock is a hollow piece of wood attached to the doorpost, into which a sliding-bolt is made to run. As soon as the bolt has been driven home a number of pins drop into holes prepared in it for their reception. To raise these pins, and so enable the bolt to be withdrawn, is to unfasten the lock. This is commonly done by means of the key (lit. "opener"), but may often be accomplished by the fingers if dipped in paste or some other adhesive substance. For such a purpose the beloved inserts his fingers here anointed with the costly unguent, which will presently distil on those of the bride when she rises to open to him.

5. *sweet smelling myrrh*] Or (as in margin) "running myrrh," that which first and spontaneously exudes, *i.e.* the freshest, finest myrrh. Even in withdrawing he has left this token of his unchanged love.

6 I opened to my beloved;
  But my beloved had withdrawn himself, *and* was gone:
  My soul failed when he spake:
  e I sought him, but I could not find him;
  I called him, but he gave me no answer.

e ch. 3. 1.

7 *f* The watchmen that went about the city found me,
  They smote me, they wounded me;
  The keepers of the walls took away my vail from me.

f ch. 3. 3.

8 I charge you, O daughters of Jerusalem,
  If ye find my beloved, ¹ that ye tell him,
  That I *am* sick of love.

9 What *is* thy beloved more than *another* beloved, *g* O thou fairest
  among women?
  What *is* thy beloved more than *another* beloved, that thou dost
  so charge us?

g ch. 1. 8

10 My beloved *is* white and ruddy,
  ² The chiefest among ten thousand.
11 His head *is as* the most fine gold,
  His locks *are* ³ bushy, *and* black as a raven.
12 *h* His eyes *are as the eyes* of doves by the rivers of waters,
  Washed with milk, *and* ⁴ fitly set.

h ch. 1. 15.
& 4. 1.

13 His cheeks *are* as a bed of spices, *as* ⁵ sweet flowers:
  His lips *like* lilies, dropping sweet smelling myrrh.
14 His hands *are as* gold rings set with the beryl:
  His belly *is as* bright ivory overlaid *with* sapphires.

---

¹ Heb. *what.*
² Heb. *a standard-bearer.*
³ Or, *curled.*
⁴ Heb. *sitting in fulness, that is, fitly placed, and set as a precious stone in*
  the foil of a ring.
⁵ Or, *towers of perfumes.*

---

8. The bride, now awake, is seeking her beloved. The dream of his departure and her feelings under it have symbolized a real emotion of her waking heart.

V. 9—VI. 3. The bride's commendation of the beloved. In the allegorical interpretations of Jewish expositors all is here spoken by exiled Israel of the Holy One Whose praise she sings "by the waters of Babylon" (Ps. cxxxvii. 1). Christian interpreters apply the description directly to the Incarnate Son, partly in His Eternal Godhead, but chiefly in His risen and glorified Humanity.

10. *My beloved is white and ruddy*] Cp. 1 Sam. xvi. 12; Dan. vii. 9. The complexion most admired in youth. Jewish interpreters remark that He Who is elsewhere called "the Ancient of Days" is here described as the Ever-Young. "White in His virginpurity," says St. Jerome, "and ruddy in His Passion."

the chiefest among ten thousand] Lit. "a bannered one among a myriad;" hence one signalized, a leader of ten thousand warriors.

11. *His head is as the most fine gold*] Perhaps in the sense of noble and precious as the finest gold. Lam. iv. 2.

bushy] Waving like branches of the palm.

12. Or, **His eyes are doves.** The comparison is to doves seen **by streams of water washing in milk** (*i.e.* milk-white), **and sitting on fulness** (*i.e.* on the full or abundant water-flood).

fitly set] This rendering supposes that the eyes within their sockets are compared to precious stones set in the foil of a ring (see marg.); but the other rendering is preferable. The milk-white doves themselves, sitting by full streams of water, or reflected in their flittings athwart the glassy surface, present images of the calm repose and vivid glances of the full pure lustrous eyes of the beloved.

13. *sweet flowers*] Better as in the margin, *i.e.* plants with fragrant leaves and flowers trained on trellis-work.

like lilies] **Are lilies dropping liquid myrrh** (see *v.* 5 note). Perhaps the fragrance of the flowers, or the delicate curl of the liplike petals, is here the point of comparison, rather than the colour.

14. *His hands* &c.] **Are golden rings** or **cylinders.** The fingers of the bent or closed hand are compared to a massive ring or set of rings; or, if outstretched or straightened, to a row of golden rods or cylinders.

the beryl] The *tarshish* (cp. Ex. xxviii. 20), probably the chrysolite of the ancients (so called from its *gold* colour), the modern topaz.

His belly &c.] **His body** (the Hebrew term applies to the whole body, from the shoulders

15 His legs *are as* pillars of marble, set upon sockets of fine gold:
His countenance *is* as Lebanon, excellent as the cedars.
16 ¹His mouth *is* most sweet: yea, he *is* altogether lovely.
This *is* my beloved, and this *is* my friend, O daughters of
Jerusalem.

a ch. 1. 8.

CHAP. 6. WHITHER is thy beloved gone, *a*O thou fairest among
women?
Whither is thy beloved turned aside? that we may seek him
with thee.

2 My beloved is gone down into his garden, to the beds of spices,
To feed in the gardens, and to gather lilies.

b ch. 2. 16.
& 7. 10.

3 *b*I *am* my beloved's, and my beloved *is* mine:
He feedeth among the lilies.

4 Thou *art* beautiful, O my love, as Tirzah,

c ver. 10.

Comely as Jerusalem,—*c*terrible as *an army* with banners.
5 Turn away thine eyes from me, for ²they have overcome me:

d ch. 4. 1.

Thy hair *is* *d*as a flock of goats that appear from Gilead.

e ch. 4. 2.

6 *e*Thy teeth *are* as a flock of sheep which go up from the washing,
Whereof every one beareth twins, and *there is* not one barren
among them.

f ch. 4. 3.

7 *f*As a piece of a pomegranate *are* thy temples within thy locks.
8 There are threescore queens, and fourscore concubines,
And virgins without number.
9 My dove, my undefiled is *but* one;
She *is* the *only* one of her mother,
She *is* the choice *one* of her that bare her.
The daughters saw her, and blessed her;
Yea, the queens and the concubines, and they praised her.

¹ Heb. *His palate.*   ² Or, *they have puffed me up.*

to the thighs) **is a piece of ivory workmanship overlaid with sapphires.** The sapphire of the ancients seems to have been the
lapis lazuli.

15. *His countenance*] Or, **his appearance**
(his whole port and mien, but especially
head and countenance) "is as the Lebanon."

16. *he is altogether lovely*] Lit. **the whole
of him desires or delights**; the plural substantive expressing the notion of the super-
lative. Theodoret, applying to our Lord
the whole description, interprets well its
last term: "Why should I endeavour to
express His beauty piecemeal when He is in
Himself and altogether the One longed-for,
drawing all to love, compelling all to love,
and inspiring with a longing (for His company) not only those who see, but also those
who hear?"

VI. 1, 2. The question put by the
Chorus, and the answer it receives from the
bride, shew that the loss and seeking are not
to be taken too seriously.

4-9. The section might be entitled,
"Renewed declaration of love after brief
estrangement."

4. *Tirzah...Jerusalem*] Named together
as the then two fairest cities of the land.
For Jerusalem compare Ps. xlviii. 2.

"Tirzah" (*i.e.* "Grace" or "Beauty") was
an old Canaanitish royal city (Josh. xii.
24). It became again a royal residence
during the reigns of Baasha and his three
successors in the kingdom of the ten tribes,
and may well therefore have been famed for
its beauty in the time of Solomon.

terrible as &c.] **Awe-inspiring as the
bannered** (hosts). The warlike image, like
others in the Song, serves to enhance the
charm of its assured peace.

5. Even for the king the gentle eyes of
the bride have an awe-striking majesty.
Such is the condescension of love. Now
follows (*vv.* 5-7) the longest of the repetitions which abound in the Song, marking
the continuance of the king's affection as
when first solemnly proclaimed (iv. 1-6).
The two descriptions belong, according to
some (Christian) expositors, to the Church
of different periods, *e.g.* to the primitive
Church in the splendour of her first voca-
tion, and to the Church under Constantine;
other (Jewish) expositors apply them to
"the congregation of Israel" under the first
and second Temples respectively.

9. The king contrasts the bride with the
other claimants for her royal estate or
favour (*v.* 8). She not only outshines them

10 Who *is* she *that* looketh forth as the morning,
Fair as the moon, clear as the sun,
g And terrible as *an army* with banners ?   *g* ver. 4.

11 I went down into the garden of nuts to see the fruits of the
valley,
And *h*to see whether the vine flourished, *and* the pomegranates   *h* ch. 7. 12.
budded.

12 ¹Or ever I was aware, my soul ²made me *like* the chariots of
Ammi-nadib.

13 Return, return, O Shulamite;
Return, return, that we may look upon thee.

What will ye see in the Shulamite?

As it were the company ³of two armies.

¹ Heb. *I knew not.*   ² Or, *set me on the chariots*   ³ Or, *of Mahanaim,*
                              of my willing people.   Gen. 32. 2.

---

all for him, but herself has received from them disinterested blessing and praise.

This passage is invaluable as a divine witness to the principle of monogamy under the Old Testament and in the luxurious age of Solomon.

FIFTH PART. VI. 10—VIII. 4.

The Chorus address the bride here only as the Shulamite, and beg her to perform for their entertainment a sacred dance (see vi. 13) of her own country. The bride, after complying with their request, while they sing some stanzas in her praise (vii. 1-5), and after receiving fresh commendations from the king (vii. 6-10), invites him to return with her to her mother's house (vii. 11–viii. 4). Many Jewish allegorists interpret the whole as referring to the times of the second Temple, and to the present dispersion of Israel, during which, God continuing to vouchsafe His mercy, Israel prays for final restoration, the coming of Messiah, and the glory of the latter day. Christian interpreters have made similar applications to the now militant Church looking for the Second Advent, or to the ancient Synagogue praying for the Incarnation.

10. *as the morning*] The glorious beauty of the bride bursts upon them like a second **dawn**, as she comes forth to meet them at the commencement of another day. Peculiar poetical words are used for "sun" (burning heat) and "moon" (white one). The same terms are applied to sun and moon in Isai. xxiv. 23, xxx. 26.

11-12. The bride's words may be paraphrased : "You speak of me as a glorious beauty ; I was lately but a simple maiden engaged in rustic toils. I went down one day into the **walnut**-garden" (the walnut abounded on the shores of Lake Gennesaret, and is still common in Northern Palestine) " to inspect the young plants of the vale " (*i.e.* the wady, or watercourse, with now verdant banks in the early spring after

the rainy season), "and to watch the budding and blossoming of vine and pomegranate." Cp. ii. 11-13 notes. "Then, suddenly, ere I was myself aware, my soul" (the love-bound heart) "had made me the chariot of a lordly people" (*i.e.* an exalted personage, one who resides on the high places of the earth ; cp. 2 K. ii. 12, xiii. 14, where Elijah and Elisha, as the spiritual leaders of the nation, are "the chariot and horsemen of Israel," cp. also Isai. xxii. 18). This last clause is another instance of the love borrowed from military similitudes in the writer of the Song.

Ammi-nadib] Lit. **my people a noble one.** The reference is either to Israel at large as a wealthy and dominant nation, under Solomon, or to the bride's people (the Shulamites) in particular, to the chief place among whom, by her union with the king, she is now exalted.

13. *Return, return*] About to withdraw, the bride is recalled by the Chorus, desiring yet a little longer to contemplate a grace and beauty which has won all hearts.

Shulamite] Probably the same as "Shunamite," *i.e.* a native of the town or district of Shunem, situated in the territory of Issachar (Josh. xix. 18), on the slopes of the Little Hermon, overlooking the plain of Jezreel. It is now called Sûlem.

see] **Look** or **gaze at.** The bride's modest reply, taking up their words, and wondering at their request. The Chorus answer with a further petition.

As it were the company of two armies] Or, rather, **the dance of Mahanaim** (see margin), a well-known sacred dance, taking its name from the locality in which it originated (Gen. xxxii. 2 ; Josh. xxi. 38). Some, taking "Mahanaim" to be an ordinary designation for "the Angels" or "Angelic Hosts," render here "a dance as it were of angel-choirs," *i.e.* one of peculiar grace and beauty. The former of these interpretations is to be preferred.

a Ps. 45. 13. **CHAP. 7.** HOW beautiful are thy feet with shoes, *a*O prince's
daughter!
The joints of thy thighs *are* like jewels,
The work of the hands of a cunning workman.

2 Thy navel *is like* a round goblet, *which* wanteth not ¹liquor:
Thy belly *is like* an heap of wheat set about with lilies.

b ch. 4. 5.   3 *b*Thy two breasts *are* like two young roes *that are* twins.

c ch. 4. 4.   4 *c*Thy neck *is* as a tower of ivory;
Thine eyes *like* the fishpools in Heshbon, by the gate of Bath-
rabbim:
Thy nose *is* as the tower of Lebanon which looketh toward
Damascus.

5 Thine head upon thee *is* like ²Carmel,
And the hair of thine head like purple;
The king *is* ³held in the galleries.

6 How fair and how pleasant art thou, O love, for delights!

7 This thy stature is like to a palm tree,
And thy breasts to clusters *of grapes.*

8 I said, I will go up to the palm tree,
I will take hold of the boughs thereof:
Now also thy breasts shall be as clusters of the vine,
And the smell of thy nose like apples;

¹ Heb. *mixture.*   ² Or, *crimson.*   ³ Heb. *bound.*

VII. 1-5. The Shulamite complies with
the request of her attendants, and as she
glides before them in the dance, they sing in
further commendation of her beauty of form
and grace of movement. The description in
the original consists, like iv. 1-5, of five
stanzas nearly coinciding with the verses
in the text.

1. *thy feet with shoes*] Or, **thy steps in
the sandals :** the bride's feet are seen in
motion in the dance. "Joints" might be
rendered **circling movements.**

prince's daughter] Or, daughter of a noble;
the bride is of honourable though not of
kingly birth.

like jewels] The image suggested is that of
large well-formed pearls or other jewels
skilfully strung or linked together.

2. Or, "Thy lap is like a moon-shaped
bowl where mixed wine faileth not." The
wine in the bowl rising to the brim adds to
the beauty of the vessel, and gives a more
pleasing image to the eye. Some interpret,
"thy girdle is like a moon-shaped bowl,"
or "bears a moon-shaped ornament" (cp.
Isai. iii. 18).

set about with lilies] The contrast is one of
colours, the flowers, it may be, representing
the purple of the robe. "The heap of wheat
is not seen because covered by the lilies."

4. *a tower of ivory*] **The tower of ivory,**
the allusion being to some particular tower,
built probably by Solomon (1 K. x. 21).

fishpools in Heshbon] Or, simply **pools.**
Among the ruins to the south of Heshbon
still remain a number of deep wells cut in
the rock, and a large reservoir of water.

The simile well sets forth the appearance of
a large clear liquid eye (cp. v. 12 note).

gate of Bath-rabbim]. Perhaps the gate
looking towards Rabbath-Ammon on the
north side of the city, though this does not
agree with the mention of Damascus; or,
the gate of the city "full of people" (Lam. i.
1); or, an expression indicating the gate itself
as the scene of numerous gatherings.

nose] Better perhaps "face" or "brow."

the tower of Lebanon] Possibly "the
house of the forest of Lebanon" or part of
it (1 K. vii. 2, ix. 19), built by Solomon in
the early part of his reign; or possibly a
watchtower erected by David to overawe
Damascus after his war with Hadadezer
(2 Sam. viii. 6).

5. Cp. and contrast with v. 15. The
rendering in the margin takes "Carmel"
as the name of a colour, equivalent to "car-
mine" (rendered "crimson" in 2 Chr. ii.
7, 14, iii. 14). This interpretation is favoured by the parallelism with "purple,"
but removes a beautiful image.

purple] A deep violet black.

the king &c.] Rather, "**A king is bound in
the tresses** or **windings** of thy hair." These
last words indicate the king's approach.

6-10. A brief dialogue; *vv.* 6-9 are
spoken by the king, *v.* 9 and *v.* 10 by the
bride.

6. A general sentiment.

**How fair, and what a charm hast thou,
O love! among delightsome things!**

Cp. ii. 7, viii. 6, 7 notes.

7. *This thy stature*] The king now ad-

9 And the roof of thy mouth like the best wine for my beloved,
    that goeth *down* [1] sweetly,
Causing the lips [2] of those that are asleep to speak.
10 [d]I *am* my beloved's, and [e]his desire *is* toward me.
11 Come, my beloved, let us go forth into the field;
    Let us lodge in the villages.
12 Let us get up early to the vineyards;
    Let us [f]see if the vine flourish, *whether* the tender grape
    [3]appear,
    And the pomegranates bud forth:
There will I give thee my loves.
13 The [g]mandrakes give a smell,
    And at our gates [h]are all manner of pleasant *fruits*, new and
    old,
Which I have laid up for thee, O my beloved.

CHAP. 8. O THAT thou *wert* as my brother, that sucked the breasts
    of my mother!
When I should find thee without, I would kiss thee;
Yea, [4]I should not be despised.
2 I would lead thee, *and* bring thee into my mother's house, *who*
    would instruct me:
I would cause thee to drink of [a]spiced wine of the juice of my
    pomegranate.
3 [b]His left hand *should be* under my head,
    And his right hand should embrace me.
4 [c]I charge you, O daughters of Jerusalem,
    [5]That ye stir not up, nor awake *my* love, until he please.

d ch. 2. 16.
& 6. 3.
e Ps. 45. 11.

f ch. 6. 11.

g Gen. 30. 14.

h Matt. 13. 52.

a Prov. 9. 2.

b ch. 2. 6.

c ch. 2. 7.
& 3. 5.

[1] Heb. *straightly.*
[2] Or, *of the ancient.*
[3] Heb. *open*
[4] Heb. *they should not despise me.*
[5] Heb. *why should ye stir up,* or, *why, &c.*

dresses the bride, comparing her to palm, vine, and apple-tree for nobility of form and pleasantness of fruit; and the utterances of her mouth to sweetest wine.

9. *for my beloved, that goeth down sweetly*] Words of the bride interrupting the king, and finishing his sentence, that goeth smoothly or pleasantly for my beloved. Cp. Prov. xxiii. 31.

10. *his desire is toward me*] All his affection has me for its object. The bride proceeds to exercise her power over his loving will.

11.-VIII. 4. Cp. iv. 8. The bride in her turn invites her beloved to revisit in her company the lowly scenes of pastoral life, out of which his grace had raised her. So in the latter day the Church of the Redeemed in heavenly places will pray for the Lord's return to earth.

12. *the tender grape appear*] Or, the vine-blossom unfold. See ii. 13 note. It is now again the same season as that in which the king had first visited the bride (ii. 8-17). This thought enhances her desire to have him with her there again.

13. *The mandrakes*] Love-apples.

all manner of pleasant fruits] Or, things, both fruits and flowers; "the new" to be freshly gathered, "the old" already laid up in store.

VIII. 1. Royal rank and splendour are grown wearisome. The king once called her "sister" and "sister-bride." Would he were indeed as a "brother," her mother's own child whom she might meet, embrace, and welcome everywhere without restraint or shame. Her love for him is simple, sacred, pure, free from the unrest and the stains of mere earthly passion.

2. *who would instruct me*] Or, thou shouldest teach me (Isai. liv. 13). Some allegorists make the whole passage (vii. 11-viii. 2) a prayer of the Synagogue for the Incarnation of the Word, like i. 2 (see note). Others, a prayer of the Church under both covenants for that complete union with the Incarnate Godhead which is still future.

3. The bride now turns to and addresses the Chorus as before (marg. ref.).

4. *that ye stir not up*] Lit. as in the margin. For "my love" read as before love. The omission of "the roes and hinds" here is noticeable. Hebrew doctors regard this charge here and elsewhere (ii. 7, iii. 5) as an admonition to Israel not to attempt obtaining a possession of, or restoration to, the Promised Land, and union or reunion there with the Holy One, before being inwardly prepared for it by the trials of the wilderness and the exile. This interpreta-

5 *d*Who *is* this that cometh up from the wilderness, leaning
upon her beloved ?

I raised thee up under the apple tree :
There thy mother brought thee forth :
There she brought thee forth *that* bare thee.

6 *e*Set me as a seal upon thine heart,
As a seal upon thine arm :
For love *is* strong as death ;
Jealousy *is* ¹cruel as the grave :
The coals thereof *are* coals of fire,
Which hath a most vehement flame.

7 Many waters cannot quench love,
Neither can the floods drown it :

*f*If a man would give all the substance of his house for love,
It would utterly be contemned.

8 *g*We have a little sister, and she hath no breasts :
What shall we do for our sister in the day when she shall
be spoken for ?

¹ Heb. *hard.*

---

tion comes very near to what appears to be
the genuine literal meaning (see ii. 7 note).
They suppose the words here to be addressed by Messiah to Israel in "the wilderness of the people" (Ezek. xx. 35), in
the latter day, and the former words (iii. 5)
by Moses in the wilderness of Sinai.

SIXTH PART. *vv.* 5–14.

5–7. The scene changes from Jerusalem
to the birthplace of the bride, where she is
seen coming up towards her mother's house,
leaning on the arm of the great king her
beloved.

5. *Who is this*] Cp. and contrast with iii.
6. In the former scene all was splendour
and exaltation, but here condescension,
humility, and loving charm.

I raised thee up &c.] **Beneath this apple-
tree I wakened thee.** The king calls the
bride's attention to a fruit-tree, which they
pass, the trysting-spot of earliest vows in
this her home and birthplace. The Masoretic pointing of the Hebrew text (the most
ancient traditional interpretation) assigns
these words to the bride, but the majority
of Christian Fathers to the king. The
whole passage gains in clearness and dramatic expression by the latter arrangement.

6, 7. The bride says this as she clings to
his arm and rests her head upon his bosom.
Cp. John xiii. 23, xxi. 20. This brief
dialogue corresponds to the longer one (iv.
7–v. 1), on the day of their espousals. Allegorical interpreters find a fulfilment of
this in the close of the present dispensation,
the restoration of Israel to the Land of
Promise, and the manifestation of Messiah
to His ancient people there, or His Second
Advent to the Church. The Targum makes
v. 6 a prayer of Israel restored to the Holy

Land that they may never again be carried
into captivity, and *v.* 7 the Lord's answering
assurance that Israel henceforth is safe.
Cp. Isai. lxv. 24, lxii. 3, 4.

6. The key-note of the poem. It forms
the Old Testament counterpart to St. Paul's
panegyric (1 Cor. xiii.) under the New.

(*a*) Love is here regarded as an universal
power, an elemental principle of all true
being, alone able to cope with the two eternal foes of God and man, Death and his
kingdom.

"For strong as death is love,
Tenacious as Sheôl is jealousy."

"Jealousy" is here another term for
"love," expressing the inexorable force
and ardour of this affection, which can
neither yield nor share possession of its
object, and is identified in the mind of the
sacred writer with Divine or true Life.
(*b*) He goes on to describe it as an all-per-
vading Fire, kindled by the Eternal One,
and partaking of His essence :

"Its brands are brands of fire,
A lightning-flash from Jah."

Cp. Deut. iv. 24. (*c*) This divine principle
is next represented as overcoming in its
might all opposing agencies whatsoever,
symbolized by water. (*d*) From all which it
follows that love, even as a human affection,
must be reverenced, and dealt with so as not
to be bought by aught of different nature ;
the attempt to do this awakening only scorn.

8–12. A brief dialogue commencing with
a question and answer probably made by
brothers of the bride concerning a younger
sister who will soon be old enough to be
asked in marriage. The answer is given in
the form of a parable : "If she be a wall,"
i.e. stedfast in chastity and virtue, one on

9 If she *be* a wall, we will build upon her a palace of silver:
　And if she *be* a door, we will enclose her with boards of cedar.

10 I *am* a wall, and my breasts like towers:
　Then was I in his eyes as one that found [1]favour.

11 Solomon had a vineyard at Baal-hamon;
　*h*He let out the vineyard unto keepers;
　Every one for the fruit thereof was to bring a thousand *pieces* of
　silver.

h Matt. 21. 33.

12 My vineyard, which *is* mine, *is* before me:
　Thou, O Solomon, *must have* a thousand,
　And those that keep the fruit thereof two hundred.

13 Thou that dwellest in the gardens,
　The companions hearken to thy voice:
　*i*Cause me to hear *it*.

i ch. 2. 14.

14 *k 2*Make haste, my beloved,
　And *l*be thou like to a roe or to a young hart
　Upon the mountains of spices.

k See Rev. 22. 17, 20.
l ch. 2. 17.

---

[1] Heb. *peace*.   [2] Heb. *Flee away*.

---

whom no light advances can be made, then let us honour and reward her. This fortress-wall shall be crowned as it were with a tower or battlement of silver. But "if she be a door," light-minded and accessible to seduction (Prov. vii. 11, 12), then let us provide against assailants the protection of a cedar-bar or panel.

10. The bride herself replies with the pride of innocence and virtue already crowned. She has shown herself to be such a fortress-wall as her brothers have alluded to, and her reward has been the royal favour.

11, 12. She next turns to the king, and commends her brothers to his favourable regard by means of another parable. Solomon owns a vineyard in Baal-hamon (possibly Báalbak, or identical with Amana [Conder]), situated in the warm and fertile plains of Cœle-Syria, overshadowed by the heights of Lebanon (iv. 8). This vineyard he has let out to tenants &c.

The bride also has a vineyard of her own (i. 6), her beauty and virtue faithfully guarded by these same brothers in time past. This vineyard now belongs to Solomon. Let him have "the thousand" which is his due—she is indeed herself henceforth entirely his—but let the faithful keepers have their meed as well. At least two hundred silverlings should be theirs—a double tithe of royal praise and honour.

13, 14. The poem having opened with the song of a Chorus in praise of the king (i. 2-4), concludes with a versicle recited by the bride, repeating the last words of her former strain (ii. 17), with one significant change. She no longer thinks of the possibility of separation. The "Mountains of Bether" (division) of ii. 17, are now "Mountains of Besamim" (spices). His haunts and hers are henceforth the same (cp. iv. 6).

JEREMIAH.

INTRODUCTION.

1. JEREMIAH was by birth a priest, and dwelt at Anathoth, a village in the tribe of Benjamin, about three miles north of Jerusalem. The name is not found till the time of David, when, however, it seems to have become common (see 1 Chr. xii. 4, 10, 13), and most probably it signifies *Jehovah shall exalt*.

It is a subject of dispute whether or not Hilkiah, the father of Jeremiah, was the High Priest of that name, who found the Book of the Law in the Temple (2 K. xxii. 8). It is at least possible that he was. The more than ordinary respect felt for the prophet by Jehoiakim and Zedekiah, and other reasons support the supposition that Jeremiah was a man of high birth.

His call to the prophetic office came in the thirteenth year of Josiah. It was a time when danger was once again gathering round the little kingdom of Judah, and to Jeremiah was assigned a more directly political position than to any other of "the goodly fellowship of the prophets;" as both the symbols shewn to him and the very words of his institution prove. If we glance back at the previous history, we find that the destruction of Sennacherib's army in the fourteenth year of Hezekiah (B.C. 693), though it had not freed the land from predatory incursions, had nevertheless put an end to all

serious designs on the part of the Assyrians to reduce it to the same condition as that to which Salmaneser had reduced Samaria. The danger of Judæa really rose from Egypt on the one hand and Babylon on the other. In Egypt Psammetichus put an end to the subdivision of the country, and made himself sole master in the seventeenth year of Assurbanipal (B.C. 649), being the twenty-fourth of Manasseh. As he reigned for fifty-four years he was—during the last eighteen or nineteen years of his life—contemporary with Josiah, but it was his successor Necho who slew Josiah at Megiddo. Meanwhile as Egypt grew in strength so Nineveh declined, partly from the effects of the Scythian invasion, but still more from the growing power of the Medes, and from Babylon having achieved its independence. Two years after the battle of Megiddo, Nineveh fell before a combined attack of the Medes under Cyaxares and the Babylonians under Nabopalassar. But Nabopalassar does not seem to have been otherwise a warlike king, and Egypt remained the dominant power till the fourth year of Jehoiakim. In that year, B.C. 586 according to the cylinders, Nebuchadnezzar defeated Necho at Carchemish. Having peaceably succeeded his father he returned to Judæa, and Jehoiakim became his vassal. After three years of servitude Jehoiakim rebelled (2 K. xxiv. 1), and died. Three months afterwards his son Jehoiachin, the queen-mother, and a large number of nobles and artificers, were carried captive to Babylon.

The growth of Egypt into a first-rate power under Psammetichus (ii. 18, 36), raised the question of a close alliance with him. The youthful Jeremiah gave his voice against it. Josiah recognised that voice as inspired, and obeyed. His obedience cost him his life at Megiddo ; but four years later Necho was defeated by Nebuchadnezzar at Carchemish. On that day the fate of the Jewish nation was decided, and the primary object of Jeremiah's mission then ceased.

The ministry of Jeremiah really belonged to the last eighteen years of Josiah's reign. Judah's probation was then going on, her salvation still possible ; though each year Judah's guilt became heavier, her condemnation more certain. But to the eye of man her punishment seemed more remote than ever. Jehoiakim was the willing vassal of Egypt, the supreme power. No wonder that, being an irreligious man, he scorned all Jeremiah's predictions of utter and early ruin : no wonder that he destroyed Jeremiah's roll, as the record of the outpourings of mere fanaticism. It was his last chance, his last offer of mercy : and as he threw the torn fragments of the roll on the fire he threw there in symbol his royal house, his doomed city, the Temple, and all the people of the land. It was in this fourth year of Jehoiakim that Jeremiah boldly foretold the greatness of Nebuchadnezzar's empire, and the wide limits over which it would extend. This pro-

phecy (ch. xxv.) placed his life in danger, so that " the Lord hid" him and Baruch (xxxvi. 26). When Jeremiah appears again Nebuchadnezzar was advancing upon Jerusalem to execute the prophecy contained in xxxvi. 30, 31. And with the death of Jehoiakim the first period of Judah's history was brought to a close. Though Jeremiah remained with Zedekiah, and tried to influence him for good, yet his mission was over. He testifies himself that the Jewish Church had gone with Jehoiachin to Babylon. Zedekiah and those who remained in Jerusalem were but the refuse of a fruit basket from which everything good had been culled (ch. xxiv.), and their destruction was a matter of course. Jeremiah held no distinctive office towards them.

Such was the political state of things in the evil days in which Jeremiah was commissioned to make Jehovah's last appeal to His Covenant-people : but to understand the prophet's position fully, the moral change which had come over the Jews, and which was the real cause of the nation's ruin, must be noted.

Up to the time of Manasseh, though there had been bad as well as good kings, and though there had probably always been a certain amount of nature-worship and of unauthorized rites upon the hill-tops, yet the service of Jehovah had been the sole established and even dominant religion of the people. But upon his accession a new order of things began ; and, in spite of his repentance, it continued throughout his long reign of fifty-five years. Not only was there the open establishment of idolatry, but a reign of terror commenced, during which not only the prophets, but all who were distinguished for religion and virtue, were cruelly murdered. The reign of Manasseh was important in another particular. During it the land was slowly recovering from its utterly exhausted state at the end of the Assyrian wars; and when Josiah came to the throne, there was both great prosperity among the people, and also a better state of feeling. Great and good men stood forward as leaders in defence of their national religion and Covenant-God : and the nation itself had become as dissatisfied with Baal and Moloch as their forefathers had been with Jehovah. In his eighteenth year Josiah entered with all his heart into the work of restoring the national religion, and laboured with a stern earnestness to remove every vestige of idol-worship from the land. This was half the work : the other half was entrusted to Jeremiah. The king could cleanse the land : the word of God speaking to their consciences could alone cleanse men's hearts. The office then of Jeremiah was to shew that a change of morals must accompany the public reformation effected by Josiah, or it would not be accepted.[1]

It was in Josiah's thirteenth year, when entire quiet prevailed in the political world, and Jeremiah was himself little more than twenty years of age, that his appointment took place, and two symbols were shewn him by which he learned the main reasons why the word of Jehovah was entrusted to his charge. By the first, the branch of an almond-tree, he was taught that judgment was awake in the land. Judah must decide at once

whether she will serve Jehovah or Baalim, and her choice must be real. If she choose Jehovah, she must prove that such is her choice by worshipping Him in purity and holiness. For, secondly, by the symbol of the seething caldron he learned that a dreadful calamity was impending over his country. There are in Jewish history two overwhelming catastrophes, the first, the destruction of the holy city and Temple by Nebuchadnezzar ; the second, the destruction of the holy city and Temple by Titus. The preaching of Jeremiah caused the first to be a new birth to the chosen people : the preaching of Christ caused the Christian Church to spring forth from the other. But had their preaching been more generally listened to, Jerusalem might each time have been saved. It was because men passed on without heeding the warning that the nation thus fell twice (Luke xix. 42).[2]

Jeremiah was not, however, one "dumb before the shearers, and that opened not his mouth" (Isai. liii. 7). Of all the prophets there is not one who so frankly lays open

---

[1] Cp. iv. 3, v. 1, vii. 9–11, ix. 4, 5.

[2] As in each case only a small minority was saved in the general ruin, the office both of Jeremiah and of our Lord is described by the same metaphor. In vi. 27–30 the prophet compares himself to a smelter, who uses all the resources of his art to extract from the ore the precious silver, but in vain. In similar terms Malachi compares our Lord to a refiner and purifier of silver (Mal. iii. 2, 3, iv. 1). The Jews understood that Jeremiah was a type of the Messiah, and surrounded his remembrance with many mythical legends (2 Macc. ii. 1–8, xv. 13–16) ; and when they asked John, "Art thou that prophet?" (John i. 21) there can be little doubt that it was Jeremiah whom they were expecting to appear again. Many Jewish and some Christian expositors see in Jeremiah the "servant of Jehovah," whose sorrows are so graphically set forth in the fifty-third chapter of Isaiah.

to us his brooding melancholy nature. He discloses to us his inmost thoughts. We find him sensitive to a most painful degree, timid, shy, hopeless, desponding, constantly complaining, and dissatisfied with the course of events, with the office which had been thrust upon him, and with the manner of the divine Providence.[3] Jeremiah was not one whose sanguine temperament made him see the bright side of things, nor did he quickly find peace and happiness in doing his Master's will. And yet we never find him rebuked, because he was doing his duty to the utmost extent of his powers. Timid in resolve he was unflinching in execution : as fearless when he had to face the whole world as he was dispirited and prone to murmuring when alone with God. He is a noble example of the triumph of the moral over the physical nature. His whole strength lay in his determination to do what was right at whatever cost. He made everything yield to that which his conscience told him he ought to do.

Danger, opposition, mockery without : fear, despondency, disappointment within, availed nothing to shake his constant mind. The sense of duty prevailed over every other consideration ; and in no saint were the words of St. Paul (2 Cor. xii. 9) better exemplified.

Much the same characteristics may be seen in Jeremiah's style of writing. He did not possess those gifts which make the orator.[4] He had none of that strength and vigour, nor of that warmth of imagination, which characterize Isaiah and Micah. His usual method is to set his main thought before the mind in a succession of images. They seldom grow out of one another, but simply form a succession of illustrations, each of which is full of poetry, but with this remarkable peculiarity, that Jeremiah never uses his picture as such, but mixes up with it words which are appropriate, not to the metaphor, but to the idea which he is illustrating (*e.g.*, i. 15, vi. 3-5). His simile is constantly dismissed almost before it has been fully presented to the mind in order that he may declare his meaning in plain and unvarnished prose. This fulness of illustration, often diffuse and inconsecutive, is exactly in harmony with Jeremiah's subject. No lot could have been more dreary to a

---

[3] *e.g.*, He accuses God of injustice because all his efforts seem to be without result. Bad men prospered (xii. 1) ; false prophets resisted those who had the divine commission (xiv. 13). No miracle was wrought by him or for him : no prediction was suddenly verified in a startling way : no demonstration of power was granted to him in common with the prophets of old, and therefore "the word of the Lord was made a reproach unto him, and a derision daily" (xx. 7). His one task was to foretell the downfall of his country because of its persistence in sin : and his reward was to be a man of strife and of contention to the whole earth : every one "doth curse me" (xv. 10 ; cp. xx. 7). And for this apparent failure he was not prepared. He contrasts the joy with which he had entered upon his office with the disappointment of his hopes (xv. 15-18, xvii. 16) ; and when put in the stocks (xx. 2), he even accuses God of deceiving him, and determines to abandon his office (do. 7-18).

[4] Jeremiah has the peculiar habit of repeating himself ; cp. :

Chap.		Chap.
ii. 28	repeated in	xi. 13.
v. 9, 29	,,	,, ix. 9.
vi. 13-15	,,	,, viii. 10-12.
vii. 14	,,	,, xxvi. 6.
xi. 20	,,	,, xx. 12.
xv. 2	,,	,, xliii. 11.
xvi. 14, 15	,,	,, xxiii. 7, 8.
xvii. 25	,	,, xxii. 4.
xxiii. 19, 20	,,	,, xxx. 23, 24.
xxx. 11	,,	,, xlvi. 28.
xxxi. 35, 36	,,	,, xxxiii. 25, 26.

man of intense patriotism like Jeremiah than to see the ruin of his country steadily approaching, to mark each step of its advance, to have to point out its causes, and to know the sole remedy, but also to know that none would heed his words. Could he but have witnessed the return of the exiles, and have known that the restoration of the Jewish Church was, humanly speaking, his work, his despondency would have given way to joy. But no such comfort was vouchsafed him. He was required to give up all the innocent joys of life (xv. 17); to abandon the most cherished privilege of a Jew, and live unmarried (xvi. 2); and to abstain even from the civilities and sympathies of society (do. 5); only to be an object of universal abhorrence. This was Jeremiah's calling; not to be a poet or orator, but to persuade men by the force of his moral character, and conquer by suffering. And his style is in keeping with the man. He spake as he thought. Ever brooding over his message to his people it presented itself to his mind in many aspects, but was in substance ever the same. We have no change of subjects in his prophecy. He has but the one cry of Woe! All he can do is to adapt his unvarying tale to the existing state of things, and present it under new images. He is a true poet, but the poet of sorrow. Though sorrow comes but occasionally, yet it comes to all, and then Jeremiah, the prophet of suffering, is full of instruction for us. Perhaps no book of Holy Scripture sets so plainly before men the great issues which depend upon right and wrong.

2. There can be little doubt that the Book of Jeremiah grew out of the roll which Baruch wrote down at the prophet's mouth in the fourth year of Jehoiakim, and which was completed and read before the king in his fifth year, in the ninth month (ch. xxxvi.). This roll contained a record of "all that God had spoken unto Jeremiah against Israel and against Judah and against all the nations" during the twenty-three years which had elapsed since the prophet's call (xxxvi. 2). But as the twenty-first chapter was written in the reign of Zedekiah, the nineteenth, with perhaps the twentieth as a sort of appendix, is the last which can have formed part of that collection. Apparently therefore we have at most only fragments of Jehoiakim's roll, the largest of which consists of chs. ii.–x. Probably also the prophecies against the Gentiles in chs. xlvi.–xlix. were contained in the roll, but were placed in their present position in order to connect them with the prophecies against Babylon (chs. l., li.) written in Zedekiah's fourth year. So also excepting ch. xiii. we must include in the roll the short prophecies which precede that of "the potter's vessel" (ch. xix.). From the twentieth chapter all signs of any general arrangement vanish. Attempts indeed have been made to shew that these later chapters are grouped together upon some sort of system, but they are far-fetched and unsatisfactory. The conclusion forced upon the mind is that Jeremiah had proposed to himself to gather into one volume all his prophecies, and that this is the reason why Jehoiakim's roll has not come down to us as a whole: but that he died in Egypt before he had been able to accomplish his design, and that at his death who-

ever had charge of his writings (probably Baruch) did not feel himself at liberty to attempt any arrangement of them. The fifty-second chapter was added to complete the history, and as it contains a notice of events more than twenty years after Jeremiah's death, it is probable that long before this time his prophecies had become current in their present disorder. The superscription of the Book of Jeremiah confirms in a remarkable manner the foregoing statements : for it bears upon its surface plain marks of repeated alterations.

The text of the Septuagint Version offers very considerable differences from that of the Masorites, contained in our Hebrew Bibles. From first to last there are innumerable variations, which sometimes affect only single letters, syllables or words, but sometimes whole verses. On the other hand the omissions are unimportant, and we nowhere find in either text anything altogether independent of the other. There is however a remarkable dislocation of the whole series of the prophecies against the nations : and not only do they hold a different place generally, but are arranged on a different plan among themselves.[5] The earlier position of the Gentile prophecies in the LXX. was probably more nearly that which they held in Jehoiakim's roll.

It was in Egypt that Jeremiah died. It is then at least probable that this Egyptian copy dates from the time when Baruch was about to depart from the country, and was transcribed (of course in Hebrew) for the private use of such Jews as believed Jeremiah to be a true prophet. It would gradually obtain currency and be copied again and again, and would in time become the authoritative form of the Book of Jeremiah among the Egyptian exiles. Its critical authority negatively is little, because of the extreme haste with which the copy was necessarily made, and because the exigencies of time required all that was not absolutely indispensable to be omitted : affirmatively its authority is very great, for it assures us that all that is common to the two texts is as old as the time when they first separated from one another. Whenever ch. lii. was added in Palestine it would not long remain unknown in Egypt. New colonists took with them copies of the fuller Hebrew text with the added appendix : but the shorter form was looked upon as that which had local authority. Patriotic Egyptian Jews doubtless held that it was the genuine text ; and as such the Alexandrian translators gave it the preference, but they could have no objection to adding to their Version so useful an annex as the fifty-second chapter.

Even independently of the evidence of this Egyptian text the genuine-

---

[5] As the dislocation thus begins at ch. xxv. 15, it follows that chs. xxv. 15-xlv. become in the LXX. chs. xxxii.-li., while the appendix, ch. lii., holds the last place in both texts. The order of the nations in the LXX. is Elam, Egypt, Babylon, the Philistines, Edom, Ammon, Kedar, Damascus, and Moab. Cp. the following table :

HEBREW. Chap.	SEPTUAGINT. Chap.
xlvi. Egypt	=xxvi.
xlvii. Philistines	=xxix. 1-7.
xlviii. Moab	=xxxi.
xlix. 1-6 Ammon	=xxx. 1-5.
,, 7-22 Edom	=xxix. 7-22.
,, 23-27 Damascus	=xxx. 12-16.
,, 28-33 Kedar & Hazor	=xxx. 6-11.
,, 34-39 Elam	=xxv. 15-20.
l., li. Babylon	=xxvii., xxviii.

ness of nearly every part of the Book of Jeremiah is so generally acknowledged that an occasional footnote on some impugned passage is all that is necessary. The value of the double text rather lies in its shewing how quickly the writings of the prophets became generally current, and how impossible it was to interpolate them or introduce falsification on a large scale. The acknowledged genuineness of the Book of Jeremiah is also valuable in another respect, because no prophet so constantly quotes the words of his predecessors. He evidently knew the other Scriptures by heart, and perpetually reproduces them, but in his own way. He never quotes them briefly and succinctly, but developes them, so as to give them something of his own soft luxuriance; but his testimony to the existence of them in the same state as that in which we have them at present, is most clear. Most numerous are his quotations from the Pentateuch, and especially from the Book of Deuteronomy. It had been so lately found (2 K. xxii. 8) that this is just what we should expect; his young mind must have been deeply penetrated by such a scene as that described in 2 K. xxiii. 1–3. And such quotations in a book of which the genuineness is acknowledged, are of the greatest possible value for the criticism of the writings from which they are taken.

THE BOOK OF THE PROPHET

JEREMIAH.

a Josh.21.18.
ch. 32. 7, 8.

b ch. 25. 3.

c ch. 39. 2.
i ch. 52. 12.
e 2 Kin. 25. 8.

f Isai. 49. 1.
g Ex. 33. 12.
h Luke 1. 15.
41.
Gal. 1. 15.
i Ex. 4. 10.
Isai. 6. 5.

CHAP. 1. THE words of Jeremiah the son of Hilkiah, of the priests 2 that *were* *a*in Anathoth in the land of Benjamin: to whom the word of the LORD came in the days of Josiah the son of Amon 3 king of Judah, *b*in the thirteenth year of his reign. It came also in the days of Jehoiakim the son of Josiah king of Judah, *c*unto the end of the eleventh year of Zedekiah the son of Josiah king of Judah, *d*unto the carrying away of Jerusalem captive 4 *e*in the fifth month.

Then the word of the LORD came unto me, saying, Before I 5 *f*formed thee in the belly *g*I knew thee; and before thou camest forth out of the womb I *h*sanctified thee, *and* I ¹ordained thee a 6 prophet unto the nations. Then said I, *i*Ah, Lord GOD ! behold, 7 I cannot speak for I *am* a child. But the LORD said unto me, Say not, I *am* a child: for thou shalt go to all that I shall

¹ Heb. *gave.*

I. 1. *The words of Jeremiah*] The usual title of the prophetical Books is the Word of the Lord : but the two Books of Amos and Jeremiah are called the words of those prophets, probably because they contain not merely prophecies, but also the record of much which belongs to the personal history of the writers. This title might therefore be translated the "life" or "acts of Jeremiah," though some understand by it a collection of the prophecies of Jeremiah. One derivation of Jeremiah's name is *God exalteth.*

Hilkiah may have been the High-Priest of that name. See p. 157.

that were] Or, **who was,** *i.e.* **dwelt.** The meaning is, that Jeremiah was a priest who dwelt at Anathoth.

2. *came*] Lit. **was** (and in *v.* 4); the phrase implies that Jeremiah possessed God's word from that time onward, not fitfully as coming and going, but constantly.

the thirteenth year of his reign] According to the ordinary reckoning this would be B.C. 629, but if the Ptolemaic canon be right in putting the capture of Jerusalem in B.C. 586, it would be two years later, namely B.C. 627. According however to the Assyrian chronology it would be B.C. 608. It was the year after that in which Josiah began his reforms.

3. The whole period contained in this verse is no less than forty years and six months, namely, eighteen years under Josiah, two periods of eleven years each under Jehoiakim and Zedekiah, and three months under each of the omitted kings Jehoahaz and Jeconiah.

in the fifth month] The capture of Jeru-

salem took place in the fourth month, but its destruction in the fifth (see marg. reff.), the ninth day of which was subsequently kept as a fast-day (Zech. vii. 3).

4. This history of Jeremiah's call to his office formed a part of his first address to the people. He claimed to act by an external authority, and to speak not his own words but those of Jehovah ; and this even when resisting the Divine call (see xv. 13, xx. 7, 14-18).

5. Rather, *Before I formed thee in the belly* **I approved of thee** [as one fit for the prophetic office], *and before thou camest forth from the womb* **I made thee holy** [dedicated thee to holy uses]; **I have appointed thee** [now by this public call to be] *a prophet unto the nations.*

unto the nations] The privileges contained in this verse are so great as in their full sense to be true only of Christ Himself, while to Jeremiah they belong as being in so many particulars a type of Christ.

6. There is no resistance on Jeremiah's part, but he shrinks back alarmed.

I cannot speak] *i.e. I cannot prophesy,* I have not those powers of oratory necessary for success. The prophets of Israel were the national preachers in religious matters, and their orators in political.

I am a child] This implies nothing very definite about Jeremiah's age. Still the long duration of his prophetic mission makes it probable that he was very young when called to the office, as also were Isaiah, Hosea, Zechariah, and others.

7. Jeremiah suggested two difficulties, the first inexperience, the second timidity. God

send thee, and *k*whatsoever I command thee thou shalt speak.
8 *l*Be not afraid of their faces : for *m*I *am* with thee to deliver thee,
9 saith the LORD.   Then the LORD put forth his hand, and *n*touched
my mouth.   And the LORD said unto me, Behold, I have *o*put
10 my words in thy mouth.   *p*See, I have this day set thee over the
nations and over the kingdoms, to *q*root out, and to pull down,
and to destroy, and to throw down, to build, and to plant.
11   Moreover the word of the LORD came unto me, saying, Jeremiah, what seest thou ?   And I said, I see a rod of an almond
12 tree.   Then said the LORD unto me, Thou hast well seen : for I
13 will hasten my word to perform it.   ¶ And the word of the LORD
came unto me the second time, saying, What seest thou ? And I
said, I see *r*a seething pot ; and the face thereof *is* ¹toward the
14 north.   Then the LORD said unto me, Out of the *s*north an evil

k Num. 22.
20, 38.
Matt. 28. 20,
l Ezek. 2. 6.
ver. 17.
m Ex. 3. 12.
Deut. 31. 6, 8.
Acts 26. 17.
Heb. 13. 6.
n Isai. 6. 7.
o Isai. 51. 16.
p 1 Kin. 19.
17.
q ch. 18. 7.
2 Cor. 10. 4, 5.
r Ezek. 11.
3, 7.
s ch. 4. 6.

¹ Heb. *from the face of the north.*

now removes the first of these. Inexperience is no obstacle where the duty is simple
obedience. His timidity is removed by the
promise given him in the next verse.

9. *touched*] **made it touch.** This was the
symbol of the bestowal of divine grace and
help, by which that want of eloquence,
which the prophet had pleaded as a dis-
qualification, was removed.

10. *I have...set thee over*] Lit. *I have made
thee Pâkeed, i.e.* deputy. This title is given
only to those invested with high authority
(*e.g.* Gen. xli. 34 ; 2 Chr. xxiv. 11 ; Jer. xx.
1, xxix. 26). From God's side the prophet is
a mere messenger, speaking what he is told,
doing what he is bid. From man's side he
is God's vicegerent, with power "to root
out, and to pull down."

root out...pull down] In the Hebr. the verbs
present an instance of the alliteration so
common in the prophets, and agreeable to
oriental taste. The former signifies the
destruction of anything planted, the latter
refers to buildings.

to throw down] More exactly **to tear in
pieces.** There are four words of destruction,
and but two of restoration, as if the message were chiefly of evil. And such was
Jeremiah's message to his contemporaries.
Yet are all God's dealings finally for the
good of His people. The Babylonian exile
was for the moment a time of chastisement :
it became also a time of national repentance (see xxiv. 5–7).

11. *what seest thou ?*] If we admit a supernatural element in prophecy, visions would
be the most simple means of communication
between God and man.

a rod of an almond tree] Many translate *a
staff of almond wood.* The vision would thus
signify that God,—like a traveller, staff in
hand—was just about to set forth upon His
journey of vengeance. But the rendering
of the A. V. is supported by Gen. xxx. 37.
The word rendered " almond " comes from
a root signifying *to be awake;* and as the
almond blossoms in January, it seems to

be awake while other trees are still sleeping,
and therefore is a fit emblem of activity.

12. *hasten*] Rather, **I watch over** *my word
to perform it.*

13. The first vision was for the support
of the prophet's own faith during his long
struggle with his countrymen : the second
explains to him the general nature of his
mission. He was to be the bearer of tidings
of a great national calamity about to break
forth from the north. He sees a **caldron.**
It was a vessel of metal (Ezek. xxiv. 11),
large enough to prepare the meal of a
numerous community (2 K. iv. 38), and
broad at the top, as it was also used for
washing purposes (Ps. lx. 8). This caldron
was boiling furiously.

the face &c.] More correctly the margin,
i.e. **toward the south.** We must suppose
this caldron set upon a pile of inflammable
materials. As they consume it settles down
unevenly, with the highest side toward the
north, so that its face is turned the other way
and looks southward. Should it still continue so to settle, the time must finally come
when it will be overturned, and will pour
the whole mass of its boiling contents upon
the south.

14. *Out of the north...*] The caldron represents the great military empires upon the
Euphrates. In Hezekiah's time Nineveh
was at their head ; but stormed by the
armies of Cyaxares and Nabopalassar it is
itself now the victim whose limbs are seething in the caldron, and the seat of empire
has been transferred to Babylon. But whoever may for the time prevail, the tide of
passion and carnage is sure finally to pour
itself upon Judæa.

an evil shall break forth] **the evil shall be
opened,** shall shew itself, be disclosed from
the north :—that special evil, which from
the days of Micah (Mic. iii. 12) all the prophets had denounced upon the Jews if they
lapsed into idolatry. At present the caldron
is fiercely boiling upon the Euphrates. As
soon as either of the parties struggling there

15 [1]shall break forth upon all the inhabitants of the land. For,
lo, I will [t]call all the families of the kingdoms of the north, saith
the LORD ; and they shall come, and they shall [u]set every one
his throne at the entering of the gates of Jerusalem, and against
all the walls thereof round about, and against all the cities of
16 Judah. And I will utter my judgments against them touching
all their wickedness, [x]who have forsaken me, and have burned
incense unto other gods, and worshipped the works of their own
17 hands. Thou therefore [y]gird up thy loins, and arise, and speak
unto them all that I command thee : [z]be not dismayed at their
18 faces, lest I [2]confound thee before them. For, behold, I have
made thee this day [a]a defenced city, and an iron pillar, and
brasen walls against the whole land, against the kings of Judah,
against the princes thereof, against the priests thereof, and
19 against the people of the land. And they shall fight against
thee ; but they shall not prevail against thee ; [b]for I am with
thee, saith the LORD, to deliver thee.

CHAP. 2. MOREOVER the word of the LORD came to me, saying,

[1] Heb. *shall be opened.*   [2] Or, *break to pieces.*

Side notes:
[t] ch. 5. 15.
& 6. 22.
[u] ch. 39. 3.
& 43. 10.

[x] Deut. 28.
20.
ch. 17. 13.

[y] 1 Kin. 18.
46.
Job 38. 3.
1 Pet. 1. 13.
[z] Ex. 3. 12.
Ezek. 2. 6.
[a] Isai. 50. 7.
ch. 6. 27.

[b] ver. 8.

---

gains the victory it will pour the whole
seething mass over other countries in the
shape of an invading army (see xxv. 17–26).

15. *I will call.*] **I am calling.** The judgment has begun. God is summoning His
hosts to the war.

families] The various races by which the
provinces of the Babylonian empire were
peopled.

they shall set every one his throne] The
chiefs of these various races come as God's
ministers to hold solemn court, and give
sentence in His name (see xxv. 9). They
therefore set each one his throne in the usual
place for administering justice, namely, the
entering in of the gates, where a large open
space was always left in cities for the purpose. Viewed in one light war is the boiling caldron of human passion, upset by
hazard, and bringing only ruin in its course ;
in the other it is God sitting in judgment,
with the kings of the earth as His assessors,
solemnly pronouncing sentence upon the
guilty.

against all the walls &c.] Sentence judicially pronounced, the nations come to execute judgment by mounting as enemies
upon her walls and storming her cities.

16. In accordance with the custom of law
courts, the crimes of the guilty city are
mentioned in the sentence. The charges
brought against her are three : first, the
desertion of the true God ; next, the offering incense to false gods, and, lastly, the
making obeisance to, or bowing down (2 K.
v. 18) before images of human workmanship.

17. *gird up thy loins*] A symbol of preparation for earnest exertion, and implying
also firm purpose, and some degree of
alacrity.

be not dismayed...] Lit. *be not dismayed at*

their faces, lest I dismay thee before their faces.
Naturally despondent and self-distrustful,
there was yet no feebleness in Jeremiah's
character. There was in him a moral superiority of the will, which made him, at any
cost to himself, faithfully discharge whatever his conscience told him was his duty.

18. Metaphorically the walls and fortifications of the city represent the prophet's
power of patiently enduring the attacks of
his enemies ; while the iron pillar, supporting the whole weight of the roof (Judg. xvi.
29 ; 1 K. vii. 21), signifies that no trials or
sufferings would crush his steadfast will.

II.–VI.—In the prophecies contained in
these chapters, we have, probably, the records of Jeremiah's earlier ministrations
during the comparatively uneventful years
of Josiah's reign. The great object of the
prophet's mission was to urge upon the
people the necessity of making use of that
final opportunity of repentance then given
them. If personal amendment followed
upon the king's reforms Judah might yet be
saved. We have then in these chapters such
portions of Jeremiah's earlier teaching,
published during Josiah's reign, as were
deemed fit also for the Church's use in all
time.

The prophecy (ii. 1–iii. 5) consists of three
parts, of which the first (ii. 1–13) contains
an appeal from God to all Israel, *i.e.* the
whole twelve tribes, proving to them His
past love, and that their desertion of Him
was without ground or reason. In the
second (ii. 14–28) the prophet shews that
Israel's calamities were entirely the result
of her apostasy. In the last (ii. 29–iii. 5)
we see Judah imitating Samaria's sin, and
hardening itself against correction.

II. **1.** *Moreover*] Lit. **And.** Notice the

2 Go and cry in the ears of Jerusalem, saying, Thus saith the LORD;
I remember [1]thee, the kindness of thy [a]youth, the love of thine
espousals, [b]when thou wentest after me in the wilderness, in a
3 land *that was* not sown. [c]Israel *was* holiness unto the LORD, *and*
[d]the firstfruits of his increase: [e]all that devour him shall offend;
4 evil shall come upon them, saith the LORD. ¶ Hear ye the word
of the LORD, O house of Jacob, and all the families of the house
5 of Israel: Thus saith the LORD, [f]What iniquity have your
fathers found in me, that they are gone far from me, [g]and have
6 walked after vanity, and are become vain? Neither said they,
Where *is* the LORD that [h]brought us up out of the land of
Egypt, that led us through [i]the wilderness, through a land of
deserts and of pits, through a land of drought, and of the shadow
of death, through a land that no man passed through, and where
7 no man dwelt? And I brought you into [2][k]a plentiful country,
to eat the fruit thereof and the goodness thereof; but when ye
entered, ye [l]defiled my land, and made mine heritage an abomi-
8 nation. The priests said not, Where *is* the LORD? and they
that handle the [m]law knew me not: the pastors also transgressed
against me, [n]and the prophets prophesied by Baal, and walked
9 after *things that* [o]do not profit. Wherefore [p]I will yet plead
with you, saith the LORD, and [q]with your children's children
10 will I plead. For pass [3]over the isles of Chittim, and see; and
send unto Kedar, and consider diligently, and see if there be

[a] Ezek. 23. 3, 8. Hos. 2. 15.
[b] Deut. 2. 7.
[c] Ex. 19. 5.
[d] Jam. 1. 18. Rev. 14. 4.
[e] ch. 12. 14. ch. 50. 7.
[f] Isai. 5. 4. Mic. 6. 3.
[g] 2 Kin. 17. 15. Jonah 2. 8.
[h] Isai. 63. 9. Hos. 13. 4.
[i] Deut. 8. 15. & 32. 10.
[k] Num. 13. 27. Deut. 8. 7.
[l] Lev. 18. 25, 27, 28. Ps. 78. 58.
[m] Mal. 2. 6. Rom. 2. 20.
[n] ch. 23. 13.
[o] ver. 11. Hab. 2. 18.
[p] Ezek. 20. 35, 36. Mic. 6. 2.
[q] Ex. 20. 5. Lev. 20. 5.

[1] Or, *for thy sake.* [2] Or, *the land of Carmel.* [3] Or, *over to.*

---

connexion between Jeremiah's call and first prophecy.

2. Up to this time Jeremiah had lived at Anathoth, he is now to make Jerusalem the scene of his ministrations.

I remember &c.] Or, **I have remembered for thee the grace** *of thy youth, the love of thine espousals,* **thy going** *after me in the wilderness* **in an unsown land.** Jeremiah contrasts the present unfriendly relations between Jehovah and His people with their past love. Israel, as often elsewhere, is represented as a young bride (Ezek. xvi. 8; Hos. ii. 20; Joel i. 8). The walking after God in the wilderness was an act of love on Israel's part. Israel did leave Egypt at Moses' bidding, and at Sinai was solemnly espoused to Jehovah.

3. Render: *Israel* **is an offering consecrated to Jehovah, His firstfruits of increase.** The firstfruits were God's consecrated property, His portion of the whole harvest. Heathen, *i.e.* unconsecrated, nations must not meddle with Israel, because it is the nation consecrated to God. If they do, they will bring such guilt upon themselves as those incur who eat the firstfruits (Lev. xxii. 10, 16).

6. Modern researches have shewn that this description applies only to limited portions of the route of the Israelites through the Sinaitic peninsula.

7. *a plentiful country*] Lit. *a land of the Carmel,* **a Carmel land** (see 1 K. xviii. 19; Isai. xxix. 17 notes).

8. The guilt of this idolatry is ascribed to the four ruling classes. The accusation brought against (*a*) the priests is indifference. (*b*) "They that handle the law" belonged also to the priestly class (Deut. xxxiii. 10). Their offence was that *they knew not God.* Cp. Mic. iii. 11. (*c*) The third class are *the pastors* or shepherds, that is the temporal rulers. Their crime is disobedience. (*d*) The fourth class are *the prophets.* It was their business to press the moral and spiritual truths of the law home to the hearts of the people: but they drew their inspiration from Baal, the Sun-god. Upon the corruption of the prophetic order at this time, see xiv. 13 note.

things that do not profit] Here idols, which are not merely unreal, but injurious. See 1 S. xii. 21; Isai. xliv. 9.

9. *plead*] The word used by the plaintiff setting forth his accusation in a law-court (see Job xxxiii. 13 note).

with you] The present generation, who by joining in Manasseh's apostasy have openly violated Jehovah's Covenant. The fathers made the nation what it now is, the children will receive it such as the present generation are now making it to be, and God will judge it according as the collective working of the past, the present, and the future tends to good or to evil.

10. Kedar signifies the whole East, and the isles of Chittim (Isai. xxiii. 12 note) the West. If then you traverse all lands from West to East, it will be impossible to find

r Mic. 4. 5.
s Ps. 115. 4.
Isai. 37. 19.
t Ps. 106. 20.
Rom. 1. 23.
u ver. 8.
x Isai. 1. 2.
ch. 6. 19.
y Ps. 36. 9.
ch. 17. 13.
John 4. 14.
z See Ex. 4.
22.
a Isai. 1. 7.
ch. 4. 7.
b ch. 43. 7.
c ch. 4. 18.
d Deut. 32.
10.
e Isai. 30. 1.
f Josh. 13. 3.
g Isai. 3. 9.
Hos. 5. 5.

11 such a thing. *r*Hath a nation changed *their* gods, which *are*
*s*yet no gods? *t*but my people have changed their glory for *u*that
12 *which* doth not profit. *x*Be astonished, O ye heavens, at this,
13 and be horribly afraid, be ye very desolate, saith the LORD. For
my people have committed two evils ; they have forsaken me tho
*y*fountain of living waters, *and* hewed them out cisterns, broken
14 cisterns, that can hold no water. ¶ *Is* Israel *z*a servant? *is* he
15 a homeborn *slave?* why is he ¹spoiled? *a*The young lions roared
upon him, *and* ²yelled, and they made his land waste : his cities
16 are burned without inhabitant. Also the children of Noph and
17 *b*Tahapanes ³have broken the crown of thy head. *c*Hast thou
not procured this unto thyself, in that thou hast forsaken the
18 LORD thy God, when *d*he led thee by the way? And now what
hast thou to do *e*in the way of Egypt, to drink the waters of
*f*Sihor? or what hast thou to do in the way of Assyria, to drink
19 the waters of the river? Thine own *g*wickedness shall correct
thee, and thy backslidings shall reprove thee : know therefore
and see that *it is* an evil *thing* and bitter, that thou hast forsaken
the LORD thy God, and that my fear *is* not in thee, saith the
20 Lord GOD of hosts. ¶ For of old time I have broken thy yoke,
and burst thy bands ; and *h*thou saidst, I will not ⁴transgress ;

h Ex. 19. 8.
Josh. 24. 18.

¹ Heb. *become a spoil?*　　³ Or, *feed on thy crown,*　　⁴ Or, *serve.*
² Heb. *gave out their voice.*　　Deut. 33. 20. Isai. 8. 8.

---

any nation guilty of such apostasy as that committed by Israel.

11. *a nation*] A Gentile nation, in strong antithesis to *people*, the appellation of Israel.

their glory] Though the worship of the one true God is a nation's greatest glory, yet it is irksome because it puts a constraint on human passions.

that which doth not profit] Israel had exchanged the prosperity which was God's reward of obedience for the calamities which resulted from idol-worship.

12. *Be astonished*] The A. V. uses this word as equivalent to *be stupefied.*

desolate] Or, *be dry.* In horror at Israel's conduct the heavens shrivel and dry up.

13. The heathen are guilty of but one sin, idolatry : the Covenant-people commit two, they abandon the true God ; they serve idols.

fountain] Not a spring or natural fountain, but a tank or reservoir dug in the ground (see vi. 7), and chiefly intended for storing living waters, *i.e.* those of springs and rivulets. The cistern was used for storing up rain-water only, and therefore the quantity it contained was limited.

14. It was Israel's glory to be Jehovah's servant (xxx. 10), and slaves born in the house were more prized than those bought with money as being more faithful (Gen. xiv. 14). Cannot Jehovah guard His own household? How happens it that a member of so powerful a family is spoiled? In the next verse the prophet gives the reason. Israel is a runaway slave, who has deserted the family to which he belongs by right of birth, and thereby brought upon himself trouble and misery.

15. *upon him*] Rather, **against him.** Israel has run away from his master's house, but only to find himself exposed to the beasts of prey in the wilderness.

they made his land waste] The prophet points to the actual results of Israel's apostasy. Not only had Israel been wasted, till the multiplication of wild beasts rendered human life unsafe (2 K. xvii. 25), but the Assyrian invasions had reduced Judæa to almost as sad a state.

burned] Others render, "levelled to the ground."

16. Noph, *i.e.* Napata, a town situated in the extreme south of Egypt. Some take it to be Memphis (see Isai. xix. 13 note).

Tahapanes] Daphne Pelusii, a border-town towards Palestine.

have broken the crown of thy head] Lit. **shall depasture the crown of thy head :** *i.e.* make it bald ; baldness was accounted by the Jews a sign of disgrace (2 K. ii. 23), and also a mark of mourning (Isai. xv. 2, xxii. 12). The Egyptians in slaying Josiah, and capturing Jerusalem, brought ruin, disgrace, and sorrow upon the Jews.

the way] Either, the journey through the wilderness, or the way of holiness.

18. *Sihor*] The Nile. To lean on Egypt was a violation of the principles of theocracy.

The two rivers are the two empires, and to drink their waters is to adopt their principles and religion. Cp. also Isai. viii. 6, 7.

19. *correct thee*] Or, *chastise* thee. Alliances with foreign powers shall bring trouble and not safety.

20. *transgress*] Rather, as in marg. If

when ⁱupon every high hill and under every green tree thou
21 wanderest, ^kplaying the harlot. Yet I had ^lplanted thee a noble
vine, wholly a right seed: how then art thou turned into ^mthe
22 degenerate plant of a strange vine unto me? For though thou
ⁿwash thee with nitre, and take thee much sope, *yet* ^othine ini-
23 quity is marked before me, saith the Lord GOD. ^pHow canst
thou say, I am not polluted, I have not gone after Baalim? see
thy way ^qin the valley, know what thou hast done: ¹*thou art a*
24 swift dromedary traversing her ways; ^r²a wild ass ³used to the
wilderness, *that* snuffeth up the wind at ⁴her pleasure; in her
occasion who can ⁵turn her away? all they that seek her will
25 not weary themselves; in her month they shall find her. Withhold thy foot from being unshod, and thy throat from thirst:
but ^sthou saidst, ⁶There is no hope: no; for I have loved
26 ^tstrangers, and after them will I go.   ¶ As the thief is ashamed
when he is found, so is the house of Israel ashamed: they, their
kings, their princes, and their priests, and their prophets, saying
27 to a stock, Thou *art* my father; and to a stone, Thou hast
⁷brought me forth: for they have turned ⁸*their* back unto me,

i Deut. 12. 2.
Isai. 57. 5.
k Ex. 34. 15.
l Ex. 15. 17.
Ps. 44. 2.
Matt. 21. 33.
m Isai. 1. 21.
n Job 9. 30.
o Deut.32.34.
Hos. 13. 12.
p Prov. 30.
12.
q ch. 7. 31.
r Job 39. 5.
ch. 14. 6.

s ch. 18. 12.
t Deut. 32.16.
ch. 3. 13.

¹ Or, *O swift dromedary.*
² Or, *O wild ass &c.*
³ Heb. *taught.*
⁴ Heb. *the desire of her heart.*
⁵ Or, *reverse it?*
⁶ Or, *Is the case desperate?*
⁷ Or, *begotten me.*
⁸ Heb. *the hinder part of the neck.*

---

the *yoke* and *bands* refer to the slavery in
Egypt from which Jehovah freed Israel,
the sense is—*For of old time I* Jehovah
broke thy yoke, I burst thy bands, not that
thou mightest be free to do thy own will,
but that thou mightest serve me: *and thou
saidst, I will not serve.*

when &c.] For...*under every leafy tree thou*
layest thyself down as a harlot. The
verb indicates the eagerness with which she
prostrates herself before the objects of her
idolatrous worship.

21. *a noble vine*] Properly, *a Sorek vine*
(see Isai. v. 2), which produced a red wine
(Prov. xxiii. 31), and had a lasting reputation (Gen. xlix. 11).

a right seed] Lit. *a seed of truth, i.e.* true,
genuine seed, not mixed with weeds, nor
with seed of an inferior quality. Cp. Matt.
xiii. 24.

how then art thou turned] Or, *How then*
hast thou changed thyself *unto me (i.e.* to
my hurt or vexation) *into the degenerate*
branches *of a strange vine?* The stock,
which was God's planting, was genuine, and
of the noblest sort: the wonder was how
such a stock could produce shoots of a
totally different kind (Deut. xxxii. 32).

22. *nitre*] Or, **natron**, a mineral alkali,
found in the Nile valley, where it effloresces
upon the rocks and surfaces of the dykes,
and in old time was carefully collected, and
used to make lye for washing (see Prov. xxv.
20).

sope] A vegetable alkali, now called
potash, because obtained from the ashes of
plants. Its combination with oils, &c., to
form soap was not known to the Hebrews
till long after Jeremiah's time, but they
used the lye, formed by passing water

through the ashes. Thus then, though
Israel use both mineral and vegetable
alkalies, the most powerful detergents
known, yet will she be unable to wash
away the stains of her apostasy.

thine iniquity is marked] *i.e.* as a stain.

23. In their defence of themselves (cp. *v.*
35), the people probably appealed to the
maintenance of the daily sacrifice, and the
Mosaic ritual: and even more confidently
perhaps to Josiah's splendid restoration of
the Temple, and to the suppression of the
open worship of Baal. All such pleas
availed little as long as the rites of Moloch
were still privately practised.

thy way in the valley] *i.e.* of Hinnom (see
2 K. xxiii. 10 note). From the time of
Ahaz it had been the seat of the worship of
Moloch, and the prophet more than once
identifies Moloch with Baal. *Way* is put
metaphorically for *conduct, doings.*

traversing] **Interlacing** *her ways.* The
word describes the tangled mazes of the
dromedary's course, as she runs hither and
thither in the heat of her passion.

24. *A wild ass used to the wilderness*] The
type of an untamed and reckless nature.

snuffeth up the wind] The wind brings
with it the scent of the male. Israel does
not wait till temptation comes of itself, but
looks out for any and every incentive to
idolatry.

occasion...month] *i.e.* the pairing season.

25. God the true husband exhorts Israel
not to run barefoot, and with parched
throat, like a shameless adulteress, **after**
strangers.

There is no hope] *i.e.* It is in vain.

27. "Stone" being feminine in Hebrew
is here represented as the mother.

v Ps. 78. 34.
Isai. 26. 16.
x Deut.32.37.
Judg. 10. 14.
y Isai. 45. 20.
z ch. 11. 13.
a ver. 23. 35.
b Isai. 1. 5.
ch. 5. 3.
c 2 Chr. 36.
16.
Acts 7. 52.
1 Thess.2.15.
d ver. 5.
e Ps. 12. 4.
f Deut.32.15.
g Ps. 106. 21.
Hos. 8. 14.
h Ps. 106. 38.
ch. 19. 4.
i ver. 23. 29.
k ver 9.
l 1 John 1.
8, 10.
m ver. 18.
ch. 31. 22.
Hos. 5. 13.
n Isai. 30. 3.
ch. 37. 7.
o 2 Chr. 28.
16, 20, 21.

and not *their* face : but in the time of their *n*trouble they will
28 say, Arise, and save us. But *x*where *are* thy gods that thou
hast made thee? let them arise, if they *y*can save thee in the
time of thy ¹trouble : for *z*according to the number of thy cities
29 are thy gods, O Judah. *a*Wherefore will ye plead with me? ye
30 all have transgressed against me, saith the LORD. In vain have
I *b*smitten your children ; they received no correction : your
own sword hath *c*devoured your prophets, like a destroying lion.
31 ¶ O generation, see ye the word of the LORD. *d*Have I been a
wilderness unto Israel? a land of darkness? wherefore say my
people, ²*e*We are lords; *f*we will come no more unto thee?
32 Can a maid forget her ornaments, *or* a bride her attire? yet
33 my people *g*have forgotten me days without number. Why
trimmest thou thy way to seek love? therefore hast thou also
34 taught the wicked ones thy ways. Also in thy skirts is found
*h*the blood of the souls of the poor innocents: I have not found
35 it by ³secret search, but upon all these. *i*Yet thou sayest,
Because I am innocent, surely his anger shall turn from me.
Behold, *k*I will plead with thee, *l*because thou sayest, I have not
36 sinned. *m*Why gaddest thou about so much to change thy way?
*n*thou also shalt be ashamed of Egypt, *o*as thou wast ashamed

¹ Heb. *evil*.　　　² Heb. *We have dominion*.　　　³ Heb. *digging*.

Arise, and save us] Whether it be idolatry or infidelity, it satisfies only in tranquil
and prosperous times. No sooner does
trouble come, than the deep conviction of
the existence of a God, which is the witness
for Him in our heart, resumes its authority,
and man prays.

28. A question of bitter irony. Things
are made for some use. Now is the time
for thy deities to prove themselves real by
being useful. When every city has its
special deity, surely among so many there
might be found one able to help his worshippers.

O Judah] Hitherto the argument had
been addressed to Israel : suddenly the
prophet charges Judah with the habitual
practice of idolatry, and points to the conclusion, that as Jerusalem has been guilty
of Samaria's sin, it must suffer Samaria's
punishment.

30. *your own sword hath devoured your
prophets*] An allusion probably to Manasseh
(2 K. xxi. 16). Death was the usual fate of
the true prophet (Neh. ix. 26 ; Matt. xxiii.
37).

31. Or, *O generation* that ye are! An
exclamation of indignation at their hardened
resistance to God.

a land of darkness] This word is written
in Hebrew with two accents, as being a
compound, signifying not merely darkness,
but *the darkness of Jehovah, i.e.*, very great
darkness.

We are lords] Others render, **We rove
about**, wander about at our will, go where
we like.

32. A bride treasures all her life the
girdle, which first indicated that she was a

married woman, just as brides now the
wedding ring ; but Israel, Jehovah's bride
(*v*. 2), cherishes no fond memorials of past
affection.

33. *Why trimmest thou thy way*] Lit. *Why
makest thou thy way good*, a phrase used here
of the pains taken by the Jews to learn the
idolatries of foreign nations.

the wicked ones...] Or, *therefore thou hast
taught* **thy ways wickednesses.**

34. *I have not found it* &c.] Rather, **thou
didst not find them breaking into thy
house.** The meaning is, that these poor
innocents had committed no crime : they
were not thieves caught in the act, whom
the Law permitted men to slay (Ex. xxii. 2),
and therefore Israel in killing them was
guilty of murder. The one crime here of
theft is put for crime generally.

upon all these] Or, **because of all this.**
Thou killedst the poor innocents, not for
any crime, but because of this thy lust for
idolatry.

35. *Because I am innocent*] Rather, **But
I am innocent**, or, *I am acquitted*. These
blood-stains cannot be upon my skirts,
because now, in king Josiah's days, the idolatry of Manasseh has been put away.

shall turn from me] Or, **has turned away
from me.**

plead] Or, **enter into judgment.**

36. *to change thy way*] The rival parties
at Jerusalem looked one to Assyria, the
other to Egypt, for safety. As one or other
for the time prevailed, the nation *changed
its way*, sending its embassies now eastward to Nineveh, now westward to Memphis.

thou also...] Lit. **also of Egypt** *shalt thou
be ashamed*. This was literally fulfilled by

37 of Assyria. Yea, thou shalt go forth from him, and *p*thine
hands upon thine head : for the LORD hath rejected thy confidences, and thou shalt not prosper in them.

CHAP. 3. THEY ¹ say, If a man put away his wife, and she go from
him, and become another man's, *a*shall he return unto her again?
shall not that *b*land be greatly polluted? but thou hast *c*played
the harlot with many lovers ; *d*yet return again to me, saith the
2 LORD.   Lift up thine eyes unto *e*the high places, and see where
thou hast not been lien with. *f*In the ways hast thou sat for
them, as the Arabian in the wilderness ; *g*and thou hast polluted the land with thy whoredoms and with thy wickedness.
3 Therefore the *h*showers have been withholden, and there hath
been no latter rain ; and thou hadst a *i*whore's forehead, thou
4 refusedst to be ashamed.   Wilt thou not from this time cry unto
5 me, My father, thou *art* *k*the guide of *l*my youth? *m*Will he
reserve *his anger* for ever? will he keep *it* to the end? Behold,
thou hast spoken and done evil things as thou couldest.

p 2 Sam. 13.
19.
a Deut. 24. 4.
b ch. 2. 7.
c Ezek. 16.
26, 28, 29.
d ch. 4. 1.
Zech. 1. 3.
e See Deut.
12. 2.
f Gen. 38. 14.
Ezek. 16.
24, 25.
g ch. 2. 7.
h Lev. 26. 19.
ch. 9. 12.
i ch. 5. 3.
Ezek. 3. 7.
Zeph. 3. 5.
k Prov. 2. 17.
l ch. 2. 2.
Hos. 2. 15.
m Ps. 77. 7.
Isai. 57. 16.

¹ Heb. *Saying.*

---

the failure of the attempt to raise the siege
of Jerusalem (xxxvii. 5).

37. *from him*] **From it,** from this Egypt,
which though fem. as a land, yet as a people
may be used as a masc. (cp. xlvi. 8). Now
that Nineveh is trembling before the armies
of Cyaxares and Nabopalassar, thou hast-
enest to Egypt, hoping to rest upon her
strength : but thou shalt retrace thy steps,
with thy hands clasped upon thy head, disgraced and discarded.

confidences] Those in whom thou con-
fidest.

in them] Lit. "with respect to them."

III. 1. *They say*] Or, **That is to say.**
The prophet has completed his survey of
Israel's conduct, and draws the conclusion
that as an adulterous wife could not be
taken back by her husband, so Israel has
forfeited her part in the Covenant with God.
Apparently the opening word, which literally means *to say,* only introduces the quotation in marg.

yet return again to me] Or, *and* thinkest
thou *to return unto me!* The whole argument is not of mercy, but is the proof that
after her repeated adulteries, Israel could
not again take her place as wife. To think
of returning to God, with the marriage-law
unrepealed, was folly.

2. These words are not the language of
consolation to the conscience-stricken, but
of vehement expostulation with hardened
sinners. They prove, therefore, the truth
of the interpretation put upon the preceding
verse.

as the Arabian &c.] The freebooting propensities of the Bedawin had passed in
ancient times into a proverb. As eager as
the desert-tribes were for plunder, so was
Israel for idolatry.

4. Or, **Hast thou** *not from this time* **called**
me, My Father, thou art the **husband** *of my*
youth! i.e. from the time of Josiah's reforms

in his eighteenth year, in opposition to "of
old time" (ii. 20).

5. Rather, *Will he,* the young husband,
retain, keep up *His anger for ever!* These
words should be joined to *v.* 4.

Behold &c.] Rather, *Behold, thou hast*
spoken thus, **but thou hast** *done evil things*
persistently. The A. V. translates as if
Judah's words and deeds were both evil.
Really her words were fair, but her deeds
proved them to be false.

And here ends the prophecy, most interesting as shewing what was the general
nature of Jeremiah's exhortations to his
countrymen, during the fourteen years of
Josiah's reign. He sets before them God
and Israel united by a covenant of marriage,
to the conditions of which Jehovah is ever
true, while Israel practises with zest every
form of idolatry. Therefore the Divine
blessing is withheld. It is an honest and
manly warning, and the great lesson it
teaches us is, that with God nothing avails
but a real and heartfelt repentance followed
by a life of holiness and sincere devotion to
His service.

III. 6–iv. 4.—*The Call to Repentance.*

The former prophecy ended with the denunciation of God's perpetual anger because
of Israel's obstinate persistence in sin. Now
there is an invitation to repentance, and
the assurance of forgiveness. The argument is as follows: Israel had been guilty
of apostasy, and therefore God had put
her away. Unwarned by this example her
more guilty sister Judah persists in the
same sins (*vv.* 6–11). Israel therefore is
invited to return to the marriage-covenant
by repentance (*vv.* 12–14), in which case she
and Judah, accepted upon the like condition,
shall become joint members of a spiritual
theocracy (*vv.*15–18). The repentance which
God requires must be real (*v.* 19–iv. 4).

6 The LORD said also unto me in the days of Josiah the king,
Hast thou seen *that* which [n]backsliding Israel hath done? she
is [o]gone up upon every high mountain and under every green
7 tree, and there hath played the harlot. [p]And I said after she
had done all these *things*, Turn thou unto me. But she returned
8 not. And her treacherous [q]sister Judah saw *it*. And I saw,
when [r]for all the causes whereby backsliding Israel committed
adultery I had [s]put her away, and given her a bill of divorce;
[t]yet her treacherous sister Judah feared not, but went and
9 played the harlot also. And it came to pass through the [1]light-
ness of her whoredom, that she [u]defiled the land, and committed
10 adultery with [x]stones and with stocks. And yet for all this her
treacherous sister Judah hath not turned unto me [y]with her
11 whole heart, but [2]feignedly, saith the LORD. ¶ And the LORD
said unto me, [z]The backsliding Israel hath justified herself more
12 than treacherous Judah. Go and proclaim these words toward
[a]the north, and say, Return, thou backsliding Israel, saith the
LORD; *and* I will not cause mine anger to fall upon you: for I
am [b]merciful, saith the LORD, *and* I will not keep *anger* for ever.
13 [c]Only acknowledge thine iniquity, that thou hast transgressed
against the LORD thy God, and hast [d]scattered thy ways to the
[e]strangers [f]under every green tree, and ye have not obeyed my
14 voice, saith the LORD. Turn, O backsliding children, saith the

[n] ver. 11. ch. 7. 24. [o] ch. 2. 20. [p] 2 Kin. 17. 13. [q] Ezek. 16. 46. [r] Ezek. 23. 9. [s] 2 Kin. 17. 6, 18. [t] Ezek. 23. 11, &c. [u] ch. 2. 7. [x] ch. 2. 27. [y] 2 Chr. 34. 33. Hos. 7. 14. [z] Ezek. 16. 51. & 23. 11. [a] 2 Kin. 17. 6. [b] Ps. 86. 15. ver. 5. [c] Lev. 26. 40. Deut. 30. 1, 2, &c. [d] ver. 2. Ezek. 16. 15, 24, 25. [e] ch. 2. 25. [f] Deut. 12. 2.

[1] Or, *fame*. [2] Heb. *in falsehood*.

---

6. *backsliding Israel*] The original is very strong: Hast thou seen Apostasy? *i.e.* Israel: as though Israel were the very personification of the denial of God.

she is gone up] Rather, **she goes**; it is her habitual practice.

7. Or, *And I said* (*i.e.* within myself), *After she has done all these things, she will return to me. But she did not return.*

treacherous] Lit. *Falsehood*, *i.e.* **false**, faithless. The character of the two sisters is plainly marked. Samaria is apostate; she abandons Jehovah's worship altogether. Judah maintains the form only; her secret desires are set upon the orgies of heathen worship.

8. Rather, *And I saw* **that because apostate** *Israel* **had** *committed adultery, I had put her away, and given her* **the writing of her divorcement,** *yet* **false** *Judah her sister feared not....* The expression, *For all the causes whereby*, is probably the actual formula with which writings of divorcement commenced.

9. *lightness*] Others render as in marg.

defiled] Rather, **profaned.** The land specially consecrated to Jehovah's service was treated by Judah as a common land.

10. *her treacherous sister Judah*] These words are a sort of refrain, thrice (*vv.* 7, 8, 10) repeated before God finally pronounces Judah more culpable than Israel.

11. *hath justified herself*] Judah had had the benefit of the warning given by Israel's example. Both abandon Jehovah's service for idolatry, but Israel is simply *apostate*, Judah is also *false*.

The verse is important, (1) as accounting for the destruction of Jerusalem so soon after the pious reign of Josiah. Manasseh's crimes had defiled the land, but it was by rejecting the reforms of Josiah that the people finally profaned it, and sealed their doom: (2) as shewing that it is not by the acts of its government that a nation stands or falls. Ahaz and Manasseh lent the weight of their influence to the cause of idolatry: Hezekiah and Josiah to the cause of truth. But the nation had to determine which should prevail. Excepting a remnant it embraced idolatry, and brought upon itself ruin: in the remnant the nation again revived (xxiv. 5, 7).

12. *the north*] The ten tribes, settled by Salmanezer in the north of Assyria.

I will not cause mine anger to fall upon you]. Lit. **I will not cause my face** *to fall upon you; i.e. I will not receive you with averted looks.* The *and* before this clause should be omitted, as also before the next clause, *I will not keep* &c.

I will not keep] All God's promises and threats are conditional upon man's conduct.

13. *acknowledge*] Lit. *know thy iniquity;* know that thy doings are iniquitous.

scattered thy ways] Wandered in search of those idolatries which foreign nations practise.

14. *children...married*] The twofold relationship gives a double certainty of acceptance. As children they were sure of a father's love, as a wife they might hope for a revival of past affection from the husband of their youth.

LORD; *o*for I am married unto you: and I will take you *h*one
of a city, and two of a family, and I will bring you to Zion:
15 and I will give you *i*pastors according to mine heart, which
16 shall *k*feed you with knowledge and understanding. And it shall
come to pass, when ye be multiplied and increased in the land,
in those days, saith the LORD, they shall say no more, The ark
of the covenant of the LORD: *l*neither shall it ¹come to mind:
neither shall they remember it; neither shall they visit *it ;*
17 neither shall ²*that* be done any more. At that time they shall
call Jerusalem the throne of the LORD ; and all the nations shall
be gathered unto it, *m*to the name of the LORD, to Jerusalem :
neither shall they *n*walk any more after the ³imagination of
18 their evil heart. In those days *o*the house of Judah shall walk
⁴with the house of Israel, and they shall come together out of
the land of *p* the north to *q*the land that I have ⁵given for an in-
19 heritance unto your fathers. But I said, How shall I put thee
among the children, and give thee *r*a ⁶pleasant land, *ᵗ*a goodly
heritage of the hosts of nations ? and I said, Thou shalt call me,

g ch. 31. 32.
Hos. 2. 19.
h Rom. 11. 5.
i ch. 23. 4.
Ezek. 34. 23.
k Acts 20. 28.

l Isai. 65. 17.

m Isai. 60. 9.
n ch. 11. 8.
o See Isai.
11. 13.
Ezek. 37.
16–22.
p ch. 31. 8.
q Amos 9. 15.
r Ps. 106. 24.
Ezek. 20. 6.
Dan. 8. 9.

¹ Heb. *come upon the heart.*
² Or, *it be magnified.*
³ Or, *stubbornness.*
⁴ Or, *to.*
⁵ Or, *caused your fathers to possess.*
⁶ Heb. *land of desire.*
⁷ Heb. *an heritage of glory,*
or, *beauty.*

one of a city, and two of a family] The
family (in Hebrew) is far larger than a city,
as it embraces all the descendants of a common ancestor. Thus the tribe of Judah
was divided into only four or five families.
However national the apostasy, it does not
involve in its guilt the few who are faithful,
and the promises are still their rightful
possession.

to Zion] To the true Church. The fulfilment of the promise began with the return
to Palestine after the Babylonian exile, but
is complete only in Christianity.

15. *pastors*] Kings, *rulers* (cp. ii. 8). Not
military usurpers (Hos. viii. 4), but true
servants of God, as David (1 S. xiii 14).

16. *in those days*] This and the phrase
"the latter days," had become under the
Messianic teaching of the prophets a regular
formula for the time of Christ's coming,
when all the nation's hopes would be fulfilled.

The Ark was the centre of the Mosaic
economy, containing within it the two tables
of the Law, as the conditions of the Covenant,
and having over it, upon the mercy-seat, the
Shechinah as the visible sign of God's presence. But "in those days" the symbol
must pass away, because God will then
dwell in His people by the gift of the Holy
Ghost (1 Cor. iii. 16), and the terms of the
Covenant will be written on their hearts
(xxxi. 33).

neither shall they visit it] Rather, *neither
shall they miss it; i.e.* they will not trouble
about it, nor regret its loss.

neither shall that be done any more] Rather,
neither shall it (the Ark) **be made any
more;** it shall not be renewed or repaired,
because the Tabernacle of God will be one
"made without hands" (Heb. ix. 11), even
the heart of His believing people.

17. *the throne of the* LORD] Jehovah's
throne shall not be the Ark, but Jerusalem,
i.e. the Christian Church (Rev. xxi. 2; Gal.
iv. 26).

to Jerusalem] The LXX. and Syriac are
probably right in omitting this word.

imagination...] **Stubbornness** (marg.). A
word always used in a bad sense, for *obstinacy.*

18. *with*] **To** (marg.). The prophet has
just described the return of the ten tribes
(*v.* 14), &c. Israel is represented as the first
to repent, and Judah must go to her, in
order that they may *come together* back to
the Holy Land, divided no longer into
Jews and Israelites, but merged into one
people.

out of the land of the north] The objection
that the Jews were not carried like the
Israelites into the northern provinces of
Assyria (*v.* 12), but into Babylonia, misin-
terprets the whole prophecy, the gist of
which is that in case of Israel's repentance,
Judah must humbly seek her out, and be
content henceforward to take the inferior
place, as having been the more guilty (see
v. 11).

19. *But I* (emphatic)] **And I.** The emphasis lies in the abundant goodness of God
contrasted with Israel's waywardness.

How...?] Rather, **How...!** *i.e.* How gloriously ! With what honour will I place thee
among the children !

goodly...of the hosts...] Rather, *a heritage
of the* **chief beauty** *of nations.* The general
sense is, that Israel possesses *the most beautiful territory of any nation.*

and I said] This clause is not the answer
to a difficulty, as in the A. V., but completes
the description of God's loving purpose. "I
said within myself that I would treat thee

s Isai. 63. 16.
t Isai. 48. 8.
ch. 5. 11.

u Isai. 15. 2.

x ver. 14.
Hos. 14. 1.
y Hos. 6. 1.

z Ps. 121. 1.
a Ps. 3. 8.
b ch. 11. 13.
Hos. 9. 10.

c Ezra 9. 7.

d ch. 22. 21.
a ch. 3. 1.
Joel 2. 12
b Deut.10.20.
Isai. 45. 23.
c Isai. 48. 1.
Zech. 8. 8.

20 *s*My father; and shalt not turn away ¹from me. Surely *as* a wife treacherously departeth from her ²husband, so *t*have ye dealt treacherously with me, O house of Israel, saith the LORD.

21   A voice was heard upon *u*the high places, weeping *and* supplications of the children of Israel: for they have perverted 22 their way, *and* they have forgotten the LORD their God. ¶ *x*Return, ye backsliding children, *and* *y*I will heal your backslidings. ¶ Behold, we come unto thee; for thou *art* the LORD our God. 23 *z*Truly in vain *is salvation hoped for* from the hills, *and from* the multitude of mountains: *a*truly in the LORD our God *is* the 24 salvation of Israel. *b*For shame hath devoured the labour of our fathers from our youth; their flocks and their herds, their 25 sons and their daughters. We lie down in our shame, and our confusion covereth us: *c*for we have sinned against the LORD our God, we and our fathers, from our youth even unto this day, and *d*have not obeyed the voice of the LORD our God.

CHAP. 4. IF thou wilt return, O Israel, saith the LORD, *a*return unto me: and if thou wilt put away thine abominations out of 2 my sight, then shalt thou not remove. *b*And thou shalt swear, The LORD liveth, *c*in truth, in judgment, and in righteousness;

¹ Heb. *from after me.*   ² Heb. *friend.*

---

as a son, and give thee a glorious inheritance : I also said, that ye would return my love, would call me Father, and be untrue to me no more."

20. *Surely as*] Rather, **Just as.**

21. *upon the high places*] Upon those bare table-lands, which previously had been the scene of Israel's idolatries (*v.* 2). The prophet supposes the offer of mercy to Israel if repentant to have been accepted, and describes Israel's agony of grief now that she is convinced of her sins.

weeping and *supplications*] Lit. *the weeping of earnest prayers for mercy.*

for they have...] Rather, **because** *they have perverted their way*, lit. made it crooked. It gives the reason of their cry for mercy.

22. Jehovah's answer to their prayer in *v.* 21 is immediately followed by their acceptance of the offer of Divine mercy.

for] Rather, **because...** This profession of faith gives the reason why they return to Jehovah. The whole description is most graphically conceived. The people weeping upon the hills: God's gracious voice bidding them return : the glad cry of the penitents exclaiming that they come : the profession of faith won from them by the divine love ; —these form altogether a most touching picture of a national repentance.

23. Rather, **Surely** *in vain from the hills* **is the revelry of the mountains.** The penitents contrast in it the uselessness of idol - worship with the salvation which Jehovah gives to His people.

24. *For...*] **And.** It is the continuation of the thought in *v.* 23. Idolatry was there described as unprofitable, here as ruinous and hurtful.

shame] Lit. **the shame** [Bosheth, per-

sonified], that is, *Baal.* The names *Bosheth* and *Baal* are constantly interchanged. Cp. Judg. vi. 31, 32.

their flocks and their herds] The temperate and sober enjoyments connected with Jehovah's sacrifices led to no excess, whereas in idol-worship the people, after sitting down "to eat and drink, rose up to play," and wasted both health and substance in licentious revelry.

their sons...] This probably refers to human sacrifices.

25. *We lie down...*] Or, **We will lie down** : we are ready to throw ourselves upon the ground in bitter humiliation.

covereth] Lit. **shall cover us.** We will hide our face from others.

IV. 1–4. The conclusion of both sides of the prophecy ; to Israel, *vv.* 1, 2 ; to Judah, *vv.* 3, 4.

1. *return*] The repentance of Israel described in iii. 21–25 was a hope, and not a reality. The return, literally, would be their restoration to their land ; spiritually, their abandoning their sins.

Verses 1 and 2 should be translated as follows :

If thou wouldst return, O Israel, saith Jehovah,
Unto Me thou shalt return :
And if thou wouldst remove thy abominations from before Me,
And not wander to and fro,
But wouldst swear truly, uprightly, and justly
By the living Jehovah ;

Then shall the heathen bless themselves &c.

*d*and the nations shall bless themselves in him, and in him shall
3 they *e*glory. For thus saith the LORD to the men of Judah and
Jerusalem, *f*Break up your fallow ground, and *g*sow not among
4 thorns. *h* Circumcise yourselves to the LORD, and take away
the foreskins of your heart, ye men of Judah and inhabitants of
Jerusalem : lest my fury come forth like fire, and burn that
none can quench *it*, because of the evil of your doings.

5 Declare ye in Judah, and publish in Jerusalem ; and say,
Blow ye the trumpet in the land : cry, gather together, and say,
*i*Assemble yourselves, and let us go into the defenced cities.
6 Set up the standard towards Zion : [1]retire, stay not : for I will
7 bring evil from the *k*north, and a great [2]destruction. *l*The lion
is come up from his thicket, and *m*the destroyer of the Gentiles
is on his way ; he is gone forth from his place *n*to make thy
land desolate ; *and* thy cities shall be laid waste, without an in-
8 habitant. For this *o*gird you with sackcloth, lament and howl :
for the fierce anger of the LORD is not turned back from us.

d Gen. 22. 18.
Gal. 3. 8.
e Isai. 45. 25.
1 Cor. 1. 31.
f Hos. 10. 12.
g Matt. 13.
7, 22.
h ch. 9. 26.
Rom. 2. 28.
Col. 2. 11.

i ch. 8. 14.

k ch. 1. 13.
& 6. 1, 22.
l 2 Kin. 24. 1.
Dan. 7. 4.
m ch. 25. 9.
n Isai. 1. 7.
ch. 2. 15.
o Isai. 22. 12.
ch. 6. 26.

[1] Or, *strengthen*.   [2] Heb. *breaking*.

---

in him] In Jehovah. Two great truths
are taught in this verse ; (1) that the
Gentiles were to be members of the Church
of the Messiah ; (2) that Israel's peculiar
office was to be God's mediator in this
great work. Thus Jeremiah is in exact
accord with the evangelical teaching of
Isaiah.

3. *to the men*] **To each man** *of Judah*.
They are summoned individually to repentance.

Break up] Lit. **Fallow for you a fallow
ground**, *i.e.* do not sow the seeds of repentance in unfit soil, but just as the husbandman prepares the ground, by clearing
it of weeds, and exposing it to the sun and
air, before entrusting to it the seed, so must
you regard repentance as a serious matter,
requiring forethought, and anxious labour.
To sow in unfallowed ground, was practically to sow on land full of thorns.

4. See Deut. x. 16 note. Nature, such as it
is in itself, unconsecrated to God, is to be
removed from our inner selves, that a new
and spiritual nature may take its place.

lest my fury...] God is long-suffering, but
unless this change take place, the time of
judgment must at length come to all as it
came to Jerusalem—*like fire* (cp. 1 Cor. iii.
13 ; Phil. ii. 12, 13).

iv. 5—vi. 30. *God's judgment upon the
Unrepentant.*

A group of prophecies now commences,
extending to ch. x. 25, but broken at
the beginning of ch. vii. by a new heading.
The subject of them all is the same,
namely, the approaching devastation of
Judæa by a hostile army in punishment
of its persistence in idolatry. The prophecy
of ch. vii. was probably written in the first
year of Jehoiakim, while as regards the
rest they probably extended over a con-

siderable period of time. This group, which
we may reasonably believe to have come
down to us much as it stood in Jehoiakim's
roll, gives us a general view of the nature of
Jeremiah's efforts during that important
period, when under Josiah a national
reformation was still possible, and the exile
might have been averted. The prophecy
(ch. vii.), spoken in the first year of
Jehoiakim, when the probation of Judah
was virtually over, was the solemn closing
of the appeal to the conscience of the
people, and a protest, while the new king
was still young upon his throne, against
that ruinous course upon which he so immediately entered.

5. Rather, **Make proclamation** *in Judah,
and in Jerusalem* **bid them hear**, *and say,
Blow the trumpet* **throughout** *the land :* **cry
aloud** *and say &c.* The prophecy begins
with a loud alarm of war. The verse well
sets forth in its numerous commands the
excitement and confusion of such a time.

6. *the standard*] A flag or signal, to which
the people were to rally.

retire, stay not] Rather, **gather your
goods together : linger not** *; for I* (emphatic,
I Jehovah) **am bringing** at this very
time &c.

7. Rather, **A** *lion...a destroyer* **of nations :**
a metaphor descriptive of the impending
calamity. A lion is just rousing himself
from his lair, but no common one. It is a
destroyer, not of men, but of nations.

is on his way] Lit. *has broken up* his en-
campment. Jeremiah uses a military term
strictly referring to the striking of tents in
preparation for the march.

without an inhabitant] The final stage of
destruction, actually reached in the utter
depopulation of Judæa consequent upon
Gedaliah's murder.

8. *is not turned...*] As long as their sins

9 And it shall come to pass at that day, saith the LORD, *that* the heart of the king shall perish, and the heart of the princes; and the priests shall be astonished, and the prophets shall wonder.

10 ¶ Then said I, Ah, Lord GOD! *p* surely thou hast greatly deceived this people and Jerusalem, *q* saying, Ye shall have peace;

11 whereas the sword reacheth unto the soul. ¶ At that time shall it be said to this people and to Jerusalem, *r* A dry wind of the high places in the wilderness toward the daughter of my people,

12 not to fan, nor to cleanse, *even* ¹a full wind from those *places* shall come unto me: now also *s* will I ²give sentence against

13 them. Behold, he shall come up as clouds, and *t* his chariots *shall be* as a whirlwind: *u* his horses are swifter than eagles.

14 Woe unto us! for we are spoiled. ¶ O Jerusalem, *x* wash thine heart from wickedness, that thou mayest be saved. How long

15 shall thy vain thoughts lodge within thee? For a voice declareth *y* from Dan, and publisheth affliction from mount

16 Ephraim. Make ye mention to the nations; behold, publish against Jerusalem, *that* watchers come *z* from a far country, and

17 give out their voice against the cities of Judah. *a* As keepers of

p Ezek. 14. 9.
2 Thess. 2. 11.
q ch. 5. 12.
& 14. 13.
r ch. 51. 1.
Ezek. 17. 10.
Hos. 13. 15.

s ch. 1. 16.

t Isai. 5. 28.

u Deut. 28.
49.
Hos. 8. 1.
Hab. 1. 8.
x Isai. 1. 16.
Jam. 4. 8.
y ch. 8. 16.

z ch. 5. 15.

a 2 Kin. 25.
1, 4.

¹ Or, *a fuller wind than those.*   ² Heb. *utter judgments.*

are unrepented of, so long must their punishment continue.

10. *Ah, Lord* GOD !] **Alas! my Lord Jehovah:** an expression of disapproval on Jeremiah's part. Jeremiah had constantly to struggle against the misgivings of his own melancholy nature, but he never let them prevent him from doing his duty. See Introd. p. 160.

Ye shall have peace] These words are generally referred to the false prophets; they rather refer to real prophecies of future blessedness promised to the Jews. Jeremiah could not reconcile the doom he was now commanded to pronounce, either with his previous prophecy, or with what he read in the writings of his predecessors. Time only could solve the difficulty. Upon the struggles of the prophets to understand their own predictions see 1 Pet. i. 10, 11.

unto the soul] The sword has reached the life. *i.e.* has inflicted a mortal wound.

11. *At that time*] See *v.* 7. Though the revelation of the certainty of Judah's ruin wrings from Jeremiah a cry of despair, yet it is but for a moment; he immediately returns to the delivery of God's message.

A dry wind] Lit. **A clear wind.** The Samûm is probably meant, a dry parching east wind blowing from the Arabian desert, before which vegetation withers, and human life becomes intolerable.

not to fan &c.] The Syrian husbandmen make great use of the wind for separating the chaff from the corn: but when the Samûm blows labour becomes impossible.— It is not for use, but for destruction.

12. Or, as in marg.; *i.e.* a wind more full, more impetuous than those winds which serve for fanning and cleansing the corn.

unto me] Rather, **for me:** to perform my will.

13. His troops move on in large masses like dark threatening clouds (Joel ii. 2).

Woe unto us! for we are spoiled] Jeremiah's own cry of grief.

14. *thy vain thoughts*] Thy **iniquitous** *thoughts.* *Aven,* the word used here, is especially applied to the sin of idolatry : thus Bethel is generally called Beth-aven by Hosea (iv. 15, v. 8 &c.), because instead of being the house of God, *El,* it was the house of an iniquity, *Aven,* the golden calf.

15. *Dan*] The border-town of Palestine on the north (Deut. xxxiv. 1).

mount Ephraim] The northern boundary of Judæa itself. The invading army presses on so rapidly, that scarcely have the news arrived of its appearance at Dan, before fresh messengers announce that it has traversed the whole length of Galilee, and is now defiling through the mountains of Samaria.

affliction] The same word, *aven,* occurs in *v.* 14, and apparently there is a play upon its double meaning : for from a root signifying worthlessness, it is used both for wickedness and for misery. Thus the *iniquity* of Judah proves also to be her *affliction,* as being the cause of the ruin inflicted by the enemy.

16. Proclaim ye to the heathen, *Behold !* **Cry aloud concerning** *Jerusalem, that watchers* **are on their way** *from a far country : and* **will** *give out their voice against the cities of Judah.* The heathen are summoned to witness the chastisement of Jerusalem, that they may take warning thereby. By *watchers* are meant besiegers, who will surround the city with a line of sentinels.

17. Jeremiah compares the tents of the

a field, are they against her round about; because she hath
18 been rebellious against me, saith the LORD. *b*Thy way and thy
doings have procured these *things* unto thee; this *is* thy wickedness, because it is bitter, because it reacheth unto thine heart.
19 ¶ My *c*bowels, my bowels! I am pained at ¹my very heart; my
heart maketh a noise in me; I cannot hold my peace, because
thou hast heard, O my soul, the sound of the trumpet, the alarm
20 of war. *d*Destruction upon destruction is cried; for the whole
land is spoiled: suddenly are *e*my tents spoiled, *and* my cur-
21 tains in a moment. How long shall I see the standard, *and*
22 hear the sound of the trumpet? For my people *is* foolish, they
have not known me; they *are* sottish children, and they have
none understanding: *f*they *are* wise to do evil, but to do good
23 they have no knowledge. *g*I beheld the earth, and, lo, *it was*
*h*without form, and void; and the heavens, and they *had* no
24 light. *i*I beheld the mountains, and, lo, they trembled, and all
25 the hills moved lightly. I beheld, and, lo, *there was* no man, and
26 *k*all the birds of the heavens were fled. I beheld, and, lo, the
fruitful place *was* a wilderness, and all the cities thereof were
broken down at the presence of the LORD, *and* by his fierce anger.
27 ¶ For thus hath the LORD said, The whole land shall be desolate;
28 *l*yet will I not make a full end. For this *m*shall the earth mourn,
and *n*the heavens above be black: because I have spoken *it*, I

b Ps. 107. 17.
Isai. 50. 1.
ch. 2. 17.

c Isai. 15. 5.
ch. 9. 1, 10.

d Ps. 42. 7.
Ezek. 7. 26.
e ch. 10. 20.

f Rom.16.19.
g Isai. 24. 19.
h Gen. 1. 2.
i Isai. 5. 25.
k Zeph. 1. 3.

l ch. 5. 10.
& 46. 28.
m Hos. 4. 3.
n Isai. 5. 30.
& 50. 3.

¹ Heb. *the walls of my heart.*

---

besiegers on guard round Jerusalem to the
booths erected by shepherds or husbandmen
for the protection of their flocks or
produce.

18. *thy wickedness*] This siege is thy
wickedness, *i.e.* in its results; or better, this
is thy wretchedness, this army and thy approaching ruin is thy misery.

because] for. To feel that one's misery is
the result of one's own doings adds bitterness to the anguish, and makes it *reach*,
penetrate to the heart.

19. The verse is best translated as a series
of ejaculations, in which the people express
their grief at the ravages committed by the
enemy:

My bowels! My bowels! **I writhe in pain!**
The walls of my heart! *My heart* moans
for me!
I cannot keep silence!
For *thou hast heard, O my soul,* **the**
trumpet's voice!
The alarm of war!

20. *Destruction* &c.] Or, **breaking upon**
breaking (*v.* 6). The news of one breaking,
one violent calamity, follows close upon
another.

my curtains] The curtains of the tent,
put here for the tents themselves. Tents
were the ordinary habitations of the
Israelites.

21. *the standard*] See *v.* 6. The alarm
caused by the invasion is graphically described. The people are dispersed over the
land following their usual pursuits, when
tidings come of the enemy's approach. The

only chance of escape is a hasty flight.
Flags stream from the hills to mark the
safest route, while the blasts of the trumpet
quicken the steps of the wavering.

23—26. In four verses each beginning
with *I beheld*, the prophet sees in vision the
desolate condition of Judæa during the
Babylonian Captivity.

23. *without form, and void*] **Desolate and**
void (see Gen. i. 2 note). The land has
returned to a state of chaos (marg. ref. note).

and the heavens] **And upward to the**
heavens. The imagery is that of the last
day of judgment. To Jeremiah's vision all
was as though the day of the Lord had
come, and earth returned to the state in
which it was before the first creative word
(see 2 Pet. iii. 10).

24. *moved lightly*] Reeled to and fro, from
the violence of the earthquake.

26. *the fruitful place*] The Carmel (ii. 7),
where the population had been most dense,
and the labours of the husbandman most
richly rewarded, has become **the wilderness.**

at the presence] *i.e.* because of, at the command of Jehovah, and because of His
anger.

27. *desolate*] **a waste.**
One of the most striking points of prophecy is, that however severe may be the
judgment pronounced against Judah, there
is always the reservation, that the ruin shall
not be complete (iii. 14).

28. *For...*] Because of this doom upon
Judah.

o Num. 23.
19.
ch. 7. 16.

p Ezek.23.40.
q ch. 22. 20.
Lam. 1. 2.

r Isai. 1. 15.
Lam. 1. 17.

a Ezek.22.30.
b Gen. 18.
23, &c.
Ps. 12. 1.
c Gen. 18. 26.
d Tit. 1. 16.
e ch. 4. 2.
f ch. 7. 9.
g 2 Chr. 16. 9.
h Isai. 1. 5.
ch. 2. 30.
i ch. 7. 28.
Zeph. 3. 2.
k ch. 8. 7.

l Mic. 3. 1.

m Ps. 2. 3.

have purposed *it*, and *o*will not repent, neither will I turn back
29 from it. The whole city shall flee for the noise of the horsemen
and bowmen; they shall go into thickets, and climb up upon the
rocks: every city *shall be* forsaken, and not a man dwell therein.
30 And *when* thou *art* spoiled, what wilt thou do? Though thou
clothest thyself with crimson, though thou deckest thee with ornaments of gold, *p*though thou rentest thy ¹face with painting,
in vain shalt thou make thyself fair; *q*thy lovers will despise
31 thee, they will seek thy life. For I have heard a voice as of a
woman in travail, *and* the anguish as of her that bringeth forth
her first child, the voice of the daughter of Zion, *that* bewaileth
herself, *that* *r*spreadeth her hands, *saying*, Woe *is* me now! for
my soul is wearied because of murderers.

Chap. 5. RUN ye to and fro through the streets of Jerusalem, and
see now, and know, and seek in the broad places thereof, *a*if ye
can find a man, *b*if there be *any* that executeth judgment, that
2 seeketh the truth; *c*and I will pardon it. And *d*though they
3 say, *e*The LORD liveth; surely they *f*swear falsely. O LORD, *are*
not *g*thine eyes upon the truth? thou hast *h*stricken them, but
they have not grieved; thou hast consumed them, *but* *i*they
have refused to receive correction: they have made their faces
4 harder than a rock; they have refused to return. Therefore I
said, Surely these *are* poor; they are foolish: for *k*they know
5 not the way of the LORD, *nor* the judgment of their God. I will
get me unto the great men, and will speak unto them; for
*l*they have known the way of the LORD, *and* the judgment of
their God: but these have altogether *m*broken the yoke, *and*

¹ Heb. *eyes.*

I have purposed it] The LXX. arrangement restores the parallelism;

For I have spoken, and will not repent,
I have purposed, and will not turn back
    from it.

29. *The whole city* &c.] Rather, **Every
city is fleeing**. All the inhabitants of the
towns flee to Jerusalem for protection, or
seek refuge in the woods and rocks.

the horsemen and bowmen] The cavalry
(iv. 13) and bowmen formed the chief
strength of the Assyrian armies.

they shall go] **They have gone.**

30. Translate, **And thou, O plundered
one, what effectest thou**, that *thou clothest
thyself with* scarlet, that *thou deckest* thyself
with ornaments of gold, **that thou enlargest
thine eyes with antimony** (2 K. ix. 30
note)? *In vain* **dost thou beautify thyself;**
thy lovers **despise** *thee, they* **seek** *thy life.*
Jerusalem is represented as a woman who
puts on her best attire to gain favour in the
eyes of her lovers, but in vain.

**31. For a cry have I heard as of one
    writhing in pain:**
    Anguish as of one that bringeth
        forth her first-born:
    The cry of the daughter of Zion.
    She gasps for breath: she stretches
        out her palms:
    Woe is me! for my soul faints before
        the murderers.

V. 1-9. The capture and the destruction
of Jerusalem was owing to its utter immorality. Josiah's reforms were frustrated by
the immorality prevalent among all classes.
The prophet sees evil triumphing, but we
must not take his words so literally as to
conclude that there were no good men then
in Jerusalem (cp. iv. 27, xxiv. 5).

1. *the broad places*] The open spaces
next the gates, and other places of concourse.

a man] Or, *any one.*

that executeth] *That* **practiseth.**

truth] **uprightness, probity** (so in *v.* 3).

2. Though they take the most binding
form of oath, they do so only as a means of
deceiving others.

3. *upon the truth*] God looks to the *faith*,
the upright purpose of the heart, and without it the nominal fealty of an oath is an
abomination.

4. *Therefore*] More simply *and.*

they are foolish] Or, **they act foolishly**
(see Num. xii. 11), not having that knowledge which would enable them to guide
their ways with discretion.

5. *they have known...*] Men of education,
who read the Scriptures, and learn from
them the nature of God's judgments.

but these] Lit. **surely they** (cp. *v.* 4).

the yoke] The Mosaic law.

and burst...] **They have torn off**, torn
themselves loose from.

6 burst the bonds. Wherefore [n]a lion out of the forest shall slay them, [o]*and* a wolf of the [1]evenings shall spoil them, [p]a leopard shall watch over their cities: every one that goeth out thence shall be torn in pieces: because their transgressions are many,
7 *and* their backslidings [2]are increased. ¶ How shall I pardon thee for this? thy children have forsaken me, and [q]sworn by *them* [r]*that are* no gods: [s]when I had fed them to the full, they then committed adultery, and assembled themselves by troops
8 in the harlots' houses. [t]They were *as* fed horses in the morning:
9 every one [u]neighed after his neighbour's wife. [x]Shall I not visit for these *things?* saith the LORD: [y]and shall not my soul
10 be avenged on such a nation as this? [z]Go ye up upon her walls, and destroy; [a]but make not a full end: take away her
11 battlements; for they *are* not the LORD's. For [b]the house of Israel and the house of Judah have dealt very treacherously
12 against me, saith the LORD. [c]They have belied the LORD, and said, [d]*It is* not he; neither shall evil come upon us; [e]neither
13 shall we see sword nor famine: and the prophets shall become wind, and the word *is* not in them: thus shall it be done unto
14 them. Wherefore thus saith the LORD God of hosts, Because ye speak this word, [f]behold, I will make my words in thy
15 mouth fire, and this people wood, and it shall devour them. Lo, I will bring a [g]nation upon you [h]from far, O house of Israel, saith the LORD: it *is* a mighty nation, it *is* an ancient nation, a nation whose language thou knowest not, neither understandeth
16 what they say. Their quiver *is* as an open sepulchre, they *are*
17 all mighty men. And they shall eat up thine [i]harvest, and thy bread, *which* thy sons and thy daughters should eat: they shall eat up thy flocks and thine herds: they shall eat up thy vines

[n] ch. 4. 7.
[o] Ps. 104. 20.
[p] Hos. 13. 7.

[q] Josh. 23, 7.
Zeph. 1. 5.
[r] Deut. 32.21.
[s] Deut. 32.15.
[t] Ezek. 22.11.
[u] ch. 13. 27.
[x] ch. 9. 9.
[y] ch. 44. 22.
[z] ch. 39. 8.
[a] ch. 4. 27.
ver. 18.
[b] ch. 3. 20.

[c] 2 Chr. 36. 16.
ch. 4. 10.
[d] Isai. 28. 15.
[e] ch. 14. 13.

[f] ch. 1. 9.

[g] Deut. 28. 49.
Isai. 5. 26.
ch. 1. 15.
[h] Isai. 39. 3.
ch. 4. 16.
[i] Lev. 26. 16.
Deut. 28. 31, 33.

---

[1] Or, *deserts.*   [2] Heb. *are strong.*

---

the bonds] The fastenings by which the yoke was fixed upon the necks of the oxen.
6. *evenings*] See marg. From its habit of skulking about in the twilight the wolf is often called the *evening wolf* (Hab. i. 8; Zeph. iii. 3), but the word used here means a sandy desert.
leopard] **panther.**
7. Rather, **Why,** for what reason should *I pardon thee?*
when &c.] Or, *though I bound them to me by oath, yet they committed adultery.*
the harlots' houses] **The harlot's house,** *i.e.* the temple of an idol ; the prophet had also in view (see *v.* 8) the unchastity which accompanied most forms of nature-worship.
8. *in the morning*] Render, **they rove about.** Some prefer, "(horses) from Mesech."
10. *her walls*] It is possible that not the city walls, but those of a vineyard are meant. Judæa is God's vineyard (Isai. v. 1-7), and God permits the enemy to enter the vineyard to destroy her.
battlements] **tendrils.** The tendrils and branches of Judah's vine are given up to ruin, but not the stock. See Isai. vi. 13 note.
12. It is *not he*] *i.e.* Who speaks by the prophets.

13. *word*] Rather, **speaker.** Lit. *And he who speaketh is not in them, i.e.* there is no one who speaketh in them ; what the prophets say has no higher authority than themselves.
thus...] *i.e.* May the evil which the prophets threaten fall upon their head.
15. Israel is not put here for the ten tribes, but for the whole house of Jacob, of which Judah was now the representative.
mighty] *permanent, enduring.* The word is the usual epithet of the rocks (Num. xxiv. 21), and of ever-flowing streams (Deut. xxi. 4. Heb.). It describes therefore a nation, whose empire is firm as a rock, and ever rolling onwards like a mighty river. The epithet *ancient* refers simply to time.
whose language thou knowest not] This would render them more pitiless, as they would not understand their cries for mercy.
16. *Their quiver*] See iv. 29, note.
17. Or,—

It shall eat *thine harvest and thy breed :*
They shall eat *thy sons and thy daughters :*
It shall eat thy sheep and thy cattle :
It shall eat *thy vines and thy fig-trees.*

and thy fig trees : they shall impoverish thy fenced cities, where-
18 in thou trustedst, with the sword.   Nevertheless in those days,
19 saith the LORD, I *k*will not make a full end with you.   ¶ And it
shall come to pass, when ye shall say, *l*Wherefore doeth the
LORD our God all these *things* unto us ? then shalt thou answer
them, Like as ye have *m*forsaken me, and served strange gods
in your land, so *n*shall ye serve strangers in a land *that is* not
20 your's.   ¶ Declare this in the house of Jacob, and publish it in
21 Judah, saying, Hear now this, O *o*foolish people, and without
*l*understanding; which have eyes, and see not; which have ears,
22 and hear not: *p*fear ye not me ? saith the LORD : will ye not
tremble at my presence, which have placed the sand *for* the
*q*bound of the sea by a perpetual decree, that it cannot pass it :
and though the waves thereof toss themselves, yet can they not
prevail; though they roar, yet can they not pass over it ?
23 ¶ But this people hath a revolting and a rebellious heart; they
24 are revolted and gone.   Neither say they in their heart, Let us
now fear the LORD our God, *r*that giveth rain, both the *s*former
and the latter, in his season : *t*he reserveth unto us the ap-
25 pointed weeks of the harvest.   *u*Your iniquities have turned
away these *things*, and your sins have withholden good *things*
26 from you.   For among my people are found wicked *men :* ²they
*x*lay wait, as he that setteth snares; they set a trap, they catch
27 men.   As a ³cage is full of birds, so *are* their houses full of
28 deceit : therefore they are become great, and waxen rich.   They

k ch. 4. 27.
l Deut. 29.
24 &c.
1 Kin. 9. 8.
ch. 13. 22.
m ch. 2. 13.
n Deut. 28.
48.
o Isai. 6. 9.
Ezek. 12. 2.
Matt. 13. 14.
p Rev. 15. 4.

q Job 26. 10.
Ps. 104. 9.

r Ps. 147. 8.
Acts 14. 17.
s Deut. 11.
14.
Joel 2. 23.
t Gen. 8. 22.
u ch. 3. 3.
x Prov. 1.
11, 17, 18.

---

¹ Heb. *heart*, Hos. 7. 11.   ² Or. *they pry as fowlers lie in wait.*   ³ Or, *coop.*

---

they shall impoverish...] Or, **It shall bat-
ter thy** *fortified cities, wherein thou* **trustest,
with weapons of war.**   There is probably
reference here to an instrument like a battering-ram, with which the Assyrians beat
down the walls of their enemies.
19. The reason why God so chastises His
people.   As they in a land specially consecrated to Jehovah had served *strange* (*i.e.*
foreign) gods, so shall they in a land belonging to others be the slaves of strangers.
20–31. Against the God (1) of Creation
(*v.* 22), and (2) of Providence (*r.* 24), they
sin, not merely by apostasy, but by a general immorality extending to all classes (*rr.*
25–28).   It is in this immorality that their
idolatry has its root.
22. The sea is the symbol of restless and
indomitable energy, chafing against all resistance, and dashing to pieces the works
whereby man endeavours to restrain its
fury.   Yet God has imposed upon it laws
which it must obey, and keeps it in its appointed place, not by barriers of iron but
by a belt of sand.   Modern science has
shewn that the resisting power of sand is
enormous.   A wave which would shatter
rocks falls powerless upon sand.
can they not prevail] The opposite of *thou
couldest* (iii. 5).   The sea, the mightiest of
God's works, cannot prevail, cannot break
God's laws, because He has not endowed it
with free-will.   Man, physically impotent,
can prevail, because, being made in God's
image, he is free.

23. The heart, or will of the Jews was
first *revolting*, lit. a will that *drew back* from
God, because it disliked His service ; and
secondly it was *rebellious*, a will that actively
resisted Him.   Cp. Deut. xxi. 18, 20.
24. As God's Providence addresses itself
chiefly to the thoughtful, Jeremiah says *in
their heart*.   By the intelligent study of
God's dealings men perceive that they are
not merely acts of power but also of love.
the appointed weeks] Lit. **He guardeth,**
maintaineth, **for us the weeks** which are
the statutes or settled laws *of the harvest.*
These were the seven weeks from the Passover to Pentecost, and were as important
for the ingathering of the crops as the rainy
seasons for their nourishment.
25. It was not that the rains did not fall,
or that the harvest weeks were less bright ;
the good was there, but the wickedness of
the community blocked up the channels,
through which it should have reached the
people.   The lawlessness and injustice of
the times kept the mass of the people in
poverty.
26. Rather, **he spieth about like the
crouching down of fowlers ; they have set
the fatal snare ;** *they catch men.*
trap] Lit. The *destroyer ;* it was probably
a gin, which strangled the birds caught in it.
27. *deceit*] The wealth gained by deceit
and fraud.
28. Fatness is admired in the East as a
sign of wealth.

are waxen *v*fat, they shine: yea, they overpass the deeds of the
wicked: they judge not *z*the cause, the cause of the fatherless,
*a*yet they prosper; and the right of the needy do they not judge.
29 *b*Shall I not visit for these *things?* saith the LORD: shall not
30 my soul be avenged on such a nation as this? ¶ ¹A wonderful and
*c*horrible thing is committed in the land; the prophets prophesy
31 *d*falsely, and the priests ²bear rule by their means; and my people *e*love *to have it* so: and what will ye do in the end thereof?

CHAP. 6. O YE children of Benjamin, gather yourselves to flee out
of the midst of Jerusalem, and blow the trumpet in Tekoa, and
set up a sign of fire in *a*Beth-haccerem: *b*for evil appeareth
2 out of the north, and great destruction. I have likened the
3 daughter of Zion to a ³comely and delicate *woman.* The shepherds with their flocks shall come unto her; *c*they shall pitch
their tents against her round about; they shall feed every one in
4 his place. *d*Prepare ye war against her; arise, and let us go up
*e*at noon. Woe unto us! for the day goeth away, for the shadows
5 of the evening are stretched out. Arise, and let us go by night,
6 and let us destroy her palaces. For thus hath the LORD of hosts

v Deut. 32.
15.
z Isai. 1. 23.
Zech. 7. 10.
a Job 12. 6.
Ps. 73. 12.
b ver. 9.
Mal. 3. 5.
c ch. 23. 14.
Hos. 6. 10.
d ch. 14. 14.
Ezek. 13. 6.
e Mic. 2. 11.

a Neh. 3. 14.
b ch. 1. 14.
& 4. 6.

c 2 Kin. 25.
1. 4.

d ch. 51. 27.
Joel 3. 9.
e ch. 15. 8.

---

¹ Or, *Astonishment and filthiness.*

² Or, *take into their hands.*

³ Or, *dwelling at home.*

---

they shine] This word is used of the sleekness of the skin, soft and smooth as ivory.

they overpass the deeds of the wicked] Lit. *They have overpassed words of wickedness, i.e.* they go to excess in wickedness.

yet they prosper] Or, **that they** (the orphans) **may prosper,** enjoy their rights.

30. Rather, **A terrible** *and horrible thing* **has happened** *in the land.*

31. *bear rule by their means*] Rather, **The** priests **rule at their hands,** *i.e.* govern according to their false prophecies, guidance, and directions.

my people love to have it *so*] False teaching lightens the yoke of God's Law, and removes His fear from the conscience: and with this, man is ready to be content.

VI. Jeremiah proceeds to unveil the judgment impending upon Jerusalem, and his description of it is divided into five parts, each beginning with the words "Thus saith Jehovah."

1. Jeremiah addresses the men of Benjamin, either as being his own tribesmen, or as a name appropriate to the people of Jerusalem, which also was situate in the tribe of Benjamin.

gather yourselves to flee] Gather your goods together to remove them to a place of safety.

blow the trumpet in Tekoa] The name of Tekoa is almost identical with the verb *to blow:* but it was not chosen merely for the alliteration, but because it was the last town in Judæa (about eleven miles south of Jerusalem), upon the very border of the desert, where the fugitives would halt.

a sign] Rather, **a signal.**

Beth-haccerem] Or, the "Vineyard-House,"

which was situated half-way between Jerusalem and Tekoa.

appeareth] **is bending over** ;—is bending forward in eagerness to seize its prey.

2. The whole verse is difficult, but should probably be translated ;—*to a pasturage, yea a luxuriant* pasturage, *have I likened* [or, *have reduced to silence, i.e.* destroyed] *the daughter of Zion.*

3. **To it shall come** *shepherds with their flocks :*
They have pitched upon it *their tents round about :*
They have pastured each his hand, *i.e. side.*

The pasture is so abundant that each feeds his flock, *i.e.* plunders Jerusalem, at the *side* of his own tent.

4. *Prepare ye war*] Rather, **Sanctify ye war against her.** War in ancient times was never undertaken without religious solemnities (see Deut. xx. 2 note). For some of these cp. Ezek. xxi. 21-23.

at noon] The midday heat is so great in the East as to be usually passed under shelter (2 Sam. iv. 5; Song of Sol. i. 7). The morning-march of an army was made fasting, and was usually over by eight or nine. But so great is the impatience of the Chaldeans for the assault that they cry, *we will make the assault at noon !*

Woe unto us !] Or,

Alas for us ! *for the day* has turned !
For the evening shadows are lengthening !

5. Up ! and **we will make the assault** *by night !*
And destroy *her palaces.*

said, Hew ye down trees, and ¹cast a mount against Jerusalem:
this *is* the city to be visited; she *is* wholly oppression in the

f Isai. 57. 20.
7 midst of her. *f*As a fountain casteth out her waters, so she
g Ps. 55. 9.
ch. 20. 8.
Ezek. 7.
11, 23.
casteth out her wickedness: *g*violence and spoil is heard in her;
8 before me continually *is* grief and wounds.　Be thou instructed,
O Jerusalem, lest *h*my soul ²depart from thee; lest I make thee
h Ezek.23.18.
Hos. 9. 12.
9 desolate, a land not inhabited.　¶Thus saith the LORD of hosts,
They shall throughly glean the remnant of Israel as a vine:
turn back thine hand as a grape-gatherer into the baskets.
10 ¶To whom shall I speak, and give warning, that they may hear?
i ch. 7. 26.
Acts 7, 51.
See Ex. 6.
12.
k ch. 20. 8.
l ch. 20. 9.
m ch. 9. 21.
behold, their *i*ear *is* uncircumcised, and they cannot hearken:
behold, *k*the word of the LORD is unto them a reproach; they
11 have no delight in it.　Therefore I am full of the fury of the
LORD; *l*I am weary with holding in: I will pour it out *m*upon
the children abroad, and upon the assembly of young men together: for even the husband with the wife shall be taken, the
n Deut. 28.
30.
ch. 8. 10.
12 aged with *him that is* full of days.　And *n*their houses shall be
turned unto others, *with their* fields and wives together: for I
will stretch out my hand upon the inhabitants of the land, saith
13 the LORD.　For from the least of them even unto the greatest
o Isai. 56. 11.
ch. 14. 18.
Mic. 3. 5.
p ch. 8. 11.
Ezek. 13. 10.
of them every one *is* given to *o*covetousness; and from the pro-
14 phet even unto the priest every one dealeth falsely.　They have
*p*healed also the ³hurt *of the daughter* of my people slightly,

¹ Or, *pour out the engine of*　² Heb. *be loosed,* or, *dis-*　³ Heb. *bruise,* or, *breach.*
shot.　　　　　　　　　　*jointed.*

The generals delay the assault till the next
morning.　The soldiers consider themselves
aggrieved at this, and clamour for a night
attack.

6. *Hew ye down trees*] Rather, **her trees:—**
for the simple purpose of clearing the approaches.

cast a mount] Lit. *pour :* the earth was
emptied out of the baskets, in which it was
carried to the required spot upon the backs
of labourers.

wholly] Or,
She *is the city* **that is visited:**
Wholly oppression **is** *in the midst of her!*
She is visited, i.e. punished; she is ripe
for punishment.

7. *As a fountain casteth out*] Better, **As a
cistern** *cooleth.*

before me...] **Before My face continually
there is disease and wounding:—**Disease as
the result of poverty and want : wounding,
or, the commission of deeds of actual violence.

8. *Be thou instructed*] **Be thou chastised:—**
learn the lesson which chastisement is intended to teach thee.

lest my soul] Lest I Myself—not *depart
from thee,* God does not willingly leave His
people, but—**be torn from thee.**

9. *They* &c.] Each word indicates the completeness of Judah's ruin.

turn back thine hand] Addressed perhaps
to Nebuchadnezzar as God's servant (xxv.
9).　He is required to go over the vine once
again, that no grapes may escape.

into the baskets] Better, *upon the tendrils.*
While the Jews carried captive to Babylon
escaped, misery gleaned the rest again and
again.

10. *give warning*] Rather **testify.**
reproach] They make the Word of God
the object of their ridicule.

11. Or, **But I am filled with** *the fury of Jehovah : I am weary with holding* it *in.* **Pour
it out** *upon the children* **in the street, and
upon the company of youths** *together;* **for
both man and** *wife shall be taken ;* **the elder
and he whose days are full.** With emphatic abruptness Jeremiah bids himself
give full utterance to God's message.　And
the message is to reach all.　Five stages
of human life are successively marked
out.

12. *turned*] Violently transferred.　Houses,
fields, wives, all they most valued, and most
jealously kept to themselves—are gone.

13. *given to covetousness*] Lit. **every one
has gained gains.** The temper of mind
which gains the world is not that which
gains heaven.

falsely] Rather, *fraudulently.*

14. *healed*] Rather, *tried to heal.*
of the daughter] These words are omitted
by a majority of MSS., but found in most
of the Versions.

slightly] Lit. *according to, i.e.* as if it were,
a trifle: making nothing of it. This cry of
peace was doubtless based upon Josiah's
reforms.

15 ^qsaying, Peace, peace; when *there is* no peace. Were they
^rashamed when they had committed abomination? nay, they
were not at all ashamed, neither could they blush: therefore
they shall fall among them that fall: at the time *that* I visit
16 them they shall be cast down, saith the LORD. ¶ Thus saith
the LORD, Stand ye in the ways, and see, and ask for the ^sold
paths, where *is* the good way, and walk therein, and ye shall
find ^trest for your souls. But they said, We will not walk
17 therein. Also I set ^uwatchmen over you, *saying*, Hearken to
the sound of the trumpet. But they said, We will not hearken.
18 Therefore hear, ye nations, and know, O congregation, what *is*
19 among them. ^xHear, O earth: behold, I will bring evil upon
this people, *even* ^ythe fruit of their thoughts, because they have
not hearkened unto my words, nor to my law, but rejected it.
20 ^zTo what purpose cometh there to me incense ^afrom Sheba,
and the sweet cane from a far country? ^byour burnt offerings
21 *are* not acceptable, nor your sacrifices sweet unto me. Therefore thus saith the LORD, Behold, I will lay stumblingblocks
before this people, and the fathers and the sons together shall
fall upon them; the neighbour and his friend shall perish.
22 ¶ Thus saith the LORD, Behold, a people cometh from the ^cnorth
country, and a great nation shall be raised from the sides of the
23 earth. They shall lay hold on bow and spear; they *are* cruel,

q ch. 4. 10.
& 23. 17.
r ch. 3. 3.

s Isai. 8. 20.
ch. 18. 15.
Luke 16. 29.
t Matt.11. 29.

u Isai. 21.11.
ch. 25. 4.
Hab. 2. 1.

x Isai. 1. 2.
y Prov. 1.31.

z Ps. 40. 6.
Amos 5. 21.
Mic. 6. 6.
a Isai. 60. 6.
b ch. 7. 21.

c ch. 1. 15
&c.

---

15. They are brought to shame because
  they have *committed abomination* :
Shame nevertheless they feel not;
To blush nevertheless they know
  not ;
  Therefore they shall fall among the
  falling ;
  At the time when *I visit them, they*
  shall **stumble,** *saith Jehovah.*

The fact is expressed that their conduct was
a disgrace to them, though they did not feel
it as such. "Abomination" has its usual
meaning of idolatry (iv. 1).
  16. The sense is:—God's prophet has declared that a great national calamity is at
hand. "Make inquiries; stand in the ways;
ask the passers by. Your country was
once prosperous and blessed. Try to learn
what were the paths trodden in those days
which led your ancestors to happiness.
Choose them, and walk earnestly therein,
and find thereby rest for your souls." The
Christian Fathers often contrast Christ the
one *goodway* with the *old tracks*, many in
number and narrow to walk in, which are
the Law and the Prophets.
  17. *watchmen*] The prophets (Isai. lii. 8).
  the sound of the trumpet] This was the
signal for flight (vi. 1; Amos iii. 6). Similarly the prophet's warning was to move
men to escape from God's judgments.
  18. God summons three witnesses to hear
His sentence. (1) The Gentiles. (2) All
mankind, Jews and Gentiles. (3) Nature
(see *v.* 19).
  what is among them] Rather, *what happens*
in them; *i.e.* "Know what great things I
will do to them."

19. The Fathers understood this to be
the decree rejecting the Jews from being
the Church.
  20. *the sweet cane*] The same as the scented
cane of Ex. xxx. 23 (see note).
  your burnt offerings] The rejection of
ritual observances is proclaimed by the two
prophets Isaiah and Jeremiah, who chiefly
assisted the two pious kings Hezekiah and
Josiah in restoring the Temple-service. God
rejects not the ceremonial service, but the
substitution of it for personal holiness and
morality. Cp. 1 Sam. xv. 22; Isai. i. 11;
Micah vi. 6-8.

  21. *Behold,* **I** *give unto this people* **causes**
    of stumbling,
  And they shall stumble against
    them :
  Fathers and sons together, *the neigh-*
    bour and his friend shall perish.

This is the natural consequence of their
conduct. Their service of Jehovah was a
systematic hypocrisy: how then could they
walk uprightly with their fellow-men?
When God lays stumblingblocks in men's
way, it is by the general action of His moral
law (James i. 13, 14), by which wilful sin
in one point reacts upon the whole moral
nature (do. ii. 10).
  22. *raised*] Or, **awakened,** to undertake
distant expeditions.
  the sides of the earth] Or **ends,** the most
distant regions (see xxv. 32).
  23. *spear*] Properly, a javelin for hurling
at the enemy (see 1 Sam. xvii. 6 note): an
ordinary weapon of the Babylonians.
  cruel] ruthless, inhuman. In the Assyrian
monuments warriors put the vanquished to

d Isai. 5. 30.

and have no mercy; their voice *c*roareth like the sea; and they ride upon horses, set in array as men for war against thee,

24 O daughter of Zion. We have heard the fame thereof: our

e ch. 4. 31.

hands wax feeble: *e*anguish hath taken hold of us, *and* pain, as

25 of a woman in travail. Go not forth into the field, nor walk by the way; for the sword of the enemy *and* fear *is* on every side.

f ch. 4. 8.
g ch. 25. 34.
Mic. 1. 10.
h Zech. 12.
10,
i ch. 1. 18.
& 15. 20.
k ch. 5. 23.
l ch. 9. 4.
m Ezek. 22.
18.
n Isai. 1. 22.

26 O daughter of my people, *f* gird *thee* with sackcloth, *g* and wallow thyself in ashes: *h* make thee mourning, *as for* an only son, most bitter lamentation: for the spoiler shall suddenly come upon us.

27 ¶ I have set thee *for* a tower *and* *i* a fortress among my people,

28 that thou mayest know and try their way. *k* They *are* all grievous revolters, *l* walking with slanders: *they are* *m* brass and iron;

29 they *are* all corrupters. The bellows are burned, the lead is consumed of the fire; the founder melteth in vain: for the

30 wicked are not plucked away. *n* 1 Reprobate silver shall *men* call them, because the LORD hath rejected them.

CHAP. 7. THE word that came to Jeremiah from the LORD, saying,

¹ Or, *Refuse silver.*

---

death; rows of impaled victims hang round the walls of the besieged towns; and men collect in heaps hands cut from the vanquished.

horses, set in array] A full stop should be put after *horses*. **It**—the whole army, and not the cavalry only—is *set in array.*

as men for war against thee] Rather, **as a warrior for battle** *against thee.*

24. The effect upon the Jewish people of the news of Nebuchadnezzar's approach.

wax feeble] **Are relaxed.** It is the opposite of what is said in *v.* 23 of the enemy, *They lay hold* &c. Terror makes the hands of the Jews hold their weapons with nerveless grasp.

25. *for the sword of the enemy*] Lit. *for to the enemy a sword*; *i.e. for the enemy is armed,* he has a commission from God to execute judgment. See xii. 12; Isai. x. 5, and Ps. xvii. 13 note.

fear is *on every side*] Mâgôr-Missâbib, Jeremiah's watchword (cp. xx. 3, 10). The *and* before it should be omitted.

26. *wallow thyself in ashes*] Violent distress is wont to find relief in eccentric actions, and thus the wallowing in ashes shews that Jerusalem's grief is unbearable.

the spoiler] Nebuchadnezzar.

27-30. Render:

27. I have set thee among My people as a prover of ore,
   And thou shalt know and try their way.

28. They are all of them rebels of rebels (*i.e.* utter rebels):
   Slander-walkers, *mere* copper and iron,
   Corrupters all of them.

29. The bellows glow: from their fire lead only!
   In vain hath the smelter smelted,
   And the wicked are not separated.

30. Refuse-silver have men called them:
   For Jehovah hath refused them.

The intermixture throughout of moral words and metallurgical terms is remarkable.

29. *The bellows are burned*] Worn out by continual blowing. The prophet has exhausted all his efforts. His heart, consumed by the heat of divine inspiration, can labour no more. Others translate *The bellows snort, i.e.* blow furiously. More probably *The bellows glow* with the strong heat of the fire.

plucked away] **Separated.** The smelter's object is to separate the metal from the dross.

30. *Reprobate*] See marg.; not really silver, but the dross.

the LORD *hath rejected them*] This then is the end. The smelter is God's prophet: the bellows the breath of inspiration: the flux his earnestness in preaching. But in vain does the fervour of prophecy essay to melt the hearts of the people. They are so utterly corrupt, that no particle even of pure metal can be found in them. All the refiner's art is in vain. They have rejected all God's gifts and motives for their repentance, and therefore *Jehovah has rejected them* as an alloy too utterly adulterate to repay the refiner's toil.

VII.—X. In these four chapters Jeremiah addresses the people as they flocked into Jerusalem from the country, to attend the solemn services in the Temple upon a fast-day. Jehoiakim (ch. xxvi.) had just ascended the throne, and was so incensed at this sermon that he would have put Jeremiah to death but for the influence of Ahikam. With the accession of Jehoiakim all hope of averting the ruin of the country had passed away. He represented the reverse of his father's policy, and belonged to

2 ^aStand in the gate of the LORD's house, and proclaim there
this word, and say, ¶Hear the word of the LORD, all *ye of*
3 Judah, that enter in at these gates to worship the LORD. Thus
saith the LORD of hosts, the God of Israel, ^bAmend your ways
and your doings, and I will cause you to dwell in this place.
4 ^cTrust ye not in lying words, saying, The temple of the LORD,
The temple of the LORD, The temple of the LORD *are* these.
5 For if ye throughly amend your ways and your doings; if ye
throughly ^dexecute judgment between a man and his neigh-
6 bour; *if* ye oppress not the stranger, the fatherless, and the
widow, and shed not innocent blood in this place, ^eneither walk
7 after other gods to your hurt: ^fthen will I cause you to dwell
in this place, in ^gthe land that I gave to your fathers, for ever
8 and ever. ¶Behold, ^hye trust in ⁱlying words, that cannot
9 profit. ^kWill ye steal, murder, and commit adultery, and swear
falsely, and burn incense unto Baal, and ^lwalk after other gods
10 whom ye know not; ^mand come and stand before me in this
house, ¹ ⁿwhich is called by my name, and say, We are delivered
11 to do all these abominations? Is ^othis house, which is called
by my name, become a ^pden of robbers in your eyes? Behold,

¹ Heb. *whereupon my name is called.*

Marginal references:

^a ch. 26. 2.

^b ch. 18. 11.
& 26. 13.

^c Mic. 3. 11.

^d cb. 22. 3.
^e Deut. 6.
14, 15.
ch. 13. 10.
^f Deut. 4. 40.
^g ch. 3. 18.
^h ver. 4.
ⁱ ch. 5. 31.
^k 1 Kin. 18.
21.
Hos. 4. 1.
Zeph. 1. 5.
^l Ex. 20. 3.
^m Ezek. 23.
39.
ⁿ ver. 11.
ch. 32. 34.
^o Isai. 56. 7.
^p Matt. 21.
13.

that faction, who placed their sole hope of deliverance in a close alliance with Pharaoh-Necho. As this party rejected the distinctive principles of the theocracy, and the king was personally an irreligious man, the maintenance of the worship of Jehovah was no longer an object of the public care. At this time upon a public fast-day, appointed probably because of the calamities under which the nation was labouring, Jeremiah was commanded by Jehovah to stand at the gate of the Temple, and address to the people as they entered words of solemn warning. The whole sermon divides itself into three parts; (1) It points out the folly of the superstitious confidence placed by the people in the Temple, while they neglect the sole sure foundation of a nation's hope. A sanctuary long polluted by immorality must inevitably be destroyed (vii. 2—viii. 3). (2) Complaints follow of a more general character, in which the growing wickedness of the nation and especially of the leaders is pointed out (viii. 4—ix. 24). (3) Lastly the prophet shews the possibility of averting the evils impending upon the nation (ix. 25—x. 25).

VII. **1, 2.** The Temple had several entrances (2 Chr. iv. 9); and the gate or door here mentioned is probably that of the *inner* court, where Baruch read Jeremiah's roll (xxxvi. 10). The prophet stood in the doorway, and addressed the people assembled in the outer court.

all ye of *Judah*] Better, lit. **all Judah** (cp. xxvi. 2).

3. If the people repented, instead of being led into captivity God would maintain their national existence. It is a promise of the continuance of an old blessing.

4. *The temple of the* LORD] Thrice re-

peated, to emphasize the rejection of the cry ever upon the lips of the false prophets. In their view the maintenance of the Temple-service was a charm sufficient to avert all evil.

these] The buildings of the Temple, to which Jeremiah is supposed to point. The Jews put their trust in the material buildings.

5–7. A summary of the conditions indispensable on man's part, before he can plead the terms of the Covenant in his favour.

6. *in this place*] *i.e.* in Jerusalem. The prophet refers to innocent blood shed there judicially. Of one such judicial murder Jehoiakim had already been guilty (xxvi. 23).

7. Why then do not the Jews still possess a land thus eternally given them? Because God never bestows anything unconditionally. The land was bestowed upon them by virtue of a Covenant (Gen. xvii. 7); — the Jews had broken the conditions of this Covenant (*vv.* 5, 6), and the gift reverted to the original donor.

10. *We are delivered*] Jeremiah accuses them of trusting in the ceremonial of the Temple instead of leading holy lives. "You break," he says, "the Ten Commandments, and then you go to the Temple; and when the service is over you say, We are delivered. We have atoned for our past actions, and may start afresh with easy minds upon a new course of wickedness."

11. *robbers*] Lit. *tearers*, those who rob with violence. The Temple was the place which sheltered them. It had been consecrated to God. Now that it harbours miscreants, must it not as inevitably be destroyed as a den of robbers would be by any righteous ruler?

q Judg. 18. 31.
r Deut.12.11.
s 1 Sam. 4. 10, 11.
t 2 Chr. 36. 15.
u Prov. 1. 24.
Isai. 65. 12.

x Ps. 78. 60.
y 2 Kin. 17. 23.
z Ps. 78. 67.
a Ex. 32. 10.
ch. 11. 14.
b ch. 15. 1.

c ch. 44. 17.

d ch. 19. 13.
e Deut. 32. 16, 21.

12 even I have seen *it*, saith the LORD. But go ye now unto q my place which *was* in Shiloh, r where I set my name at the first, and see s what I did to it for the wickedness of my people Israel.
13 And now, because ye have done all these works, saith the LORD, and I spake unto you, t rising up early and speaking, but ye
14 heard not; and I u called you, but ye answered not; therefore will I do unto *this* house, which is called by my name, wherein ye trust, and unto the place which I gave to you and to your
15 fathers, as I have done to x Shiloh. And I will cast you out of my sight, y as I have cast out all your brethren, z even the whole
16 seed of Ephraim. ¶ Therefore a pray not thou for this people, neither lift up cry nor prayer for them, neither make inter-
17 cession to me: b for I will not hear thee. Seest thou not what they do in the cities of Judah and in the streets of Jerusalem?
18 c The children gather wood, and the fathers kindle the fire, and the women knead *their* dough, to make cakes to the ¹ queen of heaven, and to d pour out drink offerings unto other gods, that
19 they may provoke me to anger. e Do they provoke me to anger? saith the LORD: *do they* not *provoke* themselves to the confusion
20 of their own faces? Therefore thus saith the Lord GOD; Behold, mine anger and my fury shall be poured out upon this place, upon man, and upon beast, and upon the trees of the field, and

¹ Or, *frame*, or, *workmanship of heaven*.

---

12. *go ye unto my place in Shiloh*] This argument roused the indignation of the people (xxvi. 8, 9, 11). The Ark, Jeremiah shews, had not always been at Jerusalem. The place first chosen, as the centre of the nation's worship, was Shiloh, a town to the north of Bethel, situated in the powerful tribe of Ephraim (Josh. xviii. 1 note). The ruin of Shiloh is ascribed (Ps. lxxviii. 58—64) to the idolatry which prevailed in Israel after the death of Joshua; a similar ruin due to similar causes should fall on Jerusalem (*v.* 14). The site of Shiloh is identified with Seilûn, the ruins of which are so insignificant as to bear out St. Jerome's remark, "At Silo, where once was the Tabernacle and Ark of the Lord, there can scarcely be pointed out the foundation of an Altar."

at the first] In the first stage, the first period of the existence of the Jewish commonwealth, Shiloh was to the Judges what Jerusalem subsequently was to the kings; and as the fall of Shiloh through the wickedness of Eli's sons marked the period when the government by Judges was to pass away, and the second stage begin; so the power of the kings perished at the fall of Jerusalem, and left the way clear for the third stage of Jewish polity, government by the scribes.

13. *rising up early and speaking*] A proverbial expression for "speaking zealously and earnestly." It is used only by Jeremiah.

15. *the whole seed of Ephraim*] *i.e.*, the whole of the nine northern tribes. Their casting out was a plain proof that the possession of the symbols of God's Presence does not secure a Church or nation from rejection, if unworthy of its privileges.

16. They had reached that stage in which men sin without any sense of guilt (see 1 John v. 16).

neither make intercession to me] In xiv. 7—9 we have an intercessory prayer offered by Jeremiah, but not heard. The intercession of Moses prevailed with God (Num. xi. 2, xiv. 13–20, xvi. 22), because the progress of the people then was upwards; the progress now was from bad to worse, and therefore in xv. 1 we read that the intercession even of Moses and Samuel (see 1 Sam. xii. 23) would profit nothing.

17. The proof of the hopeless immorality of the people is this, that they worship heathen deities (1) generally in the cities of Judah, and not in the capital only; and (2) publicly *in the streets of Jerusalem*. Such public idolatry could have been practised only in the reign of a king like Jehoiakim.

18. *children...fathers...women*] All members of the family take part in this idolatry.

cakes] Probably very similar to those offered at Athens to Artemis.

to the queen of heaven] A Persian and Assyrian deity, who was supposed to symbolize a quality possessed by moonlight of giving to nature its receptive power, as the sun represented its quickening power. The moon thus became generally the symbol of female productiveness, and was worshipped as such at Babylon. Disgraceful usages to which every woman was obliged once to submit formed part of her worship.

19. *Do they not provoke...*] Lit. **Is it not themselves** (*that they provoke*) **to the shame of their faces?**

20. *upon man, and upon beast*] All crea-

upon the fruit of the ground; and it shall burn, and shall not
21 be quenched. ¶ Thus saith the LORD of hosts, the God of Israel;
*f*Put your burnt offerings unto your sacrifices, and eat flesh.
22 *g*For I spake not unto your fathers, nor commanded them in
the day that I brought them out of the land of Egypt, ¹con-
23 cerning burnt offerings or sacrifices: but this thing commanded
I them, saying, *h*Obey my voice, and *i*I will be your God, and
ye shall be my people: and walk ye in all the ways that I have
24 commanded you, that it may be well unto you. *k*But they
hearkened not, nor inclined their ear, but *l*walked in the
counsels *and* in the ²imagination of their evil heart, and ³*m*went
25 backward, and not forward. Since the day that your fathers
came forth out of the land of Egypt unto this day I have even
*n*sent unto you all my servants the prophets, *o*daily rising up
26 early and sending *them*: *p*yet they hearkened not unto me, nor
inclined their ear, but *q*hardened their neck: *r*they did worse
27 than their fathers. Therefore *s*thou shalt speak all these words
unto them; but they will not hearken to thee: thou shalt also
28 call unto them; but they will not answer thee. But thou shalt
say unto them, This *is* a nation that obeyeth not the voice of
the LORD their God, *t*nor receiveth ⁴correction: *u*truth is
29 perished, and is cut off from their mouth. ¶ *x*Cut off thine
hair, *O Jerusalem*, and cast *it* away, and take up a lamentation
on high places; for the LORD hath rejected and forsaken the
30 generation of his wrath. For the children of Judah have done

f Isai. 1. 11.
ch. 6. 20.
g 1 Sam. 15.
22.
Ps. 51. 16.
Hos. 6. 6.
h Ex. 15. 26.
Deut. 6. 3.
i Lev. 26. 12.
k Ps. 81. 11.
l Deut. 29.19.
Ps. 81. 12.
m ch. 2. 27.
Hos. 4. 16.

n 2 Chr. 36.
15.
o ver. 13.
p ch. 11. 8.
& 25. 3, 4.
q Neh. 9.
17, 29.
r ch. 16. 12.
s Ezek. 2. 7.

t ch. 5. 3.
u ch. 9. 3.
x Job 1. 20.
Isai. 15. 2.
ch. 16. 6.
Mic. 1. 16.

---

¹ Heb. *concerning the matter of*.
² Or, *stubbornness*.
³ Heb. *were*.
⁴ Or, *instruction*.

---

tion in some mysterious way shares in man's
fall and restoration (Rom. viii. 19–22).
21. The meaning is, Increase your sacrifices as you will. Add burnt-offering to
peace-offerings. All is in vain as long as
you neglect the indispensable requirements
of obedience and moral purity. *Eat flesh* is
equivalent to *sacrifice*. The flesh of animals
offered in sacrifice was usually eaten by the
offerers, and this meal was regarded as a
symbol of reconciliation. God and man
partook of the same victim, and so were
made friends. This passage (*vv.* 21–28) is
the Haftarah, or Lesson from the Prophets
(see p. 4, note 7), after the Parashah, Lev.
vi.-viii., or Lesson from the Law. The
selection of such a Haftarah shews that the
Jews thoroughly understood that their sacrifices were not the end of the Law, but a
means for spiritual instruction.
23. *Obey* &c.] These words are not found
verbatim in the Pentateuch, but are a summary of its principles. Sacrifice is never
the final cause of the Covenant, but always
obedience (Ex. xix. 5, 6; Lev. xi. 45.
Cp. Ex. xx., Deut. xi., in which the moral
object of the Mosaic dispensation is most
clearly taught). In connexion with Jeremiah's argument, notice that Amos v. 25
(taken in conjunction with Josh. v. 2-7)
proves that the ceremonial Law was not
observed during the forty years' wandering
in the wilderness. A thing so long in abey-

ance in the very time of its founder, could
not be of primary importance.
24. *imagination*] Better, as in marg.
and went backward] Lit. as in marg.; *i.e.*
they turned their back upon Me to follow
their own devices.
27. Rather, **Though thou...yet** &c.
28. *a nation*] The *nation*. Israel holds so
unique a position among all nations that for
it to disobey God is marvellous.
truth &c.] Fidelity to God. Though they
have the name of Jehovah often upon their
lips and swear by Him (v. 2), yet it is only
profession without practice.
29-33. Jeremiah summons the people to
lament over the miserable consequences of
their rejection of God. In the valley of
Hinnom, where lately they offered their
innocents, they shall themselves fall before
the enemy in such multitudes that burial
shall be impossible, and the beasts of the
field unmolested shall prey upon their remains.
29. The daughter of Zion, defiled by the
presence of enemies in her sanctuary, and
rejected of God, must shear off the diadem
of her hair, the symbol of her consecration
to God, just as the Nazarite, when defiled
by contact with a corpse, was to shave *his
crowned head*.
take up a lamentation &c.] Or, **lift up a**
lamentation on the bare hill-sides (iii. 2).

v 2 Chr. 33.
4. 5, 7.
ch. 23. 11.
Ezek. 7. 20.
z 2 Kin. 23.
10.
a Ps. 106. 38.
b See Deut.
17. 3.
c ch. 19. 6.
d 2 Kin. 23.
10.
e Deut. 28.26.
ch. 12. 9.
f Isai. 24. 7.
ch. 16. 9.
Ezek. 26. 13.
Hos. 2. 11.
g Lev. 26. 33.
Isai. 1. 7.

evil in my sight, saith the LORD : *y*they have set their abomi-nations in the house which is called by my name, to pollute it.
31 And they have built the *z*high places of Tophet, which *is* in the valley of the son of Hinnom, to *a*burn their sons and their daughters in the fire; *b*which I commanded *them* not, neither
32 ¹came it into my heart. Therefore, behold, *c*the days come, saith the LORD, that it shall no more be called Tophet, nor the valley of the son of Hinnom, but the valley of slaughter : *d*for
33 they shall bury in Tophet, till there be no place. And the *e*carcases of this people shall be meat for the fowls of the heaven, and for the beasts of the earth; and none shall fray
34 *them* away. Then will I cause to *f*cease from the cities of Judah, and from the streets of Jerusalem, the voice of mirth, and the voice of gladness, the voice of the bridegroom, and the voice of the bride : for *g*the land shall be desolate.

CHAP. 8. AT that time, saith the LORD, they shall bring out the bones of the kings of Judah, and the bones of his princes, and the bones of the priests, and the bones of the prophets, and the bones of the inhabitants of Jerusalem, out of their graves :
2 and they shall spread them before the sun, and the moon, and all the host of heaven, whom they have loved, and whom they have served, and after whom they have walked, and whom they have sought, and *a*whom they have worshipped: they shall not be gathered, *b*nor be buried; they shall be for *c*dung upon
3 the face of the earth. And *d*death shall be chosen rather than life by all the residue of them that remain of this evil family, which remain in all the places whither I have driven them, saith the LORD of hosts.

a 2 Kin.23.5.
b ch. 22. 19.
c 2 Kin.9.36.
Ps. 83. 10.
ch. 9. 22.
d Job 3. 21.
Rev. 9. 6.

4 Moreover thou shalt say unto them, Thus saith the LORD ; Shall they fall, and not arise ? shall he turn away, and not

---

¹ Heb. *came it upon my heart.*

---

30. *they have set their abominations* &c.] Probably a reference to the reign of the fanatic Manasseh, in whose time the worship of Astarte and of the heavenly bodies was the established religion of the land (2 K. xxi. 3–5), and even the Temple was used for idolatrous services. The people had never heartily accepted Josiah's reformation.

31. *the high places*] Here, probably, not natural hills, but artificial mounts, on which the altars were erected.

Tophet (marg. ref. note) is not here a proper name ; as applied to Baal-worship the term is not an ordinary one, but almost peculiar to Jeremiah. Comparing this verse with xix. 5, xxxii. 35, it will be found that *Baal* is in those passages substituted for *Tophet.* Just as it is the practice of the prophets to substitute *Bosheth, shame,* for Baal (see iii. 24), so here Jeremiah uses *Tophet, an object of abhorrence* (cp. Job xvii. 6 note), in just the same way.

valley of the son of Hinnom] See Josh. xv. 8 note.

to burn &c.] The children were not burnt alive, but slain first (Ezek. xvi. 21).

32. *the valley of slaughter*] Where they

slew their helpless children, there shall they be slaughtered helplessly by their enemies.

till there be no place] Rather, **for want of room** elsewhere.

34. Silence and desolation are to settle upon the whole land.

VIII. **1.** Not the living only but the dead shall be exposed to the ruthless violence of the enemy, who will ransack the graves of the wealthier classes.

2. *loved ... served ... walked ... sought ... worshipped*] There is great force in the piled-up verbs by which their worship of the heavenly bodies is described. The prophet beginning with the heart's "love" describes that worship in the various stages of its development, and then contrasts its fulness with the miserable reward which ensues.

3. *this evil family*] The whole Jewish race.

which remain] The words are omitted by the LXX. and Syriac Versions.

4. The prophet here resumes from vii. 28 the main subject of his prophecy. He again invites the Jews to repentance.

Shall they fall ? The argument is that when men fall, they do not lie upon the ground,

5 return? Why *then* is this people of Jerusalem *e*slidden back
by a perpetual backsliding? *f* they hold fast deceit, *g* they refuse
6 to return. *h*I hearkened and heard, *but* they spake not aright:
no man repented him of his wickedness, saying, What have I
done? every one turned to his course, as the horse rusheth into
7 the battle. Yea, *i*the stork in the heaven knoweth her appointed times; and *k*the turtle and the crane and the swallow
observe the time of their coming; but *l*my people know not the
8 judgment of the LORD. How do ye say, We *are* wise, *m*and the
law of the LORD *is* with us? Lo, certainly *1*in vain made he *it*;
9 the pen of the scribes *is* in vain. *n 2*The wise *men* are ashamed,
they are dismayed and taken: lo, they have rejected the word

e ch. 7. 24.
f ch. 9. 6.
g ch. 5. 3.
h 2 Pet. 3. 9.

i Isai. 1. 3.
k Cant. 2. 12.
l ch. 5. 4, 5.
m Rom. 2. 17.

n ch. 6. 15.

---

1 Or, *the false pen of the scribes worketh
for falsehood*, Isai. 10. 1.

2 Or, *Have they been
ashamed &c.*

---

but endeavour to get up again : and when a
man loses his way, he does not persist in
going on, but turns round, and retraces his
steps. Israel then will be only following
the dictates of common sense in desisting
from that which she now knows to be her
ruin.

5. When men act as in *v.* 4, why is God's
own people alone an exception ?

slidden back...backsliding] The same words
as *turn* and *return* in *v.* 4. They should be
rendered, *Why doth this people of Jerusalem
turn away with a perpetual turning ?*

deceit] *i.e.* idolatry ; because men worship
in it that which is false, and it is false to
the worshippers.

refuse] From a feeling of dislike.

6. *I hearkened and heard*] God, before
passing sentence, carefully listens to the
words of the people. Cp. Gen. xi. 5, where
the Divine judgment is preceded by the
Almighty going down to see the tower.

not aright] Or, *not-right*; which in the Hebr.
idiom means that which is utterly wrong.

no man repented] The original phrase is
very striking : *No man had pity upon his
own wickedness.* If men understood the true
nature of sin, the sinner would repent out
of very pity upon himself.

as the horse rusheth] Lit. *overfloweth.* It is
a double metaphor ; first, the persistence of
the people in sin is compared to the fury
which at the sound of the trumpet seizes
upon the war-horse ; and then its rush into
the battle is likened to the overflowing of a
torrent, which nothing can stop in its destructive course.

7. Jeremiah appeals to the obedience
which migratory birds render to the law of
their natures. The *stork* arrives in Palestine about March 21, and after a six weeks'
halt departs for the north of Europe. It
takes its flight by day, at a vast height in
the air (*in the heaven*). The appearance of
the "turtle-dove" is one of the pleasant
signs of the approach of spring.

the crane and the swallow] Rather, "the
swift and the crane."

8. *the law of the* LORD] The *Torah*, or

written Law, the possession of which made
the priests and prophets so boastfully ex-
claim, *We are wise.*

Lo, certainly...] Rather, **Verily, lo ! the
lying pen** *of the scribes* **hath made it**—the
Law—**into a lie.** The mention of *scribes* in
this place is a crucial point in the argument
whether or not the Pentateuch or Torah is
the old Law-Book of the Jews, or a fabrica-
tion which gradually grew up, but was not
received as authoritative until after the return from the Captivity. It is not until the
time of Josiah (2 Chr. xxxiv. 13) that
"scribes" are mentioned except as political
officers ; here, however, they are students of
the Torah. The Torah must have existed
in writing before there could have been an
order of men whose special business it was
to study it ; and therefore to explain this
verse by saying that perhaps the scribes
were writers of false prophecies written in
imitation of the true, is to lose the whole
gist of the passage. What the scribes
turned into a lie was that Law of which they
had just boasted that they were the possessors. Moreover, the scribes undeniably became possessed of preponderating influence
during the exile : and on the return from
Babylon were powerful enough to prevent
the restoration of the kingly office. That
there should be along with the priests and
Levites men who devoted themselves to the
study of the written Law, and who in the
time of Josiah had acquired such influence
as to be recognized as a distinct class—is
just what we should expect from the rapid
progress of learning, which began with
Elisha's active management of the schools
of the prophets, and culminated in the days
of Hezekiah. Jeremiah's whole argument
depends upon the fact that there were in
his days men who claimed to be *wise* or
learned because of their study of the
Pentateuch, and is entirely inconsistent
with the assumptions that Jeremiah wrote
the book of Deuteronomy, and that Ezra
wrote parts of Exodus and the whole of
Leviticus.

9. *they have rejected the word of the* LORD]

10 of the LORD; and [1]what wisdom *is* in them? Therefore [o]will
I give their wives unto others, *and* their fields to them that
shall inherit *them*: for every one from the least even unto the
greatest is given to [p]covetousness, from the prophet even unto
11 the priest every one dealeth falsely. For they have [q]healed the
hurt of the daughter of my people slightly, saying, [r]Peace,
12 peace; when *there is* no peace. Were they [s]ashamed when
they had committed abomination? nay, they were not at all
ashamed, neither could they blush: therefore shall they fall
among them that fall: in the time of their visitation they shall
13 be cast down, saith the LORD. [2]I will surely consume them,
saith the LORD: *there shall be* no grapes [t]on the vine, nor figs
on the [u]fig tree, and the leaf shall fade; and *the things that* I
14 have given them shall pass away from them. ¶ Why do we sit
still? [x]assemble yourselves, and let us enter into the defenced
cities, and let us be silent there: for the LORD our God hath put
us to silence, and given us [y]water of [3]gall to drink, because
15 we have sinned against the LORD. We [z]looked for peace, but
no good *came*; *and* for a time of health, and behold trouble!
16 The snorting of his horses was heard from [a]Dan: the whole
land trembled at the sound of the neighing of his [b]strong ones;
for they are come, and have devoured the land, and [4]all that is
17 in it; the city, and those that dwell therein. For, behold, I
will send serpents, cockatrices, among you, which *will* not *be*
18 [c]charmed, and they shall bite you, saith the LORD. ¶ *When* I
would comfort myself against sorrow, my heart *is* faint [5]in me.
19 Behold the voice of the cry of the daughter of my people [6]be-
cause of them that dwell in [d]a far country: *Is* not the LORD in
Zion? *is* not her king in her? Why have they [e]provoked me
to anger with their graven images, *and* with strange vanities?

[o] Deut. 28. 30. ch. 6. 12. Amos 5. 11.
[p] Isai. 56. 11.
[q] ch. 6. 14
[r] Ezek. 13. 10.
[s] ch. 3. 3. & 6. 15.
[t] Isai. 5. 1. Joel 1. 7.
[u] Matt. 21. 19. Luke 13. 6.
[x] ch. 4. 5.
[y] ch. 9. 15.
[z] ch. 14. 19.
[a] ch. 4. 15.
[b] Judg. 5. 22. ch. 47. 3.
[c] Ps. 58. 4. Eccles. 10. 11.
[d] Isai. 39. 3.
[e] Deut. 32. 21. Isai. 1. 4.

[1] Heb. *the wisdom of what thing.*
[2] Or, *In gathering I will consume.*
[3] Or, *poison.*
[4] Heb. *the fulness thereof.*
[5] Heb. *upon.*
[6] Heb. *because of the country of them that are far off.*

It became in the hands of the Soferim or scribes a mere code of ceremonial observance. Cp. Mark vii. 13.

10-12. These verses are almost identical with ch. vi. 12–15.

10. *to them that shall inherit* them] Rather, **to those that shall take possession of them,** *i.e.* to conquerors who shall take them by force.

13. Or, **I will gather and sweep them away, saith Jehovah: there are** *no grapes on the vine,* **and no** *figs on the fig-tree, and the leaf* **is dry: therefore will I appoint those that shall pass over them.** Judah is a vine which bears no fruit: a tree which makes even no profession of life, for her leaf is dry. Many explain the last words of an army sweeping over the land like a flood.

14. The people rouse one another to exertion. "Why," they ask, "do we remain here to be overwhelmed?" They are ready now to follow the command given (see marg. ref.), but with the conviction that all hope is over.

let us be silent there] Rather, **let us perish there,** lit. *be put to silence.*

water of gall] *i.e.* poison. The word rendered *gall* was probably the belladonna, or night-shade, to the *berries* of which the grapes of Israel were compared.

15. *health...trouble*] Or, *rest...***terror.**

16. *Dan*] *i.e.* the northern boundary of the land.

his strong ones] *i.e. his war-horses.*

17. *I will send*] Or, **am sending.** No prophet changes his metaphors so suddenly as Jeremiah. The invading army is now compared to snakes, whom no charming can soothe, and whose bite is fatal. Cp. Num. xxi. 5, 6.

cockatrices] **vipers.** See Isai. xi. 8 note.

18. Rather, **O my comfort in** *sorrow: my heart* **faints for me.** The word translated *comfort* is by some supposed to be corrupt. With these mournful ejaculations a new strophe begins, ending with ix. 1, in which the prophet mourns over the miserable fate of his countrymen, among whom he had been earnestly labouring, but all in vain.

19. Or, *Behold the voice of the cry* **for help** *of the daughter of my people* **from a distant land:** "*Is not Jehovah in Zion? Is not her king* **there?**" "*Why have they provoked Me to anger with their* **carved** *images, with*

20 The harvest is past, the summer is ended, and we are not saved.
21 *For the hurt of the daughter of my people am I hurt ; I am   *f* ch. 4. 19.
22 *black ; astonishment hath taken hold on me. *Is there* no *h* balm   *g* Joel 2. 6.
    in Gilead; *is there* no physician there ? why then is not the   *h* Nah. 2. 10.
9 health of the daughter of my people ¹recovered ? OH ²*a*that   & Gen.37. 25.
    my head were waters, and mine eyes a fountain of tears, that I   & 43. 11.
    might weep day and night for the slain of the daughter of my   *a* Isai. 22. 4.
2 people! Oh that I had in the wilderness a lodging place of way-   ch. 4. 19.
    faring men ; that I might leave my people, and go from them !   Lam. 2. 11.
    for *b*they *be* all adulterers, an assembly of treacherous men.   *b* ch. 5. 7, 8.
3 And *c*they bend their tongues *like* their bow *for* lies : but they   *c* Ps. 64. 3.
    are not valiant for the truth upon the earth; for they proceed   Isai. 59. 4.
    from evil to evil, and they *d*know me not, saith the LORD.   *d* 1 Sam. 2.
4 ¶ *e*Take ye heed every one of his ³neighbour, and trust ye not   12.
    in any brother: for every brother will utterly supplant, and   Hos. 4. 1.
5 every neighbour will *f* walk with slanders. And they will ⁴de-   *e* ch. 12. 6.
    ceive every one his neighbour, and will not speak the truth :   Mic. 7. 5.
    they have taught their tongue to speak lies, *and* weary them-   *f* ch. 6. 28.
6 selves to commit iniquity. Thine habitation *is* in the midst of
    deceit; through deceit they refuse to know me, saith the LORD.
7 ¶ Therefore thus saith the LORD of hosts, Behold, *g* I will melt   *g* Isai. 1. 25.
            Mal. 3. 3.

    ¹ Heb. *gone up?*   ³ Or, *friend.*
    ² Heb. *Who will give my head, &c.*   ⁴ Or, *mock.*

---

foreign *vanities?*" Their complaint, *Is there no Jehovah in Zion?* is met by God demanding of them the reason why instead of worshipping Him they have set up idols.

20. *the summer*] Rather, **the fruit-gathering**, which follows the corn-harvest. The corn has failed; the fruit-gathering has also proved unproductive ; so despair seized the people when they saw opportunities for their deliverance again and again pass by, till God seemed utterly to have forgotten them.

21. *For the hurt...hurt*] Lit. *Because of the breaking...broken.* These are the words of the prophet, whose heart is crushed by the cry of his countrymen.

I am black] Or, **I go mourning.**

22. *no physician there*] *i.e.* in Gilead. Balm used to grow in Israel for the healing of the nations. Her priests and prophets were the physicians. Has Israel then no balm for herself ? Is there no physician in her who can bind up her wound? Gilead was to Israel what Israel spiritually was to the whole world.

why then is not the health...recovered ?] Or, *why then has no bandage, or plaister of balsam, been laid upon my people?*

IX. **1.** This verse is joined in the Hebrew to the preceding chapter. But any break at all here interrupts the meaning.

a fountain] Rather, *a reservoir*, in which tears had been stored up, so that the prophet might weep abundantly.

2-9. From their punishment the prophet now turns to their sins.

2. The prophet utters the wish that he might be spared his daily striving, and in

some lone wilderness give way to his sorrow, without restraint.

a lodging place] It was usual to build in the desert, either by private charity or at the public expense, caravanserais, to receive travellers for a single night, who had however to bring their own supplies with them.

an assembly] Or, **a gang.**

treacherous] Faithless towards one another.

3. Rather, *And they bend their* **tongue to be their bow of lies**, *i.e.* just as men before a battle get their bows ready, so they of set purpose make ready to do mischief, only their arrows are lying words : **neither do they rule faithfully in the land**, *i.e.* Judæa.

4. In a state of such utter lawlessness, the bonds of mutual confidence are relaxed, and suspicion takes its place.

utterly supplant] An allusion to the name of Jacob (Gen. xxvii. 36). It might be rendered, *every brother is a thorough Jacob.*

will walk with slanders] Or, **slandereth.**

6. A continuation of the warning given in *v.* 4. *Trust no one : for thou dwellest surrounded by deceit on every side.* Their rejection of God is the result of their want of honesty in their dealings with one another (1 John iv. 20).

7. *I will melt them, and try them*] The punishment is corrective rather than retributive. The terms used are those of the refiner of metals, the first being the smelting to separate the pure metal from the ore ; the second the testing to see whether the metal is pure, or still mixed with alloy. God will

them, and try them ; *h*for how shall I do for the daughter of
8 my people ? Their tongue *is as* an arrow shot out; it speaketh
*i*deceit : *one* speaketh *k*peaceably to his neighbour with his
9 mouth, but ¹in heart he layeth ²his wait. *l*Shall I not visit
them for these *things?* saith the LORD : shall not my soul be
10 avenged on such a nation as this ? ¶ For the mountains will I
take up a weeping and wailing, and *m*for the ³habitations of the
wilderness a lamentation, because they are ⁴burned up, so that
none can pass through *them ;* neither can *men* hear the voice of
the cattle ; ⁵*n*both the fowl of the heavens and the beasts are
11 fled ; they are gone. And I will make Jerusalem *o*heaps, *and*
*p*a den of dragons; and I will make the cities of Judah ⁶desolate,
12 without an inhabitant. ¶ *q*Who *is* the wise man, that may understand this ? and *who is he* to whom the mouth of the LORD hath
spoken, that he may declare it, for what the land perisheth *and*
13 is burned up like a wilderness, that none passeth through ? And
the LORD saith, Because they have forsaken my law which I set
before them, and have not obeyed my voice, neither walked
14 therein ; but have *r*walked after the ⁷imagination of their own
heart, and after Baalim, *s*which their fathers taught them :
15 therefore thus saith the LORD of hosts, the God of Israel ; Behold, I will *t*feed them, *even* this people, *u*with wormwood and
16 give them water of gall to drink. I will *x*scatter them also
among the heathen, whom neither they nor their fathers have
known : *y*and I will send a sword after them, till I have consumed
17 them. ¶ Thus saith the LORD of hosts, Consider ye, and call for
*z*the mourning women, that they may come; and send for cunning

put the nation into the crucible of tribulation, that whatever is evil being consumed
in the fire, all there is in them of good may
be purified.

for how shall I do...] Rather, *for how* **else
could I act with reference to** *the daughter of
my people ?*

8. *an arrow shot out*] Rather, *a murderous
arrow.*

in heart he layeth his wait] Rather, **inwardly** *he layeth his* **ambush.**

10–22. The punishment described in
general terms in the preceding three verses
is now detailed at great length.

10. *the habitations*] *i.e.* the temporary encampments of the shepherds (see vi. 3).

so that none can...] Or, **They are parched
up, with no man to** *pass through them ;* **neither do they** *hear the voice* **of cattle ; from
the birds of the heaven even to the beasts
they** *are fled, they are gone.*

11. *dragons*] Rather, **jackals.**

12. *for what the land perisheth...*] This is
the question proposed for consideration.
The prophet calls upon the wise man to explain his question ; that question being,
Wherefore did the land perish? He follows
it by the assertion of a fact : *It is parched
like the wilderness with no man to pass through.*

13. The cause of the chastisement about

to fall upon Jerusalem, was their desertion
of the Divine Law.

14. *imagination*] Or, as in marg.

which their fathers taught them] It was not
the sin of one generation that brought upon
them chastisement : it was a sin, which had
been handed down from father to son.

15. *I will feed them...*] Rather, **I am
feeding them.** The present participle used
here, followed by three verbs in the future,
shews that the judgment has begun, of
which the successive stages are given in the
next clause.

wormwood] See Deut. xxix. 18, note, and
for *water of gall*, viii. 14, note.

16. This verse is taken from Lev. xxvi.
33. The fulfilment of what had been so
long before appointed as the penalty for the
violation of Jehovah's Covenant is one of
the most remarkable proofs that prophecy
was something more than human foresight.

till I have consumed them] See iv. 27
note. How is this " consuming " consistent
with the promise to the contrary there
given ? Because it is limited by the terms
of *v.* 7. Previously to Nebuchadnezzar's
destruction of Jerusalem God removed into
safety those in whom the nation should
revive.

17. *the mourning women*] Hired to attend

18 *women*, that they may come: and let them make haste, and
take up a wailing for us, that ^aour eyes may run down with
19 tears, and our eyelids gush out with waters. For a voice of
wailing is heard out of Zion, How are we spoiled! we are greatly
confounded, because we have forsaken the land, because ^bour
20 dwellings have cast *us* out. Yet hear the word of the LORD, O
ye women, and let your ear receive the word of his mouth, and
teach your daughters wailing, and every one her neighbour
21 lamentation. For death is come up into our windows, *and* is
entered into our palaces, to cut off ^cthe children from without,
22 *and* the young men from the streets. Speak, Thus saith the
LORD, Even the carcases of men shall fall ^das dung upon the
open field, and as the handful after the harvestman, and none
23 shall gather *them*. ¶ Thus saith the LORD, ^eLet not the wise
man glory in his wisdom, neither let the mighty *man* glory in his
24 might, let not the rich *man* glory in his riches: but ^flet him
that glorieth glory in this, that he understandeth and knoweth
me, that I *am* the LORD which exercise lovingkindness, judgment,
and righteousness, in the earth: ^gfor in these *things* I delight,
25 saith the LORD. ¶ Behold, the days come, saith the LORD, that
^hI will ¹punish all *them which are* circumcised with the uncircum-
26 cised; Egypt, and Judah, and Edom, and the children of Ammon,
and Moab, and all *that are* ²in the ⁱutmost corners, that dwell

a ch. 14. 17.

b Lev. 18. 28.

c ch. 6. 11.

d ch. 8. 2.

e Eccles. 9. 11.

f 1 Cor. 1. 31. 2 Cor. 10. 17.

g Mic. 6. 8.

h Rom. 2. 8.

i ch. 25. 23.

¹ Heb. *visit upon.*
² Heb. *cut off into corners,*

or, *having the corners* of
their hair *polled.*

---

at funerals, and by their skilled wailings aid
the real mourners in giving vent to their
grief. Hence they are called *cunning*, lit.
wise women, wisdom being constantly used
in Scripture for anything in which people
are trained.

18. *take up a wailing for us*] *i.e.* for the
nation once God's chosen people, but long
spiritually dead.

19. *forsaken*] Or, **left**: forced to abandon
the land.

because our dwellings &c.] Rather, *because
they* **have cast down** *our dwellings.* The
whole verse is a description of their sufferings. See 2 K. xxv. 1–12.

20. The command is addressed to the women because it was more especially their
part to express the general feelings of the
nation. See 1 Sam. xviii. 6; 2 Sam. i. 24.
The women utter now the death-wail over
the perishing nation. They are to teach
their daughters and neighbours the *lamentation*, *i.e. dirge*, because the harvest of death
would be so large that the number of trained
women would not suffice.

21. *death is come up* &c.] *i.e.* death steals
silently like a thief upon his victims, and
makes such havoc that there are no children
left to go "without," nor young men to frequent the open spaces in the city.

22. The "handful" means the little bundle
of corn which the reaper gathers on his arm
with three or four strokes of his sickle, and
then lays down. Behind the reaper came
one whose business it was to gather several
of these bundles, and bind them into a sheaf.

Thus death strews the ground with corpses
as thickly as these handfuls lie upon the
reaped land, but the corpses lie there unheeded.

23. To the end of ch. x. the prophet urges
upon the people the practical conclusion to
be drawn from God's righteous dealings
with them. The three things on which men
most pride themselves are shewn in this
verse to have proved vain.

24. This is the prophet's remedy for the
healing of the nation. It is the true understanding and knowledge of God, of which
the first means the spiritual enlightenment
of the mind (1 Cor. ii. 13, 14), the other the
training of the heart unto obedience (John
viii. 31, 32). This knowledge of God is further said to find in Him three chief attributes, (1) *lovingkindness*, *i.e.* readiness to
shew grace and mercy; (2) *judgment*, a belief in which is declared in Heb. xi. 6 to be
essential to faith; (3) *righteousness*, which
is essential to religion absolutely. Unless
men believe that God's dealings with them
in life and death are right and just, they
can neither love nor reverence him.

25. *all* them which are *circumcised* &c.]
Rather, **all circumcised in uncircumcision**,
i.e. all who though outwardly circumcised
have no corresponding inward purity.

26. *all* that are *in the utmost corners*]
Really, **all who have the corners of their
hair shorn.** The people meant are those
Arabs who cut the hair close upon the forehead and temples, but let it grow long
behind. See Lev. xix. 27.

in the wilderness: for all *these* nations *are* uncircumcised, and
all the house of Israel *are* ^kuncircumcised in the heart.

k Lev. 26. 41.
Ezek. 44. 7.
Rom. 2.
28, 29.
a Lev. 18. 3.

CHAP. 10. HEAR ye the word which the LORD speaketh unto you,
2 O house of Israel: Thus saith the LORD, *"*Learn not the way of
the heathen, and be not dismayed at the signs of heaven; for
3 the heathen are dismayed at them. For the ¹customs of the

b Isai. 40-44.

people *are* vain: for *b*one cutteth a tree out of the forest, the
4 work of the hands of the workman, with the axe. They deck it

c Isai. 41. 7.

with silver and with gold; they *c*fasten it with nails and with
5 hammers, that it move not. They *are* upright as the palm tree,

d Ps. 115. 5.
Hab. 2. 19.
1 Cor. 12. 2.
e Ps. 115. 7.
Isai. 46. 1.
f Isai. 41. 23.
g Ex. 15. 11.
Ps. 86. 8.
h Rev. 15. 4.
i Ps. 89. 6.
k Ps. 115. 8.
Isai. 41. 29.
Zech. 10. 2.
Rom. 1.
21, 22.

*d*but speak not: they must needs be *e*borne, because they
cannot go. Be not afraid of them; for *f*they cannot do evil,
6 neither also *is it* in them to do good. ¶Forasmuch as *there is*
none *g*like unto thee, O LORD; thou *art* great, and thy name *is*
7 great in might. *h*Who would not fear thee, O King of nations?
for ²to thee doth it appertain: forasmuch as *i*among all the
wise *men* of the nations, and in all their kingdoms, *there is* none
8 like unto thee. But they are ³altogether *k*brutish and foolish:

¹ Heb. *statutes*, or, *ordi-*
nances are vanity.

² Or, *it liketh thee.*
³ Heb. *in one*, or, *at once.*

---

for all these *nations* are *uncircumcised*]
Or, *for all* **the heathen** *are uncircumcised.*
Circumcision probably prevailed partially
in the heathen mysteries as a sign of peculiar sanctity, but to the Jews alone it
represented their Covenant-relation to God.

X. **2.** *signs of heaven*] Extraordinary
appearances, such as eclipses, comets, and
the like, which seemed to the heathen to
portend national calamities. To attribute
importance to them is to walk in heathen
ways.

3. *the customs*] Better, as the marg., *the*
ordinances, established institutions, *of the*
peoples, *i.e.* heathen nations.

4. *They deck it*] It was covered with
plates of gold and silver, and then fastened
with nails in its place, that it might not
move, i.e. tumble down.

The agreement in this and the following
verses with the argument in Isai. xl.-xliv.
is so manifest, that no one can doubt that
the one is modelled upon the other. If,
therefore, Jeremiah took the thoughts and
phrases from Isaiah, it is plain that the last
twenty-seven chapters of Isaiah were prior
in date to Jeremiah's time, and were not
therefore written at the close of the Babylonian exile. This passage then is a crucial
one to the pseudo-Isaiah theory. Two
answers are attempted, (1) that the pseudo-
Isaiah borrowed from Jeremiah. But this
is refuted by the style, which is not that
usual with Jeremiah. (2) That it is an
interpolation in Jeremiah. But how then
are we to account for its being found in the
Septuagint Version? The only argument of
real importance is that these verses break
the continuity of thought; but the whole
chapter is somewhat fragmentary, and not
so closely connected as the previous three.

Still there is a connexion. The prophet
had just included all Israel under the ban
of uncircumcision: he now shews them their
last chance of safety by enlarging upon the
truth, that (cp. ix. 23, 24) their true glory
is their God, not an idol of wood, but the
King of nations. Then comes the sad feeling that they have rejected God and chosen
idols (*vv.* 17, 18); then the nation's deep
grief (*vv.* 19-22) and earnest prayer (*vv.* 23-
25). It is quite possible that only portions
of the concluding part of Jeremiah's Temple-
sermon were embodied in Baruch's roll, and
that had the whole been preserved, we
should have found the thoughts as orderly
in development as those in chs. vii.-ix.

5. *They* are *upright* &c.] Rather, *They are*
like a palm tree of turned work, i.e. like one
of those stiff inelegant pillars, something
like a palm tree, which may be seen in
oriental architecture. Some translate thus:
They are like pillars in a garden of cucumbers,
i.e. like the blocks set up to frighten away
the birds; but none of the ancient Versions
support this rendering.

6. *Forasmuch as*] Or, **No one is** *like unto*
thee, O Jehovah. In *vv.* 6-11, the prophet
contrasts God's greatness with the impotence of idols.

7. *O King of nations*] *i.e.* heathen nations.
Jehovah is not the national God of the Jews
only, but reigns over all mankind (Ps. xxii.
28).

it] *i.e.* everything.

in all their kingdoms] More correctly, *in*
all their **royalty** or kingship.

8. *brutish* (*v.* 21) *and foolish*] Theirs was
the brutishness of men in a savage state,
little better than mere animals: their folly
that of stupidity.

9 the stock *is* a doctrine of vanities. Silver spread into plates is brought from Tarshish, and *l* gold from Uphaz, the work of the workman, and of the hands of the founder: blue and purple *is* their clothing: they *are* all *m* the work of cunning

10 *men*. But the LORD *is* the [1] true God, he *is* *n* the living God, and an [2] *o* everlasting king: at his wrath the earth shall tremble, and the nations shall not be able to abide his indignation.

11 ¶ [3] Thus shall ye say unto them, *p* The gods that have not made the heavens and the earth, *even* *q* they shall perish from the

12 earth, and from under these heavens. He *r* hath made the earth by his power, he hath *s* established the world by his wisdom, and *t* hath stretched out the heavens by his discretion.

13 *u* When he uttereth his voice, *there is* a [4] multitude of waters in the heavens, and *x* he causeth the vapours to ascend from the ends of the earth; he maketh lightnings [5] with rain, and

14 bringeth forth the wind out of his treasures. *y* Every man [6] is *z* brutish in *his* knowledge: *a* every founder is confounded by the graven image: *b* for his molten image *is* falsehood, and

15 *there is* no breath in them. They *are* vanity, *and* the work of

16 errors: in the time of their visitation *c* they shall perish. *d* The portion of Jacob *is* not like them: for he *is* the former of all *things ;* and *e* Israel *is* the rod of his inheritance: *f* The LORD of hosts *is* his name.

17 *g* Gather up thy wares out of the land, O [7] inhabitant of the

l Dan. 10. 5.

m Ps. 115. 4.
n 1 Tim.6.17.
o Ps. 10. 16.

p See Ps.96.5.
q Isai. 2. 18.
Zech. 13. 2.
r Gen. 1. 1.
Ps. 136. 5.
ch. 51. 15.
s Ps. 93. 1.
t Job 9. 8.
Ps. 104. 2.
Isai. 40. 22.
u Job 38. 34.
x Ps. 135. 7.
y ch. 51. 17.
z Prov. 30. 2.
a Isai. 42.17.
b Hab. 2. 18.
c ver. 11.
d Ps. 119. 57.
ch. 51. 19.
e Deut. 32.9.
f Isai. 47. 4.
ch. 31. 35.
g Ezek. 12.3.
ch. 6. 1.

---

[1] Heb. *God of truth*, Ps. 31. 5.
[2] Heb. *king of eternity.*
[3] In the Chaldean language.
[4] Or, *noise.*
[5] Or, *for rain.*
[6] Or, *is more brutish than to know.*
[7] Heb. *inhabitress.*

---

the stock &c.] Rather, **the instruction of idols is a piece of wood.** That is what they are themselves, and "ex nihilo nihil fit."

9. Or, *It is a piece of wood* (v. 8 note) ; **yea, beaten silver it is,** *which is brought from Tarshish, and gold from Uphaz :* **it is the work** &c.

Tarshish...Uphaz] See marg. ref. and Gen. x. 4. Possibly Uphaz was a place in the neighbourhood of the river Hyphasis.

blue and purple] Both colours were purple, from dyes obtained from shellfish : but the former had a violet, the latter a red tinge.

11. This verse is (in the original) in Chaldee. It was probably a proverbial saying, which Jeremiah inserts in its popular form.

12. *discretion*] Or, **understanding.** The three attributes ascribed to the Creator are very remarkable. The creation of the earth, the material world, is an act of *power ;* the *establishing, i.e.* the ordering and arranging it as a place fit for man's abode, is the work of his *wisdom ;* while the spreading out the heavens over it like a tent is an act of *understanding,* or skill. Naturally, the consideration of these attributes has led many to see here an allusion to the Holy Trinity.

13. *When* &c.] *i.e.* the rushing downpour of rain follows immediately upon the thunder. The rest of the verse is identical with marg. ref. ; but probably the words belong to Jeremiah, the Psalm being of comparatively late date.

with rain] **For the rain** (Ps. cxxxv. 7).

14. *in his knowledge*] Rather, **without knowledge ;** *i.e.* on comparing his powerless idols with the terrific grandeur of a tropical thunderstorm the man who can still worship them instead of the Creator is destitute of knowledge.

every founder &c.] Or, **every goldsmith is put to shame** &c. He has exhausted his skill on what remains an image.

15. Rather, *They are vanity,* **a work of mockery,** deserving only ridicule and contempt.

16. *The portion of Jacob*] *i.e.* Jehovah. He is not like gods made by a carpenter and goldsmith.

of all things] Lit. *of the all,* the universe.

the rod of his inheritance] See Ps. lxxiv. 2 ; cp. Isai. lxiii. 17. The rod is the sceptre, and Israel the people over whom Jehovah especially rules.

17. The prophet now returns to the main subject of his sermon, the conquest of Judæa.

thy wares] Rather, **thy bundle,** which could contain a few articles for necessary use, and be carried in the hand. They are going into exile.

O inhabitant of the fortress] *i.e.* thou that art besieged, that inhabitest a besieged town.

^h 1 Sam. 25.
20.
ch. 16. 13.
ⁱ Ezek. 6. 10.
^k ch. 4. 19.
^l Ps. 77. 10.
^m Mic. 7. 9.
ⁿ ch. 4. 20.

18 fortress. For thus saith the LORD, Behold, I will ^hsling out the inhabitants of the land at this once, and will distress them.
19 ⁱthat they may find *it so.* ^kWoe is me for my hurt! my wound is grievous: but I said, ^lTruly this *is* a grief, and ^mI must
20 bear it. ⁿMy tabernacle is spoiled, and all my cords are broken: my children are gone forth of me, and they *are* not: *there is* none to stretch forth my tent any more, and to set up my
21 curtains. For the pastors are become brutish, and have not sought the LORD: therefore they shall not prosper, and all their
22 flocks shall be scattered. Behold, the noise of the bruit is come, and a great commotion out of the ^onorth country, to make the
23 cities of Judah desolate, *and* a ^pden of dragons. ¶O LORD, I know that the ^qway of man *is* not in himself: *it is* not in man
24 that walketh to direct his steps. O LORD, ^rcorrect me, but with judgment; not in thine anger, lest thou ¹bring me to nothing.
25 ^sPour out thy fury upon the heathen ^tthat know thee not, and upon the families that call not on thy name: for they have eaten up Jacob, and ^udevoured him, and consumed him, and have made his habitation desolate.

CHAP. 11. THE word that came to Jeremiah from the LORD, saying,
2 ¶ Hear ye the words of this covenant, and speak unto the men,

    ¹ Heb. *diminish me.*

---

18. *sling out*] A similar metaphor for violent ejection occurs in Isai. xxii. 18 (see note).
at this once] Or, *at this* time. Previous invasions had ended either in deliverance, or at most in temporary misfortune. God's long-suffering is exhausted, and this time Judæa must cease to be an independent nation.
that they may find it so] Omit *so*, and explain either (1) *I will distress them* with the rigours of a siege *that they may feel it, i.e.* the distress ; or, (2) *that they may find* Me, God, that which alone is worth finding.
19-25. The lamentation of the daughter of Zion, the Jewish Church, at the devastation of the land, and her humble prayer to God for mercy.
19. *grievous*] Rather, **mortal,** *i.e.* fatal, incurable.
a grief] Or, **my** *grief.*
20. *tabernacle*] *i.e. tent.* Jerusalem laments that her tent is plundered, and her children carried into exile, and so *are not,* are dead (Matt. ii. 18), either absolutely, or dead to her in the remote land of their Captivity. They can aid the widowed mother no longer in pitching her tent, or in hanging up the curtains round about it.
21. *therefore they shall not prosper*] Rather, *therefore they* **have** *not* **governed wisely.** "The pastors," *i.e.* the kings and rulers (ii. 8), having sunk to the condition of barbarous and untutored men, could not govern wisely.
22. The *great commotion* is the confused noise of the army on its march (see viii. 16).
dragons] *i.e.* **jackals** ; see marg. ref.
23. At the rumour of the enemy's approach Jeremiah utters in the name of the nation a supplication appropriate to men overtaken by the divine justice.
24. *with judgment*] In xxx. 11 ; xlvi. 28, the word "judgment" (with a different preposition) is rendered *in measure.* The contrast therefore is between punishment inflicted in anger, and that inflicted as a duty of justice, of which the object is the criminal's reformation. Jeremiah prays that God would punish Jacob so far only as would bring him to true repentance, but that he would pour forth his anger upon the heathen, as upon that which opposes itself to God (*v.* 25).
XI., XII. The prophecy contained in these two chapters seems to belong to an early period of Jeremiah's life. The Covenant (*v.* 2) was that renewed by Josiah in his eighteenth year, after the discovery of the Book of the Law in the Temple (2 K. xxiii. 3) ; while *v.* 13 apparently refers to the public establishment of idolatry by Manasseh (do. xxi. 3). The people took no hearty part in Josiah's reformation, and the prophet therefore sets before them the consequences that will inevitably follow upon their disloyalty to their Covenant-God. The prophecy was probably called forth by the conspiracy of the men of Judah and of his own relatives of Anathoth to murder Jeremiah (*vv.* 18-23 ; xii. 1-6) ; for such deeds, which but too well represented the nation's whole course, punishment must come if unrepented of.
XI. 2. *the words of this covenant*] The phrase used (2 K. xxiii. 3) to describe the contents of the Book of the Law.

3 of Judah, and to the inhabitants of Jerusalem; and say thou
  unto them, Thus saith the LORD God of Israel; *a*Cursed *be* the
4 man that obeyeth not the words of this covenant, which I commanded your fathers in the day *that* I brought them forth out
  of the land of Egypt, *b*from the iron furnace, saying, *c*Obey my
  voice, and do them, according to all which I command you:
5 so shall ye be my people, and I will be your God: that I may
  perform the *d*oath which I have sworn unto your fathers, to give
  them a land flowing with milk and honey, as *it is* this day.
6 Then answered I, and said, ¹So be it, O LORD. Then the LORD
  said unto me, Proclaim all these words in the cities of Judah,
  and in the streets of Jerusalem, saying, Hear ye the words of
7 this covenant, *e*and do them. For I earnestly protested unto
  your fathers in the day *that* I brought them up out of the land
  of Egypt, *even* unto this day, *f*rising early and protesting, say-
8 ing, Obey my voice.   *g*Yet they obeyed not, nor inclined their
  ear, but *h*walked every one in the ²imagination of their evil
  heart: therefore I will bring upon them all the words of this
  covenant, which I commanded *them* to do; but they did *them* not.
9 ¶And the LORD said unto me, *i*A conspiracy is found among
  the men of Judah, and among the inhabitants of Jerusalem.
10 They are turned back to *k*the iniquities of their forefathers,
  which refused to hear my words; and they went after other gods
  to serve them: the house of Israel and the house of Judah have
11 broken my covenant which I made with their fathers.   Therefore thus saith the LORD, Behold, I will bring evil upon them,
  which they shall not be able ³to escape; and *l*though they shall
12 cry unto me, I will not hearken unto them.   Then shall the
  cities of Judah and inhabitants of Jerusalem go, and *m*cry unto
  the gods unto whom they offer incense: but they shall not save
13 them at all in the time of their ⁴trouble.   For *according to* the
  number of thy *n*cities were thy gods, O Judah; and *according*
  to the number of the streets of Jerusalem have ye set up altars
  to *that* ⁵shameful thing, *even* altars to burn incense unto Baal.

a Deut. 27.
26.
Gal. 3. 10.

b 1 Kin. 8.
51.
c Lev. 26. 3.
ch. 7. 23.
d Deut. 7.
12, 13.
Ps. 105. 9.

e Rom. 2. 13.
Jam. 1. 22.

f ch. 7. 13.
g ch. 7. 26.
h ch. 3. 17.

i Ezek. 22.
25.
Hos. 6. 9.
k Ezek. 20.
18.

l Ps. 18. 41.
Isai. 1. 15.
Ezek. 8. 18.
Zech. 7. 13.
m Deut. 32.
37, 38.

n ch. 2. 28.

¹ Heb. *Amen*, Deut. 27.
15-26.
² Or, *stubbornness*.
³ Heb. *to go forth of*.
⁴ Heb. *evil*.
⁵ Heb. *shame*, ch. 3. 24.
Hos. 9. 10.

---

4. *from the iron furnace*] Rather, **out of**
the iron furnace, Egypt (see Deut. iv. 20).
The constant reference to Deuteronomy
shews how great had been the effect upon
Jeremiah's mind of the public recitation of
the "Book of the Covenant" found in the
Temple.

5. *as it is this day*] God had kept the terms
of the Covenant. Whether the promised
land would permanently remain the property of the Jews would depend upon their
observance of their part of the Covenant.

So be it, O LORD] Or, **Amen,** *Jehovah.*
The prophet was literally obeying the command given in Deut. xxvii. 14-26, and the
same word should be kept in both places.

6. *Proclaim* &c.] Probably Jeremiah
accompanied Josiah in his progress (2 K.
xxiii. 15-20), and everywhere read to
the people the words of the newly-found
Book.

8. *I will bring*] Rather, **I have brought.**

The breach of the Covenant upon their part
had always brought temporal calamity.
The last examples were the deportation of
the ten tribes by Salmanezer, and the
leading of Manasseh prisoner to Babylon in
chains (2 Chr. xxxiii. 11).

9. *A conspiracy*] The defection from the
Covenant was as general as if it had been the
result of preconcerted arrangement. The
decided course taken by Josiah may, however, have led the opposite party to secret
combinations against him.

10. *their forefathers*] Lit. *their fathers, the*
first ones; in allusion to the idolatries committed in the wilderness, and by the generations whose history is given in the Book
of Judges.

and they went after] Rather, **yea! they have**
walked *after other gods to serve them.* The
they refers to the men of Jeremiah's day.

11. *I will bring*] Or, **am bringing.**

13. *that shameful thing*] i.e. Baal; a

[o] Ex. 32. 10. ch. 7. 16. 1 John 5. 16.
[p] Ps. 50. 16.
[q] Ezek. 16. 25, &c.
[r] Hag. 2. 12. Tit. 1. 15.
[s] Prov. 2. 14.
[t] Ps. 52. 8. Rom. 11. 17.
[u] Isai. 5. 2. ch. 2. 21.
[x] ch. 18. 18.
[y] Ps. 83. 4.
[z] Ps. 27. 13.
[a] 1 Sam. 16. 7. Ps. 7. 9. ch. 17. 10. Rev. 2. 23.
[b] ch. 12. 5.
[c] Isai. 30. 10. Amos 2. 12. Mic. 2. 6.
[d] ch. 23. 12. Luke 19. 44.

14 Therefore [o]pray not thou for this people, neither lift up a cry
or prayer for them: for I will not hear *them* in the time that
15 they cry unto me for their [1]trouble. ¶ [p] [2]What hath my beloved
to do in mine house, *seeing* she hath [q]wrought lewdness with
many, and [r]the holy flesh is passed from thee? [3]when thou
16 doest evil, then thou [s]rejoicest. The LORD called thy name, [t]A
green olive tree, fair, *and* of goodly fruit: with the noise of a
great tumult he hath kindled fire upon it, and the branches of
17 it are broken. For the LORD of hosts, [u]that planted thee, hath
pronounced evil against thee, for the evil of the house of Israel
and of the house of Judah, which they have done against themselves to provoke me to anger in offering incense unto Baal.
18 ¶ And the LORD hath given me knowledge *of it*, and I know *it*:
19 then thou shewedst me their doings. But I *was* like a lamb *or*
an ox *that* is brought to the slaughter; and I knew not that
[x]they had devised devices against me, *saying*, Let us destroy
[4]the tree with the fruit thereof, [y]and let us cut him off from
[z]the land of the living, that his name may be no more remem-
20 bered. But, O LORD of hosts, that judgest righteously, that
[a]triest the reins and the heart, let me see thy vengeance on
21 them: for unto thee have I revealed my cause. ¶ Therefore
thus saith the LORD of the men of Anathoth, [b]that seek thy
life, saying, [c]Prophesy not in the name of the LORD, that thou
22 die not by our hand: Therefore thus saith the LORD of hosts,
Behold, I will [5]punish them: the young men shall die by the
sword; their sons and their daughters shall die by famine: and
23 there shall be no remnant of them: for I will bring evil upon
the men of Anathoth, *even* [d]the year of their visitation.

[a] Ps. 51. 4.

CHAP. 12. RIGHTEOUS [a]*art* thou, O LORD, when I plead with

[1] Heb. *evil*.
[2] Heb. *What is to my beloved in my house*.
[3] Or, *when thy evil is*.
[4] Heb. *the stalk with his bread*.
[5] Heb. *visit upon*.

---

public establishment of idolatry, such as actually took place in the reign of Manasseh (2 Chr. xxxiii. 3. Contrast 2 K. xviii. 4).

14-17. A parenthesis. As in vii. 16, all intercession is forbidden, and for this reason. Prayer for others for the forgiveness of their sins avails only when they also pray. The cry of the people now was that of the guilty smarting under punishment, not of the penitent mourning over sin.

15. This passage, like Isai. i. 12, rebukes the inconsistency of Judah's public worship of Jehovah with their private immorality and preference for idolatry. Translate; *What hath My beloved in My house to practise guile there? The great men and the holy flesh* (*i.e.* the sacrifices) *shall pass away from thee.*

16. The *goodly* or *shapely fruit*, signifies the righteousness and faith which ought to have been the result of Israel's possession of extraordinary privileges. The tree did not bear this fruit, and God now destroys it by a thunderstorm.

18. Rather, **gave** *me knowledge of it, and I* **knew** it. Jeremiah shews (*vv.* 18-23), that the general conspiracy of the people against Jehovah and the special plot against himself was revealed to him by God.

19. *like a lamb* or *an ox*] Rather, *like a* **tame** *lamb*. Jeremiah had lived at Anathoth as one of the family, never suspecting that, like a tame lamb, the time would come for him to be killed.

the tree with the fruit thereof] The words are those of a proverb or dark saying. All the Churches agree in understanding that under the person of Jeremiah these things are said by Christ.

22. *the young men*] *i.e.* those of the legal age for military service.

23. *no remnant*] 128 men of Anathoth returned from exile (Ezra ii. 23; Neh. vii. 27). Jeremiah's denunciation was limited to those who had sought his life. The year of their visitation would be the year of the siege of Jerusalem, when Anathoth being in its immediate vicinity would have its share of the horrors of war.

XII. Some divide this chapter into three extracts (*vv.* 1-6, 7-13, 14-17) from discourses of Jeremiah not preserved at length; others regard it as a connected discourse

thee: yet ¹let me talk with thee of *thy* judgments: ᵇWherefore
doth the way of the wicked prosper? *wherefore* are all they
2 happy that deal very treacherously? Thou hast planted them,
yea, they have taken root: ²they grow, yea, they bring forth
fruit: ᶜthou *art* near in their mouth, and far from their reins.
3 But thou, O LORD, ᵈknowest me: thou hast seen me, and
ᵉtried mine heart ³toward thee: pull them out like sheep for the
4 slaughter, and prepare them for ᶠthe day of slaughter. How
long shall ᵍthe land mourn, and the herbs of every field wither,
ʰfor the wickedness of them that dwell therein? ⁱthe beasts are
consumed, and the birds; because they said, He shall not see
5 our last end. ¶ If thou hast run with the footmen, and they
have wearied thee, then how canst thou contend with horses?
and *if* in the land of peace, *wherein* thou trustedst, *they wearied*
6 *thee,* then how wilt thou do in ᵏthe swelling of Jordan? For
even ˡthy brethren, and the house of thy father, even they have
dealt treacherously with thee; yea, ⁴they have called a multitude after thee: ᵐbelieve them not, though they speak ⁵fair
words unto thee.

ᵇ Job 12. 6.	
ch. 5. 28.	
Hab. 1. 4.	
Mal. 3. 15.	
ᶜ Isai. 29. 13.	
Matt. 15. 8.	
ᵈ Ps. 17. 3.	
ᵉ ch. 11. 20.	
ᶠ Jam. 5. 5.	
ᵍ ch. 23. 10.	
Hos. 4. 3.	
ʰ Ps. 107. 34.	
ⁱ ch. 4. 25.	
ᵏ Josh. 3. 15.	
1 Chr. 12.15.	
ˡ ch. 9. 4.	
ᵐ Prov. 26. 25.	

---

¹ Or, *let me reason the case with thee.*
² Heb. *they go on.*
³ Heb. *with thee.*
⁴ Or, *they cried after thee fully.*
⁵ Heb. *good things.*

---

occasioned by a drought in the days of
Josiah (cp. *v.* 4); others see in the "evil
neighbours" (*v.* 14), an allusion to the bands
of Syrians &c., who infested the land after
Jehoiakim's revolt from Nebuchadnezzar.
More probably the outburst of expostulation (*rc.* 1-4) was occasioned by the plot of
the men of Anathoth, and upon it the rest
follows naturally.

1. *yet let me talk* &c.] Rather, **yet will I
speak with thee on a matter of right.**
This sense is well given in the margin.
The prophet acknowledges the general
righteousness of God's dealings, but cannot
reconcile with it the prosperity of the conspirators of Anathoth. This difficulty was
often present to the minds of the saints of
the Old Testament, see Job xxi. 7 &c.;
Pss. xxxvii., lxxiii.
happy] Rather, **secure,** tranquil.

2. *their reins]* *i.e.* their heart. The reins
were regarded by the Jews as the seat of
the affections.

3. *thou hast seen me* &c.] Rather, **Thou
seest me and triest** *mine heart* at all times,
and knowest the sincerity of its devotion
toward Thee.
pull them out] The original is used (x. 20)
of the rending asunder of the cords of the
tent, and (Ezek. xvii. 9) of the tearing up
of roots. Jeremiah does not doubt God's
justice, or the ultimate punishment of the
wicked, but he wants it administered in a
summary way.
prepare] Lit. *sanctify, i.e.* devote.

4. The Hebrew divides this verse differently. *How long shall the land mourn,
and the herb of the* **whole** *field wither?* Because of the wickedness of them that dwell

therein **cattle** *and fowl* **have ceased to be:**
for he will not see, say they, our latter end.
The people mock the prophet, saying, In
spite of all his threatenings we shall outlive
him.
Jeremiah complained that at a time of great
general misery powerful men throve upon
the ruin of others: even the innocent cattle
and fowl suffered with the rest. To him it
seemed that all this might have been cured
by some signal display of Divine justice.
If God, instead of dealing with men by
general and slow-working laws, would tear
out some of the worst offenders from among
the rest, the land might yet be saved.

5, 6. Jehovah rebukes Jeremiah's impatience, showing him by two proverbial
sayings, that there were still greater trials
of faith in store for him. Prosperous
wickedness is after all a mere ordinary trial,
a mere "running with the footmen;" he
will have to exert far greater powers of
endurance.
and if in the land &c.] Rather, *and in a
land of peace thou art secure; but how wilt
thou do amid the pride of Jordan?* if thou
canst feel safe only where things are tranquil, what wilt thou do in the hour of
danger? The *pride of Jordan* is taken
to mean the luxuriant thickets along its
banks, famous as the haunt of lions (cp. xlix.
19, 1. 44; Zech. xi. 3). What will the
prophet do when he has to tread the tangled
maze of a jungle with the lions roaring
round him?

6. *called a multitude]* Rather, *called
aloud.* Cp. iv. 5. In all this Jeremiah
was the type of Christ (cp. Zech. xiii. 6;
Mark iii. 21; John vii. 5).

7 I have forsaken mine house, I have left mine heritage;
I have given [1]the dearly beloved of my soul into the hand of
8 her enemies. Mine heritage is unto me as a lion in the forest;
9 it [2][3]crieth out against me: therefore have I hated it. Mine
heritage *is* unto me *as* a [4]speckled bird, the birds round
about *are* against her; come ye, assemble all the beasts of
10 the field, [5][n]come to devour. Many [o]pastors have destroyed
[p]my vineyard, they have [q]trodden my portion under foot, they
11 have made my [6]pleasant portion a desolate wilderness. They
have made it desolate, *and being* desolate [r]it mourneth unto me;
the whole land is made desolate, because [s]no man layeth *it* to
12 heart. The spoilers are come upon all high places through the
wilderness: for the sword of the LORD shall devour from the
one end of the land even to the *other* end of the land: no flesh
13 shall have peace. [t]They have sown wheat, but shall reap
thorns: they have put themselves to pain, *but* shall not profit:
and [7]they shall be ashamed of your revenues because of the
fierce anger of the LORD.

14 Thus saith the LORD against all mine evil neighbours, that
[u]touch the inheritance which I have caused my people Israel to
inherit; Behold, I will [x]pluck them out of their land, and pluck
15 out the house of Judah from among them. [y]And it shall come
to pass, after that I have plucked them out I will return, and
have compassion on them, [z]and will bring them again, every
16 man to his heritage, and every man to his land. And it shall
come to pass, if they will diligently learn the ways of my people,

[n] Isai. 56. 9. ch. 7. 33.
[o] ch. 6. 3.
[p] Isai. 5. 1.
[q] Isai. 63. 18.
[r] ver. 4.
[s] Isai. 42. 25.
[t] Lev. 26. 16. Mic. 6. 15. Hag. 1. 6.
[u] Zech. 2. 8.
[x] Deut. 30. 3. ch. 32. 37.
[y] Ezek. 28. 25.
[z] Amos 9. 14.

[1] Heb. *the love.*
[2] Or, *yelleth.*
[3] Heb. *giveth out his voice.*
[4] Or, *taloned.*
[5] Or, *cause them to come.*
[6] Heb. *portion of desire.*
[7] Or, *ye.*

7–9. Jehovah shews that the downfall of the nation was occasioned by no want of love on His part, but by the nation's conduct.

left] More correctly, **cast away.**

8. Judah has not merely refused obedience, but become intractable and fierce, like an untamed lion. It has roared against God with open blasphemy. As His favour is life, so is His hatred death, *i.e.* Jerusalem's punishment shall be as if inflicted by one that hated her.

9. Rather, *Is My heritage unto Me as a speckled bird? Are the birds upon her round about? Come, assemble all the* **wild beasts: bring them** *to devour her.* By a *speckled* or parti-coloured *bird* is probably meant some kind of vulture.

10. Nebuchadnezzar and his confederate kings trampled Judah under foot, as heedless of the ruin they were inflicting as the shepherds would be who led their flocks to browse in spring upon the tender shoots of the vine.

11. *desolate*] The force of the protest lies in this word. Thrice the prophet uses it.

layeth it *to heart*] Rather, **laid it** *to heart.* The desolate land must put up its silent cry to God, because the people had refused to see the signs of the coming retribution.

12. *through*] **in.** Even these remote scaurs do not escape, polluted as they had been by the nation's idolatries.

shall devour] Or, **devoureth.** These hosts of war come as Jehovah's sword.

no flesh shall have peace] *Flesh* in Gen. vi. 3 means mankind as sinners; here, Judah. *Peace* in Hebrew has the wider signification of *welfare, happiness.* Hence their salutation in life was, "Peace be to thee," and in death "In Peace" was engraved upon their sepulchres.

13. *shall reap...shall not profit*] Rather, have **reaped...have profited nothing.** The force of the proverb is that all their labours had ended only in disappointment.

and they shall be ashamed of your revenues] Or, **yea, be ashamed of your produce**—the produce of the fields.

14. The prophet addresses the spoilers.

evil neighbours] The Syrians, Edomites, Moabites, Ammonites, and Philistines, who at all times took advantage of Judah's weakness. The special mercy to Judah was the prelude to mercy to the whole Gentile world.

16. The accomplishment of this blessing depends upon both Judah and the Gentiles reversing their past conduct. Then shall the believing Gentile be admitted within the fold of the true, because spiritual, Israel—Christ's Church.

*to swear by my name, The LORD liveth; as they taught my
people to swear by Baal; then shall they be *built in the midst
17 of my people. But if they will not *obey, I will utterly pluck
up and destroy that nation, saith the LORD.

a ch. 4. 2.
b Eph. 2. 20.
1 Pet. 2. 5.
c Isai. 60. 12.

CHAP. 13. THUS saith the LORD unto me, Go and get thee a linen
2 girdle, and put it upon thy loins, and put it not in water. So I
got a girdle according to the word of the LORD, and put *it* on
3 my loins. ¶ And the word of the LORD came unto me the
4 second time, saying, Take the girdle that thou hast got, which
is upon thy loins, and arise, go to Euphrates, and hide it there
5 in a hole of the rock. So I went, and hid it by Euphrates, as
6 the LORD commanded me. ¶ And it came to pass after many
days, that the LORD said unto me, Arise, go to Euphrates, and
take the girdle from thence, which I commanded thee to hide
7 there. Then I went to Euphrates, and digged, and took the
girdle from the place where I had hid it: and, behold, the girdle
8 was marred, it was profitable for nothing. ¶ Then the word
9 of the LORD came unto me, saying, Thus saith the LORD,
¶ After this manner *will I mar the pride of Judah, and the
10 great pride of Jerusalem. This evil people, which refuse to hear
my words, which *walk in the ¹imagination of their heart, and
walk after other gods, to serve them, and to worship them, shall
11 even be as this girdle, which is good for nothing. For as the
girdle cleaveth to the loins of a man, so have I caused to cleave
unto me the whole house of Israel and the whole house of
Judah, saith the LORD; that *they might be unto me for a
people, and *for a name, and for a praise, and for a glory: but
12 they would not hear. ¶ Therefore thou shalt speak unto them
this word: Thus saith the LORD God of Israel, ¶ Every bottle
shall be filled with wine: and they shall say unto thee, Do we
not certainly know that every bottle shall be filled with wine?
13 Then shalt thou say unto them, Thus saith the LORD, Behold,

a Lev. 26.19.

b ch. 9. 14.
& 11. 8.
& 16. 12.

c Ex. 19. 5.
d ch. 33. 9.

¹ Or, *stubbornness.*

XIII. The date of this prophecy is fixed
by the mention of the queen-mother (*v.* 18)
i.e. Nehushta, the mother of Jehoiachin.
We have in it one of those symbolical acts
by which great lessons were taught the
people more impressively than by words
After the burning of the roll in the fourth
year of Jehoiakim Jeremiah disappeared
from Jerusalem, and did not shew himself
there again for seven years. In the last few
mournful days of Jehoiakim, he was once
again seen in the streets of Jerusalem, with
his prophetic robe of black camel's hair girt
about with this girdle, mildewed and water-
stained as the symbol of the pitiable estate
of a nation which had rejected its God. His
place of refuge may have been near the
Euphrates. Many such acts alleged to have
been performed by the prophets may have
been allegories, but this we believe to have
been literally true.

1. *a linen girdle*] The appointed dress of
the priestly order (Lev. xvi. 4 &c.).
put it not in water] *i.e.* do not wash it,

and so let it represent the deep-grained
pollution of the people.

4. *in a hole of the rock*] In *a cleft of the
rock.* As there are no fissured rocks in
Babylonia, the place where Jeremiah hid
the girdle must have been somewhere in the
upper part of the river.

6. *many days*] The seventy years' Captivity.

10. This verse limits the application of
the symbol. Only the ungodly and the
idolatrous part of the people decayed at
Babylon. The religious portion was strengthened and invigorated by the exile (xxiv.
5—7).

11. The reason why the girdle was chosen
as the symbol. Similarly Israel was the
people chosen and set apart that in and by
them the Holy Ghost might work for the
salvation of mankind.

12. *bottle*] **jar**, the "potter's vessel" of
Isai. xxx. 14: a new symbol, but with the
same meaning, the approaching destruction
of Jerusalem (*v.* 14).

I will fill all the inhabitants of this land, even the kings that sit upon David's throne, and the priests, and the prophets, and all 14 the inhabitants of Jerusalem, *e* with drunkenness. And *f* I will dash them ¹one against another, even the fathers and the sons together, saith the LORD: I will not pity, nor spare, nor have 15 mercy, ²but destroy them. ¶Hear ye, and give ear; be not 16 proud: for the LORD hath spoken. *g* Give glory to the LORD your God, before he cause *h* darkness, and before your feet stumble upon the dark mountains, and, while ye *i* look for light, he turn it into *k* the shadow of death, *and* make it gross dark- 17 ness. But if ye will not hear it, my soul shall weep in secret places for *your* pride; and *l* mine eye shall weep sore, and run down with tears, because the LORD's flock is carried away cap- 18 tive. ¶ Say unto *m* the king and to the queen, Humble your- selves, sit down: for your ³principalities shall come down, *even* 19 the crown of your glory. The cities of the south shall be shut up, and none shall open *them*: Judah shall be carried away 20 captive all of it, it shall be wholly carried away captive. Lift up your eyes, and behold them *n* that come from the north: where *is* the flock *that* was given thee, thy beautiful flock? 21 What wilt thou say when he shall ⁴punish thee? for thou hast taught them *to be* captains, *and* as chief over thee: shall not 22 *o* sorrows take thee, as a woman in travail? And if thou say in thine heart, *p* Wherefore come these things upon me? For the greatness of thine iniquity are *q* thy skirts discovered, *and*

Marginal references (left column):

e Isai. 51. 17,
21. & 63. 6.
ch. 25. 27.
f Ps. 2. 9.

g Josh. 7. 19.
h Isai. 5. 30.
Amos. 8. 9.
i Isai. 59. 9.
k Ps. 44. 19.

l ch. 9. 1.
Lam. 1. 2,
16. & 2. 18.
m See
2 Kin. 24. 12.
ch. 22. 26.

n ch. 6. 22.

o ch. 6. 24.
p ch. 5. 19.
& 16. 10.
q Isai. 3. 17.
Ezek. 16.
37, 38, 39.
Nah. 3. 5.

¹ Heb. *a man against his brother.*
² Heb. *from destroying them.*
³ Or, *head tires.*
⁴ Heb. *visit upon.*

---

13. *the kings* &c.] *i.e.* his successors in general. In the fall of Jerusalem four kings in succession were crushed.

14. All orders and degrees of men in the state would be broken in indiscriminate destruction.

15. *be not proud*] Both the symbols were of a nature very humiliating to the national self-respect.

16. *the dark mountains*] Rather, *the moun- tains of twilight.* Judah is not walking upon the safe highway, but upon dangerous mountains: and the dusk is closing round her. While then the light still serves let her return unto her God.

and, while ye look &c.] Translate, *and ye wait for light, and He turn it* (the light) *into the shadow of death, yea change it into clouded darkness.*

17. *the* LORD's *flock*] The people carried away captive with Jeconiah formed the Jew- ish Church, as we are expressly told, whereas Zedekiah and the people of Jerusalem pos- sessed only the externals of the Church and not its reality. It is for this reason that the seventy years' exile counts from Jeconiah's captivity.

18. *the queen*] *i.e. the* **queen-mother**: the word signifies literally *the great lady.* The king's mother took precedence of his wives.

sit down] The usual position of slaves.

for your principalities &c.] Rather, **for the**

ornaments of your heads, *even the crown of your majesty, shall come down.*

19. *shall be shut up*] Rather, **are shut up,** *and no man* **openeth** *them.* The cities of the Negeb, the southern district of Judah, are blockaded, with no one to raise the siege. The Captivity was the inevitable result of the capture of the fortified towns. An army entering from the North would march along the Shefêlah, or fertile plain near the sea- coast, and would capture the outlying cities, before it attacked Jerusalem, almost inac- cessible among the mountains.

Judah shall be...] Translate, *Judah is....*

20. Jerusalem is asked where the cities, which once lay grouped round her, like a goodly flock of sheep, are gone? The ques- tion implies blame.

21. Translate, *What wilt thou say, O Jeru- salem, when He,* Jehovah, *shall set over thee for head those whom thou hast taught to be thy bosom friends?* The foreign powers, whose friendship she has been courting, will become her tyrants.

22. *made bare*] Rather, **ill-used,** *treated with violence.* The long flowing robes worn by ladies of rank, are to be laid aside, that they might do menial work, bare-legged, like slaves. The ill-usage to the heels is the having to tramp barefoot, a thing very pain- ful to women accustomed to the seclusion of the female apartments.

23 thy heels ¹made bare. ¶ Can the Ethiopian change his skin, or
the leopard his spots? *then* may ye also do good, that are ²ac-
24 customed to do evil. Therefore will I scatter them ʳas the
25 stubble that passeth away by the wind of the wilderness. ˢThis
is thy lot, the portion of thy measures from me, saith the LORD;
because thou hast forgotten me, and trusted in ᵗfalsehood.
26 Therefore ᵘwill I discover thy skirts upon thy face, that thy
27 shame may appear. I have seen thine adulteries, and thy
ˣneighings, the lewdness of thy whoredom, *and* thine abominations ʸon the hills in the fields. Woe unto thee, O Jerusalem!
wilt thou not be made clean? ³when *shall it* once *be?*

ʳ Ps. 1. 4,
Hos. 13. 3.
ˢ Job 20. 29.
Ps. 11. 6.
ᵗ ch. 10. 14.

ᵘ Lam. 1. 8.
Ezek. 23. 29.
Hos. 2. 10.
ˣ ch. 5. 8.
ʸ Isai 65. 7.
ch. 2. :0.
Ezek. 6. 13.

CHAP. 14. THE word of the LORD that came to Jeremiah concern-
2 ing ⁴the dearth. ¶ Judah mourneth, and ᵃthe gates thereof
languish; they are ᵇblack unto the ground; and ᶜthe cry of
3 Jerusalem is gone up. And their nobles have sent their little
ones to the waters: they came to the pits, *and* found no water;
they returned with their vessels empty; they were ᵈashamed
4 and confounded, ᵉand covered their heads. Because the ground
is chapt, for there was no rain in the earth, the plowmen were
5 ashamed, they covered their heads. Yea, the hind also calved
6 in the field, and forsook *it*, because there was no grass. And
ᶠthe wild asses did stand in the high places, they snuffed up the
wind like dragons; their eyes did fail, because *there was* no grass.
7 ¶ O LORD, though our iniquities testify against us, do thou *it* ᵍfor
thy name's sake: for our backslidings are many; we have sinned

ᵃ Isai. 3. 26.
ᵇ ch. 8. 21.
ᶜ See
1 Sam. 5.12.

ᵈ Ps. 40. 14.

ᵉ 2 Sam. 15.
30.

ᶠ ch. 2. 24.

ᵍ Ps. 25. 11.

---

¹ Or, *shall be violently taken away.* ² Heb. *taught.* ³ Heb. *after when yet?* ⁴ Heb. *the words of the dearths,* or, *restraints.*

---

23. This verse answers the question, May not Judah avert this calamity by repentance? No: because her sins are too inveterate. By the Ethiopian (Heb. *Cushite*) is meant not the Cushite of Arabia but of Africa, *i.e.* the negro.

24. *stubble*] Broken straw separated from the wheat after the corn had been trampled out by the oxen. Sometimes it was burnt as useless; at other times left to be blown away by the wind from the desert.

25. *the portion of thy measures*] *i.e.* thy *measured portion* (Job xi. 9). Others render, *the portion of thy lap,* the upper garment being constantly used for holding things (Ruth iii. 15).

in falsehood] *i.e.* in idols (see marg. ref.).

26. *Therefore will I*] Lit. *And I also;* I also must have my turn, I too must retaliate. Cp. Nahum iii. 5.

27. *and thine abominations*] **Even** *thy abominations.* The prophet sums up the three charges against Judah, viz. spiritual adultery, inordinate eagerness after idolatry (see on v. 7 note), and shameless participation in heathen orgies.

in the fields] *in the* **field,** the open, unin-closed country (see vi. 25, xii. 4).

wilt thou not...once be?] Or, *how long yet ere thou be made clean!* These words explain the teaching of v. 23. Repentance was not an actual, but a moral impossibility, and

after a long time Judah was to be cleansed. It was to return from exile penitent and forgiven.

XIV., XV. The occasion of this prophecy was a drought, the terrible effects of which are described with much force. Probably, therefore, it belongs to the early years of Jehoiakim, when Jeremiah saw all the efforts of Josiah's reign utterly frustrated.

XIV. 1. *the dearth*] Really, **the drought.**

2. *they are black unto the ground*] The people assembled at the gates, the usual places of concourse, are in deep mourning and sit humbly on the ground.

3. *little ones*] **mean ones,** the common people. The word is peculiar to Jeremiah (xlviii. 4).

the pits] *i.e.* tanks for holding water.

covered their heads] The sign of grief.

4. *is chapt*] Rather, **is dismayed.** *The ground* is used metaphorically for the people who till the ground.

in the earth] *i.e.* in the **land.**

6. *like dragons*] Like **jackals** (ix. 11).

no grass] The keen sight of the wild ass is well known, but they look around in vain for **herb.**

7. *do thou it*] Rather, **deal** *thou, act thou for Thy Name's sake, i.e.* not according to the strict measure of right and wrong, but as a God merciful and gracious.

h ch. 17. 13.

8 against thee. *h*O the hope of Israel, the saviour thereof in time of trouble, why shouldest thou be as a stranger in the land, and as a wayfaring man *that* turneth aside to tarry for a night? 9 Why shouldest thou be as a man astonied, as a mighty man *i that* cannot save? yet thou, O LORD, *k art* in the midst of us, 10 and ¹we are called by thy name; leave us not. ¶ Thus saith the LORD unto this people, *l*Thus have they loved to wander, they have not refrained their feet, therefore the LORD doth not accept them; *m*he will now remember their iniquity, and visit 11 their sins. ¶ Then said the LORD unto me, *n* Pray not for this 12 people for *their* good. *o*When they fast, I will not hear their cry; and *p*when they offer burnt offering and an oblation, I will not accept them: but *q*I will consume them by the sword, and 13 by the famine, and by the pestilence. ¶ *r* Then said I, Ah, Lord GOD! behold, the prophets say unto them, Ye shall not see the sword, neither shall ye have famine; but I will give you ²assured 14 peace in this place. ¶ Then the LORD said unto me, *s* The prophets prophesy lies in my name: *t* I sent them not, neither have I commanded them, neither spake unto them: they prophesy unto you a false vision and divination, and a thing of nought, and the de-15 ceit of their heart. Therefore thus saith the LORD concerning the prophets that prophesy in my name, and I sent them not, *u*yet they say, Sword and famine shall not be in this land; By 16 sword and famine shall those prophets be consumed. And the people to whom they prophesy shall be cast out in the streets of Jerusalem because of the famine and the sword; *x*and they shall have none to bury them, them, their wives, nor their sons, nor their daughters: for I will pour their wickedness upon them. 17 ¶ Therefore thou shalt say this word unto them; *y* Let mine eyes run down with tears night and day, and let them not cease: *z*for the virgin daughter of my people is broken with a great

h ch. 17. 13.

i Isai. 59. 1.
k Ex. 29. 45.
Lev. 26. 11.
l See ch. 2.
23, 24, 25.

m Hos. 8.
13. & 9. 9.
n Ex. 32. 10.
ch. 7. 16.
o Isai. 1. 15.
ch. 11. 11.
Mic. 3. 4.
p ch. 6. 20.
& 7. 21, 22.
q ch. 9. 16.
r ch. 4. 10.
s ch. 27. 10.

t ch. 23. 21.
& 27. 15.

u ch. 5. 12.

x Ps. 79. 3.

y ch. 9. 1.
Lam. 1. 16.

z ch. 8. 21.

¹ Heb. *thy name is called upon us*, Dan. 9. 18, 19.　　² Heb. *peace of truth.*

---

9. *astonied*] The word may possibly mean one *who is taken by surprise and loses his presence of mind.*

10. The answer is addressed to the people. Jeremiah had prayed as their representative, but he must not intercede: for to the same degree that God was determined to punish them, to the same degree ("thus") they love to continue their offence. Cp. xv. 6 note.

therefore the LORD...] Translate:

And *Jehovah hath no pleasure in them:* **Now will He** *remember their iniquity and visit their sins.*

Interference in their behalf is out of the question.

12. *their cry*] *i.e.* prayer offered aloud. *oblation*] **A meat-offering** (Lev. ii. 1).

the sword, famine, and pestilence] The two latter ever follow upon the track of the first (Ezek. v. 12), and by these God will consume them, yet so as to leave a remnant. The chastisement, which crushes those who harden themselves against it, purifies the penitent.

13. The false prophets in Jeremiah's days were so numerous and influential as to

counteract and almost nullify the influence of the true prophet. We find in Isaiah the first indications of the internal decay of the prophetic order; and Micah, his contemporary, denounces the false prophets in the strongest terms (Micah iii. 5, 11). For the secret of their power see v. 31.

14. *divination*] *i.e. conjuring,* the abuse of the less understood powers of nature. It was strictly forbidden to all Jews (Deut. xviii. 10).

a thing of nought] Probably a small idol made of the more precious metals (Isai. ii. 20). These methods the prophet declares to be *the deceit of their heart, i.e.* not self-deceit, but a wilful and intentional fraud.

16. *I will pour &c.*] *i.e.* their wickedness shall be brought home to them.

17. A message from God to the effect that the calamity would be so overwhelming as to cause perpetual weeping; it is set before the people under the representation of Jeremiah's own sorrow.

the virgin daughter of my people] The epithet testifies to God's previous care of Judah. She had been as jealously guarded from other nations as virgins are in an oriental household (cp. Song of Sol. iv. 12).

18 breach, with a very grievous blow. If I go forth into ^a the field,   ^a Ezek. 7.15.
then behold the slain with the sword! and if I enter into the
city, then behold them that are sick with famine! yea, both the
prophet and the priest ¹ go about into a land that they know
19 not. ^b Hast thou utterly rejected Judah? hath thy soul lothed   ^b Lam. 5. 22.
Zion? why hast thou smitten us, and ^c *there is* no healing for   ^c ch. 15. 18.
us? ^d we looked for peace, and *there is* no good; and for the   ^d ch. 8. 15.
20 time of healing, and behold trouble! We acknowledge, O LORD,
our wickedness, *and* the iniquity of our fathers: for ^e we have   ^e Ps. 106. 6.
21 sinned against thee. Do not abhor *us*, for thy name's sake, do   Dan. 9. 8.
not disgrace the throne of thy glory: ^f remember, break not thy   ^f Ps. 74. 2.
22 covenant with us. ^g Are there *any* among ^h the vanities of the   ^g Zech. 10.
Gentiles that can cause rain? or can the heavens give showers?   1, 2.
ⁱ *art* not thou he, O LORD, our God? therefore we will wait upon   ^h Deut. 32.
thee: for thou hast made all these *things*.   21.

                                                        ⁱ Ps. 135. 7.

CHAP. 15. THEN said the LORD unto me, ^a Though ^b Moses and ^c Samuel   Isai. 30. 23.
stood before me, *yet* my mind *could* not *be* toward this people: ch. 5. 24.
2 cast *them* out of my sight, and let them go forth. And it shall   ^a Ezek. 14.
come to pass, if they say unto thee, Whither shall we go forth?   14 &c.
then thou shalt tell them, Thus saith the LORD; ^d Such as *are* for   ^b Ex. 32. 11.
death, to death; and such as *are* for the sword, to the sword;   Ps. 99. 6.
and such as *are* for the famine, to the famine; and such as *are*   ^c 1 Sam. 7. 9.
3 for the captivity, to the captivity. And I will ^e appoint over   ^d ch. 43. 11.
them four ² kinds, saith the LORD: the sword to slay, and the   Ezek. 5. 2.
dogs to tear, and ^f the fowls of the heaven, and the beasts of the   Zech. 11. 9.
4 earth, to devour and destroy. And ³ I will cause them to be   ^e Lev. 26.
^g removed into all kingdoms of the earth, because of ^h Manasseh   16. &c.
the son of Hezekiah king of Judah, for *that* which he did in Jeru-   ^f Deut. 28.
5 salem. ¶ For ⁱ who shall have pity upon thee, O Jerusalem? or   26.
who shall bemoan thee? or who shall go aside ⁴ to ask how thou   ch. 7. 33.
6 doest? ^k Thou hast forsaken me, saith the LORD, thou art ^l gone   ^g Deut. 28.
backward: therefore will I stretch out my hand against thee,   25.
                                                          Ezek. 23.
                                                          46.
                                                          ^h 2 Kin. 21.
                                                          11, &c.
                                                          ⁱ Isai. 51. 19.
                                                          ^k ch. 2. 13.
                                                          ^l ch. 7. 24.

---

¹ Or, *make merchandise*   *acknowledge* it *not*, ch. 5.   ³ Heb. *I will give them for*
   against a land, and men   31.   *a removing.*
                     ² Heb. *families.*   ⁴ Heb. *to ask of thy peace?*

19-22. A second (cp. *vv.* 7-9) earnest intercession, acknowledging the wickedness of the nation, but appealing to the Covenant and to God's Almighty power.

lothed] More exactly, *hath thrown away as worthless.*

20. *our wickedness*, and] Omit *and*. National sin is the sin of the fathers, perpetuated generation after generation by the children.

21. This verse is in the original very emphatic, and consists of a series of broken ejaculations: *Abhor not for thy name's sake! Disgrace—lightly esteem* in Deut. xxxii. 15—*not the throne of thy glory! Remember! Break not* &c. *with us!* The throne of Jehovah's glory is Jerusalem.

22. None of the idols of the Gentiles can put an end to this present distress.

art not thou he, O LORD our God!] Rather, *art thou not Jehovah our God!*

thou hast made all these things] *i.e.* the heaven with its showers.

XV. 1. *cast them out of my sight*] Ra-

ther, **send** *them out of My* **presence**, *and let them go away.* The prophet is to dismiss them, because their mediators, Moses and Samuel, whose intercession had been accepted in old times (marg. reff.), would intercede now in vain.

3. *kinds*] Lit. as marg., *i.e.* classes of things. The first is to destroy the living, the other three to mutilate and consume the dead.

to tear] Lit. *to drag along the ground.* It forcibly expresses the contumely to which the bodies of the slain will be exposed.

4. *to be removed*] Rather, *to be* **a terror.**

because of Manasseh the son of Hezekiah] The name of the pious father intensifies the horror at the wickedness of the son.

6. This verse gives the reason of the refusal of Jehovah to hear the prophet's intercession. The punishment due has been delayed unto wearisomeness, and this seeming failure of justice has made Judah withdraw further from God.

m Hos. 13.
14.

n Isai. 9. 13.
Amos 4.
10, 11.

o 1 Sam. 2. 5.

p Amos 8. 9.

q Job 3. 1.
ch. 20. 14.

r ch. 39. 11.
& 40. 4, 5.

s Ps. 44. 12.
ch. 17. 3.

t ch. 16. 13.

7 and destroy thee; *m* I am weary with repenting. And I will fan them with a fan in the gates of the land; I will bereave *them* of ¹children, I will destroy my people, *since* *n* they return not from 8 their ways. Their widows are increased to me above the sand of the seas: I have brought upon them ²against the mother of the young men a spoiler at noonday: I have caused *him* to fall upon 9 it suddenly, and terrors upon the city. *o* She that hath borne seven languisheth: she hath given up the ghost; *p* her sun is gone down while *it was* yet day: she hath been ashamed and confounded: and the residue of them will I deliver to the sword before their enemies, saith the LORD.

10 *q* Woe is me, my mother, that thou hast borne me a man of strife and a man of contention to the whole earth! I have neither lent on usury, nor men have lent to me on usury; *yet* 11 every one of them doth curse me. The LORD said, Verily it shall be well with thy remnant; verily ³I will cause *r* the enemy to entreat thee *well* in the time of evil and in the time of affliction. 12 Shall iron break the northern iron and the steel? Thy substance 13 and thy treasures will I give to the *s* spoil without price, and *that* 14 for all thy sins, even in all thy borders. And I will make *thee* to pass with thine enemies *t* into a land *which* thou knowest not:

---

¹ Or, *whatsoever is dear.*
² Or, *against the mother city a young man spoiling,*
&c. or, *against the mother* and *the young men.*
³ Or, *I will entreat the enemy for thee.*

---

7. *I will fan them* &c.] Or, **I have win-nowed them with a winnowing shovel.** *The gates of the land* mean the places by which men enter or leave it. As God winnows them they are driven out of the land through all its outlets in every direction.

I will bereave] Rather, **I have bereaved, I have destroyed my people.** Omit *of children.*

since they return not...] Rather, *from their ways they have not returned.*

8. Translate, *I have brought upon them, even upon the mother of the young* **man, a** *spoiler* &c. The word rendered *young man* means a picked warrior. The mother has borne a valiant champion; but neither his prowess nor the numerous offspring of the other can avail to save those who gave them birth; war bereaves both alike.

at noonday] *i.e.* unexpectedly, as armies used to rest at noon (see vi. 4 note).

I have caused him...] Rather, *I have brought suddenly upon her,* the mother of the young warrior, **anguish** *and terrors.*

9. *she hath been ashamed*] Or, *is ashamed.* To a Hebrew mother to be childless was a disgrace. Many consider that *vv.* 7-9 refer to the battle of Megiddo, and depict the consternation of Jerusalem at that sad event. If so, in the sun going down while it was day, there will be a reference to the eclipse on Sept. 30, B.C. 610.

10. Jeremiah vents his sorrow at the rejection of his prayer. In reading these and similar expostulations we feel that we have to do with a man who was the reluctant minister of a higher power, whence

alone he drew strength to be content to do and suffer.

strife] More exactly, *lawsuit;* the sense is, *I am as a man who has to enter into judgment with and reprove the whole earth.*

I have neither lent &c.] *i.e.* I have no personal cause of quarrel with the people, that I should thus be perpetually at strife with them. The relations between the money-lender and the debtor were a fruitful source of lawsuits and quarrelling.

11. *shall be well with thy remnant*] Or, **thy loosing shall be for good**; in the sense of being set free, deliverance.

to entreat thee well...] Rather, **to supplicate thee** *in the time of evil* &c.; fulfilled in xxi. 1, 2, xxxvii. 3, xlii. 2.

12. *the steel*] **brass,** *i.e.* bronze. By the "iron" is meant Jeremiah's intercession; but this cannot alter the Divine purpose to send Judah into exile, which is firm as steel and brass. For *brass* see Ex. xxv. 3 note. The alloy of copper and zinc now called brass was entirely unknown to the ancients.

13. Jeremiah is personally addressed in the verse, because he stood before God as the intercessor, representing the people. (1) God would give Judah's treasures away for nothing; implying that He did not value them. (2) The cause of this contempt is Judah's sins. (3) This is justified by Judah having committed them throughout her whole land.

14. Render, *And I will make thee serve thine enemies in a land thou knewest not.*

for a [u]fire is kindled in mine anger, *which* shall burn upon you.

15 ¶ O LORD, [x]thou knowest: remember me, and visit me, and
[y]revenge me of my persecutors; take me not away in thy long-

16 suffering: know that [z]for thy sake I have suffered rebuke. Thy
words were found, and I did [a]eat them; and [b]thy word was
unto me the joy and rejoicing of mine heart: for [1]I am called

17 by thy name, O LORD God of hosts. [c]I sat not in the assembly
of the mockers, nor rejoiced; I sat alone because of thy hand:

18 for thou hast filled me with indignation. Why is my [d]pain perpetual, and my wound incurable, *which* refuseth to be healed?
wilt thou be altogether unto me [e]as a liar, and [f]as waters that

19 [2]fail? ¶ Therefore thus saith the LORD, [g]If thou return, then
will I bring thee again, *and* thou shalt [h]stand before me: and
if thou [i]take forth the precious from the vile, thou shalt be as my
mouth: let them return unto thee; but return not thou unto

20 them. And I will make thee unto this people a fenced brasen
[k]wall: and they shall fight against thee, but [l]they shall not
prevail against thee. for I *am* with thee to save thee and to de-

21 liver thee, saith the LORD. And I will deliver thee out of the
hand of the wicked, and I will redeem thee out of the hand of
the terrible.

CHAP. 16. THE word of the LORD came also unto me, saying, Thou

[u] Deut. 32.
22.
[x] ch. 12. 3.
[y] ch. 11. 20.
[z] Ps. 69. 7.

[a] Ezek. 3. 1.
Rev. 10. 9.
[b] Job 23. 12.

[c] Ps. 1. 1.

[d] ch. 30. 15.

[e] See ch. 1.
18, 19.
[f] Job 6. 15.
[g] Zech. 3. 7.
[h] ver. 1.
[i] Ezek. 22.
26.

[k] ch. 6. 27.
[l] ch. 20. 11,
12.

---

[1] Heb. *thy name is called upon me.*   [2] Heb. *be not sure?*

---

for a fire &c.] See marg. ref. The added
words shew that the punishment then predicted is about to be fulfilled.

15–18. This is the prayer of a man in
bitter grief, whose human nature cannot at
present submit to the Divine will. God's
long-suffering towards the wicked seemed to
the prophet to be the abandonment of himself
to death; justice itself required that one
who was suffering contumely for God's
sake should be delivered.

rebuke] i.e. **reproach**, contumely.

16. *Thy words were found*] Jeremiah's
summons to the prophetic office had not
been expected or sought for by him.

I did eat them] i.e. I received them with
joy. This eating of the Divine words expresses also the close union between that
which came from God and the prophet's own
being.

I am called by thy name] i.e. I am consecrated to Thy service, am ordained to be
Thy prophet.

17. Rather, *I sat not in the assembly of the
laughers, and was merry.* From the time
God's words came to Jeremiah he abstained
from things innocent, and a gravity came
over him beyond his years.

I sat alone because of thy hand] As a person *consecrated* to God he would also be
separated. See i. 5; cp. Acts xiii. 2.

with indignation] The prophet thus taught
of God sees the sins of the people as offences
against God, and as involving the ruin of
His Church.

18. *Why is my pain perpetual*] i.e. Are all
my labours to be in vain?

as a liar...] Really, *as a* **deceitful** *brook,*
a brook which flows only in the winter, the
opposite of *the perennial stream* of Amos v.
24. Jeremiah had expected that there
would be a perpetual interference of Providence in his behalf, instead whereof things
seemed to take only their natural course.

19. Jeremiah had questioned God's righteousness (see xii. 1 note); he is told, *If thou
return*, if thou repent thee of thy doubts,
and think only of thy duty, *then will I bring
thee again, then will I cause thee again to
stand before Me.* To stand before a person
means to be his chief officer or vicegerent.
It implies therefore the restoration of Jeremiah to the prophetic office.

if thou take forth the precious from the vile]
i.e. if thou cause the precious metal to come
forth from the dross. Jeremiah was to
separate in himself what was divine
and holy from the dross of human
passion. Let him abandon this mistrust,
this sensitiveness, this idea that God did
not deal righteously with him, and then *he
shall be as God's mouth*, i.e. as the organ by
which God speaks.

let them return &c.] Rather, **they shall
return unto thee, *but* thou shalt** *not return
unto them.* A flattering prophet perishes
with the people whom his soft speeches have
confirmed in their sin: but the truthful
speaking of God's word saves both.

XVI.—XVII. 1—18. In this prophecy
the punishment of the people is set forth in
even sterner terms than in the last. The
whole land is likened to a desert covered
with the bodies of the dead, who lie un-

2 shalt not take thee a wife, neither shalt thou have sons or
3 daughters in this place. For thus saith the LORD concerning
the sons and concerning the daughters that are born in this
place, and concerning their mothers that bare them, and con-
4 cerning their fathers that begat them in this land; They shall
die of *a*grievous deaths; they shall not be *b*lamented; neither
shall they be buried; *but* they shall be *c*as dung upon the face
of the earth: and they shall be consumed by the sword, and by
famine; and their *d*carcases shall be meat for the fowls of
5 heaven, and for the beasts of the earth. ¶ For thus saith the
LORD, *e*Enter not into the house of [1]mourning, neither go to
lament nor bemoan them: for I have taken away my peace
from this people, saith the LORD, *even* lovingkindness and
6 mercies. Both the great and the small shall die in this land:
they shall not be buried, *f*neither shall *men* lament for them,
nor *g*cut themselves, nor *h*make themselves bald for them:
7 neither shall *men* [2]tear *themselves* for them in mourning, to
comfort them for the dead; neither shall *men* give them the cup
of consolation to *i*drink for their father or for their mother.
8 ¶ Thou shalt not also go into the house of feasting, to sit with
9 them to eat and to drink. For thus saith the LORD of hosts, the
God of Israel; Behold, *k*I will cause to cease out of this place
in your eyes, and in your days, the voice of mirth, and the voice
of gladness, the voice of the bridegroom, and the voice of the
10 bride. ¶ And it shall come to pass, when thou shalt shew this
people all these words, and they shall say unto thee, *l*Wherefore
hath the LORD pronounced all this great evil against us? or what
is our iniquity? or what *is* our sin that we have committed
11 against the LORD our God? Then shalt thou say unto them,
*m*Because your fathers have forsaken me, saith the LORD, and
have walked after other gods, and have served them, and have
worshipped them, and have forsaken me, and have not kept my
12 law; and ye have done *n*worse than your fathers; for, behold,
*o*ye walk every one after the [3]imagination of his evil heart, that

a ch. 15. 2.
b ch. 22. 18.
& 25. 33.
c Ps. 83. 10.
ch. 8. 2.
d Ps. 79. 2.
ch. 34. 20.
e Ezek. 24.
17, 22, 23.

f ch. 22. 18.
g Lev. 19. 28.
Deut. 14. 1.
ch. 41. 5.
h Isai. 22. 12.
ch. 7. 29.
i Prov. 31.
6, 7.

k Isai. 24. 7.
Ezek. 26. 13.
Hos. 2. 11.
Rev. 18. 23.

l Deut. 29.
24.
ch. 5. 19.

m Deut. 29.
25.
ch. 22. 9.

n ch. 7. 26.

o ch. 13. 10.

---

[1] Or, *mourning feast*.
[2] Or, *break bread for them*,   as Ezek. 24. 17. Hos. 9. 4.   [3] Or, *stubbornness*.
      See Deut. 26. 14. Job 42. 11.

---

bemoaned and uncared for; and the prophet himself is commanded to abstain from the common usages of mankind that his mode of life, as well as his words, may warn the people of the greatness of the approaching calamity. There is, however, to be finally a return from exile, but only after the idolatry of the nation has been severely punished. The prophecy was probably written about the close of Jehoiakim's reign.

2. As marriage was obligatory upon the Jews, the prohibition of it to Jeremiah was a sign that the impending calamity was so great as to override all ordinary duties. Jeremiah was unmarried, but the force of the *sign* lay in its being an exception to the ordinary practice of the prophets.

in this place] The whole of Judæa.

3. The times were such that for "the present distress" it was wise for all to abstain from marriage (1 Cor. vii. 26; Matt. xxiv. 19).

6. *cut themselves,...make themselves bald*] Both these practices were strictly forbidden in the Law (marg. reff.) probably as being heathen customs, but they seem to have remained in common use. By *making bald* is meant shaving a bare patch on the front of the head.

7. *tear* themselves] Better as in margin; **break bread** *for them*. It was customary upon the death of a relative to fast, and for the friends and neighbours after a decent delay to come and comfort the mourner, and urge food upon him (2 Sam. xii. 17); food was also distributed at funerals to the mourners, and to the poor.

cup of consolation] Marg. ref. note.

11. The severe sentence passed upon them is the consequence of idolatry persisted in through many generations till it has finally deepened into national apostasy.

12. *imagination*] Read **stubbornness**.

13 they may not hearken unto me: [p]therefore will I cast you out of this land [q]into a land that ye know not, *neither* ye nor your fathers; and there shall ye serve other gods day and night;

14 where I will not shew you favour. ¶ Therefore, behold, the [r]days come, saith the LORD, that it shall no more be said, The LORD liveth, that brought up the children of Israel out of the

15 land of Egypt; but, The LORD liveth, that brought up the children of Israel from the land of the north, and from all the lands whither he had driven them: and [s]I will bring them again into

16 their land that I gave unto their fathers. ¶ Behold, I will send for many [t]fishers, saith the LORD, and they shall fish them; and after will I send for many hunters, and they shall hunt them from every mountain, and from every hill, and out of the

17 holes of the rocks. For mine [u]eyes *are* upon all their ways: they are not hid from my face, neither is their iniquity hid from

18 mine eyes. And first I will recompense their iniquity and their sin [x]double; because [y]they have defiled my land, they have filled mine inheritance with the carcases of their detestable and

19 abominable things. ¶ O LORD, [z]my strength, and my fortress, and [a]my refuge in the day of affliction, the Gentiles shall come unto thee from the ends of the earth, and shall say, Surely our fathers have inherited lies, vanity, and *things* [b]wherein *there is*

20 no profit. Shall a man make gods unto himself, and [c]they *are*

21 no gods? Therefore, behold, I will this once cause them to know, I will cause them to know mine hand and my might; and they shall know that [d]my name *is* [1]The LORD.

CHAP. 17. THE sin of Judah *is* written with a [a]pen of iron, *and*

[1] Or, *JEHOVAH*, Ps. 83. 18.

Margin notes:
[p] Deut. 4. 26, 27, 28. & 28. 36. 63.
[q] ch. 15. 14.
[r] Isai. 43. 18. ch. 23. 7, 8.
[s] ch. 24. 6. & 32. 37.
[t] Amos 4. 2. Hab. 1. 15.
[u] Job 34. 21. Prov. 5. 21. ch. 32. 19.
[x] Isai. 40. 2. 7. 9.
[y] Ezek. 43.
[z] Ps. 18. 2.
[a] ch. 17. 17.
[b] Isai. 44. 10. ch. 2. 11.
[c] Isai. 37. 19. Gal. 4. 8.
[d] Ex. 15. 3. ch. 33. 2.
Amos 5. 8.
[a] Job 19. 24.

---

13. *and there shall ye...*] Ironical, *and there ye may serve other gods day and night, since I will shew you no favour.*

14, 15. These two verses, by promising a deliverance greater than that from Egypt, implied also a chastisement more terrible than the bondage in the iron furnace there. Instead of their being placed in one land, there was to be a scattering into the North and many other countries, followed finally by a restoration.

16. The scattering of the people is to be like that of hunted animals, of which but few escape, the ancient method of hunting being to enclose a large space with beaters and nets, and so drive everything within it to some place where it was destroyed. The destruction of the whole male population was one of the horrible customs of ancient warfare, and the process is called in Herodotus "sweeping the country with a drag-net." The same authority tells us that this method could only be effectually carried out on an island. Literally understood, the fishers are the main armies who, in the towns and fortresses, capture the people in crowds as in a net, while the hunters are the light-armed troops, who pursue the fugitives over the whole country, and drive them out of their hiding places as hunters track out their game.

17. This chastisement arises not from caprice, but is decreed upon full knowledge and examination of their doings.

18. *first*] Before the return from exile.

I will recompense their iniquity...double] The ordinary rule of the Law (Isai. xl. 2 note). Sin is twofold; there is the leaving of God's will undone, and the actual wrong-doing. And every punishment is twofold: first, there is the loss of the blessing which would have followed upon obedience, and secondly, the presence of actual misery.

because they have defiled...] Rather, *because they have profaned My land with the carcases of their detestable things* (their lifeless and hateful idols, the very touch of which pollutes like that of a corpse, Num. xix. 11); *and have filled My inheritance with their abominations.*

21. *this once*] Whether we consider the greatness of the national disgrace and suffering caused by it, or its effect upon the mind of the Jews, the burning of Jerusalem by Nebuchadnezzar, followed by the Captivity of the people at Babylon, stands out as the greatest manifestation of God's "hand" in all His dealings with them.

XVII. 1-4. This section is inseparably connected with the preceding. Judah's sin had been described (xvi. 19) as one of which the very Gentiles will become

b Prov. 3. 3.
2 Cor. 3. 3.
c Judg. 3. 7.
2 Chr. 24. 18.
Isa. 1. 29.
d ch. 15. 13.

with the ¹point of a diamond: *it is* ᵇgraven upon the table of
2 their heart, and upon the horns of your altars; whilst their
children remember their altars and their ᶜgroves by the green
3 trees upon the high hills. O my mountain in the field, ᵈI will
give thy substance *and* all thy treasures to the spoil, *and* thy
4 high places for sin, throughout all thy borders. And thou, even
²thyself, shalt discontinue from thine heritage that I gave thee;

e ch. 16. 13.
f ch. 15. 14.

and I will cause thee to serve thine enemies in ᵉthe land which
thou knowest not: for ᶠye have kindled a fire in mine anger,
which shall burn for ever.

g Isai. 30. 1.
h See Isai.
31. 3.
i ch. 48. 6.
k Job 20. 17.
l Deut. 29. 23.

5   Thus saith the LORD; ᵍCursed *be* the man that trusteth in
man, and maketh ʰflesh his arm, and whose heart departeth
6 from the LORD. For he shall be ⁱlike the heath in the desert,
and ᵏshall not see when good cometh; but shall inhabit the
parched places in the wilderness, ˡ*in* a salt land and not inhabited.

m Ps. 2. 12.
Prov. 16. 20.
Isai. 30. 18.
n Job 8. 16.
Ps. 1. 3.

7   ᵐBlessed *is* the man that trusteth in the LORD, and whose
8 hope the LORD is. For he shall be ⁿas a tree planted by the
waters, and *that* spreadeth out her roots by the river, and shall
not see when heat cometh, but her leaf shall be green; and
shall not be careful in the year of ³drought, neither shall cease
from yielding fruit.

o 1 Sam. 16. 7.
Ps. 7. 9.
Prov. 17. 3.
Rom. 8. 27.
Rev. 2. 23.

9   The heart *is* deceitful above all *things*, and desperately
10 wicked: who can know it? I the LORD ᵒsearch the heart, *I* try

¹ Heb. *nail*.   ² Heb. *in thyself*.   ³ Or, *restraint*.

---

ashamed, and for which she will shortly be
punished by an intervention of God's hand
more marked than anything in her previous
history. Jeremiah now dwells upon the
indelible nature of her sin.

a pen of iron] *i.e.* an iron chisel for cutting
inscriptions upon tables of stone.

the point of a diamond] The ancients were
well acquainted with the cutting powers of
the diamond.

altars] Not Jehovah's one Altar, but the
many altars which the Jews had set up to
Baalim (xi. 13). Though Josiah had purged
the land of these, yet in the eleven years of
Jehoiakim's reign they had multiplied again,
and were the external proofs of Judah's
idolatry, as the table of her heart was the
internal witness.

2. *Whilst their children remember their
altars*] Perhaps an allusion to their sacrifices
of children to Moloch. Present perhaps at
some such blood-stained rite, its horrors
would be engraven for ever upon the
memory.

groves] *Asherahs*, *i.e.* wooden images of
Astarte (see Exod. xxxiv. 13 note).

3. *O my mountain in the field*] *i.e.* Jerusalem or Zion, called the Rock of the Plain
in xxi. 13. *The field* is the open uninclosed
country, here contrasted with the privileged
height of Zion.

for sin] *i.e.* because of thy sin.

4. The verb rendered *discontinue* is that

used of letting the land rest (Exod. xxiii.
11), and of releasing creditors (Deut. xv. 2)
in the sabbatical year. As Judah had not
kept these sabbatical years she must now
discontinue the tillage of God's inheritance
till the land had had its rest. *Even thyself*
may mean *and that through thyself*, through
thine own fault.

5–18. In the rest of the prophecy Jeremiah dwells upon the moral faults which
had led to Judah's ruin.

6. *like the heath*] Or, *like a destitute man*
(Ps. cii. 17). The verbs *he shall see* (or *fear*)
and *shall inhabit* plainly shew that a man is
here meant and not a plant.

8. *the river*] Or, *water-course* (Isai. xxx.
25), made for purposes of irrigation.

shall not see] Or, *shall not* **fear** (*v.* 6). God's
people feel trouble as much as other people,
but they do not fear it because they know (1)
that it is for their good, and (2) that God
will give them strength to bear it.

9. The train of thought is apparently
this: If the man is so blessed (*vr.* 7, 8) who
trusts in Jehovah, what is the reason why
men so generally "make flesh their arm"?
And the answer is:—Because man's heart
is incapable of seeing things in a straightforward manner, but is full of shrewd guile,
and ever seeking to overreach others.

desperately wicked] Rather, **mortally sick.**

10. The answer to the question, *who can
know it?* To himself a man's heart is an

the reins, [p]even to give every man according to his ways, *and*
11 according to the fruit of his doings. *As* the partridge [1]sitteth
on eggs, and hatcheth *them* not; *so* he that getteth riches, and
not by right, [q]shall leave them in the midst of his days, and at
his end shall be [r]a fool.

12 A glorious high throne from the beginning *is* the place of
13 our sanctuary. O LORD, [s]the hope of Israel, [t]all that forsake
thee shall be ashamed, *and* they that depart from me shall be
[u]written in the earth, because they have forsaken the LORD, the
[x]fountain of living waters.

14 Heal me, O LORD, and I shall be healed; save me, and I
15 shall be saved: for [v]thou *art* my praise. Behold, they say unto
16 me, [z]Where *is* the word of the LORD? let it come now. As for
me, [a]I have not hastened from *being* a pastor [2]to follow thee:
neither have I desired the woeful day; thou knowest: that which
17 came out of my lips was *right* before thee. Be not a terror
18 unto me: [b]thou *art* my hope in the day of evil. [c]Let them
be confounded that persecute me, but [d]let not me be confounded: let them be dismayed, but let not me be dismayed:
bring upon them the day of evil, and [3][e]destroy them with
double destruction.

[p] Ps. 62. 12.
ch. 32. 19.
Rom. 2. 6.

[q] Ps. 55. 23.

[r] Luke 12.
20.

[s] ch. 14. 8.
[t] Ps. 73. 27.
Isai. 1. 28.
[u] See Luke
10. 20.
[x] ch. 2. 13.

[y] Deut. 10.
21.
Ps. 109. 1.
[z] Issi. 5. 19.
Ezek. 12. 22.
Amos 5. 18.
[a] ch. 1. 4.
[b] ch. 16. 19.
[c] Ps. 35. 4.
& 70. 2.
[d] Ps. 25. 2.

[e] ch. 11. 20.

---

[1] Or, *gathereth* young *which
she hath not brought forth.* [2] Heb. *after thee.* [3] Heb. *break them with a
double breach.*

---

inscrutable mystery : God alone can fathom
it.

ways] Rather, **way**, his course of life. The
and must be omitted, for the last clause
explains what is meant by *man's way*, when
he comes before God for judgment. It is
the fruit, the final result *of his doings, i.e.*
his real character as formed by the acts and
habits of his life.

11. Rather, *As the partridge hath gathered
eggs which it laid not, so...* The general
sense is : the covetous man is as sure to
reap finally disappointment only as is the
partridge which piles up eggs not of her own
laying, and is unable to hatch them.

a fool] A Nabal. See 1 Sam. xxv. 25.

12, 13. Or, *Thou throne...thou place...
thou hope...Jehovah! All that forsake Thee*
&c. The prophet concludes his prediction
with the expression of his own trust in
Jehovah, and confidence that the Divine
justice will finally be vindicated by the
punishment of the wicked. The "throne
of glory" is equivalent to Him Who is enthroned in glory.

13. *shall be written in the earth*] *i.e.* their
names shall quickly disappear, unlike those
graven in the rock for ever (Job xix. 24).
A board covered with sand is used in the
East to this day in schools for giving lessons
in writing : but writing inscribed on such
materials is intended to be immediately ob-
literated. Equally fleeting is the existence
of those who forsake God. "All men are
written somewhere, the saints in heaven,
but sinners upon earth" (Origen).

15. This taunt shews that this prophecy was
written before any very signal fulfilment of
Jeremiah's words had taken place, and prior
therefore to the capture of Jerusalem at the
close of Jehoiakim's life. *Now* means *I
pray*, and is ironical.

16. *I have not hastened from*] *i.e.* I have
not sought to escape from.

a pastor to follow thee] Rather, *a shepherd* **after Thee**. "Shepherd" means *ruler,
magistrate* (ii. 8 note), and belongs to the
prophet not as a teacher, but as one invested
with authority by God to guide and direct
the political course of the nation. So Jehovah guides His people (Ps. xxiii. 1, 2), and
the prophet does so *after Him*, following
obediently His instructions.

the woeful day] Lit. *the day of mortal
sickness :* the day on which Jerusalem was to
be destroyed, and the Temple burnt.

right] Omit the word. What Jeremiah
asserts is that he spake as in God's Presence.
They were no words of his own, but had
the authority of Him before Whom he stood.
Cp. xv. 19.

17. *a terror*] Rather, *a cause of dismay*,
or consternation (i. 17). By not fulfilling
Jeremiah's prediction God Himself seemed
to put him to shame.

18. *confounded*] **Put to shame.**

destroy them...] Rather, **break them with
a double breaking** : a twofold punishment,
the first their general share in the miseries attendant upon their country's fall; the second,
a special punishment for their sin in perse-
cuting and mocking God's prophet.

19   Thus said the LORD unto me; Go and stand in the gate of
the children of the people, whereby the kings of Judah come in,
20 and by the which they go out, and in all the gates of Jerusalem;
and say unto them, *f* Hear ye the word of the LORD, ye kings of
Judah, and all Judah, and all the inhabitants of Jerusalem, that
21 enter in by these gates: Thus saith the LORD; *g* Take heed to
yourselves, and bear no burden on the sabbath day, nor bring *it*
22 in by the gates of Jerusalem; neither carry forth a burden out
of your houses on the sabbath day, neither do ye any work, but
23 hallow ye the sabbath day, as I *h* commanded your fathers. *i* But
they obeyed not, neither inclined their ear, but made their neck
24 stiff, that they might not hear, nor receive instruction. And it
shall come to pass, if ye diligently hearken unto me, saith the LORD,
to bring in no burden through the gates of this city on the
sabbath day, but hallow the sabbath day, to do no work therein;
25 *k* then shall there enter into the gates of this city kings and
princes sitting upon the throne of David, riding in chariots and
on horses, they, and their princes, the men of Judah, and the
inhabitants of Jerusalem: and this city shall remain for ever.
26 And they shall come from the cities of Judah, and from *l* the
places about Jerusalem, and from the land of Benjamin, and
from *m* the plain, and from the mountains, and from *n* the south,
bringing burnt offerings, and sacrifices, and meat offerings, and
incense, and bringing *o* sacrifices of praise, unto the house of the
27 LORD. But if ye will not hearken unto me to hallow the sabbath day, and not to bear a burden, even entering in at the gates
of Jerusalem on the sabbath day; then *p* will I kindle a fire in

f ch. 19. 3.
& 22. 2.

g Num. 15.
32, &c.
Neh. 13. 19.

h Ex. 20. 8.
Ezek. 20. 12.
i ch. 7. 24.
& 11. 10.

k ch. 22. 4.

l ch. 32. 44.

m Zech. 7. 7.
n Zech. 7. 7.

o Ps. 107. 22.
& 116. 17.
p ch. 21. 14.
Lam. 4. 11.
Amos 1. 4.

19—27. This prophecy on the observance of the Sabbath, is the first of a series of short predictions, arranged probably in chronological order among themselves, but in other respects independent of one another. Its tone is mild, and dissuasive rather of future neglect than condemnatory of past misconduct; and it may be assigned to the commencement of Jehoiakim's reign. Its similarity to the prophecy contained in xxii. 1-5 makes it probable that they were contemporaneous.

19. *the gate of the children of the people*] Perhaps the principal entrance of the outer court of the Temple. Very probably there was traffic there, as in our Lord's time, in doves and other requisites for sacrifice, and so the warning to keep the Sabbath was as necessary there as at the city gates.

21. *to yourselves*] Lit. *in your souls, i. e.* in *yourselves.* They were to be on their guard from the depths of their own conscience, thoroughly and on conviction.

bear no burden on the sabbath day] Apparently the Sabbath day was kept negligently. The country people were in the habit of coming to Jerusalem on the Sabbath to attend the Temple service, but mingled traffic with their devotions, bringing the produce of their fields and gardens with them for disposal. The people of Jerusalem for their part took (*v.* 22) their wares to the gates, and carried on a brisk traffic there with the villagers. Both parties seem to have abstained from manual labour, but did not consider that buying and selling were prohibited by the fourth commandment.

25. A picture of national grandeur. The prophet associates with the king the princes of the Davidic lineage, who in magnificent procession accompany the king as he goes in and out of Jerusalem.

shall remain for ever] Or, *shall* be in-habited *for ever*: populousness is promised.

26. The reward for keeping the Sabbath day holy consists in three things; (1) in great national prosperity, (2) in the lasting welfare of Jerusalem, and (3) in the wealth and piety of the people generally, indicated by their numerous sacrifices.

bringing sacrifices of praise] Rather, *bringing* praise. This clause covers all that precedes.

The verse is interesting as specifying the exact limits of the dominions of the Davidic kings, now confined to Judah and Benjamin. These two tribes are divided according to their physical conformation into (1) the She-fêlah, or low country lying between the mountains and the Mediterranean; (2) the mountain which formed the central region, extending to the wilderness of Judah, on the Dead Sea; and (3) the Negeb, or arid region, which lay to the south of Judah.

27. Upon disobedience follows the anger of God, which will consume like a fire all the splendour of the offending city.

the gates thereof, ᵠand it shall devour the palaces of Jerusalem, and it shall not be quenched.

ᵠ 2 Kin.25.9.
ch. 52. 13.

CHAP. 18. THE word which came to Jeremiah from the LORD,
2 saying, ¶ Arise, and go down to the potter's house, and there I
3 will cause thee to hear my words. Then I went down to the
potter's house, and, behold, he wrought a work on the ¹wheels.
4 And the vessel ²that he made of clay was marred in the hand of
the potter: so he ³made it again another vessel, as seemed good
5 to the potter to make *it*. ¶ Then the word of the LORD came to
6 me, saying, ¶ O house of Israel, ᵃcannot I do with you as this
potter? saith the LORD. Behold, ᵇas the clay *is* in the potter's
7 hand, so *are* ye in mine hand, O house of Israel. *At what* instant I shall speak concerning a nation, and concerning a king-
8 dom, to ᶜpluck up, and to pull down, and to destroy *it ;* ᵈif that
nation, against whom I have pronounced, turn from their evil,
9 ᵉI will repent of the evil that I thought to do unto them. And
at what instant I shall speak concerning a nation, and concerning
10 a kingdom, to build and to plant *it ;* if it do evil in my sight,
that it obey not my voice, then I will repent of the good, where-
11 with I said I would benefit them. ¶ Now therefore go to, speak
to the men of Judah, and to the inhabitants of Jerusalem, saying,
Thus saith the LORD ; ¶ Behold, I frame evil against you, and
devise a device against you : ᶠreturn ye now every one from his
12 evil way, and make your ways and your doings good. And they
said, ᵍThere is no hope : but we will walk after our own devices,

ᵃ Isai. 45. 9.
Rom. 9. 20.
ᵇ Isai. 64. 8.

ᶜ ch. 1. 10.
ᵈ Ezek. 18.
21.
ᵉ ch. 26. 3.
Jonah 3. 10.

ᶠ 2 Kin. 17.
13.
ch. 7. 3.
ᵍ ch. 2. 25.

---

¹ Or, *frames,* or, *seats.*   *marred, as clay in the*   ³ Heb. *returned and*
² Or, *that he made was*   *hand of the potter.*   *made.*

XVIII. In the first prophecy of the series, the fate of Jerusalem was still undeter-mined ; a long line of kings might yet reign there in splendour, and the city be inhabited for ever. This was possible only so long as it was still undecided whether Josiah's efforts would end in a national reformation or not, and before Jehoiakim threw the weight of the kingly office into the opposite balance. In the present prophecy mercy is still offered to the inhabitants of Jerusalem, but they reject it (*vv.* 11, 12). They have made their final choice : and thereupon fol-lows the third prophecy of "the broken vessel" (xix.) in which the utter overthrow of city and kingdom is foretold. We should thus place this prophecy of the potter very early in the reign of Jehoiakim ; and that of the broken vessel at the commencement of his fourth year. This internal evidence is confirmed by external proof.

2. *house*] i.e. workshop. The clay-field where the potters exercised their craft lay to the South of Jerusalem just beyond the valley of Hinnom. Cp. Zech. xi. 13, Matt. xxvii. 10.

3. *the wheels*] Lit. *the two wheels.* The lower one was worked by the feet to give motion to the upper one, which was a flat disc or plate of wood, on which the potter laid the clay, and moulded it with his fingers as it revolved rapidly.

6. *so are ye in mine hand*] When a vessel was spoilt, the potter did not throw it away, but crushed it together, dashed it back upon the wheel, and began his work afresh, till the clay had taken the predetermined shape. It was God's purpose that Judæa should become the proper scene for the manifesta-tion of the Messiah, and her sons be fit to receive the Saviour's teaching and carry the good tidings to all lands. If therefore at any stage of the preparation the Jewish nation took such a course as would have frustrated this purpose of Providence, it was crushed by affliction into an unresisting mass, in which the formative process forth-with began again.

7, 9. At what *instant*] Lit. "in a mo-ment." Here, *at one time—at another time.*

8, 10. *I will repent of the evil…I will repent of the good*] All God's dealings with man-kind are here declared to be conditional. God changeth not, all depends upon man's conduct.

11. The word rendered *frame* is a present participle, and is the same which as a noun means "a potter." God declares that He is as free to do what He will with the Jews as the potter is free to shape as he will the clay.

devise a device] *I am purposing a purpose.*

12. *And they said*] Better, **But they say.**

and we will every one do the imagination of his evil heart.
13 Therefore thus saith the LORD: [h]Ask ye now among the heathen,
who hath heard such things: the virgin of Israel hath done [i]a
14 very horrible thing.   Will *a man* leave [1]the snow of Lebanon
which cometh from the rock of the field? *or* shall the cold flowing
15 waters that come from another place be forsaken? Because my
people hath forgotten [k]me, they have burned incense to [l]vanity,
and they have caused them to stumble in their ways *from the*
16 [m]ancient paths, to walk in paths, *in* a way not cast up; to make
their land [n]desolate, *and* a perpetual [o]hissing; every one that
17 passeth thereby shall be astonished, and wag his head.   [p]I will
scatter them [q]as with an east wind before the enemy; [r]I will shew
them the back, and not the face, in the day of their calamity.
18 ¶ Then said they, [s]Come, and let us devise devices against Jeremiah; [t]for the law shall not perish from the priest, nor counsel
from the wise, nor the word from the prophet.   Come, and let
us smite him [2]with the tongue, and let us not give heed to any
19 of his words.   ¶ Give heed to me, O LORD, and hearken to the
20 voice of them that contend with me.   [u]Shall evil be recompensed
for good? for [x]they have digged a pit for my soul.   Remember
that I stood before thee to speak good for them, *and* to turn away
21 thy wrath from them.   Therefore [y]deliver up their children to

[k] ch. 2. 10.
1 Cor. 5. 1.
[i] ch. 5. 30.

[k] ch. 2. 13.
[l] ch. 10. 15.

[m] ch. 6. 16.

[n] ch. 19. 8.
[o] 1 Kin. 9. 8.
Lam. 2. 15.
Mic. 6. 16.
[p] ch. 13. 24.
[q] Ps. 48. 7.
[r] ch. 2. 27.
[s] ch. 11. 19.
[t] Lev. 10. 11.
Mal. 2. 7.
John 7. 48.

[u] Ps. 109. 4.

[x] Ps. 35. 7.
ver. 22.

[y] Ps. 109. 9.

[1] Or, *my fields for a rock,*
or for *the snow of Leba-*   *non? shall the running*
waters be forsaken for the   *strange cold* waters?
                                 [2] Or, *for the tongue.*

---

imagination] Or, **stubbornness**, see iii. 17.
13. The contrast between the chaste retirement of a virgin and Judah's eagerness
after idolatry, serves to heighten the horror
at her conduct.
14. Rather, *Will the snow of Lebanon
fail from the rock of the field?* The meaning
probably is, "Will the snow of Lebanon
fail from its rocks which tower above the
land of Israel?" The appeal of the prophet
is to the unchangeableness of one of nature's
most beautiful phenomena, the perpetual
snow upon the upper summits of Lebanon.
shall the cold &c.] Lit. *shall the strange,
i.e.* foreign, *cool, down-flowing waters be plucked
up?* The general sense is:—God is Israel's
Rock, from Whom the never-failing waters
flow (ii. 13): but men may and do abandon
the cool waters which descend from above
to seek their happiness in channels of their
own digging.
15. *Because*] **For.** Jeremiah returns to,
and continues the words of, *v.* 13.
vanity] A word meaning *falsehood*, which
signifies that the worship of idols is not
merely useless but injurious.
they have caused them to stumble] Judah's
prophets and priests were they who made
her to err (v. 31). The idols were of themselves powerless for good or evil.
in their ways &c.] Or, *in their ways*, **the
everlasting** *paths, to walk in* **byways,** *in a
road not cast up. The paths of eternity* carry
back the mind not to the immediate but to
the distant past, and suggest the good old
ways in which the patriarchs used to walk.

The *road cast up* means one raised sufficiently to keep it out of the reach of
floods &c.
16. *hissing*] Not derision, but the drawing
in of the breath quickly as men do when
they shudder.
wag his head] Or, **shake** *his* **head,** a sign
among the Jews not of scorn but of pity.
The desolation of the land of Israel is to fill
men with dismay.
I will shew them the back] The hiding of
God's face is the sure sign of His displeasure
(Isai. i. 15, lix. 2).
18. The Jews were only hardened by the
foregoing prophecy, and determined to compass Jeremiah's death.
let us devise devices] *i.e. deliberately frame
a plot* for his ruin (see *v.* 11 note).
the law shall not perish &c.] As the Law
of Moses was imperishable, the people
probably drew the conclusion that the
Levitical priesthood must also endure for
ever, and therefore that Jeremiah's predictions of national ruin were blasphemous
(cp. Acts vi. 13, 14).
let us smite him with the tongue] Their
purpose was to carry a malicious report of
what he had said to king Jehoiakim, and so
stir up his anger against him.
19. *the voice*] *i.e.* the outcry and threats.
20. Jeremiah had been labouring earnestly
to avert the ruin of his country, but the
Jews treated him as husbandmen do some
noxious animal which wastes their fields,
and for which they dig pitfalls.

the famine, and [1]pour out their *blood* by the force of the sword; and let their wives be bereaved of their children, and *be* widows; and let their men be put to death; *let* their young men *be* slain 22 by the sword in battle. Let a cry be heard from their houses, when thou shalt bring a troop suddenly upon them: for [2]they 23 have digged a pit to take me, and hid snares for my feet. Yet, LORD, thou knowest all their counsel against me [2]to slay me: [a]forgive not their iniquity, neither blot out their sin from thy sight, but let them be overthrown before thee; deal *thus* with them in the time of thine anger.

x ver. 20.

a Ps. 35. 4.
ch. 11. 20.
& 15. 15.

CHAP. 19. THUS saith the LORD, ¶Go and get a potter's earthen 2 bottle, and *take* of the ancients of the people, and of the ancients of the priests; and go forth unto [a]the valley of the son of Hinnom, which *is* by the entry of [3]the east gate, and proclaim there 3 the words that I shall tell thee, [b]and say, Hear ye the word of the LORD, O kings of Judah, and inhabitants of Jerusalem; Thus saith the LORD of hosts, the God of Israel; Behold, I will bring evil upon this place, the which whosoever heareth, his ears 4 shall [c]tingle. Because they [d]have forsaken me, and have estranged this place, and have burned incense in it unto other

a Josh. 15.8.
2 Kin. 23.10.

b ch. 17. 20.

c 1 Sam. 3. 11.
d Deut. 28. 20.
Isai. 65. 11.
ch. 17. 13.

---

[1] Heb. *pour them out.*   [2] Heb. *for death.*   [3] Heb. *the sun gate.*

---

21. *pour out...sword*] Lit. *pour them out upon the hands of the sword, i.e.* **give them up to the sword.**

put to death] Rather, **slain of death.** The prophet's phrase leaves it entirely indefinite in what way the men are to die.

22. The sack of the city follows with all the horrible cruelties practised at such a time.

23. *Yet,* LORD] Better, **But,** LORD. They conceal their plots, but God knows, and therefore must punish.

neither blot out &c.] Or, *blot not out their sin from before Thy face* **that they may be made to stumble** *before Thee.*

thus] Omit this word. As there is an acceptable time and a day of salvation, so there is a time of anger, and Jeremiah's prayer is that God would deal with his enemies at such a time, and when therefore no mercy would be shewn. On imprecations such as these, see Ps. cix. introd. note. Though they did not flow from personal vengeance, but from a pure zeal for God's honour, yet they belong to the legal spirit of the Jewish Covenant. We must not, because we have been shewn a "more excellent way," condemn too harshly that sterner spirit of justice which animated so many of the saints of the earlier dispensation.

XIX., XX. The present prophecy is to be taken in close connexion with the preceding. Jeremiah chooses a vessel baked in the fire, and therefore incapable of being re-shaped (cp. xviii. 1, 6 notes). It is the symbol of the obdurate, of those who have taken their final form (Rev. xxii. 11). In solemn procession he must bear the vessel out to the place of doom, the valley of Gehenna. There he was to break the

vessel; and just as all the art of the potter would be of no avail to restore the broken fragments, so did God proclaim the final destruction of Jerusalem such as it then was, and of that generation which inhabited it.

XIX. **1.** *get (i.e.* purchase) *a potter's earthen bottle*] The *bottle* was a flask with a long neck, and took its name from the noise made by liquids in running out.

the ancients] These *elders* were the regularly constituted representatives of the people (see xxix. 1; Num. xi. 16), and the organization lasted down to our Saviour's time (Matt. xxvi. 47). Similarly the priests had also their representatives (2 K. xix. 2). Accompanied thus by the representatives of Church and State, the prophet was to carry the earthen bottle, the symbol of their mean origin and frail existence, outside the walls of Jerusalem.

2. *the valley* &c.] See vii. 31 note.

the east gate] Others render "the pottery gate." Two gates led into the valley of Hinnom, the Fountain-gate at the South-East corner, and the Dung-gate on the South-West side of Zion; some think that "the East gate" was neither of these, but a small or postern gate, used for throwing out rubbish, the valley having been put to this degrading use from the time that Josiah defiled it (2 K. xxiii. 10). And thus the mean symbol of a proud nation was carried out through a back door to be broken upon the heaps of refuse already cast there.

3. *kings*] Plural because the message (*vv.* 3-9), related not specially to the reigning king, but to the whole royal house.

4. *have estranged this place*] They have not recognized the sanctity of this place,

gods, whom neither they nor their fathers have known, nor the kings of Judah, and have filled this place with *the blood of 5 innocents; *they have built also the high places of Baal, to burn their sons with fire *for* burnt offerings unto Baal, *which I com-6 manded not, nor spake *it*, neither came *it* into my mind: there-fore, behold, the days come, saith the LORD, that this place shall no more be called Tophet, nor *The valley of the son of 7 Hinnom, but The valley of slaughter. And I will make void the counsel of Judah and Jerusalem in this place; *and I will cause them to fall by the sword before their enemies, and by the hands of them that seek their lives: and their *carcases will I give to be meat for the fowls of the heaven, and for the beasts of 8 the earth. And I will make this city *desolate, and an hissing; every one that passeth thereby shall be astonished and hiss 9 because of all the plagues thereof. And I will cause them to eat the *flesh of their sons and the flesh of their daughters, and they shall eat every one the flesh of his friend in the siege and straitness, wherewith their enemies, and they that seek their 10 lives, shall straiten them.   ¶ *Then shalt thou break the bottle in the sight of the men that go with thee, and shalt say unto 11 them, Thus saith the LORD of hosts; *Even so will I break this people and this city, as *one* breaketh a potter's vessel, that cannot ¹be made whole again: and they shall *bury *them* in Tophet, till 12 *there be* no place to bury. Thus will I do unto this place, saith the LORD, and to the inhabitants thereof, and *even* make this 13 city as Tophet: and the houses of Jerusalem, and the houses of the kings of Judah, shall be defiled *as the place of Tophet, because of all the houses upon whose *roofs they have burned incense unto all the host of heaven, and *have poured out drink 14 offerings unto other gods.   ¶ Then came Jeremiah from Tophet, whither the LORD had sent him to prophesy; and he stood in 15 *the court of the LORD's house; and said to all the people, Thus saith the LORD of hosts, the God of Israel; Behold, I will bring upon this city and upon all her towns all the evil that I have pronounced against it, because *they have hardened their necks, that they might not hear my words.

CHAP. 20. NOW Pashur the son of *Immer the priest, who *was*

e 2 Kin. 21. 16.
ch. 2. 34.
f ch. 7. 31.
& 32. 35.
g Lev.18. 21.

h Josh. 15. 8.

i Lev. 26. 17.
Deut. 28. 25.

k Ps. 79. 2.
ch. 7. 33.

l ch. 18. 16.

m Lev.26.29.
Deut. 28. 53.
Isai. 9. 20.
Lam. 4. 10.
n So ch. 51. 63, 64.

o Ps. 2. 9.
Isai. 30. 14.

p ch. 7. 32.

q 2 Kin. 23. 10.
r ch. 32. 29.
Zeph. 1. 5.
s ch. 7. 18.

t See 2 Chr. 20. 5.

u ch. 7. 26.
& 17. 23.

a 1 Chr. 24. 14.

---

¹ Heb. *be healed.*

---

but have treated it as a strange place, by worshipping in it strange gods.

innocents] *i.e.* guiltless persons.

7. *make void*] The verb used here is that from which *bottle* (v. 1) is derived, and as it represents the sound made by the water running out, it would be better translated, *pour out*. Jeremiah perhaps carried the bottle to Tophet full of water, the symbol in the East of life (Isai. xxxv. 6, xli. 18), and at these words emptied it before the assembled elders.

11. *made whole again*] Lit. *healed.* In this lies the distinction between this symbol and that of xviii. 4.   The plastic clay can be shaped and re-shaped till the potter forms with it the vessel he had predetermined: the broken bottle is of no further use, but its fragments are cast away for ever upon the heaps of rubbish deposited in Tophet.

13. *because of all*] Lit. *with reference to all*, limiting the denunciation to those houses whose roofs had been defiled with altars.

upon whose roofs they have burned incense] See 2 K. xxiii. 12, note.

14, 15. As it was this repetition of the prophecy in the Temple which so greatly irritated Pashur, these two verses ought to be joined to the next chapter.

XX. The breaking of the bottle had been done so solemnly before witnesses of such high position, and its meaning had been so unmistakeably proclaimed in the Temple, that those in authority could endure such proceedings no longer. Roused therefore to anger by the sight of the listening crowds, Pashur, the deputy High-Priest, caused Jeremiah to be arrested, inflicted upon him the legal forty stripes save one, and made him pass a night in the stocks, exposed to

also chief governor in the house of the LORD, heard that Jere-
2 miah prophesied these things. Then Pashur smote Jeremiah the
prophet, and put him in the stocks that *were* in the high gate of
3 Benjamin, which *was* by the house of the LORD. And it came
to pass on the morrow, that Pashur brought forth Jeremiah out
of the stocks. Then said Jeremiah unto him, The LORD hath
4 not called thy name Pashur, but ¹Magor-missabib. For thus
saith the LORD, Behold, I will make thee a terror to thyself, and
to all thy friends: and they shall fall by the sword of their
enemies, and thine eyes shall behold *it*: and I will give all Judah
into the hand of the king of Babylon, and he shall carry them
captive into Babylon, and shall slay them with the sword.
5 Moreover I ᵇwill deliver all the strength of this city, and all the
labours thereof, and all the precious things thereof, and all the
treasures of the kings of Judah will I give into the hand of their
enemies, which shall spoil them, and take them, and carry them
6 to Babylon. And thou, Pashur, and all that dwell in thine
house shall go into captivity: and thou shalt come to Babylon,
and there thou shalt die, and shalt be buried there, thou, and
7 all thy friends, to whom thou hast ᶜprophesied lies. ¶ O LORD,

ᵇ 2 Kin. 20.
17. & 24.
12-16.
ch. 3. 24.

ᶜ ch. 14. 13.
& 29. 21.

¹ That is, *Fear round about*, ver. 10. ch. 46. 5 & 49. 29.

---

the jeers of the scoffers, at the most public gate of the Temple. Apparently it was Jeremiah's last public prophecy in Jehoiakim's reign, and was the cause why in the fourth year of that king it was no longer safe for him to go to the house of Jehovah (xxxvi. 5). It is probable also that Jehoiakim's roll ended with the prophecy of the potter's vessel, and the account of the contumelies to which the prophet had in consequence been exposed. One prophecy, however, at least in our present book, is of a later date, that of the linen girdle (ch. xiii.).

1. Pashur, the father probably of the Gedaliah mentioned in xxxviii. 1, was the head of the sixteenth course of priests (marg. ref.); the other Pashur (xxi. 1) belonged to the fifth course, the sons of Melchiah. Both these houses returned in great strength from the exile. See Ezra ii. 37, 38.

chief governor] Or, **deputy** *governor*. The Nâgid or governor of the Temple was the High-Priest (1 Chr. ix. 11), and Pashur was his Pâkid, *i.e.* deputy (see i. 10 note). Zephaniah held this office (xxix. 26), and his relation to the High-Priest is exactly defined (2 K. xxv. 18; Jer. lii. 24). The Nâgid at this time was Seraiah the High-Priest, the grandson of Hilkiah, or (possibly) Azariah, Hilkiah's son and Jeremiah's brother (1 Chr. vi. 13, Ezra vii. 1).

2. *Jeremiah the prophet*] Jeremiah is nowhere so called in the first nineteen chapters. In this place he thus characterizes himself, because Pashur's conduct was a violation of the respect due to the prophetical office.

the stocks] This instrument of torture comes from a root signifying *to twist*. It

thus implies that the body was kept in a distorted position. Cp. Acts xvi. 24.

the high gate...] Rather, *the* **upper** *gate of Benjamin* **in** *the house of Jehovah* (cp. 2 K. xv. 35); to be distinguished from the city gate of Benjamin leading towards the North.

3. *Magor-missabib*] See vi. 25 note. Jeremiah uses it no less than five times, having probably adopted it as his watchword from Ps. xxxi. 13.

4. *a terror to thyself, and to all thy friends*] Jeremiah plays upon the meaning of Magor-missabib saying that Pashur would be a terror to all around. It is remarkable that he prophesies no evil of Pashur (*v.* 6). His was to be the milder fate of being carried into Captivity with Jehoiachin, and dying peaceably at Babylon (*v.* 6), whereas his successor Zephaniah was put to death at Riblah (lii. 24, 27). His punishment probably consisted in this. He had prophesied "lies." When then he saw the dreadful slaughter of his countrymen, Jehoiakim put to death, his young son dragged into captivity, and the land stripped of all that was best, his conscience so condemned him as the guilty cause of such great misery that in the agonies of remorse he became a terror to himself and his friends.

5. *all the strength*] *All the* **stores.**
the labours] The gains of the citizens.

6. *thou hast prophesied lies*] Pashur belonged to the warlike party, whose creed it was, that Judæa by a close alliance with Egypt might resist the arms of Assyria.

7-18. In the rest of the chapter we have an outbreak of deep emotion, of which the first part ends in a cry of hope (*v.* 13), followed nevertheless by curses upon the day

d ch. 1. 6.
e Lam. 3. 14.
f ch. 6. 7.

g Job 32. 18.
Ps. 39. 3.
h Job 32. 18.
Acts 18. 5.
i Ps. 31. 13.
k Job 19. 19.
Ps. 55. 13.
Luke 11.
53, 54.
l ch. 1. 8, 19.
m ch. 15. 20.
n ch. 23. 40.
o ch. 17. 10.
p Ps. 54. 7.
& 59. 10.
q Ps. 35. 9.
& 109. 30.

thou hast deceived me, and I was [1]deceived: [d]thou art stronger than I, and hast prevailed: [e]I am in derision daily, every one

8 mocketh me. For since I spake, I cried out, [f]I cried violence and spoil; because the word of the LORD was made a reproach unto

9 me, and a derision, daily. ¶ Then I said, I will not make mention of him, nor speak any more in his name. But *his word* was in mine heart as a [g]burning fire shut up in my bones, and I was

10 weary with forbearing, and [h]I could not *stay*. [i]For I heard the defaming of many, fear on every side. Report, *say they*, and we will report it. [2][k]All my familiars watched for my halting, *saying*, Peradventure he will be enticed, and we shall prevail against

11 him, and we shall take our revenge on him. ¶ But [l]the LORD *is* with me as a mighty terrible one: therefore my persecutors shall stumble, and they shall not [m]prevail: they shall be greatly ashamed; for they shall not prosper: *their* [n]everlasting confusion

12 shall never be forgotten. But, O LORD of hosts, that [o]triest the righteous, *and* seest the reins and the heart, [p]let me see thy vengeance on them: for unto thee have I opened my cause.

13 Sing unto the LORD, praise ye the LORD: for [q]he hath delivered

---

[1] Or, *enticed*.　　　　　　[2] Heb. *Every man of my peace.*

---

of his birth. Was this the result of feelings wounded by the indignities of a public scourging and a night spent in the stocks? Or was it not the mental agony of knowing that his ministry had (as it seemed) failed? He stands indeed before the multitudes with unbending strength, warning prince and people with unwavering constancy of the national ruin that would follow necessarily upon their sins. Before God he stood crushed by the thought that he had laboured in vain, and spent his strength for nought.

It is important to notice that with this outpouring of sorrow Jeremiah's ministry virtually closed. Though he appeared again at Jerusalem towards the end of Jehoiakim's reign, yet it was no longer to say that by repentance the national ruin might be averted. During the fourth year of Jehoiakim the die was cast, and all the prophet henceforward could do, was to alleviate a punishment that was inevitable.

7. *thou hast deceived me...*] What Jeremiah refers to is the joy with which he had accepted the prophetic office (xv. 16), occasioned perhaps by taking the promises in i. 18 too literally as a pledge that he would succeed.

thou art stronger than I] Rather, *Thou hast taken hold of me*. God had taken Jeremiah in so firm a grasp that he could not escape from the necessity of prophesying. He would have resisted, but the hand of God prevailed.

I am in derision daily] Lit. *I am become a laughing-stock all the day*, i.e. perpetually.

8. Translate, *For as often as I speak, I must complain; I call out, Violence and spoil.*

From the time Jeremiah began to prophesy, he had had reason for nothing but lamentation. Daily with louder voice and

more desperate energy he must call out *violence and spoil;* as a perpetual protest against the manner in which the laws of justice were violated by powerful men among the people.

9. Seeing that his mission was useless, Jeremiah determined to withdraw from it.

I could not stay] Rather, *I prevailed not*, did not succeed. See *v.* 7.

10. *the defaming*] Rather, *the talking*. The word refers to people whispering in twos and threes apart; in this case plotting against Jeremiah. Cp. Mark xiv. 58.

Report, &c.] Rather, *Do you report, and we will report* **him**: *i.e.* they encourage one another to give information against Jeremiah.

my familiars] Lit. *the men of my peace* (Ps. xli. 9). In the East the usual salutation is "Peace be to thee": and the answer, "And to thee peace." Thus the phrase rather means acquaintances, than familiar friends.

enticed] Lit. *persuaded, misled*, the same word as *deceived* (*v.* 7). Cp. Mark xii. 13–17.

11. *a mighty terrible one*] Rather, *a terrible warrior*. The mighty One (Isai. ix. 6) Who is on his side is a terror to them. This change of feeling was the effect of faith, enabling him to be content with calmly doing his duty, and leaving the result to God.

for...] Rather, **because** *they* **have not acted wisely** (x. 21 note), **with an** *everlasting* **disgrace that** *shall never be forgotten.*

12. This verse is repeated almost verbatim from xi. 20.

13. *Sing*] Jeremiah's outward circumstances remained the same, but he found peace in leaving his cause in faith to God.

14 the soul of the poor from the hand of evil doers. ¶ʳCursed *be* the
day wherein I was born : let not the day wherein my mother
15 bare me be blessed. Cursed *be* the man who brought tidings to my
father, saying, A man child is born unto thee ; making him very
16 glad. And let that man be as the cities which the LORD ˢover-
threw, and repented not : and let him ᵗhear the cry in the morn-
17 ing, and the shouting at noontide ; ᵘ because he slew me not
from the womb ; or that my mother might have been my grave,
18 and her womb *to be* always great *with me.* ˣWherefore came I
forth out of the womb to ʸsee labour and sorrow, that my days
should be consumed with shame?

r Job 3. 3.
ch. 15. 10.

s Gen. 19.
25.
t ch. 18. 22.
u Job 3. 10.

x Job 3. 20.
y Lam. 3. 1.

CHAP. 21. THE word which came unto Jeremiah from the LORD,
when king Zedekiah sent unto him ªPashur the son of Melchiah,
2 and ᵇZephaniah the son of Maaseiah the priest, saying, ᶜEnquire,
I pray thee, of the LORD for us ; for Nebuchadrezzar king of
Babylon maketh war against us ; if so be that the LORD will
deal with us according to all his wondrous works, that he may
3 go up from us. ¶ Then said Jeremiah unto them, Thus shall ye
4 say to Zedekiah : Thus saith the LORD God of Israel ; Behold, I
will turn back the weapons of war that *are* in your hands,
wherewith ye fight against the king of Babylon, and *against* the
Chaldeans, which besiege you without the walls, and ᵈI will
5 assemble them into the midst of this city. And I myself will
fight against you with an ᵉoutstretched hand and with a strong
6 arm, even in anger, and in fury, and in great wrath. And I will
smite the inhabitants of this city, both man and beast : they
7 shall die of a great pestilence. And afterward, saith the LORD,
ᶠI will deliver Zedekiah king of Judah, and his servants, and the
people, and such as are left in this city from the pestilence, from
the sword, and from the famine, into the hand of Nebuchadrezzar king of Babylon, and into the hand of their enemies, and

a ch. 38. 1.
b 2 Kin. 25.
18.
ch. 29. 25.
c ch. 37. 3.

d Isai. 13. 4

e Ex. 6. 6.

f ch. 37. 17.
& 39. 5.
& 52. 9.

---

14. This sudden outbreak of impatience
after the happy faith of *v.* 13 has led to
much discussion. Possibly there was more
of sorrow in the words than of impatience ;
sorrow that the earnest labour of a life had
been in vain. Yet the form of the expression is fierce and indignant ; and the impatience of Jeremiah is that part of his
character which is most open to blame. He
does not reach that elevation which is set
before us by Him Who is the perfect pattern
of all righteousness. Our Lord was a prophet Whose mission to the men of His generation equally failed, and His sorrow was
even more deep ; but it never broke forth
in imprecations. See Luke xix. 41, 42.

16. *The cry* is the sound of the lamentation (*v.* 8) ; *the shouting* is the alarm of
war.

XXI.–XXIV. With the last verse of
ch. xx. ended the roll of Jehoiakim : with
the first verse of ch. xxi. begins a digest of
various prophecies addressed to Zedekiah
in his ninth year, and called Zedekiah's
roll. The occasion of this prophecy was the
embassy sent by Zedekiah to Jeremiah,
asking his prayers when the Chaldæan army
was advancing upon Jerusalem. So clearly

did the prophet foresee the result that he
could give the king no hope. His answer,
contained in the roll, divides itself into two
parts, in the first (xx.-xxii.), the prophet
reviews the conduct of the royal house : in
the second (xxiii. 9–40), that of the priests
and prophets ; closing with a vision (ch.
xxiv.) in which he shews the pitiable condition of Zedekiah and his people.

XXI. 1. By sending this embassy Zedekiah acknowledged that Jeremiah held the
same position in the kingdom which Isaiah
had held under Hezekiah (2 K. xix. 2).
Pashur and Zephaniah belonged to the
party who were for resisting Nebuchadnezzar by force of arms.

2. *Nebuchadrezzar*] A more correct way of
spelling the name than Nebuchadnezzar.

according to all his wondrous works] The
king and his envoys expected some such
answer as Isaiah had given on a former occasion (Isai. xxxvii. 6).

4. *without the walls*] These words are to be
joined to *wherewith ye fight.*

6. *a great pestilence*] As the result of the
excessive crowding of men and animals in a
confined space with all sanitary regulations
utterly neglected.

_g_ Deut. 28. 50.

2 Chr. 36.17.

_h_ Deut. 30. 19.

_i_ ch. 38. 2.

_k_ ch. 39. 18. & 45. 5.

_l_ Lev. 17 10. ch. 44. 11. Amos 9. 4.

_m_ ch. 38. 3.

_n_ ch. 34. 2. 22. & 37. 10.

_o_ ch. 22. 3. Zech. 7. 9.

_p_ Ps. 101. 8.

_q_ Ezek.13. 8.

_r_ ch. 49. 4.

_s_ Prov. 1. 31. Isai. 3. 10.

_t_ 2 Chr. 3 i. 19. ch. 52. 13.

into the hand of those that seek their life : and he shall smite them with the edge of the sword; _g_he shall not spare them, 8 neither have pity, nor have mercy. ¶ And unto this people thou shalt say, Thus saith the LORD ; Behold, _h_ I set before you the 9 way of life, and the way of death. He that _i_abideth in this city shall die by the sword, and by the famine, and by the pestilence : but he that goeth out, and falleth to the Chaldeans that besiege you, he shall live, and _k_his life shall be unto him for a prey. 10 For I have _l_set my face against this city for evil, and not for good, saith the LORD : _m_it shall be given into the hand of the 11 king of Babylon, and he shall _n_burn it with fire. ¶ And touching the house of the king of Judah, _say_, Hear ye the word of the 12 LORD ; O house of David, thus saith the LORD ; _o_1Execute judgment _p_in the morning, and deliver _him that is_ spoiled out of the hand of the oppressor, lest my fury go out like fire, and burn that none can quench _it_, because of the evil of your doings. 13 Behold, _q_I _am_ against thee, O 2inhabitant of the valley, _and_ rock of the plain, saith the LORD ; which say, _r_Who shall come down 14 against us ? or who shall enter into our habitations ? But I will 3punish you according to the _s_fruit of your doings, saith the LORD : and I will kindle a fire in the forest thereof, and _t_it shall devour all things round about it.

_a_ ch. 17. 20.

_b_ ch. 21. 12.

_c_ See ver.17.

_d_ ch. 17. 25.

CHAP. 22. THUS saith the LORD ; Go down to the house of the 2 king of Judah, and speak there this word, and say, _a_Hear the word of the LORD, O king of Judah, that sittest upon the throne of David, thou, and thy servants, and thy people that enter in 3 by these gates : Thus saith the LORD ; _b_Execute ye judgment and righteousness, and deliver the spoiled out of the hand of the oppressor : and _c_do no wrong, do no violence to the stranger, the fatherless, nor the widow, neither shed innocent blood in 4 this place. For if ye do this thing indeed, _d_then shall there

---

¹ Heb. _Judge._   ² Heb. _inhabitress._   ³ Heb. _visit upon._

---

8. Cp. marg. ref.; but here the alternative is a life saved by desertion to the enemy, or a death by famine, pestilence, and the sword within the walls.

9. _he that...falleth to the Chaldeans_] This was to counsel desertion, and would have been treason in an ordinary man : but the prophets spoke with an authority above that even of the king, and constantly interfered in political matters with summary decisiveness. Cp. Matt. xxiv. 16–18.

a prey] Something not a man's own, upon which he seizes in the midst of danger, and hurries away with it. So must the Jews hurry away with their lives as something more than they had a right to, and place them in the Chaldæan camp as in a place of safety.

11. Rather, _And as to the royal house of Judah, Hear ye._ Omit _say._ The words are no command to the prophet, but form his introduction to the discourse which extends to the end of xxiii. 8. The king and his officers are to hear the gist of all the messages sent to the royal house since the accession of Jehoiakim.

12. _Execute judgment_] As the administration of justice was performed in old time in person, the weal of the people depended to a great degree upon the personal qualities of the king (see 2 Sam. xv. 4). And as _the oppressor_ was generally some powerful noble, it was especially the king's duty to see that the weaker members of the community were not wronged.

13. _Inhabitant_ is fem., the population of Jerusalem being always personified as a woman, the daughter of Zion. Omit _and._ Jerusalem is at once a valley and a rock (xvii. 3). The people are described as priding themselves on the impregnability of their city.

14. _the forest_] This suggested to the Jew the idea of everything grand and stately.

XXII. **1–9.** This prophecy, like the preceding (xxi. 11–14), states the conditions upon which it was still possible for the house of David to ensure a long era of prosperity. It belongs therefore to the beginning of Jehoiakim's reign.

1. _Go down_] i.e. from the Temple to the king's house. Cp. 2 Chr. xxiii. 20.

enter in by the gates of this house kings sitting ¹upon the throne
of David, riding in chariots and on horses, he, and his servants,
5 and his people. But if ye will not hear these words, *e*I swear
by myself, saith the LORD, that this house shall become a deso-
6 lation. ¶For thus saith the LORD unto the king's house of
Judah; Thou *art* Gilead unto me, *and* the head of Lebanon: *yet*
surely I will make thee a wilderness, *and* cities *which* are not
7 inhabited. And I will prepare destroyers against thee, every
one with his weapons: and they shall cut down *f*thy choice
8 cedars, *g*and cast *them* into the fire. And many nations shall
pass by this city, and they shall say every man to his neighbour, *h*Wherefore hath the LORD done thus unto this great city?
9 Then they shall answer, *i*Because they have forsaken the covenant of the LORD their God, and worshipped other gods, and
served them.

10   Weep ye not for *k*the dead, neither bemoan him: *but* weep
sore for him *l*that goeth away: for he shall return no more,
11 nor see his native country. For thus saith the LORD touching
*m*Shallum the son of Josiah king of Judah, which reigned
instead of Josiah his father, *n*which went forth out of this place;
12 He shall not return thither any more: but he shall die in the
place whither they have led him captive, and shall see this land
no more.

13   *o*Woe unto him that buildeth his house by unrighteousness,
and his chambers by wrong; *p*that useth his neighbour's ser-
14 vice without wages, and giveth him not for his work; that saith,
I will build me a wide house and ²large chambers, and cutteth
him out ³windows; and *it is* cieled with cedar, and painted
15 with vermilion. Shalt thou reign, because thou closest *thyself*

e Heb. 6. 13, 17.

f Isai. 37. 24.
g ch. 21. 14.

h Deut. 29. 24. 25.
1 Kin. 9. 8.
i 2 Kin. 22. 17.
2 Chr. 34.25.

k 2 Kin. 22. 20.
l ver. 11.

m See
1 Chr. 3. 15.
n 2 Kin. 23. 34.

o 2 Kin. 23. 35.
p Lev. 19.13.
Deut. 24. 14, 15.
Jam. 5. 4.

¹ Heb. *for David upon his throne.*   ² Heb. *through-aired.*   ³ Or, *my windows.*

6. Omit *and. Thou art a Gilead unto me, a summit of Lebanon.*

yet *surely*] Lit. *if not,* the form of an oath with the imprecation omitted. For the full form see Num. xiv. 23.

a wilderness, and *cities*] Omit *and.* The meaning is : If the house of David does not hear God's words, though it be now grand as Lebanon, God will make it a wilderness, even uninhabited cities ; the house of David being regarded as equivalent to the kingdom of Judah.

7. *prepare*] *i.e.* **consecrate,** see vi. 4 note.

thy *choice cedars*] The chief members of the royal lineage and the leading officers of state.

10–12. In the two foregoing prophecies Jeremiah stated the general principle on which depend the rise and downfall of kings and nations. He now adds for Zedekiah's warning the history of three thrones which were not established.

The first is that of Shallum the successor of Josiah, who probably took the name of Jehoahaz on his accession (see marg. reff. notes).

10. the *dead*] *i.e.* Josiah (2 Chr. xxxv. 25).

that *goeth away*] Rather, *that is gone away.*

13. Far worse is the second example. Shallum was no heartless tyrant like Jehoiakim, who lived in splendour amid the misery of the nation, and perished so little cared for that his body was cast aside without burial.

his *chambers*] Really, *his* **upper** *chambers.* From the absence of machinery the raising of materials for the upper stories was a difficult task, especially when massive stones were used.

his *work*] Giveth him not *his* **wages.**

14. large *chambers*] spacious **upper** *chambers.*

it is *cieled*] Or, **roofing** *it.*

vermilion] The pigment which gives the deep red colour still bright and untarnished on many ancient buildings.

15. *i.e.* Will thy buildings make thy reign continue ? These words imply that Jehoiakim was looking forward to, and taking measures to secure, a long continuance of power (cp. Hab. ii. 9–13. If so, Jeremiah probably wrote this prophecy before Jehoiakim revolted (2 K. xxiv. 1); and it, therefore, probably belongs to the same date as xxxvi. 30, written in the interval between Nebuchadnezzar's first conquest of Jerusalem, and

q 2 Kin. 23. 25.
r Ps. 128. 2. Isai. 3. 10.
s Ezek. 19. 6.

in cedar? *q*did not thy father eat and drink, and do judgment
16 and justice, *and* then *r*it *was* well with him? He judged the
cause of the poor and needy; then it *was* well *with him: was*
17 not this to know me? saith the LORD. *s*But thine eyes and
thine heart *are* not but for thy covetousness, and for to shed
innocent blood, and for oppression, and for ¹violence, to do *it*.
18 Therefore thus saith the LORD concerning Jehoiakim the son of

t ch. 16. 4, 6.
u See 1 Kin. 13. 30. Fulfilled 599.
x 2 Chr. 36. 6. ch. 36. 30.

Josiah king of Judah; *t*They shall not lament for him, *saying*,
*u*Ah my brother! or, Ah sister! they shall not lament for him,
19 *saying*, Ah lord! or, Ah his glory! *x*He shall be buried with
the burial of an ass, drawn and cast forth beyond the gates of
Jerusalem.

20   Go up to Lebanon, and cry; and lift up thy voice in Bashan,
21 and cry from the passages: for all thy lovers are destroyed. I
spake unto thee in thy ²prosperity; *but* thou saidst, I will not

y ch. 3. 25.
z ch. 23. 1.
a ver. 20.

hear. *y*This *hath been* thy manner from thy youth, that thou
22 obeyedst not my voice. The wind shall eat up all *z*thy pastors,
and *a*thy lovers shall go into captivity: surely then shalt thou
23 be ashamed and confounded for all thy wickedness. O ³inha-
bitant of Lebanon, that makest thy nest in the cedars, how

b ch. 6. 24.
c See 2 Kin. 24. 6, 8. ch. 37. 1.
d Cant. 8. 6. Hag. 2. 23.

gracious shalt thou be when pangs come upon thee, *b*the pain
24 as of a woman in travail! ¶*As* I live, saith the LORD, *c*though
Coniah the son of Jehoiakim king of Judah *d*were the signet

¹ Or, *incursion*.   ² Heb. *prosperities*.   ³ Heb. *inhabitress*.

Jehoiakim's rebellion, and when Jeremiah
was out of the reach of the tyrant's power.

closest thyself *in cedar*] Rather, **viest** *in
cedar; i.e.* viest with Solomon.

did not thy father eat and drink &c.] *i.e.* he
was prosperous and enjoyed life. There is
a contrast between the life of Josiah spent
in the discharge of his kingly duties, and
that of Jehoiakim, busy with ambitious plans
of splendour and aggrandisement.

17. *covetousness*] Lit. *gain*. Besides ex-
acting forced labour Jehoiakim, to procure
the necessary means for the vast expenses he
incurred, put innocent people to death on various pretexts, and escheated their property.

18. Boldly by name is the judgment at
length pronounced upon Jehoiakim.
Dreaded by all around him, he shall soon
lie an unheeded corpse, with no one to
lament. No loving relative shall make such
wailing as when a brother or sister is carried
to the grave ; nor shall he have the respect
of his subjects, *Ah Lord! or, Ah his glory!*

19. *the burial of an ass*] *i.e.* he shall merely
be dragged out of the way, and left to decay
unheeded. Nothing is known of the fulfilment of this prophecy.

20. The third example, Jehoiachin. With
him all the best and noblest of the land
were dragged from their homes to people
the void places of Babylon.

the passages] Really, **Abarim**, a range of
mountains to the south of Gilead, opposite
Jericho (see Num. xxvii. 12; Deut. xxxii.
49). Jeremiah names the chief ranges of

mountains, which overlook the route from
Jerusalem to Babylon, in regular order,
beginning with Lebanon upon the North,
then Bashan on the North-East, and lastly
Abarim on the South-East.

thy lovers] *i.e.* the nations in alliance with
Judah, especially Egypt, whose defeat at
Carchemish (xlvi. 2) gave all western Asia
into the power of Nebuchadnezzar.

21. *prosperity*] Lit. as in marg. God spake
thus not once only, but whenever Judah
was at peace.

22. *shall eat up all thy pastors*] Lit. *shall
depasture* (ii. 16 note) *thy pastors*. Those
who used to drive their flocks to consume
the herbage shall themselves be the first
prey of war. The *pastors* mean not the
kings only, but all in authority.

23. *Lebanon* is the usual metaphor for
anything splendid, and is here put for
Jerusalem, but with especial reference to
the kings whose pride it was to dwell in
palaces roofed with cedar (*v.* 14).

how gracious shalt thou be] Or, **How wilt
thou groan!**

24. The words *king of Judah* belong to
Coniah, and prove that he was king regnant
when the prophet wrote. The prophet
gives him the name by which he was known
when in a private station (1 Chr. iii. 16) as
he had done previously with Jehoahaz.
These two kings bore their royal names for
so short a time that they probably never got
into general use.

the signet] The badge of office. To part

25 upon my right hand, yet would I pluck thee thence; *and I will *e* ch. 34. 20.
give thee into the hand of them that seek thy life, and into the
hand *of them* whose face thou fearest, even into the hand of
Nebuchadrezzar king of Babylon, and into the hand of the
26 Chaldeans. *f*And I will cast thee out, and thy mother that bare *f* 2 Kin. 24.
thee, into another country, where ye were not born; and there 15.
27 shall ye die. But to the land whereunto they ¹desire to return, 2 Chr. 36.10.
28 thither shall they not return. ¶ *Is* this man Coniah a despised
broken idol? *is he g*a vessel wherein *is* no pleasure? wherefore *g* Ps. 31. 12.
are they cast out, he and his seed, and are cast into a land which ch. 48. 38.
29 they know not? *h*O earth, earth, earth, hear the word of the *h* Deut. 32.1.
30 LORD. Thus saith the LORD, Write ye this man *i*childless, a Isai. 1. 2.
man *that* shall not prosper in his days: for no man of his seed Mic. 1. 2.
shall prosper, *k*sitting upon the throne of David, and ruling any 3. 16, 17.
more in Judah. *k* ch. 36. 30.

CHAP. 23. WOE *a*be unto the pastors that destroy and scatter the *a* ch. 10. 21.
2 sheep of my pasture! saith the LORD. Therefore thus saith Ezek. 34. 2.
the LORD God of Israel against the pastors that feed my people;
Ye have scattered my flock, and driven them away, and have
not visited them: *b*behold, I will visit upon you the evil of your *b* Ex. 32. 34.
3 doings, saith the LORD. And *c*I will gather the remnant of my *c* ch. 32. 37.
flock out of all countries whither I have driven them, and will Ezek. 34.
bring them again to their folds; and they shall be fruitful and 13, &c.
4 increase. And I will set up *d*shepherds over them which shall *d* ch. 3. 15.
feed them: and they shall fear no more, nor be dismayed, *e* Isai. 11. 1.
5 neither shall they be lacking, saith the LORD. ¶ Behold, *e*the & 40. 10, 11.
days come, saith the LORD, that I will raise unto David a ch. 33. 14.
Dan. 9. 24.
Zech. 3. 8.
John 1. 45.

¹ Heb. *lift up their mind*, ch. 44. 14.

---

with it, was to part with the royal
authority.
26. *mother*] See xiii. 18. It was her relationship, not to the dead king, but to the
king regnant, which made her powerful.
28. *idol*] Rather, *vessel*. Is Coniah a mere
piece of common earthenware in which the
potter has no pleasure, and therefore breaks
it? It is a lamentation over Jehoiachin's
hard fate, and that of his seed. This and
the two following verses may have been
written after the king had been carried into
Captivity.
29. *earth*] On the repetition cp. vii. 4
note.
30. *childless*] No child to sit on David's
throne. See 1 Chr. iii. 17 note.
Jeconiah was the last king of David's line.
His uncle indeed actually reigned after him,
but perished with his sons long before Jeconiah's death (lii. 10): and yet from so dead
a trunk, from a family so utterly fallen,
that spiritual King came forth Whose name
is "Jehovah our righteousness" (xxiii. 5, 6).
XXIII. 1. *the pastors*] **shepherds,** *i.e.*
civil rulers (ii. 8).
the sheep of My pasture] Lit. *of My pastur-
ing*, the sheep of whom I am shepherd. The
people do not belong to the rulers but to
God.
2. They had scattered them first spirit-

ually by leading them into idolatry; and
secondly, many had literally been taken to
Egypt with Jehoahaz, many in Jehoiakim's
time had fled thither, while others fell away
to the Chaldæans: and finally the best of
the land had been carried to Babylon with
Jeconiah.
driven away] *i.e. made them outcasts.* In
the East shepherds never drive their flocks,
but go before them (John x. 4, 5).
have not visited them] *i.e.* have not concerned yourselves about their conduct.
3. While there is no promise of restoration for the kings, there is for the people
(see iv. 27), because they had been led astray
by their rulers.
I have driven them] The evil shepherds
drove the people into exile by leading them
into sin: and God by inflicting punishment.
their folds] Or, *their* **pastures.**
4. *shepherds*] Men like Ezra, Nehemiah,
and the Maccabees, raised up specially by
God. It is a revocation of the promise
made to David (2 Sam. vii. 12–16) so far as
the earthly throne was concerned.
they shall fear no more...] The effect of
good government will be general security.
neither shall they be lacking] Not one sheep
shall be missing, or lost.
5. Even with the temporal kingship abolished, David's mercies are still sure.

righteous Branch, and a King shall reign and prosper, *f*and
6 shall execute judgment and justice in the earth. *g*In his days
Judah shall be saved, and Israel *h*shall dwell safely : and *i*this
is his name whereby he shall be called, ¹THE LORD OUR
7 RIGHTEOUSNESS. Therefore, behold, *k*the days come, saith
the LORD, that they shall no more say, The LORD liveth, which
8 brought up the children of Israel out of the land of Egypt ; but,
The LORD liveth, which brought up and which led the seed of
the house of Israel out of the north country, *l*and from all
countries whither I had driven them ; and they shall dwell in
their own land.

9   Mine heart within me is broken because of the prophets ;
*m*all my bones shake ; I am like a drunken man, and like a man
whom wine hath overcome, because of the LORD, and because of
10 the words of his holiness. For *n*the land is full of adulterers ;
for *o*because of ²swearing the land mourneth ; *p*the pleasant
places of the wilderness are dried up, and their ³course is evil,
11 and their force *is* not right. For *q*both prophet and priest are
profane ; yea, *r*in my house have I found their wickedness,
12 saith the LORD. *s*Wherefore their way shall be unto them
as slippery *ways* in the darkness : they shall be driven on, and
fall therein : for I *t*will bring evil upon them, *even* the year of
13 their visitation, saith the LORD. And I have seen ⁴⁵folly in
the prophets of Samaria ; *u*they prophesied in Baal, and *x*caused
14 my people Israel to err. I have seen also in the prophets of
Jerusalem ⁶an horrible thing : *y*they commit adultery, and

---

¹ *Jehovah-tsidkenu.*   ³ Or, *violence.*   ⁵ Heb. *unsavoury.*
² Or, *cursing.*   ⁴ Or, *an absurd thing.*   ⁶ Or, *filthiness.*

---

a righteous Branch] Or, *sprout, germ* (see
Isai. iv. 2 note). The sprout is that in which
the root springs up and grows, and which,
if it be destroyed, makes the root perish
also.
  and a King shall reign...] Rather, *and*
he shall reign as king. David's family is
to be dethroned (temporally), that it may
reign gloriously (spiritually). But cp. xxxiii.
17, 26 notes.
  6. *this is his name whereby he shall be
called*] From remote antiquity the person
here spoken of has been understood to be
" the righteous germ," and this alone is in
accordance with the grammar and the sense.
Nevertheless, because Jeremiah (xxxiii. 15,
16) applies the name also to Jerusalem, some
understand it of Israel.
  THE LORD OUR RIGHTEOUSNESS]
Messiah is here called (1) Jehovah, and (2)
our righteousness, because He justifies us
by His merits. Some render, *He by whom
Jehovah works righteousness.* Righteousness
is in that case personal holiness, which is
the work of the Spirit after justification.
  9. *because of the prophets*] Rather, **concerning** *the prophets.* These words should
come first, as being the title of this portion
of the prophecy (*vv.* 9-40).
  10. *because of swearing*] Rather, *because
of* **the curse** denounced against sin (xi. 3).

The mourning probably refers to the drought
(xii. 4).
  the pleasant places] **pastures.**
  their course] Their mode of life.
  their force is not right] *Their heroism,* that
on which they pride themselves as mighty
men, *is not right,* is wrong (see viii. 6 note).
  11. *For both prophet and priest are profane*]
While by their office they are consecrated to
God, they have made themselves common
and unholy by their sins. See iii. 9 note.
  yea, in my house] This may refer to sins
such as those of the sons of Eli (1 Sam. ii.
22), or that they had defiled the Temple by
idolatrous rites.
  12. Every word denotes the certainty of
their fall. *Their path is like slippery places
in darkness :* and on this path *they are pushed
with violence.* External circumstances assist
in urging on to ruin those who choose the
path of vice.
  13. *And I have seen folly...*] Rather, **Also**
I have seen. The prophet contrasts the prophets of Samaria with those of Jerusalem.
In the conduct of the former God saw folly
(lit. that which is insipid, as being unsalted).
It was stupidity to prophesy by Baal, an idol.
  in Baal] *i.e.* in the name of Baal.
  14. Rather, **But** *in the prophets of Jerusalem* &c. Their conduct is more strongly
condemned **than** that of the Baal-priests.

*walk in lies: they *a*strengthen also the hands of evildoers, that
none doth return from his wickedness: they are all of them
unto me as *b*Sodom, and the inhabitants thereof as Gomorrah.

15 ¶ Therefore thus saith the LORD of hosts concerning the prophets; Behold, I will feed them with *c*wormwood, and make
them drink the water of gall: for from the prophets of Jerusalem

16 is ¹profaneness gone forth into all the land. Thus saith the
LORD of hosts, Hearken not unto the words of the prophets that
prophesy unto you: they make you vain: *d*they speak a vision

17 of their own heart, *and* not out of the mouth of the LORD. They
say still unto them that despise me, The LORD hath said, *e*Ye
shall have peace; and they say unto every one that walketh after
the ²imagination of his own heart, *f*No evil shall come upon you.

18 For *g*who hath stood in the ³counsel of the LORD, and hath
perceived and heard his word? who hath marked his word, and

19 heard *it?* Behold, a *h*whirlwind of the LORD is gone forth in
fury, even a grievous whirlwind: it shall fall grievously upon

20 the head of the wicked. The *i*anger of the LORD shall not return,
until he have executed, and till he have performed the thoughts
of his heart: *k*in the latter days ye shall consider it perfectly.

21 *l*I have not sent these prophets, yet they ran: I have not spoken

22 to them, yet they prophesied. But if they had *m*stood in my
counsel, and had caused my people to hear my words, then
they should have *n*turned them from their evil way, and from

23 the evil of their doings. ¶ *Am* I a God at hand, saith the LORD,

24 and not a God afar off? Can any *o*hide himself in secret places
that I shall not see him? saith the LORD. *p*Do not I fill heaven

25 and earth? saith the LORD. I have heard what the prophets
said, that prophesy lies in my name, saying, I have dreamed, I

26 have dreamed. How long shall *this* be in the heart of the prophets that prophesy lies? yea, *they are* prophets of the deceit of

z ver. 26.
a Ezek. 13. 22.
b Deut. 32. 32.
Isai. 1. 9.
c ch. 8. 14.

d ch. 14. 14. ver. 21.

e ch. 6. 14.
Ezek. 13. 10.
Zech. 10. 2.
f Mic. 3. 11.
g Job 15. 8.
1 Cor. 2. 16.

h ch. 25. 32.

i ch. 30. 24.

k Gen. 49. 1.

l ch. 14. 14.

m ver. 18.

n ch. 25. 5.

o Ps. 139. 7.
Amos 9. 2.
p 1 Kin.8.27.

¹ Or, *hypocrisy.* ² Or, *stubbornness*, ch. 13. 10. ³ Or, *secret.*

---

they strengthen...] First by neglecting to warn and rebuke sinners: secondly by the direct influence of their bad example.

they are all of them] *They* **have become,** *all of them,* i.e. the people of Jerusalem, and not the prophets only.

15. *profaneness*] Desecration.

16. How were the people to know the false prophets from the true? The former bring a message that fills with vain hopes, or "speak a vision" out of their own invention.

17. *still*] **continually.** This verse gives the chief test by which the false prophet is to be detected, namely, that his predictions violate the laws of morality.

18. The prophet now applies this test to the circumstances of the times. A whirl-wind has already gone forth (*v.* 19). Had these false prophets stood in God's secret "Council" (so in *v.* 22), they like Jeremiah would have laboured to avert the danger by turning men from their evil way.

19. Rather, *Behold,* **the tempest of Jeho-vah, even** *hot anger hath gone forth* **and a whirlwind** *shall burst upon the head of the wicked.*

20. *the latter days*] The proper and final

development of any event or series of events. Thus the expression is used of the Christian dispensation as the full develop-ment of the Jewish Church. Here it means the destruction of Jerusalem, as the result of the sins of the Jews.

consider] Rather, **understand.** When Je-rusalem is destroyed, the exiles—taught by adversity—will understand that it was sin which brought ruin upon their country.

21. *ran*] *i.e.* hurried to take upon them the responsibilities of the prophetic office.

22. *they should have turned them* &c.] The work of the true prophet, which is to turn men from evil unto good.

23. *at hand*] Or, **near.** An appeal to the omnipotence of God in demonstration of the wickedness of the prophets. His power is not limited, so that He can notice only things close to Him, but is universal.

25. In Deut. xiii. 1 *a dreamer of dreams* is used in a bad sense, and with reason. God communicating His Will by dreams was a thing too easy to counterfeit for it not to be misused.

26. Some translate, *How long? Is it in the heart of the prophets that prophesy lies,*

27 their own heart; which think to cause my people to forget my
name by their dreams which they tell every man to his neigh-

q Judg. 3. 7. 28 bour, *q*as their fathers have forgotten my name for Baal. The
& 8. 33, 34.   prophet ¹that hath a dream, let him tell a dream; and he that
hath my word, let him speak my word faithfully. What *is* the

29 chaff to the wheat? saith the LORD. *Is* not my word like as a
fire? saith the LORD; and like a hammer *that* breaketh the

r Deut. 18. 30 rock in pieces? Therefore, behold, *r*I *am* against the prophets,
20.
ch. 11. 14.   saith the LORD, that steal my words every one from his neigh-

31 bour. Behold, I *am* against the prophets, saith the LORD, ²that

32 use their tongues, and say, He saith. Behold, I *am* against

s Zeph. 3. 4.   them that prophesy false dreams, saith the LORD, and do tell
them, and cause my people to err by their lies, and by *s*their
lightness; yet I sent them not, nor commanded them: therefore they shall not profit this people at all, saith the LORD.

33 ¶And when this people, or the prophet, or a priest, shall ask

t Mal. 1. 1.   thee, saying, What *is* *t*the burden of the LORD? thou shalt then
u ver. 39.   say unto them, What burden? *u*I will even forsake you, saith

34 the LORD. And *as for* the prophet, and the priest, and the people,
that shall say, The burden of the LORD, I will even ³punish

35 that man and his house. Thus shall ye say every one to his
neighbour, and every one to his brother, What hath the LORD

36 answered? and, What hath the LORD spoken? And the burden
of the LORD shall ye mention no more: for every man's word
shall be his burden; for ye have perverted the words of the

37 living God, of the LORD of hosts our God. Thus shalt thou

---

¹ Heb. *with whom* is.   ² Or, *that smooth their tongues.*   ³ Heb. *visit upon.*

---

*and prophesy the deceit of their heart — do
they purpose to make My people forget My
name by their dreams which they tell one to
another?*

27. *to his neighbour*] *i.e.* **to one another**,
to the people about him, to any one.

as their fathers &c.] Rather, *as their fathers* forgot *My name* **through** *Baal.* The
superstition which attaches importance to
dreams keeps God as entirely out of men's
minds as absolute idolatry.

28. *a dream ... faithfully*] Rather, **as** *a
dream...***as truth.** The dream is but a dream,
and is to be told as such, but God's word is
to be spoken as certain and absolute **truth.**

The dreams are the *chaff*, worthless, with
nothing in them ; the *wheat*, the pure grain
after it is cleansed and winnowed is God's
word. What have these two in common?

29. *like as a fire*] God's word is the great
purifier which destroys all that is false and
leaves only the genuine metal. Cp. Heb.
iv. 12.

like a hammer...] God's word rouses and
strengthens the conscience, and crushes
within the heart everything that is evil.

30. Jeremiah gives in succession the main
characteristics of the teaching of the false
prophets. The first is that *they steal* God's
words **from one another.** Having no message from God they try to imitate the true
prophets.

31. *that use their tongues*] Lit. *that* **take**

their tongues. Their second characteristic.
They have no message from God, but they
take their tongues, their only implement, *and
say, He saith*, using the solemn formula by
which Jehovah affirms the truth of His
words. Solemn asseverations seemed to give
reality to their emptiness.

32. The third characteristic. See *v.* 25.

lightness] Vain, empty, talk.

33. *burden*] Here a prophecy, either (1)
as being something weighty : or (2) a something said aloud. Isaiah brought the word
into general use ; Jeremiah never used it,
though his predictions were all of impending
evil. The false prophets, however, applied
it in derision to Jeremiah's prophecies, playing upon its double sense, and so turning
solemn realities into mockery (see *v.* 34).

What burden?] Or, according to another
reading, *Ye are the burden.*

I will even forsake you] Rather, *and I will*
cast you away. From the idea of a burden
the thought naturally arises of refusing to
bear it, and throwing it off.

35. The proper words for prophecy. It
is to be called an *answer* when the people
have come to enquire of Jehovah : but His
word when it is sent unasked.

36. *every man's word* &c.] Rather, **every
man's burden shall be his word ;** *i.e.* his
mocking use of the word "burden" shall
weigh him down and crush him.

perverted] *i.e.* put into a ridiculous light.

say to the prophet, What hath the LORD answered thee? and,
38 What hath the LORD spoken? But since ye say, The burden
of the LORD; therefore thus saith the LORD; Because ye say
this word, The burden of the LORD, and I have sent unto you,
39 saying, Ye shall not say, The burden of the LORD; therefore,
behold, I, even I, *will utterly forget you, and *I will forsake
you, and the city that I gave you and your fathers, *and cast*
40 *you* out of my presence: and I will bring *an everlasting
reproach upon you, and a perpetual shame, which shall not be
forgotten.

CHAP. 24. THE *LORD shewed me, and, behold, two baskets of figs
were set before the temple of the LORD, after that Nebuchadrezzar *king of Babylon had carried away captive *Jeconiah the
son of Jehoiakim king of Judah, and the princes of Judah, with
the carpenters and smiths, from Jerusalem, and had brought
2 them to Babylon. One basket *had* very good figs, *even* like the
figs *that are* first ripe: and the other basket *had* very naughty
3 figs, which could not be eaten, ¹they were so bad. ¶ Then said
the LORD unto me, What seest thou, Jeremiah? And I said,
Figs; the good figs, very good; and the evil, very evil, that
4 cannot be eaten, they are so evil. ¶ Again the word of the LORD
came unto me, saying, Thus saith the LORD, the God of Israel;
5 Like these good figs, so will I acknowledge ²them that are carried
away captive of Judah, whom I have sent out of this place into
6 the land of the Chaldeans for *their* good. For I will set mine
eyes upon them for good, and *I will bring them again to this
land: and *I will build them, and not pull *them* down; and I
7 will plant them, and not pluck *them* up. And I will give them
*an heart to know me, that I *am* the LORD: and they shall be
*my people, and I will be their God: for they shall return unto
8 me *with their whole heart. ¶ And as the evil *figs, which
cannot be eaten, they are so evil; surely thus saith the LORD,
So will I give Zedekiah the king of Judah, and his princes, and
the residue of Jerusalem, that remain in this land, and *them
9 that dwell in the land of Egypt: and I will deliver them ³to *l* be
removed into all the kingdoms of the earth for *their* hurt, *m to*

¹ Heb. *for badness.*   ² Heb. *the captivity.*   ³ Heb. *for removing,* or, *vexation.*

x Hos. 4. 6.
y ver. 33.
z ch. 20. 11.

a Amos 7. 1.
& 8. 1.
b 2 Kin. 21.
12, &c.
2 Chr. 36.10.
c ch. 22. 24.
& 29. 2.

d ch. 12. 15.
e ch. 32. 41.
f Deut. 30. 6.
ch. 32. 39.
Ezek. 11. 19.
g ch. 30. 2².
h ch. 29. 13.
i ch. 29. 17.
k See ch. 43,
& 44.
l Deut. 28.
25, 37.
1 Kin. 9. 7.
2 Chr. 7. 20.
ch. 15. 4.
m Ps. 44. 13.

---

38. *since*] Or, *But if ye say.*
39. Translate, *Therefore, behold, I will
even take you up* (or will burden you), *and I
will cast you, and the city which I gave you
and your fathers, out of my presence.*
XXIV. This prophecy is the final out-
come of what has gone before. Never perhaps has a reigning king been addressed
in such contemptuous terms. When Jeconiah was carried to Babylon, Zedekiah, the
priests, prophets, and people of Jerusalem
congratulated themselves upon being saved
from such a fate: really all that was good
among them was then culled out, and placed
in safety; and they were left behind
because they were not worth the taking.
1. Omit *were. Set before, i.e.* put in the
appointed place for offerings of firstfruits in
the forecourt of the Temple.
carpenters] **craftsmen** (see marg. ref.).

2. Fig-trees bear three crops of figs, of
which the first is regarded as a great delicacy.
4-10. The complete fulfilment of this
prophecy belongs to the Christian Church.
There is a close analogy between Jeremiah
at the first destruction of Jerusalem and
our Lord at the second. There the good
figs were those converts picked out by the
preaching of Christ and the Apostles: the
bad figs were the mass of the people left for
Titus and the Romans to destroy.
5. *acknowledge...for* their *good*] Specially
their spiritual good. Put a comma after
Chaldœans.
8. *that dwell in the land of Egypt*] Neither
those carried captive with Jehoahaz into
Egypt, nor those who fled thither, are to
share in these blessings. The new life of
the Jewish nation is to be the work only of
the exiles in Babylon.

n ch. 29. 18.

be a reproach and a proverb, a taunt *n* and a curse, in all places
10 whither I shall drive them.   And I will send the sword, the
famine, and the pestilence, among them, till they be consumed
from off the land that I gave unto them and to their fathers.

CHAP. 25. THE word that came to Jeremiah concerning all the people

a ch. 36. 1.

of Judah *a* in the fourth year of Jehoiakim the son of Josiah king
of Judah, that *was* the first year of Nebuchadrezzar king of
2 Babylon; the which Jeremiah the prophet spake unto all the
people of Judah, and to all the inhabitants of Jerusalem, saying.

b ch. 1. 2.

3 ¶ *b* From the thirteenth year of Josiah the son of Amon king of
Judah, even unto this day, that *is* the three and twentieth year,
the word of the LORD hath come unto me, and I have spoken

c ch. 7. 13.
& passim.

unto you, rising early and speaking; *c* but ye have not hearkened.
4 And the LORD hath sent unto you all his servants the prophets,

d ch. 7. 13,
& 29. 19.
e 2 Kin. 17.
13.
ch. 18. 11.
Jonah 3. 8.

d rising early and sending *them;* but ye have not hearkened, nor
5 inclined your ear to hear.   They said, *e* Turn ye again now every
one from his evil way, and from the evil of your doings, and
dwell in the land that the LORD hath given unto you and to your
6 fathers for ever and ever: and go not after other gods to serve
them, and to worship them, and provoke me not to anger with
7 the works of your hands; and I will do you no hurt.   Yet ye

f Deut. 32.
21.
ch. 7. 19.
g ch. 1. 15.

have not hearkened unto me, saith the LORD; that ye might
f provoke me to anger with the works of your hands to your own
8 hurt. ¶ Therefore thus saith the LORD of hosts; Because ye
9 have not heard my words, behold, I will send and take *g* all the

h ch. 27. 6.
& 43. 10.
See Isai.
44. 28.
i ch. 18. 16.
k Isai. 24. 7.
ch. 7. 34.
Ezek. 26. 13.
Hos. 2. 11.
Rev. 18. 23.

families of the north, saith the LORD, and Nebuchadrezzar the
king of Babylon, *h* my servant, and will bring them against this
land, and against the inhabitants thereof, and against all these
nations round about, and will utterly destroy them, and *i* make
them an astonishment, and an hissing, and perpetual desolations.
10 Moreover *1* I will take from them the *k* voice of mirth, and the

[1] Heb. *I will cause to perish from them.*

XXV. It was immediately after the
battle of Carchemish (B.C. 605) between
Egypt and Babylon, and probably before
Nebuchadnezzar and his victorious army
appeared in Palestine, that Jeremiah delivered this prophecy, orally perhaps at first
to the people, but soon afterwards committed
to writing; it formed part of Jehoiakim's
roll (xxxvi. 29). It belongs to the year
of Jeremiah's greatest activity, when he was
using his utmost efforts to detach Jehoiakim
from Egypt, and prevail upon him to accept
frankly the position of a king subject to
Nebuchadnezzar, not only as a matter of
policy but of religious duty. It was this
latter aspect of the appeal that made the
king reject it. He burnt the prophet's roll,
tried to slay the prophet, and heard the
voice of God no more during the rest of his
reign.

1. *the fourth year*] See Dan. i. 1 note.
This invasion of Judæa, in which Daniel
was carried captive to Babylon, was according to the date of the years the fourth, but
according to the actual time the third, year
of the Jewish king. Nebuchadnezzar was

not yet fully king, but associated with his
father Nabopalassar.

3. *the three and twentieth year*] *i.e.* nineteen under Josiah, and four under Jehoiakim. This prophecy divides itself into three
parts, (1) the judgment of Judah (*vv.* 3–11),
and Babylon's doom (*vv.* 12–14); (2) the
winecup of fury (*vv.* 15–29); (3) the judgment of the world (*vv.* 30–38).

5. *Turn ye*] *i.e. Repent ye;*—the great summons of God to mankind at all times (Luke
xxiv. 47; Acts ii. 38; cp. Matt. iii. 2).

9. The term *families* is probably used here
to signify the wide-spread empire of Nebuchadnezzar.

my servant] This title, so remarkable in
the Old Testament as the especial epithet.
first of Moses, and then of the Messiah, is
thrice given to Nebuchadnezzar, and marks
the greatness of the commission entrusted
to him.

10. *take from them...the sound of the millstones, and the light of the candle* (or, lamp)]
To denote the entire cessation of domestic
life. The one was the sign of the preparation
of the daily meal, the other of the assem-

voice of gladness, the voice of the bridegroom, and the voice of the bride, ^lthe sound of the millstones, and the light of the candle. ^lEccles.12.4.
11 And this whole land shall be a desolation, *and* an astonishment; 2 Kin. 24. 1.
and these nations shall serve the king of Babylon seventy years.
12 And it shall come to pass, ^mwhen seventy years are accomplished, *that* I will ¹punish the king of Babylon, and that nation, saith the LORD, for their iniquity, and the land of the Chaldeans,
13 ⁿand will make it perpetual desolations. And I will bring upon that land all my words which I have pronounced against it, *even* all that is written in this book, which Jeremiah hath prophesied
14 against all the nations. ^oFor many nations ^pand great kings shall ^qserve themselves of them also: ^rand I will recompense them according to their deeds, and according to the works of
15 their own hands. ¶ For thus saith the LORD God of Israel unto me; Take the ^swine cup of this fury at my hand, and cause all
16 the nations, to whom I send thee, to drink it. And ^tthey shall drink, and be moved, and be mad, because of the sword that I
17 will send among them. ¶ Then took I the cup at the LORD'S hand, and made all the nations to drink, unto whom the LORD
18 had sent me: *to wit,* Jerusalem, and the cities of Judah, and the kings thereof, and the princes thereof, to make them ^ua desolation, an astonishment, an hissing, and ^xa curse; as *it is* this
19 day; ^yPharaoh king of Egypt, and his servants, and his princes,
20 and all his people; and all ^zthe mingled people, and all the kings of ^athe land of Uz, ^band all the kings of the land of the Philis-
21 tines, and Ashkelon, and Azzah, and Ekron, and ^cthe remnant

m 2 Chr. 36.
21, 22.
ch. 29. 10.
Dan. 9. 2.
n Isai. 13.19.
ch. 50. 3.

o ch. 51. 27.
p ch. 50. 41.
q ch. 27. 7
r ch. 10. 29.

s Job 21. 20.
Ps. 75. 8.
Isai. 51. 17.
Rev. 14. 10.
t Ezek 23.34.
Nah. 3. 11.

u ver. 9, 11.
x ch. 24. 9.
y ch. 46. 2.
z ver. 24
a Job 1. 1.
b ch. 47. 1.
c See Isai.
20. 1.

¹ Heb. *visit upon.*

---

bling of the family after the labours of the day were over.

11. *seventy years*] The duration of the Babylonian empire was really a little short of this period. But the seventy years are usually calculated down to the time when the Jews were permitted to return to their country (cp. xxix. 10).

12. *perpetual desolations*] The ruins of Babylon form its only lasting memorial.

13. The LXX. place a full stop after *book*, and take the rest as a title "what Jeremiah prophesied against the nations," which series there immediately follows. In the Masoretic text this series is deferred to the end (chs. xlvi.-xlix.), and with chs. l., li., forms one entire series. Other reasons make it probable that the LXX. have preserved for us an earlier text, in which all direct mention of the king of Babylon is omitted and the seventy years are given as the duration of Judah's Captivity, and not of the Babylonian empire. The fuller text of the Masorites is to be explained by the dislocation which Jehoiakim's roll evidently suffered. See p. 162.

14. *shall serve themselves of them also*] *i.e.* shall impose forced labour upon the Chaldæans, and reduce them also to servitude.

15. *saith*] Or, **hath said.** This prophecy —placed by the LXX. after those against the nations—forms an impressive statement

of the manner in which the new kingdom of Babylon was to execute Jehovah's wrath upon the nations far and near.

16. *be moved*] Rather, **stagger.**

17. *Then took I the cup*] Not actually offering the wine-cup—Holy Scripture has suffered much from this materialistic way of explaining it:—but publicly proclaiming this prophecy in Jerusalem, as the central spot of God's dealings with men, and leaving it to find its way to the neighbouring states.

18. *as it is this day*] Words omitted by the LXX., and probably added by Jeremiah after the murder of Gedaliah had completed the ruin of the land.

19. The arrangement is remarkable. Jeremiah begins with the South, Egypt; next Uz on the South-East, and Philistia on the South-West; next, Edom, Moab, and Ammon on the East, and Tyre, and Sidon, and the isles of the Mediterranean on the West; next, in the far East, various Arabian nations, then northward to Media and Elam, and finally the kings of the North far and near.

20. *the mingled people*] Either *auxiliaries;* or, rather, a constituent portion of the people of Egypt, who were not of pure blood.

Azzah] *i.e.* **Gaza.**

the remnant of Ashdod] A sentence which none but a contemporary writer could have used. Psammetichus, after a siege of

d ch. 49. 7.
c ch. 48. 1.
f ch. 49. 1.
g ch. 47. 4.
h ch. 49. 23.
i ch. 49. 8.
k 2 Chr. 9.14.
l See ver. 20.
ch. 49. 31.
Ezek. 30. 5.
m ch. 49. 34.
n ch. 50. 9.
o ch. 51. 41.

22 of Ashdod, *d*Edom, and *e*Moab, and the children of *f*Ammon, and all the kings of *g*Tyrus, and all the kings of Zidon, and the 23 kings of the *i*isles which *are* beyond the *h*sea, *i*Dedan, and Tema, 24 and Buz, and all *2that are* in the utmost corners, and *k* all the kings of Arabia, and all the kings of the *l*mingled people that 25 dwell in the desert, and all the kings of Zimri, and all the kings 26 of *m*Elam, and all the kings of the Medes, *n*and all the kings of the north, far and near, one with another, and all the kingdoms of the world, which *are* upon the face of the earth : *o*and the 27 king of Sheshach shall drink after them. ¶ Therefore thou shalt say unto them, Thus saith the LORD of hosts, the God of Israel ;

p Hab. 2. 1 .
q Isai. 51.21.

*p*Drink ye, and *q*be drunken, and spue, and fall, and rise no 28 more, because of the sword which I will send among you. And it shall be, if they refuse to take the cup at thine hand to drink, then shalt thou say unto them, Thus saith the LORD of hosts : 29 Ye shall certainly drink. For, lo, *r*I begin to bring evil on the city *3s*which is called by my name, and should ye be utterly un-punished ? Ye shall not be unpunished : for *t*I will call for a sword upon all the inhabitants of the earth, saith the LORD of 30 hosts. ¶ Therefore prophesy thou against them all these words, and say unto them, ¶ The LORD shall *u*roar from on high, and utter his voice from *x* his holy habitation ; he shall mightily roar upon *y*his habitation ; he shall give *z*a shout, as they that tread 31 *the grapes*, against all the inhabitants of the earth. A noise shall come *even* to the ends of the earth ; for the LORD hath *a*a con-troversy with the nations, *b*he will plead with all flesh ; he will 32 give them *that are* wicked to the sword, saith the LORD. Thus saith the LORD of hosts, Behold, evil shall go forth from nation to nation, and *c*a great whirlwind shall be raised up from the 33 coasts of the earth. *d*And the slain of the LORD shall be at that

r Prov. 11.
31.
ch 49. 12.
Ezek. 9. 6.
Luke 23. 31.
s Dan. 9. 18.
t Ezek. 38.
21.
u Isai. 42.13.
Amos 1. 2.
x Ps. 11. 4.
ch. 17. 12.
y 1 Kin. 9. 3.
Ps. 132. 14.
z ch. 48. 33.
a Hos. 4. 1.
Mic. 6. 2.
b Isai. 66. 16.
Joel 3. 2.
c ch. 23. 19.
& 30. 23.
d Isai. 66. 16.

---

¹ Or, *region by the sea-side.*
² Heb. *cut off into corners,* or, *having the corners of* the hair *polled ;* ch. 9.26. & 49. 32.
³ Heb. *upon which my name is called.*

---

twenty-nine years, had captured and de-stroyed Ashdod, excepting a feeble rem-nant.

22. *the isles*] Rightly explained in the margin ; it probably refers here to Cyprus.

23. *Dedan*] See Isai. xxi. 13 note.

Buz] See Job xxxii. 2 note.

all that are &c.] See marg. ref. note.

24. *Arabia*] That part which bordered on Palestine, and was inhabited mainly by Ishmaelites.

the mingled people] Cp. *v.* 20 note. In Arabia there seem to have been many tribes of Cushite origin, who by intermarriage with other tribes had become of mixed blood.

25. *Zimri*] Probably a district between Arabia and Persia. " Elam " is put in Scripture for the whole of Persia.

26. *all the kingdoms of the world* &c.] In accordance with the usage of Holy Scrip-ture this universality is limited. It is moral and not geographical.

Sheshach] Jerome says that this is the name Babel written in cypher, the letters being transposed. Another example occurs in li. 1, where the words *the heart of my risers up*

become *the Chaldæans.* The LXX. omit the clause containing the name.

27. The metaphors denote the helpless-ness to which the nations are reduced by drinking the wine-cup of fury (*v.* 15).

30. Jehovah has risen like a lion from His covert, and at His roaring the whole world is filled with terror and confusion.

upon his habitation] **Against His pas-ture :** *i.e.* Judæa. Jehovah comes forth as the lion to destroy the sheep which lie terrified within the circle of the tents.

a shout] The *vintage-shout,* here used for the war-cry. Cp. Isai. xvi. 9 ; lxiii. 3.

31. *A noise*] The trampling of an army in motion. Cp. Amos ii. 2.

a controversy] *i.e.* a suit at law.

will plead], Or, *will* **hold judgment.** As judge He delivers the wicked to the sword.

32. *a great whirlwind*] Or, **storm.**

the coasts of the earth] See vi. 22 note. The thunderstorm seen first on the edge of the horizon overspreads the heaven, and travels from nation to nation in its destruc-tive course.

day from *one* end of the earth even unto the *other* end of the earth: they shall not be *e*lamented, *f*neither gathered, nor buried;
34 they shall be dung upon the ground. *g*Howl, ye shepherds, and cry; and wallow yourselves *in the ashes*, ye principal of the flock: for [1]the days of your slaughter and of your dispersions are ac-
35 complished; and ye shall fall like [2]a pleasant vessel. And [3]the shepherds shall have no way to flee, nor the principal of the
36 flock to escape. A voice of the cry of the shepherds, and an howling of the principal of the flock, *shall be heard:* for the LORD
37 hath spoiled their pasture. And the peaceable habitations are
38 cut down because of the fierce anger of the LORD. He hath forsaken *h*his covert, as the lion : for their land is [4]desolate because of the fierceness of the oppressor, and because of his fierce anger.

CHAP. 26. IN the beginning of the reign of Jehoiakim the son of Josiah king of Judah came this word from the LORD, saying,
2 Thus saith the LORD ; ¶Stand in *a*the court of the LORD's house, and speak unto all the cities of Judah, which come to worship in the LORD's house, *b*all the words that I command thee to
3 speak unto them; *c*diminish not a word: *d*if so be they will hearken, and turn every man from his evil way, that I may *e*repent me of the evil, which I purpose to do unto them because
4 of the evil of their doings. And thou shalt say unto them, Thus saith the LORD ; *f*If ye will not hearken to me, to walk in my
5 law, which I have set before you, to hearken to the words of my servants the prophets, *g*whom I sent unto you, both rising up
6 early, and sending *them*, but ye have not hearkened ; then will I make this house like *h*Shiloh, and will make this city *i*a curse
7 to all the nations of the earth. ¶So the priests and the prophets and all the people heard Jeremiah speaking these words in the
8 house of the LORD. Now it came to pass, when Jeremiah had made an end of speaking all that the LORD had commanded *him* to speak unto all the people, that the priests and the prophets and all the people took him, saying, Thou shalt surely die.
9 Why hast thou prophesied in the name of the LORD, saying, This house shall be like Shiloh, and this city shall be desolate without an inhabitant ? And all the people were gathered against Jere-

e ch. 16. 4.
f Ps. 79. 3.
ch. 8. 2.
Rev. 11. 9.
g ch. 4. 8.

h Ps. 76. 2.

a ch. 19. 14.

b Ezek. 3. 10.
Matt. 28. 20.
c Acts 20. 27.
d ch. 36. 3.
e ch. 18. 8.
Jonah 3. 8.
f Lev. 26. 14,
&c.
Deut. 28. 15.
g ch. 7. 13.
& 25. 3, 4.
h 1 Sam. 4.
10, 11.
Ps. 78. 60.
ch. 7. 12.
i Isai. 65. 15.
ch. 24. 9.

[1] Heb. *your days for slaughter.*
[2] Heb. *a vessel of desire.*
[3] Heb. *flight shall perish from the shepherds, and*
escaping from, &c.
Amos 2. 14.
[4] Heb. *a desolation.*

---

33. *lamented*] See marg. ref. and viii. 2.
34–36. *principal of the flock*] *i.e.* noble ones.
wallow yourselves in the ashes] Rather, **roll yourselves on the ground.**
for &c.] Read ; "for your days for being slaughtered are accomplished, and I will scatter you " (or, dash you in pieces).
fall like a pleasant vessel] The comparison suggests the idea of change from a thing of value into worthless fragments.
36. *hath spoiled*] Or, **spoileth.**
37. *the peaceable habitations*] *The* past-ures *of peace*, the peaceable fields where the flocks lately dwelt in security. See *v.* 30 note.
38. Jehovah has risen up, like a lion that leaves its covert, eager for prey,

that He may execute judgment upon the wicked.
XXVI. This chapter is a narrative of the danger to which Jeremiah was exposed by reason of the prophecy contained in ch. vii. and should be read in connexion with it. *Vv.* 4–6 contain a summary of the prediction contained in ch. vii., and that again is but an outline of what was a long address.
9. The charge against Jeremiah was that of prophesying falsely, for which the penalty was death (Deut. xviii. 20). They assumed that it was absolutely impossible that Jerusalem ever could become like Shiloh.
against Jeremiah] **unto** *Jeremiah.* They regularly constituted themselves **a** congregation to take part in his trial.

10 miah in the house of the LORD. ¶ When the princes of Judah
heard these things, then they came up from the king's house
unto the house of the LORD, and sat down ¹in the entry of the
11 new gate of the LORD's *house.* Then spake the priests and the
prophets unto the princes and to all the people, saying, ²This

k ch. 38. 4.

man *is* worthy to die; *k*for he hath prophesied against this city,
12 as ye have heard with your ears. ¶ Then spake Jeremiah unto
all the princes and to all the people, saying, The LORD sent me
to prophesy against this house and against this city all the words

l ch. 7. 3.

13 that ye have heard. Therefore now *l*amend your ways and your
doings, and obey the voice of the LORD your God; and the LORD

m ver. 3, 19.

will *m*repent him of the evil that he hath pronounced against

n ch. 38. 5.

14 you. As for me, behold, *n*I *am* in your hand: do with me ³as
15 seemeth good and meet unto you. But know ye for certain, that
if ye put me to death, ye shall surely bring innocent blood upon
yourselves, and upon this city, and upon the inhabitants thereof:
for of a truth the LORD hath sent me unto you to speak all these
16 words in your ears. ¶ Then said the princes and all the people
unto the priests and to the prophets; This man *is* not worthy to
die: for he hath spoken to us in the name of the LORD our God.

o See Acts
5. 34, &c.
p Mic. 1. 1.

17 ¶ *o*Then rose up certain of the elders of the land, and spake to
18 all the assembly of the people, saying, *p*Micah the Morasthite
prophesied in the days of Hezekiah king of Judah, and spake
to all the people of Judah, saying, Thus saith the LORD of hosts;

q Mic. 3. 12.

*q*Zion shall be plowed *like* a field, and Jerusalem shall become
heaps, and the mountain of the house as the high places of a
19 forest. Did Hezekiah king of Judah and all Judah put him at

r 2 Chr. 32.
26.
s Ex. 32. 14.
2 Sam.24.16.
t Acts 5. 39.

all to death? *r*did he not fear the LORD, and besought ⁴the
LORD, and the LORD *s*repented him of the evil which he had
pronounced against them? *t*Thus might we procure great evil
20 against our souls. And there was also a man that prophesied
in the name of the LORD, Urijah the son of Shemaiah of Kirjath-
jearim, who prophesied against this city and against this land

---

¹ Or, *at the door.*   *death* is *for this man.*   *right in your eyes.*
² Heb. *The judgment of*   ³ Heb. *as it is good and*   ⁴ Heb. *the face of the* LORD.

---

10. *the princes of Judah*] The priests
could scourge a man &c., but could not then
try him for his life, as the Sanhedrim subsequently did till the Romans deprived
them of the power.

the new gate] That built by Jotham (2 K.
xv. 35), and probably a usual place for
trials.

11. *This man* is *worthy to die*] Lit. *A
sentence of death is to this man, i.e.* is his
desert.

12–15. The answer of Jeremiah is simple
and straightforward. Jehovah, he affirmed,
had truly sent him, but the sole object of
his prophesying had been to avert the evil
by leading them to repentance. If they
would amend their ways God would deliver
them from the threatened doom. As for
himself he was in their hands, but if they
put him to death they would bring the guilt
of shedding innocent blood upon themselves
and upon the city.

16. *This man* &c.] Lit. *There is not to
this man a sentence of death, i.e.* he is ac-

quitted by the princes and the congregation.

17. *the elders of the land*] The heads and
spokesmen of the congregation, who added
their approval after the princes who represented the king had given their decision.

19. *Thus might we procure* &c.] Rather,
And we should commit *a great evil against
our own souls; i.e.* by putting Jeremiah to
death, we should commit a sin which would
prove a great misfortune to ourselves.

20. This narrative of Urijah's fate was
no part of the speech of the elders, who
would not be likely to contrast the beha-
viour of the reigning king so unfavourably
with that of Hezekiah. Moreover, it would
have been a precedent, not for acquitting
Jeremiah, but for putting him to death.
Jeremiah, when he reduced the narrative
to writing, probably added this history to
shew the ferocity of Jehoiakim, and the
danger to which he had been himself exposed.

21 according to all the words of Jeremiah: and when Jehoiakim the king, with all his mighty men, and all the princes, heard his words, the king sought to put him to death: but when Urijah heard it, he was afraid, and fled, and went into Egypt; and
22 Jehoiakim the king sent men into Egypt, *namely*, Elnathan the
23 son of Achbor, and *certain* men with him into Egypt. And they fetched forth Urijah out of Egypt, and brought him unto Jehoiakim the king; who slew him with the sword, and cast his
24 dead body into the graves of the [1]common people. ¶ Nevertheless "the hand of Ahikam the son of Shaphan was with Jeremiah, that they should not give him into the hand of the people to put him to death.

u 2 Kin. 22. 12, 14.

CHAP. 27. IN the beginning of the reign of Jehoiakim the son of Josiah "king of Judah came this word unto Jeremiah from the
2 LORD, saying, Thus [2]saith the LORD to me; ¶ Make thee bonds and yokes, *b*and put them upon thy neck, and send them to the
3 king of Edom, and to the king of Moab, and to the king of the Ammonites, and to the king of Tyrus, and to the king of Zidon, by the hand of the messengers which come to Jerusalem unto
4 Zedekiah king of Judah; and command them [3]to say unto their masters, Thus saith the LORD of hosts, the God of Israel; Thus
5 shall ye say unto your masters; *c*I have made the earth, the man and the beast that *are* upon the ground, by my great power and by my outstretched arm, and *d*have given it unto whom it
6 seemed meet unto me. *e*And now have I given all these lands into the hand of Nebuchadnezzar the king of Babylon, *f*my servant; and *g*the beasts of the field have I given him also to
7 serve him. *h*And all nations shall serve him, and his son, and his son's son, *i*until the very time of his land come: *k*and then many nations and great kings shall serve themselves of him.
8 And it shall come to pass, *that* the nation and kingdom which will not serve the same Nebuchadnezzar the king of Babylon, and that will not put their neck under the yoke of the king of Babylon, that nation will I punish, saith the LORD,

a Se · v. r. 3, 12, 20. ch. 28. 1.
b ch. 28. 10. So Ezek. 4. 1. & 12. 3.

e Ps. 146. 6. Isai. 45. 12.
d Dan. 4. 17.
e ch. 28. 14.
f ch. 25. 9. Ezek. 29. 18, 20.
g Dan. 2. 38.
h 2 Chr. 36. 20.
i ch. 25. 12. Dan. 5. 26.
k ch. 25. 14.

[1] Heb. *sons of the people.*
[2] Or, *hath the LORD said.*
[3] Or, *concerning their masters, saying.*

---

21. *his mighty men*] The commanders of his army; the *princes* are the civil officers.

22. *Elnathan*] Possibly the king's father-in-law (2 K. xxiv. 8).

23. *out of Egypt*] As Jehoiakim was a vassal of Egypt, he would easily obtain the surrender of a man accused of treason.

24. *Ahikam*] See marg. ref. His son Gemariah lent Jeremiah his room for the public reading of Jehoiakim's roll, and another son Gedaliah was made governor of the land by the Chaldæans (xxxix. 14); the family probably shared the political views of Jeremiah.

XXVII.—XXIX. In these three chapters we see with what energy, and yet thoughtfulness, Jeremiah enforced the lessons of ch. xxv. These chapters belong to the first four years of Zedekiah.

The spelling of certain proper names in these chapters has led some to argue that they were revised and corrected in Ezra's time, if not by Ezra himself. Others think the fact of no importance whatever.

XXVII. 1. *of Jehoiakim*] Really, *of Zedekiah*, as the Syriac reads (see *v.* 3). In the LXX. the verse is wanting. Some scribe has confused the title of this chapter with that of ch. xxvi.

2. *yokes*] Two curved pieces of wood, the one put over the neck of the ox, the other under, and then fastened together by *bonds* or cords (cp. Ps. ii. 3). Cp. marg. reff.

3. *come*] Or, *are come.* The ambassadors of these five kings had probably come to Jerusalem to consult about forming a league to throw off the Babylonian supremacy. The attempt failed.

7. *his son, and his son's son*] Evil-Merodach and Nabonadius (see Dan. v. 1 note).

shall serve themselves of him] See marg. ref. After long servitude to the Persian and Median kings, the Selucidæ ruined the remains of Babylon.

with the sword, and with the famine, and with the pestilence,
9 until I have consumed them by his hand. Therefore hearken
not ye to your prophets, nor to your diviners, nor to your
[1]dreamers, nor to your enchanters, nor to your sorcerers, which
speak unto you, saying, Ye shall not serve the king of Babylon:

l ver. 14.

10 [l]for they prophesy a lie unto you, to remove you far from your
land; and that I should drive you out, and ye should perish.
11 But the nations that bring their neck under the yoke of the king
of Babylon, and serve him, those will I let remain still in their
own land, saith the LORD; and they shall till it, and dwell

m ch. 28. 1.
& 38. 17.

12 therein. ¶ I spake also to [m]Zedekiah king of Judah according to
all these words, saying, Bring your necks under the yoke of the

n Ezek. 18.
31.

13 king of Babylon, and serve him and his people, and live. [n]Why
will ye die, thou and thy people, by the sword, by the famine,
and by the pestilence, as the LORD hath spoken against the
14 nation that will not serve the king of Babylon? Therefore
hearken not unto the words of the prophets that speak unto
you, saying, Ye shall not serve the king of Babylon: for they

o ch 14. 14.
& 23. 21.
& 29. 8, 9.

15 prophesy [o]a lie unto you. For I have not sent them, saith the
LORD, yet they prophesy [2]a lie in my name; that I might drive
you out, and that ye might perish, ye, and the prophets that
16 prophesy unto you. ¶ Also I spake to the priests and to all this
people, saying, Thus saith the LORD; Hearken not to the words

p 2 Chr. 36.
7, 10.
ch. 28. 3.
Dan. 1. 2.

of your prophets that prophesy unto you, saying, Behold, [p]the
vessels of the LORD's house shall now shortly be brought again
17 from Babylon: for they prophesy a lie unto you. Hearken not
unto them; serve the king of Babylon, and live: wherefore
18 should this city be laid waste? But if they *be* prophets, and if
the word of the LORD be with them, let them now make intercession to the LORD of hosts, that the vessels which are left in
the house of the LORD, and *in* the house of the king of Judah,
19 and at Jerusalem, go not to Babylon. For thus saith the LORD

q 2 Kin. 25.
13, &c.
ch. 52. 17.

of hosts [q]concerning the pillars, and concerning the sea, and
concerning the bases, and concerning the residue of the vessels
20 that remain in this city, which Nebuchadnezzar king of Babylon

r 2 Kin. 24.
14, 15.
ch. 24. 1.

took not, when he carried away [r]captive Jeconiah the son of
Jehoiakim king of Judah from Jerusalem to Babylon, and all the
21 nobles of Judah and Jerusalem; yea, thus saith the LORD of
hosts the God of Israel, concerning the vessels that remain *in*
the house of the LORD, and *in* the house of the king of Judah

s 2 Kin. 25.
13.
2 Chr. 36. 18.
t 2 Chr. 36.
21.
ch. 29. 10.
u Ezra 1. 7.
a ch. 27. 1.

22 and of Jerusalem; they shall be [s]carried to Babylon, and there
shall they be until the day that I [t]visit them, saith the LORD;
then [u]will I bring them up, and restore them to this place.

CHAP. 28. AND [a]it came to pass the same year, in the beginning of
the reign of Zedekiah king of Judah, in the fourth year, *and* in
the fifth month, *that* Hananiah the son of Azur, the prophet,

---

[1] Heb. *dreams.* [2] Heb. *in a lie,* or, *lyingly.*

---

9. *dreamers*] Lit., as in marg. People
dream dreams for themselves, and go to
diviners to ask the explanation of them.
10. *to remove you far...*] That would be
the result of their vaticinations.
11. *nations...*] Rather, *the nation.*
13–15. Zedekiah was restless under the
Babylonian yoke, and the false prophets

found only too ready a hearing from him.
He is addressed in the plural because his
feelings were fully shared by the mass of
the officers of state and by the people.
XXVIII. 1. *in the beginning...Zedekiah*]
Probably a gloss put into the margin to explain "the same year," whence it has crept
into the text.

which *was* of Gibeon, spake unto me in the house of the LORD,
2 in the presence of the priests and of all the people, saying, Thus
speaketh the LORD of hosts, the God of Israel, saying, I have
3 broken *b*the yoke of the king of Babylon. *c*Within ¹two full
years will I bring again into this place all the vessels of the
LORD's house, that Nebuchadnezzar king of Babylon took
4 away from this place, and carried them to Babylon: and I will
bring again to this place Jeconiah the son of Jehoiakim king of
Judah, with all the ²captives of Judah, that went into Babylon,
saith the LORD: for I will break the yoke of the king of
5 Babylon. ¶Then the prophet Jeremiah said unto the prophet
Hananiah in the presence of the priests, and in the presence of
6 all the people that stood in the house of the LORD, even the
prophet Jeremiah said, *d*Amen: the LORD do so: the LORD
perform thy words which thou hast prophesied, to bring again
the vessels of the LORD's house, and all that is carried away
7 captive, from Babylon into this place. Nevertheless hear thou
now this word that I speak in thine ears, and in the ears of all
8 the people; The prophets that have been before me and before
thee of old prophesied both against many countries, and against
9 great kingdoms, of war, and of evil, and of pestilence. *e*The
prophet which prophesieth of peace, when the word of the
prophet shall come to pass, *then* shall the prophet be known,
10 that the LORD hath truly sent him. ¶Then Hananiah the prophet
took the *f*yoke from off the prophet Jeremiah's neck, and brake
11 it. And Hananiah spake in the presence of all the people, saying, Thus saith the LORD; Even so will I break the yoke of
Nebuchadnezzar king of Babylon *g*from the neck of all nations
within the space of two full years. And the prophet Jeremiah
went his way.

12 Then the word of the LORD came unto Jeremiah *the prophet*,
after that Hananiah the prophet had broken the yoke from off
13 the neck of the prophet Jeremiah, saying, Go and tell Hananiah,
saying, Thus saith the LORD; Thou hast broken the yokes of
14 wood; but thou shalt make for them yokes of iron. For thus
saith the LORD of hosts, the God of Israel; *h*I have put a yoke of
iron upon the neck of all these nations, that they may serve
Nebuchadnezzar king of Babylon; and they shall serve him:
15 and *i*I have given him the beasts of the field also. ¶Then said
the prophet Jeremiah unto Hananiah the prophet, Hear now,
Hananiah; The LORD hath not sent thee; but *k*thou makest
16 this people to trust in a lie. Therefore thus saith the LORD;

b ch. 27. 12.
c ch. 27. 16.

d 1 Kin.1.36.

e Deut.18.22.

f ch. 27. 2.

g ch. 27.7.

h Deut. 28.
48.
ch. 27. 7.

i ch. 27. 6.

k ch. 29. 31.
Ezek. 13. 22.

¹ Heb. *two years of days.*   ² Heb. *captivity.*

Gibeon] A city of priests (Josh. xxi. 17).
Hananiah was probably a priest as well as a
prophet. He chose either a Sabbath or a new
moon, that he might confront Jeremiah not
only *in the presence of the priests*, but also *of
all the people.* He used (*v*. 2) the solemn
formula which claims direct inspiration.

3. *Within two full years*] Lit. *In yet two
years even days.* Hananiah probably was
induced to fix this date by the expectation
that the confederacy then on foot would
defeat Nebuchadnezzar.

4. *Jeconiah*] Zedekiah not being popular,

the people would have preferred the young
king, who had not reigned long enough to
make enemies. Probably also Zedekiah
had started for Babylon (li. 59).

6–9. Jeremiah's own wishes concurred
with Hananiah's prediction, but asserts that
that prediction was at variance with the
language of the older prophets.

9. *then shall the prophet* &c.] Or, "shall
be known as the prophet whom the LORD
hath truly sent."

10. The multitude would see in Hananiah's act a symbol of deliverance.

i Deut. 13. 5.
ch. 29. 32.

Behold, I will cast thee from off the face of the earth: this year
thou shalt die, because thou hast taught [1]rebellion against the
17 LORD. ¶ So Hananiah the prophet died the same year in the
seventh month.

CHAP. 29. NOW these *are* the words of the letter that Jeremiah
the prophet sent from Jerusalem unto the residue of the elders
which were carried away captives, and to the priests, and to the
prophets, and to all the people whom Nebuchadnezzar had
2 carried away captive from Jerusalem to Babylon; (after that

a 2 Kin. 24.
12, &c.
ch. 24. 26.

*a*Jeconiah the king, and the queen, and the [2]eunuchs, the
princes of Judah and Jerusalem, and the carpenters, and the
3 smiths, were departed from Jerusalem;) by the hand of Elasah
the son of Shaphan, and Gemariah the son of Hilkiah, (whom
Zedekiah king of Judah sent unto Babylon to Nebuchadnezzar
4 king of Babylon) saying, Thus saith the LORD of hosts, the God
of Israel, unto all that are carried away captives, whom I have
caused to be carried away from Jerusalem unto Babylon:

b ver. 28.

5 ¶ *b* Build ye houses, and dwell *in them;* and plant gardens, and
6 eat the fruit of them; take ye wives, and beget sons and
daughters; and take wives for your sons, and give your
daughters to husbands, that they may bear sons and daughters;
7 that ye may be increased there, and not diminished. And seek
the peace of the city whither I have caused you to be carried

c Ezra 6. 10.
1 Tim. 2. 2.

away captives, *c*and pray unto the LORD for it: for in the peace
8 thereof shall ye have peace. ¶ For thus saith the LORD of hosts,
the God of Israel; Let not your prophets and your diviners,

d ch. 14. 14.
& 23. 21.
Eph. 5. *c*.
e ver. 31.
f 2 Chr. 36.
21, 22.
ch. 27. 22.

that *be* in the midst of you, *d*deceive you, neither hearken to
9 your dreams which ye cause to be dreamed. *e*For they prophesy [3]falsely unto you in my name: I have not sent them,
10 saith the LORD. For thus saith the LORD, That after *f*seventy

---

[1] Heb. *revolt.*   [2] Or, *chamberlains.*   [3] Heb. *in a lie.*

---

16. *I will cast thee*] Rather, **I send thee
away.** God had not sent Hananiah to prophesy, but He does now send him away to
die.

taught rebellion] As Nebuchadnezzar was
Jehovah's servant, to teach rebellion against
him was to teach *rebellion* against his Master.

XXIX. Appended to this history of the
struggle with the false prophets at home is
a letter addressed to the exiles at Babylon.
There was at Babylon as at Jerusalem
the same determination of the Jews never
to submit quietly to a foreign rule. This
Jeremiah sought to quell. His words found
credence, but not without resistance on the
part of the false prophets.

1. *the residue of the elders*] *i.e.* such of the
elders as were still alive.

2. *the queen*] The queen-mother.

3. *Elasah*] Probably brother of Ahikam
(xxvi. 24), and therefore an acceptable person at the Chaldæan court. As Zedekiah
had to go in person to Babylon in his fourth
year (li. 59), this embassy was probably
sent two or three years earlier. Its date,
however, was subsequent to the vision in
ch. xxiv. It is appended therefore to ch.

xxviii., not as later in point of time, but
because of the similarity of subject.

4–7. As the exile was God's doing for
their good, they were to make the best of
their position, and acquire wealth and influence; whereas if they were always rest-
lessly looking out for the opportunity of returning home, they would rapidly fall into
poverty and dwindle away.

7. *seek the peace of the city...*] Not only
because their welfare for seventy years was
bound up with that of Babylon, but because
it would have degraded their whole moral
nature to have lived as conspirators, banded
together against the country that was for
the time their home.

8. *your prophets and your diviners*] The
evils from which the people had suffered so
cruelly at home followed them in their
exile.

dreams which ye cause to be dreamed] As
long as there was a market for dreams, so
long there would be plenty of impostors to
supply them.

10. *after seventy years*] Lit., *according to
the measure of the fulfilment of seventy years
for Babylon.* The seventy years (xxv. 11

years be accomplished at Babylon I will visit you, and perform my good word toward you, in causing you to return to this

11 place. For I know the thoughts that I think toward you, saith the LORD, thoughts of peace, and not of evil, to give you an

12 [1]expected end. Then shall ye [g]call upon me, and ye shall go

13 and pray unto me, and I will hearken unto you. And [h]ye shall seek me, and find me, when ye shall search for me [i]with all your

14 heart. And [k]I will be found of you, saith the LORD: and I will turn away your captivity, and [l]I will gather you from all the nations, and from all the places whither I have driven you, saith the LORD; and I will bring you again into the place whence I

15 caused you to be carried away captive. ¶ Because ye have said,

16 The LORD hath raised us up prophets in Babylon; *know* that thus saith the LORD of the king that sitteth upon the throne of David, and of all the people that dwelleth in this city, *and* of your

17 brethren that are not gone forth with you into captivity; Thus saith the LORD of hosts; Behold, I will send upon them the [m]sword, the famine, and the pestilence, and will make them like

18 [n]vile figs, that cannot be eaten, they are so evil. And I will persecute them with the sword, with the famine, and with the pestilence, and [o]will deliver them to be removed to all the kingdoms of the earth, [2]to be [p]a curse, and an astonishment, and an hissing, and a reproach, among all the nations whither I have

19 driven them: because they have not hearkened to my words, saith the LORD, which [q]I sent unto them by my servants the prophets, rising up early and sending *them;* but ye would not

20 hear, saith the LORD. ¶ Hear ye therefore the word of the LORD, all ye of the captivity, whom I have sent from Jerusalem to

21 Babylon: Thus saith the LORD of hosts, the God of Israel, of Ahab the son of Kolaiah, and of Zedekiah the son of Maaseiah, which prophesy a lie unto you in my name; Behold, I will deliver them into the hand of Nebuchadrezzar king of Babylon;

22 and he shall slay them before your eyes; [r]and of them shall be taken up a curse by all the captivity of Judah which *are* in Babylon, saying, The LORD make thee like Zedekiah and like

23 Ahab, [s]whom the king of Babylon roasted in the fire; because [t]they have committed villany in Israel, and have committed

Marginal references:
[g] Dan. 9. 3.
[h] Lev. 26. 39, 40, &c. Deut. 30. 1.
[i] ch. 24. 7.
[k] Deut. 4. 7. Ps. 32. 6. Isai. 55. 6.
[l] ch. 23. 3.
[m] ch. 24. 10.
[n] ch. 24. 8.
[o] Deut. 28. 25. 2 Chr. 29. 8. ch. 15. 4.
[p] ch. 26. 6.
[q] ch. 25. 4. & 32. 33.
[r] See Gen. 48. 20. Isai. 65. 15.
[s] Dan. 3. 6.
[t] ch. 23. 14.

[1] Heb. *end and expectation.*   [2] Heb. *for a curse.*

note) are primarily the length of the Babylonian empire, and only in a secondary sense that of the Jewish exile.

11. *an expected end*] Rather, *a future and a hope.* The nation shall not come to an end; the exile shall be followed by a restoration.

14. *turn away your captivity*] Or, "restore your prosperity."

16–20. These verses are not in the LXX. But the text of the LXX. is here throughout so brief and confused as to be explicable only on the supposition, that it represents what was left behind in Egypt when Jeremiah died, copied probably with extreme haste, and with no opportunity of careful collation afterwards. On the other hand the Hebrew text represents no hurried transcript, but the original manuscript, and is especially trustworthy in the case of these letters sent to Babylon (see also ch. li.), be-

cause the originals of them would be available for collation with the text preserved by Jeremiah himself. The verses were probably intended to allay excitement in Babylon consequent upon the knowledge that the representatives of various kings were assembled at that very time at Jerusalem to form a coalition against Babylon (xxvii. 3).

17. *vile*] The word does not occur elsewhere, but comes from a root signifying to shudder, and thus has an intense meaning.

22. *a curse*] There is a play here of words. which probably was the cause why the death of these men passed into a proverb. One of them was named ben-Kolaiah; and they are to be made a curse (*kᵉlâlâh*), because Nebuchadnezzar had roasted (*kâlâh*) them. Cp. marg. ref. note.

23. *villany*] Elsewhere **folly**, in the sense of *lewdness* (Judg. xx. 6), *unchastity.*

adultery with their neighbours' wives, and have spoken lying words in my name, which I have not commanded them; even I
24 know, and *am* a witness, saith the LORD. ¶ *Thus* shalt thou also speak to Shemaiah the [1]Nehelamite, saying, Thus speaketh the
25 LORD of hosts, the God of Israel, saying, Because thou hast sent letters in thy name unto all the people that *are* at Jerusalem, *u*and to Zephaniah the son of Maaseiah the priest, and to all the
26 priests, saying, The LORD hath made thee priest in the stead of Jehoiada the priest, that ye should be *x*officers in the house of the LORD, for every man *that is* *y*mad, and maketh himself a prophet, that thou shouldest *z*put him in prison, and in the
27 stocks. Now therefore why hast thou not reproved Jeremiah
28 of Anathoth, which maketh himself a prophet to you? For therefore he sent unto us *in* Babylon, saying, This *captivity is* long: *a*build ye houses, and dwell *in them;* and plant gardens,
29 and eat the fruit of them. And Zephaniah the priest read this
30 letter in the ears of Jeremiah the prophet. ¶ Then came the word
31 of the LORD unto Jeremiah, saying, Send to all them of the captivity, saying, Thus saith the LORD concerning Shemaiah the Nehelamite: Because that Shemaiah hath prophesied unto you,
32 *b*and I sent him not, and he caused you to trust in a lie: therefore thus saith the LORD; Behold, I will punish Shemaiah the Nehelamite, and his seed: he shall not have a man to dwell among this people; neither shall he behold the good that I will do for my people, saith the LORD; *c*because he hath taught [2]rebellion against the LORD.

CHAP. 30. THE word that came to Jeremiah from the LORD, say-
2 ing, Thus speaketh the LORD God of Israel, saying, ¶ Write thee
3 all the words that I have spoken unto thee in a book. For, lo, the days come, saith the LORD, that *a*I will bring again the cap-

Marginal references:
n 2 Kin. 25. 18.
ch. 21. 1.
x ch. 20. 1.
y 2 Kin.9.11.
Acts 26. 24.
z ch. 20. 2.

a ver. 5.

b ch. 28. 15.

c ch. 28. 16.

a ver. 18.
Ezek. 39. 25.
Amos 9. 14.

[1] Or, *dreamer.*   [2] Heb. *revolt.*

24–29. A narrative shewing the effects of Jeremiah's letter. Shemaiah the leader of the false prophets wrote to Zephaniah, urging him to restrain the prophet's zeal with the prison and the stocks.

24. *to Shemaiah*] Rather, **concerning.**

the Nehelamite] Not as in the margin; but *one belonging to the village of Nehlam* (unknown).

26. *officers*] *Deputy High-Priests* who had the oversight of the Temple.

mad] See 2 K. ix. 11 note. Many of the symbolical actions of the prophets, such as that of Jeremiah going about with a yoke on his neck, would be mocked at by the irreverent as passing the line between prophecy and madness.

prison] Rather, **the stocks** (xx. 2).

the stocks] Rather, **collar.**

28. *This* captivity is *long*] Rather, **It is long.** God's anger, their punishment, the exile, the time necessary for their repentance—all is long to men who will never live to see their country again.

XXX.–XXXIII. In these four chapters, not all written at the same time, are gathered together whatsoever God had revealed to Jeremiah of happier import for the Jewish people. This subject is "the New Covenant." In contrast then with the rolls of Jehoiakim and Zedekiah, we here have one containing the nation's hope. A considerable portion was written in the tenth year of Zedekiah, when famine and pestilence were busy in the city, its capture daily more imminent, and the prophet himself in prison. Yet in this sad pressure of earthly troubles Jeremiah could bid his countrymen look courageously onward to the fulfilment of those hopes, which had so constantly in his darkest hours comforted the heart and nerved the arm of the Jew. The roll consists of three portions: (1) "a triumphal hymn of Israel's salvation," chs. xxx., xxxi.; (2) ch. xxxii.; and (3) ch. xxxiii.

XXX. 2. *Write...in a book*] To be read and meditated upon by them in private. This makes it exceedingly probable that the date of these two chapters was also the tenth year of Zedekiah, immediately after the purchase of the field from Hanameel.

all the words] *i.e.* the roll was to be a summary of whatever of hope and mercy had been contained in previous predictions.

tivity of my people Israel and Judah, saith the LORD : [b]and I
will cause them to return to the land that I gave to their fathers,
4 and they shall possess it. ¶ And these *are* the words that the
5 LORD spake concerning Israel and concerning Judah. For thus
saith the LORD ; ¶ We have heard a voice of trembling, [1]of fear,
6 and not of peace. Ask ye now, and see whether [2]a man doth
travail with child ? wherefore do I see every man with his hands
on his loins, [c]as a woman in travail, and all faces are turned into
7 paleness ? [d]Alas ! for that day *is* great, [e]so that none *is* like it :
it *is* even the time of Jacob's trouble ; but he shall be saved out
8 of it. For it shall come to pass in that day, saith the LORD of
hosts, *that* I will break his yoke from off thy neck, and will burst
thy bonds, and strangers shall no more serve themselves of him :
9 but they shall serve the LORD their God, and [f]David their king,
10 whom I will [g]raise up unto them. ¶ Therefore [h]fear thou not,
O my servant Jacob, saith the LORD; neither be dismayed, O
Israel : for, lo, I will save thee from afar, and thy seed [i]from
the land of their captivity ; and Jacob shall return, and shall be
11 in rest, and be quiet, and none shall make *him* afraid. For I *am*
with thee, saith the LORD, to save thee : [k]though I make a full
end of all nations whither I have scattered thee, [l]yet will I not
make a full end of thee : but I will correct thee [m]in measure,
12 and will not leave thee altogether unpunished. ¶ For thus saith
the LORD, [n]Thy bruise *is* incurable, *and* thy wound *is* grievous.
13 *There is* none to plead thy cause, [3]that thou mayest be bound
14 up : [o]thou hast no healing medicines. [p]All thy lovers have forgotten thee ; they seek thee not ; for I have wounded thee with
the wound [q]of an enemy, with the chastisement [r]of a cruel one,
for the multitude of thine iniquity ; [s]*because* thy sins were in-
15 creased. Why [t]cryest thou for thine affliction ? thy sorrow *is*
incurable for the multitude of thine iniquity : *because* thy sins
16 were increased, I have done these things unto thee. Therefore

Marginal references:
[b] ch. 16. 15.
[c] ch. 4. 31.
[d] Joel 2. 11.
Amos 5. 18.
Zeph. 1. 14.
[e] Dan. 12. 1.
[f] Isai. 55. 3.
Ezek. 34. 23.
Hos. 3. 5.
[g] Luke 1. 69.
Acts 2. 30.
[h] Isai. 41. 13.
& 44. 2.
ch. 46. 27.
[i] ch. 3. 18.
[k] Amos 9. 8.
[l] ch. 4. 27.
[m] Ps. 6. 1.
Isai. 27. 8.
[n] 2 Chr. 36.
16.
ch. 15. 18.
[o] ch. 8. 22.
[p] Lam. 1. 2.
[q] Job 13. 24.
[r] Job 30. 21.
[s] ch. 5. 6.
[t] ch. 15. 18.

[1] Or, there is *fear, and not peace.*
[2] Heb. *a male.*
[3] Heb. *for binding up,* or, *pressing.*

---

5. Better, as in the marg. The prophet
places his hearers in the centre of Babylon,
and describes it as convulsed with terror as
the armies of Cyrus draw near. *The voice of
trembling* is the war-cry of the advancing
host : while *fear and no peace* implies that
even among the exiles there is only alarm at
the prospect of the city, where they had
so long dwelt, being destroyed.

7. *that day*] *i.e.* the day of the capture of
Babylon.

it is *even the time of Jacob's trouble*] Rather, *and it is a time of trouble to Jacob, i.e.*
of anxiety to the Jews ; for the usages of
war were so brutal that they would be in
danger when the enemy made their assault.

8. *bonds*] See xxvii. 2 note.

shall no more serve themselves] *i.e.* shall no
more exact forced labour of him (xxii. 13).

9. *David their king*] See xxiii. 5, 6 ; *i.e.*
Messiah.

10, 11. These two verses are considered
by some very similar in style to the last
twenty-seven chapters of Isaiah. The contrast, however, between the full end made

with the heathen, and the certainty that
Israel shall never so perish, is one of Jeremiah's most common topics.

11. *in measure*] See x. 24 note.

12. *incurable*] **Mortal,** fatal.

13. *that thou mayest be bound up*] Others
put a stop after " cause," and translate, **For
binding thy wound, healing plaister thou
hast none.**

14. *for the multitude* &c.] Or,

Because of *the multitude of thine iniquity,*
Because thy sins **are strong.**

Judah's lovers are the nations which once
sought her alliance (see xxii. 20, xxvii. 3).

15. Translate—

Why criest thou because of thy breaking ?
Because thy pain is grievous ?
Because of *the multitude of thine iniquity,*
Because thy sins **are strong,**
I have done these things unto thee.

16. *Therefore*] *i.e.* Because thou hast undergone thy punishment and cried out in
consciousness of thy guilt.

" Ex. 23. 22.
Isai. 33 i.
ch. 10. 25.
all they that devour thee "shall be devoured; and all thine adversaries, every one of them, shall go into captivity; and they
that spoil thee shall be a spoil, and all that prey upon thee will
ˣ ch. 33. 6.
17 I give for a prey. ˣFor I will restore health unto thee, and I
will heal thee of thy wounds, saith the LORD; because they called
thee an Outcast, *saying*, This *is* Zion, whom no man seeketh after.
ʸ ver. 3.
ch. 33. 7.
ᶻ Ps. 102. 13.
18 ¶ Thus saith the LORD; Behold, ʸI will bring again the captivity
of Jacob's tents, and ᶻhave mercy on his dwellingplaces; and
the city shall be builded upon her own ¹heap, and the palace
ᵃ Isai. 35. 10.
ch. 31. 4.
ᵇ Zech. 10. 8.
19 shall remain after the manner thereof. And ᵃout of them shall
proceed thanksgiving and the voice of them that make merry:
ᵇand I will multiply them, and they shall not be few; I will also
20 glorify them, and they shall not be small. Their children also
ᶜ Isai. 1. 26.
shall be ᶜas aforetime, and their congregation shall be established before me, and I will punish all that oppress them.
ᵈ Gen. 49.10.
ᵉ Num. 16. 5.
21 And their nobles shall be of themselves, ᵈand their governor
shall proceed from the midst of them; and I will ᵉcause him to
draw near, and he shall approach unto me: for who *is* this that
22 engaged his heart to approach unto me? saith the LORD. And
ᶠ ch. 24. 7.
Ezek. 11. 20.
ᵍ ch. 23. 19.
23 ye shall be ᶠmy people, and I will be your God. ¶ Behold, the
ᵍwhirlwind of the LORD goeth forth with fury, a ²continuing
whirlwind: it shall ³fall with pain upon the head of the wicked.
24 The fierce anger of the LORD shall not return, until he have
done *it*, and until he have performed the intents of his heart:
ʰ Gen. 49. 1.
ʰin the latter days ye shall consider it.

ᵃ ch. 30. 24.
ᵇ ch. 30. 22.
CHAP. 31. AT ᵃthe same time, saith the LORD, ᵇwill I be the God
2 of all the families of Israel, and they shall be my people. Thus
saith the LORD, The people *which were* left of the sword found
ᶜ Num.10.33.
Deut. 1. 33.
Ps. 95. 11.
Isai. 63. 14.
grace in the wilderness; *even* Israel, when ᶜI went to cause him
3 to rest. The LORD hath appeared ⁴of old unto me, *saying*, Yea,

¹ Or, *little hill.*   ² Heb. *cutting.*   ³ Or, *remain.*   ⁴ Heb. *from afar.*

---

17. *restore health*] Or, "apply a bandage"
(viii. 22 note). For *they called* read "they
call."
18–22. The prophet speaks of Judah as
the type of the Church, with Immanuel as
her king.
18. *tents*] The word suggests that a considerable portion of the people were still
nomads.
the city...the palace] Or, *each city...each
palace.* The *heap* means an artificial mount
to keep the city out of the reach of inunda-
tions, and to increase the strength of the
fortifications.
shall remain after the manner thereof]
Rather, *shall* **be inhabited** *according to its
rights, i.e.* suitably.
19. *them*] *i.e.* the city and palace. Render
the last words, **become few...become mean,**
i.e. despised, lightly esteemed.
21. Translate, *And his* glorious one *shall
spring from himself, and his ruler shall go
forth from his midst :...who is this that hath
pledged his heart, i.e.* hath staked his life,
to draw near unto Me? i.e. "Messiah shall be
revealed to them out of their own midst."
He can draw near unto God without fear of
death, because being in the form of God,

and Himself God, He can claim equality
with God (Phil. ii. 6).
22. This is the effect of Messiah's ministry. Men cannot become God's people, till
there has been revealed one of themselves,
a man, Who can approach unto God, as
being also God, and so can bridge over the
gulf which separates the finite from the Infinite.
23, 24. Cp. marg. ref. These verses would
more appropriately be attached to the next
Chapter, for which they form a suitable
introduction.
XXXI. 1. *At the same time*] Lit. **At
that time,** *i.e.* "the latter days" mentioned
in xxx. 24.
2. *The people* which were *left of the sword*]
A promise of the restoration of the ten tribes
to their land.
the wilderness] Either the desert which
lay between Assyria and Palestine; or
more probably an allusion to the wilderness
of Mount Sinai.
found grace...rest] Rather, "shall certainly find grace ; *I will go to give Israel rest.*
3. *of old*] **From afar** (marg.). See xxx.
10. To the Jew God was enthroned in
Zion, and thus when His mercy was shewn

[d]I have loved thee with [e]an everlasting love: therefore [1]with
4 lovingkindness have I [f]drawn thee. Again [g]I will build thee,
and thou shalt be built, O virgin of Israel: thou shalt again be
adorned with thy [h][2]tabrets, and shalt go forth in the dances of
5 them that make merry. [i]Thou shalt yet plant vines upon the
mountains of Samaria: the planters shall plant, and shall [3]eat
6 them as common things. For there shall be a day, that the
watchmen upon the mount Ephraim shall cry, [k]Arise ye, and
7 let us go up to Zion unto the LORD our God. ¶ For thus saith
the LORD; [l]Sing with gladness for Jacob, and shout among the
chief of the nations: publish ye, praise ye, and say, O LORD,
8 save thy people, the remnant of Israel. Behold, I will bring
them [m]from the north country, and [n]gather them from the
coasts of the earth, and with them the blind and the lame, the
woman with child and her that travaileth with child together:
9 a great company shall return thither. [o]They shall come with
weeping, and with [4]supplications will I lead them: I will cause
them to walk [p]by the rivers of waters in a straight way, wherein
they shall not stumble: for I am a father to Israel, and Ephraim
10 is my [q]firstborn. ¶ Hear the word of the LORD, O ye nations,
and declare it in the isles afar off, and say, He that scattered
Israel [r]will gather him, and keep him, as a shepherd doth his
11 flock. For [s]the LORD hath redeemed Jacob, and ransomed him
12 [t]from the hand of him that was stronger than he. Therefore
they shall come and sing in [u]the height of Zion, and shall flow
together to [x]the goodness of the LORD, for wheat, and for wine,
and for oil, and for the young of the flock and of the herd: and
their soul shall be as a [y]watered garden; [z]and they shall not
13 sorrow any more at all. Then shall the virgin rejoice in the
dance, both young men and old together: for I will turn their

[d] Mal. 1. 2.
[e] Rom. 11. 28, 29.
[f] Hos. 11. 4.
[g] ch. 33. 7.
[h] Ex. 15. 20. Ps. 149. 3.
[i] Isai. 65. 21. Amos 9. 14.
[k] Isai. 2. 3. Mic. 4. 2.
[l] Isai. 12. 5.

[m] ch. 3. 12.
[n] Ezek. 20. 34. 41.

[o] Ps. 126. 5. ch. 50. 4.

[p] Isai. 35. 8.

[q] Ex. 4. 22.

[r] Isai. 40. 11. Ezek. 34. 12, 13, 14.
[s] Isai. 41. 23.
[t] Isai. 49. 24.
[u] Ezek. 17. 23.
[x] Hos. 3. 5.

[y] Isai. 58. 11.
[z] Isai. 35. 10. Rev. 21. 4.

---

[1] Or, have I extended loving kindness unto thee.
[2] Or, timbrels.
[3] Heb. profane them, Deut. 20. 6. & 28. 30.
[4] Or, favours, Zech. 12. 10.

---

unto the exiles in Assyria it came from a distant region (2 Chr. vi. 20, 38).

with lovingkindness &c.] Rather, **I have continued** lovingkindness **unto thee.**

4. O virgin of Israel] i.e. the whole people (cp. xiv. 17 note).

5. shall eat them as common things] Rather, **shall eat the fruit.** Lit. as in marg. For three years the fruit of a newly planted tree was not to be touched, that of the fourth year was consecrated to God, but on the fifth year it was profane, i.e. unconsecrated, and so might be applied to the owner's use (Lev. xix. 23–25).

6. This verse anticipates a time when the schism caused by Jeroboam is over. Ephraimite watchmen equally with the tribe of Judah watch for the new moon that they may go up to Jerusalem to keep the appointed Feasts.

7. among] Or, **because of.** Israel is the chief or, first of the nations (Deut. xxvi. 19), and Jehovah summons mankind to rejoice, because the remnant of Israel is about to be restored to its old position.

8. the coasts of the earth] See vi. 22 note.
thither] Really, **hither.** Not to the

North country, but to Palestine, where Jeremiah wrote. A company is the word constantly used of Israel at the Exodus (Ex. xvi. 3) as an organized community.

9. weeping] For joy, not for sorrow.
supplications] The conviction that God is guiding them, encourages them to pray.
Ephraim is My firstborn] The house of Joseph is thus to be restored to its old pre-eminence.

10. the isles] The coast land of the Mediterranean, used here to shew that the most distant countries are to hear and marvel at Israel's wonderful restoration.

12. Omit together. The ten tribes are to flow like a river down from Zion's height to their own land, there to reap the rich produce of their tillage. In Jerusalem they would be occupied with religious duties, but after these are rendered to God, they are to disperse each to his own fields.
sorrow] Rather, **languish,** pine.

13. Both gives the idea of the men dancing, which is incorrect. Except at a religious solemnity (2 Sam. vi. 14), dancing was confined to women. Render and young men and old rejoice together.

mourning into joy, and will comfort them, and make them rejoice
14 from their sorrow. And I will satiate the soul of the priests
with fatness, and my people shall be satisfied with my goodness,
15 saith the LORD. ¶Thus saith the LORD; [a]A voice was heard in
[b]Ramah, lamentation, *and* bitter weeping; Rahel weeping for
her children refused to be comforted for her children, because
16 [c]they *were* not. Thus saith the LORD; Refrain thy voice from
weeping, and thine eyes from tears: for thy work shall be
rewarded, saith the LORD; and [d]they shall come again from
17 the land of the enemy. And there is hope in thine end, saith
the LORD, that thy children shall come again to their own
18 border. ¶I have surely heard Ephraim bemoaning himself
thus; Thou hast chastised me, and I was chastised, as a bullock
unaccustomed *to the yoke:* [e]turn thou me, and I shall be turned;
19 for thou *art* the LORD my God. Surely [f]after that I was turned,
I repented; and after that I was instructed, I smote upon *my*
thigh: I was ashamed, yea, even confounded, because I did
20 bear the reproach of my youth. *Is* Ephraim my dear son? *is*
he a pleasant child? for since I spake against him, I do earnestly remember him still: [g]therefore my bowels [1]are troubled
for him; [h]I will surely have mercy upon him, saith the LORD.
21 ¶Set thee up waymarks, make thee high heaps: [i]set thine heart
toward the highway, *even* the way *which* thou wentest: turn
22 again, O virgin of Israel, turn again to these thy cities. How
long wilt thou [k]go about, O thou [l]backsliding daughter? for
the LORD hath created a new thing in the earth, A woman
23 shall compass a man. ¶Thus saith the LORD of hosts, the

Marginal references:
[a] Matt. 2. 17, 18.
[b] Josh. 18. 25.
[c] Gen. 42. 13.
[d] ver. 4, 5. Ezra 1. 5. Hos. 1. 11.
[e] Lam. 5. 21.
[f] Deut. 30. 2.
[g] Deut. 32. 36. Isai. 63. 15. Hos. 11. 8.
[h] Isai. 57. 18. Hos. 14. 4.
[i] ch. 50. 5.
[k] ch. 2. 18.
[l] ch. 3. 6, 8.

[1] Heb. *sound.*

15—22. The religious character of the restoration of the ten tribes. Chastisement brought repentance, and with it forgiveness; therefore God decrees their restoration.

15. Ramah, mentioned because of its nearness to Jerusalem, from which it was distant about five miles. As the mother of three tribes, Benjamin, Ephraim, and Manasseh, Rachel is regarded as the mother of the whole ten. This passage is quoted by St. Matthew (marg. ref.) as a type. In Jeremiah it is a poetical figure representing in a dramatic form the miserable condition of the kingdom of Ephraim devastated by the sword of the Assyrians.

16. Rachel's work had been that of bearing and bringing up children, and by their death she was deprived of the joy for which she had laboured: but by their being restored to her she will receive her wages.

17. *in thine end*] *i.e.* for thy time to come (see xxix. 11 note).

18. *as a bullock unaccustomed* to the yoke] Lit. *like an untaught calf.* Cp. Hos. x. 11 note. Ephraim, like an untrained steer, had resisted Jehovah's will.

19. *after that I was turned*] *i.e. after I had turned* away from Thee. In *v.* 18 it has the sense of turning to God.

instructed] Brought to my senses by suffering. The smiting upon the thigh is a sign of sorrow. Cp. Ezek. xxi. 17.

the reproach of my youth] *i.e.* the shame brought upon me by sins of my youth.

20. Moved to compassion by Ephraim's lamentation, Jehovah shews Himself as tender and ready to forgive as parents are their spoiled (rather, **darling**) child.

for...him] Or, "that so often as I speak concerning him," *i.e.* his punishment.

my bowels are troubled] The metaphor expresses the most tender internal emotion.

21. *waymarks*] See 2 K. xxiii. 17 note.

high heaps] Or, **signposts**, pillars to point out the way.

set thine heart] Not *set thy affection,* but *turn thy thoughts* and attention (in Hebrew the heart is the seat of the intellect) *to the highway,* even *the way* by which *thou wentest.*

22. Israel instead of setting itself to return hesitates, and goes hither and thither in a restless mood. To encourage it God gives the sign following.

A woman shall compass a man] *i.e.* the *female shall protect the strong man;* the weaker nature that needs help will surround the stronger with loving and fostering care. This expresses a new relation of Israel to the Lord, a new Covenant, which the Lord will make with His people (*v.* 31 seq.). The Fathers saw in these words a prophecy of the miraculous conception of our Lord by the Virgin.

God of Israel; As yet they shall use this speech in the land of Judah and in the cities thereof, when I shall bring again their captivity; *m*The LORD bless thee, O habitation of justice, and 24 *n*mountain of holiness. And there shall dwell in Judah itself, and *o*in all the cities thereof together, husbandmen, and they 25 that go forth with flocks. For I have satiated the weary soul, 26 and I have replenished every sorrowful soul. Upon this I 27 awaked, and beheld; and my sleep was sweet unto me. ¶ Behold, the days come, saith the LORD, that *p*I will sow the house of Israel and the house of Judah with the seed of man, 28 and with the seed of beast. And it shall come to pass, that like as I have *q*watched over them, *r*to pluck up, and to break down, and to throw down, and to destroy, and to afflict; so will 29 I watch over them, *s*to build, and to plant, saith the LORD. *t*In those days they shall say no more, The fathers have eaten a 30 sour grape, and the children's teeth are set on edge. *u*But every one shall die for his own iniquity: every man that eateth 31 the sour grape, his teeth shall be set on edge. ¶ Behold, the *x*days come, saith the LORD, that I will make a new covenant 32 with the house of Israel, and with the house of Judah: not according to the covenant that I made with their fathers in the day that *y*I took them by the hand to bring them out of the land of Egypt; which my covenant they brake, ¹although I was 33 an husband unto them, saith the LORD: *z*but this shall be the covenant that I will make with the house of Israel; After those

m Ps. 122.
5, 6, 7, 8.
Isai. 1. 26.
n Zech. 8. 3.
o ch. 33. 12.

p Ezek. 36.
9, 10, 11.
Hos. 2. 23.
Zech. 10. 9.
q ch. 44. 27.
r ch. 1. 10.

s ch. 24. 6.
t Ezek. 18.
2, 3.
u Gal. 6. 5.

x ch. 32. 40.
Ezek. 37. 26.
Heb. 10. 16.

y Deut. 1. 31.

z ch. 32. 40.

¹ Or, should I have continued an husband unto them?

---

23. As yet] Or, **Again**, once more. The prophet now turns to Judah. By the mountain of holiness is meant not the Temple only, but all Jerusalem, of which the Temple was the most sacred spot, and that by which all the rest was made holy.

24. go forth] go **about**. Judah shall have its settled population and fixed abodes; and shepherds shall move about with their flocks, wherever pasture is to be found.

25. sorrowful] Or, **languishing** (v. 12).

26. The prophet, seeming to himself to awake and look up in the midst of his sleep (whether ecstatic or not we cannot tell), rejoiced in a revelation so entirely consolatory, and unlike his usual message of woe.

27-34. The prophet shews that the happiness of Israel and Judah, united in one prosperous nation, will rest upon the consciousness that their chastisement has been the result of sins which they have themselves committed, and that God's Covenant depends not upon external sanctions, but upon a renewed heart.

27. So rapid shall be the increase that it shall seem as if children and young cattle sprang up out of the ground.

29, 30. a sour grape] Better, sour **grapes**. The idea that Jeremiah and Ezekiel (marg. ref.) modified the terms of the second Commandment arises from a mistaken exegesis of their words. Cp. xxxii. 18; Deut. xxiv. 16. The obdurate Jews made it a reproach to the Divine justice that the nation was to

be sorely visited for Manasseh's sin. But this was only because generation after generation had, instead of repenting, repeated the sins of that evil time, and even in a worse form. Justice must at length have its course. The acknowledgment that each man died for his own iniquity was a sign of their return to a more just and right state of feeling.

31. A time is foretold which shall be to the nation as marked an epoch as was the Exodus. God at Sinai made a Covenant with His people, of which the sanctions were material, or (where spiritual) materially understood. Necessarily therefore the Mosaic Church was temporary, but the sanctions of Jeremiah's Church are spiritual —written in the heart—and therefore it must take the place of the former Covenant (Heb. viii. 13), and must last for ever. The prophecy was fulfilled when those Jews who accepted Jesus of Nazareth as the Messiah, expanded the Jewish into the Christian Church.

32. although &c.] i.e. although as their husband [or, "lord " (Baal, cp. Hos. ii. 16)] I had lawful authority over them. The translation in Heb. viii. 9 agrees with the LXX. here, but the balance of authority is in favour of the A. V.

33. The old Law could be broken (v. 32); to remedy this God gives, not a new Law, but a new power to the old Law. It used to be a mere code of morals, external to man, and obeyed as a duty: in Christianity

a Ps. 40. 8.
Ezek. 11.
19, 20.
2 Cor. 3. 3
b ch. 24. 7.

c Isai. 54. 13.
John 6. 45.
1 John 2. 20.
d ch. 33. 8.
Mic. 7. 18.
Acts 10. 43.
Rom. 11. 27.
e Gen. 1. 16.
Ps. 72. 5.
f Isai. 51. 15.
g ch. 10. 16.
h Ps. 148. 6.
Isai. 54. 9.
i ch. 33. 22.

k Neh. 3. 1.
Zech. 14. 10.
l Ezek. 40. 8.

m 2 Chr. 23.
15.
Neh. 3. 28.
n Joel 3. 17.

a 2 Kin. 25.
1, 2.
ch. 39. 1.

days, saith the LORD, *a*I will put my law in their inward parts, and write it in their hearts; *b*and will be their God, and they 34 shall be my people. And they shall teach no more every man his neighbour, and every man his brother, saying, Know the LORD: for *c*they shall all know me, from the least of them unto the greatest of them, saith the LORD: for *d*I will forgive 35 their iniquity, and I will remember their sin no more. ¶Thus saith the LORD, *e*which giveth the sun for a light by day, *and* the ordinances of the moon and of the stars for a light by night, 36 which divideth *f*the sea when the waves thereof roar; *g*The LORD of hosts *is* his name: *h*if those ordinances depart from before me, saith the LORD, *then* the seed of Israel also shall 37 cease from being a nation before me for ever. Thus saith the LORD; *i*If heaven above can be measured, and the foundations of the earth searched out beneath, I will also cast off all the seed of Israel for all that they have done, saith the LORD. 38 ¶Behold, the days come, saith the LORD, that the city shall be built to the LORD *k*from the tower of Hananeel unto the gate of 39 the corner. And *l*the measuring line shall yet go forth over against it upon the hill Gareb, and shall compass about to 40 Goath. And the whole valley of the dead bodies, and of the ashes, and all the fields unto the brook of Kidron, *m*unto the corner of the horse gate toward the east, *n*shall be* holy unto the LORD; it shall not be plucked up, nor thrown down any more for ever.

CHAP. 32. The word that came to Jeremiah from the LORD *a*in the tenth year of Zedekiah king of Judah, which *was* the eighteenth

---

it becomes an inner force, shaping man's character from within.

34. *I will forgive their iniquity*] The foundation of the new Covenant is the free forgiveness of sins (cp. Matt. i. 21). It is the sense of this full unmerited love which so affects the heart as to make obedience henceforward an inner necessity.

35. *divideth* &c.] Rather, **stirreth up** *the sea so that its waves roar*.

36. *If those*] **If these.** From the uniformity of God's operations in the material world, the prophet deduces the certainty of a similar uniformity in God's dealings with man in things spiritual.

a nation] **A people.** Israel has long ceased to be a nation, but it still exists as a numerous, influential, and distinct people. In Matt. xxviii. 19, 20 Jeremiah's prophecy receives its Christian application, and Israel becomes the Church, with the promise of perpetual existence. It has no national existence, but its members ought to be a strongly marked people, refusing to be merged in the world, while everywhere they pervade and influence it.

37. *all the seed*] Unworthy members of Israel may be cast away, but the race shall never entirely cease to exist.

38. *to the* LORD] Or, **for** *Jehovah* : for His dwelling in the hearts of a people prepared to be His Temple.

39. *over...Gareb*] Or, *straight along the hill*

Gareb. Probably *the hill of lepers*, outside the old walls, towards the South-West.

Goath] **Goah.** Unknown.

40. *the whole valley of the dead bodies*] Probably some part of the valley of ben-Hinnom. Comparing Zech. ii. 4, the conclusion seems evident that Jeremiah's words are to be spiritually understood. His city is one that renders holy unto Jehovah what was before unclean. Cp. St. John's new Jerusalem (Rev. xxi. 27).

XXXII. The Chaldæans were already besieging the city, the prophet was in prison for foretelling its certain capture, and yet he bought with all the proper legal solemnities an estate, of which (Lev. xxv. 25) he had the right of redemption. The price apparently was small, but was more than the land commercially was worth. Jeremiah was now verging on sixty, and only ten of the seventy years of the captivity had passed by. But though the estate was not worth the purchase, the opportunity was precious as a means of assuring the people that God would certainly bring them back. Jeremiah records, (*vv.* 16-25) how his heart misgave him, upon which (*vv.* 26-44) God unfolds to him the full meaning of the sign, and assures him of the certainty of Israel's restoration.

1. The siege of Jerusalem began in Zedekiah's ninth year (xxxix. 1), but was temporarily raised upon the approach of an Egyptian army. See chs. xxxvii., xxxviii.

2 year of Nebuchadrezzar. For then the king of Babylon's army besieged Jerusalem : and Jeremiah the prophet was shut up *b*in the court of the prison, which *was* in the king of Judah's 3 house. For Zedekiah king of Judah had shut him up, saying, Wherefore dost thou prophesy, and say, Thus saith the LORD, *c*Behold, I will give this city into the hand of the king of Baby- 4 lon, and he shall take it; and Zedekiah king of Judah *d*shall not escape out of the hand of the Chaldeans, but shall surely be delivered into the hand of the king of Babylon, and shall speak with him mouth to mouth, and his eyes shall behold his 5 eyes; and he shall lead Zedekiah to Babylon, and there shall he be *e*until I visit him, saith the LORD : *f*though ye fight with 6 the Chaldeans, ye shall not prosper. ¶ And Jeremiah said, The 7 word of the LORD came unto me, saying, Behold, Hanameel the son of Shallum thine uncle shall come unto thee, saying, Buy thee my field that *is* in Anathoth : for the *g*right of redemption *is* 8 thine to buy *it*. So Hanameel mine uncle's son came to me in the court of the prison according to the word of the LORD, and said unto me, Buy my field, I pray thee, that *is* in Anathoth, which *is* in the country of Benjamin : for the right of inheritance *is* thine, and the redemption *is* thine; buy *it* for thyself. Then 9 I knew that this *was* the word of the LORD. And I bought the field of Hanameel my uncle's son, that *was* in Anathoth, and *h*weighed him the money, *even* ¹seventeen shekels of silver. 10 And I ²subscribed the evidence, and sealed *it*, and took wit- 11 nesses, and weighed *him* the money in the balances. So I took the evidence of the purchase, *both* that which was sealed *according* 12 to the law and custom, and that which was open : and I gave the

b Neh. 3. 25.

c ch. 34. 2.
d ch. 34. 3.

e ch. 27. 22.
f ch. 21. 4.
& 33. 5.

g Lev. 25.
24, 25, 32.
Ruth 4. 4.

h Gen. 23.16.
Zech. 11. 12.

---

¹ Or, *seven shekels and ten* pieces *of silver*.   ² Heb. *wrote in the book*.

---

2. *the prison*] Or, *the* **guard,** a part of the king's palace, probably where the royal guard had its quarters.

3. For the prophecies on which the charge was grounded see xxi. 4-7, 9.

5. *I visit*] In the sense of punishment. See xxxix. 6, 7, lii. 11.

7. Hanameel was strictly the first-cousin of Jeremiah. In Hebrew all the terms of relationship are used in a more loose way than with us.

8. *the right of inheritance* is *thine*] Hanameel therefore had no children, and at his death the land would have been Jeremiah's by right of birth. According to the Law (Num. xxxv. 5) it must have been part of the suburbs of Anathoth, within less than a mile, which was all the priests and Levites might cultivate.

9. *seventeen shekels of silver*] Lit. as in marg., probably a legal formula. Jeremiah bought Hanameel's life-interest up to the year of Jubile, and no man's life was worth much in a siege like that of Jerusalem. As Jeremiah had no children, at his death the land would devolve to the person who would have inherited it had Jeremiah not bought it. He therefore bought what never was and never could have been of the slightest use to him, and gave for it what in the growing urgency of the siege might have

been very serviceable to himself. Still, **as** the next heir, it was Jeremiah's duty **to** buy the estate, independently of the importance of the act as a sign to the people **;** and evidently he gave the full value.

10, 11. Translate : *And I wrote* the particulars of the purchase *in the deed . . . And I took the purchase-deed, both that which was sealed* containing *the offer and the conditions, and that which was open* &c. There were two indentures, of which one was called *the purchase-deed,* and was signed by the purchaser and the witnesses. It was then sealed, not in our sense of appending a seal in place of signatures, but to close it up. The open deed was probably an exact copy, and was that intended for common use. In case its authenticity was called in question, the sealed copy would have to be produced before the judge, the seal opened, and if its contents agreed with those of the open deed, the decision would be in the buyer's favour.

By the *offer* is probably meant the specification. The *conditions,* lit., *the statutes,* would be the stipulations and terms of the sale, *e.g.* as to its restoration at the year of jubile, its price &c. The placing of the deeds in a jar was of course intended to preserve them from damp during the long years of the exile.

i ch. 36. 4.

k See Isai.
8. 2.

l ver. 37, 43.

m 2 K. 19.15.

n Gen. 18.14.
Luke 1. 37.
o Ex. 20. 6.
Deut. 5. 9.
p Isai. 9. 6.
q ch. 10. 16.
r Isai. 28.29.
s Job 34. 2.
Ps. 33. 13.
t ch. 17. 10.

u Ex. 9. 16.
Isai. 63. 12.
Dan. 9. 15.
x Ex. 6. 6.
Ps. 136. 11.

y Ex. 3. 8.

z Neh. 9. *6.
Dan. 9. 10—
14.

a ver. 25.
b ch. 14. 12.

c ver. 24.

d Num.16.22.
e ver. 17.
f ver. 3.

evidence of the purchase unto *i*Baruch the son of Neriah, the son of Maaseiah, in the sight of Hanameel mine uncle's *son,* and in the presence of the *k*witnesses that subscribed the book of the purchase, before all the Jews that sat in the court of the 13 prison. And I charged Baruch before them, saying, Thus saith 14 the LORD of hosts, the God of Israel; Take these evidences, this evidence of the purchase, both which is sealed, and this evidence which is open; and put them in an earthen vessel, that 15 they may continue many days. For thus saith the LORD of hosts, the God of Israel; Houses and fields and vineyards *l*shall 16 be possessed again in this land. ¶Now when I had delivered the evidence of the purchase unto Baruch the son of Neriah, I 17 prayed unto the LORD, saying, ¶Ah Lord GOD! behold, *m*thou hast made the heaven and the earth by thy great power and stretched out arm, *and* *n*there is nothing [1]too hard for thee: 18 thou shewest *o*lovingkindness unto thousands, and recompensest the iniquity of the fathers into the bosom of their children after them: the Great, *p*the Mighty God, *q*the LORD of 19 hosts, *is* his name, *r*great in counsel, and mighty in [2]work: for thine *s*eyes *are* open upon all the ways of the sons of men: *t*to give every one according to his ways, and according to the fruit 20 of his doings: which hast set signs and wonders in the land of Egypt, *even* unto this day, and in Israel, and among *other* men; 21 and hast made thee *u*a name, as at this day; and *x*hast brought forth thy people Israel out of the land of Egypt with signs, and with wonders, and with a strong hand, and with a stretched 22 out arm, and with great terror; and hast given them this land, which thou didst swear to their fathers to give them, *y*a land 23 flowing with milk and honey; and they came in, and possessed it; but *z*they obeyed not thy voice, neither walked in thy law; they have done nothing of all that thou commandedst them to do: therefore thou hast caused all this evil to come upon them: 24 behold the [3]mounts, they are come unto the city to take it; and the city *a*is given into the hand of the Chaldeans, that fight against it, because of *b*the sword, and of the famine, and of the pestilence: and what thou hast spoken is come to pass; 25 and, behold, thou seest *it.* And thou hast said unto me, O Lord GOD, Buy thee the field for money, and take witnesses; 26 [4]for *c*the city is given into the hand of the Chaldeans. ¶Then 27 came the word of the LORD unto Jeremiah, saying, ¶Behold, I *am* the LORD, the *d*God of all flesh: *e*is there any thing too 28 hard for me? Therefore thus saith the LORD; Behold, *f*I will give this city into the hand of the Chaldeans, and into the

---

[1] Or, *hid from thee.*　　[3] Or, *engines of shot,* ch.　　[4] Or, *though.*
[2] Heb. *doing.*　　　　　　　33. 4.

---

15. *possessed*] **bought.**
17 (27). *too hard*] Lit. *too* **wonderful.**
18. *recompensest*] The recompence is placed in the bosom, because in the East the garments are so arranged as to form a pocket there. Thus then men must receive and carry with them God's requital for their deeds.
20. The sense is, *Who hast set, i.e.* wrought (Exod. x. 2) *signs* &c., and hast continued working them *unto this day,* **both** *in Israel and among men (i.e.* the heathen).
23. *possessed*] See viii. 10 note.

24. *the mounts*] See vi. 6 note.
25. *for*] See marg. It is enough to place the command side by side with the state of Jerusalem to shew how contrary it is to all the rules of human prudence. The prophet is sure that God will explain to him his difficulty.
26—44. The answer is divided into two parts ; (a) *vv.* 26—35, the sins of Judah are shewn to be the cause of her punishment : (b) *vv.* 36—44, this punishment was not for Judah's destruction, but for her amendment.
28. *I will give*] Or, **I am giving.**

hand of Nebuchadrezzar king of Babylon, and he shall take it:
29 and the Chaldeans, that fight against this city, shall come and
*g*set fire on this city, and burn it with the houses, *h*upon whose
roofs they have offered incense unto Baal, and poured out drink
30 offerings unto other gods, to provoke me to anger. For the
children of Israel and the children of Judah *i*have only done
evil before me from their youth: for the children of Israel have
only provoked me to anger with the work of their hands, saith
31 the LORD. For this city hath been to me *as* ¹a provocation of
mine anger and of my fury from the day that they built it even
unto this day; *k*that I should remove it from before my face,
32 because of all the evil of the children of Israel and of the children of Judah, which they have done to provoke me to anger,
*l*they, their kings, their princes, their priests, and their prophets,
33 and the men of Judah, and the inhabitants of Jerusalem. And
they have turned unto me the ²*m*back, and not the face: though I
taught them, *n*rising up early and teaching *them*, yet they have
34 not hearkened to receive instruction. But they *o*set their abominations in the house, which is called by my name, to defile it.
35 And they built the high places of Baal, which *are* in the valley
of the son of Hinnom, to *p*cause their sons and their daughters
to pass through *the fire* unto *q*Molech; *r*which I commanded
them not, neither came it into my mind, that they should do
36 this abomination, to cause Judah to sin. ¶And now therefore
thus saith the LORD, the God of Israel, concerning this city,
whereof ye say, *s*It shall be delivered into the hand of the king
of Babylon by the sword, and by the famine, and by the pesti-
37 lence; Behold, I will *t*gather them out of all countries, whither
I have driven them in mine anger, and in my fury, and in great
wrath; and I will bring them again unto this place, and I will
38 cause them *u*to dwell safely: and they shall be *x*my people, and
39 I will be their God: and I will *y*give them one heart, and one
way, that they may fear me ³for ever, for the good of them,
40 and of their children after them: and *z*I will make an everlasting covenant with them, that I will not turn away ⁴from
them, to do them good; but *a*I will put my fear in their hearts,
41 that they shall not depart from me. Yea, *b*I will rejoice over
them to do them good, and *c*I will plant them in this land
42 ⁵assuredly with my whole heart and with my whole soul. For
thus saith the LORD; *d*Like as I have brought all this great

g ch. 21. 10.
h ch. 19. 13.

i ch. 2. 7.
Ezek. 20. 28.

k 2 Kin. 23. 27.

l Isai. 1. 4.
Dan. 9. 8.
m ch. 2. 27.
n ch. 7. 13.
o ch. 23. 11.
Ezek. 8. 5.

p ch. 19. 5.
q Lev. 18. 21.
1 Kin. 11. 33.
r ch. 7. 31.

s ver. 24.

t Deut. 30. 3
ch. 23. 3.
Ezek. 37. 21.

u ch. 33. 16.
x ch. 30. 22.
y ch. 24. 7.
Ezek. 11.
19, 20.
z Isai. 55. 3.

a ch. 31. 33.
b Deut. 30. 9.
Zeph. 3. 17.
c ch. 24. 6.
Amos 9. 15.
d ch. 31. 28.

¹ Heb. *for my anger.*
² Heb. *neck.*
³ Heb. *all days.*
⁴ Heb. *from after them.*
⁵ Heb. *in truth*, or, *sta-bility.*

30. *from their youth*] God's mighty deeds for Israel began in Egypt (*v.* 20), and so did Israel's sin.

34, 35. These verses are repeated from vii. 30, 31, but with two important varia-tions. *Baal* is put for *Tophet*, and *to Molech* instead of *in the fire*. Molech the *king* and Baal the *lord* are different names of the sun-god, but in altered relations. Molech is the sun as the mighty fire, which in pass-ing through the signs of the Zodiac burns up its own children. It is an old Canaan-itish worship, carried by the Phœnicians to all their colonies, and firmly established in Palestine at the time when the Israelites conquered the country.

39. *one heart, and one way*] Cp. iii. 13. Under the new Covenant they will with one consent walk in the one narrow path of right-doing (Matt. vii. 14). *For ever, i.e.* every day, constantly.

40. God's new Covenant (xxxi. 31) is on God's side, *I will not turn away from them to do them good, i.e.* I will never cease from doing them good. On their side, *I will put My fear in their hearts that they depart not from Me.* In these two conditions consists the certainty of the eternal duration of the Covenant (Matt. xxviii. 20).

41. *assuredly*] Lit. **in truth**, *i.e.* in verity, in reality. It refers to God's firm purpose, rather than to the safety and security of the

e ver. 15.
f ch. 33. 10.

evil upon this people, so will I bring upon them all the good
43 that I have promised them. And *e*fields shall be bought in
this land, *f*whereof ye say, It *is* desolate without man or beast;
44 it is given into the hand of the Chaldeans. Men shall buy fields
for money, and subscribe evidences, and seal *them*, and take

g ch. 17. 26.

witnesses in *g*the land of Benjamin, and in the places about
Jerusalem, and in the cities of Judah, and in the cities of the
mountains, and in the cities of the valley, and in the cities of

h ch. 33. 7.

the south: for *h*I will cause their captivity to return, saith the
LORD.

CHAP. 33. MOREOVER the word of the LORD came unto Jeremiah

a ch. 32. 2.

the second time, while he was yet *a*shut up in the court of the

b Isai. 37. 26.

2 prison, saying, ¶ Thus saith the LORD the *b*maker thereof, the

c Ex. 15. 2.
Amos 5. 8.
d Ps. 91. 15.
ch. 29. 12.

3 LORD that formed it, to establish it; [1c]the LORD *is* his name;
*d*call unto me, and I will answer thee, and shew thee great and
4 [2]mighty things, which thou knowest not. For thus saith the
LORD, the God of Israel, concerning the houses of this city, and
concerning the houses of the kings of Judah, which are thrown

e ch. 32. 24.
f ch. 32. 5.

5 down by *e*the mounts, and by the sword; *f*They come to fight
with the Chaldeans, but *it is* to fill them with the dead bodies
of men, whom I have slain in mine anger and in my fury, and
for all whose wickedness I have hid my face from this city.

g ch. 30. 17.

6 Behold, *g*I will bring it health and cure, and I will cure them,
and will reveal unto them the abundance of peace and truth.
7 And *h*I will cause the captivity of Judah and the captivity of

h ch. 30. 3.
& 32. 44.
i Isai. 1. 26.
ch. 24. 6.
k Ezek. 36. 25.
Zech. 13. 1.
Heb. 9. 13.
l ch. 31. 34.
Mic. 7. 18.
m Isai. 62. 7.
ch. 13. 11.
n Isai. 60. 5.

8 Israel to return, and will build them, *i*as at the first. And I
will *k*cleanse them from all their iniquity, whereby they have
sinned against me; and I will *l*pardon all their iniquities,
whereby they have sinned, and whereby they have transgressed
9 against me. *m*And it shall be to me a name of joy, a praise
and an honour before all the nations of the earth, which shall
hear all the good that I do unto them: and they shall *n*fear

[1] Or, *JEHOVAH*.   [2] Or, *hidden*, Isai. 48. 6.

people. The new Covenant is one of grace,
indicated by God's rejoicing over His people, and "planting them with His whole
heart."

43. *fields*] Lit. *The field*, the open unin-
closed country (iv. 17). In *v.* 44 *fields* refers
to the several portions of it which belonged
to individuals, and of which the boundaries
were shown by landmarks.

44. *subscribe evidences*] See *v.* 10. In
order to bring the certainty of the return
from exile more vividly before the mind,
the prophet enumerates the several subdi-
visions of the territory of the kings of
Judah.

XXXIII. The promises of ch. xxxii. are
confirmed, but with a more directly spiritual
meaning. The prophet foreshews in it the
happiness of the returning exiles, of which
the culminating glory is Messiah's birth
(*vv.* 15, 16), in whom both the Levitical
priesthood and the Davidic kingdom are
combined (*vv.* 17, 18), and God's Covenant
with mankind made perpetual (*vv.* 19–26).

1. *the prison*] **The guard.**

2. Or, *Thus saith Jehovah the doer of it,
Jehovah Who formeth it, that He may establish
it, Jehovah is His name.* The word *it* means
whatsoever Jehovah wills.

3. *mighty things*] Or, as in marg. The
words are probably a quotation from Isai.
xlviii. 6.

4. *by ... by*] Rather, **against ... against.**
As the works of the enemy approached the
walls, houses were pulled down to build
inner fortifications. *Swords* are mentioned
in Ezek. xxvi. 9 (translated, *axes*), as used
for breaking down the towers in the walls.
See v. 17, note.

5. Render, *They*, i.e. the Jews *come to fight
with the Chaldeans, and to fill them*, i.e. the
houses, *with the dead bodies* &c.

6. *I will bring it health and cure*] *I will
lay upon it a bandage and healing*, i.e. **a
healing bandage,** a plaister with healing
medicines.

7. *at the first*] *i.e.* before their sins had
provoked God to anger.

9. *it*] The city, Jerusalem.

they shall fear and tremble] With terror,

and tremble for all the goodness and for all the prosperity that
10 I procure unto it. ¶ Thus saith the LORD; Again there shall be
heard in this place, °which ye say *shall be* desolate without man
and without beast, *even* in the cities of Judah, and in the streets
of Jerusalem, that are desolate, without man, and without in-
11 habitant, and without beast, the ᵖvoice of joy, and the voice of
gladness, the voice of the bridegroom, and the voice of the bride,
the voice of them that shall say, ᑫPraise the LORD of hosts: for
the LORD *is* good; for his mercy *endureth* for ever: *and* of them
that shall bring ʳthe sacrifice of praise into the house of the
LORD. For ˢI will cause to return the captivity of the land, as
12 at the first, saith the LORD. ¶ Thus saith the LORD of hosts;
ᵗAgain in this place, which is desolate without man and without
beast, and in all the cities thereof, shall be an habitation of
13 shepherds causing *their* flocks to lie down. ᵘIn the cities of the
mountains, in the cities of the vale, and in the cities of the south,
and in the land of Benjamin, and in the places about Jerusalem,
and in the cities of Judah, shall the flocks ˣpass again under
14 the hands of him that telleth *them*, saith the LORD. ¶ʸBehold,
the days come, saith the LORD, that ᶻI will perform that good
thing which I have promised unto the house of Israel and to the
15 house of Judah. In those days, and at that time, will I cause
the ªBranch of righteousness to grow up unto David; and he
16 shall execute judgment and righteousness in the land. ᵇIn those
days shall Judah be saved, and Jerusalem shall dwell safely:
and this *is the name* wherewith she shall be called, ¹The LORD
17 our righteousness. For thus saith the LORD; ²David shall never
ᶜwant a man to sit upon the throne of the house of Israel;
18 neither shall the priests the Levites want a man before me to
ᵈoffer burnt offerings, and to kindle meat offerings, and to do

° ch. 32. 43

ᵖ ch. 7. 34.
Rev. 18. 23.
ᑫ 1 Chr. 16.
8, 34.
Ezra 3. 11.
Ps. 136. 1.
Isai. 12. 4.
ʳ Lev. 7. 12.
ˢ ver. 7.
ᵗ Isai. 65. 10.
ch. 31. 24.
ᵘ ch. 17. 26.

ˣLev. 27.32.
ʸ ch. 31. 27.
ᶻ ch. 29. 10.

ª Isai. 4. 2.
ᵇ ch. 23. 6.

ᶜ 2 Sam.7.16.
1 Kin. 2. 4.
Ps. 89. 29.
Luke 1. 32.
ᵈ Rom. 12. 1.
1 Pet. 2. 5.
Rev. 1. 6.

¹ Heb. *Jehovah-tsidkenu.*   ² Heb. *There shall not be cut off from David.*

---

because of the eternal opposition between
right and wrong, truth and error. The
nations of the earth as opposed to Israel
represent the world as opposed to the
Church.

10. *which ye say* shall be *desolate*] *Of
which ye say,* It is desolate... The prophet
first sees Judæa silent and desolate during
the seventy years' Captivity: and then describes the two things, men and cattle,
without which land is valueless.

11. *Praise the* LORD &c.] The customary
formula of thanksgiving in many of the later
Psalms, and from its occurrence in 2 Chr.
v. 13, vii. 3, 6 &c. probably a regular part
of the liturgical service of the Temple.

shall say...shall bring the sacrifice of praise]
Or, say...*as they bring praise, i.e.* a thank-offer-
ing (see marg. ref.) *into the house of the* LORD.

at the first] Before the Captivity, and when
still unpolluted by the sins which have
brought upon it so heavy a chastisement.

12. *an habitation*] *A shepherd's encamp-
ment.* The words, *causing* their *flocks to lie
down,* mean gathering them into the fold at
night.

13. *telleth*] *i.e.* counts the number of his
sheep.

14. *that good thing*] Better, *the good word*

(xxix. 10), with reference to the promise
already given (xxiii. 5, 6).

15, 16. Cp. marg. ref. When the good
word was spoken, the name Jehovah our
Righteousness was given to the righteous
Sprout: here it is given to Jerusalem, *i.e.*
to the Church, because it is her business
mediately to work on earth that righteousness which Christ works absolutely. Cp.
Eph. i. 23.

17, 18. Read literally, these verses promise
the permanent restoration of the Davidic
throne and of the Levitical priesthood. As
a matter of fact Zedekiah was the last king
of David's line, and the Levitical priesthood has long passed away. Both these
changes Jeremiah himself foretold (xxii. 30;
iii. 16). In what way then is this apparent
contradiction (cp. Isai. lxvi. 20–23; Ezek.
xl.–xlviii.) to be explained? The solution
is probably as follows. It was necessary
that the Bible should be intelligible to the
people at the time when it was written,
and in some degree to the writer. The
Davidic kingship and the Levitical priesthood were symbols, which represented to the
Jew all that was most dear to his heart in
the state of things under which he lived.
Their restoration was the restoration of his

19 sacrifice continually. ¶ And the word of the LORD came unto
20 Jeremiah, saying, Thus saith the LORD; *If ye can break my
covenant of the day, and my covenant of the night, and that
21 there should not be day and night in their season; *then* may also
f my covenant be broken with David my servant, that he should
not have a son to reign upon his throne; and with the Levites
22 the priests, my ministers. As *g* the host of heaven cannot be numbered, neither the sand of the sea measured: so will I multiply
the seed of David my servant, and the Levites that minister unto
23 me. ¶ Moreover the word of the LORD came to Jeremiah, say-
24 ing, Considerest thou not what this people have spoken, saying,
h The two families which the LORD hath chosen, he hath even
cast them off? thus they have despised my people, that they
25 should be no more a nation before them. ¶ Thus saith the
LORD; If *i* my covenant *be* not with day and night, *and if* I have
26 not *k* appointed the ordinances of heaven and earth; *l* then will I
cast away the seed of Jacob, and David my servant, *so* that I will
not take *any* of his seed *to be* rulers over the seed of Abraham,
Isaac, and Jacob: for *m* I will cause their captivity to return, and
have mercy on them.

CHAP. 34. THE word which came unto Jeremiah from the LORD,
a when Nebuchadnezzar king of Babylon, and all his army, and
b all the kingdoms of the earth *1* of his dominion, and all the
2 people, fought against Jerusalem, and against all the cities thereof, saying, Thus saith the LORD, the God of Israel; ¶ Go and
speak to Zedekiah king of Judah, and tell him, Thus saith the
LORD; Behold, *c* I will give this city into the hand of the king
3 of Babylon, and *d* he shall burn it with fire: and *e* thou shalt not
escape out of his hand, but shalt surely be taken, and delivered
into his hand; and thine eyes shall behold the eyes of the king
of Babylon, and *2* he shall speak with thee mouth to mouth, and
4 thou shalt go to Babylon. Yet hear the word of the LORD, O
Zedekiah king of Judah; Thus saith the LORD of thee, Thou
5 shalt not die by the sword: *but* thou shalt die in peace: and
with *f* the burnings of thy fathers, the former kings which were
before thee, *g* so shall they burn *odours* for thee; and *h* they

Marginal references:
e Ps. 89. 37.
Isai. 54. 9.
ch. 31. 36.

f Ps. 89. 34.

g Gen. 13. 16.
ch. 31. 37.

h ver. 21. 22.

i ver. 20.
Gen. 8. 22.
k Ps. 74. 16.
ch. 31. 35.
l ch. 31. 37.

m ver. 7.
Ezra 2. 1.

a 2 Kin. 25.
1, &c.
ch. 39. 1.
b ch. 1. 15.

c ch. 21. 10.
d ch. 32. 29.
ver. 22.
e ch. 32. 4.

f See 2 Chr.
16. 14.
g Dan. 2. 46.
h See ch. 22.
18.

---

1 Heb. *the dominion of his hand.*   *2* Heb. *his mouth shall speak to thy mouth.*

---

national and spiritual life. Neither was so
restored as to exist permanently. But that
was given instead, of which both were
types, the Church, whose Head is the true
Prophet, Priest and King.

21, 22. This promise also has been not
literally, but spiritually fulfilled; for in
this sense only have the seed of David and
the Levites been multiplied.

24. *Considerest thou not*] Lit. **Hast thou
not seen,** *i.e.* noticed?

this people] *i.e.* the Jews.

thus &c.] Or, **and** *My people they have despised,* **so that they are** *no more a nation*
in their sight. They say that God has
rejected Judah as well as Israel: and thus
they despise themselves in their relation to
God as His Covenant-people, by regarding
their national existence as about immediately to cease for ever.

25. *the ordinances of heaven and earth*]

i.e. the whole order of nature. Nature is
not more firmly established than God's purposes in grace.

XXXIV. The ordinary view of this
prophecy, that it is a more full account of
the narrative given in xxxii. 3-5, is not so
probable as that which takes it in connexion
with ch. xxi. Jeremiah had then informed
Zedekiah by his messengers that Jerusalem
would certainly be captured: but he was
still in a condition to obtain good terms,
and the prophet goes to him and lays before
him the alternative. Zedekiah with all the
obstinacy of a weak man chose to continue the
war, and lost kingdom, eyesight, and liberty.

1. *people*] **Peoples,** *i.e.* tribes, races, under
the rule of one man.

5. *in peace*] See xii. 12 note.

burn odours] **make a burning.** The
burning was probably that of piles of
wood, and spices were added only as an

6 will lament thee, *saying*, Ah lord! for I have pronounced the word, saith the LORD. ¶ Then Jeremiah the prophet spake all
7 these words unto Zedekiah king of Judah in Jerusalem, when the king of Babylon's army fought against Jerusalem, and against all the cities of Judah that were left, against Lachish, and against Azekah: for *i*these defenced cities remained of the cities of Judah.

8 *This is* the word that came unto Jeremiah from the LORD, after that the king Zedekiah had made a covenant with all the people which *were* at Jerusalem, to proclaim *k* liberty unto them;
9 *l*that every man should let his manservant, and every man his maidservant, *being* an Hebrew or an Hebrewess, go free; *m*that none should serve himself of them, *to wit*, of a Jew his brother.
10 Now when all the princes, and all the people, which had entered into the covenant, heard that every one should let his manservant, and every one his maidservant, go free, that none should serve themselves of them any more, then they obeyed, and let
11 *them* go. But *n*afterward they turned, and caused the servants and the handmaids, whom they had let go free, to return, and brought them into subjection for servants and for handmaids.
12 ¶ Therefore the word of the LORD came to Jeremiah from the
13 LORD, saying, Thus saith the LORD, the God of Israel; I made a covenant with your fathers in the day that I brought them forth out of the land of Egypt, out of the house of bondmen,

i 2 Kin. 18. 13.
2 Chr. 11. 5, 9.

k Ex. 21. 2.
Lev. 25. 10.
ver. 14.
l Neh. 5. 11.
m Lev. 25. 39—46.

n See ver. 21.
ch. 37. 5.

---

especial honour. It was not a Jewish custom to burn the dead. As these burnings depended upon the estimation in which the dead king was held, the verse implies a prosperous reign, such as Zedekiah might have had as an obedient vassal to Babylon.

I have pronounced the word] I have **spoken** *the word*.

7. This marks the exact time, that it was early in the campaign, while the outlying fortresses still occupied the attention of Nebuchadnezzar's army. Lachish and Azekah were strong cities in the plain towards Egypt and must be taken before the Chaldæans could march upon Jerusalem: otherwise the Egyptians might collect there and fall upon them.

8-22. It is usual with commentators to say that the laws dealing with the emancipation of the Hebrew slaves, as also that of the land resting during the sabbatical year, were not observed. The narrative teaches us the exact contrary. The manumission of the slaves on the present occasion was the spontaneous act of Zedekiah and the people. They knew of the law, and acknowledged its obligation. The observance of it was, no doubt, lax: the majority let their own selfish interests prevail: but the minority made might give way to right, and Zedekiah supported their efforts though only in a weak way.

Early in January, in the ninth year of Zedekiah, the Chaldæan army approached Jerusalem. The people made a covenant with the king, who appears as the abettor of the measure, to let their slaves go free. Possibly patriotism had its share in this: and as Jerusalem was strongly fortified, all classes possibly hoped that if the slaves were manumitted, they too would labour with a more hearty good-will in resisting the enemy. In the summer of the same year the Egyptians advanced to the rescue, and Nebuchadnezzar withdrew to meet their attack. The Jews with a strange levity, which sets them before us in a most despicable light, at once forced the manumitted slaves back into bondage. With noble indignation Jeremiah rebukes them for their treachery, assures them that the Chaldæan army will return, and warns them of the certainty of the punishment which they so richly merited.

8. As the Chaldæan army swept over the country the wealthier classes would all flee to Jerusalem, taking with them their households. And as the Mosaic Law was probably more carefully kept there than in the country, the presence in these families of slaves who had grown grey in service may have given offence to the stricter classes at the capital.

to proclaim liberty unto them] The words are those of the proclamation of the year of jubile to the people, whereupon it became their duty to set their slaves free.

9. *should serve himself of them*] Should make them serve him (see xxv. 14).

11. *they turned, and caused...to return*] But *afterwards they* **again** *made the slaves return*.

13. *the house of bondmen*] The miserable

o Ex. 21. 2.
Deut. 15. 12.

p So 2 Kin.
23. 3.
Neh. 10. 29.
q ch. 7. 10.
r Ex. 20. 7.
Lev. 19. 12.

s Matt. 7. 2.
Gal. 6. 7.
Jam. 2. 13.
t ch. 32. 24.
u Deut. 28.
25, 64.
ch. 29. 18.

x See Gen.
15. 10, 17.

y ch. 7. 33.

z See ch. 37.
5, 11.
a ch. 37. 8.
b ch. 38. 3.
c ch. 9. 11.

14 saying, At the end of *o* seven years let ye go every men his brother an Hebrew, which [1]hath been sold unto thee; and when he hath served thee six years, thou shalt let him go free from thee: but your fathers hearkened not unto me, neither inclined
15 their ear. And ye were [2]now turned, and had done right in my sight, in proclaiming liberty every man to his neighbour; and ye had *p* made a covenant before me *q* in the house [3]which is
16 called by my name: but ye turned and *r* polluted my name, and caused every man his servant, and every man his handmaid, whom he had set at liberty at their pleasure, to return, and brought them into subjection, to be unto you for servants and
17 for handmaids. ¶ Therefore thus saith the LORD; Ye have not hearkened unto me, in proclaiming liberty, every one to his brother, and every man to his neighbour: *s* behold, I proclaim a liberty for you, saith the LORD, *t* to the sword, to the pestilence, and to the famine; and I will make you [4]to be *u* removed into
18 all the kingdoms of the earth. And I will give the men that have transgressed my covenant, which have not performed the words of the covenant which they had made before me, when *x* they cut the calf in twain, and passed between the parts thereof,
19 the princes of Judah, and the princes of Jerusalem, the eunuchs, and the priests, and all the people of the land, which passed
20 between the parts of the calf; I will even give them into the hand of their enemies, and into the hand of them that seek their life: and their *y* dead bodies shall be for meat unto the fowls of the heaven, and to the beasts of the earth. And Zedekiah king
21 of Judah and his princes will I give into the hand of their enemies, and into the hand of them that seek their life, and into the hand of the king of Babylon's army, *z* which are gone up from
22 you. *a* Behold, I will command, saith the LORD, and cause them to return to this city; and they shall fight against it *b* and take it, and burn it with fire: and *c* I will make the cities of Judah a desolation without an inhabitant.

CHAP. 35. THE word which came unto Jeremiah from the LORD

[1] Or, *hath sold himself.*　　[3] Heb. *whereupon my name*　　[4] Heb. *for a removing.*
[2] Heb. *to day.*　　　　　　　*is called.*

prison in which, after being worked in the fields all day in gangs, the slaves were shut up at night.

16. *at their pleasure*] Lit. *for themselves.*

17. *I will make you to be removed into*] *I will cause you to be* a **terror unto.** Men would shudder at them.

18. *the words* &c.] The Jews spoke of "cutting" a covenant, because the contracting parties cut a calf in twain and passed between the pieces. Thus *cutting a covenant* and *cutting a calf in twain*, meant the same thing.

21. *which are gone up from you*] *i.e.* which have departed for the present, and have raised the siege.

XXXV. The Rechabites were a nomad tribe not of Jewish but of Kenite race, and connected with the Amalekites (Num. xxiv. 21; 1 Sam. xv. 6), from whom however they had separated themselves, and made a close

alliance with the tribe of Judah (Judg. i. 16), on whose southern borders they took up their dwelling (1 Sam. xxvii. 10). While, however, the main body of the Kenites gradually adopted settled habits, and dwelt in cities (1 Sam. xxx. 29), the Rechabites persisted in leading the free desert life, and in this determination they were finally confirmed by the influence and authority of Jonadab, who lived in Jehu's reign. He was a zealous adherent of Jehovah (2 K. x. 15-17), and possibly a religious reformer; and as the names of the men mentioned in the present narrative are all compounded with Jah, it is plain that the tribe continued their allegiance to Him.

The object of Jonadab in endeavouring to preserve the nomad habits of his race was probably twofold. He wished first to maintain among them the purer morality and higher feeling of the desert contrasted with

in the days of Jehoiakim the son of Josiah king of Judah, saying,
2 ¶ Go unto the house of the *a* Rechabites, and speak unto them, and bring them into the house of the LORD, into one of *b* the
3 chambers, and give them wine to drink. ¶ Then I took Jaazaniah the son of Jeremiah, the son of Habaziniah, and his brethren, and all his sons, and the whole house of the Recha-
4 bites; and I brought them into the house of the LORD, into the chamber of the sons of Hanan, the son of Igdaliah, a man of God, which *was* by the chamber of the princes, which *was* above the chamber of Maaseiah the son of Shallum, *e* the keeper of the
5 ¹door: and I set before the sons of the house of the Rechabites pots full of wine, and cups, and I said unto them, Drink ye
6 wine. But they said, We will drink no wine: for *d* Jonadab the son of Rechab our father commanded us, saying, Ye shall drink
7 no wine, *neither* ye, nor your sons for ever: neither shall ye build house, nor sow seed, nor plant vineyard, nor have *any*: but all your days ye shall dwell in tents; *e* that ye may live
8 many days in the land where ye *be* strangers. Thus have we obeyed the voice of Jonadab the son of Rechab our father in all that he hath charged us, to drink no wine all our days, we, our
9 wives, our sons, nor our daughters; nor to build houses for us
10 to dwell in: neither have we vineyard, nor field, nor seed: but we have dwelt in tents, and have obeyed, and done according to
11 all that Jonadab our father commanded us. But it came to pass, when Nebuchadrezzar king of Babylon came up into the land, that we said, Come, and let us go to Jerusalem for fear of the army of the Chaldeans, and for fear of the army of the Syrians:
12 so we dwell at Jerusalem. ¶ Then came the word of the LORD unto Jeremiah, saying, Thus saith the LORD of hosts, the God
13 of Israel; Go and tell the men of Judah and the inhabitants of Jerusalem, Will ye not *f* receive instruction to hearken to my

a 2 Kin. 10. 15.
1 Chr. 2. 55.
b 1 Kin. 6. 5.

c 2 Kin. 12. 9.
1 Chr. 9. 18, 19.

d 2 Kin. 10. 15.

e Ex. 20. 12.
Eph. 6. 2.

f ch. 32. 33.

¹ Heb. *threshold*, or, *vessel.*

---

the laxity and effeminacy of the city life; and secondly he was anxious for the preservation of their freedom. Their punctilious obedience (*v.* 14) to Jonadab's precepts is employed by Jeremiah to point a useful lesson for his own people.

The date of the prophecy is the interval between the battle of Carchemish and the appearance of Nebuchadnezzar at Jerusalem, (*v.* 11) at the end of the same year. It is consequently seventeen years earlier than the narrative in xxxiv. 8 &c.

2. *the house*] The family.

3. Jaazaniah was the chief of that portion of the tribe which had taken refuge in Jerusalem.

4. The title *man of God, i.e.* prophet, belongs to Hanan, identified by many with Hanani (2 Chr. xvi. 7). *The sons of Hanan* were probably his disciples. If so, we find a religious school or sect, regularly established in the precincts of the Temple, of whose views and modes of interpretation we know nothing. Plainly however the Hananites were friendly to Jeremiah, and lent him their hall for his purpose.

the chamber of the princes] Probably the

council-chamber in which the great officers of state met for the despatch of business.

the keeper of the door] There were three of these keepers, answering to the outer and inner courts of the Temple, and the entrance to the Temple itself. They were officers of high rank, having precedence next to the High-Priest and his deputy.

5. *pots*] **bowls,** to fill the cups.

6, 7. Wine is the symbol of a settled life, because the vine requires time for its growth and care in its cultivation, while the preparation of the wine itself requires buildings, and it then has to be stored up before it is ready for use. The drink of nomads consists of the milk of their herds.

7. *strangers*] Because not of Jewish blood, though wandering in their territory.

8, 10. *our father*] Not merely our ancestor, but the founder of our institutions.

11. *the Syrians*] The LXX. substitutes Assyrians for Syrians, but marauding bands of the Aramæans are probably meant.

13. Jeremiah, accompanied by the main body of the Rechabites, went into one of the courts of the Temple, and there addressed to the people the rebuke following.

14 words? saith the LORD. The words of Jonadab the son of
Rechab, that he commanded his sons not to drink wine, are performed; for unto this day they drink none, but obey their

g 2 Chr. 36. 15.
h ch. 25. 3.
i ch. 7. 25.
k ch. 18. 11. & 25. 5, 6.

father's commandment: *g*notwithstanding I have spoken unto
you, *h*rising early and speaking; but ye hearkened not unto me.
15 *i*I have sent also unto you all my servants the prophets, rising
up early and sending *them*, saying, *k*Return ye now every man
from his evil way, and amend your doings, and go not after
other gods to serve them, and ye shall dwell in the land which
I have given to you and to your fathers: but ye have not inclined
16 your ear, nor hearkened unto me. Because the sons of Jonadab
the son of Rechab have performed the commandment of their
father, which he commanded them; but this people hath not
17 hearkened unto me : therefore thus saith the LORD God of
hosts, the God of Israel; Behold, I will bring upon Judah and
upon all the inhabitants of Jerusalem all the evil that I have

l Prov. 1. 24
Isai. 65. 12.

pronounced against them : *l*because I have spoken unto them,
but they have not heard; and I have called unto them, but they
18 have not answered. ¶ And Jeremiah said unto the house of the
Rechabites, Thus saith the LORD of hosts, the God of Israel ;
Because ye have obeyed the commandment of Jonadab your
father, and kept all his precepts, and done according unto all
19 that he hath commanded you : therefore thus saith the LORD of
hosts, the God of Israel; ¹Jonadab the son of Rechab shall not

m ch. 15. 19.

want a man to *m*stand before me for ever.

CHAP. 36. AND it came to pass in the fourth year of Jehoiakim the
son of Josiah, king of Judah, *that* this word came unto Jeremiah

a Isai. 8. 1.
Ezek. 2. 9.
Zech. 5. 1.
b ch. 30. 2.
c ch. 25. 15.
d ch. 25. 3.

2 from the LORD, saying, Take thee *a*a roll of a book, and *b*write
therein all the words that I have spoken unto thee against Israel,
and against Judah, and against *c*all the nations, from the day I
spake unto thee, from the days of *d*Josiah, even unto this day.

¹ Heb.¹ *There shall not a man be cut off from Jona-*   *dab the son of Rechab to stand, &c.*

---

14. *are performed*] *Are* **established**, *i.e.*
are maintained in full force.

unto this day] *i.e.* for more than two hundred years.

15. *all...the prophets*] The Rechabites had
had but one lawgiver : the Jews had had a
succession of messengers from God.

19. Travellers bear witness to the existence of a large tribe who represent themselves as the descendants of the Rechabites.
The prediction was also literally fulfilled in
the Rechabites being in some way incorporated into the tribe of Levi, whose office
especially it was to *stand before* Jehovah
(Deut. x. 8).

XXXVI.-XLIV. Historical events connected with the collection of Jeremiah's
prophecies into a volume, and with his
personal history immediately before and
after the siege of Jerusalem.

XXXVI. Attached to the prophecies relating to Israel and Judah is an account of
the circumstances under which very many
of them, and also the prophecies concerning
the Gentiles, were first formed into one
volume. See Introd. p. 161.

1. *in the fourth year of Jehoiakim*] See
xxv. 1 note. The present chapter belongs
to the very end of that year. The capture
of Jerusalem by Nebuchadnezzar took place
early in Jehoiakim's fourth year, long before the writing of Jehoiakim's roll. The
humiliation seems to have sunk deeply into
the heart of Jehoiakim, and when Jeremiah
prophesied extended dominion to the Chaldæans (*v.* 29), his anger knew no bounds. It
was the fact that judgment had begun which
made it expedient to gather Jeremiah's predictions into one volume, with the object
(1) of inducing the people to repent, and
(2) of persuading the king to be a true subject of the Chaldæan empire.

2. *a roll of a book*] A parchment-roll, consisting of several skins sewn together, and
cut of an even breadth, with a piece of wood
at one end (or, in case of larger volumes, at
both ends) on which to roll them up.

write therein all the words &c.] The phrase
means that the roll was to contain "all
the counsel of God" (Acts xx. 27) upon
the special point mentioned in *v.* 3, and that
the prophet was not to keep anything back.

3 ^eIt may be that the house of Judah will hear all the evil which I ᵉ ver. 7.
purpose to do unto them; that they may ᶠreturn every man ᶠ ch. 18. 8.
from his evil way; that I may forgive their iniquity and their Jonah 3. 8.
4 sin. ¶ Then Jeremiah ᵍcalled Baruch the son of Neriah: and ᵍ ch. 32. 12.
ʰBaruch wrote from the mouth of Jeremiah all the words of the ʰ See ch.
LORD, which he had spoken unto him, upon a roll of a book. 45. 1.
5 And Jeremiah commanded Baruch, saying, I *am* shut up; I
6 cannot go into the house of the LORD: therefore go thou, and
read in the roll, which thou hast written from my mouth, the
words of the LORD in the ears of the people in the LORD's house
upon ᶦthe fasting day: and also thou shalt read them in the ears ᶦ Lev. 16. 29.
7 of all Judah that come out of their cities. ᵏIt may be ¹they will & 23. 27-32.
present their supplication before the LORD, and will return every Acts 27. 9.
one from his evil way: for great *is* the anger and the fury that ᵏ ver. 3.
8 the LORD hath pronounced against this people. And Baruch the
son of Neriah did according to all that Jeremiah the prophet
commanded him, reading in the book the words of the LORD in
9 the LORD's house. ¶ And it came to pass in the fifth year of
Jehoiakim the son of Josiah king of Judah, in the ninth month,
that they proclaimed a fast before the LORD to all the people in
Jerusalem, and to all the people that came from the cities of
10 Judah unto Jerusalem. Then read Baruch in the book the
words of Jeremiah in the house of the LORD, in the chamber of
Gemariah the son of Shaphan the scribe, in the higher court, at
the ²ˡentry of the new gate of the LORD's house, in the ears of ˡ ch. 26. 10
11 all the people. ¶ When Michaiah the son of Gemariah, the son
of Shaphan, had heard out of the book all the words of the LORD,
12 then he went down into the king's house, into the scribe's
chamber: and, lo, all the princes sat there, *even* Elishama the
scribe, and Delaiah the son of Shemaiah, and Elnathan the son
ot Achbor, and Gemariah the son of Shaphan, and Zedekiah the
13 son of Hananiah, and all the princes. Then Michaiah declared
unto them all the words that he had heard, when Baruch read
14 the book in the ears of the people. Therefore all the princes
sent Jehudi the son of Nethaniah, the son of Shelemiah, the son
of Cushi, unto Baruch, saying, Take in thine hand the roll
wherein thou hast read in the ears of the people, and come. So

---

¹ Heb. *their supplication shall fall.*   ² Or, *door.*

---

3. Cp. xxvi. 3. In point of date ch. xxvi. is immediately prior to the present.

5. *shut up*] **Hindered** from going; perhaps through fear of Jehoiakim.

6. *the fasting day*] **A** *fasting day.* Baruch was to wait for a proper opportunity (*v.* 9).

7. *they will present their supplication*] *i.e.* humbly. See marg. The phrase also contained the idea of the prayer being accepted.

8. *reading*] **To read.**

9. The ninth month answers to our December, and the fast was probably in commemoration of the capture of Jerusalem by the Chaldæans in the previous year.

10. Gemariah seems to have inherited his father's office of public scribe or secretary of state (see 2 K. xxii. 3). As brother of Ahikam, he would be favourable to Jeremiah.

the higher court] *The inner court ;* into

which it was not lawful for the people to enter, but the chamber probably itself formed one of its sides, and could be approached from the outer court.

11. Probably as his father had lent Jeremiah the hall, Michaiah had been commanded to bring Gemariah (*v.* 12) tidings, as soon as the reading was over, of the nature of the prophet's words, and the effect produced by them upon the people.

12. *the scribe's chamber*] The chancery in which the king's business was conducted. Probably Elishama was one of the "principal scribes of the host" (lii. 25), *i.e.* the secretary of state for war. The business which had brought together "all the princes" would have reference to the Chaldæan war.

14. Jehudi signifies a Jew and Cushi an Ethiopian, but it seems reasonable to conclude that they are genuine, proper names.

Baruch the son of Neriah took the roll in his hand, and came
15 unto them. And they said unto him, Sit down now, and read it
16 in our ears. So Baruch read *it* in their ears. ¶ Now it came to
pass, when they had heard all the words, they were afraid both
one and other, and said unto Baruch, We will surely tell the king
17 of all these words. And they asked Baruch, saying, Tell us now,
18 How didst thou write all these words at his mouth? Then
Baruch answered them, He pronounced all these words unto me
19 with his mouth, and I wrote *them* with ink in the book. Then
said the princes unto Baruch, Go, hide thee, thou and Jeremiah;
20 and let no man know where ye be. ¶ And they went in to the
king into the court, but they laid up the roll in the chamber of
Elishama the scribe, and told all the words in the ears of the
21 king. So the king sent Jehudi to fetch the roll: and he took it
out of Elishama the scribe's chamber. And Jehudi read it in
the ears of the king, and in the ears of all the princes which
22 stood beside the king. Now the king sat in ᵐthe winterhouse
in the ninth month: and *there was a fire* on the hearth burning
23 before him. And it came to pass, *that* when Jehudi had read three
or four leaves, he cut it with the penknife, and cast *it* into the
fire that *was* on the hearth, until all the roll was consumed in
24 the fire that *was* on the hearth. Yet they were not afraid, nor
ⁿrent their garments, *neither* the king, nor any of his servants
25 that heard all these words. Nevertheless Elnathan and Delaiah
and Gemariah had made intercession to the king that he would
26 not burn the roll: but he would not hear them. But the king
commanded Jerahmeel the son ¹of Hammelech, and Seraiah the
son of Azriel, and Shelemiah the son of Abdeel, to take Baruch
the scribe and Jeremiah the prophet: but the LORD hid them.
27 ¶ Then the word of the LORD came to Jeremiah, after that the
king had burned the roll, and the words which Baruch wrote at
28 the mouth of Jeremiah, saying, Take thee again another roll,
and write in it all the former words that were in the first roll,
29 which Jehoiakim the king of Judah hath burned. And thou
shalt say to Jehoiakim king of Judah, Thus saith the LORD;

ᵐ See Amos
3. 15.

ⁿ 2 Kin 22.
11.
Isai. 36. 22.
& 37. 1.

¹ Or, *of the king.*

---

16. *they were afraid both one and other*]
Lit. *they trembled each to his neighbour, i.e.*
they shewed their alarm by their looks and
gestures one to another. They felt that
what he had so consistently prophesied for
a period of twenty-three years would in all
probability be fulfilled.

We will surely tell] Rather, **We must tell**
the king. It was their official duty.

17. The roll might have been drawn up by
Baruch from memoranda of his own without the prophet's direct authority. The
princes therefore did not ask from curiosity,
but to obtain necessary information.

18. *He pronounced*] **He used to say
aloud,** he dictated. Baruch's office was
merely mechanical. He contributed nothing but hand, pen, and ink.

20. *the court*] *i.e.* The inner quadrangle of
the palace, in which was the royal residence.

they laid up the roll] **They left** *the roll* **in
charge,** *i.e.* in the care of some one.

22. *the winterhouse*] A separate portion of
the palace was used for residence according
to the season (marg. ref.)

and there was a fire *on the hearth*...] **And
the fire-pan** *burning before them.* On the
middle of the floor was a brazier containing
burning charcoal.

23. *leaves*] *Columns:* lit. folding-doors;
the word exactly describes the shape of the
columns of writing upon the roll.

penknife] *Scribe's knife;* used to shape the
reed for writing, and to make erasures in
the parchment.

on the hearth] Or, **in the fire-pan.** The
conduct of the king shews how violent was
his temper.

25. It is remarkable to find Elnathan
interceding for Jeremiah after the office he
had discharged towards Urijah (xxvi. 22).

26. *Hammelech*] Either a proper name or
a prince of the blood royal (see marg.;
xxxviii. 6; 1 K. xxii. 26).

Thou hast burned this roll, saying, Why hast thou written therein, saying, The king of Babylon shall certainly come and destroy this land, and shall cause to cease from thence man and beast?
30 Therefore thus saith the LORD of Jehoiakim king of Judah; °He shall have none to sit upon the throne of David: and his dead body shall be ᵖcast out in the day to the heat, and in the
31 night to the frost. And I will ¹punish him and his seed and his servants for their iniquity; and I will bring upon them, and upon the inhabitants of Jerusalem, and upon the men of Judah, all the evil that I have pronounced against them; but they
32 hearkened not. ¶ Then took Jeremiah another roll, and gave it to Baruch the scribe, the son of Neriah; who wrote therein from the mouth of Jeremiah all the words of the book which Jehoiakim king of Judah had burned in the fire: and there were added besides unto them many ²like words.

o ch. 22. 30.
p ch. 22. 19.

CHAP. 37. AND king ᵃZedekiah the son of Josiah reigned instead of Coniah the son of Jehoiakim, whom Nubuchadrezzar king of
2 Babylon made king in the land of Judah. ᵇBut neither he, nor his servants, nor the people of the land, did hearken unto the words of the LORD, which he spake ³by the prophet Jeremiah.
3 And Zedekiah the king sent Jehucal the son of Shelemiah and ᶜZephaniah the son of Maaseiah the priest to the prophet Jere-
4 miah, saying, Pray now unto the LORD our God for us. Now Jeremiah came in and went out among the people: for they had
5 not put him into prison. Then ᵈPharaoh's army was come forth out of Egypt: ᵉand when the Chaldeans that besieged Jerusalem heard tidings of them, they departed from Jerusalem.
6 ¶ Then came the word of the LORD unto the prophet Jeremiah,
7 saying, Thus saith the LORD, the God of Israel; Thus shall ye say to the king of Judah, ᶠthat sent you unto me to enquire of

a 2 Kin. 24. 17.
ch. 22. 24.
b 2 Chr. 36. 12, 14.

c ch. 21. 1, 2.
& 52. 24.

d See 2 Kin. 24. 7.
Ezek. 17. 15.
e ver. 11.
ch. 34. 21.

f ch. 21. 2.

¹ Heb. *visit upon*, ch. 23. 34.   ² Heb. *as they.*   ³ Heb. *by the hand of the prophet.*

29. *The king of Babylon* &c.] These words do not prove that Nebuchadnezzar had not already come, and compelled Jehoiakim to become his vassal. The force lies in the last words, which predict such a coming as would make the land utterly desolate: and this would be the result of the king throwing off the Chaldæan yoke.

30. *He shall have none to sit...*] The three months' reign of Jehoiakim was too destitute of real power to be a contradiction to this prediction.

32. *many like words*] The second roll was thus a more complete record of the main lessons taught by Jeremiah during the long course of his inspired ministry.

XXXVII., XXXVIII. It is evident that Zedekiah was well affected towards Jeremiah. In these two chapters, dealing with events during the siege of Jerusalem, we have an account of his relations with Jeremiah, and of the prophet's personal history up to the capture of the city.

XXXVII. 3. This embassy is not to be confounded with that (xxi. 1) which took place when Nebuchadnezzar was just march-

ing upon Jerusalem; this was in the brief interval of hope occasioned by the approach of an Egyptian army to raise the siege. The Jews were elated by this temporary relief, and miserably abused it (xxxiv. 11). Zedekiah seems to some extent to have shared their hopes, and to have expected that the prophet would intercede for the city as successfully as Isaiah had done (Isai. xxxvii. 6). Jehucal was a member of the warlike party (xxxviii. 1), as also was the deputy High-Priest Zephaniah, but otherwise he was well affected to Jeremiah.

5. *Then*] And. Pharaoh-Hophra (xliv. 30), the Apries of Herodotus, probably withdrew without giving Nebuchadnezzar battle. After a reign of 25 years he was dethroned by Amasis, but allowed to inhabit his palace at Sais, where finally he was strangled.

7–10. Jeremiah's answer here is even more unfavourable than that which is given in xxi. 4–7. So hopeless is resistance that the disabled men among the Chaldæans would alone suffice to capture the city and burn it to the ground.

me; Behold, Pharaoh's army, which is come forth to help you,

g ch. 34. 22.   8 shall return to Egypt into their own land. *g*And the Chaldeans
shall come again, and fight against this city, and take it, and
9 burn it with fire.   Thus saith the LORD; Deceive not ¹your-
selves, saying, The Chaldeans shall surely depart from us: for

h ch. 21. 4.   10 they shall not depart. *h*For though ye had smitten the whole
army of the Chaldeans that fight against you, and there remained
but ²wounded men among them, *yet* should they rise up every

i ver. 5.   11 man in his tent, and burn this city with fire.   ¶ *i*And it
came to pass, that when the army of the Chaldeans was ³broken
up from Jerusalem for fear of Pharaoh's army, then Jeremiah
12 went forth out of Jerusalem to go into the land of Benjamin, ⁴to
13 separate himself thence in the midst of the people.   And when
he was in the gate of Benjamin, a captain of the ward *was* there,
whose name *was* Irijah, the son of Shelemiah, the son of Hananiah; and he took Jeremiah the prophet, saying, Thou fallest
14 away to the Chaldeans.   Then said Jeremiah, *It is* ⁵false; I fall
not away to the Chaldeans.   But he hearkened not to him: so
15 Irijah took Jeremiah, and brought him to the princes.   Where-

k ch. 38. 26.   fore the princes were wroth with Jeremiah, and smote him, *k*and
put him in prison in the house of Jonathan the scribe: for they
16 had made that the prison.   ¶ When Jeremiah was entered into

l ch. 38. 6.   *l*the dungeon, and into the ⁶cabins, and Jeremiah had remained
17 there many days; then Zedekiah the king sent, and took him
out: and the king asked him secretly in his house, and said, Is
there *any* word from the LORD?   And Jeremiah said, There is:
for, said he, thou shalt be delivered into the hand of the king of
18 Babylon.   Moreover Jeremiah said unto king Zedekiah, What
have I offended against thee, or against thy servants, or against
19 this people, that ye have put me in prison?   Where *are* now
your prophets which prophesied unto you, saying, The king of
Babylon shall not come against you, nor against this land?
20 Therefore hear now, I pray thee, O my lord the king: ⁷let my
supplication, I pray thee, be accepted before thee; that thou
cause me not to return to the house of Jonathan the scribe, lest
21 I die there.   Then Zedekiah the king commanded that they

m ch. 32. 2.   should commit Jeremiah *m*into the court of the prison, and that
& 38. 13, 28.

---

¹ Heb. *souls*.
² Heb. *thrust through*.
³ Heb. *made to ascend*.
⁴ Or, *to slip away from thence in the midst of the people*.
⁵ Heb. *falsehood*, or, *a lie*.
⁶ Or, *cells*.
⁷ Heb. *let my supplication fall*.

---

11. *was broken up for fear of*] Or, "had
got them up from the face *of*." It was
simply a strategic movement.
12. *to separate himself thence...*] **To receive a share** *thence*. When the siege was
temporarily raised, the first object would
be food, and accordingly Jeremiah accompanied by others, who, like himself, had a
right to share in the produce of the priests'
lands at Anathoth, started thither to see
whether any stores remained which might
be available for their common use.
13. *a captain of the ward*] Captain of the
watch, whose business was to examine all
who went in and out.
the gate of Benjamin] The northern gate,
also called the gate of Ephraim.
Thou fallest away &c.] His well-known

views made Jeremiah a suspected person,
though the charge was groundless.
14. *the princes*] Not the noblemen trained
in the days of Josiah and Jeremiah's friends
(xxvi. 16), but those described in xxiv. 8.
They assumed that the accusation was true;
they first scourged and then imprisoned
Jeremiah.
15. *the house*] Probably the official residence of the secretary of state.
16. *dungeon*] Lit. *house of a cistern* or pit,
and evidently underground. In this cistern-
like excavation were several cells or arched
vaults, in one of which with little light and
less ventilation Jeremiah remained a long
time.
21. *the prison*] *the* **watch** (marg. ref.).

they should give him daily a piece of bread out of the bakers' street, *n*until all the bread in the city were spent. Thus Jeremiah remained in the court of the prison.

n ch. 38. 9.
& 52. 6.

CHAP. 38. THEN Shephatiah the son of Mattan, and Gedaliah the son of Pashur, and *a*Jucal the son of Shelemiah, and *b*Pashur the son of Malchiah, *c*heard the words that Jeremiah had spoken
2 unto all the people, saying, Thus saith the LORD, *d*He that remaineth in this city shall die by the sword, by the famine, and by the pestilence : but he that goeth forth to the Chaldeans shall live ; for he shall have his life for a prey, and shall live.
3 Thus saith the LORD, *e*This city shall surely be given into the
4 hand of the king of Babylon's army, which shall take it. Therefore the princes said unto the king, We beseech thee, *f*let this man be put to death : for thus he weakeneth the hands of the men of war that remain in this city, and the hands of all the people, in speaking such words unto them: for this man seeketh
5 not the ¹welfare of this people, but the hurt. Then Zedekiah the king said, Behold, he *is* in your hand: for the king *is* not he
6 *that* can do *any* thing against you. *g*Then took they Jeremiah, and cast him into the dungeon of Malchiah the son ²of Hammelech, that *was* in the court of the prison: and they let down Jeremiah with cords. And in the dungeon *there was* no water,
7 but mire : so Jeremiah sunk in the mire. ¶ *h*Now when Ebedmelech the Ethiopian, one of the eunuchs which was in the king's house, heard that they had put Jeremiah in the dungeon;
8 the king then sitting in the gate of Benjamin; Ebed-melech went forth out of the king's house, and spake to the king,
9 saying, My lord the king, these men have done evil in all that they have done to Jeremiah the prophet, whom they have cast into the dungeon; and ³he is like to die for hunger in the place
10 where he is: for *there is* no more bread in the city. Then the king commanded Ebed-melech the Ethiopian, saying, Take from hence thirty men ⁴with thee, and take up Jeremiah the

a ch. 37. 3.
b ch. 21. 1.
c ch. 21. 8.
d ch. 21. 9.

e ch. 21. 10.
& 32. 3.
f See ch. 26. 11.

g ch. 37. 21.

h ch. 39. 16.

¹ Heb. *peace.* ² Or, *of the king.* ³ Heb. *he will die.* ⁴ Heb. *in thine hand.*

---

a piece] Lit. *a circle, i.e.* a round cake.

the bakers' street] It is usual in oriental towns for each trade to have a special place set apart for it. Cp. Acts x. 6.

XXXVIII. The object of the princes in imprisoning Jeremiah in Jonathan's house had been to get him out of the way, as his predictions depressed the minds of the people. This purpose was frustrated by his removal to the guard-house, where he was with the soldiery, and his friends had free access to him (xxxii. 12). Therefore the princes determined upon the prophet's death. Zedekiah was powerless (*v.* 5), and Jeremiah was thrown into a miry pit.

1. *had spoken*] **Spake;** or, was speaking.

4. *for thus* &c.] **Because** he makes the men of war dispirited. No doubt this was true. Jeremiah, however, did not speak as a private person, but as the representative of the government; the temporal ruler in a theocracy being responsible directly to God.

5. All real power was in their hands, and

as they affirmed that Jeremiah's death was a matter of necessity, the king did not dare refuse it to them.

6. *the dungeon*] **The cistern.** Every house in Jerusalem was supplied with a subterranean cistern, so well constructed that the city never suffered in a siege from want of water. So large were they that when dry they seem to have been used for prisons (Zech. ix. 11).

Hammelech] See xxxvi. 26 note.

the prison] *The* **guard.** They threw Jeremiah into the nearest cistern, intending that he should die of starvation. Some have thought that Ps. lxix. was composed by Jeremiah when in this cistern.

7. *Ebed-melech*] *i.e.* the *king's slave.* By "Ethiopian" or Cushite is meant the Cushite of Africa, or negro. It seems (cp. 2 K. xxiii. 11) as if such eunuchs (or, chamberlains) took their names from the king, while the royal family and the princes generally bore names compounded with the appellations of the Deity.

10. *thirty men*] So large a number sug-

11 prophet out of the dungeon, before he die. So Ebed-melech
took the men with him, and went into the house of the king
under the treasury, and took thence old cast clouts and old
rotten rags, and let them down by cords into the dungeon to
12 Jeremiah. And Ebed-melech the Ethiopian said unto Jeremiah, Put now *these* old cast clouts and rotten rags under thine
[i] ver. 6. 13 armholes under the cords. And Jeremiah did so. [i]So they
drew up Jeremiah with cords, and took him up out of the dun-
[k] ch. 37. 21. geon: and Jeremiah remained [k]in the court of the prison.
14 ¶ Then Zedekiah the king sent, and took Jeremiah the prophet
unto him into the [1]third entry that *is* in the house of the LORD:
and the king said unto Jeremiah, I will ask thee a thing; hide
15 nothing from me. Then Jeremiah said unto Zedekiah, If I declare *it* unto thee, wilt thou not surely put me to death? and if
16 I give thee counsel, wilt thou not hearken unto me? So Zedekiah
the king sware secretly unto Jeremiah, saying, *As* the LORD
[l] Isai. 57. 16. liveth, [l]that made us this soul, I will not put thee to death,
neither will I give thee into the hand of these men that seek thy
17 life. Then said Jeremiah unto Zedekiah, Thus saith the LORD,
[m] 2 Kin. 24. 12. the God of hosts, the God of Israel; If thou wilt assuredly [m]go
[n] ch. 39. 3. forth [n]unto the king of Babylon's princes, then thy soul shall
live, and this city shall not be burned with fire; and thou shalt
18 live, and thine house: but if thou wilt not go forth to the king
of Babylon's princes, then shall this city be given into the hand
[o] ch. 32. 4. & 34. 3. ver. 23. of the Chaldeans, and they shall burn it with fire, and [o]thou shalt
19 not escape out of their hand. And Zedekiah the king said unto
Jeremiah, I am afraid of the Jews that are fallen to the Chal-
[p] 1 Sam. 31. 4. deans, lest they deliver me into their hand, and they [p]mock me.
20 But Jeremiah said, They shall not deliver *thee*. Obey, I beseech
thee, the voice of the LORD, which I speak unto thee: so it shall
21 be well unto thee, and thy soul shall live. But if thou refuse to
22 go forth, this *is* the word that the LORD hath shewed me: And,
behold, all the women that are left in the king of Judah's house
shall be brought forth to the king of Babylon's princes, and those
women shall say, [2]Thy friends have set thee on, and have prevailed against thee: thy feet are sunk in the mire, *and* they are
23 turned away back. So they shall bring out all thy wives and
[q] ch. 39. 6. & 41. 10. [q]thy children to the Chaldeans: and [r]thou shalt not escape out
[r] ver. 18. of their hand, but shalt be taken by the hand of the king of

[1] Or, *principal*. [2] Heb. *Men of thy peace*.

---

gests that Zedekiah expected some resistance. [Some read "three" men.]

11. *old cast clouts* &c.] **Rags of torn garments and rags of worn-out garments.**

14. *the third entry*] There was probably a passage from the palace to the Temple at this entry, and the meeting would take place in some private chamber close by.

15. *wilt thou not hearken...?*] Rather, **Thou wilt not hearken.**

16. *that made us this soul*] This very unusual addition to the formula of an oath (1 Sam. xx. 3) was intended to strengthen it. By acknowledging that his soul was God's workmanship Zedekiah also implied his belief in God's power over it.

19. *the Jews that are fallen to the Chaldeans*] These deserters probably formed a numerous party, and now would be the more indignant with Zedekiah for having rejected their original advice to submit.

22. *all the women that are left*] Belonging to the harems of former kings (cp. 1 K. ii. 22), attendants, and slaves.

Thy friends...] This satirical song (cp. Obad. 7) should be translated as a distich:

Thy friends have urged thee on and prevailed upon thee:
Thy feet are stuck in the mire; they have turned back.

Thy friends, lit. "men of thy peace," thy acquaintance (xx. 10). They urge Zedekiah on to a hopeless struggle with the Chaldæans, and when he gets into difficulties leave him in the lurch.

23. *So*] **And.** In addition to the ridicule, there shall be the miseries of the capture.

Babylon: and [1]thou shalt cause this city to be burned with fire.

24 ¶ Then said Zedekiah unto Jeremiah, Let no man know of these
25 words, and thou shalt not die. But if the princes hear that I
have talked with thee, and they come unto thee, and say unto
thee, Declare unto us now what thou hast said unto the king,
hide it not from us, and we will not put thee to death; also what
26 the king said unto thee: then thou shalt say unto them, [s]I presented my supplication before the king, that he would not cause
27 me to return [t]to Jonathan's house, to die there. ¶ Then came
all the princes unto Jeremiah, and asked him: and he told them
according to all these words that the king had commanded.
So [2]they left off speaking with him; for the matter was not
28 perceived. ¶ So [u]Jeremiah abode in the court of the prison
until the day that Jerusalem was taken: and he was *there* when
Jerusalem was taken.

CHAP. 39. IN the [a]ninth year of Zedekiah king of Judah, in the
tenth month, came Nebuchadrezzar king of Babylon and all his
2 army against Jerusalem, and they besieged it. *And* in the
eleventh year of Zedekiah, in the fourth month, the ninth *day*
3 of the month, the city was broken up. [b]And all the princes of
the king of Babylon came in, and sat in the middle gate, *even*
Nergal-sharezer, Samgar-nebo, Sarsechim, Rab-saris, Nergal-
sharezer, Rab-mag, with all the residue of the princes of the
4 king of Babylon. ¶ [c]And it came to pass, *that* when Zedekiah
the king of Judah saw them, and all the men of war, then they
fled, and went forth out of the city by night, by the way of the
king's garden, by the gate betwixt the two walls: and he went
5 out the way of the plain. But the Chaldeans' army pursued
after them, and [d]overtook Zedekiah in the plains of Jericho:
and when they had taken him, they brought him up to Nebuchadnezzar king of Babylon to [e]Riblah in the land of Hamath,
6 where he [3]gave judgment upon him. Then the king of Babylon
slew the sons of Zedekiah in Riblah before his eyes: also the
7 king of Babylon slew all the nobles of Judah. Moreover [f]he
put out Zedekiah's eyes, and bound him [4]with chains, to carry

ch. 37. 20.

ch. 37. 15.

*ch. 37. 21.
& 39. 14.*

*a 2 Kin. 25.
1—4.
ch. 52. 4—7.*

b ch. 38. 17.

*c 2 Kin. 25.
4, &c.
ch. 52. 7.*

*d ch. 52. 4.
& 38. 18, 23.*

*e 2 Kin. 25.
33.*

*f Ezek. 12. 13.
compared
with ch. 32. 1.*

[1] Heb. *thou shalt burn, &c.*
[2] Heb. *they were silent from him.*
[3] Heb. *spake with him judgments, ch. 4. 12.*
[4] Heb. *with two brasen
chains, or, fetters.*

---

thou shalt cause this city to be burned] Lit.
as marg. It shall be thy own act as completely as if done with thine own hand.

28. *and he was there when* &c.] These words
are altered by some to "and it came to pass
when" &c., and taken to form the opening
of ch. xxxix.

XXXIX.—*The Capture of Jerusalem.*—
The majority of the particulars given in
vv. 1–14 occur again (marg. ref.); and are
by some regarded as an interpolation. The
external evidence (that of the Versions) is,
however, in favour of their authenticity.
xxxix. 14 is to be reconciled with xl. 1–4 by
remembering that Gedaliah had left Jerusalem and gone to Mizpah (xl. 6), a city in
the immediate neighbourhood; and as he
was not at home to protect the prophet,
nothing is more probable than that Jeremiah in company with the main body of
captives was brought to Ramah in chains.

3. These princes were four (1) *Nergal-
Sharezer, i.e.* Nirgal-sar-usur (*May Nergal
protect the king*); (2) *Samgar-Nebo* (*Be gracious, O Nebo*); (3) *Sarsechim.* No explanation is given at present of this name. He
was Rab-saris, *i.e.* chief of the eunuchs (2 K.
xviii. 17 note). (4) Another *Nergal-sharezer,*
who was Rab-mag, *i.e.* chief of the Magians.
He is known in history as Neriglissar, the
son-in-law of Nebuchadnezzar, and probably his vicegerent during his seven years
of madness. Two years after his death
Neriglissar murdered Evil-Merodach, Nebuchadnezzar's son, and seized the crown,
but after a reign of four years was slain in
battle against Cyrus, when disputing with
him the crown of Media. See Dan. v. 1 note.

the middle gate] Probably that which separated the city of Zion from the lower town.

4–10. Cp. marg. ref. The differences between the two accounts are slight.

8 him to Babylon. *g*And the Chaldeans burned the king's house, and the houses of the people, with fire, and brake down the 9 walls of Jerusalem. ¶ *h*Then Nebuzar-adan the [1][2]captain of the guard carried away captive into Babylon the remnant of the people that remained in the city, and those that fell away, that 10 fell to him, with the rest of the people that remained. But Nebuzar-adan the captain of the guard left of the poor of the people, which had nothing, in the land of Judah, and gave them 11 vineyards and fields [3]at the same time. ¶ Now Nebuchadrezzar king of Babylon gave charge concerning Jeremiah [4]to Nebuzar-adan the captain of the guard, saying, Take him, and [5]look well 12 to him, and do him no harm; but do unto him even as he shall 13 say unto thee. So Nebuzar-adan the captain of the guard sent, and Nebushasban, Rab-saris, and Nergal-sharezer, Rab-mag, 14 and all the king of Babylon's princes; even they sent, *i*and took Jeremiah out of the court of the prison, and committed him *k*unto Gedaliah the son of *l*Ahikam the son of Shaphan, that he should carry him home: so he dwelt among the people.

15 ¶ Now the word of the LORD came unto Jeremiah, while he was 16 shut up in the court of the prison, saying, Go and speak to *m*Ebed-melech the Ethiopian, saying, Thus saith the LORD of hosts, the God of Israel; Behold, *n*I will bring my words upon this city for evil, and not for good; and they shall be *ac-*17 *complished* in that day before thee. But I will deliver thee in that day, saith the LORD: and thou shalt not be given into the 18 hand of the men of whom thou *art* afraid. For I will surely deliver thee, and thou shalt not fall by the sword, but *o*thy life shall be for a prey unto thee: *p*because thou hast put thy trust in me, saith the LORD.

CHAP. 40. THE word that came to Jeremiah from the LORD, *a*after that Nebuzar-adan the captain of the guard had let him go from Ramah, when he had taken him being bound in [6]chains among all that were carried away captive of Jerusalem and 2 Judah, which were carried away captive unto Babylon. ¶ And the captain of the guard took Jeremiah, and *b*said unto him,

[1] Or, *chief marshal.*
[2] Heb. *chief of the executioners,* or, *slaughtermen:*
[3] Heb. *in that day.*
[4] Heb. *by the hand of.*
[5] Heb. *set thine eyes upon him.*
[6] Or, *manicles.*

---

13. Nebuzar-adan is in the inscriptions Nabu-zir-iddina (*Nebo has given offspring*); and Nebushasban, Nabu-sizibanni (*Nebo save me*), whom some identify with Sarsechim (v. 3).

14. Jeremiah was to be taken out of the court of the watch, and placed in the palace close by.

he dwelt among the people] i.e. he was no longer in custody, but master of his own actions.

15. This prophecy probably came to Jeremiah after his interview with Zedekiah (xxxviii. 14), but is added here as a supplement in order not to break the sequence of events.

17. *of whom thou* art *afraid*] The Chaldæans. Ebed-melech apparently looked forward with much alarm to the bloodshed sure to take place at the storming of the city.

18. *a prey unto thee*] An unexpected and unlooked-for gain. He had given proof of faith in courageously delivering God's prophet.

XL. 1. As what follows is mainly a historical narrative, it seems that the title "The word &c." was appropriate not merely to a prediction of the future, but to an account of the past, if written by a prophet. The Jews regarded history as inspired if written by a seer, and thus their historical books are called "the early Prophets."

Ramah] Probably all the prisoners of note were collected at Ramah indiscriminately, and examined there.

bound in chains] The prisoners were probably fastened together in couples by one hand, and a rope passed down the centre to bind them in a long line, and prevent attempts at escape.

The LORD thy God hath pronounced this evil upon this place.

3 Now the LORD hath brought *it*, and done according as he hath said: ^cbecause ye have sinned against the LORD, and have not obeyed his voice, therefore this thing is come upon you. *c* Deut. 29. 24, 25. Dan. 9. 11.

4 And now, behold, I loose thee this day from the chains which ¹*were* upon thine hand. ^dIf it seem good unto thee to come with me into Babylon, come; and ²I will look well unto thee: but if it seem ill unto thee to come with me into Babylon, forbear: behold, ^eall the land *is* before thee: whither it seemeth *d* ch. 39. 12.

5 good and convenient for thee to go, thither go. Now while he was not yet gone back, *he said*, Go back also to Gedaliah the son of Ahikam the son of Shaphan, ^fwhom the king of Babylon hath made governor over the cities of Judah, and dwell with him among the people: or go wheresoever it seemeth convenient unto thee to go. So the captain of the guard gave him victuals *e* Gen. 20. 15.

6 and a reward, and let him go. ^gThen went Jeremiah unto Gedaliah the son of Ahikam to ^hMizpah; and dwelt with him *f* 2 Kin. 25. 22, &c.

7 among the people that were left in the land. ¶ ⁱNow when all the captains of the forces which *were* in the fields, *even* they and their men, heard that the king of Babylon had made Gedaliah the son of Ahikam governor in the land, and had committed unto him men, and women, and children, and of ^kthe poor of the land, of them that were not carried away captive to Babylon; *g* ch. 39. 14. *h* Judg. 20. 1.

8 then they came to Gedaliah to Mizpah, ^leven Ishmael the son of Nethaniah, and Johanan and Jonathan the sons of Kareah, and Seraiah the son of Tanhumeth, and the sons of Ephai, the Netophathite, and Jezaniah the son of a Maachathite, they and *i* 2 Kin. 25. 23, &c.

9 their men. And Gedaliah the son of Ahikam the son of Shaphan sware unto them and to their men, saying, Fear not ³to serve the Chaldeans: dwell in the land, and serve the king of *k* ch. 39. 10.

10 Babylon, and it shall be well with you. As for me, behold, I will dwell at Mizpah, to serve the Chaldeans, which will come unto us: but ye, gather ye wine, and summer fruits, and oil, and put *them* in your vessels, and dwell in your cities that ye *l* ch. 41. 1.

11 have taken. ¶ Likewise when all the Jews that *were* in Moab, and among the Ammonites, and in Edom, and that *were* in all the countries, heard that the king of Babylon had left a remnant of Judah, and that he had set over them Gedaliah the son

12 of Ahikam the son of Shaphan; even all the Jews returned out of all places whither they were driven, and came to the land of Judah, to Gedaliah, unto Mizpah, and gathered wine and

---

¹ Or, are *upon thine hand.*   ² Heb. *I will set mine eye upon thee.*   ³ Heb. *to stand before:* and so ver. 10. Deut. 1. 38.

---

5. *Now while he was not yet gone back*] Most modern commentators render *And as he yet answered nothing, Return then*, he said, *to Gedaliah* &c.

victuals] **A ration** *of food.*

a reward] **A present.**

7. The *men* would be the old and infirm: the *women* those whose husbands and protectors had perished in the wars (*e.g.* xli. 10). The word *children* includes all the inferior members of a household.

9, 10. *to serve the Chaldeans*] Lit. as marg.; to be their minister and lieutenant. Gedaliah supposed that officers of high rank would come from time to time from Babylon

to look after the king's interests. But whatever was ordered would be done through him, as being the prime minister.

gather ye wine] As Jerusalem was captured in the fifth month, August, it would now be autumn, and there would be fruit upon the trees, enough to maintain the scanty population during the winter.

taken] Or, **seized.** Every captain had probably occupied some place by force as his head quarters, and Gedaliah bids them retain them. He frankly accepts the whole existing state of things, as a necessary step towards re-establishing confidence.

13 summer fruits very much. ¶ Moreover Johanan the son of Kareah, and all the captains of the forces that *were* in the fields,
14 came to Gedaliah to Mizpah, and said unto him, Dost thou certainly know that *m* Baalis the king of the Ammonites hath sent Ishmael the son of Nethaniah [1] to slay thee? But Gedaliah
15 the son of Ahikam believed them not. Then Johanan the son of Kareah spake to Gedaliah in Mizpah secretly, saying, Let me go, I pray thee, and I will slay Ishmael the son of Nethaniah, and no man shall know *it*: wherefore should he slay thee, that all the Jews which are gathered unto thee should be scattered,
16 and the remnant in Judah perish? But Gedaliah the son of Ahikam said unto Johanan the son of Kareah, Thou shalt not do this thing: for thou speakest falsely of Ishmael.

CHAP. 41. NOW it came to pass in the seventh month, *a that* Ishmael the son of Nethaniah the son of Elishama, of the seed royal, and the princes of the king, even ten men with him, came unto Gedaliah the son of Ahikam to Mizpah; and there they
2 did eat bread together in Mizpah. Then arose Ishmael the son of Nethaniah, and the ten men that were with him, and *b* smote Gedaliah the son of Ahikam the son of Shaphan with the sword, and slew him, whom the king of Babylon had made governor
3 over the land. Ishmael also slew all the Jews that were with him, *even* with Gedaliah, at Mizpah, and the Chaldeans that
4 were found there, *and* the men of war. ¶ And it came to pass the second day after he had slain Gedaliah, and no man knew *it*,
5 that there came certain from Shechem, from Shiloh, and from Samaria, *even* fourscore men, *c* having their beards shaven, and their clothes rent, and having cut themselves, with offerings and incense in their hand, to bring *them* to *d* the house of the
6 LORD. And Ishmael the son of Nethaniah went forth from Mizpah to meet them, [2] weeping all along as he went: and it came to pass, as he met them, he said unto them, Come to
7 Gedaliah the son of Ahikam. And it was *so*, when they came into the midst of the city, that Ishmael the son of Nethaniah slew them, *and cast them* into the midst of the pit, he, and the
8 men that *were* with him. But ten men were found among them that said unto Ishmael, Slay us not: for we have treasures in the field, of wheat, and of barley, and of oil, and of honey. So

m See ch. 41. 10.

a 2 Kin. 25. 25. ch. 40. 6, 8.

b 2 Kin. 25. 25.

c Lev. 19. 27, 28. Deut. 14. 1. Isai. 15. 2.
d See 1 Sam. 1. 7. 2 Kin. 25. 9.

[1] Heb. *to strike thee in soul?*   [2] Heb. *in going and weeping.*

---

14. It is difficult to say what object Baalis can have had in murdering Gedaliah. As an ally of Zedekiah (xxvii. 3), he may have had a spite against the family of Ahikam for opposing, as most probably they did at Jeremiah's instigation, the league proposed (ch. xxvii.). Ishmael's motive was envy and spite at seeing a subject who had always opposed the war now invested with kingly power, in place of the royal family.

XLI. 1. *the seventh month*] Gedaliah's government lasted less than two months.

even] Rather, **and.** Ishmael was descended probably from Elishama the son of David (2 Sam. v. 16). Ten grandees each with his retinue would have aroused suspicion, but the smallness of Ishmael's following put Gedaliah completely off his guard.

5. These three towns all lay in the tribe of Ephraim, and in the district planted by Salmaneser with Cuthites; but though the fact of these men having cut themselves (see xvi. 6 note), is suspicious, yet they were probably pious Israelites, going up to Jerusalem, carrying the meat offering usual at the feast of Tabernacles, of which this was the season, and mourning over the destruction, not of the city, but of the Temple, to the repairs of which we find the members of this tribe contributing in Josiah's time (2 Chr. xxxiv. 9).

6. Ishmael's conduct seems to have been dictated by the malicious desire utterly to frustrate Gedaliah's work.

weeping] By this artifice he lured them into Mizpah. LXX. "as they were...weeping."

7. *the pit*] *the* **cistern,** and in *v.* 9.

8. *treasures*] **Hidden stores**; which would

9 he forbare, and slew them not among their brethren. Now the pit wherein Ishmael had cast all the dead bodies of the men, whom he had slain [1][2]because of Gedaliah, *was* it *e*which Asa the king had made for fear of Baasha king of Israel: *and* Ishmael the son of Nethaniah filled it with *them that were*

e 1 Kin. 15. 22.
2 Chr. 16. 6.

10 slain. Then Ishmael carried away captive all the residue of the people that *were* in Mizpah, *f even* the king's daughters, and all the people that remained in Mizpah, *g*whom Nebuzar-adan the captain of the guard had committed to Gedaliah the son of Ahikam: and Ishmael the son of Nethaniah carried them away captive, and departed to go over to *h*the Ammonites.

f ch. 43. 6.
g ch. 40. 7.

h ch. 40. 14.

11 ¶ But when Johanan the son of Kareah, and all *i*the captains of the forces that *were* with him, heard of all the evil that

i ch. 40. 7, 8, 13.

12 Ishmael the son of Nethaniah had done, then they took all the men, and went to fight with Ishmael the son of Nethaniah, and

13 found him by *k*the great waters that *are* in Gibeon. Now it came to pass, *that* when all the people which *were* with Ishmael saw Johanan the son of Kareah, and all the captains of the

k 2 Sam. 2. 13.

14 forces that *were* with him, then they were glad. So all the people that Ishmael had carried away captive from Mizpah cast about and returned, and went unto Johanan the son of Kareah.

15 But Ishmael the son of Nethaniah escaped from Johanan with

16 eight men, and went to the Ammonites. Then took Johanan the son of Kareah, and all the captains of the forces that *were* with him, all the remnant of the people whom he had re-covered from Ishmael the son of Nethaniah, from Mizpah, after *that* he had slain Gedaliah the son of Ahikam, *even* mighty men of war, and the women, and the children, and the eunuchs,

17 whom he had brought again from Gibeon: and they departed, and dwelt in the habitation of *l*Chimham, which is by Beth-le-

l 2 Sam. 19. 37, 38.

18 hem, to go to enter into Egypt, because of the Chaldeans: for they were afraid of them, because Ishmael the son of Nethaniah had slain Gedaliah the son of Ahikam, *m*whom the king of Babylon made governor in the land.

m ch. 40. 5.

CHAP. 42. THEN all the captains of the forces, *a*and Johanan the son of Kareah, and Jezaniah the son of Hoshaiah, and all the

a ch. 40. 8, 13.
& 41. 11.

2 people from the least even unto the greatest, came near, and said unto Jeremiah the prophet, [3]Let, we beseech thee, our suppli-cation be accepted before thee, and *b*pray for us unto the LORD thy God, *even* for all this remnant; (for we are left *but* *c*a few

b 1 Sam. 7. 8.
Isai. 37. 4.
Jam. 5. 16.
c Lev. 26. 22.

---

[1] Or, *near Gedaliah.* [2] Heb. *by the hand,* or, *by the side of Gedaliah.* [3] Or, *Let our supplication fall before thee.*

---

be of great value to Ishmael in his retreat back to Baalis.

9. *because of Gedaliah*] **By the side** *of Gedaliah.* Ishmael now cast beside Geda-liah's body those of the pilgrims.

12. An open pool still exists at Gibeon, and a large subterranean reservoir fed by a copious natural spring. Gibeon is about two miles North of Mizpah.

17. *the habitation of Chimham*] The He-brew text has *Geruth-Chemoham,* of which place nothing is known. The Masorites read *Geruth-Chimham,* the Khan or Cara-vanserai of Chimham, son of the rich Bar-zillai (marg. ref.). The substitution is in-

capable now of proof or disproof, but it is possibly right.

XLII. 1. Among those delivered by Jo-hanan from Ishmael had been Jeremiah and Baruch (xliii. 6); and to them now all, without exception, come for counsel.

Jezaniah] He is called Azariah in xliii. 2. The LXX. in both places call him Azariah As there is little reason for identifying him with Jezaniah the Maachathite (xl. 8), it is probable that the LXX. are right in calling him in both places Azariah, and that the reading Jezaniah arose from some scribe assuming that his name must be found in the earlier list.

3 of many, as thine eyes do behold us:) that the LORD thy God
d Ezra 8. 21.　may shew us *d* the way wherein we may walk, and the thing that
4 we may do.　¶ Then Jeremiah the prophet said unto them, I
have heard *you ;* behold, I will pray unto the LORD your God
e 1 Kin. 22.　according to your words; and it shall come to pass, *that* *e* what-
14.　soever thing the LORD shall answer you, I will declare *it* unto
f 1 Sam. 3. 18.　5 you; I will *f* keep nothing back from you.　Then they said to
Acts 20. 20.　Jeremiah, *g* The LORD be a true and faithful witness between us,
g Gen. 31. 50.　if we do not even according to all things for the which the LORD
6 thy God shall send thee to us.　Whether *it be* good, or whether
it be evil, we will obey the voice of the LORD our God, to whom
h Deut. 6. 3.　we send thee; *h* that it may be well with us, when we obey the
ch. 7. 23.　7 voice of the LORD our God.　¶ And it came to pass after ten
8 days, that the word of the LORD came unto Jeremiah.　Then
called he Johanan the son of Kareah, and all the captains of the
forces which *were* with him, and all the people from the least
9 even to the greatest, and said unto them, Thus saith the LORD,
the God of Israel, unto whom ye sent me to present your suppli-
10 cation before him; ¶ If ye will still abide in this land, then
i ch. 24. 6.　*i* will I build you, and not pull *you* down, and I will plant you,
& 31. 28.　and not pluck *you* up: for I *k* repent me of the evil that I have
k Deut. 32.　11 done unto you.　Be not afraid of the king of Babylon, of
36.　whom ye are afraid; be not afraid of him, saith the LORD:
ch. 18. 8.　*l* for I *am* with you to save you, and to deliver you from his
l Isai. 43. 5.　12 hand.　And *m* I will shew mercies unto you, that he may have
Rom. 8. 31.　mercy upon you, and cause you to return to your own land.
m Ps. 106.　13 ¶ But if *n* ye say, We will not dwell in this land, neither obey
45, 46.　14 the voice of the LORD your God, saying, No; but we will go into
n ch. 44. 16.　the land of Egypt, where we shall see no war, nor hear the sound
of the trumpet, nor have hunger of bread; and there will we
15 dwell: and now therefore hear the word of the LORD, ye remnant of Judah; Thus saith the LORD of hosts, the God of Israel;
o Deut. 17. 16.　If ye *o* wholly set *p* your faces to enter into Egypt, and go to
ch. 44. 12.　16 sojourn there; then it shall come to pass, *that* the sword, *q* which
p Luke 9. 51.　ye feared, shall *1* overtake you there in the land of Egypt, and
q Ezek. 11. 8.　the famine, whereof ye were afraid, *1* shall follow close after you
17 there in Egypt; and there ye shall die.　*2* So shall it be with all
the men that set their faces to go into Egypt to sojourn there;

1 Heb. *shall cleave after you.*　　　*2* Heb. *So shall all the men be.*

---

5. *between us*] **Against us**, as in *v.* 19
marg.
　according to all things] Lit. *according to
the whole word as to which Jehovah thy God
shall send thee to us.*
6. *we*] The form used here occurs nowhere
else in the Old Testament, but is the regular
form of the pronoun in the Talmud.　It is
one out of many instances of Jeremiah
using the popular instead of the literary
language of his times.
7. *after ten days*] On previous occasions
Jeremiah when consulted answered at once
(xxi. 3).　The present delay (cp. xxviii. 12)
was probably granted by God in order to
free the minds of the people from the panic
caused by the murder of Gedaliah and their
fear of Chaldæan vengeance.　Jeremiah
could have had no doubt that the flight into

Egypt was contrary to the tenor of his
former prophecies.
10. *I repent me*] As punishment had been
inflicted, the Divine justice was satisfied.
12. Or, **I will give you compassion**
before (*i.e.* obtain pity from) the king of
Babylon, *and he shall have mercy upon you,
and let you dwell upon your own soil.*
14. Egypt had lost the battle of Carchemish, but it had not been the scene itself of
military operations; while Judæa, from the
date of the battle of Megiddo, had perpetually been exposed to the actual horrors
of war.
16, 17. Translate, *Then* **shall** *the sword of
which ye are afraid* **reach** *you there in the
land of Egypt, and the famine whereof ye
pine shall cleave close unto you in Egypt,
and there shall ye die ;* **and** *all the men who*

they shall die *r*by the sword, by the famine, and by the pesti-
lence : and *s*none of them shall remain or escape from the evil
18 that I will bring upon them. For thus saith the LORD of hosts,
the God of Israel ; As mine anger and my fury hath been
*t*poured forth upon the inhabitants of Jerusalem ; so shall my
fury be poured forth upon you, when ye shall enter into Egypt:
and *u*ye shall be an execration, and an astonishment, and a
curse, and a reproach ; and ye shall see this place no more.
19 ¶ The LORD hath said concerning you, O ye remnant of Judah;
*x*Go ye not into Egypt: know certainly that I have ¹admonished
20 you this day. For ²ye dissembled in your hearts, when ye sent
me unto the LORD your God, saying, *y*Pray for us unto the LORD
our God; and according unto all that the LORD our God shall
21 say, so declare unto us, and we will do *it*. And *now* I have this
day declared *it* to you ; but ye have not obeyed the voice of the
LORD your God, nor any *thing* for the which he hath sent me
22 unto you. Now therefore know certainly that *z*ye shall die by
the sword, by the famine, and by the pestilence, in the place
whither ye desire ³to go *and* to sojourn.

CHAP. 43. AND it came to pass, *that* when Jeremiah had made an
end of speaking unto all the people all the words of the LORD
their God, for which the LORD their God had sent him to them,
even all these words, *a*then spake Azariah the son of Hoshaiah,
2 and Johanan the son of Kareah, and all the proud men, saying
unto Jeremiah, Thou speakest falsely : the LORD our God hath
3 not sent thee to say, Go not into Egypt to sojourn there: but
Baruch the son of Neriah setteth thee on against us, for to deliver
us into the hand of the Chaldeans, that they might put us to
4 death, and carry us away captives into Babylon. ¶ So Johanan
the son of Kareah, and all the captains of the forces, and all the
people, obeyed not the voice of the LORD, to dwell in the land of
5 Judah. But Johanan the son of Kareah, and all the captains of
the forces, took *b*all the remnant of Judah, that were returned
from all nations, whither they had been driven, to dwell in the

r ch. 24. 10.
s See ch. 44. 14, 28.

t ch. 7. 20.

u ch. 18. 16. Zech. 8. 13.

x Deut. 17. 16.

y ver. 2.

z ver. 17. Ezek. 6. 11.

a ch. 42. 1.

b ch. 40. 11, 12.

---

¹ Heb. *testified against you.*
² Or, *ye have used deceit*

against your souls.
³ Or, *to go to sojourn.*

---

have set their faces to go into Egypt to sojourn
there **shall die** ... *by the pestilence*, **nor shall**
they have *any one that is left or escaped from*
the evil which I will bring upon them.

18. *a curse*] **contempt**, or ignominy.
19. The request made in *v.* 3 has been ful-
filled : Jehovah has spoken. The prophet
now adds these four verses as a sort of epi-
logue, in which he urges upon them the
several points of the Divine message. In
the ten days which had intervened between
the request and the answer Jeremiah had
become aware that neither princes nor peo-
ple were prepared to obey unless the answer
was in accordance with their own wishes.
He does therefore his best to convince
them, but as usual it was his lot to speak
the truth to wilful men, and gain no hearing.
20. *ye dissembled in your hearts*] Or, *ye have*
led yourselves astray, i.e. your sending me to
ask counsel of God was an act of self-delu-
sion. You felt so sure that God would
direct you to go into Egypt, that now that

He has spoken to the contrary, you are un-
able to reconcile yourselves to it.
XLIII. **1-3.** These captains belonged to
the party who had all along resisted Jere-
miah's counsels, and had led Zedekiah astray.
Now however that events had proved that
the prophet's counsels had been wise and
true, they cannot for shame find fault
with him, but they affirm that he is under
the influence of Baruch, a traitor who has
sold himself to the Chaldeans, and seeks
only the hurt of the people.
4. *all the people*] Many, nevertheless,
would be unwilling agents, compelled to do
what their unscrupulous leaders forced upon
the community.
5. *all the remnant of Judah that were re-*
turned] In this way the utter depopulation
of the land was completed. Thus was ful-
filled the predictions of xxiv. 8-10, and the
sole hope of the nation now centered in the
exiles at Babylon (do. *vv.* 5-7).

c ch. 41. 10.
d ch. 39. 10.
& 40. 7.

6 land of Judah ; *even* men, and women, and children, cand the
king's daughters, dand every person that Nebuzar-adan the captain of the guard had left with Gedaliah the son of Ahikam the
son of Shaphan, and Jeremiah the prophet, and Baruch the son
7 of Neriah.   So they came into the land of Egypt: for they
obeyed not the voice of the LORD : thus came they *even* to

e ch. 41. 1.
called
Hanes,
Isai. 30. 4.

eTahpanhes.

8   Then came the word of the LORD unto Jeremiah in Tah-
9 panhes, saying, Take great stones in thine hand, and hide them
in the clay in the brickkiln, which *is* at the entry of Pharaoh's
10 house in Tahpanhes, in the sight of the men of Judah ; and say
unto them,   ¶ Thus saith the LORD of hosts, the God of Israel ;
Behold, I will send and take Nebuchadrezzar the king of Baby-

f ch. 27. 9.
& 27. 6.
g ch. 44. 13.
h ch. 15. 2.
Zech. 11. 9.

lon, fmy servant, and will set his throne upon these stones that
I have hid ; and he shall spread his royal pavilion over them.
11 gAnd when he cometh, he shall smite the land of Egypt, *and
deliver* hsuch *as are* for death to death ; and such *as are* for captivity to captivity ; and such *as are* for the sword to the sword.

i ch. 46. 25.

12 And I will kindle a fire in the houses of ithe gods of Egypt ; and
he shall burn them, and carry them away captives: and he shall
array himself with the land of Egypt, as a shepherd putteth on
13 his garment ; and he shall go forth from thence in peace.   He
shall break also the ¹images of ² Beth-shemesh, that *is* in the
land of Egypt ; and the houses of the gods of the Egyptians
shall he burn with fire.

CHAP. 44. THE word that came to Jeremiah concerning all the Jews

a Ex. 14. 2.
ch. 46. 14.

which dwell in the land of Egypt, which dwell at aMigdol, and

¹ Heb. *statues,* or, *standing images.*   ² Or, *The house of the sun.*

---

7. *Tahpanhes*] See ii. 16, note.
8. On arriving at the frontiers of Egypt,
the captains would be compelled to halt in
order to obtain the king's permission to enter
his country. Jeremiah therefore takes the opportunity to predict, first, the downfall of
Egypt ; and secondly, that of the false gods.
9. *brickkiln*] Possibly, *a pavement of brick.*
Jeremiah was to take a few large stones,
such, nevertheless, as he could carry in his
hand, and build with them, in the propylæa
before the royal palace, something that
would serve to represent the dais upon
which the seat of kings was usually placed.
By hiding them in the clay is meant plaister-
ing them over with mortar.
10. *my servant*] See xxv. 9 note.
that I have hid] *i.e.* that I have embedded
in the mortar by the instrumentality of my
prophet.
pavilion] Rather, *canopy.* It probably
means the parasol held over kings, which
had a tall and thick pole, grasped with both
hands, and in the early times a somewhat
small circular top.
11. According to each man's destiny he
will either die of famine, pestilence, or in
battle ; or he will be led captive ; or be put
to death by the executioner.
12. *I will kindle*] Or, *he shall kindle.*

he shall burn them &c.] *i.e.* he shall burn
the temples, and carry away the gods.
and he shall array] Lit. *And he shall
wrap himself in the land of Egypt as the shepherd wrappeth himself in his cloak, and shall
go forth thence in peace ; i.e.,* With as great
ease as a shepherd throws his cloak round
him when going forth to watch his flock by
night in the field, so easily shall the king of
Babylon take possession of all the glory of
Egypt, throw it round him, and depart
without anyone resisting his progress.
13. *images*] Rather, *pillars* (cp. Isai. xix.
19 note), obelisks.
Beth-shemesh] Heliopolis, famous for its
obelisks.
XLIV. Jeremiah's last prophecy, in
which he boldly rebukes the tendency of the
Jews to idolatry, which seems to have grown
only the stronger in their tribulation. The
address was evidently made to them at some
festival, and though the Jews lived in the
hope of being able soon to return to Judæa
from Egypt, yet we find that they had
spread over the whole land, representatives
of their communities having come to Pathros not only from Migdol and Tahpanhes,
but even from Noph.
1. *Migdol*] Magdolum, a strong fortress
on the northern boundary of Egypt.

at *Tahpanhes, and at *Noph, and in the country of Pathros,

2 saying, ¶ Thus saith the LORD of hosts, the God of Israel ; Ye have seen all the evil that I have brought upon Jerusalem, and upon all the cities of Judah ; and, behold, this day they *are *a*

3 desolation, and no man dwelleth therein, because of their wickedness which they have committed to provoke me to anger, in that they went *to burn incense, *and* to *serve other gods, whom they

4 knew not, *neither* they, ye, nor your fathers. Howbeit *I sent unto you all my servants the prophets, rising early and sending *them*, saying, Oh, do not this abominable thing that I hate.

5 But they hearkened not, nor inclined their ear to turn from

6 their wickedness, to burn no incense unto other gods. Wherefore *my fury and mine anger was poured forth, and was kindled in the cities of Judah and in the streets of Jerusalem ; and they

7 are wasted *and* desolate, as at this day. Therefore now thus saith the LORD, the God of hosts, the God of Israel ; Wherefore commit ye *this* great evil *against your souls, to cut off from you man and woman, child and suckling, ¹out of Judah, to leave

8 you none to remain ; in that ye *provoke me unto wrath with the works of your hands, burning incense unto other gods in the land of Egypt, whither ye be gone to dwell, that ye might cut yourselves off, and that ye might be *a curse and a reproach

9 among all the nations of the earth ? Have ye forgotten the ²wickedness of your fathers, and the wickedness of the kings of Judah, and the wickedness of their wives, and your own wickedness, and the wickedness of your wives, which they have committed in the land of Judah, and in the streets of Jerusalem ?

10 They are not ³humbled *even* unto this day, neither have they *feared, nor walked in my law, nor in my statutes, that I set

11 before you and before your fathers. ¶ Therefore thus saith the LORD of hosts, the God of Israel ; Behold, *I will set my face

12 against you for evil, and to cut off all Judah. And I will take the remnant of Judah, that have set their faces to go into the land of Egypt to sojourn there, and *they shall all be consumed, *and* fall in the land of Egypt ; they shall *even* be consumed by the sword *and* by the famine : they shall die, from the least even unto the greatest, by the sword and by the famine : and *they shall be an execration, *and* an astonishment, and a curse, and a

13 reproach. *For I will punish them that dwell in the land of Egypt, as I have punished Jerusalem, by the sword, by the

14 famine, and by the pestilence : so that none of the remnant of Judah, which are gone into the land of Egypt to sojourn there, shall escape or remain, that they should return into the land of

b ch. 43. 7.
c Isai. 19. 13.

d ch. 9. 11. & 34. 22.

e ch. 19. 4.
f Deut. 13. 6. & 32. 17.
g 2 Chr. 36. 15.
ch. 7. 25.

h ch. 42. 18.

i Num.16.38. ch. 7. 19.

k ch. 25. 6, 7.

l ch. 42. 18. ver. 12.

m Prov. 28. 14.

n Lev. 17.10. & 20. 5. ch. 21. 10. Amos 9. 4.
o ch. 42. 15.

p ch. 42. 18.

q ch. 43. 11.

---

¹ Heb. *out of the midst of Judah.*   ² Heb. *wickednesses,* or, *punishments, &c.*   ³ Heb. *contrite,* Ps. 51. 17.

---

3. *in that they went to burn incense,* and *to serve*] Or, **by going** *to burn incense to serve thereby other gods.*

4. *Howbeit I sent*] **And** *I sent.*

7. *your souls*] *i.e.* your own selves.

8. *cut yourselves off*] Rather, *cut* (them, *r.* 7) *off from you.*

9. *the wickedness of their wives*] Many accept the reading of the LXX., *the wickedness of your princes.* "The kings, the princes, the people," and finally "their wives," is a summary enumeration of all

classes, by whose united persistence in sin the ruin of their country had been consummated.

11. *all Judah*] *i.e.* all Judah in Egypt, yet even there with exceptions (see *vr.* 14, 28), while Judah in Babylon was entirely exempt from this denunciation.

14. Lit. *And there shall not be to the remnant of Judah, which are* **going** *to sojourn there in the land of Egypt, one that escapes or remains* &c. The word rendered "escapes" means one who slips away, saves himself by

Judah, to the which they ¹have a desire to return to dwell there:

r ver. 23.

15 for *r*none shall return but such as shall escape.　¶ Then all the men which knew that their wives had burned incense unto other gods, and all the women that stood by, a great multitude, even all the people that dwelt in the land of Egypt, in Pathros,

16 answered Jeremiah, saying, ¶ *As for* the word that thou hast spoken unto us in the name of the LORD, *s*we will not hearken

17 unto thee.　But we will certainly do *t*whatsoever thing goeth forth out of our own mouth, to burn incense unto the ²*u*queen of heaven, and to pour out drink offerings unto her, as we have done, we, and our fathers, our kings, and our princes, in the cities of Judah, and in the streets of Jerusalem : for *then* had we

18 plenty of ³victuals, and were well, and saw no evil.　But since we left off to burn incense to the queen of heaven, and to pour out drink offerings unto her, we have wanted all *things*, and have

19 been consumed by the sword and by the famine.　*x*And when we burned incense to the queen of heaven, and poured out drink offerings unto her, did we make her cakes to worship her, and

20 pour out drink offerings unto her, without our ⁴men ?　¶ Then Jeremiah said unto all the people, to the men, and to the women, and to all the people which had given him *that* answer, saying,

21 The incense that ye burned in the cities of Judah, and in the streets of Jerusalem, ye, and your fathers, your kings, and your princes, and the people of the land, did not the LORD remember

22 them, and came it *not* into his mind ?　So that the LORD could no longer bear, because of the evil of your doings, *and* because

s So ch. 6.
14.
t Num. 30.
12.
Deut. 23. 23.
Judg. 11. 36.
u ch. 7. 18.

x ch. 7. 18.

---

¹ Heb. *lift up their soul.*
² Or, *frame of heaven.*
³ Heb. *bread.*
⁴ Or, *husbands?*

---

a stealthy flight (Gen. xiv. 13); the word "remains," one who survives when all the rest perish (Job xviii. 19).　Of all those now going down to Egypt none shall return to Judæa except a few miserable fugitives, who shall steal away as men who flee in battle (2 Sam. xix. 3).　For many years Jewish settlers had gone to Egypt in great numbers, and these old settlers would be treated in the same way as the Egyptians, but these fugitives, with no knowledge of the Egyptian language or ways, would have no friends in the country to aid them, and would also be recognized by the Chaldæans as inveterate enemies, and mercilessly slain.

15. *had burned incense*] Omit "had"; **burned** *incense*.　This appeal of the prophet was made at a public festival held somewhere in Pathros, *i.e.* Upper Egypt : for the women are assembled in a great congregation (cp. xxvi. 9), here formed for religious purposes.　As they advance in regular procession to worship the moon-goddess, in accordance as it seems with a vow (*v.* 17), Jeremiah meets them, makes the procession halt upon its way, and pronounces in Jehovah's name words of solemn warning.　The reply that all the settlers in Egypt were formally putting themselves under the Queen of Heaven's protection was made by the heads of the congregation.

17. *whatsoever thing &c.*] Or, **the whole** *word* (or *thing*) **which hath gone forth** *out*

of our mouth; *i.e.* the vows we have made.　They would not let Jeremiah's expostulations prevent the carrying out of the special object which had brought them together : otherwise the Queen of Heaven would be offended, and avenge himself.

18. The suppression of this popular idolatry had apparently been regarded with much ill-will in Josiah's time, and many may even have ascribed to it his defeat at Megiddo.　Probably Jehoiakim had again permitted it, but Zedekiah, during the miseries of his reign, had forbidden it, and the people ascribed the fall of Jerusalem to the neglect of their favourite goddess.

19. *burned...poured...did*] Or, burn...pour ...do.

to worship her] Rather, *to represent her image*.　The cakes (vii. 18) were made in the shape of a crescent to represent the moon.

our men] *i.e.* **our husbands** (margin).　They had the authority of their husbands for what they were doing.　Jeremiah must leave them alone, and discuss the matter with those who alone had the right to interfere.

21. *them*] The various acts of idolatry involved in burning incense to an image.

22. *could no longer bear*] The prophet corrects in these words the error of their argument in *v.* 17.　God is long-suffering, and therefore punishment follows slowly upon sin.

of the abominations which ye have committed; therefore is your
land *v* a desolation, and an astonishment, and a curse, without an
23 inhabitant, *z* as at this day. Because ye have burned incense,
and because ye have sinned against the LORD, and have not
obeyed the voice of the LORD, nor walked in his law, nor in his
statutes, nor in his testimonies; *a* therefore this evil is happened
24 unto you, as at this day. ¶ Moreover Jeremiah said unto all the
people, and to all the women, Hear the word of the LORD, all
25 Judah *b* that *are* in the land of Egypt: Thus saith the LORD of
hosts, the God of Israel, saying; *c* Ye and your wives have both
spoken with your mouths, and fulfilled with your hand, saying,
We will surely perform our vows that we have vowed, to burn
incense to the queen of heaven, and to pour out drink offerings
unto her: ye will surely accomplish your vows, and surely per-
26 form your vows. Therefore hear ye the word of the LORD, all
Judah that dwell in the land of Egypt; Behold, *d* I have sworn
by my great name, saith the LORD, that *e* my name shall no more
be named in the mouth of any man of Judah in all the land of
27 Egypt, saying, The Lord GOD liveth. *f* Behold, I will watch over
them for evil, and not for good: and all the men of Judah that
are in the land of Egypt *g* shall be consumed by the sword and
28 by the famine, until there be an end of them. Yet *h* a small
number that escape the sword shall return out of the land of
Egypt into the land of Judah, and all the remnant of Judah,
that are gone into the land of Egypt to sojourn there, shall know
29 whose *i* words shall stand, ¹ mine, or their's. ¶ And this *shall be*
a sign unto you, saith the LORD, that I will punish you in this
place, that ye may know that my words shall *k* surely stand
30 against you for evil: Thus saith the LORD; Behold, *l* I will give
Pharaoh-hophra king of Egypt into the hand of his enemies, and
into the hand of them that seek his life; as I gave *m* Zedekiah
king of Judah into the hand of Nebuchadrezzar king of Babylon,
his enemy, and that sought his life.

y ch. 25. 11.
z ver. 6.

a Dan. 9. 11,
12.

b ch. 43. 7.
ver. 15.
c ver. 15.

d Gen. 22. 16.
e Ezek. 20. 39.

f ch. 1. 10.
Ezek. 7. 6.
g ver. 12.
h ver. 14.
Isai. 27. 13.

i ver. 17, 25.

k Ps. 33. 11.
l ch. 46. 25.
Ezek. 29. 3.
m ch. 39. 5.

¹ Heb. *from me,* or, *them.*

24–30. Earnest as was the preceding expostulation, Jeremiah sees that it has produced
no effect. He therefore utters his last
warning, and with this last resistance to
the sins of a debased and godless people,
his earthly ministry closed.

25. *and fulfilled with your hand*] Your
hands. Jeremiah pointed to their hands, in
which they were carrying the crescent-
shaped cakes which they had vowed to the
goddess. Their idolatry therefore was an
accomplished deed, as the symbols held in
their hands testified.

ye will surely accomplish] Or, *Accomplish
then your vows.* It is not a prediction, but
is ironical, and means that as they will take
no warning, they must needs have their
way.

26. *my name shall no more be named...*]
God swears by His own great Name that He
will be their national God no longer. Jehovah repudiates His Covenant-relation
toward them.

27. *I will watch*] **I am watching** *over them,*
not for good, but for evil: like a panther

(v. 6) lying in wait to spring upon passengers.

shall be consumed] This is the result of
Jehovah's repudiation of the Covenant.
When He was their God He watched over
them for good: now His protection is withdrawn, and He is their enemy, because of
the wickedness whereby their rejection was
made necessary. See vi. 9 note.

28. Lit. *And fugitives from the sword* (see
v. 14) *shall return from the land of Egypt to
the land of Judah, men of number, i.e.* so few
that they can be counted: *and all the remnant of Judah that* **are going** &c. So
unendurable shall be their sufferings in
Egypt, that the men now abandoning
Judæa in the hope of finding an asylum
there shall be glad to return like runaways
from a lost battle.

whose words...] *Whose* **word** *shall stand,
from Me or from them, i.e.* the one prediction,
that their descent into Egypt would be
their ruin, which they denied.

30. Pharaoh-Hophra came to the throne
the year before Jerusalem was captured.

a ch. 36. 1.

Chap. 45. THE *a* word that Jeremiah the prophet spake unto Baruch
the son of Neriah, when he had written these words in a book
at the mouth of Jeremiah, in the fourth year of Jehoiakim the
2 son of Josiah king of Judah, saying, ¶ Thus saith the LORD, the
3 God of Israel, unto thee, O Baruch; Thou didst say, Woe is me
now! for the LORD hath added grief to my sorrow; I fainted in
4 my sighing, and I find no rest. Thus shalt thou say unto him,

b Isai. 5. 5.

The LORD saith thus; Behold, *b*that which I have built will I
break down, and that which I have planted I will pluck up, even
5 this whole land. And seekest thou great things for thyself?

c ch. 25. 26.

seek *them* not: for, behold, *c*I will bring evil upon all flesh,

d ch. 21. 9.
& 39. 18.

saith the LORD: but thy life will I give unto thee *d*for a prey in
all places whither thou goest.

Chap. 46. THE word of the LORD which came to Jeremiah the

a ch. 25. 15.

prophet against *a*the Gentiles.

b 2 Kin. 23.
29.
2 Chr. 35. 20.

2   Against Egypt, *b*against the army of Pharaoh - necho king
of Egypt, which was by the river Euphrates in Carchemish,
which Nebuchadrezzar king of Babylon smote in the fourth year

c So ch. 51.
11, 12.
Nah. 2. 1.

3 of Jehoiakim the son of Josiah king of Judah. ¶ *c*Order ye
4 the buckler and shield, and draw near to battle. Harness the

---

He reigned 19 years, probably the last ten
years a prisoner. See xxxvii. 5, xlvi. 12 notes.

XLV. The long catalogue of calamities
so consistently denounced by Jeremiah
against his country, made a most painful
impression upon Baruch's mind. He was
of ambitious temperament (*v.* 5), and being
of noble birth as the grandson of Maaseiah,
the governor of Jerusalem in Josiah's time
(2 Chr. xxxiv. 8), and a scribe, he appears to
have looked forward either to high office
in the state, or far more probably to being
invested with prophetic powers. This address tells Baruch to give up his ambitious
hopes, and be content with escaping with
life only. Like the prophecy of the seventy
years of exile, it would become a prediction
of good only after many troubles had been
undergone and pride was quelled. As regards the place of this prophecy it would
come in order of time next to ch. xxxvi.,
but as that was a public, and this a private
prophecy, they would not be written upon
the same roll. When the last memorials of
Jeremiah's life were added to the history
of the fall of Jerusalem, Baruch attached to
them this prediction, which—humbled by
years, and the weight of public and private
calamity,—he now read with very different
feelings from those which filled his mind in
his youth.

1. *these words*] *i.e.* the words of Jehoiakim's roll.

3. *grief to my sorrow*] Baruch's sorrow is
caused by the sinfulness of the Jewish nation, to which God adds grief by shewing
how severely it will be punished.

I fainted in] Or, "am weary with" (Ps. vi. 6).

4. *land*] Or, *earth*. Baruch's lot was cast
in one of those troublous times when God
enters into judgment with all flesh (*v.* 5).

It was not Judæa only but the whole known
world that was thrown into turmoil by Nebuchadnezzar's energy (xxv. 26).

XLVI.-XLIX. The prophecies against
foreign nations are collected into one roll.
Cp. Isai. xiii.-xxiii.; Ezek. xxv.-xxxii.
They are arranged in two great divisions,
(*a*) xlvi.-xlix. 33, spoken in connexion with
ch. xxv.; and (*b*) chs. l., li. spoken at a subsequent date against Babylon. Between
them is placed a prophecy against Elam
(xlix. 34-39) spoken in the first year of Zedekiah. The seven earlier prophecies belonging to the fourth year of Jehoiakim
were written at the same time, and arranged
as they at present stand. It is no doubt intentional that these prophecies against the
nations are in number 7 (cp. Amos i. 3, ii. 4).

XLVI. This prophecy against Egypt
consists of two parts, (*a*) a song of triumph
because of her defeat at Carchemish (*vv.*
3-12); (*b*) a prediction that the conqueror
would invade Egypt from one end to the
other (*vv.* 14-28). Possibly a long delay intervened between these predictions.

1. *against the Gentiles*] Or, *concerning the
nations* (xlvi.-xlix. 33).

2. *Against...*] *i.e.* relating to, *concerning.*
So xlviii. 1; xlix. 1; note on *v.* 13.

Pharaoh-necho] See 2 K. xxiii. 29 note.

in (at) *Carchemish*] [The Gargamis of the
inscriptions, now Jerabis, on the Euphrates,
about 16 miles South of Birejik].

3. *Order ye...*] *i.e. prepare ye, make ready.*
The *buckler* was a small round target carried
by the light-armed troops: the *shield* belonged to the heavy-armed troops, and was
large enough to protect the whole body.

4. From the infantry the prophet proceeds to the chariots, in which the Egyptians
placed great confidence.

horses; and get up, ye horsemen, and stand forth with *your*
5 helmets; furbish the spears, *and* put on the brigandines. Wherefore have I seen them dismayed *and* turned away back? and
their mighty ones are [1]beaten down, and are[2] fled apace, and
6 look not back: *for* [d]fear *was* round about, saith the LORD. Let
not the swift flee away, nor the mighty man escape; they shall
[e]stumble, and fall toward the north by the river Euphrates.
7 Who *is* this *that* cometh up [f]as a flood, whose waters are moved
8 as the rivers? Egypt riseth up like a flood, and *his* waters are
moved like the rivers; and he saith, I will go up, *and* will cover
the earth; I will destroy the city and the inhabitants thereof.
9 Come up, ye horses; and rage, ye chariots; and let the mighty
men come forth; [3]the Ethiopians and [4]the Libyans, that handle
the shield; and the Lydians, [g]that handle *and* bend the bow.
10 For this *is* [h]the day of the Lord GOD of hosts, a day of vengeance, that he may avenge him of his adversaries: and [i]the
sword shall devour, and it shall be satiate and made drunk with
their blood: for the Lord GOD of hosts [k]hath a sacrifice in the
11 north country by the river Euphrates. [l]Go up into Gilead, and
take balm, [m]O virgin, the daughter of Egypt: in vain shalt thou
12 use many medicines; *for* [5][n]thou shalt not be cured. The nations
have heard of thy shame, and thy cry hath filled the land: for
the mighty man hath stumbled against the mighty, *and* they are
fallen both together.

[d] ch. 49. 29.

[e] Dan. 11. 19.
[f] See Isai. 8.
7, 8.
ch. 47. 2.

[g] Isai. 66. 19.
[h] Isai. 13. 6.
Joel 1. 15.
[i] Deut. 32. 42.

[k] Isai. 34. 6.
Zeph. 1. 7.
[l] ch. 51. 8.
[m] Isai. 47. 1.
[n] Ezek. 30.
21.

[1] Heb. *broken in pieces.*
[2] Heb. *fled a flight.*
[3] Heb. *Cush.*
[4] Heb. *Put.*
[5] Heb. *no cure* shall be
unto thee.

get up, ye horsemen] Or, "mount the steeds."
furbish] *i.e.* polish, sharpen.

brigandines] In old times *brigand* meant
a soldier, and we still call a division of an
army a brigade, and a commander a briga-
dier, *i.e.* a brigandier, or captain of brigands.
Similarly a brigandine means a soldier's
equipment, and is put here for a *coat of mail.*

5. Lit. *Why have I seen? They are terror-
stricken! they are giving way back!* The
Egyptian host feels that the battle is lost,
and overborne by the enemy loses heart,
and in despair, yet not without a struggle,
gives way. It is remarkable, that while
Jeremiah in his warning addressed to Jerusalem uses the most simple and unadorned
prose, his language concerning the Gentile
nations is, on the contrary, full of brilliant
poetry.

look not back] **turn** *not back.* They make
no halt, and no attempt to rally.

fear was *round about*] The prophet's watchword, Magor-missabib (see vi. 25).

6. Translate, *The swift shall not flee away,
and the hero shall not escape: in the North on
the bank of the river Euphrates they shall
stumble and fall.*

7. In *vv.* 3-6 we saw only a mighty army
marshalling for battle, and its hasty flight.
In *vv.* 7-12 the prophet tells us at whose
defeat we have been present.

a flood] *the* **Nile.** The metaphor describing the advance of the Egyptian army is
naturally drawn from the annual overflow
of their own sacred stream.

whose waters are moved...] Lit. **his waters
toss to and fro** *as the rivers,* the natural
branches of the Nile in Lower Egypt.

9. Rather, *Go up, advance, ye horses; and
drive furiously, ye chariots; and let the
mighty men go forth.* They march out of
Egypt, arranged in three divisions, cavalry,
chariots, and infantry, to begin the campaign. The armies of Egypt were composed chiefly of mercenaries. *Cush* (see
marg.), the Nubian negro, and *Phut,* the
Libyans of Mauritania, supplied the heavy-
armed soldiers (*v.* 3); and *Ludim,* the Hamite Lydians of North Africa (see Gen. x.
13 note), a weaker race, served as light-
armed troops.

10. Rather, **But that** *day belongeth to the*
LORD *Jehovah of hosts.* They march forth in
haughty confidence, *but that day,* the day to
which they are looking forward in proud
hope of victory, is Jehovah's day, a day on
which they will be the victims sacrificed in
His honour.

11. *balm*] *i.e.* **balsam,** the usual remedy
for wounds (viii. 22).

in vain shalt...] Or, *in vain* **hast thou
multiplied** *medicines:* **healing-plaister** *hast
thou none.* Nothing shall avail to heal the
blow.

12. *the land*] **The earth** ; the world rings
with the cry of grief.

against the mighty] *Against the mighty*
man, *i.e.* one mighty man against another.
The champions hired to fight Egypt's battle

13 The word that the LORD spake to Jeremiah the prophet, how
Nebuchadrezzar king of Babylon should come *and* °smite the
14 land of Egypt. ¶ Declare ye in Egypt, and publish in Migdol,
and publish in Noph, and in Tahpanhes: say ye, *p*Stand fast, and
prepare thee; for *q*the sword shall devour round about thee.
15 Why are thy valiant *men* swept away? they stood not, because
16 the LORD did drive them. He ¹made many to fall, yea, *r*one
fell upon another: and they said, Arise, and let us go again
to our own people, and to the land of our nativity, from the
17 oppressing sword. They did cry there, Pharaoh king of Egypt,
18 *is but* a noise; he hath passed the time appointed. *As* I live,
saith the King, *s*whose name *is* the LORD of hosts, Surely as
Tabor is among the mountains, and as Carmel by the sea, *so*
19 shall he come. O *t*thou daughter dwelling in Egypt, ²furnish
thyself *u*to go into captivity: for Noph shall be waste and deso-
20 late without an inhabitant. Egypt *is like* a very fair *x*heifer,
21 *but* destruction cometh; it cometh *y*out of the north. Also her
hired men *are* in the midst of her like ³fatted bullocks; for

---

¹ Heb. *multiplied the faller.*   ² Heb. *make thee instru-*   ³ Heb. *bullocks of the stall.*
                                        ments of captivity.

---

get in one another's way, and so are
slaughtered together.

13. A new prophecy, foretelling the successful invasion of Egypt by Nebuchadnezzar, has been appended to the hymn of
triumph, because they both relate to the
same kingdom. This prophecy was probably spoken in Egypt to warn the Jews
there, that the country which they were so
obstinately determined to make their refuge would share the fate of their native
land.

how...should come] Or, **concerning the
coming** of *Nebuchadrezzar.*

14. *the sword shall devour*] *The sword* hath
devoured *those round about thee.* One after
another the nations have been consumed by
Nebuchadnezzar; and now at length Tyre,
which so long had withstood him, has fallen,
and his forces are about to fall upon Egypt
(ii. 16 note). Hence the summons to arrange
themselves in their ranks, and to *prepare*
for battle by putting on their armour.

15. Translate, *Why is thy mighty one cast
down? He stood not, because Jehovah thrust
him down.* The "mighty one" is explained
by the LXX. to be the bull Apis. Thus (1)
the chief deity of Egypt (*v.* 15): (2) the army
of mercenaries (*v.* 16): (3) the king, Pharaoh
(*v.* 17), are the three upon whom the Egyptians trusted.

16. Lit. as in marg., *i.e.* Jehovah hath
made many to **stumble.**

Arise &c.] The Egyptian army being
composed of mercenaries, has no patriotic
feeling, and immediately that the battle is
lost, they propose to abandon the country
which has hired them, and return each to
his native land.

17. Translate with the Versions, *They have
called* (or, *Call ye*) *the name of Pharaoh king
of Egypt—A noise: he hath overstepped the*

appointed time. For this custom of giving
prophetic names see xx. 3; Isai. viii. 3 &c.
The words mean that Pharaoh is a mere
empty sound, and that he has allowed the
years of prosperity, which he enjoyed at
the beginning of his reign, to pass by;
having misused them, nothing now remains
but his ruin.

18. *as Tabor is*] Omit *is. He shall come
like a Tabor among the mountains, and like a
Carmel by the sea.* Tabor rises in the form of
a truncated cone to the height of about 1,350
feet above the plain of Esdraelon, its total
height above the sea-level being 1,805 feet.
Its shape and the wide extent of the plain
around it make it a far more conspicuous
object than other mountains in sight of
equal elevation. Similarly Carmel is a most
commanding mountain, because it rises
from the edge of the wide expanse of the
Mediterranean.

19. Lit. *O thou inhabitant daughter of
Egypt,* an equivalent here for Egypt and
its whole population.

furnish thyself &c.] Lit. *make for thee
vessels of banishment,* not merely the pack-
ages necessary, but their outfit generally.

20. *is like*] Or, *is.* Her god was the steer
Apis (*v.* 15), and she is the spouse.

*but destruction cometh; it cometh out of the
north*] More probably, *a gadfly from the
North has come upon her.* This is a sort of
insect which stings the oxen and drives
them to madness. Cp. Isai. vii. 18.

21. Rather, *Also her hirelings in the midst
of her are like calves of the stall.* The mercenaries of Egypt—Nubians, Moors, and
Lydians (*v.* 9)—were destroyed at the battle
of Carchemish, and their place was taken
by hirelings from Asia Minor, Carians, and
Ionians, whom Hophra took into his pay
to the number of 30,000 men. These he

they also are turned back, *and* are fled away together : they did not stand, because ᶻthe day of their calamity was come upon 22 them, *and* the time of their visitation. ᵃThe voice thereof shall go like a serpent; for they shall march with an army, 23 and come against her with axes, as hewers of wood. They shall ᵇcut down her forest, saith the LORD, though it cannot be searched; because they are more than ᶜthe grasshoppers, and 24 *are* innumerable. The daughter of Egypt shall be confounded; she shall be delivered into the hand of ᵈthe people of the north. 25 The LORD of hosts, the God of Israel, saith; Behold, I will punish the ¹²multitude of ᵉNo, and Pharaoh, and Egypt, ᶠwith their gods, and their kings; even Pharaoh, and *all* them that 26 trust in him: ᵍand I will deliver them into the hand of those that seek their lives, and into the hand of Nebuchadrezzar king of Babylon, and into the hand of his servants : and ʰafterward it shall be inhabited, as in the days of old, saith the LORD. 27 ¶ᶦBut fear not thou, O my servant Jacob, and be not dismayed, O Israel: for, behold, I will save thee from afar off, and thy seed from the land of their captivity; and Jacob shall return, and be in rest and at ease, and none shall make *him* 28 afraid. Fear thou not, O Jacob my servant, saith the LORD: for I *am* with thee; for I will make a full end of all the nations whither I have driven thee: but I will not make ᵏa full end of thee, but correct thee in measure; yet will I ³not leave thee wholly unpunished.

ᶻ Ps. 37. 13.
ch. 50. 27.
ᵃ See Isai. 29. 4.

ᵇ Isai. 10. 34.
ᶜ Judg. 6. 5.

ᵈ ch. 1. 15.

ᵉ Ezek. 30. 14, 15, 16.
Nah. 3. 8.
ᶠ ch. 43. 12.
Ezek. 30. 13.
ᵍ ch. 44. 30.
Ezek. 32. 11.
ʰ Ezek. 29.
11, 13, 14.
ᶦ Isai. 41. 13, 14.

ᵏ ch. 10. 24.

¹ Or, *nourisher.*   ² Heb. *Amon.*   ³ Or, *not utterly cut thee off.*

---

settled *in the midst* of Egypt, in the fertile lands above Bubastis, in the Delta, where, well paid and fed and with great privileges, they became as *calves of the stall.* Their mutiny cost Hophra his crown.

for they also are turned back &c.] Lit. *for they also have turned the back, they flee together, they stand not: for the day of their destruction is come upon them, the time of their visitation.*

22. *The voice thereof*] **Her voice,** *i.e.* the voice of Egypt. The word here probably means the busy sound of life and activity in the towns of Egypt, the tramping of her hosts, and the turmoil of camp and city. All this at the approach of the Chaldæan army shall depart, as the snake flees away when disturbed in its haunts by the wood-cutters.

march with an army] Advance with might.

with axes] The comparison of the Chaldæan warriors to woodcutters arose from their being armed with axes. As the Israelites did not use the battle-axe, their imagination would be the more forcibly struck by this weapon.

23. Or, *They* **have cut down** *her forest, saith Jehovah ; for it is impenetrable, i.e.* just as a pathless forest must be cleared to assist agriculture and the passage to and fro of men, so must the false worship and the material prosperity of Egypt be overthrown.

grasshoppers] The invading host advances as multitudinous as the locusts which con-

sume the whole vegetation of the land on which they alight.

24. *The daughter* &c.] *i.e.* the inhabitants *of Egypt shall be* **disgraced.**

25. *the multitude of No*] Rather, **Amon of No.** Ammon or Jupiter-Ammon was the first of the supreme triad of Thebes. He was the deity invisible and unfathomable, whose name signifies *the concealed. No-Amon,* is the sacred city of Thebes, the capital of Upper Egypt. First then Jehovah's anger falls upon the representatives of the highest divine and human powers, Amon of No and Pharaoh. It next punishes Egypt generally, *and her gods and her kings;* for each city had its special divinity, and inferior rulers were placed in the several parts of the country. Finally Pharaoh is again mentioned, with *all who trust in him, i.e.* the Jews, who had made Egypt their confidence and not God.

26. *afterward* &c.] The invasion of Nebuchadnezzar is to be a passing calamity, the severity of which will be felt chiefly by the Jews, but no subjugation of Egypt is to be attempted, and after the Chaldæan army has withdrawn things will resume their former course.

27, 28. These two verses are a repetition of xxx. 10, 11, with those slight variations which Jeremiah always makes when quoting himself. Egypt's fall and restoration have been foretold; but the prophet closes with a word of exhortation to the many

CHAP. 47. THE word of the LORD that came to Jeremiah the prophet *a*against the Philistines, *b*before that Pharaoh smote 2 ¹Gaza. ¶ Thus saith the LORD ; ¶ Behold, *c*waters rise up *d*out of the north, and shall be an overflowing flood, and shall overflow the land, and ²all that is therein ; the city, and them that dwell therein : then the men shall cry, and all the inhabitants of the 3 land shall howl. At the *e*noise of the stamping of the hoofs of his strong *horses*, at the rushing of his chariots, *and at* the rumbling of his wheels, the fathers shall not look back to *their* 4 children for feebleness of hands ; because of the day that cometh to spoil all the Philistines, *and* to cut off from *f*Tyrus and Zidon every helper that remaineth : for the LORD will spoil the Phi-5 listines, *g*the remnant of ³the country of *h*Caphtor. *i*Baldness is come upon Gaza ; *k*Ashkelon is cut off *with* the remnant of their 6 valley : how long wilt thou *l*cut thyself ? O thou *m*sword of the LORD, how long *will it be* ere thou be quiet ? ⁴put up thyself 7 into thy scabbard, rest, and be still. ⁵How can it be quiet, seeing the LORD hath *n*given it a charge against Ashkelon, and against the sea shore ? *there hath he *o*appointed it.

CHAP. 48. AGAINST *a*Moab. Thus saith the LORD of hosts, the

¹ Heb. *Azzah.*   ³ Heb. *the isle.*   ⁵ Heb. *How canst thou?*
² Heb. *the fulness thereof.*   ⁴ Heb. *gather thyself.*

---

erring Jews who dwelt there. Why should they flee from their country, and trust in a heathen power, instead of endeavouring to live in a manner worthy of the noble destiny which was their true glory and ground of confidence ?

XLVII. Pharaoh-Necho though defeated at Carchemish, was probably able to seize Gaza upon his retreat, when obviously the possession of so strong a fortress would be most useful to him to prevent the entrance of the victorious Chaldæans into Egypt.

2. *waters rise up*] A metaphor for the assembling of an army (cp. marg. reff.).

out of the north] The Chaldæan army must cross the Euphrates at Carchemish.

an overflowing flood] Or, *torrent*. To understand the metaphors of the Bible we must keep the natural phenomena of the country in mind. In Palestine rivers are torrents, dashing furiously along in the rainy seasons, and dry, or nearly so, in the summer.

all that is therein] The marg. rendering contrasts the wealth of Egypt, which forms its fulness, and the inhabitants.

3. *his strong horses*] *War-horses, chargers.*

the rushing of his chariots] Rather, **the rattling,** the crashing noise which they make by their advance.

for feebleness of hands] The Philistines flee in such panic that a father would not even turn round to see whether his sons were effecting their escape or not.

4. *Because of the day that cometh to spoil*] *Because* **the day has come** to *devastate.*

The Philistines are called Tyre's remaining (*i.e.* last) helper, because all besides who could have assisted her have already suc-

cumbed to the Chaldæan power. The judgment upon Philistia was in connexion with that upon Tyre, and it was fulfilled by expeditions sent out by Nebuchadnezzar under his lieutenants to ravage the country and supply his main army with provisions.

the country of Caphtor] *The* **coastland** *of Caphtor.* The Philistines came from the coast of the Egyptian Delta, and are called "a remnant" because they had been greatly reduced in numbers, partly by the long war of Psammetichus against Ashdod, partly by the capture of Gaza (*v.* 1), and partly by Assyrian invasions.

5. *Baldness*] Extreme mourning (see xvi. 6).

is cut off] Others render, *is speechless* through grief.

with the remnant of their valley] Others, *O remnant of their valley, how long wilt thou cut thyself? Their valley* is that of Gaza and Ashkelon, the low-lying plain, usually called the Shefēlah, which formed the territory of the Philistines. The reading of the LXX. is remarkable, *the remnant of the Anakim,* which probably would mean Gath, the home of giants (1 Sam. xvii. 4).

6. *Or,* **Alas,** *sword of Jehovah, how long wilt thou not rest !* For the answer, see *v.* 7.

XLVIII. This prophecy is an amplification of Isai. xv., xvi., and also introduces two verses 43, 44, from Isai. xxiv. 17, 18. Jeremiah's introduction of passages from older writers being accepted, it would seem that the passages borrowed are so inwoven with that which is Jeremiah's own, that they cannot be omitted as a later interpolation without destroying the whole. On the other hand in that which is the writer's own, and even in many of the alterations of

God of Israel; ¶ Woe unto *b* Nebo! for it is spoiled: *c* Kiria- ┊ *b* Num.32.38.
thaim is confounded *and* taken : ¹ Misgab is confounded and dis- ┊ *c* Num.32.37.
2 mayed. *d There shall be* no more praise of Moab: in *e* Heshbon ┊ *d* Isai. 16. 14.
they have devised evil against it; come, and let us cut it off ┊ *e* Isai. 15. 4.
from *being* a nation. Also thou shalt ² be cut down, O Madmen ;
3 the sword shall ³ pursue thee. *f* A voice of crying *shall be* from ┊ *f* ver. 5.
4 Horonaim, spoiling and great destruction. Moab is destroyed ;
5 her little ones have caused a cry to be heard. *g* For in the going ┊ *g* Isai. 15. 5.
up of Luhith ⁴ continual weeping shall go up ; for in the going
down of Horonaim the enemies have heard a cry of destruction.
6 ¶ *h* Flee, save your lives, and be like ⁵ the *i* heath in the wilderness. ┊ *h* ch. 51. 6.
7 For because thou hast trusted in thy works and in thy treasures, ┊ *i* ch. 17. 6.
thou shalt also be taken: and *k* Chemosh shall go forth into ┊ *k* Num.21.29.
8 captivity *with* his *l* priests and his princes together. And *m* the ┊ ch. 43. 12.
spoiler shall come upon every city, and no city shall escape : ┊ *l* ch. 49. 3.
the valley also shall perish, and the plain shall be destroyed, as ┊ *m* ch. 6. 26.
9 the LORD hath spoken. *n* Give wings unto Moab, that it may ┊ ver. 18.
flee and get away: for the cities thereof shall be desolate, with- ┊ *n* Ps. 55. 6.
10 out any to dwell therein. *o* Cursed *be* he that doeth the work of ┊ ver. 28.
the LORD ⁶ deceitfully. and cursed *be* he that keepeth back his ┊ *o* 1 Sam. 15.
11 sword from blood. ¶ Moab hath been at ease from his youth, ┊ 3, 9.
and he *p* hath settled on his lees, and hath not been emptied ┊ *p* Zeph. 1. 12.
from vessel to vessel, neither hath he gone into captivity : there-

---

¹ Or, *The high place.*
² Or, *be brought to silence,*
　Isai. 15. 1.
³ Heb. *go after thee.*
⁴ Heb. *weeping with weep-*
　ing.
⁵ Or, *a naked tree.*
⁶ Or, *negligently.*

---

the borrowed passages, Jeremiah's mode of
expression is so clearly to be recognized
that the whole must be acknowledged to be
his.

From Isai. xvi. 13 it has been conjectured
that Isaiah had an ancient prophecy before
him, and that Jeremiah drew from the same
source. Bearing in mind the number of
prophetical writings mentioned in the Books
of Chronicles which have not come down to
us, there is nothing unreasonable in such a
supposition.

1. *Against Moab*] **Concerning** *Moab.*
is confounded] **Is brought to shame.**

Misgab] **The high fort ;** some special fortress, probably Kir-haraseth (2 K. iii. 25).

2. *no more praise of Moab*] Lit. *The glory
of Moab is no more, i.e.* Moab has no more
cause for boasting.

Heshbon] This town now belonged to the
Ammonites (xlix. 3) but was on the border.
The enemy encamped there arranges the
plan of his campaign against Moab.

In the original there is a play of words
upon the names Heshbon and Madmen.

3. Omit *shall be.* "Spoiling and great destruction," lit. *breaking,* is the cry heard
from Horonaim (Isai. xv. 5).

4. *Moab*] Probably the city elsewhere
called Ar-Moab. See the LXX. of this verse.

5. Luhith was situated upon an eminence,
and Jeremiah describes one set of weeping
fugitives as pressing close upon another.

in the going down of Horonaim &c.] Rather,
in the descent of Horonaim they have heard
the distresses *of the cry of breaking, i.e.* the

cry of distress occasioned by the ruin inflicted by the enemy. It was situated in a
hollow, probably near the Dead Sea.

6. *like the heath*] Or, *Like a* **destitute
man.** See marg. ref. note.

7. *works*] Possibly the products of labour.
The Versions render *fortifications.*

Chemosh] As the national god of Moab
(Num. xxi. 29), he represents the whole land ;
and his being led into captivity implies the
total ruin of those under his protection.
His name here spelt *Chemish* is repeated in
Car-chemish, *i.e.* the fortress of Chemish.

8. *the valley*] The lowlands on the East
bank of the Jordan, and at the top of the
Dead Sea.

the plain] An upland pasture ; it answers
very much to *downs:* so in *v.* 21.

10. *deceitfully*] Better as in marg.

11. Moab from the time it conquered the
Emims (Deut. ii. 9, 10), and so became a
nation, had retained quiet possession of its
land, and enjoyed comparative prosperity.
From the Moabite stone we gather, that
king Mesha after the death of Ahab threw
off the yoke of Israel ; nor except for a short
time under Jeroboam II. was Israel able to
bring the Moabites back into subjection.
They gradually drove the Reubenites back,
and recovered most of the territory taken
from the Amorites by Moses, and which
originally had belonged to them.

he hath settled on his lees] Good wine was
thought to be the better for being left to
stand upon its sediment (Isai. xxv. 6), and
in all cases its flavour was rendered thereby

fore his taste [1]remained in him, and his scent is not changed.
12 Therefore, behold, the days come, saith the LORD, that I will
send unto him wanderers, that shall cause him to wander, and
13 shall empty his vessels, and break their bottles. And Moab
shall be ashamed of [q]Chemosh, as the house of Israel [r]was
14 ashamed of [s]Beth-el their confidence. ¶ How say ye, [t]We *are*
15 mighty and strong men for the war? [u]Moab is spoiled, and
gone up *out of* her cities, and [2]his chosen young men are [x]gone
down to the slaughter, saith [y]the King, whose name *is* the
16 LORD of hosts. The calamity of Moab *is* near to come, and his
17 affliction hasteth fast. All ye that are about him, bemoan him;
and all ye that know his name, say, [z]How is the strong staff
18 broken, *and* the beautiful rod! ¶ [a]Thou daughter that dost
inhabit [b]Dibon, come down from *thy* glory, and sit in thirst;
for [c]the spoiler of Moab shall come upon thee, *and* he shall
19 destroy thy strong holds. O [3]inhabitant of [d]Aroer, [e]stand by
the way, and espy; ask him that fleeth, and her that escapeth,
20 *and* say, What is done? Moab is confounded; for it is broken
down: [f]howl and cry; tell ye it in [g]Arnon, that Moab is spoiled,
21 and judgment is come upon [h]the plain country; upon Holon,
22 and upon Jahazah, and upon Mephaath, and upon Dibon, and
23 upon Nebo, and upon Beth-diblathaim, and upon Kiriathaim,
24 and upon Beth-gamul, and upon Beth-meon, and upon [i]Kerioth,
and upon Bozrah, and upon all the cities of the land of Moab,

[q] Judg. 11. 24. 1 Kin. 11. 7.
[r] Hos. 10. 6.
[s] 1 Kin. 12. 29.
[t] Isai. 16. 6.
[u] ver. 8, 9.
[x] ch. 50. 27.
[y] ch. 46. 18.
[z] See Isai. 9. 4.
[a] Isai. 47. 1. ch. 46. 19.
[b] Num. 21. 30. Isai. 15. 2.
[c] ver. 8.
[d] Deut. 2. 36.
[e] 1 Sam. 4. 13, 16.
[f] Isai. 16. 7.
[g] See Num. 21. 13.
[h] ver. 8.
[i] ver. 41. Amos 2. 2.

[1] Heb. *stood.* [2] Heb. *the choice of.* [3] Heb. *inhabitress.*

stronger (marg. ref.). By being *emptied from vessel to vessel* it became vapid and tasteless. So a nation by *going into captivity* is rendered tame and feeble. By *his taste* is meant the flavour of the wine, and so Moab's national character.

12. *I will send* **tilters** *unto him and they shall* **tilt** *him, and they shall empty his vessels, and break their* **pitchers** *in pieces. Pitchers* originally meant *skins*, but the word came to signify small earthenware jars (Isai. xxx. 14): thus the Chaldæans shall destroy of Moab everything that has contained the wine of her political life both small and great.

13. *Israel was ashamed of Beth-el*] After Salmaneser had carried Israel away, they could trust no longer in the calf of Bethel established by Jeroboam.

14. *mighty*] *Heroes*, veteran warriors.

15. Rather, *Moab is spoiled*, **and her cities have gone up**, *i.e.* in smoke, have been burnt (Josh. viii. 20, 21). Others render, *The waster of Moab and of her towns is coming up* to the attack, *and her chosen youths are gone down to the slaughter*.

16. *near to come*] Twenty-three years elapsed between the fourth year of Jehoiakim, when this prophecy was spoken, and its accomplishment by the invasion of Moab five years after the capture of Jerusalem. So slowly does God's justice move onwards.

17. The lamentation over Moab uttered by those *round about him*, *i.e.* the neighbouring nations, and those *that know his name*, nations more remote, who know little more than that there is such a people, takes the form of an elegy. The metaphorical expressions, *staff of strength*, and *rod* or *sceptre of beauty*, indicate the union of power and splendour in the Moabite kingdom.

18. *sit in thirst*] Jeremiah draws a picture of the conquered inhabitants, collected outside the walls, waiting for their captors to march them away to the slave mart. The enemy occupied with plundering the houses of Dibon thinks little of the hunger and thirst of his prisoners.

strong holds] The remains of the fortifications of Dibon are still visible.

19. *Aroer*] On the Arnon, due South of Dibon. If Dibon falls, the turn of Aroer will come next, and therefore its **inhabitants** are to be on the look out, asking for news.

20. Or, *Moab is ashamed, because she* (Dibon) *is broken* by her fortifications being battered down.

21. *Holon*] This place apparently took its name from caverns in its neighbourhood.

22. *Beth-diblathaim*] *i.e. the house of the two cakes of figs*, perhaps so called from two hills in its neighbourhood. Hos. i. 3 note.

23. *Beth-meon*] Meon is probably the Moabite Olympus, and thus Beth-Baal-Meon, the full name of this town (Josh. xiii. 17), would signify the place where the heavenly Baal was worshipped.

24. *Kerioth*] A synonym of **Ar**, the old capital of Moab. It appears to have been a considerable place, and has been identified with El-Korriât, situated on the long ridge of Mount Attarus.

Bozrah] Probably the Bosora mentioned

25 far or near. *k*The horn of Moab is cut off, and his *l*arm is
26 broken, saith the LORD. ¶ *m*Make ye him drunken: for he
magnified *himself* against the LORD: Moab also shall wallow in
27 his vomit, and he also shall be in derision. For *n*was not Israel
a derision unto thee? *o*was he found among thieves? for since
28 thou spakest of him, thou *1*skippedst for joy. O ye that dwell
in Moab, leave the cities, and *p*dwell in the rock, and be like
*q*the dove *that* maketh her nest in the sides of the hole's mouth.
29 We have heard the *r*pride of Moab, (he is exceeding proud) his
loftiness, and his arrogancy, and his pride, and the haughtiness
30 of his heart. I know his wrath, saith the LORD; but *it shall*
31 not *be* so; *s2*his lies shall not so effect *it*. ¶ Therefore *t*will I
howl for Moab, and I will cry out for all Moab; *mine heart* shall
32 mourn for the men of Kir-heres. *u*O vine of Sibmah, I will
weep for thee with the weeping of Jazer: thy plants are gone
over the sea, they reach *even* to the sea of Jazer: the spoiler is
33 fallen upon thy summer fruits and upon thy vintage. And *x*joy
and gladness is taken from the plentiful field, and from the land
of Moab; and I have caused wine to fail from the wine presses:
none shall tread with shouting; *their* shouting *shall be* no shout-
34 ing. *y*From the cry of Heshbon *even* unto Elealeh, *and even*
unto Jahaz, have they uttered their voice, *z*from Zoar *even* unto
Horonaim, *as* an heifer of three years old: for the waters also
35 of Nimrim shall be *3*desolate. Moreover I will cause to cease in
Moab, saith the LORD, *a*him that offereth in the high places, and
36 him that burneth incense to his gods. Therefore *b*mine heart
shall sound for Moab like pipes, and mine heart shall sound like

k Ps. 75. 10.
l See Ezek.
30. 21.
m ch. 25. 15,
27.
n Zeph. 2. 8.
*o*See ch.2.26.

p Ps. 55. 6.
ver. 9.
q Cant. 2. 14.
r Isai. 16. 6.

s Isai. 16. 6.
ch. 50. 36.
t Isai. 15. 5.
*u*Isai.16.8,9.

x Isai. 16. 10.

y Isai. 15. 4,
5, 6.
z Isai. 15. 5.
ver. 5.

a Isai. 15. 2.
b Isai. 16. 11.

---

1 Or, *movedst thyself.*
2 Or, *those on whom he*
    stayeth (Heb. *his Lars*) *do*
    not right.
3 Heb. *desolations.*

---

in 1 Macc. v. 26 in company with Bosor, *i.e.*
Bezer. As the word means *sheepfolds*, it
was no doubt a common name for places in
this upland region, fit only for pasturage.

25. *The horn*] *i.e.* his pride (marg. ref.);
his arm, i.e. his strength (xvii. 5).

26. *Make ye him drunken*] With the
wine-cup of God's fury, till terror deprive
him of his senses.

27. *was he found* &c.] Or, *was he found
among thieves that so often as thou speakest of
him* thou waggest thy head?—in contempt
for a fallen enemy.

28. *dwell in the rock*] See iv. 29. The
sole chance of escape is refuge in inaccessible
fastnesses.

in the sides...] On the further side *of the
mouth of the pit.* The wild rock pigeon invariably selects deep ravines for its nesting
and roosting.

30. *but it shall not be so*] Most commentators translate, *I know, saith Jehovah, his
arrogancy, and the emptiness of his boastings;
they have wrought emptiness.*

31. mine heart &c.] Rather, "there shall
be mourning for" &c.

32. Or, *More than the weeping of Jazer*
over its ruined vineyards *will I weep for
thee, O vine of Sibmah.* Cp. marg. ref.
Jazer lies in an upland valley about fifteen
miles North of Heshbon.

thy plants &c.] *Thy* **branches** *are gone over
the sea, i.e.* the power of Moab is felt even on
the western side of the Dead Sea; *they
reached* &c.

33. *vinepresses*] Rather, *wine-vats*, into
which the wine runs from the presses.

their shouting shall be *no shouting*] The
vintage shout is—silence. For the vines
have been destroyed, and desolation reigns
where once was the joyful cry of those who
tread the grapes.

34. The meaning is that, taking up the
lamentation of Heshbon, the Moabites
break forth into a wail, heard as far as
Elealeh, scarcely two miles distant (Num.
xxxii. 37), but thence spreading over the
land to towns on the southern and south-
western borders of the land.

an heifer of three years old] Applied in
Isai. xv. 5 to Zoar, but here to Horonaim.
Some take "an heifer" as a proper name,
and render, *Eglah for the third part* (cp. Isai.
xix. 24). Zoar, Horonaim, and Eglah formed
a tripolis, or confederacy of three towns,
and Eglah might therefore be put after
either one or the other.

Nimrim] Probably the Wady-en-Nemeirah
at the south-eastern end of the Dead Sea.

36. *like pipes*] A wind instrument, used
at funerals (Matt. ix. 23).

c Isai. 15. 7.
d Isai.15.2,3.
ch. 47. 5.
e Gen. 37. 34.

pipes for the men of Kir-heres: because ^cthe riches *that* he hath 37 gotten are perished. For ^devery head *shall be* bald, and every beard ¹clipped: upon all the hands *shall be* cuttings, and ^eupon 38 the loins sackcloth. *There shall be* lamentation generally upon all the housetops of Moab, and in the streets thereof: for I

f ch. 22. 28.

have broken Moab like ^fa vessel wherein *is* no pleasure, saith 39 the LORD. They shall howl, *saying*, How is it broken down! how hath Moab turned the ²back with shame! so shall Moab be 40 a derision and a dismaying to all them about him. ¶ For thus

g ch. 49. 22.
Hos. 8. 1.
Hab. 1. 8.
h Isai. 8. 8.
i ver. 24.
k Isai. 13. 8.
ch. 30. 6.
Mic. 4. 9.
l Ps. 83. 4.
Isai. 7. 8.
m Isai.24.17,
18.
n See ch. 11.
23.

saith the LORD; Behold, ^ghe shall fly as an eagle, and shall 41 ^hspread his wings over Moab. ^{i 3}Kerioth is taken, and the strong holds are surprised, and ^kthe mighty men's hearts in Moab at that day shall be as the heart of a woman in her pangs. 42 And Moab shall be destroyed ^lfrom *being* a people, because he 43 hath magnified *himself* against the LORD. ^mFear, and the pit, and the snare, *shall be* upon thee, O inhabitant of Moab, saith 44 the LORD. He that fleeth from the fear shall fall into the pit; and he that getteth up out of the pit shall be taken in the snare: for ⁿI will bring upon it, *even* upon Moab, the year of their 45 visitation, saith the LORD. They that fled stood under the

o Num.21.28.

shadow of Heshbon because of the force: but ^oa fire shall come forth out of Heshbon, and a flame from the midst of Sihon, and

p Num.24.17.
q Num.21.29.

^pshall devour the corner of Moab, and the crown of the head of 46 the ⁴tumultuous ones. ^qWoe be unto thee, O Moab! the people of Chemosh perisheth: for thy sons are taken ⁵captives, and thy 47 daughters captives. Yet will I bring again the captivity of

r ch. 49. 6.

Moab ^rin the latter days, saith the LORD. ¶ Thus far *is* the judgment of Moab.

a Ezek. 21.
28. & 25. 2.

CHAP. 49. ⁶CONCERNING ^athe Ammonites. ¶ Thus saith the

---

¹ Heb. *diminished.*   ³ Or, *The cities.*   ⁵ Heb. *in captivity.*
² Heb. *neck.*   ⁴ Heb. *children of noise.*   ⁶ Or, *Against.*

---

the riches that he hath gotten] Lit. *that which remains over, a superfluity.*

37. *cuttings*] Cp. xvi. 6, and marg. reff.

38. *generally*] Rather, **entirely.**

39. Lit. *How is it broken down! they wail! How hath Moab turned the back in shame! Yea, Moab is become a laughter and a terror* (xvii. 17) *to all who are round about him.*

40. The rapid and irresistible attack of Nebuchadnezzar is compared to the impetuous dash of the eagle on its prey (Deut. xxviii. 49).

41. *surprised*] **captured** by force.

45. *because of the force*] Rather, **without** *force.* Translate, *The fugitives have stood,* (*i.e.* halted) *powerless in the shadow of Heshbon.* As Heshbon was the capital of the Ammonites, the sense is that the defeated Moabites looked to Ammon for protection.

but a fire...] Not only will Ammon refuse aid to Moab, but her ruin is to come forth from Heshbon. To shew this Jeremiah has recourse to the old triumphal poetry of the Mosaic age (marg. ref.).

the corner] *i.e.* of the beard...*the crown of the head*] The fire of war consumes both far and near, both hair and beard, *i.e.* everything that it can singe and destroy.

the tumultuous ones] Lit. *sons of the battle-shout,* the brave Moabite warriors.

47. *bring again the captivity*] [Or, "restore the prosperity"]. A similar promise is given to Egypt, Ammon, and Elam (xlvi. 26, xlix. 6).

Thus far...Moab] An editorial note by the same hand as the last words of li. 64.

XLIX. To the North of the Moabites lay the country of the Ammonites, a closely allied nation (Gen. xix. 37, 38) who claimed that the land assigned to the tribe of Gad had originally belonged to them (Judg. xi. 13). They seem to have been far less civilized than the Moabites, and possessed but one stronghold, Rabbah, not devoting themselves to agriculture, but wandering with their flocks over the Arabian wastes. When, however, Tiglath-Pileser carried the inhabitants of Gilead into captivity, the Ammonites occupied much of the vacant land, and many of them probably adopted a more settled life; at this time they even possessed Heshbon, once the frontier town between Reuben and Gad. It is this seizure of the territory of Gad which forms the starting-point of Jeremiah's prediction. Older prophecies against Ammon are Amos i. 13–15; Zeph. ii. 8–11.

LORD; ¶ Hath Israel no sons? hath he no heir? why *then* doth
¹their king inherit *ᵇ*Gad, and his people dwell in his cities?   *ᵇ* Amos 1.13.
2 Therefore, behold, the days come, saith the LORD, that I will
cause an alarm of war to be heard in *ᶜ*Rabbah of the Ammonites;   *ᶜ* Amos 1.14.
and it shall be a desolate heap, and her daughters shall be burned
with fire: then shall Israel be heir unto them that were his
3 heirs, saith the LORD.   Howl, O Heshbon, for Ai is spoiled: *ᵈ* Isai. 32. 11.
cry, ye daughters of Rabbah, *ᵈ*gird you with sackcloth; lament,   ch. 4. 8.
and run to and fro by the hedges; for ²their king shall go into
4 captivity, *and* his *ᵉ*priests and his princes together.   Wherefore   *ᵉ* ch. 48. 7.
gloriest thou in the valleys, ³thy flowing valley, O *ᶠ*backsliding   Amos 1. 15.
daughter? that trusted in her treasures, *ᵍ*saying, Who shall   *ᶠ* ch. 3. 14.
5 come unto me?   Behold, I will bring a fear upon thee, saith the   *ᵍ* ch. 21. 13.
Lord GOD of hosts, from all those that be about thee; and ye
shall be driven out every man right forth; and none shall gather
6 up him that wandereth.   And *ʰ*afterward I will bring again the   *ʰ* So ver. 39.
captivity of the children of Ammon, saith the LORD.   & ch. 48. 47.

7   *ⁱ*Concerning Edom.   ¶ Thus saith the LORD of hosts; ¶ *ᵏ*Is   *ⁱ* Ezek.25.12.
wisdom no more in Teman? *ˡ*is counsel perished from the pru-   Amos 1. 11.
8 dent? is their wisdom vanished? *ᵐ*Flee ye, ⁴turn back, dwell   *ᵏ* Obad. 8.
deep, O inhabitants of *ⁿ*Dedan; for I will bring the calamity   *ˡ* See Isai.19.
9 of Esau upon him, the time *that* I will visit him.   If *ᵒ*grape-   11.
   ᵐ ver. 30.
   ⁿ ch. 25. 23.
   ᵒ Obad. 5.

¹ Or, *Melcom*.   ³ Or, *thy valley floweth*   ⁴ Or, *they are turned back*.
² Or, *Melcom*,1Kin.11.5.33.   *away*.

---

1. *Hath Israel no sons?*] *i.e.* the Ammonites
in seizing Gilead have acted as if the country
had no rightful owner. The sons of Israel
were to return from captivity, and the land
was their hereditary property.

their king] **Milcom** (and in *v.* 3), see marg.
The Ammonite god stands for the Ammonites just as Chemosh (xlviii. 7) is the equivalent of the Moabites.

inherit] *i.e.* **take possession of.**

2. *Rabbah*] *i.e.* the *great* city. See 2 Sam.
xii. 27 note for a distinction between Rabbah, the citadel, and the town itself, lying
below upon the Jabbok.

daughters] *i.e.* unwalled villages (and in
v. 3).

shall Israel be heir...] *i.e. shall be victor
over his victors;* cp. Micah i. 15.

3. *Ai*] Not the town on the West of the
Jordan (Josh. vii. 2); a place not mentioned
elsewhere. For Ai some read Ar.

hedges] Fields were not divided by hedges
till recent times; the term probably means
the walls which enclose the vineyards (Num.
xxii. 24).

4. *thy flowing valley*] The (fertile) valley
in which Rabbah was situated. The LXX.
again have, *in the valleys of the Anakim*,
as in xlvii. 5 (see note).

5. *every man right forth*] The Ammonites
will live in terror of the tribes which rove
in the neighbourhood, and at the slightest
alarm will flee straight away without resistance.

6. In 1 Macc. v. 6, 7, the Ammonites
appear again as a powerful nation.

7—22. Edom stretched along the south of

Judah from the border of Moab on the
Dead Sea to the Mediterranean and the
Arabian deserts, and held the same relation
to Judah which Moab held towards the
kingdom of Israel. Although expressly
reserved from attack by Moses (Deut. ii. 5),
a long feud caused the Edomites to cherish
so bitter an enmity against Judah, that they
exulted with cruel joy over the capture of
Jerusalem by the Chaldæans, and shewed
great cruelty towards those who fled to them
for refuge.

Of the prophecies against Edom the first
eight verses of Obadiah are also found in
Jeremiah (see marg. reff.). As Jeremiah
wrote before the capture of Jerusalem,
and Obadiah apparently after it (see *vv.*
13, 14), it might seem certain that Obadiah
copied from Jeremiah. Others held the
reverse view; while some consider that the
two prophets may both have made common
use of some ancient prediction. See the
Introduction to Obadiah.

The prophecy is divisible into three stro-
phes. In the first (*vv.* 7—13), the prophet
describes Edom as terror-stricken.

7. *Teman*] A strip of land on the North-
East of Edom, put here for Edom generally.
Its inhabitants were among those "children
of the East" famed for wisdom, because of
their skill in proverbs and dark sayings.

8. *dwell deep* (*v.* 30)] The Dedanites, who
were used to travel through the Edomite
territory with their caravans, are advised to
retire as far as possible into the Arabian
deserts to be out of the way of the invaders.

9. Translate, *If vintagers come to thee, they*

gatherers come to thee, would they not leave *some* gleaning grapes? if thieves by night, they will destroy [1]till they have

p Mal. 1. 3.

10 enough. *p*But I have made Esau bare, I have uncovered his secret places, and he shall not be able to hide himself: his seed

q Isai. 17. 14.

is spoiled, and his brethren, and his neighbours, and *q*he *is* not.

11 Leave thy fatherless children, I will preserve *them* alive; and

12 let thy widows trust in me. For thus saith the LORD; Behold,

r Obad. 16.

*r*they whose judgment *was* not to drink of the cup have assuredly drunken; and *art* thou he *that* shall altogether go unpunished? thou shalt not go unpunished, but thou shalt surely

s Gen. 22. 16.
Isai. 45. 23.
t Isai. 34. 6.
& 63. 1.

13 drink of *it*. For *s*I have sworn by myself, saith the LORD, that *t*Bozrah shall become a desolation, a reproach, a waste, and a curse; and all the cities thereof shall be perpetual wastes.

u Obad. 1. 2.

14 ¶I have heard a *u*rumour from the LORD, and an ambassador is sent unto the heathen, *saying*, Gather ye together, and come

15 against her, and rise up to the battle. For, lo, I will make

16 thee small among the heathen, *and* despised among men. Thy terribleness hath deceived thee, *and* the pride of thine heart, O thou that dwellest in the clefts of the rock, that holdest the

x Obad. 4.
y Job 39. 27.
z Amos 9. 2.
a ch. 18. 16.

height of the hill: *x*though thou shouldest make thy *y*nest as high as the eagle, *z*I will bring thee down from thence, saith

17 the LORD. Also Edom shall be a desolation: *a*every one that goeth by it shall be astonished, and shall hiss at all the plagues

b Gen 19. 25.
ch. 50. 40.
Amos 4. 11.
c ch. 50. 44.
d ch. 12. 5.

18 thereof. *b*As in the overthrow of Sodom and Gomorrah and the neighbour *cities* thereof, saith the LORD, no man shall abide

19 there, neither shall a son of man dwell in it. ¶*c*Behold, he shall come up like a lion from *d*the swelling of Jordan against the habitation of the strong: but I will suddenly make him run

[1] Heb. *their sufficiency*.

---

will not leave any gleaning: *if thieves by night, they will destroy their fill*.

10. *But*] For. The reason why the invaders destroy Edom so completely. *His secret places* are the hiding-places in the mountains of Seir.

his seed] Esau's seed, the Edomites; *his brethren* are the nations joined with him in the possession of the land, Amalek, and perhaps the Simeonites; *his neighbours* are Dedan, Tema, Buz.

11. As with Moab (xlviii. 47), and Ammon (xlix. 6), so there is mercy for Edom. The widows shall be protected, and in the orphans of Edom the nation shall once again revive.

12. Translate, *Behold they whose* **rule** *was not to drink of the cup* **shall** *surely drink* &c. It was not the ordinary manner of God's people to suffer from His wrath: but now when they are drinking of the wine-cup of fury (xxv. 15), how can those not in covenant with Him hope to escape?

14–18. The second strophe, Edom's chastisement.

14. *rumour*] Or, "revelation."

ambassador] Or, **messenger**, *i.e.* herald. The business of an ambassador is to negotiate, of a herald to carry a message.

15. *small* &c.] Rather, *small among the* **nations**, *i.e.* of no political importance.

16. Edom's "terribleness" consisted in her cities being hewn in the sides of inaccessible rocks, whence she could suddenly descend for predatory warfare, and retire to her fastnesses without fear of reprisals.

the clefts of the rock] Or, **the fastnesses of Sela**, the rock-city, Petra (see Isai. xvi. 1).

the hill] *i.e.* Bozrah.

17. Better, *And Edom shall become a terror: every passer by shall be terrified, and shudder* &c.

18. *neighbour* &c.] Admah and Zeboim.

a son of man] *i.e.* "Any man." From A.D. 536 onwards, Petra suddenly vanishes from the pages of history. Only in the present century was its real site discovered.

19–22. Concluding strophe. The fall of Edom is compared to the state of a flock worried by an enemy strong as a lion (iv. 7), and swift as an eagle.

19. *the swelling of Jordan*] Or, *the pride of Jordan*, the thickets on his banks (marg. ref. note).

against the habitation of the strong] Or, **to the abiding pasturage**. The lion stalks forth from the jungle to attack the fold, sure to find sheep there because of the perennial (evergreen) pasturage: *but I will suddenly make him* (the flock, Edom) *run away from her* (or *it*, the pasturage).

away from her: and who *is* a chosen *man, that* I may appoint over her? for *e*who *is* like me? and who will ¹appoint me the time? and *f*who *is* that shepherd that will stand before me? — *e* Ex. 15. 11. — *f* Job 41. 10.

20 *g*Therefore hear the counsel of the LORD, that he hath taken against Edom; and his purposes, that he hath purposed against the inhabitants of Teman: Surely the least of the flock shall draw them out: surely he shall make their habitations desolate

21 with them. *h*The earth is moved at the noise of their fall, at

22 the cry the noise thereof was heard in the ²Red sea. Behold, *i*he shall come up and fly as the eagle, and spread his wings over Bozrah: and at that day shall the heart of the mighty men of Edom be as the heart of a woman in her pangs. — *g* ch. 50. 45. — *h* ch. 50. 46. — *i* ch. 4. 13.

23 *k*Concerning Damascus. ¶ Hamath is confounded, and Arpad: for they have heard evil tidings: they are ³fainthearted; *l*there is

24 sorrow ⁴on the sea; it cannot be quiet. Damascus is waxed feeble, *and* turneth herself to flee, and fear hath seized on *her*: *m*anguish and sorrows have taken her, as a woman in travail.

25, 26 How is *n*the city of praise not left, the city of my joy! *o*Therefore her young men shall fall in her streets, and all the men of

27 war shall be cut off in that day, saith the LORD of hosts. And I will kindle a *p*fire in the wall of Damascus, and it shall consume the palaces of Benhadad. — *k* Isai. 17. 1. Amos 1. 3. Zech. 9. 1. — *l* Isai. 57. 20. — *m* Isai. 13. 8. ch. 4. 31. — *n* ch. 33. 9. — *o* ch. 51. 4. — *p* Amos 1. 4.

28 *q*Concerning Kedar, and concerning the kingdoms of Hazor, — *q* Isai. 21. 13.

¹ Or, *convent me in judgment.* ² Heb. *Weedy sea.* ³ Heb. *melted.* ⁴ Or, *as on the sea.*

---

and who is a chosen...] Better, *and* **I will appoint over it,** the abandoned land of Edom, **him who is** *chosen, i.e.* my chosen ruler Nebuchadnezzar.

who will appoint me the time?] The plaintiff, in giving notice of a suit, had to mention the time when the defendant must appear (see marg.). Jehovah identifies Himself with Nebuchadnezzar (xxv. 9), and shews the hopelessness of Edom's cause. For who is like Jehovah, His equal in power and might? Who will dare litigate with Him, and question His right? &c.

20. *Surely the least...*] Rather, *Surely* **they will worry them, the feeble ones of the flock: surely their pasture shall be** terror-stricken over them. No shepherd can resist Nebuchadnezzar (*v.* 19), but all flee, and leave the sheep unprotected. Thereupon the Chaldæans enter, and treat the poor feeble flock so barbarously, that the very fold is horrified at their cruelty.

21. *is moved*] **Quakes.**

at the cry...] The arrangement is much more poetical in the Hebrew, *The shriek—to the sea of Suph* (Exod. x. 19 note) *is heard its sound.*

22. Nebuchadnezzar shall swoop down like an eagle, the emblem of swiftness.

23. Though the superscription is confined to Damascus, the prophecy relates to the whole of Aram, called by us Syria, which was divided into two parts, the northern, of which Hamath was the capital, and the south-eastern, belonging to Damascus.

Hamath is confounded] Or, **is ashamed.** For Hamath see Isai. x. 9 note. Arpad lay about fourteen miles north of Aleppo, at a place now called Tel Erfâd.

fainthearted] The sinews are relaxed, unknit, through terror.

there is sorrow on the sea] **In** *the sea.* As the sea is used (marg. ref.) of the agitation of the thoughts of evil men, its sense here also probably is, *there is sorrow,* or rather anxiety, *in the agitated hearts* of the Syrians.

24. and *turneth*] Omit *and.* The original is a rapid sequence of unconnected sentences. *Damascus is unnerved; she turned to flee, and a trembling seized her; anguish and writhings took hold of her* &c.

25. An exclamation of sorrow wrung from the prophet at the thought of the people of Damascus remaining to be slaughtered. The words *my joy* express the prophet's own sympathy. The praise of Damascus for beauty has been universal from the days of Naaman (2 K. v. 12), to those of recent travellers.

27. See marg. ref. and 1 K. xi. 14 note.

28. Hazor, derived from a word signifying an unwalled village, is a general appellative of those Arab tribes who were partially settled, while Kedar signifies the Bedawin, who used only tents. Some think that Hazor is another way of spelling Jetor, *i.e.* Ituræa, whose inhabitants, with the Kedarenes, would naturally be called *the sons of the East.*

r Judg. 6. 3.
Job 1. 3.
s Ps. 120. 5.

t ch. 46. 5.
u ver. 8.

x Ezek. 38. 11.

y Num. 23. 9.
Mic. 7. 14.

z ver. 36.
Ezek. 5. 10.
a ch. 25. 23.
b ch. 9. 11.
Mal. 1. 3.
c ver. 18.

d ch. 25. 25.

e See Isai. 22. 6.

f ver. 32.

g ch. 9. 16.
h See ch. 43. 10.

which Nebuchadrezzar king of Babylon shall smite. ¶ Thus saith the LORD; ¶ Arise ye, go up to Kedar, and spoil *r* the
29 men of the east. Their *s* tents and their flocks shall they take away: they shall take to themselves their curtains, and all their vessels, and their camels; and they shall cry unto them, *t* Fear
30 *is* on every side. *u* Flee, ¹ get you far off, dwell deep, O ye inhabitants of Hazor, saith the LORD; for Nebuchadrezzar king of Babylon hath taken counsel against you, and hath conceived a
31 purpose against you. Arise, get you up unto *x* the *z* wealthy nation, that dwelleth without care, saith the LORD, which have
32 neither gates nor bars, *which* *y* dwell alone. And their camels shall be a booty, and the multitude of their cattle a spoil: and I will *z* scatter into all winds *a* them *that are* ³ in the utmost corners; and I will bring their calamity from all sides thereof,
33 saith the LORD. And Hazor *b* shall be a dwelling for dragons, *and* a desolation for ever: *c* there shall no man abide there, nor *any* son of man dwell in it.

34 The word of the LORD that came to Jeremiah the prophet against *d* Elam in the beginning of the reign of Zedekiah king
35 of Judah, saying, ¶ Thus saith the LORD of hosts; ¶ Behold, I
36 will break *e* the bow of Elam, the chief of their might. And upon Elam will I bring the four winds from the four quarters of heaven, and *f* will scatter them toward all those winds; and there shall be no nation whither the outcasts of Elam shall
37 not come. For I will cause Elam to be dismayed before their enemies, and before them that seek their life: and I will bring evil upon them, *even* my fierce anger, saith the LORD; *g* and I will send the sword after them, till I have consumed
38 them: and I will *h* set my throne in Elam, and will destroy

¹ Heb. *flit greatly.*
² Or, *that is at ease.*
³ Heb. *cut off into corners,* or, *that have the corners* of their hair *polled.*

---

shall smite] Or, **smote.**

29. *curtains*] The hangings of the tents.

Fear is *on every side*] *Magor-missabib* (see vi. 25 note); a cry, indicating the panic which followed the unexpected onset of the enemy.

30. *a purpose against you*] Others read "against them" (the wealthy nation, *v.* 31).

31. *the wealthy nation*] Or, *a nation* at rest, living **securely** and *in confidence.*

which *dwell alone*] **They** *dwell alone, i.e.* have neither alliances with other nations, nor intercourse by commerce.

32. *them...corners*] Or, **those who clip the corners of their beards** (cp. ix. 26).

33. *dragons*] *i.e.* **jackals.**

34. *against Elam*] Or, **concerning** *Elam.* This country, better known as Susiana, is the modern Chuzistan, and lies on the East of Chaldæa, from which it is separated by the Tigris. In the cuneiform inscriptions we find the Elamites on friendly terms with Babylon. The suggestion therefore that they served as auxiliaries in the Chaldæan army in the expedition against Judah is not improbable. It was in the first year of

Zedekiah that this prophecy was written, and thus it is a little prior to the prophecies against Babylon (li. 59), which immediately follow. The words, *the Elam,* appear in the LXX. in xxv. 14, followed by this prophecy, while in xxvi. 1 we find, *In the beginning of the reign of king Zedekiah there was this word about Elam,* followed in *v.* 2 by the prophecy (ch. xlvi. of the Hebr.) against Egypt. This is a proof simply of the confusion which existed in the Egyptian transcripts of the prophecies relating to the nations. See p. 162.

35. The bow was the national weapon of Elam, and therefore *the chief of their might,* that on which their strength in war depended.

36. In a whirlwind violent gales seem to blow from every quarter, and whatever is exposed to their fury they scatter over the whole country. With similar violence the whole nation of Elam shall be dispersed far and wide.

38. Lit. **king and princes.** Elam will lose its independence, and henceforward have no native ruler with his attendant officers.

39 from thence the king and the princes, saith the LORD. But it shall come to pass *in the latter days, *that* I will bring again the captivity of Elam, saith the LORD.   *i* ch. 48. 47.

CHAP. 50. THE word that the LORD spake *a*against Babylon *and* against the land of the Chaldeans ¹by Jeremiah the prophet.   *a* Isai. 13. 1. &21.1.&47.1.

2 ¶Declare ye among the nations, and publish, and ²set up a standard; publish, *and* conceal not: say, Babylon is taken, *b*Bel is confounded, Merodach is broken in pieces; *c*her idols are   *b* Isai. 46. 1.
3 confounded, her images are broken in pieces. *d*For out of the north there cometh up *e*a nation against her, which shall make her land desolate, and none shall dwell therein: they shall re-
4 move, they shall depart, both man and beast. ¶In those days, and in that time, saith the LORD, the children of Israel shall come, *f*they and the children of Judah together, *g*going and
5 weeping: they shall go, *h*and seek the LORD their God. They

c ch. 43. 12.
d ch. 51. 48.
e Isai. 13. 17,
'8, 20.

f Hos. 1. 11.
g Ezra 3. 12.
Ps. 126. 5.
Zech. 12. 10.
h Hos. 3. 5.

¹ Heb. *by the hand of Jeremiah.*   ² Heb. *lift up.*

---

39. *Elam*] Elam was subject to Babylon (Dan. viii. 2), and its capital Shushan a favourite residence of the Persian kings (Esther i. 2). Of its subsequent fate we know little; the Elamites continued to exist, and members of their nation were present at Pentecost among those chosen to represent the Gentile world at the first preaching of the Gospel (Acts ii. 9).

L., LI. Many critics have endeavoured to shew that this prophecy was not written by Jeremiah. Others grant that Jeremiah was the true author, yet assert that the prophecy has been largely interpolated. The arguments for its authenticity are briefly; (*a*) The superscription (l. 1), and the appended history (li. 59–64); (*b*) The general admission that the style is Jeremiah's; (*c*) The fact that the author was living at Jerusalem (l. 5, where read *hitherward*, not *thitherward*); (*d*) The Medes and not the Persians are described as the future conquerors of Babylon (li. 11, 28). The knowledge of topography and Babylonian customs is not more than Jeremiah may have learnt from the Chaldæans when they were at Jerusalem in the fourth, and again in the eleventh year of Jehoiakim: and there was constant intercourse by letter and otherwise between Babylon and Jerusalem.

The prophecy may be considered essential to the right discharge by Jeremiah of the duties of his office. He had foretold the capture and ruin of Jerusalem, not from love to Babylon, but as a necessary act of the Divine justice, and as the one remedy for Judah's sins. He recognized the Chaldæans as Jehovah's ministers; but recognizing also that they practised wanton barbarities, and claimed the glory for themselves and their gods, he proclaimed that Babylon must be punished for its cruelty, its pride, and its idolatry.

The date is fixed by li. 59. With this agrees the internal evidence.

Though deficient in arrangement the prophecy is full of grand ideas; and the similarity between passages in this prophecy and Isaiah illustrates the large knowledge which Jeremiah evidently possessed of the earlier Scriptures, and the manner in which, consciously or unconsciously, he has perpetually imitated them in his own writings.

L. 1. *against...against*] **Concerning.**

2. *confounded...confounded*] **ashamed...ashamed.**

Merodach] This deity, in the inscriptions Marduk, was the tutelary god of Babylon, and Nebuchadnezzar, who called his son Evil-Merodach, appears to have been especially devoted to his service. He was really identical with Bel, and his equivalent among the planets was Jupiter: and as such he was styled "King of heaven and earth."

3. *out of the north*] Media lay to the North-West of Babylon. This constant use of the North, the quarter where the sun never shines, and therefore the region of darkness, is symbolical of the region whence danger ever comes.

they shall remove &c.] Translate, as in ix. 10, **from man even to cattle they are fled, they are gone.**

4. The fall of Babylon is to be immediately followed by the return of the exiles homewards, in tearful procession, because they go as penitents; and yet with joy, because their faces are towards Zion. The cessation moreover of the schism between Israel and Judah is one of the signs of the times of the Messiah (Isaiah xi. 12, 13), and symbolically represents the gathering together of the warring empires of the world under the peaceful sceptre of the Church's King.

going and weeping: they shall go] Omit the colon; *i.e. they go ever onward weeping.*

shall ask the way to Zion with their faces thitherward, *saying,*

i ch. 31. 31.

Come, and let us join ourselves to the LORD in *i*a perpetual
6 covenant *that* shall not be forgotten. ¶My people hath been

k Isai. 53. 6.
1 Pet. 2. 25.
l ch. 2. 20.

*k*lost sheep: their shepherds have caused them to go astray,
they have turned them away on *l*the mountains: they have gone
from mountain to hill, they have forgotten their ¹resting-

m Ps. 79. 7.
n ch. 40. 2.
Zech. 11. 5.
o ch. 2. 3.
Dan. 9. 16.
p Ps. 90. 1.
q Ps. 22. 4.
r Isai. 48. 20.
ch. 51. 6.
Zech. 2. 6.
s ch. 15. 14.
t ver. 14. 29.

7 place. All that found them have *m*devoured them: and *n*their
adversaries said, *o*We offend not, because they have sinned
against the LORD, *p*the habitation of justice, even the LORD,
8 *q*the hope of their fathers. *r*Remove out of the midst of
Babylon, and go forth out of the land of the Chaldeans, and be
9 as the he goats before the flocks. *s*For, lo, I will raise and
cause to come up against Babylon an assembly of great nations
from the north country: and they shall *t*set themselves in
array against her; from thence she shall be taken: their arrows
shall be as of a mighty ²expert man; *u*none shall return in

u 2 Sam. 1. 22.
x Rev. 17. 16.
y Isai. 47. 6.

10 vain. And Chaldea shall be a spoil: *x*all that spoil her shall
11 be satisfied, saith the LORD. *y*Because ye were glad, because
ye rejoiced, O ye destroyers of mine heritage, because ye are

z Hos. 10. 11.

grown ³fat *z*as the heifer at grass, and ⁴bellow as bulls; your
12 mother shall be sore confounded; she that bare you shall be
ashamed: behold, the hindermost of the nations *shall be* a
13 wilderness, a dry land, and a desert. Because of the wrath of

a ch. 25. 12.
b ch. 49. 17.
c ch. 51. 2.
d ch. 49. 35.

the LORD it shall not be inhabited, *a*but it shall be wholly
desolate: *b*every one that goeth by Babylon shall be astonished,
14 and hiss at all her plagues. ¶*c*Put yourselves in array against
Babylon round about: all ye *d*that bend the bow, shoot at her,
15 spare no arrows: for she hath sinned against the LORD. Shout

e 2 Chr. 30. 8.
f ch. 51. 58.
g ch. 51. 6.

against her round about: she hath *e*given her hand: her foundations are fallen, *f*her walls are thrown down: for *g*it *is* the

---

¹ Heb. *place to lie down in.*   ³ Heb. *big,* or, *corpulent.*
² Or, *destroyer.*   ⁴ Or, *neigh as steeds.*

---

5. *thitherward*] **Hitherward**; the writer
evidently was at Jerusalem.

6. *their shepherds...mountains*] Some translate *Their shepherds, i.e.* civil rulers (ii. 8
note) *have led them astray upon the seducing
mountains:*—the mountains being the usual
places where idolatry was practised.

their restingplace] Their fold (Ps. xxiii. 2).

7. *offend not*] *i.e.* "are not guilty." Israel
having left the fold, has no owner, and may
therefore be maltreated with impunity.

habitation of justice] In xxxi. 23 applied to
Jerusalem: here, Jehovah alone is the true
pasturage, in Whom His people will find
safety, rest, and plenty.

8. So firmly did the Jews settle themselves
in Babylon under Jeremiah's counsels, that
they were the last to abandon the place.

he goats] See Isai. xiv. 9 note.

9. *I will raise*] Or, **stir up.**

an assembly of great nations] The Medo-
Persian empire was as much an aggregate
of discordant nations as that of Babylon.

from thence] From the North, *i.e.* by the
great nations coming thence.

return in vain] A proverbial expression
for ill success (cp. Isai. lv. 11). Here the
skilful warrior returns not empty.

10, 11. Or, *Chaldæa shall become a spoil...
for thou wast glad, thou exultedst, ye* **plun-
derers** *of mine heritage.*

because ye are grown fat] Rather, **for thou
leapedst, skippedst** as an animal does when
playing.

as the heifer at grass] Or, *as a heifer
threshing.* When threshing cattle were
allowed to eat their fill (Deut. xxv. 4), and
so grew playful.

bellow as bulls] Better as in marg.

12. *your mother*] *i.e.,* Babylon. *Confounded...ashamed.* Or, **ashamed**...blush.

behold &c.] Translate, *Behold she is the
hindermost of the nations, a desert, a thirsty
land, and a waste:*—the reason why Babylon
is to blush. Once the head of gold (Dan.
ii. 32), she is now the lowest of earthly
powers.

14. Place the colon after *low.*

15. *Shout*] *i.e.* spoken of the war-cry. So
in Isai. xlii. 13, where God is compared to a
warrior, it is said *He shall shout* (A. V. *cry*),
i.e. raise the war-cry.

she hath given her hand] The sign of sub-
mission (cp. 1 Chr. xxix. 24 marg.).

foundations] Or, *buttresses.* LXX. *battlements.*

vengeance of the LORD: take vengeance upon her; [h]as she
16 hath done, do unto her. Cut off the sower from Babylon, and
him that handleth the [1]sickle in the time of harvest: for fear of
the oppressing sword [i]they shall turn every one to his people, and
17 they shall flee every one to his own land. ¶ Israel is [k]a scattered
sheep; [l]the lions have driven *him* away: first [m]the king of
Assyria hath devoured him; and last this [n]Nebuchadrezzar king
18 of Babylon hath broken his bones. Therefore thus saith the
LORD of hosts, the God of Israel: Behold, I will punish the
king of Babylon and his land, as I have punished the king of
19 Assyria. [o]And I will bring Israel again to his habitation, and
he shall feed on Carmel and Bashan, and his soul shall be satis-
20 fied upon mount Ephraim and Gilead. In those days, and in
that time, saith the LORD, [p]the iniquity of Israel shall be sought
for, and *there shall be* none; and the sins of Judah, and they
shall not be found: for I will pardon them [q]whom I reserve.
21 ¶ Go up against the land [2]of Merathaim, *even* against it, and
against the inhabitants of [r][3]Pekod: waste and utterly destroy
after them, saith the LORD, and do [s]according to all that I have
22 commanded thee. [t]A sound of battle *is* in the land, and of
23 great destruction. How is [u]the hammer of the whole earth
cut asunder and broken! how is Babylon become a desolation
24 among the nations! I have laid a snare for thee, and thou art
also taken, O Babylon, [x]and thou wast not aware: thou art
found, and also caught, because thou hast striven against the
25 LORD. The LORD hath opened his armoury, and hath brought
forth [y]the weapons of his indignation: for this *is* the work of
26 the Lord GOD of hosts in the land of the Chaldeans. Come
against her [4]from the utmost border, open her storehouses:

[h] Ps. 137. 8.	
ver. 29.	
[i] Isai. 13. 14.	
[k] ver. 6.	
[l] ch. 2. 15.	
[m] 2 Kin. 17. 6.	
[n] 2 Kin. 24.	
10, 14.	
[o] Isai. 65. 10.	
Ezek. 34. 13.	
14.	
[p] ch. 31. 34.	
[q] Isai. 1. 9.	
[r] Ezek. 23. 23.	
[s] Isai. 10. 6.	
ch. 34. 22.	
[t] ch. 51. 54.	
[u] Isai. 14. 6.	
ch. 51. 20.	
[x] ch. 51. 8.	
Dan. 5. 30.	
[y] Isai. 13. 5.	

[1] Or, *scythe*.   [2] Or, *of the rebels*.   [3] Or, *Visitation*.   [4] Heb. *from the end*.

---

16. The population is to be destroyed so
utterly that the rich fields of Babylonia are
to remain untilled.

they shall turn] The full force of the words
will be seen if it be remembered that it
had been the policy of Nebuchadnezzar to
compel citizens selected from the vanquished
nations to settle in Babylonia.

17. *Israel is a scattered sheep*] i.e. is like a
flock which has been scared and driven in
all directions; for **lions have chased him.**

first the king &c.] Rather, **the first** lion *ate
him, even the king of Assyria*; *and* **this one,
the last,** *hath picked his bones, even Nebuchadrezzar* &c. The constant wasting of
the land by the Assyrians had so lessened
the number of Israel, that Nebuchadnezzar
had but the bones to pick.

19. Or, *I will bring Israel* (the scared
sheep) *back to his pasturage* (see v. 7) *and he
shall graze* &c. The places named are the
districts of Palestine most famous for their
rich herbage.

20. *those days*] The days of the Messiah.

reserve] Or, *permit to remain :* hence the
remnant, a word pregnant with meaning
in the language of the prophets. See Isai.
viii. 18 note (2).

21. *the land of Merathaim*] **of double rebellion.** Like Mitsraïm, *i.e.* the two Egypts,

Aram-Naharaïm, i.e. Syria of the two rivers,
or Mesopotamia, it is a dual. It may have
been a real name; or—the dual ending being
intensive—it may mean the land of very
great rebelliousness.

Pekod] Possibly a Babylonian town.

waste] Rather, *slay, v.* 27.

23. *the hammer*] Babylon, by whose instrumentality Jehovah had crushed the
nations, is now *cut asunder, i.e.* the head of
iron or bronze is cut away from the wooden
handle, and broken.

24. *I have laid a snare for thee*] Babylon,
the impregnable, was taken (according
to Herodotus) by Cyrus by stratagem.
Having diverted the waters of the Euphrates, he entered the city by the river
channel : but see Dan. v. 1 note.

and thou wast not aware] Better lit., **and
thou didst not know it.**

25. By a grand figure the prophet describes Jehovah arming Himself that in
person He may execute justice upon the
wicked city.

for this is *the work*] Rather, **for my Lord
Jehovah of hosts hath a work to do in the
land of the Chaldæans.**

26. *against her*] Or, **to** *her,* in order to
plunder her. *Her storehouses* (lit. **granaries**)
are to burst open, the corn piled up in

[1]cast her up as heaps, and destroy her utterly: let nothing of
27 her be left. Slay all her [z]bullocks; let them go down to the
slaughter: woe unto them! for their day is come, the time of
28 [a]their visitation. The voice of them that flee and escape out
of the land of Babylon, [b]to declare in Zion the vengeance of
29 the LORD our God, the vengeance of his temple. Call together
the archers against Babylon: [c]all ye that bend the bow, camp
against it round about; let none thereof escape: [d]recompense
her according to her work; according to all that she hath done,
do unto her: [e]for she hath been proud against the LORD, against
30 the Holy One of Israel. [f]Therefore shall her young men fall in
the streets, and all her men of war shall be cut off in that day,
31 saith the LORD. Behold, I *am* against thee, *O thou* [2]most
proud, saith the Lord GOD of hosts: for [g]thy day is come, the
32 time *that* I will visit thee. And [3]the most proud shall stumble
and fall, and none shall raise him up: and [h]I will kindle a fire
33 in his cities, and it shall devour all round about him. ¶ Thus
saith the LORD of hosts; The children of Israel and the children
of Judah *were* oppressed together: and all that took them
34 captives held them fast; they refused to let them go. [i]Their
Redeemer *is* strong; [k]the LORD of hosts *is* his name: he shall
throughly plead their cause, that he may give rest to the land,
35 and disquiet the inhabitants of Babylon. A sword *is* upon the
Chaldeans, saith the LORD, and upon the inhabitants of Babylon,
36 and [l]upon her princes, and upon [m]her wise *men*. A sword *is*
[n]upon the [4][5]liars; and they shall dote: a sword *is* upon her
37 mighty men; and they shall be dismayed. A sword *is* upon
their horses, and upon their chariots, and upon all [o]the mingled
people that *are* in the midst of her; and [p]they shall become as
women: a sword *is* upon her treasures; and they shall be
38 robbed. [q]A drought *is* upon her waters; and they shall be

[z] Ps. 22. 12. Isai. 34. 7.
[a] ch. 48. 44.
[b] ch. 51. 10.
[c] ver. 14.
[d] ver. 15. ch. 51. 56. Rev. 18. 6.
[e] Isai. 47. 10.
[f] ch. 49. 26.
[g] ver. 27.
[h] ch. 21. 14.
[i] Rev. 18. 8.
[k] Isai. 47. 4.
[l] Dan. 5. 30.
[m] Isai. 47. 13.
[n] Isai. 44. 25. ch. 48. 30.
[o] ch. 25. 20. Ezek. 30. 5.
[p] ch. 51. 30. Nah. 3. 13.
[q] Isai. 44. 27.

[1] Or, *tread her*.
[2] Heb. *pride*.
[3] Heb. *pride*.
[4] Or, *chief stays*.
[5] Heb. *bars*.

---

heaps, and finally they are to *devote her to destruction*, *i.e.* to burn her wealth with fire.

from the utmost border] [Or, "from the first of you even to the last"].

let nothing of her be left] Lit. **let her have no remnant**. Contrast v. 10.

27. *her bullocks*] Her strong youths.

28. *The voice of them...*] *i.e. There is a sound* of fugitives escaping from Babylonia. The Jews saw in the fall of Babylon Jehovah's *vengeance for His Temple*.

29. Or, *Summon ye the archers* **to** *Babylon, even all who bend the bow: encamp against* **her** &c. In this portion of the prophecy the capture of Babylon is regarded as the punishment due to her for burning the Temple (*v.*28).

31. Babylon is here called Pride, just as in *v.* 21 she was called Double-rebellion.

32. *him...his...him*] Or, **her**.

33. were *oppressed*] **are** *oppressed together: and all their captors have laid firm hold upon them: they have refused to let them go.* The restoration of Israel and Judah to their land is necessary. As Babylon will not let them go, it must be broken, and its empire destroyed.

34. *Redeemer*] *i.e.* Goel. Jehovah is Israel's next relative, bound by law to avenge him, as well as to ransom him from captivity. It was the Goel's duty also to plead his kinsman's cause. How thoroughly Jehovah will execute this duty for Israel is shewn in the Hebr. by the triple repetition of the same word; lit. *in pleading He will plead their plea.*

the land...] Rather, *the earth*. Babylon has hitherto by its ambition kept the world in unrest: now by its fall men everywhere can dwell in security.

35. Omit *is*. A summons comes from Jehovah, Israel's Goel, to the sword to fall upon all the elements of Babylon's greatness. The *princes* were her rulers at home and her generals in war. The *wise men* were those upon whose learning she so prided herself (Dan. i. 4 note).

36. *liars*] Soothsayers, fortune-tellers.

37. *the mingled people*] *i.e.* the foreigners serving as mercenaries in her army.

38. *A drought*] Rather, "a sword," *i.e.* military skill and forethought.

dried up : for it *is* the land of ^rgraven images, and they are mad
39 upon *their* idols. ^sTherefore the wild beasts of the desert with
the wild beasts of the islands shall dwell *there*, and the owls
shall dwell therein : ^tand it shall be no more inhabited for ever;
40 neither shall it be dwelt in from generation to generation. ^uAs
God overthrew Sodom and Gomorrah and the neighbour *cities*
thereof, saith the LORD; *so* shall no man abide there, neither
41 shall any son of man dwell therein. ¶^xBehold, a people shall
come from the north, and a great nation, and many kings shall
42 be raised up from the coasts of the earth. ^yThey shall hold the
bow and the lance : ^zthey *are* cruel, and will not shew mercy :
^atheir voice shall roar like the sea, and they shall ride upon
horses, *every one* put in array, like a man to the battle, against
43 thee, O daughter of Babylon. The king of Babylon hath heard
the report of them, and his hands waxed feeble : ^banguish took
44 hold of him, *and* pangs as of a woman in travail. ^cBehold, he
shall come up like a lion from the swelling of Jordan unto the
habitation of the strong: but I will make them suddenly run away
from her : and who *is* a chosen *man, that* I may appoint over
her ? for who *is* like me ? and who will ¹appoint me the time ?
45 and ^dwho *is* that shepherd that will stand before me ? Therefore
hear ye ^ethe counsel of the LORD, that he hath taken against
Babylon ; and his purposes, that he hath purposed against the
land of the Chaldeans : Surely the least of the flock shall draw
them out : surely he shall make *their* habitation desolate with
46 them. ^fAt the noise of the taking of Babylon the earth is
moved, and the cry is heard among the nations.

CHAP. 51. THUS saith the LORD; Behold, I will raise up against
Babylon, and against them that dwell in the ²midst of them that
2 rise up against me, ^aa destroying wind ; and will send unto
Babylon ^bfanners, that shall fan her, and shall empty her land :
^cfor in the day of trouble they shall be against her round about.
3 Against *him that* bendeth ^dlet the archer bend his bow, and
against *him that* lifteth himself up in his brigandine : and spare
4 ye not her young men ; ^edestroy ye utterly all her host. Thus
the slain shall fall in the land of the Chaldeans, ^fand *they that*
5 *are* thrust through in her streets. For Israel *hath* not *been*
forsaken, nor Judah of his God, of the LORD of hosts; though
their land was filled with sin against the Holy One of Israel.

r ver. 2.
ch. 51. 44.
s Isai. 13. 21,
22.
ch. 51. 37.
t Isai. 13. 20.
ch. 25. 12.
u Gen. 19. 25.
Isai. 13. 19.
ch. 49. 18.
x ch. 25. 14.

y ch. 6. 23.
z Isai. 13. 18.
a Isai. 5. 30.

b ch. 49. 24.
c ch. 49. 19.

d Job 41. 10.
ch. 49. 19.
e Isai. 14. 24,
&c.
ch. 51. 11.

f Rev. 18. 9.

a 2 Kin. 19. 7.
ch. 4. 11.
b ch. 15. 7.
c ch. 50. 14.
d ch. 50. 14.

e ch. 50. 21.
f ch. 49. 26.

---

¹ Or, *convent me to plead?*   ² Heb. *heart.*

---

they are mad upon their idols] Omit
their. The word for *idols,* lit. *terrors* (Ps.
lxxxviii. 16) is used in this one place only of
objects of worship. Probably it refers to
those monstrous forms invented as representations of their deities.

39. *wild beasts of the islands]* **Jackals.**

owls] **Ostriches** (marg. ref. note).

41-43. An application to Babylon of the
doom against Jerusalem (vi. 22-24).

41. *the coasts of the earth]* See vi. 22
note.

44-46. A similar application to Babylon
of what was said of Edom (marg. ref.).

LI. 1. *in the midst of them that rise up
against me]* Or, *in Leb-kamai,* the cipher for
Kasdim, i.e. Chaldæa. This cipher was not
necessarily invented by Jeremiah, or used

for concealment. It was probably first
devised either for political purposes or for
trade, and was in time largely employed
in the correspondence between the exiles at
Babylon and their friends at home. Thus
words in common use like Sheshach (xxv.
26) and Leb-kamai, would be known to
everybody.

2. *fanners]* Or, winnowers.

3. The man who *bends the bow,* and the
heavy-armed soldier who vaunts himself in
his coat of mail (xlvi. 4 note), represent the
Babylonians who defend the city.

4. Translate *And they, i.e.* the young men
who form her host (*v.* 3), *shall fall slain in
the land of the Chaldæans, and pierced
through in her streets, i.e.* the streets of
Babylon.

[g] ch. 50. 8. Rev. 18. 4. [h] ch. 50. 15. [i] ch. 25. 14. [k] Rev. 17. 4. [l] Rev. 14. 8. [m] ch. 25. 16. [n] Isai. 21. 9. [o] ch. 48. 20. Rev. 18. 9. [p] ch. 46. 11. [q] Isai. 13. 14. [r] Rev. 18. 5. [s] Ps. 37. 6. [t] ch. 50. 28. [u] ch. 46. 4. [x] Isai. 13. 17. [y] ch. 50. 45. [z] ch. 50. 28. [a] Nah. 2. 1. [b] Rev. 17. 1. [c] ch. 49. 13. Amos 6. 8. [d] Nah. 3. 15. [e] ch. 50. 15. [f] ch. 10. 12. [g] Job 9. 8. Ps. 104. 2. [h] ch. 10. 13.

6 [g]Flee out of the midst of Babylon, and deliver every man his
soul: be not cut off in her iniquity; for [h]this *is* the time of the
LORD's vengeance; [i] he will render unto her a recompence.
7 ¶ [k]Babylon *hath been* a golden cup in the LORD's hand, that
made all the earth drunken: [l]the nations have drunken of her
8 wine; therefore the nations [m]are mad. Babylon is suddenly
[n]fallen and destroyed: [o]howl for her; [p]take balm for her pain,
9 if so be she may be healed. We would have healed Babylon,
but she is not healed: forsake her, and [q]let us go every one into
his own country: [r]for her judgment reacheth unto heaven, and
10 is lifted up *even* to the skies. The LORD hath [s]brought forth
our righteousness: come, and let us [t]declare in Zion the work of
11 the LORD our God. ¶ [u]Make [1]bright the arrows; gather the
shields: [x]the LORD hath raised up the spirit of the kings of the
Medes: [y]for his device *is* against Babylon, to destroy it; because
it *is* [z]the vengeance of the LORD, the vengeance of his temple.
12 [a]Set up the standard upon the walls of Babylon, make the
watch strong, set up the watchmen, prepare the [2]ambushes: for
the LORD hath both devised and done that which he spake
13 against the inhabitants of Babylon. [b]O thou that dwellest
upon many waters, abundant in treasures, thine end is come,
14 *and* the measure of thy covetousness. [c]The LORD of hosts
hath sworn [3]by himself, *saying*, Surely I will fill thee with
men, [d]as with caterpillers; and they shall [4]lift [e]up a shout
15 against thee. ¶ [f]He hath made the earth by his power, he
hath established the world by his wisdom, and [g]hath stretched
16 out the heaven by his understanding. [h]When he uttereth

[1] Heb. *pure*.
[2] Heb. *liers in wait*.
[3] Heb. *by his soul*.
[4] Heb. *utter*.

---

7. Lit. *A golden cup is Babel in the hand of Jehovah, intoxicating the whole earth.* Jeremiah beholds her in her splendour, but the wine whereof she makes the nations drink is the wrath of God. As God's hammer (l. 23), Babylon was strong: as His cup of gold, she was rich and beautiful, but neither saves her from ruin.

8. *destroyed*] Lit. *broken*, as was the hammer (l. 23). The cup, though of metal, is thrown down so violently as to be shattered by the fall.

howl for her] The persons addressed are the many inhabitants of Babylon who were dragged from their homes to people its void places, and especially the Israelites. They have dwelt there long enough to feel pity for her, when they contrast her past magnificence with her terrible fall. Cp. xxix. 7.

9. Omit *would*. All was done that it was possible to do to heal her.

to the skies] Or, *to the* **clouds.**

10. Jehovah hath brought to the light those things which prove us to be righteous: *i.e.* by punishing Babylon He hath justified us.

11. *Make bright*] Rather, **Sharpen.**

The Medes (Gen. x. 2) were a branch of the great Aryan family, who as conquerors had seized upon the vast regions extending from the Caspian Sea to the eastern borders of Mesopotamia, but without being able to dispossess the Turanian tribes who had previously dwelt there. They were divided into numerous clans, each with its own local chief, the leaders of the larger sections being those who are here called kings.

12. *upon the walls of Babylon*] Or, *against the walls.* The A. V. takes the word ironically, as a summons to Babylon to prepare for her defence; others take it as a summons to the army to make the attack.

13. *upon many waters*] The great wealth of Babylonia was caused not merely by the Euphrates, but by a vast system of canals, which served for defence as well as for irrigation.

the measure of thy covetousness] *i.e.* the appointed end of thy gain. Some render *the ell of thy cutting off*, *i.e.* the appointed measure at which thou art to be cut off, at which thy web of existence is to be severed from the loom.

14. Rather, *Surely I* **have filled** *thee with men as with locusts, and they shall* **sing** *over thee* **the vintage-song.** The vintage-shout suggests the idea of trampling Babylon under foot, as the vintagers trample the grapes; a metaphor of the Divine wrath.

15–19. A transcript of x. 12–16.

his voice, *there is* a ¹multitude of waters in the heavens; and ¹he causeth the vapours to ascend from the ends of the earth: he maketh lightnings with rain, and bringeth forth the wind
17 out of his treasures. *k*Every man ²is brutish by *his* knowledge; every founder is confounded by the graven image: *l* for his molten image *is* falsehood, and *there is* no breath in them.
18 *m*They *are* vanity, the work of errors: in the time of their
19 visitation they shall perish. *n*The portion of Jacob *is* not like them; for he *is* the former of all things: and *Israel is* the rod
20 of his inheritance: the LORD of hosts *is* his name. ¶ *o*Thou *art* my battle axe *and* weapons of war: for ³with thee will I break in pieces the nations, and with thee will I destroy
21 kingdoms; and with thee will I break in pieces the horse and his rider; and with thee will I break in pieces the chariot and
22 his rider; with thee also will I break in pieces man and woman; and with thee will I break in pieces *p*old and young; and with
23 thee will I break in pieces the young man and the maid; I will also break in pieces with thee the shepherd and his flock; and with thee will I break in pieces the husbandman and his yoke of oxen; and with thee will I break in pieces captains and
24 rulers. *q*And I will render unto Babylon and to all the inhabitants of Chaldea all their evil that they have done in Zion in
25 your sight, saith the LORD. ¶ Behold, I *am* against thee, *r*O destroying mountain, saith the LORD, which destroyest all the earth: and I will stretch out mine hand upon thee, and roll thee down from the rocks, *s*and will make thee a burnt mountain.
26 And they shall not take of thee a stone for a corner, nor a stone for foundations; *t*but thou shalt be ⁴desolate for ever, saith the
27 LORD. ¶ *u*Set ye up a standard in the land, blow the trumpet among the nations, *x*prepare the nations against her, call together against her *y*the kingdoms of Ararat, Minni, and Ashchenaz; appoint a captain against her; cause the horses to come up as the
28 rough caterpillers. Prepare against her the nations with *z*the kings of the Medes, the captains thereof, and all the rulers
29 thereof, and all the land of his dominion. And the land shall

i Ps. 135. 7.

k ch. 10. 14.
l ch. 50. 2.

m ch. 10. 15.
n ch. 10. 16.

o Isai. 10. 5.
ch. 50. 23.

p So 2 Chr. 36. 17.

q ch. 50. 15.

r Isai. 13. 2.
Zech. 4. 7.

s Rev. 8. 8.

t ch. 50. 40.
u Isai. 13. 2.
x ch. 25. 14.
y ch. 50. 41.

z ver. 11.

---

¹ Or, *noise.*
² Or, *is more brutish than to know.*
³ Or, *in thee*, or, *by thee.*
⁴ Heb. *everlasting desolations.*

---

20. Or, Thou art my maul, weapons of war &c. The maul or mace (Prov. xxv. 18) only differs from the hammer (l. 23) in being used for warlike purposes.

Omit the "will" in "will I break." The crushing of the nations was going on at the time when the prophet wrote. Most commentators consider that Babylon was the mace of God.

23. *captains...rulers* (*v.* 28)] Pashas and Sagans. The prophet dwells at length upon Babylon's destructiveness.

25. *O destroying mountain*] A volcano, which by its flames and hot lava-streams *destroys the whole land.*

a burnt mountain] A burnt-out mountain, of which the crater alone remains. Such was Babylon. Its destructive energy under Nebuchadnezzar was like the first outbreak of volcanic fires; its rapid collapse under his successors was as the same volcano when its

flames have burnt out, and its crater is falling in upon itself.

26. The prophet means that (1) Babylon would never again be the seat of empire. Nor (2) would any new development of events take its rise thence.

27. Ararat, see Gen. viii. 4 note. Minni, probably the western portion of Armenia, as Ararat was that in the centre and to the East. Armenia was at this time subject to Media. Ashchenaz was between the Euxine and the Caspian Seas.

a captain] Some prefer the LXX. rendering in Nah. iii. 17, *a mingled mass of people.* [Others, a "scribe," an Assyrian term.]

the rough caterpillers] *i.e.* locusts in their third stage, when their wings are still enveloped in rough horny cases, which stick up upon their backs. It is in this stage that they are so destructive.

28. *his dominion*] This belonged not to

tremble and sorrow : for every purpose of the LORD shall be performed against Babylon, [a]to make the land of Babylon a desolation
30 without an inhabitant. The mighty men of Babylon have forborn to fight, they have remained in *their* holds: their might hath failed ; [b]they became as women : they have burned her
31 dwellingplaces ; [c]her bars are broken. [d]One post shall run to meet another, and one messenger to meet another, to shew the
32 king of Babylon that his city is taken at *one* end, and that [e]the passages are stopped, and the reeds they have burned with fire,
33 and the men of war are affrighted. For thus saith the LORD of hosts, the God of Israel ; The daughter of Babylon *is* [f]like a threshingfloor, [g][1]*it is* time to thresh her : yet a little while, [h]and
34 the time of her harvest shall come. ¶ Nebuchadrezzar the king of Babylon hath [i]devoured me, he hath crushed me, he hath made me an empty vessel, he hath swallowed me up like a dragon, he hath filled his belly with my delicates, he hath cast
35 me out. [2]The violence done to me and to my [3]flesh *be* upon Babylon, shall the [4]inhabitant of Zion say ; and my blood upon
36 the inhabitants of Chaldea, shall Jerusalem say. Therefore thus saith the LORD ; Behold, [k]I will plead thy cause, and take vengeance for thee ; [l]and I will dry up her sea, and make her
37 springs dry. [m]And Babylon shall become heaps, a dwellingplace for dragons, [n]an astonishment, and an hissing, without an

Marginal references:
[a] ch. 50. 13. ver. 43.
[b] Isai. 19. 16. ch. 50. 37.
[c] Lam. 2. 9. Nah. 3. 13.
[d] ch. 50. 24.
[e] ch. 50. 38.
[f] Isai. 21. 10. Mic. 4. 13.
[g] Hab. 3. 12.
[h] Isai. 17. 5. Hos. 6. 11. Joel 3. 13. Rev. 14. 15, 18.
[i] ch. 50. 17.
[k] ch. 50. 34.
[l] ch. 50. 38.
[m] Isai. 13. 22.
[n] ch. 25. 9.

---

[1] Or, *in the time that he thresheth her.*
[2] Heb. *My violence.*
[3] Or, *remainder.*
[4] Heb. *inhabitress.*

---

the subordinate rulers, but to the chief, *e.g.* to Cyrus.

29. The lit. translation is,

Then the earth quaked and writhed ;
For the thoughts of Jehovah against Babel have stood fast ;
To make Babel a waste without inhabitant.

30. *have forborn to fight*] Or, **have ceased to fight** : in despair when they saw that the conflict was hopeless.

holds] The word properly means an acropolis, and so any inaccessible place of refuge.

they have burned] *i.e.* the enemy have burned.

bars] *i.e.* fortifications (cp. Amos i. 5).

31. The royal palace was a strong fortification in the heart of the city. The messengers thus met one another.

at one end] Rather, *from all sides*, entirely, completely.

32. *the passages are stopped*] The ferries are **seized**, *occupied*. The historians state that when Cyrus captured the city his troops moved down the bed of the river and occupied all these ferries, finding at each of them the gates negligently left open. See Dan. v. 1 note.

the reeds] Lit. *the marshes* or pools, which formed an important part of the defences of Babylon, were dried up as completely as a piece of wood would be consumed by fire.

33. Translate, *The daughter of Babylon is as a threshing-floor* **at the time when it is**

trampled, *i.e.* trodden hard in readiness for the threshing : *yet a little while and the harvest-time* **shall come to her,** *i.e.* overtake her. In the East the corn when reaped is carried at once to the threshing-floor, a level spot carefully prepared beforehand, usually about fifty feet in diameter, and trampled hard. The grain after it has been beaten out by a sledge drawn over it by oxen is separated from the chaff and stored up in granaries.

34, 35. Lit. *Nebuchadrezzar...hath devoured us, hath crushed us, he hath set us aside as an empty vessel, he hath swallowed us like a crocodile, he hath filled his maw with my delicacies* (Gen. xlix. 20), *he hath cast us out. My wrong and my flesh be upon Babylon, shall the inhabitress of Zion say : and my blood be* &c. Nebuchadnezzar had devoured Jerusalem, had treated her as ruthlessly as a crocodile does its prey, and for this cruelty he and Babylon are justly to be punished.

36. *her sea*] Probably the great lake dug by Nitocris to receive the waters of the Euphrates.

her springs] *Her* **reservoir** ; the whole system of canals dug (*v.* 13). The wealth of Babylonia depended upon irrigation.

37. *heaps*] Of rubbish, formed in this case by the decay of the unburnt bricks of which Babylon was built. It is these heaps which have yielded such a large wealth of historical documents in our own days.

dragons] Jackals (x. 22).

38 inhabitant. They shall roar together like lions: they shall [1]yell
39 as lions' whelps. In their heat I will make their feasts, and [o]I [o] ver. 57.
will make them drunken, that they may rejoice, and sleep a per-
40 petual sleep, and not wake, saith the LORD. I will bring them
down like lambs to the slaughter, like rams with he goats.
41 ¶ How is [p]Sheshach taken! and how is [q]the praise of the whole [p] ch. 25. 26.
earth surprised! how is Babylon become an astonishment among [q] ch. 49. 25. Dan. 4. 30.
42 the nations! [r]The sea is come up upon Babylon: she is covered [r] See Isai.
43 with the multitude of the waves thereof. [s]Her cities are a deso- 7, 8.
lation, a dry land, and a wilderness, a land wherein no man [s] ch. 50. 39. ver. 29.
44 dwelleth, neither doth *any* son of man pass thereby. [t]And I [t] Isai. 46. 1.
will punish Bel in Babylon, and I will bring forth out of his ch. 50. 2.
mouth that which he hath swallowed up: and the nations shall
not flow together any more unto him: yea, [u]the wall of Babylon [u] ver. 58.
45 shall fall. ¶ [x]My people, go ye out of the midst of her, and [x] ch. 50. 8.
deliver ye every man his soul from the fierce anger of the LORD. Rev. 18. 4.
46 And [2]lest your heart faint, and ye fear [y]for the rumour that [y] 2 Kin. 19. 7.
shall be heard in the land; a rumour shall both come *one* year,
and after that in *another* year *shall come* a rumour, and violence
47 in the land, ruler against ruler. ¶ Therefore, behold, the days
come, that [z]I will [3]do judgment upon the graven images of [z] ch. 50. 2.
Babylon: and her whole land shall be confounded, and all her ver. 52.
48 slain shall fall in the midst of her. Then [a]the heaven and the [a] Isai. 44. 23.
earth, and all that *is* therein, shall sing for Babylon: [b]for the Rev. 18. 20. [b] ch. 50. 3.
spoilers shall come unto her from the north, saith the LORD.
49 [4]As Babylon *hath caused* the slain of Israel to fall, so at Babylon
50 shall fall the slain of all [5]the earth. [c]Ye that have escaped the [c] ch. 44. 28.
sword, go away, stand not still: remember the LORD afar off,
51 and let Jerusalem come into your mind. [d]We are confounded, [d] Ps. 44. 15. & 79. 4.

1 Or, *shake themselves.*
2 Or, *let not.*
3 Heb. *visit upon.*
4 Or, *Both Babylon* is *to fall, O ye slain of Israel, and with Babylon, &c.*
5 Or, *the country.*

---

38. *yell*] Or, *growl.*

39. *In their heat...*] While, like so many young lions, they are in the full glow of excitement over their prey, God prepares for them a drinking-bout to end in the sleep of death. Cp. Dan. v. 1.

40. *lambs...rams...he goats*] *i.e.* all classes of the population (see Isai. xxxiv. 6 note).

41. *Sheshach*] Babylon: see *v.* 1 note.

surprised] *i.e. seized, captured.*

42. By a grand metaphor the invading army is compared to the sea.

43. *a wilderness*] Or, **a desert** of sand.

a land wherein] Rather, *a land—no man shall dwell in them* (*i.e.* its cities), *and no human being shall pass through them.*

44. The sacred vessels plundered from Jerusalem, and laid up in the very temple of Bel, should be restored; the men and women dragged from other lands to people the city, released; and its wall falling would shew the insignificance to which it should be reduced.

45. *the fierce anger of the* LORD] *i.e.* against Babylon. The people of God are to flee away that they may not be involved in the miseries of Babylon. See l. 8 note.

46. Lit. *And* beware *lest your heart faint, and ye be afraid because of the rumour that is heard in the land: for in one year shall one rumour come, and afterwards in another year another rumour; and violence shall be in the land* &c. The fall of Babylon was to be preceded by a state of unquiet, men's minds being unsettled partly by rumours of the warlike preparations of the Medes, and of actual invasions: partly by intestine feuds. So before the conquest of Jerusalem by the Romans the Church had similar warnings (Matt. xxiv. 6, 7).

47. *Therefore*] The exiles were to note these things as signs of the approach of God's visitation.

confounded] Or, **ashamed.**

49. Render, *As Babylon caused the slain of Israel to fall, so because of Babylon have fallen the slain of* (or, *in*) *the whole earth.* Babylon has to answer for the general carnage caused by its wars.

50. *afar off*] Or, **from afar**, from Chaldæa, far away from Jehovah's dwelling in Jerusalem. The verse is a renewed entreaty to the Jews to leave Babylon and journey homewards, as soon as Cyrus grants them permission.

51. *confounded*] Or, **ashamed.** The verse

because we have heard reproach : shame hath covered our faces:
for strangers are come into the sanctuaries of the LORD's house.
52 Wherefore, behold, the days come, saith the LORD, *that I will
do judgment upon her graven images : and through all her land
53 the wounded shall groan. /Though Babylon should mount up to
heaven, and though she should fortify the height of her strength,
54 yet from me shall spoilers come unto her, saith the LORD. ¶ *A
sound of a cry *cometh* from Babylon, and great destruction from
55 the land of the Chaldeans : because the LORD hath spoiled Babylon, and destroyed out of her the great voice ; when her waves
56 do roar like great waters, a noise of their voice is uttered : because the spoiler is come upon her, *even* upon Babylon, and her
mighty men are taken, every one of their bows is broken : *for
57 the LORD God of recompences shall surely requite. *And I will
make drunk her princes, and her wise *men*, her captains, and
her rulers, and her mighty men : and they shall sleep a perpetual
sleep, and not wake, saith *the King, whose name *is* the LORD
58 of hosts. ¶ Thus saith the LORD of hosts ; ¹¹The broad walls of
Babylon shall be utterly ²broken, and her high gates shall be
burned with fire ; and *the people shall labour in vain, and the
folk in the fire, and they shall be weary.

59   The word which Jeremiah the prophet commanded Seraiah
the son of Neriah, the son of Maaseiah, when he went ³with
Zedekiah the king of Judah into Babylon in the fourth year of
60 his reign. And *this* Seraiah *was* a ⁴quiet prince. So Jeremiah
wrote in a book all the evil that should come upon Babylon,
61 *even* all these words that are written against Babylon. ¶ And
Jeremiah said to Seraiah, When thou comest to Babylon, and
62 shalt see, and shalt read all these words ; then shalt thou say,
O LORD, thou hast spoken against this place, to cut it off, that
*none shall remain in it, neither man nor beast, but that it shall
63 be ⁵desolate for ever. And it shall be, when thou hast made an
end of reading this book, *that* thou shalt bind a stone to it, and

* ver. 47.

/ ch. 49. 16.
Amos 9. 2.
Obad. 4.
ᵍ ch. 50. 22.

ʰ Ps. 94. 1.
ch. 50. 29.
ⁱ ver. 39.

ᵏ ch. 46. 18.
& 48. 15.
ˡ ver. 44.

ᵐ Hab. 2. 13.

ⁿ ch. 50. 3.
ver. 29.

* See Rev.
18. 21.

---

¹ Or, *The walls of broad Babylon.*
² Or, *made naked:*
³ Or, *on the behalf of.*
⁴ Or, *prince of Menucha,*
or, *chief chamberlain.*
⁵ Heb. *desolations.*

---

is a statement of the wrong done to the
exiles by Babylon, and so leads naturally to
Babylon's punishment (*v.* 52).
54. *a cry*] *i.e.* the war-cry.
55. Render, *For Jehovah wasteth Babylon,
and will make to cease from her the loud
noise* (of busy life) ; *and their waves* (the
surging masses of the enemy) *roar like many
waters : the noise of their shouting is given
forth, i.e.* resounds.
56. *every one* &c.] Or, *Their bows* are
*broken ; for Jehovah is a God of recompenses;
He will certainly requite.*
58. *The broad walls*] Herodotus makes
the breadth of the walls 85 English feet.
broken] See marg. *i.e.* the ground beneath
them shall be laid bare by their demolition.
the people] Or, **peoples.** Jeremiah concludes
his prophecy with a quotation from Habak-
kuk ; applying the words to the stupendous
works intended to make Babylon an eternal
city, but which were to end in such early
and utter disappointment.

59-64. Historical appendix. In his fourth
year Zedekiah journeyed to Babylon either
to obtain some favour from Nebuchadnezzar, or because he was summoned to be
present on some state occasion. Jeremiah
took the opportunity of sending to the exiles
at Babylon this prophecy.
59. *Seraiah*] Brother to Baruch.
a quiet prince] Lit. *prince of the resting-
place, i.e. quartermaster.* It was his business
to ride forward each day, and select the
place where the king would halt and pass
the night.
60. *in a book*] Lit. *in* **one** *book*, on one roll
of parchment.
61. *and shalt see, and shalt read*] Or, **then
see that thou** *read* &c.
62-64. The sinking of the roll was not
for the purpose of destroying it, but was a
symbolical act (cp. marg. ref.) ; and the
binding of a stone to it signified the certainty
of the hasty ruin of the city.

64 cast it into the midst of Euphrates: and thou shalt say, Thus shall Babylon sink, and shall not rise from the evil that I will bring upon her : *P*and they shall be weary.   *p* ver. 58.

Thus far *are* the words of Jeremiah.

Chap. 52. ZEDEKIAH *was* *a*one and twenty years old when he 1began to reign, and he reigned eleven years in Jerusalem. And his mother's name *was* Hamutal the daughter of Jeremiah of 2 Libnah. And he did *that which was* evil in the eyes of the LORD, 3 according to all that Jehoiakim had done. For through the anger of the LORD it came to pass in Jerusalem and Judah, till he had cast them out from his presence, that Zedekiah rebelled against 4 the king of Babylon. ¶ And it came to pass in the *b*ninth year of his reign, in the tenth month, in the tenth *day* of the month, *that* Nebuchadrezzar king of Babylon came, he and all his army, against Jerusalem, and pitched against it, and built forts against 5 it round about. So the city was besieged unto the eleventh year 6 of king Zedekiah. And in the fourth month, in the ninth *day* of the month, the famine was sore in the city, so that there was no 7 bread for the people of the land. Then the city was broken up, and all the men of war fled, and went forth out of the city by night by the way of the gate between the two walls, which *was* by the king's garden; (now the Chaldeans *were* by the city 8 round about:) and they went by the way of the plain. But the army of the Chaldeans pursued after the king, and overtook Zedekiah in the plains of Jericho; and all his army was scattered 9 from him. *c*Then they took the king, and carried him up unto the king of Babylon to Riblah in the land of Hamath; where he 10 gave judgment upon him. *d*And the king of Babylon slew the sons of Zedekiah before his eyes: he slew also all the princes 11 of Judah in Riblah. Then he 2put out the eyes of Zedekiah ; and the king of Babylon bound him in 3chains, and carried him to Babylon, and put him in 4prison till the day of his death.

12 ¶ *e*Now in the fifth month, in the tenth *day* of the month, *f*which *was* the nineteenth year of Nebuchadrezzar king of Babylon, *g*came Nebuzar-adan, 5 6captain of the guard, *which* 7served 13 the king of Babylon, into Jerusalem, and burned the house of the LORD, and the king's house; and all the houses of Jerusalem, and all the houses of the great *men*, burned he with fire :

*a*2 Kin. 24. 18.

b 2 Kin. 25. 1—27. ch. 39. 1. Zech. 8. 19.

c ch. 32. 4.

*d*Ezek.12.13.

e Zech. 7. 5. & 8. 19. *f* See ver. 29. *g* ch. 39. 9.

---

1 Heb. *reigned.*	4 Heb. *house of the wards.*	tioners, or, *slaughtermen.*
2 Heb. *blinded.*	5 Or, *chief marshal.*	And so ver. 14, &c.
3 Or, *fetters.*	6 Heb. *chief of the execu-*	7 Heb. *stood before.*

---

64. *Thus far* &c.] Whoever added ch. lii., evidently felt it his duty to point out that t was not written by Jeremiah.

LII. A historical appendix to the Book of Jeremiah, giving details of the capture of Babylon additional to those contained in ch. xxxix. The last words of the foregoing chapter affirm that Jeremiah was not the author, and the view adopted by most commentators is, that this chapter is taken from the 2nd Book of Kings, but that the person who added it here had access to other valuable documents, and made several modifications in it, the principal being the substitution of the account of those led captive by Nebuchadnezzar (*vv.* 28-30), for the narra-

tive given in 2 K. xxv. 22-26, where see notes.

3. *it*] *i.e.* Zedekiah's evil doing.
presence, that Zedekiah] Or, punctuate ; "presence. And Zedekiah" &c.
7. *broken up...the plain*] Or, "broken into ...the Arabah" (Deut. i. 1).
11. *put him in prison* &c.] Not found in 2 K., for in the contemporaneous history what befel Zedekiah at Riblah would alone be known. It was no doubt added by the same hand which inserted the account of the deportations to Babylon.
12. *served*] The word implies high office.
13. *houses of the great*] Rather, **every great house** ; *i.e.* the larger houses only.

h ch. 39. 9.

14 and all the army of the Chaldeans, that *were* with the captain of the guard, brake down all the walls of Jerusalem round

15 about. *h*Then Nebuzar-adan the captain of the guard carried away captive *certain* of the poor of the people, and the residue of the people that remained in the city, and those that fell away, that fell to the king of Babylon, and the rest of the multitude.

i ch. 27. 19.
k See 1 Kin.
7. 15, 23.

16 But Nebuzar-adan the captain of the guard left *certain* of the

17 poor of the land for vinedressers and for husbandmen. *i*Also the *k*pillars of brass that *were* in the house of the LORD, and the bases, and the brasen sea that *was* in the house of the LORD, the Chaldeans brake, and carried all the brass of them to Baby-

l Ex. 27. 3.
2 Kin. 25. 14,
15, 16.

18 lon. *l*The caldrons also, and the ¹shovels, and the snuffers, and the ²bowls, and the spoons, and all the vessels of brass where-

19 with they ministered, took they away. And the basons, and the ³firepans, and the bowls, and the caldrons, and the candlesticks, and the spoons, and the cups; *that* which *was* of gold *in* gold, and *that* which *was* of silver *in* silver, took the captain of

20 the guard away. The two pillars, one sea, and twelve brasen bulls that *were* under the bases, which king Solomon had made

m 1 Kin.7.47.
n 1 Kin. 7.15.
2 Kin. 25. 17

in the house of the LORD: *m*⁴the brass of all these vessels was

21 without weight. And *concerning* the *n*pillars, the height of one pillar *was* eighteen cubits; and a ⁵fillet of twelve cubits did compass it; and the thickness thereof *was* four fingers: *it was* hollow.

22 And a chapiter of brass *was* upon it; and the height of one chapiter *was* five cubits, with network and pomegranates upon the chapiters round about, all *of* brass. The second pillar also

23 and the pomegranates *were* like unto these. And there were

o See 1 Kin.
7. 20.

ninety and six pomegranates on a side; *and* *o*all the pome-

p 2Kin.25.18.
q ch. 21. 1. &
29. 25.

24 granates upon the network *were* an hundred round about. ¶And *p*the captain of the guard took Seraiah the chief priest, *q*and Zephaniah the second priest, and the three keepers of the ⁶door:

25 he took also out of the city an eunuch, which had the charge of the men of war; and seven men of them that ⁷were near the king's person, which were found in the city; and the ⁸principal scribe of the host, who mustered the people of the land; and threescore men of the people of the land, that were found in the

26 midst of the city. So Nebuzar-adan the captain of the guard

---

¹ Or, *instruments to remove the ashes.*
² Or, *basons.*
³ Or, *censers.*

⁴ Heb. *their brass.*
⁵ Heb. *thread.*
⁶ Heb. *threshold.*
⁷ Heb. *saw the face of the*

king.
⁸ Or, *scribe of the captain of the host.*

---

15. certain *of the poor of the people, and*] Omit (as in 2 K. xxv. 11), being inserted through some confusion with *v.* 16.

multitude] Possibly *workmen*. The object of Nebuchadnezzar was to people Babylon, not with paupers, but with men of a better class, artizans and workmen, who would enrich it.

16. *husbandmen*] Men who tilled little plots of ground with the mattock.

20. *twelve brasen bulls that* were *under*] Omitted in 2 K. and in xxvii. 19. Probably rightly, for what is said here of their being under the bases is a mistake. The bases were under the ten lavers. The LXX. make sense by translating, the *twelve brasen bulls under the sea.*

21. The *fillet* means a **measuring line**;

the pillars were twelve cubits, *i.e.* eighteen feet, in circumference, and thus the diameter would be 5 feet 9 inches. As the brass was four fingers, *i.e.* scarcely four inches thick, the hollow centre would be more than five feet in diameter.

23. *on a side*] The ninety-six were **towards the four winds**, twenty-four towards the North, twenty-four towards the East, and so on. Add one at each corner, and the whole hundred is made up.

25. *an eunuch...men of war*] Or, **who had charge of men of war.** The A. V. makes him commander-in-chief; he was second in command, *i.e.* a lieutenant, possibly one among many others of equal rank.

took them, and brought them to the king of Babylon to Riblah.

27 And the king of Babylon smote them, and put them to death in Riblah in the land of Hamath. Thus Judah was carried away captive out of his own land.

28 ʳThis *is* the people whom Nebuchadrezzar carried away captive: in the ˢseventh year ᵗthree thousand Jews and three and

29 twenty: ᵘin the eighteenth year of Nebuchadrezzar he carried away captive from Jerusalem eight hundred thirty and two

30 ¹persons: in the three and twentieth year of Nebuchadrezzar Nebuzar-adan the captain of the guard carried away captive of the Jews seven hundred forty and five persons: all the persons *were* four thousand and six hundred.

r 2 Kin.24. 2.
s See 2 Kin. 24. 12.
t See 2 Kin. 24. 14.
u See ver.12. ch. 39. 9.

31 ˣAnd it came to pass in the seven and thirtieth year of the captivity of Jehoiachin king of Judah, in the twelfth month, in the five and twentieth *day* of the month, *that* Evil-merodach king of Babylon in the *first* year of his reign ᵛlifted up the head of Jehoiachin king of Judah, and brought him forth out of

32 prison, and spake ²kindly unto him, and set his throne above

33 the throne of the kings that *were* with him in Babylon, and changed his prison garments: ᶻand he did continually eat bread

34 before him all the days of his life. And *for* his diet, there was a continual diet given him of the king of Babylon, ³every day a portion until the day of his death, all the days of his life.

x 2 Kin. 25. 27, 28, 29.

v Gen. 40. 13, 20.

z 2 Sam.9.13.

---

¹ Heb. *souls.*
² Heb. *good things with him.*

³ Heb. *the matter of the day in his day.*

---

28. *seventh year*] The suggestion is now generally received, that the word *ten* has dropped out before *seven*, and that the deportations mentioned here are all connected with the final war against Zedekiah. The calculation of Nebuchadnezzar's reign is different from that used elsewhere, shewing that the writer had access to a document not known to the compiler of the Book of Kings. In each date there is a difference of one year. The LXX. omits *vv.* 28-30.

The number of the exiles carried away is small compared with the 42,360 men who returned (Ezr. ii. 64, 65), leaving a large Jewish population behind at Babylon. But a continual drain of people from Judæa was going on, and the 10,000 carried away with Jehoiachin formed the nucleus and centre, and gave tone to the whole (see 2 K. xxiv. 14). When they began to thrive in Babylon, large numbers would emigrate thither of their own accord.

A comparison of this chapter with the parallel portion of 2 Kings shews that though not free from clerical errors and mistakes of copyists the body of the text is remarkably sound. Many of the differences between the two texts are abbreviations made purposely by the compiler of the Book of Kings; others are the result of negligence; and upon the whole the text of the Book of Kings is inferior to that of the Appendix to the Book of Jeremiah. Bearing in mind, however, that possibly they are not two transcripts of the same text, but the result of an independent use by two different writers of the same original authority, their complete agreement, except in trivial matters and mistakes easy of correction, is a satisfactory proof of the general trustworthiness of the Masoretic text in all more important particulars.

LAMENTATIONS.

INTRODUCTION.

THE prophecy of Jeremiah is immediately followed in the English Version by five lyric poems, the title of which in the Versions is taken from the general nature of the contents; thus the LXX. called these poems Θρῆνοι, *Threni, i.e.* Dirges, and the Syr. and Vulg. *Lamentations.* In the Hebrew Bible the Lamentations are arranged among the Cetubim, or (Holy) Writings, because of the nature of their contents : the Lamentations as being lyrical poetry are classed not with Prophecies, but with the Psalms and Proverbs. This classification is probably later than the translation of the LXX., who have appended the Lamentations to Jeremiah's prophecy, inserting between them the apocryphal book of Baruch, and in fact counting the three as only one book.

Although no name is attached to these poems in the Hebrew, yet both ancient tradition (LXX., Josephus, the Targum of Jonathan, the Talmud &c.) and internal evidence point to Jeremiah as the author. The time of the composition of these poems is certainly the period immediately after the capture of Jerusalem, and probably during the month which intervened between the capture of Jerusalem and its destruction.[1]

Their subject is the destruction of Jerusalem by the Chaldæans. In the *first* of these poems the prophet dwells upon the miseries of hunger, of death in battle, of the profanation and plundering of the sanctuary, and of impending exile, oppressed by which the city sits solitary. In the *second*, these same sufferings are described with more intense force, and in closer connexion with the national sins which had caused them, and which had been aggravated by the faithlessness of the prophets. In the *third*, Jeremiah acknowledges that chastisement is for the believer's good, and he dwells more upon the spiritual aspect of sorrow, and the certainty that finally there must be the redeeming of life for God's people, and vengeance for His enemies. In the *fourth*, Judah's sorrows are confessed to have been caused by her sins. Finally, in the *fifth*, Jeremiah prays that Zion's reproach may be taken away, and that Jehovah will grant repentance unto His people, and renew their days as of old.

The structure of the first four poems is highly artificial. They are arranged in twenty-two portions, according to the number of the letters of the Hebrew alphabet; but in the first three poems each portion is again subdivided into three double-clauses, the third differing from the first and second in that each also of these divisions

---

[1] See the passages which shew that famine and hunger were still raging in the city, i. 11, 19; ii. 19, 20; iv. 4 &c.

begins with the same letter. In ch. iv., we have again twenty-two verses beginning with the letters of the alphabet in order, but each verse is divided into only two portions. In ch. v., though there are again twenty-two verses, the alphabetical initials are discontinued. Hence some have thought that this prayer was added by the prophet to his Lamentations when in Egypt at a somewhat later time.

The book of Lamentations has always been much used in liturgical services as giving the spiritual aspect of sorrow. It is recited in the Jewish synagogues on the ninth of Ab, the day on which the Temple was destroyed. In the Church of England the whole of ch. iii., and portions of chs. i., ii., and iv. are read on the Monday, Tuesday, and Wednesday in Holy Week. For this choice two chief reasons may be given; the first, that in the wasted city and homeless wanderings of the chosen people we see an image of the desolation and ruin of the soul cast away—because of sin —from God's Presence into the outer darkness; the second and chief, because the mournful words of the prophet set Him before us Who has borne the chastisement due to human sin, and of Whom we think instinctively as we pronounce the words of i. 12.

THE
LAMENTATIONS OF JEREMIAH.

Chap. 1. (א) HOW doth the city sit solitary, *that was* full of people!

> [a] *How* is she become as a widow! she *that was* great among the nations,
> And [b] princess among the provinces, how is she become tributary!

2 (ב) She [c] weepeth sore in the [d] night, and her tears *are* on her cheeks:
> [e] Among all her lovers [f] she hath none to comfort *her:*
> All her friends have dealt treacherously with her, they are become her enemies.

3 (ג) [g] Judah is gone into captivity because of affliction, and [1] because of great servitude:
> [h] She dwelleth among the heathen, she findeth no rest:
> All her persecutors overtook her between the straits.

4 (ד) The ways of Zion do mourn, because none come to the solemn feasts:
> All her gates are desolate: her priests sigh,
> Her virgins are afflicted, and she *is* in bitterness.

5 (ה) Her adversaries [i] are the chief, her enemies prosper;
> For the LORD hath afflicted her [k] for the multitude of her transgressions:
> Her [l] children are gone into captivity before the enemy.

6 (ו) And from the daughter of Zion all her beauty is departed:
> Her princes are become like harts *that* find no pasture,
> And they are gone without strength before the pursuer.

[a] Isa. 47. 7.

[b] Ezra 4. 20.

[c] Jer. 13. 17.
[d] Job 7. 3.
Ps. 6. 6.
[e] Jer. 4. 30.
& 30. 14.
[f] ver. 9. 16,
17, 21.

[g] Jer. 52. 27.

[h] Deut. 28. 64
65.
ch. 2. 9.

[i] Deut. 28.
43. 44.
[k] Jer. 30. 14
Dan. 9. 7.
[l] Jer. 52. 28.

---

[1] Heb. *for the greatness of servitude.*

I. This poem divides itself into two equal parts; *vv.* 1–11 describe the misery which has befallen the Jews; in *vv.* 12–22, Jerusalem laments over her sufferings.

1, 2. In these two verses is the same sad image as appears in the well-known medal of Titus, struck to celebrate his triumph over Jerusalem. A woman sits weeping beneath a palm-tree, and below is the legend *Judæa capta.*

Translate *v.* 1 :—

> *How sitteth solitary the city that was full of people:*
> *She is become as a widow that was great among the nations:*
> *A princess among provinces she is become a vassal.*

tributary] In the sense of personal labour (Josh. xvi. 10).

2. *lovers...friends*] *i.e.* the states in alliance with Judæa, and all human helpers.

3. *because of...*] *i.e.* the people, not of Jerusalem only, but of the whole land, is

gone into exile to escape from the affliction and laborious servitude, to which they are subject in their own land.

persecutors...between the straits] Rather, "pursuers...in the midst of her straits." The Jews flee like deer to escape from the invading Chaldæans, but are driven by them into places whence there is no escape.

4. Zion, as the holy city, is the symbol of the religious life of the people, just as Judah in the previous verse represents their national life. The "virgins" took a prominent part in all religious festivals (Jer. xxxi. 13; Ex. xv. 20).

5. *are the chief...prosper*] Or, *are become the head...***are at rest.** Judæa is so entirely crushed that her enemies need take no precautions against resistance on her part.

children] *i.e. young children,* who are driven *before the enemy* (lit. **the adversary**), not as a flock of lambs which follow the shepherd, but for sale as slaves.

6. *her princes &c.*] Jeremiah had before his mind the sad flight of Zedekiah and his

7 (ז) Jerusalem remembered in the days of her affliction and of
   her miseries all her [1]pleasant things that she had in the days
   of old,
   When her people fell into the hand of the enemy, and none did
   help her:
   The adversaries saw her, *and* did mock at her sabbaths.

m 1 Kin. 8. 16.   8 (ח) *m*Jerusalem hath grievously sinned; therefore she [2]is re-
                        moved:

n Jer. 13. 22.   All that honoured her despise her, because *n*they have seen her
Ezek. 16. 37.   nakedness:
& 23. 29.   Yea, she sigheth, and turneth backward.

*o*Deut. 32. 29.   9 (ט) Her filthiness *is* in her skirts; she *o*remembereth not her
Isai. 47. 7.   last end;

p ver. 2. 17.   Therefore she came down wonderfully: *p*she had no comforter.
                     O LORD, behold my affliction: for the enemy hath magnified
                        himself.

q ver. 7.   10 (י) The adversary hath spread out his hand upon *q*all her [3]pleasant
                        things:

r Jer. 51. 51.   For she hath seen *that* *r*the heathen entered into her sanctuary,
s Deut. 23. 3.   Whom thou didst command *that* *s*they should not enter into
Neh. 13. 1.   thy congregation.

t Jer. 38. 9.   11 (כ) All her people sigh, *t*they seek bread;
ch. 2. 12.   They have given their pleasant things for meat [4]to relieve the
                        soul:
                     See, O LORD, and consider; for I am become vile.

                     12 (ל) [5]*Is* it nothing to you, all ye that [6]pass by?
u Dan. 9. 12.   Behold, and see *u*if there be any sorrow like unto my sorrow,
                        which is done unto me,

---

[1] Or, *desirable*, ver. 10.   [3] Or, *desirable*.   [5] Or, It is *nothing*.
[2] Heb. *is become a removing*, [4] Or, *to make the soul to*   [6] Heb. *pass by the way?*
   or, *wandering*.   *come again*.

---

men of war, and their capture within a few
miles of Jerusalem (Jer. xxxix. 4, 5).

7. *Jerusalem remembers in the days of her
   affliction, and of her homelessness,
   All her pleasant things which have been
   from the days of old:
   Now that her people fall by the hand of
   the adversary,
   And she hath no helper;
   Her adversaries have seen her,
   They have mocked at her sabbath-keep-
   ings.*

The word rendered *homelessless* means
wanderings, and describes the state of the
Jews, cast forth from their homes and about
to be dragged into exile.

sabbaths, or, **sabbath-keepings**, and the
cessation from labour every seventh day
struck foreigners as something strange, and
provoked their ridicule.

8. *grievously sinned*] Lit. *Jerusalem hath
sinned a sin*, giving the idea of a persistent
continuance in wickedness.

removed] Or, **become an abomination.**
Sin has made Jerusalem an object of horror,
and therefore she is cast away.

yea, she sigheth &c.] Jerusalem groans over

the infamy of her deeds thus brought to
open shame, and turns her back upon the
spectators in order to hide herself.

9. *Her filthiness* is *in her skirts*] Her personal defilement is no longer concealed beneath the raiment (Jer. xiii. 22).

she came down wonderfully] Jerusalem
once enthroned as a princess must sit on the
ground as a slave.

10. *her pleasant things*] Chiefly the sacred
vessels of the Temple (2 Chr. xxxvi. 10).

sanctuary...congregation] Even a Jew
might not enter the innermost sanctuary,
which was for the priests only; but now the
tramp of heathen soldiery has been heard
within its sacred precincts.

11. *sigh...seek*] **Are sighing...are seeking.** The words are present participles, describing the condition of the people. After a
siege lasting a year and a half the whole
country, far and near, would be exhausted.

to relieve the soul] See marg., *i.e.* to bring
back life to them. They bring out their
jewels and precious articles to obtain with
them at least a meal.

12-16. The lamentation of the city, personified as a woman in grief over her fate.

Wherewith the LORD hath afflicted *me* in the day of his fierce
anger.

13 (ל) From above hath he sent fire into my bones, and it pre-
vaileth against them:
He hath *ˣ*spread a net for my feet, he hath turned me back: *ˣ* Ezek. 12.
He hath made me desolate *and* faint all the day.   13. & 17. 20.

14 (נ) *ᵛ*The yoke of my transgressions is bound by his hand: they *ᵛ* Deut. 28. 48.
are wreathed,
And come up upon my neck: he hath made my strength to fall,
The Lord hath delivered me into *their* hands, *from whom* I am
not able to rise up.

15 (ס) The Lord hath trodden under foot all my mighty *men* in the
midst of me:
He hath called an assembly against me to crush my young men:
*ᶻ*The Lord hath trodden ¹the virgin, the daughter of Judah, *as*   *ᶻ* Isai. 63. 3.
in a winepress.

16 (ע) For these *things* I weep; *ᵃ*mine eye, mine eye runneth down *ᵃ* Jer. 13. 17.
with water,   ch. 2. 18.
Because *ᵇ*the comforter that should ²relieve my soul is far from   *ᵇ* ver. 2, 9.
me:
My children are desolate, because the enemy prevailed.

17 (פ) *ᶜ*Zion spreadeth forth her hands, *and* *ᵈ*there is none to com- *ᶜ* Jer. 4. 31.
fort her: *ᵈ* ver. 2, 9.
The LORD hath commanded concerning Jacob, *that* his adver-
saries *should be* round about him:
Jerusalem is as a menstruous woman among them.

¹ Or, *the winepress of the virgin, &c.*   ² Heb. *bring back.*

---

13. *it prevaileth*] Or, **hath subdued.**
he hath turned me back] Judæa, like a
hunted animal, endeavours to escape, but
finds every outlet blocked by nets, and re-
coils from them with terror and a sense of
utter hopelessness.
14. *bound by his hand*] As the ploughman
binds the yoke upon the neck of oxen, so
God compels Judah to bear the punishment
of her sins.
they are wreathed, and...] Or, **they are
knotted together,** *they come up* &c. Judah's
sins are like the cords by which the pieces
of the yoke are fastened together (Jer. xxvii.
2); they are knotted and twined like a
bunch upon the neck, and bind the yoke
around it so securely that it is impossible
for her to shake it off.
he hath made...] Or, **it hath made** *my
strength* **to stumble.** The yoke of punishment thus imposed and securely fastened,
bows down her strength by its weight, and
makes her totter beneath it.
the Lord] The third distich of the verse
begins here, and with it a new turn of the
lamentation. The title Adonai (properly,
my Lord) is in the Lamentations used
by itself in fourteen places, while the name
Jehovah is less prominent; as if in their
punishment the people felt the lordship of
the Deity more, and His Covenant-love to
them less.

15. *The Lord hath trodden under foot*]
Or, *Adonai* **hath made contemptible** (*i.e.*
put into the balance, made to go up as the
lighter weight, and so made despicable)
my war-horses (put metaphorically for
heroes).
in the midst of me] They had not fallen
gloriously in the battle-field, but remained
ignominiously in the city.
assembly] Or, "a solemn feast;" the word
especially used of the great festivals (Lev.
xxiii. 2.) Adonai has proclaimed a festival,
not for me, but against me.
the Lord hath trodden &c....] Or, *Adonai
hath trodden the winepress for the virgin
daughter of Judah.* See Jer. li. 14 note.
God by slaying Judah's young men in battle
is trampling for her the winepress of His
indignation.
17. *spreadeth forth her hands*] In prayer
(Ex. ix. 29, 33), but Zion entreats in vain.
There is no one to comfort her—not God,
for He is chastising her, nor man, for all the
neighbouring nations have become her
enemies. See *v.* 2.
that his adversaries &c.] Rather, **that
those round about him should be his adversaries;** all the neighbouring states should
regard him with aversion.
Jerusalem is &c.] *i.e.* **is become an abomination.** The words are virtually the same
as in *v.* 8.

*Neh. 9. 33.
Dan. 9. 7.
*/ 1 Sam. 12.
14, 15.

18 (צ) The LORD is *righteous; for I have *rebelled against his
   [1]commandment:
   Hear, I pray you, all people, and behold my sorrow:
   My virgins and my young men are gone into captivity.

g ver. 2.
Jer. 30. 14.

h ver. 11.

19 (ק) I called for my lovers, *but* *g*they deceived me:
   My priests and mine elders gave up the ghost in the city,
   *h*While they sought their meat to relieve their souls.

i Job 30. 27.
Isai. 16. 11.
Jer. 4. 19.

k Deut. 32.25.
Ezek. 7. 15.
l ver. 2.

20 (ר) Behold, O LORD; for I *am* in distress: my *i*bowels are
   troubled;
   Mine heart is turned within me; for I have grievously rebelled:
   *k*Abroad the sword bereaveth, at home *there is* as death.

21 (ש) They have heard that I sigh: *l*there is* none to comfort me:
   All mine enemies have heard of my trouble; they are glad that
        thou hast done *it*:

m Isai.13.&c.
Jer. 46, &c.

   Thou wilt bring *m*the day *that* thou hast [2]called, and they shall
        be like unto me.

n Ps. 109. 15.

22 (ת) *n*Let all their wickedness come before thee;
   And do unto them, as thou hast done unto me for all my trans-
        gressions:

o ch. 5. 17.

   For my sighs *are* many, and *o*my heart *is* faint.

CHAP. 2. (א) HOW hath the Lord covered the daughter of Zion
   with a cloud in his anger,

a Matt.11.23.
b 2 Sam.1.19.

   *a*And* cast down from heaven unto the earth *b*the beauty of
        Israel,

c 1 Chr. 28. 2.

   And remembered not *c*his footstool in the day of his anger!

2 (ב) The Lord hath swallowed up all the habitations of Jacob,

d ver. 17.
ch. 3. 43.

   *d*and hath not pitied:
   He hath thrown down in his wrath the strong holds of the
        daughter of Judah;

e Ps. 89. 39.

   He hath [3]brought *them* down to the ground: *e*he hath polluted
        the kingdom and the princes thereof.

3 (ג) He hath cut off in *his* fierce anger all the horn of Israel:

f Ps. 74. 11.

   *f*He hath drawn back his right hand from before the enemy,

g Ps. 89. 46.

   *g*And he burned against Jacob like a flaming fire, *which* devour-
        eth round about.

[1] Heb. *mouth*.   [2] Or, *proclaimed*.   [3] Heb. *made to touch*.

---

18. *people*] **peoples,** heathen nations.
19. *I called for...*] Rather, **to** *my lovers.*
while they sought their meat] Lit. *for they
sought food for themselves to revive their souls.*
Complete the sense by adding, *and found
none.*
20. *troubled*] Or, **inflamed** with sorrow.
turned within me] Agitated violently.
at home there is *as death*] i.e. *in the house*
there are pale pining forms, wasting with
hunger, and presenting the appearance of
death.
21. *They have heard* &c.] Or, *They heard
that I sigh,* **that I have** *no comforter.*
thou wilt bring the day...] Lit. **thou hast
brought** *the day thou hast proclaimed, and
they shall be like unto me.* The day of
Judah's punishment was the proof that the

nations now triumphing over Jerusalem's
fall would certainly be visited.
II. This poem also divides itself like ch. i.
into two nearly equal portions; in *rv.* 1–10,
the prophet describes the punishment which
has fallen upon Zion; *vv.* 11–22 are a lamentation and a prayer.
1. *How* &c.] Or, *How* **doth** *Adonai cover..*
He hath cast down &c. By God's footstool
seems to be meant the Ark. See Ps. xcix.
5 note.
2. *habitations*] The dwellings of the shepherds in the pastures (Jer. xlix. 19). These
are described as swallowed up by an earthquake, while the storm itself *throws down
the fortified cities of Judah.*
polluted] i.e. profaned it, **made common**
or unclean what before was holy.

4 (ד) [h]He hath bent his bow like an enemy : he stood with his right hand as an adversary,
And slew [1][i]all *that were* pleasant to the eye in the tabernacle of the daughter of Zion :
He poured out his fury like fire.

[h] Isai. 63. 10. ver. 5.
[i] Ezek. 24. 25.

5 (ה) [k]The Lord was as an enemy : he hath swallowed up Israel, [l]He hath swallowed up all her palaces : he hath destroyed his strong holds,
And hath increased in the daughter of Judah mourning and lamentation.

[k] ver. 4. Jer. 30. 14.
[l] 2 Kin. 25. 9. Jer. 52. 13.

6 (ו) And he hath violently [m]taken away his [2]tabernacle, [n]as *if it were of* a garden : he hath destroyed his places of the assembly :
[o]The LORD hath caused the solemn feasts and sabbaths to be forgotten in Zion,
And hath despised in the indignation of his anger the king and the priest.

[m] Ps. 80. 12.
Isai. 5. 5.
[n] Isai. 1. 8.
[o] ch. 1. 4. Zeph. 3. 18.

7 (ז) The Lord hath cast off his altar, he hath abhorred his sanctuary,
He hath [3]given up into the hand of the enemy the walls of her palaces ;
[p]They have made a noise in the house of the LORD, as in the day of a solemn feast.

[p] Ps. 74. 4.

8 (ח) The LORD hath purposed to destroy the wall of the daughter of Zion :
[q]He hath stretched out a line, he hath not withdrawn his hand from [4]destroying :
Therefore he made the rampart and the wall to lament ; they languished together.

[q] 2 Kin. 21. 13. Isai. 34. 11.

9 (ט) Her gates are sunk into the ground ; he hath destroyed and [r]broken her bars :

[r] Jer. 51. 30.

[1] Heb. *all the desirable of the eye.*
[2] Or, *hedge.*
[3] Heb. *shut up.*
[4] Heb. *swallowing up.*

---

3. As the horn is the symbol of power, the cutting off of every horn means the depriving Israel of all power of resistance. The drawing back of God's right hand signifies the withdrawal of that special Providence which used to protect the chosen people.

and he burned &c.] Or, *and* **he kindled a fire in** *Jacob :* as the active enemy of Jacob, Himself applying the torch.

4. *he stood with his right hand* &c.] i.e. that right hand so often stretched out to help now grasped a weapon ready for Judah's destruction.

were pleasant] Or, *was pleasant.* Put full stop after "eye." Begin the third distich thus: *In the tabernacle* (or, tent) *of the daughter of Zion.*

5. Lit. *Adonai* **has become** *as an enemy.*

6. *tabernacle*] Or, covert (Jer. xxv. 38), i.e. such a tent of boughs as was put up at the Feast of Tabernacles. The words mean, "the Lord hath (as) violently destroyed His booth, *as* a man might tear down a shed in a garden." Cp. Isai. i. 8.

his places of the assembly] Or, *His great festivals* (i. 15 note). It is the word rendered *solemn feasts* in the next clause, and rightly joined there with *sabbaths,* the weekly, as the other were the annual festivals. It is no longer Adonai, but the LORD (Jehovah) who lets them pass into oblivion. He had once instituted them for His own honour, now He lets them lie forgotten.

hath despised &c.] Or, *hath rejected* **king and priest.** With the destruction of the city the royal authority fell : with the ruined Temple and the cessation of the festivals the functions of the priest ceased.

7. *sanctuary*] The Holy of Holies ; *the walls of her palaces* are those of the sacred buildings.

8. *a line*] Cp. Isai. xxxiv. 11. The destruction is systematic and thorough.

9. *Her gates are sunk into the ground*] So completely destroyed, that one might suppose they had been swallowed up in an abyss.

*Deut.28.36.
2 Kin. 24. 15.
*2Chr. 15.3.
*Ps. 74. 9.
Ezek. 7. 26.
*Job 2. 13.
Isai. 3. 26.
ch. 3. 28.
*Job 2. 12.
*Isai. 15. 3.
Ezek. 7. 18.

*Her king and her princes *are* among the Gentiles:
*The law *is* no *more;* her *prophets also find no vision from the
LORD.

10 (׳) The elders of the daughter of Zion *sit upon the ground,
and keep silence :
They have *cast up dust upon their heads ; they have *girded
themselves with sackcloth ;
The virgins of Jerusalem hang down their heads to the ground.

*Ps. 6. 7.
ch. 3. 48.
*ch. 1. 20.
*Job 16. 13.
Ps. 22. 14.
*ver. 19.
ch. 4. 4.

11 (כ) *Mine eyes do fail with tears, *my bowels are troubled,
*My liver is poured upon the earth, for the destruction of the
daughter of my people ;
Because *the children and the sucklings ¹swoon in the streets of
the city.

12 (ל) They say to their mothers, Where *is* corn and wine ?
When they swooned as the wounded in the streets of the city,
When their soul was poured out into their mother's bosom.

*ch. 1. 12.
Dan. 9.12.

13 (מ) What thing shall I take to witness for thee ? *what thing
shall I liken to thee, O daughter of Jerusalem ?
What shall I equal to thee, that I may comfort thee, O virgin
daughter of Zion ?
For thy breach *is* great like the sea : who can heal thee ?

*Jer. 2. 8.
& passim :
Ezek. 13. 2.
*Isai. 58. 1.

14 (נ) Thy *prophets have seen vain and foolish things for thee :
And they have not *discovered thine iniquity, to turn away
thy captivity;
But have seen for thee false burdens, and causes of banishment.

*1 Kin. 9. 8.
Jer. 18. 16.
*Ezek. 25. 6.
*2Kin.19. 21.
Ps. 44. 14.

15 (ס) *All that pass ²by *clap *their* hands at thee ;
They hiss *and wag their head at the daughter of Jerusalem,
saying,

¹ Or, *faint.*   ² Heb. *by the way.*

---

her king] The prophet's lamentation, occupied before chiefly with the buildings of
the city and Temple, now turns to the
people, beginning with their temporal rulers.
the law is *no* more] The Jewish Law, the
Torah, came to an end when it had no
longer a local habitation. Its enactments
were essentially those not of a Catholic, but
of a national religion, and the restoration
of the nation with a material Temple was
indispensable to its continued existence. It
was only when elevated to be a Catholic
religion, by being made spiritual, that it
could do without Ark, Temple, and a separate
people.
her prophets also find...] With the Torah
the special gift of prophecy also ceased,
since both were peculiar to the Theocracy;
but it was not till the establishment of
Christianity that they were finally merged
in higher developments of grace.
11. *troubled*] See marg. ref. note.
liver] As the heart was regarded by the
Jews as the seat of the intellect, so the liver
(or *bowels*) was supposed to be the seat of the
emotions. By the pouring out of the liver
upon the ground was meant that feelings had
entirely given way under the acuteness of

sorrow, and he could no longer restrain
them.
12. *They say*] Or, "They keep saying": it
was an oft-repeated cry, even whilst expir-
ing upon their mother's bosom.
13. *equal*] *i.e.* compare. Zion's breach, *i.e.*
her destruction, is measureless, like the
ocean.
14. *Thy prophets have seen vain and foolish
things for thee*] The LXX. and Vulg. give
the true meaning, *stupidity* (see Jer. xxiii.
13 note).
to turn away thy captivity] The right sense
is, *They have not disclosed to thee thy sins,
that so thou mightest repent, and I might have
turned away thy captivity.*
burdens] Applied contemptuously to predictions which proved *false* or *empty, i.e.*
failed of accomplishment. On the deduction
to be drawn from this, see Jer. xxviii. 9.
causes of banishment] The result of the
teaching of the false prophets would be that
God would *drive out* the Jews from their
land.
Some render the words *false...banishment*
by "oracles of falsehood and seduction."
15. Cp. the scene round the cross of the
Redeemer (Matt. xxvii. 39).

Is this the city that *men* call *l*The perfection of beauty, The joy   *l* Ps. 48. 2.
of the whole earth ?

16 (ע) *m*All thine enemies have opened their mouth against thee :   *m* Job 16. 9.
They hiss and gnash the teeth : they say, *n*We have swallowed   Ps. 22. 13.
her up :   *n* Ps. 56. 2.
Certainly this *is* the day that we looked for ; we have found, *o*we   *o* Ps. 35. 21.
have seen *it.*

17 (פ) The LORD hath done *that* which he had *p*devised ; he hath   *p* Lev. 2'.
fulfilled his word that he had commanded in the days of old :   Deut. 28.
*q*He hath thrown down, and hath not pitied :   *q* ver. 2.
And he hath caused *thine* enemy to *r*rejoice over thee, he hath   *r* Ps. 38. 16.
set up the horn of thine adversaries.   & 89. 42.

18 (צ) Their heart cried unto the Lord, O *s*wall of the daughter of   *s* ver. 8.
Zion,
*t*Let tears run down like a river day and night :   *t* Jer. 14. 17.
Give thyself no rest ; let not the apple of thine eye cease.   ch. 1. 16.

19 (ק) Arise, *u*cry out in the night : in the beginning of the   *u* Ps.119.147.
watches *x*pour out thine heart like water before the face of the   *x* Ps. 62. 8.
Lord :
Lift up thy hands toward him for the life of thy young children,
*y*That faint for hunger *z*in the top of every street.   *y* ver. 11.
    z Isai. 51. 20.

20 (ר) Behold, O LORD, and consider to whom thou hast done this.   Nah. 3. 10.
*a*Shall the women eat their fruit, *and* children *1*of a span long ?   *a* Lev. 26. 29.
*b*Shall the priest and the prophet be slain in the sanctuary of the   Jer. 19. 9.
Lord ?   Ezek. 5. 10.
    b ch. 4. 13.

21 (ש) *c*The young and the old lie on the ground in the streets :   *c* 2 Chr.36.17.
My virgins and my young men are fallen by the sword ;
Thou hast slain *them* in the day of thine anger ; *d*thou hast   *d* ch. 3. 43.
killed, *and* not pitied.

22 (ת) Thou hast called as in a solemn day *e*my terrors round   *e* Jer. 46. 5.
about,
So that in the day of the LORD'S anger none escaped nor remained :

¹ Or, *swaddled with their hands ?*

---

16. *seen* it] Omit *it.* The intensity of the
enemy's exultation is shewn by the heaping
up of unconnected words. We have found
what we sought, have seen what we looked
for.

17. *that which he had devised*] Or, **what he
purposed.** Zion's ruin was the fulfilment
of God's determination, of which they had
been forewarned from the days of old (see
marg. ref.).

fulfilled] Or, **finished.**

18. *their heart*] That of the inhabitants of
Jerusalem. The prophet bids the wall, as
the representative of the people who had
dwelt secure under its protection, shed
floods of tears on their behalf. Broken up
by the enemy, it could be their guardian no
longer, but by its ruins it might still cry
unto the Lord in their behalf.

a river] Or, *a* **brook** or torrent.

rest] Properly the torpor and numbness
which follows upon excessive grief.

apple of thine eye] See Ps. xvii. 8 note.

19. *in* (or at) *the beginning of the watches*]
At the beginning of each night-watch means
all the night through. The Hebrews
divided the night into three watches.

20. The sense is : *See, Jehovah, and look !
Whom hast Thou treated thus ? Shall women
eat their fruit—children whom they must still
carry ?* the swaddled child being one still
needing to be nursed and borne in their
arms.

21. Omit *them* and *and*, which weaken the
intensity of the passage.

22. *Thou hast called as in a solemn day*]
i.e. *Thou* **callest** *like a feast day,* i.e. like the
proclaiming of a festival.

my terrors round about] The prophet's
watch-word (Jer. vi. 25 note). God now pro-
claims what Jeremiah had so often called
out before, *Magor-missabib.* On every side
were conquering Chaldæans.

f Hos. 9. 12.

*f*Those that I have swaddled and brought up hath mine enemy
consumed.

Chap. 3. (א) *I AM* the man *that* hath seen affliction
By the rod of his wrath.
2 He hath led me, and brought *me into* darkness,
But not *into* light.
3 Surely against me is he turned;
He turneth his hand *against me* all the day.

a Job 16. 8.
b Ps. 51. 8.
Jer. 50. 17.

4 (ב) *a*My flesh and my skin hath he made old;
He hath *b*broken my bones.
5 He hath builded against me,
And compassed *me* with gall and travel.

c Ps. 88. 5.
& 143. 3.
d Job 19. 8.
Hos. 2. 6.

6 *c*He hath set me in dark places,—as *they that be* dead of old.

7 (ג) *d*He hath hedged me about, that I cannot get out:
He hath made my chain heavy.

e Job 30. 20.
Ps. 22. 2.

8 Also *e*when I cry and shout,—he shutteth out my prayer.
9 He hath inclosed my ways with hewn stone,
He hath made my paths crooked.

f Job 10. 16.
Isai. 38. 13.
Hos. 5. 14.
g Hos. 6. 1.

10 (ד) *f*He *was* unto me *as* a bear lying in wait,
And *as* a lion in secret places.
11 He hath turned aside my ways, and *g*pulled me in pieces:
He hath made me desolate.

h Job 7. 20.
Ps. 38. 2.
i Job 6. 4.

12 He hath bent his bow,—and *h*set me as a mark for the arrow.

13 (ה) He hath caused *i*the ¹arrows of his quiver
To enter into my reins.

¹ Heb. *sons*.

III. This elegy is both the most elaborate
in form and the most sublime in its ideas of
the five poems which compose the Book of
Lamentations. It presents the image of the
deepest suffering, passing on to the confession of sin, the acknowledgment of God's
justice, and the prayer of faith for forgiveness. It is the ideal representation of that
godly sorrow which worketh repentance
unto salvation not to be repented of (2 Cor.
vii. 10).

1. that *hath seen affliction*] *i.e.* hath expe-
rienced, suffered it.

3. *is he turned ; he turneth*] Or, *surely
against me* **hath he turned** *his hand* **again
and again** *all the day long.*

4. *made old*] Or, **wasted:** his strength
slowly wasted as he pined away in sorrow.

he hath broken my bones] This clause completes the representation of the sufferer's
physical agonies. Here the idea is that of
acute pain.

5. *He hath builded...*] The metaphor is
taken from the operations in a siege.

gall and travel] Or "travail ;" *i.e.* bitterness and weariness (through toil).

6. Or, *He hath* **made me to dwell** *in darkness, i.e.* in Sheol or Hades, *as those* **for ever
dead.**

7. The prophet feels as if enclosed within
walls, and fettered.

8. *shout*] *i.e.* **call for help.**

shutteth out] Or, *shutteth in.* God has so
closed up the avenues to the place in which
he is immured, that his voice can find no
egress.

9. *inclosed*] Or, **hedged** (*v.* 7).

hath made crooked] Or, *hath* **turned aside.**
A solid wall being built across the main
road, Jeremiah turns aside into by-ways,
but finds them *turned aside*, so that they
lead him back after long wandering to the
place whence he started.

10–18. Having dwelt upon the difficulties
which hemmed in his path, he now shews
that there are dangers attending upon
escape.

11. The meaning is, "God, as a lion,
lying in wait, has made me turn aside from
my path, but my flight was in vain, for
springing upon me from His ambush He has
torn me in pieces."

desolate] Or, **astonied,** stupefied that he
cannot flee. The word is a favourite one
with Jeremiah.

12. This new simile arises out of the
former one, the idea of a hunter being suggested by that of the bear and lion. When
the hunter comes, it is not to save him.

14 I was a [k]derision to all my people;
  And [l]their song all the day.
15 [m]He hath filled me with [1]bitterness,
  He hath made me drunken with wormwood.
16 (ו) He hath also broken my teeth [n]with gravel stones,
  He hath [2]covered me with ashes.
17 And thou hast removed my soul far off from peace:
  I forgat [3]prosperity.
18 [o]And I said, My strength and my hope
  Is perished from the LORD:
19 (ז) [4]Remembering mine affliction and my misery,
  [p]The wormwood and the gall.
20 My soul hath *them* still in remembrance,
  And is [5]humbled in me.
21 This I [6]recall to my mind,—therefore have I hope.
22 (ח) [q]*It is of* the LORD's mercies that we are not consumed,
  Because his compassions fail not.
23 *They are new* [r]every morning:—great *is* thy faithfulness.
24 The LORD *is* my [s]portion, saith my soul;
  Therefore will I hope in him.
25 (ט) The LORD *is* good unto them that [t]wait for him,
  To the soul *that* seeketh him.
26 *It is* good that *a man* should both hope
  [u]And quietly wait for the salvation of the LORD.
27 [x]*It is* good for a man—that he bear the yoke in his youth.
28 (י) [y]He sitteth alone and keepeth silence,
  Because he hath borne *it* upon him.

[k] Jer. 20. 7.
[l] Job 30. 9.
Ps. 69. 12.
[m] Jer. 9. 15.

[n] Prov. 20. 17.

[o] Ps. 31. 22.

[p] Jer. 9. 15.

[q] Mal. 3. 6.

[r] Isai. 33. 2.
[s] Ps. 16. 5.
Jer. 10. 16.

[t] Ps. 130. 6.
Isai. 30. 18.
Mic. 7. 7.

[u] Ps. 37. 7.
[x] Ps. 94. 12.
& 119. 71.
[y] Jer. 15. 17.
ch. 2. 10.

---

[1] Heb. *bitternesses.*
[2] Or, *rolled me in the ashes.*
[3] Heb. *good.*
[4] Or, *Remember.*
[5] Heb. *lowed.*
[6] Heb. *make to return to my heart.*

---

14. Metaphor is dropped, and Jeremiah shews the real nature of the arrows which rankled in him so deeply.

15. *He hath* **filled me to the full with bitterness,** *i.e.* bitter sorrows (Job ix. 18).

16. *broken my teeth with gravel stones*] His bread was so filled with grit that in eating it his teeth were broken.

17. *prosperity*] Lit. as in marg. *i.e.* I forgot what good was, I lost the very idea of what it meant.

18. The prophet reaches the verge of despair. But by struggling against it he reaches at length firm ground.

19. *Remembering*] Or, as in marg. It is a prayer to Jehovah.

my misery] Or, *my* **homelessness** (i. 7 note).

21. *This I recall*] Rather, *This will I bring back to my heart, therefore will I hope.* Knowing that God hears the prayer of the contrite, he begins again to hope.

22-42. The centre of the present poem, as it also holds the central place in the whole series of the Lamentations. In them the riches of God's grace and mercy are set forth in the brightest colours, but no sooner are they ended than the prophet resumes the language of woe.

22. *that we*] He is speaking as the representative of all sufferers.

24. *The* LORD *is my portion*] *My portion is Jehovah*, see Num. xviii. 20; Ps. xvi. 5, &c.

therefore will I hope in him] A more full expression of the confidence present in the prophet's mind in *v.* 21, but based now upon God's faithfulness in shewing mercy.

25-27. In these three verses, each beginning in the Hebrew with the word *good*, we have first the fundamental idea that Jehovah Himself is good, and if good to all, then especially is He so to those who being in adversity can yet *wait* in confidence upon His mercy.

26. *and quietly wait*] Lit. *and be in silence,* *i.e.* abstain from all complaining.

27. *the yoke*] Or, **a** yoke. By bearing a yoke in his youth, *i.e.* being called upon to suffer in early age, a man learns betimes the lesson of silent endurance, and so finds it more easy to be calm and patient in later years.

28-30. Translate:—

Let him sit alone and keep silence;
  For He [God] hath laid the yoke *upon him.*

z Job 42. 6.

29 *z*He putteth his mouth in the dust ;
    If so be there may be hope.

a Isai. 50. 6.
Matt. 5. 39.

30 *a*He giveth *his* cheek to him that smiteth him :
    He is filled full with reproach.

b Ps. 94. 14.

31 (כ) *b*For the Lord will not cast off for ever :
32 But though he cause grief,
    Yet will he have compassion according to the multitude of his
        mercies.

c Ezek.33.11.
Heb. 12. 10.

33 For *c*he doth not afflict [1] willingly
    Nor grieve the children of men.

34 (ל) To crush under his feet—all the prisoners of the earth,
35 To turn aside the right of a man
    Before the face of [2] the most High,

d Hab. 1. 13.

36 To subvert a man in his cause,—*d*the Lord [3]approveth not.

e Ps. 33. 9.

37 (מ) Who *is* he *e*that saith, and it cometh to pass,
    When the Lord commandeth *it* not ?
38 Out of the mouth of the most High

f Job 2. 10.
Isai. 45. 7.
Amos 3. 6.
g Prov. 10. 3.
h Mic. 7. 9.

    Proceedeth not *f*evil and good ?
39 *g*Wherefore doth a living man [4]complain,
    *h*A man for the punishment of his sins ?

40 (נ) Let us search and try our ways,
    And turn again to the LORD.

i Ps. 86. 4.

41 *i*Let us lift up our heart with *our* hands
    Unto God in the heavens.

k Dan. 9. 5.

42 *k*We have transgressed and have rebelled :
    Thou hast not pardoned.

---

[1] Heb. *from his heart.*   [2] Or, *a superior.*   [3] Or, *seeth not.*   [4] Or, *murmur.*

Let him place his mouth in the dust ;
Perchance there is hope.
Let him offer his cheek to him that smiteth
    him ;
Let him be filled to the full with reproach.

It is good for a man to bear the yoke in his youth, but only if he bear it rightly. To attain this result, let him learn resignation, remembering Who has laid the yoke upon him. This reverential silence is described (*v.* 29), as putting the mouth in the dust, and so lying prostrate before the Deity ; while (*v.* 30) the harder task is imposed of bearing contumely with meekness (marg. ref.), and not shrinking from the last dregs of the cup of reproach. Many who submit readily to God are indignant when the suffering comes through men.

31–33. Reasons for the resignation urged in the previous triplet.

34–36. Neither does God approve of wanton cruelty inflicted by one man on another. Three examples are given : the treatment of prisoners of war ; the procuring an unjust sentence before a legal tribunal acting in the name of God (see Exod. xxi. 6) ; and the perversion of justice generally.

37–39. Why then does a loving God, Who disapproves of suffering when inflicted by man upon man, Himself send sorrow and misery ? *Because of sins.*

37. Lit. *Who is this that spake and it was done,* though *Adonai commanded it not !*

39. So long as God spares a man's life, why does he murmur ? The chastisement is really for his good ; only let him use it aright, and he will be thankful for it in the end.

a man for the punishment of his sins] Translate : Let *each* man sigh *for, i.e.* because of, *his sins.* Instead of murmuring because God sends him sorrow, let him rather mourn over the sins which have made punishment necessary. The sense of the A. V. is, Why does a man...murmur *for his sins ? i.e.* for the necessary results of them in chastisement.

40–42. The prophet urges men to search out their faults and amend them.

40. *and turn again to the* LORD] Or, *and return to Jehovah.* The prep. (to) in the Hebr. implies not half way, but the whole.

41. Lit. *Let us lift up our heart unto our hands unto God in heaven ;* as if the heart first lifted up the hands, and then with them mounted up in prayer to God. In real prayer the outward expression is caused by the emotion stirring within.

43 (ס) Thou hast covered with anger, and persecuted us :
    [i]Thou hast slain, thou hast not pitied.   [i]ch.2.2,17,21.
44 Thou hast covered thyself with a cloud,
    [m]That *our* prayer should not pass through.   [m] ver. 8.
45 Thou hast made us *as* the [n]offscouring   [n] 1 Cor.4.13.
    And refuse in the midst of the people.

46 (פ) [o]All our enemies have opened—their mouths against us.   [o] ch. 2. 16.
47 [p]Fear and a snare is come upon us,   [p] Jer. 48. 43.
    [q]Desolation and destruction.   [q] Isai. 51. 19.
48 [r]Mine eye runneth down with rivers of water   [r] Jer. 4. 19.
    For the destruction of the daughter of my people.   ch. 2. 11.

49 (ע) [s]Mine eye trickleth down, and ceaseth not,   [s] Ps. 77. 2.
    Without any intermission,   ch. 1. 16.
50 Till the Lord [t]look down,—and behold from heaven.   [t] Isai. 63. 15.
51 Mine eye affecteth [1]mine heart
    [2]Because of all the daughters of my city.

52 (צ) Mine enemies chased me sore,
    Like a bird, [u]without cause.   [u] Ps. 35. 7.
53 They have cut off my life [x]in the dungeon,   [x] Jer. 38. 6.
    And [y]cast a stone upon me.   [y] Dan. 6. 17.
54 [z]Waters flowed over mine head ;—*then* [a]I said, I am cut off.   [z] Ps. 69. 2.
                                                    [a] Isai. 38. 10.

55 (ק) [b]I called upon thy name, O Lord,—out of the low dungeon.   [b] Ps. 130. 1.
56 [c]Thou hast heard my voice :   Jonah 2. 2.
    Hide not thine ear at my breathing, at my cry.   [c] Ps. 3. 4.
57 Thou [d]drewest near in the day *that* I called upon thee :   [d] Jam. 4. 8.
    Thou saidst, Fear not.

58 (ר) O Lord, thou hast [e]pleaded the causes of my soul ;   [e] Ps. 35. 1.
    [f]Thou hast redeemed my life.   Jer. 51. 36.
                                        [f] Ps. 71. 23.
59 O Lord, thou hast seen my wrong :—[g]judge thou my cause.   [g] Ps. 9. 4.
60 Thou hast seen all their vengeance
    And all their [h]imaginations against me.   [k] Jer. 11. 19.

61 (ש) Thou hast heard their reproach, O Lord,
    And all their imaginations against me ;

[1] Heb. *my soul.*   [2] Or, *more than all.*

43—66. Far from pardoning, God is still actively punishing His people.

43. Rather, *Thou hast covered* **Thyself** *with wrath and pursued* (i. 3 note) *us.* The covering (here and in *v.* 44) is that of clothing and enwrapping.

45. Omit *as.*

47. *desolation*] Or, **devastation**.

48—51. The deep sympathy of the prophet, which pours itself forth in abundant tears over the distress of his people.

51. Or, *Mine eye* **causeth pain to my soul**, *i.e.* maketh my soul ache, because of the sad fate of the maidens (i. 4, 18, &c.).

52. Or, *They who without cause are mine enemies have hunted me sore like a bird.* Probably the prophet is speaking of his personal sorrows.

53. *They have cut off my life in the dungeon*] Or, *They* **destroyed** *my life in the pit, i.e.* tried to destroy it by casting me into the cistern, and covering the mouth with a stone. See marg. ref.

54. *Waters flowed over mine head*] A figurative expression for great mental trouble.

55—66. A prayer for deliverance and for vengeance upon his enemies.

55. *out of the low dungeon*] *The lowest pit* of Ps. lxxxviii. 6. Some consider that Ps. lxix. was composed by Jeremiah, and is the prayer referred to here (Jer. xxxviii. 6 note).

56. *Thou hast heard*] In sending Ebed-melech to deliver me. The next clause signifies *Hide not thine ear to my relief to my cry, i.e.* to my cry for relief.

58. God now appears as the prophet's next of kin, pleading the lawsuits of his soul, *i.e.* the controversies which concern his salvation, and rescuing his life, in jeopardy through the malice of his enemies.

59. *wrong*] Done to him by the perversion of justice.

60, 61. *imaginations*] Or, **devices**.

62 The lips of those that rose up against me,
And their device against me all the day.

i Ps. 139. 2.   63 Behold their *i*sitting down, and their rising up;
k ver. 14.   *k*I *am* their musick.

l Ps. 28. 4.   64 (ת) *l*Render unto them a recompence, O LORD,
2 Tim. 4. 14.   According to the work of their hands.

65 Give them ¹sorrow of heart,—thy curse unto them.

66 Persecute and destroy them in anger
*m*Deut. 25. 19.   *m*From under the *n*heavens of the LORD.
Jer. 10. 11.
n Ps. 8. 3.   CHAP. 4. (א) HOW is the gold become dim!
How is the most fine gold changed!
The stones of the sanctuary are poured out
a ch. 2. 19.   *a*In the top of every street.

2 (ב) The precious sons of Zion,
Comparable to fine gold,
b Isai. 30. 14.   How are they esteemed *b*as earthen pitchers,
The work of the hands of the potter!

3 (ג) Even the ²sea monsters draw out the breast,
They give suck to their young ones:
The daughter of my people *is become* cruel,
c Job 39. 14.   *c*Like the ostriches in the wilderness.

d Ps. 22. 15.   4 (ד) *d*The tongue of the sucking child
Cleaveth to the roof of his mouth for thirst:
*e*The young children ask bread,
e See ch. 2.   *And* no man breaketh *it* unto them.
11, 12.

5 (ה) They that did feed delicately
Are desolate in the streets:
They that were brought up in scarlet
f Job 24. 8.   *f*Embrace dunghills.

6 (ו) For the ³punishment of the iniquity of the daughter of my people
Is greater than the punishment of the sin of Sodom,

¹ Or, *obstinacy of heart.*   ² Or, *sea calves.*   ³ Or, *iniquity.*

---

63. *their sitting down, and their rising up*] *i.e.* all the ordinary actions of their life.
musick] Or, **song**, *the subject of it.*
64–66. The Versions render the verbs in these verses as futures, *Thou shalt render unto them a recompence*, &c.
65. *Give them sorrow of heart*] Or, *Thou wilt give them* **blindness** *of heart.*|
66. *persecute* &c.] Or, pursue them in anger and destroy them, &c.
IV. In this poem the distinctive idea is, that the miseries (*vv.* 1–11) which have befallen Judah are the punishment of her sin (*vv.* 12–20), and will therefore end—when chastisement has had its proper effect—in her restoration (*vv.* 21, 22).
1. *The stones of the sanctuary*] Or, **the hallowed stones**, lit. stones of holiness, a metaphor for the people themselves. The actual stones of the Temple would not be thus widely thrown about as to be seen everywhere, but the prophet has already affirmed this of the young children dying of hunger (cp. ii. 19).

2. *The precious sons of Zion*] The whole nation was consecrated to God, and formed " a kingdom of priests " (Exod. xix. 6): in this respect, a type of the Christian Church (1 Pet. ii. 5).
comparable to fine gold] Lit. *weighed with* **solid gold**, and so equal to their weight in it. With this is contrasted the hollow pitcher easily broken, and made of materials of no intrinsic value.
3. *sea monsters*] Rather, **jackals.**
their young ones] *Their* **whelps.** The term is applied only to the young of dogs, lions, and the like.
5. *they that were brought up in scarlet*] Lit. *those that were carried upon scarlet;* young children in arms and of the highest birth now lie on the dirt-heaps of the city.
6. Rather, *For* **the iniquity** *of the daughter of my people was greater than* **the sin** *of Sodom.* The prophet deduces this conclusion from the greatness of Judah's misery (cp. Jer. xxx. 11; see also Luke xiii. 1–5).

That was *g*overthrown as in a moment,
And no hands stayed on her.

7 (ז) Her Nazarites were purer than snow,
They were whiter than milk,
They were more ruddy in body than rubies,
Their polishing *was* of sapphire:

8 (ח) Their visage is *1h*blacker than a coal;
They are not known in the streets:
*i*Their skin cleaveth to their bones;
It is withered, it is become like a stick.

9 (ט) *They that be* slain with the sword are better
Than *they that be* slain with hunger:
For these *2*pine away,
Stricken through for *want of* the fruits of the field.

10 (י) *k*The hands of the *l*pitiful women
Have sodden their own children:
They were their *m*meat in the destruction
Of the daughter of my people.

11 (כ) The LORD hath accomplished his fury;
*n*He hath poured out his fierce anger,
And *o*hath kindled a fire in Zion,
And it hath devoured the foundations thereof.

12 (ל) The kings of the earth, and all the inhabitants of the world,
Would not have believed
That the adversary and the enemy should have entered
Into the gates of Jerusalem.

13 (מ) *p*For the sins of her prophets,
And the iniquities of her priests,
*q*That have shed the blood of the just
In the midst of her,

14 (נ) They have wandered
As blind *men* in the streets,
*r*They have polluted themselves with blood,
*3 s*So that men could not touch their garments.

g Gen. 19. 25.

h Joel 2. 6.
Nah. 2. 10.

i Ps. 102. 5.

k ch. 2. 20.
l Isai. 49. 15.
m Deut. 28. 57.
2 Kin. 6. 29.

n Jer. 7. 20.
o Deut. 32. 22.
Jer. 21. 14.

p Jer. 5. 31.
Ezek. 22. 26, 28.
Zeph. 3. 4.
q Matt. 23.
31, 37.

r Jer. 2. 34.
s Num. 19. 16.

---

¹ Heb. *darker than black-ness.*   ² Heb. *flow out.*   ³ Or, *in that they could not but touch.*

---

no hands stayed on her] Or, *no hands were round about her.* Sodom's sufferings in dying were brief: there were no starving children, no mothers cooking their offspring for food.

7. The Nazarites from their temperance were remarkable for health and personal beauty, besides being held in religious veneration.

rubies] Or, **corals.**

their polishing was of sapphire] Or, **their shape was** *a sapphire.* The allusion is no longer to colour, but to form. Their shape was exact and faultless as the cutting of a precious stone.

8. *Their visage* &c.] *Their* **form** (their whole person, see 1 Sam. xxviii. 14) &c. as in marg. See Job xxx. 30.

it is withered, it is become like a stick]

Or, **It has become dry like a piece of wood.**

10. *pitiful*] *i.e.* tender-hearted, compassionate. *Meat* is used for *food* (Ps. lxix. 21). What is here stated actually occurred during the siege of Jerusalem by Titus.

12. Though Jerusalem had been several times captured (1 K. xiv. 26; 2 K. xiv. 13, xxiii. 33–35), yet it had been so strongly fortified by Uzziah and his successors as to have been made virtually impregnable. Its present capture by Nebuchadnezzar had cost him a year and a half's siege.

13. *the blood of the just*] Jer. xxvi. 7–24 exhibits priests and prophets as the prime movers in an attempt to silence the word of God by putting Jeremiah to death. Cp. marg. ref. to Matt.

14. *They have wandered*] God's ministers,

t Lev. 13. 45.

15 (ס) They cried unto them, Depart ye; [1]*it is* *t*unclean;
Depart, depart, touch not:
When they fled away and wandered, they said among the
heathen,
They shall no more sojourn *there*.

16 (ע) The [2]anger of the LORD hath divided them;
He will no more regard them:

u ch. 5. 12.

*u*They respected not the persons of the priests,
They favoured not the elders.

x 2 Kin. 24. 7
Isai. 20. 5.
Jer. 37. 7.

17 (פ) As for us, *x*our eyes as yet failed
For our vain help:
In our watching we have watched
For a nation *that* could not save *us*.

y 2 Kin. 25.
4, 5.

18 (צ) *y*They hunt our steps,
That we cannot go in our streets:
Our end is near, our days are fulfilled;
For *z*our end is come.

z Ezek. 7. 2.
Amos 8. 2.
a Jer. 4. 13.

19 (ק) Our persecutors are *a*swifter
Than the eagles of the heaven:
They pursued us upon the mountains,
They laid wait for us in the wilderness.

b Gen. 2. 7.
ch. 2. 9.
c Jer. 52. 9.
Ezek. 12. 13.

20 (ר) The *b*breath of our nostrils, the anointed of the LORD,
*c*Was taken in their pits,
Of whom we said, Under his shadow
We shall live among the heathen.

d Like
Eccles. 11. 9.

21 (ש) *d*Rejoice and be glad, O daughter of Edom
That dwellest in the land of Uz;

e Jer. 25. 15.
Obad. 10.

*e*The cup also shall pass through unto thee:
Thou shalt be drunken, and shalt make thyself naked.

---

[1] Or, *ye polluted*.   [2] Or, *face*.

---

consecrated to His service, wandered through the city blinded by the insatiable lust of slaughter. It was a pollution to touch their garments.

15. Men cried to these priests, *Away! unclean! away! away! touch not. Unclean* was the cry of the leper whenever he appeared in public: here it is the warning shout of those who meet the murderers.

when they fled away and wandered] These priests fled away from the city, but with uncertain steps, not knowing where to find refuge. They find themselves abhorred abroad as well as at home.

It is quite possible that this verse records a real occurrence, if not during the siege, at all events during the last years of Zedekiah's reign.

16. Lit. *The countenance of Jehovah hath scattered them*, has driven these outlawed priests hither and thither, *and He will no more regard them* with favour.

17–20. A rapid sketch of the last days of the siege and the capture of the king.

17. Rather, *Still do our eyes waste away looking for our vain help*.

in our watching] Or, *on our watchtower*.

18. Or, **They hunted** *our steps that we could not go out into the streets. To hunt* means here to lie in ambush, and catch by snares; and the streets are lit. *the wide places*, especially at the gates. Towards the end of the siege the towers erected by the enemy would command these places.

19. *Our persecutors are...*] **Our pursuers** (i. 3 note) **were** *swifter than the eagles of heaven.*

they pursued us] Or, *they* **chased** *us.*

mountains...wilderness] The route in going from Jerusalem to Jericho leads first over heights, beginning with the Mount of Olives, and then descends into the plain of the Ghôr.

20. *The breath of our nostrils*] Zedekiah is not set before us as a vicious king, but rather as a man who had not strength enough of character to stem the evil current of his times. And now that the state was fallen he was as the very breath of life to the fugitives, who would have no rallying point without him.

in their pits] The words are metaphorical, suggesting that Zedekiah was hunted like a wild animal, and driven into the pitfall.

21, 22. The prophet ends his elegy with

22 (ת) *1*The punishment of thine iniquity is accomplished, O   *f* Isai. 40 . 2
daughter of Zion;
He will no more carry thee away into captivity:
*v*He will visit thine iniquty, O daughter of Edom;   *v* Ps. 137. 7.
He will *2*discover thy sins.

CHAP. 5. *a*REMEMBER, O LORD, what is come upon us: *a* Ps. 89. 50.
Consider, and behold *b*our reproach.   *b* Ps. 79. 4.
2 *c*Our inheritance is turned to strangers,—our houses to aliens.   ch. 2. 15.
3 We are orphans and fatherless,—our mothers *are* as widows.   *c* Ps. 79. 1.
4 We have drunken our water for money;
Our wood *3*is sold unto us.
5 *d**4*Our necks *are* under persecution: *d* Deut. 28 43.
We labour, *and* have no rest.   Jer. 28. 14.
6 *e*We have given the hand *f*to the Egyptians, *and to* the Assy-   *e* Gen. 24. 2.
rians,   Jer. 20. 15.
To be satisfied with bread.   *f* Hos. 12. 1.
7 *g*Our fathers have sinned, *and **h*are* not;   *g* Jer. 31. 29.
And we have borne their iniquities.   Ezek. 18. 2.
8 *i*Servants have ruled over us: *h* Gen. 42. 13.
There is none that doth deliver *us* out of their hand.   Zech. 1. 5.
     i Neh. 5. 15.

---

¹ Or, *Thine iniquity.*   *thy sins.*   ⁴ Heb. *On our necks are we*
² Or, *carry* thee *captive for*   ³ Heb. *cometh for price.*   *persecuted.*

---

the language of Messianic hope. The earthly king had fallen (*v.* 20); but Israel cannot really perish. First then Edom, the representative of the Church's foes, is ironically told to rejoice. Rejoice she did at the capture of Jerusalem (Jer. xlix. 7-22); but her punishment is quickly to follow.

22. *The punishment of thine iniquity is accomplished*] Lit. **Thy iniquity is ended.** This is the result of Judah having borne her punishment. And as it is not just to punish twice for the same thing, therefore Jeremiah adds, *He will not send thee again into captivity;* not meaning that under all circumstances Judah would have immunity from exile;—for that would depend upon her future conduct:—but that her present guilt being expiated, she would have nothing to fear on its account.

he will discover thy sins] See marg. As Edom rejoices when the Church is chastised, so is the day of the Church's triumph that also on which the wicked meet with retribution.

V. This final chapter consists of the same number of verses as there are letters in the Hebrew alphabet, but they no longer begin with the letters in regular order. Strict care is shewn in the form and arrangement of the poem, each verse being compressed into a very brief compass, consisting of two members which answer to one another both in idea and expression. It is mainly occupied with the recapitulation of sufferings (*vv.* 2-18), and finally closes with earnest prayer.

1. *what is come upon us*] Lit. *what has happened to us:* our national disgrace.

2. *turned*] *transferred.* The inheritance was the land of Canaan (Lev. xx. 24).

aliens] Or, *foreigners: i.e.* the Chaldæans upon their conquest of the country.

3. *our mothers* are *as widows*] The particle *as* suggests that the whole verse is metaphorical. Our distress and desolation is comparable only to that of fatherless orphans or wives just bereaved of their husbands.

4. Better as in marg. **cometh to us for price.** The rendering of the A. V. spoils the carefully studied rhythm of the original. The bitterness of the complaint lies in this, that it was their own property which they had to buy.

5. *Our necks &c.*] *i.e.* we were pursued so actively that our enemies seemed to be leaning over our necks ready to seize us.

we labour] **We were wearied,** *there was no rest for us:* being chased incessantly.

6. *To give the hand* means to submit oneself. Absolutely it was Babylon that had just destroyed their national existence, but Jeremiah means that all feelings of patriotism were crushed, and the sole care that remained was the desire for personal preservation. To secure this the people would readily have submitted to the yoke either of Egypt or Assyria, the great powers from which in their past history they had so often suffered.

7. and are *not; and we*...] Or, **they are not;** *we have borne their iniquities.* Our fathers who began this national apostasy died before the hour of punishment.

8. *Servants] i.e.* **Slaves.** A terrible degradation to a high-spirited Jew.

9 We gat our bread with *the peril of* our lives
  Because of the sword of the wilderness.

k Job 30. 30.
Ps. 119. 83.

10 Our *k*skin was black like an oven
  Because of the [1]terrible famine.

l Isai. 13. 16.
Zech. 14. 2.

11 *l*They ravished the women in Zion,
  And the maids in the cities of Judah.

12 Princes are hanged up by their hand:

m Isai. 47. 6.
ch. 4. 16.
n Judg.16.21.

  *m*The faces of elders were not honoured.

13 They took the young men *n*to grind,
  And the children fell under the wood.

14 The elders have ceased from the gate,
  The young men from their musick.

15 The joy of our heart is ceased;
  Our dance is turned into mourning.

o Job 19. 9.
Ps. 89. 39.

16 *o* [2]The crown is fallen *from* our head:
  Woe unto us, that we have sinned!

p ch. 1. 22.

17 For this *p*our heart is faint;

q Ps. 6. 7.

  *q*For these *things* our eyes are dim.

18 Because of the mountain of Zion, which is desolate,
  The foxes walk upon it.

r Ps. 9. 7.
Hab. 1. 12.
s Ps. 45. 6.
t Ps. 13. 1.

19 Thou, O LORD, *r*remainest for ever;
  *s*Thy throne from generation to generation.

20 *t*Wherefore dost thou forget us for ever,
  And forsake us [3]so long time?

u Ps. 80. 3.
Jer. 31. 18.

21 *u*Turn thou us unto thee, O LORD, and we shall be turned;
  Renew our days as of old.

22 [4]But thou hast utterly rejected us;
  Thou art very wroth against us.

---

[1] Or, *terrors,* or, *storms.*
[2] Heb. *The crown of our*   *head is fallen.*
[3] Heb. *for length of days?*
[4] Or, *For wilt thou utterly reject us!*

---

9. *We gat*] Or, **We get** *our bread at the peril of our lives.* This verse apparently refers to those who were left in the land, and who in gathering in such fruits as remained, were exposed to incursions of the Bedawin, here called *the sword of the desert.*

10. *Our skin* &c.] Or, **is fiery red like an oven because of the fever-blast** *of famine.*

11. *They ravished*] **They humbled.**

12. After the princes had been put to death their bodies were hung up by the hand to expose them to public contumely. Old age, again, no more availed to shield men from shameful treatment than the high rank of the princes. Such treatment of conquered enemies was not uncommon in ancient warfare.

13. *They took the young men to grind*] Or, *The young men* **have borne the mill,** a menial and laborious task usually performed by slaves (cp. Isai. xlvii. 2).

the children fell under the wood] Or, *lads have stumbled under* burdens of *wood.* By lads are meant youths up to the age of military service; another form of menial labour.

14. *the gate*] The gate was the place for public gatherings, for conversation, and the music of stringed instruments.

16. Lit. *The crown of our head is fallen,*

i.e. that which was our chief ornament and dignity is lost;—the independence of the nation, and all that gave them rank and honour.

17. *is faint* &c.] Or, **has become faint**—**have become dim.** *For this,* i.e. for the loss of our crown &c.

18. *the foxes*] Or, **jackals.** As these animals live among ruins, and shun the presence of man, it shews that Zion is laid waste and deserted.

19. *remainest*] Or, **reignest.** The earthly sanctuary is in ruins, but the heavenly throne in unchangeable glory.

22. Lit. *Unless thou hast utterly rejected us,* unless *thou art very wroth against us.* This is stated as a virtual impossibility. God's anger can be but temporary (Ps. xxx. 5), and therefore the very supposition is an indirect expression of hope.

This verse speaks of the possibility of an utter rejection through God's wrath. Therefore, to remove so painful a thought, and to make the Book more suited for public reading, v. 21 is repeated in many MSS. intended for use in the synagogue. The same rule is observed in the synagogue with the two last verses of Ecclesiastes, Isaiah, and Malachi.

EZEKIEL.

INTRODUCTION.

WE know scarcely anything of Ezekiel except what we learn from the Book that bears his name.[1] Of the date and authorship of this Book there has scarcely been any serious question. The book of Ezekiel has ever formed part of the Hebrew Canon of the Old Testament[2]; and is found in the most ancient Versions.

Ezekiel[3] (*God strengtheneth* or *hardeneth*) was the son of Buzi, a priest probably of the family of Zadok. He was one of those who went into exile with Jehoiachin (2 K. xxiv. 14), and would seem to have belonged to the higher class, a supposition agreeing with the consideration accorded to him by his fellow exiles (viii. 1, &c.). The chief scene of his ministry was Tel-Abib in Northern Mesopotamia, on the river Chebar, along the banks of which were the settlements of the exiles. He was probably born in or near Jerusalem, where he must certainly have lived many years before he was carried into exile. The date of his entering upon the prophetical office is given in i. 1; and if, as is not unlikely, he entered upon this office at the legal age of thirty, he must have been about fourteen years of age when Josiah died. In this case he could not have exercised the priestly functions at Jerusalem; but as his father was a priest (i. 3), he was no doubt brought up in the courts of the temple, and so became familiar with its services and arrangements.

Ezekiel lived in a house of his own, was married, and lost his wife in the ninth year of his exile. Of the rest of his life we know nothing.

The period during which Ezekiel prophesied in Chaldæa was signalized by the miserable reign of Zedekiah, ending in his imprisonment and death,—by the destruction of the Temple, the sack of Jerusalem, and the final deportation of its inhabitants,—by Gedaliah's short regency over the poor remnant left behind in the country, his treacherous murder, and the flight of the conspirators, conveying Jeremiah with them into Egypt,—and by Nebuchadnezzar's conquests in the neighbouring countries, and especially his prolonged siege of Tyre.

The year in which Ezekiel delivered his prophecies against Egypt

---

[1] An apocryphal tradition says that he was murdered by one of his fellow-exiles; and in the middle ages his tomb was shewn, distant a few days' journey from Bagdad.

[2] About the time of the destruction of Jerusalem, a question was raised as to the authenticity of Ezekiel on the ground of a supposed discrepancy between passages of his writings and the teaching of the Pentateuch—cp. *e.g.* xviii. 20 with Exod. xx. 5; but this was a mere critical discussion, and the difficulty was solved by reconciling the passages objected to.

[3] The name also occurs in 1 Chr. xxiv.

16.

corresponds with the first year of the reign of Pharaoh-Hophra, the Apries of Herodotus. The accession (B.C. 589) of this king to the Egyptian throne affected very materially the future of the kingdom of Judah. Since the first capture of Jerusalem by Nebuchadnezzar the Jews had found the service of the Chaldæans a hard one, and were ready at any moment to rise and shake off the yoke. Egypt was the only power from which they could hope for effectual support; and Egypt had long been inactive. The power of Necho was broken at Carchemish (B.C. 605, Jer. xlvi. 2; 2 K. xxiv. 7). Apries, during his reign of 19 years, was minded to recover the ground which his grandfather and father had lost in Palestine and in Syria. Rumours of these designs had no doubt reached the Jews, both in Jerusalem and in captivity, and they were watching their opportunity to break with Babylon and ally themselves with Egypt. Against such an alliance Ezekiel came forward to protest. He told his countrymen that their hopes of safety lay not in shaking off a yoke, which they could not do without the grossest perjury, but in repenting of their sins and turning to the God of their fathers.

The fallacy of the hopes entertained by the Jews of deliverance through Egypt was soon made manifest. In the course of the final siege of Jerusalem, Hophra attempted a diversion which proved unsuccessful. Nebuchadnezzar left the siege of Jerusalem to attack the Egyptians, who—forced to retreat over the borders—offered no further resistance to the captor of Jerusalem (Jer. xxxvii. 5–8). It was at this time that Ezekiel commenced the series of prophecies

against Egypt (xxix.–xxxii.), which were continued until the blow fell upon that country and ended in the ruin and deposition of Pharaoh-Hophra.

This Book throws much light upon the condition and the feelings of the Jews both in the Holy Land and in exile, and upon the relation of the two parties to each other.

Idolatry remained in Jerusalem, even among the priests and in the Temple (viii. 5, *seq.*), and clung to the exiles (xiv. 3, *seq.*), though probably in a less decided degree. Mixed up with this unfaithfulness to the true God there was prevalent a superstitious confidence in His disposition to protect the city and people, once His own. Utterly disregarding the conditional character of His promises, and the more spiritual nature of His blessings, men satisfied themselves that the once glorious Jerusalem never would and never could be overthrown (xiii. 2, *seq.*). Hence arose the foolish rebellions of Zedekiah, commencing in reckless perjury, and terminating in calamity and disgrace. Connected with this feeling was a strange reversal of the relative positions of the exiles and of the Jews at home. The latter, though only the meanest of the people (2 K. xxiv. 14), affected to despise their exiled countrymen (xi. 14, *seq.*); and Ezekiel had to assure his fellow-exiles that to them and not to the Jews in Palestine belonged the enduring title of God's people (xi. 16, 17, 20).

But though the voice of the prophet may have sounded back to the country which he had left, yet Ezekiel's special mission was to those among whom he dwelt. He had (*a*) to convince them of God's utter abhorrence of idolatry, and of the sure and irrevocable doom of those who practised it; (*b*) to shew that the Chaldæans were the instruments of God, and that therefore resistance to them was both hopeless and unlawful; (*c*) to destroy their presumptuous confidence in external privileges, to open their eyes to a truer sense of the nature of the Divine promises; and, lastly, to raise their drooping hearts by unfolding to them the true character of the Divine government, and the end for which it was administered. The Book of Ezekiel may be said in this respect to be the moral of the Captivity. For the Captivity was not simply a Divine judgment, but a preparation for a better state, an awakening of higher hopes. These hopes it was Ezekiel's part to direct and satisfy. He was to set before his countrymen the prospect of a restoration, reaching far beyond a return to their native soil; he was to point to an inauguration of divine worship far more solemn than was to be secured by the reconstruction of the city or Temple on its original site in its original form. Their very condition was intended, and was calculated, to stir their hearts to their inmost depths, and awaken thoughts which must find their answer in the messages characteristic of Gospel truth. In the Law there had been intimations of restoration upon repentance (Deut. xxx. 1-10): but this is expanded by Ezekiel (xviii.), and the operations of the Holy Spirit are brought prominently forward (xxxvii. 9, 10).

The mission of Ezekiel should be compared with that of his countryman, Jeremiah, who began his prophetical office earlier, but continued it through the best part of the time during which Ezekiel himself laboured. Both had to deliver much the same messages, and there is a marked similarity in their utterances. But Jeremiah's mission was incomparably the more mournful one (see p. 160). Ezekiel's task was, indeed, a bitter one; but personally he soon acquired respect and attention, and if at first opposed, was at last listened to if not obeyed. He may have been instrumental, together with Daniel, in working that reformation in the Jewish people, which certainly was to some extent effected during the Captivity.

One of the immediate effects of the Captivity was the reunion of the severed tribes of Israel. The political reasons which had sundered them were at an end; a common lot begat sympathy in the sufferers; and those of the ten tribes who even in their separation had been conscious of a natural unity, and could not but recognize in the representative of David the true centre of union, would be naturally inclined to seek this unity in amalgamation with the exiles of Judah. In the course of the years which had elapsed since their exile, the numbers of the ten tribes may well have wasted away, partly through absorption among the heathen who surrounded them; and thus the exiles from Judah may have far exceeded in number and importance those who yet remained of the exiles of Israel. Accordingly we find in Ezekiel the terms Judah and Israel applied indiscriminately to those among whom the prophet dwelt (see xiv. 1); and the sins of Israel, no less than those of Judah, are summed up in the reproof of his countrymen. All descendants

of Abraham were again being
drawn together as one people, and
this was to be effected by the
separated members gathering again
around the legitimate centre of
government and of worship, under
the supremacy of Judah. The
amalgamation of the exiles of Israel
and of Judah is in fact distinctly
predicted by Jeremiah (Jer. iii. 18);
a prediction which had its accomplishment in the restoration of the
people to their native land by the
decree of Cyrus (cp. also xxxvii. 16,
seq.). Attempts have been made
from time to time to discover the
lost ten tribes, by persons expecting to find, or thinking that they
have found, them existing still as a
separate community. According
to the foregoing view the time of
Captivity was the time of reunion.
Ezekiel's mission was *to the house
of Israel*, not only to those who
came out with him from Jerusalem
or Judah, but to those also of the
stock whom he found residing in a
foreign land, where they had been
settled for more than 100 years
(xxxvii. 16 and xlviii. 1).

The order and the character of
the prophecies which this Book
contains are in strict accordance
with the prophet's mission. His
first utterances are those of bitter
denunciation of judgment upon a
rebellious people, and these threatenings are continued until the storm
breaks in full fury upon the deserted
city. Then the note is changed.
There are yet indeed threatenings,
but they are for unfaithful shepherds, and for the enemies of God's
people. The remainder of the Book
is full of reassurances, of hopes and
promises of renovation and blessing, in which the spiritual predominates over the temporal, and
the kingdom of Christ takes the

place of the kingdom upon Mount
Zion.[1]

The prophecies are therefore in
general arranged in chronological
order. So far as the people of God

---

[1] The prophecies are divided into
groups by dates prefixed to various chapters, and we may assume that those prophecies which are without date were
delivered at the same time as the last
given date, or at any rate followed closely
upon it.

1. *The fifth year of Jehoiachin's captivity.*
Chs. i.—vii. Ezekiel's call, and predictions of the coming siege of Jerusalem.

2. *The sixth year.*
Chs. viii.—xix. An inspection of the
whole condition of the people, with predictions of coming punishment.

3. *The seventh year.*
Chs. xx.—xxiii. Fresh reproofs and
fresh predictions of the coming ruin.

4. *The ninth year.*
Ch. xxiv. The year in which the siege
began. The declarations that the city
should be overthrown.

5. *The same year.*
Ch. xxv. Prophecies against Moab,
Ammon, and the Philistines.

6. *Eleventh year.*
In this year Jerusalem was taken after
a siege of eighteen months. and the
temple destroyed.
Chs. xxvi.—xxviii. Prophecies against
Tyre.

7. *The tenth year.*
Ch. xxix. 1—16. Prophecy against
Egypt.

8. *The twenty-seventh year.*
Ch. xxix. 17—xxx.19. Prophecy against
Egypt.

9. *The eleventh year.*
Ch. xxx. 20—xxxi. 18. Prophecy against
Egypt.

10. *The twelfth year.*
Ch. xxxii. Prophecy against Egypt.

11. *The same year.*
Chs. xxxiii.—xxxiv. Reproof of unfaithful rulers.

12. *The same year, or some year between
the twelfth and twenty-fifth.*
Ch. xxxv. Judgment of Mount Seir.

13. *The same year.*
Chs. xxxvi.—xxxix. Visions of comfort.
Overthrow of Gog.

14. *The twenty-fifth year.*
Chs. xl. — xlviii. The vision of the
Temple.

were concerned, there are two chief groups, (1) those delivered before (chs. i.–xxiv.), (2) those delivered after the destruction of the city (chs. xxxiii.–xlviii.). There was an interval during which the prophet's mouth was closed so far as regarded the children of his people, from the ninth to the twelfth year of the Captivity. During this interval he was guided to utter words of threatening to the heathen nations, and these utterances find their place (chs. xxv.–xxxii.). They form a suitable transition from the declaration of God's wrath to that of His mercy towards His people, because the punishment of their enemies is in itself a part of the deliverance of His people. But the arrangement of these prophecies against the heathen is rather local than chronological, so that, as in the case of Egypt, several prophecies delivered at various times on the same subject are brought together.

The leading characteristics of Ezekiel's prophecies are, first, his use of visions; secondly, his constant reference to the earlier writings of the Old Testament. The second of these characteristics is especially seen by his application of the Pentateuch. It is not merely the voice of a priest, imbued with the Law which it was his profession to study. It is the voice of the Holy Spirit Himself, teaching us that the Law, which came from God, is ever just, wise, and holy, and preparing the way for the enlarged interpretation of the ancient testimonies, which our blessed Lord Himself afterwards promulgated.

In regard to visions, the most striking is that in which is revealed to him the majesty of God (ch. i. notes). Besides these are visions of ideal scenes (*e.g.* ch. viii.) and of symbolical actions (*e.g.* ch. iv.).[5]

The Temple and its services furnish much of the imagery and figurative language of the Book. These ordinances were but the shell containing within the kernels of eternal truth ; these were the shadows, not the substance ; and when the Spirit of God would reveal by the mouth of Ezekiel spiritual realities, He permitted the prophet to clothe them in those symbols with which he and his country were familiar. Some have insisted that the language of the prophet takes its colour from the scenes which surround him, that *the living creatures* (ch. i.), for instance, were suggested by the strange forms of Assyrian sculpture familiar to us through recent explorations. But these living creatures (like the Seraphim of Isaiah, vi. 2) have much more in common with the Cherubim of the Jewish Temple than with the winged figures of Assyria. And though here and there we find traces of the place of his sojourn (as in iv. 1), it is but seldom. By the waters of Babylon the prophet remembered Zion, and his language, like his subject, was for the most part not of Chaldæa but of Jerusalem.

The various systems of interpre-

---

[5] This form was not unknown to the earlier prophets. Isaiah has in his sixth chapter a vision resembling that with which the book of Ezekiel opens. Jeremiah has many symbolical actions similar to those of Ezekiel : but that which was heretofore kept in the background is now brought to the front, and while we find in Ezekiel direct addresses to the people, as in the older prophets, these are less frequent; while on the other hand we find no prophecy communicated to him by dreams, as was the case with Daniel. The form of his prophecy may then be said to be a kind of transition from the earlier to the later mode.

tation of Ezekiel's prophecies have been summed up under the heads of (1) historical, (2) allegorical, (3) typical, (4) symbolical, (5) Judaistical.[6]

To many the prophecy is still in the course of fulfilment; the Temple in its completeness is for the time when the kingdom of Christ shall be fully established, and He shall have put down all rule and all principalities and power, to deliver up the kingdom unto the Father, that God may be all in all (see ch. xxxvii. notes).

The relation of the visions of Ezekiel to those of the Apocalypse is very marked. So much is common to the two Books, that it is impossible to doubt that there is in the Revelation of St. John a designed reference to the older seer. It is not merely that the same images are employed, which might be supposed naturally to belong to a common apocalyptic language, but

in some of the visions there is a resemblance which can only be accounted for by an identity of subject; and as the subject is by St. John often more precisely defined, the later vision throws great light upon the former. For example, the opening visions of Ezekiel and of St. John can scarcely be otherwise than substantially identical. As there can be no doubt who is designated by St. John, we are led by an irresistible conclusion to recognize in the vision of Ezekiel the manifestation of the glory of God in the person of our Lord Jesus Christ, made Man, *in Whom dwelt all the fulness of the Godhead bodily.* But while the central object is the same there are in the two visions marked differences.[7] In Ezekiel, the various particulars are parts of one whole, which represents the manifestations of the glory of God upon *earth,* and in all the creatures of the *earth :* in St. John the scene is *Heaven.* Again, a characteristic feature of Ezekiel's prophecy is the declaration of God's judgments, first against the rebellious city, and then against the enemies of the chosen people. In the Revelation the same figures, both to denote wickedness and its punishment, which are by Ezekiel applied to idolatrous Judah, are by St. John turned upon idolatrous Babylon. The image of Babylon as *the great*

---

[6] The *historical* supposes Ezekiel's prophecies and visions to have their purpose and fulfilment in the restoration after the seventy years. The *allegorical* gathers spiritual lessons from any part according to the fancy of the interpreter. The *typical* recognizes, both in the history, and in the Temple and its services, types of the Christian Church and its ordinances (as *e.g.,* in the Epistle to the Hebrews). The *symbolical* is supplementary to the former method; the *types* were in themselves symbolical. The Tabernacle or Temple and its ordinances, its measurements and arrangements, no less than its sacrifices, had their meaning, and were intended by the Divine Lawgiver to express it. According to the *Judaistical* method the prophecies look forward to the restoration of the Jews to their native soil, to the establishment of an earthly kingdom, having Jerusalem for its capital, with a new Temple and restored services, Messiah for the King, His subjects being the whole company of believers incorporated with the twelve tribes of Israel. In this way either the Christian is to be absorbed in the Jewish, or the Jewish in the Christian Church.

[7] So, also, in the figures of a building there is a most significant difference between Ezekiel and St. John. Ezekiel, writing before the old Dispensation had passed away, is guided to represent the perfection of worship under the form of a renewed and more complete ritual; the Christian seer, writing under the new Dispensation, represents to us the true character of the worship of God (Rev. xxi. 22), foretold by our Lord Himself, " not in Jerusalem, nor in this mountain, but everywhere in spirit and in truth."

whore finds its parallel in the whoredoms of Aholah and Aholibah (ch. xxiii.), and the judgment is pronounced upon the former in the very terms which in Ezekiel are employed against the latter (cp. Rev. xvii. 16 and Ezek. xxiii. 36, &c.).[8] The repetition of such descriptions by the Christian seer must be owing to something more than the mere employment of figurative language already in use ; in fact, just as our Lord's predictions of the destruction of Jerusalem are so mixed up with those of the end of the world, that we learn to regard the destruction of the city as the type and anticipation of the final judgment, so in the adoption of Ezekiel's language and figures by St. John, we see a proof of the extended meaning of the older prophecies. It is one conflict, waged from the first, and waging still ; the conflict of evil with good, of the world with God, to be accomplished only in the final consummation, to which the Revelation manifestly conducts us.

There is one feature in the writings of Ezekiel, which deserves particular notice. This is (to use a modern term) their Eschatological character, *i.e.* their reference not merely to *an* end, but to *the* very end of all (see, *e.g.* chs. vii. and xxxvi.). There are many parts which have special reference to the circumstances of the prophet and his countrymen. The local and the temporary seem to predominate ;

but looking closely, more than this is to be found. The reiteration of the threats of the Law[9] by Ezekiel proves that the events which he predicts form part of that plan which was set forth at the commencement of the national life of the children of Israel. And as this fundamental plan of government reached beyond the time of any one visitation, so Ezekiel's predictions of siege, of slaughter, of dispersion, had not their final accomplishment in the consequences of the Chaldæan conquest. This is borne out by the history of the Jewish nation. There is no city of which such dreadful sieges are recorded as the city of Jerusalem. The horrors predicted by Moses and by Ezekiel have had their literal fulfilment on more than one occasion ; yet the discourses of our Lord (Matt. xxiv., Luke xxi.) repeat the same predictions, and manifestly look forward to the end of time, to the final judgment of the world. As, therefore, each temporal judgment foreshadows the final retribution, so one prophecy may be directly addressed to many periods of time, in all of which the immutable law illustrates itself in the history of nations and individuals. This gives the principle upon which we are to interpret even those passages in Ezekiel which seem most particularly to refer to Israel and to Jerusalem. St. John the Baptist, St. Paul, and our Lord Himself, teach us to regard believers in Christ as the true Israel, the real children of Abraham ; and this because connected with the truth, that the institution of the Church of Christ is only a continuance of the plan

[8] Further, the dirge of Babylon with its merchants and merchandize (Rev. xviii. 11 &c.), recalls forcibly the dirge of Tyre (ch. xxvii.) ; and the fowls of the air are summoned to fatten upon the carcases of the armies of Babylon in the same manner as upon those of the army of Gog (cp. Ezek. xxxix. 17 and Rev. xix. 17). The same mighty array of forces under Gog and their overthrow is found in Ezekiel (ch. xxxviii.) and in the Revelation (ch. xx.).

[9] Cp. v. 2, with Lev. xxvi. 33 ;—xiv. 21, with Lev. xxvi. 22, 25, 26 ;—xvi. 38, with Deut. xxii. 22.

according to which God called Abraham out of the world, and separated his descendants to be a peculiar people to Himself. Israel represents the visible Church, brought into special relation with God Himself. The prophetical warnings have therefore their applications to the Christian Church when neglectful of the obligations which such relation imposes. Many of the calamities of Christendom have been the direct consequence of departure from the principles of the law of Christ (cp. James iv. 1). These predictions of Ezekiel are therefore not to be interpreted simply as illustrative of, but as directly predictive of, the future of the Church, Jewish and Christian, until the end of time. This view is confirmed by the introduction of passages setting forth in the strongest terms individual responsibility (see especially ch. xviii.). Their peculiar appropriateness to such a Book as that of Ezekiel is best seen when we perceive that he is addressing, not simply the historical Israel of his own day, but the whole body who have been, like Israel of old, called forth to be God's people, and who will be called to strict account for the neglect of their consequent privileges (see xi. 19 seq.).

The parts of the Book were probably arranged by the prophet himself, who, at the same time, prefixed the dates to the several prophecies. The precision of these dates affords a clear proof that the prophecies were in the first instance orally delivered, written down at the time of their delivery, and afterwards, under the direction of the Holy Spirit, put together into one volume, to form a part of those Scriptures which God has bequeathed as a perpetual inheritance to His Church.

Some have thought that the frequent insertion of passages from older writers is characteristic rather of an author than of a prophet; but even if Ezekiel, the priest, imbued not only with the spirit, but also with the letter, of the Law engrafted it upon his predictions, this can in no degree lessen the authority of his commission as a prophet. The greater part of this Book is written in prose, although the images employed are highly poetical. Some portions, however, may be regarded as poetry ; as, for instance, the dirge of the kings (ch. xix.), the lay of the sword (xxi. 8 seq.), the dirges of Tyre (chs. xxvii., xxviii.) and of Egypt (chs. xxxi., xxxii.). The language bears marks of the later style, which was introduced at the time of the Babylonish Captivity.

Points of contact in the writings of Ezekiel, Daniel, Zechariah, and St. John, are numerous, and the principal will be found noted in the marg. reff.

THE BOOK OF THE PROPHET

EZEKIEL.

CHAP. 1. NOW it came to pass in the thirtieth year, in the fourth *month*, in the fifth *day* of the month, as I *was* among the ¹captives ªby the river of Chebar, *that* ᵇthe heavens were opened, 2 and I saw ᶜvisions of God. In the fifth *day* of the month,

¹ Heb. *captivity.*

ª ch. 3. 15.
& 10. 15.
ᵇ So Matt. 3. 16.
Acts 7. 56.
Rev. 19. 11.
ᶜ ch. 8. 3.

CHS. I.—III. contain the account of Ezekiel's call.

A mighty whirlwind issues from the North, and a dark cloud appears in that quarter of the heavens. In the midst of the cloud is an area of dazzling brightness surrounded by encircling flames. Therein are seen four beings of strange and mysterious shape standing so as to form a square, below their feet are four wheels, and over their heads a throne on which is seated the likeness of a man dimly seen, while a voice issuing from the throne summons the prophet to his office.

1. *The thirtieth year* being closely connected with *as I*, is rather in favour of considering this a personal date. It is not improbable that Ezekiel was called to his office at the age prescribed in the Law for Levites (Num. iv. 23, 30), at which age both John the Baptist and our Lord began their ministry. His call is probably to be connected with the letter sent by Jeremiah to the captives (Jer. xxix.) written a few months previously. Some reckon this date from the accession of Nabopolassar, father of Nebuchadnezzar. B.C. 625, and suppose that Ezekiel here gives a Babylonian, as in *v.* 2 a Jewish, date ; but it is not certain that this accession formed an era in Babylon and Ezekiel does not elsewhere give a double date, or even a Babylonian date Others date from the 18th year of Josiah, when Hilkiah discovered the book of the Law (supposed to be a jubilee year) : this would give B.C. 594 as the 30th year, but there is no other instance in Ezekiel of reckoning from this year.

the captives] Not in confinement, but restricted to the place of their settlement.

the fourth month] *Month* is not expressed in the original. This is the common method. Before the Captivity the months were described not by proper names but by their order, *the first, the second*, &c. ; the first month corresponding nearly with our *April*. After the Captivity the Jews brought back with them the proper names of the months, *Nisan* &c. (probably those used in Chaldæa).

Chebar] The modern *Khabour* rises near Nisibis and flows into the Euphrates near *Kerkesiah*, 200 miles north of Babylon.

visions of God] The exposition of the fundamental principles of the existence and nature of a Supreme God, and of the created Angels, was called by the Rabbis " the Matter of the Chariot " (cp. 1 Chr. xxviii. 18) in reference to the form of Ezekiel's vision of the Almighty ; and the subject was deemed so mysterious as to call for special caution in its study. The vision must be compared with other manifestations of the Divine glory (Ex. iii., xxiv. 10 ; Isai. vi. 1 ; Dan. vii. 9 ; Rev. iv. 2). Each of these visions has some of the outward signs or symbols here recorded. If we examine these symbols we shall find them to fall readily into two classes, (1) those which we employ in common with the writers of all ages and countries. *Gold, sapphire, burnished brass*, the *terrible crystal* are familiar images of majestic glory, *thunders, lightnings* and *the rushing storm* of awful power. But (2) we come to images to our minds strange and almost grotesque. That the " Four Living Creatures " had their groundwork in the Cherubim there can be no doubt. And yet their shapes were very different. Because they were symbols not likenesses, they could yet be the same though their appearance was varied.

Of what are they symbolical ? They may, according to the Talmudists, have symbolized orders of Angels and not persons ; according to others they were figures of the Four Gospels actuated by one spirit spread over the four quarters of the globe, upon which, as on pillars, the Church is borne up, and over whom the Word of God sits enthroned. The general scope of the vision gives the best interpretation of the meaning.

Ezekiel saw *the likeness of the glory of God.* Here His glory is manifested in the works of creation ; and as light and fire, lightning and cloud, are the usual marks which in inanimate creation betoken the Presence of God (Ps. xviii. 6–14)—so the four living ones symbolize animate creation. The forms are typical, *the lion* and *the ox* of the beasts of

d 2 Kin. 21.
12, 15.

e 1 Kin. 18. 46.
ch. 3. 14
f Jer. 23. 19.
g Jer. 1. 14.
& 4. 6.

h Rev. 4. 6.

i ch. 10. 8.

3 which *was* the fifth year of *d*king Jehoiachin's captivity, tho word of the LORD came expressly unto [1]Ezekiel the priest, tho son of Buzi, in the land of the Chaldeans by the river Chebar: 4 and *e*the hand of the LORD was there upon him. ¶And I looked, and, behold, *f*a whirlwind came *g*out of tho north, a great cloud, and a fire [2]infolding itself, and a brightness *was* about it, and out of the midst thereof as the colour of amber, 5 out of the midst of the fire. *h*Also out of the midst thereof *came* the likeness of four living creatures. And *i*this was their

[1] Heb. *Jehezkel.*   [2] Heb. *catching itself.*

the field (wild and tame), *the eagle* of the birds of the air, while *man* is the rational being supreme upon the earth. And the human type predominates over all, and gives character and unity to the four, who thus form one creation. Further, these four represent the constitutive parts of man's nature :—*the ox* (the animal of sacrifice), his faculty of suffering ; *the lion* (the king of beasts), his faculty of ruling ; *the eagle* (of keen eye and soaring wing), his faculty of imagination ; *the man*, his spiritual faculty, which actuates all the rest. Christ is the Perfect Man, so these four in their perfect harmony typify Him Who came to earth to do His Father's will ; and as man is lord in the kingdom of nature, so is Christ Lord in the kingdom of grace. The *wings* represent the power by which all creation rises and falls at God's will ; the *one spirit*, the unity and harmony of His works ; the free motion in all directions, the universality of His Providence. The number *four* is the symbol of the world with its *four quarters ;* the *veiled* bodies, the inability of all creatures to stand in the Presence of God ; the *noise of the wings*, the testimony borne by creation to God (Ps. xix. 1-3) ; the *wheels* connect the vision with the earth, the wings with heaven, while above them is the throne of God in heaven. As the eye of the seer is turned upward, the lines of the vision become less distinct. It is as if he were struggling against the impossibility of expressing in words the object of his vision : yet on the summit of the throne is He Who can only be described as, in some sort, the form of a man. That Jehovah, the eternal God, is spoken of, we cannot doubt ; and such passages as Col. i. 15; Heb. i. 3 ; John i. 14, xii. 41, justify us in maintaining that the revelation of the Divine glory here made to Ezekiel has its consummation or fulfilment in the person of Christ, the only-begotten of God (cp. Rev. i. 17, 18).

The vision in the opening chapter of Ezekiel is in the most general form—the manifestation of the glory of the living God. It is repeated more than once in the course of the Book (cp. viii. 2, 4 ; ix. 3 ; x. ; xi. 22; xl. 3). The person manifested is always the same, but the form of the vision is modified according to special circumstances of time and place.

2. The Jewish date. This verse and *v.* 3, which seem rather to interrupt the course of the narrative, may have been added by the prophet when he revised and put together the whole Book. The word *captivity* (as in *v.* 1) refers to the *transportation* of the king and others from their native to a foreign soil. This policy of settling a conquered people in lands distant from their home, begun by the Assyrians, was continued by the Persians and by Alexander the Great. The Jews were specially selected for such settlements, and this was no doubt a Providential preparation for the Gospel, the dispersed Jews carrying with them the knowledge of the true God and the sacred Scriptures, and thus paving the way for the messengers of the kingdom of Christ.

3. *came expressly*] The phrase marks that it was in truth a heaven-sent vision.

the hand of the LORD] A phrase in all prophecy implying a *constraining* power, because the spirit *constrains* the prophet independently of his own will.

4. *out of the north*] From this quarter the Assyrian conquerors came upon the Holy Land. The vision, though seen in Chaldæa, had reference to Jerusalem, and the seer is to contemplate judgment as it is coming upon the Holy Land. Others consider the words expressive of the special seat of the power of Jehovah. The high mountain range of Lebanon that closed in the Holy Land on the North naturally connected to the inhabitants of that country the northern region with the idea of height reaching to heaven, from which such a vision as this might be supposed to come.

infolding itself] Forming a circle of light—flames moving round and round and following each other in rapid succession, to be as it were the framework of the glorious scene.

amber] The original word occurs only in Ezekiel. The LXX. and the Vulgate have *electrum*, a substance composed by a mixture of silver and gold, which corresponds very well to the Hebrew word. The brightness, therefore, is that of shining metal, not of a transparent gum. Render, *out of the midst thereof*, **like** (& *v.* 7) **burnished gold out of the midst of fire.**

5. *living creatures*] The Hebrew word answers very nearly to the English " beings," and denotes those who live, whether Angels,

6 appearance; they had *the likeness of a man. And every one   *k* ver. 10.
7 had four faces, and every one had four wings. And their feet   ch. 10. 14.
were ¹straight feet; and the sole of their feet *was* like the sole
of a calf's foot: and they sparkled *l*like the colour of burnished   *l* Dan. 10. 6.
8 brass. *m*And *they had* the hands of a man under their wings on   Rev. 1. 15.
their four sides; and they four had their faces and their wings.   *m* ch. 10. 8.
9 *n*Their wings *were* joined one to another; *o*they turned not   *n* ver. 11.
10 when they went; they went every one straight forward. As   *o* ver. 12.
for *p*the likeness of their faces, they four *q*had the face of a   ch. 10. 11.
man, *r*and the face of a lion, on the right side: *s*and they four   *p* Rev. 4. 7.
had the face of an ox on the left side; *t*they four also had the   *q* Num. 2. 10.
11 face of an eagle. Thus *were* their faces: and their wings *were*   *r* Num. 2. 3.
²stretched upward; two *wings* of every one *were* joined one to   *s* Num. 2. 18.
12 another, and *u*two covered their bodies. And *x*they went every   *t* Num. 2. 25.
one straight forward: *y*whither the spirit was to go, they went;   *u* Isai. 6. 2.
13 *and* *z*they turned not when they went. As for the likeness of   *x* ver. 9.
the living creatures, their appearance *was* like burning coals of   ch. 10. 22.
fire, *a*and* like the appearance of lamps: it went up and down   *y* ver. 20.
among the living creatures; and the fire was bright, and out   *z* ver. 9. 17.
14 of the fire went forth lightning. And the living creatures   *a* Rev. 4. 5.
*b*ran and returned *c*as the appearance of a flash of lightning.   *b* Zech. 4, 10.
   c Matt. 24.27.

¹ Heb. *a straight foot.*   ² Or, *divided above.*

---

men (in whom is the breath of life), or inferior creatures.

6. In the Revelation of St. John each "beast" has its own distinctive character, here each unites in itself the four characters; there each has six wings, like the Seraphim (Isai. vi. 2), here only four. See p. 322.

7. The "foot" seems here to mean the lower part of the leg, including the knee, and this was *straight, i.e.* upright like a man's. The "sole" is the *foot* as distinguished from the *leg*, the leg terminated in a solid calf's hoof. This was suitable for a being which was to present a front on each of its four sides. Ezekiel was living in a country on the walls of whose temples and palaces were those strange mixed figures, human heads with the bodies of lions and the feet of calves, and the like, which we see in the Babylonian and Assyrian monuments. These combinations were of course symbolical, and the symbolism must have been familiar to Ezekiel. But the prophet is not constructing his Cherubim in imitation of these figures, the Spirit of God is revealing forms corresponding to the general rules of eastern symbolism.

8. Or, "They had the hands of a man under their wings on all four sides, just as they had wings and faces on all four sides."

9. Two of the wings were in the act of flying, so stretched out that the extremity of each touched a wing of a neighbouring living creature, similarly stretched out. This was only when they were in motion. See *v.* 24.

they went every one straight forward] The

four together formed a square, and never altered their relative position. From each side two faces looked straight out, one at each corner—and so all moved together towards any of the four quarters, towards which each one had one of its four faces directed; in whatsoever direction the whole moved the four might be said all to go *straight forward.*

10. Each living creature had four faces, in front the face of a man, that of a lion on the right side, that of an ox on the left side, and that of an eagle behind, and the "chariot" would present to the beholder two faces of a man, of a lion, of an eagle, and of an ox, according to the quarter from which he looked upon it.

11. *Thus* &c.] Rather, **And their faces and their wings were separated above.** All four formed a whole, yet the upper parts of each, the heads and the wings (though touching), rose distinct from one another. Two wings of each, as in the case of Isaiah's Seraphim, were folded down over the body; and two were in their flight (*v.* 9) "stretched upward" (parted) so as to meet, each a wing of the neighbouring living creature, just as the wings of the Cherubim touched one another over the mercy-seat of the Ark.

12. The "chariot," though composed of distinct parts, was to be considered as a whole. There was one spirit expressive of one conscious life pervading the whole, and guiding the motions of the whole in perfect harmony.

13. *lamps*] *like the appearance of* **flames.** Omit the *and* before *like.* The *bright flames* resembled *coals of fire.*

it went up] *i.e. fire went up.*

d ch. 10. 9.
15 ¶ Now as I beheld the living creatures, behold *d*one wheel upon

e ch. 10. 9.
f Dan. 10. 6.
16 the earth by the living creatures, with his four faces. *e*The appearance of the wheels and their work *was* *f*like unto the colour of a beryl: and they four had one likeness: and their appearance and their work *was* as it were a wheel in the middle

17 of a wheel. When they went, they went upon their four sides:

g ver. 12.
18 *g*and they turned not when they went. As for their rings, they were so high that they were dreadful; and their [1]rings *were*

h ch. 10. 12.
Zech. 4. 10.
i ch. 10. 16.
19 *h*full of eyes round about them four. And *i*when the living creatures went, the wheels went by them: and when the living creatures were lifted up from the earth, the wheels were lifted

k ver. 12.
20 up. *k*Whithersoever the spirit was to go, they went, thither *was their* spirit to go; and the wheels were lifted up over

l ch. 10. 17.
against them: *l*for the spirit [2]of the living creature *was* in the

m ver.19, 20.
ch. 10. 17.
21 wheels. *m*When those went, *these* went; and when those stood, *these* stood; and when those were lifted up from the earth, the wheels were lifted up over against them: for the spirit [3]of the

n ch. 10. 1.
22 living creature *was* in the wheels. ¶ *n*And the likeness of the firmament upon the heads of the living creature *was* as the colour of the terrible crystal, stretched forth over their heads

23 above. And under the firmament *were* their wings straight, the one toward the other: every one had two, which covered on this side, and every one had two, which covered on that side, their

o ch. 10. 5.
24 bodies. *o*And when they went, I heard the noise of their wings,

p ch. 43. 2.
Dan. 10. 6.
Rev. 1. 15.
q Job 37. 4.
Ps. 29. 3, 4.
*p*like the noise of great waters, as *q*the voice of the Almighty, the voice of speech, as the noise of an host: when they stood,

25 they let down their wings. And there was a voice from the

[1] Or, *strakes*.   [2] Or, *of life*.   [3] Or, *of life*.

---

15. Translate, *one wheel upon the earth by* each of *the living creatures* **on his four sides** (*i.e.* on the four sides of each of the living creatures). There was a wheel to *each* of the living creatures: it was set *by*, *i.e.* immediately *beneath* the feet of the living creature, and was constructed for direct motion in any of the four lines in which the creatures themselves moved. Their *work* or make, *i.e.* their construction, was *a wheel in the middle of a wheel*; the wheel was composed of two circumferences set at right angles to each other, like the equator and meridian upon a globe. A wheel so placed and constructed did its part alike on each side of the living creature beneath which it stood. The *ten bases* of the Temple (1 K. vii. 27-36) were constructed with lions, oxen, and Cherubim, between the ledges and wheels at the four corners attached beneath so as to move like the wheels of a chariot.

17. *upon their four sides*] *i.e.* straight in the direction towards which their faces looked. As the four quarters express all directions, the construction of the living creatures was such that they could move in each direction alike.

18. *rings*] The felloes or circumference of the wheels: **they were both high and terrible.** The *eyes* may have been no more than dazzling spots adding to their brilliancy.

But it seems more likely that they had a symbolical meaning expressing either the universal fulfilment of God's will through His creation (2 Chr. xvi. 9; cp. x. 12), or the constant and unceasing praise which His works are ever rendering to Him (Rev. iv. 8). The power of nature is no blind force, it is employed in the service of God's Providence, and the stamp of reason is impressed all over it. It is this very thing that makes the power of nature terrible to him who is at enmity with God.

20. Whithersoever the spirit of the four living creatures was to go, the wheels went: —thither was the spirit of the wheels to go. All four creatures together with their wheels are here called *the living creature*, because they formed a whole, one in motion, and in will, for one spirit was in them.

22. *The colour* (Heb. "eye") *of the terrible crystal* refers to the dazzling brightness of the *firmament*, a clear bright expanse between the *throne* and the *living creatures*, separating heaven from earth.

23. *every one had two, which covered* &c.] Or, **each one had two wings covering his body on either side.**

24. *the voice of the Almighty*] Thunder. *the voice of speech*] Rendered in Jer. xi. 16 *a great tumult*. Some take it to describe the rushing of a storm.

25. *a voice from the firmament*] Cp. iii.

firmament that *was* over their heads, when they stood, *and* had
26 let down their wings. ʳAnd above the firmament that *was*
over their heads *was* the likeness of a throne, *as the appearance
of a sapphire stone: and upon the likeness of the throne *was*
27 the likeness as the appearance of a man above upon it. ᵗAnd
I saw as the colour of amber, as the appearance of fire round
about within it, from the appearance of his loins even upward,
and from the appearance of his loins even downward, I saw as
it were the appearance of fire, and it had brightness round about.
28 ᵘAs the appearance of the bow that is in the cloud in the day
of rain, so *was* the appearance of the brightness round about.
¶ ˣThis *was* the appearance of the likeness of the glory of the
LORD. And when I saw *it*, ʸI fell upon my face, and I heard a
2. voice of one that spake. AND he said unto me, Son of man,
2 ᵃstand upon thy feet, and I will speak unto thee. ¶ And ᵇthe
spirit entered into me when he spake unto me, and set me
3 upon my feet, that I heard him that spake unto me. And he
said unto me, Son of man, I send thee to the children of Israel,
to a rebellious ¹nation that hath rebelled against me: ᶜthey and
their fathers have transgressed against me, *even* unto this very
4 day. ᵈFor *they are* ²impudent children and stiff-hearted. I do
send thee unto them; and thou shalt say unto them, Thus
5 saith the Lord GOD. ᵉAnd they, whether they will hear, or
whether they will forbear, (for they *are* a rebellious house,) yet
6 ᶠshall know that there hath been a prophet among them. And
thou, son of man, ᵍbe not afraid of them, neither be afraid of
their words, though ³ʰbriers and thorns *be* with thee, and thou
dost dwell among scorpions: ⁱbe not afraid of their words, nor
be dismayed at their looks, ᵏthough they *be* a rebellious house.

ʳ ch. 10. 1.
ˢ Ex. 24. 10.

ᵗ ch. 8. 2.

ᵘ Rev. 4. 3.
& 10. 1.
ˣ ch. 3. 23.
& 8. 4.
ʸ ch. 3. 23.
Dan. 8. 17.
Acts 9. 4.
Rev. 1. 17.
ᵃ Dan. 10. 11.
ᵇ ch. 3. 24.

ᶜ Jer. 3. 25.
ch. 20. 18.

ᵈ ch. 3. 7.

ᵉ ch. 3. 11.
26. 27.
ᶠ ch. 33. 33.
ᵍ Jer. 1. 8.
Luke 12. 4.
ʰ Isai. 9. 18.
Jer. 6. 28.
ⁱ ch. 3. 9.
Mic. 7. 4.
ⁱ ch. 3. 9.
1 Pet. 3. 14.
ᵏ ch. 3. 9.

¹ Heb. *nations.*
² Heb. *hard of face.*
³ Or, *rebels.*

12; in the midst of the tumult, are heard
articulate sounds declaring the glory of
God.

26. *sapphire*] Clear heavenly blue.

the appearance of a man] Deeply significant is the form of this manifestation.
Here is no Angel conveying God's message
to man, but the glory of the Lord Himself.
We recognise in this vision the prophetic
annunciation of the Holy Incarnation. We
are told little of the extent to which the
human form was made evident to the prophet. For the vision was rather to the
mind than to the bodily eye, and even inspired language was inadequate to convey
to the hearer the glory which eye hath not
seen or ear heard, and which only by special
revelation it hath entered into the heart of
man to conceive.

28. The rainbow is not simply a token of
glory and splendour. The *cloud* and the
day of rain point to its original message of
forgiveness and mercy, and this is specially
suited to Ezekiel's commission, which was
first to denounce judgment, and then promise restoration.

II., III. In these two chapters is contained the direct commission conveyed to
Ezekiel in connexion with the vision just

recorded. The commission was repeated
more than once, at what intervals of time
we are not told. The communication is
from without, the vision and the words are
from God.

1. *Son of man*] This phrase (which occurs
elsewhere in Scripture) is applied especially
to Ezekiel and Daniel, the prophets of the
Captivity. Ezekiel is thus reminded of his
humanity, at the time when he is especially
permitted to have intercourse with God.

2. *the spirit*] *i.e. the Spirit of God.*

nation] Lit. as in marg.—the word which
usually distinguishes the heathen from God's
people. Here it expresses that Israel is cast
off by God; and the plural is used to denote
that the children of Israel are not even *one*
nation, but scattered and disunited.

3, 4. Translate :—*I send thee to the children*
of Israel, **the** *rebellious nation that have re-*
belled against Me (*they and their fathers have*
transgressed against Me, even to this very day),
and the children *impudent and stiff-hearted :*
I do send thee unto them.

5. *a rebellious house*] A phrase employed
continually by Ezekiel in bitter irony, in
the place of *house of Israel,* as much as to
say, "House no longer of Israel, but of rebellion." Cp. Isai. xxx. 9.

l Jer. 1. 7.
m ver. 5.

n Rev. 10. 9.
o ch. 8. 3.
Jer. 1. 9.
p ch. 3. 1.

a ch. 2. 8, 9.

b Rev. 10. 9.
See Jer. 15.
16.
c Ps. 19. 10.

d Matt. 11.
21, 23.
e John 15. 20.
f ch. 2. 4.

g Isai. 50. 7.
Jer. 1. 18.
Mic. 3. 8.
h Jer. 1. 8.
ch. 2. 6.

i ch. 2. 5, 7.
ver. 27.

k ch. 8. 3.
S e 1 Kin.
18. 12.
Acts 8. 39.

7 *l*And thou shalt speak my words unto them, *m*whether they will hear, or whether they will forbear: for they *are* [1]most rebellious.

8 ¶ But thou, son of man, hear what I say unto thee; Be not thou rebellious like that rebellious house: open thy mouth, and

9 *n*eat that I give thee. And when I looked, behold, *o*an hand *was* sent unto me; and, lo, *p*a roll of a book *was* therein; and

10 he spread it before me; and it *was* written within and without: and *there was* written therein lamentations, and mourning, and woe.

CHAP. 3. MOREOVER he said unto me, Son of man, eat that thou findest; *a*eat this roll, and go speak unto the house of Israel.

2 So I opened my mouth, and he caused me to eat that roll. And

3 he said unto me, Son of man, cause thy belly to eat, and fill thy bowels with this roll that I give thee. Then did I *b*eat *it;* and

4 it was in my mouth *c*as honey for sweetness. ¶ And he said unto me, Son of man, go, get thee unto the house of Israel, and

5 speak with my words unto them. For thou *art* not sent to a people [2]of a strange speech and of an hard language, *but* to the

6 house of Israel; not to many people [3]of a strange speech and of an hard language, whose words thou canst not understand.

[4]Surely, *d*had I sent thee to them, they would have hearkened

7 unto thee. But the house of Israel will not hearken unto thee; *e*for they will not hearken unto me: *f*for all the house of Israel

8 *are* [5]impudent and hardhearted. Behold, I have made thy face strong against their faces, and thy forehead strong against their

9 foreheads. *g*As an adamant harder than flint have I made thy forehead: *h*fear them not, neither be dismayed at their looks,

10 though they *be* a rebellious house. ¶ Moreover he said unto me, Son of man, all my words that I shall speak unto thee receive

11 in thine heart, and hear with thine ears. And go, get thee to them of the captivity, unto the children of thy people, and speak unto them, and tell them, *i*Thus saith the Lord GOD;

12 whether they will hear, or whether they will forbear. Then *k*the spirit took me up, and I heard behind me a voice of a great

[1] Heb. *rebellion.*
[2] Heb. *deep of lip, and heavy of tongue;* and so ver. 6.
[3] Heb. *deep of lip, and heavy of language.*
[4] Or, *If I had sent thee, &c., would they not have*
hearken 1 unto the e?
[5] Heb. *stiff of forehead, and hard of heart.*

---

9. *was sent*] Rather, was **put forth.**

a roll of a book] The book was one of the ancient kind written on skins rolled up together. Hence our English *volume* (Ps. xl. 7). The writing was usually on one side, but in this case it was written *within and without,* on both sides, the writing as it were running over, to express the abundance of the calamities in store for the devoted people. *To eat the book* signifies to be thoroughly possessed with its contents (cp. iii. 10; Jer. xv. 16). There should be no break between *v.* 10 and ch. iii.

III. **1.** Before, there was a direct commission, now there is a symbolical action. St. John has the same vision (Rev. x. 8, *seq.*), but there that is expressed, which is here left to be inferred, viz. that *as soon as he had eaten it his belly was bitter.* The sweetness in the mouth denoted that it was good to be a messenger of the Lord (cp. marg. ref.), but the bitterness which accompanied it, denoted that the commission brought with it much sorrow.

6. *to many people*] To various nations using diverse languages.

Surely] The thought is that expressed by our Saviour Himself (marg. ref.). Some render, "but I have sent thee unto these; *they* can hearken" &c.

8. *I have made ... thy forehead strong*] I have given thee a strength superior to theirs; a metaphor taken from horned animals.

9. *adamant*] Or, *diamond* (Jer. xvii. 1), which was employed to cut flint. Ezekiel's firmness being that of a diamond, he should cut a stroke home to the hardened hearts of a rebellious people. For *though* read *for.*

11. *thy people*] *God's* people.

12. *I heard behind me*] The commission having been given, and the prophet transported to the place of his ministry, the chariot of the vision passes away with the

rushing, *saying*, Blessed *be* the glory of the LORD from his place:
13 *I heard* also the noise of the wings of the living creatures that
¹touched one another, and the noise of the wheels over against
14 them, and a noise of a great rushing. So ¹the spirit lifted me
up, and took me away, and I went ²in bitterness, in the ³heat
of my spirit; but ᵐthe hand of the LORD was strong upon me.
15 ¶ Then I came to them of the captivity at Tel-abib, that dwelt
by the river of Chebar, and ⁿI sat where they sat, and remained
16 there astonished among them seven days. And it came to pass
at the end of seven days, that the word of the LORD came unto
17 me, saying, ᵒSon of man, I have made thee ᵖa watchman unto
the house of Israel: therefore hear the word at my mouth, and
18 give them warning from me. When I say unto the wicked,
Thou shalt surely die; and thou givest him not warning, nor
speakest to warn the wicked from his wicked way, to save his
life; the same wicked *man* ᑫshall die in his iniquity; but his
19 blood will I require at thine hand. Yet if thou warn the
wicked, and he turn not from his wickedness, nor from his
wicked way, he shall die in his iniquity; ʳbut thou hast de-
20 livered thy soul. Again, When a ˢrighteous *man* doth turn
from his ⁴righteousness, and commit iniquity, and I lay a
stumblingblock before him, he shall die: because thou hast not
given him warning, he shall die in his sin, and his righteous-

l ver. 12.

m 2 Kin. 3. 15.

n Job 2. 13.
Ps. 137. 1.

o ch. 33. 7.
p Isai. 52. 8.
Jer. 6. 17.

q ch. 33. 6.
John 8. 21.

r Isai. 49. 4.
Acts 20. 26.
s ch. 18. 24.
& 33. 12.

---

¹ Heb. *kissed*.   ³ Heb. *hot anger*.
² Heb. *bitter*.   ⁴ Heb. *righteousnesses*.

---

proper tokens (i. 24, 25). *A voice from above the firmament* is now heard proclaiming the Divine glory.

from his place] The place where the glory of the Lord had revealed itself in the vision. The words are to be joined to "saying:" put a comma after LORD.

13. *that touched*] Lit. **touching.** The living creatures in their flight raised their wings, so as to touch each other.

14. *lifted me up*] We are not to suppose that the prophet was miraculously transported from one place to another in the land of his Captivity. Cp. Matt. iv. 1; Acts viii. 39. He had been in an ecstatic vision (i. 1), and now guided by the Spirit he goes forth among his countrymen.

the heat of my spirit] Full of the righteous indignation, which God inspired, against the sin which he was to denounce.

but the hand] **and** *the hand.* The Lord strengthened him for his mission.

15. *Tel-abib*, on the river Chebar was the chief seat of the Jewish exiles in Babylonia. The name *Tel-abib* (*mount of ears of corn*) was probably given on account of its fertility.

I sat where they sat] Rather, "And I saw them sitting there and I sat there."

astonished] Rather, **silent**, with fixed and determined silence (cp. Ezra ix. 3, 4). *To be silent* was characteristic of mourners (Lam. iii. 28); *to sit* their proper attitude (Isai. iii. 26; Lam. i. 1); *seven days* the set time of mourning (Job ii. 13).

16. The Lord guards both Ezekiel and

his countrymen from dwelling exclusively on the national character of his mission. In the midst of the general visitations, each individual was to stand as it were alone before Him to render account of his doings, and to be judged according to his works.

watchman] The priests and ministers of the Lord were often so called. Ezekiel is especially distinguished by this title (xxxiii. 7). The duties of a watchman are twofold, (1) to wait and watch what God will order, (2) to watch over and superintend the people. Isaiah describes and censures unfaithful watchmen (Isai. lvi. 10).

18–21. This passage anticipates the great moral principle of Divine government (ch. xviii.) that each man is individually responsible for his own actions, and will be judged according to these and these alone.

20. *I lay a stumblingblock before him*] I bring him to trial by placing difficulties and temptations in his way (cp. vii. 19; xliv. 12 marg.; xiv. 3, 4). It is true that God tempts no man in order to his destruction, but in the course of His Providence He permits men to be tried in order that their faith may be approved, and in this trial some who seem to be righteous fall.

because thou...his blood &c.] So far as the prophet was concerned, the neglect of his duty is reckoned as the cause of the seemingly righteous man's fall.

his righteousness...] Or, righteousnesses, *i.e.* acts of righteousness. The *righteous* man here is one, who had hitherto done the *acts of righteousness* prescribed by the Law, but

ness which he hath done shall not be remembered; but his
21 blood will I require at thine hand. Nevertheless if thou warn
the righteous *man*, that the righteous sin not, and he doth not
sin, he shall surely live, because he is warned; also thou hast
delivered thy soul.

22 *t*And the hand of the LORD was there upon me; and he said
unto me, Arise, go forth *u*into the plain, and I will there talk
23 with thee. Then I arose, and went forth into the plain: and,
behold, *x*the glory of the LORD stood there, as the glory which
24 I *y*saw by the river of Chebar: *z*and I fell on my face. Then
*a*the spirit entered into me, and set me upon my feet, and spake
with me, and said unto me, Go, shut thyself within thine house.
25 But thou, O son of man, behold, *b*they shall put bands upon
thee, and shall bind thee with them, and thou shalt not go out
26 among them: and *c*I will make thy tongue cleave to the roof
of thy mouth, that thou shalt be dumb, and shalt not be to
27 them ¹a reprover: *d*for they *are* a rebellious house. *e*But when
I speak with thee, I will open thy mouth, and thou shalt say
unto them, *f*Thus saith the Lord GOD: He that heareth, let
him hear; and he that forbeareth, let him forbear: *g*for they *are*
a rebellious house.

CHAP. 4. THOU also, son of man, take thee a tile, and lay it before

t ver. 14.
ch. 1. 3.
u ch. 8. 4.

x ch. 1. 28.

y ch. 1. 1.
z ch. 1. 28.
a ch. 2. 2.

b ch. 4. 8.

c ch. 24. 27.
Luke 1. 20. 22.

d ch. 2. 5, 6.
e ch. 24. 27.
& 33. 22.
f ver. 11.
g ver. 9. 26.
ch. 12. 2, 3.

¹ Heb. *a man reproving.*

---

when trial came was shewn to lack the *principle of righteousness.*

21. The repetition of the word *righteous*
is to be noted. There seems to be an inti-
mation that sin is alien to the character of
a *righteous* man. Cp. 1 John iii. 7–9.

23. A fresh revelation of the glory of the
Lord, to impress upon Ezekiel another characteristic of his mission. Now he is to
learn that there is *a time to be silent* as well
as *a time to speak*, and that both are appointed by God. This represents forcibly
the authoritative character and Divine origin
of the utterances of the Hebrew prophets.

24. "Shut" in the privacy of his own
chamber he is to receive a message from
Jehovah. This *shutting up*, however, and
the *bands* (*v.* 25, used figuratively) were signs
of the manner in which Ezekiel's countrymen would close their ears, hindering him
as far as in them lay from delivering the
message of the Lord.

With this verse commences a series of
symbolical actions enjoined to the prophet
in order to foretell the coming judgments of
Jerusalem (chs. iv., v.). Generally speaking
symbolical actions were either literal and
public, or figurative and private. In the
latter case they impressed upon the prophet's
mind the truth which he was to enforce upon
others by the description of the action as by a
figure. Difficulties have arisen, because interpreters have not chosen to recognize the
figurative as well as the literal mode of
prophesying. Hence some, who would have
all literal, have had to accept the most
strange and unnecessary actions as real;

while others, who would have all figurative,
have had arbitrarily to explain away the
most plain historical statement. There may
be a difference of opinion as to which class
one or other figure may belong; but after all,
the determination is not important, the whole
value of the parabolic figure residing in the
lesson which it is intended to convey.

26. *And I will make*] Rather, **Then will
I** *make*. One action is the consequence of
the other. Because the people would silence
the prophet, God to punish them will close
his mouth (cp. Isai. vi. 9; Matt. xiii. 14).

27. *He that heareth* &c.] The judicial
blindness of which Ezekiel speaks had
already fallen upon the great body of the
nation (xiv. 4. Cp. Rev. ii. 7, xxii. 11).

IV., V. The coming siege of Jerusalem
and dispersion of its inhabitants foretold
under divers symbols. If the 5th year of
Jehoiachins captivity be taken (as is most
probable) for the year in which Ezekiel
received this communication, it was a time
at which such an event would, according to
human calculation, have appeared improbable. It could scarcely have been expected that Zedekiah—the creature of the
king of Babylon and ruling by his authority
in the place of Jehoiachin—would have been
so infatuated as to provoke the anger of the
powerful Nebuchadnezzar. It is indeed to
infatuation that the sacred historian
ascribes the act (2 K. xxiv. 20).

1. *a tile*] Rather, **a brick.** Sun-dried or
kiln-burnt bricks were from very early times
used for building walls throughout the plain
of Mesopotamia. The bricks of Nineveh and

2 thee, and pourtray upon it the city, *even* Jerusalem : and lay siege against it, and build a fort against it, and cast a mount against it ; set the camp also against it, and set [1]*battering* rams
3 against it round about.   Moreover take thou unto thee [2]an iron pan, and set it *for* a wall of iron between thee and the city : and set thy face against it, and it shall be besieged, and thou shalt lay siege against it.   *a*This *shall be* a sign to the house of
4 Israel.   ¶ Lie thou also upon thy left side, and lay the iniquity of the house of Israel upon it : *according* to the number of the days that thou shalt lie upon it thou shalt bear their iniquity.
5 For I have laid upon thee the years of their iniquity, according to the number of the days, three hundred and ninety days : *b*so
6 shalt thou bear the iniquity of the house of Israel.   And when thou hast accomplished them, lie again on thy right side, and

a ch. 12. 6.
& 24. 24.

b Num. 14. 34.

---

[1] Or, *chief leaders*, ch. 21. 22.   [2] Or, *a flat plate*, or, *slice*.

Babylon are sometimes stamped with what appears to be the device of the king in whose reign they were made, and often covered with a kind of enamel on which various scenes are portrayed. Among the subjects depicted on such bricks discovered at Nimroud are castles and forts.

2. *lay siege against it*] The prophet is represented as doing that which he portrays. The leading features of a siege are depicted. See Jer. vi. 6 note.

the camp] **encampments.** The word denotes various hosts in various positions around the city.

fort] It was customary in sieges to construct towers of vast height, sometimes of 20 stories, which were wheeled up to the walls to enable the besiegers to reach the battlements with their arrows ; in the lower part of such a tower there was commonly a battering-ram. These towers are frequently represented in the Assyrian monuments.

battering rams] Better than the translation in the margin. Assyrian monuments prove that these engines of war are of great antiquity. These engines seem to have been beams suspended by chains generally in moveable towers, and to have been applied against the walls in the way familiar to us from Greek and Roman history. The name *ram* was probably given to describe their mode of operation ; no Assyrian monument yet discovered exhibits the ram's head of later times.

3. *an iron pan*] Another figure in the coming siege. On Assyrian sculptures from Nimroud and Kouyunjik there are sieges of cities with *forts*, *mounts*, and *rams ;* and together with these we see a kind of shield set up on the ground, behind which archers are shooting. Such a shield would be represented by the *flat plate* (marg.). Ezekiel was directed to take such a plate (part of his household furniture) and place it between him and the representation of the city.

a sign to the house of Israel] This *sign* was not necessarily acted before the people, but may simply have been described to them as

a vivid representation of the event which it foretold. *Israel* stands here for the kingdom of Judah (cp. iii. 7, 17, v. 4, viii. 6). After the Captivity of the ten tribes the kingdom of Judah represented the whole nation. Hence prophets writing after this event constantly address their countrymen as the house of Israel without distinction of tribes.

4. The siege being thus represented, the condition and suffering of the inhabitants is exhibited by the condition of one, who, bound as a prisoner or oppressed by sickness, cannot turn from his right side to his left. The prophet was in such a state.

bear their iniquity] The prophet was, in a figure, to bear their iniquities for a fixed period, in order to shew that, after the period thus foretold, the burden of their sins should be taken off, and the people be forgiven. Cp. Lev. xvi. 21, 22.

5. *according to the number of the days*] Or, "to be to thee as a number of days (even as)" &c. Cp. marg. ref. Some conceive that these "days" were the years during which Israel and Judah *sinned*, and date in the case of Israel from Jeroboam's rebellion to the time at which Ezekiel wrote (circ. 390 years) ; and in the case of Judah from Josiah's reformation. But it seems more in accordance with the other *signs*, to suppose that they represent not that which had been, but that which shall be. The whole number of years is 430 (*vv.* 5, 6), the number assigned of old for the affliction of the descendants of Abraham (Gen. xv. 13 ; Ex. xii. 40). The *forty years* apportioned to Judah (*v.* 6), bring to mind the *forty years* passed in the wilderness ; and as these were years not only of punishment, but also of discipline and preparatory to restoration, so Ezekiel would intimate the difference between the punishments of Israel and of Judah to be this, that the one would be of much longer duration with no definite hope of recovery, but the other would be imposed with the express purpose of the renewal of mercy.

thou shalt bear the iniquity of the house of Judah forty days:
7 I have appointed thee [1]each day for a year. Therefore thou
shalt set thy face toward the siege of Jerusalem, and thine arm
8 *shall be* uncovered, and thou shalt prophesy against it. *c*And,
behold, I will lay bands upon thee, and thou shalt not turn
thee [2]from one side to another, till thou hast ended the days of
9 thy siege. ¶ Take thou also unto thee wheat, and barley, and
beans, and lentiles, and millet, and [3]fitches, and put them in one
vessel, and make thee bread thereof, *according* to the number of
the days that thou shalt lie upon thy side, three hundred and
10 ninety days shalt thou eat thereof. And thy meat which thou
shalt eat *shall be* by weight, twenty shekels a day: from time to
11 time shalt thou eat it. Thou shalt drink also water by measure,
the sixth part of an hin: from time to time shalt thou drink.
12 And thou shalt eat it *as* barley cakes, and thou shalt bake it
13 with dung that cometh out of man, in their sight. And the
LORD said, Even thus *d*shall the children of Israel eat their
defiled bread among the Gentiles, whither I will drive them.
14 ¶ Then said I, *e*Ah Lord GOD! behold, my soul hath not been
polluted: for from my youth up even till now have I not eaten
of *f*that which dieth of itself, or is torn in pieces; neither came
15 there *g*abominable flesh into my mouth. Then he said unto me,

c ch. 3. 25.

d Hos. 9. 3.

e Acts 10. 14.

f Ex. 22. 31.
Lev. 11. 40.

[1] Heb. *a day for a year, a day for a year.*
[2] Heb. *from thy side to thy side.*
[3] Or, *spelt.*

---

7. *Therefore thou shalt set thy face*] Or,
"And &c." *i.e.*, direct thy mind to that
subject.

thine arm shall be *uncovered*] A sign of the
execution of vengeance (Isai. lii. 10).

8. *I will lay bands upon thee*] Contrast
marg. ref. The Lord will put constraint
upon him, to cause him to exercise his
office. In the retirement of his house,
figuratively bound and under constraint, he
shall not cease to proclaim the doom of the
city.

the days of thy siege] Those during which
he should thus foretell the approaching
calamity.

9. Two things are prefigured in the remainder of this chapter, (1) the hardships of
exile, (2) the straitness of a siege. To
the people of Israel, separated from the rest
of the nations as holy, it was a leading
feature in the calamities of their exile that
they must be mixed up with other nations,
and eat of their food, which to the Jews
was a defilement (cp. *v.* 13; Amos vii. 17;
Dan. i. 8.)

fitches] A species of wheat with shorn ears.

in one vessel] To mix all these varied
seeds was an indication that the people were
no longer in their own land, where precautions against such mixing of seeds were
prescribed.

three hundred and ninety days] The days
of Israel's punishment; because here is a
figure of the *exile* which concerns all the
tribes, not of the *siege* which concerns Judah
alone.

10. *meat*] A general term for *food*, which

in this case consists of *grain*. Instead of
measuring, it was necessary in extreme
scarcity to *weigh* it (Lev. xxvi. 26; Rev. vi.
6).

twenty shekels a day] The *shekel* contained
about 220 grains, so that 20 shekels would
be about $\frac{5}{8}$ of a lb.

from time to time] Thou shalt receive and
eat it at the appointed interval of *a day*.

11. *water by measure*] This probably corresponds to the *water of affliction* (1 K. xxii.
27; Isai. xxx. 20). The measure of the *hin*
is variously estimated by Jewish writers.
The sixth part of a *hin* will be according to
one estimate about $\frac{6}{10}$ths, according to
another $\frac{9}{10}$ths of a *pint*. The lesser estimate
is more suitable here.

12. In eastern countries where fuel is
scarce the want is supplied by dried cow-
dung laid up for the winter. Barley cakes
were (and are) baked under hot ashes without an oven. The dung here is to be burnt
to ashes, and the ashes so employed.

13. The ceremonial ordinances in relation
to food were intended to keep the nation
free from idolatrous usages; everywhere
among the heathen idol feasts formed a
leading part in their religious services, and
idol meats were partaken of in common
life. Dispersion among the Gentiles must
have exposed the Jews to much which they
regarded as common and unclean. In
Ezekiel's case there was a mitigation (*v.* 15)
of the defilement, but still legal defilement
remained, and the chosen people in exile
were subjected to it as to a degradation.

14. *abominable flesh*] Flesh that had be-

Lo, I have given thee cow's dung for man's dung, and thou
16 shalt prepare thy bread therewith. ¶ Moreover he said unto
me, Son of man, behold, I will break the *ʰstaff* of bread in
Jerusalem : and they shall *ⁱeat* bread by weight, and with care ;
and they shall *ᵏdrink* water by measure, and with astonishment :
17 that they may want bread and water, and be astonied one with
another, and *ˡconsume* away for their iniquity.

Chap. 5. AND thou, son of man, take thee a sharp knife, take
thee a barber's razor, *ᵃand* cause *it* to pass upon thine head and
upon thy beard : then take thee balances to weigh, and divide
2 the *hair*. *ᵇThou* shalt burn with fire a third part in the midst
of *ᶜthe* city, when *ᵈthe* days of the siege are fulfilled : and thou
shalt take a third part, *and* smite about it with a knife : and a
third part thou shalt scatter in the wind ; and I will draw out
3 a sword after them. *ᵉThou* shalt also take thereof a few in
4 number, and bind them in thy *¹skirts*. Then take of them
again, and *ᶠcast* them into the midst of the fire, and burn them
in the fire ; *for* thereof shall a fire come forth into all the
5 house of Israel. ¶ Thus saith the Lord GOD ; This *is* Jerusalem :
I have set it in the midst of the nations and countries *that are*
6 round about her. And she hath changed my judgments into
wickedness more than the nations, and my statutes more than

ᵒ Deut. 14. 3.
Isai. 65. 4.

ʰ Lev. 26. 26.
Ps. 105. 16.
ⁱ ver. 10.
ch. 12. 19.
ᵏ ver. 11.

ˡ Lev. 26. 39.
ch. 24. 23.

ᵃ Isai. 7. 20.
ch. 44. 20.

ᵇ ver. 12.

ᶜ ch. 4. 1.
ᵈ ch. 4. 8.

ᵉ Jer. 40. 6.
& 52. 16.

ᶠ Jer. 41. 1.
& 44. 14.

---

¹ Heb. *wings*.

---

come corrupt and foul by overkeeping. Cp.
Lev. xix. 7.

16. *the staff of bread*] Bread is so called
because it is that on which the support of
life mainly depends.

with astonishment] With dismay and
anxiety at the calamities which are befalling
them.

V. 1. Translate, **take thee a sharp sword,
for a barber's razor thou shalt take it
thee.** Even if the action were literal, the
use of an actual sword would best enforce
the symbolical meaning. The *head* represents the chief city, the *hair* the inhabitants—
its ornament and glory,—the *hair cut from
the head* the exiles cast forth from their
homes. It adds to the force of the representation that to *shave the head* was a token
of mourning (Job i. 20), and was forbidden
to the priests (Lev. xxi. 5). Thus in many
ways this action of Ezekiel *the priest* is significant of calamity and ruin. The sword
indicates the avenging power ; the shaving
of the head the removal of grace and glory ;
the scales and weights the determination of
divine justice. Cp. Zech. xiii. 8, 9.

2. *The third part burnt in the midst of the
city* represents those who perished within
the city during the siege ; *the third part
smitten about it* (the city) *with* **the sword,**
those who were killed about the city during
the same period : *the third part scattered to
the wind* those who after the siege were dispersed in foreign lands.

in the midst of the city] The prophet is in
exile, and is to do this *in the midst of Jerusalem*. His action being *ideal* is fitly assigned
to the place which the prophecy concerns.

when the days of the siege are fulfilled] *i.e.*,
"when the days of the figurative representation of the siege are fulfilled."

3, 4. Of the third part a few are yet to
be taken and kept in the fold of the garment (representing those still to remain in
their native land), and yet even of those
few some are to be cast into the fire. Such
was the fate of those left behind after
the destruction of Jerusalem (Jer. xl., xli.).
The whole prophecy is one of denunciation.

4. *thereof*] Or, **from thence,** out of the
midst of the fire. Omit *For*.

5. *I have set it in the midst of the nations*]
It was not unusual for nations to regard the
sanctuary, which they most revered, as the
centre of the earth. In the case of the Holy
Land this was both natural and appropriate.
Egypt to the South, Syria to the North,
Assyria to the East and the Isles of the
Gentiles in the Great Sea to the West,
were to the Jew proofs of the central position of his land in the midst of the nations
(cp. Jer. iii. 19). The habitation assigned
to the chosen people was suitable at the
first for separating them from the nations ;
then for the seat of the vast dominion
and commerce of Solomon ; then, when they
learnt from their neighbours idol-worship,
their central position was the source of
their punishment. Midway between the
mighty empires of Egypt and Assyria the
Holy Land became a battle-field for the
two powers, and suffered alternately from
each as for the time the one or the other
became predominant.

the countries that *are* round about her: for they have refused my judgments and my statutes, they have not walked in them.

7 Therefore thus saith the Lord GOD; Because ye multiplied more than the nations that *are* round about you, *and* have not walked in my statutes, neither have kept my judgments, *g*neither have done according to the judgments of the nations that *are* round

8 about you; therefore thus saith the Lord GOD; Behold, I, even I, *am* against thee, and will execute judgments in the midst

9 of thee in the sight of the nations. *h*And I will do in thee that which I have not done, and whereunto I will not do any more

10 the like, because of all thine abominations. Therefore the fathers *i*shall eat the sons in the midst of thee, and the sons shall eat their fathers; and I will execute judgments in thee, and the whole remnant of thee will I *k*scatter into all the winds.

11 Wherefore, *as* I live, saith the Lord GOD; Surely, because thou hast *l*defiled my sanctuary with all thy *m*detestable things, and with all thine abominations, therefore will I also diminish *thee;* *n*neither shall mine eye spare, neither will I have any pity.

12 *o*A third part of thee shall die with the pestilence, and with famine shall they be consumed in the midst of thee: and a third part shall fall by the sword round about thee; and *p*I will scatter a third part into all the winds, and *q*I will draw out

13 a sword after them. Thus shall mine anger *r*be accomplished, and I will *s*cause my fury to rest upon them, *t*and I will be comforted: *u*and they shall know that I the LORD have spoken *it* in my zeal, when I have accomplished my fury in them.

14 Moreover *x*I will make thee waste, and a reproach among the nations that *are* round about thee, in the sight of all that pass

15 by. So it shall be a *y*reproach and a taunt, an instruction and an astonishment unto the nations that *are* round about thee, when I shall execute judgments in thee in anger and in fury and in *z*furious rebukes. I the LORD have spoken *it*. When I

16 shall *a*send upon them the evil arrows of famine, which shall be for *their* destruction, *and* which I will send to destroy you: and I will increase the famine upon you, and will break your *b*staff

17 of bread: so will I send upon you famine and *c*evil beasts, and they shall bereave thee; and *d*pestilence and blood shall pass through thee; and I will bring the sword upon thee. I the LORD have spoken *it*.

CHAP. 6. AND the word of the LORD came unto me, saying, Son

Margin references:
g Jer. 2. 10. ch. 16. 47.
h Lam. 4. 6. Dan. 9. 12. Amos 3. 2.
i Lev. 26. 29. Jer. 19. 9. Lam. 2. 20.
k Deut.28.64. ch. 12. 14. Zech. 2. 6.
l 2 Chr.36.14. ch. 7. 20.
m ch. 11. 21.
n ch. 7. 4, 9.
o Jer. 21. 9. ch. 6. 12.
p Jer. 9. 16. ch. 6. 8.
q ch. 12. 14.
r Lam. 4. 11.
s ch. 21. 17.
t Isai. 1. 24.
u ch. 36. 6.
x Neh. 2. 17.
y Deut.28.^37. 1 Kin. 9. 7. Jer. 24. 9.
z ch. 25. 17.
a Deut. 32. 23, 24.
b Lev. 26. 26.
c Deut.32.24. ch. 14. 21.
d ch. 38. 22.

---

6. *they*] The inhabitants of Jerusalem.

7. *Because ye multiplied*] Some prefer: "Because ye have raged tumultuously."

neither have done according to the judgments (or, ordinances) *of the nations*] The reproach is that the Israelites have not even been as faithful to their one true God as the nations have been to their false gods (cp. 2 K. xvii. 33).

8. *execute judgments*] As upon the false gods of Egypt (Ex. xii. 12; Num. xxxiii. 4).

9. Cp. Matt. xxiv. 21. The calamities of the Babylonian were surpassed by the Roman siege, and these again were but a foreshadowing of still more terrible destruction at the last day.

12-17. The judgments of *famine, pestilence,* and the *sword,* were precisely those

which attended the coming siege of Jerusalem (Jer. xv. 2, *seq.*). The *drawing out the sword after them* indicates that the anger of God will follow them even to the land of their exile (cp. Jer. xlii. 19-22; Lev. xxvi. 25), and that the horrors of the Babylonian siege are but the beginning of the sorrows of the nation.

13. *comforted*] In the sense of *consoling one's self* and *feeling satisfaction in punishing;* hence to *avenge one's self.*

The fury is to *rest* upon them, abide, so as not to pass away. The *accomplishment* of the Divine anger is not the *completion* in the sense of bringing it to a close, but in the sense of carrying it out to the full.

VI. The former prophecies concerned the city of Jerusalem and the inhabitants of

a ch. 20. 46.
b ch. 36. 1.

c Lev. 26. 30.

d Lev. 26. 30.

e ver. 13.
ch. 7. 4, 9.
f Jer. 44. 28.
ch. 5. 2, 12.

g Ps. 78. 40.
Isai. 7. 13.
h Num.15.39.
ch. 20. 7.
i Lev. 26. 39.
Job 42. 6.
ch. 36. 31.

k ch. 21. 14.

l ch. 5. 12.

m ch. 5. 13.
n ver. 7.

o Jer. 2. 20.
p Hos. 4. 13.
q Isai. 57. 5.

2 of man, *a*set thy face toward the *b*mountains of Israel, and
3 prophesy against them, and say, ¶ Ye mountains of Israel, hear
the word of the Lord GOD; Thus saith the Lord GOD to the
mountains, and to the hills, to the rivers, and to the valleys;
Behold, I, *even* I, will bring a sword upon you, and *c*I will
4 destroy your high places. And your altars shall be desolate,
and your 'images shall be broken: and *d*I will cast down your
5 slain *men* before your idols. And I will ²lay the dead carcases
of the children of Israel before their idols; and I will scatter
6 your bones round about your altars. In all your dwellingplaces
the cities shall be laid waste, and the high places shall be
desolate; that your altars may be laid waste and made desolate,
and your idols may be broken and cease, and your images may
7 be cut down, and your works may be abolished. And the slain
shall fall in the midst of you, and *e*ye shall know that I *am* the
8 LORD. ¶ *f*Yet will I leave a remnant, that ye may have *some*
that shall escape the sword among the nations, when ye shall be
9 scattered through the countries. And they that escape of you
shall remember me among the nations whither they shall be
carried captives, because *g*I am broken with their whorish heart,
which hath departed from me, and *h*with their eyes, which go a
whoring after their idols: and *i*they shall lothe themselves for
the evils which they have committed in all their abominations.
10 And they shall know that I *am* the LORD, *and that* I have not
11 said in vain that I would do this evil unto them. ¶ Thus saith
the Lord GOD; Smite *k*with thine hand, and stamp with thy
foot, and say, Alas for all the evil abominations of the house of
Israel! *l*for they shall fall by the sword, by the famine, and by
12 the pestilence. He that is far off shall die of the pestilence;
and he that is near shall fall by the sword; and he that remaineth and is besieged shall die by the famine: *m*thus will
13 I accomplish my fury upon them. Then *n*shall ye know that I
am the LORD, when their slain *men* shall be among their idols
round about their altars, *o*upon every high hill, *p*in all the tops
of the mountains, and *q*under every green tree, and under every
thick oak, the place where they did offer sweet savour to all

¹ Or, *sun images*, and so ver. 6.   ² Heb. *give*.

Judæa. The present is addressed to the
whole land and people of Israel, which is
to be included in a like judgment. The
ground of the judgment is *idolatry*, and the
whole rests on Deut. xii. The prophecy is
against the *mountains* of Israel, because
the mountains and valleys were the seats of
idol-worship. It is also the proclamation
of the final judgment of Israel. It is the
picture of the future judgment of the world.

3. *rivers*] Or, *ravines*, which were, like
the mountains, favourite seats of idol-rites
(2 K. xxiii. 10).

4. *images*] See marg. and marg. ref., and
viii. 16 note.

idols] The Phœnicians were in the habit
of setting up *heaps* or *pillars* of stone in
honour of their gods, which renders the use
of the word more appropriate.

7. The force of the words is, "When the
slain shall fall in the midst of you, then at
last ye shall know that I am the Lord."

So in *v.* 10 where the knowledge implies a
recognition of the merciful intent of Jehovah's dispensations, and therefore a hope of
restoration.

9. *I am broken* &c.] Translate: *because* I
have broken *their whorish heart, which hath
departed from me*, and *their eyes* &c.
Since Ezekiel is addressing the Church of
God through Israel, we are to note here
that the general principle of the Divine
administration is laid down. Sin leads to
judgment, judgment to repentance, repentance to forgiveness, forgiveness to reconciliation, reconciliation to a knowledge of
communion with God.

11-14. The gleam of hope is but transitory. Darkness again gathers round, for as
yet the prophet is predicting judgment.

11. *Smite...stamp*] Well-known modes of
expressing grief.

13. *sweet savour*] Cp. Gen. viii. 21. Words,
applied to the smell of sacrifices accepted

14 their idols. So will I ʳstretch out my hand upon them, and make the land desolate, yea, ¹more desolate than the wilderness toward ˢDiblath, in all their habitations: and they shall know that I *am* the LORD.

CHAP. 7. MOREOVER the word of the LORD came unto me, say-
2 ing, Also, thou son of man, thus saith the Lord GOD unto the land of Israel; ¶ᵃAn end, the end is come upon the four corners
3 of the land. Now *is* the end *come* upon thee, and I will send mine anger upon thee, and ᵇwill judge thee according to thy ways, and will ²recompense upon thee all thine abominations.
4 And ᶜmine eye shall not spare thee, neither will I have pity : but I will recompense thy ways upon thee, and thine abominations shall be in the midst of thee : ᵈand ye shall know that I *am* the
5 LORD. ¶Thus saith the Lord GOD; An evil, an only evil,
6 behold, is come. An end is come : it ³watcheth
7 for thee; behold, it is come. ᵉThe morning is come unto thee, O thou that dwellest in the land : ᶠthe time is come, the day of trouble *is* near, and not the ⁴sounding again of the mountains.
8 Now will I shortly ᵍpour out my fury upon thee, and accom-plish mine anger upon thee: ʰand I will judge thee according to thy ways, and will recompense thee for all thine abomina-
9 tions. And ⁱmine eye shall not spare, neither will I have pity : I will recompense ⁵thee according to thy ways and thine abomi-nations *that* are in the midst of thee ; ᵏand ye shall know that
10 I *am* the LORD that smiteth. ¶Behold the day, behold, it is come : ˡthe morning is gone forth ; the rod hath blossomed,
11 pride hath budded. ᵐViolence is risen up into a rod of wicked-ness : none of them *shall remain*, nor of their ⁶multitude, nor of
12 any of ⁷theirs : ⁿneither *shall there be* wailing for them. ᵒThe time is come, the day draweth near : let not the buyer rejoice,

---

¹ Or, *desolate from the wil-*
derness.
² Heb. *give.*
³ Heb. *awaketh against thee.*
⁴ Or, *echo.*
⁵ Heb. *upon thee.*
⁶ Or, *tumult.*
⁷ Or, *their tumultuous per-sons.*

---

by God, applied here to idol-sacrifices in irony.

14. *toward Diblath*] Or, *Diblathaim*, the *Diblathan* of the Moabite stone, one of the double cities of Moab (see xxv. 9) to the East of which lay the great desert of Arabia. Some read "unto Riblah" (Jer. lii. 9) and take the marg. rendering.

VII. A dirge. Supposing the date of the prophecy to be the same as that of the preceding, there were now but four, or per-haps three, years to the final overthrow of the kingdom of Judah by Nebuchadnezzar.

3, 4. A kind of refrain, repeated in *vv.* 8, 9, as the close of another stanza.

5. *an only evil*] An evil singular and re-markable above all others.

6. *the end is come : it watcheth for thee*] The end (personified) so long slumbering now awakes and comes upon thee.

7, 10. *The morning*] Rather, *The conclu-sion :* a whole series (lit. circle) of events is being brought to a close. Others render, *Fate*.

the day of trouble &c.] Or, **The day is near; a tumult** (Zech. xiv. 13), **and not**

the echo of (or, shouting on) **the mountains.** The contrast is between the wild tumult of war and the joyous shouts of such as keep holiday.

10. *rod*] Used here for tribe (Ex. xxxi. 2). The people of Judah have blossomed into proud luxuriance. In *v.* 11 it means the rod to punish wickedness. The mean-ing of the passage is obscure, owing to the brief and enigmatic form of the utterance. We may adopt the following explanation. The Jews had ever exulted in their national privileges—everything great and noble was to be from them and from theirs ; but now Jehovah raises up the rod of the oppressor to confound and punish the rod of His people. The furious Chaldæan has become an instrument of God's wrath, endued with power emanating not from the Jews or from the multitude of the Jews, or from any of their children or people ; nay, the destruc-tion shall be so complete that none shall be left to make lamentation over them.

12. *the day*] Either of temporal or final judgment.

12. 13. It was grievous for an Israelite to

nor the seller mourn: for wrath *is* upon all the multitude
13 thereof. For the seller shall not return to that which is sold,
[1]although they were yet alive: for the vision *is* touching the
whole multitude thereof, *which* shall not return; neither shall
14 any strengthen himself [2]in [3]the iniquity of his life. They have
blown the trumpet, even to make all ready; but none goeth
to the battle: for my wrath *is* upon all the multitude thereof.
15 ¶ [p]The sword *is* without, and the pestilence and the famine
within: he that *is* in the field shall die with the sword; and he
16 that *is* in the city, famine and pestilence shall devour him. But
[q]they that escape of them shall escape, and shall be on the
mountains like doves of the valleys, all of them mourning, every
17 one for his iniquity. All [r]hands shall be feeble, and all knees
18 shall [4]be weak *as* water. They shall also [s]gird *themselves* with
sackcloth, and [t]horror shall cover them; and shame *shall be*
19 upon all faces, and baldness upon all their heads. They shall
cast their silver in the streets, and their gold shall be [5]removed:
their [u]silver and their gold shall not be able to deliver them in
the day of the wrath of the LORD: they shall not satisfy their
souls, neither fill their bowels: [6]because it is [x]the stumbling-
20 block of their iniquity. As for the beauty of his ornament, he
set it in majesty: [y]but they made the images of their abominations *and* of their detestable things therein: therefore have I
21 [7]set it far from them. And I will give it into the hands of the
strangers for a prey, and to the wicked of the earth for a spoil;
22 and they shall pollute it. My face will I turn also from them,
and they shall pollute my secret *place*: for the [8]robbers shall
23 enter into it, and defile it. ¶ Make a chain: for [z]the land is
24 full of bloody crimes, and the city is full of violence. Wherefore I will bring the worst of the heathen, and they shall possess
their houses: I will also make the pomp of the strong to cease;

[p] Deut. 32. 25. Lam. 1. 20. ch. 5. 12.
[q] ch. 6. 8.
[r] Isai. 13. 7. Jer. 6. 24. ch. 21. 7.
[s] Isai. 3. 24. Jer. 48. 37. Amos 8. 10.
[t] Ps. 55. 5.
[u] Prov. 11. 4. Zeph. 1. 18.
[x] ch. 14. 3. & 44. 12.
[y] Jer. 7. 30.
[z] 2 Kin. 21. 16. ch. 9. 9.

[1] Heb. *though their life were yet among the living.*
[2] Or, *whose life is in his iniquity.*
[3] Heb. *his iniquity.*
[4] Heb. *go (melt) into water.*
[5] Heb. *for a separation*, or, *uncleanness.*
[6] Or, *because their iniquity is their stumblingblock.*
[7] Or, *made it unto them an unclean thing.*
[8] Or, *burglers.*

---

part with his land. But now the seller need not mourn his loss, nor the buyer exult in his gain. All should live the pitiful lives of strangers in another country.

13. *although they were yet alive*] **Though they be yet among the living.**

which *shall not return* &c.] **He** (*i.e. the seller*) *shall not return;* **and, every man living in his iniquity, they shall gather no strength.** Exile being the punishment of iniquity, the exiles were said to *live in their iniquity.*

16. As doves whose natural abode is the valleys moan lamentably when driven by fear into the mountains, so shall the remnant, who have escaped actual death, moan in the land of their exile.

18. Various signs of mourning common in eastern countries. *Baldness* was forbidden to the Israelites (Deut. xiv. 1). They seem, however, in later times to have adopted the custom of foreign nations in this matter, not without permission. Cp. Isai. xxii. 12.

19. *shall be removed*] Lit. "shall be an unclean thing" (Lev. xx. 21); their gold shall be unclean and abominable in their eyes.

the stumblingblock of their iniquity] See iii. 20. Their gold and silver used in making images was the occasion of their sin.

20. Or, **And** *the beauty of his ornament, he* (the people) **turned** *it* **to pride.**

have I set it far from them] Rather, as in marg.—therefore have I made it their defilement and their disgrace.

22. *my secret* place] The inner sanctuary, hidden from the multitude, protected by the Most High.

23. *Make a chain*] **Forge the chain,** the chain of imprisonment determined for them.

24. *the worst of the heathen*] The most cruel and terrible of nations—the Chaldæans.

the pomp of the strong] Cp. Lev. xxvi. 19. *The strong* are those who pride themselves in imaginary strength.

a Deut.32.23.
Jer. 4. 20.

b Ps. 74. 9.
Lam. 2. 9.
ch. 20. 1, 3.

c ver. 4.

a ch. 14. 1.
& 33. 31.
b ch. 1. 3.
c ch. 1. 26.

d ch. 1. 4.
e Dan. 5. 5.

f ch. 3. 14.

g ch. 11. 1,
24.
h Jer. 7. 30.
ch. 5. 11.
i Deut. 32.
16, 21.
k ch. 1. 28.
& 3. 22, 23.

25 and ¹their holy places shall be defiled. ²Destruction cometh; 26 and they shall seek peace, and *there shall be* none. *a*Mischief shall come upon mischief, and rumour shall be upon rumour: *b*then shall they seek a vision of the prophet; but the law shall 27 perish from the priest, and counsel from the ancients. The king shall mourn, and the prince shall be clothed with desolation, and the hands of the people of the land shall be troubled: I will do unto them after their way, and ³according to their deserts will I judge them; *c*and they shall know that I *am* the LORD.

CHAP. 8. AND it came to pass in the sixth year, in the sixth *month*, in the fifth *day* of the month, *as* I sat in mine house, and *a*the elders of Judah sat before me, that *b*the hand of the Lord GOD 2 fell there upon me. *c*Then I beheld, and lo a likeness as the appearance of fire: from the appearance of his loins even downward, fire; and from his loins even upward, as the appearance 3 of brightness, *d*as the colour of amber. And he *e*put forth the form of an hand, and took me by a lock of mine head; and *f*the spirit lifted me up between the earth and the heaven, and *g*brought me in the visions of God to Jerusalem, to the door of the inner gate that looketh toward the north; *h*where *was* the seat of the image of jealousy, which *i*provoketh to jealousy. 4 And, behold, the glory of the God of Israel *was* there, according 5 to the vision that I *k*saw in the plain. ¶ Then said he unto me,

¹ Or, *they shall inherit their holy places.* ² Heb. *Cutting off.* ³ Heb. *with their judgments.*

---

their holy places] What elsewhere is called *God's Holy Place* is here *their holy places*, because God disowns the profaned sanctuary. In the marginal rendering *they* must mean *the worst of the heathen*.

VIII.—XIX. The prophecies contained in these chapters fall within eleven months (cp. *v.* 1 with xx. 1). Although they were not all delivered on the same day, they may be regarded as a whole. They contain in fact a review of the condition of the people of Judah, including those who were still in the Holy Land, and those who were with the prophet exiles in Chaldæa. This is first represented by a vision (viii.-xi.) in which the seer is transported in spirit to the Temple of Jerusalem; and next—the prophet having again taken his stand as a man among men—by symbolical act, parables, figures, &c., addresses his fellow-exiles.

1. *the elders of Judah*] The prophet's fellow-exiles are no longer unwilling to hear him (ch. ii.). They *sat* as mourners. The message here is not as in vi. 2, but distinctly to *Judah*, that portion of the people whose exile Ezekiel shared.

2. *the appearance of fire*] In marg. ref., seen as the *appearance of a man* enthroned upon the Cherubim. Here He stands apart from the throne revealing Himself to His servant. Cp. Dan. iii. 25 note.

amber] See marg. ref. note.

3. *in the visions of God*] Ezekiel was not transported *in the body*, but rapt *in spirit*, while he still sat amidst the elders of Judah.

the inner gate] Or, **the gate of the inner court.** This gate, leading from the outer to the inner court (the court of the priests), is called (*v.* 5) *the gate of the altar*, because it was from this side that the priests approached the brazen altar. The prophet is on the *outside* of this gate, so that the *image of jealousy* was set up in the outer or people's court over against the northern entrance to the priest's court. This image was the image of a false god provoking Jehovah to *jealousy* (Deut. xxxii. 16, 21; 1 K. xiv. 22). It may be doubted whether the scenes described in this chapter are intended to represent what actually occurred. They may be ideal pictures to indicate the idolatrous corruption of priests and people. And this is in accordance with the symbolical character of the number *four;* the four idolatries representing the idolatries in all the four quarters of the world. The false gods of heathendom are brought into the Temple in order that they may be detected and exposed by being brought face to face with the God of revelation. Still history proves that the ideal picture was supported by actual facts which had occurred and were occurring.

4. The glory of the LORD having departed from His seat between the Cherubims in the Holy of Holies (see ix. 3) rests in the threshold of the Temple, to execute vengeance before it quits the house altogether (x. 18). The *there* is the inner court, which was *full of the brightness of the LORD's glory* (x. 4), and at the gate of which Ezekiel stands.

Son of man, lift up thine eyes now the way toward the north.
So I lifted up mine eyes the way toward the north, and behold
northward at the gate of the altar this image of jealousy in the
6 entry. He said furthermore unto me, Son of man, seest thou
what they do? *even* the great abominations that the house of
Israel committeth here, that I should go far off from my sanctuary? but turn thee yet again, *and* thou shalt see greater abomi-
7 nations. ¶And he brought me to the door of the court; and
8 when I looked, behold a hole in the wall. Then said he unto
me, Son of man, dig now in the wall: and when I had digged
9 in the wall, behold a door. And he said unto me, Go in, and
10 behold the wicked abominations that they do here. So I went
in and saw; and behold every form of creeping things, and
abominable beasts, and all the idols of the house of Israel,
11 pourtrayed upon the wall round about. And there stood before
them seventy men of the ancients of the house of Israel, and in
the midst of them stood Jaazaniah the son of Shaphan, with
every man his censer in his hand; and a thick cloud of incense
12 went up. Then said he unto me, Son of man, hast thou seen
what the ancients of the house of Israel do in the dark, every
man in the chambers of his imagery? for they say, *l*the LORD   *l* ch. 9. 9.
13 seeth us not; the LORD hath forsaken the earth. ¶He said also
unto me, Turn thee yet again, *and* thou shalt see greater abomi-
14 nations that they do. Then he brought me to the door of the
gate of the LORD's house which *was* toward the north; and,
15 behold, there sat women weeping for Tammuz. Then said he
unto me, Hast thou seen *this*, O son of man? turn thee yet

---

7. *the door of the court*] The seer is
brought to another spot. In Ezekiel's time
there were sundry buildings on the space
around the inner court which formed a
court or courts, not improbably inclosed by
a wall. The idolatries here were viewed as
taking place in secret, and it is more in
accordance with the Temple arrangements
to suppose that such chambers as would
give room for those rites should belong to
the outer than to the inner court. The seer
is now outside the wall of the outer court,
by the door which leads from it out of the
Temple-boundary. By breaking through
the wall he enters into a chamber which
stands in the outer court against the wall
near the gate.

10. There is clearly a reference to the
idolatry of Egypt. Many subterranean
chambers in rocks upon the shores of the
Nile exhibit ornamentation and hierogly-
phical characters, some of which are representative of the objects of idolatrous
worship. Such chambers fitted them for
the scene of the ideal picture by which
Ezekiel represented Egyptian idolatry.
The Egyptian worship of animals is well
known.

11. *seventy men*] Cp. Ex. xxiv. 9, 10.
The vision may have pointed to the contrast between the times. The number
seven is symbolical of the Covenant between
Jehovah and His people, and so the *seventy*
men exhibit forcibly the breach of the

Covenant. It is a figure of the covert
idolatry of the whole people.

12. *in the dark*] Hidden in the secret
places which the seer dug through the wall
to discover.

chambers of his imagery] *i. e.*, chambers
painted with images.

14. The seer is now brought back to the
same gate as in *v.* 3.

It is not certain that this verse refers to any
special act of Tammuz-worship. The month
in which the vision was seen, the sixth month
(September), was not the month of the Tam-
muz-rites. But that such rites had been
performed in Jerusalem there can be little
doubt. Women are mentioned as employed
in the service of idols in Jer. vii. 18. There
is some reason for believing that the
weeping of women for Tammuz passed into
Syria and Palestine from Babylonia, Tammuz being identified with Duv-zi, whose
loss was lamented by the goddess Istar.
The festival was identical with the Greek
Adoniac. The worship of Adonis had its
head-quarters at Byblos, where at certain
periods of the year the stream, becoming
stained by mountain floods, was popularly
said to be red with the blood of Adonis.
From Byblos it spread widely over the
East and was thence carried to Greece.
The intercourse of Zedekiah with heathen
nations (Jer. xxvii. 3) may very well
have led to the introduction of an idolatry
which at this time was especially popular

again, *and* thou shalt see greater abominations than these.

16 ¶ And he brought me into the inner court of the LORD's house, and, behold, at the door of the temple of the LORD, *m*between the porch and the altar, *n*were about five and twenty men, *o*with their backs toward the temple of the LORD, and their faces toward the east; and they worshipped *p*the sun toward the east.

17 Then he said unto me, Hast thou seen *this*, O son of man ? [1]Is it a light thing to the house of Judah that they commit the abominations which they commit here? for they have *q*filled the land with violence, and have returned to provoke me to anger: and, lo, they put the branch to their nose. *r*Therefore

18 will I also deal in fury : mine *s*eye shall not spare, neither will I have pity : and though they *t*cry in mine ears with a loud voice, *yet* will I not hear them.

CHAP. 9. HE cried also in mine ears with a loud voice, saying, Cause them that have charge over the city to draw near, even

2 every man *with* his destroying weapon in his hand. And, behold,

Marginal references:
m Joel 2. 17.
n ch. 11. 1.
o Jer. 2. 27. & 32. 33.
p Deut. 4. 19. Jer. 44. 17.
q ch. 9. 9.
r ch. 5. 13.
s ch. 7. 4, 9. & 9. 5, 10.
t Isai. 1. 15. Jer. 11. 11. Mic. 3. 4. Zech. 7. 13.

[1] Or, *Is there any thing lighter than to commit.*

among the Eastern nations. This solemnity was of a twofold character, first, that of mourning, in which the death of Adonis was bewailed with extravagant sorrow; and then, after a few days, the mourning gave place to wild rejoicings for his restoration to life. This was a revival of nature-worship under another form—the death of Adonis symbolized the suspension of the productive powers of nature, which were in due time revived. Accordingly the time of this festival was the summer solstice, when in the East nature seems to wither and die under the scorching heat of the sun, to burst forth again into life at the due season. At the same time there was a connexion between this and the sun-worship, in that the decline of the sun and the decline of nature might be alike represented by the death of Adonis. The excitement attendant upon these extravagances of alternate wailing and exultation were in complete accordance with the character of nature-worship, which for this reason was so popular in the East, especially with women, and led by inevitable consequence to unbridled license and excess. Such was in Ezekiel's day one of the most detestable forms of idolatry.

16. *the inner court*] The court of the priests.

about five and twenty men] Rather, **as it were** five &c. This was the number of the heads of the twenty-four courses with the High Priest presiding over them. These then were the representatives of the priests, as the seventy were of the people. In the Temple the seat of the Divine Majesty was at the West, perhaps appointed for this very purpose, to guard against the idolatrous adoration of the rising sun. Therefore the idolatrous priests must in worshipping the false sun-god turn their backs upon the True. The worship of the heavenly bodies was one of the earliest forms of idolatry (Job

xxxi. 26, 27) and was expressly forbidden in the Law (Deut. xvii. 3). In its earliest form, it was conducted without the intervention of images, the adoration being addressed to the heavenly bodies themselves: this form, continued among the Persians, seems to have been introduced afresh into Jerusalem at the time of Ezekiel. Cp., also, 2 K. xxiii. 11, 12. The *images* (cp. vi. 4, 6) were probably columns set up in honour of the sun, not images in human form. This simpler mode of sun-worship was soon changed. The sun, or the god supposed to preside over it, was represented as a person, whose image was set up and adored.

17. *Violence* represents sin against man, *abominations* sins against God. These went hand in hand in Jerusalem.

and have returned] After the reformation effected for a time by Josiah's zeal, they have gone back to their old state.

they put the branch to their nose] An allusion to a then familiar practice, of which we find no clear traces elsewhere. Ezekiel is describing the attitude usual in such devotions, the branch held before the mouth, but wishing to represent it in contemptuous and derogatory terms, he substitutes the word *nose* for *mouth*.

IX. The punishment of the dwellers in Jerusalem.

1. *them that have charge*] The Angels who have charge to execute God's sentence. *every man*] *Angels*, not *men*.

2. *six men*] Angels of wrath—figurative of destruction. They come from the North, the quarter from which invading armies entered the Holy Land. These *six* Angels, with the *one among them*, a superior over the six, make up the number *seven*, a number symbolical of God's Covenant with His people.

six men came from the way of the higher gate, ¹which lieth toward the north, and every man ²a slaughter weapon in his hand; *and one man among them *was* clothed with linen, with a writer's inkhorn ³by his side : and they went in, and stood 3 beside the brasen altar. And *b*the glory of the God of Israel was gone up from the cherub, whereupon he was, to the threshold of the house. And he called to the man clothed with 4 linen, which *had* the writer's inkhorn by his side; and the LORD said unto him, Go through the midst of the city, through the midst of Jerusalem, and ⁴set *c*a mark upon the foreheads of the men *d*that sigh and that cry for all the abominations that 5 be done in the midst thereof. And to the others he said in ⁵mine hearing, Go ye after him through the city, and smite : 6 *e*let not your eye spare, neither have ye pity : *f*slay ⁶utterly old *and* young, both maids, and little children, and women : but *g*come not near any man upon whom *is* the mark ; and *h*begin at my sanctuary. *i*Then they began at the ancient men which 7 *were* before the house. And he said unto them, Defile the house, and fill the courts with the slain : go ye forth. And they went

a Lev. 16. 4.
ch. 10. 2, 6.
Rev. 15. 6.
b ch. 10. 4, 18.

c Ex. 12. 7.
Rev. 7. 3.
& 20. 4.
d Jer. 13. 17.
2 Pet. 2. 8.
e ch. 5. 11.
f 2 Chr. 36.
17.
g Rev. 9. 4.
h Jer. 25. 29.
1 Pet. 4. 17.
i ch. 8. 11.

¹ Heb. *which is turned.*   ³ Heb. *upon his loins.*   ⁵ Heb. *mine ears.*
² Heb. *a weapon of his*   ⁴ Heb. *mark a mark.*   ⁶ Heb. *to destruction.*
    breaking in pieces.

the higher gate] The North gate of the court of the priests. The Temple rose by platforms ; as there was a North gate to the outer and also to the inner court, the latter was probably distinguished as *the higher gate.* It was built by Jotham (2 K. xv. 35).

clothed with linen] The priestly garment (Ex. xxviii. 6, 8 ; Lev. xvi. 4). This *One Man* (Cp. Dan. x. 5 ; Rev. i. 13) was the *Angel of the Covenant,* the great High Priest, superior to those by whom He was surrounded, receiving direct communication from the Lord, taking the coals of vengeance from between the Cherubim (x. 2), but coming with mercy to the contrite as well as with vengeance to the impenitent ;— these are attributes of Jesus Christ (John v. 30 ; Luke ii. 34 ; Matt. ix. 13 ; John vi. 39).

a writer's inkhorn] Usually a flat case about nine inches long, by an inch and a quarter broad, and half an inch thick, the hollow of which serves to contain the reed pens and penknife. At one end is the ink-vessel which is twice as heavy as the shaft. The latter is passed through the girdle and prevented from slipping through by the projecting ink-vessel. The whole is usually of polished metal, brass, copper or silver. The *man with the inkhorn* has to write in the Book of Life the names of those who shall be marked. The metaphor is from the custom of registering the names of the Israelites in public rolls. Cp. Ex. xxxii. 33 ; Ps. lxix. 28 ; Isai. iv. 3 ; Philip. iv. 3 ; Rev. iii. 5.

3. *cherub*] The singular is put collectively for the *Cherubim,* which were upon the mercy-seat of the Ark in the Holy of Holies, the proper seat of the glory of the Lord in the midst of Israel. God is represented as *arising* from between the Cherubim to scatter His enemies (Num. x. 35).

4. Mercy precedes judgment. So in the case of Sodom (Gen. xix.), and in the last day (Luke xxi. 18, 28 ; Rev. vii. 1). This accords with the eschatological character of the predictions in this chapter (see Introduction, p. 323).

a mark] Lit. *Tau,* the name of the last letter of the Hebr. alphabet. The old form of the letter was that of a cross. The Jews have interpreted this sign variously, some considering that *Tau,* being the last of the Hebrew letters, and so closing the alphabet, denoted completeness, and thus the mark indicated the completeness of the sorrow for sin in those upon whom it was placed. Others again observed that *Tau* was the first letter of To-rah (*the Law*) and that the foreheads were marked as of men obedient to the Law. Christians, noting the resemblance of this letter in its most ancient form to a cross, have seen herein a reference to the cross with which Christians were signed. The custom for heathen gods and their votaries to bear certain marks furnishes instances, in which God was pleased to employ symbolism, generally in use, to express higher and Diviner truth. The sign of the cross in Baptism is an outward sign of the designation of God's elect, who at the last day shall be exempted from the destruction of the ungodly (Matt. xxiv. 22, 31).

6. *begin at my sanctuary*] The first to be punished were those who had brought idolatry nearest to the Holy Place. The "ancient men," *i.e.,* the twenty-five men who had stood with their backs to the altar (viii. 16) were the first to be slain.

7. *Defile the house*] By filling the Temple and its courts with the bodies of the slain. See Num. xix. 11.

8 forth, and slew in the city. ¶ And it came to pass, while they
were slaying them, and I was left, that I [k]fell upon my face,
and cried, and said, [l]Ah Lord God! wilt thou destroy all the
residue of Israel in thy pouring out of thy fury upon Jerusalem?

9 ¶ Then said he unto me, The iniquity of the house of Israel and
Judah *is* exceeding great, and [m]the land is [1]full of blood, and
the city full of [2]perverseness: for they say, [n]The LORD hath

10 forsaken the earth, and [o]the LORD seeth not. And as for me
also, mine [p]eye shall not spare, neither will I have pity, *but* [q]I

11 will recompense their way upon their head. And, behold, the
man clothed with linen, which *had* the inkhorn by his side,
[3]reported the matter, saying, I have done as thou hast commanded me.

CHAP. 10. THEN I looked, and, behold, in the [a]firmament that
was above the head of the cherubims there appeared over them
as it were a sapphire stone, as the appearance of the likeness of

2 a throne. [b]And he spake unto the man clothed with linen, and
said, Go in between the wheels, *even* under the cherub, and fill
[4]thine hand with [c]coals of fire from between the cherubims, and

3 [d]scatter *them* over the city. And he went in in my sight. Now
the cherubims stood on the right side of the house, when the

4 man went in; and the cloud filled the inner court. [e]Then the
glory of the LORD [5]went up from the cherub, *and stood* over
the threshold of the house; and [f]the house was filled with the
cloud, and the court was full of the brightness of the LORD's

5 glory. And the [g]sound of the cherubims' wings was heard
even to the outer court, as [h]the voice of the Almighty God when

6 he speaketh. ¶ And it came to pass, *that* when he had commanded the man clothed with linen, saying, Take fire from
between the wheels, from between the cherubims; then he went

7 in, and stood beside the wheels. And *one* cherub [6]stretched
forth his hand from between the cherubims unto the fire that
was between the cherubims, and took *thereof*, and put *it* into
the hands of *him that was* clothed with linen: who took *it*, and

8 went out. [i]And there appeared in the cherubims the form of a

9 man's hand under their wings. ¶ [k]And when I looked, behold
the four wheels by the cherubims, one wheel by one cherub,
and another wheel by another cherub: and the appearance of

10 the wheels *was* as the colour of a [l]beryl stone. And *as for* their

Marginal references:
[k] Num. 14. 5.
[l] ch. 11. 13.
[m] 2 Kin. 21. 16.
ch. 8. 17.
[n] ch. 8. 12.
[o] Ps. 10. 11. Isai. 29. 15.
[p] ch. 5. 11.
[q] ch. 11. 21.
[a] ch. 1. 22.
[b] ch. 9. 2, 3.
[c] ch. 1. 13.
[d] See Rev. 8. 5.
[e] See ver. 18. ch. 1. 28.
[f] 1 Kin. 8. 10, 11. ch. 43. 5.
[g] ch. 1. 24.
[h] Ps. 29. 3.
[i] ch. 1. 8. ver. 21.
[k] ch. 1. 15.
[l] ch. 1. 16.

[1] Heb. *filled with.*
[2] Or, *wresting* of judgment.
[3] Heb. *returned the word.*
Heb. *the hollow of thine hand.*
[5] Heb. *was lifted up.*
[6] Heb. *sent forth.*

---

8. *left*] The prophet was left alone, all
who had been around him were slain.

X. As in ch. i., the vision of the glory of
the Lord, the particulars given identifying
the two visions.

2. *he spake*] The person enthroned.

the cherub] The particular cherub who
was to hand the coals to destroy (Ps. cxx.
4; Isai. x. 16; Rev. xv. 8).

3. *on the right side*] On the South (xlvii.
2). The idolatries had been seen on the
North side. On the South stood the *Cherubim* ready to receive and bear away the
glory of the Lord.

4. A repetition of ix. 3. **Now the glory
of the Lord had gone up from the cherub
to the threshold of the house.** Verses 4—

6 describe what had occurred before the
man went in (*v.* 3).

5. *the Almighty God*] El Shaddai; cp.
Gen. xvii. 1 note.

7. *one cherub*] **The** *cherub* who stood next
the wheel by the side of which the man stood.
The representative of the priestly office now
gives up his post of reconciliation, and becomes simply a minister of wrath; another
sign that God will turn from Jerusalem.

8. An explanation following upon the
mention of the *hand*. It is characteristic of
this chapter that the narrative is interrupted by explanatory comments. The
narrative is contained in *vv.* 1—3, 6, 7, 13,
15 (first clause), 18, 19; the other verses
contain the *interposed explanations.*

appearances, they four had one likeness, as if a wheel had been
11 in the midst of a wheel. [m]When they went, they went upon [m] ch. 1. 17.
their four sides; they turned not as they went, but to the place
whither the head looked they followed it; they turned not as
12 they went. And their whole [1]body, and their backs, and their
hands, and their wings, and [n]the wheels, *were* full of eyes round [n] ch. 1. 18.
13 about, *even* the wheels that they four had. As for the wheels,
14 [2]it was cried unto them in my hearing, O wheel. [o]And every [o] ch. 1. 6, 10.
one had four faces: the first face *was* the face of a cherub, and
the second face *was* the face of a man, and the third the face of
15 a lion, and the fourth the face of an eagle. And the cherubims
were lifted up. This *is* [p]the living creature that I saw by the [p] ch. 1. 5.
16 river of Chebar. [q]And when the cherubims went, the wheels [q] ch. 1. 19.
went by them: and when the cherubims lifted up their wings
to mount up from the earth, the same wheels also turned not
17 from beside them. [r]When they stood, *these* stood; and when [r] ch. 1. 12, 20, 21.
they were lifted up, *these* lifted up themselves *also*: for the spirit
18 [3]of the living creature *was* in them. ¶ Then [s]the glory of the [s] ver. 4.
LORD [t]departed from off the threshold of the house, and stood [t] Hos. 9. 12.
19 over the cherubims. And [u]the cherubims lifted up their wings, [u] ch. 11. 22.
and mounted up from the earth in my sight: when they went
out, the wheels also *were* beside them, and *every one* stood at
the door of the east gate of the LORD'S house; and the glory of
20 the God of Israel *was* over them above. ¶ [x]This *is* the living [x] ch. 1. 22. ver. 15.

[1] Heb. *flesh*. [2] Or, *they were called in my hearing, wheel*, or, *galgal*. [3] Or, *of life*.

11. *the head*] Either "the leading wheel which the others followed," or more probably, the head of a cherub (one for all), the description passing from the wheels to the Cherubim (*v.* 12).

13. According to the marginal rendering the present verse refers back to *vv.* 2 and 6, and tells us that the name *galgal, a rolling thing* (cp. Isai. xvii. 13), was given to the wheels in the seer's hearing. But taking *v.* 14 as a description, and reading *v.* 15 immediately after *v.* 13, the meaning is clear. In the hearing of the seer a voice calls upon the wheels, and, obedient to the call, the Cherubim are lifted up and the wheels roll on. The word *galgal* would be better rendered "chariot" instead of *wheel*; "chariot" representing very well the collection of *wheels.*

14. *the first face...*] **The face of the first was the face of the cherub, and the face of the second was the face of a man, and the third the face of a lion, and the fourth the face of an eagle.** Of the four faces of each cherub, the seer names only one—the face looking in the direction in which that cherub leads the motion of the chariot. The face of the cherub which presented itself to the seer was that of *an ox.* When he looking northward first saw the chariot the *ox-face* was on the left side (i. 10). This would make the *ox-face* look eastward, and it is not unlikely that the man might approach the chariot from the south-eastern part of the inner court.

16, 17 are a repetition of the general description of the nature and connexion of the various parts of the vision, and this is the more appropriate as shewing why they were regarded as *one living creature* (*v* 15). The attributes here assigned to them shew that they were pervaded by one will—*the spirit of the living creature* (others, as in margin, *the spirit of life*) *was in them.*

19. The Cherubim (or chariot) had stood first on the threshold of the Temple-door, and there received the glory of the Lord. They then lifted their wings, rose, and left the Temple by *the East gate* of the outer court at *the entrance* of which they now for a time stood. It was by the East gate of the outer court that the glory of the Lord returned to the new Temple (xliii. 4).

and every one stood] Or, *and* **they** *stood.* The Cherubim and wheels are viewed as *one living creature.*

20. In this departure of the glory of the Lord from the Temple, the seer recognizes for the first time the full meaning of the vision which he had seen on the banks of Chebar (ch. i.). What he had seen there did indeed imply that Jehovah had forsaken His house; but now this is made clear. The Glory has left the Holy of Holies, has appeared in the court, has been enthroned on the Living Four, and with them has departed from the Temple. It is now clear that these Four (in form similar to, yet differing from, the Cherubim of the Temple) are indeed the Cherubim, in the midst of whom the Lord dwelleth.

v ch. 1. 1.
z ch. 1. 6.
ver. 14.
a ch. 1. 8.
ver. 8.
b ch. 1. 10.
c ch. 1. 12.

a ch. 3. 12.
& 8. 3.
b ch. 10. 19.
1 See ch. 8.
16.

d ch. 12. 22.
2 Pet. 3. 4.
e See Jer. 1.
13.
f ch. 2. 2.
& 3. 24.

g ch. 7. 23.
& 22. 3, 4.

h ch. 24. 3.
Mic. 3. 3.
i ver. 9.

k ch. 5. 8.
l 2 Kin. 25.
19, 20, 21.
Jer. 39. 6.
m 1 Kin. 8.
65.
n Ps. 9. 16.
ch. 6. 7.
o See ver. 3.

creature that I saw under the God of Israel *v*by the river of
21 Chebar; and I knew that they *were* the cherubims. *z*Every
one had four faces apiece, and every one four wings; *a*and the
22 likeness of the hands of a man *was* under their wings. And
*b*the likeness of their faces *was* the same faces which I saw by
the river of Chebar, their appearances and themselves: *c*they
went every one straight forward.

Chap. 11. MOREOVER *a*the spirit lifted me up, and brought me
unto *b*the east gate of the Lord's house, which looketh eastward: and behold *c* at the door of the gate five and twenty men;
among whom I saw Jaazaniah the son of Azur, and Pelatiah
2 the son of Benaiah, princes of the people. Then said he unto
me, Son of man, these *are* the men that devise mischief, and
3 give wicked counsel in this city. Which say, *1* It is not *d*near:
let us build houses: *e*this *city is* the caldron, and we *be* the
4 flesh. Therefore prophesy against them, prophesy, O son of man.
5 ¶ And *f* the Spirit of the Lord fell upon me, and said unto me,
Speak; Thus saith the Lord; Thus have ye said, O house of
Israel: for I know the things that come into your mind, *every*
6 one *of* them. *g*Ye have multiplied your slain in this city, and
7 ye have filled the streets thereof with the slain. Therefore thus
saith the Lord God; *h*Your slain whom ye have laid in the
midst of it, they *are* the flesh, and this *city is* the caldron: *i*but
8 I will bring you forth out of the midst of it. Ye have feared
the sword; and I will bring a sword upon you, saith the Lord
9 God. And I will bring you out of the midst thereof, and deliver
you into the hands of strangers, and *k*will execute judgments
10 among you. *l*Ye shall fall by the sword; I will judge you in
*m*the border of Israel; *n*and ye shall know that I *am* the Lord.
11 *o*This *city* shall not be your caldron, neither shall ye be the
flesh in the midst thereof; *but* I will judge you in the border of

1 Or, It is *not* for us *to build houses near.*

XI. **1.** *the gate*] The gate of the Temple-
court. The *gate* was the place of judgment.
five and twenty men] Not the same men
as in viii. 16. There they were representatives of the *priests*, here of the *princes*.
The number is, no doubt, symbolical, made
up, probably, of twenty-four men and the
king. The number twenty-four points to
the tribes of undivided Israel.

Jaazaniah...Pelatiah] We know nothing
more of these men. The former name was
probably common at that time (viii. 11).
In these two names there is an allusion to
the false hopes which they upheld. *Jaazaniah* (Jehovah listeneth) *son of Azur* (the
Helper); *Pelatiah* (God rescueth) *son of
Benaiah* (Jehovah buildeth). In the latter
case death (*v.* 13) turned the allusion into
bitter irony.

3. It is *not near*] In contradiction to
vii. 2.

let us build houses] To *build houses* implies
a sense of security. Jeremiah bade the
exiles *build houses* in a foreign land because
they would not soon quit it (Jer. xxix. 5;
xxxv. 7). These false counsellors promised
to their countrymen a sure and permanent

abode in the city which God had doomed
to destruction. No need, they said, to go
far for safety; you are perfectly safe at
home. The Hebrew, however, is, difficult:
lit. it means, It is *not near to build houses,*
which may be explained as spoken in
mockery of such counsel as that of Jeremiah: matters have not gone so far as to
necessitate *house-building* in a foreign land.
The same idea is expressed by the image of
the *caldron :* whatever devastation may rage
around the city, we are safe within its walls,
as flesh within a caldron is unburnt by the
surrounding fire (cp. xxiv. 6).

7. All that shall remain in the city are
the buried dead. Bloodshed and murder
were at this time rife in Jerusalem, and
these were among the chief crimes that
were bringing down judgment upon the
city. All the inhabitants that should yet
survive were destined to be carried away
into exile.

10. *in the border of Israel*] Hamath was
the northern border of Israel (marg. ref.).
At Riblah in Hamath the king of Babylon
judged and condemned Zedekiah and the
princes of Judah (Jer. lii. 9, 10).

12 Israel: and [p]ye shall know that I *am* the LORD: [1]for ye have
not walked in my statutes, neither executed my judgments, but
[q]have done after the manners of the heathen that *are* round
13 about you. ¶And it came to pass, when I prophesied, that
[r]Pelatiah the son of Benaiah died. Then [s]fell I down upon my
face, and cried with a loud voice, and said, Ah Lord GOD! wilt
14 thou make a full end of the remnant of Israel? ¶Again the
15 word of the LORD came unto me, saying, Son of man, thy
brethren, *even* thy brethren, the men of thy kindred, and all
the house of Israel wholly, *are* they unto whom the inhabitants
of Jerusalem have said, Get you far from the LORD: unto us
16 is this land given in possession. Therefore say, Thus saith
the Lord GOD; Although I have cast them far off among
the heathen, and although I have scattered them among the
countries, [t]yet will I be to them as a little sanctuary in the
17 countries where they shall come. Therefore say, Thus saith
the Lord GOD; [u]I will even gather you from the people, and
assemble you out of the countries where ye have been scattered,
18 and I will give you the land of Israel. And they shall come
thither, and [x]they shall take away all the detestable things
19 thereof and all the abominations thereof from thence. And [y]I
will give them one heart, and I will put [z]a new spirit within
you; and I will take [a]the stony heart out of their flesh, and
20 will give them an heart of flesh: [b]that they may walk in my
statutes, and keep mine ordinances, and do them: [c]and they
21 shall be my people, and I will be their God. But *as for them*
whose heart walketh after the heart of their detestable things
and their abominations, [d]I will recompense their way upon
22 their own heads, saith the Lord GOD. ¶Then did the cherubims [e]lift up their wings, and the wheels beside them; and the
23 glory of the God of Israel *was* over them above. And [f]the
glory of the LORD went up from the midst of the city, and
stood [g]upon the mountain [h]which *is* on the east side of the

[p] ver. 10.
[q] Lev. 18. 3. Deut. 12. 30, 31. ch. 8. 10.
[r] ver. 1. Acts 5. 5.
[s] ch. 9. 8.
[t] Ps. 90. 1. & 91. 9. Isai. 8. 14.
[u] Jer. 24. 5. ch. 28. 25.
[x] ch. 37. 23.
[y] Jer. 32. 39. ch. 36. 26. See Zeph. 3. 9.
[z] Ps. 51. 10. Jer. 31. 33 ch. 18. 31.
[a] Zech. 7. 12.
[b] Ps. 105. 45.
[c] Jer. 24. 7. ch. 36. 28.
[d] ch. 9. 10. & 22. 31.
[e] ch. 1. 19.
[f] ch. 8. 4.
[g] See Zech. 14. 4.
[h] ch. 43. 2.

[1] Or, *which have not walked.*

---

13. The death of Pelatiah was communicated in this vision, which represented ideally the idolatry in which Pelatiah had actually been foremost.

15. *thy kindred*] The original word is derived from a root, suggesting the ideas of *redeeming* and *avenging* as connected with the bond of *kindred.* The word, therefore, conveys here a special reproach to the proud Jews, who have been so ready to cast off the claims of blood-relationship, and at the same time a hope of restoration to those who have been rudely thrown aside.

16. *as a little sanctuary*] Rather, **I will be to them for a little while a sanctuary.** The blessing was provisional, they were to look forward to a blessing more complete. For a little while they were to be satisfied with God's special Presence in a foreign land, but they were to look forward to a renewal of His Presence in the restored Temple of Jerusalem. *Sanctuary* means here strictly the Holy Place, the Tabernacle of the Most High: Jehovah will Himself be to the exiles in the place of the local sanctuary, in which the Jews of Jerusalem so much prided themselves (cp. marg. reff.). Here is the germ from which is developed xl.—xlviii., the picture of the kingdom of God in its new form.

19–21. Cp. Rev. xxi. The identity of thought and language in Ezekiel, predicting the new kingdom of Israel, and in St John, foretelling the kingdom of heaven, forces upon us the conclusion that the prophecy of Ezekiel has an ultimate reference to that climax which St. John plainly indicates.

19. *one heart*] So long as the Israelites were distracted by the service of many gods, such unity was impossible; but now, when they shall have taken away the *abominations* from the land, they shall be united in heart to serve the true God.

stony heart...heart of flesh] The heart unnaturally hardened, and the heart reawakened to feelings proper to man.

23. *the mountain which is on the east side of the city*] The Mount of Olives. The Rabbis commenting on this passage said

i ch. 8. 3.

24 city. ¶Afterwards *i*the spirit took me up, and brought me in
   a vision by the Spirit of God into Chaldea, to them of the cap-
25 tivity. So the vision that I had seen went up from me. Then
   I spake unto them of the captivity all the things that the LORD
   had shewed me.

CHAP. 12. THE word of the LORD also came unto me, saying,

a ch. 2. 3.
b Isai. 6. 9.
Jer. 5. 21.
Matt. 13.
13, 14.
c ch. 2. 5.

2 ¶Son of man, thou dwellest in the midst of *a*a rebellious house,
   which *b*have eyes to see, and see not; they have ears to hear,
3 and hear not: *c*for they *are* a rebellious house. Therefore,
   thou son of man, prepare thee ¹stuff for removing, and remove
   by day in their sight; and thou shalt remove from thy place to
   another place in their sight: it may be they will consider,
4 though they *be* a rebellious house. Then shalt thou bring forth
   thy stuff by day in their sight, as stuff for removing: and thou
   shalt go forth at even in their sight, ²as they that go forth into
5 captivity. ³Dig thou through the wall in their sight, and carry
6 out thereby. In their sight shalt thou bear *it* upon *thy* shoulders, *and* carry *it* forth in the twilight: thou shalt cover thy

d Isai. 8. 18.
ch. 4. 3.

   face, that thou see not the ground: *d*for I have set thee *for* a
7 sign unto the house of Israel. ¶And I did so as I was commanded: I brought forth my stuff by day, as stuff for cap
   tivity, and in the even I ⁴digged through the wall with mine
   hand; I brought *it* forth in the twilight, *and* I bare *it* upon *my*
8 shoulder in their sight. ¶And in the morning came the word of

e ch. 2. 5.
f ch. 17. 12.
g Mal. 1. 1.

9 the LORD unto me, saying, Son of man, hath not the house of
   Israel, *e*the rebellious house, said unto thee, *f*What doest thou?
10 Say thou unto them, Thus saith the Lord GOD; This *g*burden
   concerneth the prince in Jerusalem, and all the house of Israel

h ver. 6.
i 2 Kin. 25.
4, 5, 7.
k Jer. 39. 4.

11 that *are* among them. Say, *h*I *am* your sign: like as I have
   done, so shall it be done unto them : ⁵*i*they shall remove *and* go
12 into captivity. And *k*the prince that *is* among them shall bear

---

¹ Or, *instruments.*   *of captivity.*   ⁴ Heb. *digged for me.*
² Heb. *as the goings forth*   ³ Heb. *Dig for thee.*   ⁵ Heb. *by removing go into captivity.*

---

the Shechinah retired to this Mount, and
there for three years called in vain to the
people with human voice that they should
repent. On that mountain Christ stood,
when He wept over the fair city so soon to
be utterly destroyed. From that mountain
he descended, amid loud Hosannas, to enter
the city and Temple as a Judge.

XII. 2. Cp. Deut. i. 26; marg. ref.;
Rom. x. 21. The repetition of such words
from age to age, shows that the prophet's
words are intended to reach beyond the
generation in which he lived.

3. *stuff*] Raiment, vessels, and the like.
The *removing* was to be of the kind that
accompanied exile. The whole account of
this transaction marks it as a real act.
The prophet was to be *a sign* to his countrymen, and the *exiles* as well as those that
remained in Judæa had need to be taught
this lesson, for though themselves far away,
they looked to Jerusalem as their home, and
were scarcely less eager for its safety than
the inhabitants themselves.

4. The particulars which Ezekiel here
foretold actually occurred (cp. 2 K. xxv.

4 : Jer. xxxix. 4) ; but at this time Zedekiah seemed to be prosperous, and the Jews
at Jerusalem expected, it is clear, a long
continuance of his prosperity (see xvii. 1
note).

The prophetical character of the passage
is undoubted (the prophet is declared to be
a sign, v. 6)—the genuineness of the Book and
of the position of the passage in the Book, are
beyond dispute ; in the historical event we
have an exact fulfilment. The only legitimate
inference is that the prophet received his
knowledge from above.

6. *thou shalt cover thy face*] A sign of
mourning (see xxiv. 17) ; also of Zedekiah's
blindness (*v.* 12).

7. In the evening the prophet was to
return to the wall, break through it, and
transport the goods from the inside to the
outside of the city.

10. *burden*] A word used to indicate a
prediction of woe to be borne by some individual or people (Isai. xiii. 1 note). Ezekiel,
bearing his *stuff* on his shoulder was a sign
of the weight of calamity coming upon king
and people.

upon *his* shoulder in the twilight, and shall go forth : they shall dig through the wall to carry out thereby : he shall cover his

13 face, that he see not the ground with *his* eyes. My *l*net also will I spread upon him, and he shall be taken in my snare: and *m*I will bring him to Babylon *to* the land of the Chaldeans; yet

14 shall he not see it, though he shall die there. And *n*I will scatter toward every wind all that *are* about him to help him, and all his bands; and *o*I will draw out the sword after them.

15 *p*And they shall know that I *am* the LORD, when I shall scatter them among the nations, and disperse them in the countries.

16 *q*But I will leave *1*a few men of them from the sword, from the famine, and from the pestilence; that they may declare all their abominations among the heathen whither they come; and they

17 shall know that I *am* the LORD. ¶ Moreover the word of the

18 LORD came to me, saying, ¶ Son of man, *r*eat thy bread with quaking, and drink thy water with trembling and with careful-

19 ness; and say unto the people of the land, Thus saith the Lord GOD of the inhabitants of Jerusalem, *and* of the land of Israel; They shall eat their bread with carefulness, and drink their water with astonishment, that her land may *s*be desolate from *2*all that is therein, *t*because of the violence of all them that

20 dwell therein. And the cities that are inhabited shall be laid waste, and the land shall be desolate; and ye shall know

21 that I *am* the LORD. ¶ And the word of the LORD came unto

22 me, saying, ¶ Son of man, what *is* that proverb *that* ye have in the land of Israel, saying, *u*The days are prolonged, and every

23 vision faileth ? Tell them therefore, Thus saith the Lord GOD; I will make this proverb to cease, and they shall no more use it as a proverb in Israel; but say unto them, *x*The days are at hand,

24 and the effect of every vision. For *y*there shall be no more any *z*vain vision nor flattering divination within the house of Israel.

25 For I *am* the LORD: I will speak, and *a*the word that I shall speak shall come to pass; it shall be no more prolonged : for in your days, O rebellious house, will I say the word, and will

26 perform it, saith the Lord GOD. ¶ Again the word of the LORD

27 came to me, saying, ¶ *b*Son of man, behold, *they of* the house of Israel say, The vision that he seeth *is* *c*for many days *to come*,

28 and he prophesieth of the times *that are* far off. *d*Therefore say unto them, Thus saith the Lord GOD; There shall none of my words be prolonged any more, but the word which I have spoken shall be done, saith the Lord GOD.

l Job 19. 6.
Lam. 1. 13.
m 2 Kin.25.7.
ch. 17. 16.
n 2 Kin. 25.
4, 5.
ch. 5. 10.
o ch. 5. 2.
p Ps. 9. 16.
ch. 6. 7, 14.

q ch. 6. 8.

r ch. 4. 16.

s Zech. 7. 14.
t Ps. 107. 34.

u ver. 27.
ch. 11. 3.

x Joel 2. 1.
Zeph. 1. 14.
y ch. 13. 23.
z Lam. 2. 14.
a Isai. 55. 11.
Dan. 9. 12.
Luke 21. 33.

b ver. 22.
c 2 Pet. 3. 4.
d ver. 23. 25.

---

[1] Heb. *men of number*.   [2] Heb. *the fulness thereof*.

---

13. Cp. Jer. lii. 9 &c.

16. *few*] Lit. as in margin ; so few, that they can easily be counted (Isai. x. 19). The few who should escape destruction should make known to all among whom they should dwell how great had been the wickedness of the people, how just their punishment.

18. Here the sign is the exhibition of such terror as the danger of a siege creates.

19. *the people of the land*] Chaldæa.

of the inhabitants] In respect to *the inhabitants*.

desolate from all that is therein] *i. e.* stripped of all its inhabitants and of all its wealth.

19, 20. At one and the same time, Jeremiah was prophesying in Jerusalem, and Ezekiel in Chaldæa; the prophecies of the former were sent to the exiles, and those of Ezekiel to the dwellers at Jerusalem, that the guiding hand of One God in different places might be made clear (Jerome).

21-28. As in ch. vii., the nearness of the judgment is foretold.

22. *The land of Israel* is put generally for the land where the children of Israel dwelt, whether at home, or in exile. There was prevalent a disregard for the true prophets, which is ever followed by a recognition of the false. First, the true prophet is re-

CHAP. 13. AND the word of the LORD came unto me, saying,

2 ¶ Son of man, prophesy against the prophets of Israel that pro-

a ver. 17.
b Jer. 14. 14.

phesy, and say thou unto *a* ¹them that prophesy out of their

3 own *b*hearts, Hear ye the word of the LORD; Thus saith the
Lord GOD; Woe unto the foolish prophets, that ²follow their

4 own spirit, ³and have seen nothing! O Israel, thy prophets

c Cant. 2. 15.
d Ps. 106.
23. 30.
ch. 22. 30.
e ch. 12. 24.

5 are *c*like the foxes in the deserts. Ye *d*have not gone up into
the ⁴gaps, neither ⁵made up the hedge for the house of Israel

6 to stand in the battle in the day of the LORD. *e*They have seen
vanity and lying divination, saying, The LORD saith: and the
LORD hath not sent them: and they have made *others* to hope

7 that they would confirm the word. Have ye not seen a vain
vision, and have ye not spoken a lying divination, whereas ye

8 say, The LORD saith *it*; albeit I have not spoken? ¶ Therefore
thus saith the Lord GOD; Because ye have spoken vanity, and
seen lies, therefore, behold, I *am* against you, saith the Lord

9 GOD. And mine hand shall be upon the prophets that see
vanity, and that divine lies:.they shall not be in the ⁶assembly

f Ezra 2.
59. 62.
Neh. 7. 5.
Ps. 69. 28.
g ch. 20. 38.
h ch. 11. 10,
12.
i Jer. 6. 14.
& 8. 11.
k ch. 22. 28.
l ch. 38. 22.

of my people, *f*neither shall they be written in the writing of
the house of Israel, *g*neither shall they enter into the land of

10 Israel; *h*and ye shall know that I *am* the Lord GOD. ¶ Because,
even because they have seduced my people, saying, *i*Peace;
and *there was* no peace; and one built up ⁷a wall, and, lo,

11 others *k*daubed it with untempered *morter:* say unto them
which daub *it* with untempered *morter*, that it shall fall: *l*there
shall be an overflowing shower; and ye, O great hailstones,

12 shall fall; and a stormy wind shall rend *it*. Lo, when the wall

---

¹ Heb. *them that are pro-*   ² Heb. *walk after.*   ⁵ Heb. *hedged the hedge.*
phets out of their own   ³ Or, *and things which*   ⁶ Or. *secret*, or, *council.*
hearts.   *they have not seen.*   ⁷ Or, *a slight wall.*
                               ⁴ Or, *breaches.*

---

jected because it is thought that his prophecies fail. Then men persuade themselves that if the prophecy be true it
respects some distant time, and that the
men of the present generation need not
disturb themselves about it. Cp. Jer. i.
11; Amos vi. 3; Matt. xxiv. 43; 1 Thess.
v. 2; 2 Pet. iii. 4. Against both these
delusions Ezekiel is commissioned to protest, and so to lead the way to his condemnation of his countrymen for their blind
reliance on false prophets.

XIII. The identity of phrases and ideas
of this chapter with Jer. xxiii. leads to the
conclusion that Ezekiel took up a well-
known prophecy to enforce and apply it to
his companions in exile. They probably
had read Jeremiah's words as referring to
others than themselves.

3. *that follow...nothing*] Better in marg.
A *true* prophet (like Ezekiel) spoke *the
word of the Lord*, and declared what he had
seen *in the visions of God*. These pre-
tenders are stigmatized in scorn "prophets
out of their own hearts," "seers of what
they have not seen."

4. *in the deserts*] Foxes find a home among
ruins &c. (Lam. v. 18). So the prophets
find their profit in the ruin of their country.

5. *for*] Or, before. In a time of siege when

there are *gaps* or *breaches* in the walls, it is
the part of the leaders to go up to defend
them, and to throw up works to stop the in-
road of the enemy. Jehovah is now assailing
His people as an enemy (cp. Isai. lxiii. 10;
Job xvi. 11–13), and where are those who
claim to be prophets, leaders of the people?

6. *and they have made* others &c.] Rather,
"and they hope for the confirmation of
their word." They come to believe their
own lies.

9. *assembly*] Here "the congregation of
the people." These false prophets were
to be struck off from "the writing" or, the
rolls, in which the names of all Israelites
were registered (cp. Ps. lxxxvii. 6; Ex.
xxxii. 32); and therefore when the restoration
(xi. 17) shall take place. these men shall not
have part in it.

10. *wall*] A partition wall; in *v.* 12, the
word used is the usual word for the outer
wall of a house or city. The fall of the partition wall would perhaps involve the fall
of the whole house.

untempered morter] Or, *whited plaster*, employed to patch up a wall, so as to give it an
appearance (without the reality) of strength
and beauty. Cp. Matt. xxiii. 27. In the
original there is a play upon a word rendered
"folly" in Jer. xxiii. 13.

is fallen, shall it not be said unto you, Where *is* the daubing
13 wherewith ye have daubed *it?* Therefore thus saith the Lord
God; I will even rend *it* with a stormy wind in my fury; and
there shall be an overflowing shower in mine anger, and great
14 hailstones in *my* fury to consume it. So will I break down the
wall that ye have daubed with untempered *morter,* and bring it
down to the ground, so that the foundation thereof shall be discovered, and it shall fall, and ye shall be consumed in the midst
15 thereof: ^mand ye shall know that I *am* the Lord. Thus will I
accomplish my wrath upon the wall, and upon them that have
daubed it with untempered *morter,* and will say unto you, The
16 wall *is* no *more,* neither they that daubed it; to *wit,* the prophets
of Israel which prophesy concerning Jerusalem, and which ⁿsee
visions of peace for her, and *there is* no peace, saith the Lord God.
17 ¶ Likewise, thou son of man, ^oset thy face against the daughters of thy people, ^pwhich prophesy out of their own heart; and
18 prophesy thou against them, and say, Thus saith the Lord God;
Woe to the *women* that sew pillow**s** to all ¹armholes, and make
kerchiefs upon the head of every stature to hunt souls! Will
19 ye ^qhunt the souls of my people, and will ye save the souls alive
that come unto you? And will ye pollute me among my people
^rfor handfuls of barley and for pieces of bread, to slay the
souls that should not die, and to save the souls alive that should
not live, by your lying to my people that hear *your* lies?
20 ¶ Wherefore thus saith the Lord God; Behold, I *am* against
your pillows, wherewith ye there hunt the souls ²to make *them*
fly, and I will tear them from your arms, and will let the souls
21 go, *even* the souls that ye hunt to make *them* fly. Your kerchiefs also will I tear, and deliver my people out of your hand,
and they shall be no more in your hand to be hunted; ^sand ye
22 shall know that I *am* the Lord. Because with lies ye have
made the heart of the righteous sad, whom I have not made

^m ver. 9. 21.
ch. 14. 8.

ⁿ Jer. 6. 14.
& 28. 9.

^o ch. 20. 46.
& 21. 2.
^p ver. 2.

^q 2 Pet. 2. 14.

^r See Prov.
28. 21.
Mic. 3. 5.

^s ver. 9.

¹ Or, *elbows.*   ² Or, *into gardens.*

17-23. A rebuke to the false prophetesses, and a declaration that God will confound them, and deliver their victims from
their snares. Women were sometimes inspired by the true God, as were Miriam, Deborah, Hannah, and Huldah; but an order
of prophetesses was unknown among the
people of God, and the existence of such a
class in the last days of the kings of Judah
was a fresh instance of declension into
heathen usages.

vv. **18-21**] Render thus :—*Woe to the*
women that put charms on every finger-
joint, that set veils upon heads of every
height to ensnare souls. *Will ye* ensnare
the souls of my people, and keep your own
souls alive, and will ye profane my name
among my people for handfuls of barley and
pieces of bread, to *slay the souls that should*
not die, and to keep alive *the souls that*
should not live, by lying to my people who
listen to *a lie? Wherefore thus saith the*
Lord God, Behold I will come upon your
charms, where ye are ensnaring the
souls like birds ; *and I will tear them from*
your arms and will let the souls go free, *even*

the souls which ye are ensnaring like
birds. *Your* veils *also will I tear, and they*
deliver my people out of your hand, and they
shall be no more in your hand to be ensnared ;
and ye shall know that I am the Lord.

Most ancient interpreters and many
modern have understood the *pillows* (or
charms) and *kerchiefs* (or veils), as ap-
pliances to which the sorcerers had resort
in order to attract notice. The veil was a
conspicuous ornament in the East,—women
whatever their "stature" (or, height) putting
them on—and it was worn by magicians in
order to seem more mysterious and awful.

19. *pollute me*] Profane Me by your false
words, which ye pretend to be from Me.

handfuls of barley] Such were the gifts
with which men. used to approach a seer
(cp. 1 Sam. ix. 7, 8 : 1 K. xiv. 3).

20. *to make them fly*] If the marginal reading *into gardens* be adopted, it must mean,
Ye entice men to the gardens or groves,
where magical arts are practised. That
groves were used for this purpose and for
idolatrous rites is notorious.

t Jer. 23. 14.

u ch. 12. 24.
Mic. 3. 6.
x ch. 14. 8.
& 15. 7.

a ch. 20. 1.

b ch. 7. 19.
ver. 4. 7.
c 2 Kin. 3. 13.

d Lev. 17. 10.
Jer. 44. 11.
e Num. 26. 10.
Deut. 28. 37.
f ch. 6. 7.

g Job 12. 16.
Jer. 4. 10.
2 Thess. 2. 11.

sad; and *t*strengthened the hands of the wicked, that he should not return from his wicked way, [12]by promising him life: 23 therefore *u*ye shall see no more vanity, nor divine divinations: for I will deliver my people out of your hand: *x*and ye shall know that I *am* the LORD.

CHAP. 14. THEN *a*came certain of the elders of Israel unto me, and 2 sat before me. And the word of the LORD came unto me, say-3 ing, Son of man, these men have set up their idols in their heart, and put *b*the stumblingblock of their iniquity before 4 their face: *c*should I be enquired of at all by them? Therefore speak unto them, and say unto them, Thus saith the Lord GOD; Every man of the house of Israel that setteth up his idols in his heart, and putteth the stumblingblock of his iniquity before his face, and cometh to the prophet; I the LORD will answer him 5 that cometh according to the multitude of his idols; that I may take the house of Israel in their own heart, because they are all 6 estranged from me through their idols. Therefore say unto the house of Israel, Thus saith the Lord GOD; Repent, and turn [3]*yourselves* from your idols; and turn away your faces from all 7 your abominations. For every one of the house of Israel, or of the stranger that sojourneth in Israel, which separateth himself from me, and setteth up his idols in his heart, and putteth the stumblingblock of his iniquity before his face, and cometh to a prophet to inquire of him concerning me; I the LORD will 8 answer him by myself: and *d*I will set my face against that man, and will make him a *e*sign and a proverb, and I will cut him off from the midst of my people; *f*and ye shall know that 9 I *am* the LORD. ¶ And if the prophet be deceived when he hath spoken a thing, I the LORD *g*have deceived that prophet, and I will stretch out my hand upon him, and will destroy him from 10 the midst of my people Israel. And they shall bear the punishment of their iniquity: the punishment of the prophet shall be

[1] Or, *that I should save his life.*   [2] Heb. *by quickening him.*   [3] Or, others.

XIV. 1–11. This prophecy is a reproof of those who consult the false prophets. Some of the chief exiles come to Ezekiel as to one who has authority; but he, endowed with the genuine prophetic spirit, sees deep into their hearts, and finds the idols of self-will and unsubmissiveness set up therein. The prophet warns them that God will not be inquired of in such a spirit as this.

1. *elders of Israel*] Some of the fellow-exiles of Ezekiel, among whom he ministered.

4. Omit *that cometh.*

according to the multitude of his idols] *i.e.* I will give him an answer as delusive as the idols which he serves. Cp. Micaiah's answer to Ahab (1 K. xxii. 15).

5. *that I may take* &c.] *i.e.* that I may take them, as in a snare, deceived by their own heart.

7. *the stranger*] They who sojourned among Israel, though they were not of Israel, were bound to abstain from idol-worship (Lev. xvii. 10, xx. 2).

by myself] Or, as in v. 4, *according to Myself.* He who comes to inquire with a heart full of idolatry shall have his answer, (1) *according to the multitude of his idols*—in delusion, (2) *according to the holiness of God*—in punishment. The inquiry was hypocritical and unreal—but God will answer not by the mouth, but by the hand, not by word but by deed, not by speech but by a scourge.

8. *will make him*] Or, I will make him amazed (xxxii. 10); or, astonished, so as to be a sign and a proverb.

9. *I the* LORD *have deceived that prophet*] A deep truth lies beneath these words, viz., that evil as well as good is under God's direction. He turns it as He will, employing it to test the sincerity of men, and thus making it ultimately contribute to the purification of His people, to the increase of their glory and felicity. The case of the false prophets who deceived Ahab (1 K. xxii.) is a striking representation of this principle. The Lord sends forth an evil spirit to persuade Ahab to his ruin. Towards the close of the kingdom of Judah false

11 even as the punishment of him that seeketh *unto him;* that the house of Israel may [h]go no more astray from me, neither be polluted any more with all their transgressions; [i]but that they may be my people, and I may be their God, saith the Lord GOD.

12, 13 The word of the LORD came again to me, saying, Son of man, when the land sinneth against me by trespassing grievously, then will I stretch out mine hand upon it, and will break the [k]staff of the bread thereof, and will send famine upon it, and
14 will cut off man and beast from it: [l]though these three men, Noah, Daniel, and Job, were in it, they should deliver *but* their
15 own souls [m]by their righteousness, saith the Lord GOD. ¶ If I cause [n]noisome beasts to pass through the land, and they [1]spoil it, so that it be desolate, that no man may pass through because
16 of the beasts : [o]*though* these three men *were* [2]in it, *as* I live, saith the Lord GOD, they shall deliver neither sons nor daughters ; they only shall be delivered, but the land shall be
17 desolate. ¶ Or *if* [p]I bring a sword upon that land, and say, Sword, go through the land; so that I [q]cut off man and beast
18 from it: [r]though these three men *were* in it, *as* I live, saith the Lord GOD, they shall deliver neither sons nor daughters, but
19 they only shall be delivered themselves. ¶ Or *if* I send [s]a pestilence into that land, and [t]pour out my fury upon it in blood,
20 to cut off from it man and beast: [u]though Noah, Daniel, and Job, *were* in it, *as* I live, saith the Lord GOD, they shall deliver neither son nor daughter ; they shall *but* deliver their own souls
21 by their righteousness. ¶ For thus saith the Lord GOD ; [3]How much more when [x]I send my four sore judgments upon Jerusalem, the sword, and the famine, and the noisome beast, and
22 the pestilence, to cut off from it man and beast? [y]Yet, behold, therein shall be left a remnant that shall be brought forth, *both* sons and daughters : behold, they shall come forth unto you, and

[h] 2 Pet. 2. 15.
[i] ch. 11. 20.

[k] Lev. 26. 26.
ch. 4. 16.
[l] Jer. 15. 1.
See Jer. 7. 16.
[m] Prov. 11. 4.
[n] Lev. 26. 22.
ch. 5. 17.

[o] ver. 14. 18.

[p] Lev. 26. 25.
ch. 5. 12.
[q] ch. 25. 13.
Zeph. 1. 3.
[r] ver. 14.

[s] 2 Sam. 24. 15.
ch. 38. 22.
[t] ch. 7. 8.
[u] ver. 14.

[x] ch. 5. 17.
& 33. 27.

[y] ch. 6. 8.

---

[1] Or, *bereave.*   [2] Heb. *in the midst of it.*   [3] Or, *Also when.*

---

prophets were especially rife. The thoughts of men's hearts were revealed, the good separated from the bad, and the remnant of the people purged from the sins by which of late years the whole nation had been defiled.

11. "God," it has been said, "punishes sins by means of sins," but the end is the re-establishment of righteousness.

12–22. Jer. xiv. xv. is a remarkable parallel to this prophecy. Here, as elsewhere, Ezekiel is commissioned to deliver to the exiles the same message which Jeremiah conveys to the inhabitants of Judæa. The answer discovers the nature of the questions which had been expressed or implied. (1) Can God cast out a people who are holy unto Himself? (2) Is it just to punish them with utter desolation? The prophet answers (1) That when a people is so corrupt as to call down national judgment, individual piety shall save none but the individuals themselves. (2) The corrupt condition of the people shall be made so manifest, that none will question the

justice of God in dealing thus severely with them.

12. Or, *When* a *land*—the case is first put in a general form, and then is brought with increased force home to Jerusalem— *sinneth against me by trespassing grievously,* **and I stretch out** *mine hand upon it,* **and break the staff of bread** *thereof,* **and send famine** *upon it and* **cut off** *man and beast :—though these three men* &c.

14. *Noah, Daniel, and Job*] Three striking instances of men who, for their integrity, were delivered from the ruin which fell upon others. Some have thought it strange that Daniel, a contemporary, and still young, should have been classed with the two ancient worthies. But the account of him (Dan. ii.) shews, that by this time Daniel was a very remarkable man (cp. xxviii. 3), and the introduction of the name of a contemporary gives force and life to the illustration. There is in the order in which the names occur a kind of climax. Noah did not rescue the guilty world, but did carry forth with him his wife, sons, and

*ch. 20. 43.

²ye shall see their way and their doings: and ye shall be comforted concerning the evil that I have brought upon Jerusalem, 23 *even* concerning all that I have brought upon it. And they shall comfort you, when ye see their ways and their doings:

a Jer. 22. 8.

and ye shall know that I have not done ªwithout cause all that I have done in it, saith the Lord GOD.

CHAP. 15. AND the word of the LORD came unto me, saying, Son of 2 man. What is the vine tree more than any tree, *or than* a branch 3 which is among the trees of the forest? Shall wood be taken thereof to do any work? or will *men* take a pin of it to hang

a John 15. 6.

4 any vessel thereon? Behold, ªit is cast into the fire for fuel; the fire devoureth both the ends of it, and the midst of it is 5 burned. ¹Is it meet for *any* work? Behold, when it was whole, it was ²meet for no work: how much less shall it be meet yet for *any* work, when the fire hath devoured it, and it is 6 burned? ¶ Therefore thus saith the Lord GOD; As the vine tree among the trees of the forest, which I have given to the fire

b Lev. 17. 10.
ch. 14. 8.
c Isai. 24. 18.
d ch. 6. 7.

7 for fuel, so will I give the inhabitants of Jerusalem. And ᵇI will set my face against them; ᶜthey shall go out from *one* fire, and *another* fire shall devour them; ᵈand ye shall know that I 8 *am* the LORD, when I set my face against them. And I will make the land desolate, because they have ³committed a trespass, saith the Lord GOD.

CHAP. 16. AGAIN the word of the LORD came unto me, saying,

a ch. 20. 4.

2 Son of man, ªcause Jerusalem to know her abominations, and

¹ Heb. *Will it prosper?*   ² Heb. *made* fit.   ³ Heb. *trespassed a trespass.*

---

sons' wives. Daniel raised only a few, but he did raise three of his countrymen with him to honour. To Job was spared neither son nor daughter.

22, 23. *ye shall be comforted* &c.] By a truer estimate of the dispensations of the Almighty. This visitation will be recognized as inevitable and just.

XV. 2. *the vine...*] The image is grounded on a well-known figure (Ps. lxxx. 8; Isai. v.). The comparison is not between the *vine* and other *trees*, but between the *wood* of the vine and the *wood* of other trees.

4. *Behold, it is cast into the fire*] The wood is in itself useless for any purpose; but what if it have been cast into the fire, and half burnt, what of it then?

7. *they shall go out* &c.] Rather, **they have gone forth from the fire, and the fire shall devour them.** The condition of the people is here depicted. The people of Israel—as a whole and as separate kingdoms —had become worthless. The branch torn from the living stem had truly been cast into the fire, which had devoured both ends of it; what remained was a brand plucked from the burning. Those who had escaped the general calamity were reserved for a like fate. Cp. John xv. 6.

XVI. Idolatry is frequently represented by the prophets under the figure of a wife's unfaithfulness to her husband. This image

is here so portrayed, as to exhibit the aggravation of Israel's guilt by reason of her origin and early history. The original abode of the progenitors of the race was the land of Canaan, defiled with idolatry and moral corruption. Israel itself was like a child born in a polluted land, abandoned from its birth, left by its parents in the most utter neglect to the chance regard of any passer-by. Such was the state of the people in Egypt (*vv.* 3-5). On such a child the Lord looked with pity, tended, and adopted it. Under His care it grew up to be comely and beautiful, and the Lord joined it to Himself in that close union, which is figured by the bonds of wedlock. The covenants made under Moses and Joshua represent this alliance (*vv.* 6-8). In the reigns of David and Solomon, Israel shone with all the glory of temporal prosperity (*vv.* 9-14). The remainder of the history of the people when divided is, in the prophet's eye, a succession of defection and degradation marked by the erection of high places (*vv.* 16-20); by unholy alliances with foreign nations (*vv.* 26-33). Such sins were soon to meet their due punishment. As an unfaithful wife was brought before the people, convicted, and stoned, so should the Lord make His people a gazing-stock to all the nations round about, deprive them of all their possessions and of their city, and

3 say, Thus saith the Lord GOD unto Jerusalem; Thy ¹birth ᵇand   ᵇ ch. 21. 30.
thy nativity *is* of the land of Canaan; ᶜthy father *was* an   ᶜ ver. 45.
4 Amorite, and thy mother an Hittite. And *as for* thy nativity,
ᵈin the day thou wast born thy navel was not cut, neither wast   ᵈ Hos. 2 3.
thou washed in water ²to supple *thee;* thou wast not salted at
5 all, nor swaddled at all. None eye pitied thee, to do any of
these unto thee, to have compassion upon thee; but thou wast
cast out in the open field, to the lothing of thy person, in the
6 day that thou wast born. ¶ And when I passed by thee, and
saw thee ³polluted in thine own blood, I said unto thee *when
thou wast* in thy blood, Live: yea, I said unto thee *when thou*
7 *wast* in thy blood, Live. ᵉI have ⁴caused thee to multiply as   ᵉ Ex. 1. 7.
the bud of the field, and thou hast increased and waxen great,
and thou art come to ⁵excellent ornaments: *thy* breasts are
fashioned, and thine hair is grown, whereas thou *wast* naked
8 and bare. Now when I passed by thee, and looked upon thee,
behold, thy time *was* the time of love; ᶠand I spread my skirt   ᶠ Ruth 3. 9.
over thee, and covered thy nakedness: yea, I sware unto thee,
and entered into a covenant with thee, saith the Lord GOD, and
9 ᵍthou becamest mine. Then washed I thee with water; yea, I   ᵍ Ex. 19. 5.
throughly washed away thy ⁶blood from thee, and I anointed   Jer. 2. 2.
10 thee with oil. I clothed thee also with broidered work, and shod
thee with badgers' skin, and I girded thee about with fine linen,
11 and I covered thee with silk. I decked thee also with ornaments,
and I ʰput bracelets upon thy hands, ⁱand a chain on thy neck.   ʰ Gen. 24.
12 And I put a jewel on thy ⁷forehead, and earrings in thine ears,   22. 47.
13 and a beautiful crown upon thine head. Thus wast thou decked   ⁱ Prov. 1. 9.
with gold and silver; and thy raiment *was of* fine linen, and

---

¹ Heb. *cutting out*, or, *habitation.*
² Or, *when I looked upon thee.*
³ Or, *trodden under foot.*
⁴ Heb. *made thee a million.*
⁵ Heb. *ornament of ornaments.*
⁶ Heb. *bloods.*
⁷ Heb. *nose*: See Isai. 3. 21.

---

cast them forth as exiles to be spoiled and destroyed in a foreign land (*rv.* 35–43).

3. *birth*] See marg. ; the word represents *origin* under the figure of *cutting out stone from a quarry* (cp. Isai. li. 1).

an Amorite] the *Amorite*, a term denoting the whole people. The Amorites, being a principal branch of the Canaanites, are often taken to represent the whole stock (Gen. xv. 16; 2 K. xxi. 11).

an Hittite] Cp. Gen. xxvi. 34. The main idea is that the Israelites by their doings proved themselves to be very children of the idolatrous nations who once occupied the land of Canaan. Cp. Deut. xx. 17.

4. *to supple* thee] *i.e.* to cleanse thee.

5. *to the lothing of thy person*] Or, "so abhorred was thy person."

6. Or, **Then I passed by thee...and I said.**

polluted] **wallowing,** "treading upon one's self."

in thy blood] may be connected either with *I said* or with *Live*. In the latter case, the state of blood and defilement is made the very cause of life, because it called forth the pity of Him Who gave life. As in the Mosaic Law *blood* was especially defiling, so was it also the special instrument of purification.

7. *I caused thee to multiply as the bud*

of the field, and thou **didst increase** *and* **wax** *great, and thou* **didst come** *to* **excellent beauty;** *thy breasts* **were** *fashioned and thine hair* **was grown, yet wast** *thou naked and bare.* The prophet has arrived at the time at which the child grew up to maturity. God preserved the life of the infant which must without His help have died (*v.* 6); and the child grew up to womanhood, but was still desolate and unprotected. This represents the sojourn in Egypt, during which the people increased, but were not bound, as a nation, to God by a covenant.

excellent ornaments] Lit. as in marg. Some render, "ornament of cheeks," *i.e.* beauty of face.

8. *Now when* &c.] Or, **Then I passed by thee...and behold.** The espousal of the damsel represents God's entering into Covenant with the people in the wilderness at Mt. Sinai (Ex. xxxiv. 27).

9. The usual purifications for marriage.

10. *badgers' skin*] Probably the skin of the dolphin or dugong (Ex. xxv. 5 note).

silk] For a robe, a turban, or (as gauze) for a transparent veil; the derivation of the word in the original is much disputed.

12. *a jewel on thy forehead*] Lit. "a nose-ring on thy nostril" (Gen. xxiv. 22 note).

silk, and broidered work ; [k]thou didst eat fine flour, and honey, and oil: and thou wast exceeding [l]beautiful, and thou didst
14 prosper into a kingdom. And [m]thy renown went forth among the heathen for thy beauty : for it *was* perfect through my comeliness, which I had put upon thee, saith the Lord GOD.
15 ¶ [n]But thou didst trust in thine own beauty, [o]and playedst the harlot because of thy renown, and pouredst out thy fornications
16 on every one that passed by ; his it was. [p]And of thy garments thou didst take, and deckedst thy high places with divers colours, and playedst the harlot thereupon : *the like things* shall
17 not come, neither shall it be *so*. Thou hast also taken thy fair jewels of my gold and of my silver, which I had given thee, and madest to thyself images [1]of men, and didst commit whoredom
18 with them, and tookest thy broidered garments, and coveredst them : and thou hast set mine oil and mine incense before them.
19 [q]My meat also which I gave thee, fine flour, and oil, and honey, *wherewith* I fed thee, thou hast even set it before them for [2]a
20 sweet savour: and *thus* it was, saith the Lord GOD. [r]Moreover thou hast taken thy sons and thy daughters, whom thou hast borne unto me, and these hast thou sacrificed unto them [3]to be
21 devoured. *Is this* of thy whoredoms a small matter, that thou hast slain my children, and delivered them to cause them to pass
22 through *the fire* for them ? And in all thine abominations and thy whoredoms thou hast not remembered the days of thy [s]youth,
[t]when thou wast naked and bare, *and* wast polluted in thy blood.
23 ¶ And it came to pass after all thy wickedness, (woe, woe unto
24 thee ! saith the Lord GOD ;) that [u]thou hast also built unto thee

Margin refs:
[k] Deut. 32. 13, 14.
[l] Ps. 48. 2.
[m] Lam. 2.15.
[n] See Deut. 32. 15. Jer. 7. 4. Mic. 3. 11.
[o] Isai. 1. 21. ch. 23. 3, 8. Hos. 1. 2.
[p] Hos. 2. 8.
[q] Hos. 2. 8.
[r] 2 Kin.16.3. Ps. 106. 37. Isai. 57. 5. Jer. 7. 31. ch. 20. 26.
[s] Jer. 2. 2. Hos. 11. 1.
[t] ver. 4, 5, 6.
[u] ver. 31.

[1] Heb. *of a male*.   [2] Heb. *a savour of rest*.   [3] Heb. *to devour*.

13. *fine flour, and honey, and oil*] These were the choicest kinds of food.
into a kingdom] This part of the description refers to the reigns of David and Solomon, when the kingdom of Israel (still undivided) attained its highest pitch of grandeur.
14. *perfect...my comeliness*] The comeliness was not natural, but the gift of God.
15. The prophet now describes the idolatries of the time of the Kings. The earlier offences in the time of the Judges are not noticed, that being an unsettled time. The conduct of the people after they had *prospered into a kingdom* is to be described.
because of thy renown] The marriages of Solomon with heathen wives, and his consequent idolatries, are a clear instance of such misuse of glory.
16. Cp. 2 K. xxiii. 7. Such decoration of idol-temples in the Holy Land shewed how the ungrateful people were devoting the wealth and energies which Jehovah had given them to the service of those false gods, in whose worship He was especially dishonoured.
the like things shall not come &c.] The abominations reached the very utmost—nothing would hereafter be so bad as these had been.
17. Possibly an allusion to the custom of

bearing about shrines. Cp. Amos v. 26; Acts vii. 43.
18. *mine oil and mine incense*] The oil was the produce of the land, the *incense* received in exchange for such produce. Both were the gifts of Jehovah and belonged to Him ; yet the oil (Ex. xxv. 6, xxix. 40) and the incense (Ex. xxx. 34), prepared for the service of God, were used in idol-worship. In nature worship the worshippers were specially lavish in vegetable products like incense.
18, 19. Allusion is here made to some rite like the Roman *Lectisternia*, in which public tables were set forth for feasts in honour of idols.
20, 21. *borne unto me*] ME is emphatic. The children of JEHOVAH have been devoted to Moloch. The rites of Moloch were twofold ; (1) The actual sacrifice of men and children as expiatory sacrifices to false gods. (2) The passing of them through the fire by way of purification and dedication. Probably the first is alluded to in *v.* 20 ; the two rites together in *v.* 21.
23. *after all* &c.] Besides these things, there was the introduction of other idolatrous rites from the nations with whom Israel had intercourse.
24. *that thou* &c.] Render, **after that thou didst build** *unto thee an eminent place, and* **didst make** *thee an high place*

an ¹eminent place, and ˣhast made thee an high place in every
25 street. Thou hast built thy high place ʸat every head of the
way, and hast made thy beauty to be abhorred, and hast opened
thy feet to every one that passed by, and multiplied thy whore-
26 doms. Thou hast also committed fornication with ᶻthe Egyptians thy neighbours, great of flesh ; and hast increased thy
27 whoredoms, to provoke me to anger. Behold, therefore I have
stretched out my hand over thee, and have diminished thine
ordinary *food*, and delivered thee unto the will of them that
hate thee, ᵃthe ²daughters of the Philistines, which are ashamed
28 of thy lewd way. ᵇThou hast played the whore also with
the Assyrians, because thou wast unsatiable ; yea, thou hast
played the harlot with them, and yet couldest not be satisfied.
29 Thou hast moreover multiplied thy fornication in the land of
Canaan ᶜunto Chaldea ; and yet thou wast not satisfied here-
30 with. ¶ How weak is thine heart, saith the Lord GOD, seeing
thou doest all these *things*, the work of an imperious whorish
31 woman ; ³in that ᵈthou buildest thine eminent place in the
head of every way, and makest thine high place in every street ;
32 and hast not been as an harlot, in that thou scornest hire ; *but*
as a wife that committeth adultery, *which* taketh strangers
33 instead of her husband! They give gifts to all whores : but
ᵉthou givest thy gifts to all thy lovers, and ⁴hirest them, that
they may come unto thee on every side for thy whoredom.
34 And the contrary is in thee from *other* women in thy whoredoms, whereas none followeth thee to commit whoredoms : and
35 in that thou givest a reward, and no reward is given unto
thee, therefore thou art contrary. ¶ Wherefore, O harlot, hear
36 the word of the LORD : Thus saith the Lord GOD ; Because thy

x Ps. 57. 5.
Jer. 2. 20.
y Prov. 3.14.

z ch. 8. 10.
& 20. 7. 8.

a 2 Chr. 28.
18, 19.
b 2 Chr. 28.
23.
Jer. 2. 18.
ch. 23. 12.

c ch. 23. 14.

d ver. 24. 39.

e Isai. 30. 6.
Hos. 8. 9.

---

¹ Or, *brothel house.*　　² Or, *cities.*　　³ Or, *In thy daughters* is *thine, &c.*　　⁴ Heb. *bribest.*

---

in every street—**after that thou didst build**
thy high place at the head of every way and
didst make...*it came to pass, that thou*
didst *also* **commit** *fornication* &c.

an eminent place] Lit., "an arched
building." Such places were used as
brothels, and so the word is used metaphorically for a place of idol-worship.

26. Egyptian idolatry, a worship of the
powers of nature, was eminently sensual.
The idolatry here spoken of is not so much
that which Israel brought with them from
Egypt, as the idolatry introduced in the
time of Solomon and Rehoboam.

27. *have diminished thine ordinary* food]
As a husband lessens the things which
minister to the luxury of an unfaithful
wife, so did the Lord cut Israel short in
consequence of her unfaithfulness.

daughters] The small cities. The Philistines have left a permanent record of
their supremacy in the name of the Holy
Land—Palestine. It was a peculiar shame
to be subjected to so small a power as that
of Philistia (see Isai. xiv. 29) ; but the very
Philistines were ashamed of Judah's unfaithfulness, and were themselves truer to
their false gods than Judah was to Jehovah.

28. Cp. marg. reff. Idolatry, spiritual
adultery, invariably accompanied these un-

holy alliances, and brought with it disaster
and ruin.

29. *in the land* &c.] Probably used in
the restricted sense of the low lands on
the coast of the western sea : occupied by
Phœnician colonies. The children of Israel
were brought into contact at first with
heathens residing within their own borders.
Then they extended their intercourse to
foreign nations, trading and forming alliances with Chaldæa, and in so doing were
attracted by the idolatries of those with
whom they carried on commerce. Some
render, "with the merchants' land, even
with Chaldæa." Cp. xvii. 4.

31. Rather, **didst build**—**didst make**—
wast not—**scornest**. In the marginal rendering, *thy daughters* must mean *thy smaller
cities or villages.*

33. The picture is heightened by the contrast between one who as a prostitute
receives hire for her shame, and one who as
a wife is so utterly abandoned as to bestow
her husband's goods to purchase her own
dishonour. Cp. 2 K. xvi. 8.

35-43. Judah is now represented as un-
dergoing the punishment adjudged to an
adulteress and murderess. Only in her
utter destruction shall the wrath of the
Lord, the jealous God, cease.

filthiness was poured out, and thy nakedness discovered through thy whoredoms with thy lovers, and with all the idols of thy abominations, and by *f*the blood of thy children, which thou
37 didst give unto them; behold, therefore *g*I will gather all thy lovers, with whom thou hast taken pleasure, and all *them* that thou hast loved, with all *them* that thou hast hated; I will even gather them round about against thee, and will discover thy nakedness unto them, that they may see all thy naked-
38 ness. And I will judge thee, ¹as *h*women that break wedlock and *i*shed blood are judged; and I will give thee blood in fury
39 and jealousy. And I will also give thee into their hand, and they shall throw down *k*thine eminent place, and shall break down thy high places: *l*they shall strip thee also of thy clothes, and shall take ²thy fair jewels, and leave thee naked and
40 bare. *m*They shall also bring up a company against thee, *n*and they shall stone thee with stones, and thrust thee through
41 with their swords. And they shall *o*burn thine houses with fire, and *p*execute judgments upon thee in the sight of many women: and I will cause thee to *q*cease from playing the harlot,
42 and thou also shalt give no hire any more. So *r*will I make my fury toward thee to rest, and my jealousy shall depart from thee, and I will be quiet, and will be no more angry.
43 ¶ Because *s*thou hast not remembered the days of thy youth, but hast fretted me in all these *things;* behold, therefore *t*I also will recompense thy way upon *thine* head, saith the Lord GOD: and thou shalt not commit this lewdness above all
44 thine abominations. Behold, every one that useth proverbs shall use *this* proverb against thee, saying, As *is* the mother, *so*
45 *is* her daughter. Thou *art* thy mother's daughter, that lotheth her husband and her children; and thou *art* the sister of thy sisters, which lothed their husbands and their children: *u*your
46 mother *was* an Hittite, and your father an Amorite. And thine elder sister *is* Samaria, she and her daughters that dwell at thy left hand: and *x*³thy younger sister, that dwelleth at thy right
47 hand, *is* Sodom and her daughters. Yet hast thou not walked after their ways, nor done after their abominations: but, ⁴as

f ver. 20.
Jer. 2. 34.
v Jer. 13.
22. 26.
Lam. 1. 8.
Hos. 2. 10.
Nah. 3. 5.

h Deut. 22. 22.
i Gen. 9. 6.

k ver. 24, 31.
l ch. 23. 26.
Hos. 2. 3.
m ch. 23. 46.
n John 8. 5.
o Deut. 13. 16.
2 Kin. 25. 9.
Jer. 39. 8.
p ch. 5. 8.
q ch. 23. 27.
r ch. 5. 13.

s Ps. 78. 42.

t ch. 9. 10.
& 11. 21.
& 22. 31.

u ver. 3.

x Deut. 32. 32.
Isai. 1. 10.

---

¹ Heb. *with judgments of.*
² Heb. *instruments of thine*
    ornament.
³ Heb. *lesser than thou.*
⁴ Or, *that was lothed as a small thing.*

---

36. *filthiness*] Or, **brass**, *i.e.* money, is lavished. The Hebrews generally speak of money as *gold* (Isai. xlvi. 6), but brass coins were not unknown in the time of the Maccabees. Cp. Matt. x. 9; Mark xii.
41. Ezekiel may here have put *brass* for *gold* contemptuously. Cp. Isai. i. 22-25, xlviii. 10.
38. *I will give thee blood in fury*] Rather, "I will make thee a bloody sacrifice to fury and jealousy." By the Law of Moses, death was the penalty for murder (Ex. xxi. 12), and for adultery (Lev. xx. 10; *e.g.* by stoning, *v.* 40). The circumstances of the siege of Jerusalem corresponded with the punishment of the adulteress; the company gathered round her were the surrounding armies, the fury of the jealous husband was the fury of the attacking army, the stripping off her ornaments the rapine of the siege, the stoning the battering-

rams, the bloody death the slaughter in the battle.
42. *So...rest*] Or, "My fury shall not rest till thou art utterly ruined."
43. *thou shalt not...abominations*] Others render, "I will not do wickedly because of all thine &c." *i.e.* by allowing Jerusalem to remain unpunished.
44. The Jews prided themselves on being under the especial protection of Jehovah. In the downfall of their neighbours, they found only additional grounds for confidence in their own security. Ezekiel now in severe rebuke places them on an equality with Sodom and Samaria. Alike have been their sins, except that Judah has had the preeminence in guilt. Alike shall be their punishment.
46. The Temple looked to the East. Samaria was on its left, and Sodom on its right hand.

if that were a very little *thing*, ^ythou wast corrupted more
48 than they in all thy ways. *As* I live, saith the Lord GOD,
^zSodom thy sister hath not done, she nor her daughters, as
49 thou hast done, thou and thy daughters. Behold, this was the
iniquity of thy sister Sodom, pride, ^afulness of bread, and
abundance of idleness was in her and in her daughters, nei-
50 ther did she strengthen the hand of the poor and needy. And
they were haughty, and ^bcommitted abomination before me:
51 therefore ^cI took them away as I saw *good*. Neither hath
Samaria committed half of thy sins; but thou hast multiplied
thine abominations more than they, and ^dhast justified thy
52 sisters in all thine abominations which thou hast done. Thou
also, which hast judged thy sisters, bear thine own shame for
thy sins that thou hast committed more abominable than they:
they are more righteous than thou: yea, be thou confounded
also, and bear thy shame, in that thou hast justified thy sisters.
53 ¶ ^eWhen I shall bring again their captivity, ^fthe captivity of
Sodom and her daughters, and the captivity of Samaria and
her daughters, then *will I bring again* the captivity of thy cap-
54 tives in the midst of them: that thou mayest bear thine own
shame, and mayest be confounded in all that thou hast done,
55 in that thou art ^ga comfort unto them. When thy sisters,
Sodom and her daughters, shall return to their former estate,
and Samaria and her daughters shall return to their former
estate, then thou and thy daughters shall return to your former
56 estate. For thy sister Sodom was not ¹mentioned by thy mouth
57 in the day of thy ²pride, before thy wickedness was discovered,
as at the time of *thy* ^hreproach of the daughters of ³Syria, and
all *that are* round about her, ⁱthe daughters of the Philistines,
58 which ⁴despise thee round about. ^kThou hast ⁵borne thy lewd-
59 ness and thine abominations, saith the LORD. For thus saith
the Lord GOD; I will even deal with thee as thou hast done,
which hast ^ldespised ^mthe oath in breaking the covenant.
60 Nevertheless I will ⁿremember my covenant with thee in the
days of thy youth, and I will establish unto thee ^oan everlasting
61 covenant. Then ^pthou shalt remember thy ways, and be ashamed,
when thou shalt receive thy sisters, thine elder and thy younger:
and I will give them unto thee for ^qdaughters, ^rbut not by thy
62 covenant. ^sAnd I will establish my covenant with thee; and

Marginal references:
y 2 Kin.21.9.
ch. 5. 6, 7.
z Matt.10.15.
a Gen. 13.10.
b Gen. 13.13.
c Gen. 19.24.
d Jer. 3. 11.
Matt. 12.
41, 42.
e See Isai.
1. 9.
f Jer. 20. 16.
g ch. 14. 22.
h 2 Kin.16.5.
Isai. 7. 1.
i ver. 27.
k ch. 23. 49.
l ch. 17. 13.
m Deut. 29.
12, 14.
n Ps. 106. 45.
o Jer. 32. 40.
p ch. 20. 43.
q Isai. 54. 1.
Gal. 4. 26.
r Jer. 31.
31, &c.
s Hos. 2. 19.

¹ Heb. *for a report*, or, *hearing.*
² Heb. *prides*, or, *excellencies.*
³ Heb. *Aram.*
⁴ Or, *spoil.*
⁵ Heb. *borne them.*

---

50. *as I saw* good] Or, "as soon as I saw
it." Omit *good*. God saw and punished.
Cp. Gen. xviii. 21.

51. *justified thy sisters*] Made them appear just in comparison with thee.

53. A denunciation of hopeless ruin.
When Sodom shall be rebuilt and shall
flourish, when Samaria shall be again a
mighty people, then, but not till then, shall
Jerusalem be restored.

54. *thou art a comfort unto them*] The
degradation of Judah would be a kind of
consolation to others. Cp. Isai. xiv.

56. *was not mentioned by thy mouth*] Was
held in utter contempt.

57. thy *reproach*] Rather, **the** *reproach*.
In his march towards Jerusalem, Nebuchad-

nezzar attacked and overthrew Damascus
and other Syrian towns. The Jews exulted, not foreseeing that this was but a
precursor of that ruin which should *discover* their own *wickedness.*

60. The promise of restoration must
almost have sounded as strangely as the
threat of punishment, including as it did
those whom Judah hated and despised (*v.*
61). The Covenant of restoration was not
to be like the old Covenant. Not *by thy
Covenant*, but *by My Covenant*. The people's
Covenant was the pledge of obedience.
That had been found ineffectual. But the
Covenant of God was by *promise* (Gal. iii.
17). See marg. ref. *r*.

f ver. 61.
u Rom. 3.19.

63 thou shalt know that I *am* the LORD: that thou mayest f remember, and be confounded, u and never open thy mouth any
more because of thy shame, when I am pacified toward thee for
all that thou hast done, saith the Lord GOD.

CHAP. 17. AND the word of the LORD came unto me, saying, Son of
2 man, put forth a riddle, and speak a parable unto the house of

a See ver.
12, &c.

3 Israel; and say, Thus saith the Lord GOD ; a A great eagle with
great wings, longwinged, full of feathers, which had 1 divers

b 2 Kin. 24.
12.

colours, came unto Lebanon, and b took the highest branch of
4 the cedar: he cropped off the top of his young twigs, and carried it into a land of traffick; he set it in a city of merchants.

c Deut. 8. 7.
d Isai. 44. 4.

5 He took also of the seed of the land, and 2 planted it in c a fruitful field; he placed *it* by great waters, *and* set it d *as* a willow

e ver. 14.

6 tree. And it grew, and became a spreading vine e of low stature,
whose branches turned toward him, and the roots thereof were
under him: so it became a vine, and brought forth branches,
7 and shot forth sprigs. ¶ There was also another great eagle

f ver. 15.

with great wings and many feathers: and, behold, f this vine
did bend her roots toward him, and shot forth her branches
toward him, that he might water it by the furrows of her plan-
8 tation. It was planted in a good 3 soil by great waters, that it
might bring forth branches, and that it might bear fruit, that it
9 might be a goodly vine. ¶ Say thou, Thus saith the Lord GOD ;

g 2 Kin. 25.7.

Shall it prosper? g shall he not pull up the roots thereof, and cut
off the fruit thereof, that it wither? it shall wither in all the
leaves of her spring, even without great power or many people
10 to pluck it up by the roots thereof. Yea, behold, *being* planted,

h ch. 19. 12.
Hos. 13. 15.

shall it prosper? h shall it not utterly wither, when the east
wind toucheth it? it shall wither in the furrows where it grew.
11 ¶ Moreover the word of the LORD came unto me, saying, Say

1 Heb. *embroidering.*　　　2 Heb. *put it in a field of seed.*　　　3 Heb. *field.*

XVII. Ezekiel, after describing by a
figure the circumstances and conditions of
the Jews and Zedekiah, the vassal of the
Assyrian monarch, warns them of the delusive character of their hopes of help from
Egypt, protests against the perfidy which
must accompany such alliance, and points
out that the restoration of the people
of God will be effected by a very different
son of David. The close of this chapter is
a striking prediction of the kingdom of the
Messiah.

3. *A great eagle…*] Probably the golden
eagle, whose plumage has the variety of
colour here depicted. The eagle (the king
of birds) is a natural representative of
monarchs (cp. Jer. xlviii. 40), and was an
Assyrian emblem.

with great wings, longwinged] Lit., "great
of wing, long of pinion," because he has
swept victoriously over widely distant
lands,—of *divers colours,* because his subjects are of various races and tongues.
Jerusalem is here called *Lebanon* because
Lebanon is the proper home of the cedar.
The *highest branch* or *topshoot* is Jeconiah,
the rightful king of Jerusalem, the *young*

twigs are his children and the princes carried by Nebuchadnezzar to Babylon.

4. *a land of traffick*] The land of Babylon.

5. *He took also of the seed of the land*]
Zedekiah the king's uncle, not a Babylonian satrap, was made king.

6. *spreading*] On the ground, not trained
to a pole, that it might have no other prop
but Nebuchadnezzar. As a vine it was
less majestic than a cedar (*v.* 3); but cp.
Ps. lxxx. 10.

whose branches &c.] Rather, **in order that
her branches should turn unto him, and
that her roots should be under him.**

7. *another great eagle*] This is the king of
Egypt, mighty indeed but not like the first.

by the furrows of her plantation] From
the beds, where it was planted to bring
forth fruit for another, it shot forth its
roots to him *that he might water it.* Zedekiah was courting the favour of Egypt
while he owed his very position to the
bounty of Assyria.

9. *her spring*] Rather, her **growth.**

even without &c.] Translate; **and not
with great power or with much people is
it to be raised up from its roots again.**

12 now to [i]the rebellious house, Know ye not what these *things* mean? tell *them*, Behold, [k]the king of Babylon is come to Jerusalem, and hath taken the king thereof, and the princes

13 thereof, and led them with him to Babylon; [l]and hath taken of the king's seed, and made a covenant with him, [m]and hath [1]taken an oath of him: he hath also taken the mighty of the

14 land: that the kingdom might be [n]base, that it might not lift itself up, [2]*but* that by keeping of his covenant it might stand.

15 But [o]he rebelled against him in sending his ambassadors into Egypt, [p]that they might give him horses and much people. [q]Shall he prosper? shall he escape that doeth such *things?* or

16 shall he break the covenant, and be delivered? *As* I live, saith the Lord GOD, surely [r]in the place *where* the king *dwelleth* that made him king, whose oath he despised, and whose covenant he brake, *even* with him in the midst of Babylon he shall die.

17 [s]Neither shall Pharaoh with *his* mighty army and great company make for him in the war, [t]by casting up mounts, and

18 building forts, to cut off many persons: seeing he despised the oath by breaking the covenant, when, lo, he had [u]given his hand, and hath done all these *things*, he shall not escape.

19 Therefore thus saith the Lord GOD; *As* I live, surely mine oath that he hath despised, and my covenant that he hath broken,

20 even it will I recompense upon his own head. And I will [x]spread my net upon him, and he shall be taken in my snare, and I will bring him to Babylon, and [y]will plead with him there

21 for his trespass that he hath trespassed against me. And [z]all his fugitives with all his bands shall fall by the sword, and they that remain shall be scattered toward all winds: and ye shall

22 know that I the LORD have spoken *it*. ¶Thus saith the Lord GOD; I will also take of the highest [a]branch of the high cedar, and will set *it;* I will crop off from the top of his young twigs [b]a tender one, and will [c]plant *it* upon an high mountain and

23 eminent: [d]in the mountain of the height of Israel will I plant it: and it shall bring forth boughs, and bear fruit, and be a goodly cedar: and [e]under it shall dwell all fowl of every wing;

24 in the shadow of the branches thereof shall they dwell. And all the trees of the field shall know that I the LORD [f]have brought

[i] ch. 2. 5.	
[k] 2 Kin. 24. 11-16.	
[l] 2 Kin. 24. 17.	
[m] 2 Chr. 36. 13.	
[n] ch. 29. 14.	
[o] 2 Kin. 24. 20.	
[p] Deut.17.16.	
Isai. 31. 1.	
[q] ver. 9.	
[r] Jer. 32. 5. ch. 12. 13.	
[s] Jer. 37. 7.	
[t] Jer. 52. 4.	
[u] 1 Chr. 29. 24. Lam. 5. 6.	
[x] ch. 12. 13.	
[y] ch. 20. 36.	
[z] ch. 12. 14.	
[a] Jer. 23. 5. Zech. 3. 8.	
[b] Isai. 53. 2.	
[c] Ps. 2. 6.	
[d] Isai. 2. 2. Mic. 4. 1.	
[e] See ch.31.6. Dan. 4. 12.	
[f] Luke 1. 52.	

[1] Heb. *brought him to an oath.*   [2] Heb. *to keep his covenant, to stand to it.*

---

17. *To cast up mounts and build forts* was the business not of the relieving but of the besieging host. Translate; **when men cast up mounts and build forts to destroy many persons.**

22. A contrast between the dealings of Nebuchadnezzar and of Jehovah. Nebuchadnezzar *cut off*, Jehovah will *set up* the topshoot; Nebuchadnezzar *carried it into a land of traffic*, Jehovah will *plant it in the mountain of the height of Israel.* Nebuchadnezzar set his favourite as a *vine*, *lowly* though not poor, in the place where such trees as the humble *willow* grow and thrive. Jehovah's favourite is like the *lofty cedar, eminent upon a high mountain.*

the highest branch of the high cedar] The rightful representative of the royal house of David, the Messiah.

tender one] The Messiah. This prophecy rests upon Isai. xi. 1, 10.

23. *in the mountain of the height of Israel*] The parallel passage (xx. 40) points to the mountain on which the Temple stood. But it is not here the actual Mount Moriah so much as the kingdom of which that mountain was the representative, the seat of the throne of the anointed Son of God (Ps. ii. 6; cp. xl. 2).

all fowl of every wing (or, of every kind) are those who flock from all lands to this kingdom. Cp. Matt. xiii. 32.

The prophet brings prominently forward the future exaltation of the king; and he furnishes us thereby with hope, encouragement, and consolation, at such times as we see the Church of Christ in like depression.

24. *the trees of the field*] The kingdoms of

down the high tree, have exalted the low tree, have dried up
the green tree, and have made the dry tree to flourish: [g]I the
LORD have spoken and have done *it*.

CHAP. 18. THE word of the LORD came unto me again, saying,
2 What mean ye, that ye use this proverb concerning the land of
Israel, saying, The [a]fathers have eaten sour grapes, and the
3 children's teeth are set on edge? *As* I live, saith the Lord GOD,
ye shall not have *occasion* any more to use this proverb in Israel.
4 Behold, all souls are mine; as the soul of the father, so also
the soul of the son is mine: [b]the soul that sinneth, it shall die.
5 ¶ But if a man be just, and do [1]that which is lawful and right,
6 [c]*and* hath not eaten upon the mountains, neither hath lifted
up his eyes to the idols of the house of Israel, neither hath
[d]defiled his neighbour's wife, neither hath come near to [e]a
7 menstruous woman, and hath not [f]oppressed any, *but* hath
restored to the debtor his [g]pledge, hath spoiled none by violence,
hath [h]given his bread to the hungry, and hath covered the
8 naked with a garment; he *that* hath not given forth upon [i]usury,
neither hath taken any increase, *that* hath withdrawn his hand
from iniquity, [k]hath executed true judgment between man and
9 man, hath walked in my statutes, and hath kept my judgments,
to deal truly; he *is* just, he shall surely [l]live, saith the Lord GOD.
10 ¶ If he beget a son *that is* a [2]robber, [m]a shedder of blood, and
11 [3]*that* doeth the like to *any* one of these *things*, and that doeth
not any of those *duties*, but even hath eaten upon the mountains,
12 and defiled his neighbour's wife, hath oppressed the poor and

[g] ch. 22. 14. & 24. 14.
[a] Lam. 5. 7.
[b] ver. 20. Rom. 6. 23.
[c] ch. 22. 9.
[d] Lev. 18.20.
[e] Lev. 18.19. & 20. 18.
[f] Lev. 19. 15.
[g] Ex. 22. 26. Deut. 24. 12, 13.
[h] Deut. 15. 7, 8. Isai. 58. 7. Matt. 25. 35, 36.
[i] Neh. 5. 7. Ps. 15. 5.
[k] Zech. 8.16.
[l] Amos 5. 4.
[m] Gen. 9. 6. Ex. 21. 12.

[1] Heb. *judgment and justice.*
[2] Or, *breaker up of an house.*
[3] Or, *that doeth to his brother besides any of these.*

---

the world as contrasted with the kingdom of God. The truth here enunciated is a general one. God gives the promise, God fulfils it.

XVIII. The last verse of ch. xvii. gives occasion for a declaration of the principle upon which God's providential dispensations proceed, viz., that every individual shall be equitably dealt with—a principle that precludes the children from either presuming on the father's merits or despairing on account of the father's guilt. This chapter is an enlargement of Jer. xxxi. 29, and sets forth fully the doctrine of individual responsibility.

2. *concerning the land of Israel*] Rather, in *the land of Israel*, *i.e.* upon Israel's soil, the last place where such a heathenish saying should be expected. The saying was general among the people both in Palestine and in exile; and expressed the excuse wherewith they ascribed their miserable condition to anyone's fault but their own—to a blind fate such as the heathen recognized, instead of the discriminating judgment of an All-holy God.

4. *all souls are mine*] Man is not simply to ascribe his existence to earthly parents, but to acknowledge as his Father Him Who created man in His own image, and Who gave and gives him the spirit of life. The relation of father to son is merged in the common relation of all (father and son alike) as sons to their Heavenly Father.

6. *eaten upon the mountains*] At the feast of idols, in contradiction to the command of Deut. xii. 17.

idols of the house of Israel] Idolatry was so popular that certain idols were counted as belonging to the people of Israel, of whom Jehovah was the true God.

8. *usury* is the profit exacted for the loan of money, *increase* that which is taken for goods; both are forbidden (Lev. xxv. 36; Deut. xxiii. 19). The placing out of capital at interest for commercial purposes is not taken into consideration. The case is that of money lent to a brother in distress.

9-13. *live...die*] In the writings of Ezekiel there is a development of the meaning of *life* and *death*. In the Holy Land the sanctions of Divine government were in a great degree temporal; so that the promise of *life* for *obedience*, the threatening of *death* for *disobedience*, in the Books of Moses, were regarded simply as temporal and national. In their exile this could not continue in its full extent, and the universality of the misfortune necessarily made men look deeper into the words of God. The word *soul* denotes a *person* viewed as an *individual*, possessing the *life* which God breathed into man when he became *a living*

needy, hath spoiled by violence, hath not restored the pledge, and
hath lifted up his eyes to the idols, hath [n]committed abomination, [n] ch. 8. 6.
13 hath given forth upon usury, and hath taken increase: shall
he then live? he shall not live: he hath done all these abomi-
nations; he shall surely die; [o]his [1]blood shall be upon him. [o] Lev. 20. 9. ch. 3. 18. Acts 18. 6.
14 ¶ Now, lo, *if* he beget a son, that seeth all his father's sins
which he hath done, and considereth, and doeth not such like,
15 [p]*that* hath not eaten upon the mountains, neither hath lifted [p] ver. 6, &c.
up his eyes to the idols of the house of Israel, hath not defiled
16 his neighbour's wife, neither hath oppressed any, [2]hath not
withholden the pledge, neither hath spoiled by violence, *but* hath
given his bread to the hungry, and hath covered the naked with
17 a garment, *that* hath taken off his hand from the poor, *that* hath
not received usury nor increase, hath executed my judgments,
hath walked in my statutes; he shall not die for the iniquity of
18 his father, he shall surely live. *As for* his father, because he
cruelly oppressed, spoiled his brother by violence, and did *that*
which *is* not good among his people, lo, even [q]he shall die in [q] ch. 3. 18.
19 his iniquity. ¶ Yet say ye, Why? [r]doth not the son bear the [r] Ex. 20. 5. Deut. 5. 9. 2 Kin. 23.26.
iniquity of the father? When the son hath done that which is
lawful and right, *and* hath kept all my statutes, and hath done
20 them, he shall surely live. [s]The soul that sinneth, it shall die. [s] ver. 4.
[t]The son shall not bear the iniquity of the father, neither shall [t] Deut. 24. 16. 2 Kin. 14. 6. Jer. 31. 29.
the father bear the iniquity of the son: [u]the righteousness of
the righteous shall be upon him, [x]and the wickedness of the [u] Isai. 3. 10.
21 wicked shall be upon him. But [y]if the wicked will turn from [x] Rom. 2. 9. [y] ver. 27. ch. 33. 12.
all his sins that he hath committed, and keep all my statutes,
and do that which is lawful and right, he shall surely live, he
22 shall not die. [z]All his transgressions that he hath committed, [z] ch. 33. 16.
they shall not be mentioned unto him: in his righteousness that
23 he hath done he shall live. [a]Have I any pleasure at all that [a] ver. 32. 1 Tim. 2. 4. 2 Pet. 3. 9.
the wicked should die? saith the Lord GOD: *and* not that he
24 should return from his ways, and live? But [b]when the righteous [b] ch. 3. 20. & 33. 12.
turneth away from his righteousness, and committeth iniquity,
and doeth according to all the abominations that the wicked
man doeth, shall he live? [c]All his righteousness that he hath [c] 2 Pet. 2. 20.
done shall not be mentioned: in his trespass that he hath trespassed, and in his sin that he hath sinned, in them shall he die.
25 ¶ Yet ye say, [d]The way of the LORD is not equal. Hear now, [d] ver. 29. ch. 33. 17.
O house of Israel; Is not my way equal? are not your ways
26 unequal? [e]When a righteous *man* turneth away from his [e] ver. 24.
righteousness, and committeth iniquity, and dieth in them; for
27 his iniquity that he hath done shall he die. Again, [f]when the [f] ver. 21.
wicked *man* turneth away from his wickedness that he hath
committed, and doeth that which is lawful and right, he shall
28 save his soul alive. Because he [g] considereth, and turneth away [g] ver. 14.
from all his transgressions that he hath committed, he shall
29 surely live, he shall not die. ¶ [h]Yet saith the house of Israel, [h] ver. 25.

[1] Heb. *bloods*. [2] Heb. *hath not pledged the pledge*, or, *taken to pledge*.

---

soul (Gen. ii. 7); *i.e.* it distinguishes *personality* from *nationality*, and this introduces that fresh and higher idea of *life* and *death*, which is not so much *life* and *death* in a future state, as *life* and *death* as equivalent to communion with or separation from God—that idea of life and death which was explained by our Lord in the Gospel of St. John (viii.), and by St. Paul in Rom. viii.

19. *Why?* &c.] Rather, "Why doth not the son bear the iniquity of the father?"

25. *equal*] Lit. "weighed out, balanced." Man's ways are arbitrary, God's ways are governed by a self-imposed Law, which makes all consistent and harmonious.

The way of the LORD is not equal. O house of Israel, are not
30 my ways equal ? are not your ways unequal ? *Therefore I will
judge you, O house of Israel, every one according to his ways,
saith the Lord GOD. *Repent, and turn ¹ *yourselves* from all
31 your transgressions : so iniquity shall not be your ruin. *Cast
away from you all your transgressions, whereby ye have transgressed ; and make you a ™new heart and a new spirit : for why
32 will ye die, O house of Israel ? For ⁿI have no pleasure in the
death of him that dieth, saith the Lord GOD : wherefore turn
² *yourselves*, and live ye.

CHAP. 19. MOREOVER ᵃtake thou up a lamentation for the
2 princes of Israel, and say, What *is* thy mother ? A lioness : she
lay down among lions, she nourished her whelps among young
3 lions. And she brought up one of her whelps : ᵇit became a
young lion, and it learned to catch the prey ; it devoured men.
4 The nations also heard of him ; he was taken in their pit, and
5 they brought him with chains unto the land of ᶜEgypt. Now
when she saw that she had waited, *and* her hope was lost, then
she took ᵈanother of her whelps, *and* made him a young lion.
6 ᵉAnd he went up and down among the lions, ᶠhe became a
young lion, and learned to catch the prey, *and* devoured men,
7 And he knew ³their desolate palaces, and he laid waste their
cities ; and the land was desolate, and the fulness thereof, by
8 the noise of his roaring. ᵍThen the nations set against him on
every side from the provinces, and spread their net over him :
9 ʰhe was taken in their pit. ⁱAnd they put him in ward ⁴in
chains, and brought him to the king of Babylon : they brought
him into holds, that his voice should no more be heard upon
10 ᵏthe mountains of Israel. ¶Thy mother *is* ⁱlike a vine ⁵in thy
blood, planted by the waters: she was ™fruitful and full of
11 branches by reason of many waters. And she had strong rods
for the sceptres of them that bare rule, and her ⁿstature was

Marginal references

i ch. 7. 3.

k Matt. 3. 2.
Rev. 2. 5.
l Eph. 4. 22.

m Jer. 32. 39.
ch. 36. 26.
n Lam. 3. 33.
ch. 33. 11.
2 Pet. 3. 9.

a ch. 26. 17.
& 27. 2.

b 2 Kin. 23.
30–33.

c 2 Chr. 36. 4.
Jer. 22. 11.

d 2 Kin. 23.
34.
e Jer. 22.
13–17.
f ver. 3.

g 2 Kin. 24. 2.

h ver. 4.
i 2 Chr. 36. 6.
Jer. 22. 18.

k ch. 6. 2.
l ch. 17. 6.
m Deut. 8.
7, 8, 9.
n So ch. 31. 3.
Dan. 4. 11.

---

¹ Or, others
² Or, others.
³ Or, *their widows.*
⁴ Or, *in hooks.*
⁵ Or, *in thy quietness,* or,
in thy likeness.

XIX. Ezekiel regarded Zedekiah as an in-
terloper (xvii. 1 note), therefore he here passes
over Jehoiakim and Zedekiah as mere creatures of Egypt and of Babylon, and recognizes
Jehoahaz and Jehoiachin as the only legitimate sovereigns since the time of Josiah.
This dirge is for them, while it warns the
usurper Zedekiah of an approaching fate
similar to that of the two earlier kings.

1. *princes of Israel*] Israel is the whole
nation over which the king of Judah was
the rightful sovereign. Cp. ii. 3, iii. 1, 7.

2. *thy mother*] The people represented by
Judah. Cp. Gen. xlix. 9 ; Num. xxiii. 24.

3, 4. Cp. marg. ref. The short reign of
Jehoahaz was marked by violence and
idolatry, and was closed by Pharaoh-Necho's carrying him captive into Egypt.

4, 9. *chains*] See marg. rendering to *v.* 9
and Isai. xxvii. 29 note.

5. *another*] Jehoiachin who soon shewed
himself no less unworthy than Jehoahaz.
The *waiting* of the people was during the
absence of their rightful lord Jehoahaz, a

captive in Egypt while Jehoiakim, whom
they deemed an usurper, was on the
throne. It was not till Jehoiachin succeeded, that they seemed to themselves to
have a monarch of their own (2 K.
xxiv. 6).

7. *their desolate palaces*] Rather, his
palaces, built upon the ground, whence he
had ejected the former owners.

8. *The nations* are here the Chaldæans :
see marg. reff.

10. *Thy mother*] Judah or Jerusalem.
Jehoiachin is still addressed.

in thy blood] *Blood* is equivalent to *life*
(Gen. ix. 4). The clause is equivalent to
"Thy mother is a vine, living in *thy blood*,"
i.e. in the life of thee and of thy children.
The excellency of a vine is in her fruitful
branches ; the glory of a mother in her
noble children. Jeremiah was to write Jehoiachin childless (see on Jer. xxii. 30) ;
Ezekiel here takes a general view of the
king and princes of the blood royal.

11. *sceptres*] Gen. xlix. 10.

exalted among the thick branches, and she appeared in her
12 height with the multitude of her branches. But she was plucked
up in fury, she was cast down to the ground, and the °east wind
dried up her fruit: her strong rods were broken and withered;
13 the fire consumed them. And now she *is* planted in the wilder-
14 ness, in a dry and thirsty ground. ᵖAnd fire is gone out of a
rod of her branches, *which* hath devoured her fruit, so that she
hath no strong rod *to be* a sceptre to rule. �qThis *is* a lamentation,
and shall be for a lamentation.

° ch. 17. 10.
Hos. 13. 15.

ᵖ Judg. 9. 15.
2 Kin. 24. 20.
ch. 17. 18.
q Lam. 4. 20.

CHAP. 20. AND it came to pass in the seventh year, in the fifth
month, the tenth *day* of the month, *that* ᵃcertain of the elders of
2 Israel came to enquire of the LORD, and sat before me. Then
3 came the word of the LORD unto me, saying, Son of man, speak
unto the elders of Israel, and say unto them, Thus saith the
Lord GOD; Are ye come to enquire of me ? *As* I live, saith the
4 Lord GOD, ᵇI will not be enquired of by you. Wilt thou ¹ᶜjudge
them, son of man, wilt thou judge *them* ? ᵈcause them to know
5 the abominations of their fathers: and say unto them, Thus
saith the Lord GOD; In the day when ᵉI chose Israel, and
²lifted up mine hand unto the seed of the house of Jacob, and
made myself ᶠknown unto them in the land of Egypt, when I
lifted up mine hand unto them, saying, ᵍI *am* the LORD your
6 God; in the day *that* I lifted up mine hand unto them, ʰto bring
them forth of the land of Egypt into a land that I had espied
for them, flowing with milk and honey, ⁱwhich *is* the glory of
7 all lands: then said I unto them, ᵏCast ye away every man
ˡthe abominations of his eyes, and defile not yourselves with
8 ᵐthe idols of Egypt: I *am* the LORD your God. But they
rebelled against me, and would not hearken unto me: they
did not every man cast away the abominations of their eyes,
neither did they forsake the idols of Egypt: then I said, I will
ⁿpour out my fury upon them, to accomplish my anger against
9 them in the midst of the land of Egypt. ᵒBut I wrought for my
name's sake, that it should not be polluted before the heathen,
among whom they *were*, in whose sight I made myself known

ᵃ ch. 8. 1.
& 14. 1.

ᵇ ver. 31.
ch. 14. 3.
ᶜ ch. 22. 2.
ᵈ ch. 16. 2.
ᵉ Ex. 6. 7.
Deut. 7. 6.
ᶠ Ex. 3. 8.
Deut. 4. 34.
ᵍ Ex. 20. 2.

ʰ Deut. 8. 7.
Jer. 32. 22.
ⁱ Ps. 48. 2.
Dan. 8. 9.
Zech. 7. 14.
ᵏ ch. 18. 31.
ˡ 2 Chr. 15. 8.
ᵐ Lev. 17. 7.
Deut. 29.
16, 17, 18.

ⁿ ch. 7. 8.
ᵒ See Ex. 32.
12.
Num. 14.
13, &c.

¹ Or, *plead for them.*   ² Or, *sware:* and so ver. 6, &c. Ex. 6. 8.

---

the thick branches] Or, **the clouds**; so xxxi.
3, 10, 14.
12. This is a dirge; and therefore that
which is foreseen by the prophet, the capture and burning of Jerusalem, is described
as already accomplished.
14. *fire is gone out*] Cp. marg. ref. Zedekiah is regarded, like Abimelech, as an
usurper and the ruin of his people.
XX.-XXIII. The prophecies of this
section were delivered nearly a year after
those of the former (viii. 1). Ezekiel in
reply to other inquiries from the chieftains
of the people, sets forth their national history, the national judgment, and the hope
of divine mercy. This leads up to the prediction of the kingdom of the Messiah.
1. *the elders of Israel*] These were as in
xiv. 1, some of Ezekiel's fellow-exiles, designated in general terms by the name of
Israel, though more properly belonging to
the kingdom of Judah.

3. *enquire*] As to the hope of deliverance
from the Babylonians.
4. *wilt thou judge them?*] We should
rather say, Wilt thou not judge them ? *i.e.*
wilt thou not pronounce sentence upon
them ? Cp. xxii. 2.
5-9. The children of Israel in Egypt
were warned to abstain from the idolatry
of the heathen. This purpose they lost
sight of, yet God spared them and brought
them into another state of probation.
5. *lifted up mine hand*] *i.e.* sware, because the hand was lifted up in adjuration.
8. *idols of Egypt*] These incidental no-
tices shew the children of Israel in Egypt
to have been addicted to idolatry. Cp.
Josh. xxiv. 14.
9. *I wrought for my name's sake*] Lest it
should appear to the Egyptians that Jehovah was a God Who would, but could not,
save.

unto them, in bringing them forth out of the land of Egypt.
10 ¶ Wherefore I [p]caused them to go forth out of the land of
11 Egypt, and brought them into the wilderness. [q]And I gave
them my statutes, and [1]shewed them my judgments, [r]which *if*
12 a man do, he shall even live in them. Moreover also I gave
them my [s]sabbaths, to be a sign between me and them, that
13 they might know that I *am* the LORD that sanctify them. But
the house of Israel [t]rebelled against me in the wilderness: they
walked not in my statutes, and they [u]despised my judgments,
which *if* a man do, he shall even live in them; and my sabbaths
they greatly [x]polluted: then I said, I would pour out my fury
14 upon them in the [y]wilderness, to consume them. [z]But I wrought
for my name's sake, that it should not be polluted before the
15 heathen, in whose sight I brought them out. ¶ Yet also [a]I
lifted up my hand unto them in the wilderness, that I would not
bring them into the land which I had given *them*, flowing with
16 milk and honey, [b]which *is* the glory of all lands; [c]because they
despised my judgments, and walked not in my statutes, but
polluted my sabbaths: for [d]their heart went after their idols.
17 [e]Nevertheless mine eye spared them from destroying them,
18 neither did I make an end of them in the wilderness. But I
said unto their children in the wilderness, Walk ye not in the
statutes of your fathers, neither observe their judgments, nor
19 defile yourselves with their idols: I *am* the LORD your God;
[f]walk in my statutes, and keep my judgments, and do them;
20 [g]and hallow my sabbaths; and they shall be a sign between me
and you, that ye may know that I *am* the LORD your God.
21 Notwithstanding [h]the children rebelled against me: they walked
not in my statutes, neither kept my judgments to do them,
[i]which *if* a man do, he shall even live in them; they polluted
my sabbaths: then I said, [k]I would pour out my fury upon
them, to accomplish my anger against them in the wilderness.
22 [l]Nevertheless I withdrew mine hand, and [m]wrought for my
name's sake, that it should not be polluted in the sight of the
23 heathen, in whose sight I brought them forth. ¶ I lifted up
mine hand unto them also in the wilderness, that [n]I would
scatter them among the heathen, and disperse them through
24 the countries; [o]because they had not executed my judgments,
but had despised my statutes, and had polluted my sabbaths,
25 and [p]their eyes were after their father's idols. Wherefore [q]I
gave them also statutes *that were* not good, and judgments

[p] Ex. 13. 18.
[q] Neh. 9. 13. Ps. 147. 19.
[r] Lev. 18. 5. Rom. 10. 5.
[s] Ex. 20. 8. Deut. 5. 12. Neh. 9. 14.
[t] Num. 14. 22. Ps. 78. 40.
[u] Prov. 1. 25.
[x] Ex. 16. 27.
[y] Num. 14. 29.
[z] ver. 9. 22.
[a] Ps. 106. 26.
[b] ver. 6.
[c] ver. 13, 24.
[d] Num. 15. 39. Amos 5. 25. Acts 7. 42.
[e] Ps. 78. 38.
[f] Deut. 5. 32.
[g] Jer. 17. 22.
[h] Num. 25. 1, 2. Deut. 9. 23.
[i] ver. 11, 13.
[k] ver. 8. 13.
[l] Ps. 78. 38.
[m] ver. 9. 14.
[n] Lev. 26. 33. Ps. 106. 27. Jer. 15. 4.
[o] ver. 13, 16.
[p] ch. 6. 9.
[q] 2 Thess. 2. 11.

[1] Heb. *made them to know.*

10–26. The probation in the wilderness. The promise was forfeited by those to whom it was first conditionally made, but was renewed to their children.

11. The *statutes* were given on Mount Sinai, and repeated by Moses before his death (Ex. xx. 1 seq.; Deut. iv. 8).

in them] Or, through them: and in *v.* 13.

12. See Ex. xxxi. 13. The Sabbath was a *sign* of a peculiar people, commemorative of the work of creation, and hallowed to the honour of Jehovah, the Covenant-God. As man honoured God by keeping the Sabbath holy, so by the Sabbath, God *sanctified* Israel and marked them as a holy people. Therefore to profane the Sabbath was to abjure their Divine Governor.

13. *my sabbaths they greatly polluted*] Not by actual non-observance of the sabbatical rest in the wilderness, but in failing to make the day holy in deed as well as in name by earnest worship and true heart service.

18. The book of Deuteronomy contains the address to *the children* of those who perished in the wilderness. The whole history of Israel was a repetition of this course. The Covenant was made with one generation, broken by them, and then renewed to the next.

25. The *judgments whereby they should not*

26 whereby they should not live; and I polluted them in their own gifts, in that they caused to pass ʳthrough *the fire* all that openeth the womb, that I might make them desolate, to the end

27 that they ˢmight know that I *am* the Lord. ¶Therefore, son of man, speak unto the house of Israel, and say unto them, Thus saith the Lord God ; Yet in this your fathers have ᵗblasphemed me, in that they have ¹committed a trespass against me.

28 *For* when I had brought them into the land, *for* the which I lifted up mine hand to give it to them, then ᵘthey saw every high hill, and all the thick trees, and they offered there their sacrifices, and there they presented the provocation of their offering: there also they made their ˣsweet savour, and poured

29 out there their drink offerings. Then ²I said unto them, What *is* the high place whereunto ye go ? And the name thereof is

30 called Bamah unto this day. ¶Wherefore say unto the house of Israel, Thus saith the Lord God ; Are ye polluted after the manner of your fathers ? and commit ye whoredom after their

31 abominations ? For when ye offer ʸyour gifts, when ye make your sons to pass through the fire, ye pollute yourselves with all your idols, even unto this day : and ᶻshall I be enquired of by you, O house of Israel ? *As* I live, saith the Lord God, I will

32 not be enquired of by you. And that ᵃwhich cometh into your mind shall not be at all, that ye say, We will be as the heathen, as the families of the countries, to serve wood and stone. ¶*As*

33 I live, saith the Lord God, surely with a mighty hand, and ᵇwith a stretched out arm, and with fury poured out, will I rule

34 over you: and I will bring you out from the people, and will gather you out of the countries wherein ye are scattered, with a mighty hand, and with a stretched out arm, and with fury

Right margin references:
ʳ 2 Kin. 17. 17. & 21. 6. Jer. 32. 35.
ˢ ch. 6. 7.
ᵗ Rom. 2. 24.
ᵘ Isai 57. 5, ch. 6. 13.
ˣ ch. 16. 19.
ʸ ver. 26.
ᶻ ver. 3.
ᵃ ch. 11. 5.
ᵇ Jer. 21. 5.

¹ Heb. *trespassed a trespass.*　　² Or, *I told them what the high place was,* or, *Bamah.*

---

live are those spoken of in *v.* 18, and are contrasted with the *judgments* in *vv.* 13, 21, laws other than Divine, to which God gives up those whom He afflicts with judicial blindness, because they have wilfully closed their eyes, (Ps. lxxxi. 12 ; Rom. i. 24).

26. *to pass through*] The word also means to *set apart*, as the firstborn to the Lord (Ex. xiii. 12). They were bidden to *set apart* their firstborn males to the Lord. They *caused them to pass through the fire* to Moloch. An instance of their perversion of God's Laws.

27–31. The probation in the land of Canaan from their entry to the day of Ezekiel.

27. *Yet in this*] It was an aggravation of their guilt that they defiled with idolatry the land given them for their glory.

29. *Bamah*] The Hebrew word for *high-place*. Another instance of the perversion of God's Laws. When the Israelites first entered Canaan they were to set up the *tabernacle* on a *high-place*, and upon this and upon no other they were to worship Jehovah (1 Sam. ix. 12, *seq.* ; 1 K. iii. 4). But the Israelites followed the custom of the country, and set up idol-worship on every high hill, and the word *high-place* (*Bamah,* plural *Bamoth*) became a by-

word (cp. *Bamoth-Baal,* Josh. xiii. 17). *Bamoth* occurs on the Moabitic stone, which records the erection of high places in honour of Chemosh. The name *Bamah* was thus a brand of the Divine displeasure, and a memorial of the people's guilt.

30, 31. The present state of the people. Those who came to inquire were the representatives of the whole people, though belonging to the exiles.

32–44. God's future dealings with His people : (1) in judgment (*vv.* 32–38) ; (2) in mercy (*vv.* 39–44).

32. The inquirers had thought that if Jerusalem were taken, and the whole people became sojourners in a foreign land, they would cease to be a separate nation. Some in their love for idolatry may have even desired this. But more probably they thought that this very consequence precluded the possibility of such a catastrophe. God answers that He will not allow them to become as the heathen, but this will only subject them to severer trial and stricter rule.

33. The expressions *a mighty hand, stretched out arm* carry back the thoughts to Egyptian bondage (Deut. iv. 34, v. 15); but then it was for deliverance, now for judgment *with fury poured out.*

c Jer. 2. 9.
ch. 17. 20.
d See Num.
14. 21, &c.
e Lev. 27. 32.
Jer. 33. 13.
f ch. 34. 17.
Matt. 25.
32, 33.

g Jer. 44. 14.
h ch. 6. 7.

i Judg.10.14.
Ps. 81. 12.
Amos 4. 4.
k Isai. 1. 13.
ch. 23. 38.
l ch. 17. 23.
Mic. 4. 1.
m Isai. 56. 7.
Zech. 8. 20.
Mal. 3. 4.
Rom. 12. 1.
n Eph. 5. 2.
Phil. 4. 18.

o ch. 36. 23.
p ch. 11. 17.

q ch. 16. 61.

r Lev. 26.39.
Hos. 5. 15.
s ver. 38.
ch. 24. 24.
t ch. 36. 22.

u ch. 6. 2.
& 21. 2.

35 poured out. And I will bring you into the wilderness of the
36 people, and there *c*will I plead with you face to face. *d*Like as
I pleaded with your fathers in the wilderness of the land of
37 Egypt, so will I plead with you, saith the Lord GOD. And I
will cause you to *e*pass under the rod, and I will bring you into
38 ¹the bond of the covenant : and *f*I will purge out from among
you the rebels, and them that transgress against me : I will
bring them forth out of the country where they sojourn, and
*g*they shall not enter into the land of Israel : *h*and ye shall
39 know that I *am* the LORD. ¶As for you, O house of Israel,
thus saith the Lord GOD ; *i*Go ye, serve ye every one his idols,
and hereafter *also*, if ye will not hearken unto me : *k*but pollute
ye my holy name no more with your gifts, and with your idols.
40 For *l*in mine holy mountain, in the mountain of the height of
Israel, saith the Lord GOD, there shall all the house of Israel,
all of them in the land, serve me : there *m*will I accept them,
and there will I require your offerings, and the ²firstfruits of
41 your oblations, with all your holy things. I will accept you
with your ³ *n*sweet savour, when I bring you out from the
people, and gather you out of the countries wherein ye have
been scattered ; and I will be sanctified in you before the heathen.
42 *o*And ye shall know that I *am* the LORD, *p*when I shall bring
you into the land of Israel, into the country *for* the which I
43 lifted up mine hand to give it to your fathers. And *q*there shall
ye remember your ways, and all your doings, wherein ye have
been defiled ; and *r*ye shall lothe yourselves in your own sight
44 for all your evils that ye have committed. *s*And ye shall know
that I *am* the LORD, when I have wrought with you *t*for my
name's sake, not according to your wicked ways, nor according
to your corrupt doings, O ye house of Israel, saith the Lord
GOD.

45, 46 Moreover the word of the LORD came unto me, saying, *u*Son

¹ Or, *a delivering.*   ² Or, *chief.*   ³ Heb. *savour of rest.*

---

35. *the wilderness of the people*] A time of
probation will follow, as before in the wilderness of Sin, so in the *wilderness of the
nations* among whom they will sojourn (not
the Babylonians) *after* that Captivity.
This period of their probation is not over.
The dispersion of the Jews did not cease
with the return under Zerubbabel ; but in our
Saviour's time they were living as a distinct
people in all the principal places in the
civilized world ; and so they live now.
God is yet pleading with them *face to face*,
calling them personally to embrace those
offers which as a nation they disregarded.

37. *to pass under the rod*] i.e. to be
gathered into the flock (Micah vii. 14).

the bond] The shepherd collects the flock,
and separates the sheep from the goats,
which are rejected. Cp.Rom. xi. 7-11.

39. Strong irony. Some prefer another
rendering : "Go ye, serve ye every one
his idols, yet hereafter ye shall surely
hearken unto me, and shall no more pollute
My Holy Name &c." In this way this verse
is introductory to what follows.

40. This points to the consummation indicated by the vision of the Temple.

in the mountain of the height] Or, *Upon a
very high mountain* (xl. 2). Cp. Isai. ii. 2, 3.

the house of Israel, all of them] All the
separation between Israel and Judah shall
cease. This points to times yet future,
when in Messiah's kingdom Jews and Gentiles alike shall be gathered into one kingdom—the kingdom of Christ. Jerusalem
is the Church of Christ (Gal. iv. 26), into
which the children of Israel shall at last be
gathered, and so the prophecy shall be fulfilled (Rev. xxi. 2).

45-49. This paragraph is in the Hebrew
text, LXX. and Vulg. the beginning of
ch. xxi. to which it belongs, as it contains a
prophecy delivered in a form which is
there explained. It may, however, be
regarded as a link between the foregoing
and following prophecies, being a general
introduction to *seven* words of judgment
about to be pronounced in development of
that which has just been delivered.

of man, set thy face toward the south, and drop *thy word* toward the south, and prophesy against the forest of the south field; 47 and say to the forest of the south, Hear the word of the LORD; Thus saith the Lord GOD; Behold, *x*I will kindle a fire in thee, and it shall devour *y*every green tree in thee, and every dry tree: the flaming flame shall not be quenched, and all faces *z*from the 48 south to the north shall be burned therein. And all flesh shall see that I the LORD have kindled it: it shall not be quenched. 49 Then said I, Ah Lord GOD! they say of me, Doth he not speak parables?

CHAP. 21. AND the word of the LORD came unto me, saying, *a*Son 2 of man, set thy face toward Jerusalem, and *b*drop *thy word* toward the holy places, and prophesy against the land of Israel, 3 and say to the land of Israel, Thus saith the LORD; Behold, I *am* against thee, and will draw forth my sword out of his sheath, and will cut off from thee *c*the righteous and the wicked. 4 Seeing then that I will cut off from thee the righteous and the wicked, therefore shall my sword go forth out of his sheath 5 against all flesh *d*from the south to the north: that all flesh may know that I the LORD have drawn forth my sword out of 6 his sheath: it *e*shall not return any more. *f*Sigh therefore, thou son of man, with the breaking of *thy* loins; and with 7 bitterness sigh before their eyes. And it shall be, when they say unto thee, Wherefore sighest thou? that thou shalt answer, For the tidings; because it cometh: and every heart shall melt, and *g*all hands shall be feeble, and every spirit shall faint, and all knees ¹shall be weak *as* water: behold, it cometh, and shall be 8 brought to pass, saith the Lord GOD. ¶ Again the word of the LORD came unto me, saying, Son of man, prophesy, and say, 9 Thus saith the LORD; Say, *h*A sword, a sword is sharpened, and 10 also furbished: it is sharpened to make a sore slaughter; it is furbished that it may glitter: should we then make mirth?

x Jer. 21. 14.
y Luke 23.31.
z ch. 21.4.

a ch. 20. 46.
b Deut. 32.2.
Amos 7. 16.
Mic. 2. 6,11.

c Job 9. 22.

d ch. 20. 47.

e So Isai. 45.
23. & 55. 11.
f Isai. 22. 4.

g ch. 7. 17.

h Deut.32.41.
ver. 15, 28.

¹ Heb. *shall go* (melt) *into water.*

46. In this verse occur three Hebrew synonyms for *South*, denoting (1) the region on the right, *Teman* (1 Sam. xxxiii. 24); (2) the region of dryness, *Negeb* (Josh. xv. 4); (3) the region of brightness, *Darom* (Deut. xxxiii. 23). The variety of terms helps the force of the application. Chebar is in the North of Babylonia; from the North the Chaldæans came upon Judæa (see i. 4 note).

47. *forest of the south*] The land of Israel. See xxi. 1, 2.

49. *parables*] Cp. xvii. 2. The meaning of the prophet was clear enough, if those whom he addressed had chosen to understand.

XXI. 1-7. The first word of judgment. Ezekiel speaks first to the people of Israel, shews the universality of the coming destructions, and indicates by a sign (that of *sighing*) the sadness of the calamity.

1, 2. The words and order of words are identical with xx. 45, 46, except that for *South*, there are substituted (1) *Jerusalem;* (2) *the Holy Place, i.e.* the Temple and its

various parts; (3) *the land of Israel.* No subterfuge is left for the people to pretend misunderstanding.

4. *The righteous and the wicked* take the place of *every green tree and every dry tree* (xx. 47); *all faces* that of *all flesh:* to shew the universality of the destructions. National judgment involves the innocent in the temporal ruin of the guilty. The equity of God is vindicated by the ruin being only *temporal.*

from the south to the north] From one end of the Holy Land to the other; the seer is in the North, and looks at once on the whole extent of the ruin.

6. The prophet was directed to let the people see him sighing and prostrate, as a sign of the sorrow and weakness about to come upon the people.

the breaking of thy *loins*] The prostration of strength; the loins being the seat of strength.

8-17. The second word of judgment: the glittering and destroying sword. The passage may be called the "Lay of the Sword;"

11 [1]it contemneth the rod of my son, *as* every tree. And he hath
given it to be furbished, that it may be handled: this sword is
sharpened, and it is furbished, to give it into the hand of [i]the
12 slayer. Cry and howl, son of man: for it shall be upon my
people, it *shall be* upon all the princes of Israel: [2]terrors by
reason of the sword shall be upon my people: [k]smite therefore
13 upon *thy* thigh. [3]Because *it is* [l]a trial, and what if *the sword*
contemn even the rod? [m]it shall be no *more*, saith the Lord
14 GOD. Thou therefore, son of man, prophesy, and [n]smite *thine*
[4]hands together, and let the sword be doubled the third time,
the sword of the slain: it *is* the sword of the great *men that are*
15 slain, which entereth into their [o]privy chambers. I have set the
[5]point of the sword against all their gates, that *their* heart may
faint, and *their* ruins be multiplied: ah! [p]*it is* made bright, *it is*
16 [6]wrapped up for the slaughter. [q]Go thee one way or other,
either on the right hand, [7]*or* on the left, whithersoever thy face
17 *is* set. I will also [r]smite mine hands together, and [s]I will cause
18 my fury to rest: I the LORD have said *it*. ¶The word of the
19 LORD came unto me again, saying, Also, thou son of man,
appoint thee two ways, that the sword of the king of Babylon
may come: both twain shall come forth out of one land: and
choose thou a place, choose *it* at the head of the way to the
20 city. Appoint a way, that the sword may come to [t]Rabbath of

[i] ver. 19.
[k] Jer. 31. 19.
[l] Job 9. 23. 2 Cor. 8. 2.
[m] ver. 27.
[n] Num. 24. 10. ch. 6. 11.
[o] 1 Kin. 20. 30.
[p] ver. 10, 28.
[q] ch. 14. 17.
[r] ver. 14. ch. 22. 13.
[s] ch. 5. 13.
[t] Jer. 49. 2. ch. 25. 5. Amos 1. 14.

[1] Or, it is *the rod of my son, it despiseth every tree.*
[2] Or, *they are thrust down to the sword with my people.*
[3] Or, *When the trial* hath been, *what then? shall they not also belong to the despising rod?*
[4] Heb. *hand to hand.*
[5] Or, *glittering,* or, *fear.*
[6] Or, *sharpened.*
[7] Heb. *set thyself, take the left hand.*

---

it is written in the form of Hebrew poetry, with its characteristic parallelism.

10. *it contemneth the rod of my son,* as *every tree*] The *rod* is the sceptre of dominion, assigned to Judah (Gen. xlix. 10). The destroying sword of Babylon despises the sceptre of Judah; it despises every tree. Others render the verse, *Shall we make mirth* (saying), *the rod of my son* (the rod which corrects my people) *contemneth* (treats with scorn, utterly confounds) *every tree* (every other nation); or, the sceptre of my people *contemneth* (proudly despises) every other nation. Proud as the people are, they shall be brought to sorrow.

12. *terrors*] Better as in marg.

smite upon thy *thigh*] A token of mourning (cp. marg. ref. note).

13. Or,

For it is put to the proof, and if it contemneth even the rod,
What shall not be? saith the Lord God.

i.e. What horrors will not arise when the sword shall cut down without regard the ruling sceptre of Judah!

14. *doubled the third time*] *i.e.*, thrice *doubled* to express its violence and force.

the sword of the slain] The sword whereby men are to be slain.

of the great men &c.] Or,

The sword of the mighty slain, which presseth hard upon them.

15. *the point of the sword*] The threatening sword or terror; as in Gen. iii. 24, *the flaming sword.*

and their *ruins be multiplied*] Lit. "to the multiplication of stumblingblocks," that is, so that the causes of their fall may be more numerous. Cp. Jer. xlvi. 16.

made bright &c.] Or,

Ah! it is prepared for a lightning-flash,
Drawn for slaughter.

16. The prophet addresses the sword,

Gather thyself up, O sword, to the right or to the left.

Another rendering is; "Turn thee backwards! get thee to the right! Set thee forwards (?)! get thee to the left! O whither is thy face appointed?

17. The Lord smites together His hands in anger (marg. ref.), man in consternation.

18-32. The third word of judgment. The king of Babylon's march upon Judæa and upon the Ammonites. Destruction is to go forth not on Judah only, but also on such neighbouring tribes as the Ammonites (cp. Jer. xxvii. 2, 3).

19. *appoint thee*] **Set before thee.**

choose thou a place, choose it] Rather, "mark a spot, mark it," as upon a map, at the head of the two roads, one leading to Jerusalem, the other to Ammon. These were the two roads by one or other of which an invading army must march from Babylon to Egypt.

21 the Ammonites, and to Judah in Jerusalem the defenced. For the king of Babylon stood at the [1]parting of the way, at the head of the two ways, to use divination: he made *his* [2]arrows
22 bright, he consulted with [3]images, he looked in the liver. At his right hand was the divination for Jerusalem, to appoint [4][5]captains, to open the mouth in the slaughter, to "lift up the voice with shouting, *x*to appoint *battering* rams against the
23 gates, to cast a mount, *and* to build a fort. And it shall be unto them as a false divination in their sight, [6]to them that *y*have sworn oaths: but he will call to remembrance the iniquity, that
24 they may be taken. ¶ Therefore thus saith the Lord GOD; Because ye have made your iniquity to be remembered, in that your transgressions are discovered, so that in all your doings your sins do appear; because, *I say*, that ye are come to re-
25 membrance, ye shall be taken with the hand. And thou, *z*pro-fane wicked prince of Israel, "whose day is come, when iniquity
26 *shall have* an end, thus saith the Lord GOD; Remove the diadem, and take off the crown: this *shall* not *be* the same: *b*exalt *him*
27 *that is* low, and abase *him that is* high. [7]I will overturn, overturn, overturn, it: *c*and it shall be no *more*, until he come

u Jer. 51. 14.
x ch. 4. 2.

y ch. 17. 13, 15, 16, 18.

z 2 Chr. 36. 13.
Jer. 52. 2.
a ch. 35. 5.
b ch. 17. 24.
Luke 1. 52.
c Luke 1. 32.
John 1. 49.

[1] Heb. *mother of the way.*
[2] Or, *knives.*
[3] Heb. *teraphim.*
[4] Or, battering *rams*, ch. 4. 2.
[5] Heb. *rams.*
[6] Or, *for the oaths made unto them.*
[7] Heb. *Perverted, perverted, perverted, will I make it.*

---

21. The Chaldæan king is depicted standing at the entrance of the Holy Land from the North, meditating his campaign, using rites of divination that really belonged to the Accadians, a primitive race which originally occupied the plains of Mesopotamia. The Accadians and the Etruscans belong through the Finnish family to the Turanian stock: this passage therefore shews a characteristic mode of divination in use among two widely separated nations; and as the Romans acquired their divination from the conquered Etruscans, so the Chaldæans acquired the same art from the races whose soil they had occupied as conquerors.

he made his arrows bright] Rather, **he shook his arrows**; a mode of divination much in practice with the Arabians. It was usual to place in some vessel three arrows, on one of which was written, "My God orders me;" on the other, "My God forbids me;" on the third was no inscription. These three arrows were shaken together until one came out; if it was the first, the thing was to be done; if the second, it was to be avoided; if the third, the arrows were again shaken together, until one of the arrows bearing a decided answer should come forth.

images] *Teraphim* (Gen. xxxi. 19 note).

he looked in the liver] It was the practice both of the Greeks and the Romans (derived from the Etruscans) to take omens from the inspection of the entrails (especially the liver) of animals offered in sacrifice.

22. *the divination for Jerusalem*] The lot fixing the campaign against Jerusalem.

23. *it shall be unto them*] The Jews in their vain confidence shall look upon the hopes gathered from the divinations by the Babylonians as false and groundless.

to them that have sworn oaths] According to some, "oaths of oaths are theirs;" *i.e.* they have the most solemn oaths sworn by God to His people, in these they trust, forgetful of the sin which broke the condition upon which these promises were given. More probably the allusion is to the oaths which the Jews had sworn to Nebuchadnezzar as vassals (xvii. 18, 19); therefore they trust he will not attack them, forgetting how imperfectly they had kept their oaths, and that Nebuchadnezzar knew this.

but he will call to remembrance the iniquity] The king of Babylon will by punishment remind them of their perjury (2 K. xxv. 6, 7; 2 Chr. xxxvi. 17).

25. *profane*] Rather, "wounded,"—not dead but—having a death-wound. The prophet, turning from the general crowd, addresses Zedekiah.

when iniquity shall have *an end*] *i.e.* at the time when iniquity shall be closed with punishment. So in *v.* 29.

26. The diadem (*the mitre*, the peculiar head-dress of the high priest) **shall be removed, and the crown taken off (this shall not be as it is), the low exalted, and the high abased.** Glory shall be removed alike from priest and king; the present glory and power attached to the government of God's people shall be quite removed.

27. *it shall be no more*] Or, "This also shall not be;" the present state of things shall not continue: all shall be confusion *until*

28 whose right it is; and I will give it *him*. ¶And thou, son of man, prophesy and say, Thus saith the Lord God ᵈconcerning the Ammonites, and concerning their reproach ; even say thou, ᵉThe sword, the sword *is* drawn : for the slaughter *it is* fur-
29 bished, to consume because of the glittering : whiles they ᶠsee vanity unto thee, whiles they divine a lie unto thee, to bring thee upon the necks of *them that are* slain, of the wicked, ᵍwhose
30 day is come, when their iniquity *shall have* an end. ¹ʰShall I cause *it* to return into his sheath ? ⁱI will judge thee in the place where thou wast created, ᵏin the land of thy nativity.
31 And I will ¹pour out mine indignation upon thee, I will ᵐblow against thee in the fire of my wrath, and deliver thee into the
32 hand of ²brutish men, *and* skilful to destroy. Thou shalt be for fuel to the fire; thy blood shall be in the midst of the land ; ⁿthou shalt be no *more* remembered : for I the Lord have spoken *it*.

ᵈ Jer. 49. 1.
ch. 25. 2,3,6.
Zeph. 2. 8.
ᵉ ver. 9, 10.
ᶠ ch. 12. 24.

ᵍ Job 18. 20.
Ps. 37. 13.
ʰ Jer. 47.6,7.
ⁱ Gen. 15.14.
ch. 16. 38.
ᵏ ch. 16. 3.
ˡ ch. 7. 8.
ᵐ ch. 22. 20.

ⁿ ch. 25. 10.

Chap. 22. MOREOVER the word of the Lord came unto me, saying,
2 Now, thou son of man, ªwilt thou ³judge, wilt thou judge ᵇthe ⁴bloody city ? yea, thou shalt ⁵shew her all her abominations.
3 Then say thou, Thus saith the Lord God, The city sheddeth blood in the midst of it, that her time may come, and maketh idols
4 against herself to defile herself. Thou art become guilty in thy blood that thou hast ᶜshed ; and hast defiled thyself in thine idols which thou hast made ; and thou hast caused thy days to draw near, and art come *even* unto thy years : ᵈtherefore have I made thee a reproach unto the heathen, and a mocking to all
5 countries. *Those that be* near, and *those that be* far from thee,
6 shall mock thee, *which art* ⁶infamous *and* much vexed. ¶Be-hold, ᵉthe princes of Israel, every one were in thee to their

ª ch. 20. 4.
& 23. 36.
ᵇ ch. 24. 6, 9.
Nah. 3. 1.

ᶜ 2 Kin. 21.
16.

ᵈ Deut. 28.
37.
1 Kin. 9. 7.
Dan. 9. 16.

ᵉ Isai. 1. 23.
Mic. 3. 1, 2.
Zeph. 3. 3.

¹ Or, *Cause it to return.*
² Or, *burning.*
³ Or, *plead for.*
⁴ Heb. *city of bloods?*
⁵ Heb. *make her know*, ch. 16. 2.
⁶ Heb. *polluted of name, much in vexation.*

He come to Whom the dominion belongs of right. Not Zedekiah but Jeconiah and his descendants were the rightful heirs of David's throne. Through the restoration of the true line was there hope for Judah (cp. Gen. xlix. 10), the promised King in Whom all power shall rest—the Son of David—Messiah the Prince. Thus the prophecy of destruction ends for Judah in the promise of restoration (as in xx. 40 &c.).

28. The burden of the Song of the Sword, also in the form of poetry, is again taken up, directed now against the Ammonites, who, exulting in Judah's destruction, fondly deemed that they were themselves to escape. For Judah there is yet hope, for Ammon irremediable ruin.

their reproach] The scorn with which they reproach Judah (marg. reff.).

the sword...the glittering] Or, *the sword is drawn for the slaughter ; it is furbished that it may devour, in order that it may glitter.* In the LXX. (and Vulg.) the sword is addressed ; *e.g.* LXX., "Arise that thou mayest shine."

29. *whiles...unto thee*] A parenthesis. The

Ammonites had their false diviners who deluded with vain hopes.

to bring thee upon the necks of them that *are slain*] To cast thee (Ammon) upon the heap of slaughtered men.

shall have an end] Shall have its final doom.

30. *Shall I cause* it *to return...*] Or, **Back to its sheath!** The work of the sword is over.

XXII. 1-16. The fourth word of judgment. The sins which have brought ruin upon Jerusalem are the sins which disgraced the heathen inhabitants of Canaan, whom the Israelites were to cast out (cp. Lev. xviii.). The commission of like sins would insure like judgment.

4. *thy days, i.e.* of judgment; *thy years, i.e.* of visitation (cp. xx. 25, 39).

a reproach...a mocking] Judah shall be like the Ammonites (xxi. 28).

5. *i.e.* Countries near and afar off shall mock thee, saying, "Ah ! defiled in name ; Ah ! full of turbulence ! "

6. Render, **Behold the princes of Israel, each according to his might** (lit. "arm") **have been in thee in order to shed blood.** They looked to might not right.

7 ¹power to shed blood. In thee have they *set light by father and mother: in the midst of thee have they *dealt by ²oppression with the stranger: in thee have they vexed the fatherless
8 and the widow. Thou hast ʰdespised mine holy things, and
9 hast ⁱprofaned my sabbaths. In thee are ³ᵏmen that carry tales to shed blood: ˡand in thee they eat upon the mountains:
10 in the midst of thee they commit lewdness. In thee have they ᵐdiscovered their fathers' nakedness: in thee have they humbled
11 her that was ⁿset apart for pollution. And ⁴one hath committed abomination ᵒwith his neighbour's wife; and ⁵another ᵖhath ⁶lewdly defiled his daughter in law; and another in thee
12 hath humbled his �q sister, his father's daughter. In thee ʳhave they taken gifts to shed blood; ˢthou hast taken usury and increase, and thou hast greedily gained of thy neighbours by
13 extortion, and ᵗhast forgotten me, saith the Lord God. ¶ Behold, therefore I have ᵘsmitten mine hand at thy dishonest gain which thou hast made, and at thy blood which hath been in
14 the midst of thee. ˣCan thine heart endure, or can thine hands be strong, in the days that I shall deal with thee? ʸI the Lord
15 have spoken *it*, and will do *it*. And ᶻI will scatter thee among the heathen, and ᵃwill consume
16 thy filthiness out of thee. And thou ⁷shalt take thine inheritance in thyself in the sight of the heathen, and ᵇthou shalt
17 know that I *am* the Lord. ¶ And the word of the Lord came unto me, saying, Son of man, ᶜthe house of Israel is to me
18 become dross: all they *are* brass, and tin, and iron, and lead, in the midst of the furnace; they are *even* the ⁸dross of silver.
19 Therefore thus saith the Lord God; Because ye are all become dross, behold, therefore I will gather you into the midst of
20 Jerusalem. ⁹*As* they gather silver, and brass, and iron, and lead, and tin, into the midst of the furnace, to blow the fire upon it, to melt *it;* so will I gather *you* in mine anger and in
21 my fury, and I will leave *you there*, and melt you. Yea, I will gather you, and ᵈblow upon you in the fire of my wrath, and
22 ye shall be melted in the midst thereof. As silver is melted in the midst of the furnace, so shall ye be melted in the midst thereof; and ye shall know that I the Lord have ᵉpoured out
23 my fury upon you. ¶ And the word of the Lord came unto
24 me, saying, Son of man, say unto her, Thou *art* the land that is not cleansed, nor rained upon in the day of indignation.
25 *f There is* a conspiracy of her prophets in the midst thereof, like a roaring lion ravening the prey; they ᵍhave devoured souls; ʰthey have taken the treasure and precious things; they have
26 made her many widows in the midst thereof. ⁱHer priests have

f Deut.27.16.	
g Ex. 22. 21.	
h ver. 26.	
i Lev. 19. 30.	
k Ex. 23. 1. Lev. 19. 16.	
l ch.18.6,11.	
m Lev. 18. 7.	
n Lev. 20.18.	
o Lev. 18. 20. Jer. 5. 8.	
p Lev. 20.12.	
q Lev. 18. 9.	
r Ex. 23. 8. Deut. 16. 19.	
s Ex. 22. 25. ch. 18. 13.	
t Deut.32.18. Jer. 3. 21.	
u ch. 21. 17.	
x See ch. 21. 7.	
y ch. 17. 24.	
z Deut. 4. 27. ch. 12. 14.	
a ch. 23. 27.	
b Ps. 9. 16.	
c Isai. 1. 22. Jer. 6. 28. See Ps. 119.	
d ch. 22. 20.	
e ch.20.8,33.	
f Hos. 6. 9.	
g Matt.23.14.	
h Mic. 3. 11. Zeph. 3. 3.	
i Mal. 2. 8.	

---

¹ Heb. *arm.*
² Or, *deceit.*
³ Heb. *men of slanders.*
⁴ Or, *every one.*
⁵ Or, *every one.*
⁶ Or, *by lewdness.*
⁷ Or, *shalt be profaned.*
⁸ Heb. *drosses.*
⁹ Heb. According *to the gathering.*

---

10. *set apart for pollution*] Or, "unclean by reason of impurity" (Lev. xii. 2).

16. *thou shalt take* &c.] Better as in marg. Thou shalt by thine own fault forfeit the privileges of a holy nation.

17-22. The fifth word of judgment. The furnace. In the besieged city the people shall be tried and purged.

18. *dross*] A frequent metaphor which denotes not only the corruption of the people, who have become like base metal, but also a future purification whereby, the *dross* being burnt away, the remnant of good may appear.

23-31. The sixth word of judgment. The special sins of princes, priests, and people.

k Lev. 22. 2.
1 Sam. 2. 29.
l Jer. 15. 19.

m Isai. 1. 23.
Mic. 3. 2, 3.
Zeph. 3. 3.
n ch. 13. 10.
o ch. 13. 6, 7.

p Jer. 5. 26.
ch. 18. 12.

q Ex. 22. 21.
Lev. 19. 33.
ch. 22. 7.
r Jer. 5. 1.
s ch. 13. 5.
t Ps. 106. 23.
u ver. 22.
x ch. 9. 10.

a Jer. 3. 7.
ch. 16. 46.
n Lev. 17. 7.
Josh. 24. 14.
ch. 20. 8.
c ch. 16. 22.

d ch. 16. 8.

e 2 Kin. 15.
19.
& 16. 7.
Hos. 8. 9.

f ver. 3.

¹violated my law, and have ᵏprofaned mine holy things: they have put no ˡdifference between the holy and profane, neither have they shewed *difference* between the unclean and the clean, and have hid their eyes from my sabbaths, and I am profaned among them. Her ᵐprinces in the midst thereof *are* like wolves ravening the prey, to shed blood, *and* to destroy souls, to get 27 dishonest gain. And ⁿher prophets have daubed them with 28 untempered *morter*, ᵒseeing vanity, and divining lies unto them, saying, Thus saith the Lord God, when the Lord hath not 29 spoken. ᵖThe people of the land have used ²oppression, and exercised robbery, and have vexed the poor and needy: yea, 30 they have ᑫoppressed the stranger ³wrongfully. ʳAnd I sought for a man among them, that should ˢmake up the hedge, and ᵗstand in the gap before me for the land, that I should not 31 destroy it: but I found none. Therefore have I ᵘpoured out mine indignation upon them; I have consumed them with the fire of my wrath: ˣtheir own way have I recompensed upon their heads, saith the Lord God.

Chap. 23. THE word of the Lord came again unto me, saying, Son 2 of man, there were ᵃtwo women, the daughters of one mother: 3 and ᵇthey committed whoredoms in ᶜtheir youth: there were their breasts pressed, 4 and there they bruised the teats of their virginity. And the names of them *were* Aholah the elder, and Aholibah her sister: and ᵈthey were mine, and they bare sons and daughters. Thus *were* their names; Samaria *is* ⁴Aholah, and Jerusalem ⁵Aholibah. 5 ¶ And Aholah played the harlot when she was mine; and she 6 doted on her lovers, on ᵉthe Assyrians *her* neighbours, *which were* clothed with blue, captains and rulers, all of them desirable 7 young men, horsemen riding upon horses. Thus she ⁶committed her whoredoms with them, with all them *that were* ⁷the chosen men of Assyria, and with all on whom she doted: with 8 all their idols she defiled herself. Neither left she her whoredoms *brought* ᶠfrom Egypt: for in her youth they lay with her, and they bruised the breasts of her virginity, and poured their 9 whoredom upon her. Wherefore I have delivered her into the

¹ Heb. *offered violence to.*
² Or, *deceit.*
³ Heb. *without right.*
⁴ That is, *His tent*, or, tabernacle.
⁵ That is, *My tabernacle in her*, 1 Kin. 8. 29.
⁶ Heb. *bestowed her whore-* doms upon them.
⁷ Heb. *the choice of the children of Asshur.*

26. *violated*] Better as in marg.; to offer *violence* to the Law is to misinterpret it. It was the special office of the priests to keep up the distinction between *holy* and *unholy*, *clean* and *unclean* (Lev. x. 10).
28. See marg. ref. note.
30. The land might be said to perish for the lack of such interpositions as saved their forefathers when Moses *stood in the gap.* This was a proof ᵉ of the general corruption, that there was not in the city sufficient righteousness to save it from utter destruction. Prince, prophet, priest, all fail.
XXIII. The seventh word of judgment. The allegory of Aholah and Aholibah.
2. *of one mother*] Israel and Judah were branches of the same stock.
4. *Aholah...and Aholibah*] More correctly

"Oholah" (" her own tent or tabernacle ") and "Oholibah" ("My tent or tabernacle is in her "): names chosen to express that after the division Israel set up her own tabernacle in the place of the Temple in which God dwelt (1 K. xii. 32), while with Judah the Temple of God still remained. The Presence of God aggravated Judah's sins. In the times of the Captivity it was customary among the Jews to give their children names connected with the Temple or tabernacle.
6. The army of the Assyrians is described. War-horses formed an important part in the armies of Assyria and Egypt; Israel was deficient in this respect (Isai. xxxvi. 8).
9. For the cause which at last brought destruction on Israel, see marg. ref.

hand of her lovers, into the hand of the *g*Assyrians, upon whom
10 she doted.   These *h*discovered her nakedness: they took her
sons and her daughters, and slew her with the sword : and she
became ¹famous among women ; for they had executed judgment
11 upon her.   ¶ And *i*when her sister Aholibah saw *this*, *k*²she was
more corrupt in her inordinate love than she, and in her whore-
12 doms ³more than her sister in *her* whoredoms.   She doted upon
the *l*Assyrians *her* neighbours, *m*captains and rulers clothed most
gorgeously, horsemen riding upon horses, all of them desirable
13 young men.   Then I saw that she was defiled, *that* they took
14 both one way, and *that* she increased her whoredoms: for when
she saw men pourtrayed upon the wall, the images of the Chal-
15 deans pourtrayed with vermilion, girded with girdles upon their
loins, exceeding in dyed attire upon their heads, all of them
princes to look to, after the manner of the Babylonians of Chal-
16 dea, the land of their nativity : *n*and ⁴as soon as she saw them
with her eyes, she doted upon them, and sent messengers unto
17 them into Chaldea.   And the ⁵Babylonians came to her into the
bed of love, and they defiled her with their whoredom, and she
was polluted with them, and *o*her mind was ⁶alienated from them.
18 So she discovered her whoredoms, and discovered her nakedness :
then *p*my mind was alienated from her, like as my mind was
19 alienated from her sister.   Yet she multiplied her whoredoms,
in calling to remembrance the days of her youth, *q*wherein she
20 had played the harlot in the land of Egypt.   For she doted upon
their paramours, *r*whose flesh *is as* the flesh of asses, and whose
21 issue *is like* the issue of horses.   Thus thou calledst to remembrance the lewdness of thy youth, in bruising thy teats by the
22 Egyptians for the paps of thy youth.   ¶ Therefore, O Aholibah,
thus saith the Lord GOD; *s*Behold, I will raise up thy lovers
against thee, from whom thy mind is alienated, and I will bring
23 them against thee on every side ; the Babylonians, and all the
Chaldeans, *t*Pekod, and Shoa, and Koa, *and* all the Assyrians
with them: *u*all of them desirable young men, captains and
rulers, great lords and renowned, all of them riding upon horses.

g 2 Kin. 17.
3, 4, 5, 6, 23.
& 18. 9, 10.
h ch. 16. 37.

i Jer. 3. 8.
k Jer. 3. 11.
ch. 16. 47.

l 2 Kin. 16.
7, 10.
2 Chr. 28
16-23.
m ver. 6, 23.

n 2 Kin. 24.1.
ch. 16. 29.

o ver. 22. 28.

p Jer. 6. 8.

q ver. 3.

r ch. 16. 26.

s ch. 16. 37.
ver. 28.

t Jer. 50. 21.
u ver. 12.

¹ Heb. *a name.*
² Heb. *she corrupted her inordinate love more than, &c.*
³ Heb. *more than the whoredoms of her sister.*
⁴ Heb. *at the sight of her eyes.*
⁵ Heb. *children of Babel.*
⁶ Heb. *loosed,* or, *disjointed.*

---

10. *famous*] Or, **infamous** *among women;* lit. as in marg., *i.e.* a byword among women.

11. The idolatries of Manasseh's reign exceeded all that had gone before either in Israel or in Judah (2 K. xxi. 1-16 ; 2 Chr. xxxiii. 1-10).

14. After Israel's captivity Judah intrigued first with Assyria, then with Babylon, courting their monarchs, imitating their customs, and learning their idolatries.

pourtrayed upon the wall] The monuments of Nineveh shew how the walls of its palaces were adorned with figures precisely answering to this description.   There is evidence that these sculptures were highly coloured with vermilion, or rather, red ochre.

16. The sending of *messengers* refers to the act of Ahaz (2 K. xvi. 7).

17. After Josiah's death and the usurpa-

tion of dominion by the Egyptians, the Babylonians were no doubt welcomed as friends (2 K. xxiv. 1).   But the Jews were soon tired of their alliance and disgusted with their friends, and this led to the rebellion of Jehoiakim and the first Captivity.

19. *Egypt*] The kings of Judah played alternately Egypt against Babylon, and Babylon against Egypt.   Jehoahaz was displaced by Necho for Jehoiakim, who then turned to the Chaldæans, and afterwards rebelling sought aid from Egypt. So Zedekiah was continually meditating help from Egypt, against which Jeremiah and Ezekiel were continually protesting.

23. *Pekod, and Shoa, and Koa*] Possibly words expressive of rank, or names of small Chaldæan tribes, selected for their resemblance to expressive Hebrew words.

24 And they shall come against thee with chariots, wagons, and wheels, and with an assembly of people, *which* shall set against thee buckler and shield and helmet round about: and I will set judgment before them, and they shall judge thee according to
25 their judgments. And I will set my jealousy against thee, and they shall deal furiously with thee: they shall take away thy nose and thine ears; and thy remnant shall fall by the sword: they shall take thy sons and thy daughters; and thy
26 residue shall be devoured by the fire. *x*They shall also strip
27 thee out of thy clothes, and take away thy [1]fair jewels. Thus *y*will I make thy lewdness to cease from thee, and *z*thy whoredom *brought* from the land of Egypt: so that thou shalt not lift up thine eyes unto them, nor remember Egypt any more.
28 ¶ For thus saith the Lord God; Behold, I will deliver thee into the hand *of them* *a*whom thou hatest, into the hand *of them*
29 *b*from whom thy mind is alienated: and they shall deal with thee hatefully, and shall take away all thy labour, and *c*shall leave thee naked and bare: and the nakedness of thy whoredoms shall be discovered, both thy lewdness and thy whoredoms.
30 I will do these *things* unto thee, because thou hast *d*gone a whoring after the heathen, *and* because thou art polluted with
31 their idols. Thou hast walked in the way of thy sister; there-
32 fore will I give her *e*cup into thine hand. Thus saith the Lord God; Thou shalt drink of thy sister's cup deep and large: *f*thou shalt be laughed to scorn and had in derision; it containeth
33 much. Thou shalt be filled with drunkenness and sorrow, with the cup of astonishment and desolation, with the cup of thy
34 sister Samaria. Thou shalt *g*even drink it and suck *it* out, and thou shalt break the sherds thereof, and pluck off thine own
35 breasts: for I have spoken *it*, saith the Lord God. Therefore thus saith the Lord God; Because thou *h*hast forgotten me, and *i*cast me behind thy back, therefore bear thou also thy
36 lewdness and thy whoredoms. ¶ The Lord said moreover unto me; Son of man, wilt thou *k*[2]judge Aholah and Aholibah? yea,
37 *l*declare unto them their abominations; that they have committed adultery, and *m*blood *is* in their hands, and with their idols have they committed adultery, and have also caused their sons, *n*whom they bare unto me, to pass for them through *the*
38 *fire*, to devour *them*. Moreover this they have done unto me: they have defiled my sanctuary in the same day, and *o*have pro-
39 faned my sabbaths. For when they had slain their children to their idols, then they came the same day into my sanctuary to profane it; and, lo, *p*thus have they done in the midst of mine
40 house. And furthermore, that ye have sent for men [3]to come

x ch. 16. 30.
y ch. 16. 41. & 22. 15.
z ver. 3, 19.
a ch. 16. 37.
b ver. 17.
c ch. 16. 39. ver. 26.
d ch. 6. 9.
e Jer. 25. 15.
f ch. 22. 4, 5.
g Ps. 75. 8. Isai. 51. 17.
h Jer. 2. 32. & 13. 25. ch. 22. 12.
i 1 Kin. 14. 9. Neh. 9. 26.
k ch. 20. 4.
i Isai. 58. 1.
m ch. 16. 38.
n ch. 16. 20, 21, 36, 45. & 20. 26, 31.
o ch. 22. 8.
p 2 Kin. 21. 4.

[1] Heb. *instruments of thy decking.*   [2] Or, *plead for.*   [3] Heb. *coming.*

24. *with chariots* &c.] Better "with armour, horsemen, and chariot."
25. *take away thy nose and thine ears*] Alluding to the barbarous custom of mutilating prisoners in the East (Dan. ii. 5). An Egyptian law prescribed this punishment for an adulteress.
fire] A mode of capital punishment (Jer. xxix. 22; Dan. iii.).
37. *blood*] One of the chief sins of Manasseh was that he *shed innocent blood* (2 K. xxi. 16, xxiv. 4).

38. *the same day*] The day when they made their offerings. See *v.* 39.
39. Jehovah was placed as it were in the list of deities, not acknowledged as the One God. Idols and idol-temples were erected close to the House of God, and yet the Temple-service went on (Jer. xxxii. 34).
40, 41. The figure is that of a woman decked in all her beauty, sitting on a couch (not *bed*) at a banquet prepared for those whom she has invited. This further offence is not one of idolatry, but that of courting

from far, ^qunto whom a messenger *was* sent; and, lo, they came: ^q Isai. 57. 9.
for whom thou didst ^rwash thyself, ^spaintedst thy eyes, and
41 deckedst thyself with ornaments, and satest upon a ¹stately
^tbed, and a table prepared before it, ^uwhereupon thou hast set
42 mine incense and mine oil. And a voice of a multitude being at
ease *was* with her: and with the men ²of the common sort *were*
brought ³Sabeans from the wilderness, which put bracelets upon
43 their hands, and beautiful crowns upon their heads. Then said
I unto *her that was* old in adulteries, Will they now commit
44 ⁴whoredoms with her, and she *with them?* Yet they went in
unto her, as they go in unto a woman that playeth the harlot:
so went they in unto Aholah and unto Aholibah, the lewd
45 women. And the righteous men, they shall ^xjudge them after
the manner of adulteresses, and after the manner of women that
shed blood; because they *are* adulteresses, and ^yblood *is* in their
46 hands. For thus saith the Lord GOD; ^zI will bring up a company upon them, and will give them ⁵to be removed and spoiled.
47 ^aAnd the company shall stone them with stones, and ⁶dispatch
them with their swords; ^bthey shall slay their sons and their
48 daughters, and burn up their houses with fire. Thus ^cwill I
cause lewdness to cease out of the land, ^dthat all women may
49 be taught not to do after your lewdness. And they shall recompense your lewdness upon you, and ye shall ^ebear the sins of
your idols: ^fand ye shall know that I *am* the Lord GOD.

^r Ruth 3. 3.
^s 2 Kin. 9. 30.
Jer. 4. 30.
^t Esth. 1. 6.
Isai. 57. 7.
Amos 2. 8.
^u ch. 16. 18.
Hos. 2. 8.

^x ch. 16. 38.

^y ver. 37.
^z ch. 16. 40.

^a ch. 16. 40.
^b 2 Chr. 36.
17, 19.
ch. 24. 21.
^c ch. 22. 15.
^d Deut. 13.
11.
2 Pet. 2. 6.
^e ver. 35.
^f ch. 20. 38.

CHAP. 24. AGAIN in the ninth year, in the tenth month, in the
tenth *day* of the month, the word of the LORD came unto me,
2 saying, Son of man, write thee the name of the day, *even* of this
same day: the king of Babylon set himself against Jerusalem

¹ Heb. *honourable.*
² Heb. *of the multitude of men.*
³ Or. *drunkards.*
⁴ Heb. *her whoredom.*
⁵ Heb. *for a removing and*
spoil.
⁶ Or, *single them out.*

---

alliances with other powers which were not
less readily made than broken.

40. *that ye have sent*] Better, "they (*i.e.*
Israel and Judah) sent."

42. *a voice* &c.] Or, **The** *voice of* **the**
tumult was stilled thereby. The tumultuous cries of the invading army were stilled
by these gifts. Others render *being at ease,*
"living carelessly."

of the common sort] See marg.,—a multitudinous crowd.

Sabeans] Better as in marg. The Chaldæans were noted for their intemperance
and revellings.

the wilderness] The desert tract which the
Chaldæans had to pass from the North of
Mesopotamia to the Holy Land. This
verse describes the temporary effects of the
alliance of Israel and Judah with the Assyrians and Babylonians. All became quiet,
the allies received gifts (incense and oil)
from Israel and Judah, and these in turn
brought riches to Palestine, *bracelets upon*
their (*i.e.* Aholah's and Aholibah's) *hands,*
and crowns *upon their heads.*

43. *Will they now commit…*] Rather, Now
shall there be **committed her whoredom,**
even this; *i.e.* when Israel and Judah

had courted these alliances God said in
wrath, "This sin too shall be committed,
and so (not *yet*) *they went in*"; the alliances
were made according to their desires, and
then followed the consequent punishment.

45–49. The judgment to be executed by
the hands of their allies.

45. *the righteous men*] Or, **righteous men.**
The allies are so called as the instruments
of God's righteous judgments.

48. *to cease*] Because they are stricken and
consumed. Cp. marg. ref.

all women] *i.e.* all countries.

XXIV. Ezekiel is commissioned to announce to his fellow-exiles that the destruction of Jerusalem, so long foretold, was
now in course of execution, that the siege
had actually begun. This he is to declare
(1) by a parable—of the boiling pot, (2) by
a symbolical act—the abstaining from the
usual outward mourning for his wife's
death.

1. The prophecies in this chapter were
delivered two years and five months after
those of the previous section (xx. 1). The
day mentioned here was the very day
on which Nebuchadnezzar completed his
arrangements for the siege, and closed in the

3 ^athis same day. ^bAnd utter a parable unto the rebellious house, and say unto them, Thus saith the Lord GOD ; ^cSet on a pot, set 4 *it* on, and also pour water into it : gather the pieces thereof into it, *even* every good piece, the thigh, and the shoulder ; fill *it* with 5 the choice bones. Take the choice of the flock, and ¹burn also the bones under it, *and* make it boil well, and let them seethe 6 the bones of it therein. ¶ Wherefore thus saith the Lord GOD ; Woe to ^dthe bloody city, to the pot whose scum *is* therein, and whose scum is not gone out of it ! bring it out piece by piece; 7 let no ^elot fall upon it. For her blood is in the midst of her ; she set it upon the top of a rock ; ^fshe poured it not upon the 8 ground, to cover it with dust ; that it might cause fury to come up to take vengeance ; ^gI have set her blood upon the top of a 9 rock, that it should not be covered. Therefore thus saith the Lord GOD ; ^hWoe to the bloody city ! I will even make the pile 10 for fire great. Heap on wood, kindle the fire, consume the flesh, 11 and spice it well, and let the bones be burned. Then set it empty upon the coals thereof, that the brass of it may be hot, and may burn, and *that* ⁱthe filthiness of it may be molten in it, *that* the 12 scum of it may be consumed. She hath wearied *herself* with lies, and her great scum went not forth out of her : her scum 13 *shall be* in the fire. In thy filthiness *is* lewdness : because I have purged thee, and thou wast not purged, thou shalt not be purged from thy filthiness any more, ^ktill I have caused my fury to rest 14 upon thee. ^lI the LORD have spoken *it :* it shall come to pass, and I will do *it ;* I will not go back, ^mneither will I spare, neither will I repent ; according to thy ways, and according to thy doings, shall they judge thee, saith the Lord GOD.

15, 16 Also the word of the LORD came unto me, saying, Son of man, behold, I take away from thee the desire of thine eyes with a stroke : yet neither shalt thou mourn nor weep, neither shall 17 thy tears ²run down. ³Forbear to cry, ⁿmake no mourning for the dead, ^obind the tire of thine head upon thee, and ^pput on

¹ Or, *heap.*　　　　² Heb. *go.*　　　　³ Heb. *Be silent.*

Marginal references

a 2 Kin. 25.1.
Jer. 52. 4.
b ch. 17. 12.
c See Jer. 1.
13.

d ch. 22. 3.

e See 2 Sam.
8. 2.
Joel 3. 3.
Obad. 11.
Nah. 3. 10.
f Lev. 17. 13.
Deut. 12. 16.
g Matt. 7. 2.
h Nah. 3. 1.
Hab. 2. 12.

i ch. 22. 15.

k ch. 5. 13.
l 1 Sam. 15.
29.
m ch. 5. 11.

n Jer. 16. 5.
o See Lev.
21. 10.
p 2 Sam. 15.
30.

---

city (marg. reff.). After the Captivity this day was regularly observed as a fast day (Zech. viii. 19).

3. *a pot*] Or, **the caldron** ; with ref. to xi.
3. The prophet indicates by the figure utter destruction. The caldron is the city, the fire is the surrounding army, the flesh and bones are the inhabitants shut in within the walls.

4. *the pieces thereof*] Or, **that belong to it ;** *i.e.* the pieces which are designed for the caldron, and belong to it as the inhabitants belong to the city. The choice pieces are the choice members of the community (xi. 3).

5. *burn*] Rather, as in marg.; the bones would serve for fuel.

6. *scum*] Better, **rust** (and in *vv.* 11, 12).

bring it out piece by piece] It, the city ; bring out the inhabitants, one by one, clear the city of them, whether by death, exile, or captivity.

let no lot fall upon it] In the captivity of Jehoiakim and in that of Jehoiachin, some

were taken, others left. Now all shall be removed.

7, 8. *the top of a rock*] The blood was poured upon a naked, dry, rock where it could not be absorbed or unnoticed.

10. *consume...spice it well*] *i.e.* " dress the flesh, and make it froth and bubble, that the bones and the flesh may be all boiled up together."

16–27. The death of Ezekiel's wife took place in the evening of the same day that he delivered the foregoing prophecy. This event was to signify to the people that the Lord would take from them all that was most dear to them ; and—owing to the extraordinary nature of the times—quiet lamentation for the dead, according to the usual forms of mourning, would be impossible.

17. The priest in general was to mourn for his dead (Lev. xxi. 1 *seq.*) ; but Ezekiel was to be an exception to the rule. The *tire* was the priest's mitre.

thy shoes upon thy feet, and ^qcover not *thy* ¹lips, and eat not
18 the bread of men. ¶ So I spake unto the people in the morning:
and at even my wife died; and I did in the morning as I was
19 commanded. And the people said unto me, ^rWilt thou not tell
20 us what these *things are* to us, that thou doest *so* ? Then I
answered them, The word of the LORD came unto me, saying,
21 Speak unto the house of Israel, Thus saith the Lord GOD;
Behold, ^sI will profane my sanctuary, the excellency of your
strength, ^tthe desire of your eyes, and ²that which your soul
pitieth ; ^uand your sons and your daughters whom ye have left
22 shall fall by the sword. And ye shall do as I have done : ^xye
23 shall not cover *your* lips, nor eat the bread of men. And your
tires *shall be* upon your heads, and your shoes upon your feet :
^yye shall not mourn nor weep; but ^zye shall pine away for
24 your iniquities, and mourn one toward another. Thus ^aEzekiel
is unto you a sign : according to all that he hath done shall
ye do : ^band when this cometh, ^cye shall know that I *am* the
25 Lord GOD. ¶ Also, thou son of man, *shall it* not *be* in the day
when I take from them ^dtheir strength, the joy of their glory,
the desire of their eyes, and ³that whereupon they set their
26 minds, their sons and their daughters, *that* ^ehe that escapeth in
that day shall come unto thee, to cause *thee* to hear *it* with *thine*
27 ears ? ^fIn that day shall thy mouth be opened to him which
is escaped, and thou shalt speak, and be no more dumb : and
^gthou shalt be a sign unto them; and they shall know that I *am*
the LORD.

CHAP. 25. THE word of the LORD came again unto me, saying,

Marginal references:
q Mic. 3. 7.

r ch. 12. 9.
& 37. 18.

s Jer. 7. 14.
ch. 7. 20, 21.
t Ps. 27. 4.
u ch. 23. 47.
x Jer. 16. 6.
ver. 17.

y Job 27. 15.
Ps. 78. 64.
z ch. 33. 10.
a Isai. 20. 3.
ch. 4. 3.
b Jer. 17. 15.
John 13. 19.
c ch. 25. 5.
d ver. 21.

e ch. 33. 21.

f ch. 3. 26.
& 33. 22.

g ver. 24.

1 Heb. *upper lip:* And so   2 Heb. *the pity of your*   3 Heb. *the lifting up of*
ver. 22. Lev. 13. 45.   *soul.*   *their soul.*

eat not the bread of men] Food supplied for
the comfort of the mourners.
23. *pine away*] Cp. Lev. xxvi. 39. The
outward signs of grief were a certain consolation. Their absence would indicate a
heart-consuming sorrow.
27. Ezekiel had been employed four years
in foretelling the calamities about to come
to pass. He had been utterly disregarded
by the inhabitants of Jerusalem, and received
with apparent respect but with real incre-
dulity by those in exile. Now until the
city had been actually taken, the voice of
prophecy should cease, so far as God's
people were concerned. Hence the inter-
vening series of predictions relating to
neighbouring and foreign nations (xxv.-
xxxii.). After which the prophet's voice
was again heard addressing his countrymen
in their exile. This accounts for the apparently parenthetic character of the next
eight chapters.
XXV.-XXXII. It was a distinct part
of scriptural prophecy to address heathen
nations. In Isaiah (xiii.-xix.), Jeremiah
(xlvi.-li.), and here, one section is specially
devoted to a collection of such prophecies.
Every such prediction had the general purpose of exhibiting the conflict ever waging
between the servants of God and the powers
of the world, the struggle in which the
Church of Christ has still to wrestle against
her foes (Eph. vi. 12), but in which she will
surely prevail.
This series of prophecies, with one exception, was delivered at the time of the fall of
Jerusalem; some shortly before, and some
shortly after, the capture of the city. They
were collected together to illustrate their
original purpose of warning the nations not
to exult in their neighbour's fall. Seven nations are addressed, which have had most intercourse with the children of Israel—on their
eastern borders Moab and Ammon, on the
South Edom, on the South-West Philistia,
northward Tyre (the merchant city) and
the more ancient Sidon, and lastly Egypt,
alternately the scourge and the false stay
of the chosen people. The number *seven*
is symbolical of completeness. *Seven* prophecies against Egypt the chief of *seven*
nations, denote the completeness of the
overthrow of the heathen power, the antagonist of the kingdom of God. While
other prophets hold out to these heathen
nations some prospect of future mercy (*e.g.*
Isai. xvi. 14 ; Jer. xlix. 6, 11), Ezekiel speaks
of their complete ruin. He was contem-
plating *national* ruin. In the case of Jerusalem there would be national restoration,

a ch. 6. 2.
b Jer. 49. 1.
ch. 21. 28.
Amos 1. 13.
Zeph. 2. 9.
c Prov. 17. 5.
ch. 26. 2.

d ch. 21. 20.
e Isai. 17. 2.
Zeph. 2. 14.
f ch. 24. 24.
g Job 27. 23.
Lam. 2. 15.
Zeph. 2. 15.
h ch. 36. 5.
Zeph. 2. 8.
i ch. 35. 3.

k Isai. 15,
& 16.
Jer. 48. 1.
Amos 2. 1.
l ch. 35. 2, 5.

2 Son of man, *a*set thy face *b*against the Ammonites, and prophesy
3 against them; and say unto the Ammonites, Hear the word of
the Lord God; Thus saith the Lord God; *c*Because thou saidst,
Aha, against my sanctuary, when it was profaned; and against
the land of Israel, when it was desolate; and against the house
4 of Judah, when they went into captivity; behold, therefore I
will deliver thee to the ¹men of the east for a possession, and
they shall set their palaces in thee, and make their dwellings in
thee: they shall eat thy fruit, and they shall drink thy milk.
5 And I will make *d*Rabbah *e*a stable for camels, and the Ammonites a couchingplace for flocks: *f*and ye shall know that I *am*
6 the Lord. For thus saith the Lord God; Because thou *g*hast
clapped *thine* ²hands, and stamped with the ³feet, and *h*rejoiced in ⁴heart with all thy despite against the land of Israel;
7 behold, therefore I will *i*stretch out mine hand upon thee, and
will deliver thee for ⁵a spoil to the heathen; and I will cut thee
off from the people, and I will cause thee to perish out of the
countries: I will destroy thee; and thou shalt know that I *am*
8 the Lord. ¶Thus saith the Lord God; Because that *k*Moab
and *l*Seir do say, Behold, the house of Judah *is* like unto all
9 the heathen; therefore, behold, I will open the ⁶side of Moab
from the cities, from his cities *which are* on his frontiers, the
glory of the country, Beth-jeshimoth, Baal-meon, and Kiria-

¹ Heb. *children.*　　³ Heb. *foot.*　　⁵ Or, *meat.*
² Heb. *hand.*　　⁴ Heb. *soul.*　　⁶ Heb. *shoulder of Moab.*

but in the case of the heathen no such recovery. The *national* ruin was irretrievable; the remnant to whom the other prophets hold out hopes of mercy were to find it as individuals gathered into God's Church, not as nations to be again set up. Ezekiel does not, like other prophets, prophesy against Babylon; it was his mission to shew that for the moment, Babylon was the righteous instrument of the Divine wrath, doing God's work in punishing His foes. In prophesying against foreign nations, Ezekiel often adopts the language of those who preceded him.

XXV. The four nations most closely connected with one another by geographical position and by intercourse, are addressed in a few brief sentences concluding with the same refrain—*Ye shall know that I am the Lord* (*e.g. v.* 5). This prophecy was delivered immediately after the capture of the city by Nebuchadnezzar, and so is later, in point of time, than some of the prophecies that follow it.

1–7. The Ammonites were inveterate foes of the descendants of Abraham.

4. *men of the east*] The wild wandering Arabs who should come in afterwards upon the ruined land. The name was a common term for the nomadic tribes of the desert. Cp. Isai. xiii. 20.

palaces] **encampments.** The tents and folds of nomadic tribes. After subjugation by Nebuchadnezzar (xxi. 28), the land was subjected to various masters. The Græco-Egyptian kings founded a city on the site

of Rabbah (*v.* 5), called Philadelphia, from Ptolemy Philadelphus. In later times, Arabs from the East have completed the doom pronounced against Rabbah.

7. *for a spoil*] Or, **for a portion.**

8. Prophecies against Moab which lay South of Ammon, and shared Ammon's implacable hostility to the children of Israel.

Seir was close to Moab. Edom is identified with Mount Seir in ch. xxxv.; and *Seir* is therefore probably coupled with *Moab* here because, being near neighbours closely leagued together, they expressed a common exultation at Jerusalem's fall.

9. *I will open the side* &c.] *i.e.* lay it open to the attack of the enemy **from the cities, from his cities, from his frontier** (or, in every quarter). There is an ironical stress on *his* cities, because these cities belonged not to Moab but to Israel, having been assigned to the Reubenites (Num. xxxii. 38; Josh. xiii. 20). They lay to the North of the river Arnon, which was the proper boundary of Moab (Num. xxi. 13). The Moabites had in the last days of the kingdom of Israel recovered this territory (Isai. xvi.). They still occupied this land in the time of Ezekiel (see Jer. xlviii.).

the glory of the country] This tract, belonging to the district called by the Arabians *Al Belka*, has been at all times highly valued on account of the excellence of its pastures for cattle. The most southern of these three cities is Kiriathaim, called on the

10 thaim, ^munto the men of the east ¹with the Ammonites, and
 will give them in possession, that the Ammonites ⁿmay not be
11 remembered among the nations. And I will execute judgments
 upon Moab; and they shall know that I *am* the LORD.
12 ¶ Thus saith the Lord GOD; ^oBecause that Edom hath dealt
 against the house of Judah ²by taking vengeance, and hath
13 greatly offended, and revenged himself upon them; therefore
 thus saith the Lord GOD; I will also stretch out mine hand upon
 Edom, and will cut off man and beast from it; and I will make
 it desolate from Teman; and ³they of Dedan shall fall by the
14 sword. And ^pI will lay my vengeance upon Edom by the hand
 of my people Israel: and they shall do in Edom according to
 mine anger and according to my fury; and they shall know my
15 vengeance, saith the Lord GOD. ¶ Thus saith the Lord GOD;
 ^qbecause ^rthe Philistines have dealt by revenge, and have taken
 vengeance with a despiteful heart, to destroy *it* ⁴for the old
16 hatred; therefore thus saith the Lord GOD; Behold, ^sI will
 stretch out mine hand upon the Philistines, and I will cut off
 the ^tCherethims, ^uand destroy the remnant of the ⁵sea coast.
17 And I will ^xexecute great ⁶vengeance upon them with furious
 rebukes; ^yand they shall know that I *am* the LORD, when I shall
 lay my vengeance upon them.

^m ver. 4.
ⁿ ch. 21. 32.

^o Ps. 137. 7.
Jer. 49. 7.
ch. 35. 2.
Amos 1. 11.
Obad. 10.

^p See Isai.
11. 14.

^q Jer. 25. 20.
& 47. 1.
Joel 3. 4.
Amos 1. 6.
^r 2 Chr.28.18.
^s Zeph. 2. 4.
^t 1 Sam. 30.
14.
^u Jer. 47. 4.
^x ch. 5. 15.
^y Ps. 9. 16.

¹ Or, *against the children*
 of Ammon.
² Heb. *by revenging re-*
 vengement.
³ Or, *they shall fall by the*
 sword unto Dedan.
⁴ Or, *with perpetual hatred.*
⁵ Or, *haven of the sea.*
⁶ Heb. *vengeances.*

Moabitic stone Kirjath, and now Kureiyat.
The dual termination of the name Kiriath-
aim is explained by the fact that Kureiyat
is situated on two sister hillocks half a
mile apart, both covered by the ancient
city. It is situated about eight miles North
of the Arnon, and seven miles East of the
shore of the Dead Sea. Baal-meon is about
ten miles north of Kureiyat — known at
present as Main. It is probable that
Kiriathaim was the *Kirjath-Huzoth* (city of
streets), and Baal-meon, the *Bamoth-Baal*
(high places of Baal), to which Balak took
Balaam (Num. xxii. 39, 41). Baal-meon
occurs on the Moabitic stone as a place
which Mesa built or fortified. He probably erected a stronghold on the old
locality, reviving the ancient name. Beth-
jeshimoth is identified with a knoll at the
north-easternmost point of the Dead Sea.

10. Ammon and Moab, of common
origin, whose lands had so often been interchanged, shall now share a common
ruin. To "the men of the East" (*v.* 4) shall
Moab with Ammon be given, that Ammon
may be remembered no more, and judgment
be executed on Moab.

12. Edom, so named from Esau, consisted of various tribes enumerated in Gen.
xxxvi. The Edomites became a powerful
nation before the Israelites came out of
Egypt. David conquered them, but in the
reign of Joram they rebelled and were not
again subdued (2 K. viii. 20). Under the
name of Idumea the land was conquered by
John Hyrcanus (cp. *v.* 14), when many of
the people adopted the religion of the Jews.

In later times the Idumean Herod became
king of Palestine, reckoning himself as a
Jew. Mount Seir, deserted by its original
inhabitants, was occupied by a tribe of
Arabians (the Nabatheans), under whom
Petra rose and continued a flourishing city
under Roman dominion, until the tide of
Mahometan conquest brought it to that
ruin in which Edom at last found the complete fulfilment of the prophecies uttered
against it (ch. xxxv.).

taking vengeance] Referring to the wrong
done by Jacob to Esau (Gen. xxvii. 36).

13. *from Teman* &c.] Or *from Teman* even
unto *Dedan, shall* they *fall.* Teman and
Dedan were districts (not cities), the former
in the South (xx. 46 note), the latter in the
North ("over the whole country").

15-17. The Philistines occupying lands
to the South of Judah were a Hamite race
(Gen. x. 14), but of a different branch from
the Canaanites. They were a powerful
people never dispossessed by the Israelites
(Josh. xiii. 3). They were a thorn in the
side of the chosen people throughout, and
joined in attacking Jerusalem in the day
of her trouble. They were much reduced
by the Assyrians (Isai. xiv. 31), and
Egyptians (Jer. xlvii.), before the time of
this prophecy, but further destruction came
upon them in the general ruin of the inhabitants of Canaan, which commenced with
the destruction of Jerusalem by Nebuchadnezzar.

16. *Cherethims*] The inhabitants of the
southern portion of Philistia (Zeph. ii. 5).

Chap. 26. AND it came to pass in the eleventh year, in the first
day of the month, *that* the word of the Lord came unto me,
2 saying, ¶ Son of man, *a*because that Tyrus hath said against
Jerusalem, *b*Aha, she is broken *that was* the gates of the people :
she is turned unto me : I shall be replenished, *now* she is laid
3 waste : therefore thus saith the Lord God ; Behold, I *am* against
thee, O Tyrus, and will cause many nations to come up against
4 thee, as the sea causeth his waves to come up. And they shall
destroy the walls of Tyrus, and break down her towers : I will
also scrape her dust from her, and *c*make her like the top of a
5 rock. It shall be *a place for* the spreading of nets *d*in the midst
of the sea : for I have spoken *it*, saith the Lord God: and it
6 shall become a spoil to the nations. And her daughters which
are in the field shall be slain by the sword : *e*and they shall
7 know that I *am* the Lord. ¶ For thus saith the Lord God :
Behold, I will bring upon Tyrus Nebuchadrezzar king of
Babylon, *f*a king of kings, from the north, with horses, and
with chariots, and with horsemen, and companies, and much
8 people. He shall slay with the sword thy daughters in the
field : and he shall *g*make a fort against thee, and ¹cast a mount
9 against thee, and lift up the buckler against thee. And he
shall set engines of war against thy walls, and with his axes he
10 shall break down thy towers. By reason of the abundance of
his horses their dust shall cover thee : thy walls shall shake at
the noise of the horsemen, and of the wheels, and of the

a Isai. 23.
Jer. 25. 22.
Amos 1. 9.
Zech. 9. 2.
b ch. 25. 3.

c ver. 14.
d ch. 27. 32.

e ch. 25. 5.

f Ezra 7. 12.
Dan. 2. 37.

g ch. 21. 22.

¹ Or, *pour out the engine of shot.*

XXVI. Prophecies against Tyre. The
siege of Tyre lasted thirteen years beginning B.C. 585, about three years after the
capture of Jerusalem. While besieging
Jerusalem, Nebuchadnezzar had driven
Pharaoh Hophra back to the borders of
Egypt. Tyre being thus relieved from a
dangerous enemy, was exulting in her own
deliverance, and in her neighbour's ruin,
when Ezekiel predicted the calamity about
to befall her. The name Tyre means *rock*,
and was given to the city in consequence
of its position. This island-rock was the
heart of Tyre, and the town upon the con-
tinent—called "Old Tyre," possibly as
having been the temporary position of the
first settlers—was the outgrowth of the
island city. The scanty records of ancient
history give no distinct evidence of the
capture of insular Tyre by Nebuchadnezzar ;
but the fact is very probable. Cp. especially *vv.* 7–12, xxix. 18. The present state
of Tyre is one of utter desolation, though
the end was long delayed (cp. Isai. xxiii.).
Tyre was great and wealthy under Persian,
Greek, Roman, and even Mahometan
masters. The final ruin of Tyre was due
to the sultan of Egypt (A.D. 1291).

in the first day of the month] The number
of the month being omitted, many suppose
" the month" to mean the month when Jerusalem was taken (*the fourth month*), called
the month, as being so well known. The
capture of the city is known to have taken
place on *the ninth day of the fourth month*,

and its destruction on *the seventh day of the
fifth month*. This prophecy therefore preceded by a few days the capture of the
city. The condition of Jerusalem in the
latter months of its siege was such that the
Tyrians may well have exulted as though it
had already fallen.

2. *gates*] *i.e.* one gate of two leaves.

the people] Or, **the peoples** (and in xxvii.
3), the plural expressing the fact that many
peoples passed through Jerusalem, as the
central place on the highway of commerce,
e.g. in the reign of Solomon. This was
viewed with jealousy by Tyre, who owed
her greatness to the same cause, and in the
true spirit of mercantile competition exulted
in the thought that the trade of Jerusalem
would be diverted into her markets. Render,
**Aha ! She is broken,—the gate of the
peoples ! She is turned unto me. I shall be
filled. She is laid waste.**

6. *her daughters* &c.] The subject states
upon the mainland, on which she at this
time relied for supplies.

7–14. The description of the siege is that
of a town invested by land.

7. *Nebuchadrezzar*] Jer. xxi. 2 note.

8. *lift up the buckler*] *i.e.* set a wall of
shields, under cover of which the walls could
be approached.

9. *engines of war*] Or, **his battering ram.**

axes] **swords.** They who would break
down the towers, rush on with their swords
to slay the defenders.

chariots, when he shall enter into thy gates, [1]as men enter into
11 a city wherein is made a breach. With the hoofs of his
horses shall he tread down all thy streets: he shall slay thy
people by the sword, and thy strong garrisons shall go down to
12 the ground. And they shall make a spoil of thy riches, and
make a prey of thy merchandise: and they shall break down
thy walls, and destroy [2]thy pleasant houses: and they shall lay
thy stones and thy timber and thy dust in the midst of the
13 water. [h]And I will cause the noise of [i]thy songs to cease; and
14 the sound of thy harps shall be no more heard. And [k]I will
make thee like the top of a rock: thou shalt be *a place* to spread
nets upon; thou shalt be built no more: for I the LORD have
15 spoken *it*, saith the Lord GOD. ¶Thus saith the Lord GOD to
Tyrus; Shall not the isles [l]shake at the sound of thy fall, when
the wounded cry, when the slaughter is made in the midst of
16 thee? Then all the [m]princes of the sea shall [n]come down from
their thrones, and lay away their robes, and put off their
broidered garments: they shall clothe themselves with [3]trem-
bling; [o]they shall sit upon the ground, and [p]shall tremble at
17 *every* moment, and [q]be astonished at thee. And they shall take
up a [r]lamentation for thee, and say to thee, How art thou
destroyed, *that wast* inhabited [4]of seafaring men, the renowned
city, which wast [s]strong in the sea, she and her inhabitants,
18 which cause their terror *to be* on all that haunt it! Now shall
[t]the isles tremble in the day of thy fall; yea the isles that *are*
19 in the sea shall be troubled at thy departure. ¶For thus saith
the Lord GOD; When I shall make thee a desolate city, like the
cities that are not inhabited; when I shall bring up the deep
20 upon thee, and great waters shall cover thee; when I shall
bring thee down [u]with them that descend into the pit, with the
people of old time, and shall set thee in the low parts of the
earth, in places desolate of old, with them that go down to the
pit, that thou be not inhabited; and I shall set glory [x]in the
21 land of the living; [y]I will make thee [5]a terror, and thou *shalt*
be no *more:* [z]though thou be sought for, yet shalt thou never be
found again, saith the Lord GOD.

CHAP. 27. THE word of the LORD came again unto me, saying,

Side notes:
h Isai. 14.11.
Jer. 7. 34.
i Isai. 23. 16.
ch. 28. 13.
Rev. 18. 22.
k ver. 4, 5.

l Jer. 49. 21.
ch. 27. 28.
m Isai. 23. 8.
n Jonah 3. 6.

o Job 2. 13.
p ch. 32. 10.
q ch. 27. 35.
r ch. 27. 32.
Rev. 18. 9.
s Isai. 23. 4.

t ver. 15.

u ch. 32. 18.

x ch. 32. 23.
y ch. 27. 36.
z Ps. 37. 36.

---

[1] Heb. *according to the enter-*
ings of a city broken up.
[2] Heb. *houses of thy desire.*
[3] Heb. *tremblings.*
[4] Heb. *of the seas.*
[5] Heb. *terrors.*

---

11. *garrisons*] **pillars**, on which stood
statues of some protecting god. Cp. 2 K. x.26.
14. The siege had been on land, but the
victory was to be completed by the subjection of the island-citadel.
15-21. The effect of the fall of Tyre.
16. *clothe themselves with trembling*]
Mourners change their bright robes for sad
garments.
17. *of seafaring men*] Lit. "from the
seas," *i.e.* occupied by men who come from
the seas. Tyre was an inhabited city rising
from out of the sea.
20. Cp. Isai. xiv. 9. The image used by
Isaiah and Jeremiah of Babylon is by Ezekiel applied to Tyre, as if to shew that Tyre
and Babylon alike represent the world-

power. So in the Apocalypse Babylon is
the kingdom of Antichrist.
the land of the living] The land of the
true God, as opposed to the land of the
dead, to which is gathered the glory of the
world. Here then, together with the utter
ruin of Tyre, rises the vision of renewed
glory to Jerusalem. The coming Messiah
is thus prophetically pointed out. The overthrow of God's enemies shall be accompanied
by the establishment of His true kingdom.
XXVII. The dirge of Tyre written in
poetical form. Tyre is compared to a
fair vessel, to whose equipment the various
nations of the world contribute, launching
forth in majesty, to be wrecked and to
perish. The nations enumerated point out

a ch. 26. 17.
& 28. 12.
b ch. 28. 2.
c Isai. 23. 3.
d ch. 28. 12.

e Deut. 3. 9.

f Jer. 2. 10.

g 1 Kin. 5. 18.
Ps. 83. 7.

h Jer. 46. 9.
ch. 30. 5.

2 Now, thou son of man, *a*take up a lamentation for Tyrus ; and say
3 unto Tyrus, ¶ *b*O thou that art situate at the entry of the sea,
which art *c*a merchant of the people for many isles, Thus saith the
Lord GOD ; O Tyrus, thou hast said, *d*I *am* [1]of perfect beauty.
4 Thy borders *are* in the [2]midst of the seas, thy builders have
5 perfected thy beauty. They have [3]made all thy *ship* boards of
fir trees of *e*Senir : they have taken cedars from Lebanon to
6 make masts for thee. *Of* the oaks of Bashan have they made
thine oars ; [4][5]the company of the Ashurites have made thy
7 benches *of* ivory, *brought* out of *f*the isles of Chittim. Fine
linen with broidered work from Egypt was that which thou
spreadest forth to be thy sail ; [6]blue and purple from the isles
8 of Elishah was that which covered thee. The inhabitants of
Zidon and Arvad were thy mariners : thy wise *men*, O Tyrus,
9 *that* were in thee, were thy pilots. The ancients of *g*Gebal and
the wise *men* thereof were in thee thy [7][8]calkers : all the ships of
the sea with their mariners were in thee to occupy thy merchan-
10 dise. They of Persia and of Lud and of *h*Phut were in thine

---

[1] Heb. *perfect of beauty.*
[2] Heb. *heart.*
[3] Heb. *built.*

[4] Or, *they have made thy hatches of ivory well trodden.*
[5] Heb. *the daughter.*

[6] Or, *purple and scarlet.*
[7] Or, *stoppers of chinks.*
[8] Heb. *strengtheners.*

Tyre as the centre of commerce between
the eastern and western world. This position, occupied for a short time by Jerusalem, was long maintained by Tyre, till the
erection of Alexandria supplanted her in
this traffic. Cp. the dirge of Babylon (Isai.
xiv. 3-23) ; in each case the city named represents the world-power antagonistic to God.

3. *entry*] Lit. "entries." Ancient Tyre
had two ports, that called the Sidonian to
the North, the Egyptian to the South ; the
former exists to the present day. The
term *entry of the sea* is naturally enough
applied to a harbour as a place from which
ships enter and return from the sea. The
city was known in the earliest times as
"Tyre the port."

5. *fir-trees* (or, cypress) *of Senir*] The
name by which the Amorites knew Mount
Hermon.

6. *the company...ivory*] Rather, "thy
benches (or, deck) made they of ivory with
boxwood" (or, larch), *i.e.* boxwood inlaid
with ivory.

the isles (or, coasts) *of Chittim* is a phrase
used constantly for Greece and the Grecian
islands. It may probably be extended to
other islands in the Mediterranean sea
(Gen. x. 5), and thither ivory may have been
brought from the coasts of North Africa.

7. Or, *Fine linen* (Gen. xli. 42) *with em-
broidery from Egypt was* **thy sail that it
might be to thee for a banner.** Sails from
Egypt were worked with various figures
upon them which served as a device. Their
boats had no separate pennons.

blue and purple] Tyrian purple was
famous. The Tyrians no doubt imported
from the neighbouring coasts the mollusks
from which they dyed the fine linen of
Egypt.

isles of Elishah] See Gen. x. 4. *Elishah* is
considered equivalent to the Greek Æolis
on the western coast of Asia Minor. This
and the islands adjacent would very naturally have commerce with the Tyrians. In
early days the supply of the murex from
the coast of Phœnicia had been insufficient
for the Tyrian manufactures. The isles of
Greece abounded in the mollusks.

that which covered thee] As an awning.

8. *Arvad*] See Gen. x. 18. An island off
the coast of Sidon, now called Ruad.

9. *Gebal*] *i.e.* Byblos (modern Gebeil) in
Phœnicia, the chief seat of the worship of
Adonis, and situated on an eminence overlooking the river Adonis, north of Beirut,
not far from the Mediterranean sea. The
ancients is a term for the council that pre-
sided over maritime cities.

10, 11. The prophet here leaves the allegory of the ship to describe the armies of
the Tyrians composed of mercenary soldiers.

10. *Persia*] The name of this people does
not occur in the more ancient Books of the
Old Testament ; but in the Books of the
exile and after the exile it is frequent.
This exactly corresponds with the record of
history. It was just at the time that Ezekiel wrote that the rude and warlike people
of Persia were rising into notice, soon about
to seize, under Cyrus, the empire of the
Asiatic world.

Lud] See Gen. x. 13. The union here of
Lud with *Phut*, an undoubtedly African
tribe (cp. xxx. 5 ; Isai. lxvi. 19) seems to
indicate *Lud* to be of Hamite, not Semitic
race. Both names occur repeatedly on
Egyptian inscriptions, especially as supply-
ing mercenary soldiers.

Phut] Libyans (see Gen. x. 6).

army, thy men of war: they hanged the shield and helmet in
11 thee; they set forth thy comeliness. The men of Arvad with
thine army *were* upon thy walls round about, and the Gammadims were in thy towers: they hanged their shields upon thy
12 walls round about; they have made [i]thy beauty perfect. [k]Tar- [i] ver. 3.
shish *was* thy merchant by reason of the multitude of all *kind of* [k] Gen. 10. 4. 2 Ch. 20. 36.
riches; with silver, iron, tin, and lead, they traded in thy fairs.
13 [l]Javan, Tubal, and Meshech, they *were* thy merchants: they [l] Gen. 10. 2.
traded [m]the persons of men and vessels of brass in thy [1]market. [m] Rev. 18.13.
14 They of the house of [n]Togarmah traded in thy fairs with horses [n] Gen. 10. 3. ch. 38. 6.
15 and horsemen and mules. The men of [o]Dedan *were* thy mer- [o] Gen. 10. 7.
chants; many isles *were* the merchandise of thine hand: they
16 brought thee *for* a present horns of ivory and ebony. Syria *was*
thy merchant by reason of the multitude of [2]the wares of thy
making: they occupied in thy fairs with emeralds, purple, and
17 broidered work, and fine linen, and coral, and [3]agate. Judah,
and the land of Israel, they *were* thy merchants: they traded in
thy market [p]wheat of [q]Minnith, and Pannag, and honey, and [p] 1 K. 5. 9, 11. Ezra 3. 7.
18 oil, and [r][4]balm. Damascus *was* thy merchant in the multitude [q] Judg. 11. 33.
of the wares of thy making, for the multitude of all riches; in [r] Jer. 8. 22.
19 the wine of Helbon, and white wool. Dan also and Javan
[5]going to and fro occupied in thy fairs: bright iron, cassia, and

1 Or, *merchandise.*
2 Heb. *thy works.*
3 Heb. *chrysoprase.*
4 Or, *rosin.*
5 Or, *Meuzal.*

---

11. *Gammadims*] Rendered by LXX. "watchmen;" by others, "brave warriors;" but more probably the name of some nation of which we have no record. The custom of hanging shields upon the walls of a town by way of ornament seems to have been of purely Phœnician origin, and thence introduced by Solomon into Jerusalem (1 K. x. 16).

12–24. The thread broken at *v.* 8 is taken up, and the various nations are enumerated which traded with Tyre.

12. *Tarshish*] Tartessus in Spain (marg. reff.). Spain was rich in the metals named.

merchant] Especially applied to those who travelled about with caravans to carry on trade (see Gen. xxiii. 16).

fairs] Or, "wares" (*v.* 33). The word occurs only in this chapter. The foreign merchants gave their wares in return for the products delivered to them by Tyre.

13. *Javan*] Greece (*Ion*), including the Grecian colonies in Sicily and Italy.

Tubal, and Meshech] The Tibareni and Moschi, whose lands were on the Caucasian highlands between the Euxine and Caspian Seas (see marg. ref.), were a fine race of men; from thence slaves have been continually sought. Greece too in ancient times was famous for furnishing slaves.

14. *Togarmah*] Armenia.

15. *Dedan*] There were two tribes (Shemite and Hamite), each bearing the name of *Dedan* (see Gen. x. 7). The Hamite (Ethiopian) Dedan may well have supplied for a payment (rather than "for a present") horns, ivory, and ebony; the Shemite (Arabians), "clothes for chariots" (see *v.* 20).

16. *Syria*] *Aram* here included Mesopotamia; and Babylon was famous for its precious stones. Many read "Edom."

emeralds] Rather, **carbuncle.**

fine linen] The word (*butz*) was used only in the times of the Captivity. It is a Phœnician word, which in Greek assumed the form "byssus," properly "cotton," as distinguished from "linen;" the Phœnicians spinning their threads from cotton wool, the Egyptians from flax.

17. *Minnith*] A city of the Ammonites, whose country was famous for wheat (2 Chr. xxvii. 5). The wheat was carried through the land of Israel to Tyre.

Pannag] This word occurs nowhere else, and has been very variously explained. Some take it to be "sweetwares." Others see in it the name of a place, fertile like *Minnith*, perhaps identical with Pingi on the road from Baalbec to Damascus.

18. *Helbon*] Chalybon, near Damascus, whose wine was a favourite luxury with Persian kings.

white wool] A product of flocks that grazed in the waste lands of Syria and Arabia.

19. *Dan also*]. Heb. *Vedan*, a place in Arabia, not elsewhere mentioned.

going to and fro] Better as in marg. a proper name, *Meuzal*, or rather, "from Uzal" which was the ancient name of Senaa the capital of Yemen in Arabia. Greek merchants would carry on commerce between Uzal and Tyre.

bright iron] Lit. "wrought iron;" iron

*Gen. 25. 3.

20 calamus, were in thy market. *Dedan was thy merchant in
21 ¹precious clothes for chariots. Arabia, and all the princes of

t Gen. 25. 13.
Isai. 60. 7.
ᵘ Gen. 10. 7.

ᵗKedar, ²they occupied with thee in lambs, and rams, and goats:
22 in these were they thy merchants. The merchants of ᵘSheba and

1 K. 10. 1.
Ps. 72. 10.
Isai. 60. 6.
*Gen. 11.31.

Raamah, they were thy merchants: they occupied in thy fairs
with chief of all spices, and with all precious stones, and gold.
23 *Haran, and Canneh, and Eden, the merchants of ʸSheba,

ʸ Gen. 25. 3.

24 Asshur, and Chilmad, were thy merchants. These were thy merchants in ³all sorts of things, in blue ⁴clothes, and broidered
work, and in chests of rich apparel, bound with cords, and made
of cedar, among thy merchandise.

*Ps. 48. 7.
Isai. 2. 16.
ᵘ ver. 4.
ᵇ Ps. 48. 7.
ᶜ Prov. 11. 4.
Rev. 18. 9.

25 *The ships of Tarshish did sing of thee in thy market: and thou
wast replenished, and made very glorious ᵃin the midst of the
26 seas. Thy rowers have brought thee into great waters: ᵇthe east
27 wind hath broken thee in the ⁵midst of the seas. Thy ᶜriches,
and thy fairs, thy merchandise, thy mariners, and thy pilots, thy
calkers, and the occupiers of thy merchandise, and all thy men
of war, that are in thee, ⁶and in all thy company which is in
the midst of thee, shall fall into the ⁷midst of the seas in the

ᵈ ch. 26. 15.

28 day of thy ruin. The ⁸suburbs ᵈshall shake at the sound of

ᵉ Rev. 18. 17,
&c.

29 the cry of thy pilots. And ᵉall that handle the oar, the mari-
30 ners, and all the pilots of the sea, shall come down from their
ships, they shall stand upon the land; and shall cause their
voice to be heard against thee, and shall cry bitterly, and shall

ᶠ Job 2. 12.
Rev. 18. 19.
ᵍ Esth. 4. 1.
Jer. 6. 26.

ᶠcast up dust upon their heads, they ᵍshall wallow themselves

¹ Heb. clothes of freedom.
² Heb. they were the mer-
chants of thy hand.
³ Or, excellent things.
⁴ Heb. foldings.
⁵ Heb. heart.
⁶ Or, even with all.
⁷ Heb. heart.
⁸ Or, waves.

---

worked into plates smooth and polished.
Yemen was famous for the manufacture of
sword-blades.

cassia] The inner bark of an aromatic
plant.

calamus] A fragrant reed-like plant (see
Ex. xxx. 23, 24). Both are specially products of India and Arabia.

20. Dedan] See v. 15. It is remarkable
that Dedan and Sheba occur both among the
descendants of Ham in Gen. x. 7, and among
the descendants of Abraham and Keturah
in Gen. xxv. 3. This seems to indicate
that there were distinct nomad tribes bearing the same names of Hamite and of
Semitic origin ; or it may be that whereas
some of the nomad Arabs were Hamite,
others Semitic, these were of mixed origin,
and so traced up their lineage alike to Ham
and Shem. Here we have, at any rate, a
number of Arabian nomad tribes mentioned together, and these tribes and their
caravans were in those days the regular
merchant travellers between East and West.
Tyre by her ships spread over Europe the
goods which by these caravans she obtained from India and China.

precious clothes] Or "clothes of covering," cloths of tapestry.

21. Kedar] The representative of the
pastoral tribes in the North-West of Arabia.

22. Sheba] Sabæa, the richest country of

Arabia, corresponded nearly with what is
now called Yemen or Arabia Felix.

Raamah] Closely connected with Sheba,
whose seat is supposed to have been in the
neighbourhood of the Persian Gulf.

23. Haran] Charræ in Mesopotamia.

Canneh] Calneh (Gen. x. 10), probably
Ctesiphon on the Tigris.

Eden] On the Euphrates (Isai. xxxvii. 12).

the merchants of Sheba] Here the towns
or tribes that traded with Sheba. Sheba
maintained a considerable trade with Mesopotamia.

Chilmad] Possibly Kalwada near Bagdad.

24. all sorts of things] See marg.

made of cedar] Rather, made fast.

25. did sing of thee] Or, were thy bulwarks, i.e. bulwarks of thy traffic. Others
render, "were thy caravans," thy merchandize.

26. the east wind] Cp. marg. ref.

27. All who have been enumerated as
sharing in, and constituting, the glory of
Tyre are now recounted as partakers in her
wreck.

28. The suburbs] Or, "precincts." Tyre
rose from the midst of the sea ; her "precincts" were the surrounding waters and
the adjoining coasts.

29. As Tyre is figured by a large vessel,
so are the subject-states by smaller boats
which accompany the great ship. These

31 in the ashes: and they shall *make themselves utterly bald for thee, and gird them with sackcloth, and they shall weep for
32 thee with bitterness of heart *and* bitter wailing. And in their wailing they shall *take up a lamentation for thee, and lament over thee, *saying,* *What *city is* like Tyrus, like the destroyed
33 in the midst of the sea? *When thy wares went forth out of the seas, thou filledst many people; thou didst enrich the kings of the earth with the multitude of thy riches and of thy mer-
34 chandise. In the time *when* *thou shalt be broken by the seas in the depths of the waters *thy merchandise and all thy com-
35 pany in the midst of thee shall fall. *All the inhabitants of the isles shall be astonished at thee, and their kings shall be sore
36 afraid, they shall be troubled in *their* countenance. The merchants among the people *shall hiss at thee; *thou shalt be ¹a terror, and ²never *shalt be* any more.

h Jer. 16. 6.
Mic. 1. 16.

i ch. 26. 17.
k Rev. 18. 18.
l Rev. 18. 19.

m ch. 26. 19.
n ver. 27.
o ch. 26. 15.

p Jer. 18. 16.
q ch. 26. 21.

Chap. 28. THE word of the LORD came again unto me, saying, Son
2 of man, say unto the prince of Tyrus, Thus saith the Lord GOD; Because thine heart *is* lifted up, and *thou hast said, I *am* a God, I sit *in* the seat of God, *in the ³midst of the seas; *yet thou *art* a man, and not God, though thou set thine heart as
3 the heart of God: behold, *thou *art* wiser than Daniel; there
4 is no secret that they can hide from thee: with thy wisdom and with thine understanding thou hast gotten thee riches, and
5 hast gotten gold and silver into thy treasures: ⁴*by thy great wisdom *and* by thy traffick hast thou increased thy riches, and
6 thine heart is lifted up because of thy riches: therefore thus saith the Lord GOD; Because thou hast set thine heart as the
7 heart of God; behold, therefore I will bring strangers upon thee, *the terrible of the nations: and they shall draw their swords against the beauty of thy wisdom, and they shall defile
8 thy brightness. They shall bring thee down to the pit, and thou shalt die the deaths of *them that are* slain in the midst of the

a ver. 9.
b ch. 27. 3, &.
c Isai. 31. 3.

d Zech. 9. 2.

e Ps. 62. 10.
Zech. 9. 3.

f ch. 30. 11.

¹ Heb. *terrors.*
² Heb. *shalt not be for ever.*
³ Heb. *heart*
⁴ Heb. *by the greatness of thy wisdom.*

terrified by the storm approach the land. Tyre is hopelessly swallowed up, crew and all, in the midst of the sea. The small crafts escape to shore.

31. *utterly bald*] See vii. 18 note.

35. The news of Tyre's ruin shall reach to distant isles, to merchant cities who trade with her. These in their selfish love of gain shall rejoice over her who was once paramount over them, hissing out against her curses and scorn.

XXVIII. 1-10. The prophecy against the prince of Tyre. Throughout the East the majesty and glory of a people were collected in the person of their monarch, who in some nations was worshipped as a god. The prince is here the embodiment of the community. Their glory is his glory, their pride his pride. The doom of Tyre could not be complete without denunciation of the prince of Tyre. Idolatrous nations and idolatrous kings were, in the eyes of the prophet, antagonists to the true God. In them was embodied the principle of evil opposing itself to the Divine govern-

ment of the world. Hence some of the Fathers saw upon the throne, not simply a hostile monarch, but *the Prince of this world, spiritual wickedness* (or *wicked spirits*) *in high places.* Whenever evil in any way domineers over good, there is a *prince of Tyrus,* against whom God utters His voice. The *mystery of iniquity* is ever working, and in that working we recognize the power of Satan whom God condemns and will destroy.

2. *thou hast said, I* am *a god*] Cp. xxix. 3; Dan. iv. 30; Acts xii. 22; 2 Thess. ii. 4.

I sit in the seat of God] Words denoting the speaker's pride; but the situation of the island-city, full of beauty, in the midst of the blue water of the Mediterranean, gives force to the expression. Cp. the words describing the lot of Tyre as having been in *Eden* (*v.* 13).

thou art a man] Rather, thou art **man.**

3. *thou* art *wiser than Daniel*] The passage is one of strong irony. Cp. xiv. 14; Dan. vi. 3.

g ver. 2.

h ch. 31. 18.
ch. 32. 19.

i ch. 27. 2.
k ch. 27. 3.
ver. 3.

l ch. 31. 8, 9.

m ch. 26. 13.

n See Ex.
25. 20.
ver. 16.
o ch. 20. 40.

p ver. 14.
q ver. 2, 5.

9 seas. Wilt thou yet *g*say before him that slayeth thee, I *am*
God? but thou *shalt be* a man, and no God, in the hand of him
10 that [1]slayeth thee. Thou shalt die the deaths of *h*the uncircumcised by the hand of strangers: for I have spoken *it*, saith
the Lord GOD.

11, 12 Moreover the word of the LORD came unto me, saying, Son
of man, *i*take up a lamentation upon the king of Tyrus, and say
unto him, Thus saith the Lord GOD; *k*Thou sealest up the sum,
13 full of wisdom, and perfect in beauty. Thou hast been in
*l*Eden the garden of God; every precious stone *was* thy covering,
the [2]sardius, topaz, and the diamond, the [3]beryl, the onyx, and
the jasper, the sapphire, the [4]emerald, and the carbuncle, and
gold: the workmanship of *m*thy tabrets and of thy pipes was
14 prepared in thee in the day that thou wast created. Thou *art*
the anointed *n*cherub that covereth; and I have set thee *so:*
thou wast upon *o*the holy mountain of God; thou hast walked
15 up and down in the midst of the stones of fire. Thou *wast*
perfect in thy ways from the day that thou wast created, till
16 iniquity was found in thee. By the multitude of thy merchandise they have filled the midst of thee with violence, and thou
hast sinned: therefore I will cast thee as profane out of the
mountain of God: and I will destroy thee, *p*O covering cherub,
17 from the midst of the stones of fire. *q*Thine heart was lifted
up because of thy beauty, thou hast corrupted thy wisdom by
reason of thy brightness: I will cast thee to the ground, I will
18 lay thee before kings, that they may behold thee. Thou hast
defiled thy sanctuaries by the multitude of thine iniquities, by
the iniquity of thy traffick; therefore will I bring forth a fire
from the midst of thee, it shall devour thee, and I will bring
thee to ashes upon the earth in the sight of all them that behold
19 thee. All they that know thee among the people shall be asto-

---

[1] Or, *woundeth.*　　[2] Or, *ruby.*　　[3] Or, *chrysolite.*　　[4] Or, *chrysoprase.*

9. *but thou* shalt be *a man*] Rather, **yet art thou man.**

10. *the uncircumcised*] The heathen idolaters as opposed to the Covenant-people.

11–19. The dirge of the prince of Tyre, answering to the dirge of the state. The passage is ironical; its main purpose is to depict all the glory, real or assumed, of *the prince of Tyrus*, in order to show how deplorable should be his ruin.

12. To *seal* the *sum* is to make up the whole measure of perfection. Cp. the LXX.

13. *Thou hast been in Eden*] *Thou* **wast** &c. The prince of Tyrus is ironically described as the first of creation; but at the same time the parallel is to be maintained in his fall from glory. Like Adam in the enjoyment of paradise, he shall be like Adam in his fall.

every precious stone] All the stones here named are found in the High Priest's breastplate (Ex. xxviii. 17-20), but their order is different, and three stones named in Exodus (the third row) are wanting. The prophet may purposely have varied the description because the number twelve (that of the tribes of Israel) had nothing to do with the

prince of Tyrus, and he wished to portray, not a High Priest, but a king, having in view a figure which was to a Jew, especially to a priest, the very type of magnificence.

Tabrets (or, drums) and *pipes* were a common expression for festivity and triumph.

14. *Thou* art] Better, *Thou* **wert.**

the anointed cherub that covereth] In the Temple the Cherubim and all holy things were consecrated and anointed with oil (Ex. xxx. 26 &c.). The prince of Tyre was also *anointed* as a sovereign priest—*covering* or protecting the minor states, like the Cherubim with outstretched wings covering the Mercy-Seat.

thou wast upon the holy mountain] As the cherub was in the Temple on the holy mountain, so the prince of Tyre was presiding over the island-city, rising like a mountain from the deep.

stones of fire] *i.e.* bright and shining. Decked with bright jewels, the prince walked among jewels in gorgeous splendour.

15. The *perfection* was false, unsuspected until the *iniquity* which lay beneath was found out.

nished at thee : ʳthou shalt be ¹a terror, and never *shalt* thou   ʳ ch. 26. 21.
be any more.

20, 21 Again the word of the LORD came unto me, saying, Son of
man, ˢset thy face ᵗagainst Zidon, and prophesy against it, and   ˢ ch. 6. 2.
22 say, Thus saith the Lord GOD ; ᵘBehold, I *am* against thee, O   ᵗ Isai. 23. 4.
Zidon ; and I will be glorified in the midst of thee : and ˣthey   Jer. 25. 22.
shall know that I *am* the LORD, when I shall have executed   ch. 32. 30.
23 judgments in her, and shall be ʸsanctified in her.   ᶻFor I will   ᵘ Ex. 14. 4.
send into her pestilence, and blood into her streets ; and the   ch. 39. 13.
wounded shall be judged in the midst of her by the sword upon   ˣ Ps. 9. 16.
her on every side ; and they shall know that I *am* the LORD.   ʸ ch. 20. 41.
24 And there shall be no more ᵃa pricking brier unto the house of   & 36. 23.
Israel, nor *any* grieving thorn of all *that are* round about them,   ᶻ ch. 38. 22.
that despised them ; and they shall know that I *am* the Lord   ᵃ Num.33.55.
25 GOD. ¶ Thus saith the Lord GOD ; When I shall have ᵇgathered   Josh. 23. 13.
the house of Israel from the people among whom they are scat-   ᵇ Isai. 11.12.
tered, and shall be ᶜsanctified in them in the sight of the heathen,   ch. 11. 17.
then shall they dwell in their land that I have given to my ser-   & 37. 21.
26 vant Jacob. And they shall ᵈdwell ²safely therein, and shall   ᶜ ver. 22.
ᵉbuild houses, and ᶠplant vineyards ; yea, they shall dwell with   ᵈ Jer. 23. 6.
confidence, when I have executed judgments upon all those that   ch. 36. 28.
³despise them round about them ; and they shall know that I   ᵉ Isai. 65. 21.
am the LORD their God.   Amos 9. 14.
ᶠ Jer. 31. 5.

CHAP. 29. IN the tenth year, in the tenth *month*, in the twelfth
day of the month, the word of the LORD came unto me, saying,
2 Son of man, ᵃset thy face against Pharaoh king of Egypt, and   ᵃ ch. 28. 21.
3 prophesy against him, and ᵇagainst all Egypt : speak, and say,   ᵇ Isai. 19. 1.
Thus saith the Lord GOD ; ¶ ᶜBehold, I *am* against thee,   Jer. 46. 2.
ᶜ Jer. 44. 30.
ch. 28. 22.

¹ Heb. *terrors.*   ² Or, *with confidence.*   ³ Or, *spoil.*

---

21. **Prophecy against Zidon.** *Zidon*
(mod. Saida) was more ancient than Tyre
and was the original metropolis of Phœnicia (Gen. x. 19), but in the times of Phœnician greatness it ever played a subordinate
part. Only once (Judg. x. 12) do wʒ find
the *Zidonians* in conflict with Israel. The
evil which they did was the seducing them
to idolatry (cp. *v.* 24), as in the case of Jeze-
bel, daughter of Ethbaal, king of the Zidonians (1 K. xvi. 31). The capture of Tyre by
Nebuchadnezzar increased the importance of
Zidon, which was a wealthy and flourishing
town when Artaxerxes Ochus destroyed it.
It has rallied from time to time, but has
never attained to any great consequence,
though not in such complete ruin as Tyre.

22. *be glorified...be sanctified*] Or, "get Me
glory...have shown Myself holy"(and in *v.*25).

25, 26. The contrast of the future of
Israel with that of the surrounding nations.
This prophecy reaches far beyond a mere
temporal restoration. It points to times of
more permanent security, when from all
nations and kingdoms the Church of
Christ, the Israel of God, shall be gathered
in, when the power of the world shall be
for ever broken, and the kingdom of Christ
shall be established for ever.

This transition from the enemies to the
people of God closes the portion of the prophecies against the nations in the immediate
vicinity of the Israelites, before passing to
the more distant Egypt.

XXIX.-XXXII.   **Prophecies against
Egypt** which, uttered (with the exception
of xxix. 17 to end) in regular succession,
predict the downfall of Pharaoh Hophra
and the desolation of Egypt.

XXIX. 1-16. **First prophecy against
Egypt** delivered some months before the
preceding prophecies against Tyre (see
xxvi. 1), the prophecies against the nations
being given, not in their chronological, but
in their geographical order, according to
their nearness to Jerusalem.

1. *the tenth year*] Jerusalem had been besieged, but not taken. Jeremiah delivered
his prophecy against Egypt, about the time
when the approach of Pharaoh Hophra's
army caused the Chaldæans for the time to
raise the siege (Jer. xxxvii. 5). This was the
solitary instance of Egypt meddling with
the affairs of Palestine or Syria after the
battle of Carchemish (cp. 2 K. xxiv. 7) ; it met
with speedy punishment.

3. The king is addressed as the embodiment of the state.

d Ps. 74. 13.
Isai. 51. 9.
ch. 32. 2.
e See ch.28.2.
f Isai. 37. 29.
ch. 38. 4.

g Jer. 8. 2.
& 25. 33.
h Jer. 7. 33.
& 34. 20.

i 2Kin.18.21.
Isai. 36. 6.
k Jer. 37. 5.
ch 17. 17.

l ch. 14. 17.
& 32. 11, 12.

m ch. 30. 12.
n ch. 30. 6.
o ch. 32. 13.

Pharaoh king of Egypt, the great *d*dragon that lieth in the midst of his rivers, *e*which hath said, My river *is* mine own, 4 and I have made *it* for myself. But *f*I will put hooks in thy jaws, and I will cause the fish of thy rivers to stick unto thy scales, and I will bring thee up out of the midst of thy rivers, 5 and all the fish of thy rivers shall stick unto thy scales. And I will leave thee *thrown* into the wilderness, thee and all the fish of thy rivers : thou shalt fall upon the ¹open fields ; *g*thou shalt not be brought together, nor gathered : *h*I have given thee for meat to the beasts of the field and to the fowls of the heaven. 6 And all the inhabitants of Egypt shall know that I *am* the LORD, because they have been a *i*staff of reed to the house of 7 Israel. *k*When they took hold of thee by thy hand, thou didst break, and rend all their shoulder : and when they leaned upon thee, thou breakest, and madest all their loins to be at a stand. 8 Therefore thus saith the Lord GOD ; Behold, I will bring *l*a 9 sword upon thee, and cut off man and beast out of thee. And the land of Egypt shall be desolate and waste ; and they shall know that I *am* the LORD : because he hath said, The river *is* 10 mine, and I have made *it*. Behold, therefore I *am* against thee, and against thy rivers, *m*and I will make the land of Egypt ²utterly waste *and* desolate, ³ⁿfrom the tower of ⁴Syene even 11 unto the border of Ethiopia. *o*No foot of man shall pass through it, nor foot of beast shall pass through it, neither shall it be in-

¹ Heb. *face of the field.*   ³ Or, *from Migdol to Syene,*   ⁴ Heb. *Seveneh.*
² Heb. *wastes of waste.*   Ex. 14. 2. Jer. 44. 1.

---

dragon] Here the crocodile, the great monster of the Nile, which was regarded very differently in different parts of Egypt. By some it was worshipped and embalmed after death, and cities were named after it (*e.g.* in the Arsinoite nome). Others viewed it with the utmost abhorrence. An animal so terrible, so venerated, or so abhorred, was an apt image of the proud Egyptian monarch—the more so, perhaps, because it was in truth less formidable than it appeared, and often became an easy prey to such as assailed it with skill and courage.

lieth in the midst of his rivers] Sais, the royal city, during the twenty-sixth dynasty was in the Delta, in the very midst of the various branches and canals of the Nile.

My river is *mine own* &c.] It was the common boast of Hophra (Apries), that " not even a god could dispossess him of power." The river was at all times the source of fertility and wealth to Egypt, but especially so to the Saite kings, who had their royal residence on the river, and encouraged intercourse with foreigners, by whose commerce the kingdom was greatly enriched.

4. *hooks in thy jaws*] Cp. Job xli. 2. The crocodile is thus rendered an easy prey.

fish of thy rivers] *i.e.* the allies of Egypt shall be involved in her ruin.

6. *staff of reed*] The reed was specially appropriate to Egypt as the natural product of its river.

7. So Egypt was continually proving to

Israel, to Jehoiakim and to Zedekiah. The tenses are present not past.

to be at a stand] Others, " to totter."

10. *from the tower of Syene*] Or, as in marg. *Migdol* (tower) was about two miles from Suez. *Syene* was the most southern town in Egypt, on the borders of Ethiopia, in the Thebaid, on the eastern bank of the Nile. The modern Assvan lies a little to the North-East of the ancient Syene.

10-12. We have no record of the circumstances of the Chaldæan invasion of Egypt, but it is possible that it did not take place till after the fall of Tyre. We gather of what nature it must have been by comparing the description of the results of Assyrian conquest (Isai. xxxvii. 25 seq.). Minute fulfilment of every detail of prophecy is not to be insisted upon, but only the general fact that Egypt would for a time, described as forty years, be in a state of collapse. No great stress is to be laid on the exact number of years. The number of years passed in the wilderness became to the Hebrews a significant period of chastisement.

Nebuchadnezzar's occupation of Egypt was of no long duration, and his ravages, though severe, must have been partial. Peace with Babylon was favourable to the development of home-works, but since the peace was in truth subjugation, it was hollow and in fact ruinous. Further, it is to be remembered that God fulfils His decree by a gradual rather than an immediate pro-

12 habited forty years. *p*And I will make the land of Egypt *p* ch. 30. 7, 26.
desolate in the midst of the countries *that are* desolate, and her
cities among the cities *that are* laid waste shall be desolate forty
years : and I will scatter the Egyptians among the nations, and
13 will disperse them through the countries. ¶ Yet thus saith the
Lord GOD ; At the *q*end of forty years will I gather the Egypt- *q* Isai. 19. 23. Jer. 46. 26.
14 ians from the people whither they were scattered : and I will
bring again the captivity of Egypt, and will cause them to return
into the land of Pathros, into the land of their ¹habitation ; and
15 they shall be there a ²*r*base kingdom. It shall be the basest of *r* ch. 17. 6.
the kingdoms; neither shall it exalt itself any more above the
nations : for I will diminish them, that they shall no more rule
16 over the nations. And it shall be no more *s*the confidence of the *s* Isai. 30. 2. & 36. 4, 6.
house of Israel, which bringeth *their* iniquity to remembrance,
when they shall look after them : but they shall know that I *am*
the Lord GOD.

17 And it came to pass in the seven and twentieth year, in the
first *month*, in the first *day* of the month, the word of the LORD
18 came unto me, saying, Son of man, *t*Nebuchadrezzar king of *t* Jer. 27. 6. ch. 26. 7, 8.
Babylon caused his army to serve a great service against Tyrus :
every head *was* made bald, and every shoulder *was* peeled : yet
had he no wages, nor his army, for Tyrus, for the service that
19 he had served against it : therefore thus saith the Lord GOD;
Behold, I will give the land of Egypt unto Nebuchadrezzar king
of Babylon ; and he shall take her multitude, and ³take her
spoil, and take her prey; and it shall be the wages for his army.
20 I have given him the land of Egypt ⁴*for* his labour wherewith
he *u*served against it, because they wrought for me, saith the *u* Jer. 25. 9.
21 Lord GOD. In that day *x*will I cause the horn of the house of *x* Ps. 132. 17.
Israel to bud forth, and I will give thee *y*the opening of the *y* ch. 24. 27.
mouth in the midst of them ; and they shall know that I *am*
the LORD.

¹ Or, *birth.*
² Heb. *low.*
³ Heb. *spoil her spoil, and prey her prey.*
⁴ Or, for *his hire.*

---

cess. The ravages of Nebuchadnezzar were
the beginning of the end, and all the desolation which followed may be looked upon as
a continuous fulfilment of God's decree. The
savage fury with which Cambyses swept
over Egypt amply realized all that Ezekiel
foretold. Many places recovered some
wealth and prosperity, but from the time of
Herodotus the kingdom never again became
really independent. Egyptian rulers gave
place to Persian, Persian to the successors of
Alexander the Great, who gave place in turn
to Rome. So thoroughly was the prophecy
of Ezekiel fulfilled (*vv.* 14, 15).

13. A similar respite was promised to
Moab (Jer. xlviii. 47), to Ammon (Jer. xlix.
6), and to Tyre (Isai. xxiii. 15).

14. *Pathros*] The Thebaid or Upper
Egypt, the original seat of the kingdom.
the land of their habitation] Rather, as
marg., *i.e.* the home of the restored exiles.

16. The false confidence of the Israelites
brought to remembrance, i.e. discovered in
the sight of God and man their *iniquity, i.e.*
their treachery and perjury to the Chal-

dæans ; their falsehood being made evident
when they *look after* (turn to) the Egyptians
and seek their aid in rebellion. The ruin
of Egypt shall put an end to all this.

17–21. The prophet places this prediction
out of chronological order, that he may
point out what had not been stated in
the foregoing prophecy, viz., that the agent
who should strike the first blow on Egypt
should be the Chaldæan king, Nebuchadnezzar.

18. *yet had he no wages*] It is not improbable that the Tyrians before they sur-
rendered their island-citadel managed to
remove much of their treasure ; but others
explain the verse ;—that the siege and capture of Tyre is to be regarded as the *work*
appointed, and the possession of Egypt as
the *reward* or *wages* for the work.

21. Egypt being the antagonist of the
people of God, her overthrow inaugurated
the triumph of good over evil.
the horn &c.] Or, "an horn to bud forth
to the house of Israel."
I will give thee the opening of the mouth]

Chap. 30. THE word of the Lord came again unto me, saying,
2 Son of man, prophesy and say, Thus saith the Lord God; [a]Howl
3 ye, Woe worth the day! For [b]the day *is* near, even the day of
the Lord *is* near, a cloudy day; it shall be the time of the
4 heathen. And the sword shall come upon Egypt, and great
[1]pain shall be in Ethiopia, when the slain shall fall in Egypt,
and they [c]shall take away her multitude, and [d]her foundations
5 shall be broken down. Ethiopia, and [2]Libya, and Lydia, and
[e]all the mingled people, and Chub, and the [3]men of the land
6 that is in league, shall fall with them by the sword. ¶ Thus
saith the Lord; They also that uphold Egypt shall fall; and
the pride of her power shall come down: [4]from the tower of
Syene shall they fall in it by the sword, saith the Lord God.
7 [g]And they shall be desolate in the midst of the countries *that*
are desolate, and her cities shall be in the midst of the cities
8 *that are* wasted. And they shall know that I *am* the Lord,
when I have set a fire in Egypt, and *when* all her helpers shall
9 be [5]destroyed. In that day [h]shall messengers go forth from
me in ships to make the careless Ethiopians afraid, and great
pain shall come upon them, as in the day of Egypt: for, lo, it
cometh.

10　　Thus saith the Lord God; [i]I will also make the multitude of
Egypt to cease by the hand of Nebuchadrezzar king of Babylon.
11 He and his people with him, [k]the terrible of the nations, shall be
brought to destroy the land: and they shall draw their swords
12 against Egypt, and fill the land with the slain. And [l]I will
make the rivers [6]dry, and [m]sell the land into the hand of the
wicked: and I will make the land waste, and [7]all that is therein,
13 by the hand of strangers: I the Lord have spoken *it*. Thus
saith the Lord God; I will also [n]destroy the idols, and I will
cause *their* images to cease out of Noph; [o]and there shall be
no more a prince of the land of Egypt: [p]and I will put a fear
14 in the land of Egypt. And I will make [q]Pathros desolate, and
will set fire in [r][8]Zoan, [s]and will execute judgments in No.

Marginal references (left column):
[a] Isai. 13. 6.
[b] ch. 7. 7.
Joel 2. 1.
Zeph. 1. 7.
[c] ch. 29. 19.
[d] Jer. 50. 15.
[e] Jer. 25. 20, 24.
[f] ch. 29. 10.
[g] ch. 29. 12.
[h] Isai. 18. 1, 2.
[i] ch 29. 19.
[k] ch. 28. 7.
[l] Isai. 19. 5.
[m] Isai. 19. 4.
[n] Jer. 43. 12.
Zech. 13. 2.
[o] Zech. 10. 11.
[p] Isai. 19. 16.
[q] ch. 29. 14.
[r] Ps. 78. 12.
[s] Nah. 3. 8, 9, 10.

[1] Or, *fear.*
[2] Heb. *Phut.* ch. 27. 10.
[3] Heb. *children.*
[4] Or. *from Migdol to Syene.*
[5] Heb. *broken.*
[6] Heb. *drought.*
[7] Heb. *the fulness thereof.*
[8] Or, *Tanis.*

When these things should begin to come to pass the prophet's mouth should be opened to declare their meaning, and to make known the end to which all was tending.

XXX. 1–19. Third prophecy against Egypt, probably to be connected with the previous verses (cp. xxx. 10 with xxix. 17-21 note). Some consider it to belong to the earlier part of xxix. (cp. xxix. 10, 12 with xxx. 5, 6).

3. *the time of the heathen*] The time when the heathen (Egyptians) shall be judged.

5. *Libya, and Lydia*] Or, as in xxvii. 10, **Phut** and **Lud.**

the mingled people] Foreigners, who settled in Egypt. The Saite dynasty of Egyptian kings were especially favourable to foreign immigrants. Hophra employed many of them in his armies, and in this way, according to Herodotus, lost the affections of his Egyptian subjects. See Jer. xxv. 20 note.

Chub] The word occurs here only. It was some tribe in alliance with Egypt, either of African race like Lud and Phut, or settlers like the *mingled people.* A not improbable suggestion connects it with *Coptos,* of which the Egyptian form was *Qeb, Qebt* or *Qabt.*

the men of the land that is in league] Rather, **the children of the land of the covenant,** *i.e.* of Israel (see xvi. 8). After the destruction of Jerusalem Jews withdrew into Egypt (Jer. xliii. 7). Many of them would naturally enough be found in the Egyptian armies. This is in favour of the later date assigned to this section.

6. See marg. ref. note.

9. *careless Ethiopians*] The Ethiopians, who were dwelling in fancied security (Zeph. ii. 15), shall tremble at Egypt's ruin.

13. *Noph*] Memphis (Isai. xix. 13).

14. *Zoan*] Tanis, a city and nome of Lower Egypt (Num. xiii. 22). See marg. ref. note.

No] Diospolis. See marg. ref. note.

15 And I will pour my fury upon ¹Sin, the strength of Egypt;
16 and *I will cut off the multitude of No. And I will "set fire   *t* Jer. 46. 25.
in Egypt: Sin shall have great pain, and No shall be rent   " ver. 8.
17 asunder, and Noph *shall have* distresses daily. The young
men of ²Aven and of ³Pi-beseth shall fall by the sword: and
18 these *cities* shall go into captivity. *At Tehaphnehes also the   *x* Jer. 2. 16.
day shall be ⁴darkened, when I shall break there the yokes of
Egypt: and the pomp of her strength shall cease in her: as for
her, a cloud shall cover her, and her daughters shall go into
19 captivity. Thus will I execute judgments in Egypt: and they
shall know that I *am* the LORD.

20   And it came to pass in the eleventh year, in the first *month*,
in the seventh *day* of the month, *that* the word of the LORD
21 came unto me, saying, ¶ Son of man, I have ᵛbroken the arm   *y* Jer. 48. 25.
of Pharaoh king of Egypt; and, lo, ᶻit shall not be bound up to   *z* Jer. 46. 11.
be healed, to put a roller to bind it, to make it strong to hold
22 the sword. Therefore thus saith the Lord GOD; Behold, I *am*
against Pharaoh king of Egypt, and will ᵃbreak his arms, the   *a* Ps. 37. 17.
strong, and that which was broken; and I will cause the sword
23 to fall out of his hand. ᵇAnd I will scatter the Egyptians   *b* ver. 26.
among the nations, and will disperse them through the countries.   ch. 29. 12.
24 And I will strengthen the arms of the king of Babylon, and
put my sword in his hand: but I will break Pharaoh's arms,
and he shall groan before him with the groanings of a deadly
25 wounded *man.* But I will strengthen the arms of the king of
Babylon, and the arms of Pharaoh shall fall down; and ᶜthey   *c* Ps. 9. 16.
shall know that I *am* the LORD, when I shall put my sword into
the hand of the king of Babylon, and he shall stretch it out
26 upon the land of Egypt. ᵈAnd I will scatter the Egyptians   *d* ver. 23.
among the nations, and disperse them among the countries;   ch. 29. 12.
and they shall know that I *am* the LORD.

CHAP. 31. AND it came to pass in the eleventh year, in the third
month, in the first *day* of the month, *that* the word of the LORD

¹ Or, *Pelusium.*   ² Or, *Heliopolis.*   ³ Or, *Pubastum.*   ⁴ Or, *restrained.*

---

17. *Aven*] The same as *On* (Gen. xli. 45),
or *Heliopolis.* The word *Aven* means also
"transgression" (cp. Hos. x. 8). Some have
thought that here too Ezekiel substituted
the word *Aven* for *On* to mark the *sin* of
idolatry there in full vogue.

Pi-beseth] The Bubastis of Herodotus.
The hieroglyphic name is "Pe-bast," the
house of Bast (the Egyptian Artemis, the
cat-headed goddess). Bubastis was situated
on the easternmost, the Pelusian, branch of
the Delta. The road from Pelusium to
Memphis lay through Bubastis and On.
In the days of Herodotus Bubastis was the
seat of one of the chief annual festivals of
the Egyptians. The Persians took the town
and razed the walls. The ruins bear the
modern name Tel-Basta.

18. *Tehaphnehes*] See marg. ref. note.
break the yokes of Egypt] i.e. break the yokes
imposed by Egypt, or break up the tyran-
nous dominion of Egypt over other lands.

20-26. Fourth prophecy against Egypt

spoken three months before the capture of
Jerusalem (xxvi. 1), and three months after
the prophecy of xxix. 1. Meantime Pharaoh-Hophra's attempt on Jerusalem had
been foiled, and the Egyptians driven back
into their own country (Jer. xxxvii. 5 note).

21. *I have broken*] Especially by the defeat at Carchemish.
a roller] Or, a bandage.

22. *the strong*] Such power as Egypt yet
retained at home and abroad.
that which was broken] The power which
Egypt aimed at ineffectually, the conquest
of Palestine and Syria.

XXXI. **1.** *in the third* month] More than
a month before Jerusalem was taken (cp.
Jer. xxxix. 2).

3-9. Fifth prophecy against Egypt: a
warning to Pharaoh from the fate of the Assyrians. The Assyrian empire, after having
been supreme in Asia for four centuries, had
been overthrown by the united forces of the
Babylonians and Medes, in the year of the

a ver. 18.
b Dan. 4. 10.

c Jer. 51. 36.

d Dan. 4. 11.

e ch. 17. 23.
Dan. 4. 12.

f Gen. 2. 8.
ch. 28. 13.

g Dan. 5. 20.

h ch. 28. 7.

i ch. 32. 5.
& 35. 8.

k Isai. 18. 6.
ch. 32. 4.

l Ps. 82. 7.
m ch. 32. 18.

2 came unto me, saying, Son of man, speak unto Pharaoh, king of
3 Egypt, and to his multitude; ¶ *a* "Whom art thou like in thy
greatness ? *b* Behold, the Assyrian *was* a cedar in Lebanon [1] with
fair branches, and with a shadowing shroud, and of an high
4 stature ; and his top was among the thick boughs. *c* The waters
[2] made him great, the deep [3] set him up on high with her rivers
running round about his plants, and sent out her [4] little rivers
5 unto all the trees of the field. Therefore *d* his height was exalted
above all the trees of the field, and his boughs were multiplied,
and his branches became long because of the multitude of waters,
6 [5] when he shot forth. All the *e* fowls of heaven made their nests
in his boughs, and under his branches did all the beasts of the
field bring forth their young, and under his shadow dwelt all
7 great nations. Thus was he fair in his greatness, in the length
8 of his branches : for his root was by great waters. The cedars
in the *f* garden of God could not hide him : the fir trees were not
like his boughs, and the chestnut trees were not like his
branches ; nor any tree in the garden of God was like unto him
9 in his beauty. I have made him fair by the multitude of his
branches : so that all the trees of Eden, that *were* in the garden
10 of God, envied him. ¶ Therefore thus saith the Lord GOD ;
Because thou hast lifted up thyself in height, and he hath shot
up his top among the thick boughs, and *g* his heart is lifted up in
11 his height ; I have therefore delivered him into the hand of the
mighty one of the heathen ; [6] he shall surely deal with him : I
12 have driven him out for his wickedness. And strangers, *h* the
terrible of the nations, have cut him off, and have left him :
i upon the mountains and in all the valleys his branches are
fallen, and his boughs are broken by all the rivers of the land ;
and all the people of the earth are gone down from his shadow,
13 and have left him. *k* Upon his ruin shall all the fowls of the
heaven remain, and all the beasts of the field shall be upon his
14 branches : to the end that none of all the trees by the waters
exalt themselves for their height, neither shoot up their top
among the thick boughs, neither their trees [7] stand up in their
height, all that drink water : for *l* they are all delivered unto
death, *m* to the nether parts of the earth, in the midst of the
15 children of men, with them that go down to the pit. ¶ Thus
saith the Lord GOD ; In the day when he went down to the

---

[1] Heb. *fair of branches.*
[2] Or, *nourished.*
[3] Or, *brought him up.*
[4] Or, *conduits.*
[5] Or, *when it sent* them *forth.*
[6] Heb. *in doing he shall do*
unto him.
[7] Or, *stand upon themselves for their height.*

---

battle of Carchemish (B.C. 605), which had
broken the power of Egypt. This gives force
to the warning to Egypt from Assyria's fall.

4. *his plants*] Rather, **her plantation.**
The water represents the riches and might
which flowed into Assyria.

5. *when he shot forth*] Or, when the deep
water sent forth its streams.

8. *garden of God*] Paradise.

10-14. Assyria's fall.

11. More accurately : Therefore I will
deliver him, &c....he shall surely deal with
him. I have driven him out, &c.

14. *their trees*] Rather, as in marg. "standing unto themselves" meaning "standing
in their own strength." The clause will
then run thus : "Neither all that drink
water stand up" in their own strength.
All that drink water means mighty princes
to whom wealth and prosperity flow in.
The Egyptians owed everything to the
waters of the Nile. The substance is, that
Assyria's fall was decreed in order that the
mighty ones of the earth might learn not to
exalt themselves in pride or to rely on themselves, seeing that they must share the common lot of mortality.

15-17. Effect of Assyria's fall.

grave I caused a mourning: I covered the deep for him, and
I restrained the floods thereof, and the great waters were stayed:
and I caused Lebanon ¹to mourn for him, and all the trees of
16 the field fainted for him. I made the nations to ⁿshake at the
sound of his fall, when I ᵒcast him down to hell with them that
descend into the pit: and ᵖall the trees of Eden, the choice and
best of Lebanon, all that drink water, �q shall be comforted in the
17 nether parts of the earth. They also went down into hell with
him unto *them that be* slain with the sword; and *they that were*
his arm, *that* ʳdwelt under his shadow in the midst of the hea-
18 then. ˢTo whom art thou thus like in glory and in greatness
among the trees of Eden? yet shalt thou be brought down with
the trees of Eden unto the nether parts of the earth: ᵗthou
shalt lie in the midst of the uncircumcised with *them that be*
slain by the sword. This *is* Pharaoh and all his multitude,
saith the Lord GOD.

ⁿ ch. 26. 15.
ᵒ Isai. 14. 15.
ᵖ Isai. 14. 8.
q ch. 32. 31.

ʳ Lam. 4. 20.
ˢ ver. 2
ch. 32. 19.
ᵗ ch. 28. 10.
& 32. 19, 21.

CHAP. 32. AND it came to pass in the twelfth year, in the twelfth
month, in the first *day* of the month, *that* the word of the LORD
2 came unto me, saying, Son of man, ᵃtake up a lamentation for
Pharaoh king of Egypt, and say unto him, ¶ ᵇThou art like a
young lion of the nations, ᶜand thou *art* as a ²whale in the seas:
and thou camest forth with thy rivers, and troubledst the waters
3 with thy feet, and ᵈfouledst their rivers. Thus saith the Lord
GOD; I will therefore ᵉspread out my net over thee with a company of many people; and they shall bring thee up in my net.
4 Then ᶠwill I leave thee upon the land, I will cast thee forth
upon the open field, and ᵍwill cause all the fowls of the heaven
to remain upon thee, and I will fill the beasts of the whole earth
5 with thee. And I will lay thy flesh ʰupon the mountains, and
6 fill the valleys with thy height. I will also water with thy
blood ³the land wherein thou swimmest, *even* to the mountains;

ᵃ ch. 27. 2.
ver. 16.
ᵇ ch. 19. 3, 6.
& 38. 13.
ᶜ ch. 29. 3.
ᵈ ch. 34. 18.
ᵉ ch. 12. 13.
Hos. 7. 12.
ᶠ ch. 29. 5.
ᵍ ch. 31. 13.
ʰ ch. 31. 12.

---

¹ Heb. *to be black.*   ² Or, *dragon.*   ³ Or, *the land of thy swimming.*

---

15. *I covered the deep*] To cover with sackcloth was an expression of mourning (xxvii.
31). The deep, the source of Assyria's prosperity (*v.* 4), was made to mourn, being
dried up instead of giving forth its waters,
its glad abundance.

for him] Upon his account.

floods...great waters] Or, rivers...the multitude of waters (as in *vv.* 4, 5).

Lebanon represents the country which Assyria governed; *the trees*, the tributary princes.

16. See marg. reff.

17. *his arm* &c.] The subject princes who
were his strength and support in war.

18. Application to Pharaoh.

the uncircumcised] The Egyptians, at
least their nobles, were circumcised. Pharaoh should thus be dishonoured with those
whom the Egyptians themselves deemed
unclean.

XXXII. 1. *in the twelfth month*] About
one year and seven months after the destruction of Jerusalem. In the meantime
had occurred the murder of Gedaliah and
the flight into Egypt of the Jews left behind by the Chaldæans (Jer. xli.-xliii.).

Jeremiah, who had accompanied them, foretold their ruin (Jer. xliv.) in a prophecy
probably contemporaneous with the present
—the sixth against Egypt, delivered in the
form of a dirge (2–16).

2. *Thou art like* &c.] Rather, **Thou
wouldest be like to** (others, "wast likened
unto") **a young lion.**

and thou art] In contrast to what thou
wouldest be.

a whale] Rather, crocodile (marg. ref. note).
Pharaoh should have been like the king of
beasts, but he is a mere sea-monster. There
is strong irony here, because the Egyptian
king was proud of the comparison between
himself and the mighty crocodile.

seas] The word is often used of the waters
of a great river, like the Nile.

thou camest forth with thy rivers] Rather,
thou didst **burst forth in** *thy rivers* as the
crocodile does from the water into which he
has plunged.

5. The prophet passes from the image of
the crocodile to that of dead bodies of the
slain heaped up on the land. Some render
height, "foulness."

7 and the rivers shall be full of thee. And when I shall ¹put thee

ⁱ Isai. 13. 10.
Amos 8. 9.
Matt. 24. 29.
Rev. 6. 12.

out, ⁱI will cover the heaven, and make the stars thereof dark ;
I will cover the sun with a cloud, and the moon shall not give
8 her light. All the ²bright lights of heaven will I make ³dark
over thee, and set darkness upon thy land, saith the Lord GOD.
9 I will also ⁴vex the hearts of many people, when I shall bring
thy destruction among the nations, into the countries which thou

ᵏ ch. 27. 35.

10 hast not known. Yea, I will make many people ᵏamazed at
thee, and their kings shall be horribly afraid for thee, when I

ˡ ch. 26. 16.

shall brandish my sword before them ; and ˡthey shall tremble
at every moment, every man for his own life, in the day of thy

ᵐ Jer. 46.26.
ch. 30. 4.
ⁿ ch. 28. 7.
ᵒ ch. 29. 19.

11 fall. ¶ ᵐFor thus saith the Lord GOD ; The sword of the king
12 of Babylon shall come upon thee. By the swords of the mighty
will I cause thy multitude to fall, ⁿthe terrible of the nations,
all of them : and ᵒthey shall spoil the pomp of Egypt, and all the
13 multitude thereof shall be destroyed. I will destroy also all the

ᵖ ch. 29. 11.

beasts thereof from beside the great waters ; ᵖneither shall the
foot of man trouble them any more, nor the hoofs of beasts
14 trouble them. Then will I make their waters deep, and cause
15 their rivers to run like oil, saith the Lord GOD. When I shall
make the land of Egypt desolate, and the country shall be
⁵destitute of that whereof it was full, when I shall smite all

ᵠ Ex. 7. 5.
ch. 6. 7.
ʳ 2 Sam.1.17.
ch. 26. 17.

them that dwell therein, ᵠthen shall they know that I am the
16 LORD. This is the ʳlamentation wherewith they shall lament
her : the daughters of the nations shall lament her : they shall
lament for her, even for Egypt, and for all her multitude, saith
the Lord GOD.

17   It came to pass also in the twelfth year, in the fifteenth day
of the month, that the word of the LORD came unto me, saying,

ˢ ch. 26. 20.

18 ¶ Son of man, wail for the multitude of Egypt, and ˢcast them
down, even her, and the daughters of the famous nations, unto
the nether parts of the earth, with them that go down into the

ᵗ ch. 31.2,18.
ᵘ ver. 21. 24.
ch. 28. 10.

19 pit. ᵗWhom dost thou pass in beauty ? ᵘgo down, and be thou
20 laid with the uncircumcised. They shall fall in the midst of
them that are slain by the sword : ⁶she is delivered to the sword :

ˣ Isai. 1. 31.
& 14. 9, 10.
ʸ ver. 19. 25.

21 draw her and all her multitudes. ˣThe strong among the mighty
shall speak to him out of the midst of hell with them that help
him : they are ʸ gone down, they lie uncircumcised, slain by the

---

¹ Or, extinguish.
² Heb. lights of the light in
  heaven.
³ Heb. them dark.
⁴ Heb. provoke to anger,
  or, grief.
⁵ Heb. desolate from the
  fulness thereof.
⁶ Or, the sword is laid.

---

9. when I shall bring thy destruction] i.e.
the news of thy destruction. The phenomena here mentioned are the accompani-
ments of the day of the Lord (Joel ii. 10 ;
Luke xxi. 25) or the day of judgment. The
fall of Pharaoh represents the fall of the
world-power before the Sovereignty of God.
14. A promise of a return of God's favour.
This concerns not the restoration of Egypt's
original power, but the establishment of the
Divine Ruler in the place of a heathen God-
opposing power.
16. daughters of the nations] Heathen kingdoms.
17–32. The seventh prophecy against
Egypt. A funeral dirge founded on xxxi.

18. The figure is the same as in Isai. xiv.,
where see notes. In this dirge Pharaoh is
especially addressed. The other nations
are represented by their kings, the nations'
overthrow being depicted by the king's body
laid low in the grave.
17. the month] i.e. the twelfth (see v. 1).
19. Whom dost thou pass in beauty ?] Thou
art not more beautiful than other nations :
thou shalt not escape their fate.
20. she is delivered to the sword] Rather,
the sword is put forth. Draw her down as
one dragged to execution.
21. The uncircumcised throughout this
dirge is equivalent to heathen viewed as
impure (xxxi. 18 note).

22 sword. ᶻAsshur *is* there and all her company: his graves *are*
23 about him: all of them slain, fallen by the sword: ᵃwhose
graves are set in the sides of the pit, and her company is round
about her grave: all of them slain, fallen by the sword, which
24 ᵇcaused ¹terror in the land of the living. There *is* ᶜElam and
all her multitude round about her grave, all of them slain, fallen
by the sword, which are ᵈgone down uncircumcised into the
nether parts of the earth, ᵉwhich caused their terror in the land
of the living; yet have they borne their shame with them that
25 go down to the pit. They have set her a bed in the midst of the
slain with all her multitude: her graves *are* round about him:
all of them uncircumcised, slain by the sword: though their
terror was caused in the land of the living, yet have they borne
their shame with them that go down to the pit: he is put in the
26 midst of *them that be* slain. ¶ There *is* ᶠMeshech, Tubal, and all
her multitude: her graves *are* round about him: all of them
ᵍuncircumcised, slain by the sword, though they caused their
27 terror in the land of the living. ʰAnd they shall not lie with
the mighty *that are* fallen of the uncircumcised, which are gone
down to hell ²with their weapons of war: and they have laid
their swords under their heads, but their iniquities shall be upon
their bones, though *they were* the terror of the mighty in the
28 land of the living. Yea, thou shalt be broken in the midst of
the uncircumcised, and shalt lie with *them that are* slain with
29 the sword. ¶There *is* ⁱEdom, her kings, and all her princes,
which with their might are ³laid by *them that were* slain by the
sword: they shall lie with the uncircumcised, and with them
30 that go down to the pit. ᵏThere *be* the princes of the north, all
of them, and all the ˡZidonians, which are gone down with the
slain; with their terror they are ashamed of their might; and
they lie uncircumcised with *them that be* slain by the sword, and
31 bear their shame with them that go down to the pit. ¶Pharaoh
shall see them, and shall be ᵐcomforted over all his multitude,
even Pharaoh and all his army slain by the sword, saith the Lord

ᶻ ver. 24. 26.
ᵃ Isai. 14. 15.

ᵇ ch. 26. 17.
ver. 27. 32.
ᶜ Jer. 49. 34.
ᵈ ver. 21.
ᵉ ver. 23.

ᶠ ch. 27. 13.

ᵍ ver. 19, 20.
ʰ ver. 21.
Isai. 14. 18.

ⁱ ch. 25. 12.

ᵏ ch. 38. 6.
& 39. 2.
ˡ ch. 28. 21.

ᵐ ch. 31. 16.

¹ Or, *dismaying.*　　²Heb. *with weapons of their war.*　　³Heb. *given,* or, *put.*

22 &c. In Jer. xxv. there is an enumeration of nations destined to be subject to the fury of the Chaldæans. Here we find those of them who had already fallen not named by Jeremiah. Asshur is the king of Assyria, representing as usual the whole nation. The king is surrounded by the graves of his people.

24. See marg. ref. Elam answers to the country known to the Greeks and Romans as Elymais, near Persia and Media. The Elamites were a fierce and warlike people. In the records of Assurbanipal his final triumph over Elam seems to have been one of his proudest boasts. Elam no doubt in the decline of Assyrian power again asserted its independence and was again crushed by the Chaldæan conqueror.

27. *And they shall not lie*] Better, "Shall they not lie?" or, "Are they not laid?" The custom of burying warriors with their swords, shields, or helmets, under their heads is well known, and common to most warlike nations.

but their iniquities &c.] They rested in all the glories of a warrior's sepulture, but their sins followed them to the grave.

30. *the princes of the north*] *i.e.* North of Palestine—The Tyrians and the Syrians.

with their terror they are ashamed of their might] *i.e.* "When their might and power were terrible to all, they were shorn of their power and delivered over to shame and confusion." There are here six nations, Asshur, Elam, Meshech, Tubal, Edom, Zidon, which added to Egypt make up SEVEN (see xxv. 1 note). The section which contains the prophecies against the heathen, closing with this description of the kings who had gone down to the grave, accords with the general purport of the whole section, viz.:—the declaration that all the powers of the world shall be annihilated to make way for the kingdom of God.

31. *comforted*] By the knowledge that his ruin is no more than that of every world-power.

32 GOD. For I have caused my terror in the land of the living:
and he shall be laid in the midst of the uncircumcised with *them*
that are slain with the sword, *even* Pharaoh and all his multitude,
saith the Lord GOD.

CHAP. 33. AGAIN the word of the LORD came unto me, saying,
2 Son of man, speak to *a*the children of thy people, and say unto
them, ¶ *b*[1]When I bring the sword upon a land, if the people of
the land take a man of their coasts, and set him for their *c*watch-
3 man : if when he seeth the sword come upon the land, he blow
4 the trumpet, and warn the people; then [2]whosoever heareth
the sound of the trumpet, and taketh not warning; if the sword
come, and take him away, *d*his blood shall be upon his own
5 head. He heard the sound of the trumpet, and took not warning : his blood shall be upon him.   But he that taketh warning
6 shall deliver his soul. But if the watchman see the sword come,
and blow not the trumpet, and the people be not warned ; if the
sword come, and take *any* person from among them, *e*he is
taken away in his iniquity; but his blood will I require at the
7 watchman's hand.   ¶ *f*So thou, O son of man, I have set thee a
watchman unto the house of Israel; therefore thou shalt hear
8 the word at my mouth, and warn them from me.   When I say
unto the wicked, O wicked *man*, thou shalt surely die; if thou
dost not speak to warn the wicked from his way, that wicked
man shall die in his iniquity; but his blood will I require at
9 thine hand.   Nevertheless, if thou warn the wicked of his way
to turn from it; if he do not turn from his way, he shall die in
10 his iniquity ; but thou hast delivered thy soul.   ¶ Therefore, O
thou son of man, speak unto the house of Israel ; Thus ye speak,
saying, If our transgressions and our sins *be* upon us, and we
11 *g*pine away in them, *h*how should we then live ? Say unto them,
As I live, saith the Lord GOD, *i*I have no pleasure in the death
of the wicked ; but that the wicked turn from his way and live :
turn ye, turn ye from your evil ways ; for *k*why will ye die, O
12 house of Israel ?   ¶ Therefore, thou son of man, say unto the
children of thy people, The *l*righteousness of the righteous shall
not deliver him in the day of his transgression : as for the wickedness of the wicked, *m*he shall not fall thereby in the day that
he turneth from his wickedness ; neither shall the righteous be
13 able to live for his *righteousness* in the day that he sinneth. When
I shall say to the righteous, *that* he shall surely live ; *n*if he trust
to his own righteousness, and commit iniquity, all his righteousnesses shall not be remembered ; but for his iniquity that he
14 hath committed, he shall die for it.   Again, *o*when I say unto
the wicked, Thou shalt surely die ; if he turn from his sin, and
15 do [3]that which is lawful and right; *if* the wicked *p*restore the
pledge, *q*give again that he had robbed, walk in *r*the statutes of

a ch. 3. 11.
b ch. 14. 17.
c 2 Sam. 18.
2 i, 25.
2 Kin. 9. 17.
Hos. 9. 8.

d ch. 18. 13.

e ver. 8.

f ch. 3. 17

g ch. 24. 23.
h So Isai.
49. 14.
ch. 37. 11.
i 2 Sam. 14.
14.
ch. 18. 23.
2 Pet. 3. 9.
k ch. 18. 31.
l ch. 18. 24.
m 2 Chr.7.14.

n ch. 3. 20.

o ch. 3. 18.
& 18. 27.
p ch. 18. 7.
q Ex. 22. 1.
Lev. 6. 2, 4.
Num. 5. 6.
Luke 19. 8.
r Lev. 18. 5.
ch. 20. 11.

[1] Heb. *A land when I bring*   [2] Heb. *he that hearing*   [3] Heb. *judgment and justice.*
   a sword upon her.   *heareth.*

---

32. *my terror*] Better "his terror," the
terror caused by him.

the land of the living] The land of God's
people. It was Jehovah Who caused Pharaoh to be terrible to His people, and now,
when the time is come, Pharaoh is fallen,
and he is laid &c.

XXXIII. to end. Ezekiel newly desig-

nated to the prophetical office, undertakes his
new duty of encouraging his countrymen to
hope for forgiveness and restoration. *vv.*
1–20 are the introduction to this third group
of prophecies.

1. *Again*] And. For *vv.* 1–20, cp. ch.
xviii. notes.

life, without committing iniquity; he shall surely live, he shall
16 not die. *None of his sins that he hath committed shall be men-   *ch. 18. 22.
tioned unto him: he hath done that which is lawful and right;
17 he shall surely live. ¶ *Yet the children of thy people say, The   *ver. 20.
way of the Lord is not equal: but as for them, their way is not   ch. 18. 25.
18 equal. "When the righteousness turneth from his righteousness,   "ch. 18. 26.
19 and committeth iniquity, he shall even die thereby. But if the
wicked turn from his wickedness, and do that which is lawful
20 and right, he shall live thereby. ¶ Yet ye say, *The way of the   *ch. 18. 25.
Lord is not equal. O ye house of Israel, I will judge you every
one after his ways.

21 And it came to pass in the twelfth year *of our captivity, in   *ch. 1. 2.
the tenth *month*, in the fifth *day* of the month, *that one that   *ch. 24. 26.
had escaped out of Jerusalem came unto me, saying, *The city   *2 Kin.25.4.
22 is smitten. Now *the hand of the LORD was upon me in the   *ch. 1. 3.
evening, afore he that was escaped came; and had opened my
mouth, until he came to me in the morning; *and my mouth   *ch. 24. 27.
23 was opened, and I was no more dumb. ¶ Then the word of the
24 LORD came unto me, saying, Son of man, *they that inhabit   *ch. 34. 2.
those *wastes of the land of Israel speak, saying, *Abraham was   *ch. 36. 4
one, and he inherited the land: *but we *are* many; the land is   *Isai. 51. 2.
25 given us for inheritance. Wherefore say unto them, Thus saith   Acts 7. 5.
the Lord GOD; *Ye eat with the blood, and *lift up your eyes   3. 11.
toward your idols, and *shed blood: and shall ye possess the   *Gen. 9. 4.
26 land? Ye stand upon your sword, ye work abomination, and   Deut. 12. 16.
ye *defile every one his neighbour's wife: and shall ye possess   *ch. 18. 6.
27 the land? Say thou thus unto them, Thus saith the Lord GOD;   *ch. 22. 6.
As I live, surely *they that *are* in the wastes shall fall by the   *ver. 24.
sword, and him that *is* in the open field *will I give to the   *ch. 39. 4.
beasts *to be devoured, and they that *be* in the forts and *in the   1 Sam. 13. 6.
28 caves shall die of the pestilence. *For I will lay the land *most   *Jer. 44. 2.
desolate, and the *pomp of their strength shall cease; and *the   ch. 36. 34.
mountains of Israel shall be desolate, that none shall pass   *ch. 7. 24.
29 through. Then shall they know that I *am* the LORD, when   *ch. 6. 2, 3.

---

¹ Heb. *to devour him.*   ² Heb. *desolation and desolation.*

---

21. The date shews an interval of 1½ years
from the taking of Jerusalem (Jer. lii. 12).
The general news that the city was taken
must have reached them, but it was only
when the messenger arrived that the prophet's mouth was opened. It is not improbable that a body of men after the destruction of the city joined their brethren
in Chaldæa; if so this would account
for the lapse of time, and supply a reason
why Ezekiel on their arrival should commence a new series of prophecies.
22. *was upon me...was opened*] For *was*
read "had been." The prophet was under
the hand of God in ecstatic trance on the
evening preceding the arrival of the messenger, and continued in this state until his
arrival.
23-33. The exhortation to repentance.
Ezekiel first addresses the remnant that still
linger in their ancient home, and warns
them against presumptuous hopes resting
on false grounds (*vv.* 23-29); then he turns his

eyes to those near him, and points out that
their apparent attention to his words was
illusory.
24. *those wastes*] The places in the Holy
Land devastated by the conqueror.
Abraham] The argument is, Abraham
was but one man, and he had the promise
of the land, though he did not at once possess it; much more shall we, the descendants of Abraham, being many, retain this
promise and possess the land, though for a
time we are depressed and subject. Cp. Matt.
iii. 9; John viii. 33, 39.
25. To *eat flesh with the blood* was forbidden (see marg. reff.). It seems to have
been connected with the idolatries of Canaan. The prohibition was, on account of
its connexion with idolatry, continued in
the enactment of the Council of Jerusalem
(Acts xv. 29).
26. *Ye stand upon your sword*] Ye put
your trust in your swords.

I have laid the land most desolate because of all their abomi-
30 nations which they have committed. ¶Also, thou son of man,
the children of thy people still are talking ¹against thee by the
walls and in the doors of the houses, and ˢspeak one to another,
every one to his brother, saying, Come, I pray you, and hear
31 what is the word that cometh forth from the LORD. And ᵗthey
come unto thee ²as the people cometh, and ³they ᵘsit before
thee *as* my people, and they hear thy words, but they will not
do them: ˣfor with their mouth ⁴they shew much love, *but*
32 ᵞtheir heart goeth after their covetousness. And, lo, thou *art*
unto them as ⁵a very lovely song of one that hath a pleasant
voice, and can play well on an instrument: for they hear thy
33 words, but they do them not. ᶻAnd when this cometh to pass,
(lo, it will come,) then ᵃshall they know that a prophet hath
been among them.

CHAP. 34. AND the word of the LORD came unto me, saying, Son
2 of man, prophesy against the ᵃshepherds of Israel, prophesy,
and say unto them, Thus saith the Lord GOD unto the shepherds; ᵇWoe *be* to the shepherds of Israel that do feed them-
3 selves! should not the shepherds feed the flocks? ᶜYe eat the
fat, and ye clothe you with the wool, ᵈye kill them that are fed:
4 *but* ye feed not the flock. ᵉThe diseased have ye not strengthened, neither have ye healed that which was sick, neither have
ye bound up *that which was* broken, neither have ye brought
again that which was driven away, neither have ye ᶠsought that
which was lost; but with ᵍforce and with cruelty have ye ruled
5 them. ʰAnd they were ⁱscattered, ⁶because *there is* no shepherd :
ᵏand they became meat to all the beasts of the field, when they
6 were scattered. My sheep wandered through all the mountains,
and upon every high hill : yea, my flock was scattered upon
all the face of the earth, and none did search or seek *after them*.
7 ¶Therefore, ye shepherds, hear the word of the LORD ; *As* I
8 live, saith the Lord GOD, surely because my flock became a
prey, and my flock ˡbecame meat to every beast of the field,
because *there was* no shepherd, neither did my shepherds search
for my flock, ᵐbut the shepherds fed themselves, and fed not

Margin references (left column):
ˢ Isai. 29. 13.
ᵗ ch. 14. 1.
ᵘ ch. 8. 1.
ˣ Ps. 78. 3ⁱ.
Isai. 29. 13.
ᵞ Matt.13.22.
ᶻ 1 Sam.3.20.
ᵃ ch. 2. 5.
ᵃ ch. 33. 24.
ᵇ Jer. 23. 1.
Zech. 11. 17.
ᶜ Isai. 56.11.
Zech. 11. 16.
ᵈ ch. 33. 25.
Mic. 3. 1.
Zech. 11. 5.
ᵉ ver. 16.
ᶠ Luke 15. 4.
ᵍ 1 Pet. 5. 3.
ʰ ch. 33. 21.
ⁱ 1 Kin.22.17.
Matt. 9. 36.
ᵏ Isai. 56. 9.
Jer. 12. 9.
ˡ ver. 5, 6.
ᵐ ver. 2, 10.

¹ Or, *of thee.*
² Heb. *according to the coming of the people.*
³ Or, *my people sit before thee.*
⁴ Heb. *they make loves,* or, *jests.*
⁵ Heb. *a song of loves.*
⁶ Or, *without a shepherd,* and so ver. 8.

30-33. God warns the prophet against
being misled by the compliance of the
people.
30. *against thee*] Rather, **about** *thee.*
by the walls] Rather, **within** *the walls.*
31. *as the people cometh*] Lit. as in marg.
i.e. in crowds. Render, **they shall come**
unto thee **like the coming of a people,** *and*
shall *sit before thee as My people* &c., *i.e.*
they assume the attitude of God's people
listening to His prophet. Cp. xiv. 1, xx. 1.
33. *And when this*] But *when* this.
XXXIV. The prophet has yet to pronounce a judgment upon unfaithful rulers,
whose punishment will further the good of
those whom they have misguided. He
shews what the rulers should have been,
what they have been, and what in the coming times they shall be when the True King

shall reign in the true kingdom. Hence
follows a description of Messiah's reign.
2. *shepherds*] Not priests or prophets, but
rulers and kings (see Jer. ii. 8 note). The
most ancient title for *ruler* is a monogram
which occurs on the oldest monuments discovered in the cuneiform character. In the Assyrian language it became RIU (cp. Heb. *roêh*=
shepherd). In the traditions of Berosus
we find that Alorus, the first king in the
world, received from the Divinity the title
of Shepherd. The title, as well as the
monogram, was preserved to the latest times
of the Assyrian monarchy. While the distress and misery of the people daily increased, the last kings of Judah exacted more
and more from their subjects and lavished
more and more on personal luxury and
show.

9 my flock; therefore, O ye shepherds, hear the word of the
10 LORD; Thus saith the Lord GOD; Behold, I *am* against the
shepherds; and ⁿI will require my flock at their hand, and
cause them to cease from feeding the flock; neither shall the
shepherds ᵒfeed themselves any more; for I will deliver my
flock from their mouth, that they may not be meat for them.
11 ¶ For thus saith the Lord GOD; Behold, I, *even* I, will both
12 search my sheep, and seek them out. ¹As a shepherd seeketh
out his flock in the day that he is among his sheep *that are* scattered; so will I seek out my sheep, and will deliver them out of
all places where they have been scattered in ᵖthe cloudy and
13 dark day. And �q I will bring them out from the people, and
gather them from the countries, and will bring them to their own
land, and feed them upon the mountains of Israel by the rivers,
14 and in all the inhabited places of the country. ʳI will feed them
in a good pasture, and upon the high mountains of Israel
shall their fold be: ˢthere shall they lie in a good fold, and *in*
15 a fat pasture shall they feed upon the mountains of Israel. I
will feed my flock, and I will cause them to lie down, saith the
16 Lord GOD. ᵗI will seek that which was lost, and bring again
that which was driven away, and will bind up *that which was*
broken, and will strengthen that which was sick: but I will destroy ᵘthe fat and the strong; I will feed them ˣwith judgment.
17 ¶ And *as for* you, O my flock, thus saith the Lord GOD; ʸBe-
hold, I judge between ²cattle and cattle, between the rams and
18 the ³he goats. *Seemeth it* a small thing unto you to have eaten
up the good pasture, but ye must tread down with your feet
the residue of your pastures? and to have drunk of the deep
19 waters, but ye must foul the residue with your feet? And *as
for* my flock, they eat that which ye have trodden with your
feet; and they drink that which ye have fouled with your feet.
20 ¶ Therefore thus saith the Lord GOD unto them; ᶻBehold, I,
even I, will judge between the fat cattle and between the lean
21 cattle. Because ye have thrust with side and with shoulder,
and pushed all the diseased with your horns, till ye have scat-
22 tered them abroad; therefore will I save my flock, and they
shall no more be a prey; and ᵃI will judge between cattle and
23 cattle. And I will set up one ᵇshepherd over them, and he

ⁿ ch. 3. 18.
Heb. 13. 17.
ᵒ ver. 2. 8.

ᵖ ch. 30. 3.
Joel 2. 2.
q Isai. 65. 9.
Jer. 23. 3.
ch. 28. 25.
& 37. 21, 22.
ʳ Ps. 23. 2.

ˢ Jer. 33. 12.

ᵗ Mic. 4. 6.
Isai. 40. 11.
Mark 2. 17.
Luke 5. 32.
ᵘ Isai.10.16.
Amos 4. 1.
ˣ Jer. 10. 24.
ʸ ch. 20. 37.
Zech. 10. 3.
Matt. 25.
32, 33.

ᶻ ver. 17.

ᵃ ver. 17.
ᵇ Isai. 40. 11.
Jer. 23. 4.
John 10. 11.
Heb. 13. 20.
1 Pet. 2. 25.

¹ Heb. *According to the
seeking.* ² Heb. *small cattle of lambs
and kids* ³ Heb. *great he goats.*

11. Jehovah is the shepherd of His people. He will do all which the shepherds should have done and did not. These promises —partially fulfilled in the return from Babylon, and in the subsequent prosperity under the Maccabees—point to the in-gathering of all nations in the Church of Christ the Good Shepherd. Cp. Matt. xviii. 11 : John x. 1-18 ; Rom. ix. 25-33.

12. *the cloudy and dark day*] Contrasted with the day in which the Lord will be among them like a shepherd to gather them together again.

16. *with judgment*] It is characteristic of Jehovah as a shepherd that He judges between sheep and sheep, rejecting the proud and accepting the penitent and broken-hearted.

20-31. Jehovah having promised to be a

Ruler of His people, the administration of the Divine kingdom is now described, as carried on by One King, the representative of David, Whose dominion should fulfil all the promises originally made to the man after God's own heart. Ezekiel does not so much add to, as explain and develope, the original promise ; and as the complete fulfilment of the spiritual blessings, which the prophets were guided to proclaim, was manifestly never realized in any temporal prosperity of the Jews, and never could and never can be realized in any earthly kingdom, we recognize throughout the Sacred Volume the one subject of all prophecy—the Right-eous King, the Anointed Prince, the Son and the Lord of David.

23. *one shepherd*] One, as ruling over an undivided people, the distinction between the

c Jer. 30. 9.
ch. 37. 24.
Hos. 3. 5.
d Ex. 29. 45.
ch. 37. 27.
e ch. 37. 22.
Luke 1. 32.
f ch. 37. 26.
g Lev. 26. 6.
Isai. 11. 6.
Hos. 2. 18.
h Jer. 23. 6.
i Isai. 56. 7.
k Gen. 12. 2.
Isai. 19. 24.
Zech. 8. 13.
l Lev. 26. 4.
m Ps. 68. 9.
Mal. 3. 10.
n Ps. 85. 12.
Isai. 4. 2.
o Jer. 2. 20.
p Jer. 25. 14.
q ch. 36. 4.
r Jer. 30. 10.
s Isai. 11. 1.
Jer. 23. 5.
t ch. 36. 3.
u ch. 37. 27.
x Ps. 100. 3.
John 10. 11.

shall feed them, *c* even my servant David; he shall feed them,
24 and he shall be their shepherd. And *d* I the LORD will be their
God, and my servant David *e* a prince among them; I the LORD
25 have spoken *it*. And *f* I will make with them a covenant of
peace, and *g* will cause the evil beasts to cease out of the land:
and they *h* shall dwell safely in the wilderness, and sleep in the
26 woods. And I will make them and the places round about *i* my
hill *k* a blessing; and I will *l* cause the shower to come down in
27 his season; there shall be *m* showers of blessing. And *n* the
tree of the field shall yield her fruit, and the earth shall yield
her increase, and they shall be safe in their land, and shall
know that I *am* the LORD, when I have *o* broken the bands of
their yoke, and delivered them out of the hand of those that
28 *p* served themselves of them. And they shall no more *q* be a
prey to the heathen, neither shall the beast of the land devour
them; but *r* they shall dwell safely, and none shall make *them*
29 afraid. And I will raise up for them a *s* plant *1* of renown, and
they shall be no more *2* consumed with hunger in the land,
30 *t* neither bear the shame of the heathen any more. Thus shall
they know that *u* I the LORD their God *am* with them, and *that*
they, *even* the house of Israel, *are* my people, saith the Lord
31 GOD. And ye my *x* flock, the flock of my pasture, *are* men, *and*
I *am* your God, saith the Lord GOD.

CHAP. 35. MOREOVER the word of the LORD came unto me,
2 saying, Son of man, *a* set thy face against *b* mount Seir, and
3 *c* prophesy against it, and say unto it, Thus saith the Lord GOD;
¶ Behold, O mount Seir, I *am* against thee, and *d* I will stretch
out mine hand against thee, and I will make thee *3* most deso-
4 late. *e* I will lay thy cities waste, and thou shalt be desolate,
5 and thou shalt know that I *am* the LORD. ¶ *f* Because thou
hast had a *4* perpetual hatred, and hast *5* shed *the blood of* the
children of Israel by the *6* force of the sword in the time of their

a ch. 6. 2.
b Deut. 2. 5.
c Jer. 49. 7.
Amos 1. 11.
Obad. 10.
d ch. 6. 14.
e ver. 9.
f ch. 25. 12.

---

1 Or, *for renown.*
2 Heb. *taken away.*
3 Heb. *desolation and deso-*

lation: So ver. 7.
Or, *hatred of old*, ch. 25.
15.

5 Heb. *poured out the*
children,
6 Heb. *hands.*

---

kingdoms of Israel and Judah having been
done away.

my servant David] David was a fit type of
the True King because he was a true and
faithful servant of Jehovah. That which
David was partially and imperfectly, Christ
is in full perfection (cp. Matt. xii. 18;
John v. 30; Heb. x. 7.)

25, 26. The blessings here foretold are
especially those of the old Covenant. The *wilderness* (or, pasture-country) and the *woods,*
the places most exposed to beasts and birds
of prey, become places of security. Under the
new Covenant Sion and the hills around are
representative of God's Church; and temporal blessings are typical of the blessings
showered down upon Christ's Church by
Him Who has vanquished the powers of
evil.

29. *a plant*] Equivalent to the *Branch,*
under which name Isaiah and Jeremiah
prophesy of the Messiah. The contrast
in this verse to hunger seems to favour
the idea that the *plant* was for food,

i.e. spiritual food, and in this sense also, ap-
plicable to the Messiah (cp. John vi. 35.)

the shame of the heathen] The shameful re-
proaches with which the heathen assail them.

31. Translate *Ye are my flock, the flock of
my pasture* (cp. Jer. xxiii. 1); ye are *men,*
and I am your God.

XXXV.—XXXVI. 15. The devastation
of Edom, and the restoration of Israel. Edom
was included among the nations against
which Ezekiel prophesied (xxv. 12–14). But
its fuller doom was reserved for this place,
because Edom was one of the surrounding
nations that profited at first by Judah's
fall, and because it helps by way of contrast to bring out in a marked way the
better future designed for Israel. Edom is
the God-hating, God-opposing power, ever
distinguished for its bitter hatred against
Israel; and so the ruin of Edom is the
triumph of Israel in the power of God.

5. *shed blood*] Omit *blood:* better as in
the marg. *i.e.* **and hast given up the children of Israel to the sword**; thou hast scat-

6 calamity, *g*in the time *that their* iniquity *had* an end: therefore, *as* I live, saith the Lord GOD, I will prepare thee unto blood, and blood shall pursue thee: *h*sith thou hast not hated blood,
7 even blood shall pursue thee. Thus will I make mount Seir ¹most desolate, and cut off from it *i*him that passeth out and
8 him that returneth. *k*And I will fill his mountains with his slain *men:* in thy hills, and in thy valleys, and in all thy rivers,
9 shall they fall that are slain with the sword. *l*I will make thee perpetual desolations, and thy cities shall not return: *m*and ye
10 shall know that I *am* the LORD. ¶ Because thou hast said, These two nations and these two countries shall be mine, and
11 we will *n*possess it; ²whereas *o*the LORD was there: therefore, *as* I live, saith the Lord GOD, I will even do *p*according to thine anger, and according to thine envy which thou hast used out of thy hatred against them; and I will make myself known among
12 them, when I·have judged thee. *q*And thou shalt know that I *am* the LORD, *and that* I have heard all thy blasphemies which thou hast spoken against the mountains of Israel, saying, They
13 are laid desolate, they are given us ³to consume. Thus *r*with your mouth ye have ⁴boasted against me, and have multiplied
14 your words against me: I have heard *them.* Thus saith the Lord GOD; *s*When the whole earth rejoiceth, I will make thee
15 desolate. *t*As thou didst rejoice at the inheritance of the house of Israel, because it was desolate, so will·I do unto thee: *u*thou shalt be desolate, O mount Seir, and all Idumea, *even* all of it: and they shall know that I *am* the LORD.

CHAP. 36. ALSO, thou son of man, prophesy unto the *a*mountains
2 of Israel, and say, ¶ Ye mountains of Israel, hear the word of the LORD: Thus saith the Lord·GOD; Because *b*the enemy hath said against you, Aha, *c*even the ancient high places *d*are our's in possession: therefore prophesy and say, Thus saith the Lord
3 GOD; ⁵Because they have made *you* desolate, and swallowed you up on every side, that ye might be a possession unto the residue of the heathen, *e*and ⁶ye are taken up in the lips of
4 talkers, and *are* an infamy of the people: therefore, ye mountains of Israel, hear the word of the Lord GOD; Thus saith the Lord GOD to the mountains, and to the hills, to the ⁷rivers, and to the valleys, to the desolate wastes, and to the cities that are forsaken, which *f*became a prey and *g*derision to the residue of
5 the heathen that *are* round about; therefore thus saith the Lord GOD; *h*Surely in the fire of my jealousy have I spoken

g Ps. 137. 7.
Dan. 9. 24.
Obad. 11.
h Ps. 109. 17.

i Judg. 5. 6.
ch. 29. 11.
k ch. 31. 12.

l Jer. 49.
17, 18.
ch. 25. 13.
Mal. 1. 3, 4.
m ch. 6. 7.
n Ps. 83. 4.
Obad. 13.
o Ps. 48. 1.
& 132. 13.
ch. 48. 35.
p Matt. 7. 2.
Jam. 2. 13.
q Ps. 9 16.
ch. 6. 7.

r 1 Sam. 2. 3.
Rev. 13. 6.

s Isai. 65.
13, 14.
t Obad. 12.
u ver. 3, 4.

a ch. 6. 2, 3.

b ch. 25. 3.

c Deut. 32. 13.
d ch. 35. 10.

e Deut. 28. 37.
1 Kin. 9. 7.
Lam. 2. 15.
Dan. 9. 16.

f ch. 34. 28.
g Ps. 79. 4.

h Deut. 4. 24.
ch. 38. 19.

---

¹ Heb. *desolation and deso-lation,* ver. 3.
² Or, *though the LORD was there.*
³ Heb. *to devour.*
⁴ Heb. *magnified.*
⁵ Heb. *Because for be-cause.*
⁶ Or, *ye are made to come upon the lip of the tongue.*
⁷ Or, *bottoms,* or, *dates.*

---

tered the children of Israel in confusion like stones poured down a mountain-side (Micah i. 6).

that their *iniquity* had *an end*] Or, "of the iniquity of the end," *i.e.* the time when by the capture of the city the iniquity of Israel came to an end (xxi. 29).

9. *return*] Or, " be inhabited."

10. *These two nations*] Israel and Judah.

XXXVI. 1-15. The contrast to the preceding. Now, when the prophet speaks, Judæa is waste. The heathen nations around, and Edom in particular, rejoice in scorn: but the land of Israel is a holy land

given by Jehovah to His people, and it shall be theirs. The promises are those of temporal blessings; and although these temporal blessings were typical of Messiah's reign, yet we may not doubt that this prophecy had for its first object the return of prosperity to the land and to the people, after their return from Babylon.

1. The *mountains of Israel* are opposed to *Seir,* the mount of Edom (xxxv. 3).

3. *the residue of the heathen*] Those of the surrounding nations which had survived Jerusalem's fall, and may have profited by it.

against the residue of the heathen, and against all Idumea,

*i*which have appointed my land into their possession with the joy of all *their* heart, with despiteful minds, to cast it out for 6 a prey. Prophesy therefore concerning the land of Israel, and say unto the mountains, and to the hills, to the rivers, and to the valleys, Thus saith the Lord GOD ; Behold, I have spoken

in my jealousy and in my fury, because ye have *k*borne the 7 shame of the heathen : therefore thus saith the Lord GOD ; I have *l*lifted up mine hand, Surely the heathen that *are* about 8 you, they shall bear their shame. ¶ But ye, O mountains of Israel, ye shall shoot forth your branches, and yield your fruit 9 to my people of Israel ; for they are at hand to come. For, behold, I *am* for you, and I will turn unto you, and ye shall be 10 tilled and sown : and I will multiply men upon you, all the house of Israel, *even* all of it : and the cities shall be inhabited,

11 and *m*the wastes shall be builded : and *n*I will multiply upon you man and beast ; and they shall increase and bring fruit : and I will settle you after your old estates, and will do better unto *you* than at your beginnings : *o*and ye shall know that I *am* 12 the LORD. Yea, I will cause men to walk upon you, *even* my

people Israel ; *p*and they shall possess thee, and thou shalt be their inheritance, and thou shalt no more henceforth *q*bereave 13 them *of men*. ¶ Thus saith the Lord GOD : Because they say unto you, *r*Thou *land* devourest up men, and hast bereaved thy 14 nations ; therefore thou shalt devour men no more, neither 15 ¹bereave thy nations any more, saith the Lord GOD. *s*Neither will I cause *men* to hear in thee the shame of the heathen any more, neither shalt thou bear the reproach of the people any more, neither shalt thou cause thy nations to fall any more, saith the Lord GOD.

16 Moreover the word of the LORD came unto me, saying, 17 ¶ Son of man, when the house of Israel dwelt in their own land,

*t*they defiled it by their own way and by their doings : their way was before me as *u*the uncleanness of a removed woman. 18 Wherefore I poured my fury upon them *x*for the blood that

¹ Or, *cause to fall.*

---

6. *the shame of the heathen*] The taunts which the heathen heaped upon them.

7. *I have lifted up mine hand*] *i.e.* I have sworn. Cp. marg. ref.

their shame] They shall find their taunts come home to themselves.

8. *they are at hand to come*] *i.e.* under Zerubbabel.

13. The judgments which God sent upon the land, had so destroyed the inhabitants that men deemed it a fatal land, which brought destruction to all that should occupy it (cp. 2 K. xvii. 25).

14. *bereave*] Or, as in marg. : *i.e.* the land shall not prove the ruin of its inhabitants by tempting them (as of old time) to the sin of idolatry.

15. *hear in thee the shame of the heathen*] Hear the heathen putting thee to shame by their contemptuous words.

the reproach of the people] Thy *people* (thy rightful possessors) shall have no cause to

reproach thee for want of fertility. Were the blessings promised here merely temporal they could not be said to be fulfilled. The land is still subject to heathen masters. The words must point to blessings yet future, spiritual blessings.

In the following chapters to the end of xxxix. the conflict between the world and God is described in its most general form, and the absolute triumph of the kingdom of God fully depicted. The honour of God is asserted in the gathering together, and the purification of, His people. As the dispersion of the children of Israel was far wider and more lasting than the sojourn in Chaldæa, so the reunion here predicted is far more extensive and complete. The dispersion yet continues, the reunion will be in those days when Israel shall be gathered into the Church of God.

16-20. The defilement of the people described in order to its removal.

they had shed upon the land, and for their idols *wherewith* they
19 had polluted it: and I ᵞscattered them among the heathen,
and they were dispersed through the countries: ᶻaccording to
20 their way and according to their doings I judged them. And
when they entered unto the heathen, whither they went, they
ᵃprofaned my holy name, when they said to them, These *are*
the people of the LORD, and are gone forth out of his land.
21 But I had pity ᵇfor mine holy name, which the house of Israel
22 had profaned among the heathen, whither they went. ¶ Therefore say unto the house of Israel, Thus saith the Lord GOD;
I do not *this* for your sakes, O house of Israel, ᶜbut for mine
holy name's sake, which ye have profaned among the heathen,
23 whither ye went. And I will sanctify my great name, which
was profaned among the heathen, which ye have profaned in
the midst of them; and the heathen shall know that I *am* the
LORD, saith the Lord GOD, when I shall be ᵈsanctified in you
24 before ¹their eyes. For ᵉI will take you from among the heathen, and gather you out of all countries, and will bring you
25 into your own land. ᶠThen will I sprinkle clean water upon
you, and ye shall be clean: ᵍfrom all your filthiness, and from
26 all your idols, will I cleanse you. A ʰnew heart also will I give
you, and a new spirit will I put within you: and I will take away
the stony heart out of your flesh, and I will give you an heart
27 of flesh. And I will put my ⁱspirit within you, and cause you
to walk in my statutes, and ye shall keep my judgments, and
28 do *them*. ᵏAnd ye shall dwell in the land that I gave to your
fathers; ˡand ye shall be my people, and I will be your God.
29 I will also ᵐsave you from all your uncleannesses: and ⁿI will

¹ Or, *your.*

y ch. 22. 15.
z ch. 7. 3.

a Isai. 52. 5.
Rom. 2. 24.
b ch. 20. 9.

c Ps. 106. 8.

d ch. 20. 41.
e ch. 34. 13.

f Isai. 52. 15.
g Jer. 33. 8.
h Jer. 32. 39.
ch. 11. 19.

i ch. 11. 19.
& 37. 14.
k ch. 37. 25.
l Jer. 30. 22.
ch. 11. 20.
m Matt.1.21.
Rom. 11. 26.
ⁿ See Ps.105.
16.

---

20. *they profaned my holy name*] Caused
it to be dishonoured by the heathen who
said in scorn, "This is the people of God."
The heathen, seeing the miserable state of
the exiles, fancied that Jehovah was no
more than a national god, powerless to
protect his subjects.

21. *I had pity for mine holy name*] Render,
I had a pitiful regard to *Mine Holy Name.*

25. Ezekiel the priest has in view the
purifying rites prescribed by the Law, the
symbolical purport of which is exhibited in
Heb. ix. 13, 14, x. 22. As the Levites were
consecrated with sprinkling of water, so
should the approved rite "sprinkling of
water" thus prescribed by the Law and
explained by the prophets, give occasion to
the use of water at the admission of prose-
lytes in later days, and so to its adoption
by John in his baptism unto repentance.
It was hallowed by our Lord when in His
discourse with Nicodemus, referring, no
doubt, to such passages as these, He shewed
their application to the Church of which He
was about to be the Founder; and when
He appointed Baptism as the Sacrament of
admission into that Church. In this Sacrament the spiritual import of the legal
ordinance is displayed,—the second birth by
water and the Spirit. As Israel throughout
the prophecy of Ezekiel prefigures the

visible Church of Christ, needing from
time to time trial or purification—so does
the renovated Israel represent Christ's
mystical Church (Eph. v. 26). The spiritual
character of the renovation presumes a
personal application of the prophet's words,
which is more thoroughly brought out
under the new Covenant (*e.g.* Heb. xi. 16).
Thus the prophecy of Ezekiel furnishes a
medium through which we pass from the
congregation to the individual, from the
letter to the spirit, from the Law to the
Gospel, from Moses to Christ. See p. 321.

28. *ye shall be my people*] Cp. 2 Cor. vi.
16-18; Heb. viii. 10. The writers of the
New Testament appropriated these and
similar phrases of the Old Testament to the
Church of Christ. Between the restoration
of the Jews (the first step) there are many
steps towards the end—the spread of
Christ's Church throughout the world, the
conversion of the Gentiles, and the acknowledgment of the true God—which justify
men in looking forward to a time when the
Gospel shall be preached in all the world,
and the earth become the kingdom of God
in a fuller sense than it has ever yet been.
But all these are *steps.* Our prophecies
look beyond all this to a new heaven to
a new earth, and to a new Jerusalem (Rev.
xxi. 3).

[o] ch. 34. 29.
[p] ch. 34. 27.
[q] ch. 16. 61.
[r] Lev. 26. 39. ch. 6. 9.
[s] Deut. 9. 5.
[t] ver. 10.
[u] Isai. 51. 3. ch. 28. 13. Joel 2. 3.
[x] ch. 17. 24. & 37. 14.
[y] See ch. 14. 3.
[z] ver. 10.

call for the corn, and will increase it, and [o]lay no famine upon
30 you. [p]And I will multiply the fruit of the tree, and the increase
of the field, that ye shall receive no more reproach of famine
31 among the heathen. Then [q]shall ye remember your own evil
ways, and your doings that *were* not good, and [r]shall lothe
yourselves in your own sight for your iniquities and for your
32 abominations. [s]Not for your sakes do I *this*, saith the Lord
GOD, be it known unto you: be ashamed and confounded for
33 your own ways, O house of Israel. ¶ Thus saith the Lord GOD;
In the day that I shall have cleansed you from all your iniquities
I will also cause *you* to dwell in the cities, [t]and the wastes shall
34 be builded. And the desolate land shall be tilled, whereas it
35 lay desolate in the sight of all that passed by. And they shall
say, This land that was desolate is become like the garden of
[u]Eden; and the waste and desolate and ruined cities *are become*
36 fenced, *and* are inhabited. Then the heathen that are left
round about you shall know that I the LORD build the ruined
places, and plant that that was desolate: [x]I the LORD have
37 spoken *it*, and I will do *it*. ¶ Thus saith the Lord GOD; [y]I will
yet *for* this be enquired of by the house of Israel, to do *it* for
38 them; I will [z]increase them with men like a flock. As the
[1]holy flock, as the flock of Jerusalem in her solemn feasts; so
shall the waste cities be filled with flocks of men: and they shall
know that I *am* the LORD.

[a] ch. 1. 3.
[b] ch. 3. 14. Luke 4. 1.
[c] 1 Sam. 2. 6. John 5. 21. Rom. 4. 17. 2 Cor. 1. 9.
[d] Ps. 104. 30.

CHAP. 37. THE [a]hand of the LORD was upon me, and carried me out
[b]in the spirit of the LORD, and set me down in the midst of the
2 valley which *was* full of bones, and caused me to pass by them
round about: and, behold, *there were* very many in the open
3 [2]valley; and, lo, *they were* very dry. And he said unto me, Son
of man, can these bones live? And I answered, O Lord GOD,
4 [c]thou knowest. ¶ Again he said unto me, Prophesy upon these
bones, and say unto them, O ye dry bones, hear the word of the
5 LORD. Thus saith the Lord GOD unto these bones; Behold, I
6 will [d]cause breath to enter into you, and ye shall live: and I
will lay sinews upon you, and will bring up flesh upon you,

[1] Heb. *flock of holy things.* [2] Or, *champaign.*

---

36. *the heathen that are left*] Gathered out of heathendom into the community of God —accepted and redeemed.

37. Their sin had prevented God's hearing them. Now their purification opens God's ears to their words.

38. *As the holy flock*] A reference to the flocks and herds brought up to Jerusalem to be consecrated and offered unto the Lord (2 Chr. xxxv. 7). Thus the idea is brought out (1) of the multiplication of the people, (2) of their dedication to the service of God.

XXXVII. **1-14.** Ezekiel sees in a vision dead men raised to life; its meaning is given (11-14). In it, the doctrine of the Resurrection of the Body is at least implied. Such a figure would only have force with those who were familiar with this idea (cp. 1 Sam. ii. 6; Job xix. 25-27; Ps. xvi. 10, 11; Dan. xii.). The vision was intended not only to comfort the despairing children of Israel—prefiguring the reinstatement of Israel now scattered and lifeless, as a community restored to their home, and reinvigorated with spiritual life—but also to impress upon them the great truth of the Resurrection, which was greatly developed in the Scriptures of the Old Testament, but found its clear and unambiguous enunciation in the New. The prophecy concerns not only the Israel after the flesh but also the Israel of God; it points to a home in heaven and to a life of immortality.

1. *the valley*] The same word as *the plain* (iii. 22, viii. 4). The *dry bones* represented the Israelites dispersed abroad, destitute of life national and spiritual.

4. *Prophesy*] Not in the sense of predicting what was to come to pass, but simply in that of speaking under the inspiration of God. In *v.* 5, not *I will cause*, but **I cause** or am causing.

and cover you with skin, and put breath in you, and ye shall live ;
7 *and ye shall know that I *am* the LORD. ¶ So I prophesied as I was   *e* ch 6. 7.
commanded : and as I prophesied, there was a noise, and behold a
8 shaking, and the bones came together, bone to his bone. And
when I beheld, lo, the sinews and the flesh came up upon them,
and the skin covered them above: but *there was* no breath in them.
9 ¶ Then said he unto me, Prophesy unto the ¹ wind, prophesy,
son of man, and say to the wind, Thus saith the Lord GOD ;
f Come from the four winds, O breath, and breathe upon these   *f* ver. 5
10 slain, that they may live. So I prophesied as he commanded
me, *g* and the breath came into them, and they lived, and stood   *g* Rev. 11. 11.
11 up upon their feet, an exceeding great army. ¶ Then he said
unto me, Son of man, these bones are the whole house of
Israel : behold, they say, *h* Our bones are dried, and our hope is   *h* Ps. 141. 7.
12 lost : we are cut off for our parts. Therefore prophesy and   Isai. 49. 14.
say unto them, Thus saith the Lord GOD ; Behold, *i* O my   *i* Isai. 26. 19.
people, I will open your graves, and cause you to come up out   Hos. 13. 14.
13 of your graves, and *k* bring you into the land of Israel. And   *k* ch. 36. 24.
ye shall know that I *am* the LORD, when I have opened your   ver. 25.
graves, O my people, and brought you up out of your graves,
14 and *l* shall put my spirit in you, and ye shall live, and I shall   *l* ch. 36. 27.
place you in your own land : then shall ye know that I the LORD
have spoken *it*, and performed *it*, saith the LORD.

15 The word of the LORD came again unto me, saying, Moreover,
16 thou son of man, *m* take thee one stick, and write upon it, For   *m* See Num.
Judah, and for *n* the children of Israel his companions : then   17. 2.
take another stick, and write upon it, For Joseph, the stick of   *n* 2 Chr. 15.
17 Ephraim, and *for* all the house of Israel his companions : and   9. & 30.
o join them one to another into one stick ; and they shall become   11, 18.
18 one in thine hand. ¶ And when the children of thy people   *o* See ver. 22.
shall speak unto thee, saying, *p* Wilt thou not shew us what thou   24.
19 *meanest* by these ? *q* Say unto them, Thus saith the Lord GOD ;   *p* ch. 12. 9.
Behold, I will take *r* the stick of Joseph, which *is* in the hand of   *q* Zech. 10. 6.
Ephraim, and the tribes of Israel his fellows, and will put them   *r* ver. 16, 17.
with him, *even* with the stick of Judah, and make them one
20 stick, and they shall be one in mine hand. And the sticks
whereon thou writest shall be in thine hand *s* before their eyes.   *s* ch. 12. 3.
21 And say unto them, Thus saith the Lord GOD ; ¶ Behold, *t* I will   *t* ch. 36. 24.

¹ Or, *breath.*

7. *bone to his bone*] *i.e.* to its proper place in
the frame.
9. *the wind*] Rather, as in marg. and as in
v. 5. The bones are the bones of the *slain*,
because the scene was one which was likely
to occur in the time of the Chaldæan invasion, and the fact of violent death reminded the prophet of the miserable condition of the people.
11. *we are cut off for our parts*] That is,
"as for us, we are cut off." The people
had fallen into despair.
16–28. A prophecy of the reunion of
Israel and Judah, the incorporation of
Israel under one Ruler, the kingdom of
Messiah upon earth and in heaven.
16. *one stick*] So in marg. ref. the names
of the tribes had been written on rods or
sticks.

For Judah &c.] To the house of David
had remained faithful, not only Judah, but
also Benjamin, Levi, and part of Simeon,
and individual members of various tribes
(2 Chr. xi. 12–16). Cp. marg. reff.
Joseph...Ephraim] Cp. Ps. lxxviii. 67;
Hos. v. 5 *seq. Joseph* is the general name
here for the ten tribes, including *Ephraim*,
the chief tribe, and his companions. Omit
for before *all. All the house of Israel* is here
the ten tribes.
19. *in the hand of Ephraim*] Because
Ephraim was the ruling tribe ; the words are
contrasted with *in mine hand.*
20. This sign was literally enacted in the
presence of the people, not, like some signs,
merely in vision (see iii. 1 note).
21. The gathering together of the children of Israel was to take effect in the first

take the children of Israel from among the heathen, whither they be gone, and will gather them on every side, and bring 22 them into their own land : and [u]I will make them one nation in the land upon the mountains of Israel ; and [x]one king shall be king to them all : and they shall be no more two nations, neither shall they be divided into two kingdoms any more at 23 all : [y]neither shall they defile themselves any more with their idols, nor with their detestable things, nor with any of their transgressions : but [z]I will save them out of all their dwelling-places, wherein they have sinned, and will cleanse them : so 24 shall they be my people, and I will be their God. ¶ And [a]David my servant *shall be* king over them ; and [b]they all shall have one shepherd : [c]they shall also walk in my judgments, 25 and observe my statutes, and do them. [d]And they shall dwell in the land that I have given unto Jacob my servant, wherein your fathers have dwelt ; and they shall dwell therein, *even* they, and their children, and their children's children [e]for ever : 26 and [f]my servant David *shall be* their prince for ever. ¶ Moreover I will make a [g]covenant of peace with them ; it shall be an everlasting covenant with them : and I will place them, and [h]multiply them, and will set my [i]sanctuary in the midst of 27 them for evermore. [k]My tabernacle also shall be with them : yea, I will be [l]their God, and they shall be my people. 28 [m]And the heathen shall know that I the LORD do [n]sanctify Israel, when my sanctuary shall be in the midst of them for evermore.

CHAP. 38. AND the word of the LORD came unto me, saying, [a]Son 2 of man, [b]set thy face against [c]Gog, the land of Magog, [1]the chief

[1] Or, *prince of the chief.*

Margin references

[u] Isai. 11. 13.
Jer. 3. 18.
Hos. 1. 11.
[x] ch. 34. 23.
John 10. 16.
[y] ch. 36. 25
[z] ch. 36. 28.
[a] Isai. 40. 11.
Jer. 23. 5.
ch. 34. 23.
Luke 1. 32.
[b] John 10. 16.
[c] ch. 36. 27.
[d] ch. 36. 28.
[e] Isai. 60. 21.
Joel 3. 20.
[f] John 12. 34.
[g] Ps. 89. 3.
Jer. 32. 40.
ch. 34. 25.
[h] ch. 36. 10.
[i] 2 Cor. 6. 16.
[k] Lev. 26. 11, 12.
John 1. 14.
[l] ch. 11. 20.
[m] ch. 36. 23.
[n] ch. 20. 12.
[a] ch. 39. 1.
[b] ch. 35. 2.
[c] Rev. 20. 8.

---

place in the return from Babylon, when the distinction of Israel and Judah should cease. The full completion concerns times still future, when all Israel shall come in to acknowledge the rule of Christ.

22. *one king*] The restoration of Israel to their native soil will lead the way to the coming of the promised King, the Son of David, Who will gather into His kingdom the true Israel, all who shall by faith be acknowledged as the Israel of God. The reign of the One King David is the reign of Christ in His kingdom, the Church.

25, 26. An enlargement of the promises. The kingdom is to be *for ever*, the Covenant *everlasting*. This looks forward to the consummation of all God's promises (1 Cor. xv. 24, 28).

27. This gives a final blessing reserved for God's accepted servants. The Tabernacle and Temple were outward symbols of His Presence. The re-erection of the Temple by Zerubbabel was the first step to a restoration of the Presence of God. The second step was the Presence of Christ, first in the flesh, then in His Church, and finally the eternal Presence of God and of the Lamb in the New Jerusalem (Rev. xxi.).

XXXVIII., XXXIX. The last conflict of the world with God, and the complete overthrow of the former. This section refers to times subsequent to the restoration of Israel. As the Church (the true Israel) waxes stronger and stronger, more distant nations will come into collision and must be overthrown before the triumph is complete. Some have thought that this prophecy is directed against the Scythians who had possession of Asia twenty-three years, and in the course of this time had overrun Syria, and had probably made their appearance in the Holy Land. But in this prophecy there is little distinctive of one nation. It is a gathering together of the enemies of Jehovah to make their last effort, and to be overthrown. The seer passes to the final struggle between Good and Evil, and the triumphant establishment of the Divine Rule. It is the same struggle which is depicted in the Book of Revelation (xx. 7-10), where St. John adopts words and phrases of Ezekiel.

There are four main divisions of this prophecy : (1) xxxviii. 1-13, describing Gog's march ; (2) xxxviii. 14-23, his punishment ; (3) xxxix. 1-16, his ruin ; (4) xxxix. 17-29, the issue of Gog's ruin in Israel's redemption and sanctification. Each division is broken up like a poem into stanzas.

XXXVIII. **2.** *Gog*, &c.] **Gog of the land**

3 prince of ^dMeshech and Tubal, and prophesy against him, and
say, Thus saith the Lord GOD ; Behold, I *am* against thee, O
4 Gog, the chief prince of Meshech and Tubal : and ^eI will turn
thee back, and put hooks into thy jaws, and I will bring thee
forth, and all thine army, horses and horsemen, ^fall of them
clothed with all sorts *of armour, even* a great company *with*
5 bucklers and shields, all of them handling swords : Persia,
Ethiopia, and ¹Libya with them ; all of them with shield and
6 helmet : ^gGomer, and all his bands ; the house of ^hTogarmah
of the north quarters, and all his bands : *and* many people with
7 thee. ⁱBe thou prepared, and prepare for thyself, thou, and
all thy company that are assembled unto thee, and be thou a
8 guard unto them. ^kAfter many days ^lthou shalt be visited : in
the latter years thou shalt come into the land *that is* brought
back from the sword, ^m*and is* gathered out of many people,
against ⁿthe mountains of Israel, which have been always waste :
but it is brought forth out of the nations, and they shall ^odwell
9 safely all of them. Thou shalt ascend and come ^plike a storm,
thou shalt be ^qlike a cloud to cover the land, thou, and all thy
10 bands, and many people with thee. ¶ Thus saith the Lord GOD ;
It shall also come to pass, *that* at the same time shall things
come into thy mind, and thou shalt ²think an evil thought :
11 and thou shalt say, I will go up to the land of unwalled villages ;
I will ^rgo to them that are at rest, ^sthat dwell ³safely, all of
them dwelling without walls, and having neither bars nor gates,
12 ⁴to take a spoil, and to take a prey ; to turn thine hand upon
^tthe desolate places *that are now* inhabited, ^uand upon the people
that are gathered out of the nations, which have gotten cattle
13 and goods, that dwell in the ⁵midst of the land. ^xSheba, and
^yDedan, and the merchants ^zof Tarshish, with all ^athe young
lions thereof, shall say unto thee, Art thou come to take a spoil ?
hast thou gathered thy company to take a prey ? to carry away
silver and gold, to take away cattle and goods, to take a great
14 spoil ? Therefore, son of man, prophesy and say unto Gog,

Marginal references:
^d ch. 32. 26.
^e ch. 29. 4.
^f ch. 23. 12.
^g Gen. 10. 2.
^h ch. 27. 14.
ⁱ Like Isai. 8. 9, 10. Jer. 46. 3.
^k Gen. 49. 1. Deut. 4. 30.
^l Isai. 29. 6.
^m ch. 34. 13.
ⁿ ch. 36. 1.
^o Jer. 23. 6. ch. 34. 25. ver. 11.
^p Isai. 28. 2.
^q Jer. 4. 13.
^r Jer. 49. 31.
^s ver. 8.
^t ch. 36. 34.
^u ver. 8.
^x ch. 27. 22.
^y ch. 27. 15.
^z ch. 27. 12.
^a ch. 19. 3.

¹ Or, *Phut,* ch. 27. 10. & 30. 5.
² Or, *conceive a mischievous*
purpose.
³ Or, *confidently.*
⁴ Heb. *To spoil the spoil,*
and to prey the prey, ch. 29. 19.
⁵ Heb. *navel,* Judg. 9. 37.

**of Magog, prince of Rosh, Meshech and
Tubal.** *Gog* is here the name of a captain
from *the land of Magog* (cp. Gen. x. 2)
the name of a people of the North, placed
between *Gomer* (the Cimmerians) and *Madai*
(the Medes). In the History of Assurbanipal
from cuneiform inscriptions, a chief of the
Saka (Scythians), called *Ga-a-gi,* is identified
by some with Gog. Rosh, if a proper name,
occurs in this connexion only.

4. *with all sorts*] Or, " gorgeously ; " see
marg. ref. Omit " of armour."

5. Libya and Ethiopia, mixed with the
northern invaders, are tribes from the
extreme South, to shew that this is a
general combination of the foes of God's
people.

7. Spoken ironically. Make all thy preparations, they will be in vain.

8. As Gog was drawn on to his attack
upon Israel in order to his ultimate ruin,
therefore his preparations were the first step
in his visitation from the Almighty.

After many days] **For** *many days.* Many
a long day shall the hand of God be upon
thee, drawing thee on to thy ruin, and in
the latter days shalt thou come.

the land] Lit. **a** *land* once laid waste by
the sword, but now delivered from it, whose
inhabitants once scattered have been gathered together from out of many peoples.

always] Rather, **a long time.** The
mountains were at the time of Gog's advance again cultivated and populous.

and they shall dwell] Rather, **and they
dwell.** It is a description of the actual
condition at the time of Gog's invasion
(cp. Judg. xviii. 7). Such was the condition of the restored Jews in their prosperous
days, after which came invasion. Such shall
be the condition of the Church previous to
the final conflict between good and evil.

11. *unwalled villages*] Cp. Zech. ii. 4, 5.

14. God will mark the prosperous security of the people, and rise up against them
as an easy prey.

b Isai. 4. 1.
c ver. 8.
d ch. 39. 2.
e ver. 6.

f ver. 9.

g ver. 8.

h Ex. 14. 4.
ch. 36. 2!.

Thus saith the Lord God; ^bIn that day when my people of
15 Israel ^cdwelleth safely, shalt thou not know *it?* ^dAnd thou
shalt come from thy place out of the north parts, thou, ^eand
many people with thee, all of them riding upon horses, a great
16 company, and a mighty army: ^fand thou shalt come up against
my people of Israel, as a cloud to cover the land; ^git shall be
in the latter days, and I will bring thee against my land, ^hthat
the heathen may know me, when I shall be sanctified in thee, O
17 Gog, before their eyes. ¶Thus saith the Lord God ; *Art* thou
he of whom I have spoken in old time ⁱby my servants the
prophets of Israel, which prophesied in those days *many* years
18 that I would bring thee against them? And it shall come to
pass at the same time when Gog shall come against the land of
Israel, saith the Lord God, *that* my fury shall come up in my

i ch. 36. 5. 6.
& 39. 25.
k Ps. 89. 46.
l Hag. 2. 6.
Rev. 16. 18.
m Hos. 4. 3.

n Jer. 4. 24.
Nah. 1. 5.

o Ps. 105. 16.
p ch. 14. 17.

q Judg. 7. 22.
1 Sam. 14.20.
r Isai. 66. 16.
Jer. 25. 31.
s ch. 5. 17.
t Ps. 11. 6.
Isai. 29. 6.
u ch. 13. 11.
Rev. 16. 21.
x ch. 36. 23.

y Ps. 9. 16.
ch. 37. 28.
a ch. 38. 2.

b ch. 38. 15.

19 face. For ⁱin my jealousy ^k*and* in the fire of my wrath have I
spoken, ^lSurely in that day there shall be a great shaking in
20 the land of Israel ; so that ^mthe fishes of the sea, and the fowls
of the heaven, and the beasts of the field, and all creeping
things that creep upon the earth, and all the men that *are* upon
the face of the earth, shall shake at my presence, ⁿand the mountains shall be thrown down, and the ²steep places shall fall, and
21 every wall shall fall to the ground. And I will ^ocall for ^pa
sword against him throughout all my mountains, saith the Lord
22 God : ^qevery man's sword shall be against his brother. And I
will ^rplead against him with ^spestilence and with blood; and ^tI
will rain upon him, and upon his bands, and upon the many
people that *are* with him, an overflowing rain, and ^ugreat hail-
23 stones, fire, and brimstone. Thus will I magnify myself, and
^xsanctify myself; ^yand I will be known in the eyes of many
nations, and they shall know that I *am* the Lord.

Chap. 39. THEREFORE, ^athou son of man, prophesy against Gog,
and say, Thus saith the Lord God ; Behold, I *am* against thee,
2 O Gog, the chief prince of Meshech and Tubal : and I will turn
thee back, and ³leave but the sixth part of thee, ^band will cause
thee to come up from ⁴the north parts, and will bring thee
3 upon the mountains of Israel : and I will smite thy bow out of

---

¹ Heb. *by the hands.*
² Or, *towers,* or, *stairs.*
³ Or, *strike thee with six*

plagues; or, *draw thee
back with an hook of six
teeth,* as ch. 38. 4.

⁴ Heb. *the sides of the
north.*

---

16. *I shall be sanctified in thee*] I shall be
shewn to be holy and just in avenging Myself of Mine enemy.

17. *Gog* is not mentioned by name in any
existing prophecy before Ezekiel's time.
The reference here shows (1) that the conflict with Gog does not represent a particular event, but one of which the prophets
in general had to speak ; (2) that in the
interpretation of Old Testament prophecy
we are to look beyond special fulfilments.
Events in the world's history come within a
prophet's ken as parts of the Divine administration whereby evil struggles against
but is overcome by good. As every such
conflict is a prelude to the final struggle,
so its prediction has reference ultimately to
the consummation here foretold.

XXXIX. The present chapter describes

the defeat of Evil and the triumph of
God and His people. As the prophet
predicted the advance of Evil under the
figure of the invasion of an actual army ;
so he declares the overthrow of Evil by the
figure of a host routed and slain, and the
consequent purification of a land, partially
overrun and disturbed. Some forgetting
that this is a *figure,* have searched history
to find out some campaign in the land of
Israel, some overthrow of invaders, on
which to fix this prophecy, and have
assigned localities to the burial-place *Hamon-
Gog* (v. 11).

2. *the chief prince*] Or, " prince of
Rosh."

and leave but the sixth part of thee] Or,
and lead thee along (LXX. and Vulg.).

thy left hand, and will cause thine arrows to fall out of thy
4 right hand. *c*Thou shalt fall upon the mountains of Israel,
thou, and all thy bands, and the people that *is* with thee: *d*I
will give thee unto the ravenous birds of every [1]sort, and *to* the
5 beasts of the field [2]to be devoured. Thou shalt fall upon [3]the
6 open field: for I have spoken *it*, saith the Lord GOD. *e*And I
will send a fire on Magog, and among them that dwell [4]care-
lessly in *f*the isles: and they shall know that I *am* the LORD.
7 *g*So will I make my holy name known in the midst of my people Israel; and I will not *let them* *h*pollute my holy name any
more: *i*and the heathen shall know that I *am* the LORD, the
8 Holy One in Israel. *k*Behold, it is come, and it is done, saith
9 the Lord GOD; this *is* the day *l*whereof I have spoken. ¶ And
they that dwell in the cities of Israel shall go forth, and
shall set on fire and burn the weapons, both the shields and the
bucklers, the bows and the arrows, and the [5]handstaves, and
10 the spears, and they shall [6]burn them with fire seven years: so
that they shall take no wood out of the field, neither cut down
any out of the forests; for they shall burn the weapons with
fire: *m*and they shall spoil those that spoiled them, and rob
11 those that robbed them, saith the Lord GOD. And it shall come
to pass in that day, *that* I will give unto Gog a place there of
graves in Israel, the valley of the passengers on the east of the
sea: and it shall stop the [7]noses of the passengers: and there
shall they bury Gog and all his multitude: and they shall call
12 *it* The valley of [8]Hamon-gog. And seven months shall the
house of Israel be burying of them, *n*that they may cleanse the
13 land. Yea, all the people of the land shall bury *them;* and it
shall be to them a renown the day that *o*I shall be glorified,
14 saith the Lord GOD. And they shall sever out [9]men of continual employment, passing through the land to bury with the
passengers those that remain upon the face of the earth, *p*to
cleanse it: after the end of seven months shall they search.
15 And the passengers *that* pass through the land, when *any* seeth
a man's bone, then shall he [10]set up a sign by it, till the buriers

Margin references:

c ch. 38. 21.
ver. 17.
d ch. 33. 27.

e ch. 38. 22.
Amos 1. 4.

f Ps. 72. 10.
g ver. 22.
h Lev. 18 21.
ch. 20. 39.
i ch. 28. 16.
k Rev.16.17.
& 21. 6.
l ch. 38. 17.

m Isai. 14. 2.

n Deut. 21.23.
ver. 14, 16.

o ch. 28. : 2.

p ver. 12.

Footnotes:

[1] Heb. *wing*.
[2] Heb. *to devour*.
[3] Heb. *the face of the field*.
[4] Or, *confidently*.
[5] Or, *javelins*.
[6] Or, *make a fire of them*.
[7] Or, *mouths*.
[8] 'l hat is, *The multitude of*
Gog.
[9] Heb. *men of continuance*.
[10] Heb. *build*.

---

6. The judgment is extended to *the isles*
(or, sea-coast) to shew that it should fall not
only on Gog and his land, but on those who
share Gog's feelings of hatred and opposition to the kingdom of God.

9, 10. *burn them with fire*] Or, "kindle fire
with them;" or, as in marg. The weapons
of the army left on the field of battle shall be
so numerous as to supply fuel for the people
of the land for *seven years*. *Seven* was a
number connected with cleansing after contact with the dead (Num. xix. 11 *seq*.), and
this purification of the land by the clearance
of heathenish spoils was a holy work (cp.
v. 12).

11. The prophet pictures to himself some
imaginary valley (cp. Zech. xiv. 5) at the
east of the sea, the Dead Sea, a place fright-
ful in its physical character, and admoni-
tory of past judgments. He calls it the

valley of the passengers (or, passers-by), because they who there lie buried were but as
a passing cloud. In *vv*. 11-15 there is a
play upon words—there were *passengers*
to be buried, *passengers* to walk over their
graves, *passengers* to bury them; [or, a
play upon the treble meaning of passing *in* (invading), passing *by*, and passing
through.]

stop the noses] The word thus rendered
occurs only once more in Scripture (Deut.
xxv. 4) where it is rendered *muzzle*. Cp.
Isai. xxxiv. 3.

Hamon-gog] See marg., cp. *v.* 16.

14. *men of continual employment*] Lit. as
marg., *i.e.* men regularly appointed to this
business. As the land of Israel represents
figuratively the Church of Christ, the purification of that land is a proper part of the
figure to indicate such a sanctification and

16 have buried it in the valley of Hamon-gog. And also the name of the city *shall be* [1]Hamonah. Thus shall they *q*cleanse the land.

17 ¶And, thou son of man, thus saith the Lord GOD; *r*Speak [2]unto every feathered fowl, and to every beast of the field, *s*Assemble yourselves, and come; gather yourselves on every side to my [3]sacrifice that I do sacrifice for you, *even* a great sacrifice *t*upon the mountains of Israel, that ye may eat flesh,

18 and drink blood. *u*Ye shall eat the flesh of the mighty, and drink the blood of the princes of the earth, of rams, of lambs,

19 and of [4]goats, of bullocks, all of them *x*fatlings of Bashan. And ye shall eat fat till ye be full, and drink blood till ye be drunken,

20 of my sacrifice which I have sacrificed for you. *y*Thus ye shall be filled at my table with horses and chariots, *z*with mighty men,

21 and with all men of war, saith the Lord GOD. ¶*a*And I will set my glory among the heathen, and all the heathen shall see my judgment that I have executed, and *b*my hand that I have

22 laid upon them. *c*So the house of Israel shall know that I *am*

23 the LORD their God from that day and forward. *d*And the heathen shall know that the house of Israel went into captivity for their iniquity: because they trespassed against me, therefore *e*hid I my face from them, and *f*gave them into the hand of

24 their enemies: so fell they all by the sword. *g*According to their uncleanness and according to their transgressions have

25 I done unto them, and hid my face from them. ¶Therefore thus saith the Lord GOD; *h*Now will I bring again the captivity of Jacob, and have mercy upon the *i*whole house of Israel, and

26 will be jealous for my holy name; *k*after that they have borne their shame, and all their trespasses whereby they have trespassed against me, when they *l*dwelt safely in their land, and

27 none made *them* afraid. *m*When I have brought them again from the people, and gathered them out of their enemies' lands, and *n*am sanctified in them in the sight of many nations;

28 *o*then shall they know that I *am* the LORD their God, [5]which caused them to be led into captivity among the heathen: but I have gathered them unto their own land, and have left none of

29 them any more there. *p*Neither will I hide my face any more from them: for I have *q*poured out my spirit upon the house of Israel, saith the Lord GOD.

q ver. 12.
r Rev. 19.17.
s Isai. 18. 6. & 34. 6. Jer. 12. 9. Zeph. 1. 7.
t ver. 4.
u Rev. 19.18.
x Deut.32.14. Ps. 22. 12.
y Ps. 76. 6. cb. 38. 4.
z Rev. 19. 18.
a ch. 38. 16, 23.
b Ex. 7. 4.
c ver. 7. 28.
d ch. 36. 18, 19, 20, 23.
e Deut.31.17. Isai. 59. 2.
f Lev. 26. 25.
g ch. 36. 19.
h Jer. 30. 3, 18. ch. 34. 13. & 36. 24.
i ch. 20. 40. Hos. 1. 11.
k Dan. 9. 16.
l Lev. 26.5,6.
m ch. 28. 25, 26.
n ch. 36. 23, 24. & 38. 16.
o ch. 34. 30. ver. 22.
p Isai. 54. 8.
q Joel 2. 28. Zech. 12.10.

[1] That is, *The multitude.*
[2] Heb. *to the fowl of every wing.*
[3] Or, *slaughter.*
[4] Heb. *great goats.*
[5] Heb. *by my causing of them, &c.*

---

cleansing of His Church, as St. Paul describes (Eph. v. 26, 27).

17-29. The purposes of the past dispensation shall be made clear to God's people themselves and to the heathen. His judgments were the consequence of their sins; and these sins once abandoned, the favour of their God will return in yet more abundance.

29. Cp. Acts ii. 17. St. Peter distinctly appropriates these prophecies (marg. reff.) to the outpouring of the Holy Spirit on the day of Pentecost, and the inauguration of the Church of Christ by that miraculous event. This was the beginning of the fulfilment. They shall find their consummation when time shall be no more.

XL.-XLVIII. The subject of the closing chapters of Ezekiel is the restitution of the kingdom of God. This is expressed by a vision, in which are displayed not only a rebuilt Temple, but also a reformed priesthood, reorganized services, a restored monarchy, a reapportioned territory, a renewed people, and, as a consequence, the diffusion of fertility and plenty over the whole earth. The return from Babylon was indeed the beginning of this work, but only a beginning, introductory to the future kingdom of Christ, first upon earth, finally in heaven. The vision must therefore be viewed as strictly *symbolical;* the symbols employed being the Mosaic ordinances. These ordinances had indeed in themselves a hidden meaning. The Tabernacle in the midst of the tents of the tribes, and afterwards the Temple in the capital of the land of inheritance, was intended to signify the dwelling of Jehovah among His people; the priesthood denoted the mediation between God and man, the monarchy the sovereignty of God, the people the saints of God, the territory their inheritance. It was probably a jubilee year when this vision was seen (see note on xl. 1). The Temple and city were in ruins, but God was pleased in this way to revive the hopes of His people.

An examination of the vision shews the insufficiency of the explanation, which conceives that Ezekiel was simply guided to leave behind patterns on the basis of which the Temple should in after days be rebuilt, and its services restored. Not only was this plan never carried out, but it was incapable of execution. The physical features of the land would not admit of the separation of precincts a mile square, surrounded by a territory sixteen miles by forty-eight (xlviii. 10). The river, though connected with the stream brought by conduit pipes into the actual Temple (sec xlvii.), soon passes into a condition wholly ideal, and the equal apportionment of the land to each of the twelve tribes is compatible neither with history nor geography.

The minuteness of the details is due to the fact that it is of the essence of a vision that the seer has before him every line, as in a carefully drawn picture. The numbers and figures employed are not without their meaning. The symbolical numbers of the Temple of Solomon were repeated in the vision of Ezekiel. Among the Hebrews the perfect figure was the square or the cube, and harmony was thought to be attained by exact equality, or by the repetition of like dimensions. Thus in the ideal Temple, as in the real, we find the fundamental measure of 100 cubits square, which is maintained in the Temple-court (A, Plan II.) and in the court of sacrifice (B). By a repetition of this measurement are formed the other courts, the outer court (o) being a square of 500 cubits, the precincts (B, Plan IV.) a square whose sides were exactly six times as long. Further, the *oblation* set apart for the priests and Levites and the city was to be *foursquare* (xlviii. 20), 25,000 reeds, and the city itself 4,500 reeds square with twelve gates, three on each side. The courts communicate with each other and with the precincts by six gates (D and G, Plan II.) equal to each other and similarly situated. The enclosing wall of the outer court has strange dimensions in order that height, width, and thickness, may all be equal. The minute details are after the same pattern. The guard-chambers, the bases of the columns, are all square. The series of chambers for the Levites and for the priests are in fixed numbers and symmetrically placed. The dimensions of the brasen Altar are changed that one part may be the double of another throughout (see xliii. 13). The number of sacrifices is in certain instances increased and made more uniform.

Most readers, when they have come to ch. xlvi., will have been struck with the small number of services described, and with the omission of one of the three great Festivals (see xlv. 25) and even of the Day of Atonement. Now if we were to expect to find in the vision directions for the re-enactment of the Temple-ritual, this would be quite unaccountable. But if we view these selected rites in relation to the Temple-building, and give to that building its true symbolical character, all is found to be just and harmonious. The vision is intended to depict the perpetual worship of the God of Heaven in the Kingdom of Christ. To the mind of an Israelite the proper figure to represent this would be the Temple and its services, with people, priest, and prince, each doing their fitting part. The most appropriate services to exhibit this worship would be those of continual recurrence, in which day by day, week by week, month by month, prayer and praise ascended to the throne of Heaven; viz. the Morning Sacrifice, the Sabbath and the New Moon Festival. Here we have the Israelite symbol of perpetual public adoration.

This will also account for the absence of all mention of the High Priest and his office. In the old dispensation the chief function of the High Priest was the performance of the great Act, which typified the Atonement wrought by the sacrifice and death of Christ for the sins of the world. This Atonement was effected once for all upon the Cross, and in the new dispensation Christ appears in the midst of His people as their Prince and Head, leading and presenting their prayers and praises day by day to His Father in Heaven.

The vision represents the coming dispensation as a kingdom (cp. xxxiv. 24). Solomon took a special part in the Temple services as king, and here there are new and remarkable provisions for the prince. Special offerings are to be made by him; there is a particular order for the prince's inheritance; and one of the gateways is reserved for him as that by which *the Lord, the God of Israel, entered in* (xliv. 2); and thus is brought forth, as a leading feature in the vision, the figure of a king reigning in righteousness, the representative of Jehovah upon earth.

EZEKIEL. XL.

PLAN I.
TEMPLE-COURT AND TEMPLE OF EZEKIEL.

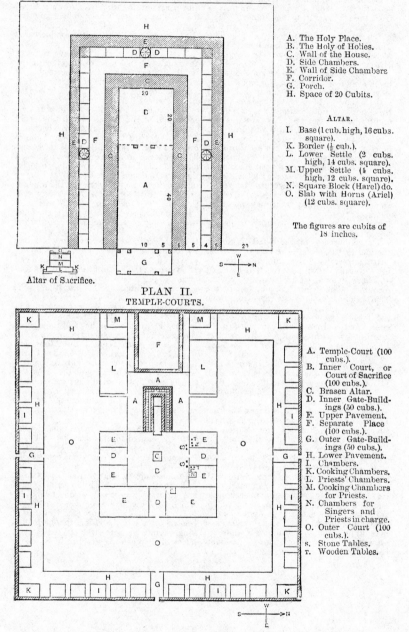

A. The Holy Place.
B. The Holy of Holies.
C. Wall of the House.
D. Side Chambers.
E. Wall of Side Chambers.
F. Corridor.
G. Porch.
H. Space of 20 Cubits.

ALTAR.

I. Base (1 cub. high, 16 cubs.
  square).
K. Border (½ cub.).
L. Lower Settle (2 cubs.
  high, 14 cubs. square).
M. Upper Settle (4 cubs.
  high, 12 cubs. square).
N. Square Block (Harel) do.
O. Slab with Horns (Ariel)
  (12 cubs. square).

The figures are cubits of
18 inches.

Altar of Sacrifice.

PLAN II.
TEMPLE-COURTS.

A. Temple-Court (100
  cubs.).
B. Inner Court, or
  Court of Sacrifice
  (100 cubs.).
C. Brasen Altar.
D. Inner Gate-Build-
  ings (50 cubs.).
E. Upper Pavement.
F. Separate Place
  (100 cubs.).
G. Outer Gate-Build-
  ings (50 cubs.).
H. Lower Pavement.
I. Chambers.
K. Cooking Chambers.
L. Priests' Chambers.
M. Cooking Chambers
  for Priests.
N. Chambers for
  Singers and
  Priests in charge.
O. Outer Court (100
  cubs.).
S. Stone Tables.
T. Wooden Tables.

CHAP. 40. IN the five and twentieth year of our captivity, in the beginning of the year, in the tenth *day* of the month, in the fourteenth year after that *ᵃ*the city was smitten, in the selfsame day *ᵇ*the hand of the LORD was upon me, and brought me 2 thither. *ᶜ*In the visions of God brought he me into the land of Israel, *ᵈ*and set me upon a very high mountain, ¹by which *was* 3 as the frame of a city on the south. And he brought me thither, and, behold, *there was* a man, whose appearance *was* *ᵉ*like the appearance of brass, *ᶠ*with a line of flax in his hand, *ᵍ*and a 4 measuring reed; and he stood in the gate. And the man said

ᵃ ch. 33. 21.
ᵇ ch. 1. 3.
ᶜ ch. 8. 3.
ᵈ Rev. 21. 10.
ᵉ ch. 1. 7.
Dan. 10. 6
ᶠ ch. 47. 3.
ᵍ Rev. 11. 1.
& 21. 15.

¹ Or, *upon which.*

PLAN III.
GATE-BUILDING OF ONE OF THE
COURTS OF EZEKIEL'S TEMPLE.

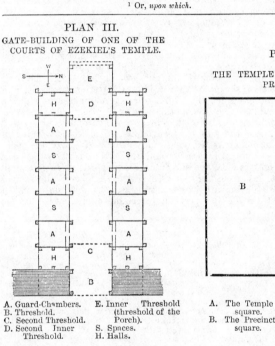

PLAN IV.

THE TEMPLE COURTS AND THE
PRECINCTS.

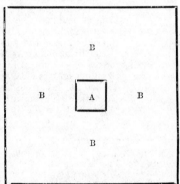

A. Guard-Chambers.
B. Threshold.
C. Second Threshold.
D. Second Inner
Threshold.
E. Inner Threshold
(threshold of the
Porch).
S. Spaces.
H. Halls.

A. The Temple and its Courts, 500 cubits
square.
B. The Precincts, 500 reeds (3000 cubits)
square.

XL. 1. *In the five and twentieth year*] This was the fiftieth year from the 18th of Josiah, the year of his memorable Passover (2 K. xxiii. 22). See i. 1 note. If that was a jubilee year, which is highly probable, this vision also falls in a jubilee year, which seems appropriate. The jubilee year began with the month of Tisri, a sufficient reason for speaking of the time as *the beginning of the year.* The tenth day of this month was the day of Atonement (Lev. xvi. 29, 30).

2. *by which*] Better as in marg. (cp. xliii. 12).

as the frame of a city] It is not *a city* which is seen, but a building (the Temple and its courts) like a city in its construction, surrounded by massive walls.

on the south] **southward,** *i.e.* on the southern slope, just as the Temple actually stood on Mount Moriah. The Temple was at the North-East corner of the city—part of the western portion of the city being more to the North, but no part directly North of the Temple.

3. *the appearance of brass*] Brightly shining.

a line of flax] For measuring the ground plan.

a measuring reed] For the walls (cp. Jer. xxxi. 38, 39). To *measure* implied a separation for sacred purposes. The measurements are (1) *exact*, to shew that the promise is certain; (2) *equal*, to denote harmony; (3) *vast*, to mark majesty and grandeur.

[h] ch. 44. 5
[i] ch. 43. 10.
[k] ch. 42. 20.

unto me, [h]Son of man, behold with thine eyes, and hear with
thine ears, and set thine heart upon all that I shall shew thee;
for to the intent that I might shew *them* unto thee *art* thou
brought hither: [i]declare all that thou seest to the house of
5 Israel. And behold [k]a wall on the outside of the house round
about, and in the man's hand a measuring reed of six cubits
long by the cubit and an hand breadth: so he measured the
breadth of the building, one reed; and the height, one reed.
6 ¶ Then came he unto the gate [1]which looketh toward the east,
and went up the stairs thereof, and measured the threshold of
the gate, *which was* one reed broad; and the other threshold *of*
7 *the gate, which was* one reed broad. And *every* little chamber
was one reed long, and one reed broad; and between the little
chambers *were* five cubits; and the threshold of the gate by the
8 porch of the gate within *was* one reed. He measured also the
9 porch of the gate within, one reed. Then measured he the
porch of the gate, eight cubits; and the posts thereof, two
10 cubits; and the porch of the gate *was* inward. And the little
chambers of the gate eastward *were* three on this side, and
three on that side; they three *were* of one measure: and the
11 posts had one measure on this side and on that side. And he
measured the breadth of the entry of the gate, ten cubits; *and*
12 the length of the gate, thirteen cubits. The [2]space also before
the little chambers *was* one cubit *on this side*, and the space
was one cubit on that side: and the little chambers *were* six
13 cubits on this side, and six cubits on that side. He measured
then the gate from the roof of *one* little chamber to the roof of
another: the breadth *was* five and twenty cubits, door against
14 door. He made also posts of threescore cubits, even unto the

[1] Heb. *whose face* was *the way toward the east.* [2] Heb. *limit,* or, *bound.*

---

5. The boundary wall of the Temple-courts. See Plan II.

a wall on the outside of the house] The wall enclosing the courts in which were the entrance gates.

by the cubit and an hand breadth] The Jews first used a cubit of fifteen inches, applying it principally to the vessels and furniture of the Temple; next a cubit of eighteen inches (*a hand-breadth* longer than the former cubit); and lastly, after the Captivity, the Babylonish cubit of twenty-one inches (a *hand-breadth* more). In the Temple measurements they used only the cubit of eighteen inches; hence the *cubit and hand-breadth* is the cubit of eighteen inches.

6-16. The East gate-building. See Plan III.

6. *stairs*] *Seven* in number (*v.* 22). **Each threshold of the gate (was) one reed broad** (or 9 ft.). The measurements are being taken from E. to W., *i.e.*, in depth.

7. every *little chamber*] **The guard-chambers** (A) for the use of the Levites who kept watch in the Temple.

the threshold of the gate by the porch] The second threshold in the easternmost gateway (C).

porch] Heb. *ulam*; the LXX. αἰλάμ; Vulg. *vestibulum*. The word probably means porch or portico, connected with *ail*=post or pillar.

9. The porch is now measured from N. to S. in *width*. The *breadth of the entry of the gate* was *ten cubits*, made up of the *eight cubits*, with a *cubit* for a *post* or pillar on each side (*v.* 11).

posts] A projection like a ram's horn; in architecture, a column projecting from the wall with its base, shaft, and capital, or it may be the *base* only (*vv.* 16, 49). Here *post* represents the lower part of the column, and the dimensions given are those of the section of the base.

10. In front of each guard-chamber were columns, whose *posts* (bases) were each one cubit square.

11. *the length of the gate*] The length of the gateway (including the porch, E.) from the court to the uncovered space. The threshold was *six cubits*, and the porch *six*. In addition one cubit was probably allowed in front of the porch, as before the porch of the Temple itself (*v.* 49).

13. This measurement is across the gate-building from N. to S. The breadth of the gate-building was exactly half its length (*v.* 15).

14. *posts of threescore cubits*] Sixty cubits were the length of a series of columns. This

15 post of the court round about the gate. And from the face of the gate of the entrance unto the face of the porch of the inner
16 gate *were* fifty cubits. And *there were* [11]narrow windows to the little chambers, and to their posts within the gate round about, and likewise to the [2]arches : and windows *were* round about
17 [3]inward : and upon *each* post *were* palm trees. ¶ Then brought he me into *m*the outward court, and, lo, *there were* *n*chambers, and a pavement made for the court round about: *o*thirty
18 chambers *were* upon the pavement. And the pavement by the side of the gates over against the length of the gates *was* the
19 lower pavement. Then he measured the breadth from the forefront of the lower gate unto the forefront of the inner court
20 [4]without, an hundred cubits eastward and northward. ¶ And the gate of the outward court [5]that looked toward the north, he
21 measured the length thereof, and the breadth thereof. And the little chambers thereof *were* three on this side and three on that side ; and the posts thereof and the [6]arches thereof were after the measure of the first gate : the length thereof *was* fifty
22 cubits, and the breadth five and twenty cubits. And their windows, and their arches, and their palm trees, *were* after the measure of the gate that looketh toward the east ; and they went up unto it by seven steps ; and the arches thereof *were*
23 before them. And the gate of the inner court *was* over against the gate toward the north, and toward the east ; and
24 he measured from gate to gate an hundred cubits. ¶ After that he brought me toward the south, and behold a gate toward the south : and he measured the posts thereof and the arches
25 thereof according to these measures. And *there were* windows in it and in the arches thereof round about, like those windows : the length *was* fifty cubits, and the breadth five and twenty

l 1 Kin. 6 4.

m Rev. 11. 2.
n 1 Kin. 6. 5.
o ch. 45. 5.

---

[1] Heb. *closed.*
[2] Or, *galleries,* or, *porches.*
[3] Or, *within.*
[4] Or, *from without.*
[5] Heb. *whose face* was.
[6] Or, *galleries,* or, *porches.*

---

gives us another feature of the gate-building. Between the porch (E) and the two most western guard-chambers was a space of five cubits (through which the road passed), forming a kind of hall with columns along the sides. This hall is called the *arches* (*v.* 16). A hall of the same dimensions was between the boundary wall and eastern guard-chambers (*v.* 31). It is probable that in one of these halls (that of the eastern gateway of the inner court) the prince *ate bread* on solemn festivals (xliv. 3).

unto the post of the court round about the gate] This hall or colonnade extended the whole breadth of the building to the *pavement* (*v.* 18, H, Plan II.). Outside the building on the pavement was a series of pillars.

15. The whole length of the gate-building was thus made up :—

Thickness of boundary wall	...	6 cubits
Hall of entrance	5	,,
Three guard-chambers (6 cubs. ea.)	18	,,
Spaces between guard-chambers	10	,,
Hall of porch	5	,,
Porch	6	,,
		50 cubits

16. The *narrow* (closed and (?) latticed) *windows* lit up both the guard-chambers and the hall. On the square base of the *post* stood the shaft in the form of a palm-tree, as we see in ancient buildings in the East.

17-19. The *outward* or outer court (O, Plan II.) corresponds to what was in Herod's temple the Court of Women, into which all Jews, but not Gentiles were admitted.

17. *chambers*] (I) See Jer. xxxv. 2.

a pavement] (H) Of mosaic work (2 Chr. vii. 3 ; Esther i. 6) which formed a border of forty-four cubits. On each side of the court in which there were gates, *i.e.* on E., N., and S. It was called the *lower pavement* to distinguish it from the pavement of the inner court ; the outer court being lower than the inner (*v.* 31).

19. There were eastern, northern, and southern gates of entrance from the outer to the inner court (B).

without] Not as in marg., but looking outwards, *i.e.* the outward front of the inner gate towards the outer court.

20-23. The gates both of the outer and of the inner court. Cp. Plan II.

26 cubits. And *there were* seven steps to go up to it, and the
arches thereof *were* before them: and it had palm trees, one on
this side, and another on that side, upon the posts thereof.
27 And *there was* a gate in the inner court toward the south: and
he measured from gate to gate toward the south an hundred cubits.
28 ¶ And he brought me to the inner court by the south gate: and
29 he measured the south gate according to these measures; and
the little chambers thereof, and the posts thereof, and the
arches thereof, according to these measures: and *there were*
windows in it and in the arches thereof round about: *it was*
30 fifty cubits long, and five and twenty cubits broad. And the
arches round about *were* [p] five and twenty cubits long, and five
31 cubits [1] broad. And the arches thereof *were* toward the utter
court; and palm trees *were* upon the posts thereof: and the
32 going up to it *had* eight steps. ¶ And he brought me into the
inner court toward the east: and he measured the gate according
33 to these measures. And the little chambers thereof, and the
posts thereof, and the arches thereof, *were* according to these
measures: and *there were* windows therein and in the arches
thereof round about: *it was* fifty cubits long, and five and
34 twenty cubits broad. And the arches thereof *were* toward the
outward court; and palm trees *were* upon the posts thereof, on
this side, and on that side: and the going up to it *had* eight steps.
35 ¶ And he brought me to the north gate, and measured *it* ac-
36 cording to these measures; the little chambers thereof, the
posts thereof, and the arches thereof, and the windows to it
round about: the length *was* fifty cubits, and the breadth five
37 and twenty cubits. And the posts thereof *were* toward the utter
court; and palm trees *were* upon the posts thereof, on this side,
38 and on that side: and the going up to it *had* eight steps. And
the chambers and the entries thereof *were* by the posts of the
39 gates, where they washed the burnt offering. And in the porch
of the gate *were* two tables on this side, and two tables on that
side, to slay thereon the burnt offering and [q] the sin offering
40 and [r] the trespass offering. And at the side without, [2] as one
goeth up to the entry of the north gate, *were* two tables; and
on the other side, which *was* at the porch of the gate, *were* two
41 tables. Four tables *were* on this side, and four tables on that
side, by the side of the gate; eight tables, whereupon they slew

[p] See ver. 21, & 25, & 33, & 36.

[q] Lev. 4. 2, 3.

[r] Lev. 5. 6. & 6. 6. & 7. 1.

[1] Heb. *breadth.*

[2] Or, *at the step.*

---

31. *utter court*] Translate **outward court** (*v.* 37, xlii. 1, 7, 14, xliv. 19, xlvi. 20, 21).

arches toward the outward court] See *v.* 14 note.

eight steps] So for the East (*v.* 34) and North gates (*v.* 37). From the precincts to the outer court were *seven* steps, from the outer to the inner court *eight*, making together the number of the Psalms (Ps. cxx.–cxxxiv.), supposed by some to have been called Psalms of Degrees, because they were sung by the choir of Levites upon the steps (*degrees*) of the Temple-courts. In later times these Psalms were used as pilgrims' songs by the Jews who went up from their abodes in foreign countries to Jerusalem on the solemn feasts.

38. *the chambers*] Render, **and chambers,** not yet described. They were North of the Altar, by the *posts* or pillars in front and along the sides of the gate-building. There were several gates in the gate-building.

39. *in the porch*] Not under the covered portico, which was only ten cubits broad (*v.* 9), but in the angles formed by the porch and gate-front. If the gate-building projected with its porch forward on to the pavement of the inner court, the tables were fitly placed for carrying out the directions of the Law.

40. On either side of the entrance of the North gate (from the inner court), were two tables on the one side and two tables on the other side of the porch.

42 *their sacrifices.* And the four tables *were* of hewn stone for the
burnt offering, of a cubit and an half long, and a cubit and an
half broad, and one cubit high: whereupon also they laid
the instruments wherewith they slew the burnt offering
43 and the sacrifice. And within *were* ¹hooks, an hand broad,
fastened round about: and upon the tables *was* the flesh
44 of the offering. And without the inner gate *were* the chambers
of ⁸the singers in the inner court, which *was* at the side of the   ⁸ 1 Chr. 6.31.
north gate; and their prospect *was* toward the south: one at
the side of the east gate *having* the prospect toward the north.
45 And he said unto me, This chamber, whose prospect *is* toward
the south, *is* for the priests, ᵗthe keepers of the ²charge of the   ᵗ Lev. 8. 35.
46 house. And the chamber whose prospect *is* toward the north *is*   1 Chr. 9. 23.
for the priests, ᵘthe keepers of the charge of the altar: these   ᵘ Num. 18.5.
are the sons of ˣZadok among the sons of Levi, which come   ch. 44. 15.
47 near to the LORD to minister unto him. So he measured the   ˣ 1 Kin. 2.35.
court, an hundred cubits long, and an hundred cubits broad,   ch. 43. 19.

¹ Or, *endirons,* or, *the two hearthstones.*   ² Or, *ward,* or, *ordinance:* And so ver. 46.

---

42. Omit *the* and *were.* These *four tables*
are not the same as those mentioned before.
The *eight tables* (T) were for slaying and preparing the victims, and were probably of
wood, these (S) were *of hewn stone.* There
may be in the number *twelve* a reference to
the twelve tribes of Israel.

43. *hooks*] The alternative renderings
given in the margin indicate the doubtful-
ness of the translation of the original word.
The form is dual, and indicates that it is
some object usually found in pairs. Some
suggest that they were borders or ledges
set, on either side of the tables, a hand-
breadth from the edges, to prevent the instruments placed on them from falling off.
If the rendering *hooks* be adopted, it is to be
explained thus: that these hooks were set
on the wall *within,* that each hook was
forked (hence the *dual* form), and projected
from the wall one span; and that on these
hooks were hung the carcases of the slain
animals.

44. *without*] Outside of the gate in the
inner court. See N, Plan II.

singers] These were Levites of particular
families, those of Heman, Asaph, and
Merari, whose genealogy is carefully traced
up to Levi (see marg. ref.). These chambers (N, Plan II.) may have been for the
singers and *priests* who were for the time
being engaged in the services of the Temple.
Other chambers (xlii. 1, seq.) were for the
use of the *priests* at other times; and the
Levites and singers, when *not* on duty,
would find accommodation in the thirty
chambers of the outer court. If there is a
departure here from the symmetry elsewhere observed, it may be accounted for by
the fact that as the sacrifices were to be
made on the *North* side of the altar, and
therefore the *tables* for the sacrifices were
on that side only, so those who had

charge of the house and its singers might
have rooms near. Others correct the Hebrew text by the LXX., and read the passage thus:—And without the *inner gate* two
chambers (*i.e.* rows of chambers) *in the inner
court,* one *at the side of the North gate, and
their prospect toward the South,* one *at the side
of the* South *gate, and the prospect towards
the North.*

45. The priests, whose chambers (L) are
here provided, were those whose business it
was to exercise this oversight which had de-
volved upon them as descendants of Aaron
(Num. iii. 32).

46. The position of the *chamber* looking
to the North commanded a view of the
brasen Altar and the sacrifices, which were
prepared at the North side of the Altar.

the sons of Zadok] The priests were all descended from one or other of the two sons of
Aaron, Eleazar and Ithamar. David distributed the priestly offices between the
families of Zadok, the representative of Eleazar, and Ahimelech, the representative of
Ithamar (1 Chr. xxiv. 3). From the time of
Solomon not only the High Priesthood, but
the priesthood itself, so far as concerned its
service, that of offering upon the two Altars,
seems to have been confined to the descendants of Zadok (see 1 Chr. vi. 49–53).
Perhaps the other offices, such as those
mentioned in *v.* 45, were performed by the
descendants of Abiathar and Ithamar. Cp.
1 Sam. ii. 36, and below, xliii. 19, xliv. 15,
xlviii. 11. The priests who had charge of
the sacrifices were distinguished from the
rest of the Levitical priests, as *they which
come near to the Lord,* and (xlii. 13) *the
priests that approach unto the Lord.*

47. *the court*] The inner court (B) where
was the brasen Altar (xliii. 13).

The new chapter would begin better at
v. 48.

48 foursquare; and the altar *that was* before the house. ¶And he
brought me to the porch of the house, and measured *each* post
of the porch, five cubits on this side, and five cubits on that
side: and the breadth of the gate *was* three cubits on this

y 1 Kin. 6. 3. 49 side, and three cubits on that side. *y*The length of the porch
was twenty cubits, and the breadth eleven cubits; and *he*
brought *me* by the steps whereby they went up to it: and *there*

z 1 Kin. 7.21. *were* *z*pillars by the posts, one on this side, and another on that
side.

CHAP. 41. AFTERWARD he brought me to the temple, and measured the posts, six cubits broad on the one side, and six cubits
broad on the other side, *which was* the breadth of the tabernacle.

2 And the breadth of the ¹door *was* ten cubits; and the sides of
the door *were* five cubits on the one side, and five cubits on the
other side: and he measured the length thereof, forty cubits:

3 and the breadth, twenty cubits. Then went he inward, and
measured the post of the door, two cubits; and the door, six

a 1 Kin. 6.20.
2 Chr. 3. 8. 4 cubits; and the breadth of the door, seven cubits. So *a*he
measured the length thereof, twenty cubits; and the breadth,
twenty cubits, before the temple: and he said unto me, This *is*

5 the most holy *place*. ¶After he measured the wall of the house,
six cubits; and the breadth of *every* side chamber, four cubits,

¹ Or, *entrance*.

48, 49. The Porch of the House. The
front of the Temple-porch (see G, Plan I.)
consisted of a central opening with two
columns on either side. Two columns with
the space between them were called *a post*
of the gate. The breadth of the gate on either
side was *a side* opening, that is, the opening between two columns. The columns
having bases of a cubit square, two columns
and the *breadth of the gate*, which we are
told was *three cubits*, made up the *five cubits*
on either side the central entrance, which,
like the entrance into the Temple itself, was
ten cubits. Thus we have twenty cubits
for the porch-front.

49. The porch of Solomon's Temple was
twenty cubits broad and ten deep (1 K. vi.
3). This corresponds nearly with the dimensions of Ezekiel's porch; the difference in
the breadth may be explained by supposing
a space of one cubit in front of the porch
(as *vv.* 11, 12). The circumstance of this
porch being approached by stairs of probably ten steps makes this more probable, a
small space in front of the porch being
naturally required.

pillars by the posts] Lit. **to** *the posts*, meaning that upon the bases (*posts*) stood shafts
(*pillars*). These shafts were probably in
the form of palm-trees (*v.* 16). The porch
with its steps must have jutted into the
inner court.

XLI. **1–11.** The Temple. See Plan I.
1. *the Temple*] Properly the Holy Place
(A), as distinguished from the porch (G) and
the Holy of Holies (B) (1 K. vi. 17, vii. 50).

the posts] The outer wall of the Temple
was six cubits thick (*v.* 5). The eastern

posts of this wall forming part of the front
of the Temple were ornamented with pillars,
six cubits on each side.

He measured the breadth] This breadth
was twenty cubits (*v.* 2). Omit *which was*.
Tabernacle is here the interior (*the covered
portion*) of the Temple.

2. The measurements are internal, the
same as in the Temple of Solomon.

3. *went he inward*] Towards the Holy of
Holies. It is not said, *he brought me in*,
but *he went in*, because the Holy of Holies
was not to be entered even by a priest like
Ezekiel, but only by the High Priest once
a year. So the *Angel* enters and announces
the measurements.

the post of the door] On either side of the
entrance was a pillar, the two together
making up two cubits. The first measurement of the door was from *post* to *post*, six
cubits; and the second measurement, *the
breadth of the door*, was the breadth of the
actual doors which shut off the Holy of
Holies (*v.* 23), and which may have been so
hung that each of the *posts* projected half a
cubit beyond the hinge of the door (which
opened inwards), so as to secure the complete closure of the Holy of Holies.

4. *The Temple* here is the Holy Place as
distinguished from the Most Holy, *the
Oracle*, which is *before* the Holy Place, inwards.

5. *the wall of the house*] This was the
outer wall of the Temple itself. Its thickness of six cubits corresponds with the
colossal proportions of the architecture of
the East.

every side chamber] **the side-chambers** (D).

6 round about the house on every side. [b]And the side chambers
were three, [1]one over another, and [2]thirty in order; and they
entered into the wall which *was* of the house for the side chambers round about, that they might [3]have hold, but they had not
7 hold in the wall of the house. And [4c]*there was* an enlarging,
and a winding about still upward to the side chambers: for the
winding about of the house went still upward round about the
house: therefore the breadth of the house *was still* upward, and
so increased *from* the lowest *chamber* to the highest by the midst.
8 I saw also the height of the house round about: the foundations
9 of the side chambers were [d]a full reed of six great cubits. The
thickness of the wall, which *was* for the side chamber without,
was five cubits: and *that* which *was* left *was* the place of the
10 side chambers that *were* within. And between the chambers
was the wideness of twenty cubits round about the house on
11 every side. And the doors of the side chambers *were* toward
the place that was left, one door toward the north, and another
door toward the south: and the breadth of the place that was
12 left *was* five cubits round about. ¶ Now the building that *was*

[b] 1 Kin 6.
5, 6.

[c] 1 Kin. 6. 8.

[d] ch. 40. 5.

[1] Heb. *side chamber over side chamber.*
[2] Or, *three and thirty times,* or, *foot.*
[3] Heb. *be holden.*
[4] Heb. *it was made broader, and went round.*

These were a marked feature in Solomon's Temple, and were probably used as store-houses for the furniture and property of the Temple. The arrangement of these side-chambers differed in some respects from that of Solomon's Temple, the object of Ezekiel's vision being throughout to bring all things to a more exact proportion.

6. *three, one over another, and thirty in order*] *i.e.* there were three stories, and each story was divided into thirty chambers.

the wall which was *of the house for the side chambers*] Not the wall of the Temple but another wall (*v.* 9) parallel to it, which might be said to be *of the house, i.e.* belonging to it. The side-chambers of Solomon's Temple were built against the Temple-wall, but in Ezekiel's vision the desire to keep the Temple still more separate and holy led to a fresh arrangement, viz., that another wall should be built at such a distance from the Temple-wall as to allow of chambers being built against it, facing the Temple-wall, and opening into a passage or corridor (F), separating them from the Temple itself.

that they might have hold, but they had not hold in the wall of the house] that they might have hold, but not have hold on the wall of the house, *i.e.* entirely separating the chambers from the Temple-wall proper.

7. *an enlarging*] The *wall for the side-chambers* had for the ground story its full thickness of five cubits (*v.* 9)—then it was diminished one cubit, so as to form a ledge whereon to rest the beams of the floor of the second story, and again was further diminished one cubit for the floor of the third story. Thus there was an *enlarging* of the second story of the chambers by one

cubit, and of the third story by two cubits beyond the breadth of the chambers on the ground-floor.

a winding about still upward] Winding stairs led *upward* from one story to another.

the winding about of the house] A collective expression for the various winding stair-cases to the side-chambers which extended on the north, west, and south sides.

and so increased &c.] Rather, "and the lowest story was such that one went by the middle story up to the highest." The winding stairs were not visible outside, so that one could not go to the upper story without passing through the middle story.

8. *the foundations of the side chambers*] Therefore the height of the side-chambers from the floor was six cubits, there being three stories, which corresponds sufficiently with the twenty cubits which was the height of the Temple. *A great cubit* is probably an architectural term to denote the line of junction between two stories, which would be that of the ceiling of the lower and the floor of the upper story.

9. *and that which* was *left*] *i.e.* the passage (F) between the side-chambers and the Temple-wall, was five cubits (*v.* 11).

the place of the side chambers that were *within*] within the side-chambers which belong to the house. The seer is giving first the height of the side-chambers (*v.* 8), and then the breadth, from the outside of the wall of these chambers to the Temple-wall.

10. See H, Plan I.

11. The doors of the side-chambers opened on to the passage or corridor, between the chambers and the Temple-wall.

before the separate place at the end toward the west *was* seventy cubits broad ; and the wall of the building *was* five cubits thick 13 round about, and the length thereof ninety cubits. So he measured the house, an hundred cubits long; and the separate place, and the building, with the walls thereof, an hundred 14 cubits long; also the breadth of the face of the house, and of 15 the separate place toward the east, an hundred cubits. ¶ And he measured the length of the building over against the separate place which *was* behind it, and the ¹galleries thereof on the one side and on the other side, an hundred cubits, with the inner

16 temple, and the porches of the court ; the door posts, and *ᵉ*the narrow windows, and the galleries round about on their three stories, over against the door, ²cieled with wood round about, ³and from the ground up to the windows, and the windows *were* 17 covered ; to that above the door, even unto the inner house, and without, and by all the wall round about within and without,

ƒ 1 Kin. 6. 29.

18 by ⁴measure. And *it was* made *ƒ* with cherubims and palm trees, so that a palm tree *was* between a cherub and a cherub ;

ᵍ See ch. 1. 10.

19 and *every* cherub had two faces ; *ᵍ* so that the face of a man *was* toward the palm tree on the one side, and the face of a young lion toward the palm tree on the other side : *it was* made through 20 all the house round about. From the ground unto above the door *were* cherubims and palm trees made, and *on* the wall of 21 the temple. The ⁵posts of the temple *were* squared, *and* the face of the sanctuary ; the appearance *of the one* as the appear-

---

¹ Or, *several walks,* or, *walks with pillars.*
² Heb. *cieling of wood.*
³ Or, *and the ground unto the windows.*
⁴ Heb. *measures.*
⁵ Heb. *post.*

---

12. *the separate place*] See F, Plan II. The word occurs only in this chapter. The name, which seems one of discredit, has led to the conjecture that the purpose of this place and its building was to receive the offal of the sacrifices and sweepings of the courts, to be carried thence by a postern gate (cp. xliii. 21). The building itself was, we are told, seventy cubits wide, with walls five cubits thick (eighty cubits in all), leaving ten cubits on each side to make up the 100 cubits from North to South. The length was ninety cubits, which, adding as before the thickness of the walls, gives 100 cubits in length. The whole Temple-building was 500 cubits from West to East, and from North to South, 500 cubits.

14. *toward the east*] The *separate place* was measured on its eastern side, for the western was not approachable for the purpose of measurement.

15. The description of certain details is introduced by a summary statement of what had been already done.

galleries] On either side of the eastern front of the building on the separate place was a gallery of ten feet, under which was an approach to the building, by which the refuse was to be carried in by openings in the North and South, and then carried out by a western postern.

16. *galleries*] The upper story of the side-

chambers was probably built in the form of an open gallery.

over against the door] The rows of the side-chambers extended to the front of the Temple, so that they were *over against* the opening, but did not extend so far as the porch.

cieled] **overlaid.** Pillars, galleries, narrow windows were overlaid with wood (1 K. vi. 15, 16).

were covered] With wood.

17. *to that* &c.] **Over above** *the door......* *within and without* **was** *by measure.* This verse asserts that all the overlaying was done by careful measurement.

18. On the symbolism of the *Cherubim* see i. 1 note &c.

every cherub had two faces] Not as in ch. i., *four faces.* Convenience of delineation upon a wall may have suggested the alteration. The cherubic devices on the curtains of the Tabernacle (Ex. xxvi. 1, xxxvi. 8) were no doubt like the Cherubim over the Ark, of which we have no reason to suppose that each had *two faces.* The symbolical character here admitted of the deviation.

21. *The posts*] Not the word used before (see xl. 9 note). These *posts* are rather pilasters forming part of the inner walls.

the appearance...other] *i.e.* the appearance in this vision was the same as in the actual Temple (cp. xliii. 3) ; [or, according to others, the front of the sanctuary resembled the front of the Holy Place].

22 ance *of the other.* [h] The altar of wood *was* three cubits high, and   [h] Ex. 30. 1.
the length thereof two cubits ; and the corners thereof, and the
length thereof, and the walls thereof, *were* of wood : and he said
23 unto me, This *is* [i] the table that *is* [k] before the LORD. [l] And   [i] ch. 44. 16.
24 the temple and the sanctuary had two doors. And the doors had   Mal. 1. 7, 12.
two leaves *apiece,* two turning leaves ; two *leaves* for the one   [k] Ex. 30. 8.
25 door, and two leaves for the other *door.* And *there were* made   [l] 1 Kin. 6
on them, on the doors of the temple, cherubims and palm trees,   31—35.
like as *were* made upon the walls ; and *there were* thick planks
26 upon the face of the porch without. And *there were* [m] narrow   [m] ch. 40. 16.
windows and palm trees on the one side and on the other side,   ver. 16.
on the sides of the porch, and *upon* the side chambers of the
house, and thick planks.

CHAP. 42. THEN he brought me forth into the utter court, the
way toward the north : and he brought me into [a] the chamber   [a] ch. 41. 12,
that *was* over against the separate place, and which *was* before   15.
2 the building toward the north. Before the length of an hundred
cubits *was* the north door, and the breadth *was* fifty cubits.
3 Over against the twenty *cubits* which *were* for the inner court,
and over against the pavement which *was* for the utter court,
4 *was* [b] gallery against gallery in three *stories.* And before the   [b] ch. 41. 16.
chambers *was* a walk of ten cubits breadth inward, a way of one
5 cubit ; and their doors toward the north. Now the upper

---

22. *The altar of wood*] The Altar for incense (marg. ref.) ; *altar of gold* (see 1 K. vii.
48).

walls] The corner pieces of the Altar,
rising into projections called in Ex. *horns,*
here *corners.*

table] *Table* and *Altar* were convertible
terms (Mal. i. 7).

23-25. See marg. ref.

25. *thick planks*] Others render, **leaves in
wood** (and in *v.* 26).

XLII. **1.** *utter court*] **outward** *court,* so
v. 3.

into the chamber...before the building] **to
the chambers** (See L, Plan II.)...**over
against** &c. *The building* is the Temple-
building, for this row of chambers was built
against eighty cubits of the wall bounding
the separate place and twenty cubits of the
wall of the Temple-court.

2. He brought me *before* a row of chambers 100 cubits long, East and West. The
door of which lay on the North side of the
chambers. The priests entered from the
outer court (o) ; the breadth of this block
of chambers was fifty cubits, North and
South (*v.* 8).

3. These *chambers* (cp. xlvi. 19) did not
reach to the western wall ; between it and
them lay a court for cooking (M), probably
forty cubits by thirty ; such court with its
approaches filled up the corner of fifty
cubits square, as in the case of the kitchen-
courts for the people. In these chambers
were dining-rooms for the priests (see *v.* 13),
and baths ; for no priest could enter upon
his daily ministry without having first
bathed. The *chambers* extended beyond
"the separate place" to the wall of the

Temple-court, on the other side of which
wall was the twenty cubits space. The
pavement (H) was no doubt continued
along the Temple-wall, so that these priests'
chambers, like the thirty chambers, stood
upon *a pavement,* and were, on the East side,
over against this *pavement.*

Translate *vv.* 1-3 : *Then he brought me
forth into the* outward *court, the way toward
the North, and he brought me* to the chambers
which **were** *over against the separate place,
and which* were over against *the building,
towards the North* along the front *of the
length of an hundred cubits,* with the door
by the North, *and the breadth fifty cubits
over against the twenty cubits which were* in
*the inner court, and over against the pave-
ment which was* in the outward *court,* gallery upon *gallery in three stories.*

4. Or, **In the front** *of the chambers* was a
gangway *of ten cubits breadth* [leading] *inward,* a path *of one cubit, and their doors
toward the north.* The *gangway* had stairs
to the upper stories, while along the North
front of the building there was a kerb of
one cubit, as before the guard-chambers
(xl. 12), on which kerb the North doors
(leading to the basement) opened. Others
follow the LXX. "And opposite the
chambers a walk 10 cubits in width to 100
cubits in length."

5. Render :—*And the upper chambers
were* shortened, for galleries took off from
them, from *the lower and* from *the middlemost* [chambers] *of the building.* The building rose in terraces, as was usual in Babylonian architecture, and so each of the two
upper stories receded from the one below it.

chambers *were* shorter: for the galleries [1]were higher than these, [2]than the lower, and than the middlemost of the build-
6 ing. For they *were* in three *stories*, but had not pillars as the pillars of the courts: therefore *the building* was straitened more
7 than the lowest and the middlemost from the ground. And the wall that *was* without over against the chambers, toward the utter court on the forepart of the chambers, the length thereof
8 *was* fifty cubits. For the length of the chambers that *were* in the utter court *was* fifty cubits: and, lo, before the temple *were*
9 an hundred cubits. And [3]from under these chambers *was* [4]the entry on the east side, [5]as one goeth into them from the utter
10 court. The chambers *were* in the thickness of the wall of the court toward the east, over against the separate place, and over

c ver. 4.

11 against the building. And *c*the way before them *was* like the appearance of the chambers which *were* toward the north, as long as they, *and* as broad as they: and all their goings out *were* both
12 according to their fashions, and according to their doors. And according to the doors of the chambers that *were* toward the south *was* a door in the head of the way, *even* the way directly before the wall toward the east, as one entereth into them.
13 ¶ Then said he unto me, The north chambers *and* the south chambers, which *are* before the separate place, they *be* holy

d Lev. 6 16,
26.
& 24. 9.
e Lev. 2 3.
Num. 18 9,
10.
f ch. 44 19.

chambers, where the priests that approach unto the LORD *d*shall eat the most holy things: there shall they lay the most holy things, and *e*the meat offering, and the sin offering, and the
14 trespass offering; for the place *is* holy. *f*When the priests enter therein, then shall they not go out of the holy *place* into the utter court, but there they shall lay their garments wherein they minister; for they *are* holy; and shall put on other garments, and shall approach to *those things* which *are* for the people.

[1] Or, *did eat of these.*
[2] Or, and *the building*   consisted *of the lower*   [4] Or, *he that brought me.*
                                                   and the middlemost.   [5] Or, *as he came.*
                                                   [3] Or, *from the place.*

---

6. The front of the higher stories was not supported on pillars, but **there was a narrowing from** the *lowest* [chambers] *and* from *the middlemost* [chambers] *from the ground.*

7. The *wall* here must be one from N. to S., fencing off from the outer court the passage along the East side of the chambers, and therefore fifty cubits long.

8. *the length*] From N. to S.

before the temple] This describes their position in a general way; more precisely they lay over against partly the *separate place* and partly the *Temple*-court (*v.* 1).

9. The entry from these chambers to the Temple-court was by a passage lying to the East fenced off by the *wall* (*v.* 7). This passage is described as lying *under* the chambers, being on the basement, and also having access by steps to the Temple-court, which was raised many steps above the outer court.

10. Render, **Breadth-wise** [was] **the wall** (*v.* 7) **towards the East; in front of the separate place and of the building** [were] **the chambers**: *i.e.* on the East was the *wall* (*geder*); along the boundary wall of *the separate place* and of the *building* (the Temple) lay the *chambers*.

11, 12. Translate: **And along the front of them—like** (lit. as the appearance of) **the chambers which were towards the North, as long as they and as broad as they, and** [like] **all their goings out, and like their fashions, and like their doors, even so were the doors of the chambers which were towards the South;** (with) **a door at the head of the way, the way of the wall adjoined eastwards as** one **entereth into them** (the chambers).

13. In Lev. x. 13 it was prescribed that the priests should eat of the sacrifices in the *holy place.* This was originally before the Altar in the inner court—now separate chambers are assigned, and these become *the holy place* for this purpose. Of the *trespass-offering* and *meat-offering* what was not consumed was eaten (Lev. vii. 6), but the *sin-offering* was burnt without the camp (xliii. 21). Probably the carcase was brought from the Altar to the chamber before being carried out.

14. Cp. Lev. xvi. 23.

those things which are *for the people*] viz. the outer court.

15 ¶ Now when he had made an end of measuring the inner house, he brought me forth toward the gate whose prospect *is* toward
16 the east, and measured it round about. He measured the east ¹side with the measuring reed, five hundred reeds, with the
17 measuring reed round about. He measured the north side, five
18 hundred reeds, with the measuring reed round about. He measured the south side, five hundred reeds, with the measuring
19 reed. He turned about to the west side, *and* measured five
20 hundred reeds with the measuring reed. He measured it by the four sides: *g*it had a wall round about, *h* five hundred *reeds* long, and five hundred broad, to make a separation between the sanctuary and the profane place.

g ch. 40. 5
h ch. 45. 2.

Chap. 43. AFTERWARD he brought me to the gate, *even* the gate
2 *a*that looketh toward the east: *b*and, behold, the glory of the God of Israel came from the way of the east: and *c*his voice *was* like a noise of many waters: *d*and the earth shined with
3 his glory. And *it was* *e*according to the appearance of the vision which I saw, *even* according to the vision that I saw ²when I came *f*to destroy the city: and the visions *were* like the vision that I saw *g*by the river Chebar; and I fell upon my face.
4 *h*And the glory of the LORD came into the house by the way of
5 the gate whose prospect *is* toward the east. *i*So the spirit took me up, and brought me into the inner court; and, behold, *k*the
6 glory of the LORD filled the house. And I heard *him* speaking
7 unto me out of the house; and *l*the man stood by me. And he

a ch. 10. 19.
b ch. 11. 23.
c ch. 1. 24.
Rev. 1. 15.
d ch. 10. 4.
Rev. 18. 1.
e ch. 1. 4, 28.
& 8. 4.
f So Jer. 1. 10.
g ch. 1. 3.
& 3. 23.
h See ch. 10. 19.
i ch. 3. 12.
& 8. 3.
k 1 Kin. 8. 10, 11.
ch. 44. 4.
l ch. 40. 3.

¹ Heb. *wind*.
² Or, *when I came to* prophesy *that*

the city should be destroyed: See ch. 9. 1, 5.

15-19. The Precincts. The Temple and its courts were surrounded by an area of exact dimensions 3000 cubits (1500 yards) square. See Plan IV.

15. *the inner house*] The Temple and its courts, all that lay within the *wall on the outside of the house* (xl. 5); *the gate* is the eastern gate of the outer court.

measured it round about] The precincts, into which he had brought the seer through the eastern gate of the outer court.

20. *The sanctuary* proper is probably here the Most Holy place as distinguished from the rest of the Temple (xli. 23, xlv. 3); but the term was capable of extension first to the whole Temple, then to all the ground that was separated to *holy* as distinguished from *profane, i.e.* common uses.

In the vision the courts rose on successive platforms, the outer court being raised seven steps above the precincts, the inner court eight steps above the outer, and the Temple itself ten steps above the court of sacrifice.

XLIII. 1 11. The consecration of the new Temple. The glory of the God of Israel must take possession of the new sanctuary, as, in time past, of the Tabernacle and of Solomon's Temple. But it is in a different form. The glory was of old veiled in a cloud resting on the Mercy-Seat of the Ark between Cherubim of carved wood. Now the glory appears in the form with which Ezekiel is familiar, in all its

symbolical significance (see i. 1 note). A personal and living God enters the sanctuary (*v.* 2), condescending to occupy it, not merely as a fixed dwelling-place, but as a centre from whence His Power and Mercy radiate freely to the utmost ends of the earth. Hence amidst the detailed preparations of the house no mention is made of the Ark or Mercy-Seat, so important a part in the former sanctuary. The living Cherubim, the firmament and the rainbow of mercy, replace the cherubic figures and the golden chest.

The Ark, having been in some way destroyed in Nebuchadnezzar's siege, was never replaced. In its stead there was within the veil a flat stone on which the High Priest poured the blood on the day of Atonement.

1. *the gate*] This was the eastern gate from the precincts to the outer court.

4. By this gate the glory of the Lord had departed. See marg. ref.

5. *the glory of the* LORD *filled the house*] Cp. marg. ref. ; Ex. xl. 34, 35.

6. *the man*] A *man*. Probably an Angel different from *the man* who had hitherto accompanied the seer. That Angel guided, measured, and explained ; this is present only to guide.

7. *he said*] *i.e.* God said. Both the LXX. and the Vulg. break this verse into two, so as to make the first half the solemn words of dedication. Place a full stop after *for*

m Ps. 99. 1.
n 1 Chr. 28.2.
Ps. 99. 5.
o Ex. 29. 45.
Ps. 68. 16.
Joel 3. 17.
John 1. 14.
2 Cor. 6. 16.
p ch. 39. 7.
q Lev. 26. 30.
Jer. 16. 18.
r See 2 Kin.
16. 14.
ch. 8. 3.
s ver. 7.
t ver. 7.
u ch. 40. 4.

x ch. 40. 2.

y ch. 40. 5.
& 41. 8.

said unto me, ¶ Son of man, *m*the place of my throne, and *n*the place of the soles of my feet, *o*where I will dwell in the midst of the children of Israel for ever, and my holy name, shall the house of Israel *p*no more defile, *neither* they, nor their kings, by their whoredom, nor by *q*the carcases of their kings in their high 8 places. ¶ *r*In their setting of their threshold by my thresholds, and their post by my posts, ¹and the wall between me and them, they have even defiled my holy name by their abominations that they have committed: wherefore I have consumed them in mine 9 anger. Now let them put away their whoredom, and *s*the carcases of their kings, far from me, *t*and I will dwell in the midst 10 of them for ever. ¶ Thou son of man, *u*shew the house to the house of Israel, that they may be ashamed of their iniquities : 11 and let them measure the ²pattern. And if they be ashamed of all that they have done, shew them the form of the house, and the fashion thereof, and the goings out thereof, and the comings in thereof, and all the forms thereof, and all the ordinances thereof, and all the forms thereof, and all the laws thereof : and write *it* in their sight, that they may keep the whole form there-12 of, and all the ordinances thereof, and do them. ¶ This *is* the law of the house ; Upon *x*the top of the mountain the whole limit thereof round about *shall be* most holy. Behold, this *is* the 13 law of the house. ¶ And these *are* the measures of the altar after the cubits : *y*The cubit *is* a cubit and an hand breadth ; even the ³bottom *shall be* a cubit, and the breadth a cubit, and the border thereof by the ⁴edge thereof round about *shall be* 14 a span : and this *shall be* the higher place of the altar. And

---

¹ Or, *for* there was but *a wall between me and*   *them.*   ³ Heb. *bosom.*
² Or, *sum*, or, *number.*   ⁴ Heb. *lip.*

---

ever; the words mark the distinction between the new and the former sanctuary.

7, 8. The palace of Solomon abutted upon the southern side of the embankment of the Temple-platform ; there was but *a wall between Jehovah and them.* When the kings gave themselves up to idolatry, this vicinity was to the Temple a pollution and defilement. Thus it has been conjectured that *the garden of Uzza* in which Manasseh and Amon were buried (2 K. xxi. 18, 26), and on which now stands the mosque of Omar, was on the Temple area itself ; if so, this would explain the mention of *high places* in connexion with the defilement by the *carcases of kings,* since the platform of the mosque of Omar at the time of Ezekiel rose to a considerable height above the Temple.

Besides this, idolatrous kings of Judah did actually introduce their idolatries into the Temple courts themselves (cp. 2 K. xvi. 11, xxi. 4).

10. Deviation from the exact rules of the Mosaic ordinances was connected with the transgression of the people. So the restoration according to the pattern of the Law was symbolical of their return to obedience.

12. xlvii. 12. The law of the ordinance of the New Sanctuary.

12. After the consecration, God pro-

nounces the *law* which is to govern the ordinances of the sanctuary (cp. 1 K. viii.), first briefly repeating the general rule that the place must be kept holy to the Lord (cp. Rev. xxi. 27), and then proceeding to specific ordinances commencing with the Altar.

13. The Altar of sacrifice which stood in the inner court, not the Altar of incense described xli. 22. In the Temple of the vision the dimensions differ from those of the Tabernacle (Exod. xxvii. 1,) and of Solomon's Temple (2 Chron. iv. 1), with a view to introduce definite propositions and symbolical numbers. See Plan I.

the bottom] The base (I) of the altar so called, because it forms with its *border* (K) a kind of socket to receive the *lower settle* (L). It was to be "a cubit" in depth.

The *breadth* is the breadth of that portion of the base which was not covered by the *lower settle.*

the higher place] the **base**, lit. back ; the base is called the back because the Altar rested upon it.

14. *the bottom*] The basement just described is now called *the bottom upon the ground.* The Altar (independently of the bottom) was composed of two stages called *settles,* the base of the *upper settle* (M) being less than that of the *lower* (L).

from the bottom *upon* the ground *even* to the lower settle *shall be* two cubits, and the breadth one cubit; and from the lesser settle *even* to the greater settle *shall be* four cubits, and the breadth *one*
15 cubit. So ¹the altar *shall be* four cubits; and from ²the altar
16 and upward *shall be* four horns. And the altar *shall be* twelve *cubits* long, twelve broad, square in the four squares thereof.
17 And the settle *shall be* fourteen *cubits* long and fourteen broad in the four squares thereof; and the border about it *shall be* half a cubit; and the bottom thereof *shall be* a cubit about; and ᶻhis
18 stairs shall look toward the east. ¶ And he said unto me, Son of man, thus saith the Lord GOD; These *are* the ordinances of the altar in the day when they shall make it, to offer burnt
19 offerings thereon, and to ᵃsprinkle blood thereon. And thou shalt give to ᵇthe priests the Levites that be of the seed of Zadok, which approach unto me, to minister unto me, saith the Lord
20 GOD, ᶜa young bullock for a sin offering. And thou shalt take of the blood thereof, and put *it* on the four horns of it, and on the four corners of the settle, and upon the border round about :
21 thus shalt thou cleanse and purge it. Thou shalt take the bullock also of the sin offering, and he ᵈshall burn it in the ap-
22 pointed place of the house, ᵉwithout the sanctuary. And on the second day thou shalt offer a kid of the goats without blemish for a sin offering; and they shall cleanse the altar, as they did
23 cleanse *it* with the bullock. When thou hast made an end of cleansing *it*, thou shalt offer a young bullock without blemish,

ᶻ See Ex. 20. 26.

ᵃ Lev. 1. 5.
ᵇ ch. 44. 15.
ᶜ Ex. 29. 10.
Lev. 8. 14.
ch. 45. 18.

ᵈ Ex. 29. 14.
ᵉ Heb. 13. 11.

---

¹ Heb. *Harel*, that is, *the mountain of God.*

² Heb. *Ariel*, that is, *the lion of God.*

---

to the lower settle] That is, to the top of *the lower settle*, which was to be *two cubits* high.

from the lesser settle…to the greater settle] *i.e.* from the top of the *lower settle* to the top of the *upper settle*, called *lesser* and *greater*, because the height of the *lower* is less than that of the *upper ; the breadth* here is the part of the lower settle not covered by the upper settle, projecting one cubit on every side.

15. *the altar…the altar*] See marg. The two words may denote, the first a square block (N) placed upon the *upper settle*, the second a slab (O), the thickness of which is not given, from which rose *four horns* (Exod. xxvii. 2); and to which it seems probable that the victims of sacrifice were at times bound. (Ps. cxviii. 27). Why the names *Harel* and *Ariel* were used must be conjectural. *Mount of God* may have been a title naturally given to the place of sacrifice as elsewhere to the place of worship (xl. 2); *Lion of God* was a term used for the Holy City itself (Isai. xxix. 1).

16. *altar*] **Ariel** was to be an exact square on all sides. Cp. Exod. xxvii. 1 ; Rev. xxi. 16.

17. *the settle*] The lower settle (L), projecting beyond the *upper settle* (M) one cubit on every side.

his stairs] Jewish tradition says that the approach to the Altar was by an inclined

plane, because to go up *by steps* was forbidden (Exod. xx. 26).

The number "twelve" was symbolical of the twelve tribes, "four," of the earth ; "sixteen" is the square of "four," and "fourteen" the double of "seven," the number of the covenant, as being composed of "three," the number of God, and of "four," the number of the world. Thus we have in the Altar a special instance of Hebrew symbolism.

18. The rites here described are not those of the regular service, but those to be observed on the day of dedication. Cp. Lev. viii. 10 seq. ; 1 K. viii. 63 seq. ; 2 Chr. vii. 4 seq. In the Tabernacle the priest slew the victims, but Moses sprinkled the blood. In the vision the seer is addressed as though he were to perform the part of Moses.

19. *the seed of Zadok*] See xl. 46 note.

21. *in the appointed place of the house*] A place within the Temple-court, but *without the sanctuary* properly so called, that is to say, without the Temple and inner court. This was probably the *separate place* (see xli. 12).

22. *they shall cleanse*] By sprinkling the blood (*v.* 18). Here *they* marks the act as that of the priests. Moses did his part before the priests were consecrated, and the seer could act through them.

23—26. There was, on each of the *seven days, a burnt-offering* of *a bullock* and *a ram*,

24 and a ram out of the flock without blemish. And thou shalt
offer them before the LORD, *f*and the priests shall cast salt upon
them, and they shall offer them up *for* a burnt offering unto the
25 LORD. *g*Seven days shalt thou prepare every day a goat *for* a
sin offering : they shall also prepare a young bullock, and a ram
26 out of the flock, without blemish. Seven days shall they purge
the altar and purify it; and they shall [1]consecrate themselves.
27 *h*And when these days are expired, it shall be, *that* upon the
eighth day, and *so* forward, the priests shall make your burnt
offerings upon the altar, and your [2]peace offerings; and I will
[i]accept you, saith the Lord GOD.

CHAP. **44.** THEN he brought me back the way of the gate of the
outward sanctuary *a*which looketh toward the east; and it *was*
2 shut. Then said the LORD unto me; This gate shall be shut, it
shall not be opened, and no man shall enter in by it; *b*because
the LORD, the God of Israel, hath entered in by it, therefore it
3 shall be shut. *It is* for the prince; the prince, he shall sit in it
to *c*eat bread before the LORD ; *d*he shall enter by the way of
the porch of *that* gate, and shall go out by the way of the same.
4 ¶ Then brought he me the way of the north gate before the
house : and I looked, and, *e*behold, the glory of the LORD filled
5 the house of the LORD : *f*and I fell upon my face. And the
LORD said unto me, *g*Son of man, [3]mark well, and behold with
thine eyes, and hear with thine ears all that I say unto thee
concerning all the ordinances of the house of the LORD, and all
the laws thereof; and mark well the entering in of the house,
6 with every going forth of the sanctuary. And thou shalt say to
the *h*rebellious, *even* to the house of Israel, Thus saith the Lord

Margin references:
f Lev. 2. 13.
g Ex. 29. 35.
Lev. 8. 33.
h Lev. 9. 1.
i Job 42. 8.
ch. 20. 40.
Rom. 12. 1.
1 Pet. 2. 5.
a ch. 43. 1.
b ch. 43. 4.
c Gen. 31. 54.
1 Cor. 10. 18.
d ch. 46. 2, 8.
e ch. 3. 23
& 43. 5.
f ch. 1. 28.
g ch. 40. 4.
h ch. 2. 5.

---

[1] Heb. *fill their hands*, Ex. 29. 24.　　[2] Or, *thank offerings*.　　[3] Heb. *set thine heart*.

---

preceded by a *sin-offereng* of a *bullock* on
the first day, and of a *kid of the goats* on
the other days.

24. Salt is here added to the *burnt-offering*
to express still more the idea of purification.
In the second Temple no sacrifice was complete without the use of salt, and the
Rabbis assert that there was a great heap
of salt close to the Altar, always ready for
use, and that the inclined plane to the Altar
was kept covered with salt. Cp. Mark ix. 49.

26. *consecrate themselves*] Lit. as in marg.
(Lev. viii. 27). The priests are already
consecrated, but the memory of their consecration was thus kept up at the dedication
of the Altar.

27. After this inauguration the regular
service shall be resumed, and be acceptable
unto God (cp. Mal. i. 11).
The Epistle to the Hebrews (viii.—x).
helps us to recognise in this vision the
symbol of the purification of the Church of
God by the cleansing blood of Christ,
Victim and Priest.

XLIV. The relation of the different
classes of people to the Temple and its
courts.

1—3. The position of the Prince.
1. *outward sanctuary*] The court of the
priests, as distinguished from the Temple
itself. This gate was reserved for the

Prince, to whom it was opened on certain
days. Only a Prince of the house of David
might sit down in the priests' court (cp. xlvi.
1, 2).

2. *the* LORD *hath entered in*] See xliii. 2.
3. *the prince*] Foretold under the name
of David (xxxiv. 24). The Rabbis understood this to be the Messiah.
to eat bread] See Lev. ii. 3 ; xxiv. 9 ; according to the old Law these feasts belonged
only to the priests ; none of the rest of the
congregation, not even the king, might
partake of them. The new system gives to
the *prince* a privilege which he did not before possess ; the prince, as the representative
of the Messiah, standing in a higher position
than the kings of old. *To eat bread* may
also include participation in the animals
sacrificed, portions of which were reserved
for those of the people who offered them.

4—16. Admonition to the ministering
priests, grounded upon former neglect.
4. *the north gate before the house*] The
North gate of the inner court. God expostu-
lates with His people in the seat of their
former idolatries (viii. 3).
5. *mark well*] The careful arrangements
made had all been intended to keep the
Temple and its surroundings from profanation. Hence attention to these particulars
is enjoined.

GOD; O ye house of Israel, 'let it suffice you of all your abomi-
7 nations, ᵏin that ye have brought *into my sanctuary* ¹¹strangers,
ᵐuncircumcised in heart, and uncircumcised in flesh, to be in my
sanctuary, to pollute it, *even* my house, when ye offer ⁿmy bread,
ᵒthe fat and the blood, and they have broken my covenant be-
8 cause of all your abominations. And ye have not ᵖkept the
charge of mine holy things : but ye have set keepers of my
9 ²charge in my sanctuary for yourselves. ¶ Thus saith the Lord
GOD; �q No stranger, uncircumcised in heart, nor uncircumcised
in flesh, shall enter into my sanctuary, of any stranger that *is*
10 among the children of Israel. ʳAnd the Levites that are gone away
far from me, when Israel went astray, which went astray away
from me after their idols ; they shall even bear their iniquity.
11 Yet they shall be ministers in my sanctuary, ˢ*having* charge at
the gates of the house, and ministering to the house : ᵗthey shall
slay the burnt offering and the sacrifice for the people, and ᵘthey
12 shall stand before them to minister unto them. Because they
ministered unto them before their idols, and ˣ³caused the house
of Israel to fall into iniquity ; therefore have I ʸlifted up mine
hand against them, saith the Lord GOD, and they shall bear their
13 iniquity. ᶻAnd they shall not come near unto me, to do the
office of a priest unto me, nor to come near to any of my holy
things, in the most holy *place :* but they shall ᵃbear their shame,
14 and their abominations which they have committed. But I will
make them ᵇkeepers of the charge of the house, for all the ser-
15 vice thereof, and for all that shall be done therein. ¶ ᶜBut the
priests the Levites, ᵈ the sons of Zadok, that kept the charge of
my sanctuary ᵉwhen the children of Israel went astray from me,
they shall come near to me to minister unto me, and they ᶠshall
stand before me to offer unto me ᵍthe fat and the blood, saith
16 the Lord GOD : they shall enter into my sanctuary, and they shall
come near to ʰmy table, to minister unto me, and they shall keep
17 my charge. ¶ And it shall come to pass, *that* when they enter in
at the gates of the inner court, ⁱthey shall be clothed with linen
garments ; and no wool shall come upon them, whiles they

¹ Heb. *children of a stranger.*
² Or, *ward,* or, *ordinance :*
³ Heb. *were for a stumbling-*

And so ver. 14 & 16, & ch. 40. 45.

block of iniquity unto, &c., ch. 14. 3, 4.

References: ⁱ ch. 45. 9. 1 Pet. 4. 3. ᵏ ch. 43. 8. Acts 21. 28. ˡ Lev. 22. 25. ᵐ Lev. 26.41. Acts 7. 51. ⁿ Lev. 21. 6. ᵒ Lev. 3. 16. & 17. 11. ᵖ Lev. 22. 2. q ver. 7. ʳ See 2 Kin. 23. 8. &c. 2 Chr. 29. 4, 5. ˢ ch. 48. 11. ˢ 1 Chr. 26. 1. ᵗ 2 Chr. 29. 34. ᵘ Num. 16. 9. ˣ Isai. 9. 16. Mal. 2. 8. ʸ P⁻ 106. 26. ᶻ Num. 18. 3. 2 Kin. 23. 9. ᵃ ch. 32. 30. ᵇ Num. 18. 4. 1 Chr. 23. 28, 32. ᶜ ch. 40. 46. ᵈ 1 Sam. 2.35. ᵉ ver. 10. ᶠ Deut. 10. 8. ᵍ ver. 7. ʰ ch. 41. 22. ⁱ Ex. 28. 39.

7. strangers] This refers especially to the sin of unauthorized and unfaithful priests ministering in the services of the Temple. Cp. marg. reff.
8. mine holy things] The Altar, its sacrifices, the sacred utensils, and the like.
for yourselves] According to your own pleasure, not My ordinances (Num. xvi. 40).
10. The Levites as a body had remained true to the Temple-service at Jerusalem (2 Chr. xi. 13) ; but individuals among them deserted to Israel probably from the first (see marg. reff.), as in later years some went over to the worship of the Samaritans on Mount Gerizim. These apostate Levites *shall bear their iniquities,* they shall not be restored to their former rank and privileges.
11. ministers] As, according to the new system, the Levites, as a body, were to receive their portion in the *oblation* (xlv. 5) ; the only manner in which the Levites of *v.*

10 could live at all, was as part of the whole body, to which they were therefore reunited, but in the lowest grade. It is remarkable that the number of Levites who returned after the captivity was very small, not exceeding 400, of whom only 74 were priests' assistants (Ezra ii. 40—42; cp. viii. 15—19). The gap in their number was filled up by 220 Nethinim (*given* ones), probably originally strangers and captives, who, although employed in the Temple services, were held by the Jews in the lowest repute.
12. lifted up mine hand] i.e. *The Lord sware* (xx. 5), that they should bear their iniquities.
17—31. Regulations as to the priests' services. The garments of the priests are defined and various rules prescribed in the Law are repeated with some additions in order to denote additional care to avoid uncleanness.

k Ex. 28. 40
42, & 39. 28.

l ch. 42 14.

m ch. 46. 20.
Matt. 23. 17,
19.
n Lev. 21. 5.
o Lev. 10. 9.

p Lev. 21. 7.

q Lev. 10. 10.
ch. 22. 26.
Mal. 2. 7.
r Deut. 17. 8.
2 Chr. 19. 8,
10.

s See ch. 22.
26.
t Lev. 21. 1.

u Num. 6. 10.

x ver. 17.

y Lev. 4. 3.

z Num. 18. 20.
Deut. 18. 1.
Josh. 13. 14.
a Lev. 6. 18.
& 7. 6.
b Lev. 27. 21,
28.
Num. 18. 14.

18 minister in the gates of the inner court, and within. *k*They shall have linen bonnets upon their heads, and shall have linen breeches upon their loins; they shall not gird *themselves* [12]with any thing
19 that causeth sweat. And when they go forth into the utter court, *even* into the utter court to the people, *l*they shall put off their garments wherein they ministered, and lay them in the holy chambers, and they shall put on other garments; and they shall
20 *m*not sanctify the people with their garments. *n*Neither shall they shave their heads, nor suffer their locks to grow long; they
21 shall only poll their heads. *o*Neither shall any priest drink
22 wine, when they enter into the inner court. Neither shall they take for their wives a *p*widow, nor her that is [3]put away: but they shall take maidens of the seed of Israel, or a
23 widow [4]that had a priest before. And *q*they shall teach my people *the difference* between the holy and profane, and cause
24 them to discern between the unclean and the clean. And *r*in controversy they shall stand in judgment; *and* they shall judge it according to my judgments: and they shall keep my laws and my statutes in all mine assemblies; *s*and they shall hallow my
25 sabbaths. And they shall come at no *t*dead person to defile themselves: but for father, or for mother, or for son, or for daughter, for brother, or for sister that hath had no husband,
26 they may defile themselves. And *u*after he is cleansed, they
27 shall reckon unto him seven days. And in the day that he goeth into the sanctuary, *x*unto the inner court, to minister in the sanctuary, *y*he shall offer his sin offering, saith the Lord God.
28 And it shall be unto them for an inheritance: I *z*am their inheritance: and ye shall give them no possession in Israel: I am
29 their possession. *a*They shall eat the meat offering, and the sin offering, and the trespass offering; and *b*every [5]dedicated thing

[1] Or, *in sweating* places.   [3] Heb. *thrust forth.*   [5] Or, *devoted.*
[2] Heb. *in*, or, *with sweat.*   [4] Heb. *from a priest.*

---

18. The material of which the four vestments of the ordinary priest were made was "linen," or, more accurately, "byssus," the cotton stuff of Egypt. The two special qualities of the byssus—white and shining—are characteristic, and on them part of the symbolic meaning depended. Cp. Rev. xix. 8.

19. *they shall not sanctify the people*] They shall not touch the people with their holy garments. The word *sanctify* is used because the effect of touching was to separate as holy the persons or things so touched (Exod. xxix. 37, xxx. 29; cp. Lev. vi. 18). The priests wore the distinctive dress, only while performing in the Temple strictly sacrificial services.

The *holy chambers*; see xlii. 1 seq.

22. Restrictions and exceptions intended to mark the holiness of the office of a priest, imposing on him additional (cp. marg. ref.) obligations to purity, and communicating it in some degree to his wife. In the Christian Church all the members are *priests* (1 Peter ii. 5; Rev. i. 6, xx. 6). Hence the directions for maintaining the holiness of the *priesthood* in the new order, represent the necessity for holiness in all Christians, and the exclusion of *the uncircumcised in heart and in flesh* is equivalent to the exclusion of *all that defileth* from the New Jerusalem (Rev. xxi. 27).

24. There was in Herod's Temple a council of priests, whose special duty it was to regulate every thing connected with the sanctuary. They did not ordinarily busy themselves with criminal questions, although they took a leading part in the condemnation of Jesus (Mark xv. 1).

28. *it shall be unto them*] The remains of the sacrifices were a chief source of the priests' support. The burnt offerings being entirely consumed, the priests had the skins, which yielded a considerable revenue; meat- and drink-offerings belonged entirely to them. Sin-offerings and trepass-offerings, except in particular cases, also belonged to the priests and were partaken of in the Temple. Of the peace-offerings a portion dedicated to the Lord by waving was left for the priests, and the rest eaten by the officers and their friends, either in the courts of the Temple, or at least within Jerusalem. The kitchen-

30 in Israel shall be their's.   And the [1c]first of all the firstfruits of
all *things*, and every oblation of all, of every *sort* of your oblations, shall be the priest's : ye [d]shall also give unto the priest the
first of your dough, [e]that he may cause the blessing to rest in
31 thine house.   The priests shall not eat of any thing that is [f]dead
of itself, or torn, whether it be fowl or beast.

CHAP. **45.** MOREOVER, [2]when ye shall [a]divide by lot the land
for inheritance, ye shall [b]offer an oblation unto the LORD, [3]an
holy portion of the land : the length *shall be* the length of five
and twenty thousand *reeds*, and the breadth *shall be* ten thousand.   This *shall be* holy in all the borders thereof round about.

2 Of this there shall be for the sanctuary [c]five hundred *in length*,
with five hundred *in breadth*, square round about ; and fifty
3 cubits round about for the [4]suburbs thereof.   And of this measure shalt thou measure the length of five and twenty thousand,
and the breadth of ten thousand : [d]and in it shall be the sanc-
4 tuary *and* the most holy *place*.   [e]The holy *portion* of the land
shall be for the priests the ministers of the sanctuary, which
shall come near to minister unto the LORD : and it shall be a
place for their houses, and an holy place for the sanctuary.

5 [f]And the five and twenty thousand of length, and the ten thousand of breadth, shall also the Levites, the ministers of the house,
have for themselves, for a possession for [g]twenty chambers.

6 [h]And ye shall appoint the possession of the city five thousand
broad, and five and twenty thousand long, over against the oblation of the holy *portion :* it shall be for the whole house of

Margin references:
[c] Ex. 13. 2.
Num. 3. 13.
[d] Num.15.20.
Neh. 10. 37.
[e] Prov. 3. 9.
Mal. 3. 10.
[f] Ex. 22. 31.
Lev. 22. 8.
[a] ch. 47. 22.
[b] ch. 48. 8.

[c] ch. 42. 20.

[d] ch. 48. 10.
[e] ver. 1.
ch. 48. 10.

[f] ch. 48. 13.

[g] See ch. 40. 17.
[h] ch. 48. 15.

[1] Or, *chief*.   [2] Heb. *when ye cause the land to fall*.   [3] Heb. *holiness*.   [4] Or, *void places*.

courts (K, Plan II. xlvi. 21—24), were
provided in order to prepare these public
meals.

30. *oblation*] *Offering*, marg. *heave-offering*
(see xlv. 1 ; Exod. xxv. 2 ; xxix. 27 ; Notes
and Pref. to Leviticus).

XLV. This chapter describes the portion
of territory reserved for the priests, in the
middle of which is to be the Temple with
its courts and precincts, for the Levites,
for the city, and for the prince.

1. *by lot*] Not by casting lots, but by *allotment*, the several portions being assigned by
rule (Josh. xiii. 6).

oblation] The oblation (properly *heave-
offering*) was regarded as the Lord's portion
(Lev. xxvii. 30).   This *oblation* is given here
as part of the provision made for the priests,
and was probably in lieu of tithes (Lev.
xxvii. 30 ; Num. xviii. 21), just as the prince
had his definite portion of land instead of
being supported by the contributions of the
people.   The priests and Levites had, in
addition, the sacrifices (xliv. 28, note).   This
provision for them, out of proportion in any
actual arrangement, is no doubt intended to
symbolize the reverence and honour due to
God, and expressed by liberality to His services and His ministers.   The LXX. read
the breadth twenty thousand ; and those who
adopt this, read *v.* 3 "and from this" whole
measure is to be deducted the priests' special
portion 25,000 from East to West, and 10,000

from North to South.   Others, retaining
the reading of the text, suppose the term
oblation here to denote the portion assigned
to the priests alone (as in xlviii. 9), and
of this measure (*v.* 3) to mean not "deducted
from this measure," but "computed by this
measure."   The A. V. rightly supplies *reeds*,
since the precincts (xlii. 20) were 500 *reeds*
square.   25,000 reeds = about 42½ statute
miles, 36½ geog. miles.

2. The *sanctuary* here probably means the
whole Temple precincts.

suburbs] Lit. as marg.   To mark out more
distinctly the sacred precincts, a vacant
space of fifty cubits was left on all sides.

5. *for a possession for twenty chambers*]
Lit. "For a possession twenty chambers,"
possibly twenty out of the thirty chambers
in the outer court (xl. 17), and assigned for
their use during residence in the sanctuary.
The LXX. reads "for cities to dwell in"
(cp. Num. xxxv. 2) which some adopt
here.

6. This portion is to belong to the whole
people, not to be subject to the encroach-
ments made by the later kings of Judah
(Jer. xxii. 13).   The Levites' portion 10,000
reeds, the priests' portion 10,000 reeds, and
the city portion 5,000 reeds, make in all
25,000 reeds from N. to S.   The measure of
each of these portions from E. to W. has
been defined to be 25,000 reeds (*v.* 1 note),
and thus we have a square of 25,000 in all.

i ch. 48. 21.
7 Israel. *i*And *a portion shall be* for the prince on the one side
and on the other side of the oblation of the holy *portion*, and
of the possession of the city, before the oblation of the holy
portion, and before the possession of the city, from the west side
westward, and from the east side eastward : and the length *shall
be* over against one of the portions, from the west border unto
8 the east border. In the land shall be his possession in Israel :
k ch. 22. 27.
& 46. 18.
and *k*my princes shall no more oppress my people ; and *the rest
of* the land shall they give to the house of Israel according to
l ch. 44. 6.
m Jer. 22. 3.
9 their tribes. ¶Thus saith the Lord GOD ; *l*Let it suffice you,
O princes of Israel : *m*remove violence and spoil, and execute
judgment and justice, take away your [1]exactions from my people,
n Lev. 19. 35.
Prov. 11. 1.
10 saith the Lord GOD. Ye shall have just *n*balances, and a just
11 ephah, and a just bath. The ephah and the bath shall be of one
measure, that the bath may contain the tenth part of an homer,
and the ephah the tenth part of an homer : the measure thereof
o Ex. 30. 13.
Lev. 27. 25.
Num. 3. 47.
12 shall be after the homer. And the *o*shekel *shall be* twenty
gerahs : twenty shekels, five and twenty shekels, fifteen shekels,
13 shall be your maneh. ¶This *is* the oblation that ye shall offer :
the sixth part of an ephah of an homer of wheat, and ye shall
14 give the sixth part of an ephah of an homer of barley : concerning the ordinance of oil, the bath of oil, *ye shall offer* the
tenth part of a bath out of the cor, *which is* an homer of ten
15 baths ; for ten baths *are an* homer : and one [2]lamb out of the
flock, out of two hundred, out of the fat pastures of Israel ; for
a meat offering, and for a burnt offering, and for [3]peace offer-
p Lev. 1. 4.
ings, *p*to make reconciliation for them, saith the Lord GOD.
16 All the people of the land [4]shall give this oblation [5]for the
17 prince in Israel. And it shall be the prince's part *to give* burnt
offerings, and meat offerings, and drink offerings, in the feasts,

[1] Heb. *expulsions.*
[2] Or, *kid.*
[3] Or, *thank offerings.*
[4] Heb. *shall be for.*
[5] Or, *with.*

7, 8. On either side of the 25,000 reeds a
strip of land, running westwards to the sea,
eastwards to the Jordan, formed the possession of the prince (see xlvi. 18 note).
For the other tribes the limits from West to
East are the Mediterranean Sea and the
Jordan (xlviii. 8).

7. *and the length* shall be *over against*] Or,
and in length *over against.*

The definition of the prince's territory
was to prevent the oppressions foretold (1
Sam. viii. 14 *seq.*), described (2 K. xxiii. 35),
and reproved (Jer. xxii.)

9. The princes are exhorted to execute
judgment, and abstain from *exaction* (lit.
"ejection"), such as that of Naboth by Ahab
(1 K. xxi. 19).

10. A general exhortation to honesty, expressed by true weights and measures (marg.
reff.) This fitly introduces the strict regula-
tion of quantities in the prescribed offerings.

11. The *ephah* was in use for dry measure,
the *bath* for liquid. The *homer* seems to
have contained about 75 gallons (see Exod.
xxix. 40 ; Lev. xix. 36, notes).

after the homer] *i.e.* according to the standard of the *homer.*

12. *the shekel*] See marg. ref.

The *maneh* shall be of true weight, but it
would seem that in Ezekiel's time there
were *manehs* of different value.

13—17. The offerings to be made by the
people through the prince for the service of
the sanctuary. In the Mosaic Law the
offerings for the sacrifices of the ordinary
festivals were left to the free will of the
people. Here they are reduced to regular
order and the amounts ordained. In later
days there were often shortcomings in these
respects (Mal. iii. 8). This is obviated, and
regularity ensured in the new order of
things. No mention is made of wine for
the drink-offering, or of bullocks for the
burnt-offering, so that the enumeration is
not complete.

14. *cor*] Translated *measure* in 1 K. v.
11, &c. Here it is a synonym of *homer.*

17. The people's gifts were to be placed
in the hands of the prince, so as to form a
common stock, out of which the prince was
to provide what was necessary for each
sacrifice. Cp. 1 K. viii. 62 ; Ezra vii. 17.
The prince handed the gifts to the priests,
whose part it was to sacrifice and offer. But
the prominent part assigned to the prince in

and in the new moons, and in the sabbaths, in all solemnities of the house of Israel: he shall prepare the sin offering, and the meat offering, and the burnt offering, and the ¹peace offerings, 18 to make reconciliation for the house of Israel. ¶ Thus saith the Lord God; In the first *month*, in the first *day* of the month, thou shalt take a young bullock without blemish, and *q* cleanse   *q* Lev. 16. 16. 19 the sanctuary: *r* and the priest shall take of the blood of the sin   *r* ch. 43. 20. offering, and put *it* upon the posts of the house, and upon the four corners of the settle of the altar, and upon the posts of the 20 gate of the inner court. And so thou shalt do the seventh *day* of the month *s* for every one that erreth, and for *him that is*   *s* Lev. 4. 27. 21 simple: so shall ye reconcile the house. ¶ *t* In the first *month*,   *t* Ex. 12. 18. in the fourteenth day of the month, ye shall have the passover,   Lev. 23. 5, 6. 22 a feast of seven days; unleavened bread shall be eaten. And   Num. 9. 2. Deut. 16. 1. upon that day shall the prince prepare for himself and for all 23 the people of the land *u* a bullock *for* a sin offering. And *x* seven   *u* Lev. 4. 14. days of the feast he shall prepare a burnt offering to the Lord,   *x* Lev. 23. 8. seven bullocks and seven rams without blemish daily the seven 24 days; *y* and a kid of the goats daily *for* a sin offering. *z* And he   *y* See Num. shall prepare a meat offering of an ephah for a bullock, and an   28. 15, 22, 30. *z* ch. 46. 5, 7. 25 ephah for a ram, and an hin of oil for an ephah. In the seventh *month*, in the fifteenth day of the month, shall he do the like in the *a* feast of the seven days, according to the sin offering, ac-   *a* Lev. 23. 34. cording to the burnt offering, and according to the meat offer-   Num. 29. 12. Deut. 16. 13. ing, and according to the oil.

Chap. 46. THUS saith the Lord God; The gate of the inner court that looketh toward the east shall be shut the six working days; but on the sabbath it shall be opened, and in the day of the new 2 moon it shall be opened. *a* And the prince shall enter by the   *a* ch. 44. 3. way of the porch of *that* gate without, and shall stand by the   ver. 8. post of the gate, and the priests shall prepare his burnt offering and his peace offerings, and he shall worship at the threshold

¹ Or, *thank offerings.*

---

makin᷈ reconciliation for the sins of the people seems to typify the union of the kingly and priestly offices in the person of the Mediator of the New Covenant.

18—25. This order of certain solemn services does not follow exactly the order of Moses, of Solomon, or of Ezra. The deviation can scarcely have been accidental, and furnishes a fresh indication that the whole vision is symbolical, representative of the times when, after the oblation of the one Sacrifice, reconciliation and sanctification were effected for man through the Presence of God dwelling in the midst of the people.

18. *in the first* day] If this is only a special Passover for the dedication, the prolongation of the festival may be compared with that under Solomon (2 Chr. vii. 8). But it is more probably a general ordinance, and, in this case, we have an addition to the Mosaic ritual (cp. Lev. xxiii. 5). Here the *first day* is marked by the rites of expiation, which are repeated on the seventh day (*v.* 20), for the purpose of including those who transgressed from ignorance rather than wilfulness.

23. Comparing this with the daily sacrifices of the Paschal week (Num. xxviii. 19—24), and those of the daily sacrifices of the week of the Feast of Tabernacles (see Num. xxix. 12 &c.), it will be seen that here the Covenant number *seven* is preserved throughout to indicate a perfect, in lieu of an imperfect, Covenant with God.

25. The Feast of Tabernacles (cp. marg. reff.). Some think that the other great festival, the Feast of Weeks, is intended.

XLVI. The prophet beholds in vision people, priest, and prince uniting in most solemn worship before the throne of God. The character of the rites here described is symbolical.

2. In the time of Solomon, priest, king, and people each took his due part in the Temple-service. Of the later kings s᷈me forsook Jehovah for false gods, some encroached upon the prerogative of the priest. Now all should be set right. The prince occupies a position analogous to that of Solomon (2 Chr. vi. 12, 13), standing in front of the porch of the eastern gate of the inner court, and at the head of his people

of the gate: then he shall go forth; but the gate shall not be
3 shut until the evening. Likewise the people of the land shall
worship at the door of this gate before the LORD in the sabbaths
4 and in the new moons. And the burnt offering that *b*the prince
shall offer unto the LORD in the sabbath day *shall be* six lambs
5 without blemish, and a ram without blemish. *c*And the meat
offering *shall be* an ephah for a ram, and the meat offering for
the lambs [1]as he shall be able to give, and an hin of oil to an
6 ephah. And in the day of the new moon *it shall be* a young
bullock without blemish, and six lambs, and a ram: they shall be
7 without blemish. And he shall prepare a meat offering, an ephah
for a bullock, and an ephah for a ram, and for the lambs according as his hand shall attain unto, and an hin of oil to an ephah.
8 ¶ *d*And when the prince shall enter, he shall go in by the way of
the porch of *that* gate, and he shall go forth by the way thereof.
9 But when the people of the land *e*shall come before the LORD
in the solemn feasts, he that entereth in by the way of the north
gate to worship shall go out by the way of the south gate; and
he that entereth by the way of the south gate shall go forth by
the way of the north gate: he shall not return by the way of the
gate whereby he came in, but shall go forth over against it.
10 And the prince in the midst of them, when they go in, shall go
11 in; and when they go forth, shall go forth. And in the feasts
and in the solemnities *f*the meat offering shall be an ephah to a
bullock, and an ephah to a ram, and to the lambs as he is able
12 to give, and an hin of oil to an ephah. Now when the prince
shall prepare a voluntary burnt offering or peace offerings volun-
tarily unto the LORD, *g*one shall then open him the gate that
looketh toward the east, and he shall prepare his burnt offering
and his peace offerings, as he did on the sabbath day: then he
shall go forth; and after his going forth *one* shall shut the gate.
13 ¶ *h*Thou shalt daily prepare a burnt offering unto the LORD *of*
a lamb [2]of the first year without blemish: thou shalt prepare it
14 [3]every morning. And thou shalt prepare a meat offering for it
every morning, the sixth part of an ephah, and the third part
of an hin of oil, to temper with the fine flour; a meat offering
15 continually by a perpetual ordinance unto the LORD. Thus

b ch. 45. 17.

c ch. 45. 24.
ver. 7, 11.

d ver. 2.

e Ex. 23. 14—
17.
Deut. 16. 16.

f ver. 5.

g ch. 44. 3.
ver. 2.

h Ex. 29. 38.
Num. 28. 3.

---

[1] Heb. *the gift of his hand,*
Deut. 16. 17.

[2] Heb. *a son of his year.*
[3] Heb. *morning by morning.*

---

to lead their worship, while the priests are
sacrificing before him.

3. *at the door of this gate*] In Herod's
Temple the place for worshipping *before the
Lord* was the court of Israel, West of the
court of Women, separated from the inner
court by a low parapet. In Ezekiel's the
worshippers were admitted into the inner
court itself. The upper pavement (E. Plan
II.) on either side of the eastern gate provided room for such worshippers.

4—15. The offerings here prescribed are
generally in excess of those enjoined by the
Law, to note not only the greater devotion
and magnificence under the new state of
things, but also the willingness (cp. Deut.
xvi. 17) of king and people ready to give
of their substance to the utmost of their
means.

5. *as he shall be able to give*] Rather, *as*

he shall be **willing** to give. So also in
v. 7.

4—6. Cp. with Num. xxviii. The enumeration of the offerings both for the Sabbath and new moon is here less complete
than there; *e.g.* the drink offerings are
passed by, and in the case of the new moon
festival no mention is made of the blowing
of trumpets (cp. Num. x. 10).

8. *that gate*] The eastern gate of the inner
court. See *v.* 2.

9. The whole body of the people gathered
together in the outer court, and from thence
bodies went in turn into the inner court to
worship, and then again out into the outer
court.

13. Cp. with marg. reff. The evening
sacrifice is here omitted, because the seer is
selecting a few only of the sacrifices of the
Law, with a particular object in view.

shall they prepare the lamb, and the meat offering, and the oil,
16 every morning *for* a continual burnt offering. ¶ Thus saith the
Lord GOD; If the prince give a gift unto any of his sons, the
inheritance thereof shall be his sons'; it *shall be* their possession
17 by inheritance. But if he give a gift of his inheritance to one
of his servants, then it shall be his to [i]the year of liberty;   [i] Lev. 25. 10.
after it shall return to the prince: but his inheritance shall be
18 his sons' for them. Moreover [k]the prince shall not take of the   [k] ch. 45. 8.
people's inheritance by oppression, to thrust them out of their
possession; *but* he shall give his sons inheritance out of his own
possession: that my people be not scattered every man from his
19 possession. ¶ After he brought me through the entry, which *was*
at the side of the gate, into the holy chambers of the priests,
which looked toward the north: and, behold, there *was* a place
20 on the two sides westward. Then said he unto me, This *is* the
place where the priests shall [l]boil the trespass offering and the   [l] 2 Chr. 35. 13.
sin offering, where they shall [m]bake the meat offering; that they   [m] Lev. 2. 4,
bear *them* not out into the outer court, [n]to sanctify the people.   5, 7.
21 ¶ Then he brought me forth into the utter court, and caused   [n] ch. 44. 19.
me to pass by the four corners of the court; and, behold, [1]in
22 every corner of the court *there was* a court. In the four corners
of the court *there were* courts [2]joined of forty *cubits* long and
23 thirty broad: these four [3]corners *were* of one measure. And
there was a row *of building* round about in them, round about
them four, and *it was* made with boiling places under the rows
24 round about. Then said he unto me, These *are* the places of
them that boil, where the ministers of the house shall [o]boil the   [o] See ver. 20.
sacrifice of the people.

CHAP. 47. AFTERWARD he brought me again unto the door of
the house; and, behold, [a]waters issued out from under the thres-   [a] Zech. 13. 1.
hold of the house eastward: for the forefront of the house   & 14. 8.
stood toward the east, and the waters came down from under   Rev. 22. 1.
from the right side of the house, at the south *side* of the altar.

---

[1] Heb. *a court in a corner*   *a corner of a court.*   [3] Heb. *cornered.*
  of a court, and a court in   [2] Or, *made with chimneys.*

16—18. The prince was to be provided with
possessions of his own, in order to prevent
exactions from his subjects; further enactments are added to prevent the alienation
of the prince's land. Any gifts made to his
servants must revert to the prince in the
"year of liberty," or jubilee (see marg. ref.
note).

19-24. The careful provision here made
to keep separate the offerings of priests and
people was to prevent collision, just as
the enactments (*vv.* 16–18) were intended
to secure their respective rights to prince
and people.

19. *at the side of the gate*] The entrance
to the inner court at the same side as the
northern gate (xlii. 9).

20. See M. Plan II.

boil] It was peculiar to the Paschal lamb,
that it was to be eaten roasted. The flesh
of the other sacrifices was to be *sodden* or
boiled (see Lev. vi. 28; 1 Sam. ii. 13; 2 Chr.
xxiv. 14 marg.). The *meat-offering* (flour and
honey) was baked (Lev. ii. 4).

21. See K. Plan II.

22. *courts joined*] **enclosed** courts, and entered by doors in the walls, which shut them
out from the great court. The marg. rendering, *made with chimnies*, is based upon
another interpretation of the word.

these four corners] Or, *these four* **corner-
courts** *were of one measure.*

XLVII. The vision of the Waters; or,
the blessings which flow from this source to
animate and refresh all the inhabitants of
the earth. Cp. Isai. xliv. 8 &c.; Joel iii. 18.
Ezekiel's description is adopted and modified by Zechariah and in Rev. (cp. marg.
reff.) Hebrew tradition speaks of a spring
of water, named Etham, said to be identical with the well-waters of Nephtoah (Josh.
xviii. 15), on the West of the Temple, whose
waters were conducted by pipes into the
Temple-courts for the uses needed in the
ministration of the priests. The waters of
Shiloah (Ps. xlvi. 4; Isai. viii. 6) flowed
from the rocks beneath the Temple-hill. It
is quite in the manner of Ezekiel's vision to

b ch. 40. 3.

2 Then brought he me out of the way of the gate northward, and
led me about the way without unto the utter gate by the way
that looketh eastward; and, behold, there ran out waters on
3 the right side. And when *b*the man that had the line in his
hand went forth eastward, he measured a thousand cubits, and
he brought me through the waters; the ¹waters *were* to the
4 ancles. Again he measured a thousand, and brought me through
the waters; the waters *were* to the knees. Again he measured
a thousand, and brought me through; the waters *were* to the
5 loins. Afterward he measured a thousand; *and it was* a river
that I could not pass over: for the waters were risen, ²waters
6 to swim in, a river that could not be passed over. ¶ And he said
unto me, Son of man, hast thou seen *this?* Then he brought
7 me, and caused me to return to the brink of the river. Now
when I had returned, behold, at the ³bank of the river *were*
8 very many *c*trees on the one side and on the other. Then said
he unto me, These waters issue out toward the east country,
and go down into the ⁴desert, and go into the sea: *which being*
9 brought forth into the sea, the waters shall be healed. And it
shall come to pass, *that* every thing that liveth, which moveth,
whithersoever the ⁵rivers shall come, shall live: and there shall
be a very great multitude of fish, because these waters shall
come thither: for they shall be healed; and every thing shall
10 live whither the river cometh. And it shall come to pass, *that*
the fishers shall stand upon it from En-gedi even unto En-

c ver. 12.
Rev. 22. 2.

¹ Heb. *waters of the ancles.* ³ Heb. *lip.* 17, & 4. 49. Josh. 3. 16.
² Heb. *waters of swimming.* ⁴ Or, *plain:* See Deut. 3. ⁵ Heb. *two rivers.*

start from an existing feature and thence proceed to an ideal picture whence to draw a spiritual lesson. The deepening of the waters in their course shows the continual deepening of spiritual life and multiplication of spiritual blessings in the growth of the kingdom of God. So long as the stream is confined to the Temple-courts, it is merely a small rill, for the most part unseen, but when it issues from the courts it begins at once to deepen and to widen. So on the day of Pentecost, the Holy Spirit descended upon the company of believers, little then but presently to develop into the infant Church in Jerusalem.

2. *out of the way of the gate northward*] Rather, **by the way of the northward gate.**

3. *the ancles*] This may coincide with the step gained in the Baptism of Cornelius (Acts x.), and the opening of the Church to the Gentiles. The dispersion which had followed the martyrdom of Stephen (Acts xi. 19), had carried believers into various countries, and so paved the way for the foundation of Gentile Churches.

4. *the knees*] The mission of St. Paul and St. Barnabas (Acts xiii. 1-4) is another marked epoch in the Church's history; and the time of St. Paul's martyrdom denotes an increase in the Gentile Church, which corresponds with the waters reaching the *loins.*

5. The rivers in Palestine were for the most part mere watercourses, dry in summer, in winter carrying the water along the wadys

to the sea. The river of the vision is to have a continuous flow.

waters to swim in] When under Constantine the Roman empire had become Christian, the Church may be contemplated as the full river, to flow on through time until the final completion of Isaiah's prophecy (xi. 9).

7. Trees naturally flourish where there is abundance of water (Ps. i. 3).

8. *The sea* is a term commonly applied to the Dead Sea. Cp. Deut. iii. 17, *the sea of the plain* (Arabah), *even the salt sea.* The more literal rendering of the verse in this sense would be, "and go into the sea; into the sea go the waters that issue forth, and the waters shall be healed."

healed] Every living thing (of which there were none before) shall abound in the *healed* waters. The absence of living creatures in the Dead Sea has been remarked by ancient and modern writers. So the water which Jesus should give should bring life to the dead in trespasses and sins. Cp. Joh. iv. 14; Rev. xxii. 2, 3.

9. *the rivers*] Lit. as in marg. Perhaps with reference to the circumstance that this *brook* or *river* is to come into the Dead Sea through the same plain as the Jordan. The one river (Jordan) always flowed, but now, when another river comes in, and *two rivers* flow into the sea, the waters shall be healed.

10. *En-gedi* (see 1 Sam. xxiii. 29) was about the middle of the western shore of the Dead Sea.

eglaim; they shall be a *place* to spread forth nets; their fish shall be according to their kinds, as the fish [d]of the great sea, 11 exceeding many. But the miry places thereof and the marishes 12 thereof [1]shall not be healed; they shall be given to salt. And [e]by the river upon the bank thereof, on this side and on that side, [2]shall grow all trees for meat, [f]whose leaf shall not fade, neither shall the fruit thereof be consumed: it shall bring forth [3]new fruit according to his months, because their waters they issued out of the sanctuary: and the fruit thereof shall be for 13 meat, and the leaf thereof [4]for [g]medicine. ¶ Thus saith the Lord GOD; This *shall be* the border, whereby ye shall inherit the land according to the twelve tribes of Israel: [h]Joseph *shall* 14 *have two* portions. And ye shall inherit it, one as well as another: *concerning* the which I [5][i]lifted up mine hand to give it unto your fathers: and this land shall [k]fall unto you for inheritance. 15 And this *shall be* the border of the land toward the north side, from the great sea, [l]the way of Hethlon, as men go to [m]Zedad; 16 [n]Hamath, [o]Berothah, Sibraim, which *is* between the border of Damascus and the border of Hamath; [6]Hazar-hatticon, which

[d] Num. 34. 6.
Josh. 23. 4.
ch. 48. 28.

[e] ver. 7.
[f] Job 8. 16.
Ps. 1. 3.
Jer. 17. 8.

[g] Rev. 22. 2.

[h] Gen. 48. 5.
1 Chr. 5. 1.
ch. 48. 4, 5.
[i] ch. 20. 5.
[k] ch. 48. 29.

[l] ch. 48. 1.
[m] Num. 34. 8.
[n] Num. 34. 8.
[o] 2 Sam. 8. 8.

---

[1] Or, *and that which shall not be healed.*
[2] Heb. *shall come up.*
[3] Or, *principal.*
[4] Or, *for bruises and sores.*
[5] Or, *swore.*
[6] Or, *the middle village.*

En-eglaim does not occur elsewhere. Its form indicates that it was one of the double cities of Moab (see xxv. 9 note). It has been identified with *Ain-el-Feshkah* to the North on the western bank of the Dead Sea. On this supposition, *from En-eglaim to En-gedi* would be the line of coast from the most northern fountain to the principal fountain southward.

11. The exception, which reserves for sterility places to which the living water does not reach, probably indicates that the life and health are solely due to the stream which proceeds from beneath the throne of God. Cp. Isai. lvii. 20, 21.

13—XLVIII. 14. Ideal reallotment of the land to the twelve tribes of Israel. See Plan opposite.

13. The special mention of Joseph's portions was in order to express that the twelve portions were to be exclusive of Levi's land, which was to be provided out of the *oblation*.

14. *as well as*] Or, **as.** Ezekiel is speaking of *tribes*, not *individuals*. Each tribe is to have an equal *breadth* of land assigned to it.

15. The borders of the land follow closely Num. xxxiv., where they begin from the South, as the people came up from Egypt; in Ezekiel, they begin from the North, as they might return from Babylon. The occupation is ideal, but is grounded, as usual, on an actual state of things.

the border of the land toward the north] Names of places in the actual northern border are given (marg. reff.) not to mark exact geographical position, but to shew that the original promise will be fulfilled.

The way of Hethlon was probably the defile between the ranges of Libanus and Anti-libanus, from the sea to Hamath. *Hamath* (Amos vi. 2), at the foot of Mount

Hermon, on the Orontes, was the ancient capital of the Hittites. Its Scripture history may be traced in Gen. x. 18; 2 Sam. viii. 9; 2 K. xviii. 34. It was never included in the possessions of Israel. The

IDEAL ALLOTMENT OF THE LAND.

| Dan |
| Asher |
| Naphtali |
| Manasseh |
| Ephraim |
| Reuben |
| Judah |
| Levites / Priests' / Sanctuary |
| Benjamin |
| Simeon |
| Issachar |
| Zebulun |
| Gad |

border ran considerably South of the town at the *entrance of Hamath*, the northern opening of Cœle-Syria.

16. *Berothah*, probably the same as *Berothai* (marg. ref.), lay between Hamath and Damascus, as did *Sibraim*.

Hazar-hatticon is probably, as in marg.,

p Num. 34. 9.
ch. 48. 1.

q Num. 20.
13.
Deut. 32. 51.
Ps. 81. 7.
ch. 48. 28.

r See Eph.
3. 6.
Rev. 7. 9, 10.
s Rom. 10. 12.
Gal. 3. 28.
Col. 3. 11.

a ch. 47. 15,
&c.

17 *is* by the coast of Hauran. And the border from the sea shall
be *p*Hazar-enan, the border of Damascus, and the north northward, and the border of Hamath. And *this is* the north side.
18 And the east side ye shall measure [1]from Hauran, and from
Damascus, and from Gilead, and from the land of Israel *by*
Jordan, from the border unto the east sea. And *this is* the east
19 side. And the south side southward, from Tamar *even* to *q*the
waters of [2]strife *in* Kadesh, the [3]river to the great sea. And
20 *this is* [4]the south side southward. The west side also *shall be*
the great sea from the border, till a man come over against
21 Hamath. This *is* the west side. So shall ye divide this land
22 unto you according to the tribes of Israel. ¶ And it shall come
to pass, *that* ye shall divide it by lot for an inheritance unto
you, *r*and to the strangers that sojourn among you, which shall
beget children among you: *s*and they shall be unto you as born
in the country among the children of Israel; they shall have
23 inheritance with you among the tribes of Israel. And it shall
come to pass, *that* in what tribe the stranger sojourneth, there
shall ye give *him* his inheritance, saith the Lord GOD.

CHAP. 48. NOW these *are* the names of the tribes. *a*From the
north end to the coast of the way of Hethlon, as one goeth to
Hamath, Hazar-enan, the border of Damascus northward, to
the coast of Hamath; for these are his sides east *and* west; *b*a

---

[1] Heb. *from between.*
[2] Or, *Meribah.*
[3] Or, *valley.*
[4] Or, *toward Teman.*
[5] Heb. *one* portion.

"the middle Hazar," to distinguish it from
Hazar-enan (*v.* 17).

17. *and the north* &c.] Or, "and on the
North, the border on the North shall be"
&c.

18. The eastern boundary is to commence
by separating off the territory of Damascus
and Hauran, and then to follow the line of
the Jordan to the Dead Sea. Further, the
land occupied by the trans-Jordanic tribes
was also to be separated off from the
land of Israel. The trans-Jordanic tribes
in fact occupied their ground (in Joshua's
allotment) by sufferance. This did not
belong to Canaan proper, the land of promise. Hence the tribes, formerly on the
east of the Jordan, have here allotments
in Canaan, though *the oblation* (xlv. 1) extends to a considerable distance beyond the
Jordan (see Plan, ch. xlviii.). The whole
arrangement being ideal and symbolical,
the vision here, as in the case of "the
waters" (xlvii. 1 note), departs from the
physical features of the land for the purpose of maintaining symbolical numbers.

19. The South border (cp. Num. xxxiv. 4)
commences with *Tamar*, probably a village
near the southern end of the Dead Sea.
The word means "palm-tree;" and is given
to more than one city in the Holy Land.

the river to the great sea] Lit. "riverward
to the great sea." By the *river* is meant
the torrent-stream entering the Mediterranean near *Rhinocolura* (El Arish).

22. *and to the strangers*] Here is quite a
new feature in the distribution of the land.

Not only the Israelites by descent, but
those who join themselves to Israel by allegiance to the true GOD, shall have a right
of inheritance. Here are opened out the
blessings which were to accrue to the Gentiles through the seed of Abraham. Cp.
Rom. ix. 24, *seq.* The difference which existed under the old Covenant between Jew
and Gentile is now at last done away.
But while heathendom thus unites itself
with God's people, Israel is still as ever the
chosen people, the centre of this union. No
new Church is founded side by side with
the old. Heathendom is absorbed in Israel
—the standard which God has set up for
the nations—*i.e.* in the One True Church,
which has subsisted from the beginning,
and will subsist in eternity.

XLVIII. The distribution of the Holy
Land in detail. The order of the original
occupation by the tribes [under Joshua is
partly, but only partly, followed. It is a
new order of things—and its ideal character
is evinced as elsewhere, by exact and equal
measurements. From N. to S. seven tribes
succeed each other. Then comes a portion,
separated as an offering to the Lord, subdivided into (1) a northern portion for the
Levites, (2) a central portion for the priests
and the Temple, (3) a southern portion for
the city and those who serve it. These
three form a square, which does not occupy
the whole breadth of the land, but is
flanked on either side, East and West, by
portions assigned to the prince. Then follow, South of the city, five portions for the

2 *portion for* Dan. And by the border of Dan, from the east side
3 unto the west side, a *portion for* Asher. And by the border of
  Asher, from the east side even unto the west side, a *portion for*
4 Naphtali. And by the border of Naphtali, from the east side
5 unto the west side, a *portion for* Manasseh. And by the border
  of Manasseh, from the east side unto the west side, a *portion*
6 *for* Ephraim. And by the border of Ephraim, from the east
7 side even unto the west side, a *portion for* Reuben. And by the
  border of Reuben, from the east side unto the west side, a *por-*
8 *tion for* Judah. ¶And by the border of Judah, from the east
  side unto the west side, shall be *b*the offering which ye shall   *b* ch. 45. 1-6.
  offer of five and twenty thousand *reeds in* breadth, and *in* length
  as one of the *other* parts, from the east side unto the west side :
9 and the sanctuary shall be in the midst of it. The oblation that

five remaining tribes—similar to those assigned to the seven. Thus the Levites, the
Temple, and city, are guarded by Judah
and Benjamin, the two tribes who had
throughout preserved their allegiance to the
true sovereignty of Jehovah, and
thus the plan expresses the Presence of Jehovah among His
people, summed up in the name
of the city, with which Ezekiel's prophecy closes, THE LORD
IS THERE.

The breadth of the portions is
not given, but since the exact
breadth of the oblation was
about 30 geog. miles (xlv. 1
note), and seven tribes were
between the entrance of Hamath
and the oblation, the *breadth* of
one portion was about 17 geog.
miles. The breadth of the Levites' portion and of the priests'
portion was in each case about
15 geog. miles. Ain-el-Weibeh,
if Kadesh, [(?), see Num. xiii. 26]
would be very nearly the southern
border.

The general lines of existing
features are followed with considerable fidelity, but accommodation is made to give the required symbolical expression.
Dan had originally an allotment
West of Benjamin, but having
colonized and given its name to
Laish in the North, was regarded
as the most northern occupant
of Canaan (Judg. xviii. 29).
Zebulun and *Issachar* are removed to the S. to make room
for the second half of *Manasseh*
brought over from the East of
Jordan. *Reuben,* brought over
from the East, is placed between
Ephraim and *Judah. Benjamin*
comes immediately South of the
city, and *Gad* is brought over
from the E. to the extreme S.

8. *Length* is throughout measured from
W. to E., as breadth is from N. to S.

The offering (*vv.* 9-22), or, *oblation,* here includes all the land given to priests, Levites,
city, and prince ; the different parts being
distinguished. All these together are to extend from W. to E. in the same way as the

THE LAND OF ISRAEL.

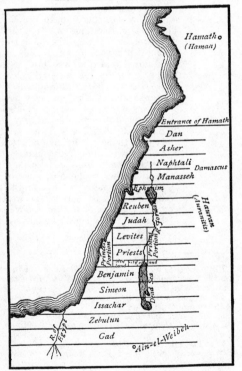

portions of the other tribes, the imaginary
Jordan being the eastern boundary of all.

ye shall offer unto the LORD *shall be* of five and twenty thousand
10 in length, and of ten thousand in breadth. And for them, *even*
for the priests, shall be *this* holy oblation; toward the north
five and twenty thousand *in length*, and toward the west ten
thousand in breadth, and toward the east ten thousand in
breadth, and toward the south five and twenty thousand in
length: and the sanctuary of the LORD shall be in the midst

 c ch. 44. 15.   11 thereof. *c* 1*It shall be* for the priests that are sanctified of the
sons of Zadok; which have kept my ²charge, which went not

d ch. 44. 10.   astray when the children of Israel went astray, *d*as the Levites
12 went astray. And *this* oblation of the land that is offered shall
be unto them a thing most holy by the border of the Levites.
13 ¶ And over against the border of the priests the Levites *shall
have* five and twenty thousand in length, and ten thousand in
breadth: all the length *shall be* five and twenty thousand, and

e Ex. 22. 29.
Lev. 27. 10,
28, 33.
f ch. 45. 6.
g ch. 42. 20.   14 the breadth ten thousand. *e*And they shall not sell of it, neither
exchange, nor alienate the firstfruits of the land: for *it is* holy
15 unto the LORD. ¶ *f*And the five thousand, that are left in the
breadth over against the five and twenty thousand, shall be *g*a
profane *place* for the city, for dwelling, and for suburbs: and
16 the city shall be in the midst thereof. And these *shall be* the
measures thereof; the north side four thousand and five hundred, and the south side four thousand and five hundred, and
on the east side four thousand and five hundred, and the west
17 side four thousand and five hundred. And the suburbs of the
city shall be toward the north two hundred and fifty, and toward
the south two hundred and fifty, and toward the east two
hundred and fifty, and toward the west two hundred and fifty.
18 ¶ And the residue in length over against the oblation of the holy
portion shall be ten thousand eastward, and ten thousand westward: and it shall be over against the oblation of the holy
portion; and the increase thereof shall be for food unto them

h ch. 45. 6.   19 that serve the city. *h*And they that serve the city shall serve it
20 out of all the tribes of Israel. All the oblation *shall be* five and
twenty thousand by five and twenty thousand: ye shall offer
the holy oblation foursquare, with the possession of the city.

i ch. 45. 7.   21 ¶ *i*And the residue *shall be* for the prince, on the one side and
on the other of the holy oblation, and of the possession of the
city, over against the five and twenty thousand of the oblation
toward the east border, and westward over against the five and
twenty thousand toward the west border, over against the por-

k ver. 8. 10.   tions for the prince: and it shall be the holy oblation; *k*and

¹ Or, *the sanctified* portion shall be *for the priests.*   ² Or, *ward,* or, *ordinance.*

---

10. *toward the north...toward the east,* &c.]
i.e. the measurements are *along the North*
and *East* sides, &c.

15. *the five thousand* &c.] The remainder
of the square of 25,000 reeds from N. to S.

profane] For common use, as distinguished from that which is *holy* unto the
Lord.

17. The city being 4500 reeds square,
250 reeds are marked off N.S.E.W. from the
city land.

18, 19. *them that serve*] *i.e.* the cultivators
or husbandmen.

19. Of old the city belonged to Benjamin

and Judah, and its inhabitants were mainly
from these tribes. Now all the tribes are
to have equal part in it, and avoid jealou-
sies (cp. 2 Sam. xix. 43).

20. *the holy...with* &c.] Or, "a fourth
part as the holy oblation, for" &c.

21. Or, *And the residue shall be for the
prince,—on the one side and on the other* **side**
*of the holy oblation and of the possession of the
city over against the 25,000 of the oblation toward the East border, and westward over
against the 25,000 toward the West border,
over against the portions* [of Judah and Benjamin, between which the oblation was in-

22 the sanctuary of the house *shall be* in the midst thereof. Moreover from the possession of the Levites, and from the possession of the city, *being* in the midst *of that* which is the prince's, between the border of Judah and the border of Benjamin, shall
23 be for the prince. ¶ As for the rest of the tribes, from the east
24 side unto the west side, Benjamin *shall have* ¹a *portion.* And by the border of Benjamin, from the east side unto the west side,
25 Simeon *shall have* a *portion.* And by the border of Simeon,
26 from the east side unto the west side, Issachar a *portion.* And by the border of Issachar, from the east side unto the west side,
27 Zebulun a *portion.* And by the border of Zebulun, from the
28 east side unto the west side, Gad a *portion.* And by the border of Gad, at the south side southward, the border shall be even from Tamar *unto* ¹the waters of ²strife *in* Kadesh, *and* to the   *l* ch. 47. 19.
29 river toward the great sea. ¶ ᵐThis *is* the land which ye shall   *m* ch. 47. 14, divide by lot unto the tribes of Israel for inheritance, and these   21, 22.
30 *are* their portions, saith the Lord GOD. ¶ And these *are* the goings out of the city on the north side, four thousand and five
31 hundred measures. ⁿ And the gates of the city *shall be* after the   *n* Rev. 21.12, names of the tribes of Israel: three gates northward; one gate   &c.
32 of Reuben, one gate of Judah, one gate of Levi. And at the east side four thousand and five hundred: and three gates; and one gate of Joseph, one gate of Benjamin, one gate of Dan.
33 And at the south side four thousand and five hundred measures: and three gates; one gate of Simeon, one gate of Issachar, one
34 gate of Zebulun. At the west side four thousand and five hundred, *with* their three gates; one gate of Gad, one gate of
35 Asher, one gate of Naphtali. *It was* round about eighteen thousand *measures.* ¶ ᵒAnd the name of the city from *that* day   *o* Jer. 33. 16. shall be, ³ᵖThe LORD *is* there.   *p* Jer. 3. 17.
Zech. 2. 10.
Rev. 22. 3.

¹ Heb. *one* portion.   ³ Heb. *Jehovah-shammah:* See
² Heb. *Meribah-kadesh.*   Exod. 17. 15, Judg. 6. 24.

---

cluded], **shall be** *for the prince; and it shall be that the holy oblation and the sanctuary of the house shall be in the midst thereof.* This exactly describes the position of the prince's allotments on the borders of the *oblation.*

30. *the goings out of the city*] The gates described in *v.* 31. *Measures* (reeds) concern the sides. Divide the verses thus :—30. *And these are the goings out of the city.* **31.** *On the north side* 4500 *measures: and the gates of the city after the names of the tribes of Israel : three gates northward* &c.

35. The circuit of the city walls, a square of 4500 reeds, was 18,000 reeds, not quite 37 English miles. The circuit of Jerusalem in the time of Josephus was reckoned by him to be about four miles.

the name &c.] The manner of expressing a spiritual meaning by giving a name to a city, a people, or the like, is familiar to the prophets (see xliii. 15 note). Jerome explains it: —"The name of the city shall be no longer Jerusalem (*the vision of peace*), but Adonaishama (*the Lord is there*) [rather, Jehovahshammah, *Jehovah is there*], because Jehovah will never again withdraw from it, as He once withdrew, but will hold it as His everlasting possession." The visible Presence of God's glory, once represented in the Tabernacle and in the Temple, had departed, and should not return in the same form. Yet Ezekiel in *visions of God* sees a Temple reconstructed to receive the glory of the Divine Presence, a prophetic vision fulfilled in Emmanuel (*God with us*), Who tabernacled among men (John i. 14). Cp. Rom. ix. 25; Rev. xxi. 2, 3.